The Legal Rights
of Handicapped Persons

Preparation and publication of this book were supported in part by a grant from the Bureau of Developmental Disabilities, Rehabilitation Services Administration, Office of Human Development Services, Department of Health, Education, and Welfare, Region III (SRS-51-P-15547). Opinions expressed herein are those of the authors and do not necessarily represent the views of the Department of Health, Education, and Welfare.

THE LEGAL RIGHTS
OF HANDICAPPED PERSONS
Cases, Materials, and Text

Edited by

Robert L. Burgdorf, Jr., J.D.
Director, Developmental Disabilities Law Project
University of Maryland School of Law
Baltimore

·P A U L·H·
BROOKES
PUBLISHERS

Baltimore • London

Paul H. Brookes, Publishers
Post Office Box 10624
Baltimore, Maryland 21204

Pages 523 and 524 reprinted from Horstman, P., ''Protective Services for the Elderly: The Limits of *Parens Patriae*,'' 40 *Missouri Law Review* 215, 231–235 (1975). Copyright 1975 by The Curators of the University of Missouri.

Typeset by The Composing Room of Michigan, Inc. (Grand Rapids)
Manufactured in the United States of America by The Maple Press Company
(York, Pennsylvania)

Library of Congress Cataloging in Publication Data
Main entry under title:

The Legal rights of handicapped persons.

Includes index.
1. Handicapped—Law and legislation—United States—
Cases. I. Burgdorf, Robert L., 1948-
KF480.A7L43   346'.73'013   79-26311
ISBN 0-933716-01-X

PREFACE

This book was developed in response to a need perceived by my wife, Marcia Pearce Burgdorf, and me during our involvement in legal education programs at the University of Maryland and University of Notre Dame schools of law—and by many other legal advocates and educators—for a formal law school casebook dealing with the legal rights of handicapped persons. I confess to having seriously underestimated the magnitude of this undertaking; early in the 1970s many of us advocates for handicapped people naively believed that all the "law" in this area could be toted around in a single file folder. The length of this book bears witness to the fact that there is actually a large and still-growing body of legal precedent and legislation dealing with the rights of handicapped individuals, and this relatively long volume resulted only after it was culled down from a manuscript over three times as extensive.

Having initially planned to complete the entire manuscript myself, I realized, after some two and one-half years of struggling, that the size of the existing body of law and the rapidity with which it was developing dictated that I enlist the aid and expertise of my professional colleagues. Subsequently, I was fortunate in obtaining the excellent assistance of the other contributors to this work (all of whom are former or present staff members of the Developmental Disabilities Law Project of the University of Maryland School of Law). By their authoring and co-authoring various chapters, they have permitted the book to take a much more comprehensive and intensive approach than my original conception.

The topics covered in the various chapters are all subject matter areas in which handicapped persons have sought equal opportunities under law. The book does not address special benefits available to handicapped persons that are unavailable to others, special Social Security benefits, for example; nor does it deal in any depth with such matters as special considerations in estate planning for handicapped persons. The scope of the book is limited, rather, to those areas in which handicapped persons have traditionally been denied some right or benefit afforded other persons in our society and have resorted to litigative activity in an effort to obtain equal treatment. The topics addressed herein are primarily civil in nature; the problems faced by handicapped persons in the criminal justice system, while very worthy of attention, are beyond the scope of this work.

The book is designed for use in law school courses, either in traditional lecture format or as a reference in clinical education contexts. Sufficient material is included for a two-semester program; for a single-semester course, the materials should be used on a selective basis. In addition to its use in the law school context, it is hoped that this book will prove to be a useful asset to practicing attorneys and other advocates for the rights of handicapped clients. Moreover, with the increasing legal sophistication of other professions, it is likely that this book will be a beneficial reference work for other professionals concerned with the rights and status of handicapped persons, at both the instructional and practitioner levels. For these latter audiences, however, a *caveat* is necessary: the book presumes a certain amount of knowledge of legal procedures and terminology; matters such as jurisdiction, *certiorari,* and mootness are not explained in the course of this volume and may be mystifying to the uninitiated.

In the interest of brevity and economy, the cases and articles included have been edited to remove extraneous and duplicative material; footnotes, except those with particular pertinence, have been deleted. The original numbering of the footnotes from these cases has been retained; those footnotes in the text added by the editor or chapter authors have been distinguished by superscript letters.

As this book was going to press, the Supreme Court of the United States has handed down three decisions relating directly to the legal rights of the handicapped persons. In *Southeastern Community College* v. *Davis,* _____U.S._____, 99 S.Ct. 2361 (1979), the Court held that a hearing-impaired woman was not an ''otherwise qualified'' handicapped individual within the coverage of a federal nondiscrimination statute, and was therefore not eligible for a university clinical nursing program. In spite of some sensationalism in news media reports of the case, the Supreme Court's opinion was rather narrowly limited to the facts of the case and did not announce any particularly damaging or helpful legal principles. In *Parham* v. *J.L.,* _____U.S._____, 99 S.Ct. 2493 (1979), the Court ruled that no formal precommitment hearing is required before parents commit their children to state mental hospitals. In an accompanying decision, *Secretary of Public Welfare* v. *Institutionalized Juveniles,* _____U.S._____, 99 S.Ct. 2523 (1979), the Court expanded the *Parham* rationale to include commitment to mental retardation facilities. The *Parham* and *Secretary of Public Welfare* decisions were significant setbacks to advocates for handicapped children and have necessitated the development of new strategies for challenging the inappropriate institutionalization of handicapped minors. Memoranda discussing the impact of these three decisions are available from the Developmental Disabilities Law Project.

The very fact, however, that the Supreme Court had occasion to decide these three cases is a testimonial to how far the civil rights movement for handicapped persons has come in the last decade. For too long the problems faced by handicapped persons in trying to find a place of dignity and achievement in our society have been ignored; the promises of equality in our laws and constitutions have been empty slogans to such citizens. These problems have now at least been brought to the eyes of the public and considered by the highest court in the land. If adequate redress for discriminatory treatment is not yet at hand in all circumstances, grievances are at least being aired. This new self-conceptualization of handicapped persons, that we are indeed full citizens of this country, protected by its laws, and entitled to resort to legal action to demand that our rights be recognized and implemented, is a most important product of the litigative and legislative activity in this area. This new vocalism and militance of handicapped persons have brought an ever-increasing need for legal advocates familiar with the problems and needs of handicapped persons. The intent of this book is to facilitate the training of attorneys and other professionals who will be vigorous and knowledgeable advocates for the legal rights of their handicapped clients.

I am indebted to a number of people for their assistance with this endeavor. The invaluable help of the contributors has already been mentioned. Special thanks are due to Julie Piper, Annette Wingfield, and Kathy Rohrbach for their typing, proofreading, copying, and correcting of the manuscript. Thanks also to Sarah Orenstein for her secretarial work on the manuscript. I am grateful to Ellen Finkelstein, Maryjane Kelley, Mary Hencke, Patrick P. Spicer, and David Holzer for their legal research and cite checking. I am especially grateful to Dawn Oxley for help at all stages; without her assistance this endeavor might never have been completed.

We are very thankful to Dean Michael J. Kelly, and the faculty and administration of the University of Maryland School of Law for their support of the work of the Developmental Disabilities Law Project, and to Elizabeth Schoenfeld, whose belief in the value of such a casebook gave us the opportunity to develop it.

Finally, I would like to dedicate this book to five ladies: to my wife, Marcia, and our daughters, Dorney, Molly, and Genevieve, and to Susan, a little girl in Ohio who died while waiting for her legal rights to be recognized.

Robert L. Burgdorf, Jr.

ACKNOWLEDGMENTS

The editor and publisher gratefully acknowledge the publishers of *Santa Clara Law Review, Columbia Journal of Law and Social Problems, Labor Law Journal, Temple Law Quarterly, Missouri Law Review, California Law Review, Leadership Series in Special Education: Audio-Visual Library Service,* and *Maryland Law Forum* for their permission to reprint material originally appearing in these journals. Full credit to the source is given at the occurrence of the excerpts in this book.

CONTRIBUTORS

Donald N. Bersoff, J.D., Ph.D.
Associate Professor, University of Maryland School of Law, 500 W. Baltimore St., Baltimore, MD 21201; Professor of Psychology, The Johns Hopkins University.

Marcia Pearce Burgdorf, J.D.
Co-Director, Developmental Disabilities Law Project, 500 W. Baltimore St., Baltimore, MD 21201; Assistant Professor, University of Maryland School of Law; Associate Professor, The Johns Hopkins University, School of Hygiene and Public Health.

Robert L. Burgdorf, Jr., J.D.
Director, Developmental Disabilities Law Project, 500 W. Baltimore St., Baltimore, MD 21201.

Beverly J. Falcon, J.D.
Staff Attorney, Developmental Disabilities Law Project, 500 W. Baltimore St., Baltimore, MD 21201.

Elizabeth E. Hogue, J.D.
National Coordinator, Developmental Disabilities Law Project, 500 W. Baltimore St., Baltimore, MD 21201.

Susan P. Leviton, J.D.
Assistant Professor, University of Maryland School of Law, 500 W. Baltimore St., Baltimore, MD 21201.

Alice K. Nelson, J.D., M.S.W.
Attorney, Bay Area Legal Services, Inc., 305 N. Morgan, Tampa, FL 33602.

W. Dawn Oxley
Legal Intern, Developmental Disabilities Law Project, 500 W. Baltimore St., Baltimore, MD 21201.

Nancy B. Shuger, J.D.
Directing Attorney, Clallam-Jefferson Office, Evergreen Legal Services, 805 East Eighth St., Port Angeles, WA 98362.

SUMMARY OF CONTENTS

TABLE OF CONTENTS

TABLE OF CASES

Principal cases are in *italic type*.

THE LEGAL RIGHTS
OF HANDICAPPED PERSONS

I

WHO ARE "HANDICAPPED" PERSONS?

Robert L. Burgdorf, Jr.

LITTLE GOOD CAN COME FROM CRIPPLES; they generally take revenge on nature, and do as little honor to her as she has done to them.[a]

A person "of unsound mind"—an idiot, for example, is, to all intellectual purposes, dead . . .[b]

I thank God for my handicaps for through them I have found myself, my work, and my God.[c]

The handicapped live among us. They have the same hopes, the same fears, and the same ambitions as the rest of us. They are children and adults, black and white, men and women, rich and poor. They have problems as varied as their individual personalities. Yet, they are today a hidden population because their problems are different from most of ours. Only the bravest risk the dangers and suffer the discomforts and humiliations they encounter when they try to live what we consider to be normal, productive lives. In their quest to achieve the benefits of our society they ask no more than equality of opportunity. But they are faced with continuing discrimination. . . . Most of us see the handicapped only in terms of stereotypes that are relevant for extreme cases. This ancient attitude is in part the result of the historical separation of our handicapped population. We have isolated them so that they have become unknown to the communities and individuals around them.[d]

I do not choose to be a common man. It is my right to be uncommon—if I can. I seek opportunity—not security. I do not wish to be a kept citizen, humbled and dulled by having the state look after me. I want to take the calculated risk; to dream and to build, to fail and to succeed. I refuse to barter incentive for a dole. I prefer the challenges of life to the guaranteed existence; the thrill of fulfillment to the stale calm of Utopia. I will not trade freedom for beneficence nor my dignity for a handout. I will never cower before any master nor bend to any threat. It is my heritage to stand erect, proud and unafraid; to think and act for myself, enjoy the benefit of my creations and to face the world boldly

---

[a]Baltasar Gracian, *The Art of Worldly Wisdom,* CCLXXIII (1647).

[b]*Jenkins* v. *Jenkins' Heirs,* 32 Ky. (2 Dana) 102, 104 (1834).

[c]Helen Keller, quoted in Harrity, R., and Martin, R., *The Three Lives of Helen Keller* 7 (1962).

[d]Senator Harrison Williams (D., N.J.) 118 Cong. Rec. 3320-3321 (Feb. 9, 1972).

and say, this I have done. For our disabled millions, for you and me, all this is what it means to be an American.[e]

They have been described as "second class citizens,"[f] "the forgotten minority,"[g] "society's stepchildren,"[h] "the most discriminated minority in our nation,"[i] "social fugitives,"[j] "the silent minority,"[k] "human discards,"[l] and "most misfortuned citizens."[m] They have been pitied and abused, occasionally deified but more frequently viewed as demoniacal;[n] they have been hidden, ignored, and generally shunned by society,[o] but recently they have engendered the concern of presidential committees and government agencies.[p] They have been the recipients of charity and special public services but have also been denied many rights and opportunities available to the general public. In literature and in real life, they have been both heroes and villains.[q]

---

[e]Sullivan, E., "Henry Viscardi and the Mislabeled Disabled", SIGN National Catholic Magazine 27 (Oct., 1967).

[f]*Hearing Before the Select Subcommittee on Education of the Committee on Education and Labor*, House of Representatives, 93rd Congress, First Session, on H.R. 17, p. 82 (Feb. 7, 1973) Statement of Elsie D. Helsel and E. Clarke Ross.

[g]Vodicka, B. E., "The Forgotten Minority: The Physically Disabled and Improving Their Physical Environment," 48 *Chicago-Kent L. Rev.* 215 (1971).

[h]"Society's Stepchildren: The Mentally Retarded," Research Report No. 112 (New Series), Commonwealth of Kentucky Legislative Research Commission, April, 1974.

[i]Sorkin, N., "Equal Access to Equal Justice: A Civil Right for the Physically Handicapped," 78 *Case & Comment* 41 (1973).

[j]Kriegel, L., "Uncle Tom and Tiny Tim: Some Reflections on the Cripple as Negro," 38 *Am. Scholar* 412, 416 (1969).

[k]President's Committee on Mental Retardation, *Silent Minority* (1973) (pamphlet published by U. S. Department of Health, Education, and Welfare, Washington, D.C.).

[l]118 Cong. Rec. 11171 (Mar. 28, 1972), remarks of Representative Michael Harrington, quoting Watson, Douglas, "Human Discards: The Problems Persist," *Washington Post,* Mar. 21, 1972.

[m]*Harrison* v. *Michigan,* 350 F.Supp. 846, 849 (E.D.Mich. 1972).

[n]Davies, S., *The Mentally Retarded in Society* 9-10 (1959).

[o]See Burgdorf, R., and Burgdorf, M., "A History of Unequal Treatment: The Qualifications of Handicapped Persons as a 'Suspect Class' Under the Equal Protection Clause," 15 *Santa Clara Lawyer* 855, 883-889 (1975).

[p]E.g., the White House Conference on Handicapped Individuals, the President's Committee on Employment of the Handicapped, the Bureau of Education for the Handicapped, the National Council on the Handicapped, and the National Institute of Handicapped Research.

[q]E.g., real life heroes: Beethoven (deaf), Homer (blind), Albert Einstein (learning disabled), Julius Caesar (epileptic), Franklin Delano Roosevelt (paralysis from polio), Helen Keller (deaf and blind), Dante (epileptic), Roy Campanella (quadriplegic), the Japanese artist Yoshikiko Yamamoto (mentally retarded), Zelda Fitzgerald (mentally ill), Napoleon Bonaparte (epileptic), Thomas Edison (hearing impaired and learning disabled), Peter Stuyvesant (amputee), Joseph Pulitzer (blind), Peter Tschaikowsky (epileptic) Lou Gehrig (amyotrophic lateral sclerosis), Goya (hearing impairment), El Greco (visual impairment), Milton (blind), Woodrow Wilson (learning disabled), Alexander the Great (epileptic), Ray Charles (blind), and Stevie Wonder (blind); fictional and literary heroes: television's Ironsides (paraplegic), Grandpa Amos McCoy (mobility impaired), and "Gunsmoke's" Chester (mobility impaired), McMurphy of *One Flew Over the Cuckoo's Nest* (insane?), the biblical Samson (blind), Charly of the book *Flowers for Algernon* and the movie *Charly* (mentally retarded), Benji Compson of Faulkner's *The Sound and the Fury* (mentally retarded), Dickens' Tiny Tim (mobility impaired), Heidi (paraplegic), Lennie in *Of Mice and Men* (mentally retarded), Phillip Carey in *Of Human Bondage* (club foot), and Don Quixote (insane?); villains: King Richard III (hunchback), King George III (insane?), Captain Ahab of *Moby Dick* (amputee), Long John Silver of *Treasure Island* (partially sighted and amputee), the "one armed man" of television's "The Fugi-

Some have made great contributions to our civilization and culture, while others have lived wasted lives in deplorable and dehumanizing conditions. They are a minority that has been present in all countries at all stages of history, and yet they have remained largely invisible.

Who are these people whom in everyday speech and in our laws we call "handicapped"?

A. GENERAL DEFINITION

The general dictionary definition of *handicap* is "a disadvantage that makes achievement unusually difficult."[r] When used generically, however, terms like *handicapped persons, handicapped children,* or *the handicapped* have a narrower meaning, referring to a particular type of "disadvantage"—a mental, physical, or emotional disability or impairment. Thus, a handicapped person is an individual who has a mental, physical, or emotional disability or impairment that makes achievement unusually difficult.[s] It should be noted that physical, mental, or emotional disabilities qualify as handicaps only if they hinder achievement. Moreover, the phrase "unusually difficult" makes it clear that the hindrance must be substantial; a slight or inconsequential disability or impairment is not a handicap.

Etymologically, the word *handicap* is thought to derive from the phrase "hand i´cap" or "hand in the cap," which is the name of a sport played in 17th century England.[t] One person would challenge some article belonging to another, for which he offered something of his own in exchange. An umpire was appointed to determine how much boot should be given, and the parties made a deposit of forfeit money held in their hands in a cap, pending the umpire's decision.[u] In the 18th century, the procedures of this sport and the word *handicap* were applied to the process of an umpire determining the extra weight to be carried by the superior horse in a horse race. This notion of "handicapping" the superior competitor was then generalized to other sports and games, and, since about 1850, the word *handicap* has been applied to any encumbrance or disability that weighs upon effort and makes success more difficult.[v]

---

tive," the Hunchback of Notre Dame, Mrs. Smallweed (mentally ill) and Mr. Smallweed (paraplegic) of Dickens' *Bleak House,* Captain Hook of *Peter Pan* (partially sighted and amputee), and Lord Chatterley of *Lady Chatterley's Lover* (paraplegic).

[r]*Webster's International Unabridged Dictionary* 1027 (3d Ed. 1966), specifically adopted by courts in *State* v. *Turner,* 3 Ohio App.2d 5, 209 N.E.2d 475, 477 (1965), and *Chicago, Milwaukee, St. Paul & Pacific R. R. Co.* v. *State Dept. of Industry, Labor & Human Relations,* 62 Wis.2d 392, 215 N.W.2d 443, 446 (1974).

[s]*The Encyclopedia Britannica* (micropedia) Vol. IV p. 885 (1974) defines "handicapped persons" as "persons having neuromotor, mental, sensory, or psychological disabilities or having such difficulties in communication as speech defects or learning disabilities." *Webster's New International Unabridged Dictionary* 1133 (2d Ed. 1942) defines "the handicapped" as those at a disadvantage in economic competition because of physical or mental defects."

[t]*The Oxford English Dictionary* 62 (1933); *Webster's New International Unabridged Dictionary* 1133 (2d Ed. 1942).

[u]*Ibid.*

[v]5 *The Oxford English Dictionary* 63 (1933).

It is only since the turn of the century, that the terminology of mental, physical, and emotional *handicaps* has emerged.[w] This is not to say that the persons whom we now call handicapped were not previously singled out and classified together as a distinct group differentiated from the rest of society. On the contrary, whether they were called defectives, degenerates, deviants, disabled, cripples, idiots, imbeciles, lunatics, the halt and the lame, morons, the afflicted, feebleminded, paralytics, deaf-mutes, epileptics, crazy, deranged, fools, incompetents, infirm, incapacitated, abnormal, or the like,[x] handicapped persons have long been meted out differential treatment from the rest of society.[y] However, it is only recently in our history that this class of persons has been afforded the denomination *handicapped*.

B. HANDICAP VERSUS DISABILITY

The term *handicap* is frequently contrasted with the word *disability*. Many commentators assert that *disability* refers to a medical condition, e.g., deafness, paraplegia, or Down's syndrome, while the word *handicap* refers to one's status as a result of a disability.[z] Thus, handicaps are perceived to be a result of a person's environment and not of the physical or mental impairment itself.[aa] Consequently, in an appropriate environment, with proper societal attitudes and supportive services, the disabled person, it is argued, need not be handicapped. "There is nothing inherent in disability to produce handicap."[bb] Elaborating upon the notion of environmental factors as agents acting upon the individual with a disability to engender handicaps, one author has declared:

> If the term *handicapped* is used, it will refer to those particular individuals who, because of some force—social, personal or otherwise—have allowed their disability to debase or debilitate them sufficiently so as to prevent them from achieving some desired goal, or preclude their faring for themselves. . . . [T]he child with a physical or mental disability, born in our society, is not, as yet, handicapped, simply disabled. Doctors, parents, teachers, psychologists, friends, relatives, all, no doubt, well-meaning, will be responsible for convincing this child, or helping him to learn, that he is handicapped.[cc]

This handicapped/disabled distinction has become something of a rallying cry for some professionals and many disabled persons. Speakers to groups of disabled people have sometimes been accosted by heated verbal attacks from individuals in the

---

[w]*Fowler's Modern English Usage* 238 (2d Ed. 1965).

[x]An example of the multiplicity of terms for describing disabilities is provided in 44 C.J.S., Insane Persons § 2, in which 43 pages are devoted to listing and defining various terms that have been employed by courts to describe insanity and related conditions.

[y]See, e.g., Burgdorf, R., and Burgdorf, M., note o, *supra*.

[z]E.g., Weiss, S., "Equal Employment and the Disabled: A Proposal," 10 Columbia J. Law & Soc. Prob. 457, 461 n. 23 (1974); Vodicka, B. E., "The Forgotten Minority: The Physically Disabled and Improving Their Physical Environment," 48 *Chicago-Kent L. Rev.* 215, 220 (1971).

[aa]E.g., Rigdon, L., "Civil Rights", Awareness paper of the White House Conference on Handicapped Individuals, p. 1 (1977); Bowe, F., *Handicapping America* 16-17 (1978).

[bb]Garfunkel, F., quoted in Blatt, B., and Kaplan, F., *Christmas in Purgatory* 117 (1974).

[cc]Buscaglia, L., *The Disabled and Their Parents: A Counseling Challenge* 18 (1975).

audience because they used the word *handicap* instead of *disability*. Many organizations of disabled individuals seek every opportunity to proclaim that persons having their particular type of disability are not handicapped. For example, the president of a state chapter of one of the national organizations of blind persons was quoted in a newspaper story as declaring that "[b]eing blind is more like an inconvenience than a handicap."[dd]

This militance against the word *handicap* has some elements of a healthy pride and self-assertion about it; it is reminiscent of the Negro/black terminological shift in the black civil rights movement in America. It may also be an attempt to escape from some of the negative connotations and stereotypes associated with the term *handicapped*.[ee] But the crusade for the handicap/disability distinction is not completely beneficent, nor, possibly, even logical.

The "I may be disabled, but I'm not handicapped" formula too often has a ring of elitism and favoritism about it. It frequently translates as, "I'm not like those 'handicapped' people. We persons with X disability are better than people with handicaps; we're much more like 'normal' folks." While denying that the individual or group is a member of the "unfortunate" class of persons with handicaps, such sentiments often lend implicit approval to the prejudice, inaccurate stereotyping, and devaluation of handicapped persons as a whole. This approach can also lead to divisiveness and infighting between various disability groups and subgroups rather than a mutually beneficial cooperation over common goals and problems faced by handicapped people.

A second difficulty with the distinctions drawn between *disability* and *handicap* is that from a purely semantic point of view the implications of the two words have been totally reversed. The word *disabled* clearly derives from roots meaning "not able," implicitly not able to do something. *Handicap,* on the other hand, in common usage, in legal contexts, and according to the dictionary, refers to a physical or mental impairment.[ff] If a person were to have a physical or mental impairment, and, through mechanical device, retraining, or other compensatory method, learned to overcome this condition so that he or she was not dis-abled from any activities, it would be logical to say that such a person was handicapped but not disabled. For instance, a person with a lower leg amputation may be able, with a proper prosthetic device, to walk, run, ski, ride a bike, kick a football, and engage in all other normal activities. Such a person is not disabled at all, in the sense of being unable to do any activity, but, for most legal and medical purposes, as well as to the average person on the street, he or she is a handicapped person.

[dd]Hall, W., "Blind Fight for Their Rights," *The Baltimore Evening Sun,* Nov. 3, 1975, p. C1. An almost identical statement, but about a double amputee, has been quoted in an editorial in a newsletter dealing with issues affecting handicapped persons: Milk, L., "Editorial: Defining Disability," 3 *Mainstream* No. 4, p. 6 (Nov.-Dec. 1978).

[ee]For a discussion of the advantages of adopting new, unsoiled terminology in describing handicapping conditions, see p. 47, below.

[ff]See, e.g., Ariz. Rev. Stat. Ann. §15-1011.3 (1974); Cal. Educ. Code § 6941 (1975); Neb. Rev. Stat. §43-604 (1974); Ohio Rev. Code Ann. § 3323.03 (1974); and nn. r and s, *supra.*

This view is reinforced by the use made of the word *disability* for purposes of eligibility for disability insurance benefits under the Social Security Act. Section 223(d) of the Act, 42 U.S.C. § 423(d) defines *disability* as "inability to engage in any substantial gainful activity by reason of any medically determinable physical or mental impairment" and then elaborates:

> an individual... shall be determined to be under a disability only if his physical or mental impairments are of such severity that he is not only unable to do his previous work but cannot, considering his age, education, and work experience, engage in any other kind of substantial gainful work which exists in the national economy....[gg]

Obviously, these provisions do not view disability as coterminous with mental and physical impairments but require the added factor of inability to do work in our competitive labor market. It seems rational, therefore, to turn the arguments against the term *handicap* inside out and to proclaim that *disability,* with its connotations of the loss or absence of ability, is a much more derogatory term than *handicap.* At the very least, such observations and reasoning undercut much of the cogency for the crusade against usage of the word *handicapped.*

Most traditional discussions of handicaps and disabilities have involved too simplistic an analysis of a highly complex phenomenon. The underlying premise has been that there are only two levels involved in analyzing the impact of physical and mental impairments, and that sharp yes or no differentiations can be made at each level. At the "disability" level, it is presumed that a person either does or does not have a physical or mental condition qualifying as a disability; perhaps medical diagnosis is to draw the line between which conditions are disabilities and which are not. Then, based upon the interaction of a disabled individual with his or her environment, the person can be adjudged handicapped or not. Under such analysis, a disabled person can escape the label of *handicapped,* if he or she is a success in the eyes of our society; disabled people who do not "make it," the failures, are the ones considered handicapped.

In reality, many more levels of complexity inhere in the assessment of handicaps, and the interaction of disabled persons with their environment. The following are among the determinations latent in the concept of *handicap:*

1. A mental or physical irregularity: The baseline criterion for the existence of a handicap is recognition that an individual has some particular physical or mental trait that makes him or her different from others. Sometimes, as in the case of amputations, paralysis, and other severe physical impairments, the irregularity may be obvious to all who come into contact with the person; in other instances, as with many epileptic conditions, some visual and hearing impairments, and various mental impairments, the irregularity may be more subtle or hidden. Traditionally, official responsibility for ascertaining the existence of such physical and mental irregularities has rested with the medical profession. More recently, psychologists, educators, and other professionals have gotten into the act as well, particularly in diagnosing such conditions as learning disabilities and emotional disorders.

[gg]For further discussion of these provisions, see *Foote* v. *Weinberger,* at p. 19, *supra.*

2. Functional impairment: Not all physical or mental irregularities have negative connotations. Physical conditions, such as double jointedness, having a rare blood type, or genetic ability to roll one's tongue, and mental conditions, such as photographic memory or extremely high intelligence, can be a significant rarity in comparison to the norm but still be considered neutral or even highly advantageous characteristics. The second factor, therefore, in analyzing the concept of *handicap* in relation to environment is that the physical or mental irregularity must have a negative impact on function, i.e., it must produce a functional impairment. Thus, because of some physical irregularity, a joint is unable to permit the proper range of motion, a muscle does not move a limb properly, the nerves do not transmit messages correctly to the brain or to the muscles, hearing or sight is impaired, and so forth. Likewise, because of some mental irregularity, a person may be unable to take in appropriate sensations and data, to interpret them properly, to make judgments, to store items in memory, or to perform similar functions that are routine in a mentally normal individual.

3. Impediment to activities: Functional impairments can lead to limitations upon activity. Thus, walking may be impossible for a person who is unable to move his or her legs. Abstract thinking may be out of the range of possibilities for a person with a particular degree of mental retardation. Driving an automobile may not be feasible for an individual who does not have sufficient sight. Taking standardized tests may be futile for persons with particular learning disabilities. Listening to the radio may be out of the question for someone who cannot hear. The general principle is that persons with functional impairments will not be able to engage in those activities in which the function that is impaired is an essential component.

4. Career limitations: Obviously, the inability to engage in certain activities can limit the choice of possible roles one can play in society. A person who cannot walk can hardly choose to be an NFL fullback. A mentally retarded person is unlikely to be a university professor. A blind person should probably not prepare for a career as a television cameraman. (Another frequently cited "red herring" is the concept of a blind bus driver.) An individual who suffers from hemiplegia would be a poor candidate for the role of professional wrestler. These ridiculous examples serve to illustrate the simple fact that certain physical and mental impairments can place realistic limitations upon the choice of careers for persons with these particular impairments. The extent, however, to which such career limitations are overstated and imposed arbitrarily upon handicapped persons by employers, job counselors, and other professionals, is the subject of subsequent discussion in Chapter 3.

5. Impact on life success: The ultimate factor in assessing the interplay between handicaps and environment is the determination of the impact of the physical or mental impairment upon the individual's success in life, that is, the individual's happiness and achievements during his or her life. In our society, success is ordinarily measured in economic terms; it is held to be synonymous with ownership, economic independence, and prosperity. The fact that a person might be very happy without such economic success is generally overlooked.

A most serious disservice done by society to handicapped persons is the assumption that there is an automatic link between the five factors just listed. It has often been presumed that mental or physical irregularities result in functional impairments, and lead, almost inevitably, to limitations upon activities, career choices, and success in life. The image of a handicapped person as one who is not able to do many things, who is unable to fill a proper role in society, and who is not a success in terms of achievements or happiness is widespread and deep-seated.

Actually, many people considered handicapped in our society do not share all or even most of the elements in this supposedly inextricable chain. A person with epilepsy, for example, clearly has a medical irregularity. If, however, the person's condition can be controlled through medication, there does not have to be any functional impairment whatever. Consequently, limitations placed upon activities, career choices, and life success need be minimal. Likewise, persons with serious cosmetic disfigurements may be considered handicapped but have no functional impairments, activity restrictions, or, except for a few occupations such as acting for which appearance is important, any career limitations; there is no intrinsic reason why such a person should not earn a full measure of success in life.

On the other hand, a person may have an actual functional impairment but learn alternative means for functioning so that there are no limitations upon the activities that can be pursued; a good example is a partial amputee with an effective prosthetic device. Even more common are instances where an individual has a functional impairment that impedes the performance of certain activities, but the individual is able to learn other activities that can be employed in place of the unavailable ones. Thus, a deaf person may learn to read lips, a blind person may learn to read and write braille, or a person with impaired use of the legs may learn to walk with crutches. Such methods allow the handicapped individual to substitute an accomplishable activity for an unfeasible one, and make it possible for handicapped people to enter vocations that might otherwise be precluded to them. While there may still be some particular career not open to them, these individuals can by and large have a wide range of career possibilities from which to choose, particularly if employers are willing to make some appropriate accommodations for their special needs and abilities. Hence, functional impairments that impede activities need not result in significant career restrictions.

Moreover, even in situations where factors 1 through 4, above, coincide and there is a mental or physical irregularity resulting in functional impairment, impediment to activities, and career limitations, there should be no automatic conclusion that life success is ruled out. In the first place, the fact that career choices are severely limited does not mean that the individual may not be able to find a single career that is perfectly suited to his or her interests and abilities. One need only to cite some well known examples, such as Helen Keller, Jill Kinmont, and astrophysicist Steven Hawking, to clarify that individuals with severe limitations upon them can find a proper niche in life where they can achieve success, fulfillment, and even fame. Second, a more philosophical question concerns the validity of our standards of life success. Supposing that a particular handicapped individual is either unable or unwilling to pursue a career (as we understand that term) or to obtain much in the way of possessions, wealth, and worldly success. Do we have the right to judge that such a person is a failure? Can the competitive, ulcerous, suburban executive decree that the mentally retarded man who is happy working as a dishwasher and living in a group home is not a success? Can we say that a person with a degenerative condition who decides to spend his or her remaining years reading the great philosophers and poets and listening to classical music is not happy? In short, does production equal success for a human being?

In any event, whatever our definition of success, the foregoing discussion illustrates that the stereotypic causal chain from physical and mental irregularities to functional limitations to impediments upon activities to career limitations to lack of life success is grossly inaccurate. Insofar as proponents of the "I'm disabled but not handicapped" school of thought are trying to awaken people to the realization that because a person has a mental or physical impairment does not presuppose that that individual will not be a competent worker or a success in life, their sentiment ought to be applauded. It appears, however, that they have chosen the wrong words to declare this sentiment. The effort should not be to show the differences between *disabled* people and *handicapped* people, but to show that such individuals, whether labeled *handicapped* or *disabled,* can lead rewarding and fruitful lives.

However much we wish it otherwise, persons having physical and mental impairments will remain *handicapped* whether they are successful or not. A blind person who becomes fabulously wealthy through a successful career and who is extremely happy with his or her lot in life will not thereby become nonhandicapped; like it or not, in general parlance and for most official purposes, that individual will still be a handicapped person; a rich, happy handicapped person to be sure, but handicapped nonetheless.

We are not in the position of Humpty Dumpty, who told Alice, "When I use a word, it means just what I choose it to mean—neither more nor less."[hh] The word *handicapped* is not an empty slate; it has a meaning given it by general usage and, more importantly, by our laws and courts. There is, as is discussed in the next section, some element of arbitrariness about the nature and degree of the physical and mental conditions considered handicaps, particularly at the outer fringes of the subclasses of impairments included (and thus, to some degree, society and its officials *do* have some of Humpty Dumpty's ability to influence the meaning given to words), but the basic content and signification of the word is generally understood and settled by social convention and legal precedent.

The attempt by some to reject the standard meaning of *handicapped*, to unilaterally assign another definition to it, and thereby to distinguish it from the term *disabled,* is perhaps fueled by the fact that, in addition to its usage to describe the class of people with physical and mental impairments, the word *handicap* has, as noted above,[ii] a more general meaning of any disadvantage that makes achievement unusually difficult. From this perspective, any number of disparate disadvantages may be termed handicaps. We may speak of persons being handicapped by poverty, ignorance, obesity, age, being female in a sexist society, lack of education, racial prejudice, religious differences, illiteracy, shyness, ethnic differences, and any number of other factors which can hinder achievement. In most medical and legal contexts, however,

---

[hh]Lewis Carroll, *Through the Looking Glass and What Alice Found There,* Chapter VI.
[ii]See text accompanying n. r, *supra.*

handicap is used in its more narrow sense to refer to mental and physical impairments, and this meaning is usually the one intended in everyday speech when someone refers to "a handicapped person" or "the handicapped."

In an attempt to find a path out of what one author has called "the semantic morass of what constitutes impairment, disability, or handicap,"[jj] the approach in the remainder of this book reflects a decision to not shy away from the use of the word *handicapped* in referring to persons with physical and mental impairments. Furthermore, if the term *disabled* is used, it will be considered as interchangeable with *handicapped*. This approach is, as statutes and court decisions on subsequent pages demonstrate, fully consistent with the choices of terminology employed by lawmakers and courts.[kk]

C. SOCIETY AS CREATOR OF HANDICAP[ll]

Up to this point, the discussion of the term *handicapped* has presupposed that a certain amount of objective reality inheres in the concept—that there really are some concrete things called handicaps and that the people we call handicapped possess characteristics that make them distinguishable from other people. Most statutory enactments and court decisions make this same assumption and accept the handicapped/nonhandicapped distinction as a precise, objective categorization. Actually, however, a large degree of artificiality and arbitrariness is inherent in the concept of handicaps, and an awareness of this fact can lend a very different perspective to the process by which the label *handicapped* is applied and to the implications that follow its imposition.

One of the most important elements in delineating who is and who is not handicapped is a social judgment; a person truly qualifies as handicapped only as a result of being so labeled by others. And the decision to impose or not to impose the *handicapped* label is ultimately grounded upon perceptions of an individual's role in society. Certain relatively severe types of impairments, such as blindness, deafness, absence or paralysis of arms or legs, or serious degrees of mental retardation or of mental illness, are nearly always considered handicaps in our society. Other impairments, such as the absence of a finger or a toe, mild mental retardation and emotional disturbance, color or night blindness, partial hearing loss, and many others, may or

---

[jj]Farrett, J. F., "Handicapped Americans—Overview," I *American Rehabilitation* 4 (No. 5, 1976).

[kk]It is worth noting the choice of words in the creation and proceedings of the White House Conference on Handicapped Individuals. The author of the Awareness Paper on Civil Rights for the conference opined that he preferred the term *disability* over *handicapped,* but ultimately adopted the other terminology: "Nevertheless, 'handicapped' is currently both the accepted everyday expression and a common statutory term for describing persons with disabilities. For the sake of uniformity, the word 'handicapped' will be used in this paper." Rigdon, L., n. aa, *supra.*

Mainstream, a newsletter dealing with issues affecting handicapped persons concluded that it would make use of both the terms *disabled* and *handicapped.* In an editorial explaining this policy decision, a reason given for not rejecting the word *handicap* was that " 'handicapped' is the only term recognized by the law and we work in the field of legal compliance assistance." Milk, L., see n. dd, *supra.*

[ll]Bartel, N., and Guskin, S., "A Handicap as a Social Phenomenon," Chapter 2 of *Psychology of Exceptional Children and Youth* 75, 77 (Cruickshank, W., ed., 1971).

may not be considered handicaps. A person can be handicapped for one purpose and not for another; for example, the "six hour mentally retarded child" is considered mentally retarded during the time he or she is in school but copes well and is considered "normal" outside the academic environment.[mm]

In a sense, therefore, *handicapped* is an artificial grouping created by the labeling process in our society.[nn] From the broad spectrum of human characteristics and capabilities certain traits have been singled out and called handicaps.[oo] The fine line between *handicapped* and *normal* has been artibrarily drawn by the "normal" majority. Frequently, the various conditions called handicaps have nothing in common except the label itself:

> Whatever characteristics such individuals may or may not have had in common prior to their classification, it is their involvement in the classification process that has generated the characteristics they all share—their social fate as members of a status category.[pp]

These labels may be imposed in a number of different ways: by one's peers (e.g., children calling another child "cripple" or "retard"), by educators (e.g., "Your child has been recommended for placement in a class for the emotionally disturbed"), by psychologists (e.g., "Her scores on the IQ test indicate moderate mental retardation"), by psychiatrists (e.g., "He's suffering from psychotic schizophrenia"), by doctors (e.g., "My diagnosis is that you have multiple sclerosis"), by rehabilitation personnel (who must certify people as disabled before they are eligible for services), and by social workers, nurses, relatives, neighbors, and, in short, by almost any member of society with whom one comes into contact. But, regardless of the person or entity applying the label in a particular instance, the existence of a status category called *handicapped* is the result of a societal value judgment:

> [W]hat is distinctive about and common to all handicapped individuals is not so much their own characteristics as the characteristic response of others to them. A handicapped person is someone whom others think is incompetent or unattractive, someone whom others want to help or protect or avoid. Physicians, psychologists, educators, and rehabilitation experts merely rationalize and institutionalize the layman's pity and antipathy. That is, professionals create terminology, organization, and treatment patterns which foster and stabilize the distinctive status relationship between handicapped persons and others.[qq]

[mm]*The Six Hour Retarded Child,* President's Committee on Mental Retardation (1969) (pamphlet published by U. S. Department of Health, Education, and Welfare).

[nn]See, e.g., Rains, P., Kitsuse, J., Duster, T., and Friedson, E., "The Labeling Approach to Deviance," 1 *Issues in the Classification of Children* 88, 91 (Hobbs, N., ed., 1975).

[oo]*Ibid.* In theory, almost everyone could be considered *handicapped* for one purpose or another, since only 1% of the population is physically able to do every kind of work, without even taking into account psychological, emotional, and intellectual impairments. Sullivan, E., "Henry Viscardi and the Mislabeled Disabled," *The Sign* 36, 37 (Oct., 1967): "Handicapped is a word Henry Viscardi never uses. 'Can you sing high C?' he likes to say. 'No? Then you are totally and permanently disabled for an opera career. You're probably not fit to pitch for the Yankees, either.' "

[pp]Rains, P., Kitsuse, J., Duster, T., and Friedson, E., n. nn, *supra,* at 91-92.

[qq]Bartel, N., and Guskin, S., n. ll, *supra,* 75.

The social judgments that draw the line between *normality* and *handicap* are necessarily arbitrary:

> The distinction is not "given," so to speak, by reality. Instead, salient and socially meaningful differences among persons (and acts) are a product of our ways of looking, our schemes for seeing and dealing with people. Thus, people are *made* different—that is, socially differentiated—by the process of being seen and treated as different in a system of social practices that crystallizes distinctions between deviant and conventional behavior and persons. For example, the legal definition of blindness is clear-cut, but it includes poorly sighted persons as well as persons who are totally impaired visually. The legal definition therefore serves to crystallize blindness as both a social status and an experience of self for those persons who might not otherwise have defined themselves as blind.[rr]

Likewise, determinations as to how much hearing loss constitutes deafness, how much motor limitation constitutes an orthopedic handicap, how much loss of contact with reality constitutes mental illness, how much difficulty with speaking constitutes speech impairment, and so on, are the result of purely arbitrary categorizations. A pertinent example of the amorphous nature of such classifications occurred in 1973 when the American Association on Mental Deficiency redefined the term *mental retardation*.[ss] Before the redefinition, *mentally retarded* included all those persons whose scores on standardized tests were one standard deviation below the norm; afterward, only those who were two standard deviations below the norm were included. By this definitional shift, about eight million persons who had been labeled "borderline mentally retarded" were no longer considered mentally retarded at all, and the incidence of mental retardation was reduced from approximately 3% to approximately 1% of the population.[tt]

Observations such as these have led some authorities to posit a social definition of handicap:

> What is a handicap in social terms? It is an imputation of difference from others: more particularly, imputation of an undesirable difference. By definition, then, a person said to be handicapped is so defined because he deviates from what he himself or others believe to be normal or appropriate.[uu]

The arbitrary nature of the categorization of individuals as "handicapped" is further complicated by the inefficiencies and inaccuracies of the techniques and procedures used to sort people into various classifications. For example, intelligence quo-

---

[rr]Rains, P., Kitsuse, J., Duster, T., and Friedson, E., n. nn, *supra*, at 94.

[ss]Blatt, B., "A Basic Kit to Confront the Human Disposal Authority, Department of Subnormal Affairs of the Monolith, in this Land of Opportunity," 3 *Leadership Series in Special Education* 15, 35 (Johnson, Gross, and Weatherman, eds., 1974); Dybwad, G., "Where Do We Go from Here?", *Developmental Disabilities: An Orientation to Epilepsy, Cerebral Palsy, and Mental Retardation* 299, 303-304 (Gordon, J., ed., 1975).

[tt]Blatt, B., n. ss, *supra*, at 37; Dybwad, G., n. ss, *supra*, at 303-304; President's Committee on Mental Retardation, *Mental Retardation . . . the known and the Unknown*, 3, 10–11 (1975).

[uu]Bartel, N., and Guskin, S., n. ll, *supra*, at 76, quoting Freidson, E., "Disability as Social Deviance," *Sociology and Rehabilitation*, 72 (Sussman, ed., 1965).

tient tests are frequently relied upon to determine mental retardation; such tests, however, not only are subject to inherent variances (depending upon the test takers' moods, physical condition, alertness or fatigue, past testing experience, and other characteristics; the weather, temperature, luxuriousness, and other attributes of the testing environment; the experience, methodology, and personalities of the persons giving and scoring the tests; and a certain degree of chance or "luck" in choosing correct or incorrect responses) and misuse and abuse of the testing instruments and scores obtained, but also tend to result in disproportionately low scores for members of racial and cultural minorities.[vv] Thus, in a number of instances, blacks, Chicanos, American Indians, and other members of minority groups have been inaccurately classified as mentally retarded, because of the cultural bias of testing instruments that have been "validated" upon samples consisting almost exclusively of white middle class people.[ww]

Moreover, impairments are frequently mistaken for one another. Communication difficulties, specific learning disabilities, autism, hearing impairments, and other disabilities have sometimes been misdiagnosed as mental retardation. Deaf people have been improperly labeled as learning disabled, autistic, mentally retarded, and brain damaged. Persons with cerebral palsy have been labeled as epileptic, mentally retarded, and aphasic. These are simply a few examples of the widespread mislabeling that occurs. One study of 280 handicapped children revealed that these children had, at one time or another, received a total of 523 inaccurate labels.[xx] This problem of the "mislabeled disabled"[yy] is a pervasive one. Not only are the definitions of *handicap* arbitrarily imposed by our society, but the classification process by which persons are assigned to the various categories of handicapping conditions are inexact and clumsy, and result in numerous errors.

Such mislabeling can be particularly harmful because a person whose condition need not be a substantial impediment may become "handicapped" if he or she is labeled and treated as handicapped by members of society. Educators and psychologists use the term *self-fulfilling prophecy* to describe a process whereby persons assigned stigmatizing labels tend to conform to the expectations created by such labels.[zz]

[vv]See, e.g., Dick, J., "Equal Protection and Intelligence Classifications," 26 *Stanford L. Rev.* 647 (1974); Kirp, D., "Schools as Sorters: The Constitutional and Policy Implications of Student Classification," 121 *U. Pa. L. Rev.* 705, 719-720 (1973); M. Sorgen, "Testing and Tracking in Public Schools," 24 *Hastings L. J.* 1129 (1973).

[ww]*Ibid.*; see *P. v. Riles,* 343 F.Supp. 1306 (N.D.Cal. 1972).

[xx]Gorham, K., DesJardins, C., Page, R., Pettis, E., and Scheiber, B., "Effect on Parents," Chapter 20 of 2 *Issues in the Classification of Children* 154, 161 (Hobbs, N., ed., 1975).

[yy]Sullivan, E., "Henry Viscardi and the Mislabeled Disabled," *The Sign* 36 (Oct., 1967). Sullivan used the phrase to express the sentiment that no one should be called "disabled." We are using the term to describe persons who have no actual disability but are inaccurately labeled as disabled and persons who have a disability but are improperly labeled as having some other disability.

[zz]Popularized by Rosenthal, R., and Jacobson, L., in *Pygmalion in the Classroom: Teacher Expectation and Pupils' Intellectual Development* (1968). See also Rains, P., Kitsuse, J., Duster, T., and Freidson, E., footnote nn, *supra,* at 97-98; Guskin, S., Bartel, N., and MacMillan, D., "Perspective of the Labeled Child," 2 *Issues in the Classification of CHildren* 189-212 (Hobbs, N., ed., 1975).

This effect may be magnified when, as in the case of handicapped persons, the label has practical and legal ramifications.

D. LEGAL AND GOVERNMENTAL DEFINITIONS OF HANDICAPS

In developing a formal definition of *handicap* and the specific conditions considered handicaps for legislative, regulatory, and judicial purposes, there are a number of different definitional approaches. First, the terms might be defined by simply listing all the particular impairments included. Thus, *handicap* might be defined by enumerating a long list of all the known handicapping conditions, or *insanity* might be defined by listing all the psychoses, neuroses, or other categories that qualify as types of insanity. A second approach would be to gear the definition into the governmental purpose of the particular statute or regulation under consideration. Thus, for purposes of eligibility for special education services, a *handicapped child* might be defined as one who because of mental or physical condition needs special education services. Or *hearing impaired* might be defined, for the purposes of eligibility for the services of an interpreter, as persons who because of their hearing impairment require the services of an interpreter. A third approach involves deferral to professional determinations. Accordingly, *mental illness* might be defined as conditions diagnosed as such by a psychiatrist. And *mentally retarded person* could be defined as a person found by a doctor or psychologist to be mentally retarded. In such circumstances, the definition does not really define; it passes the problem of definition on to one of the learned professions which is supposed to have the requisite expertise to make such determinations. Another definitional approach is the classic, pure definition model. This approach tries to follow the traditional genus and species method of defining; it seeks to avoid circularity and to give some concrete criteria for differentiating the concept being defined.

All of these definitional techniques have been tried in one or another piece of legislation, regulatory provision, or court ruling. Frequently, however, these several methods have been employed in combination with one another in an attempt to make the meaning of terms more specific or to placate political concerns raised by a particular definitional approach. For example, organizations of people with a particular disability may support and lobby for a listing of disabilities to be added to one of the other definitional types in order to assure that their disability will be explicitly included, by name, in the coverage of some statute or governmental program. This combination approach has resulted in adulterated definitions that sometimes turn out to be clear and precise and at other times give birth to obscure and cumbersome definitional formulations.

Because of the nearly interchangeable nature of the words *handicap, disability,* and *impairment,* the definition of one of these terms by reference to another is not very informative. Hence, defining a handicap as "a mental or physical disability" or "a mental or physical impairment," even though not a truly circular definition, sheds very little light on the subject. Consequently, definitions making use of such formulations usually include modifying phrases or clauses that do the real job of defining the term; it is important, therefore, that close attention be given to these modifying words.

STATE V. TURNER

Court of Appeals of Ohio, Lucas County, 1965
3 Ohio App. 2d 5, 209 N.E.2d 475

GUERNSEY, Judge.

This is an appeal on questions of law from a judgment convicting and sentencing the defendant for a violation of Section 3113.01, Revised Code, the defendant having been indicted for willfully neglecting to provide his mentally handicapped child, Robert Turner, age 18 years, with necessary food, clothing and shelter. . . .

Section 3113.01, Revised Code, reads as follows:

> *No parent* or other person charged with the maintenance of a legitimate or illegitimate child under eighteen years of age, or *of a* physically or *mentally handicapped child under twenty-one years of age,* nor the husband of a pregnant woman, living in this state, *shall fail to provide such child* or woman *with the necessary or proper home, care, food, and clothing* (Emphasis added to pertinent portions of statute.)

. . . Nowhere in the act is the term "physically handicapped child" or the term "mentally handicapped child" specifically defined. Nor do we find a specific definition of the term "mentally handicapped" at any other place in the statutes of Ohio.

Although it is basic that the power to define and classify and to prescribe punishment for felonies committed within the state is lodged in the General Assembly of the state and that, by reason thereof, the state may not issue criminal commands in vague and undefined language which would require definition by other than the General Assembly, or which would result in persons of ordinary intelligence not being informed with reasonable precision what acts the Legislature intends to prohibit, nevertheless, a statute may not be held invalid for uncertainty if any reasonable and practical construction can be given to its language. Mere difficulty in ascertaining its meaning, or the single fact that it is susceptible of different interpretations will not necessarily render it nugatory. It is the duty of courts to endeavor by every rule of construction to ascertain the meaning of, and give full force and effect to, every enactment of the General Assembly not obnoxious to constitutional prohibition. Words in common use will be construed in their ordinary acceptation and significance, and with the meaning commonly attributed to them. *Eastman* v. *State,* 131 Ohio St. 1, 1 N.E.2d 140; and 3 Sutherland, Statutory Construction, 3rd Ed. 56, Section 5606.

In Webster's Third New International Dictionary (Unabridged), the word "handicap" in its reference here is defined as "a disadvantage that makes achievement unusually difficult; *esp:* a physical disability that limits the capacity to work."

The history of the criminal legislation here involved, prior to the inclusion of the particular language with which we are concerned, is set forth at length in the case of *Seaman* v. *State,* 106 Ohio St. 177, at page 184, 140 N.E. 108, at page 110, wherein it is stated:

> The intent of this legislation was to compel persons charged by law with the support of designated dependents to meet the full measure of their obligation to such dependents and society. The converse of the proposition may be stated that it was the purpose to relieve society of a burden that properly belonged to one charged by law with its obligation. . . .

There is no reason to reach a different conclusion as to the intent of the amended legislation in its application to a mentally handicapped child. It is obvious from the amendment that the Legislature intends that parents should also have an additional burden of support for children under the age of 21 years who by reason of a mental handicap are unable by their own efforts to provide themselves "with the necessary or proper home, care, food, and clothing."

In view of the dictionary definition of handicap, in view of the legislative intent determined and expressed in *Seaman* v. *State,* 106 Ohio St. 177, 140 N.E. 108, and as a reasonable and practical construction derived from the words of the entire statutory section, it is apparent to this court, and we hold, that it is the legislative intent and definition, implicit in the provisions of Section 3113.01, Revised Code, as enacted and amended, that a mentally handicapped child is a child having a mental disability which makes, or would make, it unusually difficult for him to provide by his own efforts his necessary or proper home, care, food, and clothing. This definition operates, of course, to exclude from consideration in determining mental handicap any other limiting factors on such capability not arising from mental disability and which might be shared in common with any child, for instance, the mere fact of youth, lack of training, lack of initiative, lack of parental supervision, lack of parental or other encouragement, laziness, etc., and can operate to require a parent's support only where mental disability is the handicapping factor. Whether a child fits this definition would, of course, be a question of fact to be determined by a jury from any competent evidence bearing thereon.

We conclude, therefore, that Section 3113.01, Revised Code, in its application to the neglect of a mentally handicapped child, is not invalid for indefiniteness or uncertainty and that defendant's first assignment of error is without merit.

NOTE

The first part of the court's definition, "a mentally handicapped child is a child having a mental disability," is obviously not very significant. The remainder of the definition, referring to difficulty in obtaining home, care, food, and clothing, is an example of a definition tied closely to the statutory purpose; eligibility for the benefit provided by the statute is defined in reference to need for the benefit to be provided. While such a nebulous standard might be advantageous in the context of a federal or state program providing benefits to eligible applicants, in the context of the *Turner* case itself, where a criminal prosecution was involved, the language does seem a bit too imprecise.

CHICAGO, MILWAUKEE, S. PAUL & PACIFIC RAILROAD COMPANY v. STATE, DEPARTMENT OF INDUSTRY, LABOR, AND HUMAN RELATIONS

Supreme Court of Wisconsin, 1974
62 Wis.2d 392, 215 N.W.2d 443

Proceeding commenced by petitioner Chicago, Milwaukee, St. Paul & Pacific Railroad Company (hereinafter "Railroad") pursuant to Chapter 227, Stats. to review an order of the Department of Industry, Labor and Human Relations (hereinafter "Department") which ordered the Railroad to cease certain discriminatory practices and to reinstate Vern C. Goodwin to his former position.

On March 13, 1969, Vern C. Goodwin, age 18, was hired by the Railroad as a common laborer in the diesel house. He was given a 20 minute physical examination by a company physician on the morning of March 13, 1969 and began work during the second shift that evening. On the physical examination Goodwin disclosed a prior history of asthma and migraine headaches with dizziness. X-rays of Goodwin revealed a slight disc space narrowing at L5–S1.

Goodwin continued working in the diesel house for the next two weeks doing a variety of cleaning jobs, some of which were heavy and dirty and others easy. His work was performed to the satisfaction of the shop foreman and of the general supervisor. The superintendent of motive power for the Railroad testified that Goodwin performed his duties and assignments satisfactorily. The job and the working conditions did not bother him.

On March 26, 1969 Goodwin received notice his services were terminated effective March 28, 1969. The notice gave no reason for termination. Upon inquiry, Goodwin was told that he had a disqualifying back disease. After a private physician examined and informed Goodwin that he had no back disability, he filed a complaint with the Equal Rights Division of the Department on April 22, 1969, charging discrimination. He alleged that his employment had been terminated because of an alleged handicap which did not render him unable to physically perform the duties of the job in question.

At the hearing before Examiner Thomas W. Dale of the Department it was revealed that Goodwin's work was terminated on recommendation of its Chief Surgeon, Dr. Raymond Householder.

Dr. Householder testified his primary concern and crucial reason for recommending rejection of Goodwin as a laborer in the diesel house was the disclosed history of asthma.

The examiner recommended as a conclusion of law that complainant had established by a fair preponderance of evidence that the Railroad had committed an act of discrimination against complainant on the basis of an alleged handicap in violation of Secs. 111.31–111.37 of the Wisconsin Statutes in its termination of complainant's employment.

The Department on July 20, 1971 in a 2–1 decision, confirmed the examiner's conclusion and ordered the Railroad to cease and desist its discriminatory practices against complainant and like situated employees or applicants for employment. The Department also ordered Goodwin reinstated to his former position with the Railroad with full restoration of his seniority.

The Railroad filed a petition for review in the circuit court for Dane County. The circuit court affirmed the order of the Department and entered judgment on December 8, 1971. The Railroad appeals from the judgment.

In the instant action, the complainant charged that he was discriminated against on the basis of handicap. Thus, the burden of proof is on the complainant to prove that the reason he was terminated was because of his physical disorders. Such a finding was made by the Department and, being a finding of fact, is conclusive if supported by substantial evidence in view of the entire record. Sec. 227.20 (1)(d), Stats.; *Robertson Transport Co.* v. *Public Service Comm.* (1968), 39 Wis.2d 653, 159 N.W.2d 636.

Whether the physical disorders suffered by the complainant constitute a handicap is a conclusion of law. Errors of law are always reviewable by the reviewing court. Sec. 227.20(1)(b); *Pabst* v. *Department of Taxation* (1963), 19 Wis.2d 313, 120 N.W.2d 77.

The fact that Goodwin's employment was terminated on the basis of physical disorders—his history of asthma—is not challenged by the appellant and is supported by the substantial evidence in view of the entire record. No contrary conclusion would be possible. However, this court must determine whether asthma or the other physical disorders of the complainant constitute a handicap.

Sec. 111.32(5), Stats. fails to define what constitutes a handicap. It is the contention of the appellant that the complainant's physical disorder does not constitute a handicap. Rather, the appellant contends that, for an employee to be deemed handicapped, he must be incapacitated from normal remunerative occupation, an economic detriment to the normal employer and require rehabilitative training. We think such a reading of the statute is entirely too constrictive.

The Wisconsin Fair Employment Code was promulgated so as to encourage and foster to the fullest extent practicable the employment of all properly qualified persons. To accomplish this goal, the code restricted the employer's right to discriminate against those individuals who, though female, old, handicapped or whatever, could function efficiently on the job. If the individual can function efficiently on the job, then the mere fact that he is different from the average employee as to those statutorily proscribed bases may not be used as a basis for discrimination. To effectuate this purpose, the code is to be liberally construed. Sec. 111.31(3), Stats.

If this court were to adopt the very constricted interpretation of the appellant, an impractical result would occur. If an individual were a paraplegic and were able to efficiently perform the duties of the job, then he would be protected under Sec. 111.32(5), Stats., but if an individual were asthmatic or suffered from migraine headaches, though able to efficiently perform the duties of the job, no protection against discrimination would be found under the statute. The legislative policy of encouraging the employment of *all* properly qualified persons would not be served under such a statutory construction.

Since handicap does not have a statutory definition, the word must be given its meaning in common usage. Sec. 990.01(1), Stats. Thus, this court would define handicap as "a disadvantage that makes achievement unusually difficult: esp.: a physical disability that limits the capacity to work." Such a definition was adopted in *State* v. *Turner* (1965), 3 Ohio App.2d 5, 209 N.E.2d 475, 477 as the definition of handicap with respect to mental injuries. The Wisconsin Rehabilitative Law, Sec. 55.01(3) (a), Stats. defines "handicapped person" somewhat broader as:

> . . . any person who, by reason of a *physical or mental defect or infirmity,* whether congenital or acquired by accident, injury or disease. . . . (emphasis supplied)

In either case, it is our opinion that handicap as used in Sec. 111.32(5), Stats. must be defined as including such diseases as asthma which make achievement unusually difficult.

Since the Department found that the complainant was discriminated against on the basis of handicap, the burden of proof was on the employer to prove that his actions were exempted pursuant to Sec. 111.32(5)(f), Stats. which provides as follows:

> The prohibition against discrimination because of handicap does not apply to failure of an employer to employ or retain as an employee any person who because of a handicap is physically or otherwise unable to efficiently perform, at the standards set by the employer, the duties required in that job.

On review of the record as a whole, there is no evidence that Goodwin was unable to efficiently perform the duties of his job as a common laborer. Goodwin performed without ill effects all of the tasks assigned to him in the diesel house. In fact, there was no medical testimony that, to a reasonable degree of medical certainty, that the working conditions were or would be in the future hazardous to his health.

On the contrary, there was testimony that Goodwin successfully passed his military pre-induction physical and two other physicals necessary for strenuous jobs he held after his termination. The complainant has had no recurrence of his childhood asthmatic condition for over seven years and has continued participating in sports since high school. In fact, the record as a whole reveals that the complainant was physically qualified to efficiently perform the duties of his job as a common laborer and that the Department's finding to that effect is supported by the substantial evidence.

NOTES

1.   The court intimates that its definition of *handicap* is broad enough to include migraine headaches. Would it also include obesity? Race? Homosexuality? Alienage? Odor? Poverty? The phrase "a disadvantage that makes achievement unusually difficult" is broad indeed. By enacting a statute outlawing discrimination on the basis of handicap did the legislature really intend to forbid any and all types of discrimination against any person who can perform the job?

2.   Whatever disadvantages the court's broad interpretation may have, its approach does avoid putting handicapped individuals in the dilemma of having to prove that they are handicapped before they can avail themselves of the protection of the law. For individuals who have engaged in a lifelong struggle to avoid being labeled "crippled," "mentally retarded," or the like, the requirement of proving that one is indeed "handicapped" may be quite distasteful.

FOOTE v. WEINBERGER

United States District Court for Southern District of Texas, 1974
377 F.Supp. 1347

NOEL, District Judge.

In August of 1972, this plaintiff filed an application to establish a period of disability and for entitlement to disability insurance and benefits pursuant to Sections 216(i) and 223, respectively, of the Social Security Act, as amended. 42 U. S.C. §§ 416(i) and 423. After a hearing in April of 1973 and the receipt of additional medical evidence, the Administrative Law Judge announced his opinion that plaintiff's application should be denied. The cornerstone of the Hearing Decision appeared to be the Administrative Law Judge's conclusion that "the claimant was not under a 'disability,' as defined in the Social Security Act, at any time prior to the date of this decision."

(See page 21 of the transcript of the entire record of the administrative proceedings, hereinafter referred to as "Tr.") The Hearing Decision became final when, on October 31, 1973, the Appeals Council of the Social Security Administration approved the action of the Administrative Law Judge. This suit was brought against the Secretary of Health, Education and Welfare under Section 205(g) of theAct, 42 U.S.C. § 405(g), to review that final decision.

As to facts, the findings of the Secretary (by which is meant the final administrative determination, however made) are conclusive "if supported by substantial evidence." 42 U.S.C. § 405(g). Thus, judicial review of factual findings is strictly limited. *Celebrezze* v. *Zimmerman,* 339 F.2d 496 (5th Cir. 1964). Conflicts in the evidence are to be resolved by the Secretary, not the courts. *Martin* v. *Finch,* 415 F.2d 793 (5th Cir. 1969). "When," however, "the fact findings carry with them such operational finality as they do under this statutory plan, *we must be certain* that in arriving both at the ultimate decision and the essential subsidiary facts, the [Administrative Law Judge] has evaluated all of the evidence under proper standards." *Hayes* v. *Celebrezze,* 311 F.2d 648, 654 (5th Cir. 1963), emphasis added.

The statutory standards governing the determination of a disability are found in Section 223(d) of the Social Security Act, 42 U.S.C. § 423(d), which provides in pertinent part:

> (1) The term "disability" means—
> (A) inability to engage in any substantial gainful activity by reason of any medically determinable physical or mental impairment which can be expected to result in death or which has lasted or can be expected to last for a continuous period of not less than 12 months; ...
> (2) For purposes of paragraph (1)(A)—
> (A) an individual ... shall be determined to be under a disability only if his physical or mental impairments are of such severity that he is not only unable to do his previous work but cannot, considering his age, education, and work experience, engage in any other kind of substantial gainful work which exists in the national economy. ...
> (3) For purposes of this subsection, a 'physical or mental impairment' is an impairment that results from anatomical, physiological, or psychological abnormalities which are demonstrable by medically acceptable clinical and laboratory techniques.

Social Security Regulation No. 4 supplements the statute with the following:

> *Conclusion by physician regarding individual's disability.*
> ... The weight to be given such physician's statement depends on the extent to which it is supported by specific and complete clinical findings and is consistent with other evidence as to the severity and probable duration of the individual's impairment or impairments. 20 C.F.R. § 404.1526.

It was in the interpretation of these statutory and administrative standards that the Administrative Law Judge erred. How this was done must be explained in the context of the facts of this case.

The bulk of plaintiff's claim rested on her alleged practical inability to use her hands. This functional limitation, it was asserted, was the result of her suffering from "carpal tunnel syndrome." This diagnosis was not seriously contradicted by any medical testimony or other evidence. The primary issue on this score, as acknowledged by the Administrative Law Judge, was the severity of this condition, i. e., "the precise degree of functional loss or restriction." Tr. 16. As to this, the evidence was in conflict. In resolving this conflict the Administrative Law Judge took the approach that the legal standards quoted above required that "subjective" evidence be discounted or ignored and that "objective" evidence be the source of any conclusion.

The Hearing Decision contains several examples of this analysis being followed. In summarizing the evidence provided by Dr. Joseph Klotz, the Administrative Law Judge observed that ". . . sensory examination of this area [the hands] revealed an apparent hypesthesia over the median nerve distribution on the right. This was *subjective*." Tr. 14, emphasis supplied here and throughout. This subjectivity was presumably to be contrasted with Dr. Klotz' "*objective* clinical findings" tending to show a normal condition. Tr. 18.

When introducing his evaluation of the evidence, the Administrative Law Judge declared, "However, in order for such limitations to merit consideration and a determination of 'disability' as defined in the Social Security Act, an allegation of functional limitation must be medically determinable, that is, it must be shown that it results from *organic dysfunction or other demonstrable causes.*" Tr. 16. The Hearing Decision also carefully records that Dr. Ralph Munslow "stated that there was *subjective* evidence of pain of the right wrist and as to her left hand. . . ." Tr. 17. The diagnosis of Dr. M. C. Rittiman was discounted thus: "However, it must be noted that Dr. Rittiman's opinion is not supported by any clinical diagnostic findings of *objective* pathology." Tr. 19.

Without exception, the objective/subjective dichotomy was employed by the Administrative Law Judge to discredit testimony or other evidence favorable to plaintiff and to bolster evidence harmful to her. This was apparently made possible by the very nature of the "carpal tunnel syndrome." The Medical Advisor employed to assist the Administrative Law Judge at the hearing, Dr. W. C. McKinney, testified that the most common, and sometimes the only, symptom of this syndrome is pain—a wholly subjective symptom.

However that may be, it is clear that the applicable standards were misinterpreted. The Court of Appeals for the Fifth Circuit has decisively rejected the gloss put upon the statute and regulations in the Hearing Decision this Court now reviews. *Page* v. *Celebrezze,* 311 F.2d 757 (5th Cir. 1963). With little subtlety, the Administrative Law Judge did attempt to "restrict medical investigation, examination and opinion to only those things described as 'objectively clinical'. . . ." He did abdicate his responsibilities by looking to "that very limited field of medical science (if there is such) that deals alone with objective symptoms and demonstrable laboratory analysis." *Page, supra,* at 763.

By requiring that the severity of plaintiff's condition be established by objective evidence alone, the Administrative Law Judge applied an incorrect legal principle. *Prewitt* v. *Gardner,* 389 F.2d 993 (5th Cir. 1968). Accordingly, this case must be remanded for further proceedings at the administrative level. This Court intimates nothing regarding the proper outcome upon reconsideration by the Secretary.

NOTES

1. In linking the definition of *disability* to the ability to perform labor, § 223(d) clearly falls into the category of definitions that are drawn by reference to the context of the statutory purpose for which they will be used. Disabilities not affecting ability to work are arbitrarily tossed out of the scope of the word *disability*. Another key element of the § 223(d) definition, however, and perhaps the more important one in terms of the issues raised in the *Foote* case, is the deferral to the expertise of the medical profession. *Disability* refers to impairments that are "medically determinable" and "are demonstrable by medically acceptable clinical and laboratory techniques." Thus, disabilities are whatever conditions the medical profession says will prevent gainful employment; in short, disabilities are what the medical profession says they are.

2. A similar definitional approach, but dealing with the area of education rather than employment, can be found in § 56500 of the California Education Code, which provides:

> "Mentally retarded pupils" means all pupils under the age of 21 years who because of retarded intellectual development as determined by individual psychological examination are incapable of being educated efficiently and profitably through ordinary classroom instruction (Stats. 1976, c. 1010, § 2, operative April 30, 1977).

In this statute, the delegation of decision-making authority is made not to the medical profession but to psychologists. Views about the wisdom of such deferrals depends upon the degree of respect that one holds for the particular profession deferred to.

3. The objective/subjective distinction employed by the administrative judge could cause serious problems in many contexts other than carpal tunnel syndrome. Any physical condition for which pain is the only symptom would be impossible to qualify as a disability under such analysis. Moreover, many types of serious debilitating mental conditions have no known organic causes and are dependent upon reports of the patient as to his or her condition. If a person claims to hear strange voices, for example, there is no laboratory test for proving that the patient is being truthful or not. For many disorders, such as autism, diagnosis is more a matter of observing behavior than of running tests, and evidence of any links with physical conditions is still being sought. The best that a doctor can do in such situations is to report that the individual behaves as if he or she has the condition. The federal court opinion in *Foote* concludes that the words "demonstrable by medically acceptable clinical and laboratory techniques" embrace subjective reports of symptoms by patients and the behavioral observations made by the doctor, if such techniques are accepted by the medical profession. Is Judge Noel implicitly saying, "If the doctor believes her, who are we to disagree?"?

4. A prime example of the definitional approach of deferring to the medical professional was a New York statute, enacted in 1946, which provided that an epileptic is "a person suffering from epilepsy as defined in medical practice," N.Y. Mental Hygiene Law, § 2, N.Y. Gen. Session Laws, Chap. 751 (1946), repealed by N.Y. Gen. Session Laws, Chap. 251 (1972). This definition is, however, a great improvement over another statute dealing with epilepsy, also enacted in 1946; § 5125.14 of the Ohio Rev. Code (repealed in 1961) provided that "An epileptic is one who has epilepsy."

ARIZ. REV. STAT. ANN.

§ *15-1011.3 (Cum. Supp. 1978)*

"Handicapped child" means a child of lawful school age who due to present physical, mental or emotional characteristics or a combination of such characteristics is not afforded the opportunity for all-around adjustment and progress in regular classroom instruction and who needs special instruction, special ancillary services, or both to achieve at levels commensurate with his abilities. Handicapped child includes the following:

(a) "Educable mentally handicapped" means a child who because of his intellectual development, as determined by evaluation pursuant to § 15-1013, is incapable of being educated effectively through regular classroom instruction without the support of special classes or special services designed to promote his educational development.

(b) "Seriously emotionally handicapped" means a child who because of serious social or behavioral problems, as determined by evaluation pursuant to § 15-1013, is unable or incapable of meeting the demands of regular classroom programs in the public schools and in the opinion of diagnostic and instructional personnel the child requires special classes or special services designed to promote his educational and emotional growth and development.

(c) "Hearing handicapped" means a child who has a hearing deviation from the normal, as determined by evaluation pursuant to § 15-1013, which impedes his educational progress in the regular classroom situation without the support of special classes or special services designed to promote his educational development, and whose intellectual development is such that he is capable of being educated through a modified instructional environment.

(d) "Homebound" or "hospitalized" means a student who is capable of profiting from academic instruction but is unable to attend school due to illness, disease, accident, pregnancy or handicapping conditions, who has been examined by a competent medical doctor and is certified by that doctor as being unable to attend regular classes for a period of not less than three school months.

(e) "Multiple handicapped" means a child who has serious learning and developmental problems resulting from multiple handicapping conditions as determined by evaluation pursuant to § 15-1013, and who cannot be provided for adequately in a program designed to meet the needs of any one handicapping condition. The multiple handicapped includes a child who is autistic. Multiple handicapping conditions includes two or more of the following:

(i) Hearing handicapped.

(ii) Physically handicapped.

(iii) Trainable mentally handicapped.

(iv) Visually handicapped.

(v) One of the handicapping conditions determined pursuant to items (i) through (iv) of this subdivision existing concurrently with a condition of educable mentally handicapped, seriously emotionally handicapped or learning disabled.

(f) "Physically handicapped" means a child who has a physical handicap or disability, as determined by evaluation pursuant to § 15-1013, which impedes his educational progress in the regular classroom situation without the support of special classes or special services designed to promote his educational development, and whose intellectual development is such that he is capable of being educated through a modified instructional environment.

(g) "Learning disabled" means a child who exhibits a significant discrepancy between ability and achievement as determined by evaluation pursuant to § 15-1013, when intellectual ability, age and previous educational experience in the regular classroom are considered. Learning disabled does not include learning problems which are due primarily to visual, hearing, speech or motor handicaps, mental retardation, emotional disturbance or to environmental disadvantage.

(h) "Speech handicapped" means a child who has a communication disorder such as stuttering, impaired articulation, severe disorders of syntax, semantics or vocabulary or a voice impairment, as determined by evaluation pursuant to § 15-1013, to the extent that it calls attention to itself, interferes with communication or causes the child to be maladjusted.

(i) "Trainable mentally handicapped" means a child who because of his intellectual development, as determined by evaluation pursuant to § 15-1013, is incapable of being educated in regular classroom programs or educable mentally handicapped programs without the support of special classes or special services designed to promote his educational development.

(j) "Visually handicapped" means a child who has a vision deviation from the normal, as determined by evaluation pursuant to § 15-1013, which impedes his educational progress in the regular classroom situation without the support of special classes or special services designed to promote his educational development, and whose intellectual development is such that he is capable of being educated through a modified instructional environment.

NOTES

1. This statute contains a hodgepodge of definitional approaches. The first sentence comes close to being a "pure" definition. It is, however, along with most of the later sections, closely tied in with the statutory context of education; it could not serve as a useful definition in other contexts, such as employment or medical services. Subsections (a)–(j) are an example of definition by enumeration; they simply list various types of handicaps. At the same time, they exhibit what we have referred to as the "deferral" approach in that they predicate the determination of handicaps upon the results of a formal education evaluation. The evaluation team then ultimately determines who is and who is not handicapped.

2. Subsection (e) is hazy. It is not clear why autism is denominated a multiple handicap; it might more properly be included in one of the other categories, such as "seriously emotionally handicapped," or perhaps have been itself a separate category. Item (v) in the list of multiple handicapping conditions is obscure. It is not immediately apparent why three handicapping conditions are grouped together in item (v) rather than being (v), (vi), and (vii). A possible interpretation is that this formulation prevents the concurrence of any two of the categories educable mentally handicapped, seriously

emotionally handicapped, and learning disabled from being considered a multiple handicap. If this interpretation is accurate, it seems illogical that a trainable mental handicap plus serious emotional disturbance or a learning disability equals multiple handicap, but an educable mental handicap plus either of these latter two conditions does not add up to a multiple handicap. Another problem with this formulation is that it indicates that a multiple handicap may result from the concurrence of an educable mental handicap and a trainable mental handicap, a union that is, by definition, impossible.

3.   The archaic nature and negative implications of the terms *educable* and *trainable* are discussed in Chapter 2.

4.   The definition of *physically handicapped* in subsection (f) as "a child who has a physical handicap or disability" is to a great extent circular and unenlightening. It also seems that "hearing handicapped," "visually handicapped," and some "homebound" or "hospitalized" individuals would also be "physically handicapped" under such a definition. How far-fetched would it be to argue that a deaf child is "physically handicapped" as well as "hearing handicapped" and is, consequently, "multiply handicapped"?

§ 7 (6) OF THE REHABILITATION ACT OF 1973
P.L. 93-112, 29 U.S.C. § 706, 87 Stat. 361

The term "handicapped individual" means any individual who (A) has a physical or mental disability which for such individual constitutes or results in a substantial handicap to employment and (B) can reasonably be expected to benefit in terms of employability from vocational rehabilitation services provided pursuant to titles I and III of this Act.

NOTE

This is a very typical example of a definition geared to the statutory purpose.

§ 111(a) OF THE REHABILITATION ACT AMENDMENTS OF 1974
P.L. 93-516, 88 Stat. 1617

[Amended § 7 (6) of the Rehabilitation Act of 1973 by adding an additional sentence to the definition of "handicapped individual."]

For the purposes of titles IV and V of this Act, such term means any person who (A) has a physical or mental impairment which substantially limits one or more of such person's major life activities, (B) has a record of such an impairment, or (C) is regarded as having such an impairment.

NOTES

1.   The Title IV referred to deals with administration and program and project evaluation. Title V is a miscellaneous category, containing, among others, provisions requiring nondiscrimination against handicapped persons (§ 504, see pp. 194–213, *infra*) and affirmative action programs (§ 503, see pp. 370–409, *infra*). For the purposes of these two titles, Congress chose to provide a definition not exclusively linked to employability and ability to profit from vocational rehabilitation services.

2. Part A of the definition approaches the model of "pure" definition. A disadvantage of the formulation, however, is the vagueness of terms, such as "major life activities." The purposes of parts B and C are described in the explanatory analysis of U. S. Department of Health, Education, and Welfare regulations, pp. 29, below.

3. An interpretational "can of worms" was opened up by the suggestion that alcoholism and drug addiction might qualify as handicaps under this definition. This question was first raised formally by the Secretary of Health, Education, and Welfare in his request for public comments prior to the issuing of proposed DHEW regulations under § 504, 41 Fed. Reg. 20296 (May 17, 1976). Many handicapped individuals viewed the raising of the question of alcoholism and drug addiction qualifying as handicapping conditions as a "red herring" attempt to undermine the implementation of § 504. It was felt that many officials and members of the general public who would be sympathetic to a nondiscrimination provision aimed at traditional handicaps would shy away from supporting a measure that benefited alcoholics and drug addicts. Rumors were also circulated that this campaign for inclusion of addiction and alcoholism had been instigated by members of Congress and government officials who were alleged to have been alcoholics themselves.

The Secretary of DHEW sought and obtained from the United States Attorney General an opinion on this matter, 43 O.A.G. No. 12, U.S.G.P.O. 1978 -0267-570 (Apr. 12, 1977). Based upon the fact that addicts and alcoholics had been considered eligible for services under previous vocational rehabilitation legislation, the Attorney General concluded that there was no Congressional intent to exclude such persons from the coverage of the 1973 Act. He added, however, that the behavioral consequences of present alcoholism or drug addiction could be taken into account in determining whether a person is qualified for a particular employment opportunity.

In response to this opinion, the final HEW regulations did include persons who were alcoholics or drug abusers within the scope of the definition of "handicapped individual," see 42 Fed. Reg. 22686, Appendix A, Subpart A (4) (May 4, 1977.)

A final expression of Congressional intent in this area was provided in the Rehabilitation, Comprehensive Services, and Developmental Disabilities Amendments of 1978 (P.L. 95-602), § 122.(a) (6) (c), 92 Stat. 2985, of which adds another additional sentence to § 7(6):

> For purposes of sections 503 and 504 as such sections relate to employment, such term does not include any individual who is an alcoholic or drug abuser whose current use of alcohol or drugs prevents such individual from performing the duties of the job in question or whose employment, by reason of such current alcohol or drug abuse, would constitute a direct threat to property or the safety of others.

This addition formalizes the Attorney General's view that behavioral effects of current alcohol or drug use may disqualify alcoholics or drug addicts from the protections of the Act in regard to employment. However, by implication at least, the provision also indicates that drug addiction and alcoholism are included as handicapping conditions, and, for contexts other than employment, even current abuse of alcohol or drugs may not be used as a criterion for eligibility for programs covered by sections 503 and 504.

This question was raised in a slightly different context in a 1978 opinion of the attorney general of Maryland, 63 O. A. G. 39 (Md., Jan. 26, 1978). The Maryland attorney general was asked to decide whether alcoholism or narcotic addiction constituted a "physical or mental handicap" for purposes of a statutory prohibition on discrimination in employment. Noting that Maryland statutes had generally not treated alcoholism and addiction in the same way as traditional handicaps and that alcoholism and drug addiction are marked by a degree of voluntariness and a medically controversial status not characteristic of other conditions considered handicaps, the attorney general distinguished the United States Attorney General's opinion on this issue and ruled that narcotic addiction or alcoholism did not qualify as a "physical or mental handicap."

Is the Maryland rationale more or less convincing than that of the United States Attorney General? Is it possible that both are correct in light of their statutory contexts and legislative histories?

§ 84.3(j) OF REGULATIONS OF
THE DEPARTMENT OF HEALTH, EDUCATION, AND WELFARE ON
NONDISCRIMINATION ON THE BASIS OF HANDICAP IN
PROGRAMS AND ACTIVITIES RECEIVING OR BENEFITING FROM
FEDERAL FINANCIAL ASSISTANCE
42 Fed. Reg. 22678 (May 4, 1977)

(j) "Handicapped person." (1) "Handicapped persons" means any person who (i) has a physical or mental impairment which substantially limits one or more major life activities, (ii) has a record of such an impairment, or (iii) is regarded as having such an impairment.

(2) As used in paragraph (j)(1) of this section, the phrase:

(i) "Physical or mental impairment" means (A) any physiological disorder or condition, cosmetic disfigurement, or anatomical loss affecting one or more of the following body systems: neurological; musculoskeletal; special sense organs; respiratory, including speech organs; cardiovascular; reproductive, digestive; genito-urinary; hemic and lymphatic; skin; and endocrine; or (B) any mental or psychological disorder, such as mental retardation, organic brain syndrome, emotional or mental illness, and specific learning disabilities.

(ii) "Major life activities" means functions such as caring for one's self, performing manual tasks, walking, seeing, hearing, speaking, breathing, learning, and working.

(iii) "Has a record of such an impairment" means has a history of, or has been misclassified as having, a mental or physical impairment that substantially limits one or more major life activities.

(iv) "Is regarded as having an impairment" means (A) has a physical or mental impairment that does not substantially limit major life activities but that is treated by a recipient as constituting such a limitation; (B) has a physical or mental impairment that substantially limits major life activities only as a result of the attitudes of others toward such impairment; or (C) has none of the impairments defined in paragraph (j) (2) (i) of this section but is treated by a recipient as having such an impairment.

Subpart A(3) of Appendix A—Analysis of Final Regulation

42 Fed. Reg. 22685-22686 (May 4, 1977)

3. *"Handicapped person."* Section 84.3(j), which defines the class of persons protected under the regulation, has not been substantially changed. The definition of handicapped person in paragraph (j) (1) conforms to the statutory definition of handicapped person that is applicable to section 504, as set forth in section 111(a) of the Rehabilitation Act Amendments of 1974, Pub. L. 93-516.

The first of the three parts of the statutory and regulatory definition includes any person who has a physical or mental impairment that substantially limits one or more major life activities. Paragraph (j) (2) (i) further defines physical or mental impairments. The definition does not set forth a list of specific diseases and conditions that constitute physical or mental impairments because of the difficulty of ensuring the comprehensiveness of any such list. The term includes, however, such diseases and conditions as orthopedic, visual, speech, and hearing impairments, cerebral palsy, epilepsy, muscular dystrophy, multiple sclerosis, cancer, heart disease, diabetes, mental retardation, emotional illness, and, as discussed below, drug addiction and alcoholism.

It should be emphasized that a physical or mental impairment does not constitute a handicap for purposes of section 504 unless its severity is such that it results in a substantial limitation of one or more major life activities. Several comments observed the lack of any definition in the proposed regulation of the phrase "substantially limits." The Department does not believe that a definition of this term is possible at this time.

A related issue raised by several comments is whether the definition of handicapped person is unreasonably broad. Comments suggested narrowing the definition in various ways. The most common recommendation was that only "traditional" handicaps be covered. The Department continues to believe, however, that it has no flexibility within the statutory definition to limit the term to persons who have those severe, permanent, or progressive conditions that are most commonly regarded as handicaps. The Department intends, however, to give particular attention in its enforcement of section 504 to eliminating discrimination against persons with the severe handicaps that were the focus of concern in the Rehabilitation Act of 1973.

The definition of handicapped person also includes specific limitations on what persons are classified as handicapped under the regulation. The first of the three parts of the definition specifies that only physical and mental handicaps are included. Thus, environmental, cultural, and economic disadvantage are not in themselves covered; nor are prison records, age, or homosexuality. Of course, if a person who has any of these characteristics also has a physical or mental handicap, the person is included within the definition of handicapped person.

In paragraph (j) (2) (i), physical or mental impairment is defined to include, among other impairments, specific learning disabilities. The Department will interpret the term as it is used in section 602 of the Education of the Handicapped Act, as amended. Paragraph (15) of section 602 uses the term "specific learning disabilities" to describe such conditions as perceptual handicaps, brain injury, minimal brain dysfunction, dyslexia, and developmental aphasia.

Paragraph (j) (2) (i) has been shortened, but not substantively changed, by the deletion of clause (C), which made explicit the inclusion of any condition which is mental or physical but whose precise nature is not at present known. Clauses (A) and (B) clearly comprehend such conditions.

The second part of the statutory and regulatory definition of handicapped person includes any person who has a record of a physical or mental impairment that substantially limits a major life activity. Under the definition of ''record'' in paragraph (j) (2) (iii), persons who have a history of a handicapping condition but no longer have the condition, as well as persons who have been incorrectly classified as having such a condition, are protected from discrimination under section 504. Frequently occurring examples of the first group are persons with histories of mental or emotional illness, heart disease, or cancer; of the second group, persons who have been misclassified as mentally retarded.

The third part of the statutory and regulatory defintion of handicapped person includes any person who is regarded as having a physical or mental impairment that substantially limits one or more major life activities. It includes many persons who are ordinarily considered to be handicapped but who do not technically fall within the first two parts of the statutory definition, such as persons with a limp. This part of the definition also includes some persons who might not ordinarily be considered handicapped, such as persons with disfiguring scars, as well as persons who have no physical or mental impairment but are treated by a recipient as if they were handicapped.

NOTE

The statutory definition is notable for its breadth of scope. The DHEW regulations fill in some of the details of this general definition by listing categories of impairments included. The analysis of the regulation completes the task of fleshing out the statutory formulation by mentioning many of the specific conditions considered handicapping conditions. In concert, these three elements produce a definitional approach that is simultaneously expansive, flexible, and specific.

§ 503 (b) (1) OF THE REHABILITATION, COMPREHENSIVE SERVICES, AND DEVELOPMENTAL DISABILITIES AMENDMENTS OF 1978
P.L. 95-602 92, Stat. 3004

The term ''developmental disability'' means a severe, chronic disability of a person which—

''(A) is attributable to a mental or physical impairment or combination of mental and physical impairments;

''(B) is manifested before the person attains age twenty-two;

''(C) is likely to continue indefinitely;

''(D) results in substantial functional limitations in three or more of the following areas of major life activity: (i) self-care, (ii) receptive and expressive language, (iii) learning, (iv) mobility, (v) self-direction, (vi) capacity for independent living, and (vii) economic sufficiency; and

"(E) reflects the person's need for a combination and sequence of special, interdisciplinary, or generic care, treatment, or other services which are of lifelong or extended duration and are individually planned and coordinated."

NOTES

1. The definition of *developmental disabilities* is important because it determines eligibility for a wide range of services available under federal developmental disabilities legislation; among these services is, pursuant to § 203 of P.L. 94-103, 89 Stat. 504, an advocacy system that can pursue legal, administrative, and other appropriate remedies in order to protect and advocate the rights of developmentally disabled citizens. The most recent definition is the culmination of a long evolutionary process that began with Title I of the Mental Retardation Facilities and Community Mental Health Centers Construction Act of 1963, P.L. 88-164, 77 Stat. 282. This statute provided funds for a variety of research and service facilities for mental retardation. In 1967, the Mental Retardation Amendments of 1967, P.L. 90-170, 81 Stat. 527, expanded the range of services somewhat and increased the program funding, but retained the limitation on eligibility to the class of mentally retarded persons. However, with the enactment of the Developmental Disabilities Services and Facilities Construction Amendments of 1970, P.L. 91-517, 84 Stat. 1316, eligibility was expanded to a broader class, which was defined as follows:

> The term "developmental disability" means a disability attributable to mental retardation, cerebral palsy, epilepsy, or another neurological condition of an individual found by the Secretary to be closely related to mental retardation or to require treatment similar to that required for mentally retarded individuals, which disability originates before such individual attains age eighteen, which has continued or can be expected to continue indefinitely, and which constitutes a substantial handicap to such individual (§ 102(5), 84 Stat. 1325).

This provision, signifying expanded eligibility for federally funded services and facilities and end to the mental retardation monopoly on such services, was largely the result of vigorous lobbying on behalf of persons with cerebral palsy and epilepsy. In 1975, § 125 of the Developmentally Disabled Assistant and Bill of Rights Act, P.L. 94-103, 89 Stat. 497, expanded the definition again to the following formulation:

> The term "developmental disability" means a disability of a person which—
> (A) (i) is attributable to mental retardation, cerebral palsy, epilepsy, or autism;
> (ii) is attributable to any other condition of a person found to be closely related to mental retardation because such condition results in similar impairment of general intellectual functioning or adaptive behavior to that of mentally retarded persons or requires treatment and services similar to those required for such persons; or
> (iii) is attributable to dyslexia resulting from a disability described in clause (i) or (ii) of this subparagraph;
> (B) originates before such person attains age eighteen;
> (C) has continued or can be expected to continue indefinitely; and
> (D) constitutes a substantial handicap to such person's ability to function normally in society.

And, finally, the 1978 Act has expanded the definition once more.

2.   A major difference between the 1978 amendment and its predecessors is that it does not enumerate a list of specific impairments. The House version of the Bill had preserved such a listing approach, but the Senate's version of the Bill was ultimately adopted in a Joint Conference. The Joint Conference Report indicated, however, that the previously enumerated groups were not to be deprived of their eligibility:

> The conferees stress, however, that the definition agreed to is intended to cover everyone currently covered under the definition and is also intended to add other individuals with similar characteristics. In this definition, individuals with the conditions currently listed in the law—autism, cerebral palsy, dyslexia, epilepsy, or mental retardation—would be included if they meet the following criteria: manifestation prior to age 22, expectation of continuing indefinitely, substantial functional limitation, and need for multiple services for an extended period. It is not the intent to exclude anyone who legitimately should have been included under the definition in current law (Conference Report, 104-105).

3.   The definition of developmental disabilities requires substantial functional limitations in three or more areas of major life activity. The Rehabilitation Act definition (p. 25, *supra*) requires substantial limitation of one or more major life activities. Is there any cogent rationale for this difference? Notice also the difference in the areas of major life activity listed in the developmental disabilities definition and those listed in subsection (j) (2) (ii) of the DHEW Regulations (p. 27, *supra*).

4.   A reason for the age 22 limitation in the developmental disabilities definition (18 in preceding statutes) is presented in the Congressional finding that "individuals with disabilities occurring during their developmental period are more vulnerable and less able to reach an independent level of existence than other handicapped individuals who generally have had a normal developmental period on which to draw during the rehabilitation process" (P.L. 95-602, § 502, 92 Stat. 3004). Is such a rationale more defensible with an age 18 cutoff rather than the newly imposed age 22 limitation? Is there significant difference between a person who becomes handicapped at age 21 and one who becomes handicapped after the 22nd birthday?

5.   Is it reasonable to conclude that the newly developmental disabilities definition includes all persons whose handicaps are severe, so long as these conditions had their onset before age 22? Could not most severe handicapping conditions, of whatever sort, meet the standards of the other subsections of the definition?

E.   SPECIFIC CATEGORIES OF
CONDITIONS CONSIDERED HANDICAPS

Although there are terminological differences from state to state and in various pieces of federal legislation in enumerating and describing the particular conditions denominated "handicaps," there is a fair amount of common ground among most of the formulations. Drawing upon patterns to be found in the various statutory schemes, types of handicapping conditions recognized by legislatures, government agencies, and the courts generally tend to break down into the following categories: 1) hearing impairment, 2) visual impairment, 3) emotional disturbances and mental illness, 4) epilepsy, 5) mental retardation, 6) orthopedic and neuromotor handicaps, 7) speech impairment, 8) learning disabilities, 9) cosmetic disfigurements, and 10) other serious health impairments. The aim of this section is to discuss each of these categories and to give some general information about each, in the hope of giving the reader a very basic understanding of the meaning of, and distinctions among, various disabilities. For more detailed information about any particular impairment, professional expertise or literature should be consulted. Moreover, a great deal of information about particular handicaps can be obtained from consumer, parent, and professional organizations; for almost every major impairment, there are one or more organizations devoted to it. Many national organizations are mentioned in discussing the particular impairments, but the listing should be recognized as only a sampling of the national organizations that does not pretend to be comprehensive. Note should also be made that almost all of the national organizations have state and local chapters from which much information and assistance are available.

1. Hearing Impairment

Hearing impairment refers to any significant loss of hearing as indicated ontologically (by an ear specialist), audiometrically (as shown on an audiometer, an apparatus for measuring hearing), or functionally. The term is generally considered to include two subclassifications: deaf and hard of hearing. A person is ordinarily considered deaf when hearing loss is approximately 85 decibels (dB) or more when measured on an audiometer. Total deafness is quite rare. A person with a hearing loss of more than approximately 15 dB can be considered hard of hearing. However, although the identification of hearing loss should be established by means of audiometric evaluation that includes pure tone testing, speech reception thresholds, and speech discrimination tests, the most important, relevant assessment of hearing impairments is the manner in which a person functions in his or her daily life rather than a technical description or specification of the extent of hearing loss.

Hearing impairments may be of three types: sensorineural, conductive, or central. Conductive impairment is loss of hearing resulting from interruption of sound vibrations in the outer or middle ear before they reach the nerve endings in the inner ear. Sensorineural impairment results from a dysfunction of the inner ear or of the auditory nerve; the sound vibrations are conducted to the inner ear but the auditory messages are not transmitted properly to the brain. Central impairment refers to a dysfunction in the auditory pathways within the brain.

Some authorities break hearing impairment into five classifications according to degree: slight, mild, marked, severe, and profound. A person with a slight impairment may only have hearing difficulties in the discrimination of hearing faint sounds or distant speech or in difficult acoustic situations. An individual with mild impairment may have some difficulty in conversation, particularly if voices are faint or speakers are not close together; such an impairment may result in some defective speech patterns and vocabulary deficiencies. A person with a marked impairment will have difficulty in hearing speech in most circumstances and will misunderstand or fail to follow discussions; impaired usage of language and inappropriate articulation and voice tones will probably be exhibited. Severe impairment is characterized by inability to hear speech unless it is amplified but with ability to hear loud noises such as sirens or the honking of automobile horns; with this degree of hearing loss there will probably be a severe impairment of speech and language development. An individual with a profound impairment will generally be unable to hear speech even when amplified and usually will not develop any language ability in the absence of special training.

Causes of hearing impairments include measles, mumps, other infectious diseases, extremely loud noises, insertion of things into ears, rubella (German measles) or the taking of certain drugs during pregnancy, and some hereditary traits. Some examples of adaptive and rehabilitative techniques used by individuals with hearing impairments are hearing aids, sign language, speechreading (lipreading) interpreters, TTYs (teletypewriters, used for telephone communication by persons with hearing impairments), and "hearing ear dogs," which are trained to warn deaf people of important noises, such as doorbells, fire alarms, or sirens.

Additional information concerning deafness and impaired hearing can be obtained from the National Association of the Deaf, 814 Thayer Avenue, Silver Spring, MD 20910; the American Speech-Language-Hearing Association, 9030 Old Georgetown Road, Washington, D.C. 20014; the Deafness Research Foundation, 310 Lexington Avenue, New York, NY 10016; and the National Association of Hearing and Speech Agencies, 814 Thayer Avenue, Silver Spring, MD 20910.

2. Visual Impairment

Impaired vision is generally considered to embrace two subcategories: blindness and partial sightedness. For most legal purposes, blindness has been defined as a condition in which central visual acuity with correction is 20/200 or less in the better eye, or where the visual field has contracted so that its widest diameter is 20 degrees or less. Only a small percentage of blind persons have no vision whatsoever. A person is considered partially sighted if central visual acuity with correction falls between 20/70 and 20/200 in the better eye.

Visual impairments have a variety of causes including: accidents; glaucoma (buildup of fluid pressure inside the eye); cataracts (clouding of the lens of the eye); detached retina; infectious diseases, such as scarlet fever, small pox, and syphilis; rubella (German measles) during pregnancy; and, in some cases, hereditary conditions and other birth defects. Until recent years, two major causes of blindness in newborn children were conditions known as retrolental fibroplasia and ophthalmia neonatorum. Research has found that retrolental fibroplasia (formation of scar tissue in the lens) results from the excessive administration of oxygen during the neonatal period, and revised hospital nursery procedures have greatly reduced its incidence. Similarly, ophthalmia neonatorum, which is caused by the transmission to the infant of gonorrhea bacteria in the birth canal, has been significantly reduced by the practice of routinely putting silver nitrate in the eyes of newborns.

Some important adaptive methods for blind people include white canes and "seeing eye dogs" for assisting mobility, and the braille system of communication, based upon six raised dots that can be arranged into 63 combinations, for reading and writing. Further information about blindness can be obtained from the American Council of the Blind, Suite 506, 1211 Connecticut Avenue, N.W., Washington, D.C.

20036; the National Federation of the Blind, 1346 Connecticut Avenue, N.W., Washington, D.C. 20036; the American Foundation of the Blind, Inc., 15 West 16th Street, New York, NY 10011; National Association for the Visually Handicapped, 3201 Balboa Street, San Francisco, CA 94121; and the National Society for the Prevention of Blindness, Inc., 79 Madison Avenue, New York, NY 10016.

3. Emotional Disturbance and Mental Illness

The category of emotional disturbance and mental illness refers to disorders of the mental processes, usually evidenced by inappropriate behavior and inability to function normally in society. These disorders may be either organic or functional. Organic mental illnesses are those that are associated with some identifiable physical cause; "brain syndromes" such as delirium tremors, senility resulting from hardening of the arteries in the brain, or malfunctions resulting from brain tumors are conditions that involve some physical change in the brain structure.

Functional mental illnesses, on the other hand, cannot be pinned down to any actual organic cause, but are indicated by some abnormality in the way the individual thinks, communicates, or acts. Diagnosis of functional mental illness depends upon an assessment, usually by a psychiatrist, of the manner in which an individual's behavior deviates from what is generally expected for a person of similar age, sex, social background, and cultural group. Standards such as "deviance" and "abnormality" in examining behavioral patterns are obviously not totally objective and place a great deal of power in the discretion of psychiatrists. Some authorities have argued quite convincingly that the notion of functional mental disorders is simply a rationale for psychiatric tyranny in which, through the use of professional jargon and labels, psychiatrists are able to make judgments of other people's behavior based upon the psychiatrists' own moral values and prejudices, and that the whole mental health system is nothing other than a means for coercing people into social conformity.[aaa] Nonetheless, the concept of functional mental disorders has been generally accepted and is incorporated into many of our laws and social practices. Perhaps this acceptance is a result of the fact that, in spite of the cogent criticisms of the arbitrariness and subjectivity of psychiatric categories and the frequent ineffectiveness of psychiatric treatment, legislators and the general public want very much to believe that help is available for people who do not seem to be in touch with reality (the stereotypic example is the man who believes that he is Napoleon), or at least that such individuals can be taken away somewhere so that we "normal" people do not have to associate with them.

Psychiatrists tend to separate functional mental disorders into categories of psychophysiological reactions, psychoses, neuroses, and personality disorders. Psychophysiological (or, in more common terminology, psychosomatic) reactions refer to conditions in which an emotional disorder engenders physical symptoms, such as pain, cramps, muscle spasms, nausea, or vomiting, even though no actual physical disorder or illness can be found.

[aaa]E.g., Szasz, T., *The Myth of Mental Illness* (1961); Szasz, T., *The Manufacture of Madness: A Comparative Study of the Inquisition and the Mental Health Movement* (1970); Torrey, E., *The Death of Psychiatry* (1974); Hardisty, J., "Mental Illness: A Legal Fiction," 48 *Wash. L. Rev.* 735 (1973).

Psychoses are the most serious functional mental illnesses; they involve major emotional disorder with derangement of the personality and loss of contact with reality, often with delusions, hallucinations, or illusions. The most common type of psychosis is schizophrenia, which can be described as a split or incongruence between a person's intellect and feelings or moods. Other types of psychosis include paranoia (delusions of persecution or of grandeur) and schizoaffective reactions (greatly exaggerated swings in moods, e.g., manic-depressive).

Neurosis (sometimes called psychoneurosis) is the term used to describe an emotional disorder that can interfere with a person's ability to lead a normal, productive life, but which is less serious than psychosis. It is generally conceded that almost everyone has some tendencies that might be considered neuroses, but it is only when these tendencies tend to take over a person's entire personality that he or she is classified as a neurotic person. While a person suffering from psychosis has lost touch with reality, a neurotic individual is able to function in society, although perhaps with discomfort or with decreased efficiency. Conditions commonly labeled neuroses include depression (excessively deep and long-lasting depression), phobias (exaggerated fears, such as claustrophobia (fear of enclosed spaces) and acrophobia (fear of heights)), anxiety (extreme uneasiness without apparent reason), obsessive-compulsive neurosis (overwhelming intrusion of certain thoughts or desires in the mind coupled with an uncontrollable urge to act in certain patterns), and dissociative neurosis (conditions, such as amnesia and sleepwalking, in which parts of the personality and memory are cut off from each other).

The final category of mental illnesses is personality disorders. These are conditions that do not involve being out of touch with reality but occur when an individual's personality seems to differ significantly from the norm. Major personality disorders include psychopathy (conspicuous disregard for the rights or needs of others; predisposition to engage in criminal or antisocial conduct; absence of a "conscience"), sexual deviance, (divergence from societal norms of sexual behavior), passive-aggressive personality (expression of hostility or aggression in a passive manner), and cyclothymic personality (alternating moods of elation and dejection, but not to the extent of manic-depressive psychosis).

A more complete description of the numerous categories and subcategories of mental illness generally recognized by psychiatrists can be found in the *Diagnostic and Statistical Manual of Mental Disorders* prepared in 1968 by the Committee on Nomenclature and Statistics of the American Psychiatric Association. It should be remembered, however, that the elaborate classification systems and professional jargon frequently employed by psychiatrists assume an air of objective reality which some critics would challenge.

Treatments prescribed for mental illness include administration of drugs and dietary supplements, psychotherapy (where communication between the therapist and the patient is used as a means for understanding and modifying the patient's behavior), hypnosis, and various techniques of behavior modification. Sometimes extreme measures, such as shock therapy and psychosurgery, have been employed in attempts to treat mental illnesses.

There seems to be no meaningful distinction between the terms *mental illness* and *emotional disturbance*. It appears that there is some tendency to use the latter term more often in regard to children, particularly in educational contexts. Many school systems have classes for emotionally disturbed children; few call them classes for the mentally ill. The word *insanity* is a legal term; it is a broad and somewhat ambiguous concept that refers to unsoundness or derangement of the mind, without regard to its cause. Mental illnesses that are of sufficient severity to quality as insanity modify or abrogate the legal responsibility of the afflicted person. Insanity may be either temporary or permanent.

An important condition sometimes classified within the category of mental illnesses is autism. This condition, referred to by some psychiatrists as childhood schizophrenia, is characterized by extreme withdrawal and emotional isolation. Its onset is ordinarily during childhood, but autism is presently of unknown causation. Autistic persons seem to have a constantly functioning internal world that competes with the real world and often wins. Autistic children are unresponsive to external stimulation and usually seem to prefer proximal sensations (the sense of touch) to distal (hearing and vision). Sometimes autistic individuals engage in repetitive and self-destructive behavior patterns, such as rocking, head-banging, and self face-slapping. In recent years, some strides have been made through educational, behavior modification, dietary supplement, and other treatment programs for autism, but the underlying causes of the condition and a "cure" for it have yet to be discovered. Further information about autism can be obtained from the National Society for Autistic Children, Information and Referral Service, 306 31st Street, Huntington, WV 25702.

Additional information about other specific conditions, and mental illness and emotional disturbance in general can be obtained from the National Association for Mental Health, Inc., 1800 North Kent Street, Arlington, VA 22209; and the American Psychiatric Association, 1700 18th Street, N.W., Washington, D.C. 20009.

4. Epilepsy

Epilepsy refers to a chronic brain disorder that is characterized by recurrent seizures. A seizure is an abnormal electrical discharge by nerve cells in the brain. The effects of such electrical discharges may be very dramatic or relatively inconsequential, depending upon the number of nerve cells involved, the area of the brain in which they are located, and the length of time the discharge takes. With the most common types of seizures, the abnormal electrical discharge results in an interruption of consciousness and may also engender involuntary convulsive movements in the muscles.

Seizures can be of many different types; some of the most common categories are discussed below.

1. *Grand mal:* This type of seizure typically involves a sudden loss of consciousness, falling to the ground, a temporary interruption of breathing, and general convulsive or shaking movements. The person who has such a seizure may feel drowsy, confused, nauseous, or otherwise out of sorts afterward, or may show no aftereffects except for some muscle soreness as a result of the shaking. Grand mal seizures seldom last longer than 2 or 3 minutes. Some 80% of epileptic seizures are of the grand mal type.

2. *Petit mal:* This type of seizure can best be described as a temporary "blackout"—the person has a brief interruption of consciousness, typically from 5 to 30 seconds in duration. Although there is sometimes mild twitching of the facial or other muscles, the individual remains sitting or standing and seems to have undergone only a brief lapse of attention or a momentary period of absentmindedness or daydreaming. The individual who has a petit mal seizure usually does not recall that the seizure occurred. Petit mal seizures generally have their onset during childhood.

3. *Psychomotor:* This is a type of seizure with a relatively complex pattern of symptoms; it is believed to be linked to a disturbance in the temporal lobe of the brain. The psychomotor seizure usually begins with a period of clouded consciousness that may manifest itself as dizziness, seeing spots before the eyes, confusion, anger, ringing in the ears, fear, or a distorted sense of time, color perception, location, or self-identity. This is typically followed by the repeated performance of meaningless motions such as lip-smacking, chewing, rubbing or clapping hands, aimless walking, or pronounced inappropriate facial expressions. These purposeless motions are referred to as *automatisms.* Thereafter, the seizure may progress into a generalized convulsion, which is frequently followed by the individual falling asleep. Such seizures may be totally absent or vague, as if it had occurred in a dream.

4. *Jacksonian:* This type of seizure was named after John Hughlings Jackson, who was the first to describe it. It begins with an involuntary jerking motion in a specific group of muscles, commonly in the hand or toes, which lasts for a few seconds or minutes. This may be followed by the spreading (called Jacksonian march) of the convulsive movements to nearby parts of the body and then to the entire body, culminating in a grand mal seizure. Jacksonian seizures most often occur during adulthood.

Not all seizures are the result of epilepsy. Only those seizures that recur as a result of chronic brain disorder are considered epileptic. Thus, seizures caused by something external to the brain itself, such as hypoglycemia (low blood sugar), do not constitute epilepsy. Similarly, seizure conditions that are of temporary causation as, for example, febrile convulsions caused by high fever in young children, are not considered epilepsy.

About half of persons with epilepsy have an advance warning symptom, called an aura, which lets them know that a seizure is about to take place. The aura may consist of a tingling sensation, spots before the eyes, ringing in the ears, a sudden nauseous feeling, or any other sensation that repeatedly precedes an individual's seizure. Recognition of the aura can give a person with epilepsy an opportunity to move to a safe place, to lie down, or, in some instances, to try to forestall the seizure.

Many cases of epilepsy can be traced to brain injuries before or during birth, to brain tumors and abscesses, to nutritional deficiencies, fever, and certain diseases, to congenital disorders, and to head wounds. In a large number of other cases, however, the causes of epilepsy remain unknown.

Although epilepsy is not curable per se, tremendous advances have been made in its treatment by the proliferation of anticonvulsant drugs. With these drugs, about one-half of all persons with epilepsy are able to control their seizures completely, and another one-quarter have been able to reduce their seizures significantly.

Further information and a variety of publications about epilepsy can be obtained from the Epilepsy Foundation of America, 1828 L Street, N.W., Suite 406, Washington, D.C. 20036.

5. Mental Retardation

According to the generally recognized official definition, "mental retardation refers to significantly subaverage general intellectual functioning, existing concurrently with deficits in adaptive behavior, and manifested during the developmental period."[bbb] In simple terms, it can be described as an impairment of mental ability that results in a subnormal rate of learning and of adapting to the needs of everyday life. The label of mental retardation is only applied to impairments that occur during the developmental period; brain damage that results in similar impairment later in life is not considered mental retardation.

Before the 1970s mental retardation was viewed primarily in terms of an intellectual deficit, without regard to the level of adaptive behavior an individual exhibited. The level of intellectual functioning was (and frequently still is) measured by the score obtained on an intelligence quotient test, such as the Stanford-Binet or the Wechsler Intelligence Scale. IQ scores have also been used to divide mental retardation into subcategories by degree:

1. *Mild mental retardation:* Intelligence test scores range roughly between 2 and 3 standard deviations below the norm (a score of approximately 50–70).
2. *Moderate mental retardation:* Intelligence test scores range roughly between 3 and 4 standard deviations below the norm (a score of approximately 35–50).
3. *Severe mental retardation:* Intelligence test scores range roughly between 4 and 5 standard deviations below the norm (a score of approximately 20–35).
4. *Profound mental retardation:* Intelligence test scores are roughly more than 5 standard deviations below the norm (a score of approximately 20 or below).

It is estimated that approximately 85% of mentally retarded persons fall into the *mild* category.

Today, experts in the field of mental retardation recognize that IQ measurements are not an infallible criterion for assessing mental retardation. Of equal or perhaps greater importance is the determination of an individual's level of adaptive behavior. Adaptive behavior refers to the effectiveness or degree with which the individual can meet the standards of personal independence and social responsibility expected of his or her age, social, and cultural group. Since these expectations vary for different age groups, deficits in adaptive behavior will vary at different ages. For younger children, the adaptive behavior level is determined by a composite of measures that include the degree of self-sufficiency, sensorimotor development, language

---

[bbb]American Association on Mental Deficiency, *Manual on Terminology and Classification in Mental Retardation,* (Grossman, H., ed., 1974).

development, and socialization. For older children and adults, the adaptive behavior level is determined by the same composite of measures, augmented by measures of general domestic skills, vocational achievement, and sense of, or capability of handling, responsibility.

Unfortunately, in spite of recognition by almost all leading authorities that adaptive behavior is a key factor in evaluating mental retardation, some professionals have chosen, ostrich-like, to ignore these advances and to continue their mechanistic use of IQ tests as the sole instrument for identifying and classifying mental retardation.

Although many causative factors for mental retardation have been identified, the causes in many other cases remain unknown. The identified causes are of several types: genetic defects, prenatal damage to the fetus, injuries during the birth process (perinatal), and postnatal injuries. Two examples of genetic defects are Down's syndrome and phenylketonuria. Down's syndrome results from the presence of an extra chromosome (47 instead of 46). It is evidenced by a number of unusual physical and mental characteristics including a small flattened skull, a short, flat nose, unusual slanting of the eyes, a protruding, furrowed tongue, a short, thick neck, short broad hands with little fingers that curve inward, short, wide feet with a gap between the first and second toes, short stature, sparse hair, low voice pitch, below-average muscle tone, tendency to heart defects and respiratory disorders, and mental retardation. While persons with Down's syndrome exhibit a combination of several of these characteristics, it is rare for any one individual to exhibit all of them, and it is possible, although unusual, for an individual with Down's syndrome to have average or even superior intelligence. Phenylketonuria (PKU) is a hereditary defect that results in the inability of the body to properly metabolize a particular amino acid (phenylalanine). If untreated, the condition results in the buildup of this amino acid in the blood, which in turn causes damage to the brain resulting in mental retardation. PKU can be detected by a urine test in early infancy, and, although the condition is not curable, its damaging effects can be avoided by a special diet.

Prenatal causes of mental retardation include certain infectious diseases, including rubella (German measles), syphilis, or meningitis, contracted by the mother during pregnancy, excessive x-rays, especially during the first trimester, glandular disorders in the mother, poor prenatal care, nutritionally deficient diet, use of certain drugs during pregnancy, and damage to the fetus caused by accident or other physical injury during pregnancy. At the time of birth, mental retardation can result from lack of oxygen, prolonged labor, unusual stress, or physical injury to the fetus in the course of delivery. Premature birth has also been linked statistically to mental retardation. After birth, mental retardation may be brought about by serious injuries to the head, by metabolic disorders and glandular imbalances, by shock, by some childhood diseases, and by other serious illnesses such as encephalitis and meningitis. Mental retardation has also been linked to lack of infant stimulation, poor nutrition, inadequate medical care, cultural deprivation, and lower socioeconomic status.

Much progress has been made in the last decade in the development of educational and vocational programs designed to maximize the potential of mentally retarded persons and to enable them to be integrated into normal channels of society as much as possible. While isolation and segregation marked society's treatment of mentally retarded individuals in the past, normalization seems to be the trend of the present and the wave of the future. Additional information about mental retardation may be obtained from the National Association for Retarded Citizens, 2709 Avenue E East, P.O. Box 6109, Arlington, TX 76011; the American Association on Mental Deficiency, 5201 Connecticut Avenue, N.W., Washington, D.C. 20015; and the Joseph P. Kennedy, Jr., Foundation, 1701 K Street, N.W., Suite 205, Washington, D.C. 20006.

6. Orthopedic and Neuromotor Handicaps

The category of orthopedic and neuromotor handicaps refers to impairments of the bones, joints, muscles, and the motor (efferent) nerves, which transmit impulses from the brain and spinal cord to the muscles. Primarily, these impairments relate to the absence, improper structure, or limitations upon mobility of the limbs or digits. In terminology that is now considered outmoded, these were referred to as "crippling" disabilities. It is estimated that approximately one-half of these handicaps are the result of disease, one-third are caused by birth defects, and about one-sixth result from accidents. A variety of specific conditions are included in this general category, among which are the following:

1. *Paraplegia:* This term refers to paralysis or loss of use of both legs and frequently of the entire lower part of the body as well. It most often results from damage to the spinal cord. The paralysis may be accompanied by loss of feeling.
2. *Quadriplegia:* This condition consists of paralysis or loss of use of all the limbs of the body, frequently accompanied by loss of sensation. Quadriplegia usually is the result of damage to the spinal cord in the area of the upper vertebrae of the spine.
3. *Cerebral palsy:* This term encompasses a variety of impairments of motor skills and posture resulting from a nonprogressive defect or damage of the brain. Ordinarily, it is limited to brain injuries that occur very early in life, because the impact of these injuries on the immature brain, which has not yet mastered the complex nervous system functions involved in walking, speech, posture, and fine motor coordination, creates quite different problems than the same brain injuries to older individuals. Cerebral palsy is frequently divided into three categories: a) the spastic type, which is characterized by spasms or tightening of the muscles and exaggerated stretch reflexes, b) the athetoid type, which refers to uncontrolled movements and purposeless muscle tension, and c) the atactic type, characterized by a staggering gait with poor balance and coordination. In many instances, persons with cerebral palsy will exhibit speech impediments.
4. *Poliomyelitis:* This acute, contagious, viral disease, also called infantile paralysis or polio, was, until largely eradicated by widespread immunization with Salk and Sabin vaccines, a major cause of permanent paralysis in this country. Although only approximately one-fourth of polio victims suffer any permanent disability, epidemics of the disease, particularly in the late 1940s, resulted in many cases of motor paralysis and atrophy of skeletal muscles.
5. *Muscular dystrophy:* This term refers to a group of related muscle diseases, which are characterized by a progressive weakening and atrophy of the muscles.

The muscles are deprived of vital protein, and the muscle fibers are gradually replaced by fat and connective tissue; the word *dystrophy* means imperfect nutrition. Although not all forms of the disease are fatal, childhood muscular dystrophy, the most common form of the disease, usually results in death before the age of 20. In later stages of the disease, the voluntary muscle system becomes virtually useless. Muscular dystrophy is believed to be hereditary, at least to some degree.

6. *Multiple sclerosis:* This condition is a chronic disease characterized by the formation of patches of hardened tissue in the brain and spinal cord, which interfere with the nerve pathways in those areas. Although commonly associated with paralysis and jerking muscle tremors, the effects of multiple sclerosis vary with the portions of nervous system affected. The course of the disease varies from individual to individual; frequently, periods of improvement in condition alternate with periods of exacerbation. Visual impairments, shaking of the limbs, fatigue, speech defects, loss of balance, paralysis, and loss of bowel control are among the symptoms that can occur. Exacerbation of the disease often seems to be accelerated by other illnesses or emotional problems.

7. *Spina bifida:* The Latin words mean "a spine that is split into two parts." They refer to a birth defect that consists of a gap or improper opening between the vertebrae of the spinal column. In severe cases the spinal cord and its surrounding membranes may protrude through the gap. The resulting injuries to the spinal cord can cause permanent paralysis, loss of sensation, and loss of bowel and bladder control. Medical science has made some advances in surgical techniques for successfully closing such spinal gaps.

8. *Congenital absence, incompleteness, or malformation of limbs:* These defects are the result of imperfect formation of the body during the fetal period. Well publicized examples of such congenital defects were the children both without arms or legs, after their mothers had taken the drug thalidomide early in pregnancy. In other cases, overexposure of the developing embryo to x-rays is believed to have caused such abnormal limb formation. The causation of many other instances of congenital defects is not as clearly understood.

9. *Arthritic handicaps:* The term *arthritis* encompasses more than 100 types of diseases of the joints. These diseases are one of the chief causes of chronic disability in the United States today. Arthritis is characterized by pain, stiffness, and inflammation in the affected joints. Severe forms of arthritis may result in permanent deformity and immobility of joints. In approximately 15% of the cases of rheumatoid arthritis, the most common form of arthritis, some permanent stiffness results from the fusion of bone surfaces. There is presently no cure available for this and other common types of arthritis, although proper diagnosis and treatment can generally help to reduce the pain and lessen the chances of permanent deformities.

10. *Amputation:* This term refers to the removal of a limb or other bodily appendage. It is sometimes the direct result of a serious automobile, railroad, industrial, or wartime accident; at other times, it may be medically necessary to perform surgical amputation after irreparable injury to a limb. Gangrene, infections, and

cancer sometimes necessitate such measures. The greatest percentage of leg amputations are the result of blood vessel disorders, such as arteriosclerosis (hardening of the arteries). In addition to direct physical consequences, amputations frequently have a major psychological impact on the amputee. Proper preparation whenever possible before an amputation and a good program of rehabilitation afterward are important to help ease emotional difficulties.

11. *Dwarfism:* This condition consists of a significant underdevelopment of the body. It may result from abnormal fetal development, hormonal irregularities, nutritional deficiencies, or other disorders occurring during the growth process. The proportions of head, trunk, and limbs may be either normal or abnormal. One major form of dwarfism, achondroplasia, is a disorder of cartilage formation in the embryo which affects the growth of the bones. An achondroplastic dwarf usually has a normal size trunk but a disproportionately large head and unusually small limbs.

This list of impairments is not intended to be exclusive; other causes of neuromotor and orthopedic handicaps include Parkinson's disease, injuries during the birth process, amyotrophic lateral sclerosis (progressive degeneration of nerve cells and hardening of areas in the spinal cord resulting in a loss of nourishment to the muscles, also called Lou Gehrig's disease), myasthenia gravis (chronic disease of muscular weakness), hunchbacking conditions, osteomyelitis, tumors, meningitis, some forms of diabetes, veneral diseases, and many others. Nor are the enumerated conditions all truly distinct categories. Some, such as quadriplegia, paraplegia, and amputation, are descriptive of the physical results of some other causative condition. Others, such as poliomyelitis and arthritis, do not actually address the specific effects, but are, rather, the diseases that cause the orthopedic and neuromotor handicaps. And still other categories, such as cerebral palsy, muscular dystrophy, and multiple sclerosis, are syndromes—complex combinations of symptoms frequently occurring together and having a common causation. As a result, there is some overlap in the categories. Spina bifida, cerebral palsy, and polio can, for example, all result in paraplegia. Nonetheless, this list of conditions can be useful to the legal advocate, because these are among the most common subcategories of neuromotor and orthopedic handicaps envisaged in statutes and regulations and in everyday usage.

Important devices and techniques for dealing with various orthopedic and neuromotor handicaps include wheelchairs, canes, crutches, walkers, prosthetic devices (artificial body parts), ramps, specially adapted automobile controls, and many others. More information about orthopedic and neuromotor handicapping conditions can be obtained from the National Association of the Physically Handicapped, 12614 Flack Street, Wheaton, MD 20906; the Paralyzed Veterans of America, 4330 East West Highway, Suite 300, Washington, D.C. 20014; the American Orthotic and Prosthetic Association, 1440 N Street, N.W., Washington, D.C. 20005; the National Paraplegia Foundation, 333 North Michigan Avenue, Chicago, IL 60601; the United Cerebral Palsy Associations, 66 East 34th Street, New York, NY 10016; the Muscular Dystrophy Associations of America, 810 Seventh Avenue, New York, NY 10019; the National Multiple Sclerosis Society, 257 Park Avenue South, New York, NY 10010;

the Arthritis Foundation, 1212 Avenue of the Americas, New York, NY 10036; the National Amputation Foundation, 1245 150th Street, Whitestone, Long Island, NY 11357; the National Congress of Organizations of the Physically Handicapped, Inc., 7611 Oakland Avenue, Minneapolis, MN 55423; the National Easter Seal Society for Crippled Children and Adults, 2023 West Ogden Avenue, Chicago, IL 60612; Little People of America, Box 126, Owatonna, MN 55060; the Amyotrophic Lateral Sclerosis Society of America, 12011 San Vicente Blvd., P.O. Box 49001, Los Angeles, CA 90049; and the Myasthenia Gravis Foundation, 2 E. 103rd Street, New York, NY 10029.

7. Speech Impairment

Speaking is a very complex phenomenon. In addition to the complicated mental process involved, the uttering of a single word requires the use of over 100 muscles. Given this complexity, it is not surprising that 1 of every 20 persons reaches adulthood with a significant speech disorder. The causes of these speech impairments may be physical or they may be psychological and mental.

Cleft palate (split in the roof of the mouth) and cleft lip (split in the lip) result from failure of the tissue of the face to join properly in the early stages of fetal development. These defects may be of greater or less degree and, if untreated, they may have a correspondingly more or less severe impact on the individual's speech. Both cleft lip and cleft palate can usually be corrected by plastic surgery at an early age, and, if they are successfully corrected, there may be minimal interference with the development of normal speech. *Tongue-tie* refers to the presence of an abnormally short membrane extending from the underside of the tongue to the floor of the mouth. If not treated, tongue-tie may result in lisping or other speech impediment; fortunately, however, the condition is easily correctable by simple surgery to cut the confining membrane. Speech impairments may also result from malformations in the nasal passages, throat, larynx, and other parts of body involved in the process of speaking. Many of these defects are susceptible to surgical treatment. Poor alignment of the teeth may result in some impairment of speech. Speech may also be impaired by damage to speech centers in the brain by conditions like multiple sclerosis, syphilis, and Parkinson's disease.

In many cases, speech impairments are a secondary effect of hearing impairments. For a child who is unable to hear speech properly, it may be well nigh impossible to do the imitating of sounds that is integral to ordinary methods by which infants learn to talk. In such cases, a program by a speech therapist may be able to teach the individual to speak.

Other types of speech impairments appear to be mental or psychological in origin. Stuttering is a form of speech impediment characterized by the repetition of syllables or words, prolongation of sounds, and unduly prolonged pauses. It often involves the involuntary repetition of one sound with the apparent inability to pass on to the next sounds. Stuttering may have many causes, but some theorists trace many cases to emotional problems growing out of feelings of insecurity. Moreover, the condition may become habitual and persist long after the original cause has ceased to exist.

Aphasia is a severe communication disorder involving a disturbance of the ability to comprehend and express speech. Expressive aphasia refers to inability to speak even though the individual hears and understands things spoken to him or her and has sufficient intelligence, language skills, and control of speech muscles. Receptive aphasia refers to lack of understanding of speech and language of others as well as inability to express oneself through speaking. The person with receptive aphasia cannot use and understand speech, whether as the speaker or the one spoken to; a person with expressive aphasia can understand speech and speech concepts but cannot express himself or herself verbally. Ataxic aphasia is a form of expressive aphasia in which the individual even chooses the words to speak but is unable to verbalize them.

Some other important terms relating to speech impairments include *muteness* and *lisping*. Muteness or mutism refers to inability or refusal to speak. Most muteness is related to deafness, although in some cases it can result from damage to or removal of voice organs. Lisping refers to an inability to correctly pronounce the *s* and *z* and related sounds, frequently by giving them a *th* sound. The causes of lisping may be mechanical or psychological.

Additional information about speech impairments may be obtained from the American Speech-Language-Hearing Association, 9030 Old Georgetown Road, Washington, DC 20014; and the National Association of Hearing and Speech Agencies, 814 Thayer Avenue, Silver Spring, MD 20910.

8. Learning Disabilities

A learning disability (often referred to as a specific learning disability) is a disorder in one or more of the basic psychological processes involved in understanding or using spoken or written language. Such a disability is usually manifested by a significant discrepancy between intellectual ability and actual achievement in any of the areas of listening, thinking, speaking, reading, writing, spelling, or performing arithmetic computations. However, learning problems attributable primarily to visual, hearing, or motor handicaps, to mental retardation or emotional disturbance, or to environmental, cultural, or economic disadvantages are not considered learning disabilities. Some authorities, primarily physicians, have argued that the learning disabilities category should be limited to those conditions in which an organic cause of brain dysfunction can be demonstrated, but the term is generally accepted to apply to such learning disorders even when the causation is unknown.

Examples of learning disabilities include perceptual handicaps, brain injuries, minimal brain dysfunction (apparent malfunction of brain without evidence of specific cause), dyslexia (impairment of ability to read, sometimes manifested by reversal of letters or the order of letters), hyperactivity (excessive activity; severe inability to sit still), and hypoactivity (extreme lack of physical activity). Aphasia, discussed above as a hearing impairment, which occurs in childhood, is referred to as developmental aphasia and is classified as a learning disability.

A person with a learning disability is not impaired in general intelligence and may do quite well in areas not affected by the learning disability. For example, a person with a learning disability affecting mathematical computations might flunk mathematics courses but get high grades in all other classes.

Many advances have been made in educational programs, special diets, drug treatment, and other methods for dealing with learning disabilities. More information about learning disabilities can be obtained from the Association for Children with Learning Disabilities, 2200 Brownsville Road, Pittsburgh, PA 15210.

9. Cosmetic Disfigurement

This category does not refer to any functional disability or inherent limitation upon activities but rather to significant impairments of bodily appearance. The examples of cosmetic disfigurement that most easily come to mind are facial disfigurements—scars, structural malformations, and other facial distortions. In our society, geared to images of superficial physical attractiveness, such facial imperfections, and disfigurements of other parts of the body as well, can operate as significant barriers to social acceptance and vocational progress and can be the source of serious psychological problems.

The impairments may be present at birth, or result from automobile and other accidents, from burns, from acts of violence and war, from diseases such as smallpox, and from many other causes. Recently, mastectomy, the surgical removal of the breast, frequently performed in treatment of cases of breast cancer, has been the subject of much publicity and increased public concern.

Advances in the techniques of plastic surgery have made it possible to correct many instances of cosmetic disfigurement. Further information about some types of cosmetic disfigurement can be obtained from the Society for the Rehabilitation of the Facially Disfigured, Inc., 550 First Avenue, New York, NY 10016; and, in regard to mastectomy, from Reach to Recovery, 777 Third Avenue, New York, NY 10017.

10. Other Serious Health Impairments

This final category, other serious health impairments, includes miscellaneous conditions that do not readily fit into any of the other categories but that are substantial impairments to a person's health and may have significant ramifications in regard to a person's activities, job capabilities, or attitudes of other persons. In general, these are not short term illnesses but, rather, are prolonged or chronic conditions. It is impossible, short of producing a medical encyclopedia, to provide a detailed list of all such conditions here. However, a list is provided of some of the most common categories of these conditions along with specific examples of particular ailments included.

A major category deals with diseases of the heart, blood, and blood vessels. Heart disease is one of the leading causes of deaths in the United States, and it has been estimated that approximately 10% of our working population is afflicted with heart disease. A closely related condition is significantly high or low blood pressure. Diseases of the blood and blood vessels include arteriosclerosis (hardening of the arteries), phlebitis (inflammation of a vein), and hemophilia (hereditary, impaired clotting ability of the blood).

Respiratory diseases and impairments include asthma (a chronic disease of the bronchial passages, characterized by difficult breathing, wheezing, and feeling of constriction in the chest cavity, often caused by allergy), chronic pulmonary emphysema (a lung disease in which the bronchial terminals become plugged with mucus), tuberculosis (an infectious lung disease), and chronic bronchitis (a lung disease that results in shortness of breath and coughing and can result in infection of the bronchial tubes).

Abdominal, genitourinary, and gastrointestinal disorders include such things as ulcers, hernia, renal (kidney) diseases, disorders of the liver, diabetes (a disturbance in the body's insulin mechanism resulting in a disorder of carbohydrate metabolism), and disorders resulting in colostomy (surgical creation of an artifical opening on the surface of the abdomen for the purpose of evacuating the bowels).

Generalized disorders are those that are not limited to a single organ or system. Some examples are cancer, cystic fibrosis (hereditary condition characterized by accummulation of exceedingly thick mucus and abnormal production of saliva and sweat, often causing infections and interfering with digestion), leukemia (malignant disease of bone marrow, spleen, and lymph nodes), venereal diseases, and Hodgkin's disease (a progressive, usually fatal disorder of the spleen and lymphatic system that often begins in the neck and spreads through the body).

Further information about some of these particular conditions can be obtained from the American Heart Association, 7320 Greenville Avenue, Dallas, TX 75231; the American Cancer Society, 777 Third Avenue, New York, NY 10017; the United Cancer Council, 1803 N. Meridian Street, Indianapolis, IN 46202; the American Diabetes Association, 600 Fifth Avenue, New York, NY 10020; the International Cystic Fibrosis Association, 521 Fifth Avenue, New York, NY 10017; the Leukemia Society of America, 211 E. 43rd Street, New York, NY 10017; the National Kidney Foundation, 342 Madison Avenue, New York, NY 10017; and the National Tuberculosis and Respiratory Disease Association, 1740 Broadway, New York, NY 10019.

F. EVOLUTION OF AND PREFERENCES AMONG LABELS

The development of terminology applied to handicaps has tended to follow an evolutionary pattern. New terms are selected, generally from medical or social science, to describe a particular condition; the innovative terminology is often acclaimed as the ultimate, precise, scientific name for the condition. The new term is introduced into the vocabulary of the leading professionals and gradually is absorbed into general usage. Over the course of many years, the term becomes associated with social stereotypes and acquires derogatory connotations. Eventually, it is replaced by a new term, which does not yet have any such negative implications, and the process begins all over again.

As an example, mentally retarded persons were called *feeble-minded* in the early decades of this century. In law and in common usage, these *feeble-minded* people were divided into three subclasses: *idiots, morons,* and *imbeciles.* This terminology eventually became undesirable because the stereotypic images and social opprobrium associated with them were undermined by advances in knowledge about mental retardation. In an effort to clear the slate and employ neutral and precise terminology, the feeble-minded became *mentally deficient,* and categories of *educable, trainable,* and *subtrainable* replaced *idiots, morons,* and *imbeciles.* Another turn of this terminological wheel found the *educable, trainable,* and *subtrainable* classifications of *mental deficiency* in need of replacement because of the negative connotations these terms had acquired. The result was the currently acceptable formulation: *mental retardation* encompassing subcategories of *mild, moderate, severe,* and *profound.* Indications are that the evolution of these terms is far from completed. Already some authorities have begun to offer substitutes for the *mental retardation* phraseology, some of the suggested replacements being *delayed persons, exceptional persons,* and *individuals with special needs.* There is little doubt that these new labels will eventually pick up their own negative connotations and inaccurate stereotypes. In fact, in Massachusetts, a state which has already adopted the phraseology of *children with special needs* in relation to special education programs, there were already reports of school children referring to their handicapped classmates as "those special needs kids."

Similar patterns could be traced in the evolution of the terms *madness, lunacy,* and *mania* to *mental illness,* in the replacement of the terms *the lame and the halt* by *cripples,* and then by *orthopedically handicapped* or *mobility impaired,* and in the substitution of concepts of *handicapped* and *disabled* for *afflicted* and *defective.*

The fact that these changes of nomenclature are cyclical and apparently interminable does not imply that they are meaningless exercises. With each change of terminology some obsolete images and inaccurate connotations may be laid to rest forever. In the mental retardation example, for instance, the educable/trainable/subtrainable phraseology overthrew stereotypes of inability to learn, which had become associated with the idiot/moron/imbecile formulations. Unfortunately, this new phraseology was eventually interpreted to mean that those below the educable level could not benefit from education, and it was partially to remedy this negative implication that the educable/trainable/subtrainable formulation had to be discarded. Similarly, the terms *mental deficiency* suggest a permanent limitation on mental capacity. *Retardation,* which signifies a holding back or slower rate of progress, was chosen as a linguistic repudiation of the *deficiency* concept. Likewise, the formulation, *mental illness* undercut the notions of permanence and intrinsic abnormality, which inhered in the *maniac* terminology. And modern formulations have discarded the logic underlying the selection of the word *cripple,* which has its derivation from the root "to creep"; with its demise went the image of a helpless individual crawling and dragging himself or herself along the ground. Thus, this continuous replenishing and replacing of the terminology applied to handicapping conditions has very positive value as a means for sorting out and discarding obsolete and inaccurate images and derogatory implications that have come to be associated with certain words.

The process places a definite burden on advocates and others who deal with handicapped persons to keep up to date in regard to currently acceptable terminology. It is the aim of this section to give some guidance as to choices of terms that are generally accepted today. It should be borne in mind, however, that terminology that is in vogue today will probably sooner or later fall out of favor. Moreover, even at a single point in time, there is no unanimity among handicapped individuals as to what terms they prefer. Occasionally someone will choose to use admittedly obsolete terminology for its shock value, as in the case of the handicapped law professor who penned a law review article with a title beginning " 'Crips' Unite. . . . "[ccc] The best that

---

[ccc] Achtenberg, J., "Crips' Unite to Enfore Symbolic Laws: Legal Aid for the Disabled: An Overview," 4 *San Fernando Valley L. Rev.* 161 (1975).

can be done here is to discuss those terms that are *generally* accepted today and to caution the reader that particular individuals or organizations may disagree and, in any event, there is no guarantee that presently accepted terms will not be repudiated tomorrow.

One general principle in this area concerns the grammatical usage made of handicapping conditions. The use of a handicapping condition as a collective noun, as *the handicapped, the deaf,* or *the mentally retarded,* or as an ordinary noun describing a person, as *an epileptic,* is generally disfavored by handicapped persons and their advocates. The reasoning is that such formulations tend to imply that all persons having the same disability are alike and that such persons form a distinct group which is different from the rest of society. Adjectival or prepositional phraseology, such as *handicapped people, deaf persons, mentally retarded citizens, persons with epilepsy,* and *individuals with handicapping conditions,* is preferred. In these latter formulations, the words *person, individual,* and *citizen,* are believed to stress the common status of personhood or citizenship that handicapped persons share with others, rather than the ways in which they are different.[ddd]

Another verbal trap to beware of is the patronizing use of the word *our,* as in *our handicapped citizens* or *our disabled Americans.* Such phraseology is generally considered to be unnecessarily paternalistic and demeaning and should be avoided.

In addition to these two general principles, the remaining recommendations concerning use of terminology deal with the preference of particular terms over other less desirable terms. For the sake of brevity and clarity, these terminological preferences are presented in Table 1. These guidelines are only of *general* acceptance, and some individuals or groups may disagree with them; moreover, the currently acceptable terms may become obsolete in the future. Lest it be thought that all of this concern over choices of terms is merely fruitless quibbling, please recall that many other social movements, including those by blacks, women, native Americans, and other minority groups, have had their terminological battlefields. The power of words to affect people's lives by subtly influencing their conceptions of reality, emotional associations, and self-concepts should not be underestimated. Handicapped persons have become very militant about the terms applied to them, and it behooves their advocates and friends to attempt to be sensitive to the preferred choices of terminology.

G. SOURCES OF THE LEGAL RIGHTS MOVEMENT OF HANDICAPPED PEOPLE

The consequences of being assigned the label *handicapped,* or of one of the particular conditions considered handicaps, are significant. These effects are both attitudinal and

---

[ddd]As stated in a book on epilepsy: ". . . in order not to differentiate people with epilepsy from other people, many authorities prefer to say 'a person with epilepsy'—not 'an epileptic.' Calling a person an epileptic tends to equate him with only one of his characteristics. A person with epilepsy may also be a teacher, an athlete, a movie star, a sports fan, a music lover, an expert cook. An individual is not exclusively any one of the things he has or the things he does; he is all of them, and more. He is, above all, a person." Sands, H., and Minters, F., *The Epilepsy Fact Book* 48–49 (1977).

Table 1.   Terminology for handicapping conditions

Currently acceptable terminology	Obsolete, frowned upon terminology
Mentally retarded person	Mentally deficient; retardate; an MR, feeble-minded; retard
Mildly mentally retarded	Educable mentally retarded or EMR
Moderately mentally retarded	Trainable mentally retarded or TMR
Severely or profoundly mentally retarded	Subtrainable mentally retarded
(Now classified as normal)	Borderline mentally retarded
Down's syndrome	Mongolism; mongoloid
Seizure	Fit
Mute	Dumb
Deaf	Deaf when pronounced deef
Mental illness; emotional disturbance	Lunacy; deranged; maniac; crazy
Orthopedically handicapped; neuromotor impairment; mobility impaired	Cripple; gimp; the lame and the halt
Cleft lip	Harelip
Little people	Midgets
(Modern technology has invalidated these concepts so there are no corresponding terms)	Vegetable; basket case; "gork"

substantive. One attitudinal ramification is an uneasiness or reticence of nonhandicapped people to interact with persons who have a handicap. Discomfort or embarrassment on the part of those with whom he or she comes into contact is an everyday occurrence of many handicapped people: "He does not even possess the sense of being actively hated or feared by society, for society is merely made somewhat uncomfortable by his presence."[eee] This attitude has been exemplified in the report of one handicapped author that his own lawyer, representing him in a personal injury suit growing out of the injury that had disabled him, was terribly reluctant to associate with him and, even during trial, actively avoided having lunch with him.[fff]

Closely related to this discomfort or uneasiness on the part of nonhandicapped individuals is the concept of stigma attached to a handicap. A handicapping condition is frequently, albeit illogically, viewed as a blameworthy characteristic or a badge of disgrace. One author has observed that being labeled as having a handicap, *mental retardation* for example, is "to be burdened by a shattering stigma, . . . the ultimate horror."[ggg] A federal court has noted that stigmatization can be likened to a "sentence of death,"[hhh] and handicapped persons have described their "guilt" over their condi-

---

[eee]Kreigel, L., "Uncle Tom and Tiny Tim: Some Reflections on the Cripple as Negro," 38 *Am. Scholar* 412, 413 (1969).

[fff]Achtenberg, J., n. ccc, *supra*, at 178, n. 46.

[ggg]Edgerton, R., *The Cloak of Competence* 205–206 (1967).

[hhh]*Pennsylvania Association for Retarded Children* v. *Commonwealth of Pennsylvania*, 343 F.Supp. 279, 292 (E.D.Pa. 1972).

tion.[iii] According to many sociologists and educators, the major problem faced by handicapped persons is learning to deal with and manage this stigma.[jjj]

Another attitudinal result of being labeled *handicapped* is the process of stereotyping. Frequently the label of *handicapped* conjures up an image, and nonhandicapped persons often relate to this stereotypic image more readily than to the flesh and blood individuals with whom they come into contact. The stereotypes can take a number of different forms; the handicapped person may be viewed as subhuman, as childlike, as an object of disgust, as a threat or menace, or as a helpless supplicant for pity and charity. Whatever the particular image, these caricatures of human beings are substituted for the real thing. One physically handicapped person has described his awakening to the fact that a companion grasped only the mask of handicap and not his individual personality and characteristics: "And so I learned that I existed for him as an abstraction, that he saw me as if I, too, were smoke he was blowing through his nostrils. . . . He knew what I 'should do' because he possessed two good legs and I didn't."[kkk]

A particularly damaging aspect of these attitudes of discomfort, stigma, and stereotyping toward handicapped persons is that they have an impact upon the handicapped individual's self-conception and expectations:

> He is expected to behave in such-and-such a way; he is expected to react in the following manner to the following stimulus. And since that which expects such behavior is that which provides the stimulus, his behavior is all too often Pavlovian. He reacts as he is expected to react because he does not really accept the idea that he can react in any other way. Once he accepts, however unconsciously, the images of self that his society presents him, then the guidelines for his behavior are clear-cut and consistent.[lll]

This phenomenon has been termed "playing the disabled role,"[mmm] and the pattern involved is characterized in the following example:

> If people see a person with dark glasses and a white cane, they are more careful in how they walk near him and may offer him help in crossing a street. He may accept, despite a lack of need, because he has found that people respond more pleasantly when he lets them lead him than when he refuses their offer. His family and friends may assume that he will never be self-supporting and never marry and his attempts at courtship and independence may be rebuffed by others who can't see his competencies, only his disability. In such an instance, the social group has defined the role blind person as one similar to that of a child, and the result may be childlike role behavior, that is, withdrawal into a comfortable dependency on his parents and friends.[nnn]

This impact of the "self-fulfilling prophecy" has been substantiated in sociological

---

[iii]E.g., Kriegel, L., n. eee, *supra,* at 420.

[jjj]Bartel, N., and Guskin, S., "A Handicap as a Social Phenomenon," *Psychology of Exceptional Children and Youth* 75, 94 (Cruickshank, W., ed., 1975); Goffman, E., *Stigma: Notes on the Management of Spoiled Identity* (1963).

[kkk]Kriegel, L., footnote eee, *supra,* at 429.

[lll]*Ibid.,* at 42.

[mmm]Bartel, N., and Guskin, S., footnote jjj, *supra,* at 92.

[nnn]*Ibid.* at 87.

and educational studies.[ooo] The imposition of an unfavorable label reinforces a person's feelings of insecurity and negative self-concepts, tends to cause behavior to conform to role expectations, and results in a situation in which the individual shortchanges his or her own potential as a result of being pigeonholed by others.

This has been only the briefest overview of some of the complex attitudinal effects of handicapping conditions. It is clear, however, that these attitudes and prejudices toward handicapped persons constitute a substantial impediment to the achievement of normal relationships and positive self-conceptions by handicapped individuals. And these attitudinal barriers have led, in turn, to more substantive ramifications in societal treatment of handicapped persons.

The history of society's formal methods for dealing with handicapped people can be summed up in two words: segregation and inequality. Individuals with handicapping conditions have faced an almost universal conspiracy to shunt them aside from the mainstream of society and to deny them an equal share of benefits and opportunities available to others. The historical origins of such practices and a brief overview of the scope of such discriminatory treatment is traced in R. Burgdorf and M. Burgdorf, "A History of Unequal Treatment: The Qualifications of Handicapped Persons as a 'Suspect Class' under the Equal Protection Clause," 15 *Santa Clara Lawyer* 855 (1975). More in-depth analysis, however, of the particular types of segregation and areas of disparate treatment to which handicapped people have been subjected is the topic of the remainder of this book. The emerging legal rights of handicapped individuals have been in direct response to spheres and facets of life where they have hitherto been shortchanged. That these areas of unequal treatment of handicapped citizens are pervasive is made evident simply by noting the chapter headings of this book and realizing that the rights and issues listed affect almost every aspect of American life. At every juncture, the handicapped person has met with attempts to "push" him or her aside and to withhold that which is taken for granted by other persons.

For many years, this unfortunate situation was merely endured; more recently, it has been challenged in individuals' own consciousnesses, in the media, and, most notably, in the courts. The emergence of a legal advocacy movement for and of handicapped people has been a major motivating force in a significant reformation of attitudes toward, and in opportunities available to, handicapped persons.

The beginning of the 1950s marked the founding of many of the national organizations concerned with various handicapping conditions, although a few had been in existence and active earlier. During the next two decades these organizations went through a transition from informal gatherings where common experiences were shared,[ppp] to more organized attempts to obtain charity for their constituents, to for-

---

[ooo]*Ibid.* at 87–93; Rosenthal, R., and Jacobson, L., *Pygmalion in the Classroom: Teacher Expectation and Pupils' Intellectual Development* (1968); Rosenthal, R., "Teacher Expectations for the Disadvantaged," 218 *Scientific American* 19 (1968).

[ppp]It has been reported, for example, that in 1940 an ad placed in the *New York Times* stated: "I have a cerebral palsied child; if you have one, contact me." A meeting of those responding led to the formation of the New York Cerebral Palsy Association and ultimately to the national United Cerebral Palsy Associations.

malized national organizations that engaged in large-scale lobbying efforts to pass beneficial legislation. However, the goals of some of these organizations were frustrated when laws on the books were not enforced. Impressed by the efforts of the black civil rights movement, which proved that a minority could use the courts to raise societal consciousness and to secure the rights of its members, and reinforced by scientific and educational data that showed the reasons given for much discrimination against handicapped people to be groundless, advocates for handicapped people began to take their case to court in the early 1970s.

The start of this litigative movement is often attributed to the *Pennsylvania Association for Retarded Citizens* v. *Commonwealth of Pennsylvania*[qqq] case, which was filed on January 7, 1971. Actually, there had been a number of lawsuits filed by handicapped persons before that time, as some of the cases presented in subsequent chapters make clear. The *PARC* case is notable, however, because it was a major, statewide class action supported by a state organization, and because the publicity surrounding it placed in the public eye, for the first time, the notion that the courts could be used to secure constitutional and statutory rights for handicapped persons. After one day of testimony by expert witnesses for the plaintiffs, the case was settled by a consent order which afforded plaintiffs most of the relief they had demanded. Buoyed by this success, other advocates for handicapped people began filing lawsuits around the country. The resulting surge of litigative activity has continued to build throughout the 1970s and has produced a plethora of judicial decisions, the majority of which have been favorable to the interests of handicapped litigants. It is the aim of this book to distill the emerging legal principles from this still-bubbling cauldron of litigative activity and to suggest some likely trends in the future direction of this legal rights movement for handicapped people.

[qqq]See pp. 75–90, *infra*.

2

EQUAL EDUCATIONAL OPPORTUNITY

Robert L. Burgdorf, Jr., and Donald N. Bersoff

A. THE NATURE AND SOURCES OF THE PROBLEM

BURGDORF, M., AND BURGDORF, R., "UNEQUAL TREATMENT OF HANDICAPPED PERSONS BY PUBLIC EDUCATIONAL SYSTEMS"

Part B of "A History of Unequal Treatment: The Qualifications of Handicapped Persons as a 'Suspect Class' Under the Equal Protection Clause," 15 Santa Clara Lawyer *855, 868-875 (1975)*

EDUCATION FOR ALL HAS LONG BEEN A CHERISHED AMERICAN IDEAL. In 1846, American educator Horace Mann wrote:

> I believe in the existence of a great, immortal, immutable principle of natural law, or natural ethics,—a principle antecedent of all human institutions, and incapable of being abrogated by any ordinance of man . . . which proves the *absolute right* to an education of every human being that comes into the world, and which, of course, proves the correlative duty of every government to see that the means of that education are provided for all.

This principle that education should be equally available to all persons has been reflected in various facets of our legal system. The constitutions of about one half of the states include provisions that the public education system shall be equally available to all; constitutions of most of the remaining states declare that their educational systems must be "general, uniform and thorough," or "thorough and efficient." These constitutional mandates for education have been put into effect by specific legislation establishing and controlling the state educational systems. All of the 50 states have statutes authorizing and requiring the maintenance of a system of free public educational programs, and all but one of the states make attendance at school compulsory for persons of specified ages.

The concept of universal education has been widely recognized by judicial tribunals; numerous courts across the land have declared that opportunity for an education is a right which will be jealously safeguarded. The classic statement of this attitude appears in the decision of the United States Supreme Court in *Brown* v. *Board of Education.*

The theoretical ideal of education for all, however, has proved to be an empty promise for many persons with physical, mental and emotional handicaps. Over the years, large numbers of handicapped persons have been denied their right to equal educational opportunities and have been systematically excluded from the public schools. Some observers estimate that there are presently one million handicapped individuals of school age in this country who are totally excluded from public educational programs. When one adds to this total the approximately three million handicapped pupils attending the public schools but not being provided with special education programs suited to their needs, it is clear that unequal treatment of handicapped persons by the state public education systems is a problem of gargantuan proportions.

There is a certain irony in the denial of educational programs to so many persons while school attendance remains compulsory. In 1972, the United States Supreme Court heard arguments by the State of Wisconsin in support of compelling Amish parents to send their children to public high schools, despite their contrary religious beliefs. At the same time, 89,583 handicapped Wisconsin children were excluded from the public school system. In order to understand the full scope of the denial of public education to handicapped persons and the underlying reasons for this absence of educational opportunities, it is necessary to examine the historical development of public education and special education programs in this country.

Special Education—A Historical Perspective

In early colonial America, education was generally a private concern, frequently taking place in the context of one's home and family. There were a few formal institutions for schooling, but at first these were privately controlled and served only the wealthier colonists. It was not long, however, before the notion of public education caught on, and, by 1647, Massachusetts had developed the first public school system in this country. Other colonies followed suit and educational institutions established or supported by the colonial governments multiplied.

Teaching the "three R's" was the principal goal of early education; there were no specialized programs or grade levels. Pupils were taught only the basics of reading and mathematics, accompanied by rudimentary historical or geographical instruction.

Interestingly, the United States Constitution includes no mention of schools or educational institutions. By implication, the framers viewed public education as a matter better left to the individual states. In contrast, the constitutions of every one of the 50 states contain provisions encouraging or establishing public educational programs.

The development of public school education from the 17th century to the present is largely an evolution from the narrow concept of education as "reading, writing and arithmetic," to the broader notion that education should encompass such diverse subjects as chemistry, home economics, driver's training, foreign languages, and gym classes. Yet, the expanding scope of public education did not benefit all groups of children. Educational programs for those persons with mental, emotional, or physical handicaps lagged far behind the significant advances made in general educational programming. For many years, there were no educational strategies at all for teaching persons with mental handicaps. Educators had neither learned nor sought to learn the techniques of educating such persons.

Initially, it became apparent that certain persons did not make any significant educational progress within the "three R's" curriculum. Rather than question the appropriateness of the curriculum, the reaction of early American teachers and principals was to label such persons as incapable of profiting from education. Children who had been declared unable to profit from schooling were thenceforth excluded from attendance at school, and from the compulsory attendance laws.

Moreover, those with physical handicaps were also effectively excluded from the public school system. In the days when transportation to school was on foot or by horseback, those with serious physical disabilities understandably had tremendous difficulty in just getting to the school house. In addition, the usual techniques for teaching the "three R's" were not successful with persons who were blind or deaf or could not use their hands. Any person who deviated from the norms of what was expected of a pupil, and thereby caused extra work for the teacher, was viewed as disruptive and burdensome and thus not suited for classroom instruction. As a result of either formal policy or informal practices, most physically handicapped children did not attend the public schools.

The result of this exclusion of handicapped children from the public schools was the removal of any incentive for educators to develop programs suited to the needs of such children. Since the teachers did not have to face the problems of teaching handicapped students, there was little reason for developing curricula geared to their educational needs. Thus, the exclusion of handicapped children from the public school system greatly delayed the development of special education techniques, which, in turn, reinforced the "unable-to-be-educated" rationale for excluding them. This tragic spiral accounts for the sad fact that, for most of our history, handicapped persons had no place in American public educational systems.

It was not until the 1860s that public school special education classes for deaf children were initiated in this country, and attempts to provide public school programs for mentally retarded persons did not begin until about 1900. Actually, many of the first special classes were intended primarily to assist slow learners drawn from the population of immigrants to this country. Such programs, known as "opportunity classes," were intended to aid the non-English-speaking child in developing some English language abilities and to prepare him or her for eventual absorption into regular public school classes. Because their function was to prepare students to cope with the normal public school programs, these special classes were also known as "vestibule classes," indicating that the child was waiting to join the mainstream school program.

Eventually, these vestibule or opportunity classes evolved to a point where they had almost directly reversed their function. Instead of serving to prepare students for inclusion in regular classes, they became the dumping grounds for many students who could not fit into or manage to succeed in the normal classrooms. In addition to those with language deficiencies, these programs came to include persons with perceptual and communication problems, slow learners, and persons with other mild mental and physical handicaps.

The creation of this middle ground between regular classroom programs and total exclusion was extremely important, for it provided educators with the opportunity and incentive to develop educational strategies to meet these students' special needs.

Given the impetus, education experts did find and begin to implement such techniques.

Schooling for handicapped persons gradually became more organized. The cities of Providence, Springfield, Boston, and Chicago initiated special classes for the mentally retarded shortly before the turn of the century. In 1911, New Jersey became the first state to legislate special education by statutorily authorizing classes for the mildly mentally retarded. Formal classes for mentally retarded children were introduced in other states in the early 1920s. It is important to note, however, that these early classes included only mentally retarded individuals who functioned at a relatively high level of intelligence. Most of the children placed in such classes were the "cream of the crop," functioning at a much higher educational level than students assigned to special classes today.

The successes of these special programs led educators to divide mentally handicapped children into two groups. Those who were showing progress when put into the special classes were labeled "educable," and were increasingly included in state education systems. The remainder of the handicapped children, the "uneducable," were deemed incapable of benefiting from schooling and continued to be excluded from the public schools. Categorization was frequently based upon scores on intelligence quotient tests. If a child's score was above a certain point, he or she was "educable"; otherwise, the child was considered incapable of learning.

This educable-uneducable dichotomy was threatened in the mid-1920s when educators in St. Louis and New York City developed successful educational programs for children with an educational level below that which would have qualified them as "educable." Rather than admitting that they had been wrong in declaring such persons incapable of benefiting from education, educators responded by creating a new category: the "trainable." Since the individuals had already been labeled uneducable, it was decided to call new programs "training" rather than "education." Those who were unable to profit from these training programs were declared to be "subtrainable." Thus a changing educational reality was glossed over with a vocabulary shift.

In 1930, the White House Conference on Children and Youth adopted the educable-trainable distinction and recommended that classes be provided for both groups. These recommendations were not immediately acted upon and classes for the "trainable" mentally handicapped did not become widespread until the 1950s.

In the early 1950s, California, later followed by other states, began to require by statute that special public classes be provided for certain groups of handicapped children, generally the mentally retarded. For the most part, however, special education programs remained "permissive" undertakings at the discretion of local school officials.

The decades of the fifties and sixties were marked by an expanding scope and variety of special education programs. The number of school districts operating some type of special education program was reported to be 1,500 in 1948, 3,600 in 1958, and 5,600 in 1963. Research and experimental teaching techniques resulted in the development of new educational strategies. Educators learned how to teach those with perceptual and communication disorders; educational programs were developed for emotionally disturbed, physically handicapped, and autistic children; and eventually it was found that educational techniques could be devised for assisting even those mentally handicapped persons who had been labeled "sub-trainable."

As the number and variety of special education programs grew, it became possible to speak of "zero reject" education, a concept that involves finding instruction techniques to suit the needs and maximize the capabilities of every child. In 1971, the Council for Exceptional Children, the national organization of special education teachers, supervisors, and administrators, declared its official position:

> Education is the right of all children. The principle of education for all is based on the philosophical premise of democracy that every person is valuable in his own right and should be afforded equal opportunities to develop his full potential.

But while special education programs have grown both in number and in quality, and while lip service is paid to the idea of education for all, "zero reject" education has remained an unfulfilled promise for large numbers of handicapped citizens. Implementation of novel educational strategies has been slow and spotty. The education profession, despite numerous conferences, publications, conventions, workshops, and seminars, has not developed an effective method for the universal sharing of information and techniques. Thus, a successful educational program designed to meet the needs of children with a particular type of handicap may be developed in one locale, while in other areas of the country (or even of the same state) similar children find their educational needs unmet.

In spite of progress and important breakthroughs in the last two decades, the public education systems in this country are still a very long way from providing special educational opportunities for all handicapped children. Even today, the picture painted by statistics on special education programs is dismal. There are approximately seven million handicapped children of school age in this country who need special education programs. Of this total, approximately 17 percent, or one million children, are receiving no formal education at all: they are totally excluded from the public schools. Of the six million handicapped children who are attending the public schools, it is estimated that 3.3 million are receiving special educational services. This leaves 2.7 million handicapped children who are attending the public schools but are not provided with special education programs. Combining this figure with those totally excluded from school, the result is that 3.7 million handicapped children in this country—53 percent of all such children—need public special education services but do not receive them.

ADDITIONAL READING

Lippman, L., and Goldberg, I., *Right to Education: Anatomy of the Pennsylvania Case and Its Implications for Exceptional Children,* Teachers College Press (1973), pp. 1-15, 25-26.

Dybwad, G., "A Look at History and Present Trends in the Protection of Children's Right to Education," 2 *Leadership Series in Special Education,* University of Minnesota (R. Johnson, J. Gross, and R. Weatherman, eds., 1973), pp. 152-163.

Children's Defense Fund, *Children Out of School in America* 91-115 (1974).

Abeson, A., Burgdorf, R., Casey, P., Kunz, J., and McNeil, W., "Access to Opportunity," Chapter 24 of 2 *Issues in the Classification of Children* 270–278
(Hobbs, N., ed., 1975).

Note, "Special Education: The Struggle for Equal Educational Opportunity in Iowa,"
62 *Ia. L. Rev.* 1283, 1292–1298 (1977).

B.   THE LEGAL PERSPECTIVE IN THE PAST

Traditionally, public school superintendents and boards of education were given great
discretion in the regulation and management of educational programs. Their unfettered
authority extended to almost all areas of scholastic and school-related matters, including the exclusion of certain students if they deemed it appropriate.

1.   The Old Cases

WATSON v. CITY OF CAMBRIDGE

Supreme Judicial Court of Massachusetts, 1893
157 Mass. 561, 32 N.E. 864

KNOWLTON, J. The records of the school committee of the defendant city set
forth that the plaintiff in 1885 was excluded from the schools "because he was too
weak-minded to derive profit from instruction." He was afterwards taken again on trial
for two weeks, and at the end of that time again excluded. The records further recite
that "it appears from the statements of teachers who observed him, and from certificates of physicians that he is so weak in mind as not to derive any marked benefit from
instruction, and, further, that he is troublesome to other children, making unusual
noises, pinching others, etc. He is also found unable to take ordinary, decent, physical
care of himself." The evidence at the trial tended strongly to show that the matters set
out in the records were true.

The defendant requested the court to rule that if the facts are true which are set
forth in the records of the committee, as to the cause of the exclusion of the plaintiff
from the public schools, the determination of the school committee thereon, acting in
good faith, was final and not subject to revision in the courts. The court refused so to
rule, and submitted to the jury the question whether the facts stated, if proved, showed
that the plaintiff's presence in school "was a serious disturbance to the good order and
discipline of the school."

The exceptions present the question whether the decision of the school committee of a city or town, acting in good faith in the management of the schools, upon
matters of fact directly affecting the good order and discipline of the schools, is final,
so far as it relates to the rights of pupils to enjoy the privileges of the school, or is
subject to revision by a court. In *Hodgkins* v. *Rockport,* 105 Mass. 475, it appeared
that the school committee, acting in good faith, excluded the plaintiff from school on
account "of his general persistence in disobeying the rules of the school, to the injury
of the school." Of the plaintiff's acts of misconduct, it is said, in the opinion in that
case, that "whether they had such an effect upon the welfare of the school as to require
his expulsion was a question within the discretion of the committee, and upon which

their action is conclusive.'' The principles there laid down are decisive of the present case. It was found by the presiding justice that the alleged misconduct of the plaintiff in that case was not mutinous or gross, and did not consist of a refusal to obey the commands of the teachers, or of any outrageous proceeding, but of acts of neglect, carelessness of posture in his seat, and recitation, tricks of playfulness, inattention to study and the regulations of the school in minor matters. The only difference between the acts of disorder in that case and in this is that in this they resulted from the incapacity and mental weakness of the plaintiff, and in the other they were willful or careless,—the result in part of youthful exuberance of spirits and impatience of restraint or control. In their general effect upon the school, they were alike; and the reasons for giving the school committee, acting in good faith, the power to decide finally a question affecting so vitally the rights and interests of all the other scholars of the school, are the same in both cases.

Under the law the school committee "have the general charge and superintendence of all the public schools in the town" or city, Pub. St. c. 44, § 21. The management of the schools involves many details; and it is important that a board of public officers, dealing with these details, and having jurisdiction to regulate the internal affairs of the schools, should not be interfered with or have their conduct called in question before another tribunal, so long as they act in good faith within their jurisdiction. Whether certain acts of disorder so seriously interfere with the school that one who persists in them, either voluntarily or by reason of imbecility, should not be permitted to continue in the school, is a question which the statute makes it their duty to answer: and if they answer honestly, in an effort to do their duty, a jury composed of men of no special fitness to decide educational questions should not be permitted to say that their answer is wrong. *Spear* v. *Cummings,* 23 Pick. 224, 226. We are of opinion that the ruling requested should have been given.

Exceptions sustained.

STATE EX REL. BEATTIE v. BOARD OF EDUCATION OF CITY OF ANTIGO

Supreme Court of Wisconsin, 1919
169 Wis. 231, 172 N.W. 153

Appeal from Municipal Court, Langlade County; T. W. HOGAN, Judge.

Mandamus by the State, on the relation of William F. Beattie, to compel the Board of Education of the City of Antigo to reinstate and admit petitioner's son to the public schools of such city. From a judgment in favor of petitioner, defendant appeals. Reversed and remanded, with instructions to dismiss the petition.

This is an action of mandamus brought in the municipal court of Langlade county to compel the school board of the city of Antigo to reinstate and admit petitioner's son to the public schools of said city. From a judgment in favor of the petitioner the defendant board of education appealed.

Merritt Beattie, 13 years of age on March 27, 1918, son of petitioner, has been a resident of the city of Antigo since he was 2 years of age. Merritt has been a crippled and defective child since his birth, being afflicted with a form of paralysis which affects his whole physical and nervous make-up. He has not the normal use and control of his voice, hands, feet, and body. By reason of said paralysis his vocal cords are afflicted. He is slow and hesitating in speech, and has a peculiarly high, rasping, and disturbing tone of voice, accompanied with uncontrollable facial contortions, making it difficult for him to make himself understood. He also has an uncontrollable flow of saliva, which drools from his mouth onto his clothing and books, causing him to present an unclean appearance. He has a nervous and excitable nature. It is claimed, on the part of the school board, that his physical condition and ailment produces a depressing and nauseating effect upon the teachers and school children; that by reason of his physical condition he takes up an undue portion of the teacher's time and attention, distracts the attention of other pupils, and interferes generally with the discipline and progress of the school. He did not walk until he was 6 or 7 years of age, and did not attend school until he was 8 years old. He then entered the first grade of the Antigo Public School, and continued therein until he was through the fifth grade in 1917. It appears that he is normal mentally, and that he kept pace with the other pupils in the respective grades, although the teachers had difficulty in understanding him, and he was not called upon to recite as frequently as the others for the reason that he was slow in speech, requiring more time for him to recite than the other pupils. The city of Antigo maintains a day school under section 41.01, Statutes, "for the instruction of deaf persons or persons with defective speech." In the fall of 1916 he was placed, by the school authorities, in this department. He remained there five weeks, when he was transferred to the Fourth Ward Public School. During the school year of 1916 and 1917, a representative of the state department of public instruction visited the Antigo schools. The boy, Merritt, came under her observation, and she protested against his being in the public schools, and suggested that he be placed in the department for instruction of deaf persons or persons with defective speech. Merritt refused to attend this department, in which he was upheld by his parents and family. At the beginning of the school year in 1917, Merritt presented himself to the Second Ward Public School, but on the second day those in charge refused to accept him as a pupil. The matter was taken by the parents to the superintendent of schools, and finally laid before the board of education. On September 13, 1917, the board of education had a regular meeting to consider the demand of petitioner that his son be reinstated and admitted to the public schools. The matter was considered for an hour, during which time one member of the board moved that the boy be reinstated in the schools. This motion did not receive a second, and after some further discussion it was agreed that the matter should be presented to the state superintendent of public instruction. It appears that correspondence followed between the secretary of the school board and the state superintendent upon the question as to whether Merritt should be reinstated, but it does not appear that the state superintendent ever definitely advised the school board upon the subject, and the school board never reinstated the boy. As above stated, the petitioner brought this action to compel his reinstatement. The case was tried before a jury. A general verdict in favor of the petitioner was returned.

OWEN, J. (after stating the facts as above). The right of a child of school age to attend the public schools of this state cannot be insisted upon when its presence therein is harmful to the best interests of the school. This, like other individual rights, must be subordinated to the general welfare. It will be conceded, we think, that the foregoing statement of facts presents a fair question as to the effect of the boy's presence upon the school and the individual pupils attending the same. The question then arises as to what body or tribunal is vested with the authority of determining the question. The trial court seemed to be of the opinion that, while such authority rested with the school board in the first instance, its action in that behalf was reviewable by a jury and subordinate to the jury's opinion thereon, as indicated by its charge to the jury to the effect that, "It is incumbent upon the defendant to prove to you the needfulness of the rule in denying Merritt Beattie the privileges of the graded school by a fair preponderance of the evidence."

The power of the school board in the premises is set forth in section 101, subd. 5, of chapter 197, vol. 2, Laws of 1889, as follows:

> To have in all respects the supervision and management of the common schools of said city, and from time to time, to make, alter, modify and repeal as they may deem expedient, rules and regulations for their organization, government or instruction, . . . and the transfer of pupils from one department to another, and generally for their good order and advancement.

The situation here presented aroused the power of the board under that provision of law. Having acted, its determination should not be interfered with by the courts unless it acted illegally or unreasonably. *State ex rel. Dresser* v. *District Board,* 135 Wis. 619, 116 N.W. 232, 16 L.R.A. (N.S.) 730, 128 Am. St. Rep. 1050; *Watson* v. *City of Cambridge,* 157 Mass. 561, 32 N.E. 864; *Kinzer* v. *Directors,* 129 Iowa, 441, 105 N.W. 686, 3 L.R.A. (N.S.) 496, 6 Ann. Cas. 996. That it acted legally is without question. That it acted unreasonably cannot be said. The duty confronting the school board was a delicate one. It was charged with the responsibility of saying whether this boy should be denied a constitutional right because the exercise of that right would be harmful to the school and to the pupils attending the same. He should not be excluded from the schools except for considerations affecting the general welfare. But if his presence in school was detrimental to the best interests of the school, then the board could not, with due regard to their official oaths, refrain from excluding him, even though such action be displeasing and painful to them. The record convinces us that the board took this view of the situation and considered the question with the highest motives and with a full appreciation of its responsibility. There is no suggestion that any of the members were prompted by bad faith or considerations of ill will. The action of the board in refusing to reinstate the boy seems to have been the result of its best judgment, exercised in good faith, and the record discloses no grounds for the interference of courts with its action.

There is one other question which should be noted. It is claimed that the school board never acted as a body upon the question of the exclusion of the boy from the schools, and that its action is void within the rule that

> When a board of public officers is about to perform an act requiring the exercise of discretion and judgment the members must all meet and confer together, or must all be properly notified of such meeting, in order to make the action binding. Individual and independent action . . . will not suffice (*McNolty* v. *Board of School Directors,* 102 Wis. 261, 78 N.W. 439, 440).

It is true that the exclusion of the boy in the first instance was not the result of the action of the board of education taken at a formal meeting thereof. However, at its meeting on September 13th, the board did meet as a board and conferred upon the question as to whether he should be reinstated. A motion was made that he be reinstated, which motion received no second. This amounted to a refusal on the part of the board, acting as a board, to permit him to attend the public schools of the city. The point is not well taken.

The action of the school board, unless illegal or unreasonable, is not subject to the interference of the courts, from which it follows that the complaint of the petitioner should be dismissed.

Judgment reversed, and cause remanded, with instructions to dismiss the petition.

ESCHWEILER, J. (dissenting). I cannot agree with the result arrived at in the majority opinion in this case for two reasons:

First. Because even under the rule of law adopted by the majority as to the power vested in the school board it was still a question for the jury as to whether or not there was an unreasonable interference with plaintiff's rights; there being no evidence that as a fact this boy's presence did have any harmful influence on the other children.

Secondly, because I believe there is no such exclusive power intended to be vested in such school board.

Those who drafted the Constitution of this state evidently intended to secure to every child a substantial and fundamental right to attend the common schools. Article 10, § 3, Const., reads as follows:

> The Legislature shall provide by law for the establishment of district schools, which shall be as nearly uniform as practicable; and such schools shall be free and without charge for tuition to all children between the ages of four and twenty years; and no sectarian instruction shall be allowed therein.

Unquestionably the right of the individual child under such constitutional provision is subject to the equal rights of all other children to the same, and when the attendance of any one child in the public school is a material infringement upon the rights of other children to also enjoy the benefits of free schooling, his right must yield.

The majority opinion bases the warrant for the construction it gives to the power of the school board in this case upon the statute giving such school boards the supervision, management, and control of the common schools. I cannot agree that a statutory power can be exalted above a guaranty of the Constitution. Even were the statute to say, as it does not, that the decision of such a school board is to be exclusive and controlling, save and except the one complaining of the exercise thereof is able to show that the exercise of such power by the school board was arbitrary and unreasonable, it would be subject to the substantial objection that it placed an unwarranted burden of proof upon one deprived of a constitutional right.

I think the burden was properly laid by the instruction given by the trial court to the jury in this case, upon the defendants, to show that their action was a reasonable exercise of their statutory duty. If they were unable to convince a jury to that effect, their order should be set aside.

Not one of the cases cited in the majority opinion considered any such constitutional privilege as here suggested.

The former decision of this court cited does not mention such provision. The Iowa Constitution particularly expressly grants just such power as is contained in our statute to such board in one of the 15 subsections of article 9 of that document relating to a board of education.

The Massachusetts Constitution contains no provision like ours.

NOTES

1. While the opinion of the majority in the *Beattie* case is a traditional bowing to the authority of school boards, the dissent of Justice Eschweiler sounds two notes that are replayed with more resonance in later cases. First, the Eschweiler opinion suggests that education is a fundamental, constitutional right. Second, Justice Eschweiler focuses attention upon the procedural framework within which exclusionary decisions are made and argues that the burden of proof in justifying such exclusions ought to be upon school officials and not upon the pupil. Eschweiler's concerns are, at their source, not far from procedural due process and substantive constitutional claims that would garner much judicial attention in the future.

2. The court's ruling in the *Beattie* case should be compared with a later interpretation of Wisconsin law by the state's Attorney General, in 1967, 56 O.A.G. 82 (see p. 69 below).

2. Statutory Authorizations of Exclusions

In many instances, state statutes have expressly authorized the exclusion of handicapped children from the public schools.

11 MAINE REV. STATS. ANN., TITLE 20, SECTION 911

The superintending school committee or school directors may exclude from the public schools any child whose physical or mental condition makes it inexpedient for him to attend.

[Deleted by Ch. 510 § 21 (1975).]

NEW YORK EDUCATION LAW, TITLE 4, ART. 65, SECTION 3208

Derived from Education Law of 1910, § 624, as amended by L. 1974, c.191 § 11
(1978 Supp.)

§ 3208.   Attendance: proper mental and physical condition.

1. A person included by the provisions of part one of this article shall be required to attend upon instruction only if in proper mental and physical condition.

2. A person whose mental or physical condition is such that his attendance upon instruction under the provisions of part one of this article would endanger the health or safety of himself or of others, or who is feebleminded to the extent that he is unable to benefit from instruction, shall not be permitted to attend.

3. A person whose mental or physical condition is such that, because of the lack of facilities for his care, transportation and instruction, he is not permitted or required

to attend upon instruction, shall be deemed in proper mental and physical condition to attend, if the lacking facilities are provided.

4. If a person's mental or physical condition, by virtue of which he is not required or permitted to attend upon instruction, is due to physical defects or to a physical condition which may be remedied by the taking of reasonable measures, such mental or physical condition shall justify only the temporary failure of the person to attend.

5. The determination of mental or physical condition under the provisions of part one of this article shall be based upon actual examination made by a person or persons qualified by appropriate training and experience, in accordance with regulations of the state education department. The state education department shall designate persons having the required qualifications to make such mental or physical examinations on behalf of any local school authorities, except that in a city having a population of one million or more the superintendent of schools shall designate such persons.

OREGON LAWS, 1947, CHAPTER 463, S.B. 98

Repealed by Ch. 100 § 456 (1965)

Section 1.   The boards of directors of the several school districts of the state of Oregon hereby are authorized and empowered to exclude permanently from the public schools of such districts any child or children over ten years of age found to be mentally unable to benefit further from the instruction offered in such schools, in the manner hereinafter provided.

Section 2.   The state board of education shall establish rules and regulations governing the procedure for determining when a child is mentally unable to profit from the instruction offered in the public schools.

[Sections 3–7, omitted here, provided stringent notice, hearing, and appeal procedures, which had to be followed in making a finding of mental inability to profit from instruction.]

BOARD OF EDUCATION OF CLEVELAND HEIGHTS V. STATE, EX REL. GOLDMAN

Court of Appeals of Ohio, Cuyahoga County, 1934
47 Oh.App. 417, 191 N.E. 914

McGILL, Justice.

Beldene Goldman, a child eight years of age, was excluded from or refused admission to the public schools of Cleveland Heights city school district for the term beginning in September, 1933. This action was taken because of the alleged low mentality of the child. The child had suffered a brain injury at or about the time of birth, and there is no dispute that the child was and is subnormal. The father brought a mandamus action against the board of education of Cleveland Heights and Frank L. Wiley, superintendent of the schools, and after hearing in the common pleas court a peremptory writ of mandamus was issued commanding the board of education and the superintendent to admit the child to the schools of Cleveland Heights. Error has been prosecuted to this court.

The record discloses that in September, 1931, the board of education opened what was known as the Superior Opportunity School, which was for the accommodation of retarded children having a low intelligence quotient. This class for children of low mentality was in full operation during the school years of 1931–1932 and 1932–1933. The Goldman child was in this school.

On November 14, 1932, the board of education adopted a resolution relating to retarded children and among other things provided as follows:

> 4. That pupils now enrolled in the school having intelligence quotients below 50 be retained in the organization until the end of the current school year, but that beginning with September, 1933, all pupils below 50 I.Q., and special or custodial types, be excluded; and further that the present group of pupils of this type be excluded; and further that the present group of pupils of this type be segregated from all other school pupils at an early date, if arrangements can be made without incurring any relatively large expense.
>
> 5. That the Superintendent be authorized to set up definite regulations governing the admission and discharge of pupils from this school.

Pursuant to this resolution which was adopted by the board of education, the parents of Beldene Goldman were notified in August, 1933, that the child would not be admitted to the schools for the term beginning in September, 1933.

It is claimed, in substance, by the father of the child, that the public schools are open to all children between certain ages; that the compulsory school law requires the attendance of children in school; that this child being between six and eighteen years of age is of compulsory school age; that the expulsion of this child from the public schools is without authority in law and contrary to the provisions of section 7762-7, General Code of Ohio.

The board of education and superintendent of the schools, on the other hand, claim that under section 7762-7, General Code, the department of education of the state can prescribe standards, examinations, or tests by which it may be determined whether or not certain children of school age are incapable of profiting substantially by further instruction in the schools; that these examinations and tests were given to this child and that this child was determined to be of such low mentality as to be incapable of profiting substantially by further instruction in the schools.

It was further urged by the board that in the exercise of its sound discretion it has the right to determine that any child of school age, who is so deficient mentally as to have an intelligence quotient of not more than fifty, as determined by the Benet test, is incapable of profiting substantially by further instruction, and it is claimed that inasmuch as this child had an I.Q. of 47, the board was justified in excluding the child from the schools. It was also urged on behalf of the board and superintendent that they did not rely on the tests alone, but that they also took into consideration the lack of progress by the child over a period of two or three years.

Apparently this is a case of first impression in Ohio, and counsel have been unable to find a case anywhere in the United States which gives the right to exclude from all educational facilities any child within the prescribed ages upon the basis of an intelligence test. It is, therefore, necessary to look to the provisions of the statutes of Ohio with reference to the right to refuse this child admission to the schools, and to seek to determine the intent of the Legislature.

It is to be noted that there is a sharp conflict in the evidence concerning the results of I.Q. tests given to this particular child.

The record discloses that in September, 1932, a Miss Wager gave a test showing an I.Q. of 44. Again, in November, 1932, a Dr. Markey gave the child a test with a result of 61. The next test was made by the Brush Foundation of Cleveland, on May 8, 1933, and according to information given by the superintendent, although no representative of the Brush Foundation testified, the result was 47. On October 23, 1933, a Dr. Newcomb examined the child and found her to have an I.Q. of 55.

The authorities seem to be in agreement that a slight variation is not a determinative factor. For example, counsel for the board of education in his brief calls attention to the testimony of Dr. Henry H. Goddard, as perhaps the most learned and experienced expert who was on the stand in the court below. Among other things, Dr. Goddard testified:

> Q. Doctor, would you say that if children having an I.Q. of 50 are considered educable, that a child having an I.Q. of 47 should also be so considered? A. Of course, there is a limit to that sort of thing. I might answer yes to that question, and then you would run down three points more and I would get into trouble. The fact is, that 50, or 47, or 53 or anything in that line, in itself, is not enough. The moment you fix a point of that sort you get into difficulty. One child with an I.Q. of 40 is more educable, perhaps, than another child with an I.Q. of 50.

Turning now to the statutes of Ohio we find that General Code, section 7681, provides that the schools shall be free to all youth between six and twenty-one years of age.

Section 7690, General Code, provides that the board of education has the management and control of all schools of whatever name and character in the district.

Section 7644, General Code, provides that each board of education shall establish a sufficient number of elementary schools to provide for the free education of the youth of school age within the district under its control.

Section 7762, General Code, provides that a child between six and eighteen years of age is of compulsory school age.

The matter of the exclusion of children who may be incapable of profiting substantially by further instruction is treated in section 7762-7 of the General Code, and, although lengthy, it is quoted here in full as follows:

> A child of compulsory school age may be determined to be incapable of profiting substantially by further instruction as follows, to-wit:
> The department of education may prescribe standards and examinations or tests by which such capacity may be determined and prescribe and approve the agencies or individuals by which they shall be applied and conducted; but the capacity of a child to benefit substantially by further instruction shall be determined with reference to that available to the particular child in the public schools of the district in which he resides, and no child shall be determined to be incapable of profiting substantially by further instruction if the department of education shall find that it is feasible to provide for him in such district, or elsewhere in the public school system, special classes or schools, departments of special instruction or individual instruction through by which he might profit substantially, according to his mental capacity as so determined. In prescribing, formulating, applying and giving such standards, examinations or tests, the department of education may call for assistance and advice upon any other department or bureau of

the state government, or upon any appropriate department of any university supported wholly or partly from state appropriations.

The result of each examination or test made hereunder, with the recommendation of the agency or individual conducting the same, shall be reported to the department of education, which shall have power to make the determination herein authorized. If a child be determined hereunder to be incapable of profiting substantially by further instructions, such determination shall be certified by the department of education to the superintendent of schools of the district in which he resides, who shall place such child under the supervision of a visiting teacher or of an attendance officer, to be exercised as long as he is of compulsory school age. The department of education shall keep a record of the names of all children so determined to be incapable of profiting substantially by further instruction and a like record of all such children residing in any school district shall be kept by the superintendent of schools of such district. Upon request of the parents, guardians, or persons having the care of such child whose residence has been changed to another school district the superintendent of schools shall forward a card showing the status of such child as so determined by the superintendent of schools of the district to which the child has been moved.

Any determination made under this section may be revoked by the department of education for good cause shown.

A child determined to be incapable of profiting substantially by further instruction, as herein provided, shall not thereafter be admitted to the public schools of the state while such determination remains in force, anything in chapter four of this title to the contrary notwithstanding.

The record in this case discloses that after the board of education of Cleveland Heights determined that this child was unable to profit substantially by further instruction, the matter was submitted to the department of education at Columbus, which department at first approved the exclusion of the child. Later, the department revoked the approval or determination and finally passed the entire matter back to the local board.

As a matter of common sense it is apparent that a moron of very low type, or an idiot or imbecile who is incapable of absorbing knowledge or making progress in the schools, ought to be excluded. On the other hand, every child between the ages of six and eighteen years of age in the state of Ohio is not only entitled to be admitted to the public schools, but is compelled to attend.

There is no doubt but that school authorities possess the power to conduct the schools, and to make rules and regulations for their proper government and management. There is no doubt but that school boards in the exercise of their powers in these matters have a wide discretion, and that the courts will not interfere with that exercise of sound discretion in the absence of an abuse thereof.

It is to be borne in mind, however, that not only compulsory attendance is required by our laws, but also that the right to attend our public schools belongs to the people. Education for all youth is deemed of paramount importance. It is the foundation of popular government and is considered so essential that between certain ages children must attend our schools.

The question arises as to where the authority to exclude a child of low mentality is vested. The question in this case is whether or not this child was legally refused admission to the schools. A careful study of section 7762-7, General Code, leads us to the conclusion that the department of education may prescribe the standards, and examinations or tests, and approve the agencies or individuals by which they shall be applied and conducted, but that under that section a determination of the question must be finally made by the department of education, which counsel for the board of education concedes means the state department of education. In this case the department of education made no final determination. Without such final approval or determination by the department of education, we think that this child was not excluded in accordance with the provisions of the statute, and that the court below was right in granting a peremptory writ of mandamus.

Accordingly the judgment of the common pleas court is affirmed.

Judgment affirmed.

LIEGHLEY, P. J., and LEVINE, J., concur.

NOTES

1.   Although the *Goldman* decision upholds the authority of school officials to exclude certain pupils in compliance with statutory requirements, it does address the impropriety of hairline eligibility criteria based upon intelligence quotient tests. Note particularly the testimony of Dr. Henry H. Goddard quoted by the court.

While experts in the uses of testing have long warned against drawing black and white lines and overreliance upon IQ scores, such practices have continued. In fact, in spite of the *Goldman* holding, and in spite of an Ohio Attorney General's opinion (O.A.G. 69-040) warning that there is no precise IQ cutoff for eligibility for educational services, sharp intelligence quotient criteria continued to be employed in Ohio until the present decade (see pp. 130–143, below.)

2.   The exclusions from the public school system authorized by Ohio law resulted in a dual system whereby many of the children determined to be "incapable of profiting" were enrolled in "training centers" operated in many of the counties. Thus two systems existed: one serving those whose IQ score was 50 or above, i.e., the public schools, and one serving those who scored below 50, i.e., the training centers. Critics of the training centers claimed that many of them provided no more than custodial, "baby-sitting" services. This dual system raised the constitutional question of "separate but equal" education in an entirely new context.

3.   In *People* v. *Himmanen,* 108 Misc. 275, 178 N.Y.S. 282 (1919), a New York court ruled that a father was not required, pursuant to the state compulsory attendance law, to send his "lame" child to school, because the statute only required attendance for those "in proper physical and mental condition to attend school." (*Id.,* at 178 N.Y.S. 283.)

C.   THE BEGINNINGS OF CHANGE

As the previous material has made clear, for most of the history of education in the United States, the behavior of school officials went virtually unexamined by the legal system. Courts, pleading lack of expert knowledge, were wary of interfering in the discretion of administrators to educate their students, handicapped or otherwise. As late as 1968 the United States Supreme Court was reaffirming that understanding:

> Judicial interposition in the operation of the public school system of the Nation raises problems requiring care and restraint. . . . Courts do not and cannot intervene in the resolution of conflicts which arise in the daily operation of school systems and which do not directly and sharply implicate basic constitutional values (*Epperson* v. *Arkansas,* 393 U.S. 97, 104 [1968]).

This hands-off attitude surfaced again in 1977 when the Court upheld the use of corporal punishment in the public schools: "Assessment of the need for, and the appropriate means of maintaining school discipline is committed generally to the discretion of school authorities subject to state law" (*Ingraham* v. *Wright,* 430 U.S. 651, 681–682 [1977]).

Generally, however, judicial reluctance to overseeing and interfering with the decisions of public educators began to dissipate in the 1960s. Through the educational litigation that was a major component of the civil rights movement for blacks in this country, judges came to feel that even professional educators should be subject to judicial supervision if they failed to comply with minimal legal and constitutional requirements. As in other areas of administrative decision making, unlimited discretion in the field of public education became increasingly disfavored.

Judicial tribunals came to recognize that students do not "shed their constitutional rights . . . at the schoolhouse gate" (*Tinker* v. *Des Moines Independent Community School District,* 393 U.S. 503, 506 [1969]), that "they are 'persons' under our Constitution . . . possessed of fundamental rights which the state must respect . . ." (*id.,* at 511). In the late 1960s, there were rumblings that formerly accepted practices of summarily excluding various handicapped students from the public schools might run afoul of constitutional guarantees.

A 1967 Attorney General's Opinion in the State of Wisconsin, 56 O.A.G. 82 (April 13, 1967), marked an important advance in legal theory regarding the educational rights of handicapped people. The opinion indicated that the right to a free public education was guaranteed by the state constitution to every child, including those with handicaps. The Wisconsin attorney general cleverly skirted the holding in the *Beattie* case (*supra,* pp. 59–63) by the following reasoning:

> The obligation of the local school district or the state to such excluded children, however, does not cease with their expulsion from the district. It should be noted that in *State ex rel. Beattie* v. *Board of Education* (1919), 169 Wis. 231, 172 N.W. 153, the court did not hold that this pupil lost all rights to a free public education. The petitioner pupil sought only reinstatement in the district school rather than continuing his education in the day school established pursuant to sec. 41.01, Stat. . . .
>
> The child has not forfeited his right to a free public education through any form of misconduct. Instead, he has been unfortunate enough to be afflicted with a condition which renders his participation in the usual school program unfeasible. It is perhaps more accurate to say that his educational rights have been qualified for his own benefit and the benefit of other pupils.

Therefore, although entry to the district school might be barred in appropriate circumstances, the obligation to provide a meaningful and free public education remained. The straightforward, logical, but largely unprecedented conclusion is that the word *all* in the state constitution must include handicapped children.

WOLF v. LEGISLATURE OF THE STATE OF UTAH

Third Judicial District Court, Salt Lake County, Utah, 1969
Civ. No. 182646, Jan. 8, 1969

Findings of Fact

Plaintiff parents, Mr. and Mrs. Willard K. Paulsen and Mr. and Mrs. Fred G. Wolf, and plaintiff children, Richard Willard Paulsen and Joan Annette Wolf, are residents of the State of Utah. Plaintiff children, ages 18 and 12 respectively, are mentally retarded, having I.Q.'s in a range defining them as trainable, and have been denied admission to the regularly constituted common school system of the State of Utah. Plaintiff children are currently enrolled at day care centers, for which fees are paid by the respective plaintiff parents.

Conclusions of Law

1.   The Utah Constitution, Article X, Section 1, provides:

> The Legislature shall provide for the establishment and maintenance of a uniform system of public schools, which shall be open to *all* children of the State, and be free from sectarian control. (Emphasis added.)

There are no reported cases construing this provision with regard to whether it requires the State to provide education to retarded children. The Utah Supreme Court has, however, interpreted this provision in a very broad manner. In *Logan City School Dist.* v. *Kowallis,* 94 Utah 342, 347, 77 P.2d 348, 350 (1933), the court noted:

> The requirement that the schools must be open to all children of the state is a prohibition against any law or rule which would separate or divide the children of the state into classes or groups, and grant, allow, or provide one group or class educational privileges or advantages denied another. No child of school age, resident within the state, can be lawfully denied admission to the schools of the state because of race, color, location, religion, politics, or any other bar or barrier which may be set up which would deny to such child equality of educational opportunities or facilities with all other children of the state. This is a direction to the Legislature to provide a system of public schools to which all children of the state may be admitted.

Thus, it would seem clear that the public schools must be open to all children, including the plaintiff children.

2.   It is the public policy of this state that the financial burden of providing public education should be borne by the taxpayers of the state and not by the parents or children involved. Utah Code Annotated, Section 53-4-7 (Supp. 1967) provides:

> In each school district the public schools shall be free to all children between the ages of six and eighteen years who are residents of said district except that such schools shall also be free to persons who have not completed high school up to and including the age of twenty-one years.

It is thus abundantly clear that plaintiff children must be provided free public education within the school districts of which they are residents.

3.   The Utah Constitution, Article X, Section 8, provides:

> The general control and supervision of the public school system shall be vested in a State Board of Education . . .

The State Board of Education, therefore, is the state agency which is solely responsible for providing the plaintiff children with the public education to which they are entitled.

Judgment

This matter came regularly on for hearing before the above-entitled court on December 30, 1968; argument being presented by Bruce G. Cohne and Don W. Klingle of Summerhays, Klingle & Cohne, Attorneys for the plaintiffs, and by Mel Dayley, Assistant Attorney General, representing the Attorney General of the State of Utah and the defendants; the Court heretofore having entered its Findings of Fact and Conclusions of Law; NOW, THEREFORE, the Court does hereby enter the following written opinion and judgment:

Education, today, is probably the most important function of state and local governments. It is a fundamental and inalienable right and must be so if the rights guaranteed to an individual under Utah's Constitution and the United States Constitution are to have any real meaning. Of what value would be the right to assemble, the right to speak, the right to participate in one's own religion, if an individual were to be denied an education? Education enables the individual to exercise those rights guaranteed him by the Constitution of the State of Utah and the Constitution of the United States of America.

Utah has historically placed a premium value on education. The Supreme Court of the State of Utah re-emphasized this when it said in *Logan City School Dist.* v. *Kowallis,* 94 Utah 342, 349, 77 P.2d 348, 353 (1938).

> The history of educational development in Utah, from the first settlements to the very latests enactments, shows a devotion to the ideal of intellectual development and a constantly growing effort to insure all children in the state equality of educational opportunities and privileges as a fundamental and inalienable right, free and open to all alike. (Emphasis added.)

The Supreme Court in 1938, when the *Logan City* case (*supra*) was decided, was well aware of the vital importance of a free education. Today, 30 years later, the right to education and the need for education are no less fundamental and vital. Today it is doubtful that any child may reasonably be expected to succeed in life if he is denied the right and opportunity of an education. In the instant case the segregation of the plaintiff children from the public school system has a detrimental effect upon the children as well as their parents. The impact is greater when it has the apparent sanction of the law for the policy of placing these children under the Department of Welfare and segregating them from the educational system can be and probably is usually interpreted as denoting their inferiority, unusualness, uselessness and incompetency. A sense of inferiority and not belonging affects the motivation of a child to learn. Segregation, even though perhaps well intentioned, under the apparent sanction of law and state authority has a tendency to retard the educational, emotional and mental development of the children. The setting aside of these children in a special class affects the plaintiff parents in that under apparent sanction of law and state authority they have been told that their children are not the same as other children of the State of Utah and therefore are not to be treated like all other children of the State of Utah which, to say the least, cannot have a beneficial effect upon the parents of these plaintiff children.

The founding fathers of our state and the authors of the Utah Constitution clearly were aware of the importance of providing a free education to *all* children of the State of Utah. In Article X, Section 1, of the Utah Constitution it is provided that:

> The Legislature shall provide for the establishment and maintenance of a uniform system of public schools, which shall be open to *all* children of the state, and be free from sectarian control. (Emphasis added.)

The founding fathers and authors of the Utah Constitution were also aware that the education of children should be the primary responsibility of an educational authority for they provided in Article X, Section 8, of the Utah Constitution:

> The general control and supervision of the public school system shall be vested in a State Board of Education, ...

The legislatures and the legislators who followed the enactment of the Utah Constitution repeatedly re-affirmed the founding father's and authors' of the Utah Constitution belief in a free and equal education for all children administered under the Department of Education by enacting statutory laws that continually emphasized the public policy of the State of Utah to be the providing of a free education to all children of the State of Utah. An example of the re-affirmation of the legislators and the legislatures of the State of Utah since the enactment of the Utah Constitution is provided by Utah Code Annotated, Section 53-4-7 (Supp. 1967), wherein it provides:

> In each school district public schools shall be free to all children between the ages of six and eighteen years who are residents of said district except that such schools shall also be free to persons who have not completed high school up to and including the age of twenty-one years.

It is thus abundantly clear that the plaintiff children must be provided a free and equal education within the school districts of which they are residents, and the state agency which is solely responsible for providing the plaintiff children with a free and equal education is the State Board of Education.

WHEREFORE, the Court enters the following judgment:

1. Under the Constitution and the laws of the State of Utah, the plaintiff children and the plaintiffs' children are entitled to a free education within the framework of the public school system of the State of Utah.

2. The State Board of Education under the Constitution and the laws of the State of Utah has the primary duty and responsibility to see that the plaintiffs' children and the plaintiff children receive a free education within the framework of the public school system of the State of Utah.

NOTE

Although the *Wolf* court purports to base its decision on the Utah Constitution, much of the language in the judgment is simply a paraphrasing of the decision of the United States Supreme Court's holding in *Brown* v. *Board of Education,* 347 U.S. 483

(1954). This adaptation of equal protection analysis developed in cases involving racial discrimination to the new context of discrimination against individuals with handicaps is a significant step, probably qualifying the *Wolf* decision as the grandparent of all subsequent equal education opportunity litigation.

MARLEGA V. BOARD OF SCHOOL DIRECTORS OF THE CITY OF MILWAUKEE, WISCONSIN

United States District Court for the Eastern District of Wisconsin, 1970
Civil Action No. 70-C-8

Temporary Restraining Order of January 14, 1970

The Defendants named herein are temporarily restrained from continuing to exclude Plaintiff Douglas Marlega from public school and from excluding Plaintiff Douglas Marlega from public school in the future for alleged medical reasons without affording Plaintiff a full, fair and adequate hearing which meets the requirements of due process of law to determine if he is medically able to attend school on a full-time basis.

This order shall continue in effect until a hearing and determination of Defendants' petition to this court to vacate such temporary restraining order.

Temporary Restraining Order of March 16, 1970

The temporary restraining order issued in this cause on January 14, 1970 be modified by extending relief afforded the named Plaintiff, DOUGLAS MARLEGA, under that order to all other members of his class: specifically, that the Defendants are temporarily restrained from preventing any child enrolled in Milwaukee Public Schools from pursuing his or her education on normal, full-time daily attendance basis for alleged medical reasons without first affording such child a full, fair and adequate hearing which meets the requirements of due process of law.

Hearing Procedure, filed on July 31, 1970

The procedures for effecting a full- or part-time exemption from the Milwaukee Public School System under Section 118.15 (3), Wisconsin Statutes, are as follows:

1.   If in the opinion of the Assistant Superintendent of Pupil Personnel, it is necessary to initiate steps toward possible exclusion of a pupil, the Division of Pupil Personnel will schedule a conference with the parent(s) or legal guardian and school persons directly concerned with the case.

If after the conference, the Assistant Superintendent decides that attendance should be limited to part-time daily attendance or that the pupil should be exempted altogether, he will so inform the parent(s) or guardians and give his reasons therefor. The parent(s) will be informed in writing by registered mail of their right to a hearing, of their right to bring an attorney and will be advised of any alternative educational opportunities for their child. The parent(s) will be also informed of the opportunity of conferring directly with the Health Department medical specialists to obtain an explanation of the medical reasons for the proposed exemption. Subsequently, the parent(s) will be requested to sign a waiver of attendance. All of the above information will be given prior to any request by school officials that the parent(s) sign a waiver of the child's attendance. If the circumstances indicate that it would be appropriate, all notices will be in both Spanish and English.

2. If the parent(s) accept the decision and sign the waiver of attendance, the matter will be reported to the Board of School Directors at its next regular meeting as a matter of information giving the child's name, age and reason for exemption under regular procedures.

3. If the parent(s) do not accept the decision and do not sign the waiver of attendance, they will be notified in writing by Registered Mail, detailing the reasons for the decision and of their right to a hearing on the matter before the School Board's Committee on Appointment and Instruction. The notice will further state that if a request for a hearing is not made within seven (7) days of receipt of the notice of hearing, the hearing would be waived, and the matter would be reported to the Board of School Directors at its next regular meeting as a matter of information, giving the name and age of the student, together with the reasons for the exclusion under regular procedures. If a hearing is requested, the parent(s) will be given at least seven (7) days notice of the hearing by registered mail.

4. If the parent(s) request a hearing, the matter will be presented to the Board of School Directors through the Committee on Appointment and Instruction, and no exclusion will take place prior to official Board action. The hearing before the Committee on Appointment and Instruction would include the following procedures:

a. The parent(s) would receive notification at least seven (7) days prior to the hearing. The hearing would be in private unless otherwise requested by the parents. Attendance at the hearing would be at the committee's discretion.

b. They would have the right to be represented by counsel provided by themselves.

c. They would have the right to present evidence and witnesses on their child's behalf.

d. They would have the right to confront and cross-examine any and all witnesses.

e. The Committee's recommendation would rest upon legal rules and evidence produced at the hearing.

f. The reasons for the Committee's recommendation would be set forth in writing, together with a summary of all evidence.

g. The *Available Services Guides* manual, published by the School Board would be made available to the parent(s). This sets forth various alternatives to normal full-time daily attendance which are available to students depending on varying circumstances.

h. All parts of the child's school record available under Wisconsin law would be made available to the parent(s) prior to the hearing. Those portions of the record which the Board feels not available under Wisconsin law would be deleted, and the parent(s) would be advised if any deletions were so made.

i. A stenographic record of the hearing will be made.

5. The Committee's findings, together with the supporting file, will be submitted to the board for final action.

It is further agreed by the parties that on or before November 15, 1970, each child in the Milwaukee Public School System previously exempted from school without a hearing, will be either re-admitted to school or will be given a hearing prior to said date. Within three (3) weeks after the commencement of the fall semester of 1970, parents of those children so exempted will be notified that their child will either be given a hearing or be re-admitted by November 15th. The letter will further indicate to the parents that they will be contacted by the schools when their child's file comes up for review.

Order of September 17, 1970

A "Hearing Procedure" for effecting a full- or part-time exemption from the Milwaukee Public School System under Section 118.15 (3), Wisconsin Statutes, having been filed with the Court on July 31, 1970 pursuant to stipulation of the parties; and upon consent of the parties,

IT IS HEREBY ORDERED, that

The above-captioned action is dismissed without prejudice and without costs to either party.

D.   UNITED STATES CONSTITUTIONAL GUARANTEES OF DUE PROCESS AND EQUAL PROTECTION

The equal protection overtones of the *Wolf* case and the procedural safeguards in the *Marlega* case, reported in the previous section, presaged the direction that federal constitutional litigation would take. The Fourteenth Amendment's guarantees of "due process" and "equal protection" have been brandished as a two-pronged weapon by advocates for handicapped people seeking fairness and equality from the public school systems.

1.   The Landmark *PARC* Case

PENNSYLVANIA ASSOCIATION FOR RETARDED CHILDREN v. COMMONWEALTH OF PENNSYLVANIA

United States District Court for the Eastern District of Pennsylvania, 1972
343 F.Supp. 279

Before ADAMS, Circuit Judge, MASTERSON and BRODERICK, District Judges.

OPINION, ORDER AND INJUNCTION

MASTERSON, District Judge.

This civil rights case, a class action, was brought by the Pennsylvania Association for Retarded Children and the parents of thirteen individual retarded children on behalf of all mentally retarded persons between the ages 6 and 21 whom the Commonwealth of Pennsylvania, through its local school districts and intermediate units, is presently excluding from a program of education and training in the public schools. Named as defendants are the Commonwealth of Pennsylvania, Secretary of Welfare, State Board of Education and thirteen individual school districts scattered throughout the Commonwealth. In addition, plaintiffs have joined all other school districts in the Commonwealth as class defendants of which the named districts are said to be representative.

The exclusions of retarded children complained of are based upon four State statutes: (1) 24 Purd.Stat. Sec. 13-1375 which relieves the State Board of Education from any obligation to educate a child whom a public school psychologist certifies as uneducable and untrainable. The burden of caring for such a child then shifts to the Department of Welfare which has no obligation to provide any educational services for the child; (2) 24 Purd.Stat. Sec. 13-1304 which allows an indefinite postponement of admission to public school of any child who has not attained a mental age of five years; (3) 24 Purd.Stat. Sec. 13-1330 which appears to *excuse* any child from compulsory school attendance whom a psychologist finds unable to profit therefrom and (4) 24 Purd.Stat. Sec. 13-1326 which defines compulsory school age as 8 to 17 years but has ben used in practice to postpone admissions of retarded children until age 8 or to eliminate them from public schools at age 17.

Plaintiffs allege that Sections 1375 (uneducable and untrainable) and 1304 (mental age of 5 years) are constitutionally infirm both on their faces and as applied in three broad respects. First, plaintiffs argue that these statutes offend due process because they lack any provision for notice and a hearing before a retarded person is either excluded from a public education or a change is made in his educational assignment within the public system. Secondly, they assert that the two provisions violate equal protection because the premise of the statute which necessarily assumes that certain retarded children are uneducable and untrainable lacks a rational basis in fact. Finally, plaintiffs contend that because the Constitution and laws of Pennsylvania guarantee an education to all children, these two sections violate due process in that they arbitrarily and capriciously deny that given right to retarded children. Plaintiffs' third contention also raises a pendent question of state law, that is, whether the Pennsylvania Constitution as well as other laws of the Commonwealth already afford them a right to public education.

It is not alleged that Sections 1330 (excusal from compulsory attendance) or 1326 (definition of compulsory school age) are facially defective under the United States Constitution. Rather, plaintiffs contend that these provisions violate due process (lack of a prior hearing) and equal protection (no basis in fact to support exclusion) *as applied* to retarded children.

In addition, plaintiffs contend that the clear intent of Section 1330 is to forgive *parents* from any criminal penalty for what otherwise would be a violation of compulsory attendance requirements, and consequently, use of this provision to *exclude* retarded children constitutes an impermissible misinterpretation of state law. Likewise, plaintiffs assert that Section 1326 relates only to the obligation of *parents* (under penalty of criminal sanctions) to place their children in public schools, and its use to *exclude* retarded children contravenes the obvious meaning of the statute. To place these questions of state law before us, plaintiffs advance the principle of pendent jurisdiction.

Plaintiffs predicate jurisdiction of this court upon 28 U.S.C. § 1343(3) and their causes of action under 42 U.S.C. §§ 1981 and 1983. By way of relief, they seek both a declaratory judgment that the statutes are unconstitutional and a preliminary and permanent injunction against the enforcement of these laws by the defendants. On the basis of these pleadings, it was concluded that the case raised important and substantial federal questions requiring consideration by a three judge court under 28 U.S.C. § 2281.

Shortly after the appointment of the three judge Court by the Chief Judge of the Court of Appeals, we entered an order fixing June 15, 1971 as the hearing date on plaintiffs' motion for a preliminary injunction and June 11, 1971 as the date for prehearing conference. Between the date of our order and June 11th, however, the parties asked for an opportunity to settle amicably at least that part of the case which related to the plaintiffs' demand for due process hearings before exclusion from a public school education or a change in educational assignment within the public system is ordered. To afford them such an opportunity, we vacated our earlier order and postponed the hearing date until August 12th, 1971 and set August 2nd, 1971 as the final pre-hearing conference date.

In the interim, the parties agreed upon a Stipulation which basically provides that no child who is mentally retarded or thought to be mentally retarded can be assigned initially (or re-assigned) to either a regular or special educational status, or excluded from a public education without a prior recorded hearing before a special hearing officer. At that hearing, parents have the right to representation by counsel, to examine their child's records, to compel the attendance of school officials who may have relevant evidence to offer, to cross-examine witnesses testifying on behalf of school officials and to introduce evidence of their own. On June 18th, this Court entered an interim order approving the Stipulation.

In mid-August, as scheduled, we heard plaintiffs' evidence relating to both the due process and equal protection claims, although the evidence was particularly directed toward the unresolved question of equal protection. Following testimony by four eminent experts in the field of education of retarded children,[14a] the parties once again expressed a desire to settle the equal protection dispute by agreement rather than judicial determination. We then suspended further testimony in order to afford the parties time to resolve the remaining issues.

On October 7th, 1971 the parties submitted a Consent Agreement to this Court

---

[14a]The court heard from (1) *I. Ignacy Goldberg,* who is, *inter alia,* Professor of Education, Department of Special Education. Columbia University; member of the President's Panel on Mental Retardation (1961); consultant to the Children's Bureau, Department of Health, Education and Welfare; Scientific Advisory Board member of the Kennedy Child Study Center, New York; and author or co-author of almost 50 publications on mental retardation; (2) *James J. Gallagher,* who is, *inter alia,* the first Director of the Bureau of Education for the Handicapped and Associate Commissioner of Education, U. S. Office of Eduction, Department of Health, Education and Welfare (1967–1969); Deputy Assistant Secretary for Program Planning, Research and Education, Department of Health, Education and Welfare; Director, Frank Porter Graham Child Development Center, University of North Carolina; and author or co-author of some 30 publications on the education of retarded persons; (3) *Donald J. Steadman,* who is, *inter alia,* first Associate Director of the John F. Kennedy Center for Research on Education and Human Development, Peabody College; Professor and Chairman of the Division of Human Development in the School of Education, University of North Carolina; Associate Editor of the *Journal of Mental Deficiency*; author or co-author of some 30 publicaions on the mentally retarded; and a permanent consultant to the President's Committee on Mental Retardation; and (4) *Burton Blatt,* who is, *inter alia,* Centennial Professor and Director, Division of Special Education and Rehabilitation, Syracuse University; member of the first Connecticut State Advisory Council on Mental Retardation; member of the State of New York Committee for Children; member of the National Advisory Committee of the R & D Center for Handicapped Children of Teachers College, Columbia University; and author or co-author of almost 90 publications.

which, along with the June 18th Stipulation, would settle the entire case. Essentially, this Agreement deals with the four state statutes in an effort to eliminate the alleged equal protection problems. As a proposed cure, the defendants agreed, *inter alia,* that since "the Commonwealth of Pennsylvania has undertaken to provide a free public education for all of its children between the ages of six and twenty-one years" (Paragraph 5), therefore, "it is the Commonwealth's obligation to place each mentally retarded child in a *free, public program of education and training appropriate to the child's capacity."* (Paragraph 7.) To effectuate this result without conceding the unconstitutionality of the foregoing statutes or upsetting the existing statutory scheme, the Attorney General of the Commonwealth agreed to issue Opinions declaring in substance that: (1) Section 1375 means that "insofar as the Department of Public Welfare is charged to arrange for the care, training and supervision of a child certified to it, the Department of Public Welfare must provide a program of education and training appropriate to the capacities of that child" (Paragraph 37); (2) Section 1304 means *"only* that a school district may refuse to accept into or retain in the lowest grade of the *regular* primary school [as contrasted with a *special* primary school] any child who has not attained a mental age of five years" (Paragraph 10); (3) Section 1330(2) means *"only* that a parent may be excused from liability under the compulsory attendance provisions of the School Code when, with the approval of the local school board and the Secretary of Education and the finding by an approved school psychologist, the parent elects to withdraw the child from attendance; Section 1330(2) may not be used by defendants, contrary to parents' wishes, to terminate or in any way deny access to a free public program of education and training to any mentally retarded child." (Paragraph 20); and (4) Section 1326 means *"only* that parents of a child have a compulsory duty while the child is between eight and seventeen years of age to assure his attendance in a program of education and training; and Section 1326 does not limit the ages between which a child must be granted access to a free public program of education and training [and may not be used as such]." (Paragraph 16). Thus, possible use of these four provisions to exclude (or postpone) retarded children from a program of public education was effectively foreclosed by this Agreement. And on October 22, 1971, the Attorney General issued these agreed upon Opinions.

In addition, the Consent Agreement addresses itself to three other matters involving the education of retarded children which the plaintiffs did not specifically raise in their pleadings. First, in the area of pre-school education, the defendants agreed to cease applying 24 Purd.Stat. Sec. 13-1371 so as to deny retarded children below the age of six access to a free pre-school program of education and training appropriate to their learning capacities whenever the school districts provide such a pre-school program to *normal* children below the age of six. The Attorney General again issued an Opinion so interpreting Section 1371(1).

Next, the defendants agreed to cease applying 24 Purd.Stat. Sec. 13-1376 so as to deny tuition or tuition maintenance to any mentally retarded person. Basically, Section 1376 provides for the payment of tuition to private schools by the Commonwealth and local school districts (75% and 25%, respectively) where, with the approval of the Department of Education, a child afflicted with blindness, deafness, cerebral palsy, brain damage or muscular dystrophy is attending a private school. Prior to the

Consent Agreement, this statute was interpreted not to apply to retarded children unless they also suffered from one of the maladies mentioned above. Consequently, if the public sector excluded a retarded child (who lacked a multiple disability) under Section 1375, 1304, 1330 or 1326, his parents had to assume the full financial burden of educating and training him in a private school. Often, because of the special care required, ·this burden assumed formidable proportions.[17] Thus, the Attorney General issued an Opinion "construing the term 'brain damage' as used in Section 1376 . . . so as to include thereunder all mentally retarded persons, thereby making available to them tuition for day school and tuition and maintenance for residential school . . ." (Paragraph 27).

Finally, the defendants agreed to cease applying 24 Purd.Stat. Sec. 13-1372(3) so as "to deny [mentally retarded children] homebound instruction under that Section . . . merely because no physical disability accompanies the retardation or because retardation is not a short-term disability." (Paragraph 31.) Once again, the Attorney General issued an Opinion so construing this provision.

The lengthy Consent Agreement concludes by stating that "[e]very retarded person between the ages of six and twenty-one shall be provided access to a free public program of education and training appropriate to his capacities as soon as possible but in no event later than *September 1, 1972.*" (Paragraph 42). To implement the agreed upon relief and assure that it would be extended to all members of this class, Dennis E. Haggerty, Esq., a distinguished member of the Pennsylvania Bar who has devoted much of his energy to the welfare of retarded children, and Dr. Herbert Goldstein, an eminent expert in the education of retarded children who is Professor and Director of the Curriculum Research and Development Center in Mental Retardation at the Ferkaus

---

[17]Leonard Kalish, Esq., appearing *pro se* on behalf of his fifteen year old daughter who is a member of the plaintiff class stated that his child has been excluded from a public education all of her life. He continued:

> I would just like to call to the Court's attention what the realities of that situation are, and I think I can speak with some authority because for the last nine years, my fifteen year old daughter has been denied access to public education without due process, but consistently denied, and as a result of which we have had her in private schools for the last nine years.
>
> Now in those nine years, not counting the present year, not counting the year which started last summer, we have spent approximately forty thousand dollars on her private schooling, shall I say. At the present time we have her in a private school, a residential school where we pay a tuition of twelve thousand dollars a year, and I want to say to the Court that what I am saying here too our situation is paralleled by many other situations of many other children, and their parents.
>
> Now if a public facility were established that comes anywhere near striking distance of appropriateness for my child, Your Honors can rest assured that I will welcome that public facility with open arms. The financial burden of giving my child private education is very considerable. There is no pride or status symbol involved in having a child in a private school such as the private schools to which my child and others in the same situation would go. In other words, it isn't out of any feeling of status that I am undertaking this heavy financial burden. It is simply because there is no public facility.
>
> Now the moment a public facility is indicated, even just on the drawing board or on brochures, or papers of any kind which will look reasonably appropriate, I will assure Your Honors that ninety-five percent or more of all parents will rush to get their children in there because every one of the parents is laboring under a backbreaking financial burden. We're not talking about wealthy people here. We are talking about ordinary people, and I know a great many of them who send their children to the same school where I send mine, and I have had my child in one other school before this, and I have had her with a private tutor for a year.

Graduate School of Humanities and Social Sciences, Yeshiva University, were appointed Masters at the expense of the Commonwealth. (Paragraph 45). Next, the Consent Agreement charges defendants with the duty within 30 days, to formulate and submit to the Masters a plan to locate, evaluate and give notice to all members of the plaintiff class. (Paragraph 47). Finally, and perhaps most importantly, the Agreement states that:

> The defendants shall formulate and submit to the Masters for their approval *a plan to be effectuated by September 1, 1972,* to commence or recommence a free public program of education and training for all mentally retarded persons . . . aged between four and twenty-one years of the date of this Order, and for all mentally retarded persons of such ages hereafter. The plan shall specify the range of programs of education and training, there [sic] kind and number, necessary to provide an appropriate program of education and training to all mentally retarded children, where they shall be conducted, arrangements for their financing, and, if additional teachers are found to be necessary, the plan shall specify recruitment, hiring, and training arrangements.'' (Paragraph 49) (emphasis added).

Thus, if all goes according to plan, Pennsylvania should be providing a meaningful program of education and training to every retarded child in the Commonwealth by September, 1972.

We then entered an *interim order,* without prejudice, pending notice to the class of plaintiffs and the class of defendants, which temporarily enjoined the defendants from applying (1) 24 Purd.Stat. Sections 13-1375, 1304, 1330(2), and 1371(1) "so as to deny any mentally retarded child access to a free public program of education and training"; (2) Section 13-1376 "so as to deny tuition or tuition and maintenance to any mentally retarded person except on the same terms as may be applied to other exceptional children, including brain damaged children generally"; and (3) Section 13-1372(3) "[so as to deny] homebound instruction to any mentally retarded person merely because no physical disability accompanies the retardation or because it is not a short-term disability.''

Next, in accordance with Rule 23(e), F.R.Civ.P., a hearing was scheduled on any objections to the proposed settlement Agreements. We instructed the named plaintiffs and defendants to notify all remaining members of their respective classes (primarily by newspaper in the case of plaintiffs and by direct mailing for the defendants). Proper notice went out to the plaintiffs and only one appeared at the hearing. None of the remaining defendants appeared, however, because the Commonwealth neglected to send them any notice. Consequently, we ordered that new notice be given, and rescheduled the hearing for November 12, 1971.

Notice of that hearing went out about October 29th, and Philip Salkin, Esq. and William B. Arnold, Esq. appeared and filed objections on behalf of the Montgomery County Intermediate Unit and the Lancaster-Lebanon Intermediate Unit, respectively. In addition, John D. Killian, Esq. appeared and objected for the Pennsylvania Association of Private Schools for Exceptional Children.

Both attorneys for the Intermediate Units argued to the Court that the notice they received was inadequate to prepare their cases against both the Stipulation of June 18th and the Consent Agreement of October 7th. They also argued that many districts and intermediate units failed to appear because they did not have enough time to analyze and react to the two rather lengthy and intricate proposals. The attorneys pointed out that since most school boards meet on the first week of each month, these bodies would not even have an opportunity to review the documents until after December 1st.

To extend every element of fairness in this important litigation, we ordered that a *second individual notice* be sent to all 29 intermediate units and 569 school districts, extending them an opportunity to object and be heard at yet another hearing on December 15, 1971. Following this second notice, the Allegheny Intermediate Unit No. 3, Chester County Intermediate Unit No. 24, Schuylkill Intermediate Unit No. 29, Delaware County Intermediate Unit, and 9 individual school districts within these four Units joined the opponents of the settlement.

On December 15th and 16th, we heard from the objectors and their witnesses. Essentially, the complaining defendants challenged parts of the June 18th Stipulation (dealing with due process hearings) which they claimed were unnecessary, burdensome and administratively unwieldy and impractical. The wisdom of a few minor portions of the October 7th Consent Agreement was also questioned. Apart from questioning certain details of the Agreements, the objectors challenged our jurisdiction over the case and over themselves as purported members of a class. Finally, they raised the issue of abstention.

Following this testimony, the proponents of the settlement met with the objectors in an effort to modify the two documents so as to satisfy everyone involved. Intensive negotiations ensued. Final legal argument was scheduled for January 31, 1972.

At the request of the litigants, we postponed final argument until February 7, 1972. On that date, only *one* defendant remained—the Lancaster-Lebanon Intermediate Unit. All others had withdrawn their objections because subsequent modifications of the Stipulation and Consent Agreement by the proponents satisfied their complaints. The Pennsylvania Association of Private Schools for Exceptional Children (which is not a member of either class) also expressed dissatisfaction at that hearing.

The arguments presented by Lancaster-Lebanon are essentially legal, that is, the Intermediate Unit does not question the *fairness* of the proposed settlement to the members of either class, rather it seeks to destroy the Agreements altogether by raising the issue of jurisdiction as well as the oft-mentioned, but seldom fully understood, issue of abstention.

I.   Jurisdiction

A.   Controversy Under Article III

Preliminarily, the issue of whether the Lancaster-Lebanon Intermediate Unit can even raise jurisdictional issues at a hearing on the proposed settlement of a class action under Rule 23(e) arises. Theoretically, the scope of such a hearing is limited to an inquiry into the fairness of the settlement. See Moore's Federal Practice, § 23.80(4). Since jurisdictional issues relate to the very power of this court to hear this case and bind the parties, however, we think that the objectors must be permitted to raise them.

Although not particularly pressed at final oral argument (which was devoted primarily to absention), Lancaster-Lebanon has raised two distinct jurisdictional issues throughout this litigation. First, Lancaster-Lebanon charges that there is no controversy before this court within the meaning of Article III, Sec. 2 of the United States Constitution because of alleged collusion and total agreement on the merits between the plaintiffs and the Commonwealth in conducting this suit. Secondly, the Intermediate Unit contends that this Court lacks jurisdiction to bind it to any Consent Agreement because the Lancaster-Lebanon Unit received no notice and had no opportunity to appear when the suit was first instituted. (See Section I. B., *infra*.). We find both contentions without merit.

Undoubtedly, if two litigants commence a suit with the same goals in mind, no controversy exists to give the district court jurisdiction as required by Article III, Sec. 2. See *Moore* v. *Charlotte-Mecklenburg Board of Education,* 402 U.S. 47, 91 S.Ct. 1292, 28 L.Ed.2d 590 (1971); *United States* v. *Johnson,* 319 U.S. 302, 63 S.Ct. 1075, 87 L.Ed. 1413 (1943); *Muskrat* v. *United States,* 219 U.S. 346, 31 S.Ct. 250, 55 L.Ed. 246 (1911). But a different case arises when litigants *begin* a suit as adversaries, and then at some later point decide to compromise the dispute. In such an instance, the court does not *ipso facto* lose jurisdiction over the matter for want of a controversy. *Cf. Dixon* v. *Attorney General of Com. of Pa.,* 325 F.Supp. 966 (M.D.Pa. 1971) (Biggs, Circuit Judge). This latter rule flows from common sense as well as the fact that even in preparing a compromise, the parties may remain adversaries within the meaning of Article III.

The record in this case clearly shows that the Commonwealth did not collaborate with the plaintiffs in bringing or conducting this suit. Indeed, from January until June, 1971, the Attorney General and the thirteen named school districts vigorously contested every phase of plaintiffs' case. First, the Commonwealth filed motions to dismiss which were accompanied by elaborate briefs. The defendants denied jurisdiction, denied that a claim had been stated upon which relief might be granted, denied that plaintiffs had raised a substantial federal question, and questioned whether PARC had standing to sue. On the merits, they asserted that all of the statutes attacked were founded upon rational bases. Subsequently, the defendants filed a 13 page brief opposing plaintiffs' motion to convene a three-judge court. Moreover, in discovery, the defendants resisted the production of certain documents and the parties had to appeal to this Court for resolution of the dispute.

In June, 1971, it is true, the parties agreed to settle the issue of due process hearings. Even so, the defendants did not give the plaintiffs carte blanche to draw up any proposal of their choosing; rather the arts of negotiation and compromise were employed, with Commonwealth experts in the field of education also taking part in the discussions.

Despite negotiations on this front, the defendants steadfastly adhered to their original position on plaintiffs' equal protection claims. Indeed, it was not until after a day of testimony from four distinguished experts that the Commonwealth agreed to relent on this issue as well. Far from an indication of collusion, however, the Commonwealth's willingness to settle this dispute reflects an intelligent response to overwhelming evidence against their position.

Once the compromise was prepared, of course, plaintiffs and the named defendants shared identical interests in seeking approval of the settlement. Nevertheless, because these defendants refused to concede the unconstitutionality of the statutes and continued to enforce them, the parties remained adversaries on the constitutional issues which are critical to our jurisdiction. Hence, we conclude that a controversy exists under Article III, Sec. 2.

B. Over the Parties

Next, Lancaster-Lebanon argues that it is not bound by these Consent Agreements or the Injunction because this Court lacks jurisdiction, not necessarily over the subject matter, but over it as a party. The Intermediate Unit predicates this assertion upon the concept that under the Due Process Clause, notice at the commencement of the litigation constitutes a prerequisite to a court's jurisdiction over the parties. As applied to the facts of this case, however, we disagree.

We begin by holding that the *defendants* constitute a class under Rule 23(b) (1) (B), F.R.Civ.P. This section is appropriate because, as a practical matter, once the issues are decided against one school district within an intermediate unit, or one intermediate unit within the Commonwealth all other districts or intermediate units will ultimately be bound by the result. In other words, "adjudications with respect to individual members of the class [would] as a practical matter be dispositive of the interests of the other members not parties to the adjudication . . ." Rule 23(b) (1) (B). This result follows because (1) intermediate units have an obligation to coordinate the education of exceptional children where member school districts are unable to sustain individual programs, and (2) the Commonwealth, for reasons of economy and administration, must necessarily maintain a uniform set of rules and regulations governing the responsibilities of *all* school districts and intermediate units within the state.

The notice requirements for a (b) (1) class are set forth in Rule 23(d) (2) which provides as follows:

> (d) Orders of Conduct of Actions. In the conduct of actions to which this rule applies, the court may make appropriate orders: . . .
> (2) requiring, for the protection of the members of the class or otherwise for the fair conduct of the action, that notice be given in such manner as the court may direct to some or all of the members of any step in the action, or of the proposed extent of the judgment . . ."

Under this rule, notice of the litigation to members of the class is apparently discretionary, and "[i]n the degree that there is cohesiveness or unity in the class and the representation is effective, the need for notice to the class will tend toward a minimum." Indeed, most courts have held that where a class is adequately represented, no notice of the suit need be given under the Due Process Clause in order to bind all members of the clss. See *Management T. V. Sys. Inc.* v. *National Football League,* 52 F.R.D. 162 (E.D.Pa. 1971); *Northern Natural Gas Co.* v. *Grounds,* 292 F.Supp. 619 (D. Kan. 1968).

But we need not go this far, because the due process issue presented here is significantly different. In this case, the Lancaster-Lebanon Unit, and all 29 other intermediate units and 569 school districts received *two* notices of this proceeding and *two* opportunities to appear before this Court (November 12th and December 15th) *prior* to any final judgment on the fairness of the settlement proposals. And at these hearings, the defendants had an opportunity to recall any expert witness who testified at the August 12th hearing (at which the objectors were not present) for purposes of cross examination. Yet the defendants declined this invitation. In addition, we allowed them an opportunity to present contrary evidence on the merits, and the objecting defendants did produce the testimony which they felt was relevant. All then rested on the record. Since the defendants had an adequate notice to appear and a meaningful opportunity to present evidence *before* we rendered final judgment on the settlement, we hold that the objecting defendants were afforded every element of procedural due process. See *Armstrong* v. *Manzo,* 380 U.S. 545, 552, 85 S.Ct. 1187, 14 L.Ed.2d 62 (1965).

Further, we are satisfied that the Attorney General adequately represented the interests of all the defendants before the objectors entered the case. To the extent that inadequate representation during the early stages of litigation might constitute a denial of due process, no such denial occurred in this case. By express agreement of counsel, the Attorney General assumed the arduous task of defending this action on behalf of the thirteen named school districts as well as the named officials. And the interests of these named school districts fairly reflected the interests of all school districts in the Commonwealth. Hence, the requirement that the class representatives not have interests antagonistic to those of other members of the class whom they are representing was satisfied.

We have already reviewed the actions of the Attorney General in defending this case. And while conducting their defense, the Commonwealth kept the named parties fully informed of the progress of the litigation and advised them of the content of the proposed settlements. Considering these facts, we reject Lancaster-Lebanon's attacks upon our jurisdiction over the parties.

C. Over the Subject Matter

Although no party questions the quality of plaintiffs' constitutional claims, it is basic constitutional law that federal district courts cannot acquire jurisdiction over the subject matter of a dispute by consent. Rather our jurisdiction (power) necessarily depends upon the United States Constitution and Acts of Congress. For this reason, consensus of the parties cannot interfere with our fundamental obligation to act only where the Constitution and Congress permit. Cf. *Sibron* v. *New York,* 392 U.S. 40, 58, 88 S.Ct. 1889, 20 L.Ed.2d 917 (1968); *Young* v. *United States,* 315 U.S. 257, 258–259, 62 S.Ct. 510, 86 L.Ed. 832 (1942). Consequently, we conclude that this court has a constitutional obligation to examine the record independently and satisfy ourselves that plaintiffs' claims are not "wholly insubstantial and frivolous." *Bell* v. *Hood,* 327 U.S. 678, 682-683, 66 S.Ct. 773, 90 L.Ed. 939 (1946).

Such an inquiry becomes particularly important in the case of these defendants because we have entered an injunction which, by its terms, binds *all* school districts and intermediate units in the Commonwealth. Moreover, this injunction affects the enforcement of some half-dozen statutes by state officers. The injunctive power of this court must not be used lightly, especially when it operates against state statutes and officers.

We begin with the contention that due process requires a hearing before retarded children may be denied a public education. It is not disputed that prior to this suit, parents of retarded children who are plaintiffs were not afforded a hearing or, in many instances, even notice of their child's exclusion from public school. For example, the parents of David Tupi, a retarded child, were never officially informed of the decision to exclude him from school. Rather they were only made aware of the situation when the school bus which regularly brought him to school failed to show up. Such crass and summary treatment of these children becomes suspect, we think, because of the stigma which our society unfortunately attaches to the label of mental retardation. Dr. Goldberg testified at length concerning the historical roots of the stigma.

Organized efforts to educate the mentally retarded began about 1848 with the establishment of residential centers which were geared toward preparing mentally retarded individuals for a greater contribution to society as well as sheltering these individuals from a hostile society. About 1900, special education classes for the mentally retarded were started in public schools. These classes were originally denominated "opportunity classes," which indicated that the child was merely waiting somewhere to join the mainstream of the school life.

But Dr. Goldberg stated that in the next decade:

> [T]he wonderful idea of adjusting the individuals to our society became the dumping grounds for children who could not manage in other classes and started to be called classes for the feebleminded, classes for idiots, and so on. . . .
> And then the Eugenic Association in the United States started to raise quite a lot of cry that the American Society is going to pieces, mental retardation is hereditary, mentally retardeds are criminals, are prostitutes as the [I.Q.] tests proved. Therefore, something very drastic has to be done.
> And in 1912, the Eugenic Society, the Research Section of the Eugenic Society, namely, the American Breeders Association suggested that drastic measures be taken to prevent the Americans from becoming all feebleminded [such as] segregation or segregation during the reproductive period, for women, . . . organizing institutions for feebleminded women of child-bearing age in order to prevent them from having children, . . . compulsory sterilization law for women, and castration for men. . . . Another recommendation was euthanasia. This, of course, just introduced and I hope was not implemented. . . . I really want to point out that the days we are talking about are not so far removed, that the stigma attached to mental retardation is still with us, with the general public.

Empirical studies show that stigmatization is a major concern among parents of retarded children. Some parents liken it to a "sentence of death."

Experts agree that it is primarily the *school* which imposes the mentally-retarded label and concomitant stigmatization upon children, either initially or later on through a change in educational assignment. This follows from the fact that the school constitutes the first social institution with which the child comes into contact.

Not only is the school the institution which normally imposes the stigma; sometimes, and perhaps quite often, a child is incorrectly labeled. A recent study of 378 educable mentally retarded students from 36 independent school districts in the five county Greater Philadelphia Area found that "the diagnosis for 25% of the youngsters found in classes for the [educable mentally] retarded may be considered errone-ous. An additional 43% may be questioned.'' The authors conclude: ''[O]ne cannot help but be concerned about the consequences of subjecting these children to the 'retarded' curriculum. . . . The stigma of bearing the label 'retarded' is bad enough, but to bear the label when placement is questionable or outright erroneous is an intolerable situation.''

In the recent case of *Wisconsin* v. *Constantineau,* 400 U.S. 433, 91 S.Ct. 507, 27 L.Ed.2d 515 (1971), the United States Supreme Court considered the necessity of a due process hearing before the state stigmatizes any citizen. There the police, without notice to her or a prior hearing, had posted a notice in all retail liquor establishments forbidding sales to Mrs. Constantineau because of her ''excessive drinking.'' The Court wrote:

> The only issue present here is whether the label or characterization given a person by ''posting,'' though a mark of serious illness to some, is to others such a stigma or badge of disgrace that procedural due process requires notice and an opportunity to be heard. We agree with the district court that the private interest is such that those re-quirements . . . must be met. (*Id.* at 436, 91 S.Ct. at 509.)

Considering just *Constantineau* and the evidence presented here, we are convinced that the plaintiffs have established a colorable claim under the Due Process Clause.

Our jurisdiction over plaintiffs' equal protection claims also stands on firm ground. Without exception, expert opinion indicates that:

> [A]ll mentally retarded persons are capable of benefiting from a program of education and training; that the greatest number of retarded persons, given such education and training, are capable of achieving self-sufficiency and the remaining few, with such education and training are capable of achieving some degree of self-care; that the earlier such education and training begins, the more thoroughly and the more efficiently a men-tally retarded person will benefit from it and, whether begun early or not, that a mentally retarded person can benefit at any point in his life and development from a program of education. (Consent Agreement, Paragraph 4.)

Despite this evidence and despite the fact that Pennsylvania provides an education to most children, the State's 1965 Pennsylvania Mental Retardation Plan estimates that while 46,000 school age retarded children were enrolled in public schools, another 70,000 to 80,000 retarded children between the ages of 5 and 21 were denied access to *any* public education services in schools, home or day care or other community facilities, or state residential institutions (C.M.R.P. at 4, 92, 93, 142).

Because of an absence of adequate resources, facilities and teachers as well as the lack of a structured plan, even those whom the State serves in its institutions (i. e., residential centers, hospitals, etc.) do not always benefit. For example, Dr. Edward R. Goldman, Commissioner of the Office of Mental Retardation, Department of Welfare, testified that there are presently 4,159 children of school age in state institutions. But only 100 of these children are in a full program of education and training; 1,700 are in partial but inadequate programs, and 3,259 are in no program of any kind. Moreover, the 1965 Pennsylvania Mental Retardation Plan reports that because of a lack of space, the State housed 900 mentally retarded persons at Dallas State Correction Institution, 3,462 at State mental hospitals and 104 in Youth Development Centers. And:

Fewer than two percent of the residents of Pennsylvania's state schools leave the rolls each year; and half of those by death, rather than by discharge. A discharge rate of less than one percent has two implications: First, that beds are not opening up for persons in the community who need them; and second, that the state institutions continue to provide a program that barely rises above purely custodial care, if it rises at all.

Finally, the Report concludes:

> Nowhere is there a suitable commonwealth-supported local program for children of school age who are adjudged uneducable and untrainable by the public schools. Their normal fate is a waiting list for a state school and hospital, at which services do not conform to the spirit of the school code.

With these facts in mind, we turn to plaintiffs' equal protection argument. Plaintiffs do not challenge the separation of special classes for retarded children from regular classes or the proper assignment of retarded children to special classes. Rather plaintiffs question whether the state, having undertaken to provide public education to some children (perhaps all children) may deny it to plaintiffs entirely. We are satisfied that the evidence raises serious doubts (and hence a colorable claim) as to the existence of a rational basis for such exclusions. See, e.g., *Brown* v. *Board of Education*, 349 U.S. 294, 75 S.Ct. 753, 99 L.Ed. 1083 (1955).

One further jurisdictional matter remains. Plaintiffs' complaint contains two pendent state law claims which the Consent Agreement and our Injunction encompass. We find that, to the extent these claims involve distinct non-federal claims, this Court has jurisdiction over them because "[t]he state and federal claims . . . derive from a common nucleus of operative fact" and they are such that "[a plaintiff] would ordinarily be expected to try them all in one judicial proceeding." *United Mine Workers* v. *Gibbs,* 383 U.S. 715, 725, 86 S.Ct. 1130, 1138, 16 L.Ed.2d 218 (1966). Compare *Hurn* v. *Oursler,* 289 U.S. 238, 53 S.Ct. 586, 77 L.Ed. 1148 (1933). On the other hand, to the extent that these claims emanate from unconstitutional *results* obtained by the improper use of statutes which themselves are not unconstitutional, plaintiffs, of course, have made out a federal claim. See 42 U.S.C. § 1983.

[Section II of this opinion, in which the court discusses the issue of abstention and concludes that it would be inappropriate to abstain in the circumstances of this case, is omitted.]

III.   Fairness of the Settlement

The final matter for our consideration is whether to approve the settlement as fair and reasonable. In arriving at such a decision, we must consider its fairness to both the plaintiffs and the defendants since both groups are classes for which this Court assumes the role of guardian.

Additionally, we must dispose of the objections of the Pennsylvania Association of Private Schools for Exceptional Children (PAPSEC). Essentially, PAPSEC contends that the following paragraph is unjust *to retarded children* in private schools because it eliminates the requirement for a prior hearing.

> Whenever an additional facility or program within a School District or Intermediate Unit is submitted for approval by the Secretary of Education, then at the same time, a School

District or Intermediate Unit, upon written notice to the parent or guardian, may in writing request approval of the Director of the Bureau of Special Education, acting as the Secretary's designee, for the transfer of particular children from private schools to the additional facility or program. Any district or unit so requesting shall submit documentation of the appropriateness of the new facility or program for the particular children proposed for transfer. The parents or guardians may submit any documentation to the contrary. If after appropriate investigation the Director of the Bureau certifies the new facility or program as appropriate for those children and approves their transfers, such certification and approval shall be in lieu of individual hearings as provided above in this paragraph. (Amended Consent Agreement, Paragraph 29.)

However, since PAPSEC is neither a party nor a member of either class, we must first decide whether it has standing to raise this issue.

To confer standing under the rules of *Flast* v. *Cohen,* 392 U.S. 83, 102, 88 S.Ct. 1942, 1953, 20 L.Ed.2d 947 (1968), a party must not only establish a personal stake and interest in the outcome, it must also show "a logical nexus between the status [it asserts] and the claim sought to be adjudicated." In this case PAPSEC members no doubt have a genuine financial stake in the outcome since the Consent Agreement (particularly paragraph 29) may well tend to curtail the expansion of private schools for retarded children. However, they raise no issues relating to the welfare of private schools under the settlement. Rather PAPSEC seeks only to advance the interests and welfare of retarded children. It is not clear whether PAPSEC may do this under the doctrine of *Flast* v. *Cohen.* Compare *Pierce* v. *Society of Sisters,* 268 U.S. 510, 45 S.Ct. 571, 69 L.Ed. 1070 (1925) where the Society of Sisters alleged both a denial of their constitutional rights by a state statute which outlawed private schools as well as a denial of the constitutional rights of their patrons. But we need not decide this issue because, even if we were to consider the interests of retarded children under this paragraph of the Consent, we are convinced that it is fair to them. In this instance, certification by the Director of the Bureau of Education, the opportunity of parents to participate in determining the facility's appropriateness and automatic re-evaluation every two years are sufficient safeguards against an erroneous assignment.

Next, we consider the defendants, particularly the local districts and intermediate units which comprise the vast bulk of this class. When the objectors entered this case, they expressed alarm at the possible burdens, both administrative and financial, which the due process Stipulation and the Consent Agreement would impose. Subsequent changes in the due process Stipulation, however, eliminated most of the administrative burden, and that allayed the fears of all but the Lancaster-Lebanon Unit.

Lancaster-Lebanon continues to object to the basic concept of a prior due process hearing and asserts that injury flows to the school districts because under the Stipulation they will be unable to remove a disruptive retarded child from regular classes immediately. But this danger is more imagined than real. Dr. Sherr, Lancaster-Lebanon's own witness testified that the problem would arise, if at all, only with respect to severely retarded children. As to that group identification is rather easy; and an early identification, as required by state law, will permit a hearing and decision (if there is a dispute) well before the school year begins. In any case, the Amended Stipulation on hearings provides that in "extraordinary circumstances" the Director of the Bureau of Special Education may authorize tentative assignment to precede the hearing.

Financially, the burden of implementing this settlement falls primarily upon the Commonwealth, not the local districts or intermediate units. Dr. Ohrtman testified that the excess instruction cost required to educate a retarded child will be paid for by the Commonwealth. For example, he stated that if it costs $1,000 to educate a normal child and $1,800 for a retarded child, the State will reimburse $800 to the local district. Moreover, the Commonwealth will pay intermediate units, in advance, funds necessary to hire extra personnel such as secretaries and psychologists necessary to implement this settlement. In short, we find that both the Stipulation and Consent Agreement are fair and reasonable to the defendants.

We have absolutely no hesitation about approving the Agreements as fair and reasonable to the plaintiffs. Approval means that plaintiff retarded children who heretofore had been excluded from a public program of education and training will no longer be so excluded after September 1, 1972. This is a noble and humanitarian end in which the Commonwealth of Pennsylvania has chosen to join. Today, with the following Order, this group of citizens will have new hope in their quest for a life of dignity and self-sufficiency.

ORDER AND INJUNCTION

And now, this 5th day of May, 1972, it is ordered that the Amended Stipulation and Amended Consent Agreement are approved and adopted as fair and reasonable to all members of both the plaintiff and defendant classes.

It is further ordered that the defendants: the Commonwealth of Pennsylvania, the Secretary of the Department of Education, the State Board of Education, the Secretary of the Department of Public Welfare, the named defendant school districts and intermediate units and each of the school districts and intermediate units in the Commonwealth of Pennsylvania, their officers, employees, agents and successors are enjoined as follows:

(a) from applying Section 1304 of the Public School Code of 1949, 24 Purd.Stat. Sec. 1304, so as to postpone or in any way deny to any mentally retarded child access to a free public program of education and training;

(b) from applying Section 1326 or Section 1330(2) of the School Code of 1949, 24 Purd.Stat. Secs. 13-1326 and 13-1330(2) so as to postpone, to terminate or in any way deny to any mentally retarded child access to a free program of education and training;

(c) from Applying Section 1371(1) of the School Code of 1949, 24 Purd.Stat. Sec. 13-1371(1) so to deny to any mentally retarded child access to a free public program of education and training;

(d) from applying Section 1376 of the School Code of 1949, 24 Purd.Stat. Sec. 13-1376, so as to deny tuition or tuition and maintenance to any mentally retarded person except on the same terms as may be applied to other exceptional children, including brain damaged children generally;

(e) from denying homebound instruction under 1372(3) of the School Code of 1949, 24 Purd.Stat. Sec. 13-1372(3) to any mentally retarded child merely because no physical disability accompanies the retardation or because retardation is not a short-term disability.

(f) from applying Section 1375 of the School Code of 1949, 24 Purd.Stat. Sec. 13-1375, so as to deny to any mentally retarded child access to a free public program of education and training;

(g) to provide, as soon as possible but in no event later than September 1, 1972, to every retarded person between the ages of six and twenty-one years as of the date of this Order and thereafter, access to a free public program of education and training appropriate to his learning capacities;

(h) to provide, as soon as possible but in no event later than September 1, 1972, wherever defendants provide a preschool program of education and training for children aged less than six years of age, access to a free public program of education and training appropriate to his learning capacities to every mentally retarded child of the same age.

(i) to provide notice and the opportunity for a hearing prior to a change in educational status of any child who is mentally retarded or thought to be mentally retarded.

(j) to re-evaluate the educational assignment of every mentally retarded child not less than every two years, or annually upon the parents' request, and upon such re-evaluation, to provide notice and the opportunity for a hearing.

NOTES

1.   The *PARC* case generated a great deal of publicity and stimulated similar litigative efforts in other parts of the country. As one of the first statewide, federal, class action lawsuits brought on behalf of handicapped persons, it is often considered the cradle of the whole legal rights movement for handicapped people. The conception, development and results of the *PARC* lawsuit have been described in a book by Leopold Lippman and Ignacy Goldberg, *Right to Education* (Teachers College Press, Columbia University, N.Y., 1973).

2.   In mapping out his strategy for the Pennsylvania lawsuit, Thomas K. Gilhool, the plaintiffs' attorney, provided a blueprint for future litigation of this type. The two-barreled (due process and equal protection) attack has become standard fare in subsequent lawsuits. The legal analysis and arguments contained in the Complaint in PARC have been employed as a touchstone in the drafting of later complaints. Even though there have been a number of subsequent legal developments that have necessitated adjustments and new directions in such litigation, the impact of Gilhool's initial legal insights are difficult to overestimate.

3.   After ruling that the plaintiffs had established a colorable claim under the Due Process Clause by virtue of the *Constantineau* "stigma or badge of disgrace" theory, the court added,

> For this reason we need not consider the colorability of plaintiffs' claim that education constitutes an essential interest, and therefore it may not be disturbed by government action without a prior hearing. [Long list of citations omitted.] (343 F.Supp. at 295, n. 48).

This latter theory, that the requirements of due process attach whenever any action by public authorities denies an individual any important public benefit, e.g. *Goldberg* v. *Kelly,* 397 U.S. 254 (1970), is a more common version of due process analysis than the *Constantineau* rationale. In contexts not involving handicapped persons, courts have recognized, since at least 1961, that denial of public education requires the imposition of due process procedural protections, *Dixon* v. *Alabama State Board of Education,* 294 F.2d 150 (5th Cir. 1961). This principle has been applied in a long line of cases since that time, culminating in *Goss* v. *Lopez,* 419 U.S. 565 (1975) (see footnote 8 of that opinion for a list of such precedents). It is simple logic, therefore, to argue that the requirements of due process ought to apply to situations where handicapped children are being excluded from public school programs.

4.   The *PARC* decision was based upon a consent agreement entered into by the parties to the litigation. The original consent agreement is set out at 334 F.Supp. 1257 (E.D.Pa. 1971); an amended consent agreement was attached as Appendix B to the Opinion, Order, and Injunction included herein, along with Appendix A—Amended Stipulations (Appendix A is found at 343 F.Supp. 303 and B at 343 F.Supp. 306). The fact that the case proceeded through one day of trial, and the fact that one school district, the Lancaster-Lebanon Intermediate Unit, refused to go along with the consent agreement, made the case more adversarial than typical consent order decisions, and required the three-judge court to deal with more substantive matters than simply the usual question of whether the agreed upon resolution is "fair." For these reasons, PARC may be described as a "quasi-consensual, quasi-adversarial" decision.

5.   In the body of its opinion, the *PARC* court characterizes the plaintiffs' equal protection argument as a contention that the challenged classification "lacks a rational basis in fact." This equal protection standard, known as the "rational basis" test, was the less stringent of two levels of equal protection analysis in vogue during the Warren era. Under the alternative standard, the "strict scrutiny" test, a classification would be struck down as violative of equal protection unless the state could demonstrate a compelling interest justifying its usage. This stricter equal protection analysis was invoked by the courts whenever a classification 1) affected a "fundamental right," or 2) was based upon constitutionally "suspect" criteria, such as race or nationality. In fact, the PARC plaintiffs had argued for the application of the strict scrutiny test by alleging that education was a fundamental right and that the denial of public education programs to mentally retarded children resulted in a wealth classification (because those children whose parents could afford private school tuition would get an education while poorer children would not). In a footnote, the *PARC* court recognized these contentions by the plaintiffs, but found no need to reach them:

> But we are satisfied that the plaintiffs have established a colorable constitutional claim even under the less stringent rational basis test, and consequently we need not decide whether the Commonwealth must demonstrate a compelling state interest in order to dispose of the narrow issues presently before us (343 F.Supp. at 283 n. 8).

The question of the appropriate equal protection tests, however, would recur with more significance in some of the later equal educational opportunity lawsuits. And, as we shall see, this issue of equal protection standards retained its importance even after some subsequent criticism, revamping, and reinterpretation of the Warren Court's two-tiered equal protection theory.

ADDITIONAL READING

Gilhool, T., "The Right of Access to Free Public Schooling for All Children" 2
Leadership Series in Special Education 167, University of Minnesota (R. Johnson, J. Gross, and R. Weatherman, eds., 1973).

Weintraub, F., and Abeson, A., "Appropriate Education for All Handicapped Children: A Growing Issue," 23 *Syracuse L. Rev.* 1037 (1972).

Note, "Special Education: The Struggle for Equal Educational Opportunity in Iowa," 62 *Ia. L. Rev.* 1283, 1340-1344 (1977).

For a look at the PARC case from a different perspective, see Governor M. Shapp, "The Right to an Education for the Retarded in Pennsylvania," 23 *Syracuse L. Rev.* 1085 (1972).

2. The *Mills* Decision

MILLS v. BOARD OF EDUCATION OF THE DISTRICT OF COLUMBIA

United States District Court for the District of Columbia District, 1972
348 F.Supp. 866

WADDY, District Judge.

This is a civil action brought on behalf of seven children of school age by their next friends in which they seek a declaration of rights and to enjoin the defendants from excluding them from the District of Columbia Public Schools and/or denying them publicly supported education and to compel the defendants to provide them with immediate and adequate education and educational facilities in the public schools or alternative placement at public expense. They also seek additional and ancillary relief to effectuate the primary relief. They allege that although they can profit from an education either in regular classrooms with supportive services or in special classes adapted to their needs, they have been labelled as behavioral problems, mentally retarded, emotionally disturbed or hyperactive, and denied admission to the public schools or excluded therefrom after admission, with no provision for alternative educational placement or periodic review. The action was certified as a class action under Rule 23(b) (1) and (2) of Federal Rules of Civil Procedure by order of the Court dated December 17, 1971.

The defendants are the Board of Education of the District of Columbia and its members, the Superintendent of Schools for the District of Columbia and subordinate school officials, the Commissioner of the District of Columbia and certain subordinate officials and the District of Columbia.

The Problem

The genesis of this case is found (1) in the failure of the District of Columbia to provide publicly supported education and training to plaintiffs and other "exceptional" children, members of their class, and (2) the excluding, suspending, expelling, reassigning and transferring of "exceptional" children from regular public school classes without affording them due process of law.

The problem of providing special education for "exceptional" children (mentally retarded, emotionally disturbed, physically handicapped, hyperactive and other children with behavioral problems) is one of major proportions in the District of Columbia. The precise number of such children cannot be stated because the District has continuously failed to comply with Section 31-208 of the District of Columbia Code which requires a census of all children aged 3 to 18 in the District to be taken. Plaintiffs estimate that there are ". . . 22,000 retarded, emotionally disturbed, blind, deaf, and speech or learning disabled children, and perhaps as many as 18,000 of these children are not being furnished with programs of specialized education." According to data prepared by the Board of Education, Division of Planning, Research and Evaluation, the District of Columbia provides publicly supported special education programs of various descriptions to at least 3880 school age children. However, in a 1971 report to the Department of Health, Education and Welfare, the District of Columbia Public Schools admitted that an estimated 12,340 handicapped children were not to be served in the 1971–72 school year.

Each of the minor plaintiffs in this case qualifies as an "exceptional" child.

Plaintiffs allege in their complaint and defendants admit as follows:

PETER MILLS is twelve years old, black, and a committed dependent ward of the District of Columbia resident at Junior Village. He was excluded from the Brent Elementary School on March 23, 1971, at which time he was in the fourth grade. Peter allegedly was a "behavior problem" and was recommended and approved for exclusion by the principal. Defendants have not provided him with a full hearing or with a timely and adequate review of his status. Furthermore, Defendants have failed to provide for his reenrollment in the District of Columbia Public Schools or enrollment in private school. On information and belief, numerous other dependent children of school attendance age at Junior Village are denied a publicly-supported education. Peter remains excluded from any publicly-supported education.

DUANE BLACKSHEARE is thirteen years old, black, resident at Saint Elizabeth's Hospital, Washington, D.C., and a dependent committed child. He was excluded from the Giddings Elementary School in October, 1967, at which time he was in the third grade. Duane allegedly was a "behavior problem." Defendants have not provided him with a full hearing or with a timely and adequate review of his status. Despite repeated efforts by his mother, Duane remained largely excluded from all publicly-supported education until February, 1971. Education experts at the Child Study Center examined Duane and found him to be capable of returning to regular class if supportive services were provided. Following several articles in the Washington Post and Washington Star, Duane was placed in a regular seventh grade classroom on a two-hour a day basis without any catch-up assistance and without an evaluation or diagnostic interview of any kind. Duane has remained on a waiting list for a tuition grant and is now excluded from all publicly-supported education.

GEORGE LIDDELL, JR., is eight years old, black, resident with his mother, Daisy Liddell, at 601 Morton Street, N.W., Washington, D.C., and an AFDC recipient. George has never attended public school because of the denial of his application to the Maury Elementary School on the ground that he required a special class. George allegedly was retarded. Defendants have not provided him with a full hearing or with a timely and adequate review of his status. George remains excluded from all publicly-supported education, despite a medical opinion that he is capable of profiting from schooling, and despite his mother's efforts to secure a tuition grant from Defendants.

STEVEN GASTON is eight years old, black, resident with his mother, Ina Gaston, at 714 9th Street, N.E., Washington, D.C. and unable to afford private instruction. He has been excluded from the Taylor Elementary School since September, 1969, at which time he was in the first grade. Steven allegedly was slightly brain-damaged and hyperactive, and was excluded because he wandered around the classroom. Defendants have not provided him with a full hearing or with a timely and adequate review of his status. Steven was accepted in the Contemporary School, a private school, provided that tuition was paid in full in advance. Despite the efforts of his parents, Steven has remained on a waiting list for the requisite tuition grant from Defendant school system and excluded from all publicly-supported education.

MICHAEL WILLIAMS is sixteen years old, black, resident at Saint Elizabeth's Hospital, Washington, D.C., and unable to afford private instruction. Michael is epileptic and allegedly slightly retarded. He has been excluded from the Sharpe Health School since October, 1969, at which time he was temporarily hospitalized. Thereafter Michael was excluded from school because of health problems and school absences. Defendants have not provided him with a full hearing or with a timely and adequate review of his status. Despite his mother's efforts, and his attending physician's medical opinion that he could attend school, Michael has remained on a waiting list for a tuition grant and excluded from all publicly-supported education.

JANICE KING is thirteen years old, black, resident, with her father, Andrew King, at 233 Anacostia Avenue, N.E., Washington, D.C., and unable to afford private instruction. She has been denied access to public schools since reaching compulsory school attendance age, as a result of the rejection of her application, based on the lack of an appropriate educational program. Janice is brain-damaged and retarded, with right hemiplegia, resulting from a childhood illness. Defendants have not provided her with a full hearing or with a timely and adequate review of her status. Despite repeated efforts by her parents, Janice has been excluded from all publicly-supported education.

JEROME JAMES is twelve years old, black, resident with his mother, Mary James, at 2512 Ontario Avenue, N.W., Washington, D.C., and an AFDC recipient. Jerome is a retarded child and has been totally excluded from public school. Defendants have not given him a full hearing or a timely and adequate review of his status. Despite his mother's efforts to secure either public school placement or a tuition grant, Jerome has remained on a waiting list for a tuition grant and excluded from all publicly supported education.

Although all of the named minor plaintiffs are identified as Negroes the class they represent is not limited by their race. They sue on behalf of and represent all other District of Columbia residents of school age who are eligible for a free public education and who have been, or may be, excluded from such education or otherwise deprived by defendants of access to publicly supported education.

Minor plaintiffs are poor and without financial means to obtain private instruction. There has been no determination that they may not benefit from specialized instruction adapted to their needs. Prior to the beginning of the 1971–72 school year minor plaintiffs, through their representatives, sought to obtain publicly supported education and certain of them were assured by the school authorities that they would be placed in programs of publicly supported education and certain others would be recommended for special tuition grants at private schools. However, none of the plaintiff children were placed for the 1971 Fall term and they continued to be entirely excluded from all publicly supported education. After thus trying unsuccessfully to obtain relief from the Board of Education the plaintiffs filed this action on September 24, 1971.

There is No Genuine Issue of Material Fact

Congress has decreed a system of publicly supported education for the children of the District of Columbia. The Board of Education has the responsibility of administering that system in accordance with law and of providing such publicly supported education to all of the children of the District, including these "exceptional" children.

Defendants have admitted in these proceedings that they are under an affirmative duty to provide plaintiffs and their class with publicly supported education suited to each child's needs, including special education and tuition grants, and also, a constitutionally adequate prior hearing and periodic review. They have also admitted that they failed to supply plaintiffs with such publicly supported education and have failed to afford them adequate prior hearing and periodic review. On December 20, 1971 the plaintiffs and defendants agreed to and the Court signed an interim stipulation and order which provided in part as follows:

> Upon consent and stipulation of the parties, it is hereby ORDERED that:
> 1. Defendants shall provide plaintiffs Peter Mills, Duane Blacksheare, Steven Gaston and Michael Williams with a publicly-supported education suited to their (plaintiffs') needs by January 3, 1972.
> 2. Defendants shall provide counsel for plaintiffs, by January 3, 1972, a list showing, for every child of school age then known not to be attending a publicly-supported educational program because of suspension, expulsion, exclusion, or any other denial of placement, the name of the child's parent or guardian, the child's name, age, address and telephone number, the date of his suspension, expulsion, exclusion or denial of placement and, without attributing a particular characteristic to any specific child, a breakdown of such list, showing the alleged causal characteristics for such nonattendance and the number of children possessing such alleged characteristics.
> 3. By January 3, 1972, defendants shall initiate efforts to identify remaining members of the class not presently known to them, and also by that date, shall notify counsel for plaintiffs of the nature and extent of such efforts. Such efforts shall include, at a minimum, a system-wide survey of elementary and secondary schools, use of the mass written and electronic media, and a survey of District of Columbia agencies who may have knowledge pertaining to such remaining members of the class. By February 1, 1972, defendants shall provide counsel for plaintiffs with the names, addresses and telephone numbers of such remaining members of the class then known to them.
> 4. Pending further action by the Court herein, the parties shall consider the selection and compensation of a master for determination of special questions arising out of this action with regard to the placement of children in a publicly-supported educational program suited to their needs.

On February 9, 1972, the Board of Education passed a Resolution which included the following:

Special Education
> 7. All vacant authorized special education positions, whether in the regular, Impact Aid, or other Federal budgets, shall be filled as rapidly as possible within the capability of the Special Education Department. Regardless of the capability of the Department to fill vacant positions, all funds presently appropriated or allotted for special education, whether in the regular, Impact Aid, or other Federal budgets, shall be spent solely for special education.
> 8. The Board requests the Corporation Counsel to ask the United States District Court for an extension of time within which to file a response to plaintiffs' motion for summary

judgment in *Mills* v. *Board of Education* on the grounds that (a) the Board intends to enter into a consent judgment declaring the rights of children in the District of Columbia to a public education; and (b) the Board needs time (not in excess of 30 days) to obtain from the Associate Superintendent for Special Education a precise projection on a monthly basis the cost of fulfilling those budgets.

9. The Board directs the Rules Committee to devise as soon as possible for the purpose of *Mills* v. *Board of Education* rules defining and providing for due process and fair hearings; and requests the Corporation Counsel to lend such assistance to the Board as may be necessary in devising such rules in a form which will meet the requirements of *Mills* v. *Board of Education*.

10. It is the intention of the Board to submit for approval by the Court in *Mills* v. *Board of Education* a Memorandum of Understanding setting forth a comprehensive plan for the education, treatment and care of physically or mentally impaired children in the age range from three to twenty-one years. It is hoped that the various other District of Columbia agencies concerned will join with the Board in the submission of this plan.

It is the further intention of the Board to establish procedures to implement the finding that all children can benefit from education and, have a right to it, by providing for comprehensive health and psychological appraisal of children and the provision for each child of any special education which he may need. The Board will further require that no change in the kind of education provided for a child will be made against his wishes or the wishes of his parent or guardian unless he has been accorded a full hearing on the matter consistent with due process.

Defendants failed to comply with that consent order and there is now pending before the Court a motion of the plaintiffs to require defendants to show cause why they should not be held in contempt for such failure to comply.

On January 21, 1972, the plaintiffs filed a motion for summary judgment and a proposed order and decree for implementation of the proposed judgment and requested a hearing. On March 1, 1972 the defendants responded as follows:

1. The District of Columbia and its officers who are named defendants to this complaint consent to the entrance of a judgment declaring the rights of the plaintiff class to the effect prayed for in the complaint, as specified below, such rights to be prospectively effective as of March 1, 1972:

That no child eligible for a publicly supported education in the District of Columbia public schools shall be excluded from a regular public school assignment by a Rule, policy, or practice of the Board of Education of the District of Columbia or its agents unless such child is provided (a) adequate alternative educational services suited to the child's needs, which may include special education or tuition grants, and (b) a constitutionally adequate prior hearing and periodic review of the child's status, progress, and the adequacy of any educational alternative.

It is submitted that the entrance of a declaratory judgment to this effect renders plaintiffs' motion for summary judgment moot.

2. For response to plaintiffs' motion for a hearing, defendants respectfully request that this Court hold a hearing as soon as practicable at which defendants will present a plan to implement the above declaratory judgment and at which the Court may decide whether further relief is appropriate.

The Court set the date of March 24, 1972, for the hearing that both parties had requested and specifically ordered the defendants to submit a copy of their proposed implementation plan no later than March 20, 1972.

On March 24, 1972, the date of the hearing, the defendants not only had failed to submit their implementation plan as ordered but were also continuing in their violation of the provisions of the Court's order of December 20, 1971. At the close of the hearing on March 24, 1972, the Court found that there existed no genuine issue of a material fact; orally granted plaintiffs' motion for summary judgment, and directed defendants to submit to the Court any proposed plan they might have on or before March 31, 1972. The defendants, other than Cassell, failed to file any proposal within the time directed. However, on April 7, 1972, there was sent to the Clerk of the Court on behalf of the Board of Education and its employees who are defendants in this case the following documents:

1. A proposed form of Order to be entered by the Court.
2. An abstract of a document titled "A District of Columbia Plan for Identification, Assessment, Evaluation, and Placement of Exceptional Children."
3. A document titled "A District of Columbia Plan for Identification, Assessment, Evaluation, and Placement of Exceptional Children."
4. Certain Attachments and Appendices to this Plan.

The letter accompanying the documents contained the following paragraph:

> These documents express the position of the Board of Education and its employees as to what should be done to implement the judgment of the Honorable Joseph C. Waddy, the District Judge presiding over this civil action. The contents of these documents have not been endorsed by the other defendants in this case.

None of the other defendants have filed a proposed order or plan. Nor has any of them adopted the proposal submitted by the Board of Education. Throughout these proceedings it has been obvious to the Court that the defendants have no common program or plan for the alleviation of the problems posed by this litigation and that this lack of communication, cooperation and plan is typical and contributes to the problem.

Plaintiffs Are Entitled to Relief

Plaintiffs' entitlement to relief in this case is clear. The applicable statutes and regulations and the Constitution of the United States require it.

Statutes and Regulations

Section 31-201 of the District of Columbia Code requires that:

> Every parent, guardian, or other person residing [permanently or temporarily] in the District of Columbia who has custody or control of a child between the ages of seven and sixteen years shall cause said child to be regularly instructed in a public school or in a private or parochial school or instructed privately during the period of each year in which the public schools of the District of Columbia are in session. . . .

Under Section 31-203, a child may be "excused" from attendance only when

> . . . upon examination ordered by . . . [the Board of Education of the District of Columbia], [the child] is found to be unable mentally or physically to profit from attendance at school: Provided, however, That if such examination shows that such child may benefit from specialized instruction adapted to his needs, he shall attend upon such instruction.

Failure of a parent to comply with Section 31-201 constitutes a criminal offense, D.C.Code 31-207. The Court need not belabor the fact that requiring parents to see that their children attend school under pain of criminal penalties presupposes that an educational opportunity will be made available to the children. The Board of Education is required to make such opportunity available. It has adopted rules and regulations consonant with the statutory direction. Chapter XIII of the Board Rules contains the following:

> 1.1—All children of the ages hereinafter prescribed who are bona fide residents of the District of Columbia are entitled to admission and free tuition in the Public Schools of the District of Columbia, subject to the rules, regulations, and orders of the Board of Education and the applicable statutes.
>
> 14.1—Every parent, guardian, or other person residing permanently or temporarily in the District of Columbia who has custody or control of a child residing in the District of Columbia between the ages of seven and sixteen years shall cause said child to be regularly instructed in a public school or in a private or parochial school or instructed privately during the period of each year in which the Public Schools of the District of Columbia are in session, provided that instruction given in such private or parochial school, or privately, is deemed reasonably equivalent by the Board of Education to the instruction given in the Public Schools.
>
> 14.3—The Board of Education of the District of Columbia may, upon written recommendation of the Superintendent of Schools, issue a certificate excusing from attendance at school a child who, upon examination by the Department of Pupil Appraisal, Study and Attendance or by the Department of Public Health of the District of Columbia, is found to be unable mentally or physically to profit from attendance at school: Provided, however, that if such examination shows that such child may benefit from specialized instruction adapted to his needs, he shall be required to attend such classes.

Thus the Board of Education has an obligation to provide whatever specialized instruction that will benefit the child. By failing to provide plaintiffs and their class the publicly supported specialized education to which they are entitled, the Board of Education violates the above statutes and its own regulations.

The Constitution—Equal Protection and Due Process

The Supreme Court in *Brown* v. *Board of Education,* 347 U.S. 483, 493, 74 S.Ct. 686, 691, 98 L.Ed. 873 (1954) stated:

> Today, education is perhaps the most important function of state and local governments. Compulsory school attendance laws and the great expenditures for education both demonstrate our recognition of the importance of education to our democratic society. It is required in the performance of our most basic public responsibilities, even service in the armed forces. It is the very foundation of good citizenship. Today it is a principal instrument in awakening the child to cultural values, in preparing him for later professional training, and in helping him to adjust normally to his environment. In these days, it is doubtful that any child may reasonably be expected to succeed in life if he is denied the opportunity of an education. *Such an opportunity, where the state has undertaken to provide it, is a right which must be made available to all on equal terms.* [emphasis supplied]

Bolling v. *Sharpe,* 347 U.S. 497, 74 S.Ct. 693, 98 L.Ed. 884, decided the same day as *Brown,* applied the *Brown* rationale to the District of Columbia public schools by finding that:

> Segregation in public education is not reasonably related to any proper governmental objective, and thus it imposes on Negro children of the District of Columbia a burden

that constitutes an arbitrary deprivation of their liberty in violation of the Due Process Clause.

In *Hobson* v. *Hansen,* 269 F.Supp. 401 (D.C.C. 1967) Circuit Judge J. Skelly Wright considered the pronouncements of the Supreme Court in the intervening years and stated that ". . . the Court has found the due process clause of the Fourteenth Amendment elastic enough to embrace not only the First and Fourth Amendments, but the self-incrimination clause of the Fifth, the speedy trial, confrontation and assistance of counsel clauses of the Sixth, and the cruel and unusual clause of the Eighth." (269 F.Supp. 401 at 493, citations omitted). Judge Wright concluded "(F)rom these considerations the court draws the conclusion that the doctrine of equal educational opportunity—the equal protection clause in its application to public school education—is in its full sweep a component of due process binding on the District under the due process clause of the Fifth Amendment."

In *Hobson* v. *Hanse, supra,* Judge Wright found that denying poor public school children educational opportunities equal to that available to more affluent public school children was violative of the Due Process Clause of the Fifth Amendment. *A fortiori,* the defendants' conduct here, denying plaintiffs and their class not just an equal publicly supported education but all publicly supported education while providing such education to other children, is violative of the Due Process Clause.

Not only are plaintiffs and their class denied the publicly supported education to which they are entitled many are suspended or expelled from regular schooling or specialized instruction or reassigned without any prior hearing and are given no periodic review thereafter. Due process of law requires a hearing prior to exclusion, termination or classification into a special program. *Vought* v. *Van Buren Public Schools,* 306 F.Supp. 1388 (E.D.Mich. 1969); *Williams* v. *Dade County School Board,* 441 F.2d 299 (5th Cir. 1971); Cf. *Soglin* v. *Kauffman,* 295 F.Supp. 978 (W.D.Wis. 1968); *Dixon* v. *Alabama State Board of Education,* 294 F.2d 150 (5th Cir. 1961), cert. den., 368 U.S. 930, 82 S.Ct. 368, 7 L.Ed.2d 193 (1961); *Goldberg* v. *Kelly,* 397 U.S. 254, 90 S.Ct. 1011, 25 L.Ed.2d 287 (1970).

The Defense

The Answer of the defendants to the Complaint contains the following:

> These defendants say that it is impossible to afford plaintiffs the relief they request unless:
> (a) The Congress of the United States appropriates millions of dollars to improve special education services in the District of Columbia; or
> (b) These defendants divert millions of dollars from funds already specifically appropriated for other educational services in order to improve special educational services. These defendants suggest that to do so would violate an Act of Congress and would be inequitable to children outside the alleged plaintiff class.

This Court is not persuaded by that contention.

The defendants are required by the Constitution of the United States, the District of Columbia Code, and their own regulations to provide a publicly-supported education for these "exceptional" children. Their failure to fulfill this clear duty to include and retain these children in the public school system, or otherwise provide them with publicly-supported education, and their failure to afford them due process hearings and periodical review, cannot be excused by the claim that there are insufficient funds. In *Goldberg* v. *Kelly,* 397 U.S. 254, 90 S.Ct. 1011, 25 L.Ed.2d 287 (1969) the Supreme Court, in a case that involved the right of a welfare recipient to a hearing before termination of his benefits, held that Constitutional rights must be afforded citizens despite the greater expense involved. The Court stated at page 266, 90 S.Ct. at page 1019, that "the State's interest that his [welfare recipient] payments not be erroneously terminated, clearly outweighs the State's competing concern to prevent any increase in its fiscal and administrative burdens." Similarly the District of Columbia's interest in educating the excluded children clearly must outweigh its interest in preserving its financial resources. If sufficient funds are not available to finance all of the services and programs that are needed and desirable in the system, then the available funds must be expended equitably in such a manner that no child is entirely excluded from a publicly supported education consistent with his needs and ability to benefit therefrom. The inadequacies of the District of Columbia Public School System whether occasioned by insufficient funding or administrative inefficiency, certainly cannot be permitted to bear more heavily on the "exceptional" or handicapped child than on the normal child.

Implementation of Judgment

This Court has pointed out that Section 31-201 of the District of Columbia Code requires that every person residing in the District of Columbia ". . . who has custody or control of a child between the ages of seven and sixteen years shall cause said child to be regularly instructed in a public school or in a private or parochial school or instructed privately. . . ." It is the responsibility of the Board of Education to provide the opportunities and facilities for such instruction.

The Court has determined that the Board likewise has the responsibility for implementation of the judgment and decree of this Court in this case. Section 31-103 of the District of Columbia Code clearly places this responsibility upon the Board. It provides:

> The Board shall determine all questions of general policy relating to the schools, shall appoint the executive officers hereinafter provided for, define their duties, and direct expenditures.

The lack of communication and cooperation between the Board of Education and the other defendants in this action shall not be permitted to deprive plaintiffs and their class of publicly supported education. Section 31-104b of the District of Columbia Code dictates that the Board of Education and the District of Columbia Government must coordinate educational and municipal functions:

> (a) The Board of Education and the Commissioner of the District of Columbia shall jointly develop procedures to assure the maximum coordination of educational and other municipal programs and services in *achieving the most effective educational system and utilization of educational facilities and services to serve broad community needs.* Such procedures shall cover such matters as—
> (1) design and construction of educational facilities to accommodate civic and community activities such as recreation, adult and vocational education and training, and other community purposes;

(2) full utilization of educational facilities during nonschool hours for community purposes;

(3) utilization of municipal services such as police, sanitation, recreational, maintenance services to enhance the effectiveness and stature of the school in the community;

(4) *arrangements for cost-sharing and reimbursements on school and community programs involving utilization of educational facilities and services; and*

(5) other matters of mutual interest and concern.

(b) *The Board of Education may invite the Commissioner of the District of Columbia or his designee to attend and participate in meetings of the Board on matters pertaining to coordination of educational and other municipal programs and services and on such other matters as may be of mutual interest.* [emphasis supplied]

If the District of Columbia Government and the Board of Education cannot jointly develop the procedures and programs necessary to implement this Court's order then it shall be the responsibility of the Board of Education to present the irresolvable issue to the Court for resolution in a timely manner so that plaintiffs and their class may be afforded their constitutional and statutory rights. If any dispute should arise between the defendants which requires for its resolution a degree of expertise in the field of education not possessed by the Court, the Court will appoint a special master pursuant to the provisions of Rule 53 of the Federal Rules of Civil Procedure to assist the Court in resolving the issue.

Inasmuch as the Board of Education has presented for adoption by the Court a proposed "Order and Decree" embodying its present plans for the identification of "exceptional" children and providing for their publicly supported education, including a time table, and further requiring the Board to formulate and file with the Court a more comprehensive plan, the Court will not now appoint a special master as was requested by plaintiffs. Despite the defendants' failure to abide by the provisions of the Court's previous orders in this case and despite the defendants' continuing failure to provide an education for these children, the Court is reluctant to arrogate to itself the responsibility of administering this or any other aspect of the Public School System of the District of Columbia through the vehicle of a special master. Nevertheless, inaction or delay on the part of the defendants, or failure by the defendants to implement the judgment and decree herein within the time specified therein will result in the immediate appointment of a special master to oversee and direct such implementation under the direction of this Court. The Court will include as a part of its judgment the proposed "Order and Decree" submitted by the Board of Education, as modified in minor part by the Court, and will retain jurisdiction of the cause to assure prompt implementation of the judgment. Plaintiffs' motion to require certain defendants to show cause why they should not be adjudged in contempt will be held in abeyance for 45 days.

Judgment and Decree

Plaintiffs having filed their verified complaint seeking an injunction and declaration of rights as set forth more fully in the verified complaint and the prayer for relief contained therein; and having moved this Court for summary judgment pursuant to Rule 56 of the Federal Rules of Civil Procedure, and this Court having reviewed the record of this cause including plaintiffs' Motion, pleadings, affidavits, and evidence and arguments in support thereof, and defendants' affidavit, pleadings, and evidence and arguments in support thereof, and the proceedings of pre-trial conferences on December 17, 1971, and January 14, 1972, it is hereby ordered, adjudged and decreed that summary judgment in favor of plaintiffs and against defendants be, and hereby is, granted, and judgment is entered in this action as follows:

1. That no child eligible for a publicly supported education in the District of Columbia public schools shall be excluded from a regular public school assignment by a Rule, policy, or practice of the Board of Education of the District of Columbia or its agents unless such child is provided (a) adequate alternative educational services suited to the child's needs, which may include special education or tuition grants, and (b) a constitutionally adequate prior hearing and periodic review of the child's status, progress, and the adequacy of any educational alternative.

2. The defendants, their officers, agents, servants, employees, and attorneys and all those in active concert or participation with them are hereby enjoined from maintaining, enforcing or otherwise continuing in effect any and all rules, policies and practices which exclude plaintiffs and the members of the class they represent from a regular public school assignment without providing them at public expense (a) adequate and immediate alternative education or tuition grants, consistent with their needs, and (b) a constitutionally adequate prior hearing and periodic review of their status, progress and the adequacy of any educational alternatives; and it is further ORDERED that:

3. The District of Columbia shall provide to each child of school age a free and suitable publicly-supported education regardless of the degree of the child's mental, physical or emotional disability or impairment. Furthermore, defendants shall not exclude any child resident in the District of Columbia from such publicly-supported education on the basis of a claim of insufficient resources.

4. Defendants shall not suspend a child from the public schools for disciplinary reasons for any period in excess of two days without affording him a hearing pursuant to the provisions of Paragraph 13.f, below, and without providing for his education during the period of any such suspension.

5. Defendants shall provide each identified member of plaintiff class with a publicly-supported education suited to his needs within thirty (30) days of the entry of this order. With regard to children who later come to the attention of any defendant, within twenty (20) days after he becomes known, the evaluation (case study approach) called for in paragraph 9 below shall be completed and within 30 days after completion of the evaluation, placement shall be made so as to provide the child with a publicly supported education suited to his needs.

In either case, if the education to be provided is not of a kind generally available during the summer vacation, the thirty-day limit may be extended for children evaluated during summer months to allow their educational programs to begin at the opening of school in September.

6. Defendants shall cause announcements and notices to be placed in the *Washington Post, Washington Star-Daily News,* and the *Afro-American,* in all issues published for a three week period commencing within five (5) days of the entry of this order, and thereafter at quarterly intervals, and shall cause spot announcements to be made on television and radio stations for twenty (20) consecutive days, commencing

within five (5) days of the entry of this order, and thereafter at quarterly intervals, advising residents of the District of Columbia that all children, regardless of any handicap or other disability, have a right to a publicly-supported education suited to their needs, and informing the parents or guardians of such children of the procedures required to enroll their children in an appropriate educational program. Such announcements should include the listing of a special answering service telephone number to be established by defendants in order to (a) compile the names, addresses, phone numbers of such children who are presently not attending school and (b) provide further information to their parents or guardians as to the procedures required to enroll their children in an appropriate educational program.

7. Within twenty-five (25) days of the entry of this order, defendants shall file with the Clerk of this Court, an up-to-date list showing, for every additional identified child, the name of the child's parent or guardian, the child's name, age, address and telephone number, the date of his suspension, expulsion, exclusion or denial of placement and, without attributing a particular characteristic to any specific child, a breakdown of such list, showing the alleged causal characteristics for such nonattendance (e.g., educable mentally retarded, trainable mentally retarded, emotionally disturbed, specific learning disability, crippled/other health impaired, hearing impaired, visually impaired, multiple handicapped) and the number of children possessing each such alleged characteristic.

8. Notice of this order shall be given by defendants to the parent or guardian of each child resident in the District of Columbia who is now, or was during the 1971–72 school year or the 1970–71 school year, excluded, suspended or expelled from publicly-supported educational programs or otherwise denied a full and suitable publicly-supported education for any period in excess of two days. Such notice shall include a statement that each such child has the right to receive a free educational assessment and to be placed in a publicly-supported educational program suited to his needs. Such notice shall be sent by registered mail within five (5) days of the entry of this order, or within five (5) days after such child becomes known to any defendant. Provision of notification for non-reading parents or guardians will be made.

9. a. Defendants shall utilize public or private agencies to evaluate the educational needs of all identified "exceptional" children and, within twenty (20) days of the entry of this order, shall file with the Clerk of this Court their proposal for each individual placement in a suitable educational program, including the provision of compensatory educational services where required.

b. Defendants, within twenty (20) days of the entry of this order, shall also submit such proposals to each parent or guardian of such child, respectively, along with a notification that if they object to such proposed placement within a period of time to be fixed by the parties or by the Court, they may have their objection heard by a Hearing Officer in accordance with procedures required in Paragraph 13.e., below.

10. a. Within forty-five (45) days of the entry of this order, defendants shall file with the Clerk of the Court, with copy to plaintiffs' counsel, a comprehensive plan which provides for the identification, notification, assessment, and placement of class members. Such plan shall state the nature and extent of efforts which defendants have undertaken or propose to undertake to

(1) describe the curriculum, educational objectives, teacher qualifications, and ancillary services for the publicly-supported educational programs to be provided to class members; and,

(2) formulate general plans of compensatory education suitable to class members in order to overcome the present effects of prior educational deprivations,

(3) institute any additional steps and proposed modifications designed to implement the matters decreed in paragraph 5 through 7 hereof and other requirements of this judgment.

11.   The defendants shall make an interim report to this Court on their performance within forty-five (45) days of the entry of this order. Such report shall show:

(1) The adequacy of Defendants' implementation of plans to identify, locate, evaluate and give notice to all members of the class.

(2) The number of class members who have been placed, and the nature of their placements.

(3) The number of contested hearings before the Hearing Officers, if any, and the findings and determinations resulting therefrom.

12.   Within forty-five (45) days of the entry of this order, defendants shall file with this Court a report showing the expunction from or correction of all official records of any plaintiff with regard to past expulsions, suspensions, or exclusions effected in violation of the procedural rights set forth in Paragraph 13 together with a plan for procedures pursuant to which parents, guardians, or their counsel may attach to such students' records any clarifying or explanatory information which the parent, guardian or counsel may deem appropriate.

13.   Hearing Procedures.

a.   Each member of the plaintiff class is to be provided with a publicly-supported educational program suited to his needs, within the context of a presumption that among the alternative programs of education, placement in a regular public school class with appropriate ancillary services is preferable to placement in a special school class.

b.   Before placing a member of the class in such a program, defendants shall notify his parent or guardian of the proposed educational placement, the reasons therefor, and the right to a hearing before a Hearing Officer if there is an objection to the placement proposed. Any such hearing shall be held in accordance with the provisions of Paragraph 13.e., below.

c.   Hereinafter, children who are residents of the District of Columbia and are thought by any of the defendants, or by officials, parents or guardians to be in need of a program of special education, shall neither be placed in, transferred from or to, nor denied placement in such a program unless defendants shall have first notified their parents or guardians of such proposed placement, transfer or denial, the reasons therefor, and of the right to a hearing before a Hearing Officer if there is an objection to the placement, transfer or denial of placement. Any such hearings shall be held in accordance with the provisions of Paragraph 13.e., below.

d.   Defendants shall not, on grounds of discipline, cause the exclusion, suspension, expulsion, postponement, interschool transfer, or any other denial of access to
regular instruction in the public schools to any child for more than two days without
first notifying the child's parent or guardian of such proposed action, the reasons
therefor, and of the hearing before a Hearing Officer in accordance with the provisions
of Paragraph 13.f., below.

e.   Whenever defendants take action regarding a child's placement, denial of
placement, or transfer, as described in Paragraphs 13.b or 13.c., above, the following
procedures shall be followed.

(1)   Notice required hereinbefore shall be given in writing by registered mail to the
parent or guardian of the child.

(2)   Such notice shall:

(a)   describe the proposed action in detail;

(b)   clearly state the specific and complete reasons for the proposed action,
including the specification of any tests or reports upon which such action is
proposed;

(c)   describe any alternative educational opportunities available on a permanent
or temporary basis;

(d)   inform the parent or guardian of the right to object to the proposed action at
a hearing before the Hearing Officer;

(e)   inform the parent or guardian that the child is eligible to receive, at no
charge, the services of a federally or locally funded diagnostic center for an
independent medical, psychological and educational evaluation and shall
specify the name, address and telephone number of an appropriate local
diagnostic center;

(f)   inform the parent or guardian of the right to be represented at the hearing
by legal counsel; to examine the child's school records before the hearing,
including any tests or reports upon which the proposed action may be
based, to present evidence, including expert medical, psychological and
educational testimony; and, to confront and cross-examine any school
official, employee, or agent of the school district or public department who
may have evidence upon which the proposed action was based.

(3)   The hearing shall be at a time and place reasonably convenient to such parent or
guardian.

(4)   The hearing shall be scheduled not sooner than twenty (20) days waivable by
parent or child, nor later than forty-five (45) days after receipt of a request from
the parent or guardian.

(5)   The hearing shall be a closed hearing unless the parent or guardian requests an
open hearing.

(6)   The child shall have the right to a representative of his own choosing, including
legal counsel. If a child is unable, through financial inability, to retain counsel,
defendants shall advise child's parents or guardians of available voluntary legal
assistance including the Neighborhood Legal Services Organization, the Legal

Aid Society, the Young Lawyers Section of the D.C. Bar Association, or from some other organization.

(7) The decision of the Hearing Officer shall be based solely upon the evidence presented at the hearing.

(8) Defendants shall bear the burden of proof as to all facts and as to the appropriateness of any placement, denial of placement or transfer.

(9) A tape recording or other record of the hearing shall be made and transcribed and, upon request, made available to the parent or guardian or his representative.

(10) At a reasonable time prior to the hearing, the parent or guardian, or his counsel, shall be given access to all public school system and other public office records pertaining to the child, incuding any tests or reports upon which the proposed action may be based.

(11) The independent Hearing Officer shall be an employee of the District of Columbia, but shall not be an officer, employee or agent of the Public School System.

(12) The parent or guardian, or his representative, shall have the right to have the attendance of any official, employee or agent of the public school system or any public employee who may have evidence upon which the proposed action may be based and to confront, and to cross-examine any witness testifying for the public school system.

(13) The parent or guardian, or his representative, shall have the right to present evidence and testimony, including expert medical, psychological or educational testimony.

(14) Within thirty (30) days after the hearing, the Hearing Officer shall render a decision in writing. Such decision shall include findings of fact and conclusions of law and shall be filed with the Board of Education and the Department of Human Resources and sent by registered mail to the parent or guardian and his counsel.

(15) Pending a determination by the Hearing Officer, defendants shall take no action described in Paragraphs 13.b. or 13.c., above, if the child's parent or guardian objects to such action. Such objection must be in writing and postmarked within five (5) days of the date of receipt of notification hereinabove described.

f.   Whenever defendants propose to take action described in Paragraph 13.d., above, the following procedures shall be followed.

(1) Notice required hereinabove shall be given in writing and shall be delivered in person or by registered mail to both the child and his parent or guardian.

(2) Such notice shall
   (a) describe the proposed disciplinary action in detail, including the duration thereof;
   (b) state specific, clear and full reasons for the proposed action, including the specification of the alleged act upon which the disciplinary action is to be based and the reference to the regulation subsection under which such action is proposed;
   (c) describe alternative educational opportunities to be available to the child during the proposed suspension period;

(d) inform the child and the parent or guardian of the time and place at which the hearing shall take place;

(e) inform the parent or guardian that if the child is thought by the parent or guardian to require special education services, that such child is eligible to receive, at no charge, the services of a public or private agency for a diagnostic medical, psychological or educational evaluation;

(f) inform the child and his parent or guardian of the right to be represented at the hearing by legal counsel; to examine the child's school records before the hearing, including any tests or reports upon which the proposed action may be based; to present evidence of his own; and to confront and cross-examine any witnesses or any school officials, employees or agents who may have evidence upon which the proposed action may be based.

(3) The hearing shall be at a time and place reasonably convenient to such parent or guardian.

(4) The hearing shall take place within four (4) school days of the date upon which written notice is given, and may be postponed at the request of the child's parent or guardian for no more than five (5) additional school days where necessary for preparation.

(5) The hearing shall be a closed hearing unless the child, his parent or guardian requests an open hearing.

(6) The child is guaranteed the right to a representative of his own choosing, including legal counsel. If a child is unable, through financial inability, to retain counsel, defendants shall advise child's parents or guardians of available voluntary legal assistance including the Neighborhood Legal Services Organization, the Legal Aid Society, the Young Lawyers Section of the D.C. Bar Association, or from some other organization.

(7) The decision of the Hearing Officer shall be based solely upon the evidence presented at the hearing.

(8) Defendants shall bear the burden of proof as to all facts and as to appropriateness of any disposition and of the alternative educational opportunity to be provided any suspension.

(9) A tape recording or other record of the hearing shall be made and transcribed and, upon request, made available to the parent or guardian or his representative.

(10) At a reasonable time prior to the hearing, the parent or guardian, or the child's counsel or representative, shall be given access to all records of the public school system and any other public office pertaining to the child, including any tests or reports upon which the proposed action may be based.

(11) The independent Hearing Officer shall be an employee of the District of Columbia, but shall not be an officer, employee or agent of the Public School System.

(12) The parent or guardian, or the child's counsel or representative, shall have the right to have the attendance of any public employee who may have evidence upon which the proposed action may be based and to confront and to cross-examine any witness testifying for the public school system.

(13) The parent or guardian, or the child's counsel or representative, shall have the right to present evidence and testimony.

(14) Pending the hearing and receipt of notification of the decision, there shall be no change in the child's educational placement unless the principal (responsible to the Superintendent) shall warrant that the continued presence of the child in his current program would endanger the physical well-being of himself or others. In such exceptional cases, the principal shall be responsible for insuring that the child receives some form of educational assistance and/or diagnostic examination during the interim period prior to the hearing.

(15) No finding that disciplinary action is warranted shall be made unless the Hearing Officer first finds, by clear and convincing evidence, that the child committed a prohibited act upon which the proposed disciplinary action is based. After this finding has been made, the Hearing Officer shall take such disciplinary action as he shall deem appropriate. This action shall not be more severe than that recommended by the school official initiating the suspension proceedings.

(16) No suspension shall continue for longer than ten (10) school days after the date of the hearing, or until the end of the school year, whichever comes first. In such cases, the principal (responsible to the Superintendent) shall be responsible for insuring that the child receives some form of educational assistance and/or diagnostic examination during the suspension period.

(17) If the Hearing Officer determines that disciplinary action is not warranted, all school records of the proposed disciplinary action, including those relating to the incidents upon which such proposed action was predicated, shall be destroyed.

(18) If the Hearing Officer determines that disciplinary action is warranted, he shall give written notification of his findings and of the child's right to appeal his decision to the Board of Education, to the child, the parent or guardian, and the counsel or representative of the child, within three (3) days of such determination.

(19) An appeal from the decision of the Hearing Officer shall be heard by the Student Life and Community Involvement Committee of the Board of Education which shall provide the child and his parent or guardian with the opportunity for an oral hearing, at which the child may be represented by legal counsel, to review the findings of the Hearing Officer. At the conclusion of such hearing, the Committee shall determine the appropriateness of and may modify such decision. However, in no event may such Committee impose added or more severe restrictions on the child.

14. Whenever the foregoing provisions require notice to a parent or guardian, and the child in question has no parent or duly appointed guardian, notice is to be given to any adult with whom the child is actually living, as well as to the child himself, and every effort will be made to assure that no child's rights are denied for lack of a parent or duly appointed guardian. Again provision for such notice to non-readers will be made.

15. Jurisdiction of this matter is retained to allow for implementation, modification and enforcement of this Judgment and Decree as may be required.

NOTES

1. The *Mills* court expanded the principles applied to mentally retarded children in *PARC* by applying them to *all* handicapped children in the District of Columbia. The

D.C. court was the first to apply to handicapped individuals the phraseology of "equal educational opportunity—the equal protection clause in its application to public school education." Since *Mills* was decided subsequently to *PARC* and is commonly considered to have been predicated upon the favorable result in *PARC,* it is interesting to note that the *Mills* decision does not once cite *PARC.*

2.   Since the District of Columbia is a federal entity and not a state, it is within the authority·of the Fifth Amendment rather than the Fourteenth. The *Mills* court, however, followed the holding in *Hobson* v. *Hansen,* 269 F.Supp. 401 (D.D.C. 1967), that the Fifth Amendment's due process clause is broad enough in scope to encompass the equal protection mandate of the Fourteenth Amendment. This leads to the ironic conclusion that the plaintiffs, in addition to being deprived of due process rights to notice and a prior hearing, are denied due process because they are denied equal protection.

3.   The question of the costs of educating handicapped children, which was faced by the *Mills* court, is a recurring issue. Although such costs can be substantial, there are data that indicate that such expenditures may be economically beneficial when compared to the costs of life-long institutionalization, which can result when no education can be obtained, e.g., Conley, R., *The Economics of Mental Retardation,* (The Johns Hopkins University Press, Baltimore, 1973); 41 Fed. Reg. 20312, 20338-20360 (May 17, 1976).

   In Pennsylvania, for example, Governor Milton Shapp predicted that the *PARC* ruling would save taxpayers money by freeing thousands of young people from state institutions and hospitals (President's Committee on Mental Retardation, "P.C.M.R. Message," No. 27, Nov. 1971).

4.   For examples of other federal lawsuits along the lines of the *PARC* and *Mills* cases, see *Harrison* v. *State of Michigan,* 350 F.Supp. 846 (E.D.Mich. 1972) and *Lebanks* v. *Spears,* 60 F.R.D. 135 (E.D.La. 1973).

   In *Harrison* the United States District Court for the Eastern District of Michigan stated its clear acceptance of equal educational rights for handicapped persons:

> The plaintiffs accurately contend that providing education for some children, while not providing education for others (in this instance, handicapped children) is a denial of equal protection (350 F.Supp. at p. 848).

   The court ruled, however, that the State of Michigan was moving as fast as it could, pursuant to a recently enacted statute, to comply voluntarily with the aim of the lawsuit—to provide an appropriate education for every handicapped child in the State of Michigan. Thus, the court concluded:

> The most that should be done at this stage is to indicate clearly that, although the matter is at this time premature because the process of implementation is proceeding in good fashion, and because there is no way in which this court could proceed with implementation faster, if it should turn out either that the act is not fully and speedily implemented and funded or that procedures do not comply with due process, judicial remedies would then be available to the injured persons (350 F.Supp. at p. 849).

   In *Lebanks,* the United States District Court for the Eastern District of Louisiana approved a Consent Agreement entered into by the parties which guarantees the right of all mentally retarded children in Orleans Parish to an appropriate program of free public education. It is declared that every child who is mentally retarded or suspected of being mentally retarded is entitled to "(a) evaluation and development of a special education plan and periodic review and (b) provision of a free public program of education and training appropriate to his age and mental status," 60 F.R.D. 140, all of which is to be performed in accordance with specified, very comprehensive procedural safeguards. Compensatory education was ordered for those persons, now adults, who had been without education as children, 60 F.R.D. 140.

ADDITIONAL READING

Dimond, P., "The Constitutional Right to Education: The Quiet Revolution," 24
    Hastings L.J. 1807 (1973).
Dimond, P., "The Law of School Classification," 12 Inequality in Education No. 12,
    30 (1972).
McClung, M., "Right to Learn," 10 Trial No. 3, 22 (1974).
Schwartz, M., "The Education of Handicapped Children: Emerging Legal Doc-
    trines, " 7 Clearinghouse Review No. 3, 125 (1973).
Herr, S., "Retarded Children and the Law: Enforcing the Constitutional Rights of the
    Mentally Retarded," 23 Syracuse L. Rev. 995 (1972).
Kirp, D., Kuriloff, P., and Buss, W., "Legal Mandates and Organizational Change,"
    Chapter 26 of 2 Issues in the Classification of Children 319–61 (Hobbs, N., ed.,
    1975).

3. New York Cases

IN RE H.

Family Court, City of New York, Queens County, 1972
72 Misc. 2d 59, 337 N.Y.S. 2d 969

ISIDORE LEVINE, Judge:

Petitioner, as the mother of David H., a physically handicapped child, seeks an order from this Court directing that the City of New York pay $2,500 toward the tuition of said child, age 11, at the Lifeline Center for Child Development since he is a physically handicapped child pursuant to Sec. 232 of the Family Court Act, in that he suffers from Schizophrenia of Childhood, evidenced by a short attention span, inability to conform to classroom routines, hyperactivity and distractibility, auditory hallucinations, fears and phobias and a thinking disorder, all of which make him uneducable in the tuition-free schools of the City and State of New York.

Petitioner is a widow, age 50, whose husband died about a year and a half ago, leaving behind 3 children with petitioner, ages 20, 17, and the handicapped child age 11. The 20 year old is employed but the 17 year old attends Queensborough Community College. Petitioner is unemployed, having been a housewife during all of her married life.

[A discussion of the petitioner's financial assets is omitted.]

An analysis of the financial position of petitioner will readily reveal that the support for her 17-year-old child at Community College and the needs of the handicapped child (besides tuition), as well as her personal needs, will be a constant drain upon the petitioner and her assets and income, and with each succeeding diminution of her savings bank account will inevitably flow a reduction in bank interest, eventually reducing her income and standard of living markedly in view of the heavy and constant expenditures for the handicapped child, and will eventually result in all her assets being depleted.

Upon the entire picture herein, it would appear basically unfair to place such additional burden of tuition upon petitioner who already has her share of woe, which is aggravated by the fact that the City does not have a free school available for the education of her child. To compound her anguish by compelling her to pay tuition fees to educate her child because the Board of Education has failed to furnish suitable education facilities for her handicapped child as required by Sec. 4404, subd. 2 of the New York Education Law, while others who are more fortunate can attend school tuition free, irrespective of their assets and income, seems unfair and indecent, and perhaps even unconstitutional since depriving petitioner of the right to a free public education, as mandated by Article XI Sec. 1 of the Constitution of the State of New York, and since further depriving petitioner of the equal protection of the laws, as guaranteed by Article I Sec. 11 of the Constitution of the State of New York and the 14th Amendment to the Constitution of the United States.

In this latter connection, see *Reid* v. *Board of Education of the City of New York,* 453 F.2d 238 (U.S. Court of Appeals, 2d Circuit, December 14, 1971). However, since this Court has disposed of the case at bar by granting the petition herein on the facts, the issue of unconstitutionality need not be passed upon.

Accordingly, the Court directs and hereby signs an order directing the City of New York to pay to the Lifeline Center for Child Development the sum of $2,500 to be applied toward the cost of tuition for the handicapped child herein, David H.

IN RE DOWNEY

Family Court, City of New York, New York County, 1973
72 Misc. 2d 772, 340 N.Y.S.2d 687

MANUEL G. GUERREIRO, Judge:

This is a petition for the education of a handicapped child, pursuant to Section 234 of the Family Court Act.

Petitioner's son Rick, has been certified handicapped by the State Education Department. Furthermore the Board of Education of the City of New York has certified that there is no adequate public facility for the instruction of this child and the school which Rick Downey now attends has been approved by the State Education Department for the education of such handicapped children.

Petitioner is seeking $6,496.00 which represents the difference between tuition at the Montanari Clinical School, Inc., and the grant of $2,000 in State aid to the handicapped child. Under Section 4404 of the Education Law petitioner also seeks the cost of transportation to and from the school which is located in Florida.

The Constitution of New York, Art. XI, Sec. 1 provides: "The legislature shall provide for the maintenance and support of a system of *free* common schools, wherein *all* the children of this state may be educated." [emphasis added]

This article is implemented by the Education Law of New York. The burden is therefore on the state to assure that the educational program provided each child is appropriate to his needs. With respect to handicapped children, Section 4402 of the Education Law imposes a duty on the State Department of Education to use all means and measures necessary to adequately meet the physical and educational needs of handicapped children.

In order to assure a handicapped child the equal protection of the law, the opportunity for an education according to his needs must be available. In this context the words of the Supreme Court in the historic decision of *Brown* v. *Board of Education,* 347 U.S. 483, 493, 74 S.Ct. 686, 691, 98 L.Ed. 873 (1954), are particularly relevant.

> In these days, it is doubtful that any child may reasonably be expected to succeed in life if he is denied the opportunity of an education. Such an opportunity, where the state has undertaken to provide it, is a right which must be made available to all on equal terms.

The concept of equality has been utilized by the courts of Pennsylvania to provide the right to an education for mentally retarded children. Article 3, Section 14 of the Constitution of Pennsylvania, P.S., provides: "The General Assembly shall provide for the maintenance and support of a thorough and efficient system of public education to serve the needs of the Commonwealth." The Pennsylvania Public School Code of 1949, Purdon's Pa.Stat.Ann. Title 24 implements Article 3, Section 14, of the Pennsylvania Constitution which is substantially the same as the New York State Constitution.

In the recent decision of *Pennsylvania Associations for Retarded Children* v. *Pennsylvania,* 334 F.Supp. 1257, the Federal District Court ordered, on consent, The Commonwealth of Pennsylvania to provide every retarded person between 6 and 21 access to a free public program of education and training appropriate to his learning capacities.

In *Reid* v. *Board of Education of The City of New York,* 2 Cir., 453 F.2d 238, which is the only relevant New York case in this area, the U.S. Court of Appeals recognized the Constitutional issue presented by New York's Education Law, but abstained from considering the question pending the outcome of claims in the State Courts.

Under the Family Court Act, Section 234, the court may order contribution to the cost of educating a handicapped child by the parent or other person responsible for his care. This court has serious reservations as to the constitutionality of this provision. To order a parent to contribute to the education of his handicapped child when free education is supplied to all other children would be a denial of the constitutional right of equal protection, United States Constitution Amendment XIV; New York State Constitution Article XI, Section 1. Legislation which singles out one class for special burdens and liabilities from which all others are exempt denies equal protection of the laws. See *Matter of David H.,* 72 Misc.2d 59, 337 N.Y.S.2d 969. Equal protection does not require that all persons be dealt with identically but it does require that distinction among classes must be reasonable. Compare *Jesmer* v. *Dundon* (1971) 29 N.Y.2d 4, 323 N.Y.S.2d 417, 271 N.E.2d 905.

Furthermore it is the child who is given the right to an education, not the parent, and his right should not be abridged or limited by the willingness of a parent to become financially liable for the education. To limit the right to an education in this manner would discourage many parents from seeking the appropriate facilities for their child.

In conclusion, while at first blush this may seem like a substantial outlay of funds for one child, when compared with the dollar cost of maintaining a child in an institution all his life or on public assistance the cost is minimal; not to speak of the incalculable cost to society of losing a potentially productive adult.

For the foregoing reasons the petition is granted without considering the ability of the petitioner to contribute to the cost of educating his child.

NOTES

1. In a subsequent New York decision, *In re Kirschner,* 74 Misc.2d 20, 344 N.Y.S.2d 164, 168 (1973), the court declared:

> In the light of the advances of the last two decades in the fashioning of programs of special education for even the most severely physically handicapped and retarded children, we can no longer discriminate against them on the basis of the willingness or ability of their parents to afford them. In the context of the holding of the Supreme Court of the United States in *Brown* v. *Board of Education,* 347 U.S. 483, 74 S. Ct. 686, 98 L.Ed. 873, we can no longer demand of a parent of a handicapped child payment for the education of that child when no charge is made for the education of a non-handicapped child.
>
> It is the holding of this Court that the Constitution of the State of New York requires that all children including the handicapped are entitled to such education as is reasonably suited to their needs without charge. It is the further holding of this Court that to make a charge to a parent for the cost of educating a handicapped child while providing free public education for non-handicapped and some handicapped children violates the equal protection provisions of the Fourteenth Amendment of the United States Constitution. (*Brown* v. *Board of Education (supra): Matter of Borland,* 72 Misc.2d 766, 340 N.Y.S.2d 745; *Matter of Rick Downey,* a handicapped child, 72 Misc.2d 772, 340 N.Y.S.2d 687.)

And in *In re Lofft,* 86 Misc.2d 431, 437, 383 N.Y.S.2d 142, 147 (1976), the court declared "that it is a violation of the Equal Protection Clause of the Fourteenth Amendment to the United States Constitution to deny an educational opportunity to handicapped children while providing it to others."

2. In the *H., Downey, Lofft,* and *Kirschner* cases, the New York courts have followed the traditional judicial practice of interpreting statutes (where possible) in such a manner as to preserve their constitutionality.

4. Refined Equal Protection and Due Process Analysis

IN RE G.H.

Supreme Court of North Dakota, 1974
218 N.W.2d 441

VOGEL, Judge.

G. H., in whose interest this action was brought, was born on July 27, 1957, with severe physical handicaps which need not be detailed. She is educable, and is expected to finish her grade school education soon. At the time of her birth her family lived at Williston, Williams County, North Dakota, in Williston School District No. 1.

She spent some time at the Grafton State School (for retarded children), but did not really belong there, so she was sent to the Crippled Children's School at Jamestown, North Dakota, at the request of the superintendent of the Grafton State School. The Crippled Children's School is a private, nonsectarian, nonprofit institution. G. H. has now spent most of her 17 years of life there.

Her parents were unable to pay the charges at that school, even though approximately half of the expenses of the school are paid by charitable contributions. So the Williams County Welfare Board began paying the cost of keeping her in a foster home in Jamestown, while Williston School District No. 1 contracted with the Crippled Children's School to pay her tuition. Such contracts are authorized by Chapter 15-59, North Dakota Century Code, which provides, in substance, that a school district may contract with a private, nonsectarian, nonprofit corporation for the cost of educating handicapped children and agree to pay three times the State average per-pupil elementary or high school cost. Sixty per cent of such cost is reimbursed by the Special Education Division of the Department of Public Instruction of the State of North Dakota.

All went well until the parents of G. H. moved to Minneapolis, Minnesota, in 1969, leaving her at the Crippled Children's School in Jamestown. Williston School District No. 1 stopped paying the tuition at the school as of September 1, 1969, while the County Welfare Board continued to pay for the foster home care. The Crippled Children's School continued to provide her with educational services, without reimbursement by anyone.

On March 20, 1970, Reuben E. Carlson, an officer of the State Public Welfare Board, petitioned the district court of Stutsman County (where the Crippled Children's School is located) to make a determination concerning the care, custody, and control of G. H., and asserted that she was a deprived child without proper parental care or control; that her parents were not living together and were unable to provide a suitable home for her; that she had physical disabilities which make it necessary for her to attend the Crippled Children's School; and that her parents were unable to cope with her many needs because of her physical condition. The action was brought by Reuben E. Carlson, and the respondents were G. H. and her parents. After a hearing, the district court made findings on May 14, 1970, that G. H. is a deprived child, that her parents were unable to provide for her, that the causes of her deprivation were not likely to be remedied, that her mother was confined to a hospital for psychiatric treatment, that it was impossible for her parents to care for her, that the most suitable place for her was the Crippled Children's School, and that the parents had not established permanent residence outside the Williston area. The court further found that the Crippled Children's School had proper facilities for her education and that there were no public schools in the State of North Dakota with the necessary facilities which would accept her. The court further found that the Williams County Welfare Board was providing for her care and that up to September 1, 1969, when the parents left Williston, the Williston School District paid the tuition at the Crippled Children's School.

The court thereupon ordered that G. H. be taken under the juvenile jurisdiction of the court, that her care, custody, and control be transferred to the director of the Williams County Welfare Board, and that her father pay $55 per month to the Williams County Welfare Board if his income warranted. Williston School District No. 1 was ordered to pay the educational costs at the Crippled Children's School retroactively to September 1, 1969, and continuously thereafter so long as she remains a student at the School.

Copies of the order were served upon the administrator of the Williston school district, the area social service center at Williston, and the Crippled Children's School, as well as upon G. H.'s father.

The school district, on May 13, 1971, moved the court to vacate that portion of the order requiring it to pay for the tuition, upon grounds of (1) mistake, inadvertence, surprise or excusable neglect, and (2) fraud, misrepresentation or other misconduct of an adverse party. The motion was supported by affidavits of the register of deeds of Williams County to the effect that no real property was owned by G. H.'s father in Williams County, and of Leon Olson, the superintendent of schools of Williston, to the effect that G. H.'s father had sold his house at Williston on September 4, 1969, and her parents had moved to Minneapolis, where they had resided for 21 months. Upon a hearing on this motion, the court made certain findings as to the parents' moving to Minneapolis, but reiterated its previous findings that G. H. was a deprived child, that her parents were unable to care for her, that she was attending a crippled children's school which was a fit and proper place for her and in her best interests to attend. The court further found that her parents were then residents of Minneapolis and that her father was capable of contributing $40 per month toward her support, that G. H. was not a student of Williston School District No. 1, as that term is defined in Section 15-59-07, N.D.C.C., and that her tuition was an obligation of the Special Education Division of the State Department of Public Instruction for the year 1970–1971 and thereafter until assumed by the State of Minnesota or until further order of the court. The court vacated its prior order requiring the school district to pay the tuition and ordered the Special Education Division to do so. The responsibility of the Williams County Welfare Board for general subsistence and foster-home care was continued. Notice of the latter hearing was served upon the parents of G. H., Mr. Carlson of the Public Welfare Board, and the attorney for the Crippled Children's School; and attorneys for the school district, the Public Welfare Board, and the Crippled Children's School participated in the hearing, as did the director of the Williams County Welfare Board and others.

Thereupon the Special Education Division petitioned for the vacation of portions of the order of July 27, 1971, asserting that it was unauthorized to pay tuition except as reimbursement to school districts under Chapter 15-59, referred to above. A summons and notice to appear was served upon attorneys for the Crippled Children's School, the County Welfare Board, the Public Welfare Board for the State, the Williston school district, the Department of Public Instruction, and the parents of G. H. After a hearing, the court further amended its order to provide that the Public Welfare Board and the Williams County Welfare Board be required to pay the tuition. The specific language of the court's order is as follows:

ORDERED

I. That the above named minor child, G. H., is continued under the juvenile jurisdiction of this Court and is hereby declared to be a ward of the State; that the care,
control, custody of said child be and the same is hereby continued with the Director of
the Williams County Welfare Board, Williams County, North Dakota, and that all major
medical determinations be made with the consent of the parents.

II. It is further Ordered that . . . father of said child, G. H., is to furnish to the
Williams County Welfare Board copies of his income tax returns and that he is to report
his income to said agency each month and that if his income warrants he is to pay not
less than Forty Dollars ($40.00) per month to the Williams County Welfare Board.

III. It is further Ordered that the Williams County Welfare Board continue to be
responsible for general subsistence and foster care of said minor child, subject to reimbursement as heretofore Ordered.

IV. It is further Ordered that the Public Welfare Board of North Dakota and the
Williams County Welfare Board be and is required to pay the educational care costs of
said minor child, G. H., at the Crippled Children's School at Jamestown, North Dakota,
retroactively to the first of September, 1970, and continuously thereafter while she is a
student and inmate of said school and until the further order of this Court; and it is
further specifically ordered and determined that the additional cost of such retroactive
educational care through the year 1972 is the sum of $3908.00.

Service of the order was made upon all the parties to the present appeal, as well
as other persons.

The Williams County Welfare Board attempted to file a "Special Appearance
and Petition for Leave to be Heard and to Vacate Amended Order, dated June 5,
1973," but the trial court refused to consider it.

From the amended order the Public Welfare Board of the State of North Dakota
(now designated by statute as Social Service Board of North Dakota) appealed only
from paragraph IV of the order, and the Williams County Welfare Board appealed from
all four paragraphs of the order.

When the appeal was perfected, all parties named in the title were represented
by attorneys, except G. H. herself. On our own initiative, we requested the North
Dakota Association for Retarded Children to file a brief amicus curiae. We are grateful
to the Association for having done so and for enlisting the support of the National
Center for Law and the Handicapped, which joined in the brief and participated in the
oral argument.

Constitutional Right to Education

Two kinds of expenditures are involved in this appeal. The first is, perhaps
inadequately, described as *subsistence*. This description includes the foster home care,
including board and room of G. H., as well as payments for physical therapy and some
incidental expenses for her. These sums have been paid for years by the Williams
County Welfare Board. Although that board appealed from the order of the district
court, it continued to make payments for subsistence, and concedes that it will continue
to make the payments if no one else makes them.

The greatest disagreement arises over the second category of expenses, also
described inadequately, the so-called *tuition* at the Crippled Children's School. This
designation necessarily covers more than the ordinary kind of education, since educa-

tion of handicapped children requires a different kind of physical plant to accommodate their physical handicaps, a different kind of teaching adapted to the mental handicaps which so often accompany the physical ones, and special kinds of teachers to assist in surmounting the problems arising from all the varieties of handicaps encountered.

The first question to arise, incredibly enough, is whether G. H. is entitled to have her tuition paid by anyone. A great many handicapped children in this State have had no education at all, which might indicate that they are entitled to none. A further shadow on their claim to an education has been cast, according to some of the briefs before us, by the decision of the United States Supreme Court in *San Antonio Indepen-dent School District* v. *Rodriguez,* 411 U.S. 1, 93 S.Ct. 1278, 36 L.Ed.2d 16 (1973), which held that education is not a right mandated by the United States Constitution. We will return to the *Rodriguez* case later, but at this point we will consider whether the right to an education is a constitutional right under the Constitution of this State. We held long ago that it is, and we now reiterate that holding.

> The historic policy of this state, in common with the general policy of every other state in the Union, is to maintain a free public school system for the benefit of all children within specified age limits.
>
> This policy existed prior to statehood and is crystallized in sections 147 and 148 of the State Constitution, which read as follows:
>
> A high degree of intelligence, patriotism, integrity and morality on the part of every voter in a government by the people being necessary in order to insure the continuance of that government and the prosperity and happiness of the people, the legislative assembly shall make provision for the establishment and maintenance of a system of public schools which shall be open to all children of the state of North Dakota and free from sectarian control. This legislative requirement shall be irrevocable without con-sent of the United States and the people of North Dakota. [Sec. 147, Constitution of N.D.]
>
> The legislative assembly shall provide, at its first session after the adoption of this constitution, for a uniform system for free public schools throughout the state, begin-ning with the primary and extending through all grades up to and including the normal and collegiate course. [Sec. 148, Constitution of N.D.] *Anderson* v. *Breithbarth,* 62 N.D. 709, 245 N.W. 483, 484 (1932).

We are satisfied that all children in North Dakota have the right, under the State Constitution, to a public school education. Nothing in *Rodriguez, supra,* holds to the contrary. The State of New Jersey has held, since *Rodriguez,* that education is a right under the Constitution of that State. *Robinson* v. *Cahill,* 62 N.J. 473, 303 A.2d 273 (1973).

Handicapped children are certainly entitled to no less than unhandicapped chil-dren under the explicit provisions of the Constitution. Whether those who have been unconstitutionally deprived of education in the past have a constitutionally based claim for compensatory educational effort, we leave for future determination. See *In re H.,* 72 Misc.2d 59, 337 N.Y.S.2d 969 (Family Court, Queens County, 1972).

For the present, we say only that failure to provide educational opportunity for handicapped children (except those, if any there are, who cannot benefit at all from it) is an unconstitutional violation of the foregoing constitutional provisions, as well as Section 11 of the North Dakota Constitution and Section 20 of the North Dakota Constitution, which provide that all laws of a general nature shall have a uniform operation and that no class of citizens shall be granted privileges or immunities which upon the same terms shall not be granted to all citizens.

We find nothing in *Rodriguez, supra,* to persuade us to a different view. On the contrary, education has long been the primary responsibility of the States, and it is only natural that their constitutions should provide for a right to an education; while the Federal Constitution, as *Rodriguez* points out, is silent on the subject of education.

And even the *Rodriguez* opinion indicates that Federal constitutional questions would arise if there were a total deprivation of educational opportunities, as there would be here if none of the parties before us was paying for the education of G. H. As the Court said in *Rodriguez:*

> The argument here is not that the children in districts having relatively low assessable property values are receiving no public education; rather, it is that they are receiving a poorer quality education than that available to children in districts having more assessable wealth. (411 U.S., at p. 23, 93 S.Ct., at 1291.)
>
> Texas asserts that the Minimum Foundation Program provides an "adequate" education for all children in the State. By providing 12 years of free public school education, and by assuring teachers, books, transportation and operating funds, the Texas Legislature has endeavored to "guarantee, for the welfare of the state as a whole, that all people shall have at least an adequate program of education. This is what is meant by "A Minimum Foundation Program of Education." " The State repeatedly asserted in its briefs in this Court that it has fulfilled this desire and that it now assures "every child in every school district an adequate education." No proof was offered at trial persuasively discrediting or refuting the State's assertion. (411 U.S., at p. 24, 93 S.Ct., at 1291.)

While the Supreme Court of the United States, using the "traditional" equal-protection analysis, held that the Texas system of educational financing, which relied largely upon property taxes, was constitutional, we are confident that the same Court would have held that G. H.'s terrible handicaps were just the sort of "immutable characteristic determined solely by the accident of birth" to which the "inherently suspect" classification would be applied, and that depriving her of a meaningful educational opportunity would be just the sort of denial of equal protection which has been held unconstitutional in cases involving discrimination based on race and illegitimacy and sex. See *Frontiero* v. *Richardson,* 411 U.S. 677, 93 S.Ct. 1764, 36 L.Ed.2d 583 (1973); *New Jersey Welfare Rights Organization* v. *Cahill,* 411 U.S. 619, 93 S.Ct. 1700, 36 L.Ed.2d 543 (1973).

In *Brown* v. *Board of Education of Topeka,* 347 U.S. 483, 74 S.Ct. 686, 98 L.Ed. 873 (1954), the Supreme Court said, "In these days, it is doubtful that any child may reasonably be expected to succeed in life if he is denied the opportunity of an education. Such an opportunity, where the state has undertaken to provide it, is a right which must be made available to all on equal terms." When North Dakota undertakes to supply an education to all, and to require all to attend school, that right must be made available to all, including the handicapped, on equal terms.

The plain language of our constitutional provisions requires this conclusion. Even if it did not, the Federal Constitution would. The leading case as to the rights of the handicapped is *Pennsylvania Association for Retarded Children* v. *Commonwealth of Pennsylvania,* 334 F.Supp. 1257 (E.D.Pa. 1971), affirmed and settlement approved by a three-judge court at 343 F.Supp. 279 (1972). It is cited approvingly in *Harrison* v.

State of Michigan, 350 F.Supp. 846 (E.D.Mich. 1972). Another similar case is *Mills* v. *Board of Education of District of Columbia,* 348 F.Supp. 866 (D.C.D.C. 1972).

Even if we were disposed to avoid or evade our duty to construe the State Constitution to require educational opportunity for the handicapped (and we are not so disposed), the Federal courts would surely construe the Federal Constitution to require the same result, and properly so. See *Reid* v. *Board of Education of City of New York,* 453 F.2d 238 (2d Cir. 1971), and Federal cases *supra.*

We hold that G. H. is entitled to an equal educational opportunity under the Constitution of North Dakota, and that depriving her of that opportunity would be an unconstitutional denial of equal protection under the Federal and State Constitutions and of the Due Process and Privileges and Immunities Clauses of the North Dakota Constitution.

In fairness to the parties here, we must add that there is little disagreement among them as to the right of G. H. to an education (although one of them appears to claim that the State's duty to provide aid to welfare clients means only the duty to provide subsistence, defined as "shelter, food, clothing and medical attention and nothing else"—a view we do not share). What the parties argue about most is the identity of the agency which is to pay for the education of G. H.

Who Shall Pay?

Resolution of this question depends upon a decision as to the residence of G. H. for school purposes. That problem was exhaustively discussed in *Anderson* v. *Breithbarth, supra.* Although the statutes have been amended in many respects since then, the amendments would not change the result.

Section 15-59-07, relating to education of students with physical handicaps and learning disabilities, says nothing about residence. It tells only what is to be done if any school district "has" such a handicapped child.

The facts here are very similar to *Anderson.* In *Anderson,* a child had been more or less abandoned by her parents and left with relatives, who enrolled her in a local school. The school district challenged her right to attend the school without the payment of tuition by the district of her former residence or the district of her parents' then residence. We held that it was the residence of the child which was controlling, and that she was entitled to attend the school where she resided with relatives.

In the present case, if the Williston School District had facilities within its district to educate handicapped children such as G. H., she would no doubt still be living there, and *Anderson* would be exactly in point and controlling.

Does the fact that Williston has no such facilities, and therefore contracted with the Crippled Children's School to provide them, change the situation in any material way? We think not. A contract between a school district and the Crippled Children's School does not change the residence of the child, which remains within the contracting district.

We therefore hold that the trial court was correct in its order of May 14, 1970, in holding that Williston School District No. 1 was liable for the tuition of G. H. at the Crippled Children's School and that it erred in later modifying that order to provide that the Special Education Division of the State Department of Public Instruction be required to make such payments. [The Special Education Division will reimburse the School District for a portion of the costs, pursuant to Chapter 15-59, as it has consistently offered to do.]

We so hold, even though the child's parents have moved from the State of North Dakota and established residence elsewhere. G. H. has been determined to be a ward of the State. Her residence is separate from that of her parents. *Anderson* v. *Breithbarth, supra.* If Williston were not her residence, we would have to decide whether the responsibility for her care lay with the Social Service Board of the State.

By holding that the Public Welfare Board (now Social Service Board) is not liable for the tuition of G. H., we do not mean to agree in any sense with its position that it cannot be held liable because it has no appropriation specifically designated for that purpose or that it must first obtain approval from the Department of Health, Education, and Welfare of a "plan" to make any such provisions. We are not so federalized that a State department is not subject to the courts of the State. See *Collins* v. *State Board of Welfare,* 248 Iowa 369, 81 N.W.2d 4 (1947).

Affirmed in part and reversed in part and remanded for further proceedings consistent with this opinion.

ERICKSTAD, C. J., and TEIGEN, KNUDSON and PAULSON, JJ., concur.

NOTES

1.   The sympathy of the *G.H.* court and the New York courts in the *H., Downey,* and *Kirschner* cases to equal protection issues suggests that in some circumstances state courts may prove to be favorable forums for raising federal constitutional claims. In a state court, the federal issues may be reinforced or supplemented by claims under state statutes and constitutional provisions, thus allowing litigative efficiency by resolving all of the issues in a single action. Resort to a state court also avoids the complications and delays that might result if a federal court invokes the doctrine of abstention, e.g., *Reid* v. *Board of Education of the City of New York,* 453 F.2d 238 (2d Cir. 1971), or requires complete exhaustion of state remedies. On the other hand, if federal constitutional issues are raised in state court proceedings and the state court is not sympathetic to them, a litigant may lose his right to a federal forum, *Huffman* v. *Pursue Ltd.,* 420 U.S. 592, 605-606 (1975); *Preiser* v. *Rodriguez,* 411 U.S. 475, 497 (1973). The decision whether to go into a state or federal court is, therefore, an important strategy consideration in the development of such lawsuits.

2.   The fact pattern from which the *G.H.* case arose is a prime example of "administrative buck-passing," where a number of public agencies bicker among themselves as to who is responsible for providing an educational program for particular individuals. Fortunately for G.H. herself, the Crippled Children's School was willing to continue providing a program for her without compensation during the time it took for the case to wind its way to the North Dakota Supreme Court. Otherwise, the dispute over which agency was responsible for her education might have resulted in no one providing her such education for a significant period of time.

3.   The suggestion in *G.H.* that handicapped persons constitute a "suspect class" is a particularly important aspect of the case, with great ramifications for legal analysis in

all cases involving equal protection claims on behalf of handicapped persons. The impact and sources of such a finding are discussed below; for additional discussion and support of the concept of *handicapped* as a constitutionally suspect classification, see Burgdorf, M., and Burgdorf, R., "A History of Unequal Treatment: The Qualifications of Handicapped Persons as a 'Suspect Class' Under the Equal Protection Clause," 15 *Santa Clara Lawyer* 855 (1975)

4. A newspaper article gives more insight into the situation of Gail Hanson, the subject of the *G.H.* litigation:

> Gail is one of the 95 students at the Crippled Children's School in Jamestown, one of the 90 facilities of the Lutheran Hospitals and Homes Society. Gail has been there a long time. For her the school is home. . . .
>
> When Gail was taken to the school 14 years ago, she was a reject from the Grafton State School, but only because someone saw a glint of intelligence in the one good eye of this "retarded" mishap.
>
> Abandoned soon after her birth by her parents, who once were Williams County residents, Gail's entrance into the world seemed a mistake.
>
> She was a quadruple amputee, which means she was born without hands and feet. One eye was missing, as were teeth. She had a cleft palate, facial distortion, an inability to speak and hearing in only one ear.
>
> Almost as serious, because of what happened to Gail during her very earliest years, the school had on its hands a very emotionally disturbed child.
>
> Today Gail is a responsive, enthusiastic student, doing well in her pre-vocational training, excited about her new dormitory quarters and recalling the Winter Festival held recently by the school.
>
> The students staged a prom, with guests from the Rainbow and DeMolay groups in Jamestown, plus professional talent from the Hee-Haw Show and the Arizona Troubadours. Gail wore a formal gown and danced with her double-date escorts.
>
> Some time ago as one of a string of cosmetic and remedial operations, they split the blunt end of Gail's right arm into two thumbs. It's known as a Krukenberg operation and it gave her the ability to handle pencils, paint brushes, tableware—and to play the organ and piano.
>
> "Gail often plays the chord organ for our weekly chapel services," faculty member Mrs. Kathleen Hanson (no relation to Gail) says. Gail told a visitor she remembers as a toddler being attracted to the organ in her grandmother's home. With the thumb operation she is able to play the organ "by ear."
>
> Mrs. Hanson is Gail's counselor and art teacher and she feels industrial arts may offer a meaningful career for Gail, once she is graduated in mid-1977. The cover of the "Light of Faith" magazine, publication of Lutheran Hospitals (Jan.-Feb.) carries a winter scene drawn by her.
>
> "She's a good student," Mrs. Hanson says, listing Gail's subjects currently as consumer mathematics, home economics, art, social studies, English and industrial arts.
>
> Walter R. Hall, the school's director of development and business manager, also has praise for Gail.
>
> "She's ambitious," Hall says. "She walks, runs and rides a bike as good as anyone. She helps the other children and is good handling braces—better than many, despite her handicap."
>
> Gail Hanson receives no special attention within a population that numbers cerebral palsy, paraplegia, muscular dystrophy, arthritis, amputees and battered children among its diagnoses. . . .
>
> "Today, Gail is a confident, self-assured young lady," Hall says. "She still has frustrations when she isn't understood, but the speech and physical therapy, plus the

loving care of dozens of school workers, has made Gail virtually independent. And, more important, she has a feeling of self-worth." (Baccus, J., "Gail Hanson: Handicap No Barrier to Living," *Fargo-Moorhead Sunday Forum*, Mar. 21, 1976, p. E-4.)

5. Note the discussion of the *San Antonio School District* v. *Rodriguez* case in the *G.H.* opinion. At the time the *Rodriguez* decision was handed down, there was some gnashing of teeth among lawyers and other advocates for handicapped people who were afraid of the possible impact of the decision upon *PARC* and *Mills* types of lawsuits. Some persons felt that the whole social movement toward equal educational opportunity for handicapped individuals had come to an abrupt end as a result of the *Rodriguez* holding. *Rodriguez* was simplistically read as synonymous with the proposition that there is no right to an education; therefore, the reasoning went, there can no longer be legal actions to protect this illusory right.

As the *G.H.* case indicates, once the smoke had cleared, the *Rodriguez* decision did not prove to be much of an impediment to litigation seeking equal education for handicapped people. In *Rodriguez,* the United States Supreme Court upheld against equal protection challenge a Texas system that based public school financing on local property taxes; the Court held that the resulting unequal school expenditures did not infringe upon a fundamental right. *Rodriguez* did not involve any handicapped plaintiffs nor did it raise any issues concerning special education programs, so it is factually distinguishable from the line of cases challenging denials of education to handicapped children. But, even in terms of general principles and obiter dicta by the Court, *Rodriguez* proved, as can be seen in subsequent cases, to be more of a clarification than a setback, and, in some ways, actually assisted the battle for equal access of handicapped people to the public educational system.

FIALKOWSKI v. SHAPP

United States District Court for the Eastern District of Pennsylvania, 1975
405 F.Supp. 946

MEMORANDUM AND ORDER

HUYETT, District Judge.

Invoking 42 U.S.C. § 1983 and its jurisdictional counterpart, 28 U.S.C. § 1343, plaintiffs bring this action for damages claiming that defendant state and city officials have violated their rights to an appropriate education under the equal protection and the due process clauses of the Fourteenth Amendment to the Constitution. Plaintiffs contend that, as multiple-handicapped children, they are denied equal protection under the Constitution because unlike the programs offered to normal and less severely retarded children, the nature of the educational programs offered them is such that no chance exists that the programs will benefit. Plaintiffs then allege that all named defendants shared in some part of the duty to provide them appropriate education and that each defendant knowingly and maliciously violated this duty.

Plaintiffs in this action, represented by their parents, are Walter and David Fialkowski. At the time the complaint was filed, Walter was 21 years old with a mental age of 19 months and David was 12 years old with a mental age of 15 months. In September 1972, Walter and David were students at the Longfellow School for the multiple-handicapped. In December 1972 their parents withdrew them from school and demanded a hearing on an alternate placement since, the Fialkowskis allege, Longfellow School did no more than babysit for their sons because it offered no training appropriate to their learning capacities.[1] In accordance with the procedures established in *Pennsylvania Association for Retarded Children* v. *Commonwealth of Pennsylvania (PARC)*, 343 F.Supp. 279 (E.D.Pa. 1972), a hearing was held in May 1973 at which time the hearing examiner found Walter and David to be in need of training for the multiple-handicapped and reassigned them to Longfellow School. Apparently the Fialkowskis took no further action until they filed this lawsuit. Neither did they send their sons back to school. Walter is now past school age.

    Defendants include local school district officials of the city of Philadelphia and four officials of the Commonwealth of Pennsylvania: Milton Shapp, Governor; Israel Packel, former Attorney General; John Pittenger, Secretary of Education; and Joseph Lantzer, former Director of the Right to Education Office. Before us are four motions to dismiss.

    [The court's discussion of procedural matters is omitted.]

Constitutional Issue

    City defendants, relying on *San Antonio Independent School District* v. *Rodriguez*, 411 U.S. 1, 93 S.Ct. 1278, 36 L.Ed.2d 16 (1973), argue that plaintiffs have no claim because there is no fundamental right to education. They also argue that the question of the appropriateness of the program into which Walter and David Fialkowski were placed does not rise to a constitutional level.

    Although a broad reading of *Rodriguez* might support defendants' contention, we construe its holding more narrowly and conclude that *Rodriguez* does not foreclose plaintiffs' equal protection claim. *Rodriguez* involved an attack upon the constitutionality of a method of financing public education, partly through revenues collected from local property taxes, that resulted in differences in the per-pupil expenditures among the various school districts. Plaintiffs did not allege, however, that any student received less than an adequate education. In rejecting the attack, the Court held that when a state educational system affords minimally adequate educational opportunities to all children, that some children are afforded greater opportunities than others does not amount to a denial of equal protection so long as the differences bear a rational relation to a legitimate state interest. Based on our reading of *Rodriguez,* then, we find that the constitutional challenge in the case at bar is distinguishable from that in *Rodriguez* on several grounds.

    First, the Fialkowskis allege that their children are being completely denied educational opportunity, not that Walter and David are being afforded a lesser quality of education than other classes of children. In its discussion of the right to education in *Rodriguez,* the Court stated:

---

[1]The Fialkowskis argue that, instead of teaching their sons such essential self-help skills as how to dress, how to eat and how to walk, the school made an effort to teach the boys academic subjects.

Whatever merit appellees' argument might have if a State's financing system occasioned an absolute denial of educational opportunities to any of its children, that argument provides no basis for finding an interference with fundamental rights where only relative differences in spending levels are involved and where... no charge fairly could be made that the system fails to provide each child with an opportunity to acquire the basic minimal skills necessary for the enjoyment of the rights of speech and of full participation in the political process.[8] (411 U.S. at 37, 93 S.Ct. at 1299.)

It would thus appear not inconsistent with *Rodriguez* to hold that there exists a constitutional right to a certain minimum level of education as opposed to a constitutional right to a particular level of education.

Secondly, *Rodriguez* should be read in its peculiar factual setting involving a Texas property tax plan for financing educational facilities. The Supreme Court has recognized the great importance of education in our society. In *Brown* v. *Board of Education,* 347 U.S. 483, 493, S.Ct. 686, 691, 98 L.Ed. 873 (1954), the Court said that

education is perhaps the most important function of state and local governments. . . . In these days, it is doubtful that any child may reasonably be expected to succeed in life if he is denied the opportunity of an education. Such an opportunity, where the state has undertaken to provide it, is a right which must be made available to all on equal terms.

Rodriguez stands, then, for the proposition that equal educational opportunity is not measured in terms of equal financial expenditures. The claim of plaintiffs is on a different footing, however. Plaintiffs argue that equal educational opportunity, as a constitutional standard, should be defined to include equal access to minimal educational services. At this early stage of litigation, we cannot find this distinction invalid.

Thirdly, plaintiffs argue that we should strictly scrutinize their claims because retarded children are a suspect class. Reviewing the characteristics of a suspect class as the Supreme Court has identified them, we find a certain immediate appeal to plaintiffs' argument. The Court in *Rodriguez,* for example, set forth the following criteria for determining what constitutes a suspect class:

class... saddled with such disabilities, or subjected to such a history of purposeful unequal treatment, or relegated to such a position of political powerlessness as to command extraordinary protection from the majoritarian political process. (411 U.S. at 28, 93 S.Ct. at 1294.)

Such a test could certainly be read to include retarded children. Retarded children are precluded from the political process and have been neglected by state legislatures. Moreover, the label "retarded" might bear as great a stigma as any racial slur. In *Interest of G. H.,* 218 N.W.2d 441 (1974), the Supreme Court of North Dakota accepted the argument that the handicapped should be classified as suspect and distinguished *Rodriguez* on this basis.

---

[8]There can be no doubt that the denial of an adequate education to a retarded child is a denial of the opportunity to acquire the basic skills of citizenship, and may result in the loss of freedom from later state institutionalization. *Child's Right to an Effective Minimal Education,* 36 Ohio State L. J. 349, 363 (1975).

While the Supreme Court of the United States, using the "traditional" equal-protection analysis, held that the Texas system of educational financing, which relied largely upon property taxes, was constitutional, we are confident that the same Court would have held that G. H.'s terrible handicaps were just the sort of "immutable characteristics determined solely by the accident of birth" to which the "inherently suspect" classification would be applied, and that depriving her of a meaningful educational opportunity would be just the sort of denial of equal protection which has been held unconstitutional in cases involving discrimination based on race and illegitimacy. (218 N.W.2d at 446-47.)

Although the present posture of this case does not require us to resolve this issue, we will say that depriving retarded children of all educational benefits would appear to warrant greater judicial scrutiny than that applied in *Rodriguez*. For these reasons, we believe that *Rodriguez* is not controlling in this case.

In any event, there may be no rational basis for providing education to most children and yet denying plaintiffs instruction from which they could possibly benefit. In *PARC* this court stated that all mentally retarded children would benefit from education, 343 F.Supp. 279, 296 (E.D.Pa. 1972), and that such denial "established a colorable constitutional claim even under the less stringent rational basis test." (*Id.* at 283 and n. 8, 295.) An educational program must be assessed in terms of its capacity to equip a child with the tools needed in life. *See Wisconsin* v. *Yoder,* 406 U.S. 205, 222, 92 S.Ct. 1526, 32 L.Ed.2d 15 (1972). Placement of children with the intelligence of two year olds in a program which emphasizes skills such as reading and writing would seem inadequate for their needs. The harmful consequences of denying plaintiffs an adequate education is underscored by the fact that mentally retarded children have greater need for formal education since they are less likely than ordinary children to learn and to develop informally. Accordingly, we cannot conclude that plaintiffs' complaint lacks constitutional substance.

NOTES

1. In addition to their equal protection claims, the plaintiffs in *Fialkowski* also contended that they had suffered a violation of substantive due process; the court discussed this theory in a footnote:

> In the alternative, plaintiffs claim that by being required to attend school without being provided a minimally adequate education, they have been deprived of liberty without due process of law. Plaintiffs argue that since compulsory school attendance laws are justified by the state's interest in educating children, failing to provide a meaningful education reduces school to confinement and constitutes a serious infringement on a child's physical liberty. In making this argument, plaintiffs analogize to cases holding that mentally ill patients confined to hospitals and juveniles placed in reformatories are entitled to care and treatment in order to justify their confinement. [Citations omitted.] Nevertheless, in view of our finding regarding plaintiffs' equal protection claim, we need not presently consider the soundness of applying the due process clause to a school's failure to provide a minimally adequate education to its students. (405 F.Supp. at 959 n. 10.)

This interesting quid pro quo theory, that if you give up your liberty to get a benefit (education) from the state, due process requires that the state actually give you the promised benefit, is discussed in the case of *Lora* v. *Board of Ed. of City of New York* at pp. 147–165, below.

2. In a similar case denying defendants' motions to dismiss an equal educational opportunity lawsuit, a three-judge federal court in *Colorado Association for Retarded Children* v. *State of Colorado*, C.A. No. C-4620 (D.Colo., July 13, 1973), observed:

> [D]efendants submit that *Rodriguez, supra,* lays to rest the broader issue of whether education is a right to be afforded constitutional protection. However, the present factual posture of the matter at bar has not been developed to a point where this action can be dismissed solely on the reasoning in *Rodriguez*. In fact, the issues and purported facts surrounding the instant case are, at the moment, distinguishable from those raised in *Rodriguez*.

As in *Fialkowski,* the court in the Colorado case indicated that one of the areas needing factual development was the question of whether the plaintiff class met the three *Rodriguez* criteria for a "suspect" class.

ADDITIONAL READING

Dimond, P., and Reed, J., "*Rodriguez* and Retarded Children," 2 *J. L. & Educ.* 476 (1973).
Note, "The Right of Handicapped Children to an Education: The Phoenix of *Rodriguez,*" 59 *Cornell L. Rev.* 519 (1974).
Casey, P., "The Supreme Court and the Suspect Class," 40 *Exceptional Children* 119 (1973).
Abeson, A., "Recent Developments in the Courts," 3 *Leadership Series in Special Education* 69, University of Minnesota (R. Johnson, J. Gross, and R. Weatherman, eds., 1974).
Note, "Special Education: The Struggle for Equal Educational Opportunity in Iowa," 62 *Ia. L. Rev.* 1283, 1344-1354 (1977).

FREDERICK L. v. THOMAS

United States District Court for the Eastern District of Pennsylvania, 1976
408 F.Supp. 832

NEWCOMER, District Judge.

This case is before the Court in an unusual posture. A trial on the merits was held while there was an outstanding "motion to dismiss." We will now deny that motion. Counsel will be given an opportunity to be heard in argument on the trial record before we make findings of fact and conclusions of law.

Before setting forth our reasons for denying the motion, it is necessary to explain the basis for the unorthodox sequence of the proceedings. On January 9, 1974, a class action complaint was filed on behalf of Frederick L. and all other children with "specific learning disabilities," who are allegedly deprived of an education appropriate to their specialized needs by the defendants, the School District of Philadelphia and named officials of said District. Federal jurisdiction was based on alleged violations of the United States Constitution and of the Civil Rights Act, 42 U.S.C. § 1983, and pendant state law claims were also pleaded. The original defendants answered the complaint on April 29, 1974. The Commonwealth of Pennsylvania was given leave to intervene as a party defendant on June 15, 1974. It filed an answer to the Complaint on September 30, 1974. There was extensive pretrial discovery, together with negotiations that brought the dispute close to settlement. On September 15, 1975, the defendant-intervenor, Commonwealth of Pennsylvania, filed a "Motion to Dismiss pursuant to Rule 12(b) of the Federal Rules of Civil Procedure," in which the original defendants subsequently joined. This motion was not properly presented under Fed.R.Civ.P. 12(b), since the Commonwealth had answered the complaint almost a year earlier. The court treated the motion as it if had been made pursuant to Rule 12(c), Motion for Judgment on the Pleadings. However, Rule 12(c) provides, in pertinent part:

> After the pleadings are closed *but within such time as not to delay the trial,* any party may move for judgment on the pleadings. [emphasis supplied]

The Commonwealth filed its motion ten days after the originally scheduled trial date, and about a week before the new date, for which the court had reserved two weeks in its calendar. The court decided that at least one of the grounds asserted in the motion—abstention—raised serious issues, but they could not be thoroughly evaluated before the trial date. Unable to delay the trial but not wanting to deny the motion on a procedural ground, especially since the asserted grounds could be raised by motion at trial under Fed.R.Civ.P. 12(h)(2–3), the court took the motion under advisement and commenced the trial.

The motion asserts three grounds for dismissal of the complaint or stay of the proceedings: (a) failure to state a cause of action; (b) mootness; and (c) abstention. We will discuss each in turn. Although each ground is rejected, we have left open the possibility that partial abstention may become appropriate at some future time.

A.   Failure to State a Cause of Action

The defendants do not deny that the plaintiffs have stated a colorable claim under state statutory law. By directing their arguments at the constitutional claims in the complaint, the defendants have, in effect, attacked the federal jurisdictional basis of the case. *United Mineworkers* v. *Gibbs,* 383 U.S. 715, 86 S.Ct. 1130, 16 L.Ed.2d 218 (1966). The question before us is whether the plaintiffs, under any of their constitutional theories, have stated a colorable claim which may entitle them to relief. Their claim under the Equal Protection Clause of the Fourteenth Amendment satisfies this test, and therefore we need not inquire into the soundness of the plaintiffs' right-to-education claim under the First, Ninth and Fourteenth Amendments.

The complaint alleges that in the School District of Philadelphia, children with specific learning disabilities who are not receiving instruction specially suited to their handicaps are being discriminated against in the following respects. First, the Commonwealth and School District are providing "normal" children with a free public education appropriate to their needs, but are denying an equal educational opportunity to the plaintiffs. Admittedly, most of the plaintiffs are afforded access to the same curriculum as normal children, but it is argued that the test of *equal* treatment is the suitability of the instructional services for the educational needs of the child. Many of the plaintiffs, it is said, cannot derive *any* educational benefit from the normal curriculum if that experience is not mediated by special instruction aimed at their learning handicaps. We are told that inappropriate educational placements predictably lead to severe frustration and to other emotional disturbances which impede the learning process and erupt into anti-social behavior. On this basis it is argued that some or all of the class is constructively excluded from public educational services, because—for them—the instruction offered is virtually useless, if not positively harmful.

Second, the plaintiffs say that the Commonwealth and the School District of Philadelphia are providing mentally retarded children with a free public education especially suited to their individual needs, but are denying learning disabled children an equal educational opportunity, namely, a curriculum adapted to overcome their handicaps.

Third, it is alleged that the state and the district are unlawfully discriminating between those few learning disabled children who it is specially instructing, and the plaintiffs who are not given special instruction.

Whether the plaintiffs are to be deemed "excluded" from public education is, we think, a mixed question of fact and law. We note that the Supreme Court, in *Lau* v. *Nichols,* 414 U.S. 53, 94 S.Ct. 786, 39 L.Ed. 2d 1 (1974), did not reach the question whether non-English speaking Chinese children were, for the purposes of equal protection analysis, being constructively excluded from public educational services when they were admitted to the schools on the same basis as other children, that is, into classes conducted only in English. Furthermore, in *San Antonio School District* v. *Rodriguez,* 411 U.S. 1, 37, 93, S.Ct. 1278, 36 L.Ed.2d 16 (1973), the Court left open the possibility that the denial of a minimally adequate educational opportunity may trench upon a fundamental interest, if the state has undertaken to provide a free public education.[4] We find that the plaintiffs' legal propositions are not completely devoid of merit, and that their offer of proof on the factual question is satisfactory. Plaintiffs may be able to show that the defendants' policies must be subjected to strict scrutiny because a classification has functionally excluded them from a minimally adequate education.

The complaint also includes a colorable claim that these classifications do not satisfy the equal protection test of rationality. The appropriate test for this case would not be the traditional rationality standard. See, e.g. *Lindsley* v. *National Carbonic Gas Co.,* 220 U.S. 61, 78-79, 31 S.Ct. 337, 55 L.Ed. 369 (1911). The interests implicated in this dispute require the defendants to show that their actions have a basis in fact which rationally advances an actual purpose of the legislative scheme. *Weinberger* v. *Wiesenfeld,* 420 U.S. 636, 95 S.Ct. 1225, 43 L.Ed.2d 514 (1975); *Sosna* v. *Iowa,* 419 U.S. 393, 95 S.Ct. 553, 42 L.Ed.2d 532 (1975); *Weber* v. *Aetna Cas. & Sur. Co.,* 406 U.S. 164, 92 S.Ct. 1400, 31 L.Ed.2d 768 (1972); See also, Gunther, "Forward:

---

[4]This minimum education equal protection theory is distinct from the plaintiffs' right-to-education claim based on the First, Ninth and Fourteenth Amendments. The latter theory would impose on the state an absolute duty to provide the minimal educational services necessary to prepare children for democratic citizenship in their adult lives.

In Search of An Evolving Doctrine on a Changing Court: A Model for a Newer Equal Protection,'' 86 *Harv. L. Rev. 1* (1972).

Wiesenfeld, supra, involved a classification by sex, a quasi-suspect classification. Analogously, the instant case involves education, a quasi-fundamental interest. Moreover, although learning disabled children are not a suspect class they do exhibit some of the essential characteristics of suspect classes—minority status and powerlessness. We think that the Supreme Court, if presented with the plaintiffs' equal protection claim, would apply the as yet hard to define middle test of equal protection, sometimes referred to as "strict rationality." For example, in *Weinberger, supra,* the Court, without purporting to apply the compelling state interest test, noted that a legislative discrimination, even if it can be rationally explained and "is not entirely without empirical support," 420 U.S. at 645, 95 S.Ct. at 1232, 43 L.Ed.2d at 523, must nevertheless withstand scrutiny in light of the primary purposes of the legislative scheme of which it is a part.

The policy of the Commonwealth of Pennsylvania is to make available for every child in the state a free public education appropriate to his needs. The defendants contend that the current level and distribution of instructional services is rationally related to this goal, for the following reasons. Once the state undertakes to correct a social problem, it does not have to solve every aspect of the problem at the very beginning. The state of the art in the field of learning disabilities is uncertain both in regard to diagnosis and remedial instruction—and it is therefore rational to move more slowly in that area than in the furnishing of appropriate instruction for normal and for mentally retarded children. An additional hindrance to establishing services for the learning disabled is said to be a dearth of trained personnel. The defendant admits, that subject to the constraints just noted as well as the limiting factor of finite resources, the state and district must expend their funds equitably and without entirely excluding any child from a public education. The plaintiffs offer to prove that the factual contentions which the defendants rely on in this argument are incorrect.

It would serve no purpose for us to speculate about which combinations of facts, if proven, would support or refute the equal protection claim stated in the complaint. The defendants will have to demonstrate that their classification of learning disabled children is a means to achieving the declared legislative purpose, and that the choice of the method has a basis in fact. Since the defendants' factual contentions in this connection are disputed, we cannot grant a judgment on the pleadings.

NOTES

1. In footnote 4, the court adverts to the fact that the plaintiffs had advanced, as an alternative to their equal protection claims, the theory that the First, Ninth, and Fourteenth Amendments impose upon the states a duty to provide at least minimal educational services to enable children to fulfill duties and opportunities of citizenship. How would the arguments for this contention be formulated?

2. While seeming to lean toward the new "middle test of equal protection," the court does not preclude the possibility that the plaintiffs may be able to invoke the "strict

scrutiny" test by showing that functional exclusion from education may amount to denial of a fundamental right. In passing, however, the court indicates that learning disabled children do not constitute a suspect class. Compare this with the discussion of suspectness in *Fialkowski, supra.* Ought not a decision as to whether or not a suspect classification is involved await development of facts in relation to the "traditional indicia of suspectness" as set out in *San Antonio School District* v. *Rodriguez,* 411 U.S. 1, 28 (1973)?

3. Notice the plaintiffs' claim that learning-disabled children are being discriminated against vis-à-vis mentally retarded children, whom, it is alleged, are receiving an appropriate education in Pennsylvania. A clever way to use the *PARC* decision, *supra,* as a stepping stone to obtaining similar advances in education for children with other handicaps?

4. In regard to subsequent proceedings in *Frederick L.* v. *Thomas,* see pp. 192–193, below.

CUYAHOGA COUNTY ASSOCIATION FOR RETARDED CHILDREN & ADULTS v. ESSEX

United States District Court for the Northern District of Ohio, 1976
411 F.Supp. 46

Before WEICK, Circuit Judge, and GREEN and THOMAS, District Judges.

MEMORANDUM AND ORDER

BEN C. GREEN, District Judge.

This action presents a wide-ranging attack upon the Ohio system of education and/or training for mentally handicapped school-age children. Plaintiffs have asserted constitutional challenges to the statutes and regulations pertinent thereto on two grounds. It is alleged that the retarded are denied equal protection in that they are not afforded educational or training opportunity on the same basis as that accorded all other children of school age. It is further alleged that the retarded are denied due process in the classification procedures provided for determination of the education and/or training which they may receive. Plaintiffs seek a declaratory judgment that a number of Ohio statutes, and regulations promulgated thereunder, are unconstitutional and mandatory orders upon the defendants directing that they create and provide an educational system for the retarded upon the same terms as that offered to all other school-age children.

This action is now before the Court upon the parties' cross-motions for summary judgment. Under these motions, with the limited record before the Court, the issues for consideration must be restricted to matters of facial constitutionality. Any questions of deprivation of constitutional rights by the manner in which the statutes and/or regulaions are applied, if cognizable under the present pleadings and between the present parties, would require an evidentiary proceeding for development of the facts pertinent thereto.

It is appropriate to first deal with plaintiffs' equal protection arguments, as the issues thereunder are primary and basically arise under the Ohio statutes themselves. The issues as regards due process in the classification procedures, while presenting questions of constitutional dimension, may be considered to be secondary and arise under the regulations adopted under the statutes.

Plaintiffs contend that under the Ohio statutes all "normal" children of school age are subject to compulsory and mandatory participation in the free public educational system, but that the retarded are excluded therefrom. It is further contended that the retarded are offered only a discretionary and voluntary participation, with different programs applicable to children with I.Q.'s between 50 and 80 and those with I.Q.'s under 50. In essence, plaintiffs argue that the Ohio statutes create a three-tiered stratification, consisting of children with I.Q.'s over 80, those with I.Q.'s between 50 and 80 and those with I.Q.'s below 50, and that the latter two groupings are not granted the same rights and privileges and do not have imposed upon them the same obligations as does the first. These alleged differences are asserted as violative of the Fourteenth Amendment's guarantees, remediable under 42 U.S.C. §§ 1981 and 1983.

The question thus becomes whether the Ohio statutes do create the classifications as contended by plaintiffs, and, if so, are such classifications constitutionally impermissible.

At the outset, the interests with which we are concerned must be defined. While the Supreme Court has spoken of education as "perhaps the most important function of state and local governments," *Brown* v. *Board of Education,* 347 U.S. 483, 493, 74 S.Ct. 686, 691, 98 L.Ed. 873 (1954), recognizing that "in these days it is doubtful that any child may reasonably be expected to succeed in life if he is denied the opportunity of an education," *ibid.,* the fact remains that education has not been accorded status as a constitutionally guaranteed right, *San Antonio Independent School District* v. *Rodriguez,* 411 U.S. 1, 93 S.Ct. 1278, 36 L.Ed.2d 16 (1973), but rather is deemed a property right, *Goss* v. *Lopez,* 419 U.S. 565, 95 S.Ct. 729, 42 L.Ed.2d 725 (1975). Once a state has determined to establish and maintain a system of free public education it must do so in a framework which does not deny to its children constitutionally protected rights. *Goss* v. *Lopez, supra; Brown* v. *Board of Education, supra.*

It therefore follows that in establishing and administering a public education system a state may incorporate classifications regarding the children to be educated thereunder, so long as such classifications can withstand constitutional scrutiny. The standard which this Court determines must be met under the instant record is the "rational basis" test. *San Antonio School District* v. *Rodriguez, supra,* 411 U.S. at pp. 39–40, 93 S.Ct. at p. 1300, 36 L.Ed.2d at pp. 46–47; *Doe* v. *Laconia Supervisory Union No. 30,* 396 F.Supp. 1291, 1296 (D.N.H., 1975); *Lopez* v. *Williams,* 372 F.Supp. 1279, 1298 (S.D.Ohio, 1973); *Knight* v. *Board of Education of City of New York,* 48 F.R.D. 108, 111 (E.D.N.Y., 1969). *See also, Graham* v. *Richardson,* 403 U.S. 365, 371, 91 S.Ct. 1848, 1852, 29 L.Ed.2d 534, 541 (1971); *Dandridge* v. *Williams,* 397 U.S. 471, 485, 90 S.Ct. 1153, 1161, 25 L.Ed.2d 491, 501 (1970). In order to invalidate a classification under the "rational basis" test it must be shown that it is arbitrary, does not rest upon some ground of difference having a fair and substantial relation to the object of the legislation, or that no state of facts exists which would reasonably support a legitimate state interest therein. *Reed* v. *Reed,* 404 U.S. 71, 92 S.Ct. 251, 30 L.Ed.2d 225 (1971); *McGowan* v. *Maryland,* 366 U.S. 420, 81 S.Ct.

1101, 6 L.Ed.2d 393 (1961); *Lindsley* v. *Natural Carbonic Gas Co.,* 220 U.S. 61, 31 S.Ct. 337, 55 L.Ed. 369 (1911).

The State of Ohio has embarked upon the task of providing a free public education for its children pursuant to Sections 3313.48 and 3313.64 of the Ohio Revised Code, which, in pertinent part, provide that:

> The board of education of each city, exempted village, local, and joint vocational school district shall provide for the free education of the youth of school age within the district. . . . (O.R.C. § 3313.48)
> The schools of each city, exempted village, or local school district shall be free to all school residents between five and twenty-one years of age . . . (O.R.C. § 3313.64)

It is certain provisions of Chapters 3321 (School Attendance), 3323 (Special Classes), and 5127 (Training of Mentally Retarded Children), of the Ohio Revised Code which plaintiffs contend create constitutionally discriminatory access to the Ohio system of free public education. Those statutes, in pertinent part, provide as follows:

> O.R.C. § 3321.01
> A child between six and eighteen years of age is "of compulsory school age" for the purpose of sections 3321.01 to 3321.13, inclusive, of the Revised Code.
> O.R.C. § 3321.02
> Every child actually resident in the state shall be amenable to the laws relating to the compulsory education. . . .
> O.R.C. § 3321.03
> Except as provided in this section, the parent, guardian, or other person having the care of a child of compulsory school age *which child has not been determined to be incapable of profiting substantially by further instruction* shall cause such child to attend a school. . . . *Every child of compulsory school age who has not been determined to be incapable of profiting substantially by further instruction shall attend a school* . . . until one of the following occurs: . . .
>   (C) The child is excused from school under standards adopted by the state board of education pursuant to section 3321.04 of the Revised Code. [emphasis added]
> O.R.C. § 3321.04
> Every parent, guardian, or other person having charge of any child of compulsory school age . . . *who has not been determined to be incapable of profiting substantially by further instruction,* must send such child to a school. . . . [emphasis added]
> O.R.C. § 3321.05
> A child of compulsory school age may be determined to be incapable of profiting substantially by further instruction.
> The state board of education may prescribe standards and examinations or tests by which such capacity may be determined, . . . but the capacity of a child to benefit substantially by further instruction shall be determined with reference to that available to the particular child in the public schools of the district in which he resides, and no child shall be determined to be incapable of profiting substantially by further instruction if the superintendent of public instruction, pursuant to board standards, finds that it is feasible to provide for him in such district, or elsewhere in the public school system, special classes or schools, departments of special instruction or individual instruction through or by which he might profit substantially, according to his mental capacity as so determined. . . .
> . . . If a child is determined to be incapable of profiting substantially by further instructions, such determination shall be certified by the superintendent of public instruction to the superintendent of schools of the district in which he resides, who

shall place such child under the supervision of a visiting teacher or of an attendance officer, to be exercised as long as such child is of compulsory school age. . . .

Any determination made under this section may be revoked by the state board of education for good cause shown.

A child determined to be incapable of profiting substantially by further instruction shall not hereafter be admitted to the public schools of the state while such determination remains in force.
O.R.C. § 3323.01

The state board of education may grant permission to any board of education to establish and maintain classes for the instruction of . . . mentally handicapped persons over the age of five; and to establish and maintain . . . special instructional services, including home instruction . . . for all other persons over the age of five whose learning is retarded, interrupted or impaired by . . . mental handicaps. . . .
O.R.C. § 3323.011

Approval of state funds for the operation of programs and services provided pursuant to section 3323.01 of the Revised Code shall be contingent upon a comprehensive plan for special education approved by the state board of education no later than July 1, 1973. The state board of education shall not approve a school district's plan unless the plan proposed meets the educational needs of handicapped children in that school district and other school districts in the same general area.

Each school district shall submit such a plan to the state board of education by December 1, 1972. . . .

In approving the organization of special education, the state board of education shall provide that no school district be excluded from the statewide plan. . . .
O.R.C. § 3323.04

Upon petition by the parents or guardians of . . . eight educable mentally retarded children, in any school district, of the age named in division (A) of section 3323.01 of the Revised Code, the board of education of such district shall apply to the state board of education for permission to establish a special class for such children. . . .
O.R.C. § 5127.01

The chief of the division of mental retardation and developmental disabilities, with the approval of the director of mental health and mental retardation, shall establish in any county or district a training center or workshop, residential center, and other programs and services for the special training of mentally retarded persons, including those who have been adjudged by the proper authorities to be ineligible for enrollment in public schools under section 3321.01 or 3321.05 of the Revised Code and who are determined by the division of mental retardation and developmental disabilities to be capable of profiting by specialized training. Special attention shall be given to the establishment of a training program for the mentally retarded for the purpose of enabling them to become accepted by society and to find employment in the structure of society to the extent that they may be fitted therefor. The chief is the final authority in determining the nature and degree of mental retardation, shall decide all questions relative or incident to the establishment and operation of each training center or workshop, residential center, and other program or service, determine what constitutes special training, promulgate all rules and regulations . . . governing the approval of mentally retarded persons for such training . . . and approve the current operating costs of such program.

As used in sections 5127.01 to 5127.04, inclusive, of the Revised Code, a "mentally retarded person" means:

(A) A person who has been determined by the proper authorities to be ineligible for enrollment in a public school because of mental retardation of such nature and to such degree that the person is incapable of profiting substantially by any educational program which should be provided by such public school; . . .

O.R.C. § 5127.02

Upon petition to the county board of mental retardation in any county by the parents or guardians of eight or more mentally retarded persons of similar handicap, who are ineligible for enrollment in public school because of . . . mental retardation, the board shall forward such petition to the chief of the division of mental retardation and developmental disabilities. The chief shall take such action and make such order as he deems necessary for the special training of the mentally retarded, to the extent that funds are available.

It is plain on the face of the foregoing statutes that they do not, as contended by plaintiffs, classify children of compulsory school age by I.Q. for purposes of inclusion or exclusion from the free public school system. The statutory basis for disqualification from the system of free public education and for eligibility for admission into the training program for the mentally retarded is a determination that the particular child is "incapable of profiting substantially from further instruction."

In the Court's opinion, such a classification is sufficient to meet the rational basis test. In dealing with a system of mandatory free public education a state which determines that only those children who can derive actual benefit from a broadly based public educational system are to be included therein cannot be said to be acting arbitrarily. Statutory recognition that there are children for whom only training by persons specially qualified therefor will be of any benefit is not invidious discrimination. Whether the manner in which the State of Ohio has determined to provide for the training of children who are incapable of being benefited by instruction in the context of general or special education within the public school system is appropriate is a matter which will be considered hereinafter.

Having determined that the statutory standard for dismissal from the public school system is constitutionally permissible, the Court must now address the contention that under the statutes all children with a mental disability are automatically relegated to a discretionary education. The Court finds that, contrary to plaintiffs' allegation that the system is totally discretionary, educable mentally retarded children who require special education are within the compulsory educational system.

Section 3321.05 of the Revised Code, in defining who may be determined to be incapable of substantially profiting from further instruction, specifically provides that a child who "might profit substantially, according to his mental capacity" by instruction in "special classes" may not be excluded from the compulsory free public school system. Section 3323.01 speaks of establishing classes for children whose abilities are "retarded, interrupted or impaired." Section 3323.04 refers to establishment of classes on behalf of "educable mentally retarded" children. If there was any question as to whether such children are within the compulsory system it would certainly be resolved by reason of Regulation EDb–215–07 of the Ohio Department of Education, which includes as a criteria for eligibility for enrollment in special education units for educable mentally retarded children that the child "is capable of profiting substantially from instruction as determined by an evaluation administered by a qualified psychologist using multi-factored assessment procedures." Based on the foregoing, there can be no doubt that any child who has not been disqualified pursuant to O.R.C. § 3321.05 remains within the compulsory free public school system.

By the same token, the Court does not agree with plaintiffs' arguments that the establishment of special classes is a discretionary matter with the state. That contention is predicated upon the fact that Section 3323.01 provides that the state board of education *may* grant permission for such a program. In the Court's opinion Section 3323.01 cannot be read alone, and when construed with Sections 3323.011 and 3323.04 a conclusion can be reached which avoids the constitutional vice alleged by plaintiffs. If the statutes can be so construed, it is this Court's obligation to do so. *United States* v. *12 200-Ft Reels,* 413 U.S. 123, 130, 93 S.Ct. 2665, 2670, 37 L.Ed.2d 500, 507 (1973); *Driscoll* v. *Edison Light & Power Co.,* 307 U.S. 104, 115, 59 S.Ct. 715, 720, 83 L.Ed. 1134, 1142 (1939); *Daylo* v. *Administrator of Veterans' Affairs,* 163 U.S.App.D.C. 251, 501 F.2d 811, 819 (1974).

Section 3323.011 of the Ohio Code, which required the promulgation by the state board of education and each school district in Ohio of a comprehensive plan for special education prior to the institution of this action, provides that "in approving the organization of special education, the state board of education shall provide that no school district be excluded from the statewide plan." This Court believes that if the state board of education was to refuse to grant an application for special education classes by a local school district pursuant to O.R.C. § 3323.04, such act would constitute an exclusion from the statewide plan of special education prohibited by Section 3323.011. It is noted that in response to a request for admissions it is stated that such "permission has never been denied by the State Board of Education upon an application by a local board of education." As this Court views the overall statutory scheme, it is susceptible of the construction that Section 3323.011 required all local school districts to adopt a plan, which is not to be immediately implemented, for special education classes; that before such classes can be established permission must be secured from the state board of education pursuant to Section 3323.01; that Section 3323.04 mandates that upon petition of the parents of eight mentally retarded children the local board must apply for establishment of such classes, and; that Section 3323.011 requires that permission to implement the plan be granted if the school district's plan meets the statutory and regulatory requirements for a proper plan. Under such a system the only discretion in the state is to determine whether the local district's plan is a proper one. If it was not the state board of education could require the submission of an amended plan meeting the state's requirements.

There is one further argument of plaintiffs regarding the validity of the Ohio statutes as regards the status of the educable mentally retarded which must be considered. It is urged that the statutory scheme is rendered constitutionally impermissible by those portions of Section 3321.05 which make the determination of capability to "benefit substantially by further instruction" dependent upon the availability of instruction "to the particular child in the public schools of the district in which the child resides" or upon a determination of the superintendent of public instruction as to the "feasibility" of providing alternative instruction.

Again, if possible, this statute must be construed in such a manner as to avoid the alleged constitutional infirmity. The Court believes it can be so construed.

Section 3321.05 requires that a child shall not be excluded from the system of public education if the superintendent of public education finds it feasible to provide for such child:

> ... in such district, or elsewhere in the public school system, special classes or schools, departments of special instruction or individual instruction through or by which he might profit substantially, according to his mental capacity.

The statute has inherent in it the question of whether financial considerations may be taken into account in determining feasibility.

This Court does not believe that the question, left open by *Rodriguez, supra,* 411 U.S. at 37, 93 S.Ct. at 1299, 36 L.Ed.2d at 45, whether denial of access to educational facilities to a class of children can be sustained upon a demonstration of the inability of a particular school district to fund special programs, need be resolved in this case.

There exist statutory provisions within the Ohio Revised Code which should operate to make alternative sources or instruction financially feasible throughout the state. These provisions include cooperative school districts for purposes of special education, O.R.C. §§ 3313.841 and 3323.011; payment of tuition and transportation for special instruction, § 3323.10; allocation of excess cost for special instruction outside a district, § 3323.11; payment of boarding expenses, § 3323.12; transportation to be provided to and from school or special education classes for educable mentally retarded children, § 3327.01; and home instruction, § 3323.05. Thus it would appear highly unlikely that no educational environment would be available for a child whose capabilities are such that "substantial profit from further instruction" could be derived.

The Court has examined the regulations pertaining to inclusion or exclusion from the public school system (EDb–215–13C) and participation in the special education classes (EDb–215–07B and C), and finds that each is keyed to the statutory standard of ability to profit substantially from further instruction.[4] Thus, for purposes of classification, the regulations carry forward the constitutionally permissible standard of the statute.

The finding that the standard of the Ohio Statutes for dismissal from the compulsory school system is appropriate and that the educable mentally retarded are not excluded thereunder does not end the Court's inquiry as to equal protection under the Ohio statutes. While the Court has found fallacious the basic premise of plaintiffs' attack on the overall educational and training system for the mentally handicapped (that the law created a classification by level of I.Q.), there is implicit in plaintiffs' position

---

[4]It would appear that plaintiffs' contention that the mentally retarded are classified by I.Q. derives from the fact that regulation EDb–215–07 includes as one of the criteria for admission to special education classes that the child have an I.Q. between 50 and 80, that regulation EDb–215–13 has specific provisions for children with I.Q.'s below 50, and regulation MHh–1–18(G) provides for admission of "individuals with an I.Q. of above 50 legally excluded from the public schools" to training classes on an individual basis. Those regulations, however, are supplementary to, and not in conflict, with the statutes and regulations in which the basic standard for classification are contained. If it should develop that there is a state-wide practice of "rubber-stamping" all children with I.Q.'s below 80 out of regular classes and all children with I.Q.'s below 50 out of special education classes, and that such practice is fostered and/or condoned by the defendants in this action a question of denial of equal protection under the statutes and regulations as applied could be presented. That question is not presently before the Court, and could not be resolved on this record. If such practice exists but not on a state-wide basis or by virtue of acts attributable to these defendants it could not be remedied in the context of this suit.

the contention that the statutes pertaining to training of the mentally retarded, Chapter 5127 of the Revised Code, are in and of themselves unconstitutionally discriminatory by virtue of their permissive and discretionary character.

While it might appear from the language of Section 5127.01 of the Revised Code that there "shall" be established in any county "programs and services for the special training of mentally retarded persons" that the statute imposes a duty upon the state to create such facilities for all persons in need thereof, the overall import of Chapter 5127 and of such of the regulations adopted thereunder as are before the Court indicates that affording of the programs and services contemplated by Section 5127.01 is discretionary with the state and dependent upon available funding. Consistent with the view that training programs may not be immediately available to all who could benefit therefrom is the priority given in Section 5127.01 to "the establishment of a training program for the mentally retarded for the purpose of enabling them to become accepted by society and to find employment in the structure of society to the extent that they may be fitted therefor." Additionally, by regulation multi-handicapped children and children with lesser intellectual levels would appear to have greater problems in gaining admission, while children who are not acceptably toilet trained will not be admitted. *See,* respectively, Regulations MHh–1–18(H), MHh–1–05(A) and MHh–1–18(B)(2) and (F).

For purposes of this ruling, the Court will assume that the Ohio system of training for the mentally retarded is discretionary in both its general and individual availability, and structured so that the greatest emphasis is placed upon aiding individuals with, relatively speaking, greater intellectual capacity. The Court does not consider such a system to be constitutionally defective.

In *Dandridge* v. *Williams,* 397 U.S. 471, 90 S.Ct. 1153, 25 L.Ed.2d 491 (1970), the Supreme Court addressed itself to certain Maryland statutes which dealt unequally with a class of potential welfare recipients. The Court stated:

> In the area of economics and social welfare, a State does not violate the Equal Protection Clause merely because the classifications made by its laws are imperfect. If the classification has some "reasonable basis," it does not offend the Constitution simply because the classification "is not made with mathematical nicety or because in practice it results in some inequality." *Lindsley* v. *Natural Carbonic Gas Co.,* 220 U.S. 61, 78, 31 S.Ct. 337, 340, 55 L.Ed. 369 [377]. "The problems of government are practical ones and may justify, if they do not require, rough accommodations—illogical, it may be, and unscientific." *Metropolis Theatre Co.* v. *City of Chicago,* 228 U.S. 61, 69–70, 33 S.Ct. 441, 443, 57 L.Ed. 730 [734]. "A statutory discrimination will not be set aside if any state of facts reasonably may be conceived to justify it." *McGowan* v. *Maryland,* 366 U.S. 420, 426, 81 S.Ct. 1101, 1105, 6 L.Ed.2d 393 [399].
>
> To be sure, the cases cited, and many others enunciating this fundamental standard under the Equal Protection Clause, have in the main involved state regulation of business or industry. The administration of public welfare assistance, by contrast, involves the most basic economic needs of impoverished human beings. We recognize the dramatically real factual difference between the cited cases and this one, but we can find no basis for applying a different constitutional standard. . . .

Continuing, the Court noted that the Equal Protection Clause is not violated by legislation which is predicated upon a "solid foundation" of legitimate state interest and that the Constitution does not require that a state must choose between attacking every aspect of a problem or not attacking the problem at all. After reiterating that the key is whether the state's action is "rationally based and free from invidious discrimination," the Court concluded:

> We do not decide today that the Maryland regulation is wise, that it best fulfills the relevant social and economic objectives that Maryland might ideally espouse, or that a more just and humane system could not be devised. Conflicting claims of morality and intelligence are raised by opponents and proponents of almost every measure, certainly including the one before us. But the intractable economic, social, and even philosophical problems presented by public welfare assistance programs are not the business of this Court. The Constitution may impose certain procedural safeguards upon systems of welfare administration, *Goldberg* v. *Kelly,* 397 U.S. 254, S.Ct. 1011, 25 L.Ed.2d 287. But the Constitution does not empower this Court to second-guess state officials charged with the difficult responsibility of allocating limited public welfare funds among the myriad of potential recipients. 397 U.S. 485, 486–487, 90 S.Ct. 1162, 25 L.Ed.2d 503.

In this Court's opinion the foregoing considerations as to the state's latitude in dealing with social problems must be deemed applicable to the issue of Ohio's training system for the mentally retarded. In contrast to the public education system to which the state has by its basic legislation unconditionally committed itself so that economic considerations should not be a basis for exclusion of children from that system, Ohio has only undertaken to train the mentally retarded on a potentially limited basis commensurate with the funds allotted by the legislature for that purpose and has vested discretion in a responsible official to determine the manner in which such funds can best be used. While the Court may well agree with plaintiffs that sufficient funding should be procured so all persons suffering from mental disability can be given as much training as would be of benefit to them, or that the resources available should be used in whatever proportions necessary to reach all persons in need of training, this Court cannot substitute its judgment for that of the Ohio legislature in determining the manner in which this social welfare program is best administered.

It must be recognized that programs available pursuant to Chapter 5127 are not exclusively for the benefit of children of compulsory school age excluded from the public schools. Section 5127.01(B) specifically provides for enrollment of persons not of school age determined "to be unemployable because of mental retardation of such nature and to such degree that special training is necessary." Similarly, the regulations before the Court have provisions relating to persons not of school age. Consequently, whatever flaws may exist in the training system are not restricted to children of compulsory school age, with whose rights the Court is concerned in this litigation.

It is this Court's conclusion that Chapter 5127 of the Ohio Revised Code and the regulations adopted thereunder are sufficient to withstand plaintiffs' claim that as to the interests they represent there is a classification violative of the Equal Protection Clause.

Turning now to those aspects of this action relating to plaintiffs' claims of denial of due process, the issues presented thereunder relate to certain regulations of the Ohio Department of Education and the Ohio Department of Mental Health which govern on procedural matters relating to classification and placement. Plaintiffs' constitutional challenges pertain to the standards applicable to placement of a student in special education classes, exclusion of students from the compulsory public school system, and exclusion of individuals from training programs.

Defendants do not deny the proposition that children within a compulsory public school system must be accorded due process in matters materially affecting their education. *Goss* v. *Lopez,* 419 U.S. 565, 95 S.Ct. 729, 42 L.Ed.2d 725 (1975). It is defendants' position that their regulations are adequate to meet the minimum requirements of due process.

Regulation EDb–215–07 of the Ohio Department of Education covers the matters of eligibility for and assessment and placement of students in special education classes. In pertinent part it provides as follows:

B.   Eligibility
 1.   Any child who meets the following requirements shall be eligible for and may be placed in a special education unit for educable mentally retarded children:
  a.   Is of legal school age.
  b.   Is capable of profiting substantially from instruction as determined by an evaluation administered by a qualified psychologist using multifactored assessment procedures.
  c.   Is in the general intelligence range of 50 through 80 as determined through an individual examination by a qualified school psychologist.
  d.   Cannot meet the academic and social behavioral expectations of the regular instructional program in that school because of a significant performance deficit in the basic educational areas as determined through an educational assessment that includes standardized test and/or classroom observational data which indicates a long term need for a modified educational program.
C.   Assessment and Placement
 1.   The superintendent of the school district of attendance is responsible for the assignment of pupils to approved units.
 2.   The school district shall have written criteria to determine eligibility for, and placement of, students in approved programs and services. Such criteria shall include:
  a.   Standards adopted by the State Board of Education.
  b.   Assessment of achievement, adjustment and social adaptability.
  c.   Provisions for including additional criteria, when relevant, to the unique characteristics of the school populations.
  d.   Priorities to establish placement of students on the basis of the individual student's need.
  e.   Process for providing an opportunity for a conference with parent(s) or guardian(s) prior to placement of any student in approved programs or services.
  f.   Provisions for a systematic procedure to re-evaluate students in approved programs to assess their progress, current status and future educational needs.

In the Court's opinion the foregoing regulation is deficient in four regards. While it requires the opportunity for a conference prior to a placement, it does not oblige the school authorities to give the parent or guardian notice of the basis upon which the proposed placement is founded, affords no opportunity for review of the evidence in support thereof, grants no right to introduce into the record additional material which might be appropriate to an evaluation of the child's academic capabilities, and does not guarantee that the superintendent of the school district, the final authority on placement, will receive all pertinent information prior to rendering a decision. While due process is not an inflexible standard, it requires at the least an effective opportunity to be heard on the matter at hand. In order to have an effective hearing the persons involved must be given notice of what action is to be taken and why, an opportunity to present additional material pertinent thereto, and an assurance that evidence reasonably calculated to lead to a reliable determination of the factual issues involved will come before the person rendering the final decision. *Lopez* v. *Williams*, 372 F.Supp. 1279, 1300-1301 (S.D.Ohio, 1973), aff'd *Goss* v. *Lopez*, *supra; Mills* v. *Board of Education*, 348 F.Supp. 866, 875 (D.C., 1972); *Esteban* v. *Central Missouri State College*, 277 F.Supp. 649, 651 (W.D.Mo., 1967).

The regulation governing legal dismissal from school attendance, EDb-215-13, shares the vice of EDb-215-07. While the criteria for exclusion are more than adequate, the notice requirements and opportunity for input are sorely deficient.

Dismissal from the public education system must be approved by the Superintendent of Public Education. The application for dismissal must be signed by the superintendent of the school district in which the child resides. No application for dismissal can be submitted unless a committee is formed to evaluate all pertinent information about the minor and make recommendations concerning the most advantageous placement possible. The only portion of the regulation regarding communication with a parent or guardian by anyone related to the dismissal procedures is subdivision C-6-c which provides:

> The chairman of the committee shall have the responsibility for seeing that an opportunity for a conference is made available to the child's parent(s) or guardian(s) with school personnel having information pertinent to the school's recommendations.

Such procedure is meaningless to a fair determination as to whether a child should be dismissed from school. The conference provided by the regulation is not with any of the persons specified as a part of the decision-making process and there is no requirement that the results of the conference be transmitted to such persons. Absent a requirement of notice of the grounds upon which dismissal is being sought, a right to review the material to be submitted in support of such application and respond thereto or supplement the same, and some assurance that all pertinent information will be placed before the decision makers the required conference is a hollow formality.

It therefore follows that Regulations EDb-215-07 and EDb-215-03 must be supplemented to afford at least the minimal due process rights enunciated herein. Due process requires that a child whose educational opportunity is to be affected be afforded equal opportunity with that of the school authorities to make a presentation regarding classification and/or dismissal. Defendants will be ordered to submit proposed regulations to that end within ninety days of entry hereof.

This leaves for consideration the Ohio Department of Mental Health regulations. While the Court has found that the discretionary aspects of the Ohio statutes dealing with training of the mentally retarded do not offend any constitutional guarantees of equal protection applicable to children of compulsory school age, once such children are brought within the system they cannot be dealt with summarily.

The regulations which have been placed before the Court under the instant motions are MHh-1-04, MHh-1-05, MHh-1-06, MHh-1-18 and MHh-1-20.

Of these, Regulation "05" contains the standards of eligibility for the Community Class Program. Those persons eligible must:

1. Be at least six years of age by October 31 of the current year and not more than twenty-one years of age;
2. Be excluded from public schools if within compulsory school ages;
3. Have a minimum physical, social and intellectual level of development equal to that of an average three-year-old child;
4. Be toilet trained.

Regulation "06" provides that "all children admitted to the Community Class Program shall be on a trial basis" and provides for the dismissal of participants from the Program:

(E) If the social, physical, or mental status of a child deteriorates, he may be excluded after a conference with the parents, teacher, and administrative representative of the County Agency.

We must construe this regulation so that it meets constitutional standards if the language so permits. The Court believes it can be fairly read to mean that if a child's condition deteriorates below the minimum eligibility requirements of Regulation "05", he may be dismissed. Since Regulation "05" provides concrete standards for admission, Regulations "05" and "06" read together can be construed as providing standards for exclusion which facially comport with due process standards. Therefore, the Court concludes that the two regulations so construed are constitutionally sufficient.

Regulation "18" contains admission standards for the Workshop Program. Those eligible must:

1. Be beyond compulsory school age or sixteen years of age and ineligible for enrollment in the Community Class Program or the public schools;
2. Have a minimum physical, social and intellectual level of development equal to that of an average five-year-old child;
3. Be toilet trained.

Regulation "20" provides for the dismissal of participants from the Workshop Program in substantially the same language as quoted above from Regulation "06." Consequently, Regulation "20" can be read so as to provide for dismissal only when the participant's condition deteriorates below the minimum eligibility requirements of Regulation "18." These standards comport with due process and the Court adopts such constitutionally sufficient construction as appropriate.

However, none of the foregoing regulations provide adequate procedural safeguards to protect the program participant in the determination of whether his condition has deteriorated below the specified standards. Regulations "06" and "20" merely provide that a conference with parents is mandatory prior to dismissal and that a record of such conference be kept. The absence in these regulations of any requirements of notice as to the basis upon which exclusion may be sought, opportunity for review of the underlying material, availability of input, and a guarantee that all relevant information will reach the person responsible for final decision render the same inadequate. The defendants will be ordered to submit proposed regulations to meet such deficiencies within ninety days hereof.

In summary, the Court finds as follows:

1. That the basic standard of classification of the Ohio educational statutes excluding from the free and mandatory public school system only those children who have been found incapable of profiting substantially by further instruction does not unconstitutionally discriminate against plaintiffs or the class they represent.

2. That under the Ohio statutes the State of Ohio is obliged to utilize all resources available to it in order to provide an education to all children who might profit substantially by further instruction, according to their mental capacity as determined through proper examination and testing.

3. That all children in Ohio of compulsory school age who have not been dismissed from school under the statutory standard are subject to compulsory education, and it is the duty of the defendants to enforce the provisions of Chapter 3321 of the Ohio Revised Code as to such children.

4. That if, as plaintiffs contend, there are children of compulsory school age who have not been determined to be incapable of substantially profiting from further instruction who are not within the public school system further evidence of such fact is required; if such contingency exists and can be shown to be as a consequence of a statewide policy fostered or condoned by these defendants relief may be ordered in this action; if such contingency exists but is not as a consequence of a statewide policy fostered or condoned by these defendants but is as a consequence of acts of particular school districts relief therefrom is not available in this forum but must be sought in the state courts against such districts.

5. That if children of particular I.Q. levels are being "rubber-stamped" into special education and/or out of the public school system without regard for the detailed standards developed for classification and/or dismissal and that such action is as a consequence of statewide policies fostered or condoned by defendants such course of conduct might constitute denial of equal protection under the relevant statutes and regulations as applied and be remediable in this action, but proof of such condition will require further evidence; if such condition prevails in certain school districts, but not as a consequence of acts for which defendants may be held responsible, relief therefrom must be sought in the state courts against those responsible for such acts.

6. That Ohio Department of Education Regulations EDb-215-07 and EDb-215-03 are constitutionally deficient in that they do not contain proper provisions regarding notice, opportunity for review of the material upon which proposed action thereunder is to be taken, opportuntiy for input by the persons affected, and guarantees that all relevant material will be before the person charged with responsibility for final decision.

7. That the Ohio statutes for training of the mentally retarded, Chapter 5127 of the

Ohio Revised Code, do not deny to plaintiffs or the class they represent equal protection.

8. That Ohio Department of Mental Health Regulations MHh-1-05, MHh-1-06, MHh-1-18 and MHh-1-20 are constitutionally deficient for basically the same reasons as apply to the Department of Education regulations as specified in paragraph 6 above.

The cross-motions of the parties for summary judgment are granted in part and denied in part in accordance with the terms of this memorandum. Defendants shall within ninety days hereof submit to the Court, with service upon plaintiffs, proposed supplemental regulations as set forth herein. Plaintiffs shall within sixty days hereof advise the Court whether they intend to go forward as regards the issues which this Court has indicated required evidentiary hearing for determination.

IT IS SO ORDERED.

NOTES

1.   While one may lament the court's precipitous selection of the rational basis test as the applicable standard without any discussion of the possible fundamental rights and suspect classifications involved, even more unfortunate was a critical factual misimpression held by the court. The key factual premise of equal educational opportunity lawsuits is the fact that every child can benefit from an appropriate educational program. Yet the *Essex* court based its decision upon the notion that there are two different groups of mentally retarded children, one that can profit from an educational program and another that cannot, cf., *Maryland Association for Retarded Children* v. *State of Maryland*, pp. 182–187, below. Clearly the plaintiffs in *Essex*, and their legal counsel, did not fulfill one of the key strategic elements in such litigation—educating the judges as to the capabilities and potential of handicapped children. Permitting a summary judgment stage to be reached without having instilled this basic factual consideration into the minds of the judges is a significant error.

2.   Apart from its equal protection reasoning, wherein the court gives no indication of ever having heard of any of the other precedents dealing with equal educational opportunity for handicapped children, the *Essex* decision is not entirely negative. The court does indicate that IQ cutoffs for eligibility for education programs would be illegal. It also interprets Ohio statutes to require the provision of an educational program (in the local school district or through other arrangements) to every child not found incapable of profiting. And the plaintiffs did triumph in their procedural due process claims. Nonetheless, although the situation has been clarified for those pupils not formally excluded and while the process of making formal exclusions has been tightened up by additional procedural requirements, at its heart the *Essex* opinion stands as the only modern judicial decision expressly approving the exclusion of children from the public schools because of the degree of their mental retardation.

3.   Since the date of the decision in *Essex*, almost all of the exclusionary and segregational practices challenged by the plaintiffs have been undercut by federal legislation and changes in Ohio law.

PANITCH v. STATE OF WISCONSIN

United States District Court for the Eastern District of Wisconsin, 1977
444 F.Supp. 320

Before GORDON and REYNOLDS, U.S. District Judges, and FAIRCHILD, U.S. Circuit Judge.

DECISION and ORDER

PER CURIAM.

I. Introduction

This is an action in which the plaintiff class of handicapped children seeks a declaration that the statutes, policies and practices of the defendants deny them an education at public expense in violation of the equal protection clause of the Fourteenth Amendment to the United States Constitution. The plaintiff class also seeks an injunctive order requiring the defendants to provide them with an educational program at public expense sufficient to meet their needs.

In August, 1972, the named plaintiff, a blind and mentally retarded child, commenced this action through her guardian ad litem against the State of Wisconsin, the State Superintendent of Public Instruction, and the Joint City School District, City of Glendale and Village of River Hills (Joint City).

In a decision and order dated November 16, 1972, the following plaintiff class was certified:

> [A]ll handicapped educable children between the ages of four and twenty who are residents of Wisconsin and are presently being denied, allegedly, a program of education in public schools or in equivalent educational facilities at public expense.

The same decision and order certified a defendant class consisting of "all public school districts within the state."

In August, 1973, subchapter IV of Chapter 115, Wis.Stats. (subchapter IV) became effective. The parties agreed that subchapter IV on its face satisfied the plaintiff's constitutional demands. However, the court rejected the defendants' claim of mootness, stating that only full implementation of subchapter IV would moot the action. The court stayed further proceedings in the action pending such implementation. *Panitch v. State,* 371 F.Supp. 955 (E.D.Wis. 1974).

On September 19, 1977, we granted the plaintiff's motion to vacate the stay of proceedings after we determined that the defendants' delay in their implementation of subchapter IV proceedings had become inordinate. The plaintiff's application for certain orders on the merits was treated by the court as a motion for summary judgment. We have received briefs and heard oral argument covering the following issues:

1. Whether this court should declare that the defendants, irrespective of subchapter IV, are required under the equal protection clause of the Fourteenth Amendment to the United States Constitution to provide an education at public expense to the plaintiff class.

2. If such declaration is made, whether an injunctive order should be entered and a special master appointed to oversee its implementation.

We have concluded that summary judgment should be granted to the plaintiff and that an injunctive order should issue. The application for the appointment of a special master will be held in abeyance.

II.   Summary Judgment

Do the defendants have a constitutional duty to provide an education at public expense to the plaintiff class? In *Brown* v. *Board of Education of Topeka,* 347 U.S. 483, 493; 74 S.Ct. 686, 691, 98 L.Ed. 873 (1954), the court stated:

> Today education is perhaps the most important function of state and local governments. . . . In these days, it is doubtful that any child may reasonably be expected to succeed in life if he is denied the opportunity of an education. *Such an opportunity, where the state has undertaken to provide it, is a right which must be made available to all on equal terms.* [emphasis supplied]

The State of Wisconsin has undertaken to provide a free public school education to all children between ages 4 and 20. Wis.Const. Art. X, section 3. School attendance is compulsory by statute for both nonhandicapped and handicapped children. Wis.Stats. §§ 118.15 and 111.82.

It is clear that prior to this action meaningful education was not available to handicapped children on the same terms that it was available to nonhandicapped children. Except for those children who have been identified, placed and treated under subchapter IV since the inception of this litigation, a large number of handicapped children in Wisconsin are still being denied an education commensurate with their needs. According to the most recent information submitted by the parties, 20% of the state's handicapped children remain to be identified. Although the precise extent of the defendants' noncompliance has not been determined, there is no question that a significant portion of the plaintiff class remains to be identified, placed and specially educated.

Other courts have recognized that the equal protection clause is violated when handicapped children are denied a specialized education in the publicly-supported schools. *Mills* v. *Board of Education,* 348 F.Supp. 866 (D.C. 1972); *In Interest of G. H.,* 218 N.W.2d 441, 447 (N.D. 1974). The plaintiff and the state defendants agree that this constitutional principle controls this case.

Joint City does not deny the validity of this constitutional principle, but it argues that the plaintiff has not made the necessary showing of intentional discrimination required in equal protection actions. *Village of Arlington Heights* v. *Metropolitan Development Corp.,* 429 U.S. 252, 97 S.Ct. 555, 50 L.Ed.2d 450 (1977); *Washington* v. *Davis,* 426 U.S. 229, 96 S.Ct. 2040, 48 L.Ed.2d 597 (1976).

In our opinion, any doubt on the issue of intent has been dispelled by the fact that this case was commenced in 1972; subchapter IV became effective in 1973; yet at the end of 1977, a significant portion of the state's handicapped children has not been identified, much less placed and given an appropriate education.

The state defendants urge that the onus of noncompliance is upon the defendant class of school districts. The defendant class representative, Joint City, argues that it has fully discharged its responsibility under subchapter IV and has therefore sought dismissal from the case. Thus, all of the present active parties defendant place the blame for the delay elsewhere. This unfortunate situation persists in spite of the defendants' awareness that members of the plaintiff class have grown older and have lost with finality several important years of educational opportunity.

We therefore find that summary judgment should be granted declaring that the defendants have collectively violated the right of the plaintiff class to equal protection of the laws.

III. Injunctive Relief

The inordinate delay in the defendants' implementation of subchapter IV and the irreparable nature of the plaintiff class' loss of education compel us to grant injunctive relief. The defendants, collectively, must *promptly* provide the plaintiff class with an appropriate education at public expense.

The defendant state superintendent of public instruction is specifically directed to submit a report to the court by January 16, 1978, detailing (1) the incidence of children with exceptional educational needs; (2) the extent of compliance with subchapter IV, both statewide and by individually named school districts, in terms of identification, placement and programming; and (3) an up-dated report on the on-site and data review processes of the division of handicapped children.

The plaintiff's request for an appointment of a special master will not be granted at this time but will be reconsidered upon receipt of the superintendent's report.

In the event prompt and sufficient compliance is not made by the defendants with the affirmative injunction, this court contemplates not only the designation of a special master but also the imposition of strict sanctions and penalties upon any of the defendants found to be wilfully in noncompliance.

We note that this case is already five years old. Having previously determined that the delay is already "inordinate," we do not intend to permit any unjustified delays in obtaining full and meaningful compliance with the constitutional mandate. The failure of any defendant to accomplish total compliance in the very near future will impose on such defendant the heavy burden of attempting to justify such failure.

The parties agree that Joint City is now in full compliance with subchapter IV. Joint City will therefore be relieved of its representative status as it is no longer truly representative of the defendant class of noncomplying school districts.

Depositions and affidavits on file with the court indicate that the City of Milwaukee Public School District is in serious noncompliance. The affidavit of William W. Malloy, the assistant superintendent in charge of the division of exceptional education for the Milwaukee public school district, indicates that the current "diagnostic backlog" of children with exceptional educational needs exceeds 3000. Mr. Malloy's affidavit projects that this backlog will be reduced to 280 by August, 1978. Such projection does not include the time necessary for placement and programming. The Milwaukee Pubic School District's documented noncompliance qualifies it for substitution as the defendant class' representative, and it will be ordered to appear in such capacity in further proceedings, vice Joint City.

The City of Milwaukee Public School District is directed to submit a report to this court by January 16, 1978, specifying what progress it has made toward compliance with subchapter IV and what specific further steps it proposes to make to effectuate complete compliance.

IV. Conclusion

Therefore, IT IS ORDERED that the plaintiff's motion for summary judgment be and hereby is granted, and we declare that the policies and practices of the defendants deny the plaintiff class an education at public expense in violation of the equal protection clause of the Fourteenth Amendment to the United States Constitution.

IT IS ALSO ORDERED that the defendants be and hereby are affirmatively enjoined promptly to provide all the members of the plaintiff class with an education at public expense which is sufficient to their needs and generally equivalent to the education provided to nonhandicapped children. The defendant state superintendent is directed to submit a report in conformity with the instructions contained in the foregoing decision.

IT IS FURTHER ORDERED that the City of Milwaukee Public School District be and hereby is designated the defendant class' representative, vice Joint City. The Milwaukee Public School District is directed to submit a report in conformity with the instructions contained in the foregoing decision.

NOTES

1.   While the plaintiffs in *Panitch* won a clear victory in terms of their constitutional theories, compare the specificity of the relief orders they obtained with that imposed in other cases. Is it much of a reward after more than five years of litigation?

2.   Look closely at the description of the plaintiff class. How could the draftsmanship have been improved?

LORA v. BOARD OF ED. OF CITY OF NEW YORK
United States District Court for the Eastern District of New York, 1978
456 F.Supp. 1211

[Only a portion of the lengthy opinion is presented here; other parts of the decision are included at pp. 210–212, pp. 236–241, and pp. 283–292, below. Abbreviations used by the court include: EU, evaluation unit; COH, Committee on the Handicapped, which reviews and evaluates the status of each handicapped child in a school district; and EHA, Education for All Handicapped Children Act.]

I. Introduction

Plaintiffs complain that their constitutional and statutory rights are being denied by the procedures and facilities afforded by New York City for the education of children whose emotional problems result in severe acting-out and aggression in school, behavior which may produce danger to others as well as themselves. These children often have severe academic problems. They have been placed in special day schools for the education of the emotionally handicapped. The schools utilize smaller class size, specially trained teachers and support staff, and special facilities, designed to provide a "generally therapeutic" atmosphere.

Racial composition of the pupil population in these special day schools is 68% Black; 27% Hispanic; and 5% other, primarily White (figures as of October 31, 1977). The high percentage of "minorities" in these schools is not a recent phenomenon; rather, a disparate racial composition has remained constant for nearly 15 years. The other major services for children with emotional disturbance, "classes for emotionally handicapped" (CEH classes), have a higher proportion, 20%, of non-minority students. Still higher is the proportion of Whites in the New York City public school equivalent grades: 36% Black, 23% Hispanic and 41% "other."

Starting from this striking racial disparity plaintiffs have added extensive evidence supporting their thesis. They contend that the special day schools are intentionally segregated "dumping grounds" for minorities forced into inadequate facilities without due process. White students with the same problems, it is maintained, are treated more favorably in other settings. Defendants and their witnesses deny any racial bias. They point with considerable pride to the advantages afforded, at substantial taxpayers' expense, in an effort to bring these problem students into the mainstream of education and society.

Laid bare by the dispute is one of the most excruciating issues of our democratic society. Almost every American agrees that the ringing words of the Declaration of Independence, "all men are created equal," mean at least that: each person shall have an equal opportunity to develop and exercise his God-given talents. But many children born into deprived social, economic and psychological backgrounds lack the equality of real opportunity they would have had were their familial circumstances more fortunate. Unfavorable environment in such cases overwhelms favorable genes. To afford equality of opportunity so far as we can, we depend primarily on education. The free public system of education is the great equalizer, conceived to allow those born into the lowliest status the opportunity of rising as far as their potential talents, drive and luck will take them. But the system is—and perhaps by its nature must be—inadequate to lift fully the burden of poverty, of discrimination, and of ignorance that so many of our children carry.

Depressingly revealed by the record are some of the almost insoluble problems of educating certain of the products of this background—the socially and emotionally maladjusted children who present a physical danger to themselves and others, who cannot learn and who prevent others from learning in a regular school setting. Yet the evidence before us also illustrates how talented and devoted school personnel, sympathetic to this group of children and operating under federal, state and local laws and regulations, can help even those who appeared beyond redemption.

Hope for substantial improvements lies not in the courts but in the hands of those who control society's resources and of those who are trained and dedicated to use pedagogic and therapeutic arts. Nevertheless, since the matter has been properly placed before us for adjudication, we have, under our legal system, no alternative but to address the issues in their limited legal context. The dismal facts, the enabling aspirations, and the encouraging portents for the future have been revealed by devoted and skillful counsel for both sides.

At the time this suit was commenced in 1975, the plaintiffs could have demonstrated a violation of their rights by clear and convincing evidence. Since then, however, partly as a result of the litigation process itself, substantial improvements have been instituted by defendants. During the course of this law suit many of those charged with supervising the evaluation, placement and education of plaintiffs testified and were forced to face up to and justify shortcomings, and to modify the system as it was. For example, one day school for girls that the Court visited did not measure up to the standards enunciated by those in charge of the program. Partly as a result of colloquy between the Court and witnesses, the school was reexamined and closed. Developments on the administrative front, to be examined in more detail *infra,* have also had an ameliorating effect.

The preponderance of evidence still indicates a degree of deprivation of certain rights of some members of the plaintiff class. Yet the momentum for changes favoring plaintiffs' rights is now so strong that it cannot be said that a claim for powerful equitable relief has been substantiated. The energies of educators and therapists are best devoted to improving the education of the youngsters who need their help, rather than in litigating details of their educational practices. The record suggests that the extensive legislative and administrative regulations recently injected into the system will in due course provide adequate protections for plaintiffs. Time is needed for the educational system to absorb and adjust to the new legal standards. The case will not be dismissed but the remedies granted will be designed to have a minimal disruptive impact on personnel striving to meet plaintiffs' needs under difficult conditions.

II.   Procedural History

A.   This Case

The original complaint in this suit was filed in June 1975. The plaintiffs alleged violations of their rights under the Fourth, Eighth, Thirteenth and Fourteenth Amendments, as well as rights guaranteed by the Civil Rights Statutes, 42 U.S.C. §§ 1981, 1983, and 2000d (1974). Subsequently, the pleadings were amended to include claims under the Education of All Handicapped Children Act (20 U.S.C. §§ 1401 *et seq.* (1978)) (EHA) and the Rehabilitation Act of 1973 (29 U.S.C. §§ 701 *et seq.* (1975)).

A motion for class certification was denied by the late Judge Bruchhausen in January of 1976. In May of that year, the Court of Appeals for the Second Circuit ruled that the denial of class certification was not appealable. A request for rehearing en banc was denied in July and a petition for certiorari to the United States Supreme Court was denied in November. Subsequently, this court granted class action certification. The class includes all minority students who have been assigned to the special day schools.

In January of 1976 plaintiff moved for a preliminary injunction aimed at termination of all student placement in the special day schools without a due process hearing. This motion was denied in March of 1976 and that denial was affirmed by the Second Circuit.

In January of 1977, defendants moved for partial summary judgment on plaintiffs' due process claims and certain of their factual allegations. In addition, plaintiffs moved to compel discovery with regard to expert visits to Evaluation and Placement

Centers and access to 50 diagnostic and referral files of non-party children. Defendants' motion for partial summary judgment was denied in all respects, but plaintiffs' motion to compel discovery was granted with special limitations to protect the privacy of the children involved. 74 F.R.D. 565 (E.D.N.Y. 1977).

After various amended and supplemental complaints, there are now six plaintiffs representing the class composed of all Black or Hispanic students who have been assigned to the special day schools. The defendants include various officials of the New York City Board of Education, including Board members and administrators, as well as principals of some of the special day schools.

In their pre-trial brief plaintiffs alleged that the special day school system operates as an

> institutionalized method to perpetuate a system of education in New York City, whereby Black and Hispanic children are isolated into a racially segregated school system which does not provide them with a "special" education.

Plaintiffs' pre-trial memorandum at 5.

Plaintiffs claim, first, that the referral and assignment of students to special day schools is based upon vague and subjective criteria and that the combination of processes, practices and policies has a racially discriminatory effect on Black and Hispanic children. This, it is alleged, constitutes a violation of 42 U.S.C. § 1983 as well as section 2000d of Title VI of the Civil Rights Act of 1964, prohibiting racial discrimination under any program or activity receiving federal financial assistance. Second, plaintiffs allege that they have been denied their rights to due process, equal protection and equal educational opportunity because they have been placed in special day schools with the natural and foreseeable consequences that they will be isolated within a racially segregated system which does not provide them with suitable facilities and instruction. Third, plaintiffs charge that defendants have violated their due process rights by (1) placing students in the special day schools without giving them the opportunity for prior hearings mandated by federal and state law and regulations and (2) failure to reevaluate students already in such schools as required by state regulations, with the result that those who may be ready to return to regular schools are not able to do so. Fourth, plaintiffs invoke jurisdiction under 20 U.S.C. § 1415(e)(4) of the EHA, claiming specific violations of due process rights provided by that statute. Finally, plaintiffs claim that the special day school program affords students only inadequate educational opportunity in violation of § 791 of the Rehabilitation Act of 1973 (29 U.S.C. § 701 *et seq.*) and its accompanying regulations prohibiting discrimination against the handicapped.

This is essentially a constitutional and not a statutory case, involving racial discrimination and denial of educational rights. Defendants' strong reliance on exhaustion cases is, therefore, inappropriate.

After extensive discovery, trial commenced on May 2, 1977, and ended on March 21, 1978. There were 49 witnesses, approximately 3900 pages of transcript and over 230 groups of documents admitted in evidence; final briefs consisted of over 600 pages.

* * *

IV. Law

A. Right to Treatment

1. Theory

A right to treatment based on constitutional or statutory grounds, has been developed in several habeas corpus cases. Restraint of liberty resulting from civil commitment for the purpose of therapeutic treatment cannot be justified where no treatment is rendered. *Ragsdale* v. *Overholser,* 108 U.S.App.D.C. 308, 315, 281 F.2d 943, 950 (1960) (Fahy, J., concurring). *See O'Connor* v. *Donaldson,* 422 U.S. 563, 95 S.Ct. 2486, 45 L.Ed.2d 396 (1975); *Darnell* v. *Cameron,* 121 U.S.App.D.C. 58, 61, 348 F.2d 64, 67 (1965); "Developments in the Law—Civil Commitment," 87 *Harv. L. Rev.* 1190, 1324-29 (1974); *cf. Rouse* v. *Cameron,* 125 U.S.App.D.C. 366, 373 F.2d 451 (1966).

More recent cases have applied the right to treatment in a variety of contexts. In *Wyatt* v. *Stickney,* 325 F.Supp. 781, 334 F.Supp. 1341 (M.D.Ala. 1971) and 344 F.Supp. 373, 387 (M.D.Ala.), *aff'd sub nom., Wyatt* v. *Aderholt,* 503 F.2d 1305 (5 Cir. 1974), the court, relying on a due process rationale, found a right to adequate treatment for mentally retarded individuals committed to a state school. The suit, initially triggered by staff reductions due to budgetary restrictions, focused on the general inadequacy of treatment afforded at Alabama state mental hospitals and other facilities. In affirming the opinions and decrees of the District Court, the Court of Appeals declared that the Fifth Circuit had "established that the right to treatment arises as a matter of federal constitutional law under the due process clause of the Fourteenth Amendment." 503 F.2d at 1314. *See also Halderman* v. *Pennhurst State School and Hospital,* 446 F.Supp. 1295, 1314-20 (E.D.Pa. 1977).

In two other cases, including one from a lower court in this Circuit, the right to treatment has been applied to training schools for juveniles. *Inmates of Boys Training School* v. *Affleck,* 346 F.Supp. 1354 (D.R.I. 1972); *Martarella* v. *Kelley,* 349 F.Supp. 575 (S.D.N.Y. 1972). In *Martarella* the plaintiffs were children who had been designated "persons in need of supervision" pursuant to section 732 of the New York Family Court Act. They had committed no crimes, but had been charged with misbehavior. Many were neglected and socially maladjusted. Thus the focus was on a right to treatment for a group of individuals somewhat similar to the plaintiffs now before this court. Judge Lasker relied not only on the notion of a right to treatment for persons held in noncriminal custody, but also on cases dealing specifically with children which have emphasized an underlying assumption of juvenile justice systems— that the state is acting as parens patriae, that any noncriminal detention of a juvenile must be of a rehabilitative as opposed to penal nature. He declared:

> There can be no doubt that the right to treatment, generally, for those held in non-criminal custody (whether based on due process, equal protection or the Eighth Amendment, or a combination of them) has by now been recognized by the Supreme Court, the lower federal courts and the courts of New York.

Id. at 599.

Under *Martarella* segregation of plaintiffs in a special day school without affording them appropriate educational and therapeutic treatment would violate their constitutional rights.

2. Students in Special Day Schools

a) Due Process

Students in the special day schools are not confined or deprived of their liberty to the extent of plaintiffs in the suits described in Part IV A 1, *supra*. Nevertheless, the day schools are a "restrictive" environment. Children are segregated from their peers. They often travel far from their neighborhoods to school.

Moreover, in practice, placement is not entirely voluntary. Although parents and child are given the opportunity to contest recommended special day school placement, should the appeals process result in a decision contrary to the family's wishes, the only alternative to placement may be withdrawal of the child from the public school system. Perhaps of more significance, few, if any, of the parents whose children are referred have the means or awareness necessary to seek alternative placement. *Cf. Halderman, et al.* v. *Pennhurst State School & Hospital*, 446 F. Supp. 1295, 1310–11 (E.D.Pa. 1977) ("voluntariness" an illusory concept as applied to admission and exit from mental hospital since residents found to have no practical alternative at the time of their admission and no place else to go once admitted).

Finally, procedural safeguards are premised on the assumption that the special day schools can afford therapeutic treatment for the properly diagnosed child. Recommendation for special school placement is justified on the ground that this type of environment is the most appropriate to the child's educational needs. Without adequate treatment, therefore, the rationale for confining children in the special day schools collapses. Plaintiffs are entitled to constitutional due process protections.

b) Equal Protection

The right to treatment may also be based upon the equal protection clause. Plaintiffs claim that the acts of placing and continuing their placement in special day schools, with the natural and foreseeable consequences that such placement will isolate them within a racially segregated school sub-system without adequate provision for suitable education, deprive them of equal educational opportunity in violation of the 14th amendment. Plaintiffs also allege the deprivation of their rights as handicapped pupils to a minimally adequate education. It is urged that whether the Court chooses to apply strict scrutiny (finding handicapped children to constitute a suspect class) or an intermediate level of scrutiny (*see* G. Gunther, "The Supreme Court, 1971 Term, Forward, In Search of Evolving Doctrine in a Changing Court: A Model for a Newer Equal Protection," 86 *Harv. L. Rev.* 1 (1972), plaintiffs have been denied equal protection.

Emotionally disturbed children might be characterized as a suspect class in accordance with guidelines set by the Supreme Court as follows:

> [a] class . . . saddled with such disabilities, or subjected to such a history of purposeful unequal treatment, or relegated to such a position of political powerlessness as to command extraordinary protection from the majoritarian political process.

San Antonio School District v. *Rodriquez*, 411 U.S. 1, 28, 93 S.Ct. 1278, 1294, 36 L.Ed.2d 16. *See Fialkowski* v. *Shapp*, 405 F.Supp. 946, 958–59 (E.D.Pa. 1975) (retarded children). *But cf. New York Assoc. for Retarded Children* v. *Rockefeller*, 357

F.Supp. 752, 762–63 (E.D.N.Y. 1973) (suggesting that the mentally retarded are not to be regarded as a suspect class).

It is not necessary, however, to decide whether emotionally handicapped students should be treated as a suspect class in a constitutional sense. We deal with minority pupils who claim discrimination on the ground of race. They are entitled to suspect class treatment for that reason. The fact that these plaintiffs are emotionally disturbed children does, nevertheless, compel us to focus on the abuses to which such individuals may be subject.

The importance of an equal educational opportunity for all cannot be underestimated.

> Today, education is perhaps the most important function of the state and local governments. . . . It is required in the performance of our most basic responsibilities. . . . It is the very foundation of good citizenship. It is a principal instrument in awakening the child to cultural values, in preparing him for later professional training, and in helping him to adjust normally to his environment. It is doubtful that any child may reasonably be expected to succeed in life if he is denied the opportunity of an education. Such an education, where the state has undertaken to provide it, is a right which must be available to all on equal terms.

Brown v. *Board of Education,* 347 U.S. 483, 493, 74 S.Ct. 686, 691, 98 L.Ed. 873 (1954).

When a particular group of students has special needs the right to an adequate education has been interpreted as requiring the state to make substantial efforts toward meeting these needs. Several cases have established for the handicapped the same right of access to free public education existing under the *Brown* precedents for all "normal" children, minority and non-minority. Where, as here, the handicapped children are also from minority groups, the burden of showing a sufficient educational opportunity is especially high.

The landmark case in this area, *Hobson* v. *Hansen,* 269 F.Supp. 401 (D.D.C. 1967), *appeal dismissed,* 393 U.S. 801, 89 S.Ct. 40, 21 L.Ed.2d 85 (1968), is instructive. It involved the impact of sorting on minority pupils. The Court found that the operation of the school system, including a tracking of students at the primary and secondary levels, deprived Blacks and poor pupils of the right to an education equal to that afforded White, affluent students. This was found to violate both the equal protection and due process clauses. *Id.* at 511. The tracks at issue placed students in various curricular groups, ranging from those for "gifted" to those for "retarded" children. The latter afforded a rather limited basic education. This program was held discriminatory. The court relied on the large number of Blacks in the lower tracks, the lack of movement among tracks in spite of purported flexibility (*id.* at 464), the failure to provide remedial programs for disadvantaged and emotionally handicapped (*id.* at 468, 469–73), and the use in the referral process of standardized tests found culturally and racially biased. *Id. See also P.* v. *Riles,* 343 F.Supp. 1306 (N.D.Cal. 1972), *aff'd,* 502 F.2d 963 (9th Cir. 1974); D. Kirp, W. Buss, P. Kuriloff, "Legal Reform of Special Education: Empirical Studies and Procedural Proposals," 62 *Cal. L. Rev.* 40, 49–50 (1974).

In *Pennsylvania Association for Retarded Children* v. *Commonwealth of Pennsylvania*, 343 F.Supp. 279 (E.D.Pa. 1972), exclusion of mentally retarded children from the public education system was found violative of the equal protection clause. The court decided that the state must provide an education "appropriate to the child's capacity" whether or not the child was mentally retarded. *Id.* at 285 (citations omitted).

Still another important judicial pronouncement in this area is *Mills* v. *Board of Education*, 348 F.Supp. 866 (D.D.C. 1972). The case presented a challenge to classification and assignment of exceptional children to non-mainstream educational facilities. The court declared that since other handicapped children were given free public education, any exceptional child had a right, guaranteed under the equal protection clause, to a constructive education, including appropriate specialized instruction. Even more recently in *Panitch* v. *State of Wisconsin*, 444 F.Supp. 320, 322 (E.D.Wisconsin 1977), a district court held that a long delay in effectuating a state law designed to give equal education to the handicapped was sufficient indication of "intentional discrimination" in violation of the equal protection clause.

These cases demonstrate that the isolation of minority students in special education settings with small hope of truly fruitful education or movement into less restrictive environments constitutes a denial of equal protection. They provide persuasive support for a right to adequate treatment for plaintiffs, including adequate diagnosis and classification procedures as well as satisfactorily equipped and staffed special day schools.

Nevertheless, there is still the need to prove discrimination. Mere disproportionate impact along racial lines will not, in the absence of a finding of intent to discriminate, support a finding of a violation of equal protection guarantees. *See, e.g., Washington* v. *Davis*, 426 U.S. 229, 96 S.Ct. 2040, 48 L.Ed.2d 597 (1976). Thus in the case before us, the high proportion of Blacks and other minorities in the special day schools would not, in and of itself, require a decision for plaintiffs.

Disproportionate impact is, of course, highly relevant evidence. As Justice Stevens noted in his concurring opinion in *Washington* v. *Davis:*

> Frequently the most probative evidence of intent will be objective evidence of what actually happened rather than evidence describing the subjective state of mind of the actor. For normally the actor is presumed to have intended the natural consequences of his deeds. This is particularly true in the case of governmental action which is frequently the product of compromise, of collective decisionmaking, and of mixed motivation.

426 U.S. 229, 253, 96 S.Ct. 2040, 2054, 48 L.Ed.2d 597 (1976). Plaintiffs must demonstrate that all of the circumstances, including the statistical data, fairly support an inference of an intent to discriminate. *See also* Part IV C, *infra,* for a discussion of *Washington* v. *Davis*, 426 U.S. 229, 96 S.Ct. 2040, 48 L.Ed.2d 597 (1976) and related cases dealing with statistics, discriminatory impact and burdens of proof.

c) Statutory Rights

As in *Rouse* v. *Cameron*, 125 U.S.App.D.C. 366, 373 F.2d 451 (1967), a right to treatment may be founded on statutory grounds, specifically on the federal Education of All Handicapped Children Act, 20 U.S.C. § 1401 *et seq.* (1978), the

Rehabilitation Act of 1973, 29 U.S.C. § 701 *et seq.* (1975), and sections 4402 *et seq.* of N.Y. Educ.Law (McKinney 1978), along with applicable federal and state regulations. *See* sections III C 1 and 2, *supra*; Appendices B and C. These acts are designed to guarantee at least a minimum education for all handicapped pupils and to assure against any possibility of racial or cultural discrimination. Together they support a right to adequate treatment for plaintiffs, including entitlement to constructive services within the special day school; to proper classification for such placement; to the opportunity to contest recommended placement; and to periodic reassessment of the appropriateness of that placement.

* * *

V. Application of Law to Facts

* * *

A. Evaluation Process as Violation of Right to Treatment and Due Process

1. Right to Treatment

Since proper evaluation is recognized as central to acceptable special education, a program falling substantially below minimum established standards would constitute a violation of the right to treatment. Perfection is not expected. All deficiencies do not necessarily constitute constitutional or statutory deprivations. Nevertheless, regrettably, defendants' programs do fall short of minimally acceptable legal standards in some particulars.

Staffing shortages at the EUs necessitate extra effort on the part of those professionals who are available, but do not jeopardize plaintiffs' right to treatment. Although it is impossible for every child to have a psychiatric screening prior to referral, arrangements are made for one in cases where it is deemed essential. The evidence reveals no professional consensus on whether the failure to obtain a psychiatric report in every case is a serious deficiency. Similarly, although not all the EUs have a full-time neurologist, the EU staff is on the alert for "soft signs" of neurological impairment and examinations are conducted where necessary.

The evidence also reveals concerted efforts at eliminating linguistic barriers impeding accurate evaluation. Every EU has at least one bilingual professional. Where possible, tests are administered in the child's language; at other times, a translator may be used. Sometimes the language problem is alleviated by the use of non-verbal tests. Testimony of Elaine Thompson, transcript at 1832–34; testimony of Dolores Goidel, transcript at 1831–32. The Court takes judicial notice of the limited pool of qualified bilingual professionals.

Conceivably, the paucity of minority professionals may increase the chance of cultural bias and skewed diagnosis and referral. Although the percentages of minority staff are relatively low when compared to the percentages of minority students evaluated for special day school placement, the ratios are not compelling evidence of racial discrimination or denial of a right to treatment, particularly since good faith efforts are being made to recruit minority staff. *E.g.*, testimony of Joyce Coppin, transcript at 2527–28. Here, too, we take judicial notice of the fact that there is a relatively small pool of qualified professionals. Harm to children arguably will be

Ethnic Breakdown of Evaluation Unit
Professional Staff (as of 12/20/77)

Staff	Amer. Indian or Alaskan native	Black not of Hispanic origin	Asian or Pacific Islander	Hispanic	White not of Hispanic origin
Principals					1
Asst. principals				3	101
Teachers		1		10	140
Other professional staff		26			
Sub-totals		27		13	242
Part-time professional Staff		1		3	10
Totals		28		16	252

reduced by selcting professional staff on the basis of competence rather than on racial or ethnic grounds. We also note evidence of defendants' awareness of the danger of possible cultural bias, the efforts made not to base placement decisions on results from one type of test or a single professional's opinion, and the professional workshops which have begun to emphasize ways of avoiding cultural bias in testing.

As noted in section III F 3, *supra,* plaintiffs also charge that EU personnel employ insufficiently objective criteria in making decisions on placement, thus increasing the possibility of racial segregation. We recognize the dangers posed by the fact that the terms "handicapped" and "disabled" are socially defined categories. "Their content depends on the demands others make. . . . The fine line between "handicapped" and "normal" has been arbitrarily drawn by the 'normal' majority." S. O. Burke, "Affirmative Action Laws For People With Handicaps: Problems of Enforcement," 3 (mimeo. 1978) (citations omitted). Use of a conferencing technique in evaluation and placement recommendations, the refusal to base categorization upon a single set of tests, and other efforts observed by the Court at its visit to the EU and during the trial assure against the danger of excessive subjectivity. Moreover, the very difficulty of defining "handicapped" supports defendants' contentions that it is impracticable to reduce a combination of professional judgments to precise criteria.

With regard to ongoing evaluation or reevaluation, however, defendants have not fulfilled standards of adequacy. There is evidence of long waiting lists for the triennial evaluation mandated by the EHA. There is no showing of systematic annual review of students in special day schools by the COHs in conformance with state regulations promulgated in compliance with the EHA. The state regulations mandate that the IEP must contain, among other things:

> (ii) A statement of annual goals . . . [and] (v) Appropriate objective criteria and evaluation procedures and schedules for determining, on at least an annual basis, whether the instructional objectives are being achieved.

8 N.Y.C.R.R. § 200.4(f) 1. (1977).

Although some of the special day school principals testified about their own policies of annual reevaluation of pupils, there does not appear to be any coordinated or organized effort in this direction. Many children presently in the day schools have not had the advantage of current EU studies or of COH screening and other procedural protections. Some children may, therefore, be in day schools who would not be there had present standards been utilized. Even if triennial evaluations are eventually carried out, these children may remain in special day schools unnecessarily for some years.

Defendants seek to excuse the waiting lists for reevaluation by calling attention to the fact that in the original *Riley Reid* order (N.Y.Comm.Ed.Dec. No. 8742 (1973)) the State Commissioner of Education declared that there should be a priority in favor of "unserved" children, that is, students awaiting evaluation for special placement for the first time. This order does not constitute a valid justification for inadequate reevaluation amounting to a violation of constitutional and statutory rights.

There is also evidence indicating that children may be moved from one special educational setting to another—for example, CEH class to special day school or vice versa—in the absence of a full diagnostic work-up or clear-cut reasons for the move. This happens despite the fact that any change in placement is supposed to trigger the entire evaluative process.

Decertification is erratic and poorly defined. Some witnesses testified that it is always accompanied by full review; other testimony belied this fact. The latter testimony reflects the reality for a substantial number of students.

Plaintiffs' expert witnesses' criticism of the failure to conduct evaluation of students in the regular school constitutes no deprivation. There is no consensus of professional opinion on this point. Reports from the regular schools seem, in general, to be substantial and younger children are generally observed for at least a day in a diagnostic classroom at the EU.

In sum, the system of diagnosis and classification, so crucial to affording adequate treatment, suffers from inadequate staffing and some lack of control. There is, however, considerable evidence of good intentions and strong efforts to improve it.

2. Due Process

Conduct of the referral, evaluation and reevaluation processes also constitutes a violation of due process rights guaranteed by the Constitution and statutes. *See* discussion in section IV B, *supra*.

Defendants have made commendable efforts to comply with newly formulated due process requirements. Nevertheless, the actual notice afforded parents in the current system, taken as a whole, is not sufficient to meet its intended purposes. Defendants also state that the pupils assigned to the special schools suffer no stigma. They claim that at least since April, 1975, no child has been classified as "socially maladjusted and emotionally disturbed" (the former SMED acronym). Rather, the "severely emotionally disturbed" child (the category into which special day school students fall) is defined in applicable regulations as one

> whose emotional disturbance is so severe that the child is unable to relate to other children and may have an absence of speech, and in addition needs the support of

clinical services. A severely emotionally disturbed child is one whose condition has been determined to be such by a school psychologist, a psychiatrist, or by an approved mental health clinic.

8 N.Y.C.R.R. § 200.2(a)(3) (1977). Defendants also note that the name of the bureau in charge of the special day schools has been changed from the Bureau for Socially Maladjusted and Emotionally Disturbed to the Bureau for the Education of the Emotionally Handicapped, another effort to avoid offensive labels. Without minimizing the Board's valiant attempts to avoid stigmatization, evidence suggests that children segregated in special schools are still stigmatized to some degree. In deciding this case we assume that this, along with other considerations, is sufficient to support a triggering of due process rights.

Each of the notice steps in defendants' system of evaluation and referral is designed in literal compliance with statutory mandates. All of the steps taken together do not, however, constitute notice adequate under the circumstances involved in the placement of students in the special day schools.

Step One—Notice to parents upon initiation of referral for EU evaluation: The referring school and the COH are supposed to advise parents of their procedural due process rights, including the right to withdraw the child from the evaluation process at any time. There is no written notice at this point except for a Parental Consent and Waiver of Confidentiality Form, sent to parents prior to evaluation by the EU. This form explains the necessity for exchange of information about the child among EU professionals and apprises the parent of the opportunity to meet with the COH to discuss any change in placement. In signing the form the parent consents to the evaluation and to COH review of the EU recommendation. The form does not provide any detail of the steps involved in the evaluation and placement process nor specific information about the way to challenge a determination of placement.

Step Two—Notice at EU during initial interview: The parent who accompanies the child to the EU meets with the social worker. The social worker explains the evaluation process and gives the parent a relatively detailed booklet, "Your Child's Right to an Education." (The Court observed the booklet being given to parents again at COH hearings. See discussion in section III D 8 *supra.*) This pamphlet applies to children with any kind of handicapping condition. It includes explanations of: (1) behavior problems which may indicate certain handicaps; (2) the role of the COH and the type of notice to which parents are entitled if special education placement is recommended; (3) each school district's responsibility to identify children with handicapping conditions; (4) the evaluation process; (5) each of the special education programs; (6) the school district's obligations to guard the child's right to privacy in his school records and to give parents access to records; (7) the school's right to suspend a child from school and the child's right to a hearing if such suspension is for a period greater than five days; (8) reasons for which a child is validly excused from attendance; and (9) the way to challenge the COH's educational placement decision. The booklet is relatively long and encompasses a large range of topics. Only the section on the COH and the last section provide information on the evaluation and placement process itself, including the time and manner in which the parent can challenge placement.

The document would be overwhelming for even a well-educated layperson.

Parents of children likely to be referred to the special day schools must rely heavily on the social worker's explanation for a full understanding of the process. Yet the practice among social workers varies and there is no fixed outline for them to follow. Language and cultural barriers also inhibit comprehension.

Step Three—Meeting with social worker following case conference: Following the case conference among EU personnel, the social worker is charged with contacting the parent to discuss the findings and go over the tests used in the evaluation process. There is no written document used in this consultation or any evidence that a specific format is required or systematically utilized.

Step Four—COH notification to parents prior to review of EU determination: Notice at this stage takes the form of the "Option Letter." This letter informs the parent of the recommended placement and provides either for COH review within 45 days of (contingent) placement of the child in the special education program (Option One) or review within 10 days accompanied by possible parental pursuit of a due process hearing (Option Two). The evidence indicates that, as a practical matter, only the most aggressive and well-informed parents are capable of utilizing Option Two.

Step Five—COH notice following parental choice of Option Two: If the parent checks Option Two he is given notice from the COH including: a full description of the options considered by the EU, the reasons for rejecting certain of these, a full description of the proposed action, explanation of the tests and reports used in making the classification, notice that the school records and reports are available to the parents for review and duplication, information on obtaining both an impartial hearing challenging the COH decision and an appeal from that hearing, and information on the right to an independent evaluation of the child. (This independent evaluation will be at public expense only if the parent disagrees with the school district's evaluation and the impartial hearing officer's recommendation concurs with the parent's choice of placement.) 8 N.Y.C.R.R. § 200.5(b)(2)(vi) (1977). There is no standardized written form used in giving this notice. At the COH hearings the Court observed the chairperson trying to explain the parents' and child's rights, but it was apparent that they already were fully cognizant of them or disinterested.

The notice afforded in the course of the above five steps is inadequate for two reasons. First, there is no single document which spells out, in simple, succinct and readily understandable form, the entire process of evaluation, including the ways to challenge recommended placement. Such a document would afford realistic notice in the context of the instant case. We are dealing, by defendants' own admission, with a population from largely underprivileged, often broken homes, and with parents who are, more likely than not, poorly educated, harried, beset by their own personal problems and intimidated by authority and a plethora of forms. If there is to be any chance of realistically giving notice to a group of this type, it must be done as simply and clearly as possible.

Ms. Garfinkle has concluded from her extensive study of the problem that a

sampling of the parent consent forms presently in use, in and around New York City, raise doubts that a substantial number of parents who sign these forms do, in fact, understand what they have agreed to.

V. Garfinkle, "Recent Developments in the Law on the Education of Handicapped Children in New York State" 46 (1978) (unpub.).

Certainly a Spanish language translation, and possibly other translations, such as Italian, should be available. Illustrations and diagrams using comic book style explanations might prove helpful.

The need for a single, simple, document is most glaring when we consider the position of parents confronted with the Option Letter who may well check Option One without a full understanding of what this means. If Option One is checked, the child may be placed in the special education setting before the parent receives the benefit of COH notice as outlined in Step Five, *supra*. It is unclear if the parent who checks Option One ever gets this notice, or if so, at what point. An aggressive parent will, of course, probably be heard by the COH at any time. The Court observed one case at the COH hearing concerning a child who was already attending a school for the speech handicapped. The parent obtained a promise from the Committee that if she was dissatisfied at any time, the COH would hear her and try to correct the placement. Obviously most minority parents could exhibit no such skill.

Neither is notice afforded sufficiently early. The type of document suggested above should be distributed to parents at least at the initial stage of the process, i.e., at the point at which the parent is asked to consent to referral for evaluation. If, at this stage, one document were received which spelled out the entire process, a parent would be afforded a look at the big picture and any further notice provided along the way could act as reinforcement. Further explanations and the same or other documents might be given at later stages.

As it stands now, parents receive a barrage of papers and forms. Each item reveals bits and pieces of the whole process. There may well be a tendency for parents to consent in a piecemeal fashion, without full comprehension of the entire system. Children may be placed before they or their parents have realized fully the implications of placement or the possibility of contesting it. This impression is supported by the testimony of Grace Cavanagh, Chief Administrator of the Hearing Office for the Handicapped. Ms. Cavanagh stated at trial that of the 250 hearings completed by the Board of Education between Jan. 1 and Nov. 1, 1977, one involved a case where a child was in a special day school and the parent wanted him moved to a special class and one (a plaintiff in the instant suit) involved objection to the possibility of special day school placement. About one-half of the total number of hearings involved parents seeking, on their own initiative, placement in private schools at public expense. Transcript at 2209–11. A logical inference to be drawn from such testimony is that the type of notice afforded has not been sufficient in reaching parents of children slated for, or already in, the special day schools.

The second violation of due process guarantees involves reevaluation, including formulation of the IEP. The educational plan is considered an integral part of procedural due process rights to notice and hearing prior to initial or subsequent placement. The inadequacy of defendants' reevaluation has been covered in our discussion of the extent to which the evaluation and placement process violates a right to treatment in section V A 1, *supra*. It need not be repeated at this point. In a sense, these violations of due process are a part of the violation of a broader right to treatment.

B. *Special Day Schools as Violative of the Right to Treatment*

The heart of the treatment is found in the special day schools themselves. In this area, there is a clear consensus that deficiencies exist. First, virtually all the witnesses who testified about the schools admitted that they would benefit from increased BCG staff, guidance counselors, attendance teachers, medical personnel and the like. Although some of defendants' witnesses insisted that the smaller class size, individual attention and informality provided a "therapeutic atmosphere," there was a consensus that the disturbed children attending the special day schools should, as part of a complete treatment program, receive clinical therapy and have adequate access to guidance counselors and "crisis teachers." Bearing repetition here is the testimony of psychiatrist, Dr. Howard Weiner, a witness for the defense, who stated that adequate staff for a school of 150 pupils would consist of, at the least, part-time psychiatric services, a full-time psychologist and a full-time social worker; and that for a school of 300, an adequate staff would be even greater. Transcript at 2401. As our summary of the conditions in the schools in section III B, *supra,* makes clear, none comes close to this standard.

All witnesses agreed that the pupils in the special day schools are seriously deficient in reading and mathematics skills. Any hope of successful reentry into a regular educational setting and of realization of longer range success depends on-achievement in these basic areas. Here, too, the special day schools are deficient. Testimony reveals that remedial reading and mathematics teachers and reading and mathematics laboratories have been severely cut back with the result that not all children are served adequately. Moreover, in several schools special programs designed specifically to increase motivation and interest in learning cannot function because of inadequate supplies or faculty; despite complaints by principals, no steps have been taken to remedy these deficiencies. *See* section III F 6 *supra.*

Few of the schools have complete physical education programs. Without minimizing the importance of such activities for these children, we do not find that this lack constitutes a violation of plaintiffs' rights. It would be uneconomical to offer these pupils the full range of physical education programs available to students in larger institutions. It is this economic consideration, along with pedagogical factors, which explains the move toward union school districts in this country. In the case of the special day schools it is clear that the advantage of a small school unit outweighs any disadvantage stemming from a lack of specialized physical education facilities that might be available in larger institutions.

This deficiency is clearly distinguishable from the problem raised by shortage of clinical and other support staff discussed in section III F 5, *supra.* To skimp in the latter instance is a serious deprivation inasmuch as referral to the day school is predicated upon availability of precisely the type of therapy afforded by these professionals.

Defendants' witnesses and other personnel are obviously well-intentioned and skilled. There was no evidence of outright malevolence or indifference to the fate of the children involved. On the contrary, personnel do a fine job considering their limited resources. These positive aspects, however, do not undercut our findings of inadequate treatment. As observed in *Martarella* v. *Kelley:*

The concept of treatment as a constitutional quid pro quo for the state's right to detain . . . children, the mentally ill, for example,—involves the delivery of therapeutic services—services which must emanate from the staff. Treatment in this sense goes beyond good will and kindness, although those virtues may be indispensable to the success of the therapy.

349 F.Supp. 575, 586 (S.D.N.Y. 1972). The good intentions and helpfulness of those involved in the referral to, and treatment in, the special day schools, do not, therefore, compensate for inadequacies.

Although we do not question the educational justification for the existence of the schools as part of a continuum of services for emotionally disturbed children, they must offer suitable education and treatment to their students. Defendants' programs do not meet this standard.

VI. Defense of Lack of Funds

Throughout the course of the trial, defendants' witnesses, admitting that portions of the system of special education under attack were less than optimal, pointed to budget cuts occasioned by the current New York City fiscal crisis. New York City's monetary problems do not excuse violation of plaintiffs' rights.

This is not the first case in which lack of funds has been pleaded in answer to attacks on inadequate care. In *Wyatt* v. *Stickney,* 325 F.Supp. 781, 782-83 (M.D.Alabama 1971), 344 F.Supp. 373, 377 (M.D.Alabama 1972), *aff'd sub nom Wyatt* v. *Aderholt,* 503 F.2d 1305 (5th Cir. 1974), the State of Alabama had discharged a number of professionals due to a shortage of funds caused by a cut in the state's cigarette tax. In granting relief from inadequate treatment caused, in part, by the cuts, the court refused to countenance the use of fiscal constraints as a defense. In one of the District Court opinions in that case, Judge Johnson noted:

> . . . the unavailability of neither funds, nor staff and facilities, will justify a default by defendants in the provision of suitable treatment for the mentally ill.

344 F.Supp. at 377. Similarly, in *Mills* v. *Board of Education,* 348 F.Supp. 866, 875-76 (D.D.C.1972), it was pointed out that insufficient funds will not provide an excuse for continuing a system of special education which may result in discrimination in violation of the equal protection clause.

The current New York City fiscal crisis, therefore, provides no excuse for violations of plaintiffs' rights. In fashioning its relief, however, the Court cannot ignore the rather substantial cost of educating these children. Nor can we forget the inescapable fact that to spend substantially more on this pupil population may well necessitate a sacrifice in services now afforded children in the rest of the school system.

The amount currently spent on students in special day schools is strong evidence of lack of malevolent purpose. The per capita cost of educating a child in a special day school, based on fiscal year 1976 figures, is about $6,300 per pupil per year. The cost of a regular school education is some $2,300 per pupil per year. In addition, there are the enormous costs of the EUs, COHs and appellate processes plus the higher capital costs attributed to less heavily utilized buildings. A special day school education costs substantially more than three times a mainstream education.

New York City receives some help in meeting the expense of operating its special day schools. The EHA provides funds to New York State from which, as of March 1, 1978, the New York City Board of Education receives $55 per handicapped child—a small fraction of the cost of educating a handicapped child. State aid is allocated according to whether the program serves a population of students classified as severely or non-severely handicapped. The children in the special day schools are regarded as possessing "severe" emotional disturbance. *See* 8 N.Y.C.R.R. § 200.2(a)(3) (1977). For such severely handicapped children, New York City receives just under $3,000 per child, based not on the number of pupils on register, but on average daily attendance. The result is that the average payments for those in the special programs are considerably reduced because absentee rates tend to be high. Nevertheless, therapeutic and clinical resources must be provided for almost all the children registered even if they attend sporadically.

The City is also reimbursed for 90% of its transportation costs for handicapped children from a combination of state and federal funds. In the special day schools, however, this cost is a relatively small percentage of the total cost, $420 per child per year, again based on fiscal year 1976 figures.

While it is difficult to reconcile some of the figures, it appears that New York City receives a total of approximately $3400 from state and federal funds for each child in full attendance in a special day school. This is far less than the extra cost of educating a child in this program. Were the Court to mandate substantially increased services the fiscal burden would be absorbed wholly by the City.

VII.   Conclusion

The case is a difficult and close one. It is apparent that the plaintiffs have not established a basis for closing all special day schools, one of the main forms of relief they seek. We cannot allow any ideological promise of future statistically pure integration, however valid, to destroy the actuality of institutions that are providing, here and now, a better education for minorities. *Cf.* D. Bell, Jr., "The Legacy of W. E. B. DuBois: A Rational Model for Achieving Public School Equity for America's Black Children," 11 Creighton L.Rev. 409 (1977). Rather, preserving and improving what is good, we must aid educators in providing the equality in education that is our constitutional goal.

As it is now developing, the system does, in theory, protect adequately the procedural and substantive due process, equal protection and statutory rights of plaintiffs. In practice, however, minorities are discriminated against.

The Court has been impressed by the dedication and good faith of those charged with operation and supervision of New York City's special day schools and related services. It would be a mistake at this critical period, when procedures and programs are in the process of improvement, for the courts to impose powerful affirmative sanctions. They might so confuse and distort the system that the costs and derangements would far outweigh possible benefits. Nevertheless, as Judge Wright declared in *Hobson* v. *Hansen*, 269 F.Supp. 401, 498 (D.D.C. 1967), the fact that "a party is in the process of curing illegality, although that circumstance may affect the relief [eventually mandated by the court,] does not oust the court from its jurisdiction to declare a constitutional wrong."

The parties will meet with each other and then with the Court to attempt to work out the specific terms of a decree. *See Developments in the Law—Section 1983 and Federalism*, 90 Harv.L.Rev. 1133, 1247–50 (1977). For the purpose of focusing this discussion it is suggested that the decree might assume the following general form:

First, in view of the fact that many children presently in day schools have not had the advantage of the full protection of current statutes, regulations and procedures, all parents of children in special day schools who have not had their cases considered by the present Evaluation Units and have not had the advantage of review by a Committee on Handicapped and other procedural protections should be notified by mail of the possibility of evaluation within a specified period. Notification might be by letter in English and Spanish. *Cf. In the Matter of the Appeal of Timothy and Mary D.*, N.Y.Comm.Ed.Dec. No. 8574 (1977) (as of July 1, 1976 when the new state law took effect, parents whose children had been placed in special education programs before parental consent was required "were entitled . . . to an impartial hearing at the local level to review the appropriateness of the . . . classification."), *cited in* V. Garfinkle, "Recent Developments in the Law of the Education of Handicapped Children in New York State" (1978) (unpub.).

Second, all teachers in regular schools, administrators, clinicians and others should be notified by bulletin or otherwise of the Court's concern over the high ratio of minority persons in the special day schools. As indicated in section III 1, *supra,* there may be special need for training of parent members of COHs to avoid misunderstanding. It should be emphasized that (a) it is necessary to avoid bias in discipline and referral; (b) unnecessary use of private schools at public expense may have an indirect illegal effect of allowing middle class students to avoid programs which minority students utilize; and (c) the inability of many in the lower socio-economic groups to appreciate fully the protections and advantages or disadvantages of various alternative programs and procedures requires that they have their rights explained to them as fully as possible at every opportunity. Affirmative efforts must be made to involve parents and children in decisions affecting the children's future.

Third, an in-house training program to obtain bias-free consistency in approach and policy in EUs, COHs and day schools with respect to mainstreaming appears to be necessary. Disparity in percentages of mainstreaming among the various day schools and lack of knowledge of any policy by principals and others reflects absence of control by top administrators. It is unacceptable to have students returned to regular schools from the day schools reluctantly tolerated, or met with hostility by teachers and supervisors, as appears to be the pattern in at least some regular schools; steps to avoid such reactions need to be taken.

Fourth, an independent advocate or ombudsman system for parents and children being considered for, or assigned to, special day schools might be established. It would have the duty of representing the parents, or the child if there were a possible conflict of interest between parent and child. Referral could be made by any person with substantial grounds for belief that the child's case had not been considered adequately or that the parent or child had not understood fully or was incapable of enforcing the child's rights.

Fifth, the parties, with the assistance of the Court if requested, might call on communication experts from this city to develop readily understandable explanations to parents and children of their rights. In this great communication center of the world, with its many public-spirited and talented people, there should be no difficulty in finding people willing and able to develop materials designed to explain to the poorly educated the rights and opportunities of their children.

The Court notes with interest continuing commendable efforts of school authorities to meet this communications problem. For example, after the trial was completed, a new form of option letter was issued; explanations of due process procedures and descriptions of programs were attached. Memorandum of J. R. Coppin to COH and EU Coordinators, April 17, 1978.

Sixth, a report by defendants should be furnished to the Court by September 1979, indicating changes in the program to insure due process and adequate treatment consistent with this opinion. In addition to the selection and decertification problems referred to above, the report must address steps, required by statute, taken to correct inadequacies in IEPs. Steps taken to increase clinical staff in the day schools must be discussed. There will need to be reference to efforts made to increase minority representation in the staffs of EUs, COHs and the day schools themselves. Following the 1979 report, the parties could, if they wish, arrange for a conference with the Court to ascertain whether further relief were required.

It is requested that representatives of the New York State Commission of Education and of the United States Department of Health, Education and Welfare participate in these conferences, first with counsel and then with the Court. They should contemplate the possibility of providing funding for the advocacy proposal or its equivalent. They should also consider other ways in which federal or state agencies might assist the city in the operation of its special day school system through fiscal and other aid. Allocation of resources to education or specific forms of education are peculiarly legislative and executive tasks; the role of the Court is necessarily peripheral.

So ordered.

NOTES

1.   For additional discussion of the "right to treatment," see Chapter 6.

2.   How important was the issue of racial discrimination to the result in *Lora*? Would the decision have gone along similar lines if it had been simply a case brought by a group of white plaintiffs claiming a denial of appropriate programs for emotionally disturbed children?

3.   How blatant were the denials of equal educational opportunity in *Lora*? Was it truly, as the judge indicated, a difficult and close case?

E. STATE CONSTITUTIONAL RIGHTS

WOLF v. LEGISLATURE OF THE STATE OF UTAH

See pp. 70–72, *supra.*

IN RE G.H.

See pp. 113–120, *supra.*

NORTH CAROLINA ATTORNEY GENERAL OPINION

40 N.C.A.G. Rep. 248, 248-250 (May 28, 1969)

It is provided by Section 2 of Article IX of the Constitution of North Carolina, as follows:

> The General Assembly, at its first session under this Constitution, shall provide by taxation and otherwise for a general and uniform system of public schools, wherein tuition shall be free of charge to all children of the State between the ages of six and twenty-one years.

It is also provided in Section 27 of Article I of the State Constitution, as follows:

> The people have a right to the privilege of education, and it is the duty of the State to guard and maintain that right.

Under the Constitution the duty of providing funds by taxation or otherwise, for the maintenance of public schools is on the General Assembly, and the constitutional provision for public schools is mandatory, and being necessary expenses do not require a vote of the people. The General Assembly may, either by State appropriation or through counties as administrative agencies of the State, distribute the necessary tax burden and designate the counties and cities as administrative agencies to operate the public schools (*Tate* v. *Board of Education of McDowell County,* 192 N.C. 516; *Julian* v. *Ward,* 198 N.C. 480).

In *Bridges* v. *Charlotte,* 221 N.C. 472, it is said:

> It cannot be too often emphasized that the controlling purpose of the people of North Carolina, as declared in their Constitution, is that a State system of public schools shall be established and maintained—a system of schools supported by the State, and providing for the education of the children of the State—and that ample power has been conferred upon the General Assembly to make this purpose effective.

Further on, in this same opinion, the court stated:

> We understand that what courts appropriately refer to as the "mandate" of Article IX of the Constitution carries with it not merely the bare necessity of instructional service, but all facilities reasonably necessary to accomplish this main purpose.

It is clear that in operating the public school system counties and cities do not function as governmental units for local governmental purposes but they express the immediate power of the State as special administrative units and as agencies of the State for the performance of mandatory educational duties.

As we read all of these constitutional provisions and decisions of the Supreme

Court of North Carolina we find that the basic purpose is to provide education to the children of the State between certain ages, and no groups or classifications among children are expressed, nor are different categories of children established. The public school system is provided by the people of the State under constitutional mandate for the brilliant pupil, the mediocre pupil and also for the unfortunate mentally retarded pupil. The educational scheme, or plan, does not leave out or discriminate against the mentally retarded child nor should mentally retarded children be discriminated against in the allocation of educational funds. The tax levying authority of the State or of its administrative units in the educational field is to be exerted as much for the unfortunate mentally retarded child as it is for the normal child, whether brilliant, highly intelligent, or of a low grade of intelligence in the acquisition of educational development and skills.

It is unconstitutional and invalid, therefore, to operate the public school system in a discriminatory manner as against the mentally retarded child and to allocate funds to the disadvantage of the mentally retarded child. Often the mentally retarded child develops fair skills and abilities and becomes a useful citizen of the State but in order to do this the mentally retarded child must have his or her chance.

In re K.

Family Court, City of New York, Kings County, 1973
74 Misc.2d 872, 347 N.Y.S.2d 271 (1973)

JACOB T. ZUKERMAN, Judge.

This is an application for reimbursement of funds advanced by the parents of the handicapped child for the cost of the special education training for the 1971–1972 school year pursuant to the provisions of the Family Court Act and the Education Law. (The court has already granted that portion of this petition which dealt with the year 1972–1973.)

Arthur K. has been certified handicapped by the State Education Department. The Board of Education of New York City has certified that there is no adequate public facility for the instruction of this child and that there was none during the school year 1971–1972. The Buckingham School which Arthur now attends has been approved by the State Education Department for the education of such handicapped children. There is no question of the parents' eligibility for state aid as the Commissioner of Education has already indicated by letter from James Whitney, that he would issue a certificate of approval for state aid in the amount of $1,750 for the *1972–1973* school year if the court granted the relief (as it already has done).

The only defense by the state and the city is that the application for reimbursement for the 1971–1972 school year was not timely made. It is the state's as well as the city's position that the application for reimbursement for the 1971–1972 school year was made too late, it being after the school year and after the fiscal year. . . .

The court holds that the application for reimbursement for the 1971–1972 school year was not too late, as prior to the start of the 1971–1972 school year the state and city had notice that said claim for reimbursement would be forthcoming.

The state and city governments were both well aware in the summer of 1971, prior to the 1971–1972 school year that Arthur K. was, under the law, a handicapped child, and that Arthur was to attend Buckingham School for the 1971–1972 school year. This is evidenced by the fact that the $2,000 was paid by the state pursuant to section 4407 of the Education Law.

Since the state received the application for the $2,000 pursuant to section 4407 prior to the 1971–1972 school year and approved same and obviously based this decision on the report of the City Board of Education that there was no adequate public school facility available, the state and city governments were put on notice of the certainty of receiving in the future a petition for reimbursement for the costs of the school over and above the $2,000. Both governments could have allocated funds within the 1971–1972 fiscal year for this inevitable claim for reimbursement.

Moreover, it is this Court's opinion that even if the city and state had not received notice within the fiscal year of 1971–1972, the parents of a handicapped child have a right to reimbursement.

Section I of Article XI of the Constitution of New York State provides that the legislature shall provide for the maintenance and support of a system of free common schools where all the children of the state may be educated.

As Judge Guerreiro stated in *Matter of Downey,* 72 Misc.2d 772, 774, 340 N.Y.S.2d 687, 690, "To order a parent to contribute to the education of his handicapped child when free education is supplied to all other children would be a denial of the constitutional right of equal protection, United States Constitution Amendment XIV; New York State Constitution Article XI, Section 1." *See also Matter of Kirschner,* 74 Misc.2d 20, 344 N.Y.S.2d 164.

Judge Guerreiro further noted ". . . it is the child who is given the right to an education, not the parent and his right should not be abridged or limited by the willingness of a parent to become financially liable for the education." *Matter of Downey, supra.*

I concur that it would be a denial of the right of equal protection and morally inequitable not to reimburse the parents of a handicapped child for monies they have advanced in order that their child may attend a private school for the handicapped when no public facilities were available while other children who are more fortunate can attend public school without paying tuition and without regard to the assets and income of their parents.

Thus, this Court pursuant to Sec. 232 of the Family Court Act, orders the City of New York to reimburse the parents of Arthur K. in the amount of $1,750 for 1971–1972 school year.

NOTES

1. *Pacyna v. Board of Education, Joint Sch. Dist. #1,* 57 Wis.2d 562, 204 N.W.2d 671 (1973), involved the denial of admission to kindergarten of a 4-year-old girl. The Supreme Court of Wisconsin declared:

> Article X, Section 3, of the Wisconsin Constitution, provides a limitation upon the power and the authority of the legislature in the establishment of district schools. The Article requires district schools to be "as nearly uniform as practicable" and to be "free and without charge for tuition to all children between the ages of 4 and 20 years.". . .

We find no merit in the school board's argument that Nancy could be refused admittance to kindergarten because in the judgment of the school district psychologist she was incapable of profitably pursuing the studies of kindergarten instruction by reason of her immaturity.... Education is for all children and if a child is excluded because of immaturity or other reasons, his educational needs must be otherwise provided for by the state (at 204 N.W.2d 672, 674).

2. The state constitutional provisions relating to education discussed in the *Wolf, G. H., K.,* and *Pacyna* cases and in the North Carolina Attorney General's Opinion are typical of the constitutional mandates of about one-half of the states that declare that public education shall be equally available to all (see Burgdorf, R., and Burgdorf, M., "A History of Unequal Treatment: The Qualifications of Handicapped Persons as a 'Suspect Class' under the Equal Protection Clause," 15 *Santa Clara Lawyer* 855, 868, (1975), n. 90 and accompanying text). The constitutions of most of the remaining states specify that education shall be "general," "uniform," or "thorough"; *id.* at 868, nn. 91 and 92 and accompanying text. These provisions should be contrasted with Section 256 of Amendment 111 of the Alabama Constitution:

It is the policy of the state of Alabama to foster and promote the education of its citizens in a manner and extent consistent with its available resources, and the willingness and ability of the individual student, but nothing in this Constitution shall be construed as creating or recognizing any right to education or training at public expense, nor as limiting the authority and duty of the legislature, in furthering or providing for education, to require or impose conditions or procedures deemed necessary to the preservation of peace and order.

3. The *G. H.* decision, *In Re K.,* and the other New York cases cited in the latter rely in part upon the equal protection guarantees in the respective state constitutions. Almost every state has due process and equal protection provisions in its state constitution. Could analysis under these state equal protection and due process standards differ from that under their federal counterparts?

4. Depending on the proclivities of the state courts in applying them, state constitutional guarantees provide a hopeful alternative to federal court actions in seeking to further the educational rights of handicapped people. In states where constitutional provisions mandate education "for all," there is no need to become involved in many of the difficult analytical issues (e.g., strict scrutiny and fundamental rights) under the United States Constitution. Literal application of state constitutional language will frequently be sufficient to provide the relief sought by handicapped individuals. For discussion of additional considerations involved in the question of taking constitutional claims to state or federal court, see Note 1, p. 120, above.

ADDITIONAL READING

Note, "Special Education: The Struggle for Equal Educational Opportunity in Iowa," 62 *Ia. L. Rev.* 1285, 1360-1365 (1977).

IN RE LEVY

Court of Appeals of New York, 1976
38 N.Y.2d, 653, 382 N.Y.S.2d 13, 345, N.E.2d 556

JONES, Justice.

We hold that section 234 of the Family Court Act is constitutional notwithstanding that it authorizes Family Court in New York City to direct parents of handicapped children, other than children who are blind or deaf, to contribute to the maintenance of such children in connection with their education.

Appellants are parents of three handicapped children,[1] each of whom it is agreed is in need of special residential educational training and for none of whom does the City of New York have an appropriate educational facility. Each of the three children was attending a suitable private residential school. In each case Family Court granted the parents' applications for payment of full tuition as well as of all related transportation expenses. Three orders denied that part of the applications requesting maintenance payment, the court finding the parents of two of the children financially able to pay for board and lodging in full and accordingly directing them to make such payments. The fourth order granted the application to the extent of two-thirds of maintenance costs, directing the parent of the third child to pay the remaining third. Appellants all concede their ability to make the payments ordered. It is their contention that the statute under which they were directed to pay maintenance expenses is unconstitutional. Family Court rejected that contention in each case. The present direct appeals on constitutional grounds ensued (N.Y. Const. art. VI, § 3, subd. b, par. [2]; CPLR 5601, subd. [b], par. 2) and have been consolidated for our review.

Appellants' challenge to the statute is grounded in contentions that they have been denied equal protection of the law in two aspects. First, and principally, they urge that to require them to contribute to the maintenance component of educational expenses when no such contribution is required of the parents of deaf or blind children works a constitutionally impermissible discrimination. Secondly, they argue that, while the statutes authorize the imposition of such burden on parents of handicapped children in New York City, the same is not true with respect to children who reside outside New York City, and that this circumstance likewise constitutes a denial of equal protection.

There can be no doubt that a handicapped child has a right to a free education in the State of New York. (N.Y. Const. art. XI, § 1; Education Law, § 3202, subd. 1; *Matter of Wiltwyck School for Boys* v. *Hill,* 11 N.Y.2d 182, 227 N.Y.S.2d 655, 182 N.E.2d 268.) The handicapped child is further assured such free specialized educational training as may be required. (Education Law, § 4403; Family Ct. Act, § 231 *et seq.*)

Incident to the direct cost of education, i.e., tuition, are the expenses of main-

---

[1]Two of the four appeals are from separate orders involving the same child, but for different school years.

One child suffers from "organic brain syndrome with secondary autism manifested by moderate mental retardation, hyperactivity and language environment"; another from "schizophrenic reaction, childhood type"; and the third from "overanxious reaction of childhood with borderline features."

tenance and transportation. It is not disputed that under our State's educational program the parents of all handicapped children have no responsibility for either tuition or transportation expense. The controversy here revolves around the imposition on the parents of handicapped children, other than those who are blind or deaf, of the costs of maintenance.

The fulcrum of appellants' argument is the circumstance that in consequence of legislative enactment the State provides wholly free education, including all maintenance expense, to children who are either blind or deaf, and that the parents of such handicapped children are not required to make any contribution to the cost of maintenance regardless of their financial ability. (Education Law, arts. 85, 87, 88; §§ 4204 [deaf children], 4207 [blind children].) The assertion is that this differentiation, operating to the disadvantage of appellants, deprives them of equal protection of the law.

At the threshold of consideration of any equal protection claim is the determination of the applicable standard of review. Handicapped children as such do not constitute a "suspect classification" (cf. *Matter of Lalli,* 38 N.Y.2d 77, 378 N.Y.S.2d 351, 340 N.E.2d 721 [illegitimate children]; *Matter of Malpica-Orsini,* 36 N.Y.2d 568, 370 N.Y.S.2d 511, 331 N.E.2d 486 [illegitimate children]; contrast *Loving* v. *Virginia,* 388 U.S. 1, 87 S.Ct. 1817, 18 L.Ed.2d 1010 [race]; *Hernandez* v. *Texas,* 347 U.S. 475, 74 S.Ct. 667, 98 L.Ed. 866 [national origin]; *Matter of Griffiths,* 413 U.S. 717, 93 S.Ct. 2851, 37 L.Ed.2d 910 [alienage]). Nor is the right to education such a "fundamental constitutional right" as to be entitled to special constitutional protection (*San Antonio School Dist.* v. *Rodriguez,* 411 U.S. 1, 16, 93 S.Ct. 1278, 36 L.Ed.2d 16). Accordingly, the appropriate standard is not the so-called strict scrutiny test or anything approaching it, but rather the traditional rational basis test. (*Montgomery* v. *Daniels,* 38 N.Y.2d 41, 59, 378 N.Y.S.2d 1, 340 N.E.2d 444; cf. *Matter of Jesmer* v. *Dundon,* 29 N.Y.2d 5, 323 N.Y.S.2d 417, 271 N.E.2d 905, app. dsmd. 404 U.S. 953, 92 S.Ct. 324, 30 L.Ed.2d 270.)

A rational basis does exist for the distinction made in relieving the parents of blind and deaf children from any financial responsibility in connection with their children's education while at the same time requiring parents whose children are otherwise handicapped to contribute to the maintenance component of educational expenses.

There can be no doubt that as a matter of history and tradition our society has accorded special recognition to the blind and to the deaf in the field of education as elsewhere. In New York State since 1865 a school for the blind has been maintained by the State at Batavia (Education Law, art. 87) and a school for the deaf at Rome (Education Law, art. 88). In addition there are five other schools for the deaf and five other schools for the blind subject "to the visitation of the commissioner of education" who has broad supervisory powers in the operation of such schools (Education Law, § 4201).

In the related field of social services, assistance to the blind has long been recognized as a special category (Social Services Law, art. 5, tit. 7, prior to repeal and consolidation with other categories by L.1974, ch. 1080, § 4). Additionally the New York State Commission for the Blind and Visually Handicapped has a venerable and distinguished history (L.1913, ch. 415, as amd.; Social Services Law, § 38).

The Federal Government has also long accorded privileges and benefits to the blind which are not available to other handicapped persons—e.g., an additional exemption for income tax purposes (Internal Revenue Code, U.S. Code, tit. 26, § 151, subd. [d]); disability benefits to the blind under the Social Security Act "without regard to ability to engage in any substantial gainful activity" (U.S. Code, tit. 42, § 423; 20 CFR 404.1501[b]; see *Ferguson* v. *Celebrezze,* D.C.S.C., 232 F.Supp. 952, 955–956); free mailing privileges (U.S. Code, tit. 39, §§ 3403, 3404).

We think that the Legislature acts rationally when, in the exercise of its authority and responsibility to identify concerns of the State and to make provision with respect thereto, it takes into account distinctions which carry the imprimatur of historical authenticity, provided that such distinctions are not the reflection of invidious discrimination and have not been demonstrated to be irrational by knowledge subsequently acquired.[3] It strikes us as unintelligent to say that the decisions made in the past and the value judgments of those preceding us who were then responsible for identifying the priorities of governmental concern and response must be wholly ignored unless the determinations which were then made can be justified, *ab initio,* when measured by today's criteria and standards. This is not to say that we may today complacently accept the wisdom and the unwisdom of the past. It is to say, on the other hand, that the policy judgments and the priority determinations of our history are not totally to be rejected, especially when those judgments and determinations have enjoyed public acceptance for a long period of time. As we have said in another context: "While antiquity is not an infallible criterion for determining the scope of constitutional rights, traditional usage and understanding is helpful in defining the privilege against self-incrimination." (*People* v. *Samuel,* 29 N.Y.2d 252, 264, 327 N.Y.S.2d 321, 329, 277 N.E.2d 381, 387.)

Our Legislature in granting the preferences to parents of the blind and deaf may well have judged at the time that children with these handicaps were more educable in general than were those with other handicaps. There may also have been other politically and educationally sound predicates for the choice. The resulting educational programs manifest the historical public recognition, understanding and acceptance of human disabilities. Government, and particularly the legislative branch, acts responsibly when it reflects the concerns and interests of the governed except when to do so would be to trespass on constitutionally protected rights. Obviously choices must and will be made; priorities must and will be set. This is the essence of the legislative process. Were the financial resources available to State government unlimited, this would not be necessary and might not be desirable. It would be unthinkable, however, to suggest that confronted with economic strictures State government is powerless to move forward in the fields of education and social welfare with anything less than totally comprehensive programs. Such a contention would suggest that the only alterna-

---

[3]In passing we again observe that here we address classifications as to which the equal protections standard is that of rational basis. In instances of "suspect classifications" and "fundamental constitutional rights," where special constitutional protection is assured by application of the strict scrutiny test, historical practice would not, of course, be accorded any such significance.

tive open to the Legislature in the exercise of its policy-making responsibility, if it were to conclude that wholly free education could not be provided for all handicapped children, would be to withdraw the benefits now conferred on blind and deaf children—thus to fall back to an undifferentiated and senseless but categorically neat policy that since all could not be benefited, none would be.

As the Supreme Court of the United States has written in an associated context: "The problem of legislative classification is a perennial one, admitting of no doctrinaire definition. Evils in the same field may be of different dimensions and proportions, requiring different remedies. Or so the legislature may think. *Tigner* v. *Texas,* 310 U.S. 141, 60 S.Ct. 879, 84 L.Ed. 1124. Or the reform may take one step at a time, addressing itself to the phase of the problem which seems most acute to the legislative mind. *Semler* v. *Dental Examiners,* 294 U.S. 608, 55 S.Ct. 570, 79 L.Ed. 1086. The legislature may select one phase of one field and apply a remedy there, neglecting the others. *A. F. of L.* v. *American Sash Co.,* 335 U.S. 538, 69 S.Ct. 258, 93 L.Ed. 222. The prohibition of the Equal Protection Clause goes no further than the invidious discrimination." (*Williamson* v. *Lee Opt. Co.,* 348 U.S. 483, 489, 75 S.Ct. 461, 465, 99 L.Ed. 563.)

We conclude that there is a rational basis for the differentiation in treatment of the maintenance component of the educational expenses of blind or deaf children and children who are otherwise handicapped. (*Matter of Claire,* 44 A.D.2d 407, 355 N.Y.S.2d 399, mot. for lv. to app. dsmd. 35 N.Y.2d 706, 361 N.Y.S.2d 641, 320 N.E.2d 273.)

As to the other branch of appellants' equal protection arguments, it suffices to note that it is predicated on a false premise. There is no difference in the authority of the courts within and without New York City to direct a parent financially able to do so to contribute to the maintenance component of the expense of education of his handicapped child. Section 234 of the Family Court Act expressly grants the authority within the city. While it is true that no comparable articulation is to be found in present section 232, applicable outside the city, this has been described as a legislative oversight in the 1964 amendment and exercise of a comparable authority outside the city has been upheld as implicit in the power of the court to enter a "suitable order" under sections 232, 413, 414 and 416 of the Family Court Act (cf., also, § 415). (*Matter of Charilyn "N"* v. *County of Broome,* 46 A.D.2d 65, 66, 361 N.Y.S.2d 215, 216; *Diana L.* v. *State of New York,* 70 Misc.2d 660, 665, 335 N.Y.S.2d 3, 9.)

The orders of Family Court should be affirmed.

BREITEL, C. J., and JASEN, GABRIELLI, WACHTLER, FUCHSBERG and COOKE, JJ., concur.

In each case: Order affirmed, without costs.

NOTES

1.   Whether or not one agrees with the ultimate result in *Levy,* it is difficult to characterize the legal reasoning in the court's opinion as other than superficial and shoddy. The court cites Article XI, § 1, of the New York Constitution, which provides

for "a system of free common schools, wherein all the children of this state may be educated," for the proposition that "[t]here can be no doubt that a handicapped child has a right to a free education in the State of New York." What sort of logic could lead from there to a conclusion that education is not a "fundamental constitutional right"?

Another bald assertion by the *Levy* court is that handicapped children do not constitute a "suspect classification"; cf. *In re G. H.* and *Fialkowski* v. *Shapp, supra.* The only support offered by the court for this finding is a block citation to cases dealing with illegitimate children, race, national origin, and alienage. The decision does not mention the criteria for suspectness outlined by the Supreme Court in *San Antonio School District* v. *Rodriguez,* 411 U.S. 1, 28 (1973), nor discuss any reasons why handicapped people do not meet these criteria.

And how could the court seriously resort to a theory that equal protection scrutiny can be satisfied by waving the banner of "historical authenticity"? One can imagine guffaws if a defendant in, for example, a sex discrimination case, even one where the rational basis test was employed, e.g., *Reed* v. *Reed,* 404 U.S. 71 (1971), offered as a defense: "That's the way we've always done it." If a historical practice is a sound one, there would presumably be a rational relationship between it and a legitimate governmental purpose that prompted the practice in the first place. If there is no such rational basis, the practice, whether of long duration or not, is violative of equal protection. The pertinent consideration is the reasonable relationship to a legitimate objective, not merely the length of time involved.

2.   Would the constitutional standards and results in *Levy* have been the same if the case had involved an outright exclusion of handicapped children from any program of public education? Or if it had involved the question of reimbursement for *tuition* at private schools rather than simply board and lodging costs? Perhaps *Levy* is a concrete example of the lawyers' cliché about bad facts making bad law. In terms of strategy in the orchestration of a civil rights movement for handicapped people, did it make sense to raise the questions of equal protection standards to the highest court of a state in the context of the rather esoteric question of parents' obligation to pay room and board costs for private school placements in situations where the parents were admittedly able to afford such expenses? Moreover, how strategically desirable was it to pit the interests of plaintiffs against those of deaf and blind persons? Cf. *Frederick L.* v. *Thomas, supra.* Could the court have responded to plaintiffs' claim by invalidating the allowance of maintenance costs to parents of deaf and blind children?

3.   The *Levy* court could have reached the same result by a totally different line of reasoning. It could have sidestepped plaintiffs' "fundamental rights" argument by pointing out that this case did not at all raise the issue of denial of education, but involved only a very auxiliary issue of payment of lodging expenses. It could also have avoided the "suspect class" question by noting that the case did not raise an instance of differential treatment of handicapped versus nonhandicapped persons: Only deaf and blind persons have maintenance expenses paid for; for all others, both handicapped and not, parental payment of maintenance is the rule. For these reasons, the court could legitimately have ruled the strict scrutiny test inapplicable.

FLORIDA CONSTITUTION, ARTICLE 1

§ 2.   Basic rights.

All natural persons are equal before the law and have inalienable rights, among which are the right to enjoy and defend life and liberty, to pursue happiness, to be rewarded for industry and to acquire, possess and protect property; except that the ownership, inheritance, disposition and possession of real property by aliens ineligible for citizenship may be regulated or prohibited by law. No person shall be deprived of any right because of race, religion or physical handicap (Amended, general election, Nov. 5, 1974).

NOTE

The Florida constitutional amendment is the first of its kind. Such a provision obviously makes the battle for equal educational opportunity much easier for those with a "physical handicap."

F.   STATE STATUTES

1.   Enforcement in General

KIVELL v. NEMOINTIN

Superior Court, Fairfield County, Connecticut, 1972
No. 143913, July 8, 1972

TESTO, J.

This is an action brought in two counts by the plaintiff, mother, in behalf of her minor son.

In the first count the plaintiff seeks a mandamus directing the defendants to perform their duties toward the minor in accordance with the Statutes concerning special education to an exceptional child and in the second count monetary damages against the defendants for reimbursement to her for tuition charges she had to spend in an out-of-state educational facility.

The named defendants are all members of the Stamford Board of Education.

The plaintiff-petitioner is a minor child, aged 12, who brought this action by his mother. The minor has been a perceptually handicapped child with learning disabilities since prior to February, 1970. Commencing in February, 1970, the mother requested the defendants to identify said child as perceptually handicapped as defined in Section 10-76a through 10-76g, inclusive, and Section 10-94(a) of the Connecticut General Statutes. The reason for the identification is necessary so that the minor can qualify for benefits under our statutes.

The facts of this matter are these: The minor was enrolled in the Stamford Public School System for the year 1970–1971. It is an admitted fact that the minor could not function in a normal public school classroom. Many attempts were made by the minor through his parents to obtain the special education from the defendants to which he claimed eligibility under the statutes. These requests were made prior to the commencement of the school year in September, 1970. Eventually, the minor was seen by the diagnostic team of the Stamford Board of Education which agreed that the minor was a child who needed special education. This team recommended a program to the parents. This was done on or about September 29, 1970. After consulting with a licensed clinical psychologist who evaluated the minor and the offered program, the parents transferred their child to an out-of-state educational facility (Eagle Hill— Massachusetts). The enrollment took place on October 7, 1970. The parents, in the interim, pursued their claimed rights and sought an appeal to the Stamford Board of Education of the diagnostic team's evaluation of the educational needs of the minor. A hearing was held before the Stamford Board of Education on January 9, 1971. Said appeal was denied by the Board of Education. Subsequently, the parents appealed to the State Board of Education. An investigation was commenced by the State Agency on March 22, 1971. In a letter, dated June 21, 1971, the Commissioner of Education for the State of Connecticut advised the superintendent of the Stamford School System that the program offered to the minor for the school year 1970–1971 would not have met the minor's special educational needs. The letter further stated that if the Stamford Board of Education reversed its prior decision and assumed the cost of educating the minor at Eagle Hill School, the State Board of Education would reimburse the local board under existing legislation. The Stamford Board of Education refused to reverse its decision. The Commissioner of Education requested that a program be submitted for approval to him for the year 1971–1972. At the commencement of this action, the Commissioner of Education testified (September 28, 1971) that his office had not as yet received the requested program from Stamford. The hearing in this matter was suspended to give the Commissioner the opportunity to receive and review the program for the year 1971–1972. A letter of approval of the Stamford program was issued under date of October 14, 1971. A copy of this letter of approval was received by the parents of the minor at the end of October, 1971.

It is the mandatory duty of a parent to cause his child to receive an appropriate education. It is also a duty of the parents to see to it that his child attends a public day school regularly.

Section 10-184, Connecticut General Statutes.

Under our statutes it is also the duty of the state Board of Education to supervise and control the educational interests of the state which includes "special education."

Section 10-4, Connecticut General Statutes.

There are provisions in our law that special instruction be provided for special services where our children are unable to progress effectively in a regular school system.

Section 10-76 (a through g) Connecticut General Statutes.

In Section 10-76a, subsection (c), it provides for special education for an "exceptional child" who is suffering from an identifiable learning disability which impedes his rate of development. . . .

Further, subsection (j) of Section 10-76a provides for a definition of "learning disabilities" by the Commissioner of the State Board of Education subject to the approval of the entire state board. The Commissioner of the Board of Education has so defined "learning disability" in subsection (4) of Section 10-786-1 of the General Guidelines for Special Education Programs, Appendix 3 as a "disorder in one or more of the basic psychological processes involved in language, perception, memory or conceptualization but does not include disabilities due primarily to visual, hearing or motor handicaps or to mental retardation, emotional disturbance or cultural disadvantage.'' All of the experts who testified agreed that the minor was a learning disabled child as defined above.

Section 10-76b of the General Statutes provides that the State Board of Education shall be responsible for the development and supervision of the educational programs for children requiring special education.

Section 10-76d, subsection (b), provides that each town shall provide special education for children who require special education as described in subdivision (l) of subsection (e) of Section 10-76a.

It is well settled law in this State at this time that a local board of education is an agent of the State Board of Education, and its powers and duties are defined by Statute and regulated by its superior, the State Board of Education.

Sherman, et al. v. *Kemish,* 29 Conn. Supp. 198.

It is abundantly clear from the statutes that the regulation and supervision of special education is within the mandatory duty of the state board of education and that the local town board is its agent charged with the responsibility of carrying out the intent of the law which the minor needs and is entitled to.

The State Board of Education found the program (1970–1971) not acceptable and did not approve the local board's program for the year 1971–1972 until that school year had already commenced (October 14, 1971).

The parents of this minor were acting properly in seeking the proper educational needs for their child as defined by statute for both school years.

Therefore, this Court finds the issues for the plaintiff on the first and second counts.

Judgment may enter for the plaintiff, therefore, and she is entitled to reimbursement for the tuition charges of her minor son in the amount of Thirteen Thousand and Four Hundred Dollars ($13,400.00) for the school years of 1970–1971 and 1971–1972.

A Mandamus may also issue as requested directing the Stamford Board of Educational and Superintendent of Schools of said City to furnish the minor with the special education required by the statutes of this State. Compliance of this order shall mean the acceptance and approval by the State Board of Education of the program submitted by the local Board of Education. This Court will frown upon any unilateral action by parents in sending their children to other facilities. If a program is timely filed by a local board of education and is accepted and approved by the state board of education, then it is the duty of the parents to accept said program. A refusal by the parents in such a situation will not entitle said child to any benefits from this court.

NOTES

1.   Requiring a local school district, which has failed to provide an appropriate educational program, to pay for the costs of an out-of-state program provides a very strong incentive for the school district to deliver appropriate programming in the future. Payments made to out-of-state facilities are a definite revenue loss to the local district, without any compensation in the form of additional jobs, increased power, prestige, or

even credit for the success of the program. Therefore, the school district's self-interest will give strong motivation to future attempts to serve the pupil locally.

2. The court indicated that it would "frown upon any unilateral action by parents in sending their children to other facilities." Thus, parents may not demand that their children be sent to the best special education programs in the country but must accept adequate programs provided locally. Parents' subjective preferences are made subsidiary to the traditional authority of school officials to make decisions concerning the nature of educational programming, provided the programs comply with statutory guidelines and procedures.

RAINEY v. TENNESSEE DEPARTMENT OF EDUCATION

Chancery Court, Davidson County, Tennessee, 1976
No. A-3100, January 21, 1976

This action arises from a contempt petition filed by the original plaintiffs on September 30, 1975. The petition alleges that the defendants are in contempt of the consent decree entered on July 29, 1974, which incorporated a consent agreement executed by the parties.

The petition alleges that the defendants have violated paragraph 4, 5 and 7 of the consent agreement. Those paragraphs contain the following provisions:

4. All handicapped children ages 4 through 21, or the age of obtaining a high school diploma if prior to age 21, shall be provided access to appropriate and free special education services as soon as possible but no later than:

(a) the school year beginning in the fall of 1974 for all said children with a verified handicap;

(b) the school year beginning in the fall of 1975 for all handicapped children.

5. If by the beginning of the school year any local education agency or district is not providing, or has not arranged through other educational entities pursuant to state regulations to provide, access to appropriate special education services for all handicapped children within its responsibility, the State Department of Education will exercise its authority, pursuant to T.C.A. 49-2949 and/or other State statutes and regulations, to withhold funds from said agency and/or to directly provide, supervise and operate programs for the education of these children. Provided, that nothing in this Consent Agreement shall limit any right which any handicapped child may have to enforce the provision of appropriate educational services or compensatory education for past discrimination.

* * *

7. The parties herein agree that T.C.A. 49-1708 means only that parents of a child have a compulsory duty while the child is between seven and sixteen years of age, inclusive, to assure his or her attendance in a program of education; and that T.C.A. 49-1708 does not limit the ages between which a handicapped child must be granted access to a free program of education. Furthermore, if a parent does not discharge the duty of compulsory attendance with regard to any handicapped child between seven and sixteen years of age, inclusive, the Defendants must and shall take those steps necessary to compel the child's attendance pursuant to the appropriate state statutes and regulations. The parties request the Court to enter a declaratory judgment to this effect, and the Defendant State Board of Education agrees to issue regulations (s) pursuant thereto. Copies of the regulations shall be filed with the Court and delivered to the attorneys for the plaintiffs on or before September 15, 1974.

The proof at the hearing showed that there are at least four hundred and twelve (412) handicapped children who are totally excluded from any education and four thousand nine hundred and eighty-five (4985) handicapped children who are enrolled in school but not receiving special education services. These figures are from a census report filed on November 10, 1975, by the defendants. A similar census taken in May of 1975 showed eight hundred and five (805) in the totally excluded category and seven thousand one hundred and sixty-eight (7168) in the partially excluded category.

The record does not show any affirmative steps on the part of the State Department of Education to withhold funds from a local education agency or provide special education services itself. Neither does the record show any affirmative steps taken through the compulsory attendance laws to require all handicapped children ages seven (7) though sixteen (16) to be in school.

Therefore, it appears that the defendants are at least technically in violation of the Court's order which incorporates the Consent Agreement. The controversy then boils down to a question of whether or not the failure to comply with the Court's order is excused by the facts and circumstances surrounding the failure.

The defendants contend that they do not have the present ability to comply fully with the Consent Agreement. It appears from the record that the number of children totally excluded has been reduced by fifty (50) percent over the last two school years without any additional appropriations from the legislature. In addition the record shows that the State Department of Education's estimate of the funds needed for the full implementation of the Consent Agreement amounts to $75,000,000.00. For the past two years the legislature has appropriated only $38,000,000.00 for special education services.

The plaintiffs contend that these figures are misleading because of the various federal funds available which could be utilized for special education purposes. The defendants waited until as late as July 1, 1975, to notify the local education agencies to formulate programs to take advantage of federal funds available under Title VI B. It appears that the Department of Education knew that it had substantial Title VI B funds available for distribution as early as May 1975. In addition there is no proof in the record of any action taken after the census of November 1975 to address the problems reflected in that report.

From all of the above and all of the testimony in the record, it is the opinion of the Court that the defendants have not shown their inability to comply with the Consent Agreement. The burden of showing that is on them. *Gossett* v. *Gossett,* 34 Tenn. App. 654, 241 S.W.2d 934 (1951). The lack of coordination of programs and the delays in getting available funds into the hands of the local education agencies are found by the Court to be at least partially responsible for the lack of services extended to handicapped children. Lack of appropriations from the legislature are also a factor and are not being ignored by the Court. Regrettably, Chapter 839 of the Public Acts of 1972 is another example of a good program passed by the General Assembly without the funds to implement it. However, the Court is not convinced that lack of funds is the sole excuse for the failure to live up to the Consent Agreement. The spirit of the agreement requires the defendants to use the utmost in good faith in dealing with the problem to which the agreement is addressed. Therefore, the contempt found by the Court above, while not wilful or deliberate and while partially unavoidable, is not excusable.

The plaintiffs also urge the Court to find that the present denial of an education to some of Tennessee's handicapped children is also a denial of equal protection under the Fourteenth Amendment to the United States Constitution. The Court is of the opinion that the failure to provide an equal educational opportunity for handicapped children is a denial of equal protection and violates the section cited above. The passage of Chapter 839 of the Public Acts of 1972 is an attempt, apparently, to meet the requirements of the Constitution to provide such educational opportunities. However, the bare passage of the act without compliance by the appropriate agencies of the State, or without the funds provided by the legislature leaves handicapped children where they started.

From all of the above, the Court is of the opinion that a decree should be entered which incorporates the findings of the Court as outlined above and which includes the following provisions:

1. That the defendants report to the Court and the attorneys for the plaintiffs, within forty-five (45) days of the order to be entered in this cause, the name, age and handicap of all totally or partially excluded handicapped children within the State of Tennessee. The report should reflect the local educational agency having jurisdiction over the children and also reflect the reasons for such total partial exclusion. The report should further reflect the steps being taken to implement the Consent Agreement of July 1974. The report shall be supplemented and brought up to date on May 1, 1976. By July 1, 1976, the defendants shall provide to the Court and the plaintiffs a plan for the implementation of the Consent Agreement for the 1976–77 school year.

2. The defendants will be required to enforce the compulsory attendance requirements of this State.

The Court recognizes that the lack of funds is a serious problem confronting the defendants. However, where a shortage of funds is present the whole program must suffer without discrimination as to members of a minority class. While the Court is not ordering any re-allocation of funds and indeed does not pass on its power to do so, it is the opinion of the Court that the defendants have the power to apportion funds to meet the requirements of the Consent Agreement.

NOTES

1. The defendant school officials in *Rainey* were subsequently held in contempt of court for failure to comply with the court's order, Memorandum of January 28, 1977. The court held that defenses of lack of funds, sovereign immunity, and separation of powers did not prevent it from fashioning meaningful relief, and it enjoined the defendants from spending any public monies after July 1, 1977, for the operation of a school system unless all handicapped children were provided special education services, observing:

> This decision does not require the defendants to seek appropriations or raise additional monies to fund the program passed by the legislature in 1972. It does say to the

defendants that if the state intends to have a free public school system, it cannot discriminate against a small and politically powerless minority. Adjustments must be made in the program to fulfill the requirements of the law. Our Constitution and the Federal Constitution do not allow individuals or other branches of the government to ignore the law and discriminate against a helpless minority (See 10 Clearinghouse Review 972 (1977)).

On appeal, the Tennessee Court of Appeals agreed with the trial court's ruling that handicapped children were denied equal protection by exclusion from the public schools and its finding that the defendants were in contempt of court, No. 32435 (Tenn.Ct.App., Dec. 2, 1977); see 11 Clearinghouse Review 870, 938-939 (1978). The appellate court found, however, that the lower court's broad injunctive order created a hazard greater than the injury sought to be relieved and, therefore, reversed the trial courts relief order. *Ibid.*

2.   The *Rainey* decisions are part of a series of attempts by Tennessee advocates to persuade the public school officials to meet their statutory responsibilities. In an earlier action, *Rainey* v. *Watkins,* No. 77620-2 (Chancery Ct. Shelby Cty., Tenn., Apr. 6, 1973), a Writ of Mandamus was obtained which forced the Memphis City Board of Education to perform a census of handicapped children as required by law. Such proceedings bear witness to the fact that the mere enactment of legislation is not a cure-all; without vigorous enforcement, statutory rights may be merely empty promises.

3.   Following the cue of the Tennessee statute, many states have mandated full provision of special education services upon an incremental basis, so that educational programs for all handicapped individuals must be provided by a specified date in the future. The *Rainey* case exemplifies the sad situation in which, as the deadline date rolls around, it becomes clear that the public education system is *not* going to have programs for everyone and that some handicapped pupils will continue to be excluded beyond the date set for "zero-reject education."

Future implementation dates are based upon a consideration that it will take schools a certain amount of lead time to "gear up" to providing education for all. Teachers must be hired and trained, classrooms and equipment must be obtained, and other administrative details must be worked out. But, if the right to equal educational opportunity is of constitutional dimensions, how much delay can be allowed? The *PARC* decree allowed 11 months before full services were required. Would it, however, be unreasonable for a state to delay for 2 years or for 3 years? How about 5 years? By 1999? When does the amount of delay become unreasonable? How does the time consumed in proceeding through administrative channels balance against the harm (perhaps irreparable) suffered by the individual student because he or she is not in school? Can compensatory educational programs, designed to make up for the time a person was excluded, help to solve these problems?

4.   In 1971, the Council for Exceptional Children published "A Model Law for the Education of Seven Million Handicapped Children" (Weintraub, F., Abeson, A., and Braddock, D., *State Law and Education of Handicapped Children: Issues and Recommendations,* 1971, pp. 110-142). The Tennessee legislature enacted large chunks of the CEC "model" in 1972, resulting in the statute discussed in *Rainey.* As of May,

1977, 49 states had enacted some type of mandatory special education legislation (see Note, "Special Education: The Struggle for Equal Educational Opportunity in Iowa," 62 *Id. L. Rev.* 1285, 1367 (1977)). Unfortunately, as in *Rainey,* the adoption of such legislation has proved to be easier than enforcement.

ADDITIONAL READING

Trudeau, E. (ed.), *Digest of State and Federal Laws: Education of Handicapped Children,* Council for Exceptional Children (1972).

Weintraub, F., "Court Action and Legislation," 2 *Leadership Series in Special Education* 211, University of Minnesota (R. Johnson, J. Gross, and R. Weatherman, eds., 1973).

MARYLAND ASSOCIATION FOR RETARDED CHILDREN v. STATE OF MARYLAND

Circuit Court, Baltimore County, Maryland, 1974
Equity No. 100/182/77676, May 31, 1974

RAINE, J.

AMENDED DECREE

This Court heretofore passed a Decree on the 9th day of April, 1974. That Decree is hereby rescinded, the same not being enrolled, and the following is published as the final Decree herein.

This Court has taken extensive testimony, heard arguments by counsel, made findings of fact attached hereto, and has filed an EXPLANATORY MEMORANDUM OF DECISION attached hereto. Now, this 3rd day of May, 1974, the Court hereby ORDERS and DECREES:

1. The Court declares that it is the established policy of the State of Maryland to provide a free education to all persons between the ages of five and twenty years, and this includes children with handicaps, and particularly mentally retarded children, regardless of how severely and profoundly retarded they may be. This policy is established by Sec. 73 and Sec. 99 and Sec. 106D of Article 77 of the Annotated Code of Maryland, and by Article 59A.

2. Sec. 73 and Sec. 99 of Article 77 obligates local boards of education to provide or arrange for appropriate educational facilities and services for each mentally retarded child between the ages of five and twenty years who reside in the political sub-division of the local board.

3. Under the provisions of Article 77 referred to above the local board of education must initially determine that the educational program provided or arranged for a child is, in fact, an educational program, and that it is in fact an appropriate program for the child. When the child is placed in an educational program in a state institution it becomes the responsibility of the State to insure that the child is provided an appropriate educational program during the time the child is institutionalized. The right of the State to require the local sub-division to share the cost of such educational programs is not being adjudicated herein.

4. The following *may* constitute "appropriate provision" for a child's education for purposes of Section 92(a) of Article 77 and "appropriate educational facilities

and services" for purposes of Section 99 of Article 77, but *only* if the placement meets requirements stated herein: placement in a non-public day facility, a public or private residential facility, and home and hospital instruction.

5.   The obligations referred to above cannot be discharged by referral of a child to another governmental authority or to a non-public school or facility if no opening in programs provided by such other agency or school or facility are available for the child, and as a consequence the child cannot be enrolled but instead must wait on a waiting list for an opening.

6.   Provisions for a child's education in a facility not accredited by the Maryland State Department of Education may be appropriate if local educational authorities examine the program at the facility in sufficient detail to be able to determine that the program is in fact educational and appropriate for the child referred to the program. However, if the facility to which the child is referred is in fact educational the facility is subject to the accreditation requirements of Secs. 12 and 28 of Article 77. Therefore the Court ORDERS that appropriate standards must be promulgated by the State Department of Education, acting alone or in conjunction with the Mental Retardation Administration, for the accreditation of all educational facilities, including day-care centers and residential treatment facilities, except those church related facilities specifically exempted by Sec. 12 of Article 77. All educational programs conducted by, or subject to licensing by, the Mental Retardation Administration shall be subject to the aforesaid standards. The standards must be promulgated by September 1, 1974 and compliance with the standards must be effected by September 1, 1975.

7.   Home and hospital instruction is not an appropriate long-term educational arrangement for any child. As indicated by the bylaws of the State Board of Education, home and hospital instruction is an appropriate arrangement for the education of children who are unable, due to *physical* conditions, to attend school regularly, in cases in which a medical specialist certifies that the child should not attend school because of his physical condition. Mental retardation, however profound, is not a "physical" condition justifying referral to home and hospital instruction in lieu of instruction in school.

8.   Mental retardation, *per se,* should not be the sole reason for concluding that home and hospital instruction, or residential placement, or placement in a non-residential facility, is "appropriate" for the education of a child. The conclusion that such arrangements are appropriate must be based upon all relevant considerations.

9.   Under Article VIII of the Maryland Constitution, and under the provisions of Sections 40, 73, 92(a) and 99 of Article 77, each child in Maryland is entitled to education at no expense to the child or his parents or guardians. When the public schools provide or arrange for the education of a child outside the public schools, the program must be made available free of charge to the child and his parents or guardians. The practice of sending children to non-public schools without full funding when the public schools are unable to provide the child with a program is unlawful. When public schools provide or arrange for the education of a child in a state institution or elsewhere outside the public school system the educational program must be made available without charge to the child and his parents or guardians. The state has an obligation under Article 59A and Article 23 of the Declaration of Rights to fund

institutional educational programs that insure appropriate education, so that there is no discrimination against children in the institutions.

10. Since all appropriate educational facilities, including such non-public educational facilities as day-care centers, will be approved by the State Department of Education pursuant to Paragraph 6 of this decree it will be the obligation of the local boards of education to provide daily transportation for handicapped children to and from the appropriate facility that the boards of education have provided and arranged for, such transportation being required by Sec. 99 of Article 77. This statute only contemplates daily transportation. However, if weekend transportation is furnished by a local board to children at the Maryland School for the Blind or Maryland School for the Deaf there can be no discrimination and comparable transportation must be furnished to those children at the Rosewood State Hospital, Great Oaks and any other facility of the Mental Retardation Administration.

11. The Mental Retardation Administration is ordered to investigate and report to this Court on the extent of and appropriateness of any educational program available to Children at the Mason Lord Building of Baltimore City Hospitals.

12. There is no evidence that would justify or require the grant of any injunctive relief against the local school boards of Baltimore City, Baltimore County, Montgomery County or Prince George's County.

13. Officials of the State of Maryland have made to this Court a formal commitment of record to comply with the terms of this decree by the school year beginning in September 1975. Therefore, no specific relief with respect to funding is now ordered herein because of the Court's recognition of practical budgetary considerations. This Court retains jurisdiction over all parties to the end that any appropriate or necessary orders may be issued leading to the fulfillment of the obligations stated in this decree in the school year beginning in September 1975/76.

Memorandum

This class action began in the United States District Court, the Plaintiffs claiming violation of their rights under the United States Constitution. The Federal Court abstained until such time as a factual context could be established by the State courts, and a definitive interpretation of the Maryland Constitution and laws was made by the Court of Appeals. The pleadings here raise no federal constitutional questions, specifically reserving them for future determination in the federal courts, so this court expresses no opinion thereon. No useful purpose would be served by detailed recitation of the specific contents of the pleadings. This is a class action on behalf of all retarded children to require the state to provide a free public education for all. Their chief complaint is the failure to provide programs within the public school system for those children whose mental retardation is severe and profound. The Complainants also contend that educational programs outside the public school system are grossly inadequate. All parties to the litigation agree that all children can be benefited by some type or program of service, no matter how seriously or extensively they are retarded. This proposition is supported by eminently qualified experts who testified in this court, and it has been accepted in other cases. See *Pennsylvania Association for Retarded*

Children v. *Pennsylvania,* 334 F.Supp. 1257. The argument is over the question as to the nature of the service to be provided to the handicapped; who should bear the responsibility, and how far does that responsibility extend. The obligation of society to attempt to train or educate those unfortunate children, who are so severely and profoundly handicapped that their potential is limited to a minimal degree of self-care, involves moral and ethical considerations with which this court is not required to cope. The role of the court is to define and enforce legal rights and responsibilities.

Art. 43 of the Declaration of Rights states that the Legislature ought to "encourage the diffusion of knowledge and virtue, the extension of a judicious system of general education. . . ." In addition to this nebulous admonition Article VIII, Sec. 1 of the Constitution of Maryland provides:

> The General Assembly, at its First Session after the adoption of this Constitution, shall by law establish throughout the State a thorough and efficient System of Free Public Schools; and shall provide by taxation, or otherwise, for their maintenance.

In compliance with that constitutional mandate the General Assembly has enacted Article 77 that does provide for a Public School System. The hortatory words "thorough and efficient" contained in Article VIII of the Constitution are general and relative terms. There is nothing in the reports of the debates in the Constitutional Convention of 1867, as published by the late Philip Perlman, that suggests these words had any definite and specific meaning (the court notes that the identical words are also found in the Pennsylvania Constitution). The idea that free public education is one of the normal functions of government was not reflected in any Constitution in Maryland prior to 1864, *Niles, Maryland Constitutional Law.* No one contends that the school system is perfect and 100 percent "thorough and efficient," particularly in the area of serving all mentally retarded youth, but Article 77 sets forth a comprehensive statutory scheme or plan that is designed to create a thorough and efficient system of free education. In Maryland there have been great strides in recent years to serve the educational needs of the handicapped; new facilities have been opened, a data processing system has been initiated, more money has been spent, and more of the handicapped have been served. In 1965 the State assisted approximately three thousand children at a cost of $1,000,000. By 1973 approximately seventy-seven thousand were provided some service at a cost to the State of approximately $33,000,000. (These figures relate to the entire class of handicapped children and are not limited to the mentally retarded.) Nevertheless, with the exception of a very limited number of pilot projects, no school system has an appropriate program in the public schools for the most severely and profoundly retarded children. The main thrust of the Bill of Complaint is that this deficiency prevents the public school system from being "thorough and efficient." The Court rejects such a narrow construction, and holds that there is no violation of Article VIII of the Maryland Constitution. The question is whether the statutory enactments are being properly complied with so as to achieve the legislative goals; in other words, if the Plaintiffs are to gain any relief they will do so, not because of any violation of Article VIII, but on the grounds that the action of the Defendants contravened the statutes relating to education.

Section 40 of Article 77 directs the local boards of education to maintain a public school system "designed to provide quality education, and equal education opportunity for all youth." This would include the more than twenty-five thousand children in Maryland who suffer in some degree from mental retardation. However, it is clear that there are some children who are so far down on the broad scale of mental retardation that they cannot be benefited in the traditional and customary public school setting. This fact is recognized by the provisions of Sec. 92 of Article 77. The main thrust of this section is compulsory school attendance for all children between six and sixteen, but it does recognize that there are children so severely retarded they cannot be instructed in the public school. The local boards of education are required in such a case to "make some other appropriate provision for the child's education." Sec. 99 of Article 77 deals specifically with handicapped children, and requires the local boards to "provide or arrange for appropriate educational facilities and services." Before proceeding further it is essential that this Court adopt reasonably clear and workable definitions of words referred to in the laws. Much time has been spent in a semantic thicket. In a per curiam memorandum the United States District Court suggested that the State Court define the term "education." The definition that this Court accepts is that education is any plan or structured program administered by competent persons that is designed to help individuals achieve their full potential. The Court is aware that this definition is extremely broad, but it is a definition agreed to by Dr. Robert E. Cooke, former Director of the Kennedy Institute, and an outstanding authority in the field of mental retardation, and by Mr. Stanley Mopsik, the coordinator of Special Education of the Maryland State Department of Education. There is no distinction between the words training and education. A child may be trained to read and write, or may be educated to read and write. A child may be educated to tie his shoes or trained to tie his shoes. Every type of training is at least a sub-category of education. Care must be used in connection with the words "educable" and "trainable." They are special words used to characterize children formerly referred to as "morons" or "imbeciles." Educators refer to children with an intelligent quotient from approximately 50 to 70 as being educable, and from approximately 35 to 50 as being trainable. Those children below 35 are characterized as being severely or profoundly retarded, and it is with those children that this case is principally concerned.

At various stages of history mentally retarded children have been isolated or segregated from the general population. They have been subjected to discrimination. The General Assembly of Maryland has by recent legislation committed the State to the goal of providing beneficial services to all of the mentally retarded. In 1972, Art. 59A was enacted and it created the Mental Retardation Administration that is charged with the overall responsibility for the programs for the mentally retarded. Primary responsibility for education rests on the local boards of education, but where the retardation is so severe that there is no program available in the public school system the responsibility devolves on the Mental Retardation Administration to provide a program that will develop the ability and potential of all mentally retarded to the fullest possible extent. Since such a program must be educational in nature it should meet standards set by the State Department of Education. The chief reason why the State's responsibility to the mentally retarded had not been properly discharged is inadequate funding. No public goal, however lofty and however clearly set forth by the General Assembly, can be reached unless the State, particularly the executive budget authorities, provides adequate funding. The main thrust of the decree will be to place joint responsibility on the Mental Retardation Administration and the State Department of Education for the education of the mentally retarded, and to declare that the State of Maryland has the obligation to provide the necessary funding.

Further recognition of the State's responsibility to handicapped children is found in Ch. 359 of the Laws of 1973, now codified as Secs. 106D and 106E of Art. 77. This provides for the adoption and implementation of appropriate plans for the special education of the handicapped. The law calls for the adoption of State standards by July 1974, and the adoption of suitable local plans nine months thereafter. Implementation of the local plans would begin with the 1975 school year and would be fully implemented five years thereafter. The Complainants here object to the delay and offered evidence that suitable plans could be implemented in a shorter period of time. Perhaps this could be done on a "crash program" basis, but this Court believes the time schedule of Sec. 106D is more realistic. This Court does not believe that any decree it might pass would accelerate the institution of new and appropriate programs for the education of the mentally retarded as contemplated by Sec. 106D of Article 77, so no action will be taken in that regard.

NOTES

1.   At first blush, the court's order that the defendant school officials must comply with their obligations under the decree "by the school year beginning in September, 1975" appears to be inconsistent with the observation of the court that: "The law calls for the adoption of State standards by July, 1974, and the adoption of suitable local plans nine months thereafter. Implementation of the local plans would begin with the 1975 school year and would be fully implemented five years thereafter." Are Maryland officials required to provide education for all handicapped persons in 1975 or in 1980? The answer to this apparent contradiction is that 1980 is the deadline for implementation of a full range of special educational programming and services, while 1975 was the date specified for implementation of programs to serve all children of compulsory school age. Thus, although preschool classes, compensatory programs, and additional specialized programming for those already in school may be phased in over the 5-year period ending in 1980, no school-age child could be excluded from the public school system after September of 1975.

2.   The court's definition of "education"—"any plan or structured program administered by competent persons that is designed to help individuals achieve their full potential"—is one of the first such judicial definitions in the context of special education programs for handicapped people. Judge Raine's formulation makes it clear that education is concerned with much more than simply the "three Rs"; the definition would include instruction to teach one to dress oneself, toilet training, eating skills, and other self-help skills. This expansive definition is consonant with the proliferation of

types of courses in education generally; to the basic three-R curriculum have been added courses as diverse as driver training, home economics, woodworking, gym classes, chemistry labs, dance classes, and so on.

3. The court's holding that there is no distinction between "education" and "training" helps to silence an often heard argument that, while all children are entitled to equal educational opportunities, low functioning handicapped persons need training, not education, and such "training" is not within the scope of the public education system. Therefore, it is said, it is legitimate for the public schools to exclude those who are not able to benefit from "education." Actually, the distinction between "education" and "training" occurred because at one period in history educators had developed educational strategies for some handicapped children, but had not yet learned how to teach lower functioning individuals (see pp. 56–57, above). Judge Raine's decision helps to make it clear that such outmoded distinctions should not continue to be used today when there are educational programs for all levels of functioning. And yet the opinion seems to accept the use of the obsolete labels "educable" and "trainable" to describe levels of mental retardation.

4. Although the court expressly noted that it was not concerned with federal claims, it found that "[a]t various stages of history mentally retarded children have been isolated or segregated from the general population. They have been subjected to discrimination." This might have been very useful in establishing the existence of a "suspect classification" under the equal protection clause, if the plaintiffs had occasion to return to the federal court.

ENFORCEMENT PROBLEMS IN NEW YORK

The task of enforcing special education statutes has been especially problematic in the State of New York. Some of these problems revolve around the extremely large population, the concentration of immigrants, and other unique characteristics of New York City. Other difficulties, however, result from the unwieldy nature of the New York special education laws, which, among other things, require a court proceeding in any instance where parents seek reimbursement for private school expenses, even where there is admittedly no appropriate public school program. The court in *In re Leitner,* 40 A.D.2d 39, 337 N.Y.S.2d 267 (1972) observed that the New York statutory framework is "at best, cumbersome, and at worst, unclear and unnecessarily complex." In *In re Borland,* 72 Misc.2d 766, 340 N.Y.S.2d 745, 747 (1973), the judge noted that these statutes "are unclear and appear to create inconsistencies." And the court in *In re Daber,* 71 Misc.2d 303, 335 N.Y.S.2d 947, 948 (1972); was even more vehement: "In passing, it may be noted that the present statutory law is a mumbo-jumbo, unconsolidated and inartistically promulgated. Revision would be extremely appropriate so as to clarify the ambiguity found in the laws as they exist today."

Such ambiguity is perhaps a reason why many New York courts have been prone to resort to constitutional analysis in such circumstances (e.g., *In re H., In re Downey,* and *In re K.,* discussed above), that is, to use constitutional interpretation to provide direction in their attempts to proceed through the statutory maze.

In the early 1970s, a group of individual plaintiffs and the New York Association for Brain Injured Children attempted to remedy some of the inequities of the New York special education system by filing an action in the United States District Court for the Southern District of New York seeking equal educational opportunities for brain-injured children. The district court dismissed the action on the grounds of abstention. On appeal, the Court of Appeals for the Second Circuit held that the district court properly abstained from deciding claims based on the United States Constitution pending a determination by New York State authorities as to related but unanswered questions of New York State law, but should have retained jurisdiction pending such a determination, *Reid* v. *Board of Educ. of City of N.Y.* 453 F.2d 238 (2d Cir. 1971).

Upon refiling in the state system, the *Reid* case culminated in a favorable decision by the Commissioner of Education for the State of New York, *In re Reid,* No. 8742 (Commissioner of Education of New York, Nov. 26, 1973). The Commissioner found the following deficiencies in the special education system in New York City:

1. Undue delays in examinations and diagnostic procedures.
2. Failures to examine and diagnose handicaps.
3. Failures to place handicapped children in suitable programs.
4. Failures to provide available space and facilities for programs.
5. Children placed on home instruction in violation of the purpose of home instruction.
6. Children placed on home instruction who did not receive the required hours of personal instruction in accordance with the regulations of the Commissioner of Education.
7. Handicapped children expelled from public school education for medical reasons when such medical reasons did not preclude benefits from educational settings.
8. Incomplete or conflicting census data on the number of handicapped children residing in New York City.
9. Inadequate means of informing parents of the processes related to special education services, and inadequate plans for parent involvement in effective planning and decision-making regarding their children.
10. Suspensions of handicapped children from classes without adequate notice or provisions for alternate educational services (at p. 120).

He also found that the school system had established a "Medical Discharge Register" listing children who had been illegally suspended and were not receiving educational services. This Register operated essentially as a waiting list for educational placement that might or might not eventually occur. The Commissioner ultimately struck down the Medical Discharge Register and issued a series of orders mandating correction of the other listed deficiencies in provision of educational services to handicapped pupils. (For additional discussion of enforcement problems in New York in general and the *Reid* order in particular, see *Lora* v. *Board of Education City of New York,* 456 F.Supp. 1211, 1216-1224, 1230-1264 (E.D.N.Y. 1978).

NOTE

California's special education laws share New York's problems of complexity and ambiguity (see California Education Code, Sections 6750 to 6948; Kirp, D., Kuriloff, P., and Buss, W., "Legal Mandates and Organizational Change," Chapter 26 of 2 *Issues in the Classification of Children* 362-79 (Hobbs, N., ed., 1975).

2. Enforcement of State Law by Federal Courts

Colorado Association for Retarded Children v. State of Colorado

United States District Court for the District of Colorado, 1974
C.A. No. C-4620 (Jun. 14, 1974)

Before McWilliams, Circuit Judge; Arraj, District Judge, and Finesilver, District Judge.

Finesilver, Judge.

Plaintiffs are 18 handicapped children who range in age between 6 to 18 years. They bring this suit in behalf of themselves and all other residents of the State of Colorado who have been excluded or are threatened with exclusion from public school on the basis of a physical, educational, mental, or perceptual handicap. Pursuant to 42 U.S.C. § 1983, they allege violation of their due process and equal protection rights. They seek access to free public education and the establishment of procedural safeguards. We are proceeding on defendants' Motions to Dismiss the amended complaint.

In support of the Motion to Dismiss, the defendants assert that this suit has been rendered moot by the recent passage of the Colorado "Handicapped Children's Educational Act." C.R.S. 123-22-1 *et seq.* That act requires the school districts of the state to provide a free education for all children by July 1, 1975. Plaintiffs contend that viable issues are present and mootness is not applicable. They argue that the State legislation has not been implemented.

The pivotal question is whether plaintiffs have been afforded adequate and effective relief by the enactment of the new legislation and no viable issue remains for resolution.

In resolving this critical issue, we have considered the legislative history which provides the factual backdrop for this case. As early as 1953, the Colorado Legislature expressed its intent to supply all of the handicapped children in the state with public education. In the Education of Handicapped Children's Bill of that year, the legislature declared its purpose to "provide means for educating those children in the State of Colorado who are . . . physically or mentally handicapped." *See* 1953 C.R.S. § 123-22-1.

In spite of this declared purpose promulgated in the early fifties, it was not until 1971 that the legislature enacted legislation requiring state school districts to adopt plans for the education of all of the handicapped. The 1971 version of C.R.S. 123-22-8 (1971 Perm.Supp.) ordered the school districts to implement their plans by July 1 of 1974, allowing a full three years for the districts to put their plans into effect.

However, the state did not adhere to this schedule. In 1972, legislation was passed which delayed the mandatory implementation date for an additional two years, until July 1, 1976 (1972 Session Laws 123-22-8).

In 1973, the implementation date was once again changed. In the legislative session, the effective date of the education of all handicapped children in the state was moved back to July 1, 1975. The 1973 statute is presently applicable, and defendants are relying upon it in their claims of mootness (1973 Session Laws 123-22-6(3)).

Nevertheless, the date when the statute will ultimately be implemented remains uncertain. As plaintiffs point out in Plaintiffs' Brief in Opposition to Defendants' Motions to Dismiss (footnote 1, page 2), David C. Miles, Director of Pupil Services

Division of the State Department of Education, has publicly stated that the deadline set in the 1973 Act is "totally impractical."

In the light of the irregular and delayed implementation of legislation in the essential area of education for handicapped children, we are of the view that this case is not moot. The mere enactment of legislation without actual implementation does not render substantial legal questions moot.

Since the new legislation has not been implemented, the legal effect of earlier statutes is still a matter for determination. Thus, a question remains whether the enactment of the 1973 Act completely divested the prior statutes of their vitality.

The United States Supreme Court encountered a similar problem in the case of *Diffenderfer* v. *Central Baptist Church*, 404 U.S. 412 (1972). The statute under constitutional attack in that case was repealed and reenacted in a new form by the Florida Legislature. The Supreme Court declined to dismiss the case, allowing the plaintiffs to "demonstrate that the repealed statute retains some continuing force." *Diffenderfer, supra,* at 415. We are persuaded by the rationale expressed in *Diffenderfer*.

In addition, defendants' motions to dismiss do not take account of plaintiffs' claims for compensatory relief for past exclusions of handicapped children from school programs. The amended complaint prays for an injunction requiring defendants to "provide for plaintiffs and members of plaintiffs' class compensatory services to overcome the effects of any past wrongful suspension or exclusion." (¶j(viii) p. 49 of Amended Complaint). Thus, plaintiffs' request relief beyond that mandated in the "Handicapped Children's Educational Act." This remains an issue in the case and further supports our holding that the litigation is not moot.

For the foregoing reasons, we hold that this case is not moot, and defendants' motions to dismiss on grounds of mootness and other grounds are denied.

The defendants have also moved to dismiss the amended complaint for failure to state a claim, a contention that was disposed of in the Court's Order of July 13, 1973, with regard to the original complaint. The motions are denied for the reasons stated in the Order of July 13, 1973.

Accordingly, it is hereby ORDERED that defendants' motions to dismiss are DENIED. It is further ORDERED that defendants who have not answered the amended complaint are directed to answer before July 1, 1974.

NOTES

1. For a discussion of an earlier order of the Court, see p. 126 n.2, above.

2. Although procedurally the Colorado decision is simply a denial of a motion to dismiss for mootness, it places the federal court in an interesting position in regard to overseeing the implementation of the new state legislation. Presumably, the federal court action could still be mooted out, except for the auxiliary issue of compensatory education, by the defendants' fully implementing the new law. The federal court, however, retains the option of judging whether or not the defendants have actually fulfilled the requirements of the statute. These circumstances give the court a potent oversight function in achieving the implementation of a state law.

FREDERICK L. v. THOMAS

United States District Court for the Eastern District of Pennsylvania, 1976
419 F.Supp. 960

[Other portions of the opinion, including Findings of Fact with much information about specific learning disabilities and educational programs for pupils with learning disabilities, are omitted.]

Conclusions of Law

1. Jurisdiction over the subject matter in this case is founded on 28 U.S.C. § 1343(3) and (4); and on 28 U.S.C. § 1331. Jurisdiction over the plaintiffs' state law claims is based on the doctrine of pendent jurisdiction.

2. The plaintiffs' federal claims raise difficult constitutional issues, among them:

a) Is minimally adequate public education a fundamental right?

b) Can a handicapped child who is offered the same educational services provided to normal children, be deemed functionally excluded from school and thereby deprived of equal educational opportunity because of his inability to benefit from normal educational services?

c) Assuming that both groups are receiving minimally adequate instruction, what differences in the services provided to normal children and to exceptional children are constitutionally impermissible?[9]

3. As a general rule, a federal court should not decide federal constitutional questions where a dispositive nonconstitutional ground is available, even though the nonconstitutional claims are pendent, and standing alone, are beyond the jurisdiction of the federal court. *Hagans* v. *Lavine*, 415 U.S. 528, 546, 94 S.Ct. 1372, 39 L.Ed.2d 577 (1974).

4. Plaintiffs are entitled to relief pursuant to Pennsylvania law, as more fully set out below.

5. Abstention is not appropriate in this case because the plaintiffs have proved a set of facts establishing liability without relying on unclear parts of the state statutory scheme.

6. The Special Education State Board Regulations (1975 Regulations) were enacted in June 1975, under the authority of 24 P.S. § 13-1372(1) and have the force of law.

---

[9]The problem here is to articulate and to apply the appropriate test under the Equal Protection Clause of the Fourteenth Amendment. If there is a middle test of equal protection, its content and applicability is unsettled. *Compare Massachusetts Board of Retirement* v. *Murgia,*—U.S.—,96 S.Ct. 2562, 49 L.Ed.2d 520 (1976) *with Reed* v. *Reed,* 404 U.S. 71, 92 S.Ct. 251, 30 L.Ed.2d 255 (1971) and *Weinberger* v. *Weisenfeld,* 420 U.S. 636, 95 S.Ct. 1225, 43 L.Ed.2d 514 (1975). In recent Supreme Court cases, advocacy of a flexible equal protection test for such groups as women, illegitimates and the elderly has been limited to dissenting opinions. *See Massachusetts Board of Retirement* v. *Murgia, supra,* at—,96 S.Ct. 2562 (Marshall, J., dissenting); *Matthews* v. *Lucas,*—U.S.—,96 S.Ct. 2755, 49 L.Ed.2d 651 (1976) (Stevens, J., dissenting). *Cf. In the Matter of Levy et al.,* No. 21 *et seq.,* 38 N.Y.2d 653, 382 N.Y.S.2d 13, 345 N.E.2d 556 (1976); *Semple* v. *Miller,* 39 A.D.2d 174, 327 N.Y.S.2d 929 (1972); *Manjores* v. *Newton,* 64 Cal.2d 365, 49 Cal. Rptr. 805, 411 P.2d 901 (1968).

7. Plaintiffs, children with learning disabilities, are exceptional children pursuant to 24 P.S. § 13-1371(1). *See also* 1975 Regulations § 13.1.

8. Plaintiffs, children with learning disabilities, are entitled to proper education and training. The concept of appropriate education is defined further in the 1975 Regulations. 24 P.S. § 13 1372(1); 1975 Regulations §§ 13.1, 13.2, 13.11.

9. The School District of Philadelphia is required to identify all learning disabled students. 24 P.S. §§ 13-1371, 13-1372. 1975 Regulations §§ 13.1, 13.6, and 13.9(B).

10. Each learning disabled child does not necessarily have to be given instruction designated special education. However, a determination that a learning disabled student can receive appropriate education without receiving special education instruction, is valid only if it is made after the child's exceptionality has been identified and evaluated. 24 P.S. §§ 13-1371, 13-1372. 1975 Regulations §§ 13.1, 13.6, and 13.9(B).

11. The District is required to prepare plans for the proper education and training of all learning disabled students. The District must provide them appropriate educational services in accordance with a plan approved by the Superintendent of Public Instruction. 24 P.S. § 13-1372.

12. As part of his duty to enforce the provisions of the special education laws, the Superintendent must monitor District services to determine whether they comply with the state-approved plan. If they do not, the Superintendent must take reasonable steps to assure compliance. 24 P.S. § 1372(2) and (3).

13. The District violated its duties to identify all learning disabled students, and to provide them with appropriate education in accordance with an approved plan. The Superintendent violated his duty to enforce the special education laws. These violations establish defendants' liability. Defendants' claim that the plaintiffs are receiving appropriate educational services is relevant to the scope of relief.

14. When educational officials deviate substantially from statutorily prescribed decision-making procedures, the soundness of their ultimate policy determinations is subject to stricter judicial scrutiny than would be applied had the policy been arrived at through correct procedures.

15. Plaintiffs are not being provided appropriate educational services.

* * *

Conclusion

The District has violated the Pennsylvania special education statutes and regulations by failing to identify all learning disabled students, and by failing to implement a state-approved plan for appropriate education of the learning disabled. The Superintendent of Public Instruction has failed to carry out his duty to enforce this statutory scheme. Significant numbers of learning disabled students in the School District of Philadelphia are not receiving appropriate instruction.

In the class action aspect of this case, plaintiffs are entitled to relief under the Pennsylvania special education statutes and regulations. Further proceedings will be held to determine an appropriate remedial order.

NOTES

1.   The district court's decision was affirmed on appeal, *Frederick L.* v. *Thomas,* 557 F.2d 373 (3d Cir. 1977). In regard to a prior proceeding in the case, see p. 126, above.

2.   The *Frederick L.* and *Colorado Association for Retarded Children* opinions engender federal court involvement in the enforcement of state legislation. What combination of circumstances and legal theories is required to produce such a result?

G.   FEDERAL LEGISLATION

1.   Content and Enforcement in General

GENERAL EDUCATION PROVISIONS ACT, AMENDMENTS OF 1974

P.L. 93,380, H.R. 69, 93rd Congress, 20 U.S.C. 1221-1 (Aug. 21, 1974)
   § 801.   National Policy with Respect to Equal Education Opportunity.

   Recognizing that the Nation's economic, political, and social security require a well-educated citizenry, the Congress (1) reaffirms, as a matter of high priority, the Nation's goal of equal educational opportunity, and (2) declares it to be the policy of the United States of America that every citizen is entitled to an education to meet his or her full potential without financial barriers.

NOTE

Does this "national policy" help to make equal educational opportunity a "fundamental" right for equal protection analysis?

REHABILITATION ACT OF 1973, § 504

P.L. 93-112, 87 Stat. 394, as amended by § 119 of P.L. 95-602, 29 U.S.C. § 794

Nondiscrimination under Federal Grants and Programs

   Sec. 504.   No otherwise qualified handicapped individual in the United States, as defined in section 7(7), shall, solely by reason of his handicap, be excluded from the participation in, be denied the benefits of, or be subjected to discrimination under any program or activity receiving Federal financial assistance or under any program or activity conducted by any Executive agency or by the United States Postal Service.

* * *

HAIRSTON v. DROSICK

United States District Court for the Southern District of West Virginia, 1976
423 F.Supp. 180

   K. K. HALL, District Judge.

   This is a civil proceeding challenging the refusal of the defendants to admit the plaintiff child, Trina Evet Hairston to the regular public classroom at Gary Grade School and her exclusion therefrom as being contrary to 29 U.S.C. § 794, a section of what is commonly known as "The Rehabilitation Act of 1973," and her exclusion without procedural safeguards as being contrary to the Fourteenth Amendment to the United States Constitution.

The plaintiffs, Larry Hairston and Sheila Hairston, on behalf of their child, Trina Evet Hairston, are seeking the right of their child, Trina Evet Hairston, to attend Gary Grade School, a regular public school. The complaint alleges that the plaintiff child has a physical condition known as spina bifida and that on account of this condition her right to attend the regular public school classroom has been infringed upon; that on or about September 1, 1975, the plaintiff Sheila Hairston received a telephone call from the teacher of the class in which the plaintiff Trina Hairston was to be enrolled indicating that the plaintiff child would not be accepted into her classroom. The complaint further alleges that upon going to the school after extensive discussion it was determined by the school authorities that the plaintiff child's right to attend public school was conditioned upon the mother's attendance at such school which was an impossibility. The plaintiffs further allege that none of them had received written notice or following such written notice an opportunity to be heard and accompanying procedural safeguards to contest the exclusion or limitations upon the attendance of plaintiff Trina Evet Hairston at Gary Grade School. The plaintiffs further allege that the Board of Education of McDowell County and the schools therein are recipients of federal funds.

The plaintiffs contend that such exclusion or placement constitutes a discrimination against the named plaintiff Trina Evet Hairston on account of her handicap in violation of Title V of the "Rehabilitation Act of 1973," 29 U.S.C. § 794, which prohibits discrimination against and denial of benefits to handicapped persons in any program or activity receiving federal financial assistance. Secondly, the plaintiffs assert that the exclusion or conditional exclusion of the plaintiff child from the regular public classroom at Gary Grade School without written notice and accompanying procedural safeguards is contrary to the mandate of due process of law afforded to them by the Fourteenth Amendment to the United States Constitution.

The defendants, John R. Drosick, Jr., the superintendent of schools of McDowell County, Elizabeth Dudas, principal of Gary Grade School, and E. N. Reid, Tony J. Romeo, Ira E. Short, James R. Vilsick, and W. H. Wagner, members of the Board of Education of McDowell County, admit that the plaintiff child Trina Evet Hairston is not permitted to attend Gary Grade School without the presence of her mother on a regular daily basis. The defendants further admit in their answer that the plaintiff child is suffering from a physical condition known as spina bifida and that there is no question that the plaintiff is mentally competent to attend regular public schools. The defendants contend that at the time the child was taken to school for placement and at later discussion between the plaintiff Larry Hairston and the defendant John R. Drosick, Jr. the child was offered three alternatives with respect to school attendance, specifically, (1) that the child could be enrolled at Gary Grade School if her mother would go to the school two or three times a day to attend to the child, (2) that the child could receive homebound instruction, or (3) that the child could attend special education class at Tidewater School for physically handicapped children; and contend that under such circumstances there is no denial of educational rights or discrimination. The defendants in their answer deny that children are being placed in special education classes without adequate notice and accompanying procedural safeguards, but do not plead any prior written notice or meaningful procedural safeguards afforded the plaintiffs or others prior to placement in special education situations and the accompanying exclusion from the regular classroom.

Findings of Fact

Upon the pleadings and upon the evidence adduced the Court makes the following findings of fact:

1. The plaintiff child Trina Evet Hairston has a condition known as spina bifida which has left said plaintiff with a minor physical impairment which includes incontinence of the bowels and a noticeable limp. The child is clearly physically able to attend school in a regular public classroom. The plaintiff child is of normal mental competence and capable of performing easily in a regular classroom situation.

2. The plaintiff child, after being excluded initially from the kindergarten classroom at the direction of the defendants, was permitted to attend Gary Grade School in the regular classroom the second half of the 1974–75 school year.

3. At the time the plaintiff child was to begin this school year, the plaintiff child was not wanted in the regular classroom and it was made clear to the plaintiff Sheila Hairston that the child was not to be permitted to attend Gary Grade School without her mother's daily intermittent presence. It was clear to the defendant superintendent and other persons involved that the presence of the plaintiff Sheila Hairston at the school was an impossibility because (1) the plaintiff Sheila Hairston has an infant child at home during part of the school day which she has to supervise, (2) the mother's continued presence at home was necessary for the family's subsistence because if she were not there to take phone orders for her husband, who makes his living by delivering loads of coal for heating homes, there would be no family income, (3) during the matters involved in attempting to get this child into school, the mother of plaintiff Sheila Hairston was terminally ill and totally incapacitated, and her continued presence at home was absolutely necessary for her mother's life, and (4) the plaintiff mother does not have a driver's license and has no feasible means of transportation to the school several times a day. The requirement of the plaintiff mother's intermittent presence at Gary Grade School as a condition of her child's being permitted to attend Gary Grade School, coupled with the impossibility of this request upon the plaintiff Sheila Hairston, constituted an exclusion of the plaintiff child from Gary Grade School. Further, even if the mother's presence were circumstantially possible, the right of a child to attend school cannot be legally conditioned upon the mother's presence at the school.

4. The plaintiff Larry Hairston met with the defendant John R. Drosick, Jr. in an attempt to secure his child's admission to Gary Grade School. Following the meeting defendant John R. Drosick, Jr. caused to be forwarded to the plaintiff a letter from his assistant outlining the alternatives open to the plaintiff Larry Hairston with respect to the plaintiff child Trina Evet Hairston including only the choice of placement at Tidewater School in a physically handicapped class or homebound instruction.

5. The plaintiffs have never received any written notice or meaningful opportunity to be heard with accompanying procedural safeguards with respect to this child's exclusion from Gary Grade School.

6.   The plaintiff child was never given an examination by a medical specialist by or on behalf of the school authorities during the current school year, which examination is required by state law to serve as a basis for placement in a special education class. The most recent medical examination was performed by a specialist at the request of the parents midway in the previous school year which examination resulted in a recommendation that the plaintiff child should be permitted to attend public school.

7.   In attempt to secure the admission of plaintiff child to Gary Grade School counsel for the plaintiffs communicated with defendant Superintendent of Schools by telephone requesting admission of the child on October 9, 1975 and said defendant refused admission to the child. The defendant John R. Drosick, Jr. was aware that a child cannot be excluded from school without procedural safeguards.

8.   There are a great number of other spina bifida children throughout the State of West Virginia who are attending public schools in the regular classroom situation, the great majority of which have more severe disabilities than the plaintiff child Trina Evet Hairston including children having body braces, shunts, Cunningham clips and ostomies, and requiring the use of walkers and confinement to wheel chairs. The needless exclusion of these children and other children who are able to function adequately from the regular classroom situation would be a great disservice to these children. A child's chance in this society is through the educational process. A major goal of the educational process is the socialization process that takes place in the regular classroom, with the resulting capability to interact in a social way with one's peers. It is therefore imperative that every child receive an education with his or her peers insofar as it is at all possible. This conclusion is further enforced by the critical importance of education in this society.

9.   It is an educational fact that the maximum benefits to a child are received by placement in as normal environment as possible. The expert testimony established that placement of children in abnormal environments outside of peer situations imposes additional psychological and emotional handicaps upon children which, added to their existing handicaps, causes them greater difficulties in future life. A child has to learn to interact in a social way with his peers and the denial of this opportunity during his minor years imposes added lifetime burdens upon a handicapped individual.

10.   This educational fact that handicapped children should be excluded from the regular classroom situation only as a last resort is recognized in federal law. The federal statute providing moneys to states for special education programs mandates that every state have procedures to assure handicapped children are educated with children who are not handicapped and that "removal of handicapped children from the regular environment occurs only when the nature or severity of the handicap is such that education in regular classes with the use of supplementary aids and services cannot be achieved satisfactorily." 20 U.S.C. § 1413(a)(13)(B).

11.   The West Virginia Department of Education has promulgated regulations pursuant to state statute dealing with special education classes, the most recent edition of which are effective July 1, 1974. Among other things, these regulations provide that the age range between the youngest and oldest child in any class of physically hand-

icapped children not exceed four years. These regulations further provide that any classroom provided for physically handicapped children have at a minimum fifteen hundred square feet of floor space.

12.   The classroom at Tidewater School for placement of physically handicapped children contains children with an age difference ranging from the youngest at ten years old to the oldest at seventeen years old, an age range of seven years. Said classroom has a square footage size in gross violation of state regulation. Only two of the children presently in the classroom are ambulatory, and one of these two is legally blind. The placement of the six-year-old plaintiff child in this classroom would be in gross violation of state regulation. Moreover, such placement of the plaintiff child, who except for minor physical handicaps is a normally functioning six-year-old child, in a classroom with no child even close to her age and only two children having ambulation would work a distinct disservice to the individual needs of this child.

13.   The West Virginia Department of Education has promulgated regulations pursuant to the mandate of federal law as contained in 20 U.S.C. § 1413(a)(13) requiring that procedures be provided for insuring that handicapped children and their parents are guaranteed procedural safeguards with regard to decisions involving identification, evaluation, and educational placement of handicapped children including prior notice, opportunity to be heard, and accompanying due process procedural safeguards.

14.   The Board of Education of McDowell County, West Virginia and the schools therein are recipients of federal funds.

Conclusions of Law

The Court, after careful review of the facts and applicable law, concludes that:

1.   The exclusion of a minimally handicapped child from a regular public classroom situation without a bona fide educational reason is in violation of Title V of Public Law 93-112, "The Rehabilitation Act of 1973," 29 U.S.C. § 794. The federal statute proscribes discrimination against handicapped individuals in any program receiving federal financial assistance. To deny to a handicapped child access to a regular public school classroom in receipt of federal financial assistance without compelling educational justification constitutes discrimination and a denial of the benefits of such program in violation of the statute. School officials must make every effort to include such children within the regular public classroom situation, even at great expense to the school system.

2.   The exclusion of a child from the regular public classroom situation and placement in special education situation or otherwise without prior written notice and accompanying procedural safeguards including opportunity to be heard is contrary to the due process clause of the Fourteenth Amendment to the United States Constitution. The mandate of due process of law is satisfied by the procedural safeguards set out in West Virginia regulations, which provide:

(a) Written notice, describing in detail the proposed or requested action and a reason why such action is deemed appropriate or inappropriate for the child; specifying any tests or reports upon which the proposed or requested action is based; stating that the school files, records and other reports pertaining to the child will be available for inspection and copying at reasonable costs; giving the reasons why alternative placements are not appropriate for the child when the proposed or requested action involves placement or denial of placement; indicating the opportunity to obtain an independent evaluation of the child and including the names and addresses and telephone numbers of appropriate agencies where such services can be obtained; encouraging the parent to contact the county director of special education for a conference to discuss the matter; indicating the right to obtain a hearing if there are any objections to the proposed or requested action; listing those agencies in the community from which legal counsel may be obtained for those unable to pay for counsel; stating that the child will remain in the present educational placement until such time as there is a decision following a hearing or until a proposed educational placement is accepted by the parties.

(b) Providing for a hearing in the event that the conference with the parents does not result in an agreement as to the placement of the children including: a fifteen day written notice; assurances that the child will remain in the present educational placement until a decision is entered following the hearing; granting the parents the opportunity to obtain evaluation of the child's educational needs and giving the parents access to school reports, files and records pertaining to the child for inspection and copying at reasonable cost; the right to request the attendance at the hearing of any employee or agent of the county educational agency who might have testimony or evidence relative to the needs, abilities, or status of the child; the scheduling of the hearing within five days of the request and that the county board of education supply to the parents written notice of the time and place within at least fifteen days prior to the hearing; a verbatim record or tape recording of the proceedings to be provided by the county.

(c) That the hearing be presided over by an impartial hearing officer; that the parties have an opportunity to present their evidence and testimony; that the hearing shall be closed to the public unless the parents request an open hearing; that the parents and other persons have an opportunity to confront and question all witnesses at the hearing; that the child have the right to determine whether or not the child will attend the hearing; that the burden of proof as to the appropriateness of any proposed placement be upon the school personnel recommending the placement; that a decision be issued within thirty days of the decision in writing and forwarded by certified mail to the parents; that the decision include findings of fact, conclusions and reasons for these findings and conclusions; that such decision be based solely upon the evidence and testimony presented at the hearing; and that the parents be afforded a mechanism for administrative appeal.

Order

In conformity with the foregoing findings of fact and conclusions of law, it is hereby ORDERED that, during the pendency of this action, the defendants admit the plaintiff child to the public classroom at Gary Grade School immediately and that any attempt to exclude the child be based upon a legally justifiable reason and be conducted in a manner in accord with the mandates of due process of law, consistent with the conclusions in this ORDER. It is further ORDERED that any exclusion of the plaintiff child be reviewed by this Court prior to any such action.

The defendants hereby object to all the substance and content of the provisions of this order and approve this order as to form only.

NOTES

1.   The decision in *Hairston* v. *Drosick* was a major development in the *PARC, Mills* and *In re G. H.* line of cases. Just as the two-pronged, equal protection and due process attack initiated in *PARC* became the pattern in the progeny of *PARC,* the Rehabilitation Act and due process claims in *Hairston* became the model for subsequent cases. The *Hairston* approach avoids the complications of "fundamental rights" and "suspect class" arguments necessary in equal protection analysis.

2.   From the standpoint of legal theory, one of the most important facets of *Hairston* was the implicit holding that 29 U.S.C. § 794 (§ 504 of the Rehabilitation Act) may be enforced by an individual plaintiff in a federal court action. This ruling that § 504 creates a private cause of action has subsequently been adopted by numerous courts, e.g., *Davis* v. *Southeastern Community College,* 574 F.2d 1158 (4th Cir. 1978); *Kampmeier* v. *Nyquist,* 553 F.2d 296 (2d Cir. 1977); *Leary* v. *Crapsey,* 566 F.2d 863 (2d Cir. 1977); *Lloyd* v. *Regional Transit Authority,* 548 F.2d 1277 (7th Cir. 1977); *United Handicapped Federation* v. *Andre,* 558 F.2d 413 (8th Cir. 1977), but *Hairston* was one of the first decisions to so hold.

At the time the Rehabilitation Act of 1973 was being considered on the floor of the United States House of Representatives, Representative Vanik (D. Ohio) testified as follows:

> In December of 1971 I introduced a bill that incorporated the handicapped into the Civil Rights Act of 1964. Regardless of the fact that 60 Members of the House and 20 Members of the Senate cosponsored the civil rights bill, it was not reported to the floor by either Judiciary Committee.
>
> Senator Humphrey, who introduced my bill in the Senate, incorporated the language and intent of my bill into the Vocational Rehabilitation Act last year in the Senate.
>
> I am happy to say that my language remains in title 7, section 704 and section 705 of today's bill. 119 Congressional Record, 7114 (Mar. 8, 1973).

Drawing upon this legislative origin, arguments that § 504 creates a private cause of action have drawn analogies to the closely similar language of § 601 of the Civil Rights Act of 1964, and have relied upon the Supreme Court's implicit ruling in *Lau* v. *Nichols,* 414 U.S. 563, 566)1974), that § 601 creates a private cause of action, and upon the rulings of several lower federal courts that the Civil Rights Act of 1964 creates standing for injured parties to bring suit to enjoin discriminatory treatment. See *Lemon* v. *Bossier Parish School Bd.,* 240 F.Supp. 709 (D.C.La. 1965), motions denied 240 F.Supp. 743, affirmed 370 F.2d 847 (5th Cir. 1967), certiorari denied 388 U.S. 911; *Alvarado* v. *El Paso Independent School District,* 445 F.2d 1011 (1971); *Hicks* v. *Weaver,* 302 F.Supp. 619)1969); *Marable* v. *Alabama Mental Health B.,* 297 F.Supp. 291 (1969).

Arguments for a private cause of action under § 504 received a great boost by virtue of the Supreme Court's disposition of *Kruse* v. *Campbell,* 434 U.S. 808 (1977). That case was a class action challenge to a Virginia practice whereby handicapped children of poor parents were allegedly denied state payments for private school tuition when appropriate programs were unavailable in the public schools, except that such tuition assistance could be obtained if parents agreed to relinquish control of their children to the state welfare department. Although the plaintiffs had raised § 504 claims, a three-judge district court declined to rule on them, observing only that § 504 "constitutes the establishment of broad government policy that programs receiving Federal financial assistance shall be operated without discrimination on the basis of handicap," *Kruse* v. *Campbell*, 431 F.Supp. 180, 185 (E.D.Va. 1977). Consequently, the court reached the plaintiffs' equal protection claims, which it resolved in their favor. On October 3, 1977, the Supreme Court vacated the judgment in *Kruse* and remanded the case to the district court with directions to decide the case under § 504, 434 U.S. 808 (1977). In 1978 the plaintiffs dismissed the case voluntarily after the Governor of Virginia signed a statute providing for reimbursement for tuition in private programs as of September 1978. But the Supreme Court's action on the case is meaningful only if read as implicitly recognizing a private cause of action under § 504.

MATTIE T. v. HOLLADAY

United States District Court for the Northern District of Mississippi, Delta Division,
1977
No. DC 75-31-S, July 28, 1977

SMITH, District Judge

MEMORANDUM OF DECISION

This case is before the court for consideration of a motion by plaintiffs Bennie F. and John W. for partial summary judgment against Bill Chaney, Joe Wade, Dave Rieger, Dewey E. McNiece and John Humphreys in their respective capacities as members of the Board of Trustees of the Pearl Municipal Separate School District and against Henry P. Shepherd in his capacity as Superintendent of the Pearl Municipal Separate School District (Pearl defendants). The parties have submitted memoranda and affidavits to the court and presented argument on the motion.

Plaintiffs Bennie F. and John W. rely on the Rehabilitation Act of 1973, as amended, § 504, 29 U.S.C. § 794, which provides:

> No otherwise qualified handicapped individual in the United States, as defined in section 706(6) of this title, shall, solely by reason of his handicap, be excluded from the participation in, be denied the benefits of, or be subjected to discrimination under any program or activity receiving Federal financial assistance.

Plaintiffs contend that they are handicapped under the definition of the law, that Pearl defendants receive federal financial assistance, that Pearl defendants discriminated against plaintiffs because of their handicapped condition in the educational programs conducted by the Pearl Municipal Separate School District.

After considering the file of this case, the memoranda and oral argument of counsel, the court finds that there is no genuine issue as to the following material facts:

(1) That plaintiffs Bennie F. and John W. are otherwise qualified handicapped individuals within the definition of 29 U.S.C. § 794;

(2) That the Pearl Municipal Separate School District did receive federal financial assistance during the 1976–1977 school year;

(3) That the Pearl defendants did discriminate against plaintiffs Bennie F. and John W. in the educational programs conducted by the Pearl Municipal Separate School District solely because of their respective handicaps. The court finds that plaintiffs Bennie F. and John W. are entitled to partial summary judgment as a matter of law.

Order

Pursuant to the Memorandum of Decision entered on this day, it is hereby ORDERED AND ADJUDGED:

(1) That the motion for partial summary judgment by individual plaintiffs Bennie F. and John W. is sustained;

(2) That the defendants Billy Chaney, Joe Wade, Dave Rieger, Dewey E. McNiece and John Humphreys, as members of the Board of Trustees of the Pearl Municipal Separate School District, and Henry P. Shepherd, as Superintendent of the Pearl Municipal Separate School District, have violated the rights of the individual plaintiffs Bennie F. and John W. by failing to provide necessary educational services pursuant to the Rehabilitation Act of 1973, as amended, § 504, 29 U.S.C. § 794;

(3) That within 20 days of the date of this order, the Pearl defendants shall thoroughly and individually test and evaluate plaintiffs Bennie F. and John W. to determine each child's educational needs and within 30 days of the completion of each child's respective evaluation, provide each child with educational services appropriate to his needs;

(4) That the Pearl defendants shall submit to this court and plaintiffs' counsel a report upon the completion of the requirements of paragraph 3 of this order; and

(5) That this court shall defer ordering relief as to the proposed class and shall retain jurisdiction over all matters in this case.

NOTES

1. A simultaneous, almost identical, summary judgment ruling was made in favor of the named plaintiffs residing in another named school district.

2. The court does not discuss the issue of § 504 creating a private cause of action, but the result indicates clearly that it does. *Mattie T.* is not an example of good legal reasoning nor of a well written opinion, but it does illustrate the determinative force of § 504 in such litigation.

§ 504 REGULATIONS

[After much litigation, e.g., *Cherry* v. *Matthews,* 419 F.Supp. 922 (D.D.C. 1976), controversy, and nation-wide demonstrations, U.S. Department of Health, Education, and Welfare regulations implementing § 504 were published in 42 Fed. Reg. 22676 (1977) and became effective June 3, 1977. These regulations contained six subparts. Subpart A is primarily definitional and states in general terms that discrimination against handicapped persons is prohibited. Subpart B deals with employment, Subpart C with program accessibility (e.g., architectural barriers), and Subpart F with health, welfare, and other social service programs. Pertinent here are Subparts D and E:]

Subpart D—Preschool, Elementary, and Secondary Education

§ 84.31   Application of this subpart.

Subpart D applies to preschool, elementary, secondary, and adult education programs and activities that receive or benefit from federal financial assistance and to recipients that operate, or that receive or benefit from federal financial assistance for the operation of such programs or activities.

§ 84.32   Location and notification.

A recipient that operates a public elementary or secondary education program shall annually:

(a) Undertake to identify and locate every qualified handicapped person residing in the recipient's jurisdiction who is not receiving a public education; and

(b) Take appropriate steps to notify handicapped persons and their parents or guardians of the recipient's duty under this subpart.

§ 84.33   Free appropriate public education.

(a) *General.* A recipient that operates a public elementary or secondary education program shall provide a free appropriate public education to each qualified handicapped person who is in the recipient's jurisdiction, regardless of the nature or severity of the person's handicap.

(b) *Appropriate education.* (1) For the purpose of this subpart, the provision of an appropriate education is the provision of regular or special education and related aids and services that (i) are designed to meet individual educational needs of handicapped persons as adequately as the needs of nonhandicapped persons are met and (ii) are based upon adherence to procedures that satisfy the requirements of §§ 84.34, 84.35, and 84.36.

(2) Implementation of an individualized education program developed in accordance with the Education of the Handicapped Act is one means of meeting the standard established in paragraph (b) (1) (i) of this section.

(3) A recipient may place a handicapped person in or refer such person to a program other than the one that it operates as its means of carrying out the requirements of this subpart. If so, the recipient remains responsible for ensuring that the requirements of this subpart are met with respect to any handicapped person so placed or referred.

(c) *Free education.* (1) *General.* For the purpose of this section, the provision of a free education is the provision of educational and related services without cost to the handicapped person or to his or her parents or guardian, except for those fees that are imposed on nonhandicapped persons or their parents or guardian. It may consist either of the provision of free services or, if a recipient places a handicapped person in or refers such person to a program not operated by the recipient as its means of carrying out the requirements of this subpart, of payment for the costs of the program. Funds available from any public or private agency may be used to meet the requirements of this subpart. Nothing in this section shall be construed to relieve an insurer or similar third party from an otherwise valid obligation to provide or pay for services provided to a handicapped person.

(2) *Transportation*. If a recipient places a handicapped person in or refers such person to a program not operated by the recipient as its means of carrying out the requirements of this subpart, the recipient shall ensure that adequate transportation to and from the program is provided at no greater cost than would be incurred by the person or his or her parents or guardian if the person were placed in the program operated by the recipient.

(3) *Residential placement*. If placement in a public or private residential program is necessary to provide a free appropriate public education to a handicapped person because of his or her handicap, the program, including nonmedical care and room and board, shall be provided at no cost to the person or his or her parents or guardian.

(4) *Placement of handicapped persons by parents*. If a recipient has made available, in conformance with the requirements of this section and § 84.34, a free appropriate public education to a handicapped person and the person's parents or guardian choose to place the person in a private school, the recipient is not required to pay for the person's education in the private school. Disagreements between a parent or guardian and a recipient regarding whether the recipient has made such a program available or otherwise regarding the question of financial responsibility are subject to the due process procedures of § 84.36.

(d) *Compliance*. A recipient may not exclude any qualified handicapped person from a public elementary or secondary education after the effective date of this part. A recipient that is not, on the effective date of this regulation, in full compliance with the other requirements of the preceding paragraphs of this section shall meet such requirements at the earliest practicable time and in no event later than September 1, 1973.

§ 84.34   Educational setting.

(a) *Academic setting*. A recipient to which this subpart applies shall educate, or shall provide for the education of, each qualified handicapped person in its jurisdiction with persons who are not handicapped to the maximum extent appropriate to the needs of the handicapped person. A recipient shall place a handicapped person in the regular educational environment operated by the recipient unless it is demonstrated by the recipient that the education of the person in the regular environment with the use of supplementary aids and services cannot be achieved satisfactorily. Whenever a recipient places a person in a setting other than the regular educational environment pursuant to this paragraph, it shall take into account the proximity of the alternate setting to the person's home.

(b) *Nonacademic settings*. In providing or arranging for the provision of nonacademic and extracurricular services and activities, including meals, recess periods, and the services and activities set forth in § 84.37(a)(2), a recipient shall ensure that handicapped persons participate with nonhandicapped persons in such activities and services to the maximum extent appropriate to the needs of the handicapped person in question.

(c) *Comparable facilities*. If a recipient, in compliance with paragraph (a) of this section, operates a facility that is identifiable as being for handicapped persons, the recipient shall ensure that the facility and the services and activities provided therein are comparable to the other facilities, services, and activities of the recipient.

§ 84.35   Evaluation and placement.

(a) *Preplacement evaluation.* A recipient that operates a public elementary or secondary education program shall conduct an evaluation in accordance with the requirements of paragraph (b) of this section of any person who, because of handicap, needs or is believed to need special education or related services before taking any action with respect to the initial placement of the person in a regular or special education program and any subsequent significant change in placement.

(b) *Evaluation procedures.* A recipient to which this subpart applies shall establish standards and procedures for the evaluation and placement of persons who, because of handicap, need or are believed to need special education or related services which ensure that:

(1) Tests and other evaluation materials have been validated for the specific purpose for which they are used and are administered by trained personnel in conformance with the instructions provided by their producer;

(2) Tests and other evaluation materials include those tailored to assess specific areas of educational need and not merely those which are designed to provide a single general intelligence quotient; and

(3) Tests are selected and administered so as best to ensure that, when a test is administered to a student with impaired sensory, manual, or speaking skills, the test results accurately reflect the student's aptitude or achievement level or whatever other factor the test purports to measure, rather than reflecting the student's impaired sensory, manual, or speaking skills (except where those skills are the factors that the test purports to measure).

(c) *Placement procedures.* In interpreting evaluation data and in making placement decisions, a recipient shall (1) draw upon information from a variety of sources, including aptitude and achievement tests, teacher recommendations, physical condition, social or cultural background, and adaptive behavior, (2) establish procedures to ensure that information obtained from all such sources is documented and carefully considered, (3) ensure that the placement decision is made by a group of persons, including persons knowledgeable about the child, the meaning of the evaluation data, and the placement options, and (4) ensure that the placement decision is made in conformity with § 84.34.

(d) *Reevaluation.* A recipient to which this section applies shall establish procedures, in accordance with paragraph (b) of this section, for periodic reevaluation of students who have been provided special education and related services. A reevaluation procedure consistent with the Education for the Handicapped Act is one means of meeting this requirement.

§ 84.36   Procedural safeguards.

A recipient that operates a public elementary or secondary education program shall establish and implement, with respect to actions regarding the identification, evaluation, or educational placement of persons who, because of handicap, need or are believed to need special instruction or related services, a system of procedural safeguards that includes notice, an opportunity for the parents or guardian of the person to examine relevant records, an impartial hearing with opportunity for participation by the person's parents or guardian and representation by counsel, and a review procedure. Compliance with the procedural safeguards of section 615 of the Education of the Handicapped Act is one means of meeting this requirement.

§ 84.37   Nonacademic services.

(a) *General.* (1) A recipient to which this subpart applies shall provide nonacademic and extracurricular services and activities in such manner as is necessary to afford handicapped students an equal opportunity for participation in such services and activities.

(2) Nonacademic and extracurricular services and activities may include counseling services, physical recreational athletics, transportation, health services, recreational activities, special interest groups or clubs sponsored by the recipient, referrals to agencies which provide assistance to handicapped persons, and employment of students, including both employment by the recipient and assistance in making available outside employment.

(b) *Counseling services.* A recipient to which this subpart applies that provides personal, academic, or vocational counseling, guidance, or placement services to its students shall provide these services without discrimination on the basis of handicap. The recipient shall ensure that qualified handicapped students are not counseled toward more restrictive career objectives than are nonhandicapped students with similar interests and abilities.

(c) *Physical education and athletics.* (1) In providing physical education courses and athletics and similar programs and activities to any of its students, a recipient to which this subpart applies may not discriminate on the basis of handicap. A recipient that offers physical education courses or that operates or sponsors interscholastic, club, or intramural athletics shall provide to qualified handicapped students an equal opportunity for participation in these activities.

(2) A recipient may offer to handicapped students physical education and athletic activities that are separate or different from those offered to nonhandicapped students only if separation or differentiation is consistent with the requirements of § 84.34 and only if no qualified handicapped student is denied the opportunity to compete for teams or to participate in courses that are not separate or different.

§ 84.38   Preschool and adult education programs.

A recipient to which this subpart applies that operates a preschool education or day care program or activity or an adult education program or activity may not, on the basis of handicap, exclude qualified handicapped persons from the program or activity and shall take into account the needs of such persons in determining the aid, benefits, or services to be provided under the program or activity.

§ 84.39   Private education programs.

(a) A recipient that operates a private elementary or secondary education program may not, on the basis of handicap, exclude a qualified handicapped person from such program if the person can, with minor adjustments, be provided an appropriate education, as defined in § 84.33(b) (1), within the recipient's program.

(b) A recipient to which this section applies may not charge more for the provision of an appropriate education to handicapped persons than to nonhandicapped persons except to the extent that any additional charge is justified by a substantial increase in cost to the recipient.

(c) A recipient to which this section applies that operates special education programs shall operate such programs in accordance with the provisions of §§ 84.35 and 84.36. Each recipient to which this section applies is subject to the provisions of §§ 84.34, 84.37, and 84.38.

§ 84.40   [Reserved]

Subpart E—Postsecondary Education

§ 84.41   Application of this subpart.

Subpart E applies to postsecondary education programs and activities, including postsecondary vocational education programs and activities, that receive or benefit from federal financial assistance and to recipients that operate, or that receive or benefit from federal financial assistance for the operation of, such programs or activities.

§ 84.42   Admissions and recruitment.

(a) *General.* Qualified handicapped persons may not, on the basis of handicap, be denied admission or be subjected to discrimination in admission or recruitment by a recipient to which this subpart applies.

(b) *Admissions.* In administering its admission policies, a recipient to which this subpart applies:

(1) May not apply limitations upon the number or proportion of handicapped persons who may be admitted;

(2) May not make use of any test or criterion for admission that has a disproportionate, adverse effect on handicapped persons or any class of handicapped persons unless (i) the test or criterion, as used by the recipient, has been validated as a predictor of success in the education program or activity in question and (ii) alternate tests or criteria that have a less disproportionate, adverse effect are not shown by the Director to be available;

(3) Shall assure itself that (i) admissions tests are selected and administered so as best to ensure that, when a test is administered to an applicant who has a handicap that impairs sensory, manual, or speaking skills, the test results accurately reflect the applicant's aptitude or achievement level or whatever other factor the test purports to measure, rather than reflecting the applicant's impaired sensory, manual, or speaking skills (except where those skills are the factors that the test purports to measure); (ii) admissions tests that are designed for persons with impaired sensory, manual, or speaking skills are offered as often and in as timely a manner as are other admissions tests; and (iii) admissions tests are administered in facilities that, on the whole, are accessible to handicapped persons; and

(4) Except as provided in paragraph (c) of this section, may not make preadmission inquiry as to whether an applicant for admission is a handicapped person but, after admission, may make inquiries on a confidential basis as to handicaps that may require accommodation.

(c) *Preadmission inquiry exception.* When a recipient is taking remedial action to correct the effects of past discrimination pursuant to § 84.6(a) or when a recipient is taking voluntary action to overcome the effects of conditions that resulted in limited participation in its federally assisted program or activity pursuant to § 84.6(b), the recipient may invite applicants for admission to indicate whether and to what extent they are handicapped, *Provided,* That:

(1) The recipient states clearly on any written questionnaire used for this purpose or makes clear orally if no written questionnaire is used that the information requested is intended for use solely in connection with its remedial action obligations or its voluntary action efforts; and

(2) The recipient states clearly that the information is being requested on a voluntary basis, that it will be kept confidential, that refusal to provide it will not subject the applicant to any adverse treatment, and that it will be used only in accordance with this part.

(d) *Validity studies.* For the purpose of paragraph (b) (2) of this section, a recipient may base prediction equations on first year grades, but shall conduct periodic validity studies against the criterion of overall success in the education program or activity in question in order to monitor the general validity of the test scores.

§ 84.43   Treatment of students; general.

(a) No qualified handicapped student shall, on the basis of handicap, be excluded from participation in, be denied the benefits of, or otherwise be subjected to discrimination under any academic, research, occupational training, housing, health, insurance, counseling, financial aid, physical education, athletics, recreation, transportation, other extracurricular, or other postsecondary education program or activity to which this subpart applies.

(b) A recipient to which this subpart applies that considers participation by students in education programs or activities not operated wholly by the recipient as part of, or equivalent to, an education program or activity operated by the recipient shall assure itself that the other education program or activity, as a whole, provides an equal opportunity for the participation of qualified handicapped persons.

(c) A recipient to which this subpart applies may not, on the basis of handicap, exclude any qualified handicapped student from any course, course of study, or other part of its education program or activity.

(d) A recipient to which this subpart applies shall operate its programs and activities in the most integrated setting appropriate.

§ 84.44   Academic adjustments.

(a) *Academic requirements.* A recipient to which this subpart applies shall make such modifications to its academic requirements as are necessary to ensure that such requirements do not discriminate or have the effect of discriminating, on the basis of handicap, against a qualified handicapped applicant or student. Academic requirements that the recipient can demonstrate are essential to the program of instruction being pursued by such student or to any directly related licensing requirement will not be regarded as discriminatory within the meaning of this section. Modifications may include changes in the length of time permitted for the completion of degree requirements, substitution of specific courses required for the completion of degree requirements, and adaptation of the manner in which specific courses are conducted.

(b) *Other rules.* A recipient to which this subpart applies may not impose upon handicapped students other rules, such as the prohibition of tape recorders in classrooms or of dog guides in campus buildings, that have the effect of limiting the participation of handicapped students in the recipient's education program or activity.

(c) *Course examinations.* In its course examinations or other procedures for evaluating students' academic achievement in its program, a recipient to which this subpart applies shall provide such methods for evaluating the achievement of students who have a handicap that impairs sensory, manual, or speaking skills as will best ensure that the results of the evaluation represents the student's achievement in the course, rather than reflecting the student's impaired sensory, manual, or speaking skills (except where such skills are the factors that the test purports to measure).

(d) *Auxiliary aids.* (1) A recipient to which this subpart applies shall take such steps as are necessary to ensure that no handicapped student is denied the benefits of, excluded from participation in, or otherwise subjected to discrimination under the education program or activity operated by the recipient because of the absence of educational auxiliary aids for students with impaired sensory, manual, or speaking skills.

(2) Auxiliary aids may include taped texts, interpreters or other effective methods of making orally delivered materials available to students with hearing impairments, readers in libraries for students with visual impairments, classroom equipment adapted for use by students with manual impairments, and other similar services and actions. Recipients need not provide attendants, individually prescribed devices, readers for personal use or study, or other devices or services of a personal nature.

§ 84.45   Housing.

(a) *Housing provided by the recipient.* A recipient that provides housing to its nonhandicapped students shall provide comparable, convenient, and accessible housing to handicapped students at the same cost as to others. At the end of the transition period provided for in Subpart C, such housing shall be available in sufficient quantity and variety so that the scope of handicapped students' choice of living accommodations is, as a whole, comparable to that of nonhandicapped students.

(b) *Other housing.* A recipient that assists any agency, organization, or person in making housing available to any of its students shall take such action as may be necessary to assure itself that such housing is, as a whole, made available in a manner that does not result in discrimination on the basis of handicap.

§ 84.46   Financial and employment assistance to students.

(a) *Provision of financial assistance.* (1) In providing financial assistance to qualified handicapped persons, a recipient to which this subpart applies may not (i) on the basis of handicap, provide less assistance than is provided to nonhandicapped persons, limit eligibility for assistance, or otherwise discriminate or (ii) assist any entity or person that provides assistance to any of the recipient's students in a manner that discriminates against qualified handicapped persons on the basis of handicap.

(2) A recipient may administer or assist in the administration of scholarships, fellowships, or other forms of financial assistance established under wills, trusts, bequests, or similar legal instruments that require awards to be made on the basis of

factors that discriminate or have the effect of discriminating on the basis of handicap only if the overall effect of the award of scholarships, fellowships, and other forms of financial assistance is not discriminatory on the basis of handicap.

(b) *Assistance in making available outside employment.* A recipient that assists any agency, organization, or person in providing employment opportunities to any of its students shall assure itself that such employment opportunities, as a whole, are made available in a manner that would not violate Subpart B if they were provided by the recipient.

(c) *Employment of students by recipients.* A recipient that employs any of its students may not do so in a manner that violates Subpart B.

§ 84.47   Nonacademic services.

(a) *Physical education and athletics.* (1) In providing physical education courses and athletics and similar programs and activities to any of its students, a recipient to which this subpart applies may not discriminate on the basis of handicap. A recipient that offers physical education courses or that operates or sponsors intercollegiate, club, or intramural athletics shall provide to qualified handicapped students an equal opportunity for participation in these activities.

(2) A recipient may offer to handicapped students physical education and athletic activities that are separate or different only if separation or differentiation is consistent with the requirements of § 84.43(d) and only if no qualified handicapped student is denied the opportunity to compete for teams or to participate in courses that are not separate or different.

(b) *Counseling and placement services.* A recipient to which this subpart applies that provides personal, academic, or vocational counseling, guidance, or placement services to its students shall provide these services without discrimination on the basis of handicap. The recipient shall ensure that qualified handicapped students are not counseled toward more restrictive career objectives than are nonhandicapped students with similar interests and abilities. This requirement does not preclude a recipient from providing factual information about licensing and certification requirements that may present obstacles to handicapped persons in their pursuit of particular careers.

(c) *Social organizations.* A recipient that provides significant assistance to fraternities, sororities, or similar organizations shall assure itself that the membership practices of such organizations do not permit discrimination otherwise prohibited by this subpart.

§§84.48–84.50 [Reserved]

LORA v. BOARD OF ED. OF CITY OF NEW YORK

United States District Court for the Eastern District of New York, 1978
456 F.Supp. 1211, 1228–1230

[See pp. 147–165, above; the abbreviation EHA used by the court refers to the Education for All Handicapped Children Act.]

b. *Rehabilitation Act of 1973*

The salient features of the EHA are echoed in regulations promulgated by the Department of Health, Education and Welfare in conjunction with section 794 of the Rehabilitation Act of 1973. 29 U.S.C. §§ 701 *et seq.* (1975). Section 794 prohibits any discrimination against handicapped individuals:

> No otherwise qualified handicapped individual in the United States, as defined in section 706(6) of this title, shall, solely by reason of his handicap, be excluded from the participation in, be denied the benefits of, or be subjected to discrimination under any programs or activity receiving Federal financial assistance.

As originally promulgated, the Act focused primarily on assuring handicapped individuals vocational opportunities. But in order to assure nondiscrimination, steps must be taken prior to the actual hiring stage. Thus, in 1974, Congress amended the Act, broadening the definition of "handicapped" to extend beyond the employment context. The Senate report on the bill which contained these amendments acknowledged the importance of special emphasis on education of the handicapped:

> It was clearly the intent of the Congress in adopting section 503 (affirmative action) and section 504 (nondiscrimination) that the term "handicapped individual" in those sections was not to be narrowly limited to employment (in the case of section 504), nor to the individual's potential benefit from vocational rehabilitation services under titles I and III (in the case of both sections 503 and 504) of the Act. . . .
>
> Section 504 was enacted to prevent discrimination against all handicapped individuals, regardless of their need for, or ability to benefit from vocational rehabilitation services, in relation to Federal assistance in employment, housing, transportation, *education,* health services, or any other Federally-aided programs. Examples of handicapped individuals who may suffer discrimination in the receipt of Federally-assisted services but who may have been unintentionally excluded from the protection of section 504 by the references to enhanced employability . . . are as follows: *physically or mentally handicapped children who may be denied admission to Federally-supported school systems on the basis of their handicap;* handicapped persons who may be denied admission to Federally-assisted nursing homes on the basis of their handicap; those persons whose handicap is so severe that employment is not feasible but who may be denied the benefits of a wide range of Federal programs; and those persons whose vocational rehabilitation is complete but who may nevertheless be discriminated against in certain Federally-assisted activities.

S.Rep.No.93-1297, 93d Cong., 2nd Sess.; U.S.Code Cong. & Admin.News, pp. 6388-89 (1974) [emphasis added].

For the purposes of subchapters IV and V, which involve areas not necessarily employment related, the Act now covers "handicapped individuals," defined as:

> . . . any person who (A) has a physical or mental impairment which substantially limits one or more of such person's major life activities, (B) has a record of such an impairment, or (C) is regarded as having such an impairment.

29 U.S.C. § 706(6). H.E.W. has noted that:

> With this amended definition, it became clear that [the Act] was intended to forbid discrimination against all handicapped individuals, regardless of their need for or ability to benefit from vocational rehabilitation services.

H.E.W. Regulations, "Supplementary Information," 42 Fed.Reg. No. 86, 22676 (1977). See 42 Fed.Reg. No. 86, 22678-79 § 84.4 (1977).

Regulations promulgated under this section require, among other things, that every handicapped individual be provided with an appropriate education by recipients of federal funds. An "appropriate education" is the "provision of regular or special education and related aids and services that . . . are designed to meet individual educational needs of handicapped persons as adequately as the needs of nonhandicapped persons. . . ." Schooling must, in addition, meet requirements closely paralleling those of the EHA. Section 84.34 of the Regulations provides that a recipient of federal funds should provide for education for a handicapped individual in the least restrictive setting possible, *i.e.*, afford education, where feasible, with persons who are not handicapped. Section 84.35, dealing with evaluation and placement, requires that testing be administered by adequately trained personnel and that tests with more than a single intelligence quotient be used. In making placement decisions no one criterion or single individual's opinion is to be decisive. Section 84.36 requires recipients of federal funds to establish and implement procedural safeguards including "notice, an opportunity for the parents or guardians of the person to examine relevant records, an impartial hearing with opportunity for participation by the persons's parents or guardian, representation by counsel, and a review procedure." 42 Fed.Reg. No. 86, 22682-83 (1977).

These requirements reflect the same philosophy and concerns manifested in the EHA. This identity of purpose is specifically recognized in section 84.36 of the regulations providing that "[c]ompliance with the procedural safeguards of section 615 of the Education of the Handicapped is one means of meeting this requirement [of due process guarantees]." 42 Fed.Reg. No. 86, 22683 (1977).

The significance of the Rehabilitation Act regulations is that they make the requirements of specially tailored programs, nondiscriminatory evaluation and placement, and due process applicable to an institution receiving any federal funds. New York City schools receive substantial amounts of federal funds.

Recent cases have found violations of the Rehabilitation Act where a) a mentally retarded patient received less than adequate treatment in a state institution (*Halderman* v. *Pennhurst State School and Hospital,* 446 F.Supp. 1295, 1323-24 (E.D.Pa. 1978); and b) a mildly handicapped child was excluded from the regular classroom without a bona fide educational reason (*Hairston* v. *Drosick,* 423 F.Supp. 180, 184 (S.D.W.Va. 1976)).

NOTES

1. In addition to the *Hairston, Mattie T., Kruse* v. *Campbell,* and *Lora* cases, a number of other lawsuits have been brought seeking equal educational opportunities in the public elementary and secondary schools pursuant to § 504 (29 U.S.C. § 794). *Howard S.* v. *Friendswood Independent School District,* 454 F.Supp. 634 (S.D.Tex. 1978), is presented below at pp. 263–272. Other such cases include:

a. *Donnie R.* v. *Wood,* C.A. No. 77-11360 (D.S.C. Consent Degree entered 8/22/77)—expulsion of child with "emotional, social and mental handicaps; injunctive portion of suit settled by consent agreement.

b. *Kettler* v. *Richardson-Independent School District,* C.A. No. CA 3-78-0892-C (N.D.Tex. Agreed Order August 31, 1978)—agreement to provide due process hearings concerning provision of free appropriate public education for handicapped children.

c. *Lopez* v. *Salida School District,* C.A. No. C-73078 (D.Col. Consent Decree January 20, 1978)—agreement to provide educational program to meet needs of handicapped child; cost, including room and board, to be paid by school district.

d. *Rhode Island Society for Autistic Children* v. *Board of Regents*, C.A. No. 5081 (D.R.I. August 1, 1975)—appropriateness and quality of special education placements; amended complaint accepted over objection of defendants, and defendants' motion for postponement of trial denied; the court ruled § 794 to be applicable to the case.

e. *Sherer* v. *Waier*, 457 F.Supp. 1039 (W.D.Mo. 1977)—plaintiff sought education for child with spina bifida in regular classroom; case dismissed without prejudice for failure to exhaust administrative remedies; favorable relief subsequently obtained through HEW administrative proceeding.

f. *Wilson B.* v. *Manor Independent School District*, C.A. No. A-78-CA-168 (W.D.Tex. Agreed Judgment September 26, 1978)—agreement to provide appropriate educational program for handicapped child).

2. Section 504 and the HEW regulations have also been relied upon in several cases brought by handicapped college and postgraduate students:

a. *Davis* v. *Southeastern Community College*, 574 F.2d 1158 (4th Cir. 1978), decision below, 424 F.Supp. 1341 (E.D.N.C. 1976)—private cause of action under § 794; circuit court held that district court erred in finding person with hearing impairment was not "otherwise qualified" for nurses' training program: should focus on individual's academic and technical qualifications, not on handicap.

b. *Grimard* v. *Carlston*, 567 F.2d 1171 (1st Cir. 1978)—denial of preliminary injunction upheld; person with broken ankle temporarily withdrawn from nursing school so as not to jeopardize safety of patients.

c. *Barnes* v. *Converse College*, C.A. No. 77-116 (D.S.C. Mar. 31, 1978), previously reported 436 F.Supp. 635 (D.S.C. 1977)—action to compel college to pay for interpreter for deaf student; dismissed for failure to exhaust administrative remedies.

d. *Camenisch* v. *University of Texas*, C.A. No. A-78-CA-061 (W.D.Tex. May 17, 1978), 16 EPD ¶8336—preliminary injunction issued requiring university to provide interpreter or other necessary services for deaf student.

e. *Crawford* v. *University of North Carolina*, 440 F.Supp. 1047 (M.D.N.C. 1977)—preliminary injunction issued ordering university to provide interpreter for deaf student, conditioned upon plaintiff initiating complaint with HEW.

f. *Doe* v. *New York University*, 442 F.Supp. 522 (S.D.N.Y. 1978)—preliminary injunction denied that would have compelled university to readmit plaintiff who had a mental disability; plaintiff required to exhaust administrative remedies; no showing of irreparable harm.

EDUCATION FOR ALL HNDICAPPED CHILDREN ACT OF 1975
P.L. 94-142, 20 U.S.C. 1401 et seq., 89 Stat. 773 (Nov. 29, 1975)

Statement of Findings and Purpose

Sec. 3. (a) Section 601 of the Act (20 U.S.C. 1401) is amended by inserting "(a)" immediately before "This title" and by adding at the end thereof the following new subsections:

"(b) The Congress finds that—

"(1) there are more than eight million handicapped children in the United States today;

"(2) the special educational needs of such children are not being fully met;

"(3) more than half of the handicapped children in the United States do not receive appropriate educational services which would enable them to have full equality of opportunity;

"(4) one million of the handicapped children in the United States are excluded entirely from the public school system and will not go through the educational process with their peers;

"(5) there are many handicapped children throughout the United States participating in regular school programs whose handicaps prevent them from having a successful educational experience because their handicaps are undetected;

"(6) because of the lack of adequate services within the public school system, families are often forced to find services outside the public school system, often at great distance from their residence and at their own expense;

"(7) developments in the training of teachers and in diagnostic and instructional procedures and methods have advanced to the point that, given appropriate funding, State and local educational agencies can and will provide effective special education and related services to meet the needs of handicapped children;

"(8) State and local educational agencies have a responsibility to provide education for all handicapped children, but present financial resources are inadequate to meet the special educational needs of handicapped children; and

"(9) it is in the national interest that the Federal Government assist State and local efforts to provide programs to meet the educational needs of handicapped children in order to assure equal protection of the law.

"(c) It is the purpose of this Act to assure that all handicapped children have available to them, within the time periods specified in section 612(2) (B), a free appropriate public education which emphasizes special education and related services designed to meet their unique needs, to assure that the rights of handicapped children and their parents or guardians are protected, to assist States and localities to provide for the education of all handicapped children, and to assess and assure the effectiveness of efforts to educate handicapped children."

(b) The heading for section 601 of the Act (20 U.S.C. 1401) is amended to read as follows:

"Short Title; Statement of Findings and Purpose"

Definitions

Sec. 4. (a) Section 602 of the Act (20 U.S.C. 1402) is amended—

(1) in paragraph (1) thereof, by striking out "crippled" and inserting in lieu thereof "orthopedically impaired," and by inserting immediately after "impaired children" the following: ", or children with specific learning disabilities.":

(2) in paragraph (5) thereof, by inserting immediately after "instructional mate-

rials,'' the following: ''telecommunications, sensory, and other technological aids and devices,'';

(3) in the last sentence of paragraph (15) thereof, by inserting immediately after ''environmental'' the following: '', cultural, or economic''; and

(4) by adding at the end thereof the following new paragraphs:

''(16) The term 'special education' means specially designed instruction, at no cost to parents or guardians, to meet the unique needs of a handicapped child, including classroom instruction, instruction in physical education, home instruction, and instruction in hospitals and institutions.

''(17) The term 'related services' means transportation, and such developmental, corrective, and other supportive services (including speech pathology and audiology, psychological services, physical and occupational therapy, recreation, and medical and counseling services, except that such medical services shall be for diagnostic and evaluation purposes only) as may be required to assist a handicapped child to benefit from special education, and includes the early identification and assessment of handicapping conditions in children.

''(18) The term 'free appropriate public education' means special education and related services which (A) have been provided at public expense, under public supervision and direction, and without charge, (B) meet the standards of the State educational agency, (C) include an appropriate preschool, elementary, or secondary school education in the State involved, and (D) are provided in conformity with the individualized education program required under section 614(a) (5).

''(19) The term 'individualized education program' means a written statement for each handicapped child developed in any meeting by a representative of the local educational agency or an intermediate educational unit who shall be qualified to provide, or supervise the provision of, specially designed instruction to meet the unique needs of handicapped children, the teacher, the parents or guardian of such child, and, whenever appropriate, such child, which statement shall include (A) a statement of the present levels of educational performance of such child, (B) a statement of annual goals, including short-term instructional objectives, (C) a statement of the specific educational services to be provided to such child, and the extent to which such child will be able to participate in regular educational programs, (D) the projected date for initiation and anticipated duration of such services, and (E) appropriate objective criteria and evaluation procedures and schedules for determining, on at least an annual basis, whether instructional objectives are being achieved.

''(20) The term 'excess costs' means those costs which are in excess of the average annual per student expenditure in a local educational agency during the preceding school year for an elementary or secondary school student, as may be appropriate, and which shall be computed after deducting: (A) amounts received under this part or under title I or title VII of the Elementary and Secondary Education Act of 1965, and (B) any State or local funds expended for programs which would qualify for assistance under this part or under such titles.*

---

*20 USC 241a note, 881.

"(21) The term 'native language' has the meaning given that term by section 703(a) (2) of the Bilingual Education Act (20 U.S.C. 880b-1(a) (2).

"(22) The term 'intermediate educational unit' means any public authority, other than a local educational agency, which is under the general supervision of a State educational agency, which is established by State law for the purpose of providing free public education on a regional basis, and which provides special education and related services to handicapped children within that State."

(b) The heading for section 602 of the Act (20 U.S.C. 1402) is amended to read as follows:

"Definitions"

Assistance for Education of All Handicapped Children

Sec. 5. (a) Part B of the Act (20 U.S.C. 1411 et seq.) is amended to read as follows:

"Part B—Assistance for Education of All Handicapped Children
"Entitlements and Allocations

"Sec. 611. (a) (1) Except as provided in paragraph (3) and in section 619, the maximum amount of the grant to which a State is entitled under this part for any fiscal year shall be equal to—

"(A) the number of handicapped children aged three to twenty-one, inclusive, in such State who are receiving special education and related services;

multiplied by—

"(B) (i) 5 per centum, for the fiscal year ending September 30, 1978, of the average per pupil expenditure in public elementary and secondary schools in the United States;

"(ii) 10 per centum, for the fiscal year ending September 30, 1979, of the average per pupil expenditure in public elementary and secondary schools in the United States;

"(iii) 20 per centum, for the fiscal year ending September 30, 1980, of the average per pupil expenditure in public elementary and secondary schools in the United States;

"(iv) 30 per centum, for the fiscal year ending September 30, 1981, of the average per pupil expenditure in public elementary and secondary schools in the United States; and

"(v) 40 per centum, for the fiscal year ending September 30, 1982, and for each fiscal year thereafter, of the average per pupil expenditure in public elementary and secondary schools in the United States;

except that no State shall receive an amount which is less than the amount which such State received under this part for the fiscal year ending September 30, 1977.

"(2) For the purpose of this subsection and subsection (b) through subsection (e), the term 'State' does not include Guam, American Samoa, the Virgin Islands, and the Trust Territory of the Pacific Islands.

"(3) The number of handicapped children receiving special education and related services in any fiscal year shall be equal to the average of the number of such children receiving special education and related services on October 1 and February 1 of the fiscal year preceding the fiscal year for which the determination is made.

"(4) For purposes of paragraph (1) (B), the term 'average per pupil expenditure,' in the United States, means the aggregate current expenditures, during the second fiscal year preceding the fiscal year for which the computation is made (or, if satisfactory data for such year are not available at the time of computation, then, during the most recent preceding fiscal year for which satisfactory data are available) of all local educational agencies in the United States (which, for purposes of this subsection, means the fifty States and the District of Columbia), as the case may be, plus any direct expenditures by the State for operation of such agencies (without regard to the source of funds from which either of such expenditures are made), divided by the aggregate number of children in average daily attendance to whom such agencies provided free public education during such preceding year.

"(5) (A) In determining the allotment of each State under paragraph (1), the Commissioner may not count—

"(i) handicapped children in such State under paragraph (1) (A) to the extent the number of such children is greater than 12 per centum of the number of all children aged five to seventeen, inclusive, in such State;

"(ii) as part of such percentage, children with specific learning disabilities to the extent the number of such children is greater than one-sixth of such percentage; and

"(iii) handicapped children who are counted under section 121 of the Elementary and Secondary Education Act of 1965.

"(B) For purposes of subparagraph (A), the number of children aged five to seventeen, inclusive, in any State shall be determined by the Commissioner on the basis of the most recent satisfactory data available to him.

"(b) (1) Of the funds received under subsection (a) by any State for the fiscal year ending September 30, 1978—

"(A) 50 per centum of such funds may be used by such State in accordance with the provisions of paragraph (2); and

"(B) 50 per centum of such funds shall be distributed by such State pursuant to subsection (d) to local educational agencies and intermediate educational units in such State, for use in accordance with the priorities established under section 612(3).

"(2) Of the funds which any State may use under paragraph (1) (A)—

"(A) an amount which is equal to the greater of—

"(i) 5 per centum of the total amount of funds received under this part by such State; or

"(ii) $200,000;

may be used by such State for administrative costs related to carrying out sections 612 and 613;

"(B) the remainder shall be used by such State to provide support services and direct services, in accordance with the priorities established under section 612(3).

"(c) (1) Of the funds received under subsection (a) by any State for the fiscal year ending September 30, 1979, and for each fiscal year thereafter—

"(A) 25 per centum of such funds may be used by such State in accordance with the provisions of paragraph (2); and

"(B) except as provided in paragraph (3), 75 per centum of such funds shall be distributed by such State pursuant to subsection (d) to local educational agencies and intermediate educational units in such State, for use in accordance with priorities established under section 612(3).

"(2) (A) Subject to the provisions of subparagraph (B), of the funds which any State may use under paragraph (1) (A)—

"(i) an amount which is equal to the greater of—

"(I) 5 per centum of the total amount of funds received under this part by such State; or

"(II) $200,000;

may be used by such State for administrative costs related to carrying out the provisions of sections 612 and 613; and

"(ii) the remainder shall be used by such State to provide support services and direct services, in accordance with the priorities established under section 612(3).

"(B) The about expended by any State from the funds available to such State under paragraph (1) (A) in any fiscal year for the provision of support services or for the provision of direct services shall be matched on a program basis by such State, from funds other than Federal funds, for the provision of support services or for the provision of direct services for the fiscal year involved.

"(3) The provisions of section 613(a) (9) shall not apply with respect to amounts available for use by any State under paragraph (2).

"(4) (A) No funds shall be distributed by any State under this subsection in any fiscal year to any local educational agency or intermediate educational unit in such State if—

"(i) such local educational agency or intermediate educational unit is entitled, under subsection (d), to less than $7,500 for such fiscal year; or

"(ii) such local educational agency or intermediate educational unit has not submitted an application for such funds which meets the requirements of section 614.

"(B) Whenever the provisions of subparagraph (A) apply, the State involved shall use such funds to assure the provision of a free appropriate education to handicapped children residing in the area served by such local educational agency or such intermediate educational unit. The provisions of paragraph (2) (B) shall not apply to the use of such funds.

"(d) From the total amount of funds available to local educational agencies and intermediate educational units in any State under subsection (b) (1) (B) or subsection (c) (1) (B), as the case may be, each local educational agency or intermediate educational unit shall be entitled to an amount which bears the same ratio to the total amount available under subsection (b) (1) (B) or subsection (c) (1) (B), as the case may be, as the number of handicapped children aged three to twenty-one, inclusive, receiving special education and related services in such local educational agency or intermediate educational unit bears to the aggregate number of handicapped children aged three to twenty-one, inclusive, receiving special education and related services in all local educational agencies and intermediate educational units which apply to the State educational agency involved for funds under this part.

"(e) (1) The jurisdictions to which this subsection applies are Guam, American Samoa, the Virgin Islands, and the Trust Territory of the Pacific Islands.

"(2) Each jurisdiction to which this subsection applies shall be entitled to a grant for the purposes set forth in section 601(c) in an amount equal to an amount determined by the Commissioner in accordance with criteria based on respective needs, except that the aggregate of the amount to which such jurisdictions are so entitled for any fiscal year shall not exceed an amount equal to 1 per centum of the aggregate of the amounts available to all States under this part for that fiscal year. If the aggregate of the amounts, determined by the Commissioner pursuant to the preceding sentence, to be so needed for any fiscal year exceeds an amount equal to such 1 per centum limitation, the entitlement of each such jurisdiction shall be reduced proportionately until such aggregate does not exceed such 1 per centum limitation.

"(3) The amount expended for administration by each jurisdiction under this subsection shall not exceed 5 per centum of the amount allotted to such jurisdiction for any fiscal year, or $35,000, whichever is greater.

"(f) (1) The Commissioner is authorized to make payments to the Secretary of the Interior according to the need for such assistance for the education of handicapped children on reservations serviced by elementary and secondary schools operated for Indian children by the Department of the Interior. The amount of such payment for any fiscal year shall not exceed 1 per centum of the aggregate amounts available to all States under this part for that fiscal year.

"(2) The Secretary of the Interior may receive an allotment under this subsection only after submitting to the Commissioner an application which meets the applicable requirements of section 614(a) and which is approved by the Commissioner. The provisions of section 616 shall apply to any such application.

"(g) (1) If the sums appropriated for any fiscal year for making payments to States under this part are not sufficient to pay in full the total amounts which all States are entitled to receive under this part for such fiscal year, the maximum amounts which all States are entitled to receive under this part for such fiscal year shall be ratably reduced. In case additional funds become available for making such payments for any fiscal year during which the preceding sentence is applicable, such reduced amounts shall be increased on the same basis as they were reduced.

"(2) In the case of any fiscal year in which the maximum amounts for which States are eligible have been reduced under the first sentence of paragraph (1), and in which additional funds have not been made available to pay in full the total of such maximum amounts under the last sentence of such paragraph, the State educational agency shall fix dates before which each local educational agency or intermediate educational unit shall report to the State educational agency on the amount of funds available to the local educational agency or intermediate educational unit, under the provisions of subsection (d), which it estimates that it will expend in accordance with the provisions of this part. The amounts so available to any local educational agency or intermediate educational unit, or any amount which would be available to any other local educational agency or intermediate educational unit if it were to submit a program meeting the requirements of this part, which the State educational agency determines will not be used for the period of its availability, shall be available for allocation to those local educational agencies or intermediate educational units, in the manner provided by this section, which the State educational agency determines will need and be able to use additional funds to carry out approved programs.

"Eligibility

"Sec. 612. In order to qualify for assistance under this part in any fiscal year, a State shall demonstrate to the Commissioner that the following conditions are met:

"(1) The State has in effect a policy that assures all handicapped children the right to a free appropriate public education.

"(2) The State has developed a plan pursuant to section 613(b) in effect prior to the date of the enactment of the Education for All Handicapped Children Act of 1975 and submitted not later than August 21, 1975, which will be amended so as to comply with the provisions of this paragraph. Each such amended plan shall set forth in detail the policies and procedures which the State will undertake or has undertaken in order to assure that—

"(A) there is established (i) a goal of providing full educational opportunity to all handicapped children, (ii) a detailed timetable for accomplishing such a goal, and (iii) a description of the kind and number of facilities, personnel, and services necessary throughout the State to meet such a goal;

"(B) a free appropriate public education will be available for all handicapped children between the ages of three and eighteen within the State not later than September 1, 1978, and for all handicapped children between the ages of three and twenty-one within the State not later than September 1, 1980, except that, with respect to handicapped children aged three to five and aged eighteen to twenty-one, inclusive, the requirements of this clause shall not be applied in any State if the application of such requirements would be inconsistent with State law or practice, or the order of any court, respecting public education within such age groups in the State;

"(C) all children residing in the State who are handicapped, regardless of the severity of their handicap, and who are in need of special education and related services are identified, located, and evaluated, and that a practical method is developed and implemented to determine which children are currently receiving needed special education and related services and which children are not currently receiving needed special education and related services;

"(D) policies and procedures are established in accordance with detailed criteria prescribed under section 617(c); and

"(E) the amendment to the plan submitted by the State required by this section shall be available to parents, guardians, and other members of the general public at least thirty days prior to the date of submission of the amendment to the Commissioner.

"(3) The State has established priorities for providing a free appropriate public education to all handicapped children, which priorities shall meet the timetables set forth in clause (B) of paragraph (2) of this section, first with respect to handicapped children who are not receiving an education, and second with respect to handicapped children, within each disability, with the most severe handicaps who are receiving an inadequate education, and has made adequate progress in meeting the timetables set forth in clause (B) of paragraph (2) of this section.

"(4) Each local educational agency in the State will maintain records of the individualized education program for each handicapped child, and such program shall be established, reviewed, and revised as provided in section 614(a) (5).

"(5) The State has established (A) procedural safeguards as required by section 615, (B) procedures to assure that, to the maximum extent appropriate, handicapped children, including children in public or private institutions or other care facilities, are educated with children who are not handicapped, and that special classes, separate schooling, or other removal of handicapped children from the regular educational environment occurs only when the nature or severity of the handicap is such that education in regular classes with the use of supplementary aids and services cannot be achieved satisfactorily, and (C) procedures to assure that testing and evaluation materials and procedures utilized for the purposes of evaluation and placement of handicapped children will be selected and administered so as not to be racially or culturally discriminatory. Such materials or procedures shall be provided and administered in the child's native language or mode of communication, unless it clearly is not feasible to do so, and no single procedure shall be the sole criterion for determining an appropriate educational program for a child.

"(6) The State educational agency shall be responsible for assuring that the requirements of this part are carried out and that all educational programs for handicapped children within the State, including all such programs administered by any other State or local agency, will be under the general supervision of the persons responsible for educational programs for handicapped children in the State educational agency and shall meet education standards of the State educational agency.

"(7) The State shall assure that (A) in carrying out the requirements of this section procedures are established for consultation with individuals involved in or concerned with the education of handicapped children, including handicapped individuals and parents or guardians of handicapped children, and (B) there are public hearings, adequate notice of such hearings, and an opportunity for comment available to the general public prior to adoption of the policies, programs, and procedures required pursuant to the provisions of this section and section 613.

"State Plans

"Sec. 613. (a) Any State meeting the eligibility requirements set forth in section 612 and desiring to participate in the program under this part shall submit to the Commissioner, through its State educational agency, a State plan at such time, in such manner, and containing or accompanied by such information, as he deems necessary. Each such plan shall—

"(1) set forth policies and procedures designed to assure that funds paid to the State under this part will be expended in accordance with the provisions of this part, with particular attention given to the provisions of sections 611(b), 611(c), 611(d), 612(2), and 612(3);

"(2) provide that programs and procedures will be established to assure that funds received by the State or any of its political subdivisions under any other Federal program, including section 121 of the Elementary and Secondary Education Act of 1965 (20 U.S.C. 241c-2), section 305(b) (8) of such Act (20 U.S.C. 844a (b) (8)) or its successor authority, and section 122(a) (4) (B) of the Vocational Education Act of 1963 (20 U.S.C. 1262(a) (4) (B)), under which there is specific authority for the provision of assistance for the education of handicapped children, will be utilized by the State, or any of its political subdivisions, only in a manner consistent with the goal of providing a free appropriate public education for all handicapped children, except that nothing in this clause shall be construed to limit the specific requirements of the laws governing such Federal programs;

"(3) set forth, consistent with the purposes of this Act, a description of programs and procedures for (A) the development and implementation of a comprehensive system of personnel development which shall include the inservice training of general and special educational instructional and support personnel, detailed procedures to assure that all personnel necessary to carry out the purposes of this Act are appropriately and adequately prepared and trained, and effective procedures for acquiring and disseminating to teachers and administrators of programs for handicapped children significant information derived from educational research, demonstration, and similar projects, and (B) adopting, where appropriate, promising educational practices and materials development through such projects;

"(4) set forth policies and procedures to assure—

"(A) that, to the extent consistent with the number and location of handicapped children in the State who are enrolled in private elementary and secondary schools, provision is made for the participation of such children in the program assisted or carried out under this part by providing for such children special education and related services; and

"(B) that (i) handicapped children in private schools and facilities will be provided special education and related services (in conformance with an individualized educational program as required by this part) at no cost to their parents or guardian, if such children are placed in or referred to such schools or facilities by the State or appropriate local educational agency as the means of carrying out the requirements of this part or any other applicable law requiring the provision of special education and related services to all handicapped children within such State, and (ii) in all such instances the State educational agency shall determine whether such schools and facilities meet standards that apply to State and local educational agencies and that children so served have all the rights they would have if served by such agencies;

"(5) set forth policies and procedures which assure that the State shall seek to recover any funds made available under this part for services to any child who is determined to be erroneously classified as eligible to be counted under section 611(a) or section 611(d);

"(6) provide satisfactory assurance that the control of funds provided under this part, and title to property derived therefrom, shall be in a public agency for the uses and purposes provided in this part, and that a public agency will administer such funds and property;

"(7) provide for (A) making such reports in such form and containing such information as the Commissioner may require to carry out his functions under this part, and (B) keeping such records and affording such access thereto as the Commissioner may find necessary to assure the correctness and verification of such reports and proper disbursement of Federal funds under this part;

"(8) provide procedures to assure that final action with respect to any application submitted by a local educational agency or an intermediate educational unit shall not be taken without first affording the local educational agency or intermediate educational unit involved reasonable notice and opportunity for a hearing;

"(9) provide satisfactory assurance that Federal funds made available under this part (A) will not be commingled with State funds, and (B) will be so used as to supplement and increase the level of State and local funds expended for the education of handicapped children and in no case to supplant such State and local funds, except that, where the State provides clear and convincing evidence that all handicapped children have available to them a free appropriate public education, the Commissioner may waive in part the requirement of this clause if he concurs with the evidence provided by the State;

"(10) provide, consistent with procedures prescribed pursuant to section 617(a) (2), satisfactory assurance that such fiscal control and fund accounting procedures will be adopted as may be necessary to assure proper disbursement of, and accounting for, Federal funds paid under this part to the State, including any such funds paid by the State to local educational agencies and intermediate educational units;

"(11) provide for procedures for evaluation at least annually of the effectiveness of programs in meeting the educational needs of handicapped children (including evaluation of individualized education programs), in accordance with such criteria that the Commissioner shall prescribe pursuant to section 617; and

"(12) provide that the State has an advisory panel, appointed by the Governor or any other official authorized under State law to make such appointments, composed of individuals involved in or concerned with the education of handicapped children, including handicapped individuals, teachers, parents or guardians of handicapped children, State and local education officials, and administrators of programs for handicapped children, which (A) advises the State educational agency of unmet needs within the State in the education of handicapped children, (B) comments publicly on any rules or regulations proposed for issuance by the State regarding the education of handicapped children and the procedures for distribution of funds under this part, and (C) assists the State in developing and reporting such data and evaluations as may assist the Commissioner in the performance of his responsibilities under section 618.

"(b) Whenver a State educational agency provides free appropriate public education for handicapped children, or provides direct services to such children, such State educational agency shall include, as part of the State plan required by subsection (a) of this section, such additional assurances not specified in such subsection (a) as are contained in section 614(a), except that funds available for the provision of such education or services may be expended without regard to the provisions relating to excess costs in section 614(a).

"(c) The Commissioner shall approve any State plan and any modification thereof which—

"(1) is submitted by a State eligible in accordance with section 612; and

"(2) meets the requirements of subsection (a) and subsection (b).

The Commissioner shall disapprove any State plan which does not meet the requirements of the preceding sentence, but shall not finally disapprove a State plan except after reasonable notice and opportunity for a hearing to the State.

"Application

"Sec. 614. (a) A local educational agency or an intermediate educational unit which desires to receive payments under section 611(d) for any fiscal year shall submit an application to the appropriate State educational agency. Such application shall—

"(1) provide satisfactory assurance that payments under this part will be used for excess costs directly attributable to programs which—

"(A) provide that all children residing within the jurisdiction of the local educational agency or the intermediate educational unit who are handicapped, regardless of the severity of their handicap, and are in need of special education and related services will be identified, located, and evaluated, and provide for the inclusion of a practical method of determining which children are currently receiving needed special education and related services and which children are not currently receiving such education and services;

"(B) establish policies and procedures in accordance with detailed criteria prescribed under section 617(c);

"(C) establish a goal of providing full educational opportunities to all handicapped children, including—

"(i) procedures for the implementation and use of the comprehensive system of personnel development established by the State educational agency under section 613(a) (3);

"(ii) the provision of, and the establishment of priorities for providing, a free appropriate public education to all handicapped children, first with respect to handicapped children who are not receiving an education, and second with respect to handicapped children, within each disability, with the most severe handicaps who are receiving an inadequate education;

"(iii) the participation and consultation of the parents or guardians of such children; and

"(iv) to the maximum extent practicable and consistent with the provisions of section 612(5) (B), the provision of special services to enable such children to participate in regular educational programs;

"(D) establish a detailed timetable for accomplishing the goal described in subclause (C); and

"(E) provide a description of the kind and number of facilities, personnel, and services necessary to meet the goal described in subclause (C);

"(2) provide satisfactory assurance that (A) the control of funds provided under this part, and title to property derived from such funds, shall be in a public agency for the uses and purposes provided in this part, and that a public agency will administer such funds and property, (B) Federal funds expended by local educational agencies and intermediate educational units for programs under this part (i) shall be used to pay only the excess costs directly attributable to the education of handicapped children, and (ii) shall be used to supplement and, to the extent practicable, increase the level of State and local funds expended for the education of handicapped children, and in no case to supplant such State and local funds, and (C) State and local funds will be used in the jurisdiction of the local educational agency or intermediate educational unit to provide services in program areas which, taken as a whole, are at least comparable to services being provided in areas of such jurisdiction which are not receiving funds under this part;

"(3) (A) provide for furnishing such information (which, in the case of reports relating to performance, as in accordance with specific performance criteria related to program objectives), as may be necessary to enable the State educational agency to perform its duties under this part, including information relating to the educational achievement of handicapped children participating in programs carried out under this part; and

"(B) provide for keeping such records, and provide for affording such access to such records, as the State educational agency may find necessary to assure the correctness and verification of such information furnished under subclause (A);

"(4) provide for making the application and all pertinent documents related to such application available to parents, guardians, and other members of the general public, and provide that all evaluations and reports required under clause (3) shall be public information;

"(5) provide assurances that the local educational agency or intermediate educational unit will establish, or revise, whichever is appropriate, an individualized education program for each handicapped child at the beginning of each school year and will then review and, if appropriate, revise, its provisions periodically, but not less than annually;

"(6) provide satisfactory assurance that policies and programs established and administered by the local educational agency or intermediate educational unit shall be consistent with the provisions of paragraph (1) through paragraph (7) of section 612 and section 613(a); and

"(7) provide satisfactory assurance that the local educational agency or intermediate educational unit will establish and maintain procedural safeguards in accordance with the provisions of sections 612(5) (B), 612(5) (C), and 615.

"(b) (1) A State educational agency shall approve any application submitted by a local educational agency or an intermediate educational unit under subsection (a) if the State educational agency determines that such application meets the requirements of subsection (a), except that no such application may be approved until the State plan submitted by such State educational agency under subsection (a) is approved by the Commissioner under section 613(c). A State educational agency shall disapprove any application submitted by a local educational gency or an intermediate educational unit under subsection (a) if the State educational agency determines that such application does not meet the requirements of subsection (a).

"(2) (A) Whenever a State educational agency, after reasonable notice and opportunity for a hearing, finds that a local educational agency or an intermediate educational unit, in the administration of an application approved by the State educational agency under paragraph (1), has failed to comply with any requirement set forth in such application, the State educational agency, after giving appropriate notice to the local educational agency or the intermediate educational unit, shall—

"(i) make no further payments to such local educational agency or such intermediate educational unit under section 620 until the State educational agency is satisfied that there is no longer any failure to comply with the requirement involved; or

"(ii) take such finding into account in its review of any application made by such local educational agency or such intermediate educational unit under subsection (a).

"(B) The provisions of the last sentence of section 616(a) shall apply to any local educational agency or any intermediate educational unit receiving any notification from a State educational agency under this paragraph.

"(3) In carrying out its functions under paragraph (1), each State educational agency shall consider any decision made pursuant to a hearing held under section 615 which is adverse to the local educational agency or intermediate educational unit involved in such decision.

"(c) (1) A State educational agency may, for purposes of the consideration and approval of applications under this section, require local educational agencies to submit a consolidated application for payments if such State educational agency determines that any individual application submitted by any such local educational agency will be disapproved because such local educational agency is ineligible to receive payments because of the application of section 611(c) (4) (A) (i) or such local educational agency would be unable to establish and maintain programs of sufficient size and scope to effectively meet the educational needs of handicapped children.

"(2) (A) In any case in which a consolidated application of local educational agencies is approved by a State educational agency under paragraph (1), the payments which such local educational agencies may receive shall be equal to the sum of payments to which each such local educational agency would be entitled under section 611(d) if an individual application of any such local educational agency had been approved.

"(B) The State educational agency shall prescribe rules and regulations with respect to consolidated applications submitted under this subsection which are consistent with the provisions of paragraph (1) through paragraph (7) of section 612 and section 613(a) and which provide participating local educational agencies with joint responsibilities for implementing programs receiving payments under this part.

"(C) In any case in which an intermediate educational unit is required pursuant to State law to carry out the provisions of this part, the joint responsibilities given to local educational agencies under subparagraph (B) shall not apply to the administration and disbursement of any payments received by such intermediate educational unit. Such responsibilities shall be carried out exclusively by such intermediate educational unit.

"(d) Whenever a State educational agency determines that a local educational agency—

"(1) is unable or unwilling to establish and maintain programs of free appropriate public education which meet the requirements established in subsection (a);

"(2) is unable or unwilling to be consolidated with other local educational agencies in order to establish and maintain such programs; or

"(3) has one or more handicapped children who can best be served by a regional or State center designed to meet the needs of such children;

the State educational agency shall use the payments which would have been available to such local educational agency to provide special education and related services directly to handicapped children residing in the area served by such local educational agency. The State educational agency may provide such education and services in such manner, and at such locations (including regional or State centers), as it considers appropriate, except that the manner in which such education and services are provided shall be consistent with the requirements of this part.

"(e) Whenever a State educational agency determines that a local educational agency is adequately providing a free appropriate public education to all handicapped children residing in the area served by such agency with State and local funds otherwise available to such agency, the State educational agency may reallocate funds (or such portion of those funds as may not be required to provide such education and services) made available to such agency, pursuant to section 611(d), to such other local educational agencies within the State as are not adequately providing special education and related services to all handicapped children residing in the areas served by such other local educational agencies.

"(f) Notwithstanding the provisions of subsection (a) (2) (B) (ii), any local educational agency which is required to carry out any program for the education of handicapped children pursuant to a State law shall be entitled to receive payments under section 611(d) for use in carrying out such program, except that such payments may not be used to reduce the level of expenditures for such program made by such local educational agency from State or local funds below the level of such expenditures for the fiscal year prior to the fiscal year for which such local educational agency seeks such payments.

"Procedural Safeguards

"Sec. 615. (a) Any State educational agency, any local educational agency, and any intermediate educational unit which receives assistance under this part shall establish and maintain procedures in accordance with subsection (b) through subsection (e) of this section to assure that handicapped children and their parents or guardians are guaranteed procedural safeguards with respect to the provision of free appropriate public education by such agencies and units.

"(b) (1) The procedures required by this section shall include, but shall not be limited to—

"(A) an opportunity for the parents or guardian of a handicapped child to examine all relevant records with respect to the identification, evaluation, and educational placement of the child, and the provision of a free appropriate public education to such child, and to obtain an independent educational evaluation of the child;

"(B) procedures to protect the rights of the child whenever the parents or guardian of the child are not known, unavailable, or the child is a ward of the State, including the assignment of an individual (who shall not be an employee of the State educational agency, local educational agency, or intermediate educational unit involved in the education or care of the child) to act as a surrogate for the parents or guardian;

"(C) written prior notice to the parents or guardian of the child whenever such agency or unit—

"(i) proposes to initiate or change, or

"(ii) refuses to initiate or change,

the identification, evaluation, or educational placement of the child or the provision of a free appropriate public education to the child;

"(D) procedures designed to assure that the notice required by clause (C) fully informs the parents or guardian, in the parents' or guardian's native lanuguage, unless it clearly is not feasible to do so, of all procedures available pursuant to this section; and

"(E) an opportunity to present complaints with respect to any matter relating to the identification, evaluation, or educational placement of the child, or the provision of a free appropriate public education to such child.

"(2) Whenever a complaint has been received under paragraph (1) of this subsection, the parents or guardian shall have an opportunity for an impartial due process hearing which shall be conducted by the State educational agency or by the local educational agency or intermediate educational unit, as determined by State law or by the State educational agency. No hearing conducted pursuant to the requirements of this paragraph shall be conducted by an employee of such agency or unit involved in the education or care of the child.

"(c) If the hearing required in paragraph (2) of subsection (b) of this section is conducted by a local educational agency or an intermediate educational unit, any party aggrieved by the findings and decision rendered in such a hearing may appeal to the State educational agency which shall conduct an impartial review of such hearing. The officer conducting such review shall make an independent decision upon completion of such review.

"(d) Any party to any hearing conducted pursuant to subsections (b) and (c) shall be accorded (1) the right to be accompanied and advised by counsel and by individuals with special knowledge or training with respect to the problems of handicapped children, (2) the right to present evidence and confront, cross-examine, and compel the attendance of witnesses, (3) the right to a written or electronic verbatim record of such hearing, and (4) the right to written findings of fact and decisions (which findings and decisions shall also be transmitted to the advisory panel established pursuant to section 613(a) (12)).

"(e) (1) A decision made in a hearing conducted pursuant to paragraph (2) of subsection (b) shall be final, except that any party involved in such hearing may appeal such decision under the provisions of subsection (c) and paragraph (2) of this subsection. A decision made under subsection (c) shall be final, except that any party may bring an action under paragraph (2) of this subsection.

"(2) Any party aggrieved by the findings and decision made under subsection (b) who does not have the right to an appeal under subsection (c), and any party aggrieved by the findings and decision under subsection (c), shall have the right to bring a civil action with respect to the complaint presented pursuant to this section, which action may be brought in any State court of competent jurisdiction or in a district court of the United States without regard to the amount in controversy. In any action brought under this paragraph the court shall receive the records of the administrative proceedings, shall hear additional evidence at the request of a party, and, basing its decision on the preponderance of the evidence, shall grant such relief as the court determines is appropriate.

"(3) During the pendency of any proceedings conducted pursuant to this section, unless the State or local educational agency and the parents or guardian otherwise agree, the child shall remain in the then current educational placement of such child, or, if applying for initial admission to a public school, shall, with the consent of the parents or guardian, be placed in the public school program until all such proceedings have been completed.

"(4) The district courts of the United States shall have jurisdiction of actions brought under this subsection without regard to the amount in controversy.

"Withholding and Judicial Review

"Sec. 616. (a) Whenever the Commissioner, after reasonable notice and opportunity for hearing to the State educational agency involved (and to any local educational agency or intermediate educational unit affected by any failure described in clause (2)), finds—

"(1) that there has been a failure to comply substantially with any provision of section 612 or section 613, or

"(2) that in the administration of the State plan there is a failure to comply with any provision of this part or with any requirements set forth in the application of a local educational agency or intermediate educational unit approved by the State educational agency pursuant to the State plan,

the Commissioner (A) shall, after notifying the State educational agency, withhold any further payments to the State under this part, and (B) may, after notifying the State educational agency, withhold further payments to the State under the Federal programs specified in section 613(a) (2) within his jurisdiction, to the extent that funds under such programs are available for the provision of assistance for the education of handicapped children. If the Commissioner withholds further payments under clause (A) or clause (B) he may determine that such withholding will be limited to programs or projects under the State plan, or portions thereof, affected by the failure, or that the State educational agency shall not make further payments under this part to specified local educational agencies or intermediate educational units affected by the failure. Until the Commissioner is satisfied that there is no longer any failure to comply with the provisions of this part, as specified in clause (1) or clause (2), no further payments shall be made to the State under this part or under the Federal programs specified in section 613(a) (2) within his jurisdiction to the extent that funds under such programs are available for the provision of assistance for the education of handicapped children, or payments by the State educational agency under this part shall be limited to local educational agencies and intermediate educational units whose actions did not cause or were not involved in the failure, as the case may be. Any State educational agency, local educational agency, or intermediate educational unit in receipt of a notice pursuant to the first sentence of this subsection shall, by means of a public notice, take such measures as may be necessary to bring the pendency of an action pursuant to this subsection to the attention of the public within the jurisdiction of such agency or unit.

"(b) (1) If any State is dissatisfied with the Commissioner's final action with respect to its State plan submitted under section 613, such State may, within sixty days after notice of such action, file with the United States court of appeals for the circuit in which such State is located a petition for review of that action. A copy of the petition shall be forthwith transmitted by the clerk of the court to the Commissioner. The Commissioner thereupon shall file in the court the record of the proceedings on which he based his action, as provided in section 2112 of title 28, United States Code.

"(2) The findings of fact by the Commissioner, if supported by substantial evidence, shall be conclusive; but the court, for good cause shown, may remand the case to the Commissioner to take further evidence, and the Commissioner may thereupon make new or modified findings of fact and may modify his previous action and shall file in the court the record of the further proceedings. Such new or modified findings of fact shall likewise be conclusive if supported by substantial evidence.

"(3) Upon the filing of such petition, the court shall have jurisdiction to affirm the action of the Commissioner or to set it aside, in whole or in part. The judgment of the court shall be subject to review by the Supreme Court of the United States upon certiorari or certification as provided in section 1254 of title 28, United States Code.

"Administration

"Sec. 617. (a) (1) In carrying out his duties under this part, the Commissioner shall—

"(A) cooperate with, and furnish all technical assistance necessary, directly or by grant or contract, to the States in matters relating to the education of handicapped children and the execution of the provisions of this part;

"(B) provide such short-term training programs and institutes as are necessary;

"(C) disseminate information, and otherwise promote the education of all handicapped children within the States; and

"(D) assure that each State shall, within one year after the date of the enactment of the Education for All Handicapped Children Act of 1975, provide certification of the actual number of handicapped children receiving special education and related services in such State.

"(2) As soon as practicable after the date of the enactment of the Education for All Handicapped Children Act of 1975, the Commissioner shall, by regulation, prescribe a uniform financial report to be utilized by State educational agencies in submitting State plans under this part in order to assure equity among the States.

"(b) In carrying out the provisions of this part, the Commissioner (and the Secretary, in carrying out the provisions of subsection (c)) shall issue, not later than January 1, 1977, amend, and revoke such rules and regulations as may be necessary. No other less formal method of implementing such provisions is authorized.

"(c) The Secretary shall take appropriate action, in accordance with the provisions of section 438 of the General Education Provisions Act, to assure the protection of the confidentiality of any personally identifiable data, information, and records collected or maintained by the Commissioner and by State and local educational agencies pursuant to the provisions of this part.

"(d) The Commissioner is authorized to hire qualified personnel necessary to conduct data collection and evaluation activities required by subsections (b), (c) and (d) of section 618 and to carry out his duties under subsection (a) (1) of this subsection without regard to the provisions of title 5, United States Code, relating to appointments in the competitive service and without regard to chapter 51 and subchapter III of chapter 53 of such title relating to classification and general schedule pay rates except that no more than twenty such personnel shall be employed at any time.

"Evaluation

"Sec. 618. (a) The Commissioner shall measure and evaluate the impact of the program authorized under this part and the effectiveness of State efforts to assure the free appropriate public education of all handicapped children.

"(b) The Commissioner shall conduct, directly or by grant or contract, such studies, investigations, and evaluations as are necessary to assure effective implementation of this part. In carrying out his responsibilities under this section, the Commissioner shall—

"(1) through the National Center for Education Statistics, provide to the appropriate committees of each House of the Congress and to the general public at least annually, and shall update at least annually, programmatic information concerning programs and projects assisted under this part and other Federal programs supporting the education of handicapped children, and such information from State and local educational agencies and other appropriate sources necessary for the implementation of this part, including—

"(A) the number of handicapped children in each State, within each disability, who require special education and related services;

"(B) the number of handicapped children in each State, within each disability, receiving a free appropriate public education and the number of handicapped children who need and are not receiving a free appropriate public education in each such State;

"(C) the number of handicapped children in each State, within each disability, who are participating in regular educational programs, consistent with the requirements of section 612(5) (B) and section 614(a) (1) (C) (iv), and the number of handicapped children who have been placed in separate classes or separate school facilities, or who have been otherwise removed from the regular education environment;

"(D) the number of handicapped children who are enrolled in public or private institutions in each State and who are receiving a free appropriate public education, and the number of handicapped children who are in such institutions and who are not receiving a free appropriate public education;

"(E) the amount of Federal, State, and local expenditures in each State specifically available for special education and related services; and

"(F) the number of personnel, by disability category, employed in the education of handicapped children, and the estimated number of additional personnel needed to adequately carry out the policy established by this Act; and

"(2) provide for the evaluation of programs and projects assisted under this part through—

"(A) the development of effective methods and procedures for evaluation;

"(B) the testing and validation of such evaluation methods and procedures; and

"(C) conducting actual evaluation studies designed to test the effectiveness of such programs and projects.

"(c) In developing and furnishing information under subclause (E) of clause (1) of subsection (b), the Commissioner may base such information upon a sampling of data available from State agencies, including the State educational agencies, and local educational agencies.

"(d) (1) Not later than one hundred twenty days after the close of each fiscal year, the Commissioner shall transmit to the appropriate committees of each House of the Congress a report on the progress being made toward the provision of free appropriate public education to all handicapped children, including a detailed description of all evaluation activities conducted under subsection (b).

"(2) The Commissioner shall include in each such report—

"(A) an analysis and evaluation of the effectiveness of procedures undertaken by each State educational agency, local educational agency, and intermediate educational unit to assure that handicapped children receive special education and related services in the least restrictive environment commensurate with their needs and to improve programs of instruction for handicapped children in day or residential facilities;

"(B) any recommendations for change in the provisions of this part, or any other Federal law providing support for the education of handicapped children; and

"(C) an evaluation of the effectiveness of the procedures undertaken by each such agency or unit to prevent erroneous classification of children as eligible to be counted under section 611, including actions undertaken by the Commissioner to carry out provisions of this Act relating to such erroneous classification.

In order to carry out such analyses and evaluations, the Commissioner shall conduct a statistically valid survey for assessing the effectiveness of individualized educational programs.

"(e) There are authorized to be appropriated for each fiscal year such sums as may be necessary to carry out the provisions of this section.

"Incentive Grants

"Sec. 619. (a) The Commissioner shall make a grant to any State which—

"(1) has met the eligibility requirements of section 612;

"(2) has a State plan approved under section 613; and

"(3) provides special education and related services to handicapped children aged three to five, inclusive, who are counted for the purposes of section 611(a) (1) (A). The maximum amount of the grant for each fiscal year which a State may receive under this section shall be $300 for each such child in that State.

"(b) Each State which—

"(1) has met the eligibility requirements of section 612,

"(2) has a State plan approved under section 613, and

"(3) desires to receive a grant under this section,

shall make an application to the Commissioner at such time, in such manner, and containing or accompanied by such information, as the Commissioner may reasonably require.

"(c) The Commissioner shall pay to each State having an application approved under subsection (b) of this section the amount to which the State is entitled under this section, which amount shall be used for the purpose of providing the services specified in clause (3) of subsection (a) of this section.

"(d) If the sums appropriated for any fiscal year for making payments to States under this section are not sufficient to pay in full the maximum amounts which all States may receive under this part for such fiscal year, the maximum amounts which all States may receive under this part for such fiscal year shall be ratably reduced. In case additional funds become available for making such payments for any fiscal year during which the preceding sentence is applicable, such reduced amounts shall be increased on the same basis as they were reduced.

"(e) In addition to the sums necessary to pay the entitlements under section 611, there are authorized to be appropriated for each fiscal year such sums as may be necessary to carry out the provisions of this section.

"Payments

"Sec. 620. (a) The Commissioner shall make payments to each State in amounts which the State educational agency of such State is eligible to receive under this part. Any State educational agency receiving payments under this subsection shall distribute payments to the local educational agencies and intermediate educational units of such State in amounts which such agencies and units are eligible to receive under this part after the State educational agency has approved applications of such agencies or units for payments in accordance with section 614(b).

"(b) Payments under this part may be made in advance or by way of reimbursement and in such installments as the Commissioner may determine necessary."

(b) (1) The Commissioner of Education shall, no later than one year after the effective date of this subsection, prescribe—

(A) regulations which establish specific criteria for determining whether a particular disorder or condition may be considered a specific learning disability for purposes of designating children with specific learning disabilities;

(B) regulations which establish and describe diagnostic procedures which shall be used in determining whether a particular child has a disorder or condition which places such child in the category of children with specific learning disabilities; and

(C) regulations which establish monitoring procedures which will be used to determine if State educational agencies, local educational agencies, and intermediate educational units are complying with the criteria established under clause (A) and clause (B).

(2) The Commissioner shall submit any proposed regulation written under paragraph (1) to the Committee on Education and Labor of the House of Representatives and the Committee on Labor and Public Welfare of the Senate, for review and comment by each such committee, at least fifteen days before such regulation is published in the Federal Register.

(3) If the Commissioner determines, as a result of the promulgation of regulations under paragraph (1), that changes are necessary in the definition of the term "children with specific learning disabilities", as such term is defined by section 602(15) of the Act, he shall submit recommendations for legislation with respect to such changes to each House of the Congress.

(4) For purposes of this subsection:

(A) The term "children with specific learning disabilities" means those children who have a disorder in one or more of the basic psychological processes involved in understanding or in using language, spoken or written, which disorder may manifest itself in imperfect ability to listen, think, speak, read, write, spell, or do mathematical calculations. Such disorders include such conditions as perceptual handicaps, brain injury, minimal brain dysfunction, dyslexia, and developmental aphasia. Such term does not include children who have learning problems which are primarily the result of visual, hearing, or motor handicaps, of mental retardation, of emotional disturbance, or environmental, cultural, or economic disadvantage.

(B) The term "Commissioner" means the Commissioner of Education.

(c) Effective on the date upon which final regulations prescribed by the Commissioner of Education under subsection (b) take effect, the amendment made by subsection (a) is amended, in subparagraph (A) of section 611(a) (5) (as such subparagraph would take effect on the effective date of subsection (a)), by adding "and" at the end of clause (i), by striking out clause (ii), and by redesignating clause (iii) as clause (ii).

NOTES

1. The potential impact of P.L. 94-142 is tremendous. By requiring education for all handicapped individuals, due process notice and hearing mechanisms, individualized educational program plans, education as close to the normal classroom environment as appropriate, and nondiscriminatory testing and evaluation procedures, the statute provides definitive answers to many of the issues that have been the subjects of litigation in the past. Of particular interest to lawyers are §§ 615(e) (2) and (4), which permit an appeal of a final administrative decision, after a due process hearing, to one's choice of a state or federal court. The grant of jurisdiction over such actions to federal district courts without regard to amount in controversy is quite significant.

2. On August 23, 1977, the Bureau of Education for the Handicapped of the United States Department of Health, Education, and Welfare issued regulations implementing P.L. 94-142. These regulations, found at 42 Fed.Reg. 42474-42518 (August 23, 1977), are detailed, comprehensive, and lengthy. They will not be set out *in toto* here,

but portions will be included below in reference to some specific issues covered by
P.L. 94-142. The comprehensive definitional section of the regulations § 121a.5 (42
Fed.Reg. 12478-12479) is notable:

(a) As used in this part, the term "handicapped children" means those children
evaluated in accordance with §§ 121a.530-121a.534 as being mentally retarded, hard of
hearing, deaf, speech impaired, visually handicapped, seriously emotionally disturbed,
orthopedically impaired, other health impaired, deaf-blind, multihandicapped, or as
having specific learning disabilities, who because of those impairments need special
education and related services.

(b) The terms used in this definition are defined as follows:

(1) "Deaf" means a hearing impairment which is so severe that the child is impaired
in processing linguistic information through hearing, with or without amplification,
which adversely affects educational performance.

(2) "Deaf-blind" means concomitant hearing and visual impairments, the combination of which causes such severe communication and other developmental and educational problems that they cannot be accommodated in special education programs solely
for deaf or blind children.

(3) "Hard of hearing" means a hearing impairment, whether permanent or fluctuat-
ing, which adversely affects a child's educational performance but which is not included
under the definition of "deaf" in this section.

(4) "Mentally retarded" means significantly subaverage general intellectual functioning existing concurrently with deficits in adaptive behavior and manifested during the
developmental period, which adversely affects a child's educational performance.

(5) "Multihandicapped" means concomitant impairments (such as mentally
retarded-blind, mentally retarded-orthopedically impaired, etc.), the combination of
which causes such severe educational problems that they cannot be accommodated in
special educational programs solely for one of the impairments. The term does not
include deaf-blind children.

(6) "Orthopedically impaired" means a severe orthopedic impairment which adversely affects a child's educational performance. The term includes impairments caused
by congenital anomaly (e.g., clubfoot, absence of some member, etc.), impairments
caused by disease (e.g., poliomyelitis, bone tuberculosis, etc.), and impairments from
other causes (e.g., cerebral palsy, amputations, and fractures or burns which cause
contractures).

(7) "Other health impaired" means limited strength, vitality or alertness, due to
chronic or acute health problems such as a heart condition, tuberculosis, rheumatic
fever, nephritis, asthma, sickle cell anemia, hemophilia, epilepsy, lead poisoning,
leukemia, or diabetes, which adversely affects a child's educational performance.

(8) "Seriously emotionally disturbed" is defined as follows:

(i) The term means a condition exhibiting one or more of the following characteristics
over a long period of time and to a marked degree, which adversely affects educational
performance:

(A) An inability to learn which cannot be explained by intellectual, sensory, or health
factors;

(B) An inability to build or maintain satisfactory interpersonal relationships with peers
and teachers;

(C) Inappropriate types of behavior or feelings under normal circumstances;

(D) A general pervasive mood of unhappiness or depression; or

(E) A tendency to develop physical symptoms or fears associated with personal or
school problems.

(ii) The term includes children who are schizophrenic or autistic. The term does not
include children who are socially maladjusted, unless it is determined that they are
seriously emotionally disturbed.

(9) "Specific learning disability" means a disorder in one or more of the basic psychological processes involved in understanding or in using language, spoken or written, which may manifest itself in an imperfect ability to listen, think, speak, read, write, spell, or to do mathematical calculations. The term includes such conditions as perceptual handicaps, brain injury, minimal brain disfunction, dyslexia, and developmental aphasia. The term does not include children who have learning problems which are primarily the result of visual, hearing, or motor handicaps, of mental retardation, or of environmental, cultural, or economic disadvantage.

(10) "Speech impaired" means a communication disorder, such as stuttering, impaired articulation, a language impairment, or a voice impairment, which adversely affects a child's educational performance.

(11) "Visually handicapped" means a visual impairment which, even with correction, adversely affects a child's educational performance. The term includes both partially seeing and blind children.

LORA v. BOARD OF EDUCATION OF CITY OF NEW YORK

United States District Court for the Eastern District of New York, 1978
456 F.Supp. 1211, 1224-1228

[See pp. 147–165, above.]

a. Education of All Handicapped Children Act

The primary federal statute, the Education of All Handicapped Children Act, 20 U.S.C. §§ 1401 *et seq.* (1978) (EHA), represents the most recent statement of a strong federal policy favoring full education of all handicapped children. Congress first considered special problems involved in educating the handicapped in 1966 when it added Title VI to the Elementary and Secondary Education Act. P.L. 89-750. Title VI established the Bureau of Education for the Handicapped to function largely as a research center. In 1970, Congress repealed Title VI and created the Education of the Handicapped Act, P.L. 91-230, giving the Bureau of Education for the Handicapped power to disburse grants for studying and improving educational services for the handicapped. This funding was extended by Congress in 1973.

In 1974, Congress amended the Education of the Handicapped Act. P.L. 93-380. This represented a major change in direction. The federal government moved beyond the role of catalyst for state activities and increased its involvement in the control and funding of education for the handicapped. P.L. 93-380 set forth detailed due process procedures required for the placement and evaluation of handicapped children and required states to create programs to identify, locate, and evaluate handicapped children. In addition, the new provisions required states receiving federal funds to maintain a policy of educating all handicapped children.

Passage of P.L. 94-142 (EHA) in 1975 was meant to bring to fruition the plans and goals of the states required by P.L. 93-380. The report of the Senate Labor and Public Welfare Committee stated that EHA was designed to "carry these planning provisions into actual delivery of services." S.Rep.No. 94-168, 94th Cong., 1st Sess. at 2; U.S.Code Cong. & Admin.News, p. 1427 (1975). Congress found that existing provisions had not had sufficient impact:

> ... [of] the more than eight million children (between birth and twenty-one years of age) with handicapping conditions requiring special education and related services, only 3.9 million such children are receiving appropriate education. 1.75 million handicapped

children are receiving no educational services at all, and 2.5 million handicapped children are receiving an inappropriate education.

S.Rep.No.94-168, 94th Cong., 1st Sess., at 8; U.S.Code Cong. & Admin.News, p. 1432 (1975). Of the 1,310,000 emotionally disturbed children needing attention, over 1,000,000 or 82% were unserved by special education.

The final cost of such neglect is far greater than the expense of providing an adequate remedy. The burden is borne ultimately by the children, their families, their communities and society as a whole.

The long range implications of these statistics are that public agencies and taxpayers will spend billions of dollars over the lifetimes of these individuals to maintain such persons as dependents and in a minimally acceptable lifestyle. With proper education services, many would be able to become productive citizens, contributing to society instead of being forced to remain burdens. Others, through such services, would increase their independence, thus reducing their dependence on society.

There is no pride in being forced to receive economic assistance. Not only does this have negative effects upon the handicapped person, but it has far-reaching effects for such person's family. . .

This nation has long embraced a philosophy that the right to a free appropriate public education is basic to equal opportunity and is vital to secure the future and the prosperity of our people. It is contradictory to that philosophy when that right is not assured equally to all groups of people within the Nation. Certainly the failure to provide a right to education to handicapped children cannot be allowed to continue.

Parents of handicapped children all too frequently are not able to advocate the rights of their children because they have been erroneously led to believe that their children will not be able to lead meaningful lives. However, over the past few years, parents of handicapped children have begun to recognize that their children are being denied services which are guaranteed under the Constitution. It should not, however, be necessary for parents throughout the country to continue utilizing the courts to assure themselves a remedy. . . . The Congress must take a more active role under its responsibility for equal protection of the laws to guarantee that handicapped children are provided equal educational opportunity. It can no longer be the policy of the Government to merely establish an unenforceable goal requiring all children to be in school. [It is necessary to take . . . steps] to ensure that the rights of children and their families are protected.

S.Rep.No.94-168, 94 Cong., 1st Sess., at 9; U.S.Code Cong. & Admin.News, p. 1433 (1975). The aim of the statute resulting from this concern was:

> to assure that all handicapped children have available to them a free appropriate public education which emphasizes special education and related services designed to meet their unique needs, to assure that the rights of handicapped children and their parents or guardians are protected, to assist States and localities to provide for the education of all handicapped children, and to assess and assure the effectiveness of efforts to educate handicapped children.

20 U.S.C. § 1401 at 442 (1976).

For the first time, the exact nature of necessary services were defined; the terms "adequate" and "free appropriate public education" were given precise content, setting a standard which must be attained.

The statute provides that:

> (16) The term "special education" means specially designed instruction, at no cost to parents or guardians, to meet the unique needs of a handicapped child, including classroom instruction, instruction in physical education, home instruction, and instruction in hospitals and institutions.
>
> (17) The term "related services" means transportation, and such developmental, corrective, and other supportive services (including speech pathology and audiology, psychological services, physical and occupational therapy, recreation, and medical and counseling services, except that such medical services shall be for diagnostic and evaluation purposes only) as may be required to assist a handicapped child to benefit from special education, and includes the early identification and assessment of handicapping conditions in children.
>
> (18) The term "free appropriate public education" means special education and related services which (A) have been provided at public expense, under public supervision and direction, and without charge, (B) meet the standards of the State educational agency, (C) include an appropriate preschool, elementary, or secondary school education in the State involved, and (D) are provided in conformity with the individualized education program required under section 1414(a)(5) of this title.

20 U.S.C. § 1401(16)(17)(18). This terminology represents a clear national commitment to meet each handicapped child's special needs in as integrated and complete a way as possible.

"Handicapped children" are defined in the Act as those who are:

> ... mentally retarded, hard of hearing, deaf, speech impaired, visually handicapped, *seriously emotionally disturbed,* orthopedically impaired, or other health impaired children, or children with specific learning disabilities, who by reason thereof require special education and related services.

20 U.S.C. § 1401(1) (emphasis added). The federal regulations define "seriously emotionally disturbed" as follows:

> (i) The term means a condition exhibiting one or more of the following characteristics over a long period of time and to a marked degree which adversely affects educational performance:
>
> (A) An inability to learn which cannot be explained by intellectual, sensory or health factors:
>
> (B) An inability to build or maintain satisfactory interpersonal relationships with peers and teachers;
>
> (C) Inappropriate types of behavior or feelings under normal circumstances;
>
> (D) A general pervasive mood of unhappiness or depression; or
>
> (E) A tendency to develop physical symptoms or fears associated with personal or school problems.
>
> (ii) The term includes children who are schizophrenic or autistic. The term does not include children who are socially maladjusted, unless it is determined that they are seriously emotionally disturbed.

42 Fed.Reg. No. 163, 42478 § 121a.5(8) (1977).

To assist the states in educating the handicapped, fiscal grants are made to them. The money helps initiate, expand and improve programs and projects designed to provide full educational opportunities to all handicapped children at the pre-school, elementary and secondary school levels. 20 U.S.C. § 1411(a). Grant eligibility standards require the states to establish "a policy that assures all handicapped children the right to a free appropriate public education." 20 U.S.C. § 1412(1). *See also* 20 U.S.C. § 1414(a); 42 Fed.Reg. No. 163, 42479 § 121.a(b) 7-8 (1977).

Each state must develop a plan to assure that:

> (A) there is established (i) a goal of providing full educational opportunity to all handicapped children, (ii) a detailed timetable for accomplishing such a goal, and (iii) a description of the kind and number of facilities, personnel, and services necessary throughout the State to meet such a goal;
> (B) a free appropriate public education will be available for all handicapped children. . . .
> (C) all children residing in the State who are handicapped, regardless of the severity of their handicap, and who are in need of special education and related services are identified, located, and evaluated, and that a practical method is developed and implemented to determine which children are currently receiving needed special education and related services and which children are not currently receiving needed special education and related services;

20 U.S.C. § 1412. Moreover, the state must assure each parent and child adequate due process protections and each child's progress is to be periodically evaluated. 20 U.S.C. §§ 1412(2)(4)(5); 1414(a)(5). These features are discussed in more detail *infra*.

Of central concern to the legislature were practices and procedures which might result in misclassification of children or be discriminatory. Specifically, Congress aimed to ameliorate the following evils:

> (1) the misuse of appropriate identification and classification data within the educational process itself; (2) discriminatory treatment as the result of the identification of a handicapping condition; and (3) misuse of identification procedures or methods which results in erroneous classification of a child as having a handicapping condition.

S.Rep.No.94-168, 94 Cong., 1st Sess., at 26-27; U.S.Code Cong. & Admin.News, pp. 1450-51 (1975).

To avoid such dangers—and believing that constitutional rights to notice and hearing, as well as to equal educational opportunity, were at stake (*see* S.Rep.No. 94-168, 94 Cong., 1st Sess., at 6; U.S.Code Cong. & Admin.News, p. 1430 (1975))—Congress provided for extensive due process guarantees whenever a change in educational placement is proposed, requested or refused. The input of parent and child in the classification decision is essential under the statute. An opportunity to challenge any placement decision is a necessary check against the possibility of abusive classification and inappropriate educational services.

Pursuant to 20 U.S.C. § 1415(e) any party may appeal a decision concerning a child's placement or education to a United States District Court after exhaustion of the state administrative procedures without regard to the amount in controversy. The district court is entitled to hear additional evidence and review the record below, providing a *de novo* hearing to the parties. The court's decision is to be based upon a preponderance of the evidence and the court may grant such relief as it determines appropriate. *See also* § 1412(5).

Aware that constant monitoring and reevaluation of pupils placed in special education programs is a necessary complement to these procedural safeguards, Congress created the "Individualized Education Program" (IEP), defined as:

> (A) a statement of the present levels of educational performance of such child, (B) a statement of annual goals, including short-term instructional objectives, (C) a statement of the specific educational services to be provided to such child, and the extent to which such child will be able to participate in regular educational programs, (D) the projected date for initiation and anticipated duration of such services, and (E) appropriate objective criteria and evaluation procedures and schedules for determining, on at least an annual basis, whether instructional objectives are being achieved.

20 U.S.C. § 1401(19).

The IEP is designed to afford instruction to fit a child's unique needs. Any state applying for funds must

> provide for procedures for evaluation at least annually of the effectiveness of programs in meeting the educational needs of handicapped children (including evaluation of individualized education programs), in accordance with such criteria that the Commissioner shall prescribe pursuant to Section 1417 of this title. . . .

20 U.S.C. § 1413(a)(11). *See* 42 Fed.Reg. No. 163, 42490-91 §§ 121a.340-345 (1977). Reevaluation was viewed as "an extension of the procedural protections guaranteed . . . to parents of handicapped children . . ." S.Rep.No. 94-168, 94 Cong., 1st Sess., at 11; U.S.Code Cong. & Admin. News, p. 1435 (1975). In addition, the regulations provide that a clinical reevaluation of every child in a special education program be made at least once every three years.

Of further concern to Congress were the inadequate standards and materials used in the process of evaluating students for special education programs:

> The Committee is alarmed about the abuses which occur in the testing and evaluation of children, and is concerned that expertise in the proper use of testing and evaluation procedures falls far short of the prolific use and development of testing and evaluation tools. The usefulness and mechanistic ease of testing should not become so paramount in the educational process that the negative effects of such testing are overlooked.

S.Rep.No.94-168, 94 Cong., 1st Sess., at 29; U.S.Code Cong. & Admin.News, p. 1453 (1975).

Finally, drawing upon contemporary sociological and educational thought, Congress wrote into the law a preference in favor of "mainstreaming," a concept discussed at greater length in section III(H), *infra*. In order to be eligible for federal funding, a state, in addition to fulfilling the requirements already described, must have established,

> procedures to assure that, to the maximum extent appropriate, handicapped children, including children in public or private institutions or other care facilities, are educated with children who are not handicapped, and that special classes, separate schooling, or other removal of handicapped children from the regular educational environment occurs only when the nature or severity of the handicap is such that education in regular classes with the use of supplementary aids and services cannot be achieved satisfactorily. . . .

20 U.S.C. § 1412(5)(B). *See also* 42 Fed.Reg. No. 163, 42497 § 121a.552 (1977).

The detailed requirements set out in this federal statute take precedence over any local custom or statute. *See, e.g. Stuart* v. *Nappi,* 443 F.Supp. 1235 (D.Conn. 1978).

NOTES

1. The *Lora* court provides a good overview of P.L. 94-142 and some of its salient features. A similar succinct summary of the act is found in *Stuart* v. *Nappi,* pp. 255–262, below.

2. In *Mattie T.* v. *Holladay,* No. DC 75-31-S (N.S.Miss., July 28, 1977), the court, in addition to granting summary judgment for the plaintiffs on their claims under § 504 (see pp. 201–202, above), ordered summary judgment against the state defendants on the plaintiffs' claims under P.L. 94-142. Specifically, the court held that the defendant school officials had violated the act by denying plaintiffs their right to:

    a. procedural safeguards, including prior notice and an impartial due process hearing, to challenge decisions regarding their educational evaluation and placement, pursuant to 20 U.S.C. § 1413(a) (13) (A) (Supp. IV, 1974);

    b. a program to locate and identify all handicapped children in the state in need of special education services, pursuant to 20 U.S.C. § 1413 (b) (1) (A) (Supp. IV, 1974);

    c. racially and culturally non-discriminatory tests and procedures used to classify them as handicapped and place them in special education programs, pursuant to 20 U.S.C. § 1514 (a) (13) (c) (Supp. IV, 1974); and

    d. educational programs which are in normal school settings with non-handicapped children to the maximum extent appropriate, pursuant to 20 U.S.C. § 1514 (a) (13) (B) (Supp. IV, 1974). (*Id.* at 1-2.)

EBERLE v. BOARD OF PUBLIC EDUCATION
OF SCHOOL DISTRICT OF PITTSBURGH, PENNSYLVANIA

United States District Court for the Western District of Pennsylvania, 1977
444 F.Supp. 41

McCUNE, District Judge.

Stephen Eberle is a seven year old child with profound hearing loss. This action is brought by Stephen and his parents for review of the placement of Stephen in a special education class for the hearing impaired in the Pittsburgh Public School System. Jurisdiction is alleged under Title VI, Section 615 of the Education for All Handicapped Children Act, 20 U.S.C. § 1415.

Defendant, the Board of Public Education of the School District of Pittsburgh, Pennsylvania (School Board), has moved to dismiss this action on the basis of res judicata, their interpretation of § 615, and the impropriety of retroactive application of this act. We find the retroactivity argument meritorious, and dismiss for lack of jurisdiction. We do not reach the other arguments.

I

The parties stipulate that Stephen is a child of above average intelligence and is affected by profound hearing loss. The complaint indicates that as a result of his condition, Stephen has required special instruction from an early age to enable him to gain skills necessary for his optimal development. The School District has not, until recently, offered this instruction. Consequently, Stephen has been attending classes at the Western Pennsylvania School for the Deaf (WPSD), a private institution, at the School District's expense. Stephen has been attending WPSD since 1973.

Commencing with or sometime prior to the 1976–77 school year, the School District instituted its own program for hearing impaired children at the Beechwood School (Beechwood). The Beechwood program utilizes a method known as the "total communications program." This method is the predominant method of training deaf children in the United States, and there is no indication of inadequacy of the Beechwood program. This program centers around the use of hand signs as a means of communication.

The Beechwood program differs from the WPSD program. The WPSD program, known as the "verbotonal program," appears to be centered around the development of the child's residual hearing ability. This method is relatively new to this country. WPSD is one of the very few verbotonal schools in the United States.

With the institution of the Beechwood program, the School District began to transfer children to whom the program was thought to be appropriate from the WPSD to Beechwood. Stephen was one of the students transferred. Because Stephen had already undergone four years of verbotonal training, his parents feared that gains which Stephen had made would be lost and further gains impaired by placement in a total communications program. As a result, they oppose his transfer.

Pursuant to the regulations of the Secretary of Education of the Commonwealth of Pennsylvania, a due process hearing was held regarding this transfer on October 18, 1976. On November 5, 1976, the hearing officer submitted a decision approving the transfer. Exceptions were timely filed with the Secretary of Education. The Secretary took no action during the 1976–77 school year, and Stephen was permitted to continue at the WPSD for that term. At the completion of the term, the Eberles were informed that the School District intended to transfer Stephen to Beechwood at the beginning of the 1977–78 term. A second due process hearing was demanded, presumably due to changed circumstances, or the yearly right of hearing provided for in the Secretary's regulations. No hearing was granted. On September 8, 1977, the Secretary of Education affirmed the determination of the hearing officer as submitted on November 5, 1976. It is that decision which caused this action to be brought here.

The Eberles allege jurisdiction in this court over this action based on the Education for All Handicapped Children Act. The Education of Handicapped Children Act does contain a jurisdictional grant. However, the main purpose of the Act is the funding of special schools for the handicapped. The jurisdictional grant is one of a number of procedural safeguards attendant to the Act, insuring the equitable and efficient use of the funds by the states. Upon acceptance of federal funds, the states are required to set up certain procedures for review of administrative decisions concerning the assignment of students. These review procedures are then to be brought to this court (or a state court of competent jurisdiction) for review. The effective date of these provisions is October 1, 1977. 20 U.S.C. § 1411. The question before us is whether this court has jurisdiction over an action which has proceeded through state review prior to the effective date of the Act. The complaint in this court was filed subsequent to the effective date of the Act. To determine whether the act should be retrospectively applied, it is necessary to examine the Act in light of the allegations of the complaint.

The due process procedure to be set up by the states and our jurisdictional grant are included in Title VI, § 615 of the Act. Section 615 is a somewhat detailed provision. Only a small portion of § 615 is relevant to our jurisdiction, however. Subsection (e)(1) provides:

> A decision made in a hearing conducted pursuant to paragraph (2) of subsection (b) shall be final, except that any party involved in such hearing may appeal such decision under the provisions of subsection (c) and paragraph (2) of this subsection. . . .
> (2) Any party aggrieved by the findings and decision made under subsection (b) of this section who does not have the right to an appeal under subsection (c) of this section, and any party aggrieved by the findings and decision under subsection (c) of this section, shall have the right to bring a civil action with respect to the complaint presented pursuant to this section, which action may be brought in any State court of competent jurisdiction or in a district court of the United States without regard to the amount in controversy. In any action brought under this paragraph the court shall receive the records of the administrative proceedings, shall hear additional evidence at the request of a party, and, basing its decision on the preponderance of the evidence, shall grant such relief as the court determines is appropriate.

Subsection (e)(1) cannot be fully understood without reference to paragraph (2) of subsection (b):

> (2) Whenever a complaint has been received under paragraph (1) of this subsection, the parents or guardian shall have an opportunity for an impartial due process hearing which shall be conducted by the State education agency or by the local educational agency or intermediate educational unit, as determined by State law or by the State educational agency. No hearing conducted pursuant to the requirements of this paragraph shall be conducted by an employee of such agency or unit involved in the education or care of the child.

Subsection (c) is also referred to in Subsection (e)(1); that subsection merely refers to an optional appeal procedure, allowing appeal to the Secretary of Education prior to the review of the determination by an appropriate court.

These subsections provide the basic structure for the establishment of a review procedure by the states. More elaborate due process guarantees may be instituted by individual states. At a minimum, however, a parent must be given notice of the assignment of his child to a special program; he must be given a right to a hearing on that assignment; and he is allowed an appeal to this court or an appropriate state court. This procedure must be available to parents if a state accepts funds from the federal government for handicapped children's education.

The question of whether Pennsylvania due process procedures conform to the requirements of the Education of Handicapped Children Act is not before this court. The existence of these procedures is, however, significant. If they were instituted prior to the effective date of § 615 and were instituted pursuant to § 615, then it would be apparent the Secretary of Education expected § 615 to have retrospective effect.

Our research shows that the Pennsylvania procedures which have been followed by the litigants in this action are not procedures instituted as a result of § 615. These procedures were established pursuant to a consent decree entered into by the Commonwealth on October 8, 1971. *Pennsylvania Association for Retarded Children* v. *Pennsylvania*, 334 F.Supp. 1257 (E.D.Pa. 1971). Interestingly, this decree was in part, the motivation § 615. See 2 U.S.Code Cong. & Admin.News, p. 1430 (1975). Since both the Pennsylvania procedures and § 615 are motivated by the *Pennsylvania Association for Retarded Children* consent decree, it is impossible to determine when the Secretary of Education believed that § 615 required the due process procedures.

It is, of course, the intent of Congress and not the Secretary of Education which controls our decision here. That intent is made clear by both the form and legislative history of § 615.

Section 615 is attached to a funding act. It is logical to conclude that Congress intended the scope of § 615 to be coextensive with the Education of Handicapped Children Act itself. Since the power base of the act is the funding of state programs, § 615 cannot become binding on the states prior to the funding to which it is attached. The due process procedures were only a condition of funds received after October 1, 1977. The due process procedure prior to that date were procedures pursuant to § 615. Since our jurisdiction is over complaints made "pursuant to" § 615, we have no jurisdiction over this action.

The legislative history of § 615 supports this interpretation. In the Joint Explanatory Statement of the Committee of Conference, it is noted that "[a]ll of the procedural safeguards [§ 615] are established as a condition of a state's eligibility to receive funds under this part." 2 U.S.Code Cong. & Admin.News, pp. 1480, 1501 (1975). The safeguards are not intended as independent of funding, but are imposed as a condition of funding. As a result, these conditions cannot be imposed prior to funding made conditional upon them. They should not be retrospectively applied.

The practical effect of this decision may be somewhat temporary. Our reading of the Secretary's regulations leads us to believe that Stephen would be entitled to a second due process hearing based upon the decision to transfer him for the school year 1977–78. Whether the result of that hearing, occurring after October 1, 1977, but based on a decision made prior to October 1, 1977, furnishes the basis for an appeal to this court of which we would have jurisdiction, is not now decided. Whether the doctrine of res judicata applies to the second proceeding is not decided. The Secretary's regulations appear to entitle parents to a hearing each year. It is thus apparent that there may be multiple hearings related to the same subject.

Whether there should be modifications of the regulations and whether they should be promulgated pursuant to § 615, is left to the Secretary.

NOTE

While the legal import of *Eberle* is primarily the ruling that P.L. 94-142 procedural requirements are not retroactive (*accord, Stemple* v. *Board of Education of Prince George's County*, C.A. No. Y-78-55 (D.Md. Sept. 26, 1978)), the opinion touches on an interesting factual issue—the parents' disagreement with the school district over the proper method for educating a child with a profound hearing loss. The debate between the "total communication" approach and the "verbotonal" method in *Eberle* is similar to a common difference of opinion among deaf people over the relative merits of total communication versus what is termed the "oral" method. The oral method is an approach for teaching deaf persons that stresses the use of speechreading (lipreading) and the development of speech skills by deaf individuals. In contrast, in the total communication method, oral communication techniques are supplemented by the use of sign language. Proponents of the oral method claim that sign language is an unnecessary crutch which hinders the development of speechreading and speaking skills. Advocates of total communication argue that the inability of deaf children to communicate until they have mastered oral speech and speechreading skills results in emotional problems and social and academic backwardness in comparison to their peers; moreover, some deaf students never succeed in mastering the oral method and are condemned to frustration, failure, and almost complete inability to communicate. The debate between these two camps is long-standing and vehement. Both total communication and oralism can number well qualified experts among their adherents, although in modern times the weight of authority seems to favor the total communication approach, as attested to by the fact that the national organizations of deaf persons advocate total communication. For additional information about these issues, see, e.g., Switzer, M., and Williams, B., "Life Problems of Deaf People," 15 *Archives of Environmental Health* 249-56 (1967); Vernon, M., "Potential, Achievement, and Rehabilitation in the Deaf Population," 31 *Rehabilitation Literature* 258-67 (1970); Williams, B., and Sussman, A., "Social and Psychological Problems of Deaf People," *Counseling with Deaf People* 13, 16-19 (1971); Greenberg, J., and Doolittle, G., "Can Schools Speak the Language of the Deaf?" *N.Y. Times Magazine*, p. 50 (Dec. 11, 1977); and Nix, G. (ed.), *Mainstream Education for Hearing Impaired Children and Youth* (1976).

For a case in which parents refused to send their child to the Western Pennsylvania School for the Deaf because of their belief that it employed the total communication approach, and were held to have thereby committed child neglect, see *In Re Wingard Petition*, 7 D.&C.2d 522 (Pa. 1956). And in a similar case in Iowa, parents who had insisted that their deaf child remain in the local "country" school were ordered to send him to the Iowa School for the Deaf, *In re Petty*, 214 Ia. 523, 41 N.W.2d 672 (1950). Would the results in such situations be affected by the provisions of P.L. 94-142?

ADDITIONAL READING

Note, "The Education for All Handicapped Children Act: Opening the Schoolhouse Door," 6 *N.Y.U. Rev. of Law & Soc. Change* 43, 50-62 (1976).
Note, "The Education of All Handicapped Children Act of 1975," 10 *J. Law Ref.* 110 (1976).

2. Specific Issues

The provisions of the Education for All Handicapped Children Act of 1975 and § 504 of the Rehabilitation Act of 1973 have been invoked in the attempted resolution of many specific problem areas, some of which had been the subject of much previous litigative activity.

a. Due Process Procedural Rights

Regulations for Implementation of P.L. 94-142

42 Fed. Reg. 42473, 42494-42496 (Aug. 23, 1977), 45 C.F.R. § 121a

Subpart E—Procedural Safeguards
Due Process Procedures for Parents and Children

§ 121a.500 Definitions of "consent," "evaluation," and "personally identifiable."

As used in this part: "Consent" means that: (a) The parent has been fully informed of all information relevant to the activity for which consent is sought, in his or her native language, or other mode of communication;

(b) The parent understands and agrees in writing to the carrying out of the activity for which his or her consent is sought, and the consent describes that activity and lists the records (if any) which will be released and to whom; and

(c) The parent understands that the granting of consent is voluntary on the part of the parent and may be revoked at any time.

"Evaluation" means procedures used in accordance with §§ 121a.530-121a.534 to determine whether a child is handicapped and the nature and extent of the special education and related services that the child needs. The term means procedures used selectively with an individual child and does not include basic tests administered to or procedures used with all children in a school, grade, or class.

"Personally identifiable" means that information includes:

(a) The name of the child, the child's parent, or other family member;

(b) The address of the child;

(c) A personal identifier, such as the child's social security number or student number; or

(d) A list of personal characteristics or other information which would make it possible to identify the child with reasonable certainty.

(20 U.S.C. 1415, 1417 (c).)

§ 121a.501 General responsibility of public agencies.

Each State educational agency shall insure that each public agency establishes and implements procedural safeguards which meet the requirements of §§ 121a.500-121a.514.

(20 U.S.C. 1415(a).)

§ 121a.502 Opportunity to examine records.

The parents of a handicapped child shall be afforded, in accordance with the procedures in §§ 121a.562-121a.569 an opportunity to inspect and review all education records with respect to:

(a) The identification, evaluation, and educational placement of the child, and

(b) The provision of a free appropriate public education to the child.

(20 U.S.C. 1415(b) (1) (A).)

§ 121a.503 Independent educational evaluation.

(a) *General.* (1) The parents of a handicapped child have the right under this part to obtain an independent educational evaluation of the child, subject to paragraphs (b) through (e) of this section.

(2) Each public agency shall provide to parents, on request, information about where an independent educational evaluation may be obtained.

(3) For the purposes of this part:

(i) "Independent educational evaluation" means an evaluation conducted by a qualified examiner who is not employed by the public agency responsible for the education of the child in question.

(ii) "Public expense" means that the public agency either pays for the full cost of the evaluation or insures that the evaluation is otherwise provided at no cost to the parent, consistent with § 121a.301 of Subpart C.

(b) *Parent right to evaluation at public expense.* A parent has the right to an independent educational evaluation at public expense if the parent disagrees with an evaluation obtained by the public agency. However, the public agency may initiate a hearing under § 121a.506 of this subpart to show that its evaluation is appropriate. If the final decision is that the evaluation is appropriate, the parent still has the right to an independent educational evaluation, but not at public expense.

(c) *Parent initiated evaluations.* If the parent obtains an independent educational evaluation at private expense, the results of the evaluation:

(1) Must be considered by the public agency in any decision made with respect to the provision of a free appropriate public education to the child, and

(2) May be presented as evidence at a hearing under this subpart regarding that child.

(d) *Requests for evaluations by hearing officers.* If a hearing officer requests an independent educational evaluation as part of a hearing, the cost of the evaluation must be at public expense.

(e) *Agency criteria.* Whenever an independent evaluation is at public expense, the criteria under which the evaluation is obtained, including the location of the evaluation and the qualifications of the examiner, must be the same as the criteria which the public agency uses when it initiates an evaluation.
(20 U.S.C. 1415(b) (1) (A).)

§ 121a.504   Prior notice; parental consent.

(a) *Notice.* Written notice which meets the requirements under § 121a.505 must be given to the parents of a handicapped child a reasonable time before the public agency:

(1) Proposes to initiate or change the identification, evaluation, or educational placement of the child or the provision of a free appropriate public education to the child, or

(2) Refuses to initiate or change the identification, evaluation, or educational placement of the child or the provision of a free appropriate public education to the child.

(b) *Consent.* (1) Parental consent must be obtained before:

(i) Conducting a preplacement evaluation; and

(ii) Initial placement of a handicapped child in a program providing special education and related services.

(2) Except for preplacement evaluation and initial placement, consent may not be required as a condition of any benefit to the parent or child.

(c) *Procedures where parent refuses consent.* (1) Where State law requires parental consent before a handicapped child is evaluated or initially provided special education and related services, State procedures govern the public agency in overriding a parent's refusal to consent.

(2) (i) Where there is no State law requiring consent before a handicapped child is evaluated or initially provided special education and related services, the public agency may use the hearing procedures in §§ 121a.506-121a.508 to determine if the child may be evaluated or initially provided special education and related services without parental consent.

(ii) If the hearing officer upholds the agency, the agency may evaluate or initially provide special education and related services to the child without the parent's consent, subject to the parent's rights under §§ 121a.510-121a.513.

(20 U.S.C. 1415(b) (1) (C). (D).)

Comment. 1. Any changes in a child's special education program, after the initial placement, are not subject to parental consent under Part B, but are subject to the prior notice requirement in paragraph (a) and the individualized education program requirements in Subpart C.

2. Paragraph (c) means that where State law requires parental consent before evaluation or before special education and related services are initially provided and the parent refuses (or otherwise withholds) consent, State procedures, such as obtaining a court order authorizing the public agency to conduct the evaluation or provide the education and related services, must be followed.

If, however, there is no legal requirement for consent outside of these regulations, the public agency may use the due process procedures under this subpart to obtain a decision to allow the evaluation or services without parental consent. The agency must notify the parent of its actions, and the parent has appeal rights as well as rights at the hearing itself.

§ 121a.505   Content of notice.

(a) The notice under § 121a.504 must include:

(1) A full explanation of all of the procedural safeguards available to the parents under Subpart E;

(2) A description of the action proposed or refused by the agency, an explanation of why the agency proposes or refuses to take the action, and a description of any options the agency considered and the reasons why those options were rejected;

(3) A description of each evaluation procedure, test, record, or report the agency uses as a basis for the proposal or refusal; and

(4) A description of any other factors which are relevant to the agency's proposal or refusal.

(b) The notice must be:

(1) Written in language understandable to the general public, and

(2) Provided in the native language of the parent or other mode of communication used by the parent, unless it is clearly not feasible to do so.

(c) If the native language or other mode of communication of the parent is not a written language, the State or local educational agency shall take steps to insure:

(1) That the notice is translated orally or by other means to the parent in his or her native language or other mode of communication;

(2) That the parent understands the content of the notice, and

(3) That there is written evidence that the requirements in paragraph (c) (1) and (2) of this section have been met.

(20 U.S.C. 1415(b) (1) (D))

§ 121a.506   Impartial due process hearing.

(a) A parent or a public educational agency may initiate a hearing on any of the matters described in § 121a.504(a) (1) and (2).

(b) The hearing must be conducted by the State educational agency or the public agency directly responsible for the education of the child, as determined under State statute, State regulation, or a written policy of the State educational agency.

(c) The public agency shall inform the parent of any free or low-cost legal and other relevant services available in the area if:

(1) The parent requests the information; or

(2) The parent or the agency initiates a hearing under this section.

(20 U.S.C. 1416(b) (2).)

Comment: Many States have pointed to the success of using mediation as an intervening step prior to conducting a formal due process hearing. Although the process of mediation is not required by the statute or these regulations, an agency may wish to suggest mediation in disputes concerning the identification, evaluation, and educational placement of handicapped children, and the provision of a free appropriate public education to those children. Mediations have been conducted by members of State educational agencies or local educational agency personnel who were not previously involved in the particular case. In many cases, mediation leads to resolution of differences between parents and agencies without the development of an adversarial relationship and with minimal emotional stress. However, mediation may not be used to deny or delay a parent's rights under this subpart.

§ 121a.507   Impartial hearing officer.

(a) A hearing may not be conducted:

(1) By a person who is an employee of a public agency which is involved in the education or care of the child, or

(2) By any person having a personal or professional interest which would conflict with his or her objectivity in the hearing.

(b) A person who otherwise qualifies to conduct a hearing under paragraph (a) of this section is not an employee of the agency solely because he or she is paid by the agency to serve as a hearing officer.

(c) Each public agency shall keep a list of the persons who serve as hearing officers. The list must include a statement of the qualifications of each of those persons.

(20 U.S.C. 1414(b) (2).)

§ 121a.508   Hearing rights.

(a) Any party to a hearing has the right to:

(1) Be accompanied and advised by counsel and by individuals with special knowledge or training with respect to the problems of handicapped children;

(2) Present evidence and confront, cross-examine, and compel the attendance of witnesses;

(3) Prohibit the introduction of any evidence at the hearing that has not been disclosed to that party at least five days before the hearing;

(4) Obtain a written or electronic verbatim record of the hearing;

(5) Obtain written findings of fact and decisions. (The public agency shall transmit those findings and decisions, after deleting any personally identifiable information, to the State advisory panel established under Subpart F).

(b) Parents involved in hearings must be given the right to:

(1) Have the child who is the subject of the hearing present; and

(2) Open the hearing to the public.

(20 U.S.C. 1415(d).)

§ 121a.509   Hearing decisions; appeal.

A decision made in a hearing conducted under this subpart is final, unless a party to the hearing appeals the decision under § 121a.510 or § 121a.511.

(20 U.S.C. 1415(c).)

§ 121a.510   Administrative appeal; impartial review.

(a) If the hearing is conducted by a public agency other than the State educational agency, any party aggrieved by the findings and decision in the hearing may appeal to the State educational agency.

(b) If there is an appeal, the State educational agency shall conduct an impartial review of the hearing. The official conducting the review shall:

(1) Examine the entire hearing record;

(2) Insure that the procedures at the hearing were consistent with the requirements of due process;

(3) Seek additional evidence if necessary. If a hearing is held to receive additional evidence, the rights in § 121a.508 apply;

(4) Afford the parties an opportunity for oral or written argument, or both, at the discretion of the reviewing official;

(5) Make an independent decision on completion of the review; and

(6) Give a copy of written findings and the decision to the parties.

(c) The decision made by the reviewing official is final, unless a party brings a civil action under § 121a.512.

(20 U.S.C. 1415 (c), (d); H. Rep. No. 94-664, at p. 49 (1975).)

Comment. 1. The State educational agency may conduct its review either directly or through another State agency acting on its behalf. However, the State educational agency remains responsible for the final decision on review.

2. All parties have the right to continue to be represented by counsel at the State administrative review level, whether or not the reviewing official determines that a further hearing is necessary. If the reviewing official decides to hold a hearing to

receive additional evidence, the other rights in section 121a.508, relating to hearings, also apply.

§ 121a.511   Civil action.

Any party aggrieved by the findings and decision made in a hearing who does not have the right to appeal under § 121a.510 of this subpart, and any party aggrieved by the decision of a reviewing officer under § 121a.510 has the right to bring a civil action under section 615(e) (2) of the Act.
(20 U.S.C. 1415.)

§ 121a.512   Timeliness and convenience of hearings and reviews.

(a) The public agency shall insure that not later than 45 days after the receipt of a request for a hearing:

(1) A final decision is reached in the hearing; and

(2) A copy of the decision is mailed to each of the parties.

(d) The State educational agency shall insure that not later than 30 days after the receipt of a request for a review:

(1) A final decision is reached in the review; and

(2) A copy of the decision is mailed to each of the parties.

(c) A hearing or reviewing officer may grant specific extensions of time beyond the periods set out in paragraphs (a) and (b) of this section at the request of either party.

(d) Each hearing and each review involving oral arguments must be conducted at a time and place which is reasonably convenient to the parents and child involved.
(20 U.S.C. 1415.)

§ 121a.513   Child's status during proceedings.

(a) During the pendency of any administrative or judicial proceeding regarding a complaint, unless the public agency and the parents of the child agree otherwise, the child involved in the complaint must remain in his or her present educational placement.

(b) If the complaint involves an application for initial admission to public school, the child, with the consent of the parents, must be placed in the public school program until the completion of all the proceedings.
(20 U.S.C. 1415(e) (3).)

Comment. Section 121a.513 does not permit a child's placement to be changed during a complaint proceeding, unless the parents and agency agree otherwise. While the placement may not be changed, this does not preclude the agency from using its normal procedures for dealing with children who are endangering themselves or others.

§ 121a.514   Surrogate parents.

(a) *General.* Each public agency shall insure that the rights of a child are protected when:

(1) No parent (as defined in § 121a.10) can be identified;

(2) The public agency, after reasonable efforts, cannot discover the whereabouts of a parent; or

(3) The child is a ward of the State under the laws of that State.

(b) *Duty of public agency.* The duty of a public agency under paragraph (a) of this section includes the assignment of an individual to act as a surrogate for the parents. This must include a method (1) for determining whether a child needs a surrogate parent, and (2) for assigning a surrogate parent to the child.

(c) *Criteria for selection of surrogates.* (1) The public agency may select a surrogate parent in any way permitted under State law.

(2) Public agencies shall insure that a person selected as a surrogate:

(i) Has no interest that conflicts with the interests of the child he or she represents; and

(ii) Has knowledge and skills, that insure adequate representation of the child.

(d) *Non-employee requirement; compensation.* (1) A person assigned as a surrogate may not be an employee of a public agency which is involved in the education or care of the child.

(2) A person who otherwise qualifies to be a surrogate parent under paragraph (c) and (d) (1) of this section, is not an employee of the agency solely because he or she is paid by the agency to serve as a surrogate parent.

(e) *Responsibilities.* The surrogate parent may represent the child in all matters relating to:

(1) The identification, evaluation, and educational placement of the child, and

(2) The provision of a free appropriate public education to the child.

(20 U.S.C. 1415(b) (1) (B).)

NOTES

1. These regulations supplement, modify, and explain the statutory provisions regarding procedural safeguards outlined in § 615 of P.L. 94-142; see pp. 227–229, above.

2. Compare the procedural requirements of the regulations with the procedures imposed by the courts in the *Marlega, PARC,* and *Mills* cases.

LORA v. BOARD OF EDUCATION OF CITY OF NEW YORK

United States District Court for the Eastern District of New York, 1978
456 F.Supp. 1211, 1278, 1279
[See pp. 147–165, above.]

B. *Right to Due Process in Procedures*

Plaintiffs claim a violation of their due process rights in that pupils have been, and continue to be, transferred to special day schools without adequate prior notice and an opportunity to be heard. This, it is argued, constitutes a violation not only of the due process clause of the 14th Amendment, but also of due process guarantees included in federal and state statutes and regulations. Defendants have two answers to these charges. First, they claim there is no right to notice and hearing prior to a change in educational placement; second, assuming the existence of such a right, they deny that their practices have violated it in any way.

The argument that there is no right to notice and hearing prior to a change in educational setting is without merit; it flies in the face of judicial pronouncements as well as the congressional and state policies outlined in the statutes and regulations. *See* section III C 1 and 2, *supra;* Appendices B and C. Placement of children out of the mainstream requires procedural due process protection. The law supports plaintiffs' contention that the following abuses—if established by the evidence—would constitute a violation of due process: (a) use of surreptitious means to obtain parental consent for special day school placement by mailing uninformed parents forms which are signed without full realization of what is involved; (b) denial of plaintiffs' right to a hearing by not appointing a surrogate parent to represent the interests of the child should the parent disagree with the child's objection to placement in a special school or be disinterested in the matter; (c) failure to reevaluate students already placed in these schools without the benefit of the due process protections built into the current regulations; (d) failure to carry out an annual and triennial review of all students currently in the special day schools as provided in the regulations; and (e) failure to provide parents with clinical records upon which recommendations for special day school placement are made so that they are unable to prepare for a hearing to contest the placement.

In *Mills* v. *Board of Education*, 348 F.Supp. 866, 875 (D.D.C. 1972) the court noted that "[d]ue process of law requires a hearing prior to exclusion, termination or classification into a special program" (citations omitted). The court also ordered periodic review of each child's status and of the soundness of present placement. *Id* at 878. *See Hairston* v. *Drosick,* 423 F.Supp. 180, 184-85 (S.D.West Virginia 1976) (exclusion of a handicapped child from the regular classroom without procedural safeguards is a violation of constitutional rights as well as of the Rehabilitation Act of 1973.)

Pennsylvania Association for Retarded Children v. *Pennsylvania,* 343 F.Supp. 279 (E.D.Pa. 1972) was resolved by a consent decree providing for public education for all retarded children and guaranteeing both prior notice of suggested non-mainstream placement and the opportunity for a hearing to contest the recommendation. In its opinion, the court acknowledged the danger of stigma in labeling a child mentally retarded; it emphasized the need for due process hearings in any instance where the state's action may result in stigmatization. *Id.* 295. *See New York Association for Retarded Children, Inc.* v. *Rockefeller,* 357 F.Supp. 752, 762 (E.D.N.Y. 1973).

Legal commentators have recognized the dangers of misclassification in special education placement, whether due to misuse of proper criteria, invalidity of such criteria, or the vulnerability of minority group and behavioral problem pupils to misclassification because of impatient or innately biased teachers, and the possibility of stigma attached to special education placement. These possibilities mandate a hearing, involving parent, student, educator and administrator, prior to placement. *See, e.g.,* S. L. Ross, H. G. DeYoung, J. S. Cohen, "Confrontation: Special Education and the Law," in R. E. Schmid, J. Moneypenny, and R. Johnston, *Contemporary Issues in Special Education,* 20 (1977); D. Kirp, Wm. Buss, and P. Kuriloff, "Legal Reform of Special Education: Empirical Studies and Procedural Proposals," 62 *Cal. L. Rev.* 40, 117-55 (1974); Kirp, "Student Classification, Public Policy and the Courts," 44 *Harv. Educational Review* 7 (1974); Jones, "Coercive Behavior Control in the Schools: Reconciling 'Individually Appropriate' Education with Damaging Changes in Educational Status," 29 *Stan. L. Rev.* 93, 111 (1976). Parents must have adequate access to all records and the opportunity to obtain an independent evaluation of the child should it be desired. D. Kirp, Wm. Buss, and P. Kuriloff, *supra* at 128.

Finally, adequate notice is an essential part of due process. As the Supreme

Court noted in *Goss* v. *Lopez,* a case involving due process requirements prior to school suspension:

> The fundamental requisite of due process of law is the opportunity to be heard . . . a right that has little reality or worth unless one is informed that the matter is pending and can choose for himself whether to . . . contest. . . . Parties whose rights are to be affected are entitled to be heard; and in order that they may enjoy that right they must first be notified.

419 U.S. 565, 579, 95 S.Ct. 729, 738, 42 L.Ed.2d 725 (1974) (citations omitted).

There is no general rule on the details of required notice. Rather, "the timing and content of notice . . . will depend on appropriate accommodation of the competing interests involved." *Goss* v. *Lopez, supra,* 419 U.S. at 579, 95 S.Ct. at 738-39. *See also Morrissey* v. *Brewer,* 408 U.S. 471, 481, 92 S.Ct. 2593, 2600, 33 L.Ed.2d 484 (1972). "The very nature of due process negates any concept of inflexible procedures universally applicable to every imaginable situation." *Cafeteria & Restaurant Workers Union* v. *McElroy,* 367 U.S. 886, 895, 81 S.Ct. 1743, 1748, 6 L.Ed.2d 1230 (1961), *cited in Goss* v. *Lopez, supra,* 419 U.S. at 578, 95 S.Ct. at 738.

Reinforcing this case law are, of course, the statutory and regulatory requirements already referred to outlining the contours of due process rights to notice and hearing as well as to periodic reevaluations of the appropriateness of special education placement.

NOTES

1. In *Goss* v. *Lopez,* 419 U.S. 565 (1974), cited by the *Lora* court, the Supreme Court held that suspending students from the public schools for misconduct without notice and a prior hearing was a violation of the Due Process Clause. The two constitutional bases relied upon by the Court for mandating due process procedures in the factual situation of *Goss* v. *Lopez* were the "property" interest in entitlement to public education and the "liberty" interest in one's reputation. These considerations, as the *Lora* case indicates, are at least equally valid in the context of denials of public education to handicapped individuals. In fact, the "stigma" attached to the labels *handicapped, mentally retarded, crippled,* and the like, and the resulting segregation from one's peers (see discussion of stigma in Chapter 1) makes the possibility of damage to reputation even more likely than in the *Goss* situation. The *Goss* decision seems, therefore, to validate the reasoning in the earlier educational due process cases, such as *PARC, Mills,* and *Marlega.* In fact, in a block citation in footnote 8 of its opinion, the *Goss* v. *Lopez* Court cited *Mills* v. *Board of Education of the District of Columbia,* see pp. 92–108, *supra,* with approval. It is interesting to note that Mr. Peter Roos, attorney for the plaintiff students in *Goss* has also been an advocate for equal educational rights of handicapped individuals; for example, he represented a statewide class of handicapped children in *Rhode Island Society for Autistic Children* v. *Board of Regents,* (see note 1(d) on p. 213, *supra*), a § 504 education case.

2. In a dissenting opinion in *Goss,* Justice Powell expressed great concern about judicial intervention in the operation of the public schools. Justice Powell's viewpoint prevailed in *Ingraham* v. *Wright,* 430 U.S. 651 (1977), in which the Court upheld the

use of "reasonable" corporal punishment. Writing for the 5–4 majority in *Ingraham,* Justice Powell declared: "Assessment of the need for, and the appropriate means of maintaining, school discipline is committed generally to the discretion of school authorities subject to state law. '[T]he court has repeatedly emphasized the need for affirming the comprehensive authority of the States and of school officials, consistent with fundamental constitutional safeguards, to prescribe and control conduct in the schools.' (citation omitted)." *Id.* at 681-682.

The Court reiterated its preference for administrative discretion in *Board of Curators of Univ. of Mo.* v. *Horowitz,* 435 U.S. 78, 98 S. Ct. 948 (1978), turning aside a challenge by a fourth year medical student that her dismissal by the medical school for academic reasons without a prior hearing violated the due process clause of the Fourteenth Amendment. In what ways are *Goss, Mills,* and *Lora* distinguishable from *Ingraham* and *Horowitz?*

ADDITIONAL READING

Abeson, A., Bolic, N., Hass, J., *A Primer on Due Process: Educational Decisions for Handicapped Children,* Council for Exceptional Children (1975).
Buss, W., Kirp, D., and Kuriloff, P., "Exploring Procedural Modes of Special Classification," in 2 *Issues in the Classification of Children* 386 (Hobbs, N., ed. 1975).
Kirp, D., "Proceduralism and Bureaucracy: Due Process in the School Setting," 28 *Stan. L. Rev.* 841 (1976).
Bersoff, D., Procedural Safeguards 82-83 (Bureau of Education for the Handicapped Monograph, 1978).
See also the articles cited in *Lora* v. *Board of Education of City of New York.*

b. Dealing with Handicaps as Disciplinary Problems

STUART V. NAPPI

United States District Court for the District of Connecticut, 1978
443 F.Supp. 1235

DALY, District Judge.

Plaintiff, Kathy Stuart, is in her third year at Danbury High School. The records kept by the Danbury School System concerning plaintiff tell of a student with serious academic and emotional difficulties. They describe her as having deficient academic skills caused by a complex of learning disabilities and limited intelligence. Not surprising, her record also reflects a history of behavioral problems. It was precisely for handicapped children such as plaintiff that Congress enacted the Education of the Handicapped Act (Handicapped Act), 20 U.S.C. § 1401 *et seq. See* 20 U.S.C. § 1401(1).

Plaintiff seeks a preliminary injunction of an expulsion hearing to be held by the Danbury Board of Education. She claims that she has been denied rights afforded her by the Handicapped Act. Her claims raise novel issues concerning the impact of recent regulations to the Handicapped Act on the disciplinary process of local schools.

The Handicapped Act was passed in 1970 and amended in 1975. Its purpose is to provide states with federal assistance for the education of handicapped children. *See*

45 C.F.R. § 121a at 374 (Appendix § 2.1) (1976). The regulations on which this decision turns became effective on October 1, 1977. *See* 42 Fed.Reg. 42,473 (1977) (to be codified in 45 C.F.R. § 121a). State eligibility for federal funding under the Handicapped Act is made contingent upon the implementation of a detailed state plan and upon compliance with certain procedural safeguards. *See* 20 U.S.C. §§ 1413, 1415. The state plan must require all public schools within the state to provide educational programs which meet the unique needs of handicapped children. *See Kruse* v. *Campbell*, 431 F.Supp. 180, 186 (E.D. Va.), *vacated and remanded*, 434 U.S. 808, 98 SCt. 38, 54 L.Ed.2d 65 (October 4, 1977); *cf. Cuyahoga County Association for Retarded children and Adults* v. *Essex*, 411 F.Supp. 46, 61 n. 7 (N.D. Ohio 1976). Connecticut's plan has been approved and the state presently receives federal funds. As a handicapped student in a recipient state, plaintiff is entitled to a special education program that is responsive to her needs and may insist on compliance with the procedural safeguards contained in the Handicapped Act. After scrutinizing the recent regulations to the Handicapped Act and reviewing both plaintiff's involved school record and the evidence introduced at the preliminary injunction hearing, this Court is persuaded that a preliminary injunction should issue.

The events leading to the present controversy began in 1975 when one of plaintiff's teachers reported to the school guidance counselor that plaintiff was "academically unable to achieve success in his class." As a result of this report and corroboration from her other teachers, it was suggested that plaintiff be given a psychological evaluation and that she be referred to a Planning and Placement Team (PPT). The members of a PPT are drawn from a variety of disciplines, but in all cases they are "professional personnel" employed by the local board of education. The PPT's functions are to identify children requiring special education, to prescribe special education programs, and to evaluate these programs.

A meeting of the PPT was held in February of 1975, at which plaintiff was diagnosed as having a major learning disability. The PPT recommended that plaintiff be scheduled on a trial basis in the special education program for remediating learning disabilities and that she be given a psychological evaluation. Although the PPT report specifically stated that the psychological evaluation be given "at the earliest feasible time," no such evaluation was administered.

A second PPT meeting was held in May in order to give plaintiff the annual review mandated by Conn.Reg. § 10-76b-7(b). The PPT reported plaintiff had made encouraging gains, but she suffered from poor learning behaviors and emotional difficulties. A psychological evaluation was again recommended. Her continued participation in the special educational program was also advised, but it was made contingent upon the results of the psychological evaluation.

When school commenced in September of 1975, the PPT requested an immediate psychological evaluation. The PPT stated that an evaluation was essential in order to develop an appropriate special education program. For reasons which have not been explained to the Court, the psychological evaluation was not administered for some time, and the clinical psychologist's report of the evaluation was not completed until January 22, 1976. The report stated that plaintiff had severe learning disabilities derived from either a minimal brain dysfunction or an organically rooted perceptual disorder. It recommended her continued participation in the special education program and concluded: "I can only imagine that someone with such deficit and lack of development must feel utterly lost and humiliated at this point in adolescence in a public school where other students . . . are performing in such contrast to her." The report of plaintiff's psychological evaluation was reviewed at a March, 1976 PPT meeting. The PPT noted that plaintiff was responding remarkably well to the intensive one-to-one teaching she received in the special education program, and recommended that she continue the program until the close of the 1975–1976 school year.

The first indication that the special education program was no longer appropriate came in May of 1976. At that time plaintiff's special education teacher reported that plaintiff had all but stopped attending the program. The teacher requested a PPT meeting to consider whether plaintiff's primary handicap was an emotional disability rather than a learning disability. Despite this request, plaintiff's schedule was not changed nor was a PPT meeting held to review her program before the close of the school year.

At the beginning of the 1976–1977 school year, plaintiff was scheduled to participate in a learning disability program on a part-time basis. Her attendance continued to decline throughout the first half of the school year. By late fall she had completely stopped attending her special education classes and had begun to spend this time wandering the school corridors with her friends. Although she was encouraged to participate in the special education classes, the PPT meeting concerning plaintiff's program, which had been requested at the end of the previous school year, was not conducted in the fall of 1976.

In December of 1976 plaintiff was involved in several incidents which resulted in a series of disciplinary conferences between her mother and school authorities. These conferences were followed by a temporary improvement in plaintiff's attendance and behavior. In light of these improvements, the annual PPT review held in March of 1977 concluded that plaintiff should continue to participate in the special education program on a part-time basis for the remaining three months of the school year. The PPT also recommended that in the next school year plaintiff be scheduled for daily special education classes and that she be considered for a special education vocational training program. The PPT report stated that it was of primary importance for plaintiff to be given a program of study in the 1977–1978 school year which was based on a realistic assessment of her abilities and interests.

Despite the PPT recommendation, plaintiff has not been attending any learning disability program this school year. It is unclear whether this resulted from the school's failure to schedule plaintiff properly or from plaintiff's refusal to attend the program. Regardless of the reason, the school authorities were on notice in the early part of September that the program prescribed by the PPT in March of 1977 was not being administered. In fact, a member of the school staff who was familiar with plaintiff requested that a new PPT review, be conducted. This review has never been undertaken.

On September 14, 1977 plaintiff was involved in school-wide disturbances which erupted at Danbury High School. As a result of her complicity in these disturbances, she received a ten-day disciplinary suspension and was scheduled to appear at a disciplinary hearing on November 30, 1977. The Superintendent of Danbury Schools recommended to the Danbury Board of Education that plaintiff be expelled for the remainder of the 1977–1978 school year at this hearing.

Plaintiff's counsel made a written request on November 16, 1977 to the Danbury Board of Education for a hearing and a review of plaintiff's special education program in accordance with Conn.Gen.Stat. § 10-76h. On November 29, 1977 plaintiff obtained a temporary restraining order from this Court which enjoined the defendants from conducting the disciplinary hearing. This order was continued on December 12, 1977 at the conclusion of the preliminary injunction hearing. Between the time the first temporary restraining order was issued and the preliminary injunction hearing was held plaintiff was given a psychological evaluation. However, the results of this evaluation were unavailable at the time of the hearing. A PPT review of plaintiff's program has not been conducted since March of 1977, nor has the school developed a new special education program for plaintiff. Furthermore, there was no showing at the hearing that plaintiff's attendance at Danbury High School would endanger her or others.

Plaintiff is entitled to a preliminary injunction enjoining Danbury Board of Education from conducting a hearing to expel her. The standard which governs the issuance of a preliminary injunction is well-settled. Plaintiff must demonstrate either (1) probable success on the merits of her claim and possible irreparable injury, or (2) sufficiently serious questions going to the merits of her claim and a balance of hardship tipping decidedly in her favor. *Triebwasser & Katz* v. *American Tel. & Tel. Co.*, 535 F.2d 1356, 1358 (2d Cir. 1976); *Sonesta Int'l Hotels Corp.* v. *Wellington Associates*, 483 F.2d 247, 250 (2d Cir. 1973); *City of Hartford* v. *Hills*, 408 F.Supp. 879, 882 (D.Conn. 1975). In *Triebwasser, supra,* at 1359 the Second Circuit stated that a demonstration of possible irreparable harm is required under both of these alternatives.

Plaintiff has made a persuasive showing of possible irreparable injury. It is important to note that the issuance of a preliminary injunction is contingent upon *possible* injury. The irreparable injuries claimed by plaintiff are those which will result from her expulsion at the Board of Education hearing. In this situation the Court must assume that she will, in fact, be expelled, and then proceed to consider the probable consequences of her expulsion. If plaintiff is expelled, she will be without any educational program from the date of her expulsion until such time as another PPT review is held and an appropriate educational program is developed. In light of past delays in the administration of plaintiff's special education program, the Court is concerned that some time may pass before plaintiff is afforded the special education to which she is entitled. However, even assuming her new program is developed with dispatch, for a period of time plaintiff will suffer the injury inherent in being without any educational program. The second irreparable injury to which plaintiff will be subjected derives from the fact that her expulsion will preclude her from taking part in any special education programs offered at Danbury High School. If plaintiff is expelled, she will be restricted to placement in a private school or to homebound tutoring. Regardless of whether these two alternatives are responsive to plaintiff's needs, the PPT will be limited to their use in fashioning a new special education program for plaintiff. Of particular concern to the Court is the possibility that an appropriate private placement will be unavailable and plaintiff's education will be reduced to some type of homebound tutoring. Such a result can only serve to hinder plaintiff's social development and to perpetuate the vicious cycle in which she is caught. *See Hairston* v. *Drosick,* 423 F.Supp. 180, 183 (S.D.W. Va. 1976) (holding that it is "imperative that every child receive an education with his or her peers insofar as it is at all possible"). The Court is persuaded that plaintiff's expulsion would have been accompanied by a very real possibility of irreparable injury.

Plaintiff has also demonstrated probable success on the merits of four federal claims. The Handicapped Act and the regulations thereunder detail specific rights to which handicapped children are entitled. Among these rights are: (1) the right to an "appropriate public education"; (2) the right to remain in her present placement until the resolution of her special education complaint; (3) the right to an education in the "least restrictive environment"; and (4) the right to have all changes of placement effectuated in accordance with prescribed procedures. Plaintiff claims she has been or will be denied these rights.

Plaintiff argues with no little force that she has been denied her right to an "appropriate public education." The meaning of this term is clarified in the definitional section of the Handicapped Act. Essentially, it is defined so as to require Danbury High School to provide plaintiff with an educational program specially designed to meet her learning disabilities. *See* 20 U.S.C. § 1401(1), (15)-(19). The record before this Court suggests that plaintiff has not been provided with an appropriate education. Evidence has been introduced which shows that Danbury High School not only failed to provide plaintiff with the special education program recommended by the PPT in March of 1977, but that the high school neglected to respond adequately when it learned plaintiff was no longer participating in the special education program it had provided. The Court cannot disregard the possibility that Danbury High School's handling of plaintiff may have contributed to her disruptive behavior. The existence of a causal relationship between plaintiff's academic program and her anti-social behavior was supported by expert testimony introduced at the preliminary injunction hearing. *Cf. Frederick L.* v. *Thomas,* 408 F.Supp. 832, 935 (E.D.Pa. 1976) (argument that inappropriate educational placement caused anti-social behavior is raised). If a subsequent PPT were to conclude that plaintiff has not been given an appropriate special education placement, then the defendant's resort to its disciplinary process is unjustifiable. The Court is not making a final determination of whether plaintiff has been afforded an appropriate education. The resolution of this question is beyond the scope of the present inquiry. In order to sustain a preliminary injuction plaintiff need only demonstrate probable success on the merits of her claim. She has satisfied this standard.

Plaintiff also claims that her expulsion prior to the resolution of her special education complaint would be in violation of 20 U.S.C. § 1415(e)(3). This subsection of the Handicapped Act states: "During the pendency of any proceedings conducted pursuant to this section, unless the state or local educational agency and the parents or guardian otherwise agree, the child shall remain in the then current educational placement of such child ... until all such proceedings have been completed." Plaintiff qualifies for the protection that this subsection provides. She has filed a complaint pursuant to 20 U.S.C. § 1415(b)(1)(E) requesting a hearing and a review of her special education placement. Moreover, there has been no agreement to leave her present special education placement voluntarily. Thus, plaintiff has a right to remain in this placement until her complaint is resolved. The novel issue raised by plaintiff arises from the fact that the right to remain in her present placement directly conflicts with Danbury High Schools's disciplinary process. If the high school expels plaintiff during the pendency of her special education complaint, then her placement will be changed in contravention of 20 U.S.C. § 1415(e)(3). The Court must determine whether this subsection of the Handicapped Act prohibits the expulsion of handicapped children during the pendency of a special education complaint.

This is a case of first impression. Although there are no decisions in which the relation between the special education processes and disciplinary procedures is discussed, the regulations promulgated under the new law are helpful. The Department of Health, Education and Welfare (HEW) released regulations in August of this year that are aimed at facilitating the implementation of the Handicapped Act. See 42 Fed.Reg. 42,473 (1977) (to be codified in 45 C.F.R. § 121a). Contained therein is a comment addressing the conflict between 20 U.S.C. § 1415(e)(3) and the disciplinary procedures of public schools. The comment reiterates the rule that after a complaint proceeding has been initiated, a change in a child's placement is prohibited. It then states: ''While the placement may not be changed, this does not preclude a school from using its normal procedures for dealing with children who are endangering themselves or others.'' 42 Fed.Reg. 42,473, 42,496 (1977) (to be codified in 42 C.F.R. § 121a.513). This somewhat cryptic statement suggests that subsection 1415(e)(3) prohibits disciplinary measures which have the effect of changing a child's placement, while permitting the type of procedures necessary for dealing with a student who appears to be dangerous. This interpretation is supported by a comment-to-the-comment which states that the comment was added to make it clear that schools are permitted to use their regular procedures for dealing with emergencies. See 42 Fed.Reg. 42,473, 42,512 (1977) (to follow the codification at 45 C.F.R. § 121a.513). There is no indication in either the regulations or the comments thereto that schools should be permitted to expel a handicapped child while a special education complaint is pending.

The Court concurs with HEW's reading of subsection 1415(e)(3). As will be discussed, the Handicapped Act establishes procedures which replace expulsion as a means of removing handicapped children from school if they become disruptive. Furthermore, school authorities can deal with emergencies by suspending handicapped children. Suspension will permit the child to remain in his or her present placement, but will allow schools in Connecticut to exclude a student for up to ten consecutive school days. See Conn.Gen.Stat. § 10-233a(c) and note 3 supra. Therefore, plaintiff's expulsion prior to the resolution of her complaint would violate the Handicapped Act.

Plaintiff makes a third claim that the Handicapped Act prohibits her expulsion even after her complaint proceedings have terminated. She bases this claim on her right to an education in the ''least restrictive environment'' and on the overall design of the Handicapped Act. An important feature of the Handicapped Act is its requirement that children be educated in the ''least restrictive environment.'' This requirement entitles handicapped children to be educated with nonhandicapped children whenever possible. See 20 U.S.C. § 1412(5)(B); 42 Fed.Reg. 42,473, 42,497, 42,513 (1977) (to be codified in 45 C.F.R. § 121a.550). The right of handicapped children to an education in the "least restrictive environment" is implemented, in part, by requiring schools to provide a continuum of alternative placements. *See* 20 U.S.C. § 1412(5)(B); 42 Fed.Reg. 42,473, 42,497 (1977) (to be codified in 45 C.F.R. § 121a.551). These alternatives include instruction in regular classes, special classes, private schools, the child's home and other institutions. By providing handicapped children with a range of placements, the Handicapped Act attempts to insure that each child receives an education which is responsive to his or her individual needs while maximizing the child's opportunity to learn with nonhandicapped peers. *See* 42 Fed.Reg. 42,473, 42,497 (1977) (to be codified in 45 C.F.R. § 121a.552).

The right to an education in the least restrictive environment may be circumvented if schools are permitted to expel handicapped children. An expulsion has the effect not only of changing a student's placement, but also of restricting the availability of alternative placements. For example, plaintiff's expulsion may well exclude her from a placement that is appropriate for her academic and social development. This result flies in the face of the explicit mandate of the Handicapped Act which requires that all placement decisions be made in conformity with a child's right to an education in the least restrictive environment. *See* 42 Fed.Reg. 42,473, 42,497 (1977) (to be codified in 45 C.F.R. § 121a.533(a)(4)).

The expulsion of handicapped children not only jeopardizes their right to an education in the least restrictive environment, but is inconsistent with the procedures established by the Handicapped Act for changing the placement of disruptive children. The Handicapped Act prescribes a procedure whereby disruptive children are transferred to more restrictive placements when their behavior significantly impairs the education of other children. *See* 42 Fed.Reg. 42,473, 42,497 (1977) (to be codified in 45 C.F.R. § 121a.552). The responsibility for changing a handicapped child's placement is allocated to professional teams, such as Connecticut's PPTs. *See* 42 Fed.Reg. 42,473, 42,497 (1977) (to be codified in 45 C.F.R. § 121a.533(a)(3)). Furthermore, parents of handicapped children are entitled to participate in and to appeal from these placement decisions. *See* 42 Fed.Reg. 42,473, 42,490 (1977) (to be codified in 45 C.F.R. § 121a.345); 20 U.S.C. § 1415(b)(1)(C), (c). Thus, the use of expulsion proceedings as a means of changing the placement of a disruptive handicapped child contravenes the procedures of the Handicapped Act. After considerable reflection the Court is persuaded that any changes in plaintiff's placement must be made by a PPT after considering the range of available placements and plaintiff's particular needs.

It is important that the parameters of this decision are clear. This Court is cognizant of the need for school officials to be vested with ample authority and discretion. It is, therefore, with great reluctance that the Court has intervened in the disciplinary process of Danbury High School. However, this intervention is of a limited nature. Handicapped children are neither immune from a school's disciplinary process nor are they entitled to participate in programs when their behavior impairs the education of other children in the program. First, school authorities can take swift disciplinary measures, such as suspension, against disruptive handicapped children. Secondly, a PPT can request a change in the placement of handicapped children who have demonstrated that their present placement is inappropriate by disrupting the education of other children. The Handicapped Act thereby affords schools with both short-term and long-term methods of dealing with handicapped children who are behavioral problems.

Defendants contend that their disciplinary procedures are beyond the purview of this Court. They are mistaken. It has long been fundamental to our federalism that public education is under the control of state and local authorities. *See Epperson* v. *Arkansas,* 393 U.S. 97, 104, 89 S.Ct. 266, 21 L.Ed.2d 228 (1968); *Buck* v. *Board of Education of City of New York,* 553 F.2d 315, 320 (2d Cir. 1977). Although there is little doubt that the judgment of state and local school authorities is entitled to considerable deference, it is equally clear that even a school's disciplinary procedures are subject to the scrutiny of the federal judiciary. *See, e.g., Goss* v. *Lopez,* 419 U.S. 565, 95 S.Ct. 729, 42 L.Ed.2d 725 (1974); *Tinker* v. *Des Moines School Dist.,* 393 U.S. 503, 89 S.Ct. 733, 21 L.Ed.2d 731 (1969); *Board of Educ.* v. *Barnette,* 319 U.S. 624; 63 S.Ct. 1178, 87 L.Ed. 1628 (1942). *Cf. Yoo* v. *Moynihan,* 28 Conn.Sup. 375, 262 A.2d 814 (1969) (temporary injunction issued by state court against expulsion of student for violation of dress code). In the instant case judicial intervention in Danbury High School's disciplinary procedures is Congressionally mandated. The Handicapped Act vests jurisdiction in federal district courts over all claims of noncompliance with the Act's procedural safeguards, regardless of the amount in controversy. *See* 20 U.S.C. § 1415(e)(4).

Defendants' principal objection to the issuance of a preliminary injunction is that the procedures for securing a special education are distinct from disciplinary procedures and therefore one process should not interfere with the other. This contention is based on a non sequitur. The inference that the special education and disciplinary procedures cannot conflict, does not follow from the premise that these are separate processes. Defendants are really asking the Court to refuse to resolve an obvious conflict between these procedures. This Court will not oblige them.

Danbury Board of Education is HEREBY ORDERED to require an immediate PPT review of plaintiff's special education program and is preliminarily enjoined from conducting a hearing to expel her. Furthermore, any changes in her placement must be effectuated through the proper special education procedures until the final resolution of plaintiff's claims.

NOTES

1. In asserting that "... there are no decisions in which the relation between the special education processes and disciplinary procedures is discussed," the *Stuart* v. *Nappi* court overlooks *Mills* v. *Board of Education of the District of Columbia,* pp. 92–108, above, where this issue was dealt with, particularly in sections 4, 13d and 13f of the court's Judgment and Decree. Review also the descriptions of the named plaintiffs in *Mills* to see the factual situations from which this issue arose.

2. Is the preliminary result in *Stuart* v. *Nappi* a coherent means for reconciling the expulsion mechanism with the requirements of equal educational opportunity for handicapped children?

HOWARD S. v. FRIENDSWOOD INDEPENDENT SCHOOL DISTRICT

United States District Court for the Southern District of Texas, 1978
454 F.Supp. 634

STATEMENT OF REASONS FOR PRELIMINARY INJUNCTION

COWAN, Judge.

Pursuant to the mandate of Rule 65(d), Fed.R.Civ.Proc., this Court states herein its reasons for the preliminary injunction issued on June 21, 1978.

These findings of fact and conclusions of law are made solely for the purpose of determining the plaintiffs' rights to obtain preliminary injunctive relief pursuant to Rule 65, Fed.R.Civ.Proc. These findings of fact and conclusions of law are not findings upon the merits. The merits are reserved for trial at a later date, if necessary.

Douglas S. (hereinafter "Douglas"), the minor plaintiff in this case, is an Anglo-American male born in the State of California on November 16, 1961. In 1962, he was hospitalized and tested for meningitis. Although his mother was eventually able to furnish him a stable family background, the first three years of his life were unsettled, chaotic and traumatic. Competent medical evidence establishes that these two events created a situation in which Douglas has minimal brain damage, a definite learning disability, and at least temporarily, a severe emotional disturbance. Medical testimony establishes that these events in his early childhood are probably the most significant, although not the most immediate, causes of the difficulties which have precipitated this litigation.

Douglas went through the first five years of his schooling in California, where he was diagnosed as having minimal brain damage, and placed in special education classes.

Douglas' parents moved to Friendswood in 1973, and Douglas was enrolled in the public schools maintained by defendant FISD (Friendswood Independent School District). During his first year of school in FISD, his teachers noted his short attention span, hyperactivity and demands for attention. In May of 1974, while enrolled at the Friendswood Junior High School, he was evaluated for th FISD by competent, independent, outside consultants, who noted that despite his normal intelligence, he had made markedly slow progress in school and that probable organic brain damage as well as anxiety interfered with his ability to concentrate, remember and perceive accurately. The consultants recommended that Douglas "... continue in a resource program in which he can receive special help with basic subjects ... and that "efforts should be made by the school counselor to establish a warm relationship with Douglas ..."

During his junior high years, Douglas was placed in a special education program in which he was, for the most part "mainstreamed," i. e., placed in classes with nonhandicapped children, but still nevertheless, given special help by a "resource teacher."

In November of 1974, Mrs. Patricia Burton worked out a program for Douglas involving special help, and this program apparently produced reasonably good results during his junior high years.

In mid-August of 1976, Douglas was enrolled in the Friendswood High School. Although FISD's program with reference to Douglas had been reasonably successful in dealing with his problems during junior high, this success ended abruptly when Douglas entered high school. He immediately began to develop behavior problems, characterized by truancy and wandering in the halls. The Assistant Principal, Mr. Fred Nelson, regarded these difficulties as discipline problems and not special education problems and failed to notify the special education department of Douglas' difficulties in adjusting to high school.

These difficulties in high school were clearly forseeable. All of the experts who have testified have agreed that a young man with Douglas' handicaps, when confronted with the challenge of adjusting to a high school environment and coping with the strains of puberty, is likely to develop severe difficulties. FISD had coped with Douglas' difficulties fairly up until August of 1976, but FISD did not cope adequately with Douglas' difficulties from August 1976 until December of that year.

Douglas' difficulties at school were paralleled by difficulties in adjusting at home. In November 1976, he was referred to Dr. Grace Jamison at the John Sealy Hospital in Galveston. Dr. Jamison, a child psychiatrist, began to treat Douglas. In December 1976, just before or during the Christmas holidays, Douglas made a suicide attempt which resulted in his being confined in the Graves Unit at John Sealy Hospital for several weeks.

After Douglas was released from the Graves Unit, Dr. Jamison recommended his placement in the Oakes Unit of the Brown School, a private school in Austin. Both Dr. Jamison and Dr. Boynton from the Brown School have testified credibly that Douglas, at the present time, is not able to return to FISD in a normal classroom setting, but that he is capable of receiving an education, and that if he is allowed to remain in a setting like the Brown School another 12 to 24 months, he has a reasonable chance of developing into a reasonably well-adjusted person who can lead a productive life. If removed from the Brown School or some similar facility, his prognosis is, the doctors agree, very poor.

The undersigned has concluded that since August of 1976, when Douglas entered high school, FISD has failed to provide him a free, appropriate public education and that this failure was a contributing and a proximate cause (although certainly not the sole or even the predominant cause) of Douglas' severe emotional difficulties which culminated in his suicide attempt and confinement in the Graves Unit of John Sealy Hospital in December of 1976.

Although it is a harsh conclusion, the undersigned must reluctantly conclude that following the development of Douglas' difficulties in adjusting to high school, FISD engaged in a calculated, deliberate effort to avoid and evade its legal responsibility. FISD's activities in this regard violate its legal obligations under the Rehabilitation Act of 1973 (29 U.S.C. § 794) and the Fifth and Fourteenth Amendments to the Constitution of the United States.

The most important deficiencies, in connection with FISD's conduct occurred during the period from August of 1976 until December 1976 and from January 1977 until July 6, 1977. During that period Douglas had been classified as a minimal brain damaged child who needed and was entitled to receive special education. Despite this, when he developed disciplinary difficulties and was wandering the halls, the special education department was never notified. Dr. Wren, the head of special education, was never told that Douglas was having difficulties; instead, Douglas' difficulties were handled entirely and solely as disciplinary problems. No effort was made to determine whether or not his disciplinary problems were related to his diagnosed handicaps. This pattern continued despite expressions of interest and concern by Howard S. and Judy S. (Douglas' parents) to the school administration.

On January 18, 1977, while Douglas was in the Graves Unit of the John Sealy Hospital in Galveston, FISD, without notice to Douglas or his parents, "officially dropped" Douglas from FISD. This effective and constructive expulsion occurred without notice to the parents, without a hearing of any kind, and is a clear violation of the FISD's obligation under the Constitution of the United States. See *Goss v. Lopez*, 419 U.S. 565, 95 S.Ct. 729, 42 L.Ed.2d 725 (1974).

On February 15, 1977, Mrs. S. met with FISD's superintendent, the assistant principal of the high school, and the head of special education; informed these officials of Douglas' difficulties; delivered to them a handwritten letter indicating that Douglas was only temporarily out of school; advised that Mrs. S. was seeking a suitable educational program for him in the light of his handicaps; and advised that she wished to participate in a scheduled ARD (Admissions, Review and Dismissal) meeting to determine if a suitable program could be developed for Douglas in FISD.

Three days later, on February 18, 1977, the ARD meeting occurred. Mrs. S. was not given an opportunity to be present. The ARD committee "dismissed" Douglas from the special education program "following the usual procedure of Friendswood ISD regarding students who move. . . ." This conduct was a subterfuge. Douglas and his family had not moved. Douglas had been placed in a hospital. The hospital had referred him to a special school because of his handicaps and his severe emotional disturbance. By no stretch of the imagination can it be contended that he had "moved." FISD here clearly violated the duties placed upon it by the Constitution of the United States. See *Goss v. Lopez, supra.*

Ultimately in May 1977, Mr. and Mrs. S. retained counsel and requested an impartial due process hearing. Mr. and Mrs. S. were entitled to this due process hearing under the provisions of both the United States Constitution and the Rehabilitation Act of 1973 (29 U.S.C. § 794). Continuing its previous pattern, however, FISD intentionally evaded and avoided its responsibility to provide an impartial due process hearing.

A gathering which can best be described as a meeting occurred on July 6, 1977. This "meeting" cannot accurately be described as a hearing. The meeting was chaired by FISD's retained counsel. The designated decision maker was the school superintendent. There was no formal introduction of evidence, no formal presentation of arguments, no notice of the issues to be decided at the meeting, no impartial due process hearing examiner, no findings of fact or conclusions of law, and no real decision of any kind rendered at or after the meeting.

It is true that in July 1977 the Education for All Handicapped Children Act of 1975 (20 U.S.C. § 1401 *et seq.*) had not become fully operative, and the regulations pursuant to that statute had not been published; the plan of the State of Texas for compliance with that Act had not been approved; however, FISD was still obligated to comply with the Rehabilitation Act of 1973 (29 U.S.C. § 794) and with the Constitution of the United States.

The Rehabilitation Act of 1973 (Public Law 93-112 codified at 29 U.S.C. § 794) provides in its pertinent parts as follows:

> No otherwise qualified handicapped individual in the United States, as defined in § 706(6) of this title, shall, solely by reason of his handicap, be excluded from the participation in, be denied the benefits of, or be subjected to discrimination under any program or activity receiving Federal financial assistance.

FISD at all material times has received federal financial assistance.

On May 4, 1977, the Secretary of Health, Education and Welfare, had published in 45 C.F.R. § 84.36 the regulations issued pursuant to the Rehabilitation Act of 1973. This regulation states:

> § 84.36 Procedural safeguards.
> A recipient that operates a public elementary or secondary education program shall establish and implement, with respect to actions regarding the identification, evaluation, or educational placement of persons who, because of handicap, need or are believed to need special instruction or regulated services, a system of procedural safeguards that includes notice, an opportunity for the parents or guardian of the person to examine relevant records, an impartial hearing with opportunity for participation by the person's parents or guardian and representation by counsel, and a review procedure. Compliance with the procedural safeguards of section 615 of the Education of the Handicapped Act is one means of meeting this requirement.

Section 615 of the Education of the Handicapped Act (Public Law 94-142 codified at 20 U.S.C. § 1415) sets forth detailed provisions concerning procedural safeguards and clearly provides that: "... no hearing conducted pursuant to the requirements of this paragraph shall be conducted by an employee of such agency or unit involved in the education or care of the child. ..."

This meeting of July 6, 1977, did not meet the requirements of the regulations published under the Rehabilitation of the Handicapped Act of 1973 (specifically 42 C.F.R. § 84.36) and was not consistent with the procedures promulgated in § 615 of Public Law 94-142 (codified in 20 U.S.C. § 1415, passed on November 29, 1975). In addition, the meeting (if it is claimed to have been a hearing) was not consistent with the due process clause of the Fourteenth Amendment to the Constitution of the United States. See *Lau* v. *Nichols,* 414 U.S. 563, 94 S.Ct. 786, 39 L.Ed.2d 1 (1973); *Goss* v. *Lopez,* 419 U.S. 565, 95 S.Ct. 729, 42 L.Ed.2d 725 (1974); *Morrisey* v. *Brewer,* 408 U.S. 471, 92 S.Ct. 2593, 33 L.Ed.2d 484 (1972); *Mathews* v. *Eldridge,* 424 U.S. 319 (see particularly the analysis at 335), 96 S.Ct. 893, 47 L.Ed.2d 18; *Sullivan* v. *Houston ISD,* 307 F.Supp. 1328, 333 F.Supp. 1149 (1969–71). While factually distinguishable, the analysis of Chief Justice Burger in *Hortonville JSD No. 1* v. *Hortonville Education Assn.,* 426 U.S. 482, 96 S.Ct. 2308, 49 L.Ed.2d 1 (1976) supports the conclusion that, even without reference to the recent Congressional enactments, the meeting of July 6, 1977 (if argued to be a hearing) did not meet the requirements of substantive and procedural due process.

After they had employed counsel, Mr. and Mrs. S. took virtually all action which could conceivably have been taken to attempt to obtain administrative relief. Numerous letter were written to the Texas Educational Agency (hereinafter "TEA") to no avail. Similar entreaties were made to the Department of Health, Education and Welfare (HEW), which launched or said that it launched an investigation in July 1977. Apparently, from the record here, nothing has been heard further from this investigation in the eleven intervening months.

Arguably, an "appeal" could have been taken from the meeting of July 6, 1977 to the FISD Board of Trustees; however, there was no decision to appeal from. In addition, this Court finds from the pleadings and arguments asserted in this cause that an appeal from the "meeting of July 6, 1977" to the Board of Trustees of FISD would have been a futile gesture. The Board's retained counsel was fully cognizant of and an active participant in the meeting of July 6, 1977. The school superintendent and the director of special education (who was also one of the principal administrators in the school system) participated actively in events after January of 1977. It is clear, and the Court finds, that the Board of Trustees ratified the actions of the school administrators at the time of and after Douglas' constructive expulsion in January of 1977 and the further actions relating to Douglas up to July 6, 1977.

A hearing before the Board of Trustees would not have satisfied the requirements of 29 U.S.C. § 794 and the regulations promulgated pursuant thereto. Specifically, 45 C.F.R. § 84.36 would not have been satisfied, and the procedures promulgated by the Education for All Handicapped Children Act of 1975 (Public Law 94-142 § 615 codified at 20 U.S.C. § 1415) would not have been met.

This Court has concluded that the Board of Trustees of FISD has received extremely poor advice concerning its legal obligations and the possible liability of individual administrators and Trustees for intentional violation of plaintiffs' constitutional rights. In this connection, the attention of the Board of Trustees is respectfully directed to the possibility of personal liability being imposed upon school board members for failure to comply with their legal obligations. See Justice White's language in *Wood* v. *Strickland,* 420 U.S. 308 at 321, 95 S.Ct. 992 at 1000, 43 L.Ed.2d 214, where he stated:

> . . . The official, himself, must be acting sincerely and with a belief that he is doing right, but an act violating a student's constitutional rights can be no more justified by ignorance or disregard of settled, indisputable law on the part of one entrusted with the supervision of students' daily lives, than by the presence of actual malice. . . .

See also *Burnaman* v. *Bay City Independent School District,* 445 F.Supp. 927 (S.D.Tex. 1978).

In July 1977 there *may* have been some justification for lack of information concerning the Trustee's legal obligations. There is no like justification now.

The foregoing constitutes the Court's general findings of fact and conclusions of law applicable to this case. In addition the Court makes the following specific findings of fact and conclusions of law:

1. Plaintiffs have taken all reasonable and practicable steps to exhaust administrative remedies in this cause.

2. The procedures employed by FISD in connection with the constructive expulsion of Douglas and the other procedures relating to Douglas from January 1977 until the present date have denied Douglas and his parents substantive and procedural due process in violation of the guarantees of the Fifth and Fourteenth Amendments to the Constitution of the United States.

3. Mr. and Mrs. S were caught in a typical governmental "Catch 22" situation. FISD purported to have expelled Douglas because he "moved from the system." Thereafter, FISD refused to give him an impartial due process hearing, and took the position that nothing further could be done with the child until he was re-enrolled in FISD. It was impossible to re-enroll him because he had been placed, because of his severe emotional difficulties, in a school outside the jurisdiction of FISD. This removal of Douglas to the Brown School occurred because of FISD's refusal to comply with its legal obligations and its refusal to attempt to work out an appropriate educational plan to afford Douglas a free, appropriate public education.

4. At the pertinent times, no adequate mechanisms have existed to afford the plaintiffs a full administrative hearing, or a meaningful administrative remedy. In this connection, see plaintiffs' exhibits 7, 8, 15, 16, 18 and 23 (particularly TEA's letter of November 30, 1977 to Mr. Reed Martin).

5. The undersigned, in determining whether or not to grant a preliminary injunction, has balanced the interests of the parties. The Court concludes that the consequences of denying relief to Douglas and his parents could be disastrous, and that the denial of relief could destroy Douglas' chances to lead a normal life. On the contrary, the relief granted against FISD merely creates, for FISD, an expense and inconvenience—moreover this expense and inconvenience is an expense and inconvenience which is imposed upon FISD by law and which FISD has a legal obligation to undertake. In addition, the Trustees' failure to meet their legal obligations promptly could well result in substantial personal liability.

6. Douglas at all material times has been a "handicapped child" as that term is defined in the Education for All Handicapped Children Act of 1975 (Public Law 94-142 codified at 20 U.S.C. § 1401 *et seq.*) Since December 1976, Douglas has been seriously emotionally disturbed and that serious emotional disturbance is compounded by a specific learning disability.

7. At all material times Douglas has been a "handicapped" child, as that term is defined in § 4(a) of Public Law 94-142 [20 U.S.C. § 1401(1)] because he has been seriously emotionally disturbed and handicapped by a specific learning disability.

8. At all material times Douglas has been a child with specific learning disabilities, as that term is used in the Education for All Handicapped Children Act of 1975 (Public Law 94-142 codified at 20 U.S.C. § 1401 *et seq.*) in that he has suffered from minimal brain dysfunction and probable organic brain damage.

9. At all material times Douglas has been a "qualified handicapped individual" as that term is used in the Rehabilitation Act of 1973 (Public Law 93-112 codified at 29 U.S.C. § 794) and since August of 1976, he has in fact been excluded from participation in and denied the benefits of, and subjected to discrimination under a program or activity receiving federal financial assistance, i.e., the operation of FISD.

10. Since August of 1976, FISD has failed to afford Douglas a free, appropriate public education and has thus discriminated against him.

11. FISD has failed to provide, since August of 1976, an individualized education program for Douglas which meets his unique needs. This failure commenced in August of 1976 and continues to this date.

12. At all material times, Douglas has been a "handicapped child" as that term is defined in 45 C.F.R. § 128.5 in that he has, since December of 1976, suffered from a severe, emotional disturbance, compounded by a specific learning disability.

13. For some periods of time since June of 1977, Douglas has suffered from a handicap which made placement in a public or private residential program necessary in order for him to have the benefit of a free, appropriate public education. The Court does not hold that such placement will be necessary in the indefinite future, and this determination (it is hoped) will be made by the administrative process functioning through an impartial due process hearing of the type contemplated by § 615 of Public Law 94-142 (20 U.S.C. § 1415) and the regulations promulgated under the Rehabilitation Act of 1973 (specifically the regulation appearing at 45 C.F.R. § 84.36).

14. During the period from January 1977 until the present date, the State of Texas has not afforded Douglas and his parents a feasible or practicable administrative remedy because TEA has not established procedures to afford an impartial due process hearing in this type of case, or an appeal or review of the type contemplated by § 615 of the Education for All Handicapped Children Act of 1975 [20 U.S.C. § 1415(c)].

15. There is no legal impediment in the State of Texas to the establishment of the procedural safeguards mandated by the Education for All Handicapped Children Act of 1975 (Public Law 94-142, codified at 20 U.S.C. § 1415). This is true because although there may be legal requirements which require that binding action of certain types be taken only by the Boards of Trustees of school districts, it is common knowledge that the Board of Trustees of Independent School Districts cannot make independent determinations of every question of every conceivable nature presented for decision. For example, employment decisions in reality, are made by the administrators of the Independent School Districts and ratified by the Boards of Trustees. There is no legal impediment to the establishment of an impartial due process hearing procedure such as that set forth in plaintiffs' exhibit 24 (Administrative Procedure Concerning Special Education approved by the Houston Independent School District Board of Education on October 21, 1977).

16. The regulations issued by the Secretary of Health, Education and Welfare under the Rehabilitation Act of 1973 (codified at 29 U.S.C. § 794), the Education for All Handicapped Children Act of 1975, and the Amendments of 1974 (codified at 20 U.S.C. § 1401 et seq.) are reasonably related to the purposes of the enabling legislation. See concurring opinion by Mr. Justice Stewart in Lau v. Nichols, 414 U.S. 563, at 569, 94 S.Ct. 786, 39 L.Ed.2d 1.

17. Douglas became seriously emotionally disturbed in December of 1976. This emotional upheaval was the precipitating factor which led to his hospitalization and necessitated his enrollment at the Brown School. This emotional disturbance was the result of multiple factors. Medical evidence established that the predominant cause

was probably related to organic brain damage and environmental factors in the first three years of his life. On the other hand, the fact that he was not afforded free, appropriate public education during the period from the time he enrolled in high school until December of 1976, was, this Court finds, a contributing and proximate cause of his emotional difficulties and emotional disturbance.

18. 42 U.S.C. § 1983 and the Rehabilitation Act of 1973 (29 U.S.C. § 794) do afford the plaintiffs a private cause of action. *Lau* v. *Nichols,* 414 U.S. 563, 94 S.Ct. 786, 39 L.Ed.2d 1 (1973).

Conclusion

On the basis of the findings of fact and conclusions of law set forth above, the Court has concluded that there is a high probability that plaintiffs will succeed in the trial of this case on the merits. The Court has further concluded that the plaintiffs will suffer irreparable injury if not given preliminary injunctive relief. The Court has also balanced the irreparable harm which the plaintiffs will suffer against the inconvenience to the defendants and has determined that the irreparable and grave nature of the harm which will be suffered by the plaintiffs greatly outweighs the inconvenience and expense which will be imposed upon the defendants by preliminary injunctive relief. The Court has also determined that the public interest will be served by the entering of a preliminary injunction for the reason that such preliminary injunction will afford the plaintiffs their statutory and constitutional rights, and will encourage compliance with the law.

Reference to the legislative history reveals that it was the judgment of the Congress that the apparently substantial expense of compliance with the Education for all Handicapped Children Act of 1975 (Public Law 94-142, 20 U.S.C. § 1401) is actually much less than cost of life-long institutionalization. Senate Report 94-168, U.S.Code Cong. & Admin.News 1975, pp. 1425, 1433 says:

> The long range implications of these statistics are that public agencies and taxpayers will spend billions of dollars over the lifetimes of these individuals to maintain such persons as dependents and in a minimally acceptable lifestyle. With proper education services, many would be able to become productive citizens, contributing to society instead of being forced to remain burdens. Others, through such services, would increase their independence, thus reducing their dependence on society.

The Court finds the foregoing language to be directly, squarely applicable to the facts of this case.

For the reasons stated herein, the Court, after hearing argument of counsel on the form of the injunctive relief, has entered a preliminary injunction in compliance with the terms and provisions of Rule 65, Fed.R.Civ.Proc. (see copy attached as Exhibit A).

Preliminary Injunction

On the 18th day of May, 1978, the above-entitled and numbered cause was filed seeking a temporary restraining order. Plaintiffs and their counsel appeared in chambers and the Court, after hearing argument, declined to issue a temporary restraining order, but set a hearing for the purpose of determining whether or not a preliminary injunction should issue. This hearing occurred on various dates, culminating in a hearing on June 21, 1978. All parties were allowed to introduce all evidence tendered, present authorities and present full arguments. In compliance with Rule 65(a)(2), Fed.R.Civ.Proc., the Court has considered a consolidation of the extensive hearing with trial on the merits but has declined to do so because to do so might deny the parties their rights to a trial by jury of contested issues of fact. The Court has stated into the record its detailed findings of fact and conclusions of law supporting the granting of this preliminary relief and incorporates such findings of fact and conclusions of law in this preliminary injunction.

Reasons

In compliance with Rule 65(d), the Court states, in summary form, the following reasons for the issuance of this injunction:

Exhibit A

1. Plaintiffs have been denied rights guaranteed to them by the Rehabilitation Act of 1973 (Public Law 93-112 § 504, codified at 29 U.S.C. § 794) in that Douglas S., a qualified handicapped individual, has been excluded from participation in and denied the benefits of a free, appropriate public education in the Friendswood Independent School District (hereinafter FISD); and has been subjected to discrimination under an activity receiving federal financial assistance.

2. Douglas S. has been denied the rights to procedural and substantive due process guaranteed by the Fourteenth Amendment to the Constitution of the United States and has been constructively expelled from FISD without being afforded the procedural and substantive due process required by the Constitution of the United States.

3. Plaintiffs have shown a probability of success on the merits at final trial and that plaintiffs will be irreparably injured if temporary injunctive relief is not granted. The public interest will be served by the granting of a preliminary injunction. The certainty of harm to plaintiffs outweighs the inconvenience and expense to the defendants occasioned by the granting of injunctive relief.

Relief Granted as to FISD

1. Defendants FISD, Ted L. Thomas, J. L. Birdwell, Riley Ross, Harold Whitaker, Bill N. Allen, C. W. Cline, William P. Jones, Dickie K. Warren (hereinafter called "FISD defendants") will forthwith cause an immediate and comprehensive evaluation of Douglas S. and determine his special educational needs. This evaluation may be conducted by a competent, independent, professional evaluator retained by the FISD defendants and need not be done in consultation with the Brown School, but must be done in consultation with Douglas S.'s parents and must be done in such manner as to take advantage of the work of the Brown School and to avoid disturbing Douglas S.'s current placement in the Brown School.

2. After such consultation and evaluation, the FISD defendants will immediately develop an individual educational plan which specifies Douglas S.'s needs and all services required to meet those needs.

3. The FISD defendants will thereafter provide directly or arrange to contract for provision of, appropriate educational services for plaintiff Douglas S. without cost,

affording contact with non-handicapped children in a normal setting to the maximum extent appropriate.

4. Douglas S. will remain in the Brown School until such new placement is available, and the FISD defendants must pay the cost of the Brown School on behalf of Douglas S. from January 18, 1977, the date of his constructive expulsion without due process, until Douglas S. is afforded a new placement or until appropriate administrative bodies have afforded Douglas S. and his parents the impartial due process hearing and review of such impartial due process hearing required by 29 U.S.C. § 794 and described in detail in 20 U.S.C. § 1416.

5. The FISD defendants shall, while the foregoing steps are in progress, create an impartial due process hearing system so that future complaints about or concerning plaintiff Douglas S.'s educational placement may be processed administratively. The FISD defendants shall, in creating and administering this system, comply with the requirements of 20 U.S.C. § 1415 and the applicable regulations published pursuant to the Rehabilitation Act of 1973 and the Education for All Handicapped Children Act of 1975.

6. The FISD defendants will take all action necessary and appropriate to insure that Douglas S. will not be denied treatment and education in his present educational placement (i. e., the Brown School) until full due process has been afforded Douglas S. and his parents, including payment of the Brown School charges during the period from January 18, 1977 until the date when due process is fully afforded to Douglas S. and his parents. The FISD defendants' obligation to pay the costs and charges of the Brown School with reference to Douglas S. shall continue until terminated by written agreement of the parties or further order of this Court.

Relief Granted as to "State Defendants"

Defendants M. L. Brockette, L. Harlan Ford, Don L. Partridge, and Joe Kelly Butler (hereinafter called "State Defendants") shall, during the period when the FISD defendants are complying with the injunctive relief granted above, insure that the State Defendants are prepared to afford a review of a decision made with reference to Douglas S. by the FISD defendants and in doing so, shall comply with the procedures required by 20 U.S.C. § 1415(c) and all regulations issued applicable thereto.

Security

In compliance with Rule 65(c), the Court will require Howard S. and Judy S. to post a security bond in the amount of $500 for the payment of such costs and damages as may be incurred or suffered by any party who is found to have been wrongfully enjoined or restrained. In this connection, the Court acknowledges that such security is a mere token and required solely to comply with Rule 65(c), but the Court also acknowledges that the acquisition of a bond of the type which would be required to fully protect the FISD defendants from any loss resulting from this injunction would be virtually impossible and could probably be obtained only by posting cash or negotiable securities equal to the amount of money which the FISD defendants will be required to expend in compliance with this preliminary injunction. The requirement of an excessive or greater bond would in effect deny Howard S. and Douglas S. the statutory and constitutional rights which this Court is attempting here to protect.

NOTES

1. Unusual aspects of the *Howard S.* ruling include the court's indication that the defendants' failure to provide an appropriate educational program was a contributing and proximate cause of the plaintiff child's emotional difficulties and attempted suicide, that the defendant school district had engaged in a "calculated, deliberate effort to avoid and evade its legal responsibility," that the defendants had received "extremely poor advice" concerning legal obligations and potential liability, and that the defendants should be apprised of the possibility of personal liability of school board members for failing to fulfill their legal duties. While some of these comments were gratuitous *obiter dicta* by the court, they certainly indicate that the court views the defendants' conduct as egregious and do not bode well for the defendants in the resolution of the case on the merits. Indeed, the court's finding of plaintiffs' likelihood of success on the merits seems almost an understatement. What procedural step is suggested to the defendants by this result?

2. What constituted a "constructive expulsion" in *Howard S.*? Compare this with the factual situation in *Stuart* v. *Nappi, supra.*

    c. Placement Alternatives   The principle that every handicapped individual is entitled to a public educational program does not answer the question of where in the spectrum of such programs a particular handicapped person shall be placed. Within the public education system, there are numerous types of programs and settings available for persons with varying kinds and degrees of handicaps. These include variations on regular classroom placements, such as the addition of special counseling services or itinerant teachers, part- or full-time special classes in a "normal" school, separate special public schools, private educational programs paid for by public funds, and residential schools.

    Generally, decisions as to the appropriate placements and programs for specific pupils are considered to be educational matters, best left to the discretion of public education officials, and courts have hesitated to meddle. The judicial system has neither the time nor the expertise to direct and manage the daily operation of the schools. The public schools, however, do operate within the limitations of statutory and constitutional provisions, and some court opinions dealing with various placement alternatives have been handed down. Ideally, the law ought to set up a framework and some broad guidelines, within which public educators can exercise their professional discretion in selecting an educational program and placement designed to meet the needs of each individual handicapped student.

STATE V. GHRIST

Supreme Court of Iowa, 1936
222 Ia. 1069, 270 N.W. 376

RICHARDS, Justice.

    Information was filed charging defendant with violating section 4410, Code 1935, which reads:

4410. *Attendance requirement.* Any person having control of any child over seven and under sixteen years of age, in proper physical and mental condition to attend school, shall cause said child to attend some public or private school for at least twenty-four consecutive school weeks in each school year, commencing with the first week of school after the first day of September, unless the Board of school directors shall determine upon a later date, which date shall not be later than the first Monday in December.

The board may, by resolution, require attendance for the entire time when the schools are in session in any school year.

In lieu of such attendance such child may attend upon equivalent instruction by a competent teacher elsewhere than at school.

Section 4411 is as follows:

4411. *Exceptions.* Section 4410 shall not apply to any child:
1. Who is over the age of fourteen and is regularly employed.
2. Whose educational qualifications are equal to those of pupils who have completed the eighth grade.
3. Who is excused for sufficient reason by any court of record or judge.
4. While attending religious services or receiving religious instructions.

Upon the trial the following testimony was uncontroverted: Defendant, a resident of the Ames Independent School District, had control of his son, whose age was fourteen years at time of the trial. This child entered the kindergarten of the Ames public schools in September, 1926. In September, 1927, he entered the first grade of said public schools where he remained continuously for three school years. In September, 1930, he entered the second grade, remaining there one year. Entering the third grade in September, 1931, and his school work being not satisfactory, he dropped out in February, 1932, and entered a parochial school where he was a pupil until he returned to the public schools of Ames in September, 1934, entering then the fifth grade. During the school year commencing in September, 1934, he failed to maintain the required standard of scholarship. Thereafter in the summer of 1935, the school board determined that the child should attend, beginning in September, 1935, what is known as the Franklin School. Defendant refused to cause the child to attend the Franklin School and demanded that the child continue as a student in the same grade school that he had been attending. The board refused to permit the child so to do and made it known that the Franklin School was the only school of the Ames Independent School District at which the child could attend. The trial court adjudged defendant not guilty. The State has appealed.

As one reason for the judgment, the trial court held that the Legislature had not conferred on this school board the power to establish the Franklin School. This holding appellant assigns as error. Facts pertaining to this alleged error are these: About twelve years previously the Franklin School had been established by the school board as a part of the Ames public schools. There was an attendance of between sixteen and twenty pupils. The school was originally housed in one of the large grade school buildings, but had been removed to a separate frame structure built originally for residential purposes. In the Franklin School all subjects required by statute were taught and, in addition, there was work in industrial arts, wood work, sewing, cooking, and a little gardening. The distinguishing feature of the school lay in the fact that it was not graded. That is, instead of the pupils being grouped in classes and required as members of such classes to accomplish a fixed amount of study with a prescribed degree of efficiency during a certain period of time, the school work required of each pupil in the Franklin School was determined on an individual basis, and was dependent on the proficiency of the child, each being permitted to go forward in his studies as rapidly as he might be able. One purpose of the Franklin School was to afford education to children who had difficulty in doing the work as required in the classes of the regular grades. Such difficulty was often because of mental handicaps, sometimes because of defects that are physical, such as defects of speech. After attending the Franklin School for a period of time, some pupils were transferred back to the grades.

It was because the Franklin School differed from the remaining schools of the district in being an ungraded school that the trial court held its establishment was unauthorized. Upon that question, article 9 of our present State Constitution placed the educational interests of the State, including common schools and other educational institutions, under the management of a constitutional board of education. Although by constitutional authority the Legislature later abolished such board, yet while existent it was vested with a qualified power of legislation. One of the early laws enacted by this board, December 24, 1859, found in chapter 88 of the Revision of 1860 (section 2022 et seq.), provided that each civil township then or thereafter organized in the several counties of the State should constitute a school district, and that in each subdistrict there should be taught one or more schools for at least twenty-four consecutive weeks in each year excepting in certain contingencies. The then somewhat pioneer period of development of the State dictated the civil township as the instrumentality for providing educational opportunities. At the same time the board recognized that there were localities of concentrated population and enacted that cities or towns of not less than 300 inhabitants may be constituted as separate school districts. Such provision is found in chapter 172 of the Acts of the Ninth General Assembly amendatory of an earlier act, contemplating the same end. Naturally, increasing population made desirable in localities a more developed type of school, and there is found in section 2037 of the Revision of 1860 a provision that the duties of the district board of directors shall include the establishment of graded or union schools wherever they may be necessary. Section 1726, Code 1873, provides that the board of directors "may establish graded or union schools wherever they may be necessary." Section 2835, McClain's Annotated Code of 1888, contains the same provision. In the Code of 1897, section 2776 provided that the board may establish graded or union schools. Section 4267, 1935 Code, provides: "The board may establish graded and high schools." These statutes with respect to establishing graded schools are definitely permissive. Naturally the earlier statutes were so, as the ungraded subdistrict school was the original and generally accepted conception of a public school, from which any change for improvement would start. But the changing to a graded school was permissive and in the language of the present Code it still so remains. Our attention has not been called to any mandatory legislation that graded schools be established, nor that all schools in the district be graded, if any. Though graded schools may have become quite generally adopted in towns and cities, the fact remains that the Legislature has seen fit to leave unchanged the original character of its enactments. That fact compels the conclusion that it was not beyond the powers of the Ames board of directors to maintain in their district an ungraded school.

The trial court also made the following finding: "In view of the fact that, the school which the board ordered this pupil to attend, was a special one, separate and distinct from the general public school, in view of the other evidence as to its nature, and in view of the terms of the statute itself, I am of the opinion, and so hold, that the defendant did not violate this law when he refused to compel his son to attend the school in question." This finding appears to be assigned as error. The school district having had authority to maintain this ungraded school as one of the schools of the district, and it not being separate and distinct from the general public schools of the district, but a part thereof, there was error in a contrary holding.

The defendant was demanding that his child be permitted to continue to attend the graded school from which he had been transferred to the Franklin School. The trial court was of he opinion that from such fact it was necessary to find defendant not guilty. Although the trial court correctly held that this criminal statute should be strictly construed, yet the conclusion just mentioned was not tenable in view of section 4227, Code 1935, which reads:

> 4227. *Number of schools—attendance—terms.* The board of directors shall determine the number of schools to be taught, divide the corporation into such wards or other divisions for school purposes as may be proper, determine the particular school which each child shall attend, and designate the period each school shall be held beyond the time required by law.

Exercising the authority found in this section, the board had designated the Franklin School for attendance by this child if defendant chose to select the public schools for his child's attendance. Defendant questions such interpretation of section 4227, claiming that this section authorizes the board to determine the school each child shall attend only by dividing the district into wards, the school to be attended being then determined by the ward in which the child may reside. We need not discuss whether such might have been the legislative meaning as expressed in the corresponding section 1725, Code of 1873, which provides that the board "shall determine where pupils may attend school, and for this purpose may divide their district into such sub-districts as may by them be deemed necessary." However that may have been, the revised manner of expression as found in the 1935 Code, section 4227, appears to indicate a legislative intent to extend a wider authority, and in this case authorizing the board to designate the Franklin School for attendance by defendant's child irrespective of the division of the district into school wards.

The assigning of defendant's child to the Franklin School does not appear to be amenable to attack on the ground that it was an unreasonable exercise of authority. There was evident inability on the part of the child to meet the standards of the graded schools. It is in the record that he was an unfortunate victim of infantile paralysis, and that he suffers continually from pain. True, the child is sensitive and it was the fear of defendant that, being compelled to attend the Franklin School, the child might become embittered against attending any school on account of the fact that children in the graded schools were inclined to refer to the Franklin School as the "dumb school" and to treat discourteously the pupils there attending. Defendant also made objection to the Franklin School because it was housed in a two-story frame building, inferior to the grade school buildings, without fire escapes and having equipment inferior to that used in the grade schools. Explanations concerning these complaints are in the evidence and need not be recounted except to say these matters when explained are not of serious moment. From the entire record, there does not appear unreasonableness such as would warrant holding that the board exceeded the authority intended to be granted to school boards to determine where pupils may attend school.

The trial court seems to have looked upon the information as charging that defendant committed an offense because he had refused to permit the child to attend the particular school designated by the school board. The information was so inaptly drawn that the court's attitude had some foundation. But we have viewed the case as one in which the information was intended to charge violation of section 4410, Code 1935, as modified by section 4411, and have looked upon the issue as being based on the fact that defendant failed to cause the child to attend either the Franklin School or some private school or to attend private instruction, alternatives that appear to have been open to defendant.

No claim is made that the child was not in proper physical and mental condition to attend school, nor that the child had been excused from school attendance for sufficient reason by a court of record or judge. While there is here an unhappy and unfortunate situation, yet the uncontroverted facts presented and the provisions the Legislature has made left no room for an acquittal. This conclusion, of course, does not subject defendant to further prosecution upon the information.

Reversed.

PARSONS, C. J., and STIGER, HAMILTON, DONEGAN, KINTZINGER, ANDERSON, and ALBERT, J. J., concur.

NOTES

1. Although Mr. Ghrist's decision to keep his child out of school seems extreme, prior to the evolution of due process procedural mechanisms there were not many alternatives for challenging an allegedly inappropriate placement.

2. Parental disfavor to having their children assigned to the "dumb school" is an understandably common phenomenon. Frequently, opposition to such segregation from the child's peers is justified, but in some cases the parents' attitude is the result of a refusal to face the fact that their child does have educational problems that necessitate special attention.

WOLF v. LEGISLATURE OF THE STATE OF UTAH

[See pp. 70–73, above.]

NOTE

The *Wolf* court seems to imply that educational segregation is totally impermissible. By equating the legal status of segregation of handicapped pupils with racial segregation, the court is led to the conclusion that such segregation is constitutionally forbidden. But the notion that separate educational facilities are inherently unequal may be too simplistic when applied to the special education context. Most professional educators believe that separated classes may be necessary, at least for limited periods of time, in dealing with certain types of educational problems; they would urge that students be educated in a setting as close to the normal classroom environment as appropriate, but not that all children should always be in the regular classroom situation.

The *Wolf* holding that no separate classes are allowed is at the other extreme from the ruling in the *Ghrist* case that the placement decisions of school officials are controlling. A better resolution would appear to fall somewhere between these two extremes, with educators being given some discretion, in recognition of their professional expertise, but with parents being allowed a chance to have input in the placement process, as well as some mechanisms for challenging disputed placements.

HAIRSTON v. DROSICK

[See pp. 194–200, above.]

NOTE

Compare the result in *Hairston* with that in *State* v. *Ghrist*, pp. 273–277, above. Is there any justification under the *Hairston* rationale for the segregation of pupils with orthopedic handicaps?

BURGDORF, R., "THE DOCTRINE OF THE LEAST RESTRICTIVE ALTERNATIVE"

4 Leadership Series in Special Education *143, 147-151, University of Minnesota (R. Johnson, R. Weatherman, and A. Rehmann, eds., 1975)*

As long ago as 1819, Chief Justice Marshall of the United States Supreme Court, in the early landmark case of *McCulloch* v. *Maryland,* indicated that regulation affecting citizens of a state should be both "appropriate" and "plainly adapted" to the end sought to be achieved. This concept gradually expanded through the next century and a half, until by 1960 the Supreme Court could say:

> In a series of decisions this Court has held that, even though the governmental purpose be legitimate and substantial, that purpose cannot be pursued by means that broadly stifle fundamental personal liberties when the end can be more narrowly achieved. The breadth of the legislative abridgement must be viewed in the light of less drastic means for achieving the same basic purpose.[12]

This principle has received a number of judicial forms of phrasing. In the case just cited, the Supreme Court spoke of "less drastic means for achieving the same basic purpose." Other courts have referred to the "least restrictive means,"[13] the "least burdensome method,"[14] and the way we are embracing it herein, "the least restrictive alternative."[15]

These majestic-sounding phrases have a fairly straightforward meaning. In very

---

[12] *Shelton* v. *Tucker,* 364 U.S. 479, 483 (1960).

[13] *Smith* v. *Sampson,* 349 F.Supp. 268, 271 (D.N.H. 1972).

[14] *Ramirez* v. *Brown,* 9G.3d 199, 104 Ca. R. 137, 507 P.2d 1345, 1353 (1973).

[15] E.g., *Covington* v. *Harris,* 419 F.2d 617, 623 (D.C.Cir. 1969).

simple terms, the principle of least restrictive alternative means that state laws and state officials (and here would be included public education officials and public school teachers) should be no nastier than they absolutely have to be. An attorney friend refers to the least restrictive alternative as the principle of the flyswatter instead of the shotgun. He reasons that it might be reasonable for a person to use a flyswatter or a roll of newspaper to swat a pesky fly. But if one took out a shotgun and started blasting away at a fly, that would be too drastic an alternative, and therefore an improper course of conduct.

Least restrictive alternative first developed in this country in relation to civil commitment of mentally handicapped persons to residential institutions. The courts, fairly early, ruled that in giving treatment for people within these institutions, such treatment has to be provided in as unrestrictive an environment as can be arranged. An extension of that principle requires that where no less restrictive alternatives are available, the state and state officials are responsible for creating less restrictive alternatives; and further, the state and its officials have the burden of demonstrating what other alternatives were investigated and why these other alternatives were not appropriate.

In recent years, least restrictive alternative has come to apply to education. There appear to be two basic reasons why this occurred, both of which are historical. The first was that the courts became aware that the concept and practice of segregation does not make sense simply from an educational point of view. This insight was first drawn from experiences in the area of racial segregation. In *Brown* v. *Board of Education*,[16] the United States Supreme Court stated its conclusion:

> We conclude that in the field of public education the doctrine of "separate but equal" has no place. Separate educational facilities are inherently unequal. Therefore, we hold that the plaintiffs and others similarly situated for whom the actions have been brought are, by reason of the segregation complained of, deprived of the equal protection of the laws guaranteed by the Fourteenth Amendment.

So, first of all, from an educational viewpoint, the courts became convinced that segregation makes no sense.

Secondly, the courts heard testimony from numerous expert education professionals who declared that the separating of children into isolated groups and labeling them "mentally retarded," "mentally deficient," "untrainable" or even some of the more avant-garde terms such as "exceptional" or "special," has a stigmatizing effect upon those children. The recognition of this social stigma occurred in educational and sociological theory and thence was absorbed as a judicial theory.

Finally these notions converged and in a 1969 case which was actually the grandfather of all the special education lawsuits, the court made a very important decision. Drawing upon the Supreme Court's decision in *Brown* v. *Board of Education*, a Utah court declared:

> Today it is doubtful that any child may reasonably be expected to succeed in life if he is denied the right and opportunity of an education. In the instant case the segregation of the plaintiff children from the public school system has detrimental effects upon the

---

[16]347 U.S. 483, 495 (1954).

children as well as their parents. The impact is greater when it has the apparent sanction of the law for the policy of placing these children under the Department of Welfare and segregating them from the educational system can be and probably is usually interpreted as denoting their inferiority, unusualness, uselessness and incompetency. A sense of inferiority and not belonging affects the motivation of a child to learn. Segregation, even though perhaps well intentioned, under the apparent sanction of law and state authority has a tendency to retard the educational, emotional and mental development of the children.[17]

But while segregation or separation is generally harmful, it may sometimes be appropriate. The law has never stated that equal treatment means identical treatment for different types of persons. So how is this doctrine of the least restrictive alternative to be applied?

The courts have answered by saying that it is a presumption; it is a presumption of how things will take place. It is not an absolute, black-and-white law. To illustrate how the courts have reacted to this concept, it is useful to examine the language of the various decisions. In the *Pennsylvania Association for Retarded Children* case, the decree stated:

> It is the Commonwealth's obligation to place each mentally retarded child in a free, public program of education and training appropriate to the child's capacity, within the context of a presumption that, among the alternative programs of education and training required by statute to be available, placement in a regular public school class is preferable to placement in special public school class and placement in special public school classes is preferable to placement in any other type of program of education and training.[18]

A shortened, partial version of the presumption was outlined by the court in the *Mills* case in the District of Columbia. The court declared:

> Each member of the plaintiff class is to be provided with a publicly-supported educational program suited to his needs, within the context of a presumption that among the alternative programs of education, placement in a regular public school class with appropriate ancillary services is preferable to placement in a special school class.[19]

Similarly, in the *Lebanks* decision in New Orleans, it was ordered:

> All evaluations and educational plans, hearings, and determinations of appropriate programs of education and training hereinafter provided for shall be made in the context of a presumption that, among alternative programs and plans, placement in regular public school class with the appropriate support services is preferable to placement in special public school class and placement in a special public school class is preferable to placement in a community training facility and placement in a community training facility is preferable to placement in a residential institution or other program of education outside the Orleans Parish public schools.[20]

Likewise, the Consent Order in the *Rainey* case in Tennessee includes the following provision:

---

[17] *Wolf* v. *Legislature of the State of Utah,* Civil No. 182646 (3rd Jud.Dist.Ct.Utah, Jan. 8, 1969).

[18] 334 F.Supp. 1257, 1260 (E.D.Pa. 1971).

[19] 348 F.Supp. 866, 880 (D.D.C. 1972).

[20] 60 F.R.D. 135, 140 (E.D.La. 1973).

Furthermore, the parties are in agreement with the requirement in the mandatory education law that handicapped children shall be provided special education services in as normal an educational environment as possible and that the labeling of individual children should be minimized and eliminated. Thus, placement of a child in the regular classroom is preferable to placement in separate special classes, and placement of a child in a special class is preferable to any other educational assignment such as institutional or private school placement.[21]

These cases are exemplary of the court decisions dealing with the concept of least restrictive alternative as it applies to the education of those with special educational needs. The principle of least restrictive alternative has also been incorporated into a very great number of state statutory enactments.

REGULATIONS FOR THE IMPLEMENTATION OF P.L. 94-142
42 Fed.Reg. 42473, 42497-42498 (Aug. 23, 1977), 45 C.F.R. § 121a

Least Restrictive Environment

§ 121a.550   General.

(a) Each State educational agency shall insure that each public agency establishes and implements procedures which meet the requirements of §§ 121a.550-121a.556.

(b) Each public agency shall insure:

(1) That to the maximum extent appropriate, handicapped children, including children in public or private institutions or other care facilities, are educated with children who are not handicapped, and

(2) That special classes, separate schooling or other removal of handicapped children from the regular educational environment occurs only when the nature or severity of the handicap is such that education in regular classes with the use of supplementary aids and services cannot be achieved satisfactorily.

§ 121a.551   Continuum of alternative placements.

(a) Each public agency shall insure that a continuum of alternative placements is available to meet the needs of handicapped children for special education and related services.

(b) The continuum required under paragraph (a) of this section must:

(1) Include the alternative placements listed in the definition of special education under § 121a.13 of Subpart A (instruction in regular classes, special classes, special schools, home instruction, and instruction in hospitals and institutions), and

(2) Make provision for supplementary services (such as resource room or itinerant instruction) to be provided in conjunction with regular class placement.

§ 121a.552   Placements.

Each public agency shall insure that:

(a) Each handicapped child's educational placement:

(1) Is determined at least annually,

(2) Is based on his or her individualized education program, and

---

[21]Consent Agreement, p. 2, approved by Chancery Court on July 29, 1974.

(3) Is as close as possible to the child's home;

(b) The various alternative placements included under § 121a.551 are available to the extent necessary to implement the individualized education program for each handicapped child:

(c) Unless a handicapped child's individualized education program requires some other arrangement, the child is educated in the school which he or she would attend if not handicapped; and

(d) In selecting the least restrictive environment, consideration is given to any potential harmful effect on the child or on the quality of services which he or she needs.

Comment. Section 121a.552 includes some of the main factors which must be considered in determining the extent to which a handicapped child can be educated with children who are not handicapped. The overriding rule in this section is that placement decisions must be made on an individual basis. The section also requires each agency to have various alternative placements available in order to insure that each handicapped child receives an education which is appropriate to his or her individual needs.

The analysis of the regulations for Section 504 of the Rehabilitation Act of 1973 (45 CFR Part 84—Appendix, Paragraph 24) includes several points regarding educational placements of handicapped children which are pertinent to this section:

1. With respect to determining proper placements, the analysis states: "... it should be stressed that, where a handicapped child is so disruptive in a regular classroom that the education of other students is significantly impaired, the needs of the handicapped child cannot be met in that environment. Therefore regular placement would not be appropriate to his or her needs. . . ."

2. With respect to placing a handicapped child in an alternate setting, the analysis states that among the factors to be considered in placing a child is the need to place the child as close to home as possible. Recipients are required to take this factor into account in making placement decisions. The parent's right to challenge the placement of their child extends not only to placement in special classes or separate schools, but also to placement in a distant school, particularly in a residential program. An equally appropriate education program may exist closer to home; and this issue may be raised by the parents under the due process provisions of this subpart.

§ 121a.553   Nonacademic settings.

In providing or arranging for the provision of nonacademic and extracurricular services and activities, including meals, recess periods, and the services and activities set forth in § 121a.306 of Subpart C, each public agency shall insure that each handicapped child participates with nonhandicapped children in those services and activities to the maximum extent appropriate to the needs of that child.

Comment. Section 121a.553 is taken from a new requirement in the final regulations for Section 504 of the Rehabilitation Act of 1973. With respect to this requirement, the analysis of the Section 504 Regulations includes the following statement: "[A new paragraph] specifies that handicapped children must also be provided nonacademic services in as integrated a setting as possible. This requirement is especially important for children whose educational needs necessitate their being solely with other handicapped children during most of each day. To the maximum extent appropriate, children in residential settings are also to be provided opportunities for participation with other children.'' (45 CRF part 84—Appendix, Paragraph 24.)

§ 121a.554   Children in public or private institutions.

Each State educational agency shall make arrangements with public and private institutions (such as a memorandum of agreement or special implementation procedures) as may be necessary to insure that § 121a.550 is effectively implemented.

Comment. Under section 612(5) (B) of the statute, the requirement to educate handicapped children with nonhandicapped children also applies to children in public and private institutions or other care facilities. Each State educational agency must insure that each applicable agency and institution in the State implements this requirement. Regardless of other reasons for institutional placement, no child in an institution who is capable of education in a regular public school setting may be denied access to an education in that setting.

§ 121a.555   Technical assistance and training activities.

Each State educational agency shall carry out activities to insure that teachers and administrators in all public agencies:

(a) Are fully informed about their responsibilities for implementing § 121a.550, and

(b) Are provided with technical assistance and training necessary to assist them in this effort.

§ 121a.556   Monitoring activities.

(a) The State educational agency shall carry out activities to insure that § 121a.550 is implemented by each public agency.

(b) If there is evidence that a public agency makes placements that are inconsistent with § 121a.550 of this subpart, the State educational agency:

(1) Shall review the public agency's justification for its actions, and

(2) Shall assist in planning and implementing any necessary corrective action.

STUART v. NAPPI

[See pp. 255–262, above.]

NOTE

The factual situation of *Stuart* v. *Nappi* epitomizes the "child must fit the program" attitude common among old-line educators; if a child is out of step with academic or behavioral expectations, the child is to be booted out. The concept of least restrictive environment, on the other hand, mandates that efforts be made to adapt the program to the special needs of the child so that the child can be educated, if possible, in the regular setting, and, if not, in an environment as close to the regular classroom situation as can be made educationally appropriate.

LORA v. BOARD OF EDUCATION OF CITY OF NEW YORK

United States District Court for the Eastern District of New York, 1978
456 F.Supp. 1211, 1264-1271

[See pp. 147–165, above.]

H.   Mainstreaming

1. Theory

Briefly, "mainstreaming" involves the integration of handicapped children into the regular classroom to the greatest degree possible. A discussion of this approach and the problems and legal implications it raises is essential to an understanding of the special day schools.

As a general proposition all agree that children with special educational needs, including the socially maladjusted and emotionally disturbed, should be served in regular classrooms and neighborhood schools insofar as these arrangements are conducive to good educational progress. In addition, it is acknowledged that supplementary services for exceptional children, or their removal from part or all of the regular school environment may be required. The continuum of acceptable educational programs designed to meet the needs of exceptional children, arranged from least to most restrictive, has traditionally been: 1) regular classroom; 2) regular classroom with specialist consultation; 3) regular classroom with itinerant teachers; 4) regular classroom plus resource room; 5) part-time special class; 6) full-time special class; 7) special day school; and 8) residential institutions. M. C. Reynolds, "A Framework for Considering Some Issues In Special Education," in J. P. Glavin, *Major Issues In Special Education,* 13, 14 (1973).

A standard conceptual approach to the utilization of these resources has been the "Cascade System." It has been described as follows:

> The flow of service provisions in the cascade progresses from minimal to maximal. The regular classroom is the level at which the least amount of special resources are needed. There are, however, three modifications of the regular classroom which allow the minimally handicapped child the maximum opportunity to obtain and participate in a normal educational experience.
>
> Modification I provides the regular classroom teacher with the opportunity to obtain consultation with a number of educational and related specialists in instructional materials, reading, psychology, guidance, speech, and others. In this situation, the regular classroom teacher, who is ultimately responsible for the child, is searching for a better understanding of the child and his problems, and is seeking improved instructional and management techniques. Modification II involves itinerant specialists and differs from I in that these individuals actually work with the child. Modification III includes the placement of the child in a regular classroom, but with some time spent in a special resource area where specific remedial instruction occurs. Specialists working in this area confer with the classroom teacher, and together they plan appropriate programs for the child.
>
> Children who cannot participate or achieve in one of the above modifications of the regular classroom can split their school day by spending part of it in the regular class and the remainder in a special class. In this program option, the special class is staffed by a trained special educator who works with the child in a special adaptation of the regular classroom program as well as other specialized instructional areas. Also in this situation, the special education and regular classroom teachers confer, and jointly plan to insure that the child is provided with a meaningful and coordinated education.
>
> If a child is unable to participate successfully in most regular classroom activities, he may be placed in a full-time special education class where all of his education, with the exception of non-academic areas such as physical education, art, shop, and music, will be provided. In this placement the total curriculum is adapted to each child's individual

needs. The special class teacher in this program is ultimately responsible for the children.

Special day schools for handicapped children offer facilities and programs generally unavailable in the regular school. These include . . . smaller pupil-teacher ratios, and the availability of greater amounts of supportive personnel. The children live at home and are frequently transported from large geographic areas extending beyond single school districts.

F. J. Weintraub and A. R. Abeson, "Appropriate Education for All Handicapped Children: A Growing Issue," 23 *Syracuse L.Rev.* 1037, 1040-41 (1972).

Recently, this scheme has been challenged by increasing numbers of special educators who feel that special day schools and other programs that remove mildly handicapped children from the "mainstream" may in many instances represent an unnecessary and undesirable educational tool, not part of a defensible and acceptable education scheme.

The following definition is a useful starting point for a discussion of mainstreaming as it bears on the issues before us.

Mainstreaming Is:
—providing the most appropriate education for each child in the least restrictive setting.
—looking at the educational needs of children instead of clinical or diagnostic labels such as mentally handicapped, learning disabled, physically handicapped, hearing impaired, or gifted.
—looking for and creating alternatives that will help general educators serve children with learning or adjustment problems in the regular setting. Some approaches being used to help achieve this are consulting teachers, methods and materials specialists, itinerant teachers, and resource room teachers.
—uniting the skills of general education and special education so all children may have equal educational opportunity.
Mainstreaming Is Not:
—wholesale return of all exceptional children in special classes to regular classes.
—permitting children with special needs to remain in regular classrooms without the support services they need.
—ignoring the need of some children for a more specialized program than can be provided in the general education program.
—less costly than serving children in special self-contained classrooms.

J. L. Paul, A. P. Turnbull, Wm. M. Cruickshank, *Mainstreaming, A Practical Guide,* vii-viii (1977) (citations omitted).

The movement reflects dissatisfaction with the way that special education programs have been handled to permit regular teachers to avoid problems they should be capable of dealing with. The following criticisms are typical:

Special education is part of the arrangement for cooling out students. It has helped to erect a parallel system which permits relief of institutional guilt and humiliation stemming from the failure to achieve competence and effectiveness in the task given to it by society. Special education is helping the regular school maintain its spoiled identity when it creates special programs (whether psychodynamic or behavioral modification) for the "disruptive child" and the "slow learner," many of whom, for some strange reason, happen to be Black and poor and live in the inner city.

J. L. Johnson, "Special Education and the Inner City: A Challenge For the Future or Another Means for Cooling the Mark Out?," *The Journal of Special Education* 241, 245 (1969).

> The conscience of special educators needs to rub up against morality. In large measure we have been at the mercy of the general education establishment in that we accept problem pupils who have been referred out of the regular grades. In this way, we contribute to the delinquency of the general educators since we remove the pupils that are problems for them and thus reduce their need to deal with individual differences. Because of these pressures from the school system, we have been guilty of fostering quantity with little respect for quality of special education instruction. . . . Our first responsibility is to have an abiding commitment to the less fortunate children we aim to serve.

M. Dunn, "Special Education for the Mildly Retarded—Is Much of It Justifiable?," 35 *Exceptional Children* 5, 20 (1968).

Generally shared by thoughtful proponents of this approach is a commitment to encouraging acceptance of diversity. Average children are considered to benefit as much from having the handicapped in their classrooms as are exceptional pupils.

> . . . The special educator's function in mainstreaming . . . becomes twofold: (1) education of the general public and the educational community with respect to normalization—that is, including child diversity and deviation in the social and institutional mainstreaming and (2) changing the educational structures and processes to embrace diversity and pluralism.

W. C. Rhodes, "Beyond Abnormality: Into the Mainstream," in A. G. Pappanikou and J. L. Paul, *Mainstreaming Emotionally Disturbed Children,* 37 (1977). *See also* M. J. Trippe, "The Social Psychology of Exceptional Children, Part II" in J. P. Glavin, *Major Issues in Special Education,* 17-21 (1973).

Moreover, it has been found that "mildly" disturbed exceptional children often do better in regular classes than in settings where they are segregated from their "normal" peers. *See* G. Calhoun, Jr., and R. N. Elliot, Jr. "Self-Concept and Academic Achievement of Educable Retarded and Emotionally Disturbed Pupils," 43 *Exceptional Children* 379, 380 (1970); G. O. Johnson, "Special Education for the Mentally Handicapped-Paradox," 29 *Exceptional Children* 62-66 (1962).

Suggested programs for accomplishing integration of exceptional with "normal" pupils are founded on the premise that properly trained regular teachers, supported and counseled by special educators, can adapt classroom practices and procedures to serve adequately both normal and exceptional children. Effective mainstreaming involves training of teachers along with the presence of support personnel in regular classes, including consultants, crisis or resource room teachers, psychologists, and psychiatrists. In sum, mainstreaming of pupils cannot occur in a vacuum; to whatever extent implemented, it must involve many coordinated changes in the system as a whole. As one study has put it, the system itself must be "mainstreamed." J. L. Paul, "Mainstreaming Emotionally Disturbed Children," in A. J. Pappanikou, J. L. Paul, *Mainstreaming Emotionally Disturbed Children,* 11, 16 (1977). *See also* J. P. Glavin, H. C. Quay, F. R. Annesley, J. S. Werry, "An Experimental Resource Room for

Behavior Problem Children,'' in J. P. Glavin, *Major Issues in Special Education* 165 (1973).

Mainstreaming includes a movement away from rigid labelling. Categorizing children is viewed as destructive because it stigmatizes, promotes a sense of negative self-worth and may result in pigeonholing rather than in efforts to improve a child's condition or a classroom situation. Labelling is also feared because it may be erroneous, either as a result of misapplication of agreed upon criteria or use of criteria of questionable validity. Rigid labels are to be replaced by more flexible definitions of exceptional children, definitions designed to emphasize specific learning needs rather than defects. The child is to be placed in the least restrictive environment possible to meet these needs. It has been noted that

> [a]busive classification of children should be as much a target of the freeing impulse of mainstreaming as special class placement. Both inappropriate labelling and placement of a child compromise the integrity and freedom of the child.

J. L. Paul, "Mainstreaming Emotionally Disturbed Children," in A. J. Pappanikou, J. L. Paul, *Mainstreaming Emotionally Disturbed Children*, 1, 8 (1977). *See also* R. M. Smith and J. T. Niesworth, "Special Education: A Changing Field; Careers in Special Educational and Definitions," in R. E. Schmid, J. Moneypenny, R. Johnston, *Contemporary Issues in Special Education*, 6, 8-9 (1977); D. Kirp, W. Buss, P. Kuriloff, "Legal Reform of Special Education: Empirical Studies and Procedural Proposals," 62 Cal.L.Rev. 40, 44-45 (1974); D. Kirp, "School as Sorters, The Constitutional and Policy Implications of Student Classification," 121 *U.Penn.L.Rev.* 705, 719, 731-37 (1973).

It should be noted that mainstreaming does not necessarily call for the eradication of all special education settings. Some educators do take an extreme position, sometimes termed a "zero reject" model, aimed at making it virtually impossible to switch mildly disturbed or behaviorally disoriented children out of the regular classroom, but providing support and special training to the regular teacher. *E.g.,* M. S. Lilly, "A Training Based Model for Special Education," in J. P. Glavin, *Major Issues in Special Education,* 219 (1973). *See also* testimony of Dr. Rachel Lauer, transcript at 1142-45. Most take a less absolutist stance, and are critical of the "zero reject" model.

> Some very peculiar things have happened in the name of education in the United States, and this movement toward integration into the regular grades is among them. Tens of thousands of children are involved as well as thousands of teachers. However, the literature is devoid of any reasonable research which demonstrates the positive gains to both exceptional and normal children under this arrangement. Overnight, educational leadership has advocated integration. No solid facts exist to support their claims. The literature is full of opinions, but not fact born of careful longitudinal research under relatively controlled conditions—essentials in this significant issue. . . .
> Caution is recommended, for the needs of a generation of children are at stake. Those things which can be considered good in the special class should be retained and further perfected. Those elements which give rise to sound hope for integration should immediately be put to the test. The culling from both should provide the base for a rich educational plan for the next generation of exceptional children.

* * *

1. For the child, it is desirable to provide service outside the regular classroom . . . when his needs cannot reasonably be met within the flexibility possible in the regular classroom. Meeting needs does not include children who exist, even placidly in a regular class, but whose problems are such that educational growth fails. The fact that they present no problem to the group or the teacher is not enough. They must benefit by remaining.

2. It must be remembered that the normal pupils have rights too. The usual school operates on a large group basis and has goals which are set in terms of a broad normal range. The exceptional child with bizarre behavior, excessive aggression, or an all-out belligerent attitude may upset the group or require an inordinate amount of teacher time so that the other pupils are left with too little help. In other words, it may be asking the class to take on more than it can when a disturbed pupil remains. When the group is being sacrificed for the individual, resources outside the classroom are needed.

3. Some teachers handle a trying child well, others do not. Some have high tolerance, some low tolerance. There is nothing to be gained by saying that every teacher should be able to accept one such child or two. When the disturbed child takes up the teacher's psychic energy and reduces her effectiveness, removal is necessary.

Wm. M. Cruikshank, G. O. Johnson, *Education of Exceptional Children and Youth,* 82, 84, 597-98 (3d Edition 1975). *See also* F. Christoplos, P. Renz, "A Critical Examination of Special Education Programs," 3 *Journal of Special Education* 371, 373-74 (1969) (no reliable evidence either way as to effect on learning of "normal" or exceptional children from inclusion of the latter in the regular class.)

Criticism and skepticism of mainstreaming has stemmed also from a fear that the process may advance without adequate changes in the system and that the results will be disastrous. A recent study of the impact of mainstreaming on deaf children pointed out the dangers incurred in forcing untrained teachers in overcrowded classrooms to deal with a new group of students who are tragically vulnerable educationally, psychologically and socially. "The dream is equality and social acceptance. The fact is that nine out of ten deaf children will receive neither. For some, mainstreaming may be catastrophic." J. Greenberg, G. Doolittle, "Can Schools Speak the Language of the Deaf," *N.Y. Times Sunday Magazine,* 50, Dec. 11, 1977.

The controversy over mainstreaming of emotionally disturbed and behaviorally maladjusted students is especially intense. The disruptive behavior so often manifested by these children presents more of a threat to the integrity of the regular classroom than do under-achievement or physical handicaps. Unlike the latter problems, "acting out" is not easily accommodated by special academic materials or adjustment of the physical plant. A. J. Pappanikou, J. L. Paul, *Mainstreaming Emotionally Disturbed Children,* xii-xiii (1977); Wm. C. Morse "The Psychology of Mainstreaming Socio-Emotionally Disturbed Children," in A. J. Pappanikou and J. L. Paul, *supra* at 18, 22.

One defense witness, psychologist Dr. Florence Halpern, was particularly critical of the movement towards education of these children in the least restrictive environment possible.

A. . . ., for the . . . reason that the large school is not the atmosphere for these kids and they are discriminated against by the other kids.
Q. You would much prefer to put them in a special school?
A. Where the school is there and they are comfortable there.

Transcript at 3095.

The predominant view seems to be that special day schools and classes are merely the beginning of treatment; that the aim is referral out of these settings as soon as possible. On the other hand, they should not necessarily be abandoned.

> Mainstreaming is no more than a *preference* in favor of regular educational placement. Because mainstreaming reflects a preference, it is not, nor should it become, an inflexible rule; rather, it should be a guide for conduct, not a rule of conduct. As a guide, *it should not prohibit alternatives to mainstream placement.*

H. R. Turnbull III, "Legal Implications," in A. P. Pappanikou, J. L. Paul, *Mainstreaming Emotionally Disturbed Children,* 43, 45 (1977) (emphasis in original).

The testimony supports a nondogmatic, pragmatic approach. Plaintiffs' as well as defendants' witnesses admitted that special day schools are desirable for at least some of the students currently being referred to these schools. For instance, Dr. Steven Weiss, Associate Professor of Education at New York University, favors the "least restrictive environment" approach, but did note that a properly constituted special day school program can play a useful role in special education. *E.g.,* transcript at 1485. Dr. Kenneth B. Clark testified on this point as follows:

> THE COURT: Well, do you have a professional view with respect to whether there is a need[, . . .] a usefulness in the spectrum of special services available[, . . .] for a well-run day school with small classes, extra service, more guidance, and . . . specially trained teachers? . . . In other words, you wouldn't on a theoretical basis . . . eliminate this end of the spectrum?
> THE WITNESS: No. . . . A well-run system in which . . . the problems presented by this child are such . . . that a panel of professionals with high standards would say, look, this child needs a special kind of care short of hospitalization, short of institutionalization, and . . . these services would be provided in the context of other things which the child needs, such as a family situation.
> Yes, there is room, there is a place for children whose problems are beyond those that can be handled in the classroom or for that matter handled in an out-patient sort of service such as the Child Guidance centers, Jewish Board of Guardians, or Northside. . . .—I am not objecting to the special facilities for children who need [them]—I'm objecting to just using the facilities as a catchall and pushing children in without regard to a serious study of whether they need it or not, and without regard to what you're doing for those who need it.

Transcript at 1701-02.

The Commissioner of Education of the State of New York seems fully sensitive to the nuances of the mainstreaming controversy. As he has noted, while "mainstreaming to the maximum extent possible is the goal for all handicapped children, it is not sound educational programming to place a child in a 'mainstreaming' setting in the absence of some evidence that the needs of the child can be met there." *In the Matter of the Appeal of Cornelia,* N.Y. Comm.Ed.Dec. No. 9575 (1977), *cited in* V. Garfinkle, "Recent Developments in the Law on the Education of Handicapped Children in New York State," 27 (1978) (unpub.).

In light of the weight of professional opinion, it is impossible for the Court to conclude that special day schools are unacceptable educational alternatives for socially maladjusted and emotionally disturbed children. Nor can we realistically mandate that a specific number of children be mainstreamed over a specific period of time. As has already been noted, mainstreaming involves a multitude of coordinated changes in the educational system as a whole. There are a variety of ways in which the generally recognized goal of smoother transition and increased continuity among all levels of services provided for exceptional children can be implemented. These must vary in accordance with the specifics of the system involved. Moreover, the dynamics of the process involve professional judgments only educators and administrators can make in considering resources provided by legislators and executives. In fulfilling an appropriate judiciary role in this suit, it would be inappropriate to require extensive structural overhaul of the special education system for emotionally disturbed children in New York City.

Nevertheless, there are discrete areas of special education, highlighted by the mainstreaming movement, into which the judiciary must venture because of statutory and constitutional mandates. Due process rights to notice and hearing prior to special education placement to provide safeguards against misclassification, along with the appropriate education of all handicapped children once placed as part of a right to equal educational opportunity, have been recognized repeatedly in the course of studies in the education of exceptional pupils. *See, e.g.,* N. Hobbs, *The Futures of Children,* 156-179 (1975); H. R. Turnbull III, "Legal Implications," in A. J. Pappanikou and J. L. Paul, *Mainstreaming Emotionally Disturbed Children,* 43 (1977). There must be adequate safeguards against unnecessary referral of children to these schools. It is crucial, not only that proper identification of pupils for possible referral take place in the first instance, but also that reevaluations be undertaken with sufficient frequency to assure that children are assigned to the least restrictive environment suitable for their educational needs. To the extent that children are placed in the restrictive setting of a special day school, they must be provided with adequate facilities, educational materials and therapeutic support staff.

2. Alleged Lack of Consistent Use of Special Day Schools

Part of the criticism leveled against the special schools is that insufficient efforts are made to refer students to other, less restrictive educational environments. In a 1973 report on the special day schools it was noted that reluctance of principals accounted for the failure to meet the stated aim of return to the mainstream. Principals stated, however, that the practice of holding students in the schools was usually agreed to by the child and parent. J. D. Goldman, "Special Day Schools for Socially Maladjusted and Emotionally Disturbed Children," 27 (mimeo. 1973).

The process of returning a child from a special school has been described in section III E, *supra*. As was noted there are no written criteria used in this process. Rather, the decision stems from an observation of the pupil's progress—both emotional and academic—in the special school. One principal testified that the average stay for a child in her school was from one to two years. She has instituted a program in which the students are instructed that they may apply on their own initiative for re-entrance into the regular school. Their applications are screened by school personnel and then referred to the COH. Although pupils may apply at any time, this principal feels that a stay of at least six months is necessary before anything can be gained from the special day school experience. Testimony of Marjorie Louer, transcript at 2440. Another witness testified that he uses a similar method. Testimony of Dr. Julian Schtierman, transcript at 2812-15. Dr. Dorothy Arnsten, a school psychologist, noted that although students could take the initiative on mainstreaming, the actual decision to return to a regular school setting should not be left entirely in his hands. Often a child who could function in a regular school feels reluctant to leave the comfortable setting of the special day school. In such a case efforts must be made to help him overcome these fears so that he learns to cope with a more normal existence. Transcript at 2898-99.

The decision to return the child may depend in part on the availability of special services, including a resource room or BCG staff. One of defendants' witnesses admitted that the paucity of BCG staff in the regular school may deter mainstreaming. Testimony of Dr. Gerald Davis, transcript at 2104.

During the period June 1, 1976 to May 31, 1977, 344 or approximately 10% of the total special day school population at that time, were sent back to the regular school. Only 17 students were discharged to a CEH class. Although these classes, housed in the same building as the regular school, are commonly considered less restrictive than the self-contained special day school, they are not truly in the mainstream. Moreover, there was testimony suggesting that the progression back to the mainstream does not necessarily run from special to regular school via a CEH class. Testimony of Dr. Martin Groveman, transcript at 2322. Other witnesses object to any special class placement at all and have expressed the opinion that these special classes are at least as restrictive as the special school. *E.g.,* Testimony of Dr. Florence Halpern, transcript at 3097. There was also testimony supporting the view that transfers into the freshman class at a new school are more desirable than transfers into the mid-grades. Avoidance of the latter alleviates the strain of entering a setting where peers are already adjusted and faculty might look askance at a new "problem" student. Whatever the weight of any of these considerations, they can properly be taken into account by sensitive educators and therapists concerned with the welfare of special day school students.

Differences of professional opinion are reflected in the variance in the numbers of students mainstreamed from each of the special schools in existence during the period June 1, 1976 through May 31, 1977:

School	Total number of students	Number of students returning to regular classes
Intermediate school		
P 12X	162	9
P 75Q	244	45
P 23Q	134	17
P 9Q	182	30
P 4Q	139	1
P 371K	246	58
P 369K	205	32
P 36K	224	34
P 82M	107	12
P 169M	215	49

(continued)

School	Total number of students	Number of students returning to regular classes
High school		
P 58M	462	32
P 8M (Girls)	163	1
P 8M (Boys)	234	9
P 141K	129	8
P 85K	488	3

NOTE

The term *mainstreaming,* used by the *Lora* court, is an educational term which is analogous to the legal concept of the least restrictive alternative; it signifies the principle that handicapped pupils should be educated in a setting as close to the regular classroom situation as possible. Unfortunately, however, there has not been unanimity or consistency in the educational terminology. A number of terms and phrases with similar meanings have cropped up and caused confusion regarding this concept.

> A number of catch phrases and slogans have been associated with or used interchangeably with the term mainstreaming. For example, mainstreaming has been interpreted as an attempt to provide services to special education students in the "least restrictive program alternative." The least restrictive alternative has been defined as the delivery of special education services under the highest possible degree of "normalization." "Normalization" has been referred to as an attempt to organize special education services in a way that allows maximum opportunities for "integration." Finally, "integration" is said to be an attempt to provide programs and services to handicap students in the "mainstream" !!! Special education has obviously gone full circle with its mainstream related jargon and as a result definitions for each of these terms have become blurred (Gross, J., and Vance, V., "Mainstream Educator Training in a Cooperative Joint Agreement and Intermediate Unit District," 4 *Leadership Series in Special Education 103,* 106-7, University of Minnesota (R. Johnson, R. Weatherman, and A. Rehmann, eds., 1975).

To avoid such terminological problems and the resultant confusion, many education administrators have created schematic diagrams to illustrate the range of alternative programs and the interrelationships between them. One of the first such constructs was the "Cascade System," developed by Maynard Reynolds:

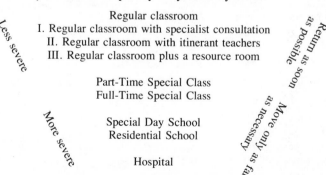

Regular classroom
I. Regular classroom with specialist consultation
II. Regular classroom with itinerant teachers
III. Regular classroom plus a resource room

Part-Time Special Class
Full-Time Special Class

Special Day School
Residential School

Hospital

Less severe — *More severe* — *Return as soon as possible* — *Move only as necessary as far*

From: Reynolds, M., "A Framework for Considering Some Issues in Special Education," 28 *Exceptional Children* 367-370 (1962).

A student's educational placement moves vertically in the diagram only if he or she cannot be effectively served at one of the higher levels. Thus, a pupil should be considered for a full-time special class only if a part-time special class or one of the variations of the regular class cannot meet the pupil's educational needs. Similarly, a student should be considered for a special day school only if none of the regular classroom or special class alternatives can serve the student effectively. Moreover, pupils should be returned to the more normal placements as soon as possible.

Other educators have developed similar schematic diagrams, and recent models have become increasingly more complex than Reynolds' scheme; see, e.g., Deno, E., "Special Education as Developmental Capitol," 37 *Exceptional Children* 229-237 (1971); Gross, J., and Vance, V., "Mainstream Educator Training in a Cooperative Joint Agreement and Intermediate Unit District," 4 *Leadership Series in Special Education* 103, 108, University of Minnesota (R. Johnson, R. Weatherman, and A. Rehmann, eds., 1975).

All of these models are, however, simply attempts to illustrate that there is a range of educational alternatives and that there should be safeguards for ensuring that each individual student is served in an educational environment as close to the "normal" or "mainstream" classroom setting as the student's educational needs permit; in short, that pupils are educated in the "least restrictive alternative."

ADDITIONAL READING

Abeson, A., Burgdorf, R., Casey, P., Kunz, J., and McNeil, W., "Access to Opportunity," Chapter 24 of 2 *Issues in the Classification of Children* 270, 274-278 (Hobbs, N., ed., 1975).

"Handicapped Youth and the Mainstream Educator," 4 *Leadership Series in Special Education* 1-186, University of Minnesota (R. Johnson, R. Weatherman, and A. Rehmann, eds., 1975).

d. Payment for Private School Programs   A number of cases have dealt with the propriety of public funding for private educational programs for handicapped children. Frequently, when no appropriate public school program is provided, payment for private school tuition has been approved by the courts, e.g., *Kivell* v. *Nemoitin,* pp. 175-177, above; *In re H.,* pp. 110-111, above; *In re Downey,* pp. 111-*113, above; In re G.H.,* pp. 113-120, above; *In re H.,* 66 Misc.2d 1097, 323 N.Y.S.2d 302 (1971); *In re Saberg,* 87 Misc.2d 848, 386 N.Y.S.2d 592 (1976); *In re Kaye,* 54 A.D.2d 907, 388 N.Y.S.2d 620 (1976); and *In re Patrick P.,* 85 Misc.2d 829, 380 N.Y.S.2d 877 (1976). In other circumstances, some courts have disapproved such payments, e.g., *Serotte* v. *State Education Department,* 63 Misc.2d 999, 314 N.Y.S.2d 114 (1970) (no showing that there was not an adequate public school program); *Doe* v. *Laconia Supervisory Union,* 369 F.Supp. 1291 (D.N.H. 1975) (inadequate legislative funding; resulting denial of education held not a violation of equal protection); *In re L.,* 39 N.Y.2d 434, 384 N.Y.S.2d 392, 348 N.E.2d 867 (1976) (parental claims for reimbursement not timely submitted); *In re Richard G.,* 52

A.D.2d 924, 383 N.Y.S.2d 403 (1976) (summer camp not shown to be for educational purposes). Cf. *Halderman* v. *Pittenger,* 391 F.Supp. 872 (E.D.Pa. 1975).

Since their enactment, P.L. 94-142 and § 504 of the Rehabilitation Act of 1973 have resolved much of the controversy over these issues.

HEW REGULATIONS IMPLEMENTING § 504 OF THE REHABILITATION ACT OF 1973

42 Fed. Reg. 22682 (May 4, 1977), 45C.F.R. 84 et seq.

§ 84.33 Free appropriate public education.

(a) *General.* A recipient that operates a public elementary or secondary education program shall provide a free appropriate public education to each qualified handicapped person who is in the recipient's jurisdiction, regardless of the nature or severity of the person's handicap.

* * *

(c) *Free education*—(1) *General.* For the purpose of this section, the provision of a free education is the provision of educational and related services without cost to the handicapped person or to his or her parents or guardian, except for those fees that are imposed on nonhandicapped persons or their parents or guardian. It may consist either of the provision of free services or, if a recipient places a handicapped person in or refers such person to a program not operated by the recipient as its means of carrying out the requirements of this subpart, of payment for the costs of the program. Funds available from any public or private agency may be used to meet the requirements of this subpart. Nothing in this section shall be construed to relieve an insurer or similar third party from an otherwise valid obligation to provide or pay for services provided to a handicapped person.

(2) *Transportation.* If a recipient places a handicapped person in or refers such person to a program not operated by the recipient as its means of carrying out the requirements of this subpart, the recipient shall ensure that adequate transportation to and from the program is provided at no greater cost than would be incurred by the person or his or her parents or guardian if the person were placed in the program operated by the recipient.

(3) *Residential placement.* If placement in a public or private residential program is necessary to provide a free appropriate public education to a handicapped person because of his or her handicap, the program, including nonmedical care and room and board, shall be provided at no cost to the person or his or her parents or guardian.

(4) *Placement of handicapped persons by parents.* If a recipient has made available, in conformance with the requirements of this section and § 84.34, a free appropriate public education to a handicapped person and the person's parents or guardian choose to place the person in a private school, the recipient is not required to pay for the person's education in the private school. Disagreements between a parent or guardian and a recipient regarding whether the recipient has made such a program available or otherwise regarding the question of financial responsibility are subject to the due process procedures of § 84.36.

NOTES

1. Compare with § 613 (a)(4)(A) of P.L. 94-142, p. 222, above.

2. The regulations do not answer all of the questions about apportionment of expenses. For example, the Attorney General of Maryland has ruled that it is permissible for the state to require parents to pay for "raw food costs" for children placed in private residential educational programs if these costs are equal to or less than the expenses the parents would incur if they were able to feed the children at home, 62 O.A.G. 353 (Md. 1977). What other costs might be legitimately chargeable to parents whose children are placed in educational programs away from home?

3. In *State ex. rel. Warren* v. *Nusbaum,* 64 Wis.2d 314, 219 N.W.2d 577 (1974), a Wisconsin statute providing for contracts with private schools for special education services was upheld against the charge that it violated the "establishment of religion" and "free exercise" clauses of the First Amendment; see *Meek* v. *Pittenger,* 421 U.S. 349 (1975); *Wolman* v. *Walter,* 433 U.S. 229 (1977).

H. SCHOOL RECORDS

THE FAMILY EDUCATIONAL RIGHTS AND PRIVACY ACT,

20 U.S.C. § 1232g

Conditions for availability of funds to educational agencies or institutions; inspection and review of education records; specific information to be made available; procedure for access to educational records; reasonableness of time for such access; hearings; written explanations by parents; definitions

(a)(1)(A) No funds shall be made available under any applicable program to any educational agency or institution which has a policy of denying, or which effectively prevents, the parents of students who are or have been in attendance at a school of such agency or at such institution, as the case may be, the right to inspect and review the education records of their children. If any material or document in the education record of a student includes information on more than one student, the parents of one of such students shall have the right to inspect and review only such part of such material or document as relates to such student or to be informed of the specific information contained in such part of such material. Each educational agency or institution shall establish appropriate procedures for the granting of a request by parents for access to the education records of their children within a reasonable period of time, but in no case more than forty-five days after the request has been made.

(B) The first sentence of subparagraph (A) shall not operate to make available to students in institutions of postsecondary education the following materials:

(i) financial records of the parents of the student or any information contained therein;

(ii) confidential letters and statements of recommendation, which were placed in the education records prior to January 1, 1975, if such letters or statements are not used for purposes other than those for which they were specifically intended;

(iii)   if the student has signed a waiver of the students' right of access under this subsection in accordance with subparagraph (C), confidential recommendations—

(I)   respecting admission to any educational agency or institution,

(II)   respecting an application for employment, and

(III)   respecting the receipt of an honor or honorary recognition.

(C) A student or a person applying for admission may waive his right of access to confidential statements described in clause (iii) of subparagraph (B), except that such waiver shall apply to recommendations only if (i) the student is, upon request, notified of the names of all persons making confidential recommendations and (ii) such recommendations are used solely for the purpose for which they were specifically intended. Such waivers may not be required as a condition for admission to, receipt of financial aid from, or receipt of any other services or benefits from such agency or institution.

(2) No funds shall be made available under any applicable program to any educational agency or institution unless the parents of students who are or have been in attendance at a school of such agency or at such institution are provided an opportunity for a hearing by such agency or institution, in accordance with regulations of the Secretary, to challenge the content of such student's education records, in order to insure that the records are not inaccurate, misleading, or otherwise in violation of the privacy or other rights of students, and to provide an opportunity for the correction or deletion of any such inaccurate, misleading, or otherwise inappropriate data contained therein and to insert into such records a written explanation of the parents respecting the content of such records.

(3)For the purposes of this section the term "educational agency or institution" means any public or private agency or institution which is the recipient of funds under any applicable program.

(4)(A) For the purposes of this section, the term "education records" means, except as may be provided otherwise in subparagraph (B), those records, files, documents, and other materials which—

(i)   contain information directly related to a student; and

(ii)   are maintained by an educational agency or institution or by a person acting for such agency or institution.

(B) The term "education records" does not include—

(i)   records of instructional, supervisory, and administrative personnel and educational personnel ancillary thereto which are in the sole possession of the maker thereof and which are not accessible or revealed to any other person except a substitute;

(ii)   if the personnel of a law enforcement unit do not have access to education records under subsection (b)(1) of this section, the records and documents of such law enforcement unit which (I) are kept apart from records described in subparagraph (A), (II) are maintained solely for law enforcement purposes, and (III) are not made available to persons other than law enforcement officials of the same jurisdiction.

(iii)   in the case of persons who are employed by an educational agency or institution but who are not in attendance at such agency or institution, records made and maintained in the normal course of business which relate exclusively to such person in that person's capacity as an employee and are not available for use for any other purpose; or

(iv) records on a student who is eighteen years of age or older, or is attending an institution of postsecondary education, which are made or maintained by a physician, psychiatrist, psychologist, or other recognized professional or paraprofessional acting in his professional or paraprofessional capacity, or assisting in that capacity, and which are made, maintained, or used only in connection with the provision of treatment to the student, and are not available to anyone other than persons providing such treatment, except that such records can be personally reviewed by a physician or other appropriate professional of the student's choice.

(5)(A) For the purposes of this section the term "directory information" relating to a student includes the following: the student's name, address, telephone listing, date and place of birth, major field of study, participation in officially recognized activities and sports, weight and height of members of athletic teams, dates of attendance, degrees and awards received, and the most recent previous educational agency or institution attended by the student.

(B) Any educational agency or institution making public directory information shall give public notice of the categories of information which it has designated as such information with respect to each student attending the institution or agency and shall allow a reasonable period of time after such notice has been given for a parent to inform the institution or agency that any or all of the information designated should not be released without the parent's prior consent.

(6) For the purposes of this section, the term "student" includes any person with respect to whom an eductional agency or institution maintains education records or personally identifiable information, but does not include a person who has not been in attendance at such agency or institution.

Release of educational records; parental consent requirement; exceptions; compliance with judicial orders and subpoenas; audit and evaluation of Federally-supported education programs; record-keeping

(b)(1) No funds shall be made available under any applicable program to any educational agency or institution which has a policy or practice of permitting the release of education records (or personally identifiable information contained therein other than directory information, as defined in paragraph (5) of subsection (a) of this section) of students without the written consent of their parents to any individual, agency, or organization, other than to the following—

(A) other school officials, including teachers within the educational institution or local educational agency, who have been determined by such agency or institution to have legitimate educational interests;

(B) officials of other schools or school systems in which the student seeks or intends to enroll, upon condition that the student's parents be notified of the transfer, receive a copy of the record if desired, and have an opportunity for a hearing to challenge the content of the record;

(C) authorized representatives of (i) the Comptroller General of the United States, (ii) the Secretary, (iii), an administrative head of an education agency (as defined in section 1221e-3(c) of this title) or (iv) State educational authorities, under the conditions set forth in paragraph (3) of this subsection:

(D) in connection with a student's application for, or receipt of, financial aid;

(E) State and local officials or authorities to whom such information is specifically required to be reported or disclosed pursuant to State statute adopted prior to November 19, 1974;

(F) organizations conducting studies for, or on behalf of, educational agencies or institutions for the purpose of developing, validating, or administering predictive tests, administering student aid programs, and improving instruction, if such studies are conducted in such a manner as will not permit the personal identification of students and their parents by persons other than representatives of such organizations and such information will be destroyed when no longer needed for the purpose for which it is conducted;

(G) accrediting organizations in order to carry out their accrediting functions;

(H) parents of a dependent student of such parents, as defined in section 152 of Title 26; and

(I) subject to regualtions of the Secretary, in connection with an emergency, appropriate persons if the knowledge of such information is necessary to protect the health or safety of the student or other persons.

Nothing in clause (E) of this paragraph shall prevent a State from further limiting the number or type of State or local officials who will continue to have access thereunder.

(2) No funds shall be made available under any applicable program to any educational agency or institution which has a policy or practice of releasing, or providing access to, any personally identifiable information in education records other than directory information, or as is permitted under paragraph (1) of this subsection unless—

(A) there is written consent from the student's parents specifying records to be released, the reasons for such release, and to whom, and with a copy of the records to be released to the student's parents and the student if desired by the parents, or

(B) such information is furnished in compliance with judicial order, or pursuant to any lawfully issued subpoena, upon condition that parents and the students are notified of all such orders or subpoenas in advance of the compliance therewith by the educational institution or agency.

(3) Nothing contained in this section shall preclude authorized representatives of (A) the Comptroller General of the United States, (B) the Secretary, (C) an administrative head of an education agency or (D) State educational authorities from having access to student or other records which may be necessary in connection with the audit and evaluation of Federally-supported education program, or in connection with the enforcement of the Federal legal requirements which relate to such programs: *Provided,* That except when collection of personally identifiable information is specifically authorized by Federal law, any data collected by such officials shall be protected in a manner which will not permit the personal identification of students and their parents by other than those officials, and such personally identifiable data shall be destroyed

when no longer needed for such audit, evaluation, and enforcement of Federal legal requirements.

(4)(A) Each educational agency or institution shall maintain a record, kept with the education records of each student, which will indicate all individuals (other than those specified in paragraph (1)(A) of this subsection), agencies, or organizations which have requested or obtained access to a student's education records maintained by such educational agency or institution, and which will indicate specifically the legitimate interest that each such person, agency, or organization has in obtaining this information. Such record of access shall be available only to parents, to the school official and his assistants who are responsible for the custody of such records, and to persons or organizations authorized in, and under the conditions of, clauses (A) and (C) of paragraph (1) as a means of auditing the operation of the system.

(B) With respect to this subsection, personal information shall only be transferred to a third party on the condition that such party will not permit any other party to have access to such information without the written consent of the parents of the student.

Surveys or data-gathering activities; regulations

(c) The Secretary shall adopt appropriate regulations to protect the rights of privacy of students and their families in connection with any surveys or data-gathering activities conducted, assisted, or authorized by the Secretary or an administrative head of an education agency. Regulations established under this subsection shall include provisions controlling the use, dissemination, and protection of such data. No survey or data-gathering activities shall be conducted by the Secretary, or an administrative head of an education agency under an applicable program, unless such activities are authorized by law.

Students' rather than parents' permission or consent

(d) For the purposes of this section, whenever a student has attained eighteen years of age, or is attending an institution of postsecondary education the permission or consent required of and the rights accorded to the parents of the student shall thereafter only be required of and accorded to the student.

Informing parents or students of rights under this section

(e) No funds shall be made available under any applicable program to any educational agency or institution unless such agency or institution informs the parents of students, or the students, if they are eighteen years of age or older, or are attending an institution of postsecondary education, of the rights accorded them by this section.

Enforcement; termination of assistance

(f) The Secretary, or an administrative head of an education agency, shall take appropriate actions to enforce provisions of this section and to deal with violations of this section, according to the provisions of this chapter, except that action to terminate assistance may be taken only if the Secretary finds there has been a failure to comply with the provisions of this section, and he has determined that compliance cannot be secured by voluntary means.

Office and review board; creation; functions

(g) The Secretary shall establish or designate an office and review board within the Department of Health, Education, and Welfare for the purpose of investigating, processing, reviewing, and adjudicating violations of the provisions of this section and complaints which may be filed concerning alleged violations of this section. Except for the conduct of hearings, none of the functions of the Secretary under this section shall be carried out in any of the regional offices of such Department.

NOTES

1. The Family Educational Rights and Privacy Act (FERPA) resulted from a last minute amendment to the Education of the Handicapped Amendments of 1974, P.L. 93-380. Popularly called the Buckley Amendment after the former New York Senator who introduced it, it has been heralded by parents, students, and civil libertarians as an invaluable safeguard against encroachment of privacy by the state bureaucracies, and has been denounced as a disaster by some education administrators. By and large, however, relatively few parents have actually gone to the schools and looked at their children's files.

2. On June 17, 1976, the U.S. Department of Health, Education, and Welfare published detailed regulations implementing FERPA, 41 Fed.Reg. 24662 (1976), 45 C.F.R. § 99 *et seq.*

3. Litigation under FERPA has been sparse. In *Girardier* v. *Webster College,* 563 F.2d 1267 (8th Cir. 1977), college students brought suit to enjoin a college from refusing to release transcripts of credits to students who had not repaid their student loans. The court held that FERPA did not give rise to a private cause of action. In two other cases, *Rios* v. *Read,* 73 F.R.D. 589 (E.D.N.Y. 1977), and *Mattie T.* v. *Johnston,* 74 F.R.D. 498 (N.D.Miss. 1976), FERPA was used as a defense by educators who did not wish to release school records sought in discovery by plaintiffs. In each of these cases the education officials were ordered by the court to produce the requested records.

4. In reference to the confidentiality aspects of FERPA, one commentator has noted that "the law has given some educators a much sought-after basis for refusing to turn over files to probation officers, police, the armed services and the FBI," Cudlipp, K., "The Family Educational Rights and Privacy Act Two Years Later," 11 *U. Rich. L. Rev.* 33, 39 (1976).

REGULATIONS IMPLEMENTING § 615 OF P.L. 94-142

20 U.S.C. § 1415, 42 Fed. Reg. 42498-42499
(Aug. 23, 1977), 45 C.F.R. 121a.560 et seq.

Confidentiality of Information

§·121a.560   Definitions.

As used in this subpart:

"Destruction" means physical destruction or removal of personal identifiers from information so that the information is no longer personally identifiable.

"Education records" means the type of records covered under the definition of "education records" in Part 99 of this title (the regulations implementing the Family Educational Rights and Privacy Act of 1974).

"Participating agency" means any agency or institution which collects, maintains, or uses personally identifiable information, or from which information is obtained, under this part.
(20 U.S.C. 1412(2) (D); 1417(c).)

§ 121a.561   Notice to parents.

(a) The State educational agency shall give notice which is adequate to fully inform parents about the requirements under § 121a.128 of Subpart B, including:

(1) A description of the extent to which the notice is given in the native languages of the various populations groups in the State:

(2) A description of the children on whom personally identifiable information is maintained, the types of information sought, the methods the State intends to use in gathering the information (including the sources from whom information is gathered), and the uses to be made of the information;

(3) A summary of the policies and procedures which participating agencies must follow regarding storage, disclosure to third parties, retention, and destruction of personally identifiable. information; and

(4) A description of all of the rights of parents and children regarding this information, including the rights under section 438 of the General Education Provisions Act and Part 99 of this title (the Family Educational Rights and Privacy Act of 1974, and implementing regulations).

(b) Before any major identification, location, or evaluation activity, the notice must be published or announced in newspapers or other media, or both, with circulation adequate to notify parents throughout the State of the activity.
(20 U.S.C. 1412(2) (D); 1417(c).)

§ 121a.562   Access rights.

(a) Each participating agency shall permit parents to inspect and review any education records relating to their children which are collected, maintained, or used by the agency under this part. The agency shall comply with a request without unnecessary delay and before any meeting regarding an individualized education program or hearing relating to the identification, evaluation, or placement of the child, and in no case more than 45 days after the request has been made.

(b) The right to inspect and review education records under this section includes:

(1) The right to a response from the participating agency to reasonable requests for explanations and interpretations of the records;

(2) The right to request that the agency provide copies of the records containing the information if failure to provide those copies would effectively prevent the parent from exercising the right to inspect and review the records; and

(3) The right to have a representative of the parent inspect and review the records.

(c) An agency may presume that the parent has authority to inspect and review records relating to his or her child unless the agency has been advised that the parent does not have the authority under applicable State law governing such matters as guardianship, separation, and divorce.
(20 U.S.C. 1412(2) (D); 1417(c).)

§ 121a.563   Record of access.

Each participating agency shall keep a record of parties obtaining access to education records collected, maintained, or used under this part (except access by parents and authorized employees of the participating agency), including the name of the party, the date access was given, and the purpose for which the party is authorized to use the records.
(20 U.S.C. 1412(2) (D); 1417(c).)

§ 121a.564   Records on more than one child.

If any education record includes information on more than one child, the parents of those children shall have the right to inspect and review only the information relating to their child or to be informed of that specific information.
(20 U.S.C. 1412(2) (D); 1417(c).)

§ 121a.565   List of types and locations of information.

Each participating agency shall provide parents on request a list of the types and locations of education records collected, maintained, or used by the agency.
(20 U.S.C. 1412(2) (D); 1417(c).)

§ 121a.566   Fees.

(a) A participating education agency may charge a fee for copies of records which are made for parents under this part if the fee does not effectively prevent the parents from exercising their right to inspect and review those records.

(b) A participating agency may not charge a fee to search for or to retrieve information under this part.
(20 U.S.C. 1412(2) (D); 1417(c).)

§ 121a.567   Amendment of records at parent's request.

(a) A parent who believes that information in education records collected, maintained, or used under this part is inaccurate or misleading or violates the privacy or other rights of the child, may request the participating agency which maintains the information to amend the information.

(b) The agency shall decide whether to amend the information in accordance with the request within a reasonable period of time of receipt of the request.

(c) If the agency decides to refuse to amend the information in accordance with the request it shall inform the parent of the refusal, and advise the parent of the right to a hearing under § 121a.568.

(20 U.S.C. 1412(2) (D); 1417(c).)

§ 121a.568   Opportunity for a hearing.

The agency shall, on request, provide an opportunity for a hearing to challenge information in education records to insure that it is not inaccurate, misleading, or otherwise in violation of the privacy or other rights of the child.

(20 U.S.C. 1412(2) (D); 1417(c).)

§ 121a.569   Result of hearing.

(a) If, as a result of the hearing, the agency decides that the information is inaccurate, misleading or otherwise in violation of the privacy or other rights of the child, it shall amend the information accordingly and so inform the parent in writing.

(b) If, as a result of the hearing, the agency decides that the information is not inaccurate, misleading, or otherwise in violation of the privacy or other rights of the child, it shall inform the parent of the right to place in the records it maintains on the child a statement commenting on the information or setting forth any reasons for disagreeing with the decision of the agency.

(c) Any explanation placed in the records of the child under this section must:

(1) Be maintained by the agency as part of the records of the child as long as the record or contested portion is maintained by the agency; and

(2) If the records of the child or the contested portion is disclosed by the agency to any party, the explanation must also be disclosed to the party.

(20 U.S.C. 1412(2) (D); 1417(c).)

§ 121a.570   Hearing procedures.

A hearing held under § 121a.568 of this subpart must be conducted according to the procedures under § 99.22 of this title.

(20 U.S.C. 1412(2) (D); 1417(c).)

§ 121a.571   Consent.

(a) Parental consent must be obtained before personally identifiable information is:

(1) Disclosed to anyone other than officials of participating agencies collecting or using the information under this part, subject to paragraph (b) of this section; or

(2) Used for any purpose other than meeting a requirement under this part.

(b) An educational agency or institution subject to Part 99 of this title may not release information from education records to participating agencies without parental consent unless authorized to do so under Part 99 of this title.

(c) The State educational agency shall include policies and procedures in its annual program plan which are used in the event that a parent refuses to provide consent under this section.

(20 U.S.C. 1412(2) (D); 1417(c).)

§ 121a.572   Safeguards.

(a) Each participating agency shall protect the confidentiality of personally identifiable information at collection, storage, disclosure, and destruction stages.

(b) One official at each participating agency shall assume responsibility for insuring the confidentiality of any personally identifiable information.

(c) All persons collecting or using personally identifiable information must receive training or instruction regarding the State's policies and procedures under § 121a.129 of Subpart B and Part 99 of this title.

(d) Each participating agency shall maintain, for public inspection, a current listing of the names and positions of those employees within the agency who may have access to personally identifiable information.

(20 U.S.C. 1412(2) (D); 1417(c).)

§ 121a.573   Destruction of information.

(a) The public agency shall inform parents when personally identifiable information collected, maintained, or used under this part is no longer needed to provide educational services to the child.

(b) The information must be destroyed at the request of the parents. However, a permanent record of a student's name, address, and phone number, his or her grades, attendance record, classes attended, grade level completed, and year completed may be maintained without time limitation.

(20 U.S.C. 1412(2) (D); 1417(c).)

Comment. Under section 121a.573, the personally identifiable information on a handicapped child may be retained permanently unless the parents request that it be destroyed. Destruction of records is the best protection against improper and unauthorized disclosure. However, the records may be needed for other purposes. In informing parents about their rights under this section the agency should remind them that the records may be needed by the child or the parents for social security benefits or other purposes. If the parents request that the information be destroyed, the agency may retain the information in paragraph (b).

§ 121a.574   Children's rights.

The State educational agency shall include policies and procedures in its annual program plan regarding the extent to which children are afforded rights of privacy similar to those afforded to parents, taking into consideration the age of the child and type or severity of disability.

(20 U.S.C. 1412(2) (D); 1417(c).)

Comment. Note that under the regulations for the Family Educational Rights and Privacy Act (45 CFR 99.4(a)), the rights of parents regarding education records are transferred to the student at age 18.

§ 121a.575   Enforcement.

The State educational agency shall describe in its annual program plan the policies and procedures, including sanctions, which the State uses to insure that its policies and procedures are followed and that the requirements of the Act and the regulations in this part are met.

(20 U.S.C. 1412(2) (D); 1417(c).)

§ 121a.576   Office of Education.

If the Office of Education or its authorized representatives collect any personally identifiable information regarding handicapped children which is not subject to 5
U.S.C. 552a (The Privacy Act of 1974), the Commissioner shall apply the requirements of 5 U.S.C. section 552a(b) (1)–(2), (4)–(11); (c); (d); (e) (1), (2), (3), (A), (B),
and (D), (5)–(10); (h); (m); and (n), and the regulations implementing those provisions
in Part 5b of this title.
(20 U.S.C. 1412(2) (D); 1417(c).)

NOTES

1.   Section 615 of P.L. 94–142, implemented by these regulations, mandates that
parents and guardians of handicapped children have an "opportunity to examine all
relevant records with respect to the identification, evaluation, and educational placement of the child . . .," 20 U.S.C. § 1415.

2.   Prior to P.L. 94–142 and FERPA, questions of access to educational records had
to be resolved under common law or state statutes. *Van Allen* v. *McCleary,* 27
Misc.2d 81, 211 N.Y.S.2d 501 (1961), raised the question of a common law right to
examine records; the court concluded that "absent constitutional, legislative or administrative permission or prohibition, a parent is entitled to inspect the records of his child
maintained by the school authorities as required by law." In *Citizens for Better Ed.* v.
Board of Ed. of Camden, 124 N.J.Super. 523, 308 A.2d 35 (1973), a concerned
citizens group was found to be entitled to obtain the results of standardized achievement tests on a school-by-school and grade-by-grade basis pursuant to a New Jersey
Right-to-Know Law. Like New Jersey, many other states have statutes dealing specifically with access to educational records, e.g., 2 C Laws of Mass., Chapter 71B, § 3;
Mich. Comp. L. Ann. § 600.2165; Cal. Educ. Code § 10931 *et seq.*, Cal. Sen. Bill
No. 182, Chap. 816, § 4 (Sept. 17, 1975).

ADDITIONAL READING

Note, "Buckley Amendment: Opening School Files for Student and Parental Review,"
      24 *Catholic U.L. Rev.* 588 (1975).
Carey, S., "Students, Parents, and the School Record Prison: A Legal Strategy for
      Preventing Abuse," 3 *J.L. & Educ.* 365 (1974).
Note, "Protecting the Privacy of School Children and their Families through the
      Family Educational Rights and Privacy Act of 1974," 14 *J. Family L.* 255
      (1975).
Cudlipp, K., "The Family Educational Rights and Privacy Act Two Years Later," 11
      U. Rich. L. Rev. 33 (1976).

I. OTHER PROBLEMS

1. Transportation

The issue of providing transportation for handicapped pupils to and from school has
been the subject of some litigative activity, e.g., *Berry* v. *School Board of Barrington,*

78 N.H. 30, 95 A. 952 (1915) (school district's refusal to provide transportation to physically handicapped plaintiff held not an abuse of discretion); *Christman* v. *Board of Education,* 347 Ill.App. 324, 106 N.E.2d 846 (1952) (deaf child sent to neighboring school for educational program held entitled to reimbursement for transportation costs, but only to limit set in state statute); *Thomason* v. *County of Suffolk,* 66 Misc.2d 926, 322 N.Y.S.2d 762 (1971) (transportation of some children to school, but not emotionally disturbed children, is violation of equal protection).

The holding in *Berry* that handicapped children are not entitled to transportation to educational programs, the ruling in *Christman* that transportation is required to the extent authorized by statute and agreed to by school officials, and the *Thomason* holding that transportation for handicapped pupils is mandated by equal protection outline the spectrum of judicial responses to the question of the rights of handicapped individuals to public school transportation. Until the recent emergence of the equal protection theory, most of the previous cases were of the *Christman* mold, centering around the issue of the extent of statutory responsibility; see, e.g., *Schutte* v. *Decker,* 164 Neb. 582, 83 N.W.2d 69 (1957); *Los Angeles City School Dist.* v. *Simpson,* 112 C.A.2d 970, 245 P.2d 629 (1952); *Knauff* v. *Board of Ed. of Union Free Sch. Dist. No. 1,* 57 Misc.2d 456, 293 N.Y.S.2d 133 (1968).

The question of transportation costs figured in a number of decisions previously found in these materials. See *Cuyahoga County Ass'n for Retard. Ch. & Adults* v. *Essex,* 411 F.Supp. 46 (N.D.Ohio 1976) (pp. 130–143, above); *Levy* v. *City of New York,* 382 N.Y.S.2d 13 (Ct. of App. 1976) (pp. 170–173, above); *Md. Ass'n for Retard. Ch.* v. *State of Md.,* Equity No. 100/182/77676 (Cir. Ct., Baltimore County, May 31, 1974) (pp. 182–187, above); *In re Leitner,* 40 A.D.2d 38, 337 N.Y.S.2d 267 (1972) (p.188, above).

The issue has basically now been settled by federal statute and regulation. Under P. L. 94-142 parents and their handicapped children are entitled to special education and related services at no cost.

> (17) The term "related services" means transportation, and such developmental, corrective, and other supportive services (including speech pathology and audiology, psychological services, physical and occupational therapy, recreation, and medical and counseling services, except that such medical services shall be for diagnostic and evaluation purposes only) as may be required to assist a handicapped child to benefit from special education, and includes the early identification and assessment of handicapping conditions in children (20 U.S.C. 1401(17)).

The implementing regulations further define the meaning of transportation:

> (13) "Transportation" includes:
> (i) Travel to and from school and between schools.
> (ii) Travel in and around school buildings and
> (iii) Specialized equipment (such as special or adapted buses, lifts, and ramps), if required to provide special transportation for a handicapped child (45 C.F.R. § 121a13(b) (13)).

Finally, the implementing regulations to § 504 of the 1973 Rehabilitation Act state:

§ 84.33   Free appropriate public education.

(a) *General*. A recipient that operates a public elementary or secondary education program shall provide a free appropriate public education to each qualified handicapped person who is in the recipient's jurisdiction, regardless of the nature or severity of the person's handicap.

* * *

(2) *Transportation*. If a recipient places a handicapped person in or refers such person to a program not operated by the recipient as its means of carrying out the requirements of this subpart, the recipient shall ensure that adequate transportation to and from the program is provided at no greater cost than would be incurred by the person or his or her parents or guardian if the person were placed in the program operated by the recipient (45 C.F.R. § 84.33).

2. Misclassification

One of the earliest and one of the most controversial issues in special education was the misclassification of minority children as handicapped. It was charged that black and Mexican-American children, among others, had been labeled mentally retarded when proper assessment would have shown that these children were not mentally retarded at all, but misdiagnosed because those responsible for evaluating them had inappropriately relied on tests that were grounded in the white, middle class culture.

BERSOFF, D., AND OAKLAND, T., "THE ROLE OF LAW IN DEFINING PSYCHOLOGICAL ASSESSMENT PRACTICES"

Unpublished manuscript, 1979

Testing is a pervasive activity in schools. More than 250 million standardized tests of academic aptitude and ability plus additional tests of perceptual and motor abilities, emotional and social characteristics, and vocational interests and aptitudes are used yearly in our public schools (Brim, Glass, Neulinger, Firestone, and Lerner, 1969). No pupil in our country remains untouched by a school's assessment program. The characteristics of an assessment program must reflect local needs and resources and also must reflect standards established at the state and national levels. . . .

Legal Considerations

Litigation

* * *

The first significant legal challenge to the practice of using tests to label and place school children was *Hobson* v. *Hansen* (1967) in which the tracking system in the Washington, D.C. public schools was attacked. The decision ordered the abolition of tracking but did not invalidate ability grouping as such. Rather, what caused the constitutional inquiry in *Hobson* was the fact that there was a significantly disproportionate number of black children in the lower tracks and significantly fewer in the upper of college bound tracks. The court said that only if such disparity in treatment could be justified would it be maintained. Otherwise, the risks in classification become "wholly irrational and . . . unconstitutionally discriminatory" (fn. 211). And the court found that the means for placing these children were, indeed, discriminatory and thus constitutionally infirm:

The evidence shows that the method by which track assignments were made depends essentially on standardized aptitude tests which, although given on a system-wide basis, are completely inappropriate for use with a large segment of the student body. Because these tests are standardized primarily on and are relevant to a white middle class group of students, they produce inaccurate and misleading test scores when given to lower class and Negro students (p. 514).[3]

In *Hobson* the attack was on group ability tests. But, it did not take long before individually administered intelligence tests were also challenged. In 1970, a suit was brought on behalf of nine Mexican-American children who were placed in classes for educably mentally retarded students primarily on the basis of scores derived from the Stanford-Binet or WISC. All the students were from homes having Spanish as the primary language. One of the plaintiffs in the case, Diana, (*Diana* v. *State Bd. of Educ.*, C.A.N. C-70 37 RFP (N.D.Cal. Feb. 3, 1970) had been judged to have an IQ of 30 when given a test by an English speaking examiner. When re-examined in Spanish and English by a bilingual psychologist, she scored 49 points higher, several points above the cut-off score in California for placement in an EMR class. When eight other Mexican-American children randomly selected from EMR classes were retested in the same way all but one scored above the retarded level. An out-of-court agreement was reached which resulted in major changes in the California school code with regard to assessment and placement of children in EMR programs.

However, it was not long before California, EMR placement, and IQ testing were back in the courts in a case known as *P.* v. *Riles* (1972). This time the plaintiffs were black children in the San Francisco elementary schools who were placed in EMR classes after scoring below 75 on one of several tests authorized by the State Department of Education. The plaintiffs produced evidence that racial imbalance existed in these classes. For example, black children constituted about 29% of all students in the San Francisco school system but 66% of the students in the EMR program. In California as a whole, while black children comprised 9% of the school population, they comprised about 28% of all children in EMR classes. Having presented these data, the plaintiffs argued that the burden had been shifted to the school system to explain this racial disparity. If the San Francisco school system could not successfully explain this disparity on some reasonable basis, then it should be enjoined (order to refrain) from using the IQ tests to place black children in EMR classes.

This strategy concerning shifting the burden of proof to the defendants was borrowed from *Griggs* v. *Duke Power Co.* (1971), a case decided by the Supreme Court the previous year. There, in an action brought under Title VII of the 1964 Civil Rights Act (which prohibits discrimination in employment because of race, color, religion, sex, or national origin), black employees challenged the use of intelligence tests as a condition of employment or transfer to certain positions for which they were otherwise qualified. The employers claimed that, while the test criterion may have had a discriminatory effect in that fewer blacks were hired or promoted, there was no intent

---

[3]Another finding in *Hobson* was that of 1272 students examined by school psychologists and then assigned to special education or the lowest track, two-thirds of them had been improperly classified (Kirp, 1973).

to discriminate. The courts, however, interpreted Title VII as proscribing "not only overt discrimination but also practices that are fair in form, but discriminatory in operation" (p. 431). Thus, the court would look at the *consequences* of the practice in question, not simply to the motivation. Once the discriminatory effect was shown, the burden was then on the employer to show "that any given requirement . . . have a manifest relationship to the employment in question" (p. 432).[4]

This reasoning from *Griggs* was persuasive in *P.* v. *Riles.* The school system offered the explanation that black children were more frequently found in EMR, not because of inherited differences in intelligence, but rather because of the poor nutrition of their mothers, and that the school system had followed California's education code in using a number of measures besides IQ scores to place children. Nevertheless, the court agreed to enjoin the administration of IQ tests for purposes of placing black children in classes for the educably retarded. The court found that substantial emphasis was placed on the IQ test score resulting in such disproportionality as to constitute a denial of equal protection.

In the two years following the Court's issuance of the injunction in *Riles,* there were more court maneuvers. However, in early 1975 the State of California issued a memorandum and accompanying resolution stating that until further notice none of the IQ tests then on its approved list (containing among others, the WISC and Stanford-Binet) could be used in placing any child, *of any race,* in EMR classes.

Issues regarding educational opportunities and the use of tests with minority group children reappeared in a second major court case involving the San Francisco school district, *Lau* v. *Nichols* (1974). Plaintiffs, Chinese students, charged that the school district failed to provide bilingual language instruction to all children in need of these programs. Ruling in favor of the plaintiffs the Supreme Court recommended that a task force be created to set forth procedures which insured the proper use of educational programs and assessment techniques with bilingual or non-English-speaking students. Their report, issued by the Office for Civil Rights (OCR) in the summer of 1975, recommended that information from home interviews, observations of children in school, and/or a test of language dominance be used to determine whether a child is a (1) non-English-speaking monolingual, (2) predominantly non-English-speaking and somewhat fluent in English, (3) bilingual, (4) predominantly English-speaking but somewhat fluent in another language, (5) or English-speaking monolingual. Further, information acquired from other diagnostic and prescriptive measures which identify

---

[4]Recently, in *Washington* v. *Davis* (1976), The Supreme court indicated that the test of discriminatory effect was not of constitutional stature. Unsuccessful black applicants for positions as police officers in Washington, D.C. claimed that certain tests were racially discriminatory because it excluded a disproportionately high number of black applicants. The Court said that the standard applicable to equal employment opportunity cases under Title VII (i.e., the standard that plaintiffs need show only discriminatory effect to shift the burden to defendants) was not applicable to cases brought under the due process clause of the Constitution. It held that a law is not unconstitutional solely because it has a racially disproportionate impact regardless of whether it reflects a racially discriminatory purpose. Thus, a test neutral on its face having a discriminatory effect did not warrant the conclusion that without a showing of intent to discriminate, the test violates the Constitution. This case indicates why new federal laws regarding the handicapped are so important. Handicapped plaintiffs and those misclassified as such need not depend on a Constitutional remedy but can rely on statutes passed by Congress.

the nature of each student's educational needs should be utilized to implement an educational program which meets the diagnosed needs of each child. The assessment and instructional personnel are required to be linguistically and culturally familiar with the students' backgrounds and the programs must be free of discrimination in terms of course content and enrollment and cannot be racially or ethnically identifiable. Due process provisions addressed by the Buckley amendment and P.L. 93-380 generally are adhered to. The provisions are described in the following section of this chapter.

Because of the dangers of misclassification, the potential for racial disproportionality, and concern that all children do not become needlessly categorized and labeled, courts also began insisting that rather extensive procedures be developed to accord with due process. Most notably in *Pennsylvania Ass'n. for Retarded Children* v. *Commonwealth* (1972) and in *Mills* v. *D.C. Bd. of Educ.* (1972), the court required that parents had right, among others, to a hearing, including representation, the right to call witnesses, and present evidence before the school could lawfully place children in education programs.

But, the controversy concerning the use of tests (summarized in the legal literature most comprehensively by Kirp (1973) and Sorgen (1973) and in the psychological literature by Bersoff (1973), Cronbach (1975), and Oakland and Laosa (1976) is rarely considered in the courts of this time. Courts are now entertaining what might be called "second generation" issues, most notably the right to an appropriate effective education especially with regard to those children denominated as "learning disabled."

NOTES

1. The order granting plaintiffs a preliminary injunction in *P.* v. *Riles,* 343 F.Supp. 1306 (N.D.Cal. 1972), was affirmed on appeal, 502 F.2d 963 (9th Cir. 1974).

2. *Hobsen* v. *Hansen,* 269 F.Supp. 401 (D.D.C. 1967) is also discussed in *Mills* v. *Board of Education of District of Columbia,* pp. 92-108, above.

3. As with many other matters, federal legislation now controls the evaluation of children suspected to be, or already denominated, as handicapped.

a.   P.L. 94-142, 20 U.S.C. § 1412

> Sec. 812.   In order to qualify for assistance under this part in any fiscal year, a State shall demonstrate to the Commissioner that the following conditions are met:
>
> * * *
>
> (5) The State has established . . .
> (C) procedures to assure that testing and evaluation materials and procedures utilized for the purposes of evaluation and placement of handicapped children will be selected and administered so as not to be racially or culturally discriminatory. Such materials or procedures shall be provided and administered in the child's native language or mode of communication, unless it clearly is not feasible to do so, and no single procedure shall be the sole criterion for determining an appropriate educational program for a child.

b.   Regulations Implementing P. L.94-142, 42 Fed. Reg. 42496-42497 (Aug. 23, 1977), 45 C.F.R. § 121a.530 *et seq.*

Protection in Evaluation Procedures

§ 121a.530   General.

(a) Each State educational agency shall insure that each public agency establishes and implements procedures which meet the requirements of §§ 121a. 530–121a.534.

(b) Testing and evaluation materials and procedures used for the purposes of evaluation and placement of handicapped children must be selected and administered so as not to be racially or culturally discriminatory.

§ 121a.531   Preplacement evaluation.

Before any action is taken with respect to the initial placement of a handicapped child in a special education program, a full and individual evaluation of the child's educational needs must be conducted in accordance with the requirements of § 121a.532.

§ 121a532   Evaluation procedures.

State and local educational agencies shall insure, at a minimum, that:

(a) Tests and other evaluation materials:

(1) Are provided and administered in the child's native language or other mode of communication, unless it is clearly not feasible to do so;

(2) Have been validated for the specific purpose for which they are used; and

(3) Are administered by trained personnel in conformance with the instructions provided by their producer;

(b) Tests and other evaluation materials include those tailored to assess specific areas of educational need and not merely those which are designed to provide a single general intelligence quotient;

(c) Tests are selected and administered so as best to ensure that when a test is administered to a child with impaired sensory, manual, or speaking skills, the test results accurately reflect the child's aptitude or achievement level or whatever other factors the test purports to measure, rather than reflecting the child's impaired sensory, manual, or speaking skills (except where those skills are the factors which the test purports to measure);

(d) No single procedure is used as the sole criterion for determining an appropriate educational program for a child; and

(e) The evaluation is made by a multidisciplinary team or group of persons, including at least one teacher or other specialist with knowledge in the area of suspected disability.

(f) The child is assessed in all areas related to the suspected disability, including, where appropriate, health, vision, hearing, social and emotional status, general intelligence, academic performance, communicative status, and motor abilities.

Comment. Children who have a speech impairment as their primary handicap may not need a complete battery of assessments (e.g., psychological, physical, or adaptive behavior). However, a qualified speech-language pathologist would (1) evaluate each speech impaired child using procedures that are appropriate for the diagnosis and appraisal of speech and language disorders. and (2) where necessary, make referrals for additional assessments needed to make an appropriate placement decision.

§ 121a.533   Placement procedures.

(a) In interpreting evaluation data and in making placement decisions, each public agency shall:

(1) Draw upon information from a variety of sources, including aptitude and achievement tests, teacher recommendations, physical condition, social or cultural background, and adaptive behavior;

(2) Insure that information obtained from all of these sources is documented and carefully considered;

(3) Insure that the placement decision is made by a group of persons, including persons knowledgeable about the child, the meaning of the evaluation data, and the placement options; and

(4) Insure that the placement decision is made in conformity with the least restrictive environment rules in §§ 121a.550–121a.554.

(b) If a determination is made that a child is handicapped and needs special education and related services, an individualized education program must be developed for the child in accordance with §§ 121a.340–121a.349 of Subpart C.

* * *

§ 121a.534   Reevaluation

Each State and local educational agency shall insure:

(a) That each handicapped child's individualized education program is reviewed in accordance with §§ 121a.340–121a.349 of Subpart C, and

(b) That an evaluation of the child, based on procedures which meet the requirements under § 121a.532, is conducted every three years or more frequently if conditions warrant or if the child's parent or teacher requests an evaluation.

Additional Procedures for Evaluating Specific Learning Disabilities

§ 121a.540   Additional team members.

In evaluating a child suspected of having a specific learning disability, in addition to the requirements of § 121a.532, each public agency shall include on the multidisciplinary evaluation team:

(a)(1) The child's regular teacher; or

(2) If the child does not have a regular teacher, a regular classroom teacher qualified to teach a child of his or her age; or

(3) For a child of less than school age, an individual qualified by the State educational agency to teach a child of his or her age; and

(b) At least one person qualified to conduct individual diagnostic examinations of children, such as a school psychologist, speech-language pathologist, or remedial reading teacher.

§ 121a.541   Criteria for determining the existence of a specific learning disability.

(a) A team may determine that a child has a specific learning disability if:

(1) The child does not achieve commensurate with his or her age and ability levels in one or more of the areas listed in paragraph (a)(2) of this section, when provided with learning experiences appropriate for the child's age and ability levels; and

(2) The team finds that a child has a severe discrepancy between achievement and intellectual ability in one or more of the following areas:

(i) Oral expression;

(ii) Listening comprehension;

(iii) Written expression;

(iv) Basic reading skill;

(v) Reading comprehension;

(vi) Mathematics calculation; or

(vii) Mathematics reasoning.

(b) The team may not identify a child as having a specific learning disability if the severe discrepancy between ability and achievement is primarily the result of:

(1) A visual, hearing, or motor handicap;

(2) Mental retardation;

(3) Emotional disturbance; or

(4) Environmental, cultural or economic disadvantage.

§ 121a.542   Observation.

(a) At least one team member other than the child's regular teacher shall observe the child's academic performance in the regular classroom setting.

(b) In the case of a child of less than school age or out of school, a team member shall observe the child in an environment appropriate for a child of that age.
(20 U.S.C. 1411 note.)

§ 121a.543   Written report.

(a) The team shall prepare a written report of the results of the evaluation.

(b) The report must include a statement of:

(1) Whether the child has a specific learning disability;

(2) The basis for making the determination;

(3) The relevant behavior noted during the observation of the child;

(4) The relationship of that behavior to the child's academic functioning;

(5) The educationally relevant medical findings, if any;

(6) Whether there is a severe discrepancy between achievement and ability which is not correctable without special education and related services; and

(7) The determination of the team concerning the effects of environmental, cultural, or economic disadvantage,

(c) Each team member shall certify in writing whether the report reflects his or her conclusion. If it does not reflect his or her conclusion, the team member must submit a separate statement presenting his or her conclusions.
(20 U.S.C. 1411 note.)

c.   Regulations Implementing § 504 of the Rehabilitation Act of 1973, 42 Fed.Reg. 22682–22683 (May 4, 1977) 45 C.F.R. § 84.35

§ 84.35   Evaluation and placement.

(a) *Preplacement evaluation.* A recipient that operates a public elementary or secondary education program shall conduct an evaluation in accordance with the requirements of paragraph (b) of this section of any person who, because of handicap, needs or is believed to need special education or related services before taking any action with respect to the initial placement of the person in a regular or special education program and any subsequent significant change in placement.

(b) *Evaluation procedures.* A recipient to which this subpart applies shall establish standards and procedures for the evaluation and placement of persons who, because of handicap, need or are believed to need special education or related services which ensure that:

(1) Tests and other evaluation materials have been validated for the specific purpose for which they are used and are administered by trained personnel in conformance with the instructions provided by their producer;

(2) Tests and other evaluation materials include those tailored to assess specific areas of educational need and not merely those which are designed to provide a single general intelligence quotient; and

(3) Tests are selected and administered so as best to ensure that, when a test is administered to a student with impaired sensory, manual, or speaking skills, the test results accurately reflect the student's aptitude or achievement level or whatever other factor the test purports to measure, rather than reflecting the student's impaired sensory, manual, or speaking skills (except where those skills are the factors that the test purports to measure).

(c) *Placement procedures.* In interpreting evaluation data and in making placement decisions, a recipient shall (1) draw upon information from a variety of sources, including aptitude and achievement tests, teacher recommendations, physical condition, social or cultural background, and adaptive behavior, (2) establish procedures to ensure that information obtained from all such sources is documented and carefully considered,

(3) ensure that the placement decision is made by a group of persons, including persons knowledgeable about the child, the meaning of the evaluation data, and the placement options, and (4) ensure that the placement decision is made in conformity with § 84.34.

(d) *Reevaluation.* A recipient to which this section applies shall establish procedures, in accordance with paragraph (b) of this section, for periodic reevaluation of students who have been provided special education and related services. A reevaluation procedure consistent with the Education for the Handicapped Act is one means of meeting this requirement.

ADDITIONAL READING

Bersoff, D., "Legal Constraints on Psychological Assessment in the Public Schools," 3 *Perspectives in Law and Psychology* (Sales, B., and Novick, M., eds., 1979).

Kirp, D., "Schools as Sorters: The Constitutional and Policy Implications of Student Classification," 121 *U. Pa. L. Rev.* 705 (1973).

Sorgen, M., "Testing and Tracking in Public Schools," 24 *Hastings L. J.* 1129 (1973).

Comment, "Educational Testing: A Challenge for the Courts," *U. Ill. L. Forum* 375 (1973).

Comment, "Equal Protection and Standardized Testing," 44 *Miss. L. J.* 900 (1973).

Comment, "Constitutional Law—Limiting the Use of Standardized Intelligence Tests for Ability Grouping in Public Schools," 51 *N.C.L. Rev.* 1564 (1973).

Note, "Constitutional Requirements for Standardized Ability Tests Used in Education," 26 *Vand. L. Rev.* 789 (1973).

Cronbach, L., "Five Decades of Public Controversy over Mental Testing," *American Psychologist* 1 (January 1975).

3. Residency Questions

IN RE G. H.
[See pp. 113–120, above.]

NOTES

1. Is the *G.H.* decision a satisfactory resolution of the question of which school district was the child's residence?

2. In *State ex rel. Doe* v. *Kingery,* 203 S.E.2d 358 (W. Va. 1974), the plaintiff was a resident of a state hospital in a different county from that in which she had resided before coming to the facility. The court held that the school district in which the institution was located was required to provide an educational program for the girl: "[A]ll children in this state have the right to attend public school in the district in which they live, even if they are only temporary residents of such district."

3. In *Michigan Association for Retarded Citizens* v. *State Board of Education of the State of Michigan,* No. G-74-385 C.A.5 (W.D. Mich. 1974), the defendant public school officials agreed to issue regulations to the effect that residence, for educational purposes of a child in a residential institution, is in the school district in which the child resided before coming to the institution.

4. Since most local educational programs are funded by property taxes, school districts in which large residential institutions are located are understandably unwilling to

pay for the instruction of all of the students who have come from other school districts to reside at the institution. Thus, a simple rule that a child's residence for school purposes is in the district in which he or she actually lives is not acceptable, because it places a disproportionate burden upon school districts having residential institutions within their boundaries. A better rule would seem to be that a child "resides" where the parents reside. But what if the parents have died, or, as in *In re G.H.,* they have moved to another state? Moreover, if parents living in one school district send their child to live with friends or relatives in another district, should the first district, which was willing to educate the child locally, be required to pay the second school district for the child's instruction?

5.   P.L. 94-142 2 614, 20 U.S.C. § 1414 states, in pertinent part:

> (a) A local educational agency or an intermediate educational unit . . . shall—
> (1) provide satisfactory assurance that payments under this part will be used for excess costs directly attributable to programs which
> provide that all children *residing within the jurisdiction* of the local eductional agency or the intermediate educational unit who are handicapped . . . will be identified, located, and evaluated . . . [emphasis added]

(See also 45 C.F.R. § 121a.220.)

With regard to children in private schools not placed or referred by public agencies, the local educational agency still has the responsibility to "provide special education and related services designed to meet the needs of private school handicapped children residing in the jurisdiction of the agency," 45 C.F.R. § 121a.452(a).

Section 84.33 of the "504 Regulations" states:

> § 84.33   Free appropriate public education
> (a) *General.* A recipient that operates a public elementary or secondary education program shall provide a free appropriate public education to each qualified handicapped person *who is in the recipient's jurisdiction,* regardless of the nature or severity of the person's handicap (42 Fed.Reg. 22682 (May 4, 1977), 45 C.F.R. § 84.33). [emphasis added]

3

EMPLOYMENT

Robert L. Burgdorf, Jr., and Beverly J. Falcon

A. THE NATURE AND SOURCES OF THE PROBLEM

1. Examples of Problem Situations

A BLIND WOMAN, WITH EXCEPTIONAL ACADEMIC CREDENTIALS, completed the requirements for and obtained a state teaching certification. The local public school system, however, refused to consider her for a teaching position, claiming that she would be unable to maintain classroom discipline or to grade the students' written work.

A MAN WITH EPILEPSY APPLIED AND WAS HIRED as a stockboy at a local drugstore, which was part of a large drugstore chain. On the employment application form, the man replied honestly to the question, "Have you ever had any fits or seizures?" and answered that he had a seizure five years before, but that his condition was under control and he had had no seizures since then. He worked at the job for over a month, successfully performing his duties, and earned the manager's praise for his work; in the meantime, his application was processed and ultimately sent to the main office of the drugstore chain. The main office notified the local manager that the employee had to be terminated immediately because the company had a policy against hiring epileptics.

A WOMAN IN A WHEELCHAIR OBTAINED A JOB in a factory, but was forced to quit when she found that there were no restrooms that would accommodate her wheelchair.

A MENTALLY RETARDED MAN confined in a state residential institution does maintenance and gardening work for the institution but receives no pay whatsoever for his labor.

A MAN WITH SIGHT IN ONLY ONE EYE applied for a clerical position, but the employer refused to consider his application because he felt that the man would be unable to read numbers in small print.

MENTALLY RETARDED MEN AND WOMEN ARE EMPLOYED at a "sheltered workshop" but receive only two dollars a week in salary, even though the products they manufacture are sold commercially for a substantial profit.

A DEAF MAN WAS REFUSED A JOB because the employer doubted his ability to safely operate a motor vehicle.

HAROLD KRENTZ, A BLIND ATTORNEY who inspired "Butterflies Are Free," has described his problems in finding employment:

> When "Butterflies" opened somebody at Harvard said, "Now you'll have no trouble getting a job. Your grades are good, you've worked hard, and with that extra publicity you're all set."
>
> Well, I was turned down by over 40 law firms. Some of them turned me down twice. One turned me down before I'd even applied, because of a rumor that I was thinking of applying. The problems of getting a job were some of the most disillusioning of my life. I could get on the talk shows of Mike Douglas and Dick Cavett, and talk about my blindness. But I wanted to punch anybody in the mouth who said to me, "I saw you on TV. You're fantastic. Have you ever thought of becoming a comedian?" I didn't bust myself for three years at Harvard Law School to become a comedian.

2. Scope of the Problem

The preceding examples of discrimination in employment against handicapped persons are not isolated instances. Only a small percentage of the handicapped Americans who could work if given the opportunity are actually employed.[a] Transportation, physical barriers, and employers' prejudices have combined to deny the handicapped person access to many avenues of employment available to other citizens.[b] It is estimated that only one-third of blind persons of working age in the United States have jobs.[c] Only 47% of paraplegic persons of working age are employed.[d] Between 15% and 25% of working age persons with epilepsy are employed.[e] Only a handful of persons of working age with cerebral palsy have been able to secure employment.[f]

These figures are dismal indeed when one considers that the majority of unemployed handicapped persons, if given the chance, are quite capable of taking their places in the job market.[g] In fact, numerous studies indicate that the handicapped worker, when assigned an appropriate position, performs as well as or better than his nonhandicapped fellow workers.[h] Yet employers continue to discriminate against handicapped job applicants because of stereotypes, prejudices, and misconceptions.[i]

---

[a]Note, "Abroad in the Land: Legal Strategies to Effectuate the Rights of the Physically Disabled," 61 *Geo. L. J.* 1501, 1512 (1973) hereinafter cited as Note, "Abroad in the Land."

[b]*Id.* at 1513.

[c]118 *Cong. Rec.* 3321 (1972).

[d]*Id.*

[e]*Id.*

[f]*Id.*

[g]*Id.* at 3320. It is estimated that 9 out of 10 mentally retarded persons could work if given proper training and opportunities. *Ibid.*

[h]Note, "Abroad in the Land," *supra* n. a, at 1513.

[i]*Ibid.* One common misconception is that hiring handicapped workers may cause an increase in workmen's compensation insurance rates. Statistics indicate that handicapped persons have 8% fewer accidents than nonhandicapped workers; thus, the hiring of handicapped employees may actually decrease the insurance rates. *Id.* at 1513.

Denial of employment opportunities is especially outrageous in regard to handicapped veterans. While the unemployment rate for Vietnam era veterans at the end of 1971 was estimated at 8.8%, 87.7% of handicapped veterans were unable to find jobs. The disabled Vietnam veteran "seeks employment and is rebuffed either by the private employer as incompetent, or by his Government as being essentially unplaceable."[j]

An additional problem is that those handicapped persons who do manage to find employment tend to be channeled into unskilled, low paying positions involving monotonous tasks.[k]

B. THE LEGAL PERSPECTIVE IN THE PAST

IN RE MORTON

Appellate Court of Indiana, Division No. 1, 1922
79 Ind. App. 5, 137 N.E. 62

REMY, J. On September 11, 1922, John Morton, age 14, having completed the fifth grade of the public schools of his school district, was by the school superintendent of such district, excluded from such schools on the ground that he was mentally unfit for school attendance. The order of exclusion was certified to by a physician of good standing. On September 18, 1922, upon the request of an operator of a woolen mill in the school district in which Morton resided, and upon the application of Morton and his father, a certificate was issued to Morton purporting to authorize him to take employment with such operator, and to work in the woolen mill. On October 3, 1922, while the public schools of said district were in session, Morton received a personal injury from an accident arising out of and in the course of his employment. For the injuries thus received, Morton filed with the Industrial Board his application for compensation. The claim was made both against the operator of the woolen mill and the insurance carrier. To the application for compensation, the insurance carrier has filed a motion to dismiss, setting up all the facts hereinabove stated, which facts are not in dispute.

The Industrial Board submits for the decision of this court the following question:

"Does the Industrial Board have jurisdiction to hear and determine the claim of the said John Morton for compensation?"

The question involves the construction of certain sections of the act of March 7, 1921, "concerning the school attendance and employment of minors." Acts 1921, p. 337.

Section 5 of the act of 1921, *supra,* provides:

That "unless otherwise provided herein, every child between the ages of seven and sixteen years shall attend" school "each year during the entire time the public schools are in session in the school district in which such child resides," and that "the school superintendent of any attendance district" may have such children examined,

---

[j]118 *Cong. Rec.* 2998 (1972) (remarks of Congressman Vanik).

[k]See, e.g., *Diminished People: Problems and Care of the Mentally Retarded* 32 (Bernstein, N., ed., 1970).

and "may exclude or excuse from school any child found mentally or physically unfit for school attendance, provided such exclusion or excuse is approved and certified to by a physician of good standing, and providing further that such exclusion or excuse shall be valid for not longer than the school year during which it is issued."

Morton, having been excluded from school under this section of the law because of mental incapacity, and having been given an employment certificate by the issuing officer of his school district, was employed to work in the woolen mill where a few days later, and while in the line of his employment, he received the injury for which compensation is claimed. If Morton was lawfully employed at the time of his injury, he is entitled to compensation under the Workmen's Compensation Act. The legality of his employment depends upon the validity of the certificate purporting to authorize his employment.

Section 19 of the act under consideration makes unlawful the employment of a minor between the ages of 14 and 18 to work in any "gainful occupation," except "to perform farm labor and domestic service," unless the employer shall first have secured and placed on file an employment certificate issued by the issuing officer of the school corporation in which such minor resides. The section further specifically provides that the officer authorized to issue employment certificates shall issue no such certificate except to "a minor whose employment is necessary and not prohibited by law, and only upon the receipt of the following four documents herein referred to as proof of age, proof of physical fitness, proof of schooling, and proof of prospective employment." Then follow statements as to what the documents as to "proof of age," "proof of physical fitness," "proof of schooling" and "proof of prospective employment" shall include. The paragraph of the section setting forth what is required as to "proof of schooling," in so far as it applies to the question under consideration, is as follows:

"The requisite, prescribed schooling of any minor herein contemplated shall be proved by a certificate signed by the superintendent, principal or teacher of the school last attended showing that the minor can read and write correctly sentences in the English language and showing that he has satisfactorily completed the eighth grade of the common schools, or its equivalent."

No further or different authority for the issuance of employment certificates is provided in section 19, or in any other section of the act. There is no authority given for the issuance of employment certificates to minors between the ages of 14 and 16 who have been excluded from school because of mental incapacity. We have no authority to read into the law what the lawmakers have omitted. It follows that the issuance of the employment certificate to Morton was without authority, and his employment unlawful.

The question submitted is answered in the negative.

NOTE

The court's decision places persons such as John Morton in a predicament similar to that of a swimmer whose hands are tied behind his back and then is told not to kick his feet. Excluded from school and then prohibited from obtaining employment because he has not completed his schooling, what is John supposed to do? Run the streets and get into trouble? The situation discourages rather than assists John in becoming a responsible, contributing member of society.

KLETZING v. YOUNG

United States Court of Appeals for the District of Columbia Circuit, 1954
210 F.2d 729

Before EDGERTON, WILBUR K. MILLER, and DANAHER, Circuit Judges.
PER CURIAM.

With the aid of readers the appellant, who is blind, passed Civil Service examinations for certain government positions the duties of which he would not have been able to perform without employing readers. The Civil Service Commission, after entering his name on the resulting registers of eligibles, told him his eligibility was being cancelled because of his handicap. He asserted a right to be restored to the registers, and asked for injunctive and declaratory relief. His complaint alleged, among other things, that the cancellation of his eligibility violated 62 Stat. 351, 5 U.S. C.A. § 633(2)9, which forbids the Commission to discriminate against a physically handicapped person "with respect to any position the duties of which, in the opinion of the Civil Service Commission, may be efficiently performed by a person with such a physical handicap. . . ."

Since the registers to which appellant seeks to be restored have expired under the Commission's usual practice, the District Court rightly dismissed the complaint as moot. The fact that the legal question appellant seeks to raise may recur in the future does not defeat the defense of mootness. *Eastern Air Lines, Inc.* v. *Civil Aeronautics Board,* 341 U.S. 901, 71 S.Ct. 613, 95 L.Ed. 1341, reversing 87 U.S.App.D.C. 331, 185 F.2d 426.

Affirmed.

NOTES

1.   Is it unfair to say that a court which was sympathetic to Mr. Kletzing's claim could have found sufficient reasons for avoiding a finding of mootness? Does not the case present a "question that is 'capable of repetition, yet evading review,' *Southern Pacific Terminal Co.* v. *Interstate Commerce Commission,* 219 U.S. 498, 515 (1911); *Roe* v. *Wade,* 410 U.S. 113, 125 (1973), and is thus amenable to federal adjudication even though it might otherwise be considered moot," *DeFunis* v. *Odegaard,* 416 U.S. 312, 318-319 (1974)?

2.   While it does not go to the heart of the substantive issues, the *Kletzing* decision does construct a strong procedural roadblock against the resolution of the plaintiff's claims.

CHAVICH v. BOARD OF EXAM. OF BD. OF ED. OF CITY OF N.Y.

Supreme Court of New York, Appellate Division, Second Department, 1965
23 A.D.2d 57, 258 N.Y.S.2d 677

Before BELDOCK, P. J., and UGHETTA, CHRIST, HILL and RABIN, JJ.
BELDOCK, Presiding Justice.

Petitioner passed all the written, interview, and performance tests in connection with his examination for license as a regular teacher of music in the New York City junior high schools. However, he failed the required physical and medical examinations solely because he is blind. The regulations of the appellant Board of Examiners of the Board of Education of the City of New York require at least 20/30 vision in one eye, with or without glasses. This proceeding under article 78 of the CPLR was brought to compel certification of petitioner for eligibility on the ground that appellants' regulation with respect to sight violates section 3004 of the Education Law (as amd. by L.1960, ch. 270). This section, as amended, prohibits the State Commissioner of Education from prescribing, for all the public schools of the State, regulations to disqualify, solely by reason of blindness, any blind person otherwise qualified for a position as teacher. Special Term granted the application.

In my opinion, the statute (Education Law, § 3004, as amd. by L.1960, ch. 270) is inapplicable to appellants for a number of reasons:

(1) The statute (Education Law, § 3004) provides that the State Commissioner of Education shall prescribe regulations governing the examination and certification of teachers employed in all public schools of the State. However, the Commissioner's certification qualifies a teacher to teach only in public schools outside New York City. To qualify as a teacher in the New York City public schools, certification by the State Commissioner of Education is not required. What is required is a certification by the New York City Superintendent of Schools (Education Law, § 3008, § 2566, subd. 8) after examination conducted by the Board of Examiners of the Board of Education (Education Law, § 2569, subd. 1). The provisions of the statute (Education Law, § 3004) which prohibit the State Commissioner of Education from prescribing regulations with respect to blindness as a disqualification for obtaining the Commissioner's certification to teach cannot be applicable to teachers who do not require his certificate.

(2) The Education Law authorizes the State Commissioner of Education to prescribe minimum qualifications to teach in the public schools of the State. At present, such minimum requirements relate only to the academic standards. However, subdivision 9 of section 2573 of the Education Law provides that the New York City Board of Education may prescribe additional or higher qualifications for persons employed as teachers in the New York City school system. In accordance with such specific statutory power, the New York City Board of Education has prescribed additional or higher qualifications—academic, physical and medical, among others. One of these additional or higher requirements relates to sight, which petitioner failed to meet. A condition precedent to employment as a teacher in the New York City public schools is compliance with the additional or higher requirements prescribed by the New York City Board of Education (*Matter of Joseph,* 55 State Dept. Reports 507).

(3) Subdivision 2 of section 2554 of the Education Law gives the New York City Board of Education the exclusive right to determine the qualifications for teachers in the New York City school system. That right is not curtailed by section 3004 of the Education Law, which in express language curtails only the power of the State Commissioner of Education.

(4) Any other interpretation would make section 3004 of the Education Law inconsistent with section B 20–42.0 of the Administrative Code of the City of New York. This section provides for retirement of a teacher for physical incapacity for the

performance of duty. Although under the Administrative Code provisions a teacher who becomes blind may be retired for physical disability, yet, in the view of the minority, a new teacher who is blind could be granted a license.

(5) The State Commissioner of Education, who is charged with the administration of section 3004 of the Education Law, has interpreted the statute not to apply to teachers in the New York City schools. In 1963 the Commissioner determined that a person not blind, but not possessing the extent of vision required by the New York City Board of Education, is not entitled to be licensed as a teacher (*Matter of Bart*, 2 Education Dept. Reports 512). The minority view would require the New York City Board of Education to license not only blind teachers, but also teachers not blind who do not possess the required vision.

The New York City Board of Education has determined that an applicant who does not possess at least 20–30 vision in one eye, with or without glasses, cannot satisfactorily perform the duties of a teacher in the New York City schools and that such a condition may endanger the health or safety of pupils. Subsequent to the enactment of amended section 3004 of the Education Law, the State Commissioner of Education held that the Board of Education vision requirements are not so unrelated to the performance of teachers' duties as to be unreasonable or arbitrary (*Matter of Bart*, *supra*).

That the determination by the Board of Education with respect to vision requirements is reasonable is clear when the multitude of duties of a New York City junior high school teacher is considered, e.g., maintaining discipline in a class of approximately 30 children, aged 12 to 15; preventing them from fighting or from throwing pencils or erasers at each other (of which there have been many instances resulting in tort actions against the Board of Education, involving serious injury to pupils); marking roll books, examinations, or other written work; preventing cheating on examinations; writing on the blackboard; fire drills; going up and down stairs quickly in emergencies; use of textbooks; keeping the room clean; performing other administrative duties during non-teaching periods, etc.

Whether a blind teacher may satisfactorily perform classroom duties in a particular school may not be left for the determination of the school principal or other supervisory official, as the minority opinion suggests. The statute requires the Board of Examiners to determine whether an applicant has the ability to perform satisfactorily the duties of a teacher. The Board of Education is concerned with the effective performance of duties by a teacher both inside and outside the classroom. Although my sympathies are with this petitioner because of his unfortunate affliction, it is my opinion that the refusal to certify petitioner as eligible for a teaching license was within the power of the Board of Examiners.

The judgment should be reversed on the law and the facts, without costs, and the petition dismissed, without costs. Findings of fact implicit or contained in the opinion of Special Term which may be inconsistent herewith should be reversed and new findings made as indicated herein.

Judgment reversed on the law and the facts, without costs, and petition dismissed, without costs. Findings of fact implicit in or contained in the opinion at Special

Term which may be inconsistent herewith are reversed, and new findings made as indicated herein.

UGHETTA and HILL, JJ., concur.

SAMUEL RABIN, Justice (dissenting).

* * *

At the core of this controversy stands the statute (Education Law, § 3004, as amd. by L.1960, ch. 270). The relevant portion of this statute reads as follows:

> § 3004. *Regulations governing certification of teachers.*
>
> The commissioner of education shall prescribe, subject to approval by the regents, regulations governing the examination and certification of teachers employed in all public schools of the state . . . *but no such regulations shall hereafter prohibit, prevent or disqualify any person, who is otherwise qualified, from competing, participating and registering for such examination nor from obtaining a teacher's certificate or from qualifying for a position as a teacher solely by reason of his or her blindness, ...* (Emphasis supplied.)

* * *

In my view, the 1960 amendment to section 3004 of the Education Law effected a state-wide declaration of broad public policy that no blind person was hereafter to be deprived of the privilege of employment as a teacher "solely by reason of his or her blindness" (L.1960, ch. 270). It is inconceivable that when the Legislature directed the commissioner of education not to disqualify blind persons, it meant to exempt from that mandate the local school authorities under his jurisdiction and supervision. On a matter affecting so vitally and equally all of the people of the State, it would indeed be an anomaly to hold that the Legislature intended to set up different standards for different portions of the State. For such dual standards would exclude New York City—the most populous area of the State—and would thus devitalize the new policy and render the amendment self-defeating.

* * *

There is no factual foundation for the majority's view that—in advance of petitioner's attempted performance of his duties as a music teacher—the Board unilaterally may now conclude that a blind person cannot fulfill such duties and that petitioner therefore must be summarily rejected, regardless of his conceded satisfactory demonstration that he is in every respect fit and qualified to teach music.

That view is also untenable because it is based primarily on collateral factors which have no necessary connection with the teaching of music and which are wholly incidental to teaching. For instance, the majority points out that a blind teacher cannot possibly: (1) maintain proper discipline in the classroom or prevent altercations between students, so as to avoid consequent law suits against the City; (2) mark the attendance rolls or grade the written test papers; (3) supervise or direct fire drills and proper use of stairways in emergencies; and (4) perform other administrative duties during non-teaching periods.

All this may readily be conceded. But what the majority overlooks is that none of these disciplinary, administrative or clerical duties relates in the slightest degree to the basic qualifications or fitness to teach. These duties are incidental or peripheral;

they are wholly unrelated to the essential ability to teach. True, these incidental duties must be performed. But the Board, in furtherance of the fundamental policy of the State with respect to the employment of blind teachers otherwise qualified, may easily arrange for their performance by other sighted persons, whether such sighted persons be teachers, clerks or more mature students. Essentially, the situation is simply one of mutual accommodation and adjustment by all concerned.

In any event, the disciplinary, administrative and clerical duties envisaged by the majority present no insoluble problems or insuperable obstacles to a Board of Education willing to meet them and willing to adopt regulations and measures appropriate to the needs of the occasion. Surely, the intelligence and the ingenuity of the members of the Board of Education of the City of New York are equal to the task.

The efficacy of the blind teacher at all levels of instruction in the public schools is attested by the undisputed facts in this record. Equally important, it is further attested by the facts of history: Since the 16th century the utilization of blind teachers has gained acceptance throughout the civilized world and has produced teachers of renown in every field of endeavor, especially music in which the blind have proved themselves most proficient.

In sum, it is my view that the learned Special Term properly ruled that the Board of Examiners acted arbitrarily in this case because it disqualified petitioner from eligibility upon the basis of its own prior visual standards which had been rendered illegal by the 1960 amendment (ch. 270) to section 3004 of the Education Law. The Board acted "in violation of the legal rights" of petitioner (*Cheasty* v. *Board of Examiners*, Sup., 230 N.Y.S.2d 234, 238).

It may also be noted that the two rulings of the State Commissioner of Education, adverted to by the Board in its brief (*Matter of Kerr*, 2 Education Dept. Reports, 287–288; *Matter of Bart*, 2 Education Dept. Reports, 512, 513) lend no aid to the Board here. In neither decision did the Commissioner of Education take any position as to the application of section 3004 of the Education Law (as amd. by L.1960, ch. 270), although in the *Bart* case he was specifically invited to do so. Moreover, both these decisions involved sighted persons neither of whom had obtained a certification as a legally blind person, as had the petitioner here.

By its action the Board has subverted the fundamental educational policy of the State. Obviously, no political subdivision of the State and no board of education of any such subdivision should be empowered to undermine or thwart the educational policy established by the State itself.

Accordingly, the judgment under review should be modified so as to delete the direction to the Board to issue a license to petitioner; and as so modified, the judgment should be affirmed.

CHRIST, J., concurs in the dissenting opinion of SAMUEL RABIN, J.

NOTE

The majority opinion in *Chavich* is a traditional bowing to the discretion of employers. The dissent, arguing that there should be no blanket disqualification of blind applicants but rather a determination on an individual case-by-case basis as to an applicant's qualifications, anticipates the tone of later decisions.

C. THE BEGINNINGS OF CHANGE

KING-SMITH v. AARON

United States District Court for the Western District of Pennsylvania, 1970
317 F.Supp. 164, reversed at 455 F.2d 378 (3rd Circ. 1972), which follows
immediately at p. 329

OPINION

GERALD J. WEBER, District Judge.

Plaintiff is blind. The law of compensation, however, has endowed her with a remarkable facility for learning diverse and unrelated foreign languages. Her academic credentials are certified by degrees from two prestigious universities. Even more to her merit, she does not flaunt the ubiquitous doctorate whose glut on today's market makes it more of a substitute for rather than a recognition of genuine intellectual competence.

She is fully qualified and certified to teach in the public schools of Pennsylvania. A state certificate is required to teach in any public school in Pennsylvania. (24 P.S. 12-1201). Plaintiff, to have acquired such state certificate, must have secured a physician's certificate of no major physical disability, unless such person submits a certificate from her university certifying that the applicant can perform the duties notwithstanding the impediment. (24 P.S. 12-1209).

Plaintiff applied to be placed on the eligibility list to teach in the Pittsburgh public schools. She took the physical examination required by the provisions of the state statute for appointment in the school districts of the first class (i.e., Pittsburgh) (24 P.S. 21-2108), under which it is provided that applicant must present a physician's certificate setting forth that applicant is not physically disqualified by reason of any acute physical defect from successfully performing the duties of a teacher.

The examining physician noted such physical defect but recommended that it be waived in view of plaintiff's extraordinary qualifications.

Plaintiff was not placed on the eligible list. She brings this action against a large number of defendants allegedly the membership of the Board of Education of the City of Pittsburgh, in their individual capacity, and three employees of the Board, the Superintendent and two Assistant Superintendents.

Plaintiff claims jurisdiction in this court under the Civil Rights Act, 42 U.S.C. 1983 and 1985. Plaintiff alleges that the refusal of defendants to place her on the eligibility list solely on the basis of a physical handicap constitutes a denial of substantial due process of law and of the equal protection of the law. Plaintiff adds vaguely pleaded conspiracy counts under 42 U.S.C. 1985.[1]

---

[1] An uninvited and largely useless "amicus curiae" brief ascribes this action to "disaffection for blind persons." We think this is a clearly unwarranted aspersion on the defendants. The requirement of sight may be a very valid qualification in today's public high schools, where the teacher may be more likely to be called on to fulfill the functions of a babysitter, a policeman, and a referee for a free-for-all, than the traditional role of teacher, and where the first principle of pedagogy is now reported to be, "Always keep your back to the blackboard."

On the other hand, lest the court be accused of such disaffection, let us note our admiration for the genius of Homer and Milton, and our recollection of John F. Maher, the blind tutor, who taught Latin, Greek and mathematics to George Wharton Pepper and who later became an outstanding student of Pepper's at the University of Pennsylvania Law School. (Pepper, G. W., "Philadelphia Lawyer," Lippincott, 1944, p. 28).

Defendants have moved to dismiss for failure of the complaint to state a cause of action under the Civil Rights Act and for failure to plead a cause of action in conspiracy.

While there are probable defects in pleading such as misnomer, possible misjoinder of parties, and a failure to plead the conspiracy count with specificity, these might be cured by amendment. The other matters raised by defendants' motion are more critical, going to the sufficiency of the Civil Rights Act allegations which alone give us jurisdiction.

However, it becomes immediately apparent from plaintiff's pleading and brief that we do not need to meet these questions at this point. A conflict of state law is made immediately apparent in that plaintiff alleges that "defendants violated the letter and spirit of 24 P.S. 12-1209." This contention is made because plaintiff claims that the general provisions of the Pennsylvania School Code, Article XII, control and that the provisions of Article XXI concerning the powers of the local school board are governed by the general provisions of the code. If this is so, a determination of this by the state courts or the administrative processes would dispose of the alleged civil rights claim.

This is a clear case for application of the doctrine of abstention. If the state courts should hold the action of defendants as unauthorized under state law it will not be necessary for the federal court to pass upon the Civil Rights or constitutional claim.

The abstention doctrine has been based, in part, on federal-state comity;

> "This now well-established procedure is aimed at the avoidance of unnecessary interference by the federal courts with proper and validly administered state concerns, a course so essential to the balanced working of our federal system. To minimize the possibility of such interference a 'scrupulous regard for the rightful independence of state governments . . . should at all times actuate the federal courts,' *Matthews* v. *Rodgers,* 284 U.S. 521, 525, 52 S.Ct. 217, 76 L.Ed. 447, as their 'contribution . . . in furthering the harmonious relation between state and federal authority . . .' *Railroad Commission of Texas* v. *Pullman Co., 312 U.S. 496, 501, 61 S.Ct. 643, 85 L.Ed. 971.* In the service of this doctrine which this Court has applied in many different contexts, no principle has found more consistent or clear expression than that the federal courts should not adjudicate the constitutionality of state enactments fairly open to interpretation until the state courts have been afforded a reasonable opportunity to pass upon them." (citations omitted). *Harrision* v. *N.A.A.C.P.* 360 U.S. 167, 176, 79 S.Ct. 1025, 1030, 3 L.Ed.2d 1152 (1959).

We think there is something more than comity involved today. We note that the United States District Courts are flooded with claims allegedly arising under the Civil Rights Act. Every act, every administrative decision of every state and local official is today threatened by federal litigation. This extends to every organization or institution that receives some financial support from state or local government sources. If state and local governments are to remain viable instruments of government and not become administrative agencies of the federal court system, there must remain some avenue by which local concerns are solved locally through the democratic process. Using the federal Civil Rights Act as a vehicle to threaten every exercise of discretion in matters legitimately within the area of a state's competence is not the purpose of this grant of jurisdiction to the federal courts. Plaintiff's complaint does not reveal a deliberate, calculated state assault upon a constitutionally guaranteed freedom. It merely contests the application of a certain standard of fitness for teaching as to whether that standard is authorized by state law, and whether that standard is reasonable. The state has a right to make a legitimate inquiry into the competency of its teachers. *Shelton* v. *Tucker*, 364 U.S. 479, 81 S.Ct. 247, 5 L.Ed.2d 231 (1960).

Plaintiff may submit her federal claims to the state court along with the contention that defendants' acts were contrary to state law. State court judges are sworn to uphold the Constitution of the United States, as well as federal district judges. In such case the avenue of appeal leads to the United States Supreme Court. Or plaintiff may reserve the federal question in state court action and seek only the interpretation of the conflicting state statute. Cf. *England* v. *Louisiana State Bd. of Medical Examiners*, 375 U.S. 411, 84 S.Ct. 461, 11 L.Ed.2d 440 (1964).

An illustration of what we deem a proper procedure in this case is illustrated by the only reported case presenting the same factual situation. New York State had a dual system of teacher certification, one for the state at large except for New York City, and one for New York City. The state-wide statute prohibited disqualification for blindness, the city regulations prescribed a visual test. An action was filed in the New York Courts contesting the City's visual requirement on the grounds that it violated the state statute, but, the Court held the City's requirement valid in view of the powers granted the City by the state statute. *Chavich* v. *Bd. of Examiners,* 16 N.Y.2d 810, 263 N.Y.S.2d 7, 210 N.E.2d 359 (1965). No question of federal constitutional rights was raised. Thereafter the state statute was amended to make the state-wide standard applicable to the City. Thus the local problem was solved by the local legislative process after the judicial construction had been determined.

We find no barrier to applying the abstention doctrine. This is not a case where the state law is settled and clear. *County of Allegheny* v. *Frank Mashuda Co.,* 360 U.S. 185, 79 S.Ct. 1060, 3 L.Ed.2d 1163 (1959), nor is it a case where state action threatens a "protected" activity; i.e., the exercise of rights of free expression under the First Amendment. *Dombrowski* v. *Pfister,* 380 U.S. 479, 85 S.Ct. 1116, 14 L.Ed.2d 22 (1965).

Having determined that abstention is proper here our question now is the proper determination of this case. As stated in *Urbano* v. *Board of Mgrs. of N.J. State Prison,* 415 F.2d 247, 254 (3rd Cir., 1969):

> "Professor Wright has also noted, quite significantly, that 'where the federal court defers to avoid interference with state activities, *dismissal of the action,* rather than retention of jurisdiction pending a state determination, *is normally appropriate.'*" (Emphasis added.);

citing Wright, Federal Courts [1963 Ed.] p. 173. The opinion cites Wright further in a footnote:

> "... If the state court to which deference is thus shown prejudices any federal rights of the parties, this can be redressed by review of the state decision in the United States Supreme Court." *Op. cit.,* p. 173.

ORDER

Now this 7th day of October, 1970, in accordance with the foregoing Opinion, the Motion of Defendants is granted, and the within action is dismissed.

KING-SMITH V. AARON

United States Court of Appeals for the Third Circuit, 1972
455 F.2d 378

OPINION OF THE COURT

VAN DUSEN, Circuit Judge.

This case involves the alleged right of a blind woman, with exceptional academic credentials,[1] to serve as a teacher in the Pittsburgh public school system. In 1968, plaintiff completed a formal application to teach in the Pittsburgh public schools and had several interviews. After passing the required physical examination, she was granted a provisional teacher's certificate by the Department of Public Instruction of the Commonwealth of Pennsylvania. Plaintiff then made a request to take the physical examination required by the Board of Education of the City of Pittsburgh. Although this initial request was refused, plaintiff was permitted to teach on a voluntary basis at a Pittsburgh public high school and was later permitted to take the physical examination. Despite the recommendation of the examining physician that the visual requirement be waived, she was not recommended for employment by the Medical Service Division. Plaintiff was called to act as a substitute teacher on three occasions in 1969, but all requests to be placed on the eligibility list were declined. On May 22, 1970, the instant action was filed in the district court based on 42 U.S.C. §§ 1983 and 1985, alleging a violation of plaintiff's due process and equal protection rights. After reviewing briefs submitted on defendants' motion to dismiss, the motion was granted by the district court. That court, in its opinion of October 7, 1970, 317 F.Supp. 164, relied on the abstention doctrine in dismissing the action and cited the existence of state law issues which might avoid the Federal Constitutional issues as the predicate for relying on that doctrine. We disagree and remand for a hearing on the merits of plaintiff's complaint.

A federal court should abstain when a decision concerning a question of state law is necessary to a disposition of the case and the answer to the state question involves unclear state law, especially where a matter of paramount interest to the state is involved. There is no uncertain state law question in this case.

We do not agree with the district court's determination that a controlling and unclear question of state law was presented due to a conflict in the provisions of 24 P.S. § 12-1209 and 24 P.S. § 21-2102. The theory that the constitutional question could be avoided by a resolution of unclear state law questions is based on the following interpretation of the Pennsylvania School Code:

(1) § 21-2103 grants authority to the Board to set standards for the hiring of teachers.

(2) § 21-2108 extends that authority to disqualifying persons who have physical defects which would prohibit them from successfully performing the duties of a teacher.

---

[1] As the district court judge pointed out, plaintiff has been endowed with a remarkable facility to master diverse and unrelated foreign languages. While a student at Stanford University, she majored in Russian and did minor study in German and Chinese. Plaintiff graduated from Stanford in three academic years with great distinction, ranking sixth in her class, and was elected to Phi Beta Kappa. Plaintiff did graduate studies at the Monterey Institute of Foreign Studies, the Warsaw University in Poland, and received a Master's Degree in Education with a Russian concentration from Harvard University. She took the National Teachers' Examination in March 1969 and received a score of 769 out of a possible 800.

(3) However, the authority granted by these sections is expressly made subject to the other provisions of the Act by § 21-2102.

(4) One such provision is contained in § 12-1209, which provides for the certification of teachers having major physical disabilities by the state.

Defendants suggest that since plaintiff, having such a disability, has received a state certification, her disqualification under the physical defects provision of § 21-2108 would controvert the policy expressed in § 12-1209 to hire such teachers and is thus inconsistent with the "provisions of the Act." § 21-2103.

Reading the various provisions of Article XII and Article XXI of the Public School Code of 1949 (Act of March 10, 1949, P.L. 30) as a whole, it is clear that a prospective teacher is required not only to secure provisional approval from the Commonwealth authorities under Article XII of the Act of 1949 but is also required to receive the approval of the City of Pittsburgh Board of Education under Article XXI. The statute, read as a whole, places authority in the local school boards to pass reasonable regulations to insure that prospective teachers are physically qualified to carry out their teaching assignments. Even though a prospective teacher with a serious physical handicap has received her state certification (a prerequisite required by the Act), she is still subject to the independent discretion of the local board as to whether her physical defect would prohibit her from successfully performing her duties as a teacher. Therefore, no conflict among the above-mentioned sections of the Act exists. In a case such as this, it is the duty of the federal courts to exercise jurisdiction. Plaintiff has alleged that she has been deprived of her civil rights in violation of the Fourteenth Amendment and 42 U.S.C. § 1983 by an arbitrary, discriminatory and unreasonable classification of blind persons as being unfit for teaching positions in the public schools. We express no opinion on the merits of this claim but, in view of the motion to dismiss, are bound to accept the allegations of the complaint as being true. For these reasons, we reverse the district court order of October 7, 1970, and remand the case for further proceedings consistent with this opinion.

NOTES

1. Despite the disclaimer of "disaffection" in footnote 1 of the district court's opinion, the hostility of the district judge toward Ms. King-Smith's civil rights claim is apparent throughout his opinion. Invoking the doctrine of abstention appears merely to have been a simple way to remove this undesirable piece of litigation from the court's docket.

2. The decision of the Circuit Court in no way addresses the merits of the plaintiff's constitutional claims but merely orders the district court to consider such claims. Clearly, however, the opinion of the Third Circuit does not exhibit any of the repugnance toward plaintiff's civil rights allegations, which characterized the ruling of the district judge.

3. *Parolisi* v. *Board of Examiners of City of New York,* 285 N.Y.S.2d 936, 55 Misc.2d 546 (1967), involved an overweight person denied a license as a substitute teacher solely because of overweight. Observing that "obesity, standing alone, is not

reasonably and rationally related to ability to teach" at 285 N.Y.S.2d 940, the court held that a weight standard for employment was "arbitrary and capricious."

While obesity is not a type of physical disability that has traditionally been considered a "handicap," it is apparent that the legal reasoning in *Parolisi* could apply to handicaps as well. The proper question for an employer to ask is not whether a person fits this or that label (e.g., overweight, epileptic, deaf) but whether the prospective employee can or cannot do the job for which he or she is being considered.

Heumann v. *Board of Education of the City of New York,* 320 F.Supp. 623 (S.D.N.Y. 1970), dealt with the denial to the plaintiff of a license to teach in the New York City schools "on the ground that, being confined to a wheelchair as a result of poliomyelitis, she was physically and medically unsuited for teaching, *id.* at 624. The complaint, seeking declaratory, monetary, and injunctive relief, was ultimately dismissed as moot after the Board of Education reversed itself and granted the plaintiff a license and a teaching position. This outcome should be contrasted with *Kletzing* v. *Young,* p. 321, above. While Judy Heumann's case was dismissed as moot because she had already obtained the relief she sought, Mr. Kletzing was thrown out of court without obtaining anything.

D. STATE LAW

1. Statutory Provisions

WEISS, S., "EQUAL EMPLOYMENT AND THE DISABLED: A PROPOSAL"

10 Columbia J. L. & Soc. Problems 457, 459-465 (1974)
The State and the Disabled

1. *Equal Employment Opportunities.* Despite a growing recognition that the disabled need statutory protection in the area of employment, most states fail to provide such protection. Presently only twenty-one states[16] and the District of Columbia[17] have amended existing anti-discrimination laws to require equal employment opportunity for

---

[16]Alaska Stat. §§ 18.80.220-.300 (Supp. 1973) (separate act); Cal. Labor Code §§ 1410-33 (West Supp. 1973); Conn. Gen. Stat. Ann. §§ 311-122 to -128 (Supp. 1973); Ill. Ann. Stat. ch. 38, §§ 65-21 to -30 (Smith-Hurd Supp. 1974) (separate act); Iowa Code Ann. § 601A (1970); Law of Feb. 22, 1974, ch. 209, Kan. Sess. Laws 759-68; Law of Feb. 26, 1974, ch. 705, Me. Laws 76-81; Mass. Ann. Laws ch. 149, § 24K (Supp. 1972) (separate act); Minn. Stat. Ann. §§ 363.01-.13 (Supp. 1973); Mont. Rev. Codes Ann. §§ 64-301 to -312 (Supp. 1974); Neb. Rev. Stat. §§ 48-1101 to -25 (Supp. 1973); Nev. Rev. Stat. §§ 613.310-.430 (1971); N.J. Stat. Ann. § 10:5-4.1 (Supp. 1973); N.M. Stat. Ann. §§ 4-33-7 to -12 (Supp. 1973); Law of Sept. 1, 1974, ch. 988, McKinney's Session Laws of N.Y. 1575-80; N.C. Gen. Stat. § 128-15.3 (Supp. 1973); R.I. Gen. Laws Ann. §§ 28-5-2 to -38 (Supp. 1973); Vt. Stat. Ann. tit. 21, § 498 (Supp. 1974); Wash. Rev. Code Ann. §§ 49.60.010-.320 (Supp. 1974); W. Va. Code Ann. §§ 5-11-3 to -16 (Supp. 1974); Wis. Stat. Ann. §§ 111.31-.37 (1974).

The remedies for discrimination in most of these states are injunctive relief, damages, and, in some cases, affirmative action. In Massachusetts, however, the exclusive remedy for discrimination against the disabled is a fine of not less than 25, not more than 200 dollars. Mass. Ann. Laws ch. 149, § 24K (Supp. 1972). For a brief discussion of criminal penalties in employment discrimination, see notes 46-48 *infra* and accompanying text.

[17]D.C. Code Ann. §§ 6-1501 to -1508 (1973). A violation is punishable as a misdemeanor.

the disabled in both the public and private sectors. These laws, however, provide the disabled with uncertain remedies when discrimination occurs in hiring, promotions, or firing. Furthermore, since state civil rights commissions, which are responsible for enforcing the existing laws, have not aggressively pursued claims of discrimination against minorities,[18] the disabled cannot expect strict enforcement of these laws in their favor.

Finally, the existing state laws are uneven in scope and quality. Some statutes reach only the physically disabled,[19] while others include the mentally disabled as well.[20] Many of the statutes are either vague or overly strict in defining disability.

The Iowa law,[21] though otherwise excellently drafted, defines disability as "a substantial handicap . . . unrelated to one's ability to engage in a particular occupation."[22] In defining disability as a "handicap," this provision is both circular and conclusory. Whether a disability is in fact a handicap to job performance should be the very issue to be determined in each case. Iowa law unfortunately blurs the distinction.[23]

By contrast, New York City's Human Rights Law[24] defines physical disability as an individual's reliance on crutches, braces, and other aid devices,[25] thereby seemingly excluding persons such as epileptics and asthmatics. The Nebraska statute

---

[18]Cooper & Rabb, Equal Employment Law and Litigation, Employment Rights Project 50, (1972) (unpublished text) (hereinafter cited as Cooper & Rabb).

[19]Alaska, California, Connecticut, Maine, Massachusetts, Montana, Nevada, New Jersey, North Carolina, Rhode Island, Vermont, Wisconsin. West Virginia's statute protects only the blind. See note 16 supra.

[20]Illinois, Iowa, Kansas, Minnesota, Nebraska, New Mexico, New York, Oregon, Washington. See note 16 supra.

[21]Iowa Code Ann., § 601A (1974).

[22]Id. at § 601A.2(11).

[23]There is some logic to this definition. "Disability" refers to a medical condition, e.g., blindness or deafness, while the word "handicap" refers to one's status due to the disability. For example, paralysis is a disability. While it is not a handicap to reading, it may be a handicap to free movement, and therefore will probably be one to obtaining employment because it may cause discriminatory treatment by employers. Thus the protected class is defined as being handicapped by a disability, though the definition stresses that this class is not handicapped in its ability to do a job. Therefore the employer is not being forced to hire workers unqualified for the job due to their impairment. Unfortunately, this phrase fails to serve as an adequate statutory definition, since it does not make clear precisely who is protected. Consequently neither the civil rights commission, the courts, nor an employer can determine precisely what constitutes a statutory violation.

[24]New York, N.Y., Admin. Code Ann. § B1-1 (Human Rights Law) (1971).

[25]"The term 'physically handicapped' means a person who, because of accident, illness, or congenital condition may depend upon a brace, crutch, cane, seeing eye dog, hand controlled car or other such device or appliance in performance of his daily responsibilities as a self-sufficient, productive, and complete human being." Id. at § B-2.16.
The scope of jurisdiction conferred by this definition is unclear. By saying "may depend upon," the law implies that the Commission may have jurisdiction over a disabled person not employing a device if someone with a similar disability uses one. Thus, a totally deaf person who cannot benefit from a hearing aid might be protected by the law because other deaf people who do use hearing aids are incorporated.
A proposed amendment to the Code would broaden the definition to include anyone with a "physical or neurological condition which results in . . . a physical impairment of his capacity to function physically in the manner of a normal person." A Local Law to Amend the Administrative Code of New York, New York, N.Y., Admin. Code Ann. § B1-1 (Human Rights Law) (1971).

defines the classification in the most comprehensive fashion.[26] Although cumbersome and lengthy, the Nebraska definition of the protected class[27] has the advantage of being detailed enough to give an employer notice of what constitutes a statutory violation. Additionally, it encompasses a broader class than that protected by the well-defined but narrower New York City law.

The distinctions in the various state statutory definitions magnify the need for a uniform federal law, for even if all states were to include the disabled in their anti-discrimination laws, the degree of protection would depend on the scope[28] of each statutory definition.

2. *Scope of Protection.* Many laws dealing with discrimination against the disabled contain exceptions which are never applied to other minorities protected by equal employment laws, and which clearly reflect the prejudices with which the disabled must contend.[29] In equal employment laws, states typically impose the limitation

---

[26]Neb. Rev. Stat. §§ 48-1101 to -25 (Supp. 1973).

[27] "Disability shall mean any physical condition, infirmity, malformation, or disfigurement which is caused by bodily injury, birth defect, or illness, including epilepsy or seizure disorders, and which shall include, but not be limited to, any degree of paralysis, amputation, lack of physical coordination, blindness or physical impediment, deafness or hearing impediment, muteness or speech impediment, or physical reliance on a dog guide, wheelchair, or other remedial device and shall also mean the physical or mental condition which constitutes a substantial handicap as determined by a physician, but is unrelated to such person's ability to engage in a particular occupation." Neb. Rev. Stat. § 48-1102 (Supp. 1973).

The last clause of the Nebraska definition contains language similar to that of the Iowa definition, *supra* note 23 and accompanying text.

The Rhode Island and New Jersey statutes contain definitions with similar language. However, their definitions are shorter and applicable only to the physically disabled.

[28]The scope of statutory definition of disability varies from state to state. For example, a mentally disabled person in Nebraska could claim statutory protection. Neb. Rev. Stat. § 48-1101 to -25 (Supp. 1973), but not in California, where only the physically disabled are included in the law, Cal. Labor Code § 1410-33 (West Supp. 1973). A diabetic would be covered in New Jersey, with its comprehensive definition of disability, N.J. Stat. Ann. § 10:5-4.1 (Supp. 1973); but probably not in New York City, New York, N.Y., Admin. Code Ann. § B1-1 (Human Rights Law) (1971). It is unclear if a legally blind person in New York City who did not use a cane would receive the same protection as one who, because of total blindness, was forced to rely on such a device. *See* note 25 *supra* and accompanying text.

[29]*E.g.* Cal. Labor Code § 1420 (West Supp. 1973) ("Nothing in this bill shall prohibit an employer from refusing to hire or discharge a physically handicapped person . . . where the employee, because of his physical handicap . . . is unable to perform his duties in a manner which would not endanger his health or the health and safety of others. . . ."); Alaska Stat. § 18.80.220 (Supp. 1973) (forbidding discrimination ". . . when the reasonable demands of the position do not require . . . physical handicap . . . distinctions."); Ill. Ann. Stat. ch. 38, § 65-23 (Supp. 1974) (". . . unless it can be shown that the particular handicap prevents the performance of the employment involved."); Mont. Rev. Codes § 64-301 (Supp. 1974) ("There is no discrimination where . . . the handicap reasonably precludes the performance of the particular employment or where the particular employment may subject the handicapped or his fellow employees to physical harm."); N.J. Stat. Ann. § 10:4-4.1 (Supp. 1972) (". . . unless the nature and extent of the handicap reasonably precludes the performance of the particular employment").

The New Mexico statute provides: "An employee shall execute as a condition of employment a certificate of preexisting physical or mental handicap." N.M. Stat. Ann. § 4-33-7.1 (1974).

The problem with these exceptions is that they focus on disability as a classification to justify discrimination. The purpose of fair employment laws should be to force the employer to focus on the capacity of the *individual* to do the job regardless of the class to which he belongs.

In contrast, the Iowa Code forbids an employer from automatically assuming that the disabled cannot perform a certain job: "If a disabled person is qualified to perform a particular occupation, by reason of

that to justify a discriminatory hiring practice, the employer must prove that the particular handicap prevents adequate job performance.[30] Yet, prior to the passage of the amendment[31] to include the disabled in the New York State Human Rights Law,[32] the New York State Assembly considered several bills[33] which would not have found discrimination unlawful if the State Division of Human Rights determined that the physical handicap unreasonably interfered with the "duties" of other workers.[34] Additionally, the Commission could permit discriminatory job exclusion in the interest of public safety or in the interest of the well-being of the physically handicapped person.[35] The wording of these bills was vague in defining "unreasonable interference" and "public safety." By allowing an exception for non-hiring in terms other than ability to perform the job, these bills would have had the effect of creating an exclusion which is not only invidious and debilitating, but also superfluous. The discrimination ostensibly made unlawful by fair employment laws is not the discrimination against qualified workers, but against members of a protected group.[36] Presumably, any worker who interferes with the duties of others or undermines the public safety would be unqualified for the job. Yet this exception was written in the proposed bills to apply only to the disabled, and not to other groups covered by the state Human Rights Law. By singling out the disabled, these bills would have created the psychological impression that there is something peculiar about the disabled which distinguishes them from other protected minorities. Furthermore, allowing an employer to discriminate against disabled applicants who might represent a "danger to themselves"[37] exemplifies the very paternalism of which the disabled complain. The New York bills would have undermined the notion of equal employment for the disabled by distinguishing even those disabled who are qualified for employment from other minority groups.

Even in jurisdictions without such statutory distinctions, guidelines have yet to be drawn to determine discrimination. It is conceivable that in cases brought under these statutes, courts will allow as much leeway in justifying exceptions to discrimination against the disabled as these New York bills would have allowed. With greatly divergent state fair employment legislation being enacted, it seems federal legislation is necessary to adequately protect the rights of the disabled.

---

training or experience, the nature of the occupation shall not be the basis for exception to the unfair or discriminating practices prohibited by this subsection." Iowa Code Ann. § 601A.7(1)(a)(1970).

[30] *See* note 29 *supra*.

[31] Law of Sept. 1, 1974, ch. 988, McKinney's Session Laws of N.Y. 1575-80.

[32] N.Y. Exec. Law, §§ 290-301 (McKinney 1972).

[33] S. 3818—A. 6836 (1973); S. 3773—A. 5931 (1973).

[34] *See* note 33 *supra*.

[35] *See* note 33 *supra*.

[36] *See, e.g., Diaz* v. *Pan Am. World Airways, Inc.,* 442 F.2d 385 (5th Cir.), *cert. denied,* 404 U.S. 950 (1971) (discriminating against males when hiring flight attendants violated Title VII of the Civil Rights Act of 1964, 42 U.S.C. § 2000e (1964)). "Pan Am can take into consideration the ability of *individuals* to perform the non-mechanical functions of the job. But Pan Am cannot exclude *all* males simply because most males may not perform adequately." *Id.* at 388 (emphasis added).

[37] S. 3818—A. 6836 (1973); S. 3773—A. 5931 (1973).

3. *Other Related State Laws.* In addition to the laws passed in some states to protect the disabled from discrimination in public employment,[39] twenty-nine states[40] have passed, either in whole or in part, a statute known as the Model White Cane Law.[41] Although drafted primarily to insure the rights of the blind to safe streets, public accommodations, and housing,[42] the Law contains a clause on equal rights in public employment which covers all physically disabled persons.[43] The White Cane Law, however, is unimpressive in both reach and enforceability. Unlike the previously mentioned fair employment laws,[44] the White Cane Law does not cover the private sector. Although the first paragraph of the Law suggests extension beyond public employment, its wording is merely hortatory.[45] Furthermore, the enforcement provisions are extremely unclear. The public facilities section of the Law is enforceable in most states by a misdemeanor provision; however, with exceptions in only a few

---

[39]New York State, for example, prohibits employment discrimination against the blind in education. New York Educ. Law § 3004 (McKinney 1973). Similarly, New York Civ. Ser. Law § 55 (McKinney 1973) prohibits discrimination in the civil service solely on the basis of blindness or physical handicap, unless the condition prevents performance of the duties for which the individual is seeking employment. However, even if the blind or otherwise disabled person passes the civil service exam, he is not assured of a job until the State Commission for the visually handicapped, or the state education department, certifies his ability to perform. *Id* § 55(3).

[40]Alaska Stat. §§ 18.06.010-.050 (Supp. 1973); Ariz. Rev. Stat. Ann. § 24-411 (Supp. 1973); Ark. Stat. Ann. § 82-2901 *et seq.* (Supp. 1973); Cal. Gov't Code § 3550 (West Supp. 1973); Colo. Rev. Stat. Ann. § 25-4-1(c) (Cum. Supp. 1971); Fla. Stat. Ann. § 413.08 (Supp. 1972); Hawaii Rev. Stats. § 347-20 (Supp. 1973); Idaho Code Ann. § 56-707 (Supp. 1973); Ill. Ann. Stat. ch. 23, § 3365 (Smith-Hurd Supp. 1973); Ind. Ann. Stat. §§ 16-7-5-1 to -7 (Burns Supp. 1974); Iowa Code Ann. § 601D.2 (Supp. 1973); Kan. Stat. Ann. § 39.1101 *et seq.* (1973); Me. Rev. Stat. Ann. tit. 17, § 1316 (Supp. 1973); Md. Ann. Code art. 30, § 33 (Supp. 1973) (applicable only to the blind); Minn. Stat. Ann. § 246C.01 (1971); Miss. Code Ann. § 43-6-1 *et seq.* (Supp. 1974); Mont. Rev. Codes Ann. § 71-1304 (1971); Neb. Rev. Stat. § 20-131 (Supp. 1972); Nev. Rev. Stat. § 284.012 (1971); N.H. Rev. Stat. Ann. § 167-C:5 (Supp. 1973); N.M. Stat. Ann. § 12-26-7 (Supp. 1973); N.D. Cent. Code § 24-13-05 (1970); R.I. Gen. Laws. Ann. § 25-2-13 (Supp. 1973); S.C. Code Ann. § 71-300.56 (Supp. 1974); Tex. Rev. Civ. Stat. art. 4419e (Supp. 1973); Utah Code Ann. § 26-28-3 (Supp. 1973); Va. Code Ann. § 63.1-71.6)1973); Wash. Rev. Code Ann. § 70.84.080 (Supp. 1972); W. Va. Code Ann. § 5-25-7 (1971).

[41]The Model White Cane Law was drafted by Professor Jacobus tenBroek, who was himself blind. For the full text of the Act see tenBroek, *supra* note 10, at 918-19.

[42]Of the states that have adopted the White Cane Law, seventeen have yet to adopt the housing provisions: Alaska, Arizona, Colorado, Hawaii, Idaho, Illinois, Maine, Mississippi, Montana, Nebraska, New Hampshire, New Mexico, Rhode Island, Texas, Utah, Washington, and West Virginia. *See* note 40 *supra.*

[43]Section 6 of the Model White Cane Law states: "It is the policy of this State that the blind, the visually handicapped, and the *otherwise physically disabled* shall be employed in the State Service, the service of the political subdivisions of the State, in the public schools, and in all other employment supported in whole or in part by public funds on the same terms and conditions as the ablebodied unless it is shown that the particular disability prevents the performance of the work involved." [emphasis added]

The laws of Alaska and Texas do not contain section 6. The Mississippi law, on the other hand, contains a section similar to section 6, but phrased in terms of a mandate not to discriminate, as opposed to a statement of policy. *See* note 40 *supra.*

[44]*See* note 16 *supra.*

[45]"It is the policy of this state to encourage and enable the blind, the visually handicapped, and the otherwise physically disabled to participate fully in the social and economic life of the state and to engage in remunerative employment."

jurisdictions,[46] this protection is not available for discrimination in public employment.[47] The result is to reduce the employment section of the Law to a policy statement. Even in the few jurisdictions where the misdemeanor does apply to public employment, the remedy is inadequate. The misdemeanor penalty is a negative enforcement mechanism. To be effective, relief for discrimination requires civil remedies, such as injunctive relief, damages, and in some instances quota hiring.[48] Furthermore, unlike the misdemeanor penalty, these civil penalties would be available to a private plaintiff. Even the minor criminal penalties mandated by the White Cane Law can be sought solely by a state prosecutor, who may be reluctant to bring such an action against a state agency. It will therefore take more than misdemeanor provisions to open the job market to the disabled.

CHICAGO, MILWAUKEE, ST. PAUL & PACIFIC R.R. CO. v. STATE, DEPT. OF
INDUSTRY, LABOR & HUMAN RELATIONS

Supreme Court of Wisconsin, 1974
62 Wis.2d 392, 215 N.W.2d 443
(See pp. 16–19 supra)

NOTES

1.   This case is one of the few court decisions dealing with enforcement of state legislation forbidding discrimination against individuals with handicaps.

2.   The definition of *handicap* adopted by the court and the reasoning of the court in support of such a broad interpretation would seem to apply to any type of medical problem that makes achievement more difficult; the court indicates that even migraine headaches would be included. This interpretation does not limit the effect of the statute to simply remedying discrimination against those traditionally labeled "handicapped," but rather takes an affirmative step toward discouraging all medically related employment criteria.

2.   State Constitutional Provisions

ILLINOIS CONSTITUTION ARTICLE 1 § 19

§ 19.   No Discrimination against the Handicapped.

All persons with a physical or mental handicap shall be free from discrimination in the sale or rental of property and shall be free from discrimination unrelated to ability in the hiring and promotion practices of any employer.

---

[46] *See, e.g.,* Arkansas, California, Iowa, Maryland, *supra* note 40.

[47] The penalty clause specifies that it relates to those sections of the law dealing with public accommodations and rights of the blind on public thoroughfares.

[48] *Carter v. Gallagher,* 452 F.2d 315 (8th Cir. 1971), *modified on rehearing en banc,* 452 F.2d 327, *cert. denied,* 406 U.S. 950 (1972).

1972 ILLINOIS ATTORNEY GENERAL OPINION 69
No. S-435 (March 24, 1972)

HON. BERNARD L. OLTMAN, State's Attorney, Tazewell County, Pekin, Illinois.

I have your letter of recent date wherein you state:

> Tazewell County has for several years maintained a group hospitalization insurance policy on behalf of its employees. All those persons employed by Tazewell County are eligible for coverage under this policy. The premium for this policy however has increased tremendously and the Insurance Committee of the County Board is seeking a way to reduce the cost of this insurance program.

> Under the plan, elected county officers and their dependents are required to pay for their insurance coverage; but, employees of the county are covered at no cost to them and they can pay a premium and thereby cover the dependent members of their families. One of the methods the committee is considering is to require new employees to submit to and pass a physical examination prior to employment or in lieu thereof waive their rights to coverage under the plan.

> The question for which they desire an answer is whether or not the County Board of Supervisors can in any way curtail or prevent a county officer from employing a person who cannot pass the required physical examination and who refuses to waive his coverage under the insurance plan.

The question of the power of a County Board of Supervisors to control selection of their employees by individual county officers need not be discussed here inasmuch as the action that you contemplate is not permissible, regardless of which county officer might be involved.

Article I, section 19 of the Illinois Constitution of 1970 reads as follows:

> All persons with a physical or mental handicap shall be free from discrimination in the sale or rental of property and shall be free from discrimination unrelated to ability *in the hiring and promotion practices of any employer.* (Emphasis added.)

Discrimination has been defined as "particular privileges on a class arbitrarily selected from a large number of persons, all of whom stand in the same relation to privileges granted and between whom and those not favored no reasonable distinction can be found." *Franchise Motor Freight Association* v. *Seavey,* 196 Cal. 77, 235 P. 1000.

Section 3 of "An Act to prohibit unjust discrimination in the sale or rental of property because of physical or mental handicap, and in employment because of physical or mental handicap unrelated to ability, and providing for penalties" (Ill. Rev. Stat. 1971, ch. 38, par. 65-23) reads, in part:

> *It is an unlawful employment practice for an employer:*
> (1) to refuse to hire, to discharge, or otherwise to discriminate against any individual with respect to his *terms, conditions, or privileges of employment* otherwise lawful, because of such individual's physical or mental handicap, unless it can be shown that the particular handicap prevents the performance of the employment involved; (Emphasis added.)

Included in the "terms" of any employment is the compensation received therefrom. Any employee hospitalization benefits financed by an employer is part of this compensation. To ask any employee to waive coverage under such a policy would be discriminatory as to the terms of employment.

Section 22 of said Act reads, in part, as follows:

> The term "employer" means a person or *governmental unit or officer in this State* having in his or its employ one or more individuals; and any person acting in the interest of an employer, directly or indirectly. (Emphasis added.)

It is, therefore, my opinion that the County Board cannot prevent a county officer from employing a person who cannot pass the required physical examination for group hospitalization insurance and who refuses to waive his coverage under the insurance plan, if the handicap is not related to the ability to perform the employment involved.

NOTES

1.   The Illinois constitutional amendment is the first of its kind, although Texas and other states are considering similar provisions. Florida has a constitutional amendment forbidding discrimination on the basis of physical handicap, see p. 175, above.

2.   Some states have constitutional provisions that, although not specifically addressing discrimination against handicapped individuals, do provide some constitutional status to employment rights. Section 23 of the North Dakota Constitution, for example, provides: "Every citizen of this state shall be free to obtain employment wherever possible, and any person, corporation, or agent thereof, maliciously interfering or hindering in any way, any citizen from obtaining or enjoying employment already obtained, from any other corporation or person, shall be deemed guilty of a misdemeanor." Such provisions remain largely untested in relation to denials of employment to handicapped people.

E.   THE UNITED STATES CONSTITUTION

1.   The Fourteenth Amendment

When state agencies engage in discrimination against handicapped persons in relation to employment, the Fourteenth Amendment's guarantees of "equal protection" and "due process of law" provide likely bases for legal theories to challenge such discrimination.

    a.   Equal Protection.   Much of the equal protection analysis discussed in Chapter 2 in regard to public education (see pp. 75–165) is equally applicable to employment problems. Like the right to equal educational opportunity, we may speak of a right to equal employment opportunities. The Warren Court's two-tiered analysis, the "rational basis" and "compelling state interest" tests (pp. 91–92 above), are again relevant.

    An important factor in determining if the strict scrutiny standard will apply is the question of whether or not there is a fundamental right to public employment. In 1914, the United States Supreme Court declared:

Life, liberty, property and the equal protection of the law, grouped together in the Constitution, are so related that the deprivation of any one of those separate and independent rights may lessen or extinguish the value of the other three. In so far as a man is deprived of the right to labor, his liberty is restricted, his capacity to earn wages and acquire property is lessened, and he is denied the protection which the law affords those who are permitted to work. Liberty means more than freedom from servitude, and the constitutional guarantee is an assurance that the citizen shall be protected in the right to use his powers of mind and body in any lawful calling (*Smith* v. *Texas,* 233 U.S. 630, 636 [1914].)

The following year, the court held that

... the right to work for a living in the common occupations of the community is of the very essence of the personal freedom and opportunity that it was the purpose of [the Fourteenth] Amendment to secure (*Truax* v. *Raich,* 239 U.S. 33, 41 [1915].)

Based upon such reasoning, some courts have held that the right to pursue lawful occupations is a fundamental right and that classifications interfering with this right must be strictly scrutinized: *Sail' er Inn, Inc.* v. *Kirby,* 95 Cal.Rptr. 329, 5 Cal.3d 1, 485 P.2d 529 (1971); *Purifoy* v. *State Board of Education,* 30 Cal.App.3d 197, 106 Cal.Rptr. 201 (1973); see also *Arrington* v. *Massachusetts Bay Transportation Authority,* 306 F.Supp. 1355, 1358 (D.Mass. 1969).

Most courts, however, have ruled that the right to public employment is not fundamental, e.g., *Koelfgen* v. *Jackson,* 355 F.Supp. 243, 250 (D.Minn. 1972); *Whitner* v. *David,* 410 F.2d 24, 30 (9th Cir. 1969). In *Schware* v. *Board of Bar Examiners,* 353 U.S. 232 (1957), the court chose not to employ a strict scrutiny standard in analyzing an employment case.

But whether or not there is a right to employment *per se,* the courts are in agreement that public employment opportunities do fall within the purview of the equal protection clause; i.e., there is a right to equal employment opportunity.

While there may be no constitutional right to public employment as such, there is a constitutional right to be free from unreasonably discriminatory practices with respect to such employment (*Whitner* v. *Davis,* 410 F.2d 24, 30 [9th Cir. 1969]).

The Supreme Court has declared:

We need not pause to consider whether an abstract right to public employment exists. It is sufficient to say that constitutional protection does extend to the public servant whose exclusion ... is patently arbitrary or discriminatory (*Wieman* v. *Updegraff,* 344 U.S. 183, 192 [1952]).

In addition, the task of challenging employment discrimination would be greatly eased if handicapped plaintiffs were found to be members of a "suspect class" (see p. 120, n.3, above).

In spite of the seeming applicability of equal protection analysis to the problem of employment discrimination against handicapped individuals, the cases employing such analysis are few. Both *Heumann* v. *Board of Education of the City of New York* (p. 331, above) and *King-Smith* v. *Aaron* (pp. 326–330 above) involved allegations of denials of equal protection, but neither of these cases reached a decision on the merits.

And a favorable decision on the merits in *Duran* v. *City of Tampa,* (pp. 355–356, below) elicited only a one-sentence mention of equal protection, perhaps unwittingly. One reason for this scarcity of equal protection precedents dealing with employment problems is that the concept of and impetus behind the struggle of handicapped persons for equality in employment have only recently emerged; the battle for equal employment is a relatively new phenomenon. In addition, the need for equal protection analysis has been sidestepped somewhat by the enactment of federal and state antidiscrimination legislation. For these reasons, the potential of equal protection theory in the area of employment practices that discriminate against those with handicaps remains largely untested. For a case in which exclusion of rehabilitated drug addicts from public employment was held to be a violation of equal protection, see *Davis* v. *Bucher,* pp. 416–424, below.

b. Due Process. The Fourteenth Amendment provides that no state shall "deprive any person of life, liberty, or property without due process of law." If a person can show that denial of an employment opportunity by a public agency results in the deprivation of "liberty" or "property," the constitutional requirement of procedural due process attaches and mandates that such a person have an opportunity for notice and a hearing, *Board of Regents* v. *Roth,* 408 U.S. 564, 571 (1972); *Perry* v. *Sindermann,* 408 U.S. 593, 599 (1972).

In regard to property interests in employment, the Supreme Court has declared that such rights may arise from statutory guarantees, tenure arrangements, formal contracts, and from "a clearly implied promise of continued employment," *Board of Regents* v. *Roth, supra,* at 577. On the other hand:

> To have a property interest in a benefit, a person clearly must have more than an abstract need or desire for it. He must have more than a unilateral expectation of it. He must, instead, have a legitimate entitlement to it. It is a purpose of the ancient institution of property to protect those claims upon which people rely in their daily lives, reliance that must not be arbitrarily undermined (*Board of Regents* v. *Roth, supra,* at 577).

So while a handicapped person who is already employed or who has an employment contract may have a property interest in continued employment, a prospective new employee probably does not gain a property interest in employment simply by applying for a job.

Regarding "liberty" interests in employment, the courts have declared:

> The concept of liberty recognizes two particular interests of a public employee: 1) the protection of his good name, reputation, honor and integrity, and 2) his freedom to take advantage of other employment opportunities (*Board of Regents* v. *Roth, supra,* at 573–574, 92 S.Ct. 2701. *Lipp* v. *Board of Education of City of Chicago,* 470 F.2d 802, 805 [7th Cir. 1972]).

So, if the denial of employment opportunities to a handicapped individual occasions either a foreclosure of employment elsewhere or damage to the individual's good name and reputation (as by the imposition of a stigmatizing label), procedural due process rights to notice and a hearing would be mandated.

BEVAN v. N.Y. STATE TCHRS. RETIREMENT SYSTEM

Supreme Court of New York, Special Term, Albany County, 1973
74 Misc.2d 443, 345 N.Y.S.2d 921

HAROLD J. HUGHES, Justice:

This is a motion by plaintiff for a preliminary injunction. Defendants have cross-moved for an order (1) vacating the temporary restraining orders previously granted by Mr. Justice Edward S. Conway; (2) dismissing the complaint for insufficiency pursuant to CPLR 3211 (subd. [a], par. [7]); or alternatively granting summary judgment dismissing the complaint pursuant to CPLR 3211 (subd. [c]). On the return date of the order to show cause, April 6, 1973, this court vacated the temporary restraining orders.

The plaintiff is a public school teacher. He was appointed to the position of elementary school teacher within the city school district of the City of Poughkeepsie in September, 1962 and obtained tenure in September, 1965. Thereafter, in the summer of 1970, plaintiff began experiencing difficulty with his vision and took an extended sick leave effective September, 1970. Plaintiff subsequently became totally blind. He thereafter successfully concluded a rehabilitation program operated by the New York Association for the Blind, which program was designed to help him return to teaching.

In March, 1972, plaintiff advised the school district that he would be returning to his classroom duties in September, 1972. The superintendent of schools requested that plaintiff submit to a medical examination by the school district's medical supervisor. Upon completion of said examination, the medical supervisor concluded that plaintiff was capable of working, with limitations. Plaintiff was advised by letter dated July 14, 1972 from the school district's superintendent of schools that the Board of Education at a meeting held on July 13, 1972 adopted a resolution placing plaintiff on medical disability retirement as of July 1, 1972. In September, 1972, plaintiff reported for his teaching assignment and was advised there was no such assignment. On every school day thereafter, plaintiff has reported for assignment.

On January 22, 1973, plaintiff was examined by Dr. Sydney N. Miller, who stated in a report to the Board of Education that plaintiff should not return to his classroom duties. The recommendation was based solely on the fact of blindness.

Defendant is a member of the New York State Teachers' Retirement System. The New York State Teachers' Retirement Board is vested by virtue of article 11 of the Education Law with the general administrative authority and responsibility for the proper operation of the retirement system. The medical board of the retirement system is a body of three physicians. One of their duties is to review applications for medical disability retirement purposes and to make recommendations thereon (Education Law, § 507, subd. 6).

On February 19, 1973, the Board of Education authorized the submission of an application to the retirement system to effect plaintiff's disability retirement. Pursuant to subdivision 1 of section 511 of the Education Law, members who have obtained the requisite years of service may be retired on account of disability upon the application of the employer, if the retirement board, after a medical examination of the member, shall determine upon the basis of the report of the examining physician or physicians that the member is physically or mentally incapacitated for the performance of duty, that he was incapacitated at the time he ceased teaching and that said member ought to be retired. Plaintiff did not consent to the filing of said application and opposes retirement. On February 19, 1973, the Board of Education terminated plaintiff's sick leave with pay.

The plaintiff received a letter from the retirement system, dated March 2, 1973, advising him that on February 23, 1973 the retirement system had received an application from the school district requesting plaintiff's retirement on account of disability. Plaintiff was advised that the retirement system could make the retirement effective March 25, 1973.

Plaintiff commenced an appeal to the Commissioner of Education, pursuant to section 310 of the Education Law. Plaintiff contended in his petition that the Board of Education was acting in violation of sections 2509 and 3004 of the Education Law in refusing to reinstate him to his former position. Plaintiff asked that the Commissioner order the Board of Education to reinstate him with all benefits, effective September 5, 1972, and that the Board be enjoined from placing plaintiff on medical disability retirement. By decision dated March 5, 1973, the Commissioner of Education ordered that the plaintiff herein be reinstated as a teacher pending a final determination on the matter or until such time as the disability retirement requirements set forth in section 511 of the Education Law have been fully complied with.

Plaintiff's underlying action in the case at bar is for a declaratory judgment and a permanent injunction. He seeks: to have declared unconstitutional sections 503 and 511 and all existing provisions of the Education Law pertaining to the involuntary retirement of teachers; a declaration that the actions of the city school district of the City of Poughkeepsie in refusing to reinstate plaintiff to his tenured teaching position since September, 1973 were a violation of plaintiff's constitutionally protected rights; a permanent injunction enjoining the school district from refusing to reinstate plaintiff to his former teaching position and directing it to remunerate plaintiff with all back pay and other benefits as of the first day of the 1972–73 school year; and, finally, a permanent injunction enjoining the other defendants from further processing the application for disability retirement.

The court first notes that the fact that plaintiff has pursued an administrative appeal to the Commissioner of Education does not deprive this court of jurisdiction under the present circumstances. The underlying issue in the present case involves the constitutionality of a State statute and it is clear that the Commissioner has no power to determine constitutionality.

Since the defendants seek a dismissal of the complaint for legal insufficiency or, in the alternative, summary judgment, the court will go directly to the merits. There is no question but that this plaintiff, a tenured teacher, possesses constitutionally protected interests in "liberty" and "property" within the meaning of the Fourteenth Amendment; specifically plaintiff has an interest in continued employment that is safeguarded by due process (see *Board of Regents* v. *Roth*, 408 U.S. 564, 92 S.Ct. 2701, 33 L.Ed.2d 548; *Perry* v. *Sindermann*, 408 U.S. 593, 92 S.Ct. 2694, 33

L.Ed.2d 570). Before this plaintiff may be deprived of employment, either by dismissal or enforced retirement, procedural due process requires that he first be afforded a hearing (see *Board of Regents* v. *Roth, supra; Perry* v. *Sinderman, supra; Fuentes* v. *Shevin,* 407 U.S. 67, 92 S.Ct. 1983, 32 L.Ed.2d 556). While there are extraordinary situations that justify postponing an opportunity for a hearing, such as when there is a countervailing State interest of overriding significance (see *Boddie* v. *Connecticut,* 401 U.S. 371, 91 S.Ct. 780, 28 L.Ed.2d 113; *Matter of Sanford* v. *Rockefeller,* 40 A.D.2d 82, 337 N.Y.S.2d 688, affd. 32 N.Y.2d 788, 345 N.Y.S.2d 543, 298 N.E.2d 681 [May 3, 1973]), it has not been suggested such a situation exists here. Indeed, plaintiff reported for assignment in September, 1972 and it was not until February 19, 1973 that the Board of Education made formal application for his retirement.

Based on the above decisions, this court holds that insofar as subdivision 1 of section 511 of the Education Law allows for the enforced retirement of a tenured teacher without a prior adversary hearing, it violates the due process clause of the Fourteenth Amendment. (See *Snead* v. *Dept. of Social Services of the City of New York,* 355 F.Supp. 764, decided March 12, 1973.)

Defendants argue that in the present case there is no need for a factual hearing since it is conceded that plaintiff is blind. It is contended that if such a hearing were to be afforded plaintiff, ''it would amount to no more than an inquest on a default.'' With this contention this court cannot agree.

The question to be decided at the hearing will not be whether plaintiff is blind but whether he is physically incapacitated from performing his duties as a teacher. The articles in the appendices to plaintiff's memorandum of law reveal that there are numerous teachers throughout the United States who are both successful and competent, notwithstanding their lack of sight. This court will not rule, as defendants implicitly urge, that blindness per se disqualifies one to teach. Indeed, such a ruling would be directly contrary to the express policy of the Legislature as expressed in section 3004 of the Education Law.

Section 3004, insofar as it pertains to blindness, provides that no regulation established by the Commissioner or by any school district shall disqualify any person, otherwise qualified, from qualifying for a position as a teacher solely by reason of his or her blindness or physical handicap, provided such physical handicap does not interfere with such person's ability to perform teaching duties. While the applicability and construction of this section is not at this time before this court, it might be useful to make some comments thereon. Whether directly applicable or not, the section expresses a strong legislative policy that a teacher shall not be denied a position because of blindness. It is also apparent from a reading of the present section and its predecessor that the words, ''provided such physical handicap does not interfere with such person's ability to perform teaching duties,'' pertain only to a physical handicap other than blindness. In other words, it is premised in the statute itself that blindness per se will not interfere with a person's ability to perform teaching duties.

The case cited by defendants, *Matter of Chavich* v. *Board of Examiners of Bd. of Educ. of City of N.Y.,* 23 A.D.2d 57, 258 N.Y.S.2d 677, affd. 16 N.Y.2d S10. 263 N.Y.S.2d 7, 210 N.E.2d 359, merely holds that section 3004 is not applicable to teachers in the New York City public schools. While the dissenters were not upheld on the issue of applicability, much of what they said may serve as rebuttal to one of the contentions of the defendants herein, that plaintiff will not be able to carry out incidental supervisory functions, or to maintain discipline in the classroom or supervise fire drills or to carry out the dozens of other administrative jobs that fall to the classroom teacher. As the minority there aptly pointed out:

> That view is also untenable because it is based primarily on collateral factors which have no necessary connection with the teaching of music and which are wholly incidental to teaching. For instance, the majority points out that a blind teacher cannot possibly: (1) maintain proper discipline in the classroom or prevent altercations between students, so as to avoid consequent lawsuits against the city; (2) mark the attendance rolls or grade the written test papers; (3) supervise or direct fire drills and proper use of stairways in emergencies; and (4) perform other administrative duties during non-teaching periods.
>
> All this may readily be conceded. But what the majority overlooks is that none of these disciplinary, administrative or clerical duties relates in the slightest degree to the basic qualifications or fitness to teach. These duties are incidental or peripheral; they are wholly unrelated to the essential ability to teach. True, these incidental duties must be performed. But the board, in furtherance of the fundamental policy of the State with respect to the employment of blind teachers otherwise qualified, may easily arrange for their performance by other sighted persons, whether such sighted persons be teachers, clerks or more mature students. Essentially, the situation is simply one of mutual accommodation and adjustment by all concerned.
>
> In any event, the disciplinary, administrative and clerical duties envisaged by the majority present no insoluble problems or insuperable obstacles to a Board of Education willing to meet them and willing to adopt regulations and measures appropriate to the needs of the occasion. Surely, the intelligence and the ingenuity of the members of the Board of Education of the City of New York are equal to the task. (*Matter of Chavich* v. *Board of Examiners of Bd. of Educ. of City of N.Y.*, 23 A.D.2d 57, 67–68, 258 N.Y.S.2d 677, 687, *supra*.)

Since defendants have moved for summary judgment and since there are no issues of fact on plaintiff's causes of action and since this court may grant summary judgment to either party (CPLR 3212, subd. [b]), the court hereby declares that portion of subdivision 1 of section 511 of the Education Law which authorizes the involuntary retirement of a tenured teacher because of alleged physical or mental incapacity upon application of the employer, without a hearing, either before the employer board of education or the retirement board, to be unconstitutional. The court directs that plaintiff be reinstated to his former position and be remunerated with all back pay and other benefits of the first day of the 1972–73 school year. The motion of the plaintiff for a preliminary injunction is denied as moot. The motions of the defendants are denied, all without costs.

NOTE

This decision is an amalgam of traditional procedural due process and the rationale of the *Chavich* dissent. Could the former have prevailed in *Bevan* in the absence of the latter?

GURMANKIN v. COSTANZO

United States Court of Appeals for the Third Circuit, 1977
556 F.2d 184

Before FORMAN, GIBBONS and ROSENN, Circuit Judges.
OPINION OF THE COURT.
GIBBONS, Circuit Judge.

In these appeals we review two injunctive orders entered by the district court in an action charging that the defendants, officials of the Philadelphia School District, discriminated against the plaintiff, Judith Gurmankin, because she is a blind person.[1] Ms. Gurmankin is an English teacher. She holds a Professional Certificate from the Pennsylvania Department of Education as a teacher of Comprehensive English in Pennsylvania Public Schools. In 1969 she attempted to obtain employment in the Philadelphia School District. At that time the District's medical and personnel policy excluded blind teachers from teaching sighted students in the public schools. Applicants who were certified as having a "chronic or acute physical defect," including blindness, were prevented from taking the Philadelphia Teachers Examination. Ms. Gurmankin was examined by the District's Director of Medical Services, and rejected for any position teaching sighted students because of her blindness. Ms. Gurmankin persisted in her attempts to take the examination and with the assistance of counsel at Community Legal Services, Inc., in the spring of 1974 she was admitted, and passed.

When her name was reached on the eligibility list the District offered her several positions, none of which she accepted, because they were not accompanied by an agreement that she would be afforded seniority as of the time she should properly have been admitted to the examination. Ms. Gurmankin filed this suit in November 1974, and on March 31, 1976 the district court ruled in her favor. The court ordered defendants to offer her employment

> as a secondary school English teacher, with seniority rights and all other rights accruing to a secondary school English teacher commencing employment in September, 1970. Specifically, the plaintiff is to have the same rights under the School District's teacher transfer policy as a teacher who commenced employment in September, 1970.

The effect of this injunction was to require her employment, with a September 1970 seniority date. The court reserved decision on class aspects of the litigation and on back pay and attorney's fees.

Both the defendants and Ms. Gurmankin appealed from the injunction. The defendants contend that no order should have been entered. Ms. Gurmankin contends that the court fixed a seniority date later than that to which she was entitled. The defendants attempted unsuccessfully to obtain a stay pending appeal.

Despite the absence of a stay, ten months after the injunction issued Ms. Gurmankin still was not employed by the District as an English teacher. Several offers of employment had been made to her, but she rejected them as not reflecting the seniority awarded her by the court. In January, 1977, she filed a motion to amend the

---

[1] The district opinion is reported. *Gurmankin v. Costanzo*, 411 F.Supp. 982 (E.D.Pa. 1976).

injunction. She contended that the District had offered her only the least attractive schools in the system, while teachers with less seniority were placed in more attractive schools. The court permitted limited discovery on that contention, found it to be meritorious, and concluded:

> The School District's continued refusal over the past ten months to place Ms. Gurmankin in an appropriate position has prevented the court's order from accomplishing its purpose. Moreover, the School District has indicated that it will not make any further offers to the plaintiff unless compelled by court order. This court is under a duty to insure that its orders provide full and adequate relief, and if an order is inadequate, it should be modified accordingly.

It then amended the injunction to provide:

> Within thirty (30) days of the date of this order, the defendants shall provide the plaintiff with a position as an English teacher at one of the six schools designated by plaintiff in Plaintiff's Supplemental Interrogatory, or at some other school acceptable to the plaintiff.

From this order the defendants again appealed, and again unsuccessfully sought a stay. The appeals were consolidated. In each we affirm.

I. The Original Injunction

The defendants contend that the court erred in finding a due process violation in the District's pre-1974 policy of refusing to allow blind persons to take the Philadelphia Teachers Examination. They also contend that an award of seniority is beyond the equitable powers of a federal court. Ms. Gurmankin defends the injunction not only for the constitutional reasons on which the district court relied, but also on equal protection grounds and on a statutory supremacy ground. The statutory supremacy argument refers to § 504 of the Rehabilitation Act of 1973, P.L. 93-112, 87 Stat. 357, 29 U.S.C. § 794:

> [n]o otherwise qualified handicapped individual in the United States, as defined in section 706(6) of this title, shall, solely by reason of his handicap, be excluded from participation in, be denied the benefits of, or be subjected to discrimination under any program or activity receiving Federal financial assistance.

It was apparently in response to this statute that in 1974 the District changed its policy and permitted Ms. Gurmankin to take the examination. If the statutory supremacy claim would suffice to sustain the injunction we would be obliged to rest on it rather than reach the due process ground on which the district court relied. But as that court noted, the Rehabilitation Act of 1973 did not become effective until December, 1973. P.L. 93-112, § 500(a), 29 U.S.C. § 790(a). Ms. Gurmankin concedes that it would not apply to pre-1974 injuries. The same would appear to be true of the later Pennsylvania statutes. The seniority relief afforded by the injunction is designed to remedy pre-1974 discrimination. Thus, that relief requires that we consider the district court's constitutional holding.

Relying on *Cleveland Board of Education* v. *LaFleur,* 414 U.S. 632, 94 S.Ct. 791, 39 L.Ed.2d 52 (1974), the court held that the District policy of preventing blind teachers from teaching sighted students created an irrebuttable presumption that blind persons could not be competent teachers, in violation of due process. In *LaFleur* the Supreme Court ruled that mandatory leaves for pregnant teachers, five months before the birth of their children created an irrebuttable presumption of physical incompetency to teach after the fourth month of pregnancy. The court held that denying pregnant teachers the opportunity to present evidence of continued competency violated due process. The challenge was not to the requirement that teachers be sufficiently healthy for the rigors of the classroom, but to the denial of the opportunity to show that they were. In this case, as well, Gurmankin's complaint is not addressed to the requirement that Philadelphia teachers pass a qualifying examination, which she eventually passed, but rather to the pre-1974 denial of the opportunity to demonstrate her competency. We agree with the district court that *Cleveland Board of Education* v. *LaFleur, supra,* controls.[5] The refusals by the District to permit her to take the examination violated due process by subjecting Ms. Gurmankin to an irrebuttable presumption that her blindness made her incompetent to teach sighted students.

In *LaFleur,* of course, the court dealt with employed teachers, and thus with some continued expectation of employment based on state law. Ms. Gurmankin had no contract of employment, but she had an expectation, based on state law, of being admitted to the qualifying examination. In July 1970 she was issued a Professional Certificate, No. 190-34-3597, by the Pennsylvania Department of Education, certifying her as a qualified teacher of Comprehensive English. Under the rules of the Philadelphia School District this certificate was the only requirement for entrance to the examination. She was, by virtue of the irrebuttable presumption of incompetency, deprived of the opportunity to take it between 1970 and 1974. The right to take the examination is a right arising under state law, and its deprivation in an arbitrary manner violated due process.

---

[5]Appellant School District relies on *Weinberger* v. *Salfi,* 422 U.S. 749, 95 S.Ct. 2457, 45 L.Ed.2d 522 (1975), contending that it overrules *LaFleur. Weinberger* v. *Salfi* rejected an "irrebuttable presumption" attack on the duration-of-relationship requirements of the Social Security Act, 42 U.S.C. §§ 416(c)(5) and (e)(2). However, in that case the Court was able to rely on the prior authority of *Flemming* v. *Nestor,* 363 U.S. 603, 611, 80 S.Ct. 1367, 1373, 4 L.Ed.2d 1435 (1960), which established a different due process standard for evaluating classification under the Social Security Act:

". . . we must recognize that the Due Process Clause can be thought to interpose a bar only if the statute manifests a patently arbitrary classification, utterly lacking in rational justification."

Salfi is distinguishable because it is a government benefits case. While this is not a distinction we would draw if writing on a clean slate, it is plainly the one drawn by the Supreme Court. *Flemming* v. *Nestor* was decided fourteen years before *LaFleur.* The Supreme Court evidently was content that *Flemming* and *LaFleur* coexist, even as recently as *Salfi.* There, Justice Rehnquist wrote, after discussing *Flemming* v. *Nestor* and several other "benefits" cases (422 U.S. at 768–770, 95 S.Ct. 2457):

"These cases quite plainly lay down the governing principle for disposing of constitutional challenges . . . *in this type of social welfare legislation.*" *Id.* at 770, 95 S.Ct. at 2469 (emphasis added).

In distinguishing *Salfi* from the *LaFleur* line, Justice Rehnquist noted that in *Salfi:*

". . . appell[ees] are completely free to present evidence that they meet the specified requirements; failing in this effort, their only constitutional claim is that the test they cannot meet is not so rationally related to a legitimate legislative objective that it can be used to deprive them of benefits available to those who do satisfy that test." *Id.* at 772, 95 S.Ct. at 2470.

The very point of this case is that denying Gurmankin the *opportunity* to take a qualifying exam, the defendants deprived her of the opportunity to present evidence of her qualifications. This is not a case challenging the competency requirements for teachers. It challenges the deprivation of the right to present evidence of competency. It is quite different from *Salfi,* and the district court was correct to regard it as controlled by *LaFleur.*

The District urges that even if we agree that there was a due process violation, the trial court lacked the power to cure it by the award of rightful place seniority. It distinguishes cases such as *Franks* v. *Bowman Transp. Co.*, 424 U.S. 747, 96 S.Ct. 1251, 47 L.Ed.2d 444 (1976) and *United States* v. *Int'l Union of Elevator Constructors,* 538 F.2d 1012 (3d Cir. 1976) as confined solely to remedies for violations of Title VII of the Civil Rights Act of 1964. 42 U.S.C. § 2000e *et seq.* But the language of Title VII in § 706(g), 42 U.S.C. § 2000e-5(g), on which the courts have relied in affording seniority relief is merely ". . . any other equitable relief as the court deems appropriate.'' There is no distinction in the law of equitable remedies between suits brought under Title VII and suits brought in reliance on 42 U.S.C. § 1983, or directly on the fourteenth amendment.

> [W]here federally protected rights have been invaded, it has been the rule from the beginning that courts will be alert to adjust their remedies so as to grant the necessary relief.

Bell v. *Hood,* 327 U.S. 678, 684, 66 S.Ct. 773, 777, 90 L.Ed. 939 (1946); *Bivens* v. *Six Unknown Federal Narcotics Agents,* 403 U.S. 388, 392, 91 S.Ct. 1999, 29 L.Ed.2d 619 (1971). The equitable relief of an award of a retroactive seniority date was, on the record before us, entirely appropriate.

Because the district court's due process analysis was necessary to the decision and adequately sustains the injunction there is no reason for us to address Ms. Gurmankin's equal protection contentions. For the same reason we need not consider whether those contentions should, as the School District urges, be rejected on the authority of *Mass. Bd. of Retirement* v. *Murgia,* 427 U.S. 307, 96 S.Ct. 2562, 49 L.Ed.2d 520 (1976) (*per curiam*). Nor do we have any occasion in this case to determine whether § 504 of the Rehabilitation Act of 1973 confers affirmative rights enforceable in private lawsuits. Courts which have considered that question have noted the similarity of language between § 504 and § 601 of the Civil Rights Act of 1964, 42 U.S.C. § 2000d. The latter statute was construed in *Lau* v. *Nichols,* 414 U.S. 563, 94 S.Ct. 786, 39 L.Ed.2d 1 (1974) to imply a private cause of action. *See Lloyd et al.* v. *Regional Transportation Authority and Chicago Transit Authority,* 548 F.2d 1277, 1280-1281 (7th Cir. filed Jan. 18, 1977), and cases therein cited, holding, on the authority of *Lau* v. *Nichols, supra,* that a private cause of action in favor of the handicapped is implied from § 504. The amici, The American Coalition of Citizens with Disabilities, Inc., The American Council of the Blind, The National Association of Blind Teachers, and the Counsel for Handicapped People, urge that this is an appropriate cause in which to adopt that position. We conclude that the question is not properly before us since the disputed issue, seniority, is unaffected by § 504.

II. Ms. Gurmankin's Appeal

The District Court fixed Ms. Gurmankin's seniority date as September, 1970. In her cross appeal she contends that she should have been awarded a seniority date of June, 1968, when she graduated from college. We find no error. The court found that she first sought a Philadelphia employment opportunity in 1969, and that if she had then been admitted to the examination, she would have been offered suitable employment by September, 1970. These findings are not clearly erroneous.

III.   The Supplemental Order

To support her contention that job offers made to her following the March 31, 1976 injunction were not in compliance with the injunction's seniority provisions, Ms. Gurmankin sought discovery of all secondary school English teachers hired from 1970 to 1977 and a list of the schools at which they are now teaching. The School District resisted discovery and moved for a protective order. The court ruled that

> [e]vidence that teachers hired since 1970 have managed to obtain positions at more desirable schools might indicate that the offers that have been made to the plaintiff have not given her the same rights as a teacher who commenced teaching in September, 1970. Thus, the plaintiff should be able to obtain some information on this subject. However, in light of the School District's representation that the plaintiff's request is burdensome and possibly could not be complied with in less than a year, we believe that the plaintiff can obtain useful information through a more narrow request. Consequently, at this time we will require the School District to provide the following information for any six schools to be selected by the plaintiff: (1) Are there any English teachers who were hired by the School District in or after 1970 presently assigned to that school? (2) If so, how and when were those teachers assigned to that school? This information should indicate whether recently hired teachers have been able to transfer to more desirable schools, and the School District should be able to provide the information without having to check an unnecessarily large number of personnel files.

When the limited discovery was completed it disclosed that numerous persons hired after September, 1970 were teaching English at the six high schools selected by the plaintiff as more attractive, although Ms. Gurmankin was not offered a position in any of the six. The court concluded that the School District's refusal over ten months to place Ms. Gurmankin in an appropriate position commensurate with her September, 1970, seniority date had prevented the order from accomplishing its purpose, and entered the supplemental order quoted above.

The School District objects to that order because its implementation may require that some other teacher be "bumped." It made no showing by affidavit or testimony that in any of the six specific schools to which the supplemental order applies any "bumping" will occur. Nor has there been any showing that any teacher who may be "bumped" was placed in the position he or she occupies prior to the entry of the March 31, 1976 injunction. Certainly the School Board cannot be heard to claim equities of third parties, particularly when any such equities were created by its disobedience of the court's order. Moreover, even if the original order, by giving Ms. Gurmankin a competitive seniority date of September, 1970, put her in a position to bid for a more desirable school and "bump" teachers hired after that date (on this record a matter of speculation), it is settled that a court of equity has discretion to make such an order in a discrimination case. *Franks* v. *Bowman Transp. Co., Inc., supra; United States* v. *Int'l Union of Elevator Constructors, supra.* The School District's objections to the supplemental order are in essence the same objections it makes to the March 31, 1976 injunction. We reject them for the same reasons.

Conclusion

The orders appealed from will be affirmed.

Costs taxed in favor of appellee Gurmankin in Nos. 76-1730 and 77-1273. Costs taxed in favor of the appellees in No. 76-2297.

NOTES

1. The "irrebuttable presumption" analysis employed in *Gurmankin* is an old legal doctrine which has recently undergone something of a rebirth. In the 1920s and 1930s, several tax statutes were struck down by the United States Supreme Court on the ground that they contained "conclusive presumptions" in violation of the due process clause, *Heiner* v. *Donnan*, 285 U.S. 312 (1932); *Schlesinger* v. *Wisconsin*, 270 U.S. 230 (1926); *Hoeper* v. *Tax Comm'n*, 284 U.S. 206 (1931).

> [A] statute creating a presumption which operates to deny a fair opportunity to rebut it violates the due process clause of the Fourteenth Amendment (*Heiner* v. *Donnan, supra*, at 285 U.S. 329).

After the 1930s the concept of "irrebuttable presumption" fell into disuse, and it has only returned to prominence in the present decade, in such cases as *Bell* v. *Burson*, 402 U.S. 535 (1971); *Stanley* v. *Illinois*, 405 U.S. 645 (1972); *Vlandis* v. *Kline*, 412 U.S. 441 (1973); *United States Department of Agriculture* v. *Murry*, 413 U.S. 508 (1973); and *Cleveland Board of Education* v. *LaFleur*, 414 U.S. 632 (1974).

The renaissance of the doctrine has been criticized as a return to the discarded concept of substantive due process, *Vlandis* v. *Kline*, 412 U.S. 441, 467-468 (1973) (Rehnquist, J., dissenting), and as equal protection analysis under the guise of due process, Note, "The Irrebuttable Presumption Doctrine in the Supreme Court," 87 *Harv. L. Rev.* 1534, 1534-1536 (1974). The *Weinberger* v. *Salfi* decision discussed in *Gurmankin* may indicate a new shying away from irrebuttable presumption analysis. In his dissenting opinion in *Salfi*, Justice Brennan suggested that the *Salfi* decision "is flatly contrary to several recent decisions," at 422 U.S. 802.

It may be, however, that the doctrine of "irrebuttable presumptions" is a justifiable extension of traditional due process theory. Since the remedy delineated by the Supreme Court in irrebuttable presumption cases is simply the provision of a hearing for the aggrieved party (see Note, "The Irrebuttable Presumption Doctrine in the Supreme Court," *supra*, at 1536), many such decisions could have reached the same results through procedural due process analysis; i.e., a party is being denied liberty or property, so the due process clause mandates an opportunity for a hearing. The limitation upon such analysis is that there must be a clear showing of deprivation of a liberty or property interest; traditionally, if a person applies for and is denied some public benefit (such as food stamps, *United States Department of Agriculture* v. *Murry, supra*, or public employment, *Gurmankin* v. *Costanzo*), there is generally no deprivation of liberty or property.

Perhaps through its irrebuttable presumption analysis, the Supreme Court is suggesting that some public benefits are so important in our society that they may not be denied in the absence of a hearing, whether or not the denial of the public benefit interferes with a liberty or property interest in the traditional sense, especially where the difficulty involved in providing an individualized determination is clearly out-weighed by the importance of the benefit at stake. Such reasoning could be used to reconcile the *Salfi* ruling with the earlier irrebuttable presumption cases. *Salfi* could be read to mean that the importance of social security benefits is not sufficiently great to outweigh the administrative difficulty involved in providing hearings to determine whether the marriages of social security applicants were entered into collusively, while in the other irrebuttable presumption cases, the difficulty of providing individual hear-ings was not substantial enough to counterbalance the importance of the benefit in-volved. This is precisely the type of analysis employed by the trial court in *Gurmankin* where the court declared:

> [T]he importance of the plaintiff's interest and the ease with which a hearing can be provided distinguish this case from most other challenges to legislative classifications, and make this an appropriate case for applying irrebuttable presumption analysis (At 411 F.Supp. 992).

2.   The results in *Gurmankin* should be contrasted with *Coleman* v. *Darden*, 13 E.P.D. 6788 (D.Colo. 1977) where a blind law school graduate asserted an irrebuttable presumption claim under the Fifth Amendment due process clause after being denied a job as a research assistant with (ironically) the U.S. Equal Employment Opportunity Commission. The court denied this claim and stated:

> It is not arbitrary or capricious for a government agency to establish physical require-ments which are job related and there can be no question here that sufficient visual acuity to enable the employee to read has a direct relationship to the job of assisting lawyers in the preparation of evidence and data in discrimination investigations.

ADDITIONAL READING

"The Irrebuttable Presumption Doctrine in the Supreme Court," 87 *Har. L. Rev.* 1534 (1974).
"Irrebuttable Presumptions: An Illusory Analysis," 27 *Stan. L. Rev.* 449 (1975).
"Irrebuttable Presumptions as an Alternative to Strict Scrutiny: From *Rodriguez* to *LaFleur*," 62 *Geo. L. J.* 1173 (1974).

DURAN v. CITY OF TAMPA

United States District Court for the Middle District of Florida, Tampa Division, 1977
430 F.Supp. 75

KRENTZMAN, District Judge.

Background

The Court has for consideration the plaintiff's motion for preliminary injunc-tion. The Court has jurisdiction pursuant to 28 U.S.C. §§ 1331(a) and 1343(3). Two hearings were held on this matter and on both occasions the Court received testimony. The basis of the plaintiff's complaint alleges that the defendants violated both the plaintiff's fourteenth amendment due process rights and his rights pursuant to 29 U.S.C. §§ 793 and 794 by failing to hire him for the position of policeman because of his history of epilepsy.

Facts

In April, 1975, the plaintiff, who is a twenty-eight year old male, applied to the defendant, City of Tampa, for the position of policeman. Soon thereafter the City administered both a written and oral examination to the plaintiff and also gave him a polygraph test. The plaintiff satisfactorily completed all of the defendant's examinations. In October, 1975, the City placed the plaintiff's name on an eligibility list for the position of policeman. On December 19, 1975, the plaintiff was requested by the City to appear for a physical examination. Later the same day the defendant contacted the plaintiff and informed him that a physical examination would not be necessary because his past history of epilepsy would automatically exclude him from service as a policeman. The plaintiff attempted through several avenues to have the defendants reverse its decision but to no avail. The plaintiff filed this suit on August 26, 1976.

The plaintiff's history of epilepsy consisted of four episodes of grand mal seizures in 1958 and several petit mal seizures or blank staring episodes during 1959. The plaintiff has not experienced any seizures of either variety since 1959 and discontinued any medication related to epilepsy in July, 1966.

At the hearings the plaintiff called two expert witnesses both of whom were physicians who specialize in neurological disorders and both of whom had personally examined the plaintiff and his medical history. The unrebutted testimony of both physicians was that the plaintiff had a history of epilepsy as a child which he had outgrown and was at present perfectly able to serve from a medical perspective as a policeman. The testimony also indicated Mr. Duran's likelihood of having a seizure in the future was equal to that of any person in the general population (i.e., the plaintiff's proclivity for having seizures was in no way increased by his past history of epilepsy). Both physicians concluded that Mr. Duran could no longer be considered an epileptic and he suffered no continuing effects from his childhood experiences with seizures.

The plaintiff also called Marshall B. Jesse, the deputy personnel director for the City of Tampa. Mr. Jesse testified that the City of Tampa Civil Service Board Medical Standards automatically excluded an applicant for a Group I position (firefighter or policeman) if he or she had a history of epilepsy. Mr. Jesse also stated that the medical standards used by the Civil Service Board had been designed in 1952 and had not undergone substantial review since 1966. The review in 1966 was by the City's retirement board which determined disabilities relating to pensions and not qualifications for persons who were applying for new positions.

The defendant presented only one witness, Dr. Harold Sutker, the City of Tampa Physician. Dr. Sutker testified that he had not examined the plaintiff and to his knowledge no other City physician had done so.

Motion for Preliminary Injunction

In order for the Court to grant a preliminary injunction four essential prerequisites must be proved:

1. A substantial likelihood the plaintiff will prevail on the merits.
2. The threatened injury to the plaintiff outweighs the threatened harm the injunction may do to the defendant.

3. Granting the preliminary injunction will not disserve the public interest.
4. A substantial threat that the plaintiff will suffer irreparable harm if the injunction is
    not granted.

Morgan v. *Fletcher,* 518 F.2d 236, 239 (5th Cir. 1975).

Element 1: The plaintiff's complaint alleges the defendants have violated the
plaintiff's fourteenth amendment equal protection and due process rights, his rights
pursuant to 29 U.S.C. §§ 793 and 794 and various Florida Statutes. A thorough
analysis of the sparse case law in this area indicates that the plaintiff does have a
substantial likelihood he will prevail on the merits of at least two of the grounds
asserted.

The Supreme Court's analysis in *Cleveland Board of Education* v. *LaFleur,*
414 U.S. 632, 94 S.Ct. 791, 39 L.Ed.2d 52 (1974) can readily be applied to the
plaintiff's case. In *LaFleur* the Court found the mandatory maternity leave policy
under which a pregnant teacher in the Cleveland school system was forced to take
maternity leave without pay at a period five months prior to delivery was a violation of
her due process rights. The School Board in *LaFleur* argued that since "at least some
teachers become physically incapable of adequately performing certain of their duties
during the latter part of pregnancy," the mandatory maternity leave policy assured a
physically capable instructor in the classroom and protected the health of the mother
and her unborn child. *Id.* at 641, 94 S.Ct. at 797. The Court rejected such an argument
and found that the mandatory cutoff dates established an irrebuttable presumption about
the teacher's competence during pregnancy and could not pass muster under the due
process clause.

In *Stanley* v. *Illinois,* 405 U.S. 645, 92 S.Ct. 1208, 31 L.Ed.2d 551 (1972) the
Supreme Court was presented with a situation in which a state statute established a
similar irrebuttable presumption. In *Stanley* an Illinois law set forth an irrebuttable
determination that unmarried fathers were unsuitable and neglectful parents. The Supreme Court found the Illinois statute which promoted efficient and certain determination of guardianship issues was violative of the due process clause. The Court in
Stanley found:

> Procedure by presumption is always cheaper and easier than individualized determina-
> tion. But when, as here, the procedure forecloses the determination of issues of com-
> petence and care, when it specially disdains present realities in deference to past
> formalities, it needlessly risks running roughshod over important interests of both the
> parent and the child. It therefore cannot stand. *Id.* at 656-7, 92 S.Ct. at 1215.

The City of Tampa Civil Service Board's Medical Standards lists as the principal objective of the standards to "select candidates for City employment who are
physically fit and who can reasonably be expected to remain so." Given this noble
purpose, the Board promulgated Standard K(4)(a) which states, "Not Acceptable for
Group I, Epilepsy." The Board has further interpreted Standard K(4)(a) to automatically exclude from employment an applicant with a history of epilepsy even prior to
medical examination. Thus, the Medical Standards have created an irrebuttable presumption to exclude all individuals from employment who have suffered from
epilepsy.

The Court is of the opinion that the Medical Standards sweep too broadly and include within their ambit those individuals like the plaintiff, whose history of epilepsy in no way infringes upon their present ability to perform the duties and tasks required by the position to which they have applied. Thus, the Court is of the opinion the absolute presumption established by Standard K(4)(a) as applied to the plaintiff is violative of his due process rights. At minimum, the due process clause mandates that the defendants provide the plaintiff with an individual determination of his medical status. Accordingly, it is the judgment of the Court that the plaintiff has a substantial likelihood of prevailing on the merits of his due process claim.

[The discussion of plaintiff's claim under 29 U.S.C. § 794 is omitted here; see pp. 410–411 below.]

Elements 2 and 3: The Court will deal with these two elements together because of their intimate interrelationship in the context of this case. In light of the fact that no evidence was adduced which indicated the plaintiff had an increased likelihood of seizures or that his past history of epilepsy would present any future restrictions on his employment as a policeman, the Court is convinced the threatened and existing injury to the plaintiff far outweighs any threatened harm the injunction may do to the defendants. The Court is also certain the public interest is not disserved by injunctions which ferret out discrimination against individuals whose past handicap continues to affect their present ability to find and retain employment.

As in the other discrimination contexts, the Court is especially predisposed against irrebuttable presumptions which are inextricably intertwined with prerequisites of public employment and which are without basis in fact. This is especially true when practical and inexpensive alternatives can facilitate the elimination of such discrimination. The public interest demands that all individuals capable of performing a particular task be placed on an equal footing in acquiring such positions, and society is indeed diminished when the valuable contributions of such individuals are not put to good use.

Element 4: The final prerequisite which the plaintiff must prove is that irreparable injury will result from the denial of a preliminary injunction. In the instant case, the plaintiff has not shown such irreparable injury. A mere loss of income or damage of reputation would fall short of the type of irreparable injury upon which a preliminary injunction must be predicated. *Sampson* v. *Murray,* 415 U.S. 61, 91, 94 S.Ct. 937, 39 L.Ed.2d 166; *Morgan* v. *Fletcher,* 518 F.2d 236 (5th Cir. 1975); *Virginia Petroleum Jobbers Assn.* v. *Federal Power Commission,* 104 U.S.App.D.C. 106, 259 F.2d 921 (1958). The Court in *Virginia Petroleum Jobbers* stated, "The possibility that adequate compensatory or other corrective relief will be available at a latter date, in the ordinary course of litigation, weighs heavily against a claim of irreparable harm." In light of the remedies which are available to fully assist the plaintiff at the completion of this litigation and because of the possibility of prejudice and harm to the defendant prior to full hearing, the Court is of the opinion the plaintiff has not shown the requisite irreparable injury. Also of significance to the Court in its determination is the fact that an almost immediate trial of these issues is anticipated. Accordingly, it is ORDERED:

1. The plaintiff's motion for preliminary injunction is DENIED.
2. The defendants' motion to dismiss, on all the asserted grounds, is DENIED consistent with this Court's statements at hearing.

3. The Clerk of the Court is directed to schedule this case for trial on the Court's April trial calendar.
4. Both parties are directed to file a memorandum of law addressed to whether the defendant has a right to a jury trial on the issues presented.

DURAN V. CITY OF TAMPA

United States District Court for the Middle District of Florida, Tampa Division, 1978
451 F.Supp. 954

KRENTZMAN, District Judge.

Plaintiff applied with the City of Tampa for the position of policeman in April, 1975. He passed a written and oral examination and a polygraph test. His name was placed on an eligibility list in October, 1975. On December 19, 1975 he was directed to appear for a physical examination, the last prerequisite to employment. Before he was able to do so he was advised that he would not be employed because of the statement in his application concerning his childhood history of epilepsy.

On August 24, 1976 this suit was filed alleging violation of plaintiff's fourteenth amendment due process rights and his rights pursuant to 29 U.S.C., §§ 793 and 794, the Rehabilitation Act of 1973. The plaintiff sought declaratory, preliminary and permanent injunctive relief, and award of lost pay, allowances and attorney's fees.

After hearing on plaintiff's motion for preliminary injunction the Court found that plaintiff had a substantial likelihood of prevailing on the merits but denied preliminary relief on the ground that plaintiff had not proved the irreparable injury requisite thereto. Memorandum Opinion and Order, March 15, 1977. *Duran* v. *City of Tampa,* 430 F.Supp. 75 (M.D.Fla. 1977).

Thereafter, at final hearing the plaintiff relied on the evidence produced at the preliminary injunction hearing. See Rule 65(a)(2) Fed.R.Civ.P. The defendant presented one additional witness, Deputy Police Chief Jim Diamond. Diamond testified that there were often times when policemen experienced considerable stress because of abnormal working hours and the nature of the job. The Diamond testimony in no way refutes or reduces the medical evidence presented at the preliminary injunction hearing. Thus, the Court is convinced that the defendant City of Tampa has violated the plaintiff's equal protection rights and his rights under the Rehabilitation Act of 1973 by refusing to hire him because of his childhood experience with epilepsy.

Upon consideration, it is ORDERED:

1. The defendant City of Tampa is directed to provide a physical examination for the plaintiff on or before July 15, 1978. The defendant is directed not to consider the plaintiff's history of epilepsy as a disqualifying medical condition.
2. If the plaintiff successfully passes his medical examination, the defendant is directed to employ the plaintiff as a policeman on or before August 1, 1978.
3. The defendant City of Tampa is directed to compensate the plaintiff through an award of back pay for the period December 19, 1975 through August 1, 1978, less the amount plaintiff has earned in the same period. The plaintiff is directed to supply the Court within ten (10) days of the date of this order with information regarding his earned income during the relevant period. The defendant is directed to supply the Court within ten days of the date of this order with information

regarding the compensation of policemen during the relevant period. The information regarding compensation should include, but is not limited to, base pay, normal pay raises, insurance, health, and pension benefits.

4. The defendant City of Tampa is directed to award the plaintiff seniority rights as if he were employed as of December 19, 1975.

5. The plaintiff's counsel are entitled to a reasonable attorneys' fee for the representation they have rendered to the plaintiff. Plaintiff's counsel are directed to file within ten (10) days of the date of this order affidavits relative to their fees. *See Johnson* v. *Georgia Highway Express,* 488 F.2d 714, 717-9 (5th Cir. 1974) [twelve criteria for attorneys' fees]. The defendant shall have ten days thereafter to respond to the plaintiff's affidavits.

6. The Court will direct the entry of final judgment after consideration of the questions of back pay compensation and attorneys' fees.

IT IS SO ORDERED at Tampa, Florida this 15th day of June, 1978.

NOTES

1. The *Duran* holding is particularly forceful in light of the fact that it involved the police force, an agency of government service that is frequently permitted extraordinary discretion in its rulemaking in the interest of public safety.

2. The preliminary injunction opinion dealt with plaintiff's due process (irrebuttable presumption) and Rehabilitation Act claims. The second paragraph of the subsequent order mentioned these same two claims. Unexpectedly, however, the fourth paragraph of that order ruled that the plaintiff had successfully proved his *equal protection* and Rehabilitation Act charges, and makes no mention of due process claims nor the irrebuttable presumption theory. Did the court change legal theory horses in midstream, or was this more likely an inadvertent clerical error?

2. The Thirteenth Amendment

The Thirteenth Amendment provides:

> §1   Neither slavery nor involuntary servitude, except as a punishment for crime whereof the party shall have been duly convicted, shall exist within the United States, or any place subject to their jurisdiction.
> §2   Congress shall have power to enforce this article by appropriate legislation.

a.   Scope of the Amendment.   While liberation of black slaves in post–Civil War America was the primary goal in the ratification of the Thirteenth Amendment, the scope of the amendment is not limited to blacks. There is historical evidence that supporters of the Thirteenth Amendment expected it to address the plight of oppressed whites as well:

> The whites considered in need of such national protection were the poor white Southerner, "impoverished, debased, dishonored by the system that makes toil a badge of disgrace," and the loyal southern whites, "who have been reduced from men almost to chattels because of their fidelity to our flag, to our constitution, and to this country" (Cummings, E., "Civil Rights—Protection Under the Thirteenth Amendment—Housing

Discrimination," 20 *Case Western Reserve L. Rev.* 448, 458, n. 70 [1969], quoting tenBroek, J., *The Antislavery Origins of the Fourteenth Amendment* 146, 162 [1951]).

Hence, the courts have not construed the Thirteenth Amendment to be merely a racial provision:

> While the immediate concern was with African slavery, the Amendment was not limited to that. It was a charter of universal civil freedom for all persons, of whatever race, color or estate, under the flag (*Bailey* v. *Alabama,* 219 U.S. 219, 240-241 [1911]).
>
> While the inciting cause of the Amendment was the emancipation of the colored race, yet it is not an attempt to commit that race to the care of the Nation. It is the denunciation of a condition and not a declaration in favor of a particular people. It reaches every race and every individual, and if in any respect it commits one race to the Nation it commits every race and every individual thereof. Slavery or involuntary servitude of the Chinese, of the Italian, of the Anglo-Saxon are as much within its compass as slavery or involuntary servitude of the African. Of this Amendment it was said by Mr. Justice Miller in *Slaughter House Cases,* 16 Wall. 36, 69, "Its two short sections seem hardly to admit of construction." And again: "To withdraw the mind from the contemplation of this grand yet simple declaration of the personal freedom of all the human race within the jurisdiction of this Government . . . requires an effort, to say the least of it" (*Hodges* v. *United States,* 203 U.S. 1, 16-17 [1906], overruled on other grounds, *Jones* v. *Alfred H. Mayer Co.,* 392 U.S. 409, 441 n. 78 [1968]).

Numerous cases have applied the Thirteenth Amendment to situations not involving the issue of race: e.g., *United States* v. *Reynolds,* 235 U.S. 133 (1914); *Clyatt* v. *United States,* 197 U.S. 207 (1905); *Taylor* v. *Georgia,* 315 U.S. 25 (1942); *Bailey* v. *Alabama, supra; Johnston* v. *Ciccone,* 260 F.Supp. 553 (W.D.Mo. 1966); *Tyler* v. *Harris,* 226 F.Supp. 852 (W.D.Mo. 1964); *Ex parte Lloyd,* 13 F.Supp. 1005 (E.D.Ky. 1936); and *Stone* v. *City of Paducah,* 120 Ky. 322, 86 S.W. 531, 533 (1905).

The Thirteenth Amendment is also broad in that it is not limited to "state action," but applies to the acts of private citizens as well.

> This amendment denounces a status or condition, irrespective of the manner or authority by which it is created. The prohibitions of the Fourteenth and Fifteenth Amendments are largely upon the acts of the States, but the Thirteenth Amendment names no party or authority, but simply forbids slavery and involuntary servitude. . . (*Clyatt* v. *United States, supra,* at 197 U.S. 216).

The Court has declared further:

> As its text reveals, the Thirteenth Amendment "is not a mere prohibition of state laws establishing or upholding slavery, but an absolute declaration that slavery or involuntary servitude shall not exist in any part of the United States." Civil Rights Cases, 109 U.S. 3, 20, 3 S. Ct. 18, 28, 27 L.Ed. 835. It has never been doubted, therefore, "that the power vested in Congress to enforce the article by appropriate legislation," *ibid.,* includes the power to enact laws "direct and primary, operating upon the acts of individuals, whether sanctioned by state legislation or not." *Id.,* at 23, 3 S.Ct., at 30 (*Jones* v. *Alfred H. Mayer Co., supra,* at 392 U.S. 438).

A third way in which the Thirteenth Amendment is very broad in scope is that it is both self-executing and yet authorizes additional Congressional action:

This Amendment, as well as the Fourteenth, is undoubtedly self-executing without any ancillary legislation, so far as its terms are applicable to any existing state of circumstances. By its own unaided force and effect it abolished slavery, and established universal freedom. Still, legislation may be necessary and proper to meet all the various cases and circumstances to be affected by it, and to prescribe proper modes of redress for its violation in letter or spirit. And such legislation may be primary and direct in its character; for the amendment is not a mere prohibition of state laws establishing or upholding slavery, but an absolute declaration that slavery or involuntary servitude shall not exist in any part of the United States (*Clyatt* v. *United States, supra,* at 197 U.S. 216-217; Civil Rights Cases, 109 U.S. 3, 20 [1883]).

Or, more succinctly:

While the Amendment was self-executing, so far as its terms were applicable to any existing condition, Congress was authorized to secure its complete enforcement by appropriate legislation (*Bailey* v. *Alabama, supra,* at 219 U.S. 241).

For a discussion of the applicability of legislation enacted by Congress to enforce the Thirteenth Amendment see section 4, pp. 436–438 below.

b. Effect of the Amendment. The direct impact of the Thirteenth Amendment is straightforward; it "forbids slavery and involuntary servitude" (*Clyatt* v. *United States, supra,* at 197 U.S. 216). The terms "slavery" and "involuntary servitude" are difficult to define with particularity, but the Supreme Court has explained the general tenor of their meaning:

Slavery implies involuntary servitude—a state of bondage; the ownership of mankind as a chattel, or at least the control of the labor and services of one man for the benefit of another, and the absence of a legal right to the disposal of his own person, property and services. This amendment was said in the *Slaughter House Cases,* 16 Wall. 36, to have been intended primarily to abolish slavery, as it had been previously known in this country, and that it equally forbade Mexican peonage or the Chinese coolie trade, when they amounted to slavery or involuntary servitude, and that the use of the word "servitude" was intended to prohibit the use of all forms of involuntary slavery, of whatever class or name (*Clyatt* v. *United States, supra,* at 197 U.S. 218).

And further:

The words involuntary servitude have a "larger meaning than slavery." "It was very well understood that in the form of apprenticeship for long terms, as it had been practiced in the West India Islands, on the abolition of slavery by the English government, or by reducing the slaves to the condition of serfs attached to the plantation, the purpose of the article might have been evaded, if only the word slavery had been used." *Slaughter House Cases,* 16 Wall. p. 69. The plain intention was to abolish slavery of whatever name and form and all its badges and incidents; to render impossible any state of bondage; to make labor free, by prohibiting that control by which the personal service of one man is disposed of or coerced for another's benefit which is the essence of involuntary servitude (*Bailey* v. *Alabama, supra,* at 219 U.S. 241).

In regard to handicapped persons, therefore, it seems clear that the Thirteenth Amendment forbids any type of forced labor, state of bondage, or other kind of involuntary servitude. Like African slavery, Mexican peonage, the Chinese coolie trade, West Indian "apprenticeship" and plantation serfdom, the coerced labor of handicapped individuals is prohibited by the Amendment. Mandatory, unpaid labor by residents of mental health facilities quickly comes to mind as a close analog of traditional slavery, and would clearly seem to fall within the proscription of the Amendment.

Perhaps as a vestige of the self-supporting "farm colony" concept of residential facilities,[1] the residents of state institutions have frequently been viewed as an available pool of labor for tasks to be performed at or by the institution. The types of labor required of residents have ranged across a wide spectrum of purposes, degrees of difficulty, and expenditures of time: from simple, personal housekeeping chores, such as making one's bed or tidying one's room, to 40 hours or more of work in the institution's laundry or in landscaping, sanitation, and other maintenance jobs. In many instances, institutions have taken in commercial work to be performed by the inmates at a profit to the institution. Payment for the resident's labor is often only nominal, or paid in "tokens," which must be redeemed for products or services at the institution; in many cases, residents receive no payment at all for their labor.

The legal sufficiency of Thirteenth Amendment challenges to such practices has been upheld in several cases: *Jobson* v. *Henne,* 355 F.2d 129 (2d Cir. 1966); *Downs* v. *Department of Public Welfare,* 368 F.Supp. 454, 465 (E.D.Pa. 1973), consent decree approved, 65 F.R.D. 557, 559 (E.D.Pa. 1974); *Stone* v. *City of Paducah,* 120 Ky. 322, 86 S.W. 531, 533 (1905); and *Dale* v. *State,* 44 A.D.2d 384, 355 N.Y.A.2d 485 (1974); although in *Dale,* the court held, after trial, that the plaintiff had failed to sustain her burden of proof in establishing such a claim.

In addition to this negative aspect—the abolition of slavery and involuntary servitude—an argument can be framed that the Thirteenth Amendment has an implicit positive corollary—the establishment of universal freedom (see "Abroad in the Land: Legal Strategies to Effectuate the Rights of the Physically Disabled," 61 *Georgetown L. J.* 1501, 1515 (1973); *Jones* v. *Alfred H. Mayer, Co., supra,* at 392 U.S. 439). Based upon precedents like the Supreme Court's characterization of the Thirteenth Amendment as "a charter of universal freedom," whose "plain intention was to abolish slavery of whatever name and form *and all its badges and incidents*" and "to make labor free, by prohibiting that control by which the personal service of one man is disposed of or coerced for another's benefit" (*Bailey* v. *Alabama, supra,* at 219 U.S. 240-241 [emphasis added]), one can contend that the sweep of the Amendment is broad enough to encompass the area of employment discrimination generally, and not merely the classic slavery or servitude situation.

Coupling this expansive interpretation of the effect of the Thirteenth Amendment with a contention that handicapped individuals have been treated as harshly as southern black slaves in our society produces a somewhat cogent argument that discrimination against handicapped persons, especially in the area of employment, violates the Thirteenth Amendment.

---

[1] E.g., Wolfensberger, W., "The Origin and Nature of Our Institutional Models," in *Changing Patterns in Residential Services for the Mentally Retarded* 59, 118-119, 125 (Kugel, R., and Wolfensberger, W., eds., 1969).

The validity of this argument and the breadth of the Amendment remain, at present, undetermined. It is clear, however, that Congress, pursuant to the second section of the Amendment, does have broad power to address the "badges and incidents of slavery" and is not limited to simply prohibiting slavery or involuntary servitude itself. The present state of the law in this area was probably best summed up by the Supreme Court in 1968, when it declared:

> "By its own unaided force and effect," the Thirteenth Amendment "abolished slavery, and established universal freedom." *Civil Rights Cases,* 109 U.S. 3, 20, 3 S.Ct. 18, 28. Whether or not the Amendment itself did any more than that—a question not involved in this case—it is at least clear that the Enabling Clause of that Amendment empowered Congress to do much more (*Jones* v. *Alfred H. Mayer Co., supra,* at 392 U.S. 439).

ADDITIONAL READING

"Abroad in the Land: Legal Strategies to Effectuate the Rights of the Physically Disabled," 61 *Georgetown L. J.* 1501, 1512-1519 (1973).

Cummings, E., "Civil Rights—Protection Under the Thirteenth Amendment—Housing Discrimination," 20 *Case Western Reserve L. Rev.* 448-459 (1969).

F. FEDERAL LEGISLATION AND REGULATIONS

1. Jobs with United States Government Agencies

FEDERAL PERSONNEL MANUAL
REGULATIONS OF THE UNITED STATES CIVIL SERVICE COMMISSION
5 C.F.R. § 713.401

§ 713.401   Equal opportunity without regard to politics, marital status, or physical handicap.

(a) *In appointments and position changes.* In determining the merit and fitness of a person for competitive appointment or appointment by noncompetitive action to a position in the competitive service, an appointing officer shall not discriminate on the basis of the person's political affiliations, except when required by statute, or marital status, nor shall he discriminate on the basis of a physical handicap with respect to any position the duties of which may be efficiently performed by a person with the physical handicap.

(b) *In adverse actions and termination of probationers.* An agency may not take an adverse action against an employee covered by Part 752 of this chapter, nor effect the termination of a probationer under Part 315 of this chapter, (1) for political reasons, except when required by statute, (2) that is based on discrimination because of marital status, or (3) for physical handicap with respect to any position the duties of which may be efficiently performed by a person with the physical handicap.

SMITH v. FLETCHER

United States District Court for the Southern District of Texas, 1975
393 F.Supp. 1366, aff'd 559 F.2d 1014

COURT'S FINDINGS OF FACT AND CONCLUSIONS OF LAW

SINGLETON, District Judge.

Findings of Fact

1. Plaintiff Charlotte R. Smith is a female and is a paraplegic confined to a wheelchair because of a childhood disease.

2. Plaintiff is employed by the National Aeronautics and Space Administration, an executive agency of the United States, and has been so employed since February 12, 1962.

3. Plaintiff at the time of her being employed by NASA in 1962 held a Master of Science degree in Physiology and had done research work related to the Space Program, and at that time, she was employed at a grade of GS-7.

4. Plaintiff was promoted to a grade of GS-9 effective November 24, 1963, was subsequently reached by a reduction in force and reduced to a GS-5 in 1971, and was repromoted to GS-7 in 1973, was promoted to a GS-9 in February, 1974, and presently holds that grade of GS-9.

5. A male, named James M. Waligora, was hired in June of 1963, at a grade of GS-9, although he had no better qualifications than plaintiff, having received a Master of Science degree from the same institution and having worked with the same graduate advisor as plaintiff.

6. Another male, named William Carter Alexander, who was hired in the same year as plaintiff, also holding a Master's degree in Physiology, was hired as a GS-9 and promoted to GS-11 three months later because he was given credit for research work related to the Space Program.

7. Waligora was promoted to a grade of GS-11 in July, 1964; to GS-12 in January, 1966; and to GS-13 in January or February of 1968.

8. Alexander was promoted to GS-12 in 1965, was granted a leave with pay to get his Doctor's degree from 1966 to 1968, and was promoted to GS-13 in July of 1969.

9. Plaintiff because of her sex was given routine clerical assignments, while males hired with comparable qualifications were given assignments in research or advanced programs.

10. Plaintiff filed a formal complaint of discrimination on December 1, 1971, alleging discrimination against her as a result of her being a physically-handicapped female.

11. A hearing was held before an examiner of the Civil Service Commission on the complaint of discrimination on the basis of sex. The examiner ruled that testimony as to possible discrimination on the basis of physical handicap would be admitted only for the purpose of showing a possible motive, other than sex discrimination, for the denial of promotions to plaintiff and her separation from her professional field of Physiology.

12. The examiner, in a written decision found that plaintiff had not been discriminated against on the basis of sex but that the plaintiff had been severely mistreated as a result of her first supervisor making an arbitrary and unfounded decision as to her physical capabilities, a decision which was carried forward by subsequent supervisors until the assignments of plaintiff deteriorated to menial clerical tasks.

13. The examiner recommended that the Agency accept the responsibility for making the plaintiff whole but left the specific relief to the Agency. The examiner recommended that the Agency not require the plaintiff to go through the regular grievance machinery to obtain relief, and the Agency, adopted the findings and recommendations of the examiner in their entirety.

14. The Agency and plaintiff could not agree on adequate relief, and plaintiff asked the Commission to specify the relief to which she was entitled. As a result of an appeal to the then Board of Appeals and Review of the Commission, plaintiff obtained an additional decision of the Commission. The decision supported the findings of the examiner as to discrimination because of physical handicap but merely noted that the Agency had accepted responsibility for making the plaintiff whole again not specifying any relief.

15. Plaintiff because of her physical handicap was denied opportunity for assignment to positions which she could physically perform and in which she could have gained promotion and advancement.

16. Applicable regulations of the United States Civil Service Commission prohibit denial of appointment by noncompetitive action to positions in the competitive service on the basis of physical handicap, when an employee is physically able to efficiently perform in the subject positions.

17. In the administrative processing of plaintiff's complaint, both the National Aeronautics and Space Administration and the United States Civil Service Commission erroneously concluded that Chapter 713 of the Federal Personnel Manual did not at that time cover discrimination because of physical handicap. Thus, both NASA and the Civil Service Commission were given the opportunity to hear the complaint regarding the alleged discrimination because of physical handicap, but declined to hear the complaint.

18. The regulation adopted by the United States Civil Service Commission was promulgated pursuant to a statute which provides the President the discretion to prohibit discrimination on the basis of physical handicap.

19. Defendant James C. Fletcher issued a decision adversely affecting plaintiff in that he did not provide for promotion and retroactive back pay upon a finding of discrimination on the basis of physical handicap.

20. Defendant Commissioners of the United States Civil Service Commission issued decisions which adversely affected plaintiff in that they did not provide for promotion and retroactive back pay upon a finding of discrimination because of physical handicap.

21. Defendant Commissioners of the United States Civil Service Commission failed to process the complaint of plaintiff in keeping with the purposes of applicable statutes and regulations, in the following respects:

a. By failing to order an independent and separate investigation of plaintiff's complaint of employment discrimination and utilizing the file of a prior investigation involving a reduction-in-force action rather than the issue of failure to promote.

b. By refusing to include the issue of discrimination because of physical handicap in the investigation.

c. By failing to instruct the hearing examiner to enforce all applicable regulations, resulting in the examiner's recommending no specific relief for the discrimination because of physical handicap.

d. By failing, upon review of the examiner's and agency's decisions, to enforce its own regulation pertaining to discrimination on the basis of physical handicap.

22. Plaintiff, had it not been because of discrimination against her because of her sex and her physical handicap, would have been promoted to a grade of GS-13 in February of 1974, at which time she was promoted to a GS-9.

23. In order to protect her interests under the Equal Employment Opportunity Act of 1972, 42 U.S.C. § 2000e-16, it was necessary for plaintiff to retain the services of David T. Lopez, Esquire, a member of the bar of this court.

24. A hearing should be held to determine the reasonable fee of plaintiff's attorney, Mr. David Lopez.

Conclusions of Law

1. The court has full and complete jurisdiction of all the parties and the subject matter herein.

2. Under the circumstances of this case, it was appropriate to permit the plaintiff to supplement the administrative record with additional evidence.

3. The failure of the National Aeronautics and Space Administration and the United States Civil Service Commission to order the promotion with back pay of plaintiff subjected the plaintiff to a legal wrong and an adverse effect within the meaning of 5 U.S.C. § 7153 and regulations promulgated pursuant thereto, so as to entitle the plaintiff to judicial review under 5 U.S.C. § 702.

4. This court is empowered by 5 U.S.C. § 706 to compel the National Aeronautics and Space Administration to retroactively promote plaintiff with back pay.

5. The provisions contained in the regulations of the United States Civil Service Commission found at 5 C.F.R. § 713.401 were applicable to the plaintiff and the denial to plaintiff of promotion to higher positions in the competitive service because of her physical handicap was in violation of that regulation.

6. The court is empowered in equity to grant plaintiff an order directing the National Aeronautics and Space Administration to appoint her to a GS-13 position effective February, 1974, and such an order is appropriate for this court to grant and it should be granted and, accordingly, plaintiff should be ordered promoted to GS-13, effective February, 1974.

7. The court is empowered in equity to grant plaintiff an order directing the National Aeronautics and Space Administration to pay to plaintiff the difference between payments made to her since February, 1974, and the amounts she would have been paid as a GS-13 since that same date as compensation for the damages suffered as

a result of unlawful discrimination against her by the said Agency, and such an order is appropriate for this court to grant and it should be granted.

8. In order to effectuate the purposes of the Act, plaintiff should be granted relief in this regard by appointment to GS-13, Step 1, as of February, 1974, with the appropriate step increases.

9. Plaintiff is entitled to relief under the provisions of both the Equal Employment Opportunity Act of 1972 and the provisions of the Administrative Procedures Act.

10. Given the fact that the Commissioners of the United States Civil Service Commission were given the opportunity to hear plaintiff's complaint pertaining to discrimination on the basis of physical handicap and refused to do so and that this court has already heard testimony on that complaint, the interests of justice would not be served by remanding the case to the United States Civil Service Commission.

11. The court is empowered to grant to plaintiff the costs of this litigation and such costs should be granted, including an award to plaintiff's attorney of his reasonable fee, to be determined at a hearing set by this court.

12. The court is empowered to grant to plaintiff an injunction against the Commissioners of the United States Civil Service Commission, enjoining the said Commissioners from failing to abide by applicable statutes and regulations, in any of the following ways:

a. By failing to order separate and independent investigation of any complaint of discrimination.

b. By refusing to include the issue of discrimination because of physical handicap in the investigation of complaints of discrimination under Chapter 713 of the Federal Personnel Manual, 5 C.F.R. Part 713.

e. By failing to instruct the hearing examiner to enforce all applicable regulations.

d. By failing, upon review of the examiner's and agency's decisions, to enforce its own regulation pertaining to discrimination on the basis of physical handicap.

NOTE

§ 713.401 and, consequently, the *Smith* v. *Fletcher* holding are limited to physical handicaps. There do not appear to be any sound reasons for not including mentally handicapping conditions as well, and, as we shall see subsequently, discrimination on the basis of mental handicap is also prohibited by statute and regulation.

29 U.S.C. § 791 (b);

§ 501 (b) OF THE REHABILITATION ACT OF 1973

Federal Agencies: Affirmative Action Program Plans

(b) Each department, agency, and instrumentality (including the United States Postal Service and the Postal Rate Commission) in the executive branch shall, within one hundred and eighty days after September 26, 1973, submit to the Civil Service Commission and to the Committee an affirmative action program plan for the hiring, placement, and advancement of handicapped individuals in such department, agency, or instrumentality. Such plan shall include a description of the extent to which and methods whereby the special needs of handicapped employees are being met. Such plan shall be updated annually, and shall be reviewed annually and approved by the Commission, if the Commission determines, after consultation with the Committee, that such plan provides sufficient assurances, procedures and commitments to provide adequate hiring, placement, and advancement opportunities for handicapped individuals.

RYAN v. FEDERAL DEPOSIT INSURANCE CORPORATION

United States Court of Appeals for the District of Columbia Circuit, 1977
565 F.2d 762

Before WRIGHT, ROBINSON, AND MACKINNON, Circuit Judges.
PER CURIAM:

Appellant Mary Ryan, an attorney at the Federal Deposit Insurance Corporation (FDIC), alleges that she has been refused certain job assignments and denied promotion to the GS-14 level because of her physical disability. The District Court, after holding that her claim failed to state a cause of action and that she had failed to exhaust administrative remedies, ordered the agency to make available to her all relevant administrative procedures. This appeal followed.

Two statutes are addressed to discrimination against handicapped federal employees: 5 U.S.C. § 7153 (1970) and Section 501 of the Rehabilitation Act of 1973, 29 U.S.C. § 791 (Supp. V 1975). Section 7153 authorizes the President to prescribe rules prohibiting discrimination because of physical handicap in Executive agencies or the competitive service. Acting under authority delegated to it by the President pursuant to this provision, the Civil Service Commission in 1969 promulgated a regulation requiring equal opportunity without regard to physical handicap. 5 C.F.R. § 713.401 (1977) provides:

> (a) *In appointments and position changes.* In determining the merit and fitness of a person for competitive appointment or appointment by noncompetitive action to a position in the competitive service, an appointing officer shall not discriminate on the basis of a physical handicap with respect to any position the duties of which may be efficiently performed by a person with the physical handicap.
> (b) *In adverse actions and termination of probationers.* An agency may not take an adverse action against an employee . . . for physical handicap with respect to any position the duties of which may be efficiently performed by a person with the physical handicap.

In addition, under Section 501 of the Rehabilitation Act of 1973 every agency in the Executive Branch is required to submit to the Civil Service Commission and to the Interagency Committee on Handicapped Employees, established by the Act, ''an affirmative action program plan for the hiring, placement, and advancement of handicapped individuals'' within the agency. Plans are to be updated annually and approved by the Commission if it determines ''that such plan provides sufficient assurances, procedures and commitments to provide adequate hiring, placement, and advancement opportunities for handicapped individuals.''

Appellant argues that these provisions afford a basis for implication of a private right of action for disability discrimination. But we need not go so far in this case. For it is clear to us that the quoted provisions impose a duty upon federal agencies to structure their procedures and programs so as to ensure that handicapped individuals are afforded equal opportunity in both job assignment and promotion. If an agency fails to comply with its duty, then the aggrieved individual is entitled to seek judicial review of the agency action under 28 U.S.C. § 1331(a) (1970), *as amended,* Pub. L. No. 94-574, 90 Stat. 2721 (1976), *see Califano* v. *Sanders,* 430 U.S. 99, 97 S.Ct. 980, 51 L.Ed.2d 192 (1977), and the Administrative Procedure Act, 5 U.S.C. §§ 701-706 (1970). *See generally McNutt* v. *Hills,* 426 F.Supp. 990 (D.D.C. 1977).

In this case, however, we are unable, on the record as it is now before us, to determine whether or not the FDIC is in compliance with all of its statutory obligations. If, as appellant has alleged, neither the FDIC nor the Civil Service Commission provides any opportunity for an individual to raise a claim that he has been denied promotion on the basis of a physical handicap, then we think it clear that the agency plan does not "provide[] sufficient assurances, procedures and commitments to provide adequate . . . advancement opportunities for handicapped individuals," 29 U.S.C. § 791(b) (Supp. V 1975). Beyond that, however, we are unable to reach any conclusions on agency compliance in its treatment of appellant. This is so both because appellant failed to test the agency's procedures for resolving such claims through its grievance process and, more generally, because she has, throughout most of this litigation, considered the agency's affirmative action plan and its compliance with the requirements of Section 501 to be irrelevant to her claim.

Under the circumstances, we affirm that portion of the District Court's order which directs the FDIC, upon a prompt request by appellant, to make available to her all applicable administrative processes including those afforded by 5 C.F.R. § 713.401 (1977), the FDIC Employee Grievance Procedures, and the FDIC's Affirmative Action Program Plan for the Employment of the Handicapped for Fiscal Year 1976 (FDIC Circular 2000.10). If these procedures and Plan do not provide a remedy for discrimination in promotion because of physical handicap, the FDIC should amend the procedures and Plan to so provide. And if appellant is aggrieved by the action taken by the agency, she may seek judicial review at that point.

So ordered.

NOTES

1. *McNutt* v. *Hills,* 426 F.Supp. 990 (D.D.C. 1977) involved the claim of a blind man that he had been denied a promotion at the United States Department of Housing and Urban Development because of discrimination on the basis of handicap, and also that HUD had failed to meet affirmative action obligations toward handicapped employees. The court upheld the plaintiff on the substance of both these claims, although it refused to grant plaintiff an award of back pay, which it held was barred by sovereign immunity. The plaintiff was, however, held entitled to retroactive promotion, and HUD was ordered to submit to the court a department-wide report of plans to bring the agency into compliance with affirmative action obligations.

2. Lawsuits such as *Ryan* and *McNutt* put pressure on various government agencies

to take real, concrete steps to increase employment opportunities for handicapped people. In addition to the formulation of affirmative action plans, a very important measure for dealing with discrimination on the basis of handicap is the development of specific administrative enforcement mechanisms for handling complaints of such discrimination.

5 C.F.R. PART 713—EQUAL OPPORTUNITY

[Administrative Complaints Procedure]
43 Fed. Reg. 12293-12296 (March 24, 1978)

Subpart G—Prohibition Against Discrimination
Because of a Physical or Mental Handicap

General Provisions
§ 713.701   Purpose and applicability.

(a)   *Purpose.*   This subpart sets forth the policy under which an agency shall establish a continuing program to assure nondiscrimination on account of physical or mental handicap and the regulations under which an agency will process complaints of discrimination based on a physical or mental handicap.

(b)   *Applicability.*   (1) This subpart applies to executive agencies as defined in section 105 of Title 5 of the United States Code and to those positions in the legislative and judicial branches of the Federal Government and the government of the District of Columbia which are in the competitive service. (2) This subpart applies to the U.S. Postal Service and Postal Rate Commission. (3) This subpart applies only to applicants and employees who have a handicap as defined in § 713.702(a).

§ 713.702   Definitions.

(a)   "Handicapped person" is defined for this subpart as one who: (1) Has a physical or mental impairment which substantially limits one or more of such person's major life activities, (2) has a record of such an impairment, or (3) is regarded as having such an impairment.

(b)   "Physical or mental impairment" means (1) any physiological disorder or condition, cosmetic disfigurement, or anatomical loss affecting one or more of the following body systems: Neurological; musculoskeletal; special sense organs; cardiovascular; reproductive; digestive; genito-urinary; hemic and lymphatic; skin; and endocrine; or (2) any mental or psychological disorder, such as mental retardation, organic brain syndrome, emotional or mental illness, and specific learning disabilities.

(c)   "Major life activities" means functions, such as caring for one's self, performing manual tasks, walking, seeing, hearing, speaking, breathing, learning, and working.

(d)   "Has a record of such an impairment" means has a history of, or has been classified (or misclassified) as having a mental or physical impairment that substantially limits one or more major life activities.

(e)   "Is regarded as having such an impairment" means (1) has a physical or mental impairment that does not substantially limit major life activities but is treated by an employer as constituting such a limitation; (2) has a physical or mental impairment that substantially limits major life activities only as a result of the attitude of an employer toward such impairment; (3) or has none of the impairments defined in (b) of this section but is treated by an employer as having such an impairment.

(f) "Qualified handicapped person" means with respect to employment, a handicapped person who, with or without reasonable accommodation, can perform the essential functions of the position in question without endangering the health and safety of the individual or others and who, depending upon the type of appointing authority being used: (1) Meets the experience and/or education requirements (which may include passing a written test) of the position in question, or (2) meets the criteria for appointment under one of the special appointing authorities for handicapped persons.

§ 713.703 General policy.

Agencies shall give full consideration to the hiring, placement, and advancement of qualified mentally and physically handicapped persons. The Federal Government shall become a model employer of handicapped individuals. An agency shall not discriminate against a qualified physically or mentally handicapped person.

§ 713.704 Reasonable accommodation.

(a) An agency shall make reasonable accommodation to the known physical or mental limitations of a qualified handicapped applicant or employee unless the agency can demonstrate that the accommodation would impose an undue hardship on the operation of its program.

(b) Reasonable accommodation may include, but shall not be limited to: (1) Making facilities readily accessible to and usable by handicapped persons, and (2) job restructuring, part-time or modified work schedules, acquisition or modification of equipment or devices, appropriate adjustment or modification of examinations, the provision of readers and interpreters, and other similar actions.

(c) In determining pursuant to paragraph (a) of this section whether an accommodation would impose an undue hardship on the operation of the agency in question, factors to be considered include: (1) The overall size of the agency's program with respect to the number of employees, number and type of facilities and size of budget; (2) the type of agency operation, including the composition and structure of the agency's work force; and (3) the nature and the cost of the accommodation.

§ 713.705 Employment criteria.

(a) An agency may not make use of any employment test or other selection criterion that screens out or tends to screen out qualified handicapped persons or any class of handicapped persons unless: (1) The test score or other selection criterion, as used by the agency, is shown to be job-related for the position in question, and (2) alternative job-related tests or criteria that do not screen out or tend to screen out as many handicapped persons are not shown by the Civil Service Commission's Director of Personnel Research and Development Center to be available.

(b) An agency shall select and administer tests concerning employment so as to insure that, when administered to an applicant or employee who has a handicap that impairs sensory, manual, or speaking skills, the test results accurately reflect the applicant's or employee's ability to perform the position or type of positions in question rather than reflecting the applicant's or employee's impaired sensory, manual, or speaking skills (except where those skills are the factors that the test purports to measure).

§ 713.706   Preemployment inquiries.

(a) Except as provided in paragraph (b) of this section, an agency may not conduct a preemployment medical examination and may not make preemployment inquiry of an applicant as to whether the applicant is a handicapped person or as to the nature or severity of a handicap. An agency may, however, make preemployment inquiry into an applicant's ability to meet the medical qualification requirements, with or without reasonable accommodation, of the position in question, i.e., the minimum abilities necessary for safe and efficient performance of the duties of the position in question. The Civil Service Commission may also make an inquiry as to the nature and extent of a handicap for the purpose of special testing.

(b) Nothing in this section shall prohibit an agency from conditioning an offer of employment on the results of a medical examination conducted prior to the employee's entrance on duty, *Provided,* That: (1) All entering employees are subjected to such an examination regardless of handicap or when the preemployment medical questionnaire used for positions which do not routinely require medical examination indicates a condition for which further examination is required because of the job-related nature of the condition, and (2) the results of such an examination are used only in accordance with the requirements of this part. Nothing in this section shall be construed to prohibit the gathering of preemployment medical information for the purposes of special appointing authorities for handicapped persons.

(c) Information obtained in accordance with this section as to the medical condition or history of the applicant shall be collected and maintained according to the existing maintenance, use, and disposition schedules for medical records, except that: (1) Supervisors and managers may be informed regarding necessary accommodations; (2) first aid and safety personnel may be informed, where appropriate, if the condition might require emergency treatment.

§ 713.707   Physical access to buildings.

(a) An agency shall not discriminate against qualified handicapped applicants or employees due to the inaccessibility of its facility.

(b) For the purpose of this subpart, a facility shall be deemed accessible if it is in compliance with the Architectural Barriers Act of 1968.

Agency Regulations for Processing
Complaints of Discrimination

§ 713.708   General.

An agency shall provide regulations governing the acceptance and processing of complaints of discrimination based on a physical or mental handicap which subject to § 713.710, comply with principles and requirements in §§ 713.213 through 713.271 and §§ 713.601 through 713.614 and §§ 713.631 through 713.632. Nothing in the foregoing shall be construed to postpone the effective date of this rule.

§ 713.709   Coverage.

(a) An agency shall provide in its regulations for the acceptance of a complaint from any aggrieved employee or applicant for employment who believes that he or she has been discriminated against because of a handicap as defined in § 713.702.

(b) An agency must process complaints of discrimination based on acts or actions that occurred 1 year prior to the effective date of these regulations *Provided:* (1) The complaint of discrimination was brought to the attention of the agency within 30 calendar days of the alleged discriminatory act, or, if a personnel action, within 30 calendar days of its effective date, (2) the complaint of discrimination was not adjudicated under some other grievance or appeals procedure, and (3) the complaint of discrimination is filed within 180 calendar days of the effective date of these regulations. Complaints of discrimination based on alleged discriminatory acts or personnel actions that occurred on or after the effective date of these regulations are subject to the time restraints set forth in § 713.214(a).

§ 713.710   Exclusions.

The remedies provided in § 713.271 shall apply to this subpart except that no back pay may be awarded to an applicant for employment.

NOTES

1.   The reference to remedies provided in § 713.271 includes retroactive hiring, back pay, retroactive promotion, cancellation of employment sanctions, and expurgation of records. The failure to allow back pay for job applicants (§ 713.710) while permitting it for employees was explained as follows:

> Many commenters were concerned about the lack of a back pay provision for applicants. There presently exists no express statutory authority for back pay to persons who can establish that they were discriminated against because of a physical or mental handicap in Federal employment. However, there is generalized authority contained in the Back Pay Act to provide an employee with backpay relief when he or she is the subject of an unwarranted or improper personnel action. The Commission takes the position that discrimination because of handicap can give rise to a backpay award under the Back Pay Act (5 U.S.C. 5596) and the regulations implementing the Act (5 CFR Part 550). However, since the Act creates a backpay entitlement for employees only, the Commission has no authority under existing law to extend such relief to applicants for employment (43 Fed. Reg. 12294).

2.   Preemployment inquiries have always been a major concern of handicapped job applicants (see, e.g., *Duran* v. *City of Tampa,* pp. 351–356, *supra.*) Does § 713.706 provide a workable solution to this problem?

2.   Federal Government Contracts

29 U.S.C. § 793

§ 503 OF THE REHABILITATION ACT OF 1973

§ 793.   Employment under Federal contracts.

Amount of contracts or subcontracts; provision for employment and advancement of qualified handicapped individuals; regulations.

(a) Any contract in excess of $2,500 entered into by any Federal department or agency for the procurement of personal property and nonpersonal services (including construction) for the United States shall contain a provision requiring that, in employing persons to carry out such contract the party contracting with the United States shall take affirmative action to employ and advance in employment qualified handicapped individuals as defined in section 706(6) of this title. The provisions of this section shall apply to any subcontract in excess of $2,500 entered into by a prime contractor in carrying out any contract for the procurement of personal property and nonpersonal services (including construction) for the United States. The President shall implement the provisions of this section by promulgating regulations within ninety days after September 26, 1973.

Administrative enforcement; complaints; investigations; departmental action.

(b) If any handicapped individual believes any contractor has failed or refuses to comply with the provisions of his contract with the United States, relating to employment of handicapped individuals, such individual may file a complaint with the Department of Labor. The Department shall promptly investigate such complaint and shall take such action thereon as the facts and circumstances warrant, consistent with the terms of such contract and the laws and regulations applicable thereto.

Waiver by President; national interest special circumstances for waiver of particular agreements.

(c) The requirements of this section may be waived, in whole or in part, by the President with respect to a particular contract or subcontract, in accordance with guidelines set forth in regulations which he shall prescribe, when he determines that special circumstances in the national interest so require and states in writing his reasons for such determination.

NOTES

1. Pursuant to Executive Order No. 11758 of January 15, 1974, 39 Fed. Reg. 2075, as amended by Executive Order No. 11784 of May 30, 1974, 39 Fed. Reg. 19443, the President's authority to prescribe regulations, under § 793(a), and to issue guidelines or regulations for waiver of § 793, as provided in § 793(c), is delegated to the Secretary of Labor.

2. 38 U.S.C. § 2012 requires, as a component of contracts with the federal government, an affirmative action program for the hiring of disabled veterans.

ROGERS V. FRITO-LAY, INC.

United States District Court for the Northern District of Texas, 1977
433 F.Supp. 200

WILLIAM M. TAYLOR, JR., District Judge.

The complaint in this action as amended alleges causes of action under Sections 503 and 504 of the Rehabilitation Act of 1973, 29 U.S.C. §§ 793 and 794, with jurisdiction under 28 U.S.C. §§ 1331(a), 1337, 1343(4), 2201, and 2202. Plaintiff also alleges pendent jurisdiction over a claim under the Texas Workmen's Compensation Act. Defendant filed a motion to dismiss for lack of subject matter jurisdiction, which, in view of the affidavit, requests for production, interrogatories, and responses which have been filed, is treated as a motion for summary judgment and granted for the reasons stated hereinafter.

Section 793

I conclude that a private cause of action for handicapped employees should not be implied under 29 U.S.C. § 793. This statute requires that federal contracts worth more than $2,500 contain a provision obligating the contractor to "take affirmative action to employ and advance in employment qualified handicapped individuals." Section 793 was intended to cover that large number of private businesses whose only receipts of federal funds involve transactions in which goods or services are sold to the government for their fair market value. Congress intended by § 793 to direct federal agencies to exercise their purchasing power in such a way as to bring about improved employment opportunities for the handicapped.

Under the standards laid down in *Cort v. Ash*, 422 U.S. 66, 78, 95 S.Ct. 2080, 45 L.Ed.2d 26 (1975), this court cannot imply a private right of action for handicapped employees of federal contractors under § 793. To do so would be to go far beyond the intent of Congress.

Plaintiff alleges, as she must, that she is a handicapped individual, that she is qualified for a specific job from which she was terminated by Frito-Lay, and that Frito-Lay is a government contractor. Since § 793 applies only to "qualified handicapped individuals," and the burden of proof of statutory coverage is on the complainant, the complainant must prove all three allegations before the contractor is subject to a § 793 duty. "[S]ection 503 itself relates solely to employment and thus the adjective 'qualified' in modification of 'handicapped individual' in that section clearly requires that the 'employability' of the handicapped individual in question is a prerequisite to section 503 application." S.Rep.No. 93-1297, 93d Cong., 2d Sess., *reprinted in* [1974] U.S.Code Cong. & Admin. News pp. 6373, 6390. Assuming for purposes of this motion to dismiss that the allegations of the complaint are true, however, plaintiff is "one of the class for whose *especial* benefit" § 793 was enacted, and satisfies the first of the four *Cort* tests.

The second of the four tests, evidence of legislative intent, weighs strongly against plaintiff. Section 793(b) explicitly provides a procedure for administrative enforcement of a contractor's affirmative action obligations, to be initiated by private complaints. Investigation and enforcement responsibilities are specifically delegated to the Department of Labor. Furthermore, Congress has rejected the perennial attempts to amend Title VII to give handicapped employees and applicants a private right of action. The following proposed amendments to the Civil Rights Act of 1964 have never mustered sufficient support for passage: H.R. Nos. 264, 461, 1107, 1200, 1995, 95th Cong., 1st Sess. (1977); S. Nos. 1311, 1757, H.R. Nos. 1346, 1886, 2515, 3497, 4624, 4625, 4626, 5016, 7061, 7754, 7758, 7946, 8028, 8417, 12,541, 94th Cong. (1975–76); S. 1780, H.R. Nos. 1120, 2685, 10,960, 11,986, 11,987, 12,654, 12,916, 13,199, 13,200, 93d Cong. (1973–74); H.R. 10,962, 92d Cong. (1972). The repeated defeats of efforts to amend Title VII to add coverage for handicapped persons, coupled with the explicit grant of a private administrative remedy in § 793(b), make it quite clear that Congress did not intend to bestow a private right to bring suit in court upon qualified handicapped employees. *National Railroad Passenger Corp.* v. *National Association of Railroad Passengers,* 414 U.S. 453, 458, 94 S.Ct. 690, 693, 38 L.Ed.2d 646, teaches that "when legislation expressly provides a particular remedy or remedies, courts should not expand the coverage of the statute to subsume other remedies."

Implication of a private right of action would be inconsistent with the purpose of § 793 for several reasons. The statute does not use the term "discrimination," and legal analysis based on comparative treatment of "the handicapped" as a group and the non-handicapped seems inappropriate, at least in the individualized job context. There is no readily identifiable and homogeneous class of handicapped persons, handicaps often affect job abilities and productivity; and different treatment of the handicapped normally stems from sympathetic rather than intolerant motives. Furthermore, courts may not presume that the administrative scheme established by § 793(b) and the companion regulations of the Department of Labor will be inadequate without resort to private federal actions. Such suits might impair and delay the orderly development of enforcement precedent in this new and uncharted field, and interfere with conciliation efforts. The third *Cort* test thus weighs against the plaintiff.

The fourth *Cort* criterion counsels restraint in interfering with state regulation. Texas Rev.Civ.Stat.Ann. Art. 4419e (1975) prohibits employment discrimination on the basis of handicap "if the person's ability to perform the task required by a job is not impaired by the handicap and the person is otherwise qualified for the job." An implied federal private right of action might thus duplicate available state remedies and substantially increase the possibility of inconsistent judgments by federal courts, federal administrative agencies, state courts, and state administrative agencies.

Having considered all the relevant facts of the *Cort* test, I conclude that a private right of action should not be implied under § 793.

Section 794

Plaintiff also claims an implied private cause of action under 29 U.S.C. § 794, which provides:

> No otherwise qualified handicapped individual in the United States, as defined in section 706(6) of this title, shall, solely by reason of his handicap, be excluded from the participation in, be denied the benefits of, or be subjected to discrimination under any program or activity receiving Federal financial assistance.

The Seventh Circuit has held that there is an implied private right under § 794 for a class of handicapped individuals to seek judicial review of decisions by public authorities which perpetuate the inaccessibility of a public transportation system to the mobility-disabled. *Lloyd* v. *Regional Transportation Authority,* 548 F.2d 1277 (7th Cir. 1977). The court construed the legislative history of § 794 as contemplating "judicial review of an administrative proceeding as contradistinct from an independent cause of action in federal court." *Id.,* at 1286. Any private cause of action under § 794 appears to be limited to entities which receive federal grants in the nature of gifts to support activities deemed to be in the public interest or for the public welfare. The term "federal financial assistance" as used in § 794 does not comprehend government procurement contracts but rather refers to the form of grant assistance that goes primarily to public entities.

Plaintiff has conducted discovery on the issue of whether Frito-Lay receives any such federal financial assistance or has received such assistance since the effective date of § 794. Frito-Lay's sworn responses show that it had not. Treating Frito-Lay's motion to dismiss as a motion for summary judgment, therefore, I grant the motion in favor of defendant.

Other Alleged Jurisdictional Grounds

Since plaintiff's complaint does not show that she has a federal right under § 793 or § 794, neither 28 U.S.C. § 1331(a), (federal question) nor § 1343(4) (federal civil right) confers federal court jurisdiction. Likewise, claims under 28 U.S.C. § 2201 and § 2202 are not cognizable, since "the declaratory judgment statute is not a jurisdictional act. It provides only a remedy in cases in which the court has jurisdiction from other sources." *National Foundation* v. *City of Fort Worth, Texas,* 307 F.Supp. 177, 179 (N.D.Tex. 1967), *aff'd,* 415 F.2d 41 (5th Cir. 1969); *Skelly Oil Co.* v. *Phillips Petroleum Co.,* 339 U.S. 667, 671, 70 S.Ct. 876, 879, 94 L.Ed. 1194 (1950). Nor can 28 U.S.C. § 1337 provide a basis for plaintiff's claims. *See B. F. Goodrich Co.* v. *Northwest Industries, Inc.,* 424 F.2d 1349, 1354 (3d Cir.), *cert. denied,* 400 U.S. 822, 91 S.Ct. 41, 27 L.Ed.2d 50 (1970) ("Although § 1337 creates jurisdiction, it does not create a cause of action."); *Russo* v. *Kirby,* 453 F.2d 548, 551 (2d Cir. 1971); *Colorado Labor Council, AFL-CIO* v. *American Federation of Labor and Congress of Industrial Organizations,* 481 F.2d 396, 400 (10th Cir. 1973); *Weigand* v. *Afton View Apartments,* 473 F.2d 545, 548-49 (8th Cir. 1973); *Potomac Passengers Assoc.* v. *Chesapeake and Ohio Ry. Co.,* 171 U.S.App.D.C. 359, 520 F.2d 91 (1975). Finally, there is no pendent jurisdiction over state law claims where there is no substantive federal jurisdiction. *United Mine Workers of America* v. *Gibbs,* 383 U.S. 715, 86 S.Ct. 1130, 16 L.Ed.2d 218 (1966).

For the foregoing reasons this action is hereby dismissed with prejudice. Costs are to be taxed against plaintiff.

NOTES

1. For a discussion of the distinctions between § 503 and § 504, see Ochoa, V., "Sections 503 and 504: New Employment Rights for Individuals with Handicaps," 2 *Amicus* 38 (Sept. 1977).

2. *Moon* v. *Roadway Express, Inc.,* 439 F.Supp. 1308 (N.D.Ga. 1977), relied upon the *Rogers* case to reach a similar holding that § 793 does not create a private cause of action.

DRENNON V. PHILADELPHIA GENERAL HOSPITAL

United States District Court for the Eastern District of Pennsylvania, 1977
428 F.Supp. 809

OPINION

A. LEON HIGGINBOTHAM, District Judge.

I. Introduction

The defendants in this action have filed a Motion to Dismiss both the Complaint and the Amended Complaint for: (1) lack of subject matter jurisdiction; (2) for failure to state a claim upon which relief can be granted; (3) for lack of specificity; and (4) for failure to exhaust both state and federal administrative remedies. The plaintiff contends that she is a highly qualified laboratory technician denied employment at Philadelphia General Hospital solely by reason of her epilepsy. It is claimed that Philadelphia General Hospital and the City of Philadelphia had a policy to deny employment to anyone who had experienced an epileptic seizure within two years from the date of his or her job application. Ms. Drennon was within this group of individuals allegedly denied employment for the above reason. The plaintiff asserts that the procedures and policies of the various defendants deprived her of due process and equal protection under the 14th Amendment, abridged her right to be free from discrimination as a result of a non-job-related disability—a statutory claim under the Rehabilitation Act of 1973, 29 U.S.C. §§ 793 and 794—and violated her rights under 42 U.S.C. § 1983. Along with her response to the defendants' Motion to Dismiss, the plaintiff has filed a Motion to Compel Answers to Interrogatories. After full consideration of the parties' respective motions and briefs filed in support of and in opposition thereto, I must DENY the Motion to Dismiss but STAY these proceedings pending consideration of plaintiff's claims by the Department of Labor. Because of my decision to STAY the present proceedings, I will, at this time, DENY plaintiff's Motion to Compel Answers to Interrogatories, without prejudice to its renewal should plaintiff be entitled to relief in this Court after her administrative remedies have been exhausted.

[Section II of the Opinion, dealing with the validity of plaintiff's Amended Complaint and the court's jurisdiction over the defendants, is omitted.]

III. Does the Plaintiff State a Cause of Action
Under the 14th Amendment and § 1983?

In recent years there have been increasing tensions in attempting to define with specificity the rights which persons are guaranteed by the equal protection and due process provisions of the 14th Amendment. As one reads the abstract pronouncements in behalf of liberty, due process and property or the condemnation against governmental arbitrariness there is very little guidance for those cases which courts have not previously considered and probably never anticipated. On the level of pure abstraction we can find language in cases, always arising in quite different factual situations, which state that "The touchstone of due process is protection of the individual against arbitrary action of government." *Wolff* v. *McDonnell,* 418 U.S. 539, 558, 94 S.Ct.

2963, 2976, 41 L.Ed.2d 935 (1974); See also *Zannino* v. *Arnold*, 531 F.2d 687, 690 (3d Cir. 1976). But the "arbitrary actions of government" in *Wolff* v. *McDonnell* pertained to a prisoner's losing good time credit or the imposition of solitary confinement—thus a different milieu than the present case.

In contrast to the broad condemnation of arbitrary conduct by the government as announced in *Wolff*, only last term a majority of the Supreme Court said that:

> The federal court is not the appropriate forum in which to review the multitude of personnel decisions that are made daily by public agencies. We must accept the harsh fact that numerous individual mistakes are inevitable in the day-to-day administration of our affairs. The United States Constitution cannot feasibly be construed to require federal judicial review of every such error. In the absence of any claim that the public employer was motivated by a desire to curtail or to penalize the exercise of an employee's constitutionally protected rights, we must presume that official action was regular and, if erroneous, can best be corrected in other ways. The Due Process Clause of the Fourteenth Amendment is not a guarantee against incorrect or ill-advised personnel decisions. (footnote omitted) *Bishop* v. *Wood*, 426 U.S. 341, 96 S.Ct. 2074, 2080, 48 L.Ed.2d 684 (1976).

Thus, in this case, was the conduct of the City of Philadelphia and Philadelphia General Hospital an "arbitrary act of government" as condemned in *Wolff*, or was it merely an "ill-advised personnel decision" or one of the "numerous individual mistakes . . . inevitable in the day to day administration of our affairs" which are not "constitutionally protected rights?"

The Court is faced in this case with the precise issue whether the City of Philadelphia and Philadelphia General Hospital's alleged flat prohibition against the employment of persons who had epileptic seizures less than two years prior to the date of application is a violation of the plaintiff's substantive due process and equal protection rights and those of the purported class members. Although this specific plaintiff may not have a right to public employment, that is not the question in this case; the issue is only whether the government acted lawfully in denying her employment. That certain arbitrary classifications denying employment are prohibited has clearly been set forth by the U.S. Supreme Court in *Cleveland Board of Education* v. *LaFleur*, 414 U.S. 632, 94 S.Ct. 791, 39 L.Ed.2d 52 (1974) and in *Turner* v. *Dept. of Employment Sec. and Bd. of Review of Indus. Commission of Utah*, 423 U.S. 44, 96 S.Ct. 249, 46 L.Ed.2d 181 (1975). Obviously pregnant persons are not the only individuals entitled to challenge state action as a violation of an individual's 14th Amendment right to substantive due process and equal protection of the laws. Recently, the Court of Appeals for the Third Circuit held that an action brought by a handicapped person charging arbitrary, unreasonable and discriminatory classification of blind persons, in alleged violation of both 42 U.S.C. § 1983 and the 14th Amendment, stated a cause of action and would withstand a motion to dismiss lodged by individual defendants. See *King-Smith* v. *Aaron*, 455 F.2d 378, 381–382 (3d Cir. 1972); see also *Frederick L.* v. *Thomas*, 408 F.Supp. 832 (E.D.Pa. 1976), in which Judge Newcomer found that a cause of action had been stated and denied a motion to dismiss (treated as a motion for judgment on the pleadings), after a trial of a 14th Amendment claim brought by children with specific learning disabilities against the School District of Philadelphia. Finally Judge Newcomer recently entertained and tried an action brought by the visually handicapped in which the School

District of Philadelphia was charged with abridging the 14th Amendment, and individual defendants were charged with violations of both the 15th Amendment and § 1983, *Gurmankin* v. *Costanzo,* 411 F.Supp. 982 (E.D.Pa. 1976). Just as the Court of Appeals in *King-Smith* v. *Aaron, supra,* stated that it expressed no opinion on the merits of the claim, I cannot here conclude that plaintiff has no cause of action, nor do I conclude that plaintiff will ultimately prevail. I find that within the context of this Motion to Dismiss, plaintiff's Amended Complaint states a cause of action, but this judgment is without prejudice to reconsidering this issue after the City and PGH have come forward with evidence explaining their policies, if there are any, with respect to epileptics. At this stage, plaintiff has a cause of action under the 14th Amendment, and, in the case of the individual defendants, under § 1983.

IV.   Plaintiff States A Colorable Cause of Action
Under 29 U.S.C. §§ 793 and 794

The United States Supreme Court, in an opinion by Mr. Justice Brennan, recently outlined the standards for determining whether a statute authorized an implicit private action in court. In *Cort* v. *Ash,* 422 U.S. 66, 95 S.Ct. 2080, 2088, 45 L.Ed.2d 26 (1975), Mr. Justice Brennan held:

> In determining whether a private remedy is implicit in a statute not expressly providing one, several factors are relevant. First, is the plaintiff "one of the class for whose *especial* benefit the statute was enacted" . . . that is, does the statute create a federal right in favor of the plaintiff? Second, is there any indication of legislative intent, explicit or implicit, either to create such a remedy or to deny one. Third, is it consistent with the underlying purposes of the legislative scheme to imply such a remedy for the plaintiff? And finally, is the cause of action one traditionally relegated to state law, in an area basically the concern of the states, so that it would be inappropriate to infer a cause of action based solely on federal law? (citations omitted; emphasis in the original)

That persons with epilepsy are considered handicapped is too self-evident to be contested. See Epilepsy Foundation of America, *Behind the Stigma of Epilepsy* (1975); Epilepsy Foundation of America, *Basic Statistics on the Epilepsies* (1975). See 29 U.S.C. § 706(6) for a definition of the handicapped individual. It is also clear from the statement of the Committee on Labor and Public Welfare, in its report to the Senate on the Amendment of the Rehabilitation Act of 1973, that the legislators anticipated and approved of inclusion of a private right of action as a means to enforce 29 U.S.C. § 794:

> This approach to implementation of Section 504 which closely follows the models of the above cited antidiscrimination provisions [i.e. Section 601 of the Civil Rights Act of 1964, 42 U.S.C. 2000d, and Section 903 of the Education Amendments of 1972, 20 U.S.C. 1683], would insure administrative due process (right to hearing, right to review) provide for administrative consistency within the Federal government as well as relative ease of implementation and *permit a judicial remedy through a private action* (emphasis added). 120 Cong.Rec. 30534.

Although the legislative history does not mention § 793, that factor does not negate the existence of a private cause of action under that statute. Mr. Justice Brennan in *Court* v. *Ash, supra,* held that:

in situations in which it is clear that federal law has granted a class of persons certain rights, it is not necessary to show an intention to *create* a private cause of action, although an explicit purpose to *deny* such cause of action would be controlling. 95 S.Ct. at 2090 (emphasis in the original; footnote omitted).

The remedy sought in this case, the employment of plaintiff and members of her class in positions from which they were purportedly excluded in violation of the Rehabilitation Act, could not better foster the goals of the legislation in question. And, finally, that the area was one not traditionally controlled by the State of Pennsylvania is evidenced by the inclusion, only recently, of the employment of handicapped persons as one of the goals to be fostered by the Pennsylvania Human Relations Act. Courts have previously recognized the federal government's interest in preventing discrimination, on the basis of race, color or national origin, in employment in federally assisted activities and programs and, consequently, have implied a right of action under Title VI of the Civil Rights Act of 1964, 42 U.S.C. § 2000d. See *U.S. by Clark* v. *Frazer,* 297 F.Supp. 319 (M.D.Ala. 1968) where the court held that the Attorney General had standing to bring an action to enforce federal statutes and regulations which required state personnel, engaged in the administration of federally financed grant-in-aid programs, to recruit, hire and promote or demote personnel on merit, without regard to race or color, *supp'd. sub nom. U.S. by Mitchell* v. *Frazer,* 317 F.Supp. 1079 (M.D.Ala. 1970) where the court held for plaintiff on the merits; *supp'd. sub nom. NAACP* v. *Allen,* 340 F.Supp. 703 (M.D.Ala. 1972), *aff'd* 493 F.2d 614 (5th Cir. 1974); See also *Wade* v. *Mississippi Co-op. Extension Service,* 372 F.Supp. 126 (D.Miss. 1974), *aff'd in part and rem'd in part,* 528 F.2d 508 (5th Cir. 1976), an action against a state agency operating an agricultural and home economic extension service, and other defendants for declaratory and injunctive relief to eliminate statewide racial discrimination in employment and promotion practices of the agency, among other claims.

Other judges have found an implied right of action under 29 U.S.C. § 794. See *Gurmankin* v. *Costanzo, supra;* see also *Rhode Island Society for Autistic Children* v. *Board of Regents for Education for the State of Rhode Island,* Civil Action No. 5081 (D.R.I. filed August 1, 1975). Given this overwhelming data in favor of implying a cause of action under both 29 U.S.C. §§ 793 and 794, it cannot be disputed that Ms. Drennon has stated such a cause of action, but is not entitled to judicial relief because of her failure to exhaust her federal administrative remedies.

V. Exhaustion of Administrative Remedies,
the Doctrine of Primary Jurisdiction and
the Court's Present Inability to Grant Relief

A. State Remedies

The defendants argue that this entire action should be barred from consideration because of plaintiff's failure to exhaust her prior state and federal administrative remedies. As for the claim that state remedies were not exhausted, at the time plaintiff alleges that she was initially injured, no state administrative remedy existed. The Pennsylvania Human Relations Act did not foster the employment of handicapped individuals "in accordance with their fullest capacities" regardless of their disability until December 19, 1974—more than eleven months after plaintiff took the qualifying examination to become a lab technician. 43 P.S. § 951 and 952, as amended. There is no indication in the legislative history that the statute is to be retroactively applied. In fact, Pennsylvania has a provision on statutory construction which states:

> No statute shall be construed to be retroactive unless clearly and manifestly so intended by the General Assembly. 1 Pa.C.S.A. § 1926.

Since there is no clear indication that the amendment to the Pennsylvania Human Relations Act should be given retroactive application, and given that the statute is substantive, rather than procedural and remedial, in nature (in that it adds a new category of individuals to those protected under the statute in question), the plaintiff cannot be required to resort to the state administrative tribunal for assistance—the statute cannot be given retroactive effect. Failure to exhaust now-existing federal administrative remedies poses a different problem for the Court.

B. Federal Remedies

Since this Court clearly has jurisdiction under the 14th Amendment and § 1983 without implication of jurisdiction under 29 U.S.C. §§ 793 and 794, the implication of a judicial remedy under §§ 793 and 794 seems consistent with the principles articulated in *Cort* v. *Ash, supra,* and the administrative remedy afforded under 29 U.S.C. § 793 does not appear to be exclusive, the defendant actually raises the doctrine of primary jurisdiction as a present bar to consideration of the plaintiff's claims by the Court. The Court of Appeals for the Third Circuit clearly articulated the doctrine of primary jurisdiction in an opinion by Judge Van Dusen, *MCI Communications Corporation* v. *American Telephone & Telegraph Co.,* 496 F.2d 214, 220 (3d Cir. 1974):

> The doctrine of primary jurisdiction has been developed by courts in order to avoid conflict between the courts and an administrative agency arising from either the court's lack of expertise with the subject matter of the agency's regulation or from contradictory rulings by the agency and the court. Under the doctrine, a court should refer a matter to an administrative agency for resolution, *even if the matter is otherwise properly before the court,* if it appears that the matter involves technical or policy considerations which are beyond the court's ordinary competence and within the agency's particular field of expertise. (emphasis added)

Later, in that same opinion, Judge Van Dusen found that *even if the matters raised in the complaint are within the ordinary experience of the judiciary* "the Supreme Court has indicated that the primary jurisdiction doctrine may be applicable in such a situation." *MCI Communications Corp.* v. *American Telephone & Telegraph Co., supra,* 496 F.2d at 223.

Even though district courts often consider claims of arbitrary and unreasonable actions on the part of the government, § 1983 violations, and equal protection claims, and courts within this very district have considered cases involving 29 U.S.C. § 794, this Court must defer decision on the plaintiff's various claims until such time as the Department of Labor has had the opportunity to consider those matters.

The administrative agency is not precluded from considering the plaintiff's claims, despite the fact that no remedies were available at the time this lawsuit was filed. In *Cort* v. *Ash, supra,* the Supreme Court considered the claim of a stockholder seeking both injunctive relief and damages for an alleged violation of a criminal statute prohibiting corporate expenditures in campaigns for federal office. At the time the lawsuit was filed there was no statutory provision for civil enforcement of the act in question. However, prior to the Supreme Court's decision of the matter, the Congress established a Federal Election Commission which had an administrative procedure for processing private complaints of alleged violations of the criminal statute governing federal elections. The Supreme Court, reiterating a long-established principle, held that:

> "a court is to apply the law in effect at the time it renders its decision, unless doing so would result in manifest injustice or there is statutory direction or legislative history to the contrary." There is no "statutory direction or legislative history to the contrary" in or respecting the Amendments, nor is there any possible "manifest injustice" in requiring respondent to pursue with respect to alleged violations which have yet to occur the statutory remedy for injunctive relief created by the Amendments.

Cort v. *Ash, supra,* 95 S.Ct. at 2087. In this case the procedure for enforcing 29 U.S.C. § 793 was not promulgated until April 16, 1976, whereas the complaint in this action was filed on January 26, 1976. Although the regulation under which the plaintiff would seek relief in this case specifies a 180 day limitation for the filing of claims, the regulation also specifies that the director may extend the time for filing a claim upon "good cause shown." 41 C.F.R. § 60-741. 26(a). No more "good cause" can be imagined than that apparent in this case, namely that the regulation had not been adopted at the time the alleged injury was suffered. As in *Cort* v. *Ash,* the plaintiff in this case also has recourse to injunctive relief. In *Cort,* if the Federal Election Commission found that some form of violation existed, the Commissioner could petition the Attorney General to seek injunctive relief in federal court. In the present action, the Director of the Department of Labor has the authority to "seek appropriate judicial action to enforce the contractual provisions set forth in 41 C.F.R. § 60-741.28(b)." There is no "manifest injustice" in requiring plaintiff to seek administrative relief in the first instance, since the Court is retaining jurisdiction of this action. The Court of Appeals for the Third Circuit has previously held that:

> The requirement that Barnes exhaust his administrative remedies thus affects only the timing, not the effectiveness of judicial review. The delay, of course, is not without cost and we regret the additional pecuniary hardship and stress imposed upon Barnes. We are bound, however, by the holding of the Supreme Court that such costs do not constitute irreparable injury.

Barnes v. *Chatterton,* 515 F.2d 916, 921 (3d Cir. 1975). Certainly the holding in the above case would apply with more force in this instance, for the plaintiff is not only assured of judicial review of an administrative determination should agency remedies prove inadequate, but also may be entitled to a *de novo* consideration of the issues raised on the administrative level because of the existence of an independent cause of action under the 14th Amendment and § 1983. Finally, there is no indication that retroactive application of the statute was found to be undesirable by the legislature.

The necessity for administrative consideration of the plaintiff's claim is particularly acute in this case, since the nature of the federal contractual arrangement between Philadelphia General Hospital and the government is, to date, unclear. While the plaintiff alleges that Philadelphia General Hospital receives in excess of $2500 in "federal financial assistance for its clinical and research activities" from the federal government (Plaintiff's Complaint, Doc. # 11, ¶ 11), and this Court notes that the non-personal services covered under § 793 of the Rehabilitation Act of 1973 include research, 41 C.F.R. § 60-741.2, the defendant draws a distinction between federal contracts and *federal grants*. A construction of the agency statute would be particularly helpful in disposing of plaintiff's claims.

Finally, although no administrative remedy is yet prescribed under 29 U.S.C. § 794, and the ambit of § 794 is different from that of § 793, see 41 C.F.R. § 60-741.1, nonetheless there are common issues which permeate plaintiff's claims under both sections of the Rehabilitation Act. One of the purposes of the doctrine of primary jurisdiction, namely the avoidance of contradictory agency and judicial determinations, would seem to be thwarted by an immediate consideration by this Court of plaintiff's claims under 29 U.S.C. § 794. The complaint under both sections of the Rehabilitation Act arises from the same event—the denial of municipal employment by reason of plaintiff's epileptic seizures. Although the standards to be applied under each section of the statute may differ, the critical facts for consideration are the same in each instance and would best be detailed in an agency proceeding.

In light of the doctrine of primary jurisdiction, the present action is STAYED and the plaintiff's claim is REMANDED to the Director of the Department of Labor for consideration without regard to the 180 limitation appearing in 41 C.F.R. § 60-741.26(a).

NOTES

1. Did LaVon Drennon win or lose her case? The court held that § 793 does create a private cause of action for aggrieved parties but then tossed the case to the Department of Labor for possible resolution. Perhaps the outcome of *Drennon* is best described by the male football coaches' age-old cliche concerning tie games: "It's like kissing your sister—nice but not very exciting."

2. The plaintiff can hope that the Department of Labor's awareness that the jurisdiction of a federal court is lurking in the background may spur the Department to take quick and decisive action on her case. Inevitably, however, pursuance of remedies within the federal bureaucracy will occasion significant delays in ultimate resolution of the matter.

WOOD v. DIAMOND STATE TELEPHONE COMPANY

United States District Court for the District of Delaware, 1977
440 F.Supp. 1003

OPINION

STAPLETON, District Judge:

Robert Spencer Wood brought this action against The Diamond State Telephone Company, a Delaware corporation (hereinafter "Diamond"), The Bell Telephone Company of Pennsylvania, a Pennsylvania corporation, The American Telephone and Telegraph Company, a New York corporation, and The American Telephone and Telegraph Company of Delaware, a Delaware corporation. Pursuant to a stipulation among the parties, the action has been dismissed with prejudice as to the latter two corporations.

The original complaint alleges that Wood, a veteran with a disability of 30% or more, is entitled to damages flowing from Diamond's refusal to hire him. He applied for employment with Diamond and was subsequently interviewed and scheduled for a medical examination on February 5, 1974. Shortly after the examination, according to the complaint, Wood was told that he would not be hired because "in ten or twenty years . . . [he] might develop some condition related to his present disability" which would subject Diamond to a disability pension claim.

The plaintiff's first theory of recovery is grounded upon Section 503 of the *Vietnam Era Veteran's Readjustment Act of 1972*, 38 U.S.C. § 2012 (1972), as it existed prior to its amendment in December of 1974. Section 503 then provided:

> (a) Any contract entered into by any department or agency for the procurement of personal property and non-personal services (including construction) for the United States, shall contain a provision requiring that, in employing persons to carry out such contract, the party contracting with the United States shall give special emphasis to the employment of qualified disabled veterans and veterans of the Vietnam era. The provisions of this section shall apply to any subcontract entered into by a prime contractor in carrying out any contract for the procurement of personal property and nonpersonal services (including construction) for the United States. The President shall implement the provisions of this section by promulgating regulations within 60 days after the date of enactment of this section, which regulations shall require that (1) each such contractor undertake in such contract to list immediately with the appropriate local employment service office all of its suitable employment openings, and (2) each such local office shall give such veterans priority in referral to such employment openings.
>
> (b) If any disabled veteran or veteran of the Vietnam era believes any contractor has failed or refuses to comply with the provisions of his contract with the United States, relating to giving special emphasis in employment to veterans, such veteran may file a complaint with the Veterans' Employment Service of the Department of Labor. Such complaint shall be promptly referred to the Secretary who shall promptly investigate such complaint and shall take such action thereon as the facts and circumstances warrant consistent with the terms of such contract and the laws and regulations applicable thereto.

Sometime before the initiation of this lawsuit, the plaintiff resorted to the administrative remedy provided by subsection (b) above. His decision to bring suit before the Department of Labor's final determination was apparently due to his fear that the applicable time period within which he might bring this action might expire in the interim. In October, 1976, the Assistant Regional Administrator of the Office of Federal Contract Compliance Programs, Department of Labor, without mentioning the Veteran's Readjustment Act claim, determined that Diamond, "by refusing to hire [Wood], ha[d] violated its obligations under affirmative action provision of *The Vocational Rehabilitation Act of 1973*, 29 U.S.C. § 793." That Act, in relevant part, provides that:

> (a) Any contract in excess of $2,500 entered into by any Federal department or agency for the procurement of personal property and nonpersonal services (including construction) for the United States shall contain a provision requiring that, in employing persons

to carry out such contract the party contracting with the United States shall take affirmative action to employ and advance in employment qualified handicapped individuals as defined in section 706(6) of this title. The provisions of this section shall apply to any subcontract in excess of $2,500 entered into by a prime contractor in carrying out any contract for the procurement of personal property and nonpersonal services (including construction) for the United States. The President shall implement the provisions of this section by promulgating regulations within ninety days after September 26, 1973.

(b) If any handicapped individual believes any contractor has failed or refuses to comply with the provisions of his contract with the United States, relating to employment of handicapped individuals, such individual may file a complaint with the Department of Labor. The Department shall promptly investigate such complaint and shall take such action thereon as the facts and circumstances warrant, consistent with the terms of such contract and the laws and regulations applicable thereto.

On January 3, 1977 the plaintiff was permitted to amend his complaint to include a second count relating to this latter statutory provision.

The matter presently before the Court is the defendants' motion to dismiss both counts of the complaint on the ground that neither states a claim upon which relief can be granted.

I.   The Vietnam Era Veteran's Readjustment Act of 1972 Claim

Defendants maintain that there is no private cause of action under Section 503 of the Veteran's Readjustment Act. I find it unnecessary to reach that issue, however. Plaintiff does not allege that defendants breached Diamond's contract with the government by failing "to list . . . with the appropriate local employment service office all of its suitable employment openings" or by refusing to consider referrals resulting from such listings. Rather, he alleges that the defendants breached their duty by failing to accord plaintiff a "job preference" and by applying an employment criterion which had a disparate impact on disabled veterans. I reluctantly conclude that, because of the meaning given to the requisite "special emphasis" by the other terms of Section 503, the scope of the defendants' duties under Diamond's contract did not include an obligation to afford the plaintiff a job preference or to refrain from applying a criterion having a disparate impact.

The Report of the Senate Committee on the Vietnam Era Veteran's Readjustment Act of 1972 indicates that Section 503 "is a logical extension of the President's Executive Order No. 11598 issued on June 16, 1971. . . ." That Order required "Government contracts . . . to contain assurances that the contractor . . . shall, to the maximum extent feasible, list all of its suitable employment openings with the appropriate office of the state employment service system. . . ." The Senate Report noted that the increase in listings as a result of this Order had not been as great as anticipated and that Section 503 was "intended to achieve more effectively the intent of the President's Executive Order." The "logical extension" referred to was the deletion of the phrase "to the maximum extent feasible," the addition of a requirement that each local employment office "give such veterans priority in referral to such employment openings" and the creation of an administrative remedy for violations of the duties imposed.

This view of Section 503 is consistent with the contemporaneous understanding of those charged with the responsibility of implementing that section. The implementing regulations specify a contract clause to be inserted in every federal contract over $2,500. That clause provided only that "the contractor, to provide special emphasis to the employment of qualified disabled veterans and veterans of the Vietnam era, agrees that all suitable employment openings . . . shall be offered for listing at an appropriate local office of the State employment service system . . . and to provide such reports to such local offices regarding employment openings and hires [sic] as may be required." 41 C.F.R. § 50-250.6. The contract clause goes on to explain that, while the duty imposed "shall involve . . . the acceptance of referrals of veterans and non-veterans, the listing of employment openings does not require the hiring of any particular job applicant or from any particular group of job applicants."

In summary, I conclude that the scope of Section 503 of the Vietnam Era Veteran's Readjustment Act, as it existed prior to December 3, 1974, was limited to assuring the listing of job openings with State employment agencies and to the preference of certain veterans in referrals by those agencies. It imposed no duties and created no rights with respect to the employer's decision to hire or not to hire. Accordingly, Count I of the complaint must be dismissed.

II. The Rehabilitation Act of 1973 Claim

Section 503 of The Rehabilitation Act of 1973, which I shall refer to by its Code section number, Section 793, to avoid confusion with Section 503 of the Veterans Act, has been set forth above. A review of the implementing regulations is helpful by way of supplement. Section 60-741.4 of those regulations provides in part:

> Each agency and each contractor and subcontractor shall include the following affirmative action clause in each of its covered government contracts or subcontracts (and modifications, renewals, or extensions thereof if not included in the original contract).
> AFFIRMATIVE ACTION FOR HANDICAPPED WORKERS
> (a) The contractor will not discriminate against any employee or applicant for employment because of physical or mental handicap in regard to any position for which the employee or applicant for employment is qualified. The contractor agrees to take affirmative action to employ, advance in employment and otherwise treat qualified handicapped individuals without discrimination based upon their physical or mental handicap in all employment practices such as the following: employment, upgrading, demotion or transfer, recruitment, advertising, layoff or termination, rates of pay or other forms of compensation, and selection for training, including apprenticeship.
> (b) The contractor agrees to comply with the rules, regulations, and relevant orders of the Secretary of Labor issued pursuant to the Act.
> (c) In the event of the contractor's non-compliance with the requirements of this clause, actions for non-compliance may be taken in accordance with the rules, regulations and relevant orders of the Secretary of Labor issued pursuant to the Act.

41 C.F.R. § 60-741.4

Section 60-741.26 specifies the procedures which are to be followed when a complaint is filed with the Labor Department under subsection (b) of Section 793. It provides that the Labor Department "shall institute a prompt investigation of each complaint" and develop "a complete case record" which is to include "recommended findings and resolution.'' If the investigation shows no violation or if the Agency decides not to initiate ''administrative or legal proceedings against the contractor,'' the complainant is notified and, within thirty days, may request a review by the Agency. If the investigation shows a violation, ''conciliation and persuasion'' is attempted. If these efforts fail, the contractor is entitled to a formal hearing before any sanctions may be imposed.

Section 60-741.28 provides:

> (a) *General*. In every case where any complaint investigation indicates the existence of a violation of the affirmative action clause or these regulations, the matter should be resolved by informal means, including conciliation, and persuasion, whenever possible. This will also include establishing a corrective action program in accordance with § 60-741.26(g)(2). Where the apparent violation is not resolved by informal means, the Director or the agency shall proceed in accordance with the enforcement procedures contained in this Part.
>
> (b) *Judicial enforcement*. In addition to the administrative remedies set forth herein, the Director may, within the limitations of applicable law, seek appropriate judicial action to enforce the contractual provisions set forth in § 60-741.4 including appropriate injunctive relief.

The administrative remedies referred to include the withholding of progress payments, contract termination, and ''debarment . . . from receiving future contracts.'' § 60-741.28(c)–(e).

The question for resolution is whether a private cause of action should be implied for violations of Section 793 and the implementing regulations. The parties agree that the standards to be applied in answering this question are found in *Cort* v. *Ash*, 422 U.S. 66, 95 S.Ct. 2080, 45 L.Ed.2d 26 (1975). The Supreme Court there identified four ''relevant'' factors:

> First, is the plaintiff ''one of the class for whose *especial* benefit the statute was enacted,'' . . . that is, does the statute create a federal right in favor of the plaintiff? Second, is there any indication of legislative intent, explicit or implicit, either to create such a remedy or to deny one? . . . Third, is it consistent with the underlying purposes of the legislative scheme to imply such a remedy for the plaintiff? . . . And finally, is the cause of action one traditionally relegated to state law, in an area basically the concern of the States, so that it would be inappropriate to infer a cause of action based solely on federal law?
>
> . . . . .

422 U.S. at 78, 95 S.Ct. at 2088.

Because I must accept plaintiff's allegation that he is a ''qualified handicapped individual'' as defined in 29 U.S.C. § 706(6), the proposition that he is ''one of the class for whose *especial* benefit'' Section 793 was enacted seems self-evident. *Rogers* v. *Frito-Lay, Inc.*, 433 F.Supp. 200, 14 F.E.P. Cases 1752 (N.D.Tex. 1977).

As a sister court in this Circuit has observed, the legislative history is not helpful in determining whether or not Congress contemplated an independent, private cause of action under Section 793. *Drennon* v. *Philadelphia General Hospital*, 428 F.Supp. 809 (E.D.Pa. 1977). While plaintiff has suggested that the legislative history concerning a companion provision, Section 794, is of significance in determining this issue, I conclude that it is not. After describing the contemplated administrative methods of implementing Section 794, the Senate Report expresses the view that "[t]his approach to implementation of section [794] . . . would ensure administrative due process . . . , provide for administrative consistency within the Federal government as well as relative ease of implementation, and permit a judicial remedy through a private action." 1974 U.S. Code Cong. & Admin.News p. 6391. This reference to a judicial remedy through a private action is said to be of significance because, the Senate Report also observes that "[i]t is intended that sections [793 and 794] . . . be administered in such a manner that a consistent, uniform, and effective Federal approach to discrimination against handicapped persons would result." *Id.* at 6391. As will appear from the following discussion, however, there are important distinctions between the approach taken by Congress in Sections 793 and 794 and they have different legislative histories. Moreover, as the Seventh Circuit Court of Appeals has observed, the Committee's reference to a private judicial remedy, when read in context, suggests "judicial review of an administrative proceeding as contradistinct from an independent cause of action in federal court. . . ." *Lloyd* v. *Regional Trans. Authority,* 548 F.2d 1277, 1286 (7th Cir. 1977). This kind of judicial review is quite a different remedy than the one plaintiff asks this Court to imply from Section 793. I conclude, therefore, that the recited legislative history of Section 794 is of no aid in determining whether a private cause of action should be implied from Section 793.

Nor is the fourth factor mentioned in the *Cort* decision helpful in this context. Implication of a federal remedy under Section 793 would not involve an inappropriate intrusion into an area of peculiar State interest and concern.

In a situation of this kind, I believe the crucial inquiry relates to the third *Cort* factor—would an independent private cause of action be consistent with the underlying purposes of the legislative scheme? This question is not answered simply by pointing out that handicapped persons are the intended beneficiaries of the Act and that implication of private cause of action would provide such individuals with an additional remedy. We must inquire further to determine whether an independent private cause of action would be consistent with the overall legislative scheme including the manner in which Congress provided its goals should be furthered and its legislation enforced.

Before turning to the elements of legislative scheme it is helpful to recognize what the practical significance of implying an independent private cause of action would be insofar as the administration of the Act is concerned. The question before this Court does not involve the issue of whether there will be judicial control of the administration of the Act or whether there will be judicial enforcement of sanctions upon contractors who have violated the Act. Section 793 and the regulations implementing it expressly contemplate that the agency may seek judicial enforcement of sanctions and, as the *Lloyd* opinion suggests, there may well be judicial review of agency determinations for or against a complainant.

Similarly the issue before the Court does not involve the question of whether the agency will be permitted to define the somewhat nebulous terms of the statute and develop a uniform body of national law by applying those definitions to individual cases. If an independent private cause of action is implied, it is to be expected that the federal courts, after determining that they have jurisdiction to entertain such a case, will invoke the doctrine of primary jurisdiction, to stay the proceedings before them, and give great deference to any agency determinations thereafter made. The *Drennon* court, which implied a private cause of action, recognized this fact. *Drennon* v. *Philadelphia General Hospital, supra.* While this does not mean that the role of the agency would be precisely the same as it would be if no private cause of action is implied, it suggests that the weight placed by the defendants on the desirability of uniformity is exaggerated.

Insofar as the administration of the Act is concerned, it seems to me that the principal differences between implying an independent cause of action, while at the same time recognizing primary jurisdiction in the agency, and refusing to imply such a cause of action relate (1) to whether contractors will be exposed to the burdens of *de novo* litigation, and (2) whether the remedies fashioned in cases of violations will be limited to those which the agency, in its discretion, deems appropriate. The importance of these differences becomes evident when the legislative scheme is analyzed.

Section 793 does not make discrimination against handicapped persons in the private sector illegal. Rather, it requires that an "affirmative action" covenant be inserted in all government contracts which exceed the modest amount of $2,500. Any contractor who chooses to enter such a contract is put on notice by Congress that, in the event of a violation, the Department of Labor will take "such action . . . as the facts and circumstances [determined by the Department] warrant, consistent with the terms of such contract and the laws and regulations applicable thereto." This Congressional approach, in my judgment, suggests that the duties imposed are to be duties assumed by contract and that the exposure of the contractor is to be limited to the terms of his contract and of any statutes and regulations applicable thereto. Given this approach, in the absence of any legislative history so suggesting, I conclude that a court should not infer an intent to subject contractors to independent federal actions at the instance of individuals and to remedies other than those determined appropriate by the agency in accordance with the contract and the rules, regulations, and relevant orders of the Secretary.

Also of importance is the emphasis in the legislative scheme on the resolutions of disputes by conciliations and persuasion. I think it apparent that the existence of independent federal litigation, even if stayed during the administrative process, and the possibility of relief independently fashioned by a federal court is likely to impair the effectiveness of the administrative conciliation process. Indeed, this case offers an excellent example of the potential mischief. After the Department of Labor found Diamond to be in violation of Section 793, it initiated conciliation efforts. The record reflects that the principal reason these efforts have been unsuccessful is a dispute between the parties as to whether recovery for "mental anguish, pain and suffering" is available in this proceeding.

Because I find independent federal litigation at the initiative of private individuals to be inconsistent with the legislative scheme fashioned by Congress, I conclude that no private right of action should be implied under Section 793.

* * *

NOTES

1. The plaintiff's claim under the Vietnam Era Veteran's Readjustment Act has not been the subject of much litigative activity. Notice that under the Act federal contractors have to promise two things: 1) to "provide special emphasis to the employment of qualified disabled veterans and veterans of the Vietnam era," and 2) to list job openings with the state employment service. The court's interpretation of the statute seems to ignore the former requirement, thereby emasculating the Congressional intent to promote the hiring of disabled veterans and veterans of the Vietnam era.

2. The *Wood* court summarized some of the pertinent provisions of the Department of Labor's regulations for implementing § 793 (§ 503). The full text of these regulations follows.

RULES OF THE DEPARTMENT OF LABOR, EMPLOYMENT STANDARDS ADMINISTRATION

41 C.F.R. Part 60-741, 41 Fed. Reg. 16147, April 16, 1976

Part 60-741—Affirmative Action Obligations of
Contractors and Subcontractors for Handicapped Workers

Subpart A—Preliminary Matters, Affirmative Action Clause, Compliance

Sec.

60-741.1   Purpose and application.
60-741.2   Definitions
60-741.3   Coverage and waivers.
60-741.4   Affirmative action clause.
60-741.5   Applicability of the affirmative action program requirement.
60-741.6   Affirmative action policy, practices and procedures.
60-741.7   Determination of handicap.
60-741.8   Listing of employment openings.
60-741.9   Labor unions and recruiting and training agencies.

Subpart B—General Enforcement and Complaint Procedure

Sec.

60-741.20   Subcontracts.
60-741.21   Adaptation of language.
60-741.22   Incorporation by reference.
60-741.23   Incorporation by operation of the Act and agency regulations.
60-741.24   Duties of agencies.
60-741.25   Evaluations by the Director.
60-741.26   Complaint procedures.
60-741.27   Noncompliance with the affirmative action clause.
60-741.28   Actions for noncompliance.
60-741.29   Formal hearings.
60-741.30   Notification of agencies.
60-741.31   Contractor ineligibility list.
60-741.32   Disputed matters related to the affirmative action program.

Subpart C—Ancillary Matters

Authority: Sec. 503, Pub. L. 93-1112, 87 Stat. 393 (20 U.S.C. 793), as amended by sec. 111, Pub. L. 93-516, 88 Stat. 1619 (29 U.S.C. 706) and Executive Order 11758.

Source: 41 FR 16148, Apr. 16, 1976, unless otherwise noted.

Subpart A—Preliminary Matters, Affirmative Action Clause, Compliance

§ 60-741.1 Purpose and application.

The purpose of the regulations in this Part is to assure compliance with section 503 of the Rehabilitation Act of 1973, which requires government contractors and subcontractors to take affirmative action to employ and advance in employment qualified handicapped individuals. The regulations in this Part apply to all government contracts and subcontracts for the furnishing of supplies or services or for the use of real or personal property (including construction) for $2,500 or more. Compliance of a contractor with the provisions of this Part will not necessarily determine its compliance with the requirements of section 504 of the Rehabilitation Act of 1973 and compliance with section 504 will not necessarily determine compliance with section 503 and the regulations in this Part.

§ 60-741.2 Definitions.

"Act" means the Rehabilitation Act of 1973, Pub. L. 93-112, as amended by the Rehabilitation Act Amendments of 1974, Pub. L. 93-516.

"Affirmative action clause" means the contract provisions set forth in § 60-741.4.

"Agency" means any contracting and/or compliance agency of the government.

"Assistant Secretary" means the Assistant Secretary of Labor for Employment Standards or his or her designee.

"Compliance agency" means any agency which the Director requests to conduct investigations and such other responsibilities in connection with the administration of the Act as the Director may request, as appropriate, including the responsibility to ensure that contractors are fully cognizant of their obligations under the Act and this Part and to provide the Director with any information which comes to its attention that the contractor is not in compliance with the Act or this Part.

"Construction" means the construction, rehabilitation, alteration, conversion, extension, demolition, or repair of buildings, highways, or other changes or improvements to real property, including facilities providing utility services. The term also includes the supervision, inspection, and other onsite functions incidental to the actual construction.

"Contract" means any government contract.

"Contracting agency" means any department, agency, establishment or instrumentality of the United States, including any wholly owned government corporation, which enters into contracts.

"Contractor" means, unless otherwise indicated, a prime contractor or subcontractor.

"Director" means the Director of the Office of Federal Contract Compliance Programs of the United States Department of Labor.

"Government" means the government of the United States of America.

"Government contract" means any agreement or modification thereof between any contracting agency and any person for the furnishing of supplies or services or for the use of real or personal property including lease arrangements. The term "services," as used in this section includes, but is not limited to the following services: utility, construction, transportation, research, insurance, and fund depository, irrespective of whether the government is the purchaser or seller. The term "government contract" does not include (1) agreements in which the parties stand in the relationship of employer and employee, and (2) federally-assisted contracts.

"Handicapped individual" means any person who (1) has a physical or mental impairment which substantially limits one or more of such person's major life activities, (2) has a record of such impairment or (3) is regarded as having such an impairment. For purposes of this Part, a handicapped individual is "substantially limited" if he or she is likely to experience difficulty in securing, retaining or advancing in employment because of a handicap. (See Appendix A attached for guidelines on the applications of this definition.)

"Modification" means any alteration in the terms and conditions of a contract, including supplemental agreements, amendments, and extensions.

"Person" means any natural person, corporation, partnership or joint venture, unincorporated association, state or local government, and any agency, instrumentality, or subdivision of such a government.

"Prime contractor" means any person holding a contract, and, for the purposes of Subpart B of this Part, includes any person who has held a contract subject to the Act.

"Qualified handicapped individual" means a handicapped individual as defined in § 60-741.2 who is capable of performing a particular job, with reasonable accommodation to his or her handicap.

"Recruiting and training agency" means any person who refers workers to any contractor or subcontractor, or who provides or supervises apprenticeship or training for employment by any contractor or subcontractor.

"Rules, regulations, and relevant orders of the Secretary of Labor," as used in paragraph (b) of the affirmative action clause means rules, regulations, and relevant orders of the Secretary of Labor of his or her designee issued pursuant to the Act.

"Secretary" means the Secretary of Labor, U.S. Department of Labor.

"Subcontract" means any agreement or arrangement between a contractor and any person (in which the parties do not stand in the relationship of an employer and an employee):

(1) For the furnishing of supplies or services or for the use of real or personal property, including lease arrangements, which, in whole or in part, is necessary to the performance of any one or more contracts; or

(2) Under which any portion of the contractor's obligation under any one or more contracts is performed, undertaken, or assumed.

"Subcontractor" means any person holding a subcontract and, for the purpose of Subpart B of this Part, any person who has held a subcontract subject to the Act.

"United States" as used herein shall include the several States, the District of Columbia, the Virgin Islands, the Commonwealth of Puerto Rico, Guam, the Panama Canal Zone, American Samoa and the Trust Territory of the Pacific Islands.
[41 FR 16148. Apr. 16, 1976; 42 FR 3307, Jan. 18, 1977]

§ 60-741.3   Coverage and waivers.

(a) *General.* (1) Transactions for less than $2,500. Contracts and subcontracts for less than $2,500 are not covered by the Act. No agency, contractor or subcontractor shall procure supplies or services in less than usual quantities to avoid the applicability of the affirmative action clause.

(2) Contracts and subcontracts for indefinite quantities. With respect to indefinite delivery-type contracts and subcontracts (including, but not limited to, open end contracts, requirement-type contracts, Federal Supply Schedule contracts, "call-type" contracts, and purchase notice agreements), the affirmative action clause shall be included unless the contracting agency has reason to believe that the amount to be ordered in any year under such contract will be less than $2,500. The applicability of the affirmative action clause shall be determined at the time of award for the first year, and annually thereafter for succeeding years, if any. Notwithstanding the above, the affirmative action clause shall be applied to such contract whenever the amount of a single order is $2,500 or more. Once the affirmative action clause is determined to be applicable, the contract shall continue to be subject to such clause for its duration, regardless of the amounts ordered, or reasonably expected to be ordered in any year.

(3) Work outside the United States. The requirements of the affirmative action clause are waived with respect to contracts and subcontracts with regard to work performed outside the United States by employees who were not recruited within the United States.

(4) Contracts with state or local governments. The requirements of the affirmative action clause in any contract or subcontract with a state or local government (or any agency, instrumentality or subdivision thereof) shall not be applicable to any agency, instrumentality or subdivision of such government which does not participate in work on or under the contract or subcontract.

(5) Facilities not connected with contracts. The Director may waive the requirements of the affirmative action clause with respect to any of a prime contractor's or subcontractor's facilities which he or she finds to be in all respects separate and distinct from activities of the prime contractor or subcontractor related to the performance of the contract or subcontract, provided that he or she also finds that such a

waiver will not interfere with or impede the effectuation of the Act. Such waivers shall be considered only upon the request of the contractor or subcontractor.

(b) *Waivers*. (1) Specific contracts and classes of contracts. The head of an agency, with the concurrence of the Director, may waive the application to any contract or subcontract of any part of or all the affirmative action clause when he or she deems that special circumstances in the national interest so require. The agency head, with the concurrence of the Director, may also grant such waivers to groups or categories of contracts or subcontracts of the same type where it is (i) in the national interest, (ii) found impracticable to act upon each request individually, and (iii) where such waiver will substantially contribute to convenience in administration of section 503 of the Act.

(2) National security. Any requirement set forth in the regulations in this Part shall not apply to any contract or subcontract whenever the head of the contracting agency determines that such contract or subcontract is essential to the national security and that its award without complying with such requirements is necessary to the national security. Upon making such a determination the head of the agency will notify the Director in writing within 30 days.

(c) *Withdrawal of waiver*. When a waiver has been granted for any class of contracts or subcontracts under this section other than contracts granted waivers under paragraph (b)(2) of this section, the Director may withdraw the waiver for a specific contract or subcontract or group of contracts or subcontracts to be awarded, when in his or her judgment such action is necessary or appropriate to achieve the purposes of the Act. The withdrawal shall not apply to contracts or subcontracts awarded prior to the withdrawal, except that in procurements entered into by formal advertising, or the various forms of restricted formal advertising, such withdrawal shall not apply unless the withdrawal is made more than 10 calendar days before the date set for the opening of the bids.

§ 60-741.4   Affirmative action clause.

Each agency and each contractor and subcontractor shall include the following affirmative action clause in each of its covered government contracts or subcontracts (and modifications, renewals, or extensions thereof if not included in the original contract).

Affirmative Action for Handicapped Workers

(a) The contractor will not discriminate against any employee or applicant for employment because of physical or mental handicap in regard to any position for which the employee or applicant for employment is qualified. The contractor agrees to take affirmative action to employ, advance in employment and otherwise treat qualified handicapped individuals without discrimination based upon their physical or mental handicap in all employment practices such as the following: employment, upgrading, demotion or transfer, recruitment, advertising, layoff or termination, rates of pay or other forms of compensation, and selection for training, including apprenticeship.

(b) The contractor agrees to comply with the rules, regulations, and relevant orders of the Secretary of Labor issued pursuant to the Act.

(c) In the event of the contractor's noncompliance with the requirements of this clause, actions for noncompliance may be taken in accordance with the rules, regulations and relevant orders of the Secretary of Labor issued pursuant to the Act.

(d) The contractor agrees to post in conspicuous places, available to employees and applicants for employment, notices in a form to be prescribed by the Director, provided by or through the contracting officer. Such notices shall state the contractor's obligation under the law to take affirmative action to employ and advance in employment qualified handicapped employees and applicants for employment, and the rights of applicants and employees.

(e) The contractor will notify each labor union or representative of workers with which it has a collective bargaining agreement or other contract understanding, that the contractor is bound by the terms of section 503 of the Rehabilitation Act of 1973, and is committed to take affirmative action to employ and advance in employment physically and mentally handicapped individuals.

(f) The contractor will include the provisions of this clause in every subcontract or purchase order of $2,500 or more unless exempted by rules, regulations, or orders of the Secretary issued pursuant to section 503 of the Act, so that such provisions will be binding upon each subcontractor or vendor. The contractor will take such action with respect to any subcontract or purchase order as the Director of the Office of Federal Contract Compliance Programs may direct to enforce such provisions, including action for noncompliance.

§ 60-741.5   Applicability of the affirmative action program requirement.

(a) Within 120 days of the commencement of a contract every government contractor or subcontractor holding a contract of $50,000 or more and having 50 or more employees shall prepare and maintain an affirmative action program at each establishment which shall set forth the contractor's policies, practices and procedures in accordance with § 60-741.6 of this Part. This program may be integrated into or kept separate from other affirmative action programs of the contractor. Contractors presently holding government contracts shall update their affirmative action programs within 120 days of the effective date of this Part.

(b) The affirmative action program shall be reviewed and updated annually. If there are any significant changes in procedures, rights or benefits as a result of the annual updating, those changes shall be communicated to employees and applicants for employment.

(c) (1) The contractor shall invite all applicants and employees who believe themselves covered by the Act and who wish to benefit under the affirmative action program to identify themselves to the contractor. The invitation shall state that the information is voluntarily provided, that it will be kept confidential, that refusal to provide it will not subject the applicant or employee to any adverse treatment, and that it will be used only in accordance with the Act and the regulations in this Part. If an applicant or employee so identifies himself or herself the contractor should also seek the advice of the applicant or employee regarding proper placement and appropriate accommodation. (An acceptable form for such an invitation is set forth in Appendix B attached.)

(2) Nothing in this section shall preclude an employee from informing a contractor at any future time of his or her desire to benefit under the program.

(3) Nothing in this section shall relieve a contractor of its obligation to take affirmative action with respect to those applicants or employees of whose handicap the

contractor has actual knowledge: *Provided,* that the contractor is not obligated to search the medical files of any applicant or employee to determine the existence of a handicap.

(4) Nothing in this section shall relieve a contractor from liability for discrimination under the Act.

(d) The full affirmative action program shall be available for inspection to any employee or applicant for employment upon request. The location and hours during which the program may be obtained shall be posted at each facility.

[41 FR 16148, Apr. 16, 1976; 42 FR 3307, Jan. 18, 1977]

§ 60-741.6   Affirmative action policy, practices and procedures.

(a) *General requirements.* Under the affirmative action obligation imposed by section 503 of the Rehabilitation Act of 1973, contractors are required to take affirmative action to employ and advance in employment qualified handicapped individuals at all levels of employment, including the executive level. Such action shall apply to all employment practices, including, but not limited to, the following: hiring, upgrading, demotion or transfer, recruitment or recruitment advertising, layoff or termination, rates of pay or other forms of compensation, and selection for training, including apprenticeship.

(b) *Proper consideration of qualifications.* Contractors shall review their personnel processes to determine whether their present procedures assure careful, thorough and systematic consideration of the job qualifications of known handicapped applicants and employees for job vacancies filled either by hiring or promotion, and for all training opportunities offered or available. To the extent that it is necessary to modify their personnel procedures, contractors shall include the development of new procedures for this purpose in their affirmative action program required under this Part. These procedures must be designed so as to facilitate a review of the implementation of this requirement by the contractor or the government. (Appendix C attached is an example of an appropriate set of procedures. The procedures in Appendix C are not required and contractors may develop other procedures which are appropriate to their circumstances.)

(c) *Physical and mental qualifications.* (1) The contractor shall provide in its affirmative action program, and shall adhere to, a schedule for the review of all physical or mental job qualification requirements to ensure that, to the extent qualification requirements tend to screen out qualified handicapped individuals, they are job related and are consistent with business necessity and the safe performance of the job.

(2) Whenever a contractor applies physical or mental job qualification requirements in the selection of applicants or employees for employment or other change in employment status such as promotion, demotion or training, to the extent that qualification requirements tend to screen out qualified handicapped individuals, the requirements shall be related to the specific job or jobs for which the individual is being considered and shall be consistent with business necessity and the safe performance of the job. The contractor shall have the burden to demonstrate that it has complied with the requirements of this paragraph.

(3) Nothing in this section shall prohibit a contractor from conducting a comprehensive medical examination prior to employment provided that the results of such

an examination shall be used only in accordance with the requirements of this section. Whenever a contractor inquires into an applicant's or employee's physical or mental condition or conducts a medical examination prior to employment or change in employment status information obtained in response to such inquiries or examination shall be kept confidential except that:

(i) Supervisors and managers may be informed regarding restrictions on the work or duties of handicapped individuals and regarding accommodations; and

(ii) First aid and safety personnel may be informed, where and to the extent appropriate, if the condition might require emergency treatment; and

(iii) Government officials investigating compliance with the Act shall be informed.

(d) *Accommodation to physical and mental limitations of employees.* A contractor must make a reasonable accommodation to the physical and mental limitations of an employee or applicant unless the contractor can demonstrate that such an accommodation would impose an undue hardship on the conduct of the contractor's business. In determining the extent of a contractor's accommodation obligations, the following factors among others may be considered: (1) Business necessity and (2) financial cost and expenses.

(e) *Compensation.* In offering employment or promotions to handicapped individuals, the contractor may not reduce the amount of compensation offered because of any disability income, pension or other benefit the applicant or employee receives from another source.

(f) *Outreach, positive recruitment, and external dissemination of policy.* Contractors shall review their employment practices to determine whether their personnel programs provide the required affirmative action for employment and advancement of qualified handicapped individuals. Based upon the findings of such reviews, contractors shall undertake appropriate outreach and positive recruitment activities, such as those listed below. It is not contemplated that contractors will necessarily undertake all the listed activities or that their activities will be limited to those listed. The scope of a contractor's efforts shall depend upon all the circumstances, including the contractor's size and resources and the extent to which existing employment practices are adequate.

(1) The contractor should develop internal communication of its obligation to engage in affirmative action efforts to employ qualified handicapped individuals in such a manner as to foster understanding, acceptance and support among the contractor's executive, management, supervisory and all other employees and to encourage such persons to take the necessary action to aid the contractor in meeting this obligation.

(2) The contractor should develop reasonable internal procedures to ensure that its obligation to engage in affirmative action to employ and promote qualified handicapped individuals is being fully implemented.

(3) The contractor should periodically inform all employees and prospective employees of its commitment to engage in affirmative action to increase employment opportunities for qualified handicapped individuals.

(4) The contractor should enlist the assistance and support of recruiting sources (including state employment security agencies, state vocational rehabilitation agencies or facilities, sheltered workshops, college placement officers, state education agencies,

labor organizations and organizations of or for handicapped individuals) for the contractor's commitment to provide meaningful employment opportunities to qualified handicapped individuals. (A list of numerous national organizations serving the handicapped, many of which have state or local affiliates, is found in the "Directory of Organizations Interested in the Handicapped" published by the Committee for the Handicapped People-to-People Program, Washington, D.C.)

(5) The contractor should engage in recruitment activities at educational institutions which participate in training of the handicapped, such as schools for the blind, deaf, or retarded.

(6) The contractor should establish meaningful contracts with appropriate social service agencies, organizations of and for handicapped individuals, vocational rehabilitation agencies or facilities, for such purposes as advice, technical assistance and referral of potential employees. Technical assistance from the resources described in this paragraph may consist of advice on proper placement, recruitment, training and accommodations contractors may undertake, but no such resource providing technical assistance shall have the authority to approve or disapprove the acceptability of affirmative action programs.

(7) The contractor should review employment records to determine the availability of promotable and transferable qualified known handicapped individuals presently employed, and to determine whether their present and potential skills are being fully utilized or developed.

(8) The contractor should include handicapped workers when employees are pictured in consumer, promotional or help wanted advertising.

(9) The contractor should send written notification of company policy to all subcontractors, vendors and suppliers, requesting appropriate action on their part.

(10) The contractor should take positive steps to attract qualified handicapped persons not currently in the work force who have requisite skills and can be recruited through affirmative action measures. These persons may be located through the local chapters of organizations of and for handicapped individuals described in paragraph (f)(4).

(g) *Internal dissemination of policy.* A strong outreach program will be ineffective without adequate internal support from supervisory and management personnel and other employees, who may have had limited contact with handicapped persons in the past. In order to assure greater employee cooperation and participation in the contractor's efforts, the contractor should adopt, implement and disseminate this policy internally as follows:

(1) Include it in the contractor's policy manual.

(2) Publicize it in the company newspaper, magazine, annual report and other media.

(3) Conduct special meetings with executive, management, and supervisory personnel to explain the intent of the policy and individual responsibility for effective implementation, making clear the chief executive officer's attitude.

(4) Schedule special meetings with all employees to discuss policy and explain individual employee responsibilities.

(5) Discuss the policy thoroughly in both employee orientation and management training programs.

(6) Meet with union officials to inform them of the contractor's policy, and request their cooperation.

(7) Include nondiscrimination clauses in all union agreements, and review all contractual provisions to ensure they are nondiscriminatory.

(8) Include articles on accomplishments of handicapped workers in company publications.

(9) Post the policy on company bulletin boards, including a statement that employees and applicants are protected from coercion, intimidation, interference or discrimination for filing a complaint or assisting in an investigation under the Act.

(10) When employees are featured in employee handbooks or similar publications for employees, include handicapped employees.

(h) *Responsibility for implementation.* An executive of the contractor should be designated as director or manager of company affirmative action activities under these regulations. His or her identity should appear on all internal and external communications regarding the company's affirmative action programs. This executive should be given necessary top management support and staff to manage the implementation of this program, including the following activities:

(1) Develop policy statements, affirmative action programs, and internal and external communication techniques. The latter techniques should include regular discussions with local managers, supervisors and employees to be certain the contractor's policies are being followed. In addition, supervisors should be advised that:

(i) Their work performance is being evaluated on the basis of their affirmative action efforts and results, as well as other criteria.

(ii) The contractor is obligated to prevent harassment of employees placed through affirmative action efforts, as set forth in § 60-741.51.

(2) Identify problem areas in conjunction with line management and known handicapped employees, in the implementation of the affirmative action programs, and develop solutions. This is particularly important for the accommodations requirements.

(3) Design and implement audit and reporting systems that will:

(i) Measure effectiveness of the contractor's programs.

(ii) Indicate need for remedial action.

(iii) Determine the degree to which the contractor's objectives have been attained.

(iv) Determine whether known handicapped employees have had the opportunity to participate in all company sponsored educational, training, recreational and social activities.

(v) Ensure that each location is in compliance with the Act and the regulations in this Part.

(4) Serve as liaison between the contractor and enforcement agencies.

(5) Serve as liaison between the contractor and organizations of and for handicapped persons, and arrange for the active involvement by company representatives in the community service programs of local organizations of and for the handicapped.

(6) Keep management informed of the latest developments in the entire affirmative action area.

(7) Arrange for career counseling for known handicapped employees.

(i) *Development and execution of affirmative action programs.* (1) Job qualification requirements reviewed pursuant to paragraph (c) of this section should be made available to all members of management involved in the recruitment, screening, selection, and promotion process.

(2) The contractor should evaluate the total selection process including training and promotion to ensure freedom from stereotyping handicapped persons in a manner which limits their access to all jobs for which they are qualified.

(3) All personnel involved in the recruitment, screening, selection, promotion, disciplinary, and related processes should be carefully selected and trained to ensure that the commitments in its affirmative action program are implemented.

(4) Formal briefing sessions should be held, preferably on company premises, with representatives from recruiting sources. Plant tours, clear and concise explanations of current and future job openings, position descriptions, worker specifications, explanations of the company's selection process, and recruiting literature should be an integral part of the briefings. Formal arrangements should be made for referral of applicants, follow up with sources, and feedback on disposition of applicants.

(5) A special effort should be made to include qualified handicapped persons on the personnel relations staff.

(6) Handicapped employees should be made available for participation in career days, youth motivation programs, and related activities in their communities.

(7) Recruiting efforts at all schools should incorporate special efforts to reach handicapped students.

(8) An effort should be made to participate in workstudy programs with rehabilitation facilities and schools which specialize in training or educating handicapped individuals.

(9) The contractor should use all available resources to continue or establish on the job training programs.

(j) *Sheltered workshops.* Contracts with sheltered workshops do not constitute affirmative action in lieu of employment and advancement of qualified handicapped individuals in the contractor's own workforce. Contracts with sheltered workshops may be included within an affirmative action program if the sheltered workshop trains employees for the contractor and the contractor is obligated to hire trainees at full compensation when such trainees become qualified as "qualified handicapped individuals" as defined in § 60-741.2.

[41 FR 16148, Apr. 16, 1976; 42 FR 3307, Jan. 18, 1977]

§ 60-741.7 Determination of handicap.

(a) Any handicapped individual filing a complaint with the Director under this Part shall submit with his or her complaint a signed statement specifying the handicapping impairment or situation (see § 60-741.2 definition of "handicapped individual"). If the Director determines that further documentation is necessary, he or she may require the complainant to provide additional information.

(b) Any contractor requiring a determination of an applicant's or employee's handicap may require the applicant or employee to provide medical documentation of the impairment or, in the alternative, may require the applicant or employee to undergo a medical examination at the contractor's expense.

(c) Any determination of handicap required pursuant to paragraph (b) of this section must meet the requirements of § 60-741.5(c) and must be for the purpose of affirmative action and proper job placement. Information obtained therefrom shall not be used to exclude or otherwise limit the employment opportunities of qualified handicapped individuals.

(d) All medical documentation required under this section shall be based upon the American Medical Association Guides to the Evaluation of Permanent Impairment, provided that the Guides shall be used only to determine the existence of impairment without regard to the degree of impairment.

§ 60-741.8   Listing of employment openings.

Contractors should request state employment security agencies to refer qualified handicapped individuals for consideration under their affirmative action programs.

§ 60-741.9   Labor unions and recruiting and training agencies.

(a) Whenever performance in accordance with the affirmative action clause or any matter contained in the regulations in this Part may necessitate a revision of a collective bargaining agreement, the labor union or unions which are parties to such agreements shall be given an adequate opportunity to present their views to the agency, or to the Director.

(b) The Director shall use his or her best efforts, directly or through contractors, subcontractors, local officials, vocational rehabilitation facilities, and all other available instrumentalities, to cause any Labor union, recruiting and training agency or other representative of workers who are or may be engaged in work under contracts and subcontracts to cooperate with, and to assist in, the implementation of the purposes of the Act.

Subpart B—General Enforcement and Complaint Procedure
§ 60-741.20   Subcontracts.

Each nonexempt prime contractor and subcontractor shall include the affirmative action clause prescribed in § 60-741.4 in each of their nonexempt subcontracts. The clause may be incorporated by reference in accordance with § 60-741.22.
[41 FR 16148, Apr. 16, 1976; 42 FR 3307, Jan. 18, 1977]

§ 60-741.21   Adaptation of language.

Such necessary changes in language may be made to the affirmative action clause (see § 60-741.4) as shall be appropriate to identify properly the parties and their undertakings.
[41 FR 16148, Apr. 16, 1976; 42 FR 3307, Jan. 18, 1977]

§ 60-741.22   Incorporation by reference.

The affirmative action clause and the regulations contained in this Part may be incorporated by reference in all contracts and subcontracts.

§ 60-741.23   Incorporation by operation of the Act and agency regulations.

By operation of the Act, the affirmative action clause shall be considered to be a part of every contract and subcontract required by the Act and the regulations in this Part to include such a clause, whether or not it is physically incorporated in such contracts and whether or not there is a written contract between the agency and the contractor.

§ 60-741.24   Duties of agencies.

(a) General responsibility. Each agency shall cooperate with the Director in the performance of his or her responsibilities under the Act. Such cooperation shall include the responsibility to ensure that contractors are fully cognizant of their obligations under the Act and this Part, to provide the Director with any information which comes to its attention that the contractor is not in compliance with the Act or this Part, and to take such actions for noncompliance as set forth in § 60-741.28 as may be ordered by the Director.

(b) Designation of agency official. The head of each agency, or his or her designee, shall identify and submit to the Director the name, address and telephone number of the official within the agency who is primarily responsible for implementation of this program within the agency.
[41 FR 16148, Apr. 16, 1976; 42 FR 3307, Jan. 18, 1977]

§ 60-741.25   Evaluations by the Director.

The Director shall be primarily responsible for undertaking such investigations of complaints and other matters as well as evaluations of contractor and agency performance as may be necessary to assure that the purposes of section 503 of the Rehabilitation Act of 1973 are being effectively carried out.

§ 60-741.26   Complaint procedures.

(a) *Place and time of filing.* Any applicant for employment with a contractor or any employee of a contractor may, personally or by an authorized representative, file a written complaint with the Director alleging a violation of the Act or the regulations in this Part. Such complaint must be filed within 180 days from the date of the alleged violation, unless the time for filing is extended by the Director for good cause shown.

(b) *Referral to contractor.* When a complaint is filed by an employee of a contractor and the contractor has an applicable internal review procedure, the complaint shall be referred to the contractor for processing under that procedure. The complaint and all actions taken thereunder shall be kept confidential by the contractor. If there has not been a resolution of the complaint under that procedure satisfactory to the complainant within 60 days of the referral, the Department of Labor or the designated agency will proceed as provided in this section.

(c) *Contents of complaints.* Complaints must be signed by the complainants or their authorized representatives and must contain the following information: (1) Name and address (including telephone number) of the complainant, (2) name and address of the contractor or subcontractor who committed the alleged violation, (3) a description of the act or acts considered to be a violation, (4) a signed statement that the individual is handicapped or has a history of a handicap or other documentation of impairment or was regarded by the contractor as having an impairment, and (5) other pertinent information available which will assist in the investigation and resolution of the complaint, including the name of any known federal agency with which the employer has contracted.

(d) *Incomplete information.* Where a complaint contains incomplete information, the Director or the agency designated by the Director for investigation of the complaint shall seek the needed information from the complainant. If the information is not furnished to the agency or the Director within 60 days of the date of such request, the case may be closed.

(e) *Investigations.* The Department of Labor or the designated agency shall institute a prompt investigation of each complaint, and shall be responsible for developing a complete case record. A complete case record consists of the following: (1) Name and address of each person interviewed, (2) a summary of his or her statement, (3) copies or summaries of pertinent documents, (4) a narrative summary of the evidence disclosed in the investigation as it related to each charge, and (5) recommended findings and resolution.

(f) *Responsibilities of agencies.* Agencies shall conduct investigations of complaints in accordance with specific requests of the Director.

(g) *Resolution of matters.* (1) If the complaint investigation shows no violation of the Act or regulations in this Part, or if the agency or the Director decides not to initiate administrative or legal proceedings against the contractor, the complainant shall be so notified. Within 30 days, the complainant may request review by the Director of such a finding or decision.

(2) Where an investigation indicates that the contractor has not complied with the requirements of the Act or this Part, efforts shall be made to secure compliance through conciliation and persuasion within a reasonable time. Before the contractor or subcontractor can be found to be in compliance, it must make a specific commitment, in writing, to take corrective action to meet the requirements of the Act and this Part. The commitment must indicate the precise action to be taken and dates for completion. The time period allowed should be no longer than the minimum period necessary to effect such changes. Upon approval of such commitment by the Director or the agency, the contractor may be considered in compliance on condition that the commitments are kept. Where the matter has been referred to an agency for investigation and resolution, the contractor and the complainant shall be advised that the resolution is subject to review by the Director and may be disapproved if it is determined that such resolution is not sufficient to achieve compliance.

(3) Where the complaint investigation indicates a violation of the Act or regulations in this Part (and the complaint has not been resolved by informal means), the Director, or the agency with the approval of the Director, shall afford the contractor an opportunity for a hearing in accordance with § 60-741.29.

§ 60-741.27   Noncompliance with the affirmative action clause.

Noncompliance with the prime contractor's or subcontractor's obligations under the affirmative action clause is a ground for taking appropriate action for noncompliance as set forth in § 60-741.28 by the agency, the Director, prime contractor,

or subcontractor. Any such noncompliance shall be reported in writing to the Director by the agency as soon as practicable after it is identified.
[41 FR 16148, Apr. 16, 1976; 42 FR 3307, Jan. 18, 1977]

§ 60-741.28   Actions for noncompliance.

(a) *General.* In every case where any complaint investigation indicates the existence of a violation of the affirmative action clause or these regulations, the matter should be resolved by informal means, including conciliation, and persuasion, whenever possible. This will also include establishing a corrective action program in accordance with § 60-741.26(g)(2). Where the apparent violation is not resolved by informal means, the Director or the agency shall proceed in accordance with the enforcement procedures contained in this Part.

(b) *Judicial enforcement.* In addition to the administrative remedies set forth herein, the Director may, within the limitations of applicable law, seek appropriate judicial action to enforce the contractual provisions set forth in § 60-741.4 including appropriate injunctive relief.

(c) *Withholding progress payments.* With the prior approval of the Director so much of the accrued payment due on the contract or any other contract between the government prime contractor and the federal government may be withheld as necessary to correct any violations of the provisions of the affirmative action clause.

(d) *Termination.* A contract or subcontract may be cancelled or terminated, in whole or in part, for failure to comply with the provisions of the affirmative action clause.

(e) *Debarment.* A prime contractor or subcontractor or a prospective contractor or subcontractor may be debarred from receiving future contracts for failure to comply with the provisions of the affirmative action clause.

§ 60-741.29   Formal hearings.

(a) *Hearing opportunity.* An opportunity for a formal hearing shall be afforded to a prime contractor or a subcontractor or a prospective prime contractor or subcontractor by the agency or Director in any of the following circumstances:

(1) An apparent violation of the affirmative action clause by a contractor or subcontractor, as shown by any investigation, is not resolved by informal means and a hearing is requested; or

(2) The Director, or an agency upon prior notification to the Director, proposes to cancel or terminate the contract or withhold progress payments, or cause the contract to be canceled or terminated or progress payments to be withheld, in whole or in part, on a contract or contracts, or to require cancellation or termination of a contract or subcontract or withholding of progress payments; or

(3) The Director, or an agency with the approval of the Director, proposes to declare a prime contractor or subcontractor ineligible for further contracts or subcontracts under the Act.

(b) *Hearing practice and procedure.* (1) All hearings conducted under section 503 of the Rehabilitation Act of 1973, as amended, and the regulations in this Part shall be governed by the Rules of Practice for Administrative Proceedings to Enforce Equal Opportunity Under Executive Order 11246 contained in 41 CFR Part 60-30 except that complaints shall be issued by the Associate Solicitor, Division of Labor Relations and Civil Rights, Office of the Solicitor, rather than by the Solicitor of Labor.

(2) For the purposes of hearings pursuant to this Part 60-741, references in 41 CFR Part 60-30 to "Executive Order 11246" shall mean section 503 of the Rehabilitation Act of 1973, as amended; to "equal opportunity clause" shall mean the affirmative action clause published at 41 CFR 60-741.4; and to "regulations" shall mean the regulations contained in this Part 60-741.

(3) The administrative Law Judge's recommended findings, conclusions and decision shall be certified to the Assistant Secretary, Employment Standards Administration rather than to the head of the compliance agency or to the Secretary (see 41 CFR 60-30.27). Accordingly, exceptions to the recommended decision (41 CFR 60-30.28) shall be filed with the Assistant Secretary, Employment Standards Administration, and the final Administrative Order contemplated by 41 CFR 60-30.30 shall be issued by the Assistant Secretary, Employment Standards Administration. Except for these changes in procedure, all the other provisions of the rules of practice cited in this 41 CFR 60-741.29(b) shall remain in full force and effect.

[41 FR 16148, Apr. 16, 1976, as amended at 42 FR 19146, Apr. 12, 1977]

§ 60-741.30 Notification of agencies.

The Director shall notify the heads of all agencies of any action for non-compliance taken against any contractor after such actions have been taken. No agency may issue a waiver under § 60-741.3(b)(1) to any contractor subject to such action without prior approval of the Director.

[41 FR 16148, Apr. 16, 1976; 42 FR 3307, Jan. 18, 1977]

§ 60-741.31 Contractor ineligibility list.

The Director shall distribute periodically a list to all executive departments and agencies giving the names of prime contractors and subcontractors who have been declared ineligible under the regulations in this Part and the Act.

§ 60-741.32 Disputed matters related to the affirmative action program.

The procedures set forth in the regulations in this Part govern all disputes relative to a contractor's compliance with the affirmative action clause and the requirements of this Part. Any disputes relating to issues other than compliance, including contract costs arising out of the contractor's efforts to comply, shall be determined by the disputes clause of the contract.

Subpart C—Ancillary Matters

§ 60-741.50 Reinstatement of ineligible contractors and subcontractors.

Any prime contractor or subcontractor debarred from further contracts or subcontracts under the Act may request reinstatement in a letter directed to the Director. In connection with the reinstatement proceedings, the prime contractor or subcontractor shall be required to show that it has established and will carry out employment policies and practices in compliance with the affirmative action clause.

§ 60-741.51 Intimidation and interference.

The sanctions and penalties contained in this regulation may be exercised by the agency or the Director against any prime contractor or subcontractor, who fails to take all necessary steps to ensure that no person intimidates, threatens, coerces, or discriminates against any individual for the purpose of interfering with the filing of a complaint, furnishing information, or assisting or participating in any manner in an investigation, compliance review, hearing, or any other activity related to the administration of the Act.

§ 60-741.52   Recordkeeping.

(a) Each contractor and a subcontractor shall maintain for a period not less than one year records regarding complaints and actions taken thereunder, and such employment or other records as required by the Director or agency or by this Part and shall furnish such information in the form required by the Director or agency or as the Director deems necessary for the administration of the Act and regulations issued under this Part.

(b) Failure to maintain complete and accurate records as required under this section or failure to update annually the affirmative action program as required by § 60-741.5(b) constitutes noncompliance with the contractor's or subcontractor's obligations under the affirmative action clause and is a ground for the imposition of appropriate sanctions.

[41 FR 16148, Apr. 16, 1976; 42 FR 3307, Jan. 18, 1977]

§ 60-741.53   Access to records of employment.

Each prime contractor and subcontractor shall permit access during normal business hours to its places of business, books, records and accounts pertinent to compliance with the Act, and all rules and regulations promulgated pursuant thereto for the purposes of complaint investigations, and investigations of performance under the affirmative action clause of the contract or subcontract. Information obtained in this manner shall be used only in connection with the administration of the Act.

§ 60-741.54   Rulings and interpretations.

Rulings under or interpretations of the Act and the regulations contained in this Part 741 shall be made by the Secretary or his or her designee.

Appendix A—Guidelines on the Application of the Definition "Handicapped Individual"

The Rehabilitation Act of 1973, as amended, defines a handicapped individual for the purposes of the program as any person who has a physical or mental impairment which substantially limits one or more of such person's major life activities, has a record of such impairment, or is regarded as having such an impairment.

"Life activities" may be considered to include communication, ambulation, selfcare, socialization, education, vocational training, employment, transportation, adapting to housing, etc. For the purpose of section 503 of the Act, primary attention is given to those life activities that affect employability.

The phrase *"substantially limits"* means the degree that the impairment affects employability. A handicapped individual who is likely to experience difficulty in securing, retaining or advancing in employment would be considered substantially limited.

"Has a record of such an impairment" means that an individual may be completely recovered from a previous physical or mental impairment. It is included

because the attitude of employers, supervisors, and coworkers toward that previous impairment may result in an individual experiencing difficulty in securing, retaining, or advancing in employment. The mentally restored, those who have had heart attacks or cancer often experience such difficulty. Also, this part of the definition would include individuals who may have been erroneously classified and may experience discrimination based on this misclassification. This group may include persons such as those who have been misclassified as mentally retarded or mentally restored.

"*Is regarded as having such an impairment*" refers to those individuals who are perceived as having a handicap, whether an impairment exists or not, but who, because of attitudes or for any other reason, are regarded as handicapped by employers, or supervisors who have an effect on the individual securing, retaining or advancing in employment.

Appendix B

1. This employer is a government contractor subject to section 503 of the Rehabilitation Act of 1973, which requires government contractors to take affirmative action to employ and advance in employment qualified handicapped individuals. If you have such a handicap and would like to be considered under the affirmative action program, please tell us. Submission of this information is voluntary and refusal to provide it will not subject you to discharge or disciplinary treatment. Information obtained concerning individuals shall be kept confidential, except that (i) supervisors and managers may be informed regarding restrictions on the work or duties of handicapped individuals, and regarding necessary accommodations, (ii) first aid and safety personnel may be informed, when and to the extent appropriate, if the condition might require emergency treatment, and (iii) government officials investigating compliance with the Act shall be informed.

2. If you are handicapped, we would like to include you under the affirmative action program. It would assist us if you tell us about (1) any special methods, skills and procedures which qualify you for positions that you might not otherwise be able to do because of your handicap, so that you will be considered for any positions of that kind, and (2) the accommodations which we could make which would enable you to perform the job properly and safely, including special equipment, changes in the physical layout of the job, elimination of certain duties relating to the job, or other accommodations.

Appendix C

The following is a set of procedures which contractors may use to meet the requirements of § 60-741.6(b).

(1) The application or personnel form of each known handicapped applicant should be annotated to identify each vacancy for which the applicant was considered, and the form should be quickly retrievable for review by the agency, the Department of Labor and the contractor's personnel officials for use in investigations and internal compliance activities.

(2) The personnel or application records of each known handicapped employee should include (i) the identification of each promotion for which the handicapped

employee was considered, and (ii) the identification of each training program for which the handicapped employee was considered.

(3) In each case where a handicapped employee or applicant is rejected for employment, promotion or training, a statement of the reasons should be appended to the personnel file or application form. This statement should include a comparison of the qualifications of the handicapped applicant or employee and the person(s) selected, as well as a description of the accommodations considered. This statement should be available to the applicant or employee concerned upon request.

(4) Where applicants or employees are selected for hire, promotion or training and the contractor undertakes any accommodation which makes it possible for him or her to place a handicapped individual on the job, the application form or personnel record should contain a description of that accommodation.

DeLURY, B., ASSISTANT SECRETARY OF LABOR FOR EMPLOYMENT STANDARDS, "EQUAL JOB OPPORTUNITY FOR THE HANDICAPPED MEANS POSITIVE THINKING AND POSITIVE ACTION"

26 Labor L. J. *679, 681-685 (1975)*

How Does a Contractor Take Affirmative Action?

Section 503 requires that each nonexempt federal contract contain a special clause, set forth by regulation, saying the contractor will take affirmative action to employ and advance in employment qualified handicapped individuals. Under the June 11, 1974, regulations, three different clauses stipulating different affirmative action requirements are used depending on contract amount and/or length of performance. However, under the proposed regulations the same clause stating affirmative action obligation will be included in all contracts over $2,500.

Also, the new regulations propose that any employer with a federal contract or subcontract of $50,000 or more and 50 or more employees be additionally required to prepare and maintain at each establishment a *written* affirmative action program for employment of the handicapped. Such a program should set forth the policies, practices and procedures the employer intends to use to implement the affirmative action obligation. Although the program need not be submitted to the federal government for approval, it should be available for inspection on request.

Affirmative action should apply to employment practices including, but not limited to, employment, upgrading, demotion or transfer, recruitment or recruitment advertising, layoff or termination, rates of pay or other forms of compensation, and selection for training, including apprenticeship. I mentioned a few examples of specific affirmative action steps in the introduction to this article. The proposed regulations list in detail a number of other examples. These involve: outreach and positive recruitment efforts; accommodation to the physical and mental limitations of employees; proper consideration of job applicant and employee qualifications; reevaluation of physical standards required for a job; compensation policy; and internal and external dissemination of affirmative action policy.

Particular emphasis is placed on accommodations for handicapped workers. For one, accommodation should be made in terms of access to the building, the work area, the lunchroom, and the restrooms. Secondly, accommodation may be made in the work area itself. For example, a handicapped person should be able to use tools and equipment necessary for the job. And thirdly, jobs may be restructured for handicapped workers if the employer considers their potential and assigns job responsibilities based on that potential.

Affirmative action efforts will depend on the nature of the business and on the involved handicapped job applicants and employees. All of the suggestions in the new regulations need not be used; yet the list is certainly not exhaustive. The Section 503 program encourages initiative and originality. It is up to the contractor to evaluate the particular work situation and to institute those affirmative action policies, practices, and procedures which will be the most effective.

How Is Section 503 Enforced?

A handicapped employee or job applicant, or a representative of that person, may file with a contractor a written complaint alleging violation under Section 503. The contractor should use internal review procedures to resolve the complaint within 60 days. If the decision is adverse to the employee or job applicant, or if the matter is not resolved by the contractor within 60 days, the complainant may file with the Department of Labor.

When a contractor does not have an internal review procedure, complainants should file directly with the Department of Labor. Complaints filed with the Department should be sent to the nearest office of the Employment Standards Administration, Office of Federal Contract Compliance Programs, not later than 180 days from the date of the alleged violation (unless an extension is granted by the Assistant Secretary for Employment Standards).

Complainants or their authorized representatives must sign the complaints. They should indicate: (1) name, address, and telephone number of the complainant; (2) name and address of the contractor or subcontractor who committed the alleged violation; (3) a description of the act or acts considered a violation; (4) a brief statement on the complainant's job skills or training, job experience or other qualifications for the position; (5) a statement of the complainant's disability or handicap; and (6) other pertinent information which will assist in the investigation and resolution of the complaint, including the name of the federal agency with which the employer contracted.

ESA may refer complaints to the compliance agency for that contractor, or it may investigate directly. If the compliance agency investigates and resolution is in favor of the contractor, the complainant may appeal to ESA. When it is determined that a contractor has violated the affirmative action requirements of Section 503, the matter will be resolved by informal means, including conciliation and persuasion, whenever possible.

Complaints have been filed by individuals across the country based on a variety of handicaps such as arthritis, asthma, cancer, gastrointestinal problems, and vision and hearing disabilities. To date, some 330 complaints have been received and about one-third of these are resolved. The following three cases provide examples of successful resolutions.

1. In Fort Worth, Texas, a man seeking a job as an aerosystems engineer was refused employment because of diabetes. The employer felt this person was not taking precautions to control his condition. After several months of conciliation the complainant was hired in the position originally offered.
2. In Boston, Massachusetts, a job applicant was viewed as handicapped by an employer after she stated that earlier in her life she had suffered a fractured knee. Because this clerical job required much sitting, the employer felt that her leg could not tolerate the bent position. A medical consultant assisted the Labor Department representative in conciliation and the job applicant was hired.
3. In San Francisco, California, a young man applied for a job which required reading numbers in small print. The employer felt he could not do this because he had only one eye and simply refused to consider his application. A Labor Department representative subsequently met with the employer and explained Section 503. After short deliberation the man was hired.

Of the 75 persons ESA is hiring to work on the Section 503 program, the majority will be in the field, assigned to the ten Labor Department regional offices. Complaint investigation is a primary responsibility of this staff.

What Is the Penalty for Violating Section 503?

If informal resolution is not reached, payment due the contractor may be withheld until the violation is corrected. Also, the contract or subcontract may be cancelled or terminated, in whole or in part, for failure to comply with the affirmative action clause; and the contractor may be debarred from receiving future contracts. Finally, the government may take action in the courts to enforce the contract.

The employer may request a formal hearing if an apparent violation is not resolved by informal means or if contract cancellation, contract termination, or debarment is proposed. An administrative law judge shall preside over the hearing and make recommendations to the Assistant Secretary for Employment Standards, who shall make the final decision. A debarred contractor may be reinstated if employment policies and practices have been established in compliance with the Section 503 program.

Complex Problems Still Remain

Even after the new regulations are finalized, implementation of the Section 503 program will not be an easy task. Complex problems which still exist in the administration of the program must be resolved.

For example, how much should an employer be able to demand as to medical information? The contractor needs to make employment decisions, but at the same time the handicapped person's privacy must be protected.

Standards to define a substantial barrier to employment do not exist. What may be a barrier to one job will not deter the handicapped person from another job. For example, a foot deformity or a knee injury may prevent taking on the occupation of mail deliverer; but will it make any difference to a bookkeeper who sits at a desk?

What about health insurance and medical benefits? Must the employer provide the same health insurance to a handicapped employee under constant medical care which is provided nonhandicapped employees? Should handicapped employees be covered by the same insurance eligibility rules as all other employees? What about life insurance? Must it be provided to very seriously ill employees not expected to have a working life as long as most doing the work?

Such problems in the Section 503 program must be worked out if it is to be successfully administered. However, we in ESA are gaining more experience every day about the needed assistance which can be offered to handicapped workers. With our new experience and the cooperation of contractors and the handicapped, we hope to meet this challenge.

We are also looking to the President's Committee on Employment of the Handicapped for assistance in administering the Section 503 program. The President's Committee seeks to promote employment of the handicapped throughout the work force.

All of us who promote employment of the handicapped recognize that they are a rich resource for our economy—but too often a wasted resource. Department of Labor studies prove that handicapped persons have better safety records than the nonhandicapped; that the handicapped show a slightly higher productivity rate than the nonhandicapped; and that handicapped and nonhandicapped workers are absent from work about the same amount of time.

In our efforts to provide greater job opportunity for the handicapped, we urge employers to take account of these facts and to hire on the basis of ability. We also urge employers to think positively about these handicapped workers—to make affirmative action and to make accommodations—so society can benefit from their talents and skills.

3. Programs Receiving Federal Financial Assistance

29 U.S.C. § 794
§ 504 of THE REHABILITATION ACT OF 1973, AS AMENDED

Nondiscrimination Under Federal Grants and Programs

Sec. 504. No otherwise qualified handicapped individual in the United States, as defined in Section 7(7), shall, solely by reason of his handicap, be excluded from the participation in, be denied the benefits of, or be subjected to discrimination under any program or activity receiving Federal financial assistance or under any program or activity conducted by any Executive agency or by the United States Postal Service. The head of each such agency shall promulgate such regulations as may be necessary to carry out the amendments to this section made by the Rehabilitation, Comprehensive Services, and Developmental Disabilities Act of 1978. Copies of any proposed regulation shall be submitted to appropriate authorizing committees of the Congress, and such regulation may take effect no earlier than the thirtieth day after the date on which such regulation is so submitted to such committees. . . .

NOTES

1. A declared purpose of the Rehabilitation Act of 1973 was to "promote and expand employment opportunities in the public and private sectors for handicapped individuals and to place such individuals in employment" (P.L. 93-112 § 2 [8]). It is apparent, therefore, that outlawing discrimination in employment in programs receiving federal grants was one of the primary goals of Section 794. In light of the pervasiveness of federal financial assistance, especially in educational, scientific, literary, and social welfare matters, this section is potentially a very powerful tool in eliminating employment discrimination against those with handicaps. (For a more extensive discussion of the general scope and enforcement of Section 794, see pp. 194-213, above.)

2. See *Rogers* v. *Frito-Lay, Inc.*, pp. 371-374, *supra*, in regard to the differences between § 793 and § 794. The general language of § 794, "receiving Federal financial assistance," is usually interpreted, as in *Rogers*, to apply only to grants, while § 793 applies only to contracts.

GURMANKIN V. COSTANZO

United States Court of Appeals for the Third Circuit, 1977
556 F.2d 184

[See pp. 345-350, above.]

NOTES

1. It is probable that if the challenged discrimination had occurred after enactment of the Rehabilitation Act of 1973, the case could have been resolved by section 794 with no need to resort to constitutional analysis. This may forecast the direction of subsequent decisions: due process, equal protection, and other constitutional theories for challenging employment discrimination may be rendered obsolete by the broad proscription of section 794.

2. In a similar factual situation, a blind teacher who was denied a position in the public school filed an action in a federal court in Indiana in reliance on section 794, *Garshwiller* v. *Marion Community Schools*, Cause No. F-75-134 (N.D.Ind., dismissed Feb. 10, 1976). Subsequent to the filing of the suit, the parties agreed to a voluntary settlement providing the plaintiff with a teaching position; dismissal of the case was then mutually stipulated.

DURAN V. CITY OF TAMPA

United States District Court for the Middle District of Florida, Tampa Division, 1977
430 F.Supp. 75

[The facts and other parts of the court's opinions are set out above at pp. 351-356.]
    The Court is also of the opinion the plaintiff's second claim pursuant to 29 U.S.C. §§ 793 and 794 is meritorious. The Rehabilitation Act of 1973 states in part:

> No otherwise qualified handicapped individual in the United States, as defined in section 706(6) of this title, shall solely by reason of his handicap, be excluded from the

participation in, be denied the benefits of, or be subjected to discrimination under any program or activity receiving Federal financial assistance.

Section 706(6) defines a handicapped individual as:

> . . . any person who (a) has a physical or mental impairment which substantially limits one or more of such person's major life activities, (b) has a record of such impairment, or (c) is regarded as having such an impairment.

The plaintiff clearly fits within the definition of handicapped in category (c) and the parties have stipulated to the fact that the City of Tampa Police Department receives in excess of $2500 from the federal government, a prerequisite to the application of this statute.

Although the provisions of 29 U.S.C. §§ 793 and 794 have rarely been interpreted, one decision clearly discusses the issues presented herein. In *Gurmankin* v. *Costanzo,* 411 F.Supp. 982 (E.D.Penn. 1976) Judge Newcomer construed the Rehabilitation Act of 1973 to offer a remedy to a blind woman who had been automatically excluded from a teaching position because of her handicap. Although the Court in *Gurmankin* only tangentially dealt with the statute because the plaintiff therein had not shown she was "otherwise qualified," it did find the statute to require a nondiscriminatory evaluation of the competence of the applicant.

In the instant case, the defendants determined the plaintiff's abilities and qualifications through a battery of tests and balked at hiring him only when presented with his history of epilepsy. Thus the plaintiff, who is "otherwise qualified," was refused a physical examination and employment based on the defendants' presumption of unfitness. The Rehabilitation Act of 1973 is applicable in this instance and the plaintiff's claim has a substantial likelihood of success.

NOTE

The federal financial assistance in *Duran* amounted to only $2,500 out of the large budget of an urban police department. This should be compared with the result in *Simon* v. *St. Louis City Police Dept.,* 14 F.E.P. Cases 1363, No. 76-963 C(2) (E.D.Mo., May 2, 1977) where a former police officer filed a § 794 suit after the police department refused to rehire him because of his paraplegia resulting from a gunshot wound received in the line of duty. In the process of dismissing his complaint for failure to state a claim, the court observed:

> In an attempt to bring the defendants within the coverage of the Act [§ 794] plaintiff has alleged that the Police Department is a recipient of federal aid. However, the complaint does not allege that plaintiff was denied *all* employment by the Department, but, rather, that the defendants refused to rehire him to his position within the Department as a *commissioned police officer* "with reasonable accommodations for his paraplegia." In this situation plaintiff must allege that the *particular* job category in which he was allegedly discriminated was a program or activity receiving federal financial assistance.

This question of the degree to which federal funds need to be traced in order to invoke the coverage of § 794 is of critical importance in the drafting of pleadings and the securing of appropriate evidence.

RULES AND REGULATIONS, DEPARTMENT OF HEALTH, EDUCATION, AND WELFARE

Subpart B §§ 84.11-84.14, 42 Fed. Reg. 22676, 22680-22681, May 4, 1977

General Administration—Nondiscrimination on the Basis of Handicap in Programs and Activities Receiving or Benefiting from Federal Financial Assistance

Subpart B—Employment Practices

§ 84.11 Discrimination prohibited.

(a) *General.* (1) No qualified handicapped person shall, on the basis of handicap, be subjected to discrimination in employment under any program or activity to which this part applies.

(2) A recipient that receives assistance under the Education of the Handicapped Act shall take positive steps to employ and advance in employment qualified handicapped persons in programs assisted under that Act.

(3) A recipient shall make all decisions concerning employment under any program or activity to which this part applies in a manner which ensures that discrimination on the basis of handicap does not occur and may not limit, segregate, or classify applicants or employees in any way that adversely affects their opportunities or status because of handicap.

(4) A recipient may not participate in a contractual or other relationship that has the effect of subjecting qualified handicapped applicants or employees to discrimination prohibited by this subpart. The relationships referred to in this subparagraph include relationships with employment and referral agencies, with labor unions, with organizations providing or administering fringe benefits to employees of the recipient, and with organizations providing training and apprenticeship programs.

(b) *Specific activities.* The provisions of this subpart apply to:

(1) Recruitment, advertising, and the processing of applications for employment;

(2) Hiring, upgrading, promotion, award of tenure, demotion, transfer, layoff, termination, right of return from layoff, and rehiring;

(3) Rates of pay or any other form of compensation and changes in compensation;

(4) Job assignments, job classifications, organizational structures, position descriptions, lines of progression, and seniority lists;

(5) Leaves of absence, sick leave, or any other leave;

(6) Fringe benefits available by virtue of employment, whether or not administered by the recipient;

(7) Selection and financial support for training, including apprenticeship, professional meetings, conferences, and other related activities, and selection for leaves of absence to pursue training;

(8) Employer sponsored activities, including social or recreational programs; and

(9) Any other term, condition, or privilege of employment.

(c) A recipient's obligation to comply with this subpart is not affected by any inconsistent term of any collective bargaining agreement to which it is a party.

§ 84.12 Reasonable accommodation.

(a) A recipient shall make reasonable accommodation to the known physical or mental limitations of an otherwise qualified handicapped applicant or employee unless the recipient can demonstrate that the accommodation would impose an undue hardship on the operation of its program.

(b) Reasonable accommodation may include: (1) making facilities used by employees readily accessible to and usable by handicapped persons, and (2) job restructuring, part-time or modified work schedules, acquisition or modification of equipment or devices, the provision of readers or interpreters, and other similar actions.

(c) In determining pursuant to paragraph (a) of this section whether an accommodation would impose an undue hardship on the operation of a recipient's program, factors to be considered include:

(1) The overall size of the recipient's program with respect to number of employees, number and type of facilities, and size of budget;

(2) The type of the recipient's operation, including the composition and structure of the recipient's workforce; and

(3) The nature and cost of the accommodation needed.

(d) A recipient may not deny any employment opportunity to a qualified handicapped employee or applicant if the basis for the denial is the need to make reasonable accommodation to the physical or mental limitations of the employee or applicant.

§ 84.13 Employment criteria.

(a) A recipient may not make use of any employment test or other selection criterion that screens out or tends to screen out handicapped persons or any class of handicapped persons unless: (1) the test score or other selection criterion, as used by the recipient, is shown to be job-related for the position in question, and (2) alternative job-related tests or criteria that do not screen out or tend to screen out as many handicapped persons are not shown by the Director to be available.

(b) A recipient shall select and administer tests concerning employment so as best to ensure that, when administered to an applicant or employee who has a handicap that impairs sensory, manual, or speaking skills, the test results accurately reflect the applicant's or employee's job skills, aptitude, or whatever other factor the test purports to measure, rather than reflecting the applicant's or employee's impaired sensory, manual, or speaking skills (except where those skills are the factors that the test purports to measure).

§ 84.14 Preemployment inquiries.

(a) Except as provided in paragraphs (b) and (c) of this section, a recipient may not conduct a preemployment medical examination or may not make preemployment inquiry of an applicant as to whether the applicant is a handicapped person or as to the nature or severity of a handicap. A recipient may, however, make preemployment inquiry into an applicant's ability to perform job-related functions.

(b) When a recipient is taking remedial action to correct the effects of past discrimination pursuant to § 84.6 (a), when a recipient is taking voluntary action to overcome the effects of conditions that resulted in limited participation in its federally assisted program or activity pursuant to § 84.6(b), or when a recipient is taking affirmative action pursuant to section 503 of the Act, the recipient may invite applicants for employment to indicate whether and to what extent they are handicapped, *Provided,* That:

(1) The recipient states clearly on any written questionnaire used for this purpose or makes clear orally if no written questionnaire is used that the information requested is intended for use solely in connection with its remedial action obligations or its voluntary or affirmative action efforts; and

(2) The recipient states clearly that the information is being requested on a voluntary basis, that it will be kept confidential as provided in paragraph (d) of this section, that refusal to provide it will not subject the applicant or employee to any adverse treatment, and that it will be used only in accordance with this part.

(c) Nothing in this section shall prohibit a recipient from conditioning an offer of employment on the results of a medical examination conducted prior to the employee's entrance on duty, *Provided,* That: (1) All entering employees are subjected to such an examination regardless of handicap, and (2) the results of such an examination are used only in accordance with the requirements of this part.

(d) Information obtained in accordance with this section as to the medical condition or history of the applicant shall be collected and maintained on separate forms that shall be accorded confidentiality as medical records, except that:

(1) Supervisors and managers may be informed regarding restrictions on the work or duties of handicapped persons and regarding necessary accommodations;

(2) First aid and safety personnel may be informed, where appropriate, if the condition might require emergency treatment; and

(3) Government officials investigating compliance with the Act shall be provided relevant information upon request.

NOTES

1. These regulations are modeled after other job discrimination provisions, such as the Department of Health, Education, and Welfare's regulations implementing Title IX of the Education Amendments of 1972 (45 C.F.R. Part 86), and rely heavily on Department of Labor regulations under § 793 (see pp. 388–406, above).

2. Central to these regulations is the requirement that employers must make "reasonable accommodation" to the handicapping conditions of job applicants unless the employer can show that such accommodation would impose an "undue hardship." Questions as to how much accommodation is reasonable and what types of burdens are undue are the probable battlegrounds in future administrative and judicial proceedings under these regulations.

3. By Executive Order 11914, issued April 28, 1976, the Department of Health, Education, and Welfare is designated as the central coordinating agency to assist other federal departments in implementing § 794. In furtherance of this purpose, on January 13, 1978, DHEW issued rules, based in large part upon its own substantive regulations under § 794, to define and eliminate discrimination on the basis of handicap in all federal agencies, 43 Fed. Reg. 2132, 45 C.F.R. Part 85 (Jan. 13, 1978). The employment provisions are set out below.

Employment

§ 85.52   General prohibitions against employment discrimination.

(a) No qualified handicapped person shall, on the basis of handicap, be subjected to discrimination in employment under any program or activity that receives or benefits from federal financial assistance.

(b) A recipient shall make all decisions concerning employment under any program or activity to which this part applies in a manner which ensures that discrimination on the basis of handicap does not occur and may not limit, segregate, or classify applicants or employees in any way that adversely affects their opportunities or status because of handicap.

(c) The prohibition against discrimination in employment applies to the following activities:

(1) Recruitment, advertising, and the processing of applications for employment;

(2) Hiring, upgrading, promotion, award of tenure, demotion, transfer, layoff, termination, right of return from layoff, and rehiring;

(3) Rates of pay or any other form of compensation and changes in compensation;

(4) Job assignments, job classifications, organizational structures, position descriptions, lines of progression, and seniority lists;

(5) Leaves of absence, sick leave, or any other leave;

(6) Fringe benefits available by virtue of employment, whether or not administered by the recipient;

(7) Selection and financial support for training, including apprenticeship, professional meetings, conferences, and other related activities, and selection for leaves of absence to pursue training;

(8) Employer sponsored activities, including social or recreational programs; and

(9) Any other term, condition, or privilege of employment.

(c) A recipient may not participate in a contractual or other relationship that has the effect of subjecting qualified handicapped applicants or employees to discrimination prohibited by this subpart. The relationships referred to in this paragraph include relationships with employment and referral agencies, with labor unions, with organizations providing or administering fringe benefits to employees of the recipient, and with organizations providing training and apprenticeship programs.

§ 85.53   Reasonable accommodation.

A recipient shall make reasonable accommodation to the known physical or mental limitations of an otherwise qualified handicapped applicant or employee unless the recipient can demonstrate that the accommodation would impose an undue hardship on the operation of its program.

§ 85.54   Employment criteria.

A recipient may not use nonjob-related employment tests or criteria that discriminate against handicapped persons and shall ensure that employment tests are adapted for use by persons who have handicaps that impair sensory, manual, or speaking skills.

§ 85.55   Preemployment inquiries.

A recipient may not conduct a preemployment medical examination or make a preemployment inquiry as to whether an applicant is a handicapped person or as to the nature or severity of a handicap except under the circumstances described in 45 CFR 84.14.

Davis v. Bucher

United States District Court for the Eastern District of Pennsylvania, 1978
451 F.Supp. 791

Cahn, District Judge.

Plaintiffs have brought this action on behalf of themselves and others similarly situated to challenge the hiring practices of the City of Philadelphia (hereinafter "City") regarding job applicants with prior histories of drug abuse. The named plaintiffs, Woolworth Davis, Salvatore D'Elia, and Herbert Sims, Jr., claim they were denied employment solely on the basis of former drug use, without regard to their qualifications, present rehabilitative status or the nature of the job for which they had applied. Defendants are various City officials entrusted with the authority to develop and implement employment practices.

Plaintiffs allege that the hiring policy of the City of Philadelphia unlawfully discriminates against former drug abusers in violation of the Equal Protection Clause and the Due Process Clause of the United States Constitution. The plaintiffs also allege violations of the Federal Rehabilitation Act of 1973, 29 U.S.C. § 794, and the Civil Rights Act of 1871, 42 U.S.C. § 1983.

Plaintiffs have moved for summary judgment and class certification. The City has not opposed the class certification motion but has contested the merits of plaintiffs' legal claims. After careful consideration of the contentions of the parties and an independent review of the appropriateness of class certification, I grant both motions.

Facts

Since this is a summary judgment motion, I base my decision on undisputed facts and view these facts in the light most favorable to the party opposing the motion. The affidavits, depositions, and documentatry evidence establish the following facts.

At various times, plaintiffs filed job applications with the City of Philadelphia. Plaintiff Davis reported for a medical examination on January 27, 1977, at the Municipal Medical Dispensary after having been notified by the City that he had been selected for the next class of firemen. (Davis Affidavit, Par. 5-7). During the examination the physician noticed a scar. Davis explained that during a four month period in 1972 he had used nonnarcotic amphetamines injected intravenously, but that he had not engaged in drug use since that time. The doctor agreed that the scar was old. (Davis Affidavit, Par. 3, 8). Nevertheless, plaintiff was told that he could not be employed in any city job because the City would not hire anyone with a past drug history. It is undisputed that but for the scar on plaintiff's forearm and his admission of prior drug use, plaintiff Davis would have been hired as a fireman with the Philadelphia Fire Department. (Davis Affidavit, Par. 10, 11).

Salvatore D'Elia is a former narcotics addict who has been enrolled in a methadone program. (D'Elia Affidavit, Par. 2). Random urine samples required by federal law showed that he was using no drugs other than methadone. (D'Elia Affidavit, Par. 8). D'Elia applied for a position with the City of Philadelphia under Title II of the Comprehensive Employment and Training Act (CETA), 29 U.S.C. § 841, *et seq.* (D'Elià Affidavit, Par. 10). He was referred for employment to both the Museum of Art as a security guard and the Philadelphia Civic Center as a laborer. On both occasions he was denied employment because of his history of drug use. (D'Elia Affidavit, Par. 11–12). Next he was referred for a job as a physical property maintenance worker. He was accepted for employment and sent to the dispensary for a medical examination. At this time he was again rejected because of his former drug use. (D'Elia Affidavit, Par. 15). Thus, on three separate occasions he was refused employment solely on the basis of his drug history.

Plaintiff Herbert Sims is a former user of morphine and heroin. He took these drugs near the end of his two year tour of duty with the armed services. (Sims Affidavit, Par. 2). He has been totally drug free since 1975. (Sims Affidavit, Par. 3–4). Sims was accepted for employment by the Department of Streets subject to his passing a medical examination. (Sims Affidavit, Par. 7–8). At the examination, plaintiff was told that pursuant to city personnel policy he was rejected for employment because of his admitted former drug abuse. (Sims Affidavit, Par. 9).

The facts, as demonstrated by the undisputed affidavits, show that Davis, D'Elia, and Sims are rehabilitated. They were all fully qualified for the positions for which they applied. At oral argument, counsel for the defense stipulated that but for the old scars and admissions of prior drug use the applicants would have been hired by the City of Philadelphia.

Discussion

I.   The Summary Judgment Motion

A.   The City's Policy Regarding Employment of Substance Abusers

The City's policy concerning employment of narcotic substance abusers has been interpreted by the medical dispensary staff (Lawlor Deposition at pp. 10, 13–20, 17–19) to include past or present drug use, abuse, or addiction. According to the City, the policy is grounded in the City Civil Service Regulations 8.0233:

> The Director may refuse to examine an applicant or may disqualify a candidate at any time prior to appointment either during or after an examination . . . who is addicted to the intemperate use of intoxicating liquors, or the use of harmful drugs, . . .

and 10.0910:

> The name of an eligible shall be removed from an eligible list for any of the following reasons: . . . Addiction to the intemperate use of intoxicating liquors or to the use of harmful drugs.

and in Section XIV of "Procedures & Policies Regarding Medical Examination":

> Generally, emotional instability, immaturity, psychosis, alcoholism, or drug addiction, are disqualifying for all positions.

The medical examination through which this policy is enforced is the last stage in the process of screening job applicants. The purpose of the medical examination is to determine whether a job applicant is medically qualified for the position for which he has applied. (Lawlor Deposition at p. 7). Counsel for the City has represented that the medical examiners have the discretion to overlook past drug use as a disqualifying characteristic for city employment. Counsel stipulates, however, that this discretion was not exercised with respect to the plaintiffs and the three nonparty affiants in the instant case and that an absolute bar to employment due to former drug use was imposed. In excluding plaintiffs from employment because of past drug use, the medical dispensary staff did not consider whether such a history of substance abuse medically disqualified a person from performing a particular job. At least with respect to the named plaintiffs and the three nonparty affiants, the effect of the City's policy was that, once it was revealed a prospective employee formerly used drugs, he would not be employed.

   B.   *Defendant's Policy Is Violative of § 504 of the Rehabilitation Act, 1973, 29 U.S.C. § 794*

Plaintiffs claim that former drug addicts fall within the protection of the Rehabilitation Act of 1973, 29 U.S.C. § 701 *et seq.* (hereinafter "Act") and that the Act provides them with a remedy for the discrimination alleged here. Section 504 of the Act provides in pertinent part:

> No otherwise qualified handicapped individual in the United States, . . . shall, solely by reason of his handicap, be excluded from the participation in, be denied the benefits of, or be subject to discrimination under any program or activity receiving Federal financial assistance.

29 U.S.C. § 794. The City contends that Congress did not intend drug addicts to be included within the definition of handicapped for purposes of § 504. However, although there are no cases on point, I am persuaded that the clear words of the statute do encompass drug addiction.

   29 U.S.C. § 706(6) defines a handicapped individual as:

> [A]ny person . . . who (a) has a physical or mental impairment which substantially limits one or more of such person's major life activities, (b) has a record of such impairment, or (c) is regarded as having such an impairment.

It is undisputed that drug addiction substantially affects an addict's ability to perform major life activities, defined by Department of Health, Education and Welfare regulations supplementing the Act, 42 Fed. Reg. 22686 *et seq.* (May 4, 1977) (hereinafter "the Regulations") as "caring for one's self, performing manual tasks, walking, seeing, hearing, speaking, breathing, learning, and working." Regulations § 84.2(j)(2)(ii). Furthermore, prior addiction and drug use clearly fall within the definition of having a "record of such impairment," 29 U.S.C. § 706(6)(C), as defined in § 84.2(j)(2)(iii) of the Regulations.

   Counsel for the City might reasonably have argued, absent any indication to the contrary, that Congress must have intended to differentiate drug use from other physical and mental handicaps because (1) it is a handicap voluntarily created by the handicapped person; and (2) drug possession and use are generally illegal and Congress could not have wished to compensate users for criminal activity. This argument, however, loses all force in view of the Department of Health, Education and Welfare analysis of the Act accompanying the Regulations. The analysis, at 42 Fed.Reg. 22686 (May 4, 1977) directly addresses and disposes of the issue of whether drug addicts are encompassed by the Act.

> The Secretary has carefully examined the issue and has obtained a legal opinion from the Attorney General. That opinion concludes that drug addiction and alcoholism are "physical or mental impairments" within the meaning of section 7(6) of the Rehabilitation Act of 1973, as amended, and that drug addicts and alcoholics are therefore handicapped for purposes of section 504 if their impairment substantially limits one of their major life activities. The Secretary therefore believes that he is without authority to exclude these conditions from the definition. There is a medical and legal consensus that alcoholism and drug addiction are diseases although there is disagreement as to whether they are primarily mental or physical. In addition while Congress did not focus specifically on the problems of drug addiction and alcoholism in enacting section 504, the committees that considered the Rehabilitation Act of 1973 were made aware of the Department's long-standing practice of treating addicts and alcoholics as handicapped individuals eligible for rehabilitation services under the Vocational Rehabilitation Act.

The conclusion that Congress intended to include past drug users within the protections of the Act is reasonable as a matter of public policy as well. Drug addiction is a serious public problem. It is therefore not surprising that Congress would wish to provide assistance for those who have overcome their addiction and give some support and incentive for those who are attempting to overcome it. The HEW regulations including drug addicts as handicapped individuals for purposes of § 504 merely recognize these realities. I therefore conclude that persons with histories of drug use, including present participants in methadone maintenance programs, are "handicapped individuals" within the meaning of the statutory and regulatory language.

The City treats drug users as if they were handicapped, yet discriminates against them. The Regulations provide that even pre-employment inquiries into handicaps are prohibited for purposes other than to determine "an applicant's ability to perform job-related functions." Regulations § 84.14(a). Although plaintiffs had met the requirements of all selection criteria except the medical examination, they were disqualified at the very final stage of the hiring process solely because of their former drug abuse. Furthermore, plaintiffs submitted uncontested evidence that persons with a history of substance abuse, and in particular ex-heroin addicts, could be employed successfully. (Affidavit of Thomas W. Collins, par. 14; Woody Affidavit, par. 29–34; Dodson Affidavit, par. 11). *See also Beazer* v. *New York City Transit Authority,* 399 F.Supp. 1032, 1037, 1048–1049, 1058 (S.D.N.Y.1975), *aff'd* 558 F.2d 97 (2d Cir. 1977). Thus, by virtue of the absolute exclusion from consideration for city employment, the City denied them the benefits of a program receiving federal financial assistance (e.g. CETA funds) in direct violation of the Act.[4]

---

[4] I emphasize, however, that the statute and regulation apply only to discrimination against qualified handicapped persons solely by reason of their handicap. If in any individual situation it can be shown that a particular addiction or prior drug use prevents successful performance of a job, the applicant need not be provided the employment opportunity in question. As stated in the HEW analysis of the Act:

The Secretary wishes to reassure recipients that inclusion of addicts and alcoholics within the scope

Having determined that plaintiffs fall within the ambit of § 504 and that the City has discriminated against them, I turn now to a consideration of whether a private cause of action may be inferred from the Act to vindicate plaintiffs' rights. The Act itself provides no specific enforcement mechanism. However, one of the clear purposes of the statute, as set forth in 29 U.S.C. § 701(8), is to prevent employment discrimination against and expand employment opportunities for handicapped individuals. I believe that since plaintiffs are handicapped individuals subject to the protection of the statute they are entitled to a remedy under it.

The Supreme Court's decision in *Cort* v. *Ash,* 422 U.S. 66, 78, 95 S.Ct. 2080, 2088, 45 L.Ed.2d 26 (1975), prescribes an analysis for determining when a private enforcement remedy should be inferred:

> First, is the plaintiff 'one of the class for whose *especial* benefit the statute was en-acted,'. . . that is, does the statute create a federal right in favor of the plaintiff? Second, is there any indication of legislative intent, explicit or implicit, either to create such a remedy or to deny one? Third, is it consistent with the underlying purposes of the legislative scheme to imply such a remedy for the plaintiff? And finally, is the cause of action one traditionally relegated to state law, in an area basically the concern of the States, so that it would be inappropriate to infer a cause of action based solely on federal law? (Citations omitted.)

Lloyd v. *Regional Transportation Authority,* 548 F.2d 1277, 1284-5 (7th Cir. 1977) offers an exhaustive discussion of the import of *Cort* v. *Ash* in the present context. There, the court concluded that § 504 extended affirmative rights to all handicapped individuals and held that such rights are enforceable in the courts by a private right of action. The court further held that *Lau* v. *Nichols,* 414 U.S. 563, 94 S.Ct. 786, 39 L.Ed.2d 1 (1974) was controlling in the 504 context:

> Because of the near identity of language in § 504 of the Rehabilitation act of 1973 and § 601 of the Civil Rights Act of 1964, *Lau* is dispositive. Therefore, we hold that § 504

---

of the regulation will not lead to the consequences feared by many commenters. It cannot be emphasized too strongly that the statute and the regulation apply only to discrimination against qualified handicapped persons solely by reason of their handicap. The fact that drug addiction and alcoholism may be handicaps does not mean that these conditions must be ignored in determining whether an individual is qualified for services or employment opportunities. On the contrary, a recipient may hold a drug addict or alcoholic to the same standard of performance and behavior to which it holds others, even if any unsatisfactory performance or behavior is related to the person's drug addiction or alcoholism. In other words, while an alcoholic or drug addict may not be denied services or disqualified from employment soley because of his or her condition, the behavioral manifestations of the condition may be taken into account in determining whether he or she is qualified.

With respect to the employment of a drug addict or alcoholic, if it can be shown that the addiction or alcoholism prevents successful performance of the job, the person need not be provided the employment opportunity in question. For example, in making employment decisions, a recipient may judge addicts and alcoholics on the same basis it judges all other applicants and employees. Thus, a recipient may consider— for all applicants including drug addicts and alcoholics—past personnel records, absenteeism, disruptive, abusive, or dangerous behavior, violations of rules and unsatisfactory work performance. Moreover, employers may enforce rules prohibiting the possession or use of alcohol or drugs in the work-place, provided that such rules are enforced against all employees.
42 Fed.Reg. 22686 (May 4, 1977). In this case, however, the City concedes that prior drug abuse and/or present maintenance on methadone are factors which alone do not detract from an applicant's qualifications.

of the Rehabilitation Act, at least when considered with the regulations which now implement it, establishes affirmative rights and permits this action to proceed.

548 F.2d at 1281.

I am in full agreement with the Court of Appeals for the Seventh Circuit. The named plaintiffs are among the class specifically benefited by the enactment of the statute. Thus plaintiffs met the standard established by the first criterion in the *Cort* analysis.

The legislative history of 1974 Amendments to the Rehabilitation Act evidences the legislative intention to create a private cause of action. In considering the Act, the Committee on Labor and Public Welfare emphasized the parallels between the Act and the 1964 Civil Rights Act, 42 U.S.C. § 2000d. As noted in the Committee Report to the Senate, the legislature endorsed the inclusion of a private right of action as a means of enforcing 29 U.S.C. § 794:

> This approach to implementation of section 504, which closely follows the models of the above-cited anti-discrimination provisions, would ensure administrative due process (right to hearing, right to review), provide for administrative consistency within the Federal government as well as relative ease of implementation, and *permit a judicial remedy through a private action*. (Emphasis supplied).

4 U.S. Code Cong. & Admin. News, p. 6391 (1974).

As to the third requirement of *Cort,* it is consistent with the underlying scheme to infer such a remedy. Indeed, one of the explicitly detailed purposes of the Rehabilitation Act of 1973 was the enhancement of employment possibilities for handicapped individuals. A private right of action for plaintiffs is therefore not only compatible with the legislative intent, but also is necessary to secure the Act's remedial purposes.

Finally, resort to federal law in this context does not infringe upon the state by encouraging a federal action in an area traditionally and appropriately reserved to the states. A major aspect of the Rehabilitation Act was the creation of federal standards and enforcement mechanisms to eliminate discrimination against the handicapped. The legislative scheme parallels the federal government's programs for dealing with race and sex discrimination and other causes of action ordinarily grounded in the Federal Civil Rights Act, 42 U.S.C. § 1981, *et seq*. In addition, this does not appear to be an area which the state of Pennsylvania has traditionally shown a major interest in regulating.

In view of the fact that all four *Cort* tests are satisfied, I hold that § 504 implicitly provides a private cause of action. *See Kampmeier* v. *Nyquist,* 553 F.2d 296, 299 (2d Cir. 1977). Having concluded that plaintiffs are entitled to a remedy on this statutory basis, I would ordinarily not consider their constitutional claims. However, since this is a case of first impression in this Circuit concerning the Rehabilitation Act and my decision may well be subject to reconsideration on appeal, in the interests of sound judicial administration I will consider plaintiffs' constitutional arguments as well.

    C. Defendant's Policy is Violative of the Equal Protection and Due Process Clauses of the Fourteenth Amendment to the United States Constitution

    1. Equal Protection: Plaintiffs contend that the City's refusal to hire them violates equal protection. They claim that the City's absolute bar to employing former

drug users results from an illegal classification of plaintiffs which is unrelated to the City's purpose of hiring qualified employees. The City counters with the argument that the regulation barring the employment of drug users is discretionary in that it is couched in the terms of "may" disqualify and that this discretion has on several occasions been applied. Thus it contends that no classification whatsoever has been created.

Unfortunately, counsel for the City has missed the point. He does not contest that as to the three named plaintiffs, the three plaintiffs who filed affidavits, and a substantial number of other former drug users, the regulations have been used to deny jobs on the sole basis of prior drug use. Therefore, even if the regulations create no arbitrary and absolute classification on their face, a classification of the class of potential employees which plaintiffs seek to represent has been created by the City's method of applying the statute.

There are various standards for testing such a classification under the equal protection clause. Because I believe the issues are clear, I will indulge in applying the standard most favorable to defendants; that is, whether there is a rational relationship between the classification and the legitimate governmental purpose for which it is used. *Johnson* v. *Robison*, 415 U.S. 361, 94 S.Ct. 1160, 39 L.Ed.2d 389 (1974); *Eisenstadt* v. *Baird*, 405 U.S. 438, 92 S.Ct. 1029, 31 L.Ed.2d 349 (1972). I find that no rational relationship whatsoever exists.

There is no doubt that the City, as an employer, has a legitimate interest in hiring individuals who are qualified to perform particular duties. But defendants have failed to demonstrate that this interest would in fact be threatened by employment of *former* drug users. The hiring policy applied to the named plaintiffs serves as an absolute exclusion of them. No consideration is given to individual factors such as recent employment history, successful maintenance on a methadone program, or evidence of freedom from drug use. It is undisputed that plaintiff Davis has not used drugs since 1972. Plaintiff Sims has been drug free since 1975. Whatever undesirable characteristics may attach to current drug use—such as a possible inability to perform on the job or untrustworthiness due to an addict's need to support his addiction—there is absolutely no basis for concluding that those characteristics will in every case persist after the use has ceased. Thus, I have no hesitancy in terming a regulation which bars former users and addicts from city employment, without any consideration of the merits of each individual case, overbroad and irrational. Such a policy bears no connection whatsoever to the City's interest in maintaining the quality of its work force and assuring that its employees perform their tasks. *Thompson* v. *Gallagher*, 489 F.2d 443 (5th Cir. 1973). *See also Cleveland Board of Education* v. *LaFleur*, 414 U.S. 632, 651, 94 S.Ct. 791, 39 L.Ed.2d 52 (1974) (Powell, J. concurring); *Beazer* v. *New York City Transit Authority, supra.*

2. Due Process: Plaintiffs also allege a due process violation. They base their claim on the majority opinion in *Cleveland Board of Education* v. *LaFleur, supra,* where the Supreme Court struck down a mandatory requirement that public school teachers take leaves of absence from their employment at a fixed stage in their pregnancies. The court reasoned that this absolute policy created an irrebuttable presumption of physical incompetency due to pregnancy and thus violated due process

because it did not provide for individualized determinations of that incompetency. *Cf. Vlandis* v. *Kline*, 412 U.S. 441, 93 S.Ct. 2230, 37 L.Ed.2d 63 (1973); *Stanley* v. *Illinois*, 405 U.S. 645, 92 S.Ct. 1208, 31 L.Ed.2d 551 (1972); *Schware* v. *Board of Examiners*, 353 U.S. 232, 77 S.Ct. 752, 1 L.Ed.2d 796 (1957). Defendants again argue that the regulation does not create an irrebuttable presumption because the City has on occasion hired past drug users. As noted above, however, the City has applied the policy inflexibly to the named plaintiffs and other members of the class they seek to represent. Thus the City has established a conclusive presumption that drug addiction will affect their job performance. This presumption is "irrebuttable" within the meaning of *LaFleur*.

In *LaFleur* the challenged regulation was found unconstitutional because it created a conclusive presumption that every teacher who is four or five months pregnant is physically incapable of continuing her duties, despite the fact that a pregnant woman's ability to continue past a fixed pregnancy period is an individual matter. The reasoning of *LaFleur* dictates that a city employment policy may not constitutionally exclude all former drug abusers as poor employment risks for all jobs without any determination that the former drug use will affect job performance.

The City must make individual evaluations of each applicant in light of the demands of the position in question. The plaintiffs in this case were in fact found to meet all the present requirements for City employment and were excluded only because of the conclusive operation of the challenged policy. I believe that as a matter of due process the City had an obligation to at least give plaintiffs an opportunity to show that their former drug use would not have affected their ability to work to the City's satisfaction. *See Sugarman* v. *Dougall*, 413 U.S. 634, 93 S.Ct. 2842, 37 L.Ed.2d 853 (1973).

I make this ruling fully cognizant of the fact that there is a significant distinction between *LaFleur* and this case. In *LaFleur*, the plaintiff teachers at the time of their termination were already working, and prior case law had made it clear that they had a procedural due process right to a hearing before their termination. Here plaintiffs had not yet commenced their employment at the time the irrebuttable presumption was applied. I do not hold that before a hiring decision a plaintiff is entitled to a full hearing with respect to all job-qualifying characteristics. But if the City establishes a policy which is as facially arbitrary as the one in the case at bar and seeks to apply it in a conclusive manner, then plaintiffs should, at a minimum, be given an opportunity to demonstrate that the policy is inappropriate in their case. *Cf. Scott* v. *Macy*, 121 U.S.App.D.C. 205, 208, 349 F.2d 182, 185 (1965) (McGowan, J., concurring) (exclusion of homosexuals from civil service).

Beazer v. *New York City Transit Authority, supra,* is on point. The court in *Beazer* held that an absolute ban against public employment by a municipal transit authority of present and past methadone maintained persons was a violation of due process and equal protection. The court reasoned that, even assuming a rational basis for concluding that some such applicants would pose employment risks, a conclusive bar based on an irrebuttable presumption of incompetency is unconstitutional:

> It is perfectly clear that there are substantial numbers of present or past methadone maintained persons who would be capable of performing many of the jobs at the TA.

Individual consideration, or narrower rules rationally related to certain classifications of jobs, are constitutionally required.

399 F.Supp. at 1058. I agree with *Beazer*, and believe that its reasoning is even more compelling in the case at bar, where the City's policy is applied to persons who are admitted to have no current connection with drugs whatsoever.

D. Conclusion

I have held that because the City's exclusion of former drug users bears no rational relationship to the City's goal of hiring competent employees, the City must make individual evaluations of each applicant's qualifications in light of the demands of the position in question. The uncontradicted facts establish that the plaintiffs were found to meet all the present requirements for City employment and were excluded only because of the automatic operation of the City's policy against former drug users. This court has been presented with no evidence to contradict plaintiffs' position that former drug abuse does not make plaintiffs less qualified for City employment than other applicants.

The City's employment policy bears no rational relationship to the demands of jobs for which plaintiffs applied. The regulation which bars the class of persons plaintiffs seek to represent from City employment without any consideration of the merits of each individual's application violates the Equal Protection and Due Process Clauses of the United States Constitution, as well as the Federal Rehabilitation Act. Accordingly, plaintiffs' Motion for Summary Judgment will be granted.

[The remainder of the opinion, in which the court discussed and granted the plaintiffs' motion for class certification, is omitted.]

NOTES

1. As to the inclusion of drug addiction as a handicapping condition, see n.3, pp. 26–27, above.

2. The three legal theories relied upon in *Davis*—§ 794, equal protection, and due process—are the standard claims found in most complaints of employment discrimination on the basis of handicap. When an employment practice is found to be discriminatory in violation of § 794, is it a foregone conclusion that it will also constitute a denial of equal protection? An irrebuttable presumption? When might one of these theories be applicable in the absence of the other two?

WHITAKER v. BOARD OF HIGHER EDUCATION OF THE CITY OF NEW YORK

United States District Court for the Eastern District of New York, 1978
461 F.Supp. 99

MISHLER, CH. J.

Seeking both injunctive and monetary relief, plaintiff, a former professor of African Studies at Brooklyn College, commenced this suit against the College, several members of its faculty and administration, and the Board of Higher Education, charging that the defendants violated 42 U.S.C. §§ 1981 and 1983 and § 504 of the Rehabilitation Act of 1973, 29 U.S.C. § 794 (section 504). Specifically, the plaintiff claims that the defendants' conduct, which culminated in their decisions to deny him tenure and to prohibit him from using the title "Martin Luther King Distinguished

Professor'' (MLKDP), violated plaintiff's due process rights. Furthermore, plaintiff, an admitted alcoholic who characterizes his alcoholism as a "handicap," alleges that the defendants' conduct was proscribed by § 504, which prohibits recipients of federal financial assistance from discriminating against "otherwise qualified handicapped individual[s]."

Plaintiff has moved for a preliminary injunction ordering that the defendants treat him as a tenured Brooklyn College faculty member and restraining them from interfering with his use of the title "MLKDP" pending the final on-the-merits determination of the action. Defendants have cross-moved to dismiss the complaint, stressing, in the main, 3 points: (i) that the plaintiff fails to state a claim upon which relief can be granted under sections 1981 or 1983 since the defendants' actions did not affect any cognizable "property" or "liberty" interest entitled to due process protection; (ii) that the court lacks subject-matter jurisdiction over, and that the plaintiff has failed to state a claim under, the Rehabilitation Act since no private right of action exists under section 504; and (iii) that even if a private right of action does exist, the plaintiff should be required to exhaust certain administrative remedies prior to bringing suit. For the reasons stated below, both the plaintiff's and the defendants' motions are in all respects denied. . . .

Discussion

1. The Due Process Claim

The defendants contend that the plaintiff has failed to state a claim under sections 1981 and 1983. We note that the plaintiff's complaint is hardly a model of draftsmanship. We are also not unmindful of this Circuit's admonition that "[o]f all fields, which the federal courts should hesitate to invade and take over, education and faculty appointments at a University level are probably the least suited for federal court supervision." *Faro* v. *New York University*, 502 F.2d 1229, 1231-32, (2d Cir. 1974). Yet, we must apply the accepted rule that a "complaint should not be dismissed for insufficiency unless it appears to a certainty that the plaintiff is entitled to no relief under any state of facts which could be proved in support of the claim." 2A Moore's Federal Practice, ¶ 12.08 at 2271-74. Application of this standard warrants, at least at this stage of the litigation, that defendants' motion be denied.

Admittedly, the complaint contains many allegations which are hardly of a constitutional nature, sounding in defamation, and perhaps, breach of contract. Yet, the complaint also alleges that the defendants' actions "were intended to interfere with plaintiff's rightful expectency, property, and liberty, and were in violation of his constitutional . . . rights." Complaint, page 7, ¶ 5. As we read that statement, in the factual context described in the complaint and outlined above, it reflects a charge that the defendants denied the plaintiff tenure, and prohibited him from using the title MLKDP, without due process of law. While the precise nature of the denial of due process is not specified, the liberal reading of the complaint which is required in determining such a motion reveals that the plaintiff is complaining of having been deprived of his tenure and title on the basis of untrue charges relating to his competency. That is, it appears as if the denial of the due process complained of is the defendants' having taken their adverse action for arbitrary and capricious reasons as a result of a mistaken belief that the plaintiff, who was an alcoholic, was unfit to teach. If plaintiff was deprived of a "property" or "liberty" interest in an arbitrary or capricious manner or for arbitrary or capricious reasons, he has been denied due process. *See Simard v. Board of Educ.*, 473 F.2d 988 (2d Cir. 1973). *See also Schware v. Board of Bar Examiners*, 353 U.S. 232, 77 S.Ct. 752 (1957); *Wieman v. Updegraff*, 344 U.S. 183, 192, 73 S.Ct. 215 (1952). *Cf. Jeffries v. Turkey Run Consol. School Dist.*, 492 F.2d 1 (7th Cir. 1974) (Stevens, J.).

In any case, apparently recognizing the essence of plaintiff's constitutional claim, the defendants do not attack his pleadings by arguing that they insufficiently define the nature of the alleged due process deprivation. Rather, defendants ground their motion on the contention that neither the plaintiff's "property" nor "liberty" interests have been affected by their actions and that the plaintiff therefore cannot avail himself of the protections of the due process clause. While the defendants may ultimately prove those points, in this case resolution of those issues implicates factual questions and a judgment on the pleadings is therefore inappropriate.

The defendants are of course correct in their assertion that in *Board of Regents v. Roth*, 408 U.S. 564, 92 S.CT. 2701 (1972), the Supreme Court held that a party must show that a challenged action has deprived him of a constitutionally cognizable "property" or "liberty" interest before the procedural protections of the due process clause are implicated. A similar showing must be made in a case, such as this one appears to be, where a party complains that he has been deprived of a right or interest for arbitrary, irrational reasons, *i.e.*, where he claims that he has been deprived of "substantive" due process. *See, e.g., McGhee v. Draper*, 564 F.2d 902, 912-13 (10th Cir. 1977); *Weathers v. West Yuma County School Distr. R-J-1*, 530 F.2d 1335, 1340-42 (10th Cir. 1976); *Jeffries v. Turkey Run Consol. School Distr., supra. See also Simard v. Board of Educ., supra*, at 994-95.

Plaintiff's complaint indicates that the "property" rights at issue were his alleged rights to tenure and to the continued use of the title "MLKDP." The defendants, however, turn to *Roth* in an effort to defeat plaintiff's claim. There, in holding that a non-tenured professor could not use the due process clause as a vehicle with which to challenge a university's decision not to renew his employment contract, the Court wrote: "To have a property interest in a benefit, a person clearly must have more than an abstract need or desire for it. He must have more than a unilateral expectation of it. He must, instead, have a legitimate claim of entitlement to it." 408 U.S. at 577, 92 S.Ct. at 2709. Focusing on the fact that the plaintiff in that action, under the terms of his employment contract and under state law, had no "legitimate claim" to reemployment, the Court held that the dismissed teacher had not been deprived of a constitutionally cognizable property right.

The defendants attempt to fit the instant case into the *Roth* mold. In brief, they contend that the plaintiff had not actually been hired in 1974 to fill the seat of MLK Visiting Professor. Rather, they claim that the Board of Higher Education, which is the body that actually enters into employment contracts on behalf of the College, officially employed plaintiff as a full professor without any other special title. Furthermore, while admitting that members of the Department of Africana Studies continued to refer to plaintiff as MLKDP, defendants contend that upon his subsequent yearly reappointments the plaintiff likewise held only the title of full professor. Accordingly, they argue that plaintiff could not have been deprived of a right to a title which he never possessed.

Similarly, defendants also contend that plaintiff has no claim to tenure. They point out that while early tenure is sometimes granted, under established procedures a professor is generally granted tenure only after 5 years of continuous service. Furthermore, while officials of the College may recommend tenure, only the Board of Higher Education may actually confer it. In the instant case, because the plaintiff did not serve for 5 years continuously and because the Board of Higher Education did not at any point agree to grant him tenure, he had no legitimate claim of entitlement to it.

As is seen, defendants bottom their arguments on the official procedures followed by the Board of Higher Education, and the absence of formal agreements between the Board and the plaintiff. However, *Roth's* companion case, *Perry* v. *Sindermann*, 408 U.S. 593, 92 S.Ct. 2694 (1972), clearly teaches "that the lack of a contractual or tenure right to reemployment [does not], taken alone, defeat [a] claim that the nonrenewal of [a] contract violated the . . . Fourteenth Amendment." *Id.* at 596, 92 S.Ct. at 2697. There, in reversing a grant of summary judgment in favor of a university which had discharged a professor who had not been officially granted tenure, the Court recognized that the "absence of . . . an explicit contractual provision may not always foreclose the possibility that a teacher has a 'property' interest in reemployment. . . . A teacher . . . who has held his position for a number of years, might be able to show from the circumstances of this service—and from other relevant facts—that he has a legitimate claim of entitlement to job tenure." *Id.* at 601-02, 92 S.Ct. at 2699-2700. Other courts have followed suit and recognized that while not officially tenured, a party may possess "de facto" tenure. *See, e.g., Gentile* v. *Wallen*, 562 F.2d 193, 197 n. 5 (2d Cir. 1977); *Weathers* v. *West Yuma County School Board, supra,* at 1336 (10th Cir. 1976). *See also Bishop* v. *Wood*, 426 U.S. 341, 344, 96 S.Ct. 2074, 2077 ("A property interest in employment can, of course, be created by . . . an implied contract").

In the instant action, if we take the facts in plaintiff's pleadings as true, the plaintiff has alleged, as did the plaintiff in *Sindermann*, "the existence of . . . understandings . . . fostered by state officials, that may justify his legitimate claim of entitlement," 408 U.S. at 602, 92 S.Ct. at 2700, to tenure and use of the MLKDP title. Moreover, even if we treat this motion to dismiss as one for summary judgment, *see* Rule 12(b)(6), and go beyond the pleadings to the conflicting affidavits regarding the nature of the plaintiff's employment, we are confronted with serious fact questions. Accordingly, because plaintiff should be given an opportunity to prove that under state law, *see Roth, supra,* at 577, 92 S.Ct. at 2709; *Sindermann, supra,* at 602 n. 7, 92 S.Ct. at 2700 n. 7, he had a property interest in the expectation of tenure and the use of the MLKDP title, a judgment at this time would be inappropriate.

Similarly, plaintiff should be given an opportunity to prove that he has been deprived of a "liberty" interest. As this Circuit has stated, *Roth* made clear "that where [an individual's] 'good name, reputation, honor, or integrity is at stake' or 'the State in declining to reemploy [that individual], imposed on him a stigma or other disability that foreclosed his freedom to take advantage of other employment opportunities,'... he may claim a deprivation of 'liberty' under the due process clause of the fourteenth amendment.'' *Lombard* v. *Board of Educ.*, 502 F.2d 631, 637 (2d Cir. 1974), *cert. denied*, 420 U.S. 976, 95 S.Ct. 1400 (1975), quoting *Board of Regents* v. *Roth*, 408 U.S. at 573, 92 S.Ct. at 2707. Other Supreme Court decisions have refined the *Roth* formula so that where one claims that official action in connection with an employment decision has resulted in the imposition of a stigma, that action will

> constitute deprivation of a liberty interest, [when] the stigmatizing information [is] both false, *Codd* v. *Velger*, 429 U.S. 624, 97 S.Ct. 882, 51 L.Ed. 2d 92 (1977) (per curiam), and made public, *Bishop* v. *Wood*, 426 U.S. 341, 348, 96 S.Ct. 2074, 48 L.Ed.2d 684 (1976), by the offending governmental entity, *see Paul* v. *Davis*, 424 U.S. 693, 708-10, 96 S.Ct. 1155, 47 L.Ed.2d 405 (1976); *Wisconsin* v. *Constantineau*, 400 U.S. 433, 437, 91 S.Ct. 507, 27 L.Ed.2d 515 (1971). *Gentile* v. *Wallen*, 562 F2d 193, 197 (2d Cir. 1977).

In the instant action, defendants submit that plaintiff is in no position to contend that he was "stigmatized." First, they argue that no reason whatsoever was given to explain his being denied tenure since no official action was ever taken regarding his claim to tenure. Accordingly, he could not have been denied tenure on "stigmatizing" grounds. Second, they contend, as mentioned above, that plaintiff was ordered to stop using the title MLKDP simply because he never held that title. Again, these allegations simply raise factual questions. Plaintiff's complaint, if taken as true, complains of adverse action taken on the basis of the untrue charges that because he was an alcoholic he could not meet his teaching responsibilities. Further, he alleges that these charges were communicated to members of the faculty under circumstances unrelated to confidential or necessary discussions regarding his teaching competency. *Cf. Bishop* v. *Wood*, 426 U.S. 341, 348-49, 96 S.Ct. 2074, 2079 (1976). Lastly, he contends that the challenged action has seriously damaged his employment opportunities. Thus, while plaintiff may not be able to prove his charges, he has stated a claim that he has been deprived of liberty without due process of law.

II. The Rehabilitation Act Claim

Section 504 of The Rehabilitation Act of 1973, 29 U.S.C. § 794 provides:

> No otherwise qualified handicapped individual in the United States, as defined in section 7(6) of this title, shall, solely by reason of his handicap, be excluded from participation in, be denied the benefits of, or be subjected to discrimination under any program or activity receiving Federal financial assistance.

As noted at the outset, plaintiff admits that he is an alcoholic, but alleges that his alcoholism is under control and that it has not interfered with the successful performance of any of his assigned teaching responsibilities. Thus, characterizing his alcoholism as a "handicap," and himself as an "otherwise qualified handicapped individual," he alleges that the defendants in effect denied him tenure and prohibited him from using the MLKDP title solely because of his alcoholism and thereby violated § 504. The defendants, while not challenging plaintiff's characterization of his alcoholism have moved to dismiss his claim on the ground that no private right of action exists by which an individual can seek redress for an alleged violation of section 504. Furthermore, they submit that even if such a private right of action does exist, plaintiff should be required to exhaust certain administrative remedies prior to bringing suit. The American Council on Education has filed an amicus curiae brief in support of this position. The Department of Justice has filed an amicus brief on this point in which it joins in the plaintiff's contention that a private cause of action exists and that this suit may be maintained without prior resort to administrative proceedings. We adopt this latter view.

In *Lloyd v. Regional Transp. Auth.*, 548 F.2d 1277 (7th Cir. 1977), the Seventh Circuit was confronted with a class action brought under section 504 by individuals who were confined to wheelchairs or were otherwise "mobility-disabled." The plaintiffs there sought to restrain the defendants, which were entities responsible for mass transit in the northeastern region of Illinois, from purchasing transportation equipment which would be inaccessible to members of the plaintiff class. After carefully reviewing the legislative history of the Act, and after analyzing section 504 against the standards laid down by the Supreme Court in *Cort v. Ash*, 422 U.S. 66, 95 S.Ct. 2080 (1975), for determining whether a private cuase of action is impliedly granted by a statute, the Court concluded that "it is plain that the rights of the handicapped [are] meant to be enforced at some point through the vehicle of a private cause of action." 548 F.2d at 1286. The court noted that section 504 confers affirmative rights upon handicapped individuals, *id.* at 1281, and that "[w]hen administrative remedial machinery does not exist to vindicate an affirmative right, there can be no objection to an independent cause of action in the federal courts," *id.* at 1286. Since *Lloyd*, every circuit court which has considered the question, including our own, has sustained the existence of a private cause of action under section 504. *See Davis v. Southeastern Community College*, C.A. 77-1237 (4th Cir. March 28, 1978); *Kampmeier v. Nyquist*, 553 F.2d 296 (2d Cir. 1977); *United Handicapped Federation v. Andre*, 558 F.2d 413 (8th Cir. 1977); *Leary v. Crapsey*, 566 F.2d 863 (2d Cir. 1977).

Defendants point out, however, that since the time *Lloyd* was decided, the H.E.W., pursuant to Executive Order 11914, 41 F.R. 17871 (1976), has promulgated regulations designed to insure compliance with section 504, and that the existence of these regulations removed one of the underpinnings of the *Lloyd* decision. That is, *Lloyd's* holding was premised on the unavailability of administrative remedies by which aggrieved parties could seek redress for violations of section 504, with the Seventh Circuit specifically noting that "assuming a meaningful administrative enforcement mechanism, the private cause of action under Section 504 should be limited to *a posteriori* judicial review." 548 F.2d at 1286 n. 29. Defendants argue that with the promulgation of these regulations, "a meaningful administrative enforcement mechanism" has been established and that such a mechanism is meant to be the exclusive means by which violations of section 504 are to be rectified. Aside from the fact that the Second Circuit, in *Leary, supra,* sustained the existence of a private cause of action—admittedly without extensive discussion—after the regulations were promulgated, a review of those regulations reveals that they do not provide an effective means whereby an individual may vindicate his rights under section 504.

The regulations, which appear in 45 C.F.R. §§ 84.1-84.47, are designed to insure that recipients of federal funds do not violate the strictures of section 504. To that end, adopting in 45 C.F.R. § 84.61 those procedures utilized to assure compliance with Title VI of the Civil Rights Act of 1964 which are contained in 45 C.F.R. §§ 80.6-80.10 and Part 81, the regulations provide that the H.E.W. will, when learning of a possible section 504 violation, institute an investigation. If it is determined that a violation has occurred, voluntary compliance by way of remedial action will be sought. If these efforts at voluntary compliance are unsuccessful, the H.E.W., after a hearing, can cut off the federal funds which had been flowing to the transgressing institution.

This cutting off of funds is, effectively, the only sanction that H.E.W. can impose. Nowhere is the H.E.W. authorized to issue a binding order that damages be paid to an individual who has suffered by reason of a section 504 violation. Nor is the H.E.W. authorized to order the reinstatement of an individual who has been discharged in violation of that section. Moreover, while an individual may file a complaint and thereby possibly trigger an H.E.W. investigation, he does not become a party to any proceedings between the H.E.W. and the alleged violator. 45 C.F.R. § 81.23. Indeed, the only relationship that he may have with these proceedings is the receipt of a notice that an administrative hearing is going to be held to determine whether funds should be cut off. In short, while the administrative process may effectively provide, by way of the threat of a funding termination, an incentive to comply with section 504, it provides no means by which an individual can obtain personal redress for a section 504 violation. Thus, by their very terms, the regulations do not provide a "meaningful enforcement mechanism" for the vindication of personal rights. Moreover, as a practical matter, the H.E.W. itself, in an affidavit submitted with the Justice Department's amicus brief, has represented to the court that there is "a large backlog of [section 504] complaints and there is no guarantee that any newly filed complaint can be investigated and resolved in an expeditious manner." Accordingly, since there clearly is still no effective administrative enforcement mechanism, we find no reason to distinguish the holding of *Lloyd* as it has been adopted in *Leary* and *Kampmeier*.

For essentially the same reasons, we reject the defendants' contention that exhaustion of the H.E.W. procedures is a necessary prerequisite to the institution of such an action. As the *Lloyd* court stated, "There being no administrative remedy open to th[is] plaintiff, neither the exhaustion nor primary jurisdiction doctrine applies." 548 F.2d at 1287, *citing Rosado* v. *Wyman*, 397 U.S. 397, 405-06, 90 S.Ct. 1207, 1214-15 (1970). *See also Simon* v. *St. Louis County*, C.A. 77-1140(c)(4) (E.D.Mo. Jan. 31, 1978); *Michigan Paralyzed Veterans of America* v. *Coleman*, C.A. 5-7114 (E.D.Mich. Nov. 3, 1977).

Admittedly, in *Doe* v. *New York University*, 442 F.Supp. 522 (S.D.N.Y. 1978), the court did require a plaintiff bringing a section 504 action to first exhaust the H.E.W.'s administrative procedures. However, the basis of that court's decision was that because the H.E.W. regulations had been recently promulgated, "On paper, it now appears that, in the words of the Seventh Circuit in *Lloyd*, 'meaningful administrative enforcement' is available for complaints under section 504." *Id.* at 523. The court stated that "it is simply too early to find th[e] administrative remedy inadequate." *Id.* As we have noted, to the extent that the *Doe* court found that the promulgated regulations on their face provide an adequate remedy to vindicate individual rights, we disagree. Moreover, as a practical matter, the H.E.W. in its affidavit has stated that its handling of complaints is not efficient and that, as a matter of policy, it believes grievants should be entitled to institute suits without exhausting the Department's own complaint investigation procedures established pursuant to 45 C.F.R. § 80.7. Accordingly, we choose not to follow the holdings of *Doe* and other cases which have required exhaustion.

III.   The Preliminary Injunction Motion

Plaintiff has sought to preliminarily restrain the defendants from not treating him as a tenured member of the Brooklyn College faculty or from interfering with his use of the title MLKDP. Because the plaintiff, who left the Brooklyn College faculty after the institution of this suit and obtained a faculty position at another college, . . . has not shown that he will suffer any harm that can be categorized as "irreparable,'' and because it is too late to preserve the status quo ante, we find that the issuance of a preliminary injunction would be inappropriate. *See Triebwasser & Katz* v. *American Telephone & Telegraph Co.,* 535 F.2d 1356, 1358-59 (2d Cir. 1976); *Checker Motors Corp.* v. *Chrysler Corp.,* 405 F.2d 319 (2d Cir. 1969), *cert. denied,* 394 U.S. 999, 89 S.Ct. 1595 (1969). Accordingly, the motion is denied.

Conclusion

The defendants' motion to dismiss the complaint and the plaintiff's motion for a preliminary injunction are dened and IT IS SO ORDERED.

NOTES

1.   One of the court's reasons for upholding the sufficiency of plaintiff's due process claim was the "stigma'' theory—that a liberty interest may be at stake when official actions result in damage to a person's reputation or good name. It should be noted that one of the cases cited by the *Whitaker* court in support of this ground, *Wisconsin* v. *Constantineau,* 400 U.S. 433 (1971), directly involved the issue of labeling a person as an alcoholic, although not in an employment context. Could this same legal theory be applied to other more traditional handicapping conditions? Since the court noted that Mr. Whitaker admits his alcoholism, is it really the label or the refusal of employment which constitutes the stigma?

2.   The court's reasons for not requiring exhaustion of HEW administrative remedies stands as a fairly comprehensive critique of the shortcomings of the HEW procedures. It is notable that the Justice Department and HEW agreed with the court that § 794 creates a private cause of action and that no exhaustion of administrative remedies ought to be required.

SECTION 505 OF THE REHABILITATION ACT

29 U.S.C. § 795, added by § 120(a) of P.L. 95-602 (Nov. 6, 1978)

Sec. 505.(a)(1).   The remedies, procedures, and rights set forth in section 717 of the Civil Rights Act of 1964 (42 U.S.C. 2000e-16), including the application of sections 706(f) through 706(k) (42 U.S.C. 2000e-5(f) through (k)), shall be available, with respect to any complaint under section 501 of this Act, to any employee or applicant for employment aggrieved by the final disposition of such complaint, or by the failure to take final action on such complaint. In fashioning an equitable or affirmative action remedy under such section, a court may take into account the reasonableness of the cost of any necessary work place accommodation, and the availability of alternatives therefore or other appropriate relief in order to achieve an equitable and appropriate remedy.

(b) The remedies, procedures, and rights set forth in Title VI of the Civil Rights Act of 1964 shall be available to any person aggrieved by any act or failure to act by any recipient of Federal assistance or Federal provider of such assistance under section 504 of this act.

(c) In any action or proceeding to enforce or charge a violation of a provision of this title, the court, in its discretion, may allow the prevailing party, other than the United States, a reasonable attorney's fee as part of the costs.

NOTE

The addition of § 505 to the Rehabilitation Act as part of the 1978 Amendments (P.L. 95-602) is significant for several reasons. The authorization of court-awarded attorneys' fees will improve access to legal services for disabled persons. Note that such fees may be awarded for actions brought under any section of Title V of the Rehabilitation Act.

The application of Title VI remedies to actions brought under § 504 and of Title VII to those under § 501 may enlarge the scope of available remedies. But see one early analysis of the impact of § 505 in the *Trageser* case which follows.

TRAGESER v. LIBBIE REHABILITATION CENTER, INC.
United States Court of Appeals for the Fourth Circuit, 1978
590 F.2d 89

BUTZNER, Circuit Judge:

Novella H. Trageser appeals the district court's dismissal of her complaint alleging that the termination of her employment at Libbie Rehabilitation Center constituted handicap discrimination in violation of § 504 of the Rehabilitation Act of 1973, the fifth and fourteenth amendments to the Constitution, and 42 U.S.C. § 1983. We affirm because § 120(a) of the Comprehensive Rehabilitation Services Amendments of 1978 foreclose her claim under the Rehabilitation Act of 1973, and lack of governmental action precludes recovery on the other grounds.

I

Libbie, a private corporation, operates a nursing home for profit in Richmond, Virginia. It receives substantial income from the state and federal governments in the form of Medicare, Medicaid, Veterans Administration, and welfare payments. The purpose of these payments is to compensate for treatment of specified patients who are entitled to the benefits. The home is subject to inspection by the Virginia Department of Health.

Trageser, a registered nurse, was hired in 1971 and promoted to director of nurses in 1975. Her sight is impaired by a condition known as retinitis pigmentosa, which is hereditary and progressive.

On April 28, 1976, the certification officer from the Virginia Department of Health conducted a regular inspection of the nursing home. The inspector told the administrator of the home that Trageser's eyesight had deteriorated since the last inspection and asked what the home intended to do about it. The administrator relayed these comments to the board of directors. At its meeting on June 7, 1976, the board resolved to dismiss her. Upon learning of this decision, Trageser resigned.

Trageser then brought this action seeking reinstatement, back pay, and an injunction against payment of federal financial assistance to the home unless she was reinstated. The district court treated the termination of her employment as tantamount to discharge, but it granted Libbie's motion to dismiss the complaint for failure to state a claim upon which relief could be granted. *See Trageser* v. *Libbie Rehabilitation Center*, 16 E.P.D. ¶ 8117, 17 F.E.P. Cases 938 (E.D.Va. 1977).

II

Trageser bases her claim on § 504 of the Rehabilitation Act of 1973 which provides as follows:

No otherwise qualified handicapped individual in the United States . . . shall, solely by reason of his handicap, be excluded from the participation in, be denied the benefits of, or be subjected to discrimination under any program or activity receiving Federal financial assistance.

In § 120(a) of the Comprehensive Rehabilitation Services Amendments of 1978, Congress added, among other provisions, § 505(a)(2) which states:

The remedies, procedures, and rights set forth in title VI of the Civil Rights Act of 1964 shall be available to any person aggrieved by any act or failure to act by any recipient of Federal assistance or Federal provider of such assistance under § 504 of this Act.

Title VI contains the prototype of § 504 of the Rehabilitation Act. *See Lloyd* v. *Regional Transportation Authority,* 548 F.2d 1277, 1280 and n. 9 (7th Cir. 1977). Section 601 of Title VI provides as follows:

No person in the United States shall, on the ground of race, color, or national origin, be excluded from participation in, be denied the benefits of, or be subjected to discrimination under any program or activity receiving Federal financial assistance.

The broad prohibition of § 601 is, however, qualified by § 604, which creates the following limitation:

Nothing contained in this subchapter shall be construed to authorize action under this subchapter by any department or agency with respect to any employment practice of any employer, employment agency, or labor organization except where a primary objective of the Federal financial assistance is to provide employment.

Although § 604 expressly curtails the authority of federal departments and agencies, it also restricts private suits. Thus, because of § 604, Title VI does not provide a judicial remedy for employment discrimination by institutions receiving federal funds unless (1) providing employment is a primary objective of the federal aid, or (2) discrimination in employment necessarily causes discrimination against the primary beneficiaries of the federal aid.

Title VII of the Civil Rights Act of 1964 provides the primary statutory remedies for racial and ethnic discrimination in employment. Recognizing this, Congress supplemented the Rehabilitation Act by including in § 120(a) of the 1978 amendments a new subsection 505(a)(1) which makes the pertinent remedies, procedures, and rights of Title VII available to federal employees who complain of handicap discrimination in employment in violation of § 501 of the Rehabilitation Act. Congress also could have utilized Title VII to define the rights and remedies of a person in Trageser's position who must rely on § 504. Instead, for employees of private institutions receiving federal financial aid, § 120(a) of the 1978 amendments makes available only the remedies, procedures, and rights of Title VI, which, as we have noted above, contains the restriction of § 604. The distinction that § 120(a) draws between the relief available to federal employees and that available to employees of private institutions receiving federal assistance could not have been inadvertent. We therefore conclude that we must apply the limitation contained in § 604 of Title VI to § 504 of the Rehabilitation Act in literal compliance with § 120(a) of the 1978 amendments.

We cannot accept Trageser's contention that the 1978 amendments are inapplicable to her 1976 dismissal. We must decide this case in accordance with the law as it exists at the time we render our decision " 'unless doing so would result in manifest injustice or there is statutory direction or legislative history to the contrary.' " *Cort* v. *Ash*, 422 U.S. 66, 76-77 (1975). In the absence of legislative history to the contrary, the explicit incorporation of § 604 of Title VI simply confirms a plausible reading of § 504 as originally enacted. *See, e.g.*, Guy, The Developing Law on Equal Employment Opportunity for the Handicapped: An Overview and Analysis of the Major Issues, 7 U. Balt. L. Rev. 183, 207 (1978). We therefore find no manifest injustice in applying the amendments to illuminate this case which was pending when they were enacted.

A private action under § 504 to redress employment discrimination therefore may not be maintained unless a primary objective of the federal financial assistance is to provide employment. There has been no such allegation in this case; nor could there be one. Viewing the complaint in the light most favorable to Trageser, in compliance with Federal Rule of Civil Procedure 12(b)(6), we nevertheless hold that she cannot prevail on her § 504 claim.

III

Trageser also based her complaint on 42 U.S.C. § 1983, the fourteenth amendment, and the equal protection component of the due process clause in the fifth amendment. We conclude, however, that the district court correctly granted Libbie's motion to dismiss these claims.

Section 1983 requires Trageser to show that Libbie acted under color of either a state law or regulation or a state-enforced custom. *Adickes* v. *S. H. Kress & Co.*, 398 U.S. 144, 148, 161-69 (1970). To establish a denial of equal protection of the laws in violation of the fifth and fourteenth amendments, Trageser is required to do more than merely allege governmental regulation of the nursing home. She must demonstrate that Libbie's ostensibly private conduct was in reality an act of either the state or federal government. There must exist "a sufficiently close nexus between the State and the challenged action of the regulated entity so that the action of the latter may be fairly treated as that of the State itself.'' *Jackson* v. *Metropolitan Edison Co.*, 419 U.S. 345, 351 (1974). To satisfy this requirement, Trageser relies on (1) Libbie's receipt of public funds and (2) the state inspector's role in Libbie's decision to dismiss her.

Libbie did not participate in the Hill-Burton construction program which ''subjects hospitals to an elaborate and intricate pattern of governmental regulations, both state and federal.'' *See Simkins* v. *Moses H. Cone Memorial Hospital*, 323 F.2d 959, 964 (4th Cir. 1963). Consequently, our decision in *Simkins* which detected state action in the operation of participating hospitals does not control here. Moreover, we have previously held that the receipt of Medicaid funds does not convert private medical care to state action. *Walker* v. *Pierce*, 560 F.2d 609 (4th Cir. 1977). For similar reasons, we decline to ascribe state action to Libbie's receipt of Medicare and Veterans Administration benefits.

To show state action, Trageser also relies on the query of the state inspector who, noting that her eyesight had deteriorated, asked what Libbie intended to do about it. The inspector did not include this observation about Trageser among the deficiencies found at the home, and Trageser does not allege that the state would or could impose any sanctions on Libbie if it continued to employ her. Libbie's subsequent decision to dismiss her, therefore, cannot be considered an action of the state itself. *See Jackson* v. *Metropolitan Edison Co.*, 419 U.S. 345, 351 (1974).

Consequently, neither Libbie's receipt of patients' benefits nor Virginia's regulation of the home constitutes state action sufficient to sustain the § 1983 and constitutional claims.

The judgment of the district court is affirmed.

NOTES

1. As *Gurmankin, Duran, Davis, Whitaker,* and most of the other cases in this chapter have indicated, a private cause of action under § 794 for employment discrimination was well established before *Trageser*. Yet the *Trageser* court concludes that by giving Title VI remedies Congress precluded the right to a private cause of action. If a person is legally entitled to A, does the passage of a law giving him or her B automatically destroy entitlement to A? The logic of the *Trageser* court seems even more inverted when one recalls that pursuant to § 604 of Title VI, the Title provides no remedies whatever, administrative or otherwise, for employment discrimination in most federal programs. Thus, this is not a case of Congress substituting one remedy for another, but rather the court's interpretation means that Congress has taken away a solidly established right to a court action, and in return has given nothing. If this had been the Congressional intent (which it obviously was not), would not this purpose have been indicated more explicitly?

2. Is a possible rationale for the *Trageser* court's hostility to plaintiff's § 794 claim, and a possible distinguishing feature of the case, the indirect nature of the federal funds received? Is this an example of a reaction against too many federal strings attached to too little money?

3. Can the *Trageser* and *Whitaker* holdings be reconciled?

4. Right to Contract for Employment Generally—Section 1981

As noted above in the discussion of the Thirteenth Amendment to the United States Constitution (pp. 356–360, above), the Enabling Clause of that Amendment empowers Congress "to pass all laws necessary and proper for abolishing all badges and incidents of slavery in the United States," *Jones* v. *Alfred H. Mayer Co.*, 392 U.S. 409, 439 (1968); Civil Rights Cases, 109 U.S. 3, 20 (1883). Pursuant to that power, Congress passed the Civil Rights Act of 1866, which contained a section that is now 42 U.S.C. § 1981:

> All persons within the jurisdiction of the United States shall have the same right in every State and Territory to make and enforce contracts, to sue, be parties, give evidence, and to the full and equal benefit of all laws and proceedings for the security of persons and property as is enjoyed by white citizens, and shall be subject to like punishment, pains, penalties, taxes, licenses, and exactions of every kind, and to no other.

Although § 1981 is worded as protecting the same contractual and other rights "as [are] enjoyed by white citizens," some courts have held that its scope is not limited to racial discrimination, e.g., *Scher* v. *Board of Education of Town of West Orange*, 424 F.2d 741, 743 (3rd Cir. 1970).

> Sections 42 U.S.C. §§ 1981–1985 are sometimes called the Reconstruction Civil Rights Acts. . . . While it is obvious that these statutes were passed primarily to insure the rights of non-whites, nothing in the statutes limits their application to situations where the civil rights of non-whites are being violated. The statutes are phrased in terms such as "all persons" and "all citizens," and the courts are bound to give these sections "a sweep as broad as (their) language." *Gannon* v. *Action*, 303 F.Supp. 1240, 1244 (E.D.Mo. 1969), *aff'd in part*, on other grounds, *Action* v. *Gannon*, 450 F.2d 1227 (8th Circ. 1971).

Thus, the United States Supreme Court has recognized that § 1981 protects the rights of aliens, *Takahashi* v. *Fish and Game Commission*, 334 U.S. 410, 419 (1948).

There is little doubt that one of the rights protected by § 1981 is the right to enter into contracts for employment; in *Jones* v. *Alfred H. Mayer Co.*, *supra*, the Court specifically characterized "the right to contract for employment" as "a right secured by 42 U.S.C. § 1981," at 392 U.S. 440 n.78. Moreover, the *Jones* decision expressly overruled *Hodges* v. *United States* 203 U.S. 1 (1906), which had held that § 1981 did not prohibit private acts interfering with employment opportunities, 392 U.S. 440 n.78. Since *Jones*, the lower courts have uniformly held that § 1981 protects against interference with the right to contract for employment: *Young* v. *International Telephone & Telegraph Co.*, 438 F.2d 757 (3rd Cir. 1971); *Waters* v. *Wisconsin Steel Wks. of Internat'l Harvester Co.*, 427 F.2d 476, 482 (7th Cir. 1970), cert. denied, sub. nom. *International Harvester Co.* v. *Waters*, 400 U.S. 911 (1970); *Sanders* v. *Dobbs Houses, Inc.*, 431 F.2d 1097 (5th Cir. 1970), cert. denied, 401 U.S. 948 (1971); *Brady* v. *Bristol-Meyers, Inc.*, 459 F.2d 621 (8th Cir. 1972). As the *Young* court observed:

> In the context of the Reconstruction it would be hard to imagine to what contract right the Congress was more likely to have been referring. (At 438 F.2d. 760.)

If applied to situations involving employment discrimination against handicapped persons, § 1981 could have a dramatic impact in combating such discrimination. The effect of such legal analysis would be particularly far-reaching in light of the fact that § 1981 is not limited to "state action," but extends to private acts of discrimination as well, *Runyon* v. *McCrary,* 427 U.S. 160 (1976). But, although the use of § 1981 as a possible remedy for discrimination against handicapped individuals in regard to employment opportunities has been suggested by some authorities (e.g., "Abroad in the Land: Legal Strategies to Effectuate the Rights of the Physically Disabled," 61 *Georgetown L.J.* 1501, 1514-1519 (1973), such a theory has not yet been tested in the courts.

5. The Fair Labor Standards Act and the Problem of Forced Institutional Labor: A Reformational Dead End

As noted above (see pp. 356–360), practices of forced labor in residential institutions may be challenged as "involuntary servitude" prohibited by the Thirteenth Amendment. Another reformational approach, however, has been an attempt to bring the labor of institutional residents within the regulation of the Fair Labor Standards Act. Among other things, the F.L.S.A. sets a minimum wage (29 U.S.C. § 206) and requires additional compensation for overtime work (29 U.S.C. § 207): these requirements apply to any employee who "is employed in an enterprise engaged in commerce or in the production of goods for commerce."

When employers fail to comply with its provisions, the F.L.S.A. provides for two types of remedies. First, 29 U.S.C. § 216(b) provides:

> Any employer who violates the provisions of section 206 [wages] or section 207 [hours] of this title shall be liable to the employee or employees affected in the amount of their unpaid minimum wages, or their unpaid overtime compensation as the case may be, and in an additional equal amount as liquidated damages. Action to recover such liability may be maintained . . . in any court . . . of competent jurisdiction.

Second, the Act authorizes suits by the Secretary of Labor to recover unpaid minimum wages or overtime compensation, 29 U.S.C. § 216(c), and for injunctive relief against violations, 29 U.S.C. § 217.

In 1966, Congress amended the F.L.S.A. to expand its coverage to include public and private hospitals, schools, and institutions serving handicapped people. 29 U.S.C. § 203(s) provides:

> "Enterprise engaged in commerce or in the production of goods for commerce" means an enterprise which has employees engaged in commerce or in the production of goods for commerce, or employees handling, selling, or otherwise working on goods or materials that have been moved in or produced for commerce by any person, and which— . . . is engaged in the operation of a hospital, an institution primarily engaged in the care of the sick, the aged, the mentally ill or defective who reside on the premises of such institution, a school for mentally or physically handicapped or gifted children, a preschool, elementary or secondary school, or an institution of higher education (regardless of whether or not such hospital, institution, or school is public or private or operated for profit or not for profit); . . .

In *Maryland* v. *Wirtz,* 392 U.S. 183 (1968), the United States Supreme Court upheld these amendments against the constitutional challenge that they were beyond the authority of Congress. The Court's reasoning took an expansive view of Congressional power to regulate commerce:

> Congress may by appropriate legislation regulate intrastate activities where they have a substantial effect on interstate commerce (392 U.S. at 189).

The Court held that, because of the large amounts of imported products used by hospitals, schools, and institutions, and because of the large labor force employed there, such "enterprises" could rationally be said to have substantial impact upon interstate commerce and therefore were properly subject to F.L.S.A. regulation.

It was only a short step from application of F.L.S.A. standards to employees of hospitals, institutions, and schools to their application to labor performed by the clients or residents of such agencies. After the *Wirtz* decision, advocates for reform of mental institutions embraced the 1966 amendments as potent tools regulating the job tasks assigned to patients and in requiring that a minimum wage be paid for such tasks. The first half decade of the 1970s saw an assortment of litigative activity seeking to have the mandates of the F.L.S.A. enforced in regard to patient labor in various mental health and mental retardation facilities: *Souder* v. *Brennan,* 367 F.Supp. 808 (D.D.C. 1973); *Brennan* v. *State of Iowa,* 494 F.2d 100 (8th Cir. 1974); *Clover Bottom Hospital and School* v. *Townsend,* 513 S.W.2d 505 (Tenn. 1974), cert. denied, 421 U.S. 1007 (1975); *Roebuck* v. *Florida Dept. of Health & Rehab. Serv., Inc.,* 502 F.2d 1105 (5th Cir. 1974); *Wyatt* v. *Stickney,* 344 F.Supp. 373, 381, 402–403 (M.D.Ala. 1972). By and large, such lawsuits were successful in establishing the application of federal labor regulations to institution residents and in obtaining injunctive remedies, often quite detailed, clarifying the types of activities to which minimum wage and overtime compensation provisions would apply. For more discussion of such litigation, see P. Friedman, "The Mentally Handicapped Citizen and Institutional Labor," 87 *Harv. L. Rev.* 567 (1974); D. Ferleger, "Loosing the Chains: In-Hospital Civil Liberties of Mental Patients," 13 *Santa Clara Lawyer* 447, 477-483 (1973).

The broad successes of this reform strategy, however, were only short-lived. In 1976, the Supreme Court reversed its ruling in *Maryland* v. *Wirtz,* and held that the authority granted to Congress by the Commerce Clause was not so extensive as to permit the federal regulation of state employees, *National League of Cities* v. *Usery,* 426 U.S. 833 (1976). The sovereignty of the states would, therefore, bar such attempts at regulatory activities that "operate to directly displace the States' freedom to structure integral operations in areas of traditional governmental functions," at 426 U.S. 852.

National League of Cities v. *Usery* apparently marks the Waterloo of attempts to reform institutional labor practices in state-run facilities through the instrumentality of the Fair Labor Standards Act. The *Usery* holding, however, would seemingly not apply to private residential facilities, and such institutions may therefore still be subject to F.L.S.A. regulation; see, e.g., *Weidenfeller* v. *Kidulis,* 380 F.Supp. 445 (E.D.Wis. 1974).

4

ACCESS TO BUILDINGS AND TRANSPORTATION SYSTEMS

Marcia Pearce Burgdorf and W. Dawn Oxley

A. THE NEED FOR ACCESSIBILITY

TENBROEK, J., "THE RIGHT TO LIVE IN THE WORLD: THE DISABLED IN THE LAW OF
TORTS"

54 Cal. L. Rev. 841–842 (1966)

Movement, we are told, is a law of animal life. As to man, in any event, nothing could
be more essential to personality, social existence, economic opportunity—in short, to
individual well-being and integration into the life of the community—than the physical
capacity, the public approval, and the legal right to be abroad in the land.

Almost by definition, physical disability in many of its forms entails difficulties
in getting about, and this is so quite regardless of the particular surroundings. Such is
the case of the cripple, the paraplegic, and the legless. The word "halt" itself is a
description of disability in terms of limitation on mobility. Some difficulties in getting
about arise out of the conditions of the modern world in combination with the particular
disability, as in the case of the deaf person in traffic. However different from what they
are widely supposed to be, there are travel problems inherent in blindness and these are
to some extent increased, to some extent diminished, by the structures and conditions
of modern urban life and activities.

* * *

The actual physical limitations resulting from the disability more often than not
play little role in determining whether the physically disabled are allowed to move
about and be in public places. Rather, that judgment for the most part results from a
variety of considerations related to public attitudes, attitudes which not infrequently are
quite erroneous and misconceived. These include public imaginings about what the
inherent physical limitations must be; public solicitude about the safety to be achieved
by keeping the disabled out of harm's way; public feelings of protective care and
custodial security; public doubts about why the disabled should want to be abroad
anyway; and public aversion to the sight of them and the conspicuous reminder of their
plight. For our purposes, there is no reason to judge these attitudes as to whether they

do credit or discredit to the human head and heart. Our concern is with their existence and their consequences.

To what extent do the legal right, the public approval, and the physical capacity coincide? Does the law assure the physically disabled, to the degree that they are physically able to take advantage of it, the right to leave their institutions, asylums, and the houses of their relatives? Once they emerge, must they remain on the front porch, or do they have the right to be in public places, to go about in the streets, sidewalks, roads and highways, to ride upon trains, buses, airplanes, and taxi cabs, and to enter and to receive goods and services in hotels, restaurants, and other places of public accommodation? If so, under what conditions? What are the standards of care and conduct, of risk and liability, to which they are held and to which others are held with respect to them? Are the standards the same for them as for the able-bodied? Are there legal as well as physical adaptations; and to what extent and in what ways are these tied to concepts of custodialism or integrationism?

NOTE

The tenBroek article, written by a blind law professor, is an important starting point in any examination of physical accessibility and the law; it was a precursor of the organized efforts by handicapped people to eliminate architectural barriers and to achieve equality in American society. The portion of the article included here is from an introductory section. The body of the article examined specific precedents in personal injury law involving handicapped victims, and sought to determine general implications of these decisions in regard to the rights of handicapped people to move about in society. Although some of the terminology used to describe various handicapping conditions is outmoded and inexpedient, most of tenBroek's observations and questions have remained timely.

"REPORT OF THE UNITED NATIONS EXPERT GROUP MEETING ON BARRIER-FREE DESIGN"
26 Int. Rehabil. Rev. 3 (1975)

[D]espite everything we can do, or hope to do, to assist each physically or mentally disabled person achieve his or her maximum potential in life, our efforts will not succeed until we have found the way to remove the obstacles to this goal directed by human society—*the physical barriers* we have created in public buildings, housing, transportation, houses of worship, centers of social life, and other community facilities—*the social barriers* we have evolved and accepted against those who vary more than a certain degree from what we have been conditioned to regard as normal. More people are forced into limited lives and made to suffer by these man-made obstacles than by any specific physical or mental disability.

NOTE, "THE FORGOTTEN MINORITY: THE PHYSICALLY DISABLED AND IMPROVING THEIR PHYSICAL ENVIRONMENT"
48 Chi.-Kent L. Rev. 215, 221 (1971)

Countless buildings still have no ramps for wheelchairs, no readily accessible elevators, narrow or revolving doorways, too narrow aisles, inadequate toilet facilities, drinking fountains and light switches that are too high, fire alarm boxes that cannot be reached and countless other deficiencies. Just a few improvements such as hand rails, ground level entrance ramps, doors that open automatically, raised letters and numbers on doors and in elevators so that the blind can read them, danger signals equipped with light and sound so that the deaf can be warned, toilet stalls with grab rails and accessible telephone booths would make a whole new world available to the disabled. Public transportation is generally without facilities such as level station platforms to eliminate steps to trains, luggage carts that the handicapped can handle, turnstiles through which the disabled can pass, elevators to subway stations, lift platforms for buses, and interstate highway rest areas with adequate accommodations. These are but a few illustrations of the environmental barriers faced by the physically disabled in attempting to achieve normalcy.

COMMENT, "ACCESS TO BUILDINGS AND EQUAL EMPLOYMENT OPPORTUNITY FOR THE DISABLED: SURVEY OF STATE STATUTES"

50 Temple L. Q. *1067–1068 (1977)*

Presently, much of our physical environment is designed for the "ideal user"[3] and is relatively inaccessible to the disabled. Yet it is not only the "handicapped" who are disadvantaged by this system: the young, the elderly, and the ill also experience varied degrees of mobility limitation. Nor is the problem one which only affects a small group of people. Statistical data on the number of physically disabled are not readily available, but estimates range from eighteen to sixty-eight million nationally.

Architectural barriers are a primary obstacle in limiting the ability of the disabled to live independent lives. These barriers confront the handicapped in places of residence, employment, recreation, entertainment, public accommodation, and, most significantly, public transportation. It is difficult to see how the disabled can achieve equal employment, fair housing, and full independent lives when they are effectively denied entrance to privately and publicly owned restaurants, theatres, places of employment, and business or public accommodations.

Although the public policy articulated in federal and state legislation has favored social integration entitling the disabled to full participation in society, architectural barriers have not been removed. Inaccessibility, essentially an apolitical issue, remains a significant problem even though resolution is not only technologically feasible but can be obtained with relative ease. In addition, the cost of providing barrier-free design in new construction has been estimated to be between one-tenth of one percent and one-half of one percent of the total construction cost of new buildings. One author has explained that the reasons for this neglect are rooted in erroneous public attitudes toward the disabled among which are misconceptions regarding their inherent physical limitations, misplaced public solicitude concerning their safety, a *parens patriae* notion of protective care and custodial security, skepticism concerning their desire to be mobile, and public aversion to the constant and conspicuous reminder of the plight of

---

[3]Morgan, *"Beyond Disability: A Broader Definition of Architectural Barriers," Am. Inst. Arch. J.* 50, 50 (May 1976).

the disabled.[13] Architectural barriers perpetuated by society's indifference to the disabled have physically and psychologically hindered them in demanding their legally protected rights.

NOTE

In regard to the use of handicapping conditions as collective nouns in the two previous articles, see p. 48, above.

B. ACCESS TO TRANSPORTATION: UNDERLYING LEGAL PRINCIPLES

1. Nature of the Problem

ACHTENBURG, J., "LAW AND THE PHYSICALLY DISABLED:
AN UPDATE WITH CONSTITUTIONAL IMPLICATIONS"

8 S.W.U.L. Rev. 847, 865–866 (1976)

... [P]ersonal liberty consists in a power of locomotion, of changing situations, or removing one's person to whatever place one's own inclination may direct, without imprisonment or restraint, unless by due course of law.[56]

From the earliest times, it has been recognized that mobility is the key to social integration, job flexibility, and a vital ingredient to a productive and useful life. It is not surprising that the second major target area of the disabled has been urban mass transit. The inability to use mass transit affects every aspect of a disabled person's life. Without either a private car or a very expensive van, a mobility-impaired person often is deprived of the opportunity to go to school, to explore job opportunities or to enjoy recreational facilities. Without sufficient education and flexibility in finding housing the disabled person may be relegated to a nonproductive life.

BARTELS v. BIERNAT

United States District Court for the Eastern District of Wisconsin, 1975
405 F. Supp. 1012, 1017–1018

* * *

Certainly the public has a need for the most modern and efficient public transit system that money can buy; the evils of mass transportation by means of the privately owned and operated automobile are manifest. On the other hand, society has a distinct interest in utilizing every possible source of human skill and ingenuity, including the skills and talents of mobility-handicapped individuals. When effectively confined to a single floor, building or city block, not only are the handicapped deprived of the myriad benefits of society, but society is deprived of the valuable contributions of these otherwise normal human beings. And this deprivation is compounded by the fact that, when unable to fend for themselves, the handicapped must depend upon the public

---

[13][tenBroek, J., "The Right to Live in the World: The Disabled in the Law of Torts," 54 *Cal. L. Rev.* 841 (1966)] at 842.

[56]Blackstone, I. W., *Commentaries* 230–31 (Jones, ed., 1916).

purse for their sustenance. This is a burden that should be inflicted upon neither the mobility handicapped nor society in general.

* * *

BURGDORF, R., AND BURGDORF, M., "A HISTORY OF UNEQUAL TREATMENT: THE QUALIFICATIONS OF HANDICAPPED PERSON AS A 'SUSPECT CLASS' UNDER THE EQUAL PROTECTION CLAUSE"

15 Santa Clara Lawyer *855, 865–866 (1975)*

Transportation is another major area of current discrimination against individuals with handicaps. In our mobile society, handicapped people are all too frequently denied access to public transportation.

The Air Traffic Conference, the trade association for air carriers, has promulgated the following rule concerning service to handicapped passengers by member airlines: "Persons who have malodorous conditions, gross disfigurement, or other unpleasant characteristics so unusual as to offend fellow passengers should not be transported by any member."[72] Who determines what is "unpleasant," "unusual" or offensive to fellow passengers? Such vagueness permits airlines to effect policies of discrimination toward handicapped persons. For example, one airline will not allow an unaccompanied blind person to sit next to a person of the opposite sex; another refuses to accept persons with epilepsy as passengers; at least seven airlines refuse service to mentally ill passengers; and one airline expressly excludes mentally retarded people from passenger service.[73]

Moreover, a Civil Aeronautics Board regulation[74] has been interpreted by most airlines to require that an attendant accompany all passengers in wheelchairs, whether or not these passengers are capable of caring for themselves in flight.[75]

Similar discriminatory practices occur in surface transportation systems:

Bus lines plead lack of trained personnel in helping the passenger off and on the bus, and insist that the bus aisles are too narrow for any sort of manipulation equipment. While there is no evidence that their ruling is enforced to the letter consistently, Greyhound has an official policy that . . . if an individual cannot walk onto the bus on his own power he cannot ride the bus.[76]

Railroads have also been guilty of unequal treatment of handicapped persons, particularly in requiring that a fare-paying attendant accompany all passengers in wheelchairs, regardless of the passenger's ability to fend for himself.

Even where transportation agencies do not have active policies which restrict the travel rights of handicapped passengers, architectural impediments and physical obstacles may render use of transportation facilities impossible for various groups of handicapped citizens. The "fundamental right to travel" has little meaning if architec-

---

[72] *Air Traffic Conference of America, Trade Practices Manual* (1962), *quoted in* 118 *Cong. Rec.* 11363 (1972).

[73] 118 *Cong. Rec.* 11363 (1972) (remarks of Congressman Vanik).

[74] Specifically, Rule 15 of C.A.B. No. 142(2).

[75] 18 *Cong. Rec.* 11362-63 (1972).

[76] *Id.* at 11363.

tural barriers render a person unable to enter buses, trains, planes or transportation terminals. New York Judge Nathanial Sorkin, himself a handicapped person, has observed:

> The physically handicapped are de facto barred from using the city's subways and to an only slighter degree from the city's surface transportation system. They are not merely relegated to the back of the bus, they are totally excluded.[81]

2. Common Law Principles

a. Duty of Common Carriers to Transport Handicapped Passengers

HOGAN v. NASHVILLE INTERURBAN RY. CO.

Supreme Court of Tennessee, 1915
131 Tenn. 244, 174 S.W. 1118

WILLIAMS, J. this case stands for trial on bill of complaint and a demurrer thereto; the appeal being that of complainant, Hogan from a decree of the chancery court of Davidson county sustaining the demurrer.

The complainant in his bill alleges that he is about 26 years of age, and resides near the city of Nashville; that he is a student and instructor in Vanderbilt University in that city, and has been accustomed to use the cars of the defendant company almost daily since the line of that company was constructed for transportation into the city; that he has since infancy been lame as a result of infantile paralysis, and has been forced to walk ever since with two crutches; that for the last 10 years he has continually traveled alone and unattended, riding trains, street cars, interurban cars, and goes everywhere a sound and healthy man can go; that in the use of defendant company's cars he was never injured but once, and that then his injury was due to the gross negligence of the servants of defendant; that in so riding he has never caused any trouble, or asked or received any assistance; that he "acts as other passengers, and has been treated as such"; that when ordinary care is exercised "there is no more danger of injuring him than any other person"; that, following the injury above referred to, complainant brought suit against defendant; that thereafter rumors reached him that the defendant was about to withdraw from him the right of passage on its cars; that yet later a communication was received by him from the company's general manager, as follows:

Nashville, Tenn., April 23, 1914.

Mr. Woodall Hogan, R. F. D. #2, Brentwood, Tenn.—Dear Sir: We regret to notify you that on and after May 1st, 1914, we will decline to convey you as a passenger on our line, unless you are at all times accompanied by an attendant. Your physical infirmity is of such a nature as to cause a continued source of possible injury to yourself and as a possible liability as against us. You are also advised that our trainmen and ticket agents will be notified not to receive you as a passenger unless you are accompanied by an

---

[81]See Sorkin, ["Equal Access to Equal Justice: A Civil Right for the Physically Handicapped," 78 *Case and Comment* 41 (1973)] at 41.

attendant. We regret that conditions are such as require this action but deem it necessary, as well for your protection as for the protection of ourselves.

Very truly yours,

[Signed] Meade Frierson,
General Manager.

The bill of complaint further recites: That on May 1, 1914, complainant tendering the usual fare, demeaning himself properly and offering to comply with all the usual and necessary conditions to become a passenger, presented himself to defendant for carriage on its line, but was absolutely refused; that in his work he is compelled to go into Nashville every day, and that his only means of transportation is defendant's line; that defendant is a common carrier.

That the refusal to receive him as a passenger is a persecution of complainant for not dropping the above-mentioned suit and an attempted intimidation, with a view to forcing him to abandon his legal rights, and arbitrary and in violation of defendant's charter.

The demurrer interposed set out the following grounds:

(1) That the bill discloses such physical infirmity on the part of complainant as that it was not a part of defendant's duty at common law to receive him for passage.

(2) That by force of a valid statute defendant had a right to decline to carry complainant for any reason whatever deemed sufficient by it.

(3) That there is no case made for resort to injunctive process; complainant having an ample remedy at law.

The chancellor sustained the several grounds of the demurrer.

The rule, broadly stated, is that any person desiring transportation shall be entitled to be received as a passenger on payment of the fare, notwithstanding a seeming incapacity on his part to take care of himself, if, in point of fact, he "is competent to travel alone without requiring other care than that which the law requires the carrier to bestow on all persons alike." Hutchinson on Carriers (3d Ed.) § 966.

In the application of the rule to concrete instances the authorities are not in exact agreement, but the points of difference are narrow ones.

The disability claimed to disqualify may be mental or physical. Thus, while a common carrier may not lawfully refuse absolutely to carry persons who are insane, it may do so where the proposing passenger is not properly attended or guarded. *Owens v. Macon, etc., R. Co.,* 119 Ga. 230, 46 S.E. 87, 63 L.R.A. 946; *Meyer v. St. Louis, etc., R. Co.,* 54 Fed. 116, 4 C.C.A. 221.

In respect to physical disability, the carrier is not under obligation to receive as a passenger a person who without an attendant is unable, because of extreme age or tender years, to care for himself; and the same test applies to other physical limitations. The carrier may refuse to carry unless the applicant be in charge of one fit to serve as attendant.

The clearest and most comprehensive statement of the rules governing is that of the Supreme Court of Mississippi in a series of cases dealing with blind persons who offered themselves for passage. Blindness is by that court held to be *prima facie* a disqualification; that presumedly the affliction of blindness unfits a person for safe travel by railway, if unaccompanied; that a showing of experience or ability to travel alone on the part of the offerer brought to the knowledge of the railroad company's agent may serve as a basis of liability on the part of the carrier for a refusal to accept him.

That court, on a point pertinent to the case in hand, said:

> We are asked to hold that a regulation that no blind person whatever shall travel unaccompanied by an assistant, no matter how skillful or expert a traveler he may have been, or may be, and no matter how perfectly qualified in every other respect to travel on cars unaccompanied, is a reasonable rule. This cannot be sound. Each case must depend on its own facts, and the reasonableness of the refusal to sell the blind person a ticket must, on principle, depend, not on a universal, arbitrary, and undiscriminating rule like this one, but on the capacity to travel unaccompanied of the particular blind person.

It was therefore held, where a blind person sued, and in his declaration averred that for several years he had traveled on defendant company's cars in the transaction of current business, and had never given cause of complaint to any of its servants, and that no objection had been offered to his riding on the company's train before the date of the exclusion complained of, that this statement of his cause of action was not demurrable, the court holding that it was sufficiently shown that plaintiff was able to take care of himself as a passenger. *Zackery* v. *Mobile & Ohio R. Co.,* 74 Miss. 520, 21 South. 246, 36 L.R.A. 546, 60 Am.St.Rep. 529; *Id.,* 75 Miss. 746, 23 South. 434, 41 L.R.A. 385, 65 Am.St.Rep. 617; *Illinois Cent. R. Co.* v. *Smith,* 85 Miss. 349, 37 South. 643, 70 L.R.A. 642, 107 Am.St.Rep. 293. And see, also, *Illinois Cent. R. Co.* v. *Allen,* 121 Ky. 138, 89 S. W. 150, 11 Ann.Cas. 970.

We have not been cited any case that deals with a disability claimed to exist because of lameness or infirmity of the two lower limbs, making the use of crutches necessary. But we think it clear that the reasoning in behalf of disqualification of such a person for acceptance must be less obvious than in the case of a blind person. It is a matter of common knowledge that, where a man is deprived of the use of his lower limbs, the enforced constant use of his arms increases their strength, enabling him, especially in the case of a youth, to handle himself with considerable facility and safety on crutches. Such persons are seldom attended, and seldom need to be. To deny the right to be so carried to such as complainant is shown to be by the bill of complaint would be to put an unwarranted handicap on a class of men capable of being service-able to society, and therefore on society itself, which the defendant company, if a common carrier, is under obligation to serve.

We readily decline to give assent to the contention of the railway company that, as a proposition of law, a man may be denied passage merely because fate has placed on him the necessity of using two crutches in locomotion; and we hold that the bill of complaint makes a case of improper exclusion of Hogan.

But it is insisted by the defendant company that it is not under the common-law duty of a common carrier in respect of the matter of accepting complainant as a passenger. This contention is based on a statute passed by the Legislature of this state in 1875, doubtless to operate by way of a hedge against the enforcement of the "Civil Rights Bill" passed by the Congress of the United States, which bill at that date had not been declared unconstitutional by the Supreme Court of the United States.

Acts 1875, c. 130 (Shannon's Code, § 3046), is as follows:

> The rule of the common law giving a right of action to any person excluded from any hotel, or public means of transportation, or place of amusement, is hereby abrogated; and hereafter no keeper of any hotel, or public house, or carrier of passengers for hire, or conductors, drivers, or employés of such carrier or keeper, shall be bound, or under any obligation to entertain, carry, or admit any person whom he shall, for any reason whatever, choose not to entertain, carry, or admit to his house, hotel, carriage, or means of transportation, or place of amusement; nor shall any right exist in favor of any such person so refused admission, but the right of such keepers of hotels and public houses, carriers of passengers, and keepers of places of amusement and their employés to control the access and admission or exclusion of persons to or from their public houses, means of transportation, and places of amusement, shall be as perfect and complete as that of any private person over his private house, carriage, or private theater, or places of amusement for his family.

On the other hand, it is urged by complainant that, if this act be constitutional, it was impliedly repealed by a later statute (Acts 1897, c 10), which undertakes to regulate railroads as carriers of passengers and freight. In section 14 of this last-named act it is provided that all corporations, trustees, receivers, and lessees operating railroads in this state are declared to be common carriers. A later section makes it unlawful for any corporation to subject any person to any undue or unreasonable prejudice or disadvantage.

We are of opinion that, if the defendant company be a railroad within the meaning of this statute, it, along with commercial railroads, was classed as, and onerated by the last-quoted statute with the duties of, a common carrier.

What, then, is the necessary import of the statutory phrase declaring railroad companies to be "common carriers"?

> 'Common,' in its legal sense, used as a description of the carrier and his duty and the correlative right of the public, contains the whole doctrine of the common law on the subject. The defendants are common carriers. That is all that need be said. All beyond that can be no more than an explanation or application of the legal meaning of "common" in that connection. *McDuffee* v. *Portland, etc., R. Co.,* 52 N. H. 430, 457, 13 Am.Rep. 72; *Indianapolis Traction, etc., Co.* v. *Lawson,* 143 Fed. 834, 74 C.C.A. 630, 5 L.R.A. (N.S.) 721, 6 Ann.Cas. 666.

The true test of the character of a party, as to whether he is a common carrier or not, is his legal duty and obligation with reference to transportation. Is it optional with him whether he will or will not carry; or must he carry for all? If it be his legal duty to carry for all alike, then he is subject to all those stringent rules which, for wise ends, have long since been adopted and uniformly enforced, both in England and all the states, upon common carriers. *Piedmont Mfg. Co.* v. *Columbia, etc., R. Co.,* 19 S. C. 353, 364.

The court, in *McGregor* v. *Gill,* 114 Tenn. 521, 86 S.W. 318, 108 Am.St.Rep. 919, in drawing the distinction between public or common carriers and private carriers, said that a common carrier of passengers is one who undertakes for hire to carry all passengers indifferently who may apply for passage.

The result of the declaration in the act of 1897 was to place on railroad companies at least the burdens of common carriers as those burdens are defined and prescribed by the common law. No longer may that particular class of carriers claim the benefit of the act of 1875 abrogating the rule of the common law touching the acceptance of those offering to become passengers.

But is the defendant, an interurban railway company, to be treated as being in the class with ordinary trunk or commercial railroad companies thus regulated? Here, again, the Legislature has given the answer.

By Acts 1907, c. 433, it is provided that any interurban railroad company incorporated under the laws of this state shall have and possess the same powers and privileges as are conferred by the general incorporation act upon railroad companies, and subject to the same general duties and obligations. The classification thus made by our Legislature is in line with a strong tendency manifested by the courts of several states to judicially declare interurban railroads to belong to this class [citations omitted].

We come now to the consideration of complainant's right to the remedy of injunction by which to restrain defendant company from excluding him from its passenger cars.

It is said in 6 Pom. Eq. Juris. § 633, that a writ of injunction, sometimes even mandatory in form is granted to compel a carrier to transport freight or to furnish proper transportation facilities, and that unjust and illegal discrimination on the part of public service corporations may be so relieved against, and our case of *Memphis News Pub. Co.* v. *Southern R. Co.*, 110 Tenn. 684, 75 S.W. 941, 63 L.R.A. 150, is cited.

In that case the bill of complaint was one for injunctive process to compel a common carrier to desist from discrimination, but the form of the injunction sought is not disclosed in the opinion, and it does not discuss that phase of the litigation; any disposition of the point being *sub silentio.*

However, in *Coe* v. *L. & N. Railroad (C.C.)* 3 Fed. 775, Baxter, Circuit Judge, held that even a mandatory injunction was grantable to require a railroad company defendant to extend transportation facilities to complainant; and see *Chicago, etc., R. Co.* v. *N. Y., etc., Railroad Co. (C.C.)*, 24 Fed. 516; *Chicago, etc., R. Co.* v. *Burlington, etc., R. Co.* (C.C.), 34 Fed. 481.

In several cases injunctions were granted to compel a public service corporation defendant to furnish a supply of gas, water, etc., to the complainant, which supply had been wrongfully cut off [citations omitted].

These cases relate to the protection of a complainant in his property rights. We are cited no case which approves of the issuance of injunctive process to protect one in his right to be accepted and carried as a passenger by a public carrier; but we have not that bald question to decide.

The bill of complaint presents two phases in its allegations which, if sustained by proof to the satisfaction of a chancellor, might warrant the award of an interlocutory injunction:

First, it is alleged that the carrier's refusal to accept complainant for carriage is a persecution of complainant for having brought a suit for damages against the company and an attempted intimidation. This would, if established, evidence a palpable abuse of a public franchise that a court of equity should not hesitate to restrain by the exercise of its highest prerogative with promptitude.

Again, it is shown by the bill of complaint that the carrier threatens to continue the wrongful acts described therein. The modern authorities make it manifest that the rules of equity have grown less strict in respect to interference by a court of equity by way of injunction to restrain repeated wrongful acts, and even purely mandatory injunctions are now granted on clear showing made, where a defendant is guilty of a continuing wrong or threatens repeated perpetration of wrongs which would for remedy at law give rise to a multiplicity of suits, pending the determination of which the wrongs would continue. If a threatened wrong consist of a single act, which will be temporary in effect, the complainant may well be left to his remedy at law for damages. But if persistent repetition of a wrong is threatened, especially by a quasi public corporation involving discrimination as between citizens, equity will move to afford in a single action its more adequate remedy of injunction [citations omitted].

Here the remedy sought may be by an injunction prohibitory in form operating on future conduct, and not, strictly speaking, to restore a status by undoing a past act, and when this may be done a court of equity is less chary in exercising the power. It should, of course, in granting interlocutory injunctions of this character, act only after each party, complainant and defendant, has had an opportunity to present his case by affidavits, in an effort by the court to prevent an abuse of its process.

Deeming the bill of complaint to be framed in a manner that will admit of such procedure and relief, we are of opinion that the court below erred in sustaining this and the several grounds of demurrer interposed by the defendant company, and discussed in this opinion.

Reversed, with remand to the court below for further proceedings not inconsistent with the rulings herein embodied.

NOTE

The Mississippi cases relied upon in *Hogan* actually represent a wavering on the issues by the Supreme Court of Mississippi. In *Zackery* v. *Mobile & Ohio R. Co.*, 74 Miss. 520, 21 So. 246 (1897); 75 Miss. 746, 23 S. 434 (1898), the court ruled emphatically in favor of a claim by a blind man who had ridden the train for several years but had suddenly been refused passage by the defendant railroad, unless he were to be accompanied by an attendant.

> It is not every sick or crippled or infirm person whom a railroad regulation can exclude, but one who is sick or so crippled or so infirm as not to be able to travel without aid. And so it is not every blind person, but one who, though blind, is otherwise incompetent to travel alone on the cars; otherwise, we would be compelled to hold that one suffering from sickness, no matter how slight, or one who had lost an arm or leg, or one, no matter how active physically, and no matter how expert a traveler, if merely blind, could be shut out by such a rule. And this ought not to be, and cannot be sound law. (*Id.* at 23 S. 435).

These rulings seemed to indicate that a handicapped person is entitled to passage unless the carrier demonstrates that the individual is unable to travel unaccompanied. Seven years later, however, the same court backed down from its stand in *Zackery* and left intact a rule providing that blind people are presumed to be unfit to travel alone. In *Illinois Cent. R. Co.* v. *Smith*, 85 Miss. 349, 37 So. 643 (1905) the court declared:

> Primarily the affliction of blindness unfits every person for safe travel by rail-
> way, if unaccompanied. No blind person without previous experience could possibly
> accommodate himself to the many exigencies incident to travel by railroad, or guard
> himself against peril in boarding and alighting from trains; changing from one train to
> another, or threading his way in safety across the railway tracks at crowded stations.
> Hence the rule which provides that every blind person is presumed to be, in the absence
> of proof of experience, unfit to travel alone, is not unreasonable. Nor do we consider
> such a regulation a hardship upon the persons afflicted with blindness or other disabling
> physical infirmity. It is rather a safeguard thrown around them for their own protection
> (*Id.* at 37 So. 644).

Although such a presumption could be rebutted, it helped create a "Catch-22"
situation for the handicapped traveler. In effect, the only way to convince the railroad
of one's ability to travel unaccompanied was to demonstrate that one had done so
previously.

The common law rule that emerged from such cases was that railroads had a
duty to transport an unaccompanied disabled person if, in fact, that person could
sufficiently demonstrate his or her ability to travel alone. Implicitly, there was also a
duty to transport handicapped people who were determined to be incapable of traveling
alone, provided that such person was accompanied by an attendant who assumed full
responsibility for the disabled person's care en route.

Owens v. Macon & B. R. Co.

Supreme Court of Georgia, 1903
119 Ga. 230, 46 S.E. 87

Under a writ of lunacy in Troup county, before a jury, of which the ticket agent
of the railroad was a member, Josh Owens was adjudged insane, and committed to the
State Sanatorium at Milledgeville. Being sometimes violent, he was handcuffed and
taken to the railroad station by his brother, the plaintiff in error, and another friend,
acting as guards. Three tickets from Mountville to Macon were purchased. The train
stopped. The insane man was taken toward the passenger car, but the conductor
instructed that he should be placed in the apartment ahead of the smoking car. Josh
Owens violently resisted being put on the car, though it appears that he was not making
any noise or outcry. The general manager of the railroad company happened to be on
the train, and, seeing the condition and conduct of the insane person, gave instructions
that he could not be carried on the train. The plaintiff replied that the lunatic would be
quiet if they could get him on a seat, at which Josh Owens himself, with great noise and
vehemence, began swearing, saying that he would not be quiet; and, in reply to the
continued objection of the general manager to allow him passage, plaintiff stated that
he would be willing to take his brother in the baggage car, which was also declined;
witness for the railroad stating at the trial that it was used for carrying express and
breakables, and was not in a condition for the transportation of the insane man. The
company's agent agreed, however, to transport him in the cab of a freight car due
shortly thereafter, which offer was declined on the ground that that train did not make
connection at Macon, the point it was necessary to go to in order to reach Mil-

ledgeville. There was evidence that, after the refusal to transport, the passage money was tendered and declined, and that plaintiff was obliged to take his brother in a buggy across the country to another railroad, by which he was subsequently carried to Milledgeville. There was evidence on the part of the company that there were only two passenger coaches, in one of which there were ladies, and the other was divided into two compartments, one end of which was used as a smoker, all the seats of which were occupied by passengers, the other end being used for colored people, and in which there was a colored woman passenger; that the general manager offered to carry the insane man on the next day, if he was then quiet, or he would carry him in the cab of the freight train that passed for Macon a few hours later on the same day. The petition alleged that it was the usual custom of the company to transport lunatics and persons adjudged insane, over its line to Macon, en route to the State Sanatorium, to which allegation the defendant answered that it never refused to transport lunatics when they were quiet and not in such a condition as to render themselves dangerous to passengers, and that it would have transported Josh Owens, had he not been resisting those attempting to put him on the cars, and uttering vulgar language in a loud and boisterous manner, and that when the tickets were sold, prior to the arrival of the train, Josh Owens appeared to be quiet. At the conclusion of the evidence the court directed a verdict for the defendant, and the plaintiff excepted.

LAMAR, J. This was a suit by one of the guards in charge of a lunatic, but it was conceded on the argument here that he could not recover if the company was justified in refusing to transport the lunatic, and we shall therefore consider what was the carrier's obligation to the insane man. The relation of carrier and passenger creates reciprocal duties. One is bound safely to transport; the other, to conform to all reasonable regulations, and so to conduct himself as not to incommode other passengers who have an equal right to a safe and comfortable passage. Those who so act as to be obnoxious may be refused transportation or ejected. The payment of fare and the possession of a ticket do not require the carrier to transport those who are noisy or boisterous, or who threaten the safety of, or occasion inconvenience to, others on the train. But in the case of unfortunates who are not responsible for their disorderly conduct, and who, at best, are involuntary passengers, a different question is presented, calling in each case for the exercise of a wise discretion. On the one hand, regard must be had for the safety and comfort of other travelers, and, on the other, to the fact that in losing his mind the lunatic has not lost the right to be transported. It may be vitally important that he be taken to a place where he can receive the attention and confinement rendered necessary by his mental state. The carrier cannot absolutely refuse transportation to insane persons, but it may in all cases insist that he be properly attended, safely guarded, and securely restrained. And even where such precautions have been taken, it is not bound to afford him, if violent, transportation in the cars in which other travelers are being conveyed. And while there may be cases in which the convenience of other passengers should yield to the necessities of the unfortunate, the company may decline to receive one who at the time of entering the train exhibits signs of violence which indicate that his presence and conduct would tend to the manifest annoyance of others. So to do would ordinarily be better than to receive him on the promise of his attendants that he would be quiet, and, on the disorder continuing, force upon the carrier the duty of deciding whether he should be ejected at a station where there might not be proper accommodations. Where, however, it becomes essential to transport one who, though violent and noisy, is not responsible for his actions, the company is entitled to seasonable notice, in order that it may make proper arrangements. The action of the defendant in the present case in offering transportation on a later train, whereon others would not be incommoded, was in strict fulfillment of its double duty to the lunatic and the general public. It could not be required to place him in the baggage car, which was not intended for passengers. If the attendants were unwilling for him to be taken in the cab of the freight train, they were at least bound to give the carrier an opportunity to make other arrangements.

Although the ticket agent was on the jury inquiring as to the lunacy of Owens, and had notice of his mental state, the latter was not exhibiting any signs of violence when the ticket was sold; and, though the company was accustomed to convey persons insane, it was not bound to admit to its cars one boisterous, cursing, and using obscene language at the time.

There was no error of law committed, and the verdict was demanded by the evidence. Judgment affirmed. All the Justices concur.

b. Special Rules Regarding Air Travel   The balancing act performed by the Georgia Supreme Court in *Owens* v. *Macon and B. R. Co.*, between the railroad's duty to transport the disabled person and its responsibility to provide a safe and convenient trip for other passengers, has been repeated in the context of air travel. As the mode of transportation has changed with time, many of the issues have remained the same.

CASTEEL V. AMERICAN AIRWAYS, INC.

Court of Appeals of Kentucky, 1935
261 Ky. 818, 88 S.W.2d 976

STANLEY, Commissioner.

These cases are of first impression. They are consolidated suits for damages for ejection of passengers from an airplane.

Ford Casteel and wife, Mrs. Frieda Casteel, were citizens of Laurel county, Ky. He was afflicted with tuberculosis, and they had been residing for some time in New Mexico. On October 5, 1933, they took passage on appellee's air line from El Paso, Tex., to Louisville, Ky. He was permitted to travel in pajamas and a robe. It is alleged in the petitions that they were carried to Fort Worth, Tex., and without just or legal cause wrongfully removed from the plane and put off in a strange city without means and compelled to wait there for five hours until they were transported at the defendant's expense by railroad to Louisville. The petitions charged that because of the wrongful act of the defendant each was weakened and permanently impaired in health due to the change and prolonged transportation. Humiliation, exposure, and mental and physical distress and discomfort were averred.

In the petition of Ford Casteel's administrator it was further charged that the defendant allowed and suffered another passenger on the ship to impose and mistreat the decedent by leaning against him, and that the defendant so operated the plane for at least 200 miles "in an improper manner by suddenly and unnecessarily shunting it upward and instantly shifting its course downward in such a way and manner as to jerk and shake" him unnecessarily, and "endeavored in divers ways to make it so uncomfortable and unpleasant as to try to cause him to ask to leave said airship of his own accord," but he refused to do so, and protested against removal.

The answers presented a traverse, justification, and consent by the passengers to discontinuance of the journey by plane. The defendant also pleaded a regulation promulgated by the Treasury Department of the United States governing transportation in interstate commerce by air and placing a quarantine upon passengers afflicted with pulmonary tuberculosis; but this went out on demurrer, it appearing that the regulation, filed as an exhibit, did not prohibit the transport of such afflicted persons if certain provisions for their care and the protection of other passengers should be made, and the pleading did not negative the existence of such provisions.

After the joint trial had commenced, amended petitions were tendered which alleged certain profane language intended to apply to the plaintiffs, mistreatment during passage by another passenger, and negligence in failing to provide suitable protection for the sick man from exposure to inclement weather. The court properly refused to allow the amendments to be filed at the stage of the case. We shall therefore consider only the evidence coming within the pleadings and pass over that pertaining to circumstances apparently embraced by the amendments, which, it was said, indicated a hostile attitude or atmosphere of displeasure over the presence of the sick man.

The carrier sold the tickets with full knowledge of Casteel's condition. We state the testimony of Mrs. Casteel: Before reaching Fort Worth, the pilot navigated the ship up and down and sideways in a rough manner, which made her husband sick. But neither of them made complaint. Change in planes was to be made at Fort Worth. When the machine arrived there, Casteel was carried into the port. A doctor felt his pulse and advised that he should not continue by plane, but ought to finish the journey by rail. Both she and her husband protested. She told the doctor that her husband's physician had administered medicine to prepare and enable him to make the journey by plane, that he could not stand the long trip by train, which was the reason they were traveling that way. She asked to be allowed to go on, but was told she could not. An agent asked to see the tickets, and when she gave them to him he stated they could not be taken farther and her money would be refunded. Neither consented to the surrender of the tickets nor to continuing by train. A check was given her representing the proportionate fare to Louisville, and she signed a refund receipt. The company had them taken to a first-class hotel and bore all expenses. The company made arrangements for the railroad tickets and paid for them out of the refund check. The amount was something less. It also provided transportation to the station. They traveled in a pullman drawing room and changed trains only at Memphis. They arrived in Louisville the next afternoon, experiencing a delay of about 29 hours. The company had sent a message to those awaiting their arrival by plane. Mr. and Mrs. Casteel remained in Louisville five days because he was unable to go on to his home in Laurel county. He was taken there by automobile, a distance of 150 miles, and died a week later of tuberculosis.

Mrs. Casteel testified to humiliation because of her experiences and of having been worried and made nervous, weak, and exhausted. Their expense in Louisville was about $40. A local doctor testified that when Casteel arrived home he was in a serious condition, and in response to a hypothetical question expressed the opinion that the experience had hastened his death. However, the doctor had no personal knowledge of travel by air.

According to the defendant's evidence, the dispatcher at El Paso advised against the sick man embarking and informed him and his wife that it would depend on how he stood the trip as to whether or not he would be taken off at Big Springs or Fort Worth or carried to his destination. They were told of the conditions which might be expected and the ill effects likely to ensure; but they insisted on going on. The plane was delayed a few minutes on this account. This evidence was contradicted by Mrs. Casteel. En route the pilots observed the effect on the sick man and did the best they could to avoid disturbance by changing altitude gradually and otherwise operating the plane in an unusually careful manner. El Paso is 3,900 feet above sea level, and it was necessary to ascend 6,500 or 7,000 feet through the mountains and descend to 650 feet, the elevation of Fort Worth. During the last six minutes the ship encountered head winds. The station at Fort Worth was radioed to have a doctor meet the plane.

The man was very ill and in a helpless condition. He was carried into the station and Dr. W. H. McKnight, a well-qualified physician, made a careful examination of his heart and lungs. He found him in the last stages of tuberculosis and experiencing considerable distress in breathing. He had a very poor heart action and looked as if he would die soon. The doctor advised that he was not able to continue, that it would be dangerous for him to go on by air and much safer to finish the journey by rail. The evidence of the defendant is that the passengers acquiesced and appeared satisfied that the best thing to do was to go by train. The doctor gave professional reasons why it would not have been safe for a man in his condition to travel by plane. Courtesy and due attention were shown the passengers.

Mrs. Casteel denied the testimony of the several witnesses as to agreement or consent of herself and husband.

At the beginning of the trial the defendant's offer to confess judgment in each case for $50 was declined. At the conclusion of all the evidence, the court directed the jury peremptorily to find verdicts for the defendant. The appeals are from judgments entered thereon.

The nature of the defendant's business is, obviously, conceded to be that of a common carrier of passengers. It has been several times so declared. "Transportation, as its derivation denotes, is a carrying across, and, whether the carrying be by rail, by water or by air, the purpose in view and the thing done are identical in result." *Curtiss-Wright Flying Service* v. *Glose (C.C.A.)*, 66 F.(2d) 710, 712; *Conklin* v. *Canadian-Colonial Airways*, 266 N.Y. 244, 194 N.E. 692.

The obligation of a common carrier to receive and transport passengers and freight without discrimination in choice or accommodations has come down to us from medieval England, where, because of the communal and feudal life or political and social conceptions, many trades and businesses were required to serve alike all who applied, such as the miller, the victualler, the clothier, the farrier, and the innkeeper. Travel and transportation of goods being hazardous, the merchant was dependent upon the caravaneer, hoyman, and lighterman, so that it was early decided that the carrier was liable in damages for refusing to accept goods for transport. The logical development was to make the same application in respect of travelers. The word "common" addressed itself to the exercise of a public calling, so they became "common carriers."

Succeeding periods of history witnessed the overthrow of the feudal system and the destruction in whole or in part of other governmental and economic theories. In the evolution there was a tendency to depart from the control or interference in private business affairs by the government in behalf of the public. The Colonies, fresh from England, framed their Constitutions in such a way as to preserve much greater freedom to individual property rights than had theretofore been enjoyed. However, it was still found necessary to adhere to many of the traditions of the mother country, so that when private property was used for a purpose which became essential to public welfare, it became impressed with the duty to serve the public just as were the industries of the same class in ancient times, the reasons remaining practically the same.

So, from the beginning of our jurisprudence it has been recognized as the duty of a common carrier to accept and carry without discrimination those who offer themselves for transportation because of the dependence of the public and the demands of its welfare, presupposing, of course, the tender of the proper compensation by one to whom there could be no legal objection. It is, as well, the recognized duty of a carrier to transport its passengers safely to their destination. This extraordinary responsibility of private business, based upon considerations of public policy, has survived the great change in the conditions and circumstances under which they first arose where there was entire monopoly and extreme limitation of facilities. It has been adapted to the revolutionary changes in the mode of transportation with some deviations required by the peculiar facilities. It is a long way from the sailing vessel to the palatial liner, from the ancient caravan to the modern railroad train, from the ox cart to the automobile, from the stage coach to the airplane. But after all, each is merely a form of transportation, is subject to the same general law controlling public service, and must be held, in general, to the same principles and responsibilities. However, special and distinctive rules are imperative because of the physical differences in the carriages.

In general, while a common carrier is bound to receive all persons who desire to become passengers, this demand of the public interest is of necessity subject to some exceptions; thus, there may be justification for refusal of carriage for want of room in the vehicle. Furthermore, "A carrier of passengers not only has the power, but it is its duty, to adopt such rules and regulations as will enable it to perform its duties to the traveling public with the highest degree of efficiency, and to secure to its passengers all possible convenience, comfort, and safety." *Brumfield* v. *Consolidated Coach Corporation,* 240 Ky. 1, 40 S.W.(2d) 356, 361. Manifestly, those rules must be reasonable, according to the judgment of the courts, and they will be deemed reasonable if they redound to the comfort, convenience, safety, and health of the traveling public in general. Indeed, it is the duty of the carrier to adopt such rules and the duty of the passenger to obey them. A carrier's duty to other passengers cannot be lost sight of in observing the rights of an individual traveler. *Chesapeake & Ohio Ry. Co.* v. *Spiller,* 157 Ky. 222, 162 S.W. 815, 50 L.R.A.(N.S.) 394, Ann.Cas. 1915D, 186; *Brumfield* v. *Consolidated Coach Corporation, supra;* Hutchinson on Carriers, § 1077.

Among the recognized exceptions applicable to railroad and steamship carriers is that they may decline to receive for transportation one afflicted with contagious diseases whose presence would endanger the health of the passengers. *Bogard's Adm'r.* v. *Illinois Cent. R. Co.,* 144 Ky. 649, 139 S.W. 855, 36 L.R.A.(N.S.) 337; Hutchinson on Carriers, § 966. It is also the law that one who is so mentally or physically infirm as to be unable to take care of himself, or who may become a burden upon his fellow passengers or demand medical attention, may be refused passage. But the rule cannot be too rigorously enforced, and its application has been denied where the passenger has an attendant or has made provision for his own care. Hutchinson on Carriers, §§ 966, 992; *Conolly* v. *Crescent City R. Co.,* 41 La.Ann. 57, 5 So. 259, 6 So. 526, 3 L.R.A. 133, 17 Am.St.Rep. 389.

Continuing our consideration of these general principles of the law of carriers to a closer relation to the case in hand, regard must be had for the contract of carriage in process of execution.

Extreme infirmity from an infectious disease existed. It was held in *Pullman Car Co.* v. *Krauss* 145 Ala. 395, 40 So. 398, 4 L.R.A.(N.S.) 103, 8 Ann.Cas. 218, that if after making a contract to carry a person with an infectious or contagious disease the carrier becomes aware of his condition it may put an end to the contract and decline to admit or carry him as a passenger. Should an infirm passenger be voluntarily accepted, his inability to care for himself being apparent or made known at the time of his acceptance, a greater duty ensues in caring for him, and the carrier will be held responsible if such care and assistance are not afforded. Hutchinson on Carriers, § 992. After having entered upon his journey, if the passenger becomes sick or in a helpless condition, it is the duty of the carrier to exercise the reasonable and necessary offices of humanity toward him until some suitable provision be made. This may require that he be removed and left at a suitable place until he becomes able to resume his journey or until he shall obtain proper aid and assistance. Michie on Carriers, §§ 2976, 3020; Hutchinson on Carriers, § 992. Or where a passenger's conduct or condition is such as to render his presence dangerous to fellow passengers and such as will occasion serious annoyance and discomfort, it is not only a right but a duty of the carrier to exclude him, having due regard always for the rights of such passenger. This duty to exercise reasonable care and diligence toward him does not end with removal, but it must continue in providing temporarily for his safety. Hutchinson on Carriers, § 992; *Atchison, T. & S. F. Ry. Co.* v. *Parry,* 67 Kan. 515, 73 P. 105; *Atchison, T. & S. F. Ry. Co.* v. *Weber,* 33 Kan. 543, 6 P. 877, 52 Am.Rep. 543; *Railway Co.* v. *Valleley,* 32 Ohio St. 345, 30 Am.Rep. 601. These rules, in their application to particular situations, may require that one who accompanies such disabled passenger, though he may not himself be objectionable or incapacitated, be ejected if it is necessary that he remain with the other. *Braun* v. *Northern Pacific Ry. Co.,* 79 Minn. 404, 82 N.W. 675, 49 L.R.A. 319, 79 Am.St.Rep. 497.

The right or power of ejection of a passenger for these reasons is, obviously, hedged about with certain limitations regardless of the justification for exercising it. Thus, in the absence of a statute, it must be done in a proper manner so as to avoid violating the duty of considerate treatment, which continues until there is an actual ejectment, and at a point where the passenger will not be subjected to peril. If it be wrongful in any particular, it follows that the carrier is liable for damages proximately resulting from the tort. Michie on Carriers, §§ 3016, 3408; *Cincinnati, N. O. & T. P. Ry. Co.* v. *Carson,* 145 Ky. 81, 140 S.W. 71; *Louisville & N. R. Co.* v. *Tuggle's Adm'r,* 151 Ky. 409, 152 S.W. 270. Where the ejectment is caused by the misfortune of the passenger and his condition of illness or helplessness, so much the more must these obligations to care for him in a high degree of prudence and care for his safety be observed. Michie, § 3020; *Eidson* v. *Southern Ry. Co.* (Miss.) 23 So. 369; *Connolly* v. *Crescent City R. Co.,* 41 La.Ann. 57, 5 So. 259, 6 So. 526, 3 L.R.A. 133, 17 Am.St.Rep. 389.

In order to avoid liability for ejectment at an intermediate station, there must first be a tender or return of fare less that from the point of origin. Michie, § 3022.

The foregoing historical narrative and reference to railroad and steamship companies and to the law of carriers generally, some of which may be regarded as of the nature of obiter dictum, has seemed helpful as an approach to the decision of the case at bar. In this changing world, we have come far from the modal conditions of transportation out of which came the genesis and development of our law of common carriers, although perhaps as measured by these latter day conceptions not so far from the original doctrine of regulation of public agencies. In adapting the general principles to the newest mode of transportation, it is not altogether "putting new wine in old bottles." Although the same principles must obtain and be applied, the law of aeronautics cannot be completely synchronized with the law pertaining to other agencies, for it must be modified to meet the traffic problems of the novel method. The inherent nature of the facilities of an airplane cannot be disregarded. In respect of those things we have been considering, it demands an extension or broadening of the powers of the proprietors, or to be exact, a lessening of the powers of control or interference with a private enterprise. Transportation has become highly competitive and other reasons for some of the older rules of compulsion, such as dependence by travelers, have lost their force. The nature of the method of transportation imposes different and distinct duties pertaining to the safety and comfort of those served.

The reasonableness of the rules of the air carrier must be measured accordingly. Although the safety of the passengers, individually and collectively, must ever be regarded as the prime criterion, provision for their convenience and comfort is more essential aboard an airplane in flight with its restrictions and limitations of space than on surface carriers where passengers may move about with some degree of freedom. The right to reject or eject passengers from an airplane must be sustained not only upon grounds deemed justifiable where older methods of carriage are used, but other reasonable grounds as well because of the necessarily close personal proximity of the passengers. We think the statement of the learned author of the article, "Airline Passenger Discrimination," appearing in the *Journal of Air Law,* vol. 3, p. 479 (acknowledgement being here made of its value in the preparation of the opinion) is sound law, pertinent to the case at bar, namely: "Diseased persons, who are likely to be repulsive to passengers, or persons who may communicate a disease should, of course, be refused. The carrier owes the duty to its passengers not only to protect them from dangers incident to transportation, but to avoid placing anything among them which might injure them. The quarters are so crowded aboard an airplane that the opportunities for contamination or repulsion are usually more imminent than on board surface carriers.''

The nature of the business and the machine make it almost necessary that the courts sanction a reasonable discretion in these matters on the part of the operators, and that their judgment, if exercised in good faith and upon reasonable grounds, should be accepted *prima facie* as justification. This must be particularly so in relation to sick and invalid persons or others whose presence may demand such extraordinary individual care as to interfere with the discharge of duties owing to other passengers.

And though such a person shall have been accepted for transportation in the reasonable belief that he is able to make the journey to his destination without inconvenience or danger, if en route he becomes so sick that not only his own health and life are endangered, but the convenience, comfort, and health of other passengers are imperiled, it seems to us the carrier has the duty and the right to remove such passenger from the plane. Of course, due regard must be had for its concomitant and commensurate duty of humane and considerate treatment and the several obligations resting upon carriers generally in relation to the manner and place of ejectment and the refund of the proportionate fare.

In the case at bar, the carrier had accepted Casteel as a passenger when he was known to be afflicted with a highly infectious disease, although then assured that he was able to make the journey. After having proceeded some distance, he was found to be suffering from the effects of air travel, and a physician of high standing and qualification pronounced him unable because of the atmospheric conditions and changing altitudes to go farther by plane. The carrier was in a situation of necessity rather than of choice. Even though we give strict interpretation of the testimony of Mrs. Casteel that it was against their will, the carrier showed the unfortunate passengers every consideration and gave them the best of care and attention. It is our conclusion that the ejectment was justified under the law, and that no tort was committed.

As to the individual case of Mrs. Casteel, it is apparent that she acted voluntarily, and quite naturally, in choosing to remain with her sick husband. But if it be regarded otherwise, she proved no recoverable damage by reason of her ejectment.

The court properly directed verdicts for the defendant.

Judgments affirmed.

Whole court sitting.

NOTE

The reasoning in *Casteel* was upheld more than 35 years later by a Louisiana appellate court in *Austin* v. *Delta Air Lines, Inc.,* 246 So.2d 894 (La. 1971). In *Austin,* the plaintiff sought to recover damages for the airline's refusal to sell him a ticket. The airline asserted that it had done so because the plaintiff appeared to be drunk. Subsequent testimony revealed that the plaintiff's behavior was caused by medication he had taken as treatment for a serious medical problem. In holding that the defendants' actions were reasonable and had been made in good faith, the court relied on a Civil Aeronautics Board ruling that an airline should refuse to transport any person whose

mental or physical condition is such as to—
  (a) render him incapable of caring for himself without assistance, unless—

(i)   he is accompanied by an attendant who will be responsible for caring for
       him enroute, and
(ii)   with the care of such attendant, he will not require unreasonable attention
       or assistance from employees of the carrier.
Local and Joint Passenger Rules Tariff No. Pr-5 published in C.A.B. Number 117.

HEUMANN v. NATIONAL AIRLINES, INC.
United States District Court for the District of Columbia, 1975
13 Aviation Cases 17, 912

GESELL, District Judge: Plaintiff seeks damages claiming that defendant's decision to deny transportation to her as an unaccompanied paraplegic and to remove her from its plane at Kennedy Airport was arbitrary and without reasonable justification. National has moved for summary judgment claiming that on the admittedly undisputed facts the proceedings are barred by the doctrine of primary jurisdiction developed in *Nader* v. *Allegheny Airline, Inc.* 512 F.2d 527 (D.C.Cir. 1975). The issue has been fully briefed and argued.

National's tariff, adopted and filed pursuant to the Federal Aviation Act, 49 U.S.C. § 1511, provides that the carrier will refuse to transport, or will remove, any passenger whose physical condition is such that he cannot care for himself, or where such action is necessary for the reasonable safety or comfort of other passengers or where the passenger presents an unusual hazard or risk to himself or to other persons or to property. The company's rules implement this tariff provision by requiring a medical certificate for unaccompanied paraplegics to the general effect that the prospective passenger is able to travel by air. The actual practice in this regard is uneven and the company rule has not always been observed.

National's tariff is not questioned. It is simply claimed that the carrier has applied its tariff in a discriminatory manner by invoking the medical certificate requirement as to some paraplegic passengers, including plaintiff, but ignoring the requirement in other instances. There is no claim that National acted in this instance out of any malice, or other improper motivation such as race. Under these circumstances, an action based on discrimination cannot be mounted solely because the company did not always apply a company rule where the rule is itself reasonably related to enforcement of a lawful tariff.

Thus the issue is reduced to whether the company's medical certificate rule is reasonable. This is a highly technical, policy question involving much expertise and is presently the subject of extensive, detailed rule-making proceedings which have been in progress before the Federal Aviation Administration since 1973, looking toward a universal regulation to be incorporated in all tariffs designed to establish suitable standards governing transportation of paraplegics and others with infirmities. Carrier and public comments have been received, tests conducted and the rule is being finally formulated. Some form of medical certificate is under consideration and regulations will issue shortly. Thus, *Nader* controls. See 512 F.2d at 539.

This Circuit, in *Nader,* fashioned a broad rule of primary jurisdiction applicable in these situations which in effect forecloses common law remedies for injuries arising out of a carrier's reasonable compliance with its approved tariff rules, thus leaving the remedy to administrative rule-making and other procedures. The area in controversy is now, and in the future will be, directly regulated through tariff provisions.

The common law count sounding in false arrest and the claim for conspiracy to deprive of federal civil rights raise again the issue of the reasonableness *vel non* of enforcement of the tariff, which the Court has already held to be barred under *Nader*. There is no claim of excessive force or malice, and, in fact, plaintiff's deposition makes clear she refused to leave the plane voluntarily and demanded to be arrested in order to provoke the issue. Defendant's motion for summary judgment as to these counts is granted on the ground the undisputed facts fail to state a claim on which relief may be granted.

Defendant's motion for summary judgment is granted and the entire complaint is dismissed without prejudice to plaintiff pursuing any further remedies she may have after appropriate consideration of the issues by the agency.

So ordered.

NOTES

1.   Is Judge Gesell correct in invoking the doctrine of primary jurisdiction rather than ruling on the reasonableness of the tariff? Can FAA rule-making procedures provide an adequate remedy to plaintiff in the circumstances of this case?

2.   Several airlines have been severely criticized recently for their policies requiring blind passengers to "stow" their canes during flight. Various groups representing blind persons are attempting to refute the airlines' assertion that the canes could present dangers to other passengers. Those advocating the abolition of this policy cite the dependency of a blind person on the use of his or her cane for increasing mobility, a factor particularly vital during emergencies. See *National Federation for the Blind* v. *Federal Aviation Administration,* Civil Action No. H-78-938 (D.Md. filed May 26, 1978).

c.   **Standard of Care Owed to Handicapped Passengers**   An issue involved in many early cases was the degree of care owed to the handicapped traveler by the common carrier. Generally, precedents concerning this matter arose from traditional negligence actions in which a disabled person sued to recover damages for an injury suffered while traveling. Often the carrier asserted the affirmative defense of contributory negligence, arguing that the plaintiff had failed to take reasonable care to prevent the injury. Out of such cases grew some generally accepted legal precepts. Some of the pertinent principles include the following: 1) a common carrier is held to the highest degree of care for passengers, but the carrier is not an insurer of the safety of passengers under all circumstances; (2) if a passenger has a physical disability that should be reasonably apparent to the employees of the carrier, or of which they have notice, then it is the carrier's duty to render such assistance in boarding and alighting as is reasonably necessary under the circumstances, provided that the passenger must give the employees of the carrier a reasonable opportunity of rendering such needed assistance; and (3) in a negligence action, the negligence of the carrier must be the proximate cause of the injury to the plaintiff, and a plaintiff may be barred from recovering damages if he or she takes unnecessary risks or fails to exercise reasonable care under the circumstances. *Singletary* v. *Atlantic Coast Line R. Co.*, 217 N.C. 212, 60 S.E.2d 305, 307–308 (1950).

The *Singletary* case involved the negligence claim of a man, described in his complaint as "visibly deformed and a crippled midget," *id.* at 305, against a railroad for injuries sustained when he fell from a stool used for a step when alighting from the train. The plaintiff claimed that the railroad was negligent in not providing him with assistance in getting off the train, but the court held that the plaintiff was contributorily negligent in failing to ask for assistance from a conductor standing nearby and in deciding to take the risk of alighting without such assistance:

> The respondent, who was not a stranger to traveling by train, knew his physical limitations better than anyone else, and it is difficult for us to see why the conductor of the train should have been required to take more precautions for the safety of the respondent than he himself took (*Id.* at 60 S.E.2d 310).

The situation and results in *Singletary* are in contrast to those in *Denver & R. G. R. Co.* v. *Derry*, 47 Colo. 584, 108 P. 172 (1910), where a blind passenger was successful in a negligence suit against a railroad because of failures of the railroad's employees to shut a safety gate and to assist the plaintiff into a Pullman Car, as a result of which he fell from the car's platform onto the tracks.

> It may . . . be true that the care to be observed by one who is blind, traveling alone upon railroad trains, is greater than that required of one without such infirmity. But when the railroad company accepts as a passenger one whom it knows to be incapable of taking proper care of himself, and who has no attendant, it must certainly use at least reasonable care and diligence for his safety, and, if it fails to do so, it is negligent (*Id.* at 108 P. 174).

In *Texas and P. Ry. Co.* v. *Reid*, 74 S.W. 99 (Civ.App.Tex. 1903), the plaintiff was injured when she fell while disembarking from a train at night. The railroad defended solely on the ground that the plaintiff, an elderly deaf and "crippled" woman, was contributorily negligent for traveling without an attendant. On appeal, the court refused to accept the affirmative defense and ruled that the plaintiff had the same right as able-bodied passengers to rely on the defendant to provide a safe place to step off the train.

The cases discussed here are simply a few examples of an extensive body of judicial decisions arising from negligence actions by handicapped passengers. For more discussion of such decisions, see tenBroek, J., "The Right to Live in the World: The Disabled in the Law of Torts," 54 *Cal. L. Rev.* 841 (1966).

3. Constitutional Theories

The Supreme Court long ago recognized the significance of the right to travel. As early as 1849, Chief Justice Taney stated, "We are all citizens of the United States; and, as members of the same community, must have the right to pass and repass throughout every part of it without interruption, as freely as in our own States" (*The Passenger Cases*, 7 How. 283, 492 (1849)). Although not explicitly mentioned in the Constitution, the source of this right has been ascribed to many separate provisions, e.g., the

Commerce Clause (*Edwards* v. *California*, 314 U.S. 160 (1941), and the *Passenger Cases*, 7 How. 283 (1849)); the Fifth Amendment due process clause (*Kent* v. *Dulles*, 357 U.S. 116 (1958), and *Zemel* v. *Rusk*, 381 U.S. 1 (1965)); the privilege and immunity clause of Art. IV, § 2 (*Ward* v. *Maryland*, 12 Wall. 418 (1870)); and the privileges and immunities clause of the Fourteenth Amendment (*Twining* v. *New Jersey*, 211 U.S. 78 (1908)).

In *Shapiro* v. *Thompson*, 394 U.S. 618 (1969), the Court held that movement from jurisdiction to jurisdiction was a "constitutional right and any classification which serves to penalize the exercise of that right, unless shown to be necessary to promote a compelling governmental interest, is unconstitutional" (*Id.* at 634).

These decisions have given rise to the argument that actions by state officials that effectively deny handicapped individuals the opportunity to use mass transit systems are violative of the equal protection and due process clauses of the Fifth and Fourteenth Amendments. Such official state action might be found, for example, in decisions by local transit officers to purchase buses that are not accessible to wheelchair-bound individuals, or to approve designs for subway stations that deny access to individuals with mobility impairments.

Thus far, however, courts that have ruled on the merits of these lines of reasoning have refused to accept their validity. In *Snowden* v. *Birmingham-Jefferson County Transit Authority*, 407 F.Supp. 394 (N.D.Ala. 1975), aff'd. mem. op 551 F.2d 862 (5th Cir. 1976), the court merely required that the defendants have a rational basis for denying disabled individuals access to transportation. Judge Guin stated, "Plaintiff cannot credibly maintain that access to public transportation facilities is a 'fundamental right' on a parity with the right to education at public expense which must be made available to all on equal terms" (*Id.* at 398). Does this statement explain any defects the court apparently saw in the plaintiff's argument, or does it merely state the court's conclusion without an adequate rationale?

In *United Handicapped Federation* v. *Andre*, 409 F.Supp. 1297, rev'd. 558 F.2d 413 (8th Cir. 1977), the court declined to rule that the defendant had created a "suspect classification" of wheelchair users who are unable to effectively use the local bus system, thereby refusing to apply the compelling state interest test in evaluating the defendants' actions. (See pp. 120–121 n.3, above, for further explanation of the concept of handicapped individuals as a suspect class. Also, see Burgdorf, R., and Burgdorf, M., "A History of Unequal Treatment: The Qualifications of Handicapped Persons as a 'Suspect Class' under the Equal Protection Clause," 15 *Santa Clara Lawyer* 855 (1975).

In addition, the *Andre* Court refused to hold that "travel by intrastate . . . bus involves a 'fundamental right'" (*Id.* at 1302). Is the constitutional right to travel limited to interstate travel or does it also apply to movement within the state? At least one circuit court of appeals has held this right to be applicable to travel within the state as well as without. See *King* v. *New Rochelle Municipal Housing Authority*, 314 F.Supp. 427 (S.D.N.Y. 1970), aff'd. 442 F.2d 646 (2d Cir. 1971).

In at least one case, a handicapped plaintiff has argued that the denial of access to certain governmental offices because of architectural barriers, effectively chills a handicapped individual's exercise of the right to travel. See *Friedman* v. *County of*

Cuyahoga, C.A. No. 895961, (Consent Judgment, Court of Common Pleas, Cuyahoga County, Ohio, 1972), discussed in the following section.

C. ACCESS TO BUILDINGS: UNDERLYING LEGAL PRINCIPLES

1. Constitutional Theories

SUMMARY OF ARGUMENT, BRIEF FOR THE PLAINTIFF, FRIEDMAN V. COUNTY OF CUYAHOGA

Court of Common Pleas, Cuyahoga County, Ohio, 1972
Civil Action No. 895, 961, Brief pp. 2–3

[Plaintiff Jeffrey H. Friedman was elected to the University Heights, Ohio city council in 1971. He found he was unable to use his own office because of his confinement to a wheelchair. He was also unable to enter several other county government buildings. He brought a class action suit seeking declaratory judgment and injunctive relief against the County and the County Commissioners.]

I

The building and maintaining of County buildings which are inaccessible to plaintiff without assistance denies him, and all others similarly situated, their constitutional right of reasonable access to the Cuyahoga County Courts. The lack of any reasonable access to the County Courts has, at the least, a chilling effect on the exercise by plaintiff of his right of accesss to all courts, and also tends to make his exercise of this right costly. Right of reasonable access is protected by both the privilege and immunities and the due process clauses of the fourteenth amendment to the United States Constitution. In addition, the right of reasonable access to all courts can be considered so fundamental of a right as to be included within the purview of the ninth amendment to the United States Constitution. This right has been recognized in forty-two state constitutions, including Ohio's art. 1, § 16.

II

Defendants are denying to the plaintiff and members of his class their right to equal protection of the laws as guaranteed by the fourteenth amendment to the United States Constitution and by the Ohio Constitution, art. 1, §§ 1 and 2. Failure to make county buildings accessible to plaintiff and his class denies them their right to equal opportunity employment. The defendants have neither a compelling interest nor a rational basis as a justification of their denial of access to plaintiff and his class. Where fundamental rights are involved, as they are here, the state must show a compelling interest. Even if no fundamental right were involved, the state must still have a rational basis for its action. In this case, the minimal cost that the County would expend in building the ramps, when balanced against the physical, financial, and psychological burdens that large numbers of disabled and elderly citizens must bear, shows that the state does not have even a rational basis for its continued denial of plaintiff's constitutional rights.

III

Defendants are denying to plaintiff and his class their right of access to the seats of government. The right of access to the seats of government is mandated by the right to petition the government for a redress of grievances. Defendants' actions have a chilling effect on plaintiff's right to petition protected by the first amendment to the United States Constitution and by the Ohio Constitution, art. 1, § 3. This right to petition, and the system of government set up by the Constitution, demands access to both federal and state seats of government, and is protected against infringement by either the federal or state governments.

IV

Defendants are depriving plaintiff and his class of their right to travel and freedom of movement. The right to travel does not depend on the interstate nature of the travel; the right to travel intrastate is just as basic as the right to travel interstate. The freedom of movement is protected by the ninth amendment and the privileges and immunities and liberty clauses of the fourteenth amendment to the United States Constitution, and by article one, sections one and twenty of the Ohio Constitution.

V

Defendants have an affirmative duty to provide plaintiff and his class with equal access to Cuyahoga County buildings. Just as school boards or county commissioners have been required to take immediate affirmative action to correct a denial of constitutional rights, Cuyahoga County has a duty to correct the denials of the constitutional rights of plaintiff and his class by providing some means of access to the County buildings. The County must exercise its police power, as is its right and duty, to protect and promote public health and welfare.

NOTES

1. Elaborate upon Mr. Friedman's federal constitutional arguments. Which are the most persuasive? Notice that many of Mr. Friedman's arguments are alternatively grounded upon state constitutional provisions.

2. The plaintiff in *Friedman* eventually succeeded in having the buildings mentioned in the suit made accessible to mobility-handicapped persons, as the case was settled by consent agreement. Unfortunately, several years later, Mr. Friedman again found himself back in court when the county began plans to build a new courthouse to replace the antiquated facilities that were the subject of the first litigation. See *Friedman* v. *Graver, Patrick and Pindles,* Civil Action No. C-77-607 (N.D.Ohio, filed 1977).

3. Several other suits have been filed regarding the accessibility of local courthouses. See *Wargowsky* v. *Novak,* Civil No. C-72-138 (W.D.Ohio, consent decree, March 30, 1973) and *Cassilly* v. *Anderson,* Civil No. K-76-1691 (D. Md., filed 1976).

4. For some disabled people, the difficulties through which they must go to enter public buildings engender only a small amount of frustration and humiliation. For many others, however, such denial of access can constitute a shattering, self-image-destroying experience. For such persons, the encountering of barriers appears to rein-

force feelings of inadequacy and rejection by an uncaring society. Is this a legal issue? Can it be made into one?

5.   Formulate a legal argument for access to public buildings based upon First Amendment rights to freedom of assembly and to petition the government for redress of grievances. What other constitutional bases can be found for the right of equal access to public buildings?

6.   Cases involving the right of handicapped persons to accessible polling places are discussed below at pp. 1037–1041. Unfortunately, the constitutional issues in such cases have frequently been clouded by the availability of absentee voting procedures.

7.   Frequently the constitutional theories regarding accessibility of public buildings are superfluous in light of state laws and local ordinances mandating such accessibility. See, e.g., *In re Fenton*, p. 468, below.

2.   State and Local Architectural Barriers Laws

a.   Overview   Almost every state and many local jurisdictions have some form of architectural barriers laws. There is great variety among the laws. Some laws apply only to new structures, while others apply to any renovated building; some even require all buildings, existing and new, to be brought into compliance by a specific date. In addition, some laws deal only with public buildings, others with both public and private. There is also frequently a lack of clarity as to whether temporary facilities are covered by the access statutes. Only a small proportion of such statutes specifically require temporary buildings to be accessible.

Compliance with these laws also varies greatly. Not only are there differing standards of strictness in the waiver provisions of the laws but variations as to which agency is responsible for enforcing compliance are also common. Many statutes give the enforcement responsibility to local building authorities, most of whom have little or no experience with the needs of disabled people.

b.   Standards

Comment, "Access to Buildings and Equal Employment Opportunity for the disabled: Survey of State Statutes"

50 Temple L. Q. *1067, 1074–1078 (1977)*

Perhaps the most critical provisions of an architectural barrier statute are the standard-setting sections. In 1961, the American Standards Association[45] approved recommendations, known as ANSI standards, "for use in the construction of all buildings . . . so that those individuals with permanent physical disabilities might pursue their interests and aspirations, develop their talents, and exercise their skill."[46] These

---

[45]United States of America Standards Institute, American Standard Specifications for Making Buildings and Facilities Accessible to and Usable by the Physically Handicapped, A117.1–1961. These standards were reaffirmed in 1971 and in June 1974, the Department of Housing and Urban Development contracted with Syracuse University to provide a revision and expansion of the ANSI standards.

[46]*Id.*

ANSI standards provide minimum design criteria for sixteen different aspects of building construction including doors and doorways, restrooms, parking lots, walks, entrances, and grading. Although a variety of inadequacies have been detected in the ANSI standards, many states have utilized these incomplete minimum standards. However, if the ANSI standards are updated and revised, this uniformity of high standards will promote adequate architectural design for the disabled.

Sixteen states have incorporated by reference the ANSI standards and all revisions. Thirteen states do not use or mention the ANSI standards at all: rather, these states have delegated the authority to prescribe standards to an administrative agency without requiring that agency to adopt or consider the ANSI standards. However, another fifteen states have prescribed standards in their legislation. Of these fifteen states, ten have adopted the language of the ANSI standards almost verbatim. Five of those fifteen states have adopted standards which partially conform to ANSI. While five other states delegate authority to prescribe standards to an administrative agency, the legislation in these states provides that the ANSI standards are at least to be considered. The advantages of incorporating the ANSI standards by reference are uniformity as well as the automatic update and revision which the ANSI standards undergo. Those states which have delegated complete authority to prescribe standards to various agencies with little or no legislative guidance and no requirement to consider the ANSI standards have retained all of the inherent disadvantages of delegation of authority to administrative agencies—the lack of uniformity, the interposition of administrative discretion, and an absence of legislative guidance which could render the statute virtually ineffective. However, an advantage to this approach is the possibility of a more practical and detailed set of standards designed to adapt to changing needs.

Those states in which the legislatures have delegated authority to prescribe standards and have also given some legislative guidance by providing that the ANSI standards should at least be considered have retained the flexibility and practicality of delegation of authority, while indicating that the ANSI standards are considered appropriate minimum standards. The disadvantages to states which have adopted the language of the ANSI standards almost verbatim, is that these standards require new legislation in order to be revised while incorporation by reference generally includes the ANSI revisions and updating without legislative action. In addition, the adoption of basic ANSI standards insures that *ad hoc* legislative or administrative determinations of standards will not occur. Finally, for those few states which have only partially adopted the ANSI standards, the disadvantages differ depending upon the manner and degree to which the adopted standards vary from the ANSI standards.

An important factor which may limit the effectiveness of the standards is the availability of a waiver. Even when the standards are sufficiently detailed and efficacious, if a waiver is easily obtained many buildings will still be inaccessible. In many cases a waiver or exception may be necessary to avoid hardship or infeasibility. Therefore, the state legislatures should limit the degree of administrative discretion in granting waivers by specifying standards to balance the impracticability of requiring access against the need of the disabled to achieve it. Only seventeen states lack specific waiver clauses in their architectural barriers legislation. Of the states which have specific waiver clauses, nine impose a requirement of substantial compliance or reasonable availability of alternative facilities, and four provide for waiver in the discretion of the administering authority, usually upon the basis of impracticability, extreme hardship, or disproportionate expense. Even in those states where no waiver is legislatively supplied, it is reasonable to assume that waivers may be granted by the enforcing agencies. Therefore, it may be most effective to have in the statute an explicit waiver clause which provides the guidelines for administrative discretion and the prerequisites to attaining a waiver.

Perhaps the most crucial aspect of access statutes is the legislative provisions for enforcement. Twenty states have statutes which provide that one agency or official shall have supervisory or enforcement powers. The statutes of twenty-five states provide that two or more officials or agencies shall have enforcement responsibilities. Only two states have statutes which give the enforcement responsibility to a specially created architectural barriers compliance board. However, six other states have created specialized agencies, such as barrier-free design boards, which are given minimum enforcement responsibility.

Specialized compliance boards are an efficient method for enforcing the architectural barrier statutes. Generally, these boards include representatives of the disabled to make the boards more sensitive and responsive to the problems and needs of that group. Furthermore, a specialized compliance board will develop expertise in its sole function of enforcing and evaluating the architectural barriers statutes. Concentration of enforcement powers in one compliance board will also provide the uniformity in enforcement which cannot be achieved when diverse agencies or officials are given enforcement powers.

Another desirable method of enforcement of the access statutes is to allow private parties to sue and recover damages for noncompliance. To date, only one state has a statutory provision allowing recovery of damages in private suits for violations of the barriers statute although six states have statutes which designate violations of the barrier statutes as misdemeanors. As one author has stated, legislation has not been a panacea for the disabled: "[T]he one element running throughout the developments of the 1960's and 1970's is that the laws and regulations that were passed have seen little or no effective enforcement."[67] Such inaction suggests that allowing recovery of damages by private individuals for violations of these statutes is the most significant step which should be taken in the near future.

NOTES

1.   Currently, the nonuniformity of standards means that in some places "accessible" doorways, for example, measure 34" or 32½" or even 36". This discrepancy in standards, added to the problem that standards are applied differently to existing buildings, buildings to be built, and buildings undergoing remodeling and renovations, has made it almost meaningless to say that a structure is "accessible." The ANSI standards are an

---

[67]Achtenberg, J., ["Law and the Physically Disabled: An Update with Constitutional Implications," 8 *S.W.U.L. Law Rev.* 847 (1976)] at 855. The author indicated that because city officials interpreted facilities as excluding sidewalks, an amendment was required to make the standards applicable to sidewalks. *Id.* at 855 and nn. 25–27.

attempt at federal leadership in achieving some standardization in this area. The critical next step is the incorporation of these uniform standards into the various pieces of state and local legislation so that the term *accessibility* will have a real and consistent meaning throughout the land.

2. In footnote 67, mention is made of Achtenberg's observation about the failure of legislation to address the need for curb cuts in sidewalks. The fact that curbs are overlooked as architectural barriers because they are not part of a building, *per se,* has sometimes caused them to be omitted from accessibility legislation. Many states have, however, specifically addressed the problem of ensuring that sidewalks and crosswalks are accessible, e.g., 78A Ann. Code Md. § 51 (g) (1974). See p. 507, below, for a discussion of a federal curb cut mandate. The terribly sad and ironic end to Achtenberg's pioneering work in seeking curb cut laws has been described by his sister:

> Last September, at age thirty-five, Jack Achtenberg was struck by a van in the street in front of his home. Jack was riding in the street in his wheelchair because, in that area, Los Angeles County had failed to provide sidewalks with usable curb cuts. The driver of the van sped away without summoning help for the man who lay dying in the street. The driver has never been identified.
>
> After lingering in the hospital for two weeks in a coma from which he never awoke, Jack died—a victim of a careless driver and an even more careless society. Jack's fight was against such carelessness. In part, his death illustrates the fact that though not lost, the fight is far from won.[a]

c. Application to Public Buildings

In re Fenton

Supreme Court of New York, Suffolk County, 1977
18 N.Y.L.J. No. 107, P. 14, Dec. 6, 1977

Lazer, Judge

In this article 78 proceeding, a resident of the Town of Brookhaven seeks judgment directing the Supervisor, Town Clerk and Town Board of the Town (collectively hereafter, the "Town") not to hold public meetings at the Brookhaven Town Hall until facilities are installed which would permit "barrier-free" access by the physically handicapped. Petitioner lost his lower left leg during combat service with the United States Marines during World War II and has difficulty in walking and climbing stairs, with or without his crutches. Meetings of the Brookhaven Town Board usually are held on the second floor of the Town Hall in a meeting room which is accessible only by ascending a winding staircase which has more then twenty steps. Although ramp access to the Town Hall building itself has been constructed, the ramp is at the rear of the building and petitioner alleges that the door to which the ramp leads is kept locked. Petitioner further claims that his physical handicap has prevented and continues to prevent him for access to and participation in public hearings and meetings conducted by the Town Board "or its departments or boards, including the Zoning Board, at Town Hall." Neither the Zoning Board of Appeals nor any other Town

---

[a]Achtenberg, R., "Dedication," 50 Temple L.Q. 941 (1977).

agency apart from the Town Board and the named co-defendants have been joined as respondents.

At issue is the meaning of and the degree of imperative implied by the language used by the Legislature in sections 93(b) and 74-a of the Public Officers Law (L. 1977, c. 368) which became effective on Sept. 1, 1977. These sections read as follows:

> Section 93. Open meetings and executive sessions.
> (b) Public bodies shall make or cause to be made all reasonable efforts to ensure that meetings are held in facilities that permit barrier-free physical access to the physically handicapped, as defined in subdivision five of section fifty of the public buildings law.
> Section 74-a. Duty of public officers regarding the physically handicapped.
> It shall be the duty of each public officer responsible for the scheduling or sitting of any public hearing to make reasonable efforts to ensure that such hearings are held in facilities that permit barrier-free physical access to the physically handicapped, as defined in subdivision five of section fifty of the public buildings law.

Section 50, subdivision 5 of the public buildings law referred to in the quoted sections defines "physically handicapped," *inter alia,* as follows:

> (a) impairment requiring confinement to a wheel chair; or
> (b) impairment causing difficulty or insecurity in walking or climbing stairs or requiring the use of braces, crutches or other artificial supports, or impairment caused by amputation . . . or other ills rendering the individual semi-ambulatory.

Petitioner's proceeding followed quick upon the effective date of the new enactments and during oral argument on Sept. 20, 1977 he sought immediate proscription of further public meetings at the Town Hall. The Town's response was that it was moving expeditiously to obtain specifications and bids for the construction of an elevator which would resolve the problem. In its law memorandum, the Town has pointed to continuing efforts on its part to meet the legislative command such as the undertaking of feasibility studies and by providing for the presence of members of the Auxiliary Police at public meetings to assist handicapped persons to the meeting rooms. In a supplemental affirmation submitted on Nov. 21, 1977, the Town asserts that specifications have been drawn and that it is about to bid out the contracts for the construction of an elevator in Town Hall. In addition, the Town appears to have written to five schools in the Town seeking the use of their facilities for public meetings. The Town thus concludes that it is making the "reasonable efforts" referred to by the Legislature.

Although it is apparent that the town is moving expeditiously to alter the Town Hall, the papers submitted contain no indication as to when the elevator will be completed, nor is there any clue as to the response from the schools which have been solicited. Barrier-free access to public meetings still is not a reality despite the statutory command which became effective last summer. The question is whether the Town's laudable movement in the direction of architectural revision and its letters to various schools may be deemed to constitute "reasonable efforts" to insure that meetings are held in barrier-free facilities.

The term "reasonable efforts" was criticized as being ambiguous in several communications from state agencies prior to the Governor's approval of the statutory amendments (see Governor's Bill Jacket) and this proceeding cannot be determined without construction of the language utilized. Section 93(b) of the Public Officers Law constitutes an amendment to the Open Meetings Law first enacted last year (see Public Officers Law, Article 7, L. 1976, c. 511). In section 90 of the Open Meetings Law, the Legislature declared that it was "essential to a democratic society that citizens . . . be . . . able to observe the performance of public officials and attend and listen to the deliberations and decisions that go into the making of public policy." Section 93(b) extends the benefits of the Open Meetings Law to the handicapped by making special provisions for their access to such meetings.

Not only should a statute be construed as a whole and all parts of an act be read and construed together to determine the legislative intent (*Levine* v. *Bornstein,* 4 N.Y.2d 241, 173 N.Y.S.2d 599), but basic to the interpretation of any statute is the general spirit and purpose underlying its enactment and that consideration is to be preferred which furthers its object, spirit and purpose (*Williams* v. *Williams,* 23 N.Y.2d 592, 298 N.Y.S.2d 473; *Rankin* v. *Shanker,* 23 N.Y.2d. 111, 295 N.Y.S.2d 625; *People* v. *Kaye,* 212 N.Y. 407, rearg. den., 213 N.Y. 648; McKinney's sec. 96). Where a statute is ambiguous, it should be construed according to its apparent general purpose with a view to executing the design and purpose of the act (*Drew* v. *Village of White Plains,* 157 App. Div. 394, 142 N.Y.W. 577) and, indeed, its inherent purpose should point the direction of its interpretation (*Farrell* v. *New York Evening Post,* 167 Misc. 412, 3 N.Y.S.2d 1018).

That the enactment of sections 93(b) and 74-a of the Public Officers Law reflected a legislative intent to compel public bodies to reasonably accommodate their meetings to the needs of the physically handicapped is obvious. Since the terms for compliance with that intent were stated in section 74-a, however, the almost redundant insertion of essentially similar language in section 93(b) of the Open Meetings Law tends to establish the strength of public policy considerations underlying the Legislature's action and the fact that the statutes are not merely precatory. The "reasonable efforts" required to meet the statutory command must be viewed in the light of that public policy and the statutes must be interpreted with a view to accomplishing the legislative goal. Plainly, reasonable efforts can take the form of altering existing owned meetings facilities which contain barriers, moving to other available facilities or combining these options when necessary. The Town Board's efforts to alter the Town Hall have been quite expeditious, but considering the effective date of the statutes involved, the failure to move Town Board meetings to other available barrier-free facilities requires judicial intervention particularly because there has been no showing that such movement would in any fashion disrupt governmental operations. Indeed, judicial notice will be taken of the fact that over the years numerous meetings of the Town Board have been held in public school facilities. Under the circumstances, the time for achievement of the Legislature's purpose has arrived.

Commencing Jan. 1, 1978 the Town Board of Brookhaven is directed to conduct all of its meetings with the exception of executive sessions (as defined in section 92 of the Public Officers Law) at barrier-free facilities. The judgment to be entered hereon shall not apply to meetings already advertised. Settle judgment.

d. Application to Private Buildings

MARSH V. EDWARDS THEATRES CIRCUIT, INC.

Court of Appeals of California, Second District, Division 2, 1976
64 Cal.App.3d 881, 134 Cal.Rptr. 844

COMPTON, Associate Justice.

Plaintiff is a quadriplegic confined to a wheelchair. He commenced this action against the defendant, an owner and operator of a chain of motion picture theatres, alleging that the latter unlawfully discriminated against him because of his physical handicap by denying him admission to its Newport Cinema Theatre.

The complaint alleged that defendant's conduct violated various provisions of the United States Constitution as well as federal and state statutes. The prayer was for compensatory, statutory and punitive damages and an injunction against future violations.

The case was tried, and properly so, on the basis of California statutory law. Defendant's business is a private venture. No public funds are involved nor is there any governmental action or participation in the maintenance or operation of defendant's theatres. Furthermore, in this case, defendant did not seek to invoke state action in the form of judicial process against the plaintiff. The court was not asked to enforce a discriminatory state law nor to lend judicial assistance to discrimination by a private person. (Cf. *Shelley* v. *Kraemer,* 334 U.S. 1, 68 S.Ct. 836, 92 L.Ed. 1161; *Marsh* v. *Alabama,* 326 U.S. 501, 66 S.Ct. 276, 90 L.Ed. 265; *Amalgamated Food Employees* v. *Logan Valley Plaza,* 391 U.S. 308, 88 S.Ct. 1601, 20 L.Ed.2d 603; *Lloyd Corp.* v. *Tanner,* 407 U.S. 551, 92 S.Ct. 2219, 33 L.Ed.2d 131; see also *Diamond* v. *Bland,* 11 Cal.3d 331, 113 Cal.Rptr. 468, 521 P.2d 460; *Newby* v. *Alto Riviera Apartments,* 60 Cal.App.3d 288, 131 Cal.Rptr. 547.)

Federal anti-discrimination statutes are no broader in application to the circumstances here involved than are the California statutes. Federal law in a manner similar to California law, generally prohibits discrimination on the basis of race, color, religion or national origin in public accommodations. (See 42 U.S.C.A., § 2000a *et seq.*; 42 U.S.C.A., § 1983.)

Hence plaintiff, if he is to prevail, must establish that defendant's conduct violated those statutes by which California, under its police power, has barred certain forms of discrimination by privately operated business accommodations. Our resolution of this case is based on an interpretation of those statutes.

In the court below the jury returned a verdict in favor of the plaintiff declaring that defendant had discriminated against him but awarding plaintiff no damages of any kind. The trial judge denied plaintiff's request for an injunction but did award the plaintiff $250 statutory damages pursuant to Civil Code section 52.[1]

---

[1]Civil Code section 52 provides as follows: "Whoever denies, or who aids, or incites such denial, or whoever makes any discrimination, distinction or restriction on account of sex, color, race, religion, ancestry, or national origin contrary to the provisions of Section 51 of this code, is liable for each and every such offense for the actual damages, and two hundred fifty dollars ($250) in addition thereto, suffered by any person denied the rights provided in Section 51 of this code.

Civil Code section 51 itself provides: "This section shall be known, and may be cited, as the Unruh

Plaintiff appeals from that portion of the judgment which makes no award for compensatory or punitive damages and denies injunctive relief. Defendant cross-appeals from the judgment with respect to the finding of discrimination, the award of $250 statutory damages and the award of costs to plaintiff.

There is no significant dispute as to the facts. On April 21, 1972, the plaintiff accompanied by his father and mother arrived at the Newport Cinema Theatre in the City of Newport Beach. The theatre had been built in 1968 in conformance with then applicable building laws. It contained no special facilities for persons in wheelchairs.

The theatre manager, who was acting as box office cashier, informed plaintiff's father that plaintiff would have to leave his wheelchair and occupy a regular seat since the fire regulations prohibited anyone from sitting in the aisles. As an alternative, the manager offered plaintiff a space in front of the regular seats a short distance from the screen.

Plaintiff was unwilling to risk injury by being lifted from his wheelchair into a theatre seat and did not wish to be placed near the screen. He left the theatre with feelings of frustration and humiliation. Beyond being upset, he suffered no monetary loss or physical harm as a result of the incident.

Plaintiff advances a number of claims of error in procedural and evidentiary rulings. The significance of these contentions, however, is totally dependent on the determination of the correctness of his basic premise which is that defendant in constructing and maintaining a building without the modifications necessary to accommodate persons suffering from physical handicaps, violated those laws which prohibit discrimination by operators of public accommodations such as theatres.

The question then is—does California law which prohibits discrimination against the physically handicapped in access to public accommodations require the operator of such accommodations, absent specific legislation mandating it, to make structural modifications in order to facilitate access. Under the present state of the law the answer is "No."

In 1968, the Legislature had enacted Civil Code sections 54.1 and 54.3.

> (a) Blind persons, visually handicapped persons, and other physically disabled persons shall be entitled to *full and equal access, as other members of the general public,* to accommodations, advantages, facilities, and privileges of all common carriers, airplanes, motor vehicles, railroad trains, motorbuses, streetcars, boats or any other public conveyances or modes of transportation, hotels, lodging places, places of public accommodation, amusement or resort, and other places to which the general public is invited, *subject only to the conditions and limitations established by law,* or state or federal regulation, and applicable alike to all persons. [Emphasis added.]

Civil Code section 54.3 provided:

> Any person or persons, firm or corporation who denies or interferes with admittance to or enjoyment of the public facilities as specified in Sections 54 and 54.1 or

---

Civil Rights Act. All persons within the jurisdiction of this state are free and equal, and no matter what their sex, race, color, religion, ancestry, or national origin are entitled to the full and equal accommodations, advantages, facilities, privileges, or services in all business establishments of every kind whatsoever. This section shall not be construed to confer any right or privilege on a person which is conditioned or limited by law or which is applicable alike to persons of every sex, color, race, religion, ancestry, or national origin."

otherwise interferes with the rights of a totally or partially blind person or other disabled person under Sections 54, 54.1 and 54.2 shall be guilty of a misdemeanor.

Under these provisions discrimination against handicapped persons was declared to be a crime. The effect of such declaration was to invoke the threat of criminal prosecution as a deterrent to such discrimination while at the same time vesting the public prosecutor with the responsibility for determining whether or not in each case access was equally available to all members of the public and whether a particular denial of access was based on legally established conditions and limitations.

These statutes created no private cause of action. This conclusion is compelled by the fact that in 1974 the Legislature did enact Civil Code section 55 which provides a private remedy as follows:

> Any person who is aggrieved or potentially aggrieved by a violation of Section 54 or 54.1 of this code, Chapter 7 (commencing with Section 4450) of Division 5 of Title 1 of the Government Code, or Part 5.5 (commencing with Section 19955) of Division 13 of the Health and Safety Code may bring an action to enjoin the violation. The prevailing party in the action shall be entitled to recover reasonable attorney's fees.

Concern about the effect of the design and construction of buildings and sidewalks on the ability of handicapped persons to have access to and use *public buildings* led in 1968 to the enactment of Government Code section 4450. That section provided for the establishment of standards for buildings constructed with *public funds*. These standards which were to adhere to the American Standards Association specifications were designed to insure such accessibility.

Effective July 1, 1970, public accommodations and facilities thereafter constructed with *private funds* were with certain limited exceptions required to conform to the above referenced standards. (Health & Saf.Code, §§ 19995, 19956.)

Health and Safety Code section 19959 enacted in 1971 provided a limitation to the standards set out in Government Code section 4450 and Health and Safety Code section 19955, as follows:

> Every existing public accommodation constructed prior to July 1, 1970, which is not exempted by Section 19956, shall be subject to the requirements of this chapter when any alterations, structural repairs or additions are made to such public accommodation. This requirement shall only apply to the area of specific alteration, structural repair or addition and shall not be construed to mean that the entire building or facility is subject to this chapter.

Present public accommodation laws prohibit gross and invidious discrimination. They do not impose affirmative duties of the type which plaintiff seeks to impose. Government Code section 4450 and Health and Safety Code sections 19955, 19956, 19959 make clear the legislative intent. That intent is that affirmative conduct is required only when directed by those sections dealing with construction of new facilities or with the repair and alteration of existing facilities.

This court is not insensitive to the hardships suffered by persons who are afflicted with the wide range of physical disabilities that exist in our society. Many of these disabilities are suffered by persons who served their country in one or more of the three recent debilitating wars in which this country has been involved. Our society's traditional concern for the less fortunate among us requires that we take all appropriate measures to lessen the burden of handicapped persons.

The varied and distinctive nature of the numerous handicaps from which so many people suffer suggests, however, that the problem is one for which the legislative branch of government is uniquely equipped to solve. It is in the legislative halls where the numerous factors involved can be weighed and where the needs can be properly balanced against the economic burdens which of necessity will have to be borne by the private sector of the economy in providing a proper and equitable solution to the problem.

Plaintiff argues that the Legislature has already spoken with sufficient force to permit judicial remedy by way of damages and injunction for his particular situation. He reasons that the Unruh Civil Rights Act, Civil Code section 51 (fn. 1, *ante*) is designed to address all forms of invidious discrimination even when that discrimination takes a form other than those specifically enumerated, i.e., race, sex, color, religion or national origin, citing *In re Cox,* 3 Cal.3d 205, 90 Cal.Rptr. 24, 474 P.2d 992. According to plaintiff it then follows that Civil Code section 52 provides for actual as well as statutory damages in the event of a violation of section 51, and Code of Civil Procedure section 526 permits issuance of an injunction to prevent a multiplicity of judicial proceedings or in situations where pecuniary compensation is inadequate.

Thus he contends that the court below correctly awarded him statutory damages and that he should be entitled to have the entire matter of actual damages resubmitted to the jury because of their failure to award even those statutory damages. He further contends that the trial court erred in refusing to grant an injunction directing the defendant to take the necessary steps to accommodate him in the future. This is all based on the fact that the jury found that the defendant had discriminated against the plaintiff.

There are several answers to this argument. First it is premised on the contention that the jury was correct in its finding that defendant's conduct amounted to actionable discrimination. We are of the opinion, however, that that determination by the jury has no support in the evidence or law.

In re Cox, supra, held that the Unruh Civil Rights Act, Civil Code section 51, was broad enough to prohibit all forms of arbitrary discrimination by a business enterprise. The court also stated at page 212, 90 Cal.Rptr. at page 27, 474 P.2d at page 995, that: "... this broad interdiction of the act is not absolute; the [business enterprise] may establish reasonable regulations that are rationally *related to the ... facilities provided.*" [Emphasis added.] The Unruh Civil Rights Act itself contains a limiting clause which excepts from its application situations where access is conditioned or limited by a law applicable to all persons alike.

Because of the limitation enunciated by the Court in *Cox* and the limitation in the language of the statute, Civil Code section 51 is of little aid to the plaintiff here. Beyond that we conclude that section 51 and the remedies provided in Civil Code section 52 have no application to discrimination against the physically handicapped.

It must be remembered that *In re Cox* did not involve an action brought under Civil Code section 51. That case involved a petition for habeas corpus filed by a person who had been charged with a criminal offense for refusing to leave business premises when ordered to do so. The particular city ordinance which he was alleged to have violated specifically excepted instances where its application would violate Civil Code section 51. The *Cox* ruling was pretrial and simply stated the general proposition that petitioner could successfully defend the criminal action by establishing that his expulsion from the business premises was the result of any form of arbitrary discrimination.

The legislative intent is clearly contrary to plaintiff's position. Civil Code section 54.1 was enacted after Civil Code section 51 and deals specifically with discrimination against the physically handicapped. A special statute dealing expressly with a particular subject controls and takes precedent over a more general statute covering the same subject. (*Simpson* v. *Cranston,* 56 Cal.2d 63, 13 Cal.Rptr. 668, 362 P.2d 492.) Both sections 51 and 54.1 deal with forms of discrimination in public accommodations. As to the physically handicapped, section 54.1 is specific.

Plaintiff's case then is governed solely by Civil Code section 54.1. That latter section, in a manner similar to the Unruh Civil Rights Act, excepts from its interdiction, limitations or conditions of access based on laws or regulations applicable to all persons, and we again emphasize that *Cox, supra,* recognized the right of a proprietor of public accommodations to impose reasonable restrictions.

One of the limitations to which all persons are subject is the requirement that they be able to avail themselves of public accommodations without violating fire regulations. It is a well known fact that fire insurance carriers often rely on violations of fire regulations to avoid payment of benefits. This, of course, is a factor which a proprietor can reasonably consider in regulating access to his premises.

Section 6503 of Title 10, California Administrative Code prohibits obstruction of the minimum clear width of all exits, aisles, ramps, corridors and passageways by ticket offices, turnstiles, chairs, other equipment or persons.

Further, Newport Beach Municipal Code section 9.08.010 adopts by reference provisions of the fire prevention code promulgated by the National Board of Fire Underwriters. The relevant subdivision entitled "Obstruction to Means of Egress" reads as follows:

> c. No aisle, passageway or stairway in any mercantile occupancy shall be obstructed with tables, showcases or other obstructions during hours such occupancy is open to the public.

The foregoing fire regulations apply to all persons equally and the definition of prohibited obstructions would include persons seated in wheelchairs. It necessarily follows that the plaintiff in this case as well as all other persons entering the threatre were subject to the fire regulations. Treating plaintiff in the same manner as any other person who entered the theatre does not amount to actionable discrimination.

Finally, the enactment of Civil Code sections 54.3 and 55 providing for public prosecution and private injunctive relief for violations of Civil Code section 54.1 evidences a legislative intent that those remedies are to be exclusive and that the damages provided for in section 52 are not recoverable for a violation of Civil Code section 54.1.

Where a statute on a particular subject omits a particular provision, the inclusion of such a provision in another statute concerning a related matter indicates an intent that the provision is not applicable to the statute from which it was omitted. (*City of Burbank* v. *Metropolitan Water District,* 180 Cal.App.2d 451, 4 Cal.Rptr. 757.)

We need not decide whether section 55 should have prospective or retroactive application since plaintiff has failed to establish a violation of section 54.1, a necessary prerequisite to injunctive relief. Section 54.1 does not require affirmative action by way of modifying existing structures. This conclusion is borne out by the fact that section 55 also specifically includes references to violations of the provisions of those Government Code and Health and Safety Code sections which established building standards and requirements in this area. If the Legislature had intended injunctive enforcement of section 54.1 to apply to structural modifications then the inclusion in section 55 of reference to Health and Safety Code sections 19955 and 19959 would be redundant.

We conclude that the operator of a business of a type enumerated in Civil Code section 54.1 is not required by the force of that section *alone* to modify its facilities to allow for their use by handicapped persons. That statute requires only that the operator open its doors on an equal basis to all that can avail themselves of the facilities without violation of other valid laws and regulations.

The judgment is reversed and the trial court is directed to enter a judgment for the defendant along with an award of costs. Defendant is to recover costs on this appeal.

Fleming, Acting P. J., and Beach, J., concur.

NOTES

1. Before the handing down of the appellate decision, one article summarized the factual background and lower court proceedings in the *Marsh* case:

> In late June 1975, the *Edwards Theatre* case was tried. This suit was one of the first recorded "discrimination" cases brought against a private defendant. The case involved an ex-Marine, Marsh, who had become a high paraplegic as a result of an auto accident. His disability had led to a state of depression and to a marital breakdown. His parents, in order to cheer him up, decided to take him to a motion picture theatre. Upon arrival at the theatre, he tendered the appropriate fee, and at that point he was told by the manager that unless he could sit in a regular seat he would not be allowed admittance. The manager stated that to allow him to remain in his wheelchair would violate fire regulations, and, moreover, there simply was no room for a wheelchair. His parents offered to sit with him in the back of the theatre so that he could be removed immediately in case of emergency. The manager informed them that this was not acceptable. He threatened to call the police if there were any further disturbance. Marsh was so humiliated and outraged by these events that he immediately fell into a state of total depression. Although three years have elapsed, he has yet to attend a theatre.
>
> In arguing this case the plaintiff asked for, and received, jury instructions that the disabled are covered under the California general civil rights statutes. This was highly significant for two reasons. Initially, after a five year delay, the case of *In re Cox,* upon which the judge substantially relied, was finally used to aid the disabled. In *Cox,* the court found that there was a violation of the plaintiffs' civil rights when two long haired teenagers were denied access to a retail shopping center *solely* because of their appearance. The importance of *Cox,* however, is that the California supreme court held that the seemingly narrow general civil rights statute was not restricted to the enumerated

categories of race, color, religion, ancestry, or national origin, but also included *any* instances of invidious discrimination by a business establishment.

The second important aspect of *Edwards* concerns damages. California's Civil Rights Statutes for the Handicapped seemingly provide for only reasonable attorney's fees in actions brought to enjoin discriminatory activities under California Civil Code Sections 54 and 54.1 or violations of the Architectural Barrier Laws. The general civil rights statute, the Unruh Act, provides for claims of plaintiff's *actual* damages, as well as $250 penalty damages. By allowing *actual* damages, the incentive for private attorneys to bring valid suit is increased greatly. This is exemplified by the result of the *Edwards* case.

Although only minimum statutory damages were awarded, *Edwards* constitutes a major moral and legal victory and establishes an important precedent. The jury found that there was room in the theatre for the wheelchair, that the claimed violation of the fire ordinance was only a pretense, and by a nine to three vote decided that they would have awarded $90,000 in damages, both compensatory and punitive. They refrained from awarding this amount because they concluded that Marsh really wanted an injunction so that, in the future, disabled persons would not be excluded from places of public amusement. They assumed the judge would issue such a decree.

While the jury was deliberating, the judge, in the process of trying the equitable issues, decided that there was a present, speedy, and adequate remedy at law (damages) and refused to issue the injunction. The members of the jury, upon learning of the judge's decision, were furious. [b]

2. Is the *Marsh* decision in harmony with the spirit of the statutes it interpreted? Cf. *In re Fenton,* pp. 468–470, above. In the event of a fire in the theatre, is Mr. Marsh in a worse position in the aisle in his wheelchair or in a theatre seat?

3. For a discussion of the state architectural barriers statutes whose language can be interpreted to cover private buildings, see Comment, "Access to Buildings and Equal Employment Opportunity for the Disabled: Survey of State Statutes," 50 *Temple L. Q.* 1067, 1069–1071 (1977). For a comprehensive summary of barriers legislation in each of the states, see Michigan Center for a Barrier-Free Environment, *Access to America* (1976).

D. FEDERAL STATUTORY REQUIREMENTS

In contrast to other legal issues for which U.S. Congressional recognition of rights occurred only after significant judicial victories were won by handicapped people, in the areas of architectural barriers and transportation Congress demonstrated a relatively early awareness of problems facing disabled people. Initial legislation in these areas was partially a reflection of developments in education and employment. Accessibility was a prerequisite to equal education and employment opportunities; it does little good to provide employment opportunities and vocational rehabilitation services for handicapped individuals if they are unable to travel to and from work. See, for example, S. Rep. No. 538, 90th Cong., 2d Sess., 1962 U.S.C.C. & A.N. 3214, 3215 (1968).

---

[b]Achtenberg, J., "Law and the Physically Disabled: An Update with Constitutional Implications," 8 S.W.U.L. Rev. 847, 863–865 (1976).

Because of the prompt Congressional action, litigation in this field has focused primarily on enforcing and implementing previously enacted statutes and regulations. Frequently, this task has proved to be far more difficult than an initial reading of the statutes would indicate.

This section explores several of these statutes and presents the major cases that have sought their implementation. The bulk of recent litigation has dealt with the accessibility of local transit vehicles and systems. Several factors are responsible for this trend and are noteworthy.

First, the energy crisis has dictated a new respect for the economic benefits to be gained from efficient mass transportation systems. As major revisions have been undertaken to increase transit ridership, the opportunity to accommodate the needs of elderly and handicapped persons has arisen. Second, handicapped people may have a greater need for access to mass transportation than the general population; see Urban Mass Transportation Administration and Transportation Systems Center for the United States Department of Transportation, *Technical Report, The Handicapped and Elderly Market for Urban Mass Transit* 6, 7 (1973). Fewer handicapped individuals own automobiles, either because of their incapacity to drive or the expense of owning a car, and mass transportation usually represents the least expensive, most convenient, and often the only alternative.

Finally, the issue of access to mass transit has come to the fore because rapid technological advances have made it possible to eliminate many of the mobility limitations previously associated with handicapping conditions and have rendered it technologically feasible to make transportation systems remarkably accessible to handicapped persons. The motorized wheelchair, for example, has given a great deal of mobility to many persons whose mobility was hitherto extremely limited; now, able to move about their neighborhoods, such people are demanding that modern technology be applied to allow them to get on public buses.

1. 29 U.S.C. § 794

The history and effects of 29 U.S.C. § 794, § 504 of the Rehabilitation Act of 1973 (P.L. 93-112 as amended by the Rehabilitation, Comprehensive Services, and Developmental Disabilities Amendments of 1978, P.L. 95-602), are discussed generally at pp. 194–213, above.

a. Early Judicial Distortion

Snowden v. Birmingham-Jefferson County Transit Authority

United States District Court, for the Northern District of Alabama, Southern Division,
1975
407 F.Supp. 394, aff'd. mem., 551 F.2d 862 (5th Cir. 1977)
Guin, District Judge.

This action came on further to be heard on April 11, 1975, upon the motions for summary judgment filed by defendants Birmingham-Jefferson County Transit Authority (BJCTA) and William T. Coleman, Jr., Secretary of Transportation of the United States of America (USDOT), the affidavits and other documentary evidence filed by the parties, the testimony taken herein on April 1, 1975, and the briefs of counsel. This court on April 1, 1975, entered an order refusing plaintiff's motions for a temporary restraining order and for a preliminary injunction. That order is hereby incorporated by reference in this memorandum opinion.

Plaintiff Jane Snowden is a physically handicapped resident of the Birmingham metropolitan area who, by reason of her handicap, is forced to ambulate by means of a wheelchair. She, on her own behalf and on behalf of all others similarly situated, sues BJCTA and USDOT, contending that BJCTA's development and operation of a public mass transportation bus system in Birmingham, and the furnishing of federal financial assistance therefor by USDOT, when such bus system is not accessible to physically handicapped persons including those confined to wheelchairs, violates Section 504 of the Rehabilitation Act of 1973 (29 U.S.C. § 794), Section 16(a) of the Urban Mass Transportation Act of 1964 as amended (49 U.S.C. § 1612(a)) and the fifth and fourteenth amendments to the Constitution of the United States. Plaintiff seeks a declaration of her rights and an injunction restraining USDOT from extending further federal financial assistance to BJCTA and restraining BJCTA from acquiring any new buses or other mass transportation vehicles which are not accessible to the handicapped, including those confined to wheelchairs, until adequate and effective public mass transportation has been made available to them.

1. Statement of the Facts

The following facts appear to be undisputed and are therefore found for purposes of this action:

The program of federal assistance to urban mass transportation systems, authorized by the Urban Mass Transportation Act of 1964 as amended (49 U.S.C. § 1601 *et seq.*) (the UMT Act), is administered by the Secretary of Transportation, presently William T. Coleman, Jr., pursuant to Reorganization Plan No. 2 of 1968 (33 F.R. 6965, 82 Stat. 1369). All of the powers of the secretary under the UMT Act and related laws pertaining to federal assistance to urban mass transportation systems have been delegated to the Urban Mass Transportation Administrator (UMTA), presently Frank C. Herringer (49 C.F.R. § 1.50).

On May 21, 1974 UMTA approved a capital facilities grant to BJCTA under Section 3 of the UMT Act (49 U.S.C. § 1602) for Project No. AL-03-0003, which includes the purchase of 22 new 45-passenger diesel transit buses, a bus garage and office complex, and related items. The buses involved had been advertised for public competitive bidding, an award was made to the low bidder, A. M. General Corporation, and the buses were scheduled to be delivered at some time beginning about the end of April, 1975. These buses were not to be specially designed or equipped to enable passengers confined to wheelchairs to board, ride and alight with convenience and safety for themselves and other passengers, but were to include certain special equipment and features such as stanchions, grab-rails, step-well lighting, power-assisted doors, etc., designed to make them more readily and safely usable by elderly and physically handicapped persons other than those confined to wheelchairs. At the present time no manufacturer in the United States produces a standard size (45-passenger) diesel transit bus designed and equipped for safe and convenient use by passengers confined to wheelchairs. Neither has any smaller vehicle designed and equipped for safe and convenient use by persons confined to wheelchairs been manufactured and tested in regular line haul urban mass transportation service in the United States.

The Urban Mass Transportation Administration has, pursuant to Section 16 of the UMT Act (49 U.S.C. § 1612) carried on a substantial program of technical studies projects and research, development and demonstration projects designed to ascertain the nature and extent of the need of elderly and physically handicapped persons for mass transportation service, and to develop and demonstrate facilities, equipment and operating techniques to meet that need. Such program includes one major project known as "TRANSBUS," designed to develop a new generation of buses for general use in federally assisted urban mass transportation service in the United States. As part of that project, three prototype standard-size diesel transit buses, each designed and equipped to accommodate passengers confined to wheelchairs, have been developed and built, and are presently being demonstrated and tested in actual revenue service in four major cities to determine their safety, reliability and economy, and their acceptability and attractiveness to all segments of the public, including the elderly and the physically handicapped. At present these prototypes are not available for manufacture and sale and distribution to meet the needs of mass transportation.

BJCTA does not at the present time have any mass transit vehicles designed and equipped to accommodate passengers confined to wheelchairs, but permits such passengers to ride on its regular transit vehicles when they are able, alone or with the assistance of others, to do so.

2.   Urban Mass Transportation Act of 1964 as Amended

* * *

[The discussion of Section 16(a) of the Urban Mass Transportation Act is omitted. See Section 2, UMTA, pp. 497–502, below.]

* * *

3.   Section 504 of the Rehabilitation Act of 1973

Section 504 of the Rehabilitation Act of 1973 (29 U.S.C. § 794), upon which plaintiff also relies, is, like section 16(a) of the UMT Act, a statement of federal policy. It reads as follows:

> No *otherwise qualified* handicapped individual in the United States, as defined in section 706(6) of this title, shall, *solely by reason of his handicap,* be excluded from participation in, be denied the benefits of, or be subjected to discrimination under any program or activity receiving Federal financial assistance. [Emphasis supplied.]

The affidavit of Charles W. Croft, resident manager of BJCTA, dated March 31, 1975, and attached to the defendant's motion for summary judgment, pointed out that persons confined to wheelchairs are permitted to ride as passengers on BJCTA vehicles. Although it is necessary for persons handicapped in this manner to arrange for someone to help them board and alight from the bus, these persons are allowed to use the transportation vehicles in question. Thus, it cannot be said that persons who ambulate by wheelchair are excluded from using the defendant's transportation system. For this reason, the court finds no violation of the Rehabilitation Act of 1973 on the part of BJCTA or on the part of UMTA, and hence that act provides plaintiff and the class she represents with no cause of action.

4. The Equal Protection Clause of the 14th Amendment

Plaintiff also contends that she and the class she represents are being deprived by defendants of rights under the fifth and fourteenth amendments to the Constitution of the United States, presumably the "due process" or "equal protection" clauses. This unconstitutional deprivation is claimed to result not from plaintiff and her class being prohibited from riding, but from defendants' failure to provide vehicles specially designed and equipped so that they and their wheelchairs can ride on defendants' buses safely and conveniently.

The court has not been directed to any case which holds that a local governmental body is under an affirmative duty grounded in and arising from the Constitution of the United States to provide any special class or type of physical facilities to accommodate any special class or type of citizen, in the absence of a statute which so requires. In a somewhat analogous case involving public housing, the Supreme Court of the United States recently said:

> We do not denigrate the importance of decent, safe, and sanitary housing. But the Constitution does not provide judicial remedies for every social and economic ill. We are unable to perceive in that document any constitutional guarantee of access to dwellings of a particular quality. . . . Absent constitutional mandate, the assurance of adequate housing and the definition of landlord-tenant relationship are legislative, not judicial, functions. *Lindsey et al.* v. *Normet et al.,* 405 U.S. 56, 74, 92 S.Ct. 862, 874, 31 L.Ed.2d 36 (1972); see also *Gautreaux* v. *Romney,* 363 F.Supp. 690, 691 (N.D.Ill.1973), rev'd on other grounds 503 F.2d 930 (7th Cir. 1974).

Plaintiff cannot credibly maintain that access to public transportation facilities is a "fundamental right" on a parity with the right to an education at public expense which must be made available to all on equal terms. *Brown* v. *Board of Education,* 347 U.S. 483, 493, 74 S.Ct. 686, 98 L.Ed. 873 (1954); *Mills* v. *Board of Education,* 348 F.Supp. 866, 874, 875 (D.D.C.1972). That being so, the Constitution merely requires a rational basis for any discrimination among persons similarly situated. *Yick Wo* v. *Hopkins,* 118 U.S. 356, 6 S.Ct. 1064, 30 L.Ed. 220 (1886); *Shapiro* v. *Thompson,* 394 U.S. 618, 89 S.Ct. 1322, 22 L.Ed.2d 600 (1969). The facts of this case do not appear to involve any invidious discrimination against similarly situated persons. Such discrimination as may in fact exist results from technological and operational difficulties in designing, producing and operating the kind of special vehicles needed to allow plaintiff and the class she represents to utilize BJCTA's bus system with safety and convenience for themelves and other passengers. The affidavits of UMTA Administrator Herringer and BJCTA Resident Manager Croft, which are uncontroverted, show that there is no device presently developed and proven reliable for use in a standard full-size urban transit bus which would make that bus fully accessible to plaintiff and her class. As the Supreme Court noted in *Yakus* v. *United States.* "The Constitution as a continuously operative charter of government does not demand the impossible or the impracticable." 321 U.S. 414, 424, 64 S.Ct. 660, 88 L.Ed. 834 (1944).

For the foregoing reasons, the motion for summary judgment filed by the defendants are granted and this action is dismissed.

NOTES

1.   The *Snowden* case perhaps best exemplifies one of the ironies facing those handicapped persons who are actively seeking enforcement of their civil rights. "In the 1960's there was a political and legal revolution because a significant minority of the population had to sit at the back of the bus. Today it is realized that a significant minority cannot even get on the bus" (Achtenburg, J., "Law and the Physically Disabled: An Update with Constitutional Implications," 8 *S.W.U.L. Rev.* 847, 850 (1976)). The lack of accessible transportation systems has helped to effectively segregate handicapped individuals not only from the mainstream of society but from each other as well. One result has been to deter "the militancy necessary for demanding legally protected rights" (*Id.* at 852).

See also Kriegal, L., "Uncle Tom and Tiny Tim: Reflections on the Cripple as Negro," 38 *Am. Scholar* 412 (1969).

2.   Several other early opinions based on § 504 followed the lead set by the *Snowden* court. Section 504 was thought to be only another statement of national policy and not to confer affirmative rights. See *United Handicapped Federation* v. *Andre*, 409 F.Supp. 1297 (D.Minn. 1976), rev'd. 558 F.2d 113 (8th Cir. 1977), pp. 491–493, below, but cf. *Bartels* v. *Biernat*, 405 F.Supp. 1012 (E.D.Wis. 1975).

In *Martin* v. *Seattle-King County Metropolitan Transit Commission,* Civil Action No. 795806 (Wash. Superior Ct., June 26, 1975), the court dismissed the plaintiffs' suit to enjoin the purchase of inaccessible buses. In finding that no civil rights violation had occurred, the court stated:

> [W]e have testimony that [the defendant] would transport people in wheelchairs around if there could be some way they could be put on the bus. The reason they are not being transported is the disability of the person; it is not the cooperation of [the defendant]. They have not intentionally or maliciously or in any other way discriminated against people who are in wheelchairs (*Id.* at 7).

Summary judgment was granted for the defendants in *Webb* v. *Miami Valley Regional Transit Authority,* Civil Action No. C-3-75-67 (S.D.Ohio, January 19, 1976), another suit involving the purchase of inaccessible buses. Although relying on the precedent set by *Snowden,* the court awarded the plaintiffs attorneys' fees noting that during the pendency of the litigation, the defendant had contracted to purchase a number of buses that complied with the accessibility standards desired by the plaintiffs.

3.   The Fifth Circuit Court of appeals affirmed the *Snowden* decision without opinion, 551 F.2d 862 (5th Cir. 1977). As one of the first circuit decisions on the issue of access to transportation, the *Snowden* ruling might have been expected to be a major factor in affecting the subsequent direction of law in this area. Actually, however, technological advances and more cogent legal analysis in subsequent cases have almost totally undermined the precedental value of the *Snowden* decision.

b.   Later Judicial Perspectives

LLOYD V REGIONAL TRANSPORTATION AUTHORITY

United States Court of Appeals for the Seventh Circuit, 1977
548 F.2d 1277

CUMMINGS, Circuit Judge.

This class action was filed under the Civil Rights Act of 1871 (42 U.S.C. § 1983), the Rehabilitation Act of 1973 (29 U.S.C. §§ 701 *et seq.*), the Architectural Barriers Act of 1968 (42 U.S.C. §§ 4151 and 4152), and unspecified regulations promulgated under the statutes. Plaintiffs also relied on various sections of the Constitution but now rest their constitutional argument only on the Equal Protection Clause of the Fourteenth Amendment.

The named plaintiffs are George A. Lloyd, a quadriplegic who has been confined to a wheelchair since 1953, and Janet B. Wolfe, who is "mobility-disabled" because of a chronic pulmonary dysfunction. They sued on behalf of a class of all mobility-disabled persons in the northeastern region of Illinois. The two defendants are the Regional Transportation Authority (RTA), which provides public transportation and assists in the public mass transportation system in that region, and the Chicago Transit Authority (CTA`, which operates a mass transportation system in the Chicago metropolitan area. The complaint alleges that the suing class is unable to use defendants' public transportation system because of physical disabilities. Plaintiffs aver on information and belief that defendants are in the process of planning for the purchase of new transportation equipment utilizing federal funds and that, unless defendants are compelled to take affirmative action, the transportation system will continue to be inaccessible to the mobility-disabled.

The complaint sets out four causes of action. First, plaintiffs assert that defendants have violated Section 16 of the Urban Mass Transportation Act of 1964 (49 U.S.C. § 1612) because they have not met the transportation needs of handicapped persons. Secondly, plaintiffs charge that defendants have violated Section 504 of the Rehabilitation Act of 1973 (29 U.S.C. § 794) because, by reason of their handicaps, plaintiffs have been denied the meaningful usage of defendants' federally financed mass transportation facilities. Thirdly, plaintiffs claim that defendants have not complied with Sections 1 and 2 of the Architectural Barriers Act of 1968 (42 U.S.C. §§ 4151 and 4152) because they have not designed vehicular facilities permitting ready access to physically handicapped persons. Finally, defendants' denial of public transportation system access to plaintiffs and their class is said to violate the Fourteenth Amendment's Equal Protection Clause.

The plaintiffs sought a preliminary injunction to prevent the defendants from designing or placing into operation any new federally funded facilities unless the facilities were accessible to all mobility-disabled persons. Plaintiffs also prayed for a mandatory injunction compelling the defendants to make the existing transportation system accessible to the mobility-disabled.

The district court filed a memorandum opinion granting the defendants' motions to dismiss on the ground that the three statutes in question do not confer a private right of action. The opinion stated that the only substantial constitutional claim of plaintiffs was founded on the Equal Protection Clause but that it was inapplicable because

> [d]efendants have not created any inequalities of treatment. They are not alleged to be providing handicapped persons with any lesser facilities than other persons.

We vacate and remand.

Section 504 Confers Affirmative Rights

Plaintiffs and two *amici curiae* rely on Section 504 of the Rehabilitation Act of 1973 as giving plaintiffs the right to file a private action to enforce compliance with the statutes relied upon in the complaint and the recent regulations of the Urban Mass Transportation Administration.[8] Section 504 provides:

> No otherwise qualified handicapped individual in the United States, as defined in section 7(6), shall, solely by reason of his handicap, be excluded from the participation in, be denied the benefits of, or be subjected to discrimination under any program or activity receiving Federal financial assistance (29 U.S.C. § 794).

This provision closely tracks Section 601 of the Civil Rights Act of 1964,[10] which was construed in *Lau* v. *Nichols,* 414 U.S. 563, 94 S.Ct. 786, 39 L.Ed.2d 1. There a unanimous Supreme Court held that Section 601 provided a private cause of action. See also *Bossier Parish School Board* v. *Lemon,* 370 F.2d 847, 852 (5th Cir. 1967), certiorari denied, 388 U.S. 911, 87 S.Ct. 2116, 18 L.Ed.2d 1350. While adverting to regulations and guidelines issued by the Department of Health, Education and Welfare (HEW) pursuant to Section 602 of the Act[11] and the respondent school district's contractual agreement to comply with Title VI of the Civil Rights Act of 1964 and the regulations thereunder, Justice Douglas (speaking for himself and Justices Brennan, Marshall, Powell and Rehnquist) stated, in reversing the court of appeals, that "[w]e do not reach the Equal Protection Clause argument which has been advanced but rely solely on § 601." 414 U.S. at 566, 94 S.Ct. at 788. The concurring opinion of Justice Stewart (with whom the Chief Justice and Justice Blackmun joined) relied on Section 601 and the HEW regulations and guidelines and mentioned that plaintiffs there could concededly sue as third-party beneficiaries of said contract. Finally, Justice Blackmun (with whom the Chief Justice joined) stated that because the plaintiff class involved

---

[8]Those regulations were issued on April 27, 1976, and made effective May 31, 1976. They appear in 49 C.F.R. §§ 609.1–609.25 and 613.204 and in 41 F.R. 18239–18241 and 18234 (April 30, 1976). Two appendices were also added. 49 C.F.R. §§ 609.15(a), (b) and (c) were revised effective October 12, 1976. 41 F.R. 45842 (October 18, 1976).

[10]Section 601 of the Civil Rights Act of 1964 provides: "No person in the United States shall, on the ground of race, color, or national origin, be excluded from participation in, be denied the benefits of, or be subjected to discrimination under any program or activity receiving Federal financial assistance" (42 U.S.C. § 2000d).

[11]Section 602 provides: "Each Federal department and agency which is empowered to extend Federal financial assistance to any program or activity, by way of grant, loan, or contract other than a contract of insurance or guaranty, is authorized and directed to effectuate the provisions of section 2000d of this title with respect to such program or activity by issuing rules, regulations, or orders of general applicability which shall be consistent with achievement of the objectives of the statute authorizing the financial assistance in connection with which the action is taken . . . " (42 U.S.C. § 2000d–1).

2800 school children, he concurred in the holding that the San Francisco School District could not continue to teach students in English without teaching English to Chinese-speaking children or giving their classes in the Chinese language. Because of the near identity of language in Section 504 of the Rehabilitation Act of 1973 and Section 601 of the Civil Rights Act of 1964, *Lau* is dispositive. Therefore, we hold that Section 504 of the Rehabilitation Act, at least when considered with the regulations which now implement it, establishes affirmative rights and permits this action to proceed.

Judge Flaum held that *Lau* was not controlling because this case was devoid of analogs to the HEW guidelines there involved. In the district court's view, the "obligation to provide special programs did not flow from the cited statutory language [Section 601 of the Civil Rights Act of 1964], but rather from Health, Education and Welfare guidelines which were enacted pursuant to the additional statutory section, § 2000d-1 [Section 602 of the Civil Rights Act of 1964]." Even though the opinion of the Court in *Lau* can be read as authority for allowing this action to proceed under Section 504 of the Rehabilitation Act alone, developments subsequent to the district court's opinion have provided a virtual one-to-one correspondence between the conceptual props supporting the concurring opinions in *Lau* and the elements of the instant case.

Here the conceptual analog of Section 602 of the Civil Rights Act of 1964 came into being on April 28, 1976, in the form of Executive Order 11914, 41 F.R. 17871 (April 29, 1976). The Executive Order authorizes HEW and other federal agencies dispensing financial assistance to adopt rules, regulations and orders to ensure that recipients of federal aid are in compliance with Section 504. If compliance cannot be secured voluntarily, it may be compelled by suspension or termination of federal assistance after a hearing or by "other appropriate means authorized by law." HEW is given the responsibility of establishing standards for who are "handicapped individuals" and for determining what are "discriminatory practices" as well as coordinating the implementation of Section 504 by all federal agencies. While the Rehabilitation Act itself contains no express directive to issue regulations, the 1974 Amendments to the Act generated a legislative history which indicates that Congress contemplated speedy implementation of Section 504 through regulations. See S.Rep. No. 93-1139, 93d Cong., 2d Sess. 24–25 (1974); H.R.Rep. No. 32-1457, 93d Cong., 2d Sess. 27–28 (1974); S.Rep. No. 32-1297, 93d Cong., 2d Sess. 39–40 (1974). "In review of the foregoing, [it can be concluded] that the [HEW] Secretary is required to promulgate regulations effectuating § 504." *Cherry* v. *Mathews,* 419 F.Supp. 922 (D.D.C., 1976).

Forty days after the district court's opinion was issued, the Urban Mass Transportation Administrator promulgated final regulations, in part under the authority of Section 504. These regulations and various accompanying guidelines are squarely couched in affirmative language. Thus new regulation 49 CFR § 613.204 provides:

> *Additional criteria for Urban Mass Transportation Administrator's approvals under 23 CFR 450.320.*
>
> The Urban Mass Transportation Administrator will grant project approvals pursuant to 23 CFR 450.320(a)(3) *only if:*

(a) *The urban transportation planning process exhibits satisfactory special efforts in planning public mass transportation facilities and services that can be utilized by elderly and handicapped persons;* and

(b) The annual element of the transportation improvement program developed pursuant to 23 CFR 450.118 and submitted after September 30, 1976, contains projects or project elements designed to benefit elderly and handicapped persons, *specifically including wheelchair users and those with semi-ambulatory capabilities;* and

(c) After September 30, 1977, *reasonable progress* has been demonstrated in implementing previously programmed projects. [Emphasis supplied.]

Advisory information issued simultaneously, to be added to the appendix to 23 CFR Part 450, Subpart A, sets forth general guidance on the meaning of "special efforts" in planning:

> The urban transportation planning process must include special efforts to plan public mass transportation facilities and service that can effectively be utilized by elderly and handicapped persons. As used in this guidance, the term "special efforts" refers both to service for elderly and handicapped persons in general and specifically to service for wheelchair users and semiambulatory persons. *With regard to transportation for wheelchair users and others who cannot negotiate steps, "special efforts" in planning means genuine, good-faith progress in planning service for wheelchair users and semiambulatory handicapped persons that is reasonable by comparison with the service provided to the general public and that meets a significant fraction of the actual transportation needs of such persons within a reasonable time period.* [Emphasis supplied.]

Further advisory information published as an appendix to 49 CFR Part 613, Subpart B, gives several examples of a level of effort that will be deemed to satisfy the special efforts requirement. While the guidelines do not purport to be regulatory standards or minimums, they do suggest a commitment to an affirmative remedial program of substantial scope. The most recently issued Urban Mass Transportation Administrator's regulation (49 CFR § 609.15(b), 41 F.R. 45842 (October 18, 1976)) provides in pertinent part that:

> procurement solicitations shall provide for a bus design which permits the addition of a wheelchair accessibility option and shall require an assurance from each bidder that it offers a wheelchair accessibility option for its buses. The term "wheelchair accessibility option" means a level change mechanism (e.g., lift or ramp), sufficient clearances to permit a wheelchair user to reach a securement location, and at least one wheelchair securement device.

Indeed, in oral argument the CTA conceded that the regulations created an affirmative duty on federal grant recipients.

Four months after the district judge's opinion, HEW issued proposed regulations implementing Section 504. Paralleling 45 CFR § 80.3(b)(1)(ii) and (iv), the provisions explicitly mentioned by eight Justices in *Lau*, proposed regulations 49 CFR §§ 84.4(b)(1)(ii) and (iv) specify that recipients of federal financial assistance may not

> (ii) Provide a qualified handicapped person with aid, benefit, or service which is not *as effective as that provided to others;*
>
> * * * *
>
> (iv) Otherwise limit a qualified handicapped person in the enjoyment of any right, privilege, advantage or opportunity enjoyed by others receiving an aid, benefit or service. [Emphasis supplied.]

Moreover § 84.4(b)(2) establishes that

> A recipient may not provide different or separate aid, benefits or services to handicapped persons unless such action is necessary to provide qualified handicapped persons with aid, benefits, or services *which are as effective as those provided to others.* [Emphasis supplied.]

Finally, pending the adoption of a new procedural regulation consolidating all of the enforcement procedures implementing the civil rights statutes for which HEW has enforcement responsibilities, the "procedural provisions of the title VI regulation, which may be found at 45 CFR Part 80, will be incorporated by reference into the section 504 regulations for use during the interim." 41 F.R. 29548 (July 16, 1976). The regulations thus reduce to concrete terms the abstract words of section 504.

Taken together with the numerosity of the class, every element of the two concurring opinions in *Lau* is also satisfied under the statutory and administrative framework of the instant case. The existence of affirmative rights under Section 504 necessarily follows, for, to paraphrase Justice Douglas in *Lau*:

> Under these [federal] standards there is no equality of treatment merely by providing [the handicapped] with the same facilities [as ambulatory persons] . . . ; for [handicapped persons] who [can] not [gain access to such facilities] are effectively foreclosed from any meaningful [public transportation] (414 U.S. at 566, 94 S.Ct. at 788).

Cf. *Griggs* v. *Duke Power Co.,* 401 U.S. 424, 431, 91 S.Ct. 849, 28 L.Ed.2d 158.

Private Right of Action

Having demonstrated that *Lau* v. *Nichols* is conclusive on the question of the existence of affirmative rights under Section 504 and the regulations, we now turn to a consideration whether a private cause of action may be implied to vindicate these rights. As the parties have acknowledged, *Cort* v. *Ash,* 422 U.S. 66, 78, 95 S.Ct. 2080, 2087, 45 L.Ed.2d 26, sets out the four factors relevant to determining whether a private remedy is implicit in a statute not expressly providing one. They are:

> First, is the plaintiff "one of the class for whose *especial* benefit the statute was enacted," [emphasis supplied]—that is, does the statute create a federal right in favor of the plaintiff? Second, is there any indication of legislative intent, explicit or implicit, either to create such a remedy or to deny one? Third, is it consistent with the underlying purposes of the legislative scheme to imply such a remedy for the plaintiff? And finally, is the cause of action one traditionally relegated to state law, in an area basically the concern of the States, so that it would be inappropriate to infer a cause of action based solely on federal law? [Citations omitted.]

Applying the *Cort* factors here leads to the conclusion that a private cause of action must be implied from Section 504.

(1) Plaintiffs of course are among the class specifically benefited by the enactment of the statute. As demonstrated above, Section 504 establishes affirmative private rights. In particular, these rights apply to transportation barriers impeding handicapped individuals. 29 U.S.C. § 701(11).

(2) While the 1973 legislative history of Section 504 is bereft of much explanation, the legislative history of the Rehabilitation Act Amendments of 1974 casts light

on the original Congressional intent. These amendments, *inter alia,* redefined the term "handicapped individual" as used in Section 504 and, as clarifying amendments, have cogent significance in construing Section 504. See *Red Lion Broadcasting Co., Inc.* v. *Federal Communications Commission,* 395 U.S. 367, 380–381, 89 S.Ct. 1794, 23 L.Ed.2d 371. It is noteworthy that the Senate Report was submitted on November 26, 1974, and the *Lau* opinion construing Section 601 of the Civil Rights Act of 1964 was handed down on January 21 of that year and certainly known by the Senate Committee. Indeed, the report of the Senate Labor and Public Welfare Committee notes that the

> new definition applies to section 503, as well as to section 504, in order to avoid limiting the affirmative action obligation of a Federal contractor to only that class of persons who are eligible for vocational rehabilitation services. . . . Where applicable, section 504 is intended to include a requirement of affirmative action as well as a prohibition against discrimination (4 U.S.Code Cong. & Admin. News, p. 6390 (1974)).

The Committee continues by stating that Section 504's similarity to Section 601 of the Civil Rights Act of 1964 was not accidental:

> Section 504 was patterned after, and is almost identical to, the antidiscrimination language of section 601 of the Civil Rights Act of 1964, 42 U.S.C. 2000d-1 (relating to race, color, or national origin), and section 901 of the Education Amendments of 1972, 42 U.S.C. 1683 (relating to sex). The section therefore constitutes the establishment of a broad government policy that programs receiving Federal financial assistance shall be operated without discrimination on the basis of handicap. It does not specifically require the issuance of regulations or expressly provide for enforcement procedures, but it is clearly mandatory in form, and such regulations and enforcement are intended (4 U.S.Code Cong. & Admin. News, p. 6390 (1974).)

Further, the scope of the enforcement mechanism to result from such conscious parallelism did not escape comment:

> The language of section 504, in followig [sic] the above-cited Acts, further envisions the implementation of a compliance program which is similar to those Acts, including promulgation of regulations providing for investigation and review of recipients of Federal financial assistance, attempts to bring non-complying recipients into voluntary compliance through informal efforts such as negotiation, and the imposition of sanctions against recipients who continue to discriminate against otherwise qualified handicapped persons on the basis of handicap. Such sanctions would include, where appropriate, the termination of Federal financial assistance to the recipient or other means otherwise authorized by law. Implementation of section 504 would also include pre-grant analysis of recipients to ensure that Federal funds are not initially provided to those who discriminate against handicapped individuals. Such analysis would include pre-grant review procedures and a requirement for assurances of compliance with section 504. This approach to implementation of section 504, which closely follows the models of the above-cited anti-discrimination provisions, would ensure administrative due process (right to hearing, right to review), provide for administrative consistency within the Federal government as well as relative ease of implementation, and *permit a judicial remedy through a private action. Id.* at pp. 6390–6391. [Emphasis supplied.]

While the above language contemplates judicial review of an administrative proceeding as contradistinct from an independent cause of action in federal court, still it is plain that the rights of the handicapped were meant to be enforced at some point through the vehicle of a private cause of action. When administrative remedial machinery does not exist to vindicate an affirmative right, there can be no objection to an independent cause of action in the federal courts.[29] See *Steele* v. *Louisville & N. R. Co.*, 323 U.S. 192, 206–207, 65 S.Ct. 226, 89 L.Ed. 173. In any event, under the second prong of the *Cort* test, there is surely an indication of legislative intent to create such a remedy and none to deny it.

(3) It is certainly consistent with the underlying purposes of the legislative scheme to imply such a remedy. Indeed, one of the explicitly detailed purposes of the Rehabilitation Act of 1973 was to "enforce statutory and regulatory standards and requirements regarding barrier-free construction of public facilities and study and develop solutions to existing architectural and transportation barriers impeding handicapped individuals." 29 U.S.C. § 701(11). Moreover, since a private cause of action in this case serves to enforce the uniform substantive standards laid down by the UMTA and HEW regulations, the unseemly vista of a spotty application of *ad hoc* remedies in lawsuits in various regions of the country is not presented here. And no objection to local implementation of these substantive standards can prevail since the nationwide Urban Mass Transportation Administrator's regulations which set out standards for meeting the needs of the handicapped in transportation only serve as a guide for the local implementation of transportation opportunities for the mobility-disabled. 41 F.R. 18234 (April 30, 1976).

(4) Affording a private remedy under Section 504 of the Rehabilitation Act of 1973 would not be the kind of suit traditionally relegated to state law in an area basically the concern of the States. In fact, both the RTA and CTA conceded below that it was the intent of Congress to deal with the transportation needs of the handicapped on a national basis.

Because all four *Cort* tests are satisfied, we are reinforced in our holding that Section 504 implicitly provides a private remedy. Therefore, we need not and do not consider whether the Equal Protection Clause (together with 28 U.S.C. § 1343) and the other statutes cited in the complaint also confer jurisdiction on the district court.

Defendants rely principally on *Cannon* v. *University of Chicago* (7th Cir. Nos. 76-1238 and 1239, decided August 27, 1976), in arguing that Section 504 does not provide for a private right of action. There a panel of this Court held that Title IX of the Education Amendments of 1972 (20 U.S.C. § 1681) does not permit a private cause of action. However, the Court noted that in contradistinction to *Lau*, *Cannon* involved only an individual plaintiff who had not exhausted her administrative remedies (slip op. 11–16). Here we have a huge class, and plaintiffs and *amicus* Urban Mass Transportation Administrator have not persuaded us that any administrative remedy is yet avail-

---

[29]We expressly leave open as premature the question whether, after consolidated procedural enforcement regulations are issued to implement Section 504, the judicial remedy available must be limited to post-administrative remedy judicial review. In any event, the private cause of action we imply today must continue at least in the form of judicial review of administrative action. And until effective enforcement regulations are promulgated, Section 504 in its present incarnation as an independent cause of action should not be subjugated to the doctrine of exhaustion. Cf. *Hardy* v. *Leonard*, 377 F. Supp. 831 (N.D. Cal. 1974); *Southern Christian Leadership Conference, Inc.* v. *Connolly*, 331 F. Supp. 940 (E.D.Mich. 1971). See also Albert, L. "Standing to Challenge Administrative Action: An Inadequate Surrogate for Claims of Relief," 83 *Yale L.J.* 425, 451–456 (1974). But assuming a meaningful administrative enforcement mechanism, the private cause of action under Section 504 should be limited to a *posteriori* judicial review.

able to plaintiffs and their class, nor has Congress provided other means of enforcement. Furthermore, it should be noted that the *Cannon* opinion is not final, for the panel granted the petition for rehearing in part on November 30, 1976, and now again has the case *sub judice*. There HEW's most recent brief quotes legislative history of Section 504 to show that a private right of action should be inferred (Br. 15–16).

Defendants and the *amicus* Urban Mass Transportation Administrator also rely on *Bradford School Bus Transit, Inc.* v. *Chicago Transit Authority*, 537 F.2d 943, 948 (7th Cir. 1976), in claiming that here plaintiffs must exhaust their administrative remedies before seeking judicial relief. There we applied the primary jurisdiction doctrine because the regulations specifically provided "for judicial review of administrative actions regarding school bus operations after certain procedures have been exhausted." No comparable regulations presently exist with respect to the problem at hand. There being no administrative remedy open to these plaintiffs, neither the exhaustion nor primary jurisdiction doctrine applies. *Rosado* v. *Wyman*, 397 U.S. 397, 405–406, 90 S.Ct. 1207, 25 L.Ed.2d 442.

Upon remand, defendants may of course be able to show that they are in compliance with the statutes on which plaintiffs rely and the regulations thereunder. The affidavit filed in the district court by defendant CTA's general operations manager tends in that direction although it may already be partly obsolete in view of the Transbus developments (41 F.R. 15735, 32286–32287, 45842 (April 14, 1976; August 2, 1976; October 18, 1976)). See also notes 17–18 and accompanying text *supra*. Our opinion expresses no view on the ultimate merits of plaintiffs' case because the undeveloped record does not show whether RTA and CTA are following the statutes and regulations.

In concluding, we cannot fault the district court for its dismissal order. Without the benefit of any regulations, it is difficult to perceive what relief could have been afforded at that stage. However, the Urban Mass Transportation Administrator's regulations were issued before this appeal was briefed and argued and of course apply to our deliberations. *Thorpe* v. *Housing Authority*, 393 U.S. 268, 281–282, 89 S.Ct. 518, 21 L.Ed.2d 474; *United States* v. *Fitzgerald*, 545 F.2d 578, 581 (7th Cir. 1976). Since the plaintiffs may now be able to show that they are entitled to remedial action, the case must be returned to the district court for appropriate further proceedings. If effective by then, consideration will also have to be given to HEW's proposed regulations.

Vacated and remanded.

NOTE

Judge Cummings' excellent analysis of Section 504 has been accepted by every court to subsequently consider its applicability to transportation systems, as the cases that follow demonstrate. His reasoning has also been applied to many other areas touched by Section 504 as well. See, for example, *Davis* v. *Southeastern Community College*, 574 F.2d 1158 (4th Cir. 1978) (education); *Kampmeier* v. *Nyquist*, 553 F.2d 296 (2d Cir. 1977) (recreation); *Whitaker* v. *Board of Higher Education of City of New York*, 461 F.Supp. 99 (E.D.N.Y. 1978) (employment).

UNITED HANDICAPPED FEDERATION V. ANDRE

United States Court of Appeals for the Eighth Circuit, 1977
558 F.2d 413

LAY, Circuit Judge.

This is a civil action brought by the United Handicapped Federation, the National Paraplegia Foundation, and six mobility handicapped individuals against officials of the Metropolitan Transit Commission (MTC), the Secretary of the United States Department of Transportation, the Administrator of the Urban Mass Transportation Administration (UMTA), and the AM General Corporation. The complaint alleges that the defendants failed to make urban mass transit equipment purchased with federal financial aid fully accessible to all handicapped persons. Plaintiffs allege that the defendants have violated the Fourteenth Amendment to the United States Constitution, § 504 of the Rehabilitation Act of 1973, § 16(a) of the Urban Mass Transportation Act of 1964 as amended, §§ 105(a) and (b) of the Federal-Aid Highway Amendments of 1974, § 315 of the Department of Transportation and Related Agencies Appropriations Act of 1975, Minn.Stat.Ann. Ch. 256C, and 42 U.S.C. §§ 1983 and 1985(3).

Plaintiffs originally sought preliminary injunctive relief to restrain MTC and UMTA from the purchase of 338 standard size buses which were to be used in a seven-county metropolitan area and which were not equipped to transport passengers confined to wheelchairs. The district court denied a preliminary injunction and the buses were subsequently delivered and payment made. The plaintiffs continued to seek declaratory and other injunctive relief.

On March 11, 1976, the district court, the Honorable Donald D. Alsop, granted defendants' motion for summary judgment, ruling that none of the statutes relied on by plaintiffs required that every standard size bus purchased with federal assistance be specially equipped to transport passengers confined to wheel chairs. He further held that defendants had made "special efforts" to aid the elderly and handicapped in utilization of the mass transportation system. Finding no violations of the statutes or of the Constitution, the district court stated:

> UMTA has, in accordance with the mandate of Congress pursuant to the Urban Mass Transportation (UMT) Act of 1964, as amended, 49 U.S.C. § 1601 *et seq.*, carried on extensive research, planning, and design of mass transportation services and facilities to provide for effective utilization of mass transportation by the elderly and physically handicapped. Included in these efforts are the ongoing research and development of facilities and services, approval of grants for the purchase of vans and small buses equipped to meet the needs of the elderly and handicapped, development of the "TRANSBUS," publication of Notice of Rulemaking, and a requirement in grant approvals that the elderly and handicapped be charged reduced rates during non-peak hours. *United Handicapped Federation* v. *Andre,* 409 F.Supp. 1297, 1299 (D.Minn. 1976).

Although Judge Alsop found that defendants were in full compliance with the "special efforts" requirements under the laws, we note that his decision was rendered prior to the issuance of UMTA regulations, in part under the authority of § 5(.

Judge Alsop's opinion does not discuss whether the plaintiffs have any standing to bring a private claim for relief or whether any of the statutes place affirmative duties on the defendants. We assume the district court felt it did not have to pass on these issues since, in any event, it found that defendants had complied with the statutes.

In *Lloyd v. Illinois Regional Transp. Authority,* No. 75-C-1834 (N.D.Ill., filed Mar. 16, 1976), rev'd, 548 F.2d 1277 (7th Cir., 1977), the district court granted defendant's motion for summary judgment under a complaint similar to the one filed here. The Seventh Circuit reversed finding that § 504 did place affirmative duties on the mass public transportation systems in that region, and that plaintiffs (who were defined as a class of mobility disabled persons in the northeastern region of Illinois) had standing to seek declaratory and injunctive relief under § 504 and regulations. See *Lloyd v. Regional Transp. Authority,* 548 F.2d 1277 (7th Cir., 1977).

Although the postures at the time of appeal of the *Lloyd* case and the present one appear different (in *Lloyd* the district court dismissed the complaint for failure to state a claim for relief; here the district court granted summary judgment on the merits), they are parallel in that all plaintiffs are denied relief. In one sense, the district court's action here is more final than in *Lloyd* since no further relief can be forthcoming. After reviewing the Seventh Circuit's reversal in the *Lloyd* case we find we must remand to the district court for reconsideration of defendants' duties under the statutes and administrative regulations and guidelines.

We adhere to the reasoning of Judge Cummings in his excellent analysis in the *Lloyd* appeal, and find that § 504 does create an affirmative duty on the part of these defendants. We also agree that plaintiffs do have standing to bring a private cause of action.

Subsequent to the district court's decision, regulations and accompanying guidelines were promulgated and became effective May 31, 1976. See 49 C.F.R. 609.1–609.25 and 613.204. One regulation provides that the UMTA administrator will grant project approvals only if:

> (a) The urban transportation planning process exhibits satisfactory *special efforts* in planning public mass transportation facilities and services that can be utilized by elderly and handicapped persons; and
> (b) The annual element of the transportation improvement program developed pursuant to 23 CFR 450.118 and submitted after September 30, 1976, contains projects or project elements designed to benefit elderly and handicapped persons, *specifically including wheelchair users and those with semi-ambulatory capabilities;* and
> (c) After September 30, 1977, *reasonable progress* has been demonstrated in implementing previously programmed projects. 49 C.F.R. § 613.204 [emphasis added].

Guidance on the meaning of special efforts in planning is set forth in 23 C.F.R. Part 450, Subpart A, issued simultaneously with the above regulations:

> The urban transportation planning process must include *special efforts* to plan public mass transportation facilities and service that can effectively be utilized by elderly and handicapped persons. As used in this guidance, the term "special efforts" refers both to service for elderly and handicapped persons in general and specifically to service for wheelchair users and semiambulatory persons. *With regard to transportation for wheelchair users and others who cannot negotiate steps, "special efforts" in planning means genuine, good-faith progress in planning service for wheelchair users and semiambulatory handicapped persons that is reasonable by comparison with the service provided to the general public and that meets a significant fraction of the actual transportation needs of such persons within a reasonable time period.* [Emphasis added].

Examples of what affirmative duties will satisfy "special efforts" requirements are given in 49 C.F.R. Part 613, Subpart B. In addition to these positive examples, proposed regulations of the Health, Education, and Welfare Department indicate what recipients of federal assistance may not do. See 45 C.F.R. § 84.4.

On the basis of the record before the district court, if it were not for the subsequent promulgation of the administrative guidelines and regulations, we would agree with the district court's result. However, we feel that the denial of relief to the plaintiffs cannot be justified in light of these recent definitions and guidelines. Although the buses in question here have been purchased and placed in service, because of the recent developments the defendants now have the burden to take affirmative action to conform to the regulations and guidelines. It is difficult to assess the record and the statutes in any other light.

Under the circumstances we vacate the grant of summary judgment and remand to the district court for further proceedings. The district court, upon receiving further evidence, should reappraise defendants' compliance with the statutes, regulations and guidelines, and fashion whatever equitable relief it deems necessary.

LEARY v. CRAPSEY

United States Court of Appeals for the Second Circuit, 1977
556 F.2d 863

PER CURIAM:

The eight individual plaintiffs in this class action each suffer from severe physical handicaps; seven are confined to wheelchairs and the other must use crutches. All plaintiffs appeal from a decision of the United States District Court for the Western District of New York granting summary judgment to defendants, various federal and local officials who are responsible for, or administer, mass transportation programs in the area of Rochester, New York. The complaint was filed in July 1976 and alleged that defendants' failure to provide plaintiffs an accessible bus transportation system violated the Urban Mass Transportation Act of 1964, as amended, 49 U.S.C. § 1601 *et seq.*, and section 504 of the Rehabilitation Act of 1973, 29 U.S.C. § 794, and various constitutional rights of plaintiffs. The complaint sought equitable and declaratory relief and damages.

The district judge, after enjoining discovery, granted summary judgment to defendants in March 1977, and dismissed the action. The judge's brief opinion held in conclusory fashion that defendants had not violated any federal statutory or constitutional provisions and that the action was barred by the doctrines of laches, primary jurisdiction and failure to exhaust administrative remedies. This appeal followed.

In the district court, defendants took the position that section 504 of the Rehabilitation Act did not create a private cause of action, a view which the district court apparently accepted *sub silentio*. In this court, however, defendants concede that mobility-handicapped persons, who are denied the use of a public transportation system, do have a private cause of action under section 504. The concession is well warranted. See *Lloyd* v. *Regional Transportation Authority*, 548 F.2d 1277 (7th Cir. 1977); *United Handicapped Federation* v. *Andre*, 558 F.2d 413 (8th Cir. 1977);

Vanko v. *Finley*, No. C76-1305, 440 F.Supp. 656 (N.D.Ohio 1977); see also *Kampmeier* v. *Nyquist*, 553 F.2d 296, 299 (2d Cir. 1977). Defendants do not, however, concede that the facts in this case warrant the conclusion that defendants have violated plaintiffs' rights. Indeed, defendants overwhelm us with a wealth of information regarding the bus transportation system in Rochester, the relevant applications by the local defendants for federal funding and the details of subsequent administrative proceedings thereon, the applicable statutes and regulations, the state of technology regarding the manufacture of buses designed to aid the mobility-handicapped, and the efforts of the local and federal defendants to meet various federal requirements, none of which was discussed in the summary disposition of the trial court. We are also told that two of the applications that plaintiffs attack are somewhere in the administrative process of the UMTA. However, the district court opinion fails to inform us what has delayed action upon these applications and whether the specific aid applied for is consistent with the newest regulations promulgated by the UMTA. Appellees stress that these regulations were brought to the attention of the district court, but we cannot tell whether the judge considered them—nowhere does the opinion analyze the "special efforts" of the local defendants in planning for the needs of the handicapped, which these regulations require.

In light of the above and since the two pending applications are part of the overall planning of the transportation system complained of, we think it appropriate to remand this case for a detailed examination of the local defendants' special efforts, taking into consideration the new regulations and the development of Transbus. See *United Handicapped Federation* v. *Andre*, 558 F.2d 413 (8th Cir. 1977) (remand for failure to consider new regulations). Additionally, the district court may retain jurisdiction of this case pending final UMTA action on the applications still before it, cf. *Bartels* v. *Biernat*, 427 F.Supp. 226, 233 (E.D.Wis. 1977), and if this action is found to be unduly delayed, the district court may compel agency action under the Administrative Procedure Act, 5 U.S.C. § 706(1). Furthermore, we hope that close supervision of this action by the district court may bring about a plan which effectively deals with the needs of the handicapped in Rochester and is acceptable to all sides.

The judgment of the court below is reversed and the case remanded to the district court for further proceedings.

c. Regulations under § 504

45 CFR §§ 84.21–84.23

42 Fed.Reg. 22681 (May 4, 1977)

Subpart C—Program Accessibility

§ 84.21 Discrimination prohibited.

No qualified handicapped person shall, because a recipient's facilities are inaccessible to or unusable by handicapped persons, be denied the benefits of, be excluded from participation in, or otherwise be subjected to discrimination under any program or activity to which this part applies.

§ 84.22   Existing facilities.

(a)   *Program accessibility.* A recipient shall operate each program or activity to which this part applies so that the program or activity, when viewed in its entirety, is readily accessible to handicapped persons. This paragraph does not require a recipient to make each of its existing facilities or every part of a facility accessible to and usable by handicapped persons.

(b)   *Methods.* A recipient may comply with the requirement of paragraph (a) of this section through such means as redesign of equipment, reassignment of classes or other services to accessible buildings, assignment of aides to beneficiaries, home visits, delivery of health, welfare, or other social services at alternate accessible sites, alteration of existing facilities and construction of new facilities in conformance with the requirements of § 84.23, or any other methods that result in making its program or activity accessible to handicapped persons. A recipient is not required to make structural changes in existing facilities where other methods are effective in achieving compliance with paragraph (a) of this section. In choosing among available methods for meeting the requirement of paragraph (a) of this section, a recipient shall give priority to those methods that offer programs and activities to handicapped persons in the most integrated setting appropriate.

(c)   *Small health, welfare, or other social service providers.* If a recipient with fewer than fifteen employees that provides health, welfare, or other social services finds, after consultation with a handicapped person seeking its services, that there is no method of complying with paragraph (a) of this section other than making a significant alteration in its existing facilities, the recipient may as an alternative, refer the handicapped person to other providers of those services that are accessible.

(d)   *Time period.* A recipient shall comply with the requirement of paragraph (a) of this section within sixty days of the effective date of this part except that where structural changes in facilities are necessary, such changes shall be made within three years of the effective date of this part, but in any event as expeditiously as possible.

(e)   *Transition plan.* In the event that structural changes to facilities are necessary to meet the requirement of paragraph (a) of this section, a recipient shall develop, within six months of the effective date of this part, a transition plan setting forth the steps necessary to complete such changes. The plan shall be developed with the assistance of interested persons, including handicapped persons or organizations representing handicapped persons. A copy of the transition plan shall be made available for public inspection. The plan shall, at a minimum:

(1)   Identify physical obstacles in the recipient's facilities that limit the accessibility of its program or activity to handicapped persons;

(2)   Describe in detail the methods that will be used to make the facilities accessible;

(3)   Specify the schedule for taking the steps necessary to achieve full program accessibility and, if the time period of the transition plan is longer than one year, identify steps that will be taken during each year of the transition period; and

(4)   Indicate the person responsible for implementation of the plan.

(f)   *Notice.* The recipient shall adopt and implement procedures to ensure that interested persons, including persons with impaired vision or hearing, can obtain information as to the existence and location of services, activities, and facilities that are accessible to and usable by handicapped persons.

§ 84.23   New construction.

(a) *Design and construction*. Each facility or part of a facility constructed by, on behalf of, or for the use of a recipient shall be designed and constructed in such manner that the facility or part of the facility is readily accessible to and usable by handicapped persons, if the construction was commenced after the effective date of this part.

(b) *Alteration*. Each facility or part of a facility which is altered by, on behalf of, or for the use of a recipient after the effective date of this part in a manner that affects or could affect the usability of the facility or part of the facility shall, to the maximum extent feasible, be altered in such manner that the altered portion of the facility is readily accessible to and usable by handicapped persons.

(c) *American National Standards Institute accessibility standards*. Design, construction, or alteration of facilities in conformance with the "American National Standard Specifications for Making Buildings and Facilities Accessible to, and Usable by, the Physically Handicapped," published by the American National Standards Institute, Inc. (ANSI A117.1-1961 (R1971)), which is incorporated by reference in this part, shall constitute compliance with paragraphs (a) and (b) of this section. Departures from particular requirements of those standards by the use of other methods shall be permitted when it is clearly evident that equivalent access to the facility or part of the facility is thereby provided.

NOTE

Pursuant to Executive Order 11914, the U.S. Department of Health, Education, and Welfare is responsible for coordinating regulations promulgated under § 504 by other federal agencies. In the regulations promulgated by DHEW to implement the Executive Order, the standards reprinted below on program accessibility were directed to other agencies for use in developing their § 504 regulations.

45 CFR § 85.56–85.58

43 Fed.Reg., 2132 (Jan. 13, 1978)

Program Accessibility

§ 85.56   General requirement concerning program accessibility.

No qualified handicapped person shall, because a recipient's facilities are inaccessible to or unusable by handicapped persons, be denied the benefits of, be excluded from participation in, or otherwise be subjected to discrimination under any program or activity that receives or benefits from federal financial assistance.

§ 85.57   Existing facilities.

(a)   A recipient shall operate each program or activity so that the program or activity, when viewed in its entirety, is readily accessible to and usable by handicapped persons. This paragraph does not necessarily require a recipient to make each of its existing facilities or every part of an existing facility accessible to and usable by handicapped persons.

(b) Where structural changes are necessary to make programs or activities in existing facilities accessible, such changes shall be made as soon as practicable, but in no event later than three years after the effective date of the agency regulation: *Provided,* That, if the program is a particular mode of transportation (e.g., a subway system) that can be made accessible only through extraordinarily expensive structural changes to, or replacement of, existing facilities and if other accessible modes of transportation are available, the federal agency responsible for enforcing section 504 with respect to that program may extend this period of time, but only for a reasonable and definite period, such period to be set forth in the agency's regulation.

(c) In the event that structural changes to facilities are necessary to meet the requirement of paragraph (a) of this section, a recipient shall develop, within a definite period to be established in each agency's regulation, a transition plan setting forth the steps necessary to complete such changes. The plan shall be developed with the assistance of interested persons, including handicapped persons or organizations representing handicapped persons.

§ 85.58   New construction.

(a) Except as provided in paragraph (b) of this section, new facilities shall be designed and constructed to be readily accessible to and usable by handicapped persons. Alterations to existing facilities shall, to the maximum extent feasible, be designed and constructed to be readily accessible to and usable by handicapped persons.

(b) The Department of Transportation may defer the effective date for requiring all new buses to be accessible if it concludes on the basis of its section 504 rulemaking process that it is not feasible to require compliance on the effective date of its regulation: *Provided,* That comparable, accessible services are available to handicapped persons in the interim and that the date is not deferred later than October 1, 1979.

2.   UMTA

THE URBAN MASS TRANSPORTATION ACT OF 1964, SECTION 16(A) AS AMENDED BY THE URBAN MASS TRANSPORTATION ASSISTANCE ACT OF 1970

49 U.S.C. 1612

Congressional Declaration of Policy

(a) It is hereby declared to be the national policy that elderly and handicapped persons have the same right as other persons to utilize mass transportation facilities and services; that special efforts shall be made in the planning and design of mass transportation facilities and services so that the availability to elderly and handicapped persons of mass transportation which they can effectively utilize will be assured; and that all Federal programs offering assistance in the field of mass transportation (including the programs under this chapter) should contain provisions implementing this policy.

NOTE

Despite the seemingly clear and unequivocal language of this passage, the judiciary has not considered Section 16(a) of the Urban Mass Transportation Act, as amended, as determinative of the accessibility issue.

Its most controversial element is the "special efforts" requirement. The vagueness of this term, coupled with the lack of specific enforcement mechanism, has generated a greal deal of confusion among the courts that have attempted to apply it to specific fact situations. In *Snowden* v. *Birmingham-Jefferson County Transit Authority,* 407 F.Supp. 394 (N.D.Ala. 1975), aff'd. mem. 551 F.2d 862 (5th Cir. 1977), above at pp. 478–482, for example, the defendants were deemed to have met the special efforts requirement through the installation of "features such as stanchions, grab-rails, step-well lighting, power-assisted doors, etc., to aid handicapped persons other than those confined to wheelchairs in boarding and alighting from its buses" (*Id.* at 397).

The primary limitation on early court implementation of Section 16(a) appears to have been technological problems in the development of accessible vehicles. ". . . [N]o bus manufacturer in the United States presently produces a standard-size transit bus that is totally accessible to passengers confined to wheelchairs and which could transport them with safety for themselves and all other passengers" (*United Handicapped Federation* v. *Andre,* 409 F.Supp. 1297, 1300 (D.Minn. 1976), rev'd. 558 F.2d 413 (8th Cir. 1977), above at pp. 491–493.

Furthermore, early regulations promulgated by the Urban Mass Transportation Administration did not require full accessibility. They merely restated the "special efforts" requirement for those programs receiving federal funds. 49 C.F.R. 613.204 (1976).

In 1977, new hopes were raised that Section 16(a) could be used to require full and immediate accessibility after the Secretary of Transportation's decision that all new buses purchased with UMTA funds after September, 1979, must meet accessibility standards. (See pp. 509–514, below, dealing with Transbus.) Judicial reluctance to rely solely on Section 16(a) still exists, however. As the case below indicates, this section remains most effective when used in conjunction with Section 504 of the Rehabilitation Act of 1973, as amended.

MICHIGAN PARALYZED VETERANS v. COLEMAN

United States District Court for the Eastern District of Michigan, Southern Division,
1977
451 F.Supp. 7

KEITH, Chief Judge.

The federal defendants have moved, in a motion joined in by the state and municipal defendants, to dismiss the action pursuant to Rule 12(b)(6) of the Federal Rules of Civil Procedure for failure to state a claim upon which relief can be granted, or, in the alternative, for summary judgment pursuant to Rule 56 on the ground that there is no genuine issue as to any material fact and they are entitled to judgment as a matter of law. Briefs, supplemental briefs, affidavits and exhibits were filed in support of and in opposition to this motion. The matter came on for a hearing on October 26, 1976. At the conclusion of the hearing, the Court announced it would deny the motion to dismiss, and take under advisement the motion for summary judgment. Additional information regarding the issues raised by this action and the motion under consideration were brought to the Court's attention by each party after the hearing had been held and while the summary judgment motion was under advisement. The Court received a supplemental memorandum from the plaintiffs on April 19, 1977, and copies of the amendments to the Urban Mass Transportation Administration regulations from the federal defendants on September 27, 1977. The Court is now fully advised in the premises.

This action was brought by and on behalf of elderly and handicapped persons seeking injunctive and declaratory relief to prevent the Southeastern Michigan Transportation Authority (SEMTA) from planning, approving, issuing money for, contracting for, or fulfilling existing contracts for, the purchase of any diesel transit buses, other public transportation vehicles or related facilities which are inaccessible to mobility handicapped persons where said purchases are to be funded in whole or in part by the United States Department of Transportation, unless and until the defendants comply with those federal and state laws and agency regulations designed to protect the rights of the mobility handicapped to public transportation facilities. Complaint at 1-2. On June 19, 1975, the Court denied plaintiffs' request for a temporary restraining order to halt SEMTA's procurement of buses with funds derived from Urban Mass Transportation Capital Improvement Grant No. MI-03-0030. The defendants subsequently filed their motion to dismiss or for summary judgment.

The Complaint alleges seven causes of action. Plaintiffs assert that the defendants have violated: 1) section 16(a) of the Urban Mass Transportation Act, 84 Stat. 962, 49 U.S.C. § 1612(a) (1970); 2) section 504 of the Rehabilitation Act of 1973, 29 U.S.C. § 794; 3) Public Law 90-480, 42 U.S.C. §§ 4151 et seq.; 4) the Federal Aid Highway Amendments of 1974, 88 Stat. 2283, Public Law 93-643; 5) the Department of Transportation and Related Agencies Appropriations Act of 1975, 88 Stat. 768, Public Law 93-391; 6) Act 327 of Michigan Public Acts of 1972, M.S.A. § 9.1097(10c), M.C.L.A. § 247.660b; and 7) the due process and equal protection clauses of the United States and Michigan Constitutions. In Lloyd v. Regional Transportation Authority, 548 F.2d 1277 (7th Cir. 1977), a case decided subsequent to the hearing on defendants' motion to dismiss or for summary judgment, the Court held that section 504 of the Rehabilitation Act of 1973 does confer upon private parties a cause of action to compel compliance by government authorities with the Urban Mass Transportation Act and the regulations promulgated thereunder, 548 F.2d at 1284-1287, and that doctrines of primary jurisdiction and prior administrative agency review do not bar consideration of such claims by a federal district court. 548 F.2d at 1287. See Lau v. Nichols, 414 U.S. 563, 94 S.Ct. 786, 39 L.Ed.2d 1 (1974) (opinion construing section 601 of the Civil Rights Act of 1964, an analogous predecessor statute to section 504 of the Rehabilitation Act of 1973, as providing a private cause of action); Cort v. Ash, 422 U.S. 66, 95 S.Ct. 2080, 45 L.Ed.2d 26 (1975) (opinion setting out the four factors relevant to a determination of whether a private remedy is implicit in a statute which does not specifically provide for one). Thus, defendants' motion to dismiss this action was properly denied by this Court.[1]

In support of their alternative motion for summary judgment the defendants contend that neither section 16(a) of the UMT Act nor section 504 of the Rehabilitation Act of 1973 require every transit bus purchased by a local transit authority in whole or in part with federal funds to be fully accessible to the mobility handicapped. Instead, they assert, these acts only require them to make "special efforts" to assure the effective utilization by the elderly and the handicapped to mass transportation facilities (section 16(a)), and that no otherwise qualified handicapped individual be denied, solely because of his handicap, the benefits of, or be subjected to discrimination under, any program or activity receiving federal assistance (section 504). The plaintiffs respond by asserting that buses which are accessible to the mobility handicapped (called Transbus) do exist, and are available for purchase by SEMTA with UMTA funds. Pls'. Exhibit B attached to their Reply to Defs'. Supp.Memo. They assert that SEMTA's failure to purchase such buses is a failure to make the special efforts required by section 16(a), and the plaintiffs are therefore being discriminated against in federally funded public transportation programs in violation of section 504.

In *United Handicapped Federation* v. *Andre,* 409 F.Supp. 1297 (D.Minn. 1976), vacated and remanded, 558 F.2d 413 (8th Cr. 1977), and *Snowden* v. *Birmingham-Jefferson County Transit Authority,* 407 F.Supp. 394 (N.D.Ala. 1975), affirmed, 551 F.2d 862 (5th Cir. 1977), cases relied upon the federal defendants in their supplemental brief, the district courts found that the state of the art in transit bus technology was such that the defendants therein could not be required to purchase buses which were completely accessible to mobility handicapped persons. In *Andre* the court noted:

> It would seem unreasonable to interpret the statute [section 16(a)] as requiring total accessibility since no bus manufacturer in the United States presently manufactures a standard-size transit bus especially equipped to transport, with safety, those confined to wheelchairs.

409 F.Supp. at 1300. And in *Snowden*, the court stated:

> Special efforts have been made by BJCTA by the installation of special equipment and features such as stanchions, grab-rails, step-well lighting, power-assisted doors, etc., to aid handicapped persons other than those confined to wheelchairs in boarding and alighting from its buses. Modern technology has not progressed to the point of doing any more for those persons confined to a wheelchair than is already being done by BJCTA. In view of the present state of available bus technology, as above described, it would seem inherently unreasonable to bring all new bus procurement to a halt while new equipment is being designed, developed, tested and produced. Such a course of action would harm the general public without in any way aiding plaintiff and the class she represents.

---

[1]In holding that this action should not be dismissed for failure to state a claim upon which relief can be granted, the Court finds that the action is properly brought pursuant to section 16(a) of the Urban Mass Transportation Act, 49 U.S.C. §§ 1612(a), 49 U.S.C.A. § 1612(a) (1976), and section 504 of the Rehabilitation Act of 1973, 29 U.S.C. § 794, 29 U.S.C.A. § 794 (1975). [Remainder of footnote omitted.]

407 F.Supp. at 397. But since these cases were decided, at least one municipal transportation authority, the Southern California Rapid Transit District, did receive bids from three bus manufacturers in the United States for buses which had wheelchair accessible options. Pls'. Exhibit B attached to their Reply to Defs'. Supp.Memo. Also, on May 19, 1977, Secretary of Transportation Brock Adams announced at a press conference on Transbus that the Department of Transportation was going to require all new buses purchased with DOT grants to be designed for easy access by elderly and handicapped persons. He acknowledged that there was some opposition to the Transbus concept on the ground that it was not within the capacity of the industry to produce a low-floor, ramped bus which could operate safely and efficiently in day-to-day transit service. *Statement* of Secretary Adams, Press Conference on Transbus, May 19, 1977, at 2. But he supported the Transbus idea:

> A review of the record convinces me that, at a minimum the three major domestic bus manufacturers could begin Transbus deliveries within 3½ years. This date allows almost 2½ years for development before bidding would begin, and approximately 15 months thereafter before the buses are actually delivered.

Ibid. at 2. See 123 Cong.Rec. S-10556-S-10567 (June 23, 1977). Thus, the technology which did not exist when *Andre, supra,* and *Snowden, supra,* were decided in the district courts now exists. The question remains whether the defendants are required by the Urban Mass Transportation Act or the regulations promulgated thereunder to order such buses immediately.

In addition, the Urban Mass Transportation Administration has amended its regulations regarding the transportation of elderly and handicapped persons to conform to the aforementioned decision of the Secretary of Transportation. These amendments provide that as of September 9, 1977, the effective date of the amendments, all procurement solicitations made on or before September 30, 1979, by UMTA grantees for new, standard, full-size buses must provide for a bus design which permits the addition of a wheelchair accessible option for each bus, and the bidder must provide assurances that it offers wheelchair accessibility options for its buses. All procurement solicitations by UMTA grantees containing UMTA approved specifications issued after September 30, 1979, for new standard, full-size urban transit buses must utilize the Transbus Procurement Requirements of UMTA's bid package.

It remains for the Court to consider the effect of these amendments to 49 CFR § 609.15 (1976) on this action. The Court must review the sufficiency of these regulations in light of section 16 of the Urban Mass Transportation Act, taking into account the discretion conferred by this Act upon the Secretary of Transportation to implement the Congressional policy. Should these regulations be sustained as being neither arbitrary, capricious, or an abuse of discretion, the question is presented whether SEMTA is in fact soliciting bids on buses which do permit the addition of the wheelchair accessibility option.

For the foregoing reasons, the Court is of the opinion that defendants' motion for summary judgment is premature and must be denied without prejudice.

The Court will allow the plaintiffs to amend their complaint to add or delete causes of action in conformity with this opinion and in light of developments in the law since this motion was argued.

IT IS SO ORDERED.

NOTE

In *Atlantis Community, Inc.* v. *Adams,* 453 F.Supp. 825 (D.Col. 1978), the plaintiffs sought to enjoin delivery of mass transit buses that were not equipped with accessibility features, specifically wheelchair lifts. While the court recognized that Section 16(a) of the Urban Mass Transportation Act of 1964 and Section 504 of the Rehabilitation Act of 1973 place affirmative action requirements upon recipients of federal funds to provide accessible transportation systems for handicapped and elderly citizens, it refused to grant relief. Citing enormous difficulties inherent in forming and implementing effective judicial remedies to the problems of mass transportation, Judge Matsch found that the above-cited federal statutes did not give sufficient definition of the affirmative requirements imposed to enable the court to fashion relief.

> A far more appropriate and effective method for achieving the proclaimed objective of providing transportation opportunities for the handicapped would be for the Congress to maintain an oversight of administrative action and to provide such direction as may be needed (*Id.* at 831).

3. Architectural Barriers Act

ARCHITECTURAL BARRIERS ACT OF 1968, AS AMENDED

42 U.S.C. §§ 4151-4157

§ 4151. Definitions

As used in this chapter, the term "building" means any building or facility (other than (A) a privately owned residential structure not leased by the Government for subsidized housing programs and (B) any building or facility on a military installation designed and constructed primarily for use by able bodied military personnel) the intended use for which either will require that such building or facility be accessible to the public, or may result in the employment or residence therein of physically handicapped persons, which building or facility is—

(1) to be constructed or altered by or on behalf of the United States;

(2) to be leased in whole or in part by the United States after August 12, 1968;

(3) to be financed in whole or in part by a grant or a loan made by the United States after August 12, 1968, if such building or facility is subject to standards for design, construction, or alteration issued under authority of the law authorizing such grant or loan; or

(4) to be constructed under authority of the National Capital Transportation Act of 1960, the National Capital Transportation Act of 1965, or title III of the Washington Metropolitan Area Transit Regulation Compact.

§ 4152. Standards for design, construction, and alteration of buildings; Secretary of Health, Education, and Welfare

The Administrator of General Services, in consultation with the Secretary of Health, Education, and Welfare, shall prescribe standards for the design, construction,

nd alteration of buildings (other than residential structures subject to this chapter and
uildings, structures, and facilities of the Department of Defense and of the United
States Postal Service subject to this chapter) to insure whenever possible that physically
andicapped persons will have ready access to, and use of, such buildings.

§ 4153.   Standards for design, construction, and alteration of buildings; Sec-
etary of Housing and Urban Development

The Secretary of Housing and Urban Development, in consultation with the
Secretary of Health, Education, and Welfare, shall prescribe standards for the design,
construction, and alteration of buildings which are residential structures subject to this
chapter to insure whenever possible that physically handicapped persons will have
eady access to, and use of, such buildings.

§ 4154.   Standards for design, construction, and alteration of buildings; Sec-
etary of Defense

The Secretary of Defense, in consultation with the Secretary of Health, Educa-
ion, and Welfare, shall prescribe standards for the design, construction, and alteration
of buildings, structures, and facilities of the Department of Defense subject to this
chapter to insure whenever possible that physically handicapped persons will have
eady access to, and use of, such buildings.

§ 4154a.   Standards for design, construction and alteration of buildings;
United States Postal Service

The United States Postal Service, in consultation with the Secretary of Health,
Education, and Welfare, shall prescribe such standards for the design, construction,
and alteration of its buildings to insure whenever possible that physically handicapped
persons will have ready access to, and use of, such buildings.

§ 4155.   Effective date of standards

Every building designed, constructed, or altered after the effective date of a
standard issued under this chapter which is applicable to such building, shall be
designed, constructed, or altered in accordance with such standard.

§4156.   Waiver and modification of standards

The Administrator of General Services, with respect to standards issued under
section 4152 of this title, and the United States Postal Service with respect to standards
issued under section 4154a of this title, and the Secretary of Housing and Urban
Development, with respect to standards issued under section 4153 of this title, and the
Secretary of Defense with respect to standards issued under section 4154 of this title,—

(1)   is authorized to modify or waive any such standard, on a case-by-case
basis, upon application made by the head of the department, agency, or instrumentality
of the United States concerned, and upon a determination by the Administrator or
Secretary, as the case may be, that such modification or waiver is clearly necessary,
and

(2)   shall establish a system of continuing surveys and investigations to insure
compliance with such standards.

§ 4157.   Reports to Congress and congressional committees

(a)   The Administrator of General Services shall report to Congress during the
first week of January of each year on his activities and those of other departments,

agencies, and instrumentalities of the Federal Government under this chapter during the preceding fiscal year including, but not limited to, standards issued, revised, amended, or repealed under this chapter and all case-by-case modifications, and waivers of such standards during such year.

(b)　The Architectural and Transportation Barriers Compliance Board established by section 792 of Title 29 shall report to the Public Works and Transportation Committee of the House of Representatives and the Public Works Committee of the Senate during the first week of January of each year on its activities and actions to insure compliance with the standards prescribed under this chapter.

NOTES

1.　What are the strengths of the act? Its weaknesses?

2.　The Architectural and Transportation Barriers Compliance Board, mentioned in § 4157(b), is described below at p. 514.

3.　For regulations under the Architectural Barriers Act, see 41 C.F.R. §§ 101-19.6 *et seq.*

WASHINGTON URBAN LEAGUE, INC. v. WASHINGTON METROPOLITAN AREA TRANSIT
AUTHORITY, INC.

United States District Court for the District of Columbia, 1973
Civil Action No. 776-72, Order of June 29, 1973

JONES, Judge

This matter came on to be heard on plaintiffs' motion for summary judgment and defendant's cross-motion for summary judgment, and the Court having considered the memoranda in support of and in opposition to the respective motions, and having heard argument of counsel, it is this 29th day of June, 1973,

ORDERED

That partial summary judgment be entered in favor of the plaintiffs to the extent that this Court declares that the Act of Congress of August 12, 1968, as amended by the Act of Congress of March 5, 1970 (42 U.S.C. § 4151), and the regulations adopted pursuant thereto by the General Services Administration (41 C.F.R. §§ 101-17.7, *et seq.*) be and the same are applicable to the construction of subway stations and facilities related thereto by defendant;

FURTHER ORDERED that this Court retains jurisdiction over this action and that on October 8, 1973, the parties through their counsel shall appear before this Court at 2 P.M. and counsel for defendant at that time shall advise the Court of the progress of the construction of the subway stations and related facilities and the installation and construction of elevators and all other things required by the regulations adopted by the General Services Administration as set forth in 41 C.F.R. §§ 101-17.9 *et seq.*; and

FURTHER ORDERED that this Court defers taking any action with respect to the injunctive relief sought by plaintiffs in this action until on or after October 8, 1973.

WASHINGTON URBAN LEAGUE, INC. v. WASHINGTON METROPOLITAN AREA TRANSIT
AUTHORITY, INC.

United States District Court for the District of Columbia, 1973
Civil Action No. 776-72, Order of Final Judgment, October 23, 1973
JONES, Judge.

This matter came on to be heard for final judgment pursuant to this Court's
order of June 29, 1973, granting partial summary judgment to plaintiffs, deferring
action on requested injunctive relief, and retaining jurisdiction over this action. Upon
consideration of the pleadings; the cross-motions for summary judgment; the briefs,
affidavits and exhibits submitted in support of and in opposition thereto; and the
appearance by counsel for the parties before this Court on October 9, 1973, it appearing that there is no genuine issue of material fact, full summary judgment including the
partial summary judgment granted in the aforementioned order of June 29, 1973, is
granted to plaintiffs as the final order on all issues in this action, and it is this 23rd day
of October, 1973,

ORDERED that defendant is enjoined from commercially operating any station of
the Metro railway transportation system until defendant installs and makes operational
all those facilities, including elevators, as may be necessary to ensure that physically
handicapped persons will have ready access to, and use of, such Metro railway system
station, in compliance with 42 U.S.C. 4151 and 41 C.F.R. 101-17.7.

NOTES

1. Some of the factual situation from which the *Metro* case arose is described in
Achtenberg, J., "Law and the Physically Disabled: An Update with Constitutional
Implications," 8 *S.W.U.L. Rev.* 847, 860–861 (1976):

> In the District of Columbia an action was commenced by *pro bono* private
> attorneys to require the newly formed Washington Metropolitan Area Transit Authority
> (W.M.T.A.) to adhere to the Federal Architectural Barrier Law. Transit facilities, such
> as stations and platforms, last for decades. Nevertheless, these facilities were being built
> without complying with any architectural barrier laws. If the project had been built
> completely without access, the disabled effectively would have been excluded from
> using this public transportation for generations. . . . The defendants argued that the funds
> needed to make the facility accessible had to be provided by Congress, and since
> Congress had not done so, it was impermissible to impose upon a joint federal-state
> compact the added costs of building facilities accessible to all. The Transit District
> contended that Congress' effort to place W.M.T.A. nonrolling stock under the Federal
> Architectural Barrier Law was, therefore, meaningless. The federal district court held
> that W.M.T.A. was specifically cited by name in an amendment to the Federal Architec-
> tural Barrier Law which required the subway to be made accessible. Consequently, the
> court decided that accessibility was not dependent upon special appropriations. Since the
> original federal court decision, however, the judge has been asked to require that
> specific stations be actually accessible before they are opened to the public [and he has
> so ruled]. Thus, the Transit Authority has been unable to place certain parts of the line in
> service before appropriate steps are taken to assure ready access.

For an interesting history of litigation concerning Metro, see Heddinger, R., "The
Twelve Year Battle for a Barrier Free Metro," May/June *American Rehabilitation* 7
(1976).

2. Are the words "ready access" used by Judge Jones sufficiently specific? See, Achtenberg, J., *supra* note 1, at 861, footnote 42.

3. The *Metro* case is an instance of an architectural barriers statute being applied to transportation facilities. The issues of access to buildings and to transportation systems are frequently interrelated. Accessible vehicles lose much of their value if terminals are not accessible or if the traveler is frustrated by stairs, curbs, or other architectural barriers blocking entry to his or her ultimate destination. Accessible buildings, on the other hand, are less useful if there is no accessible transportation to permit handicapped persons to get to these buildings.

The converse of the *Metro* situation, and an odd result, occurred in *Philadelphia Council of Neighborhoods* v. *Coleman,* 437 F.Supp. 1341 (E.D.Pa. 1977), where the plaintiffs sought to stop construction of a commuter train tunnel because it was not accessible. In finding the tunnel itself to meet accessibility standards, the court ruled that neither Section 504 of the Rehabilitation Act nor the Architectural Barriers Act would be applied to the preexisting stations that provided the only means of ingress and egress to the tunnel itself. The fact that the stations at both ends were inaccessible to mobility-impaired persons did not deter the court from ruling that the tunnel had met accessibility requirements.

4. The regulations cited in the *Metro* decision have been recodified at 41 C.F.R. 101-19.6

4. Federal-Aid Highway Act

The Federal-Aid Highway Act of 1973, Section 165(b), as Amended by the Federal-Aid Highway Amendments of 1974.

23 U.S.C. § 142, note

(b) The Secretary of Transportation shall require that projects receiving Federal financial assistance under (1) subsection (a) or (c) of section 142 of title 23, United States Code, (2) paragraph (4) of subsection (e) of section 103, title 23, United States Code, or (3) section 147 of the Federal-Aid Highway Act of 1973 shall be planned, designed, constructed, and operated to allow effective utilization by elderly or handicapped persons who, by reason of illness, injury, age, congenital malfunction, or other permanent or temporary incapacity or disability, including those who are nonambulatory wheelchair-bound and those with semiambulatory capabilities, are unable without special facilities or special planning or design to utilize such facilities and services effectively. The Secretary shall not approve any program or project to which this section applies which does not comply with the provisions of this subsection requiring access to public mass transportation facilities, equipment, and services for elderly or handicapped persons.

NOTE

In contrast to the broad statement of policy contained in Section 16(a) of the Urban Mass Transportation Act as amended, this passage provides a specific directive to the Secretary of Transportation. The Secretary is forbidden from funding any program under the Federal-Aid Highway Act that does not enable "effective utilization" by handicapped persons.

While it appears plain from the language and legislative history of this act that its intent was to provide total accessibility in Federal-Aid Highway Projects, S. Rep. No. 93-1111, 93d Cong. 2d Sess. 7-8 (1974), one court that considered this issue was not willing to give force to this broad mandate, apparently feeling that total accessibility was technologically infeasible. See *United Handicapped Federation* v. *Andre,* 409 F.Supp. 1297, 1300 (D.Minn. 1976), rev'd. 558 F.2d 413 (8th Cir. 1977). pp. 491–493, above.

A second limitation impeding the applicability of this section is that substantially fewer programs are funded under the Federal-Aid Highway Act than under the Urban Mass Transportation Act. Thus, the scope of Section 165(b) is narrowly circumscribed by the necessity of tracing Federal-Aid Highway funds into a project.

THE FEDERAL-AID HIGHWAY ACT OF 1973, AS AMENDED BY THE FEDERAL-AID HIGHWAY AMENDMENTS OF 1974

23 U.S.C. § 402(b)(1)

The Secretary shall not approve any State highway safety program under this section which does not—

* * *

(F)   provide adequate and reasonable access for the safe and convenient movement of physically handicapped persons, including those in wheelchairs, across curbs constructed or replaced on or after July 1, 1976, at all pedestrian crosswalks throughout the State.

NOTE

Like the requirements of Section 165(b), the highway safety programs outlined in Section 402(b)(1) are a federal funding prerequisite. It is the closest thing we have to a federal curb-cut law.

5.   Amtrak

AMTRAK IMPROVEMENT ACT OF 1974, AS AMENDED 1976

45 U.S.C. § 545(c)

The Corporation is authorized to take all steps necessary to insure that no elderly or handicapped individual is denied intercity transportation on any passenger train operated by or on behalf of the Corporation, including but not limited to, acquiring special equipment and devices and conducting special training for employees; designing and acquiring new equipment and facilities and eliminating architectural and other barriers in existing equipment and facilities to comply with the highest standards for the design, construction, and alteration of property for the accommodation of elderly and handicapped individuals; and providing special assistance while boarding and alighting and in terminal areas to elderly and handicapped individuals.

NOTE

Examine closely the language of this provision to determine how strong a mandate it is.

6. Federal Income Tax Deduction

§ 2122(a) of the Tax Reform Act of 1976

26 U.S.C. § 190

Expenditures to remove architectural and transportation barriers to the handicapped and elderly

(a) Treatment as expenses.—

(1) In general.—A taxpayer may elect to treat qualified architectural and transportation barrier removal expenses which are paid or incurred by him during the taxable year as expenses which are not chargeable to capital account. The expenditures so treated shall be allowed as a deduction.

(2) Election.—An election under paragraph (1) shall be made at such time and in such manner as the Secretary prescribes by regulations.

(b) Definitions.—For purposes of this section—

(1) Architectural and transportation barrier removal expenses.—The term "architectural and transportation barrier removal expenses" means an expenditure for the purpose of making any facility or public transportation vehicle owned or leased by the taxpayer for use in connection with his trade or business more accessible to, and usable by, handicapped and elderly individuals.

(2) Qualified architectural and transportation barrier removal expense.—The term "qualified architectural and transportation barrier removal expense" means, with respect to any such facility or public transportation vehicle, an architectural or transportation barrier removal expense with respect to which the taxpayer establishes, to the satisfaction of the Secretary, that the resulting removal of any such barrier meets the standards promulgated by the Secretary with the concurrence of the Architectural and Transportation Barriers Compliance Board and set forth in regulations prescribed by the Secretary.

(3) Handicapped individual.—The term "handicapped individual" means any individual who has a physical or mental disability (including, but not limited to, blindness or deafness) which for such individual constitutes or results in a functional limitation to employment, or who has any physical or mental impairment (including, but not limited to, a sight or hearing impairment) which substantially limits one or more major life activities of such individual.

(c) Limitation.—The deduction allowed by subsection (a) for any taxable year shall not exceed $25,000.

(d) Regulations.—The Secretary shall prescribe such regulations as may be necessary to carry out the provisions of this section within 180 days after the date of the enactment of the Tax Reform Act of 1976.

NOTE

Regulations under this section are found at 26 CFR §§ 7.190-1 to 7.109-3.

7. Public Works Grants Requirement

PUBLIC WORKS EMPLOYMENT ACT OF 1977

42 U.S.C. § 6705(g)

Accessibility Standards for Handicapped and Elderly

No grant shall be made under this chapter for any project for which the applicant does not give assurances satisfactory to the Secretary that the project will be designed and constructed in accordance with the standards for accessibility for public buildings and facilities to the handicapped and elderly under the Act entitled ''An Act to insure that certain buildings financed with Federal funds are so designed and constructed as to be accessible to the physically handicapped,'' approved August 12, 1968. The Architectural and Transportation Barriers Compliance Board established by the Rehabilitation Act of 1973 is authorized to insure that any construction and renovation done pursuant to any grant made under this chapter complies with the accessibility standards for public buildings and facilities issued under the Act of August 12, 1968.

NOTES

1.   The 1968 act to which reference is made by its complete title is more often referred to as the Architectural Barriers Act of 1968; see pp. 502–506 above. The Architectural and Transportation Barriers Compliance Board, to which reference is also made, is discussed at pp. 514–520, below.

2.   The purpose of the Public Works Employment Act is to provide employment opportunities in areas of high unemployment by federal grants for construction or renovation of useful public works.

3.   Another source of funds for the removal of architectural barriers is § 6(a) of the Education for All Handicapped Children Act of 1975 (P.L. 94-142), 20 U.S.C. § 1406, pursuant to which the Commissioner of the Bureau of Education for the Handicapped is authorized to make grants to state and local education agencies for the elimination of barriers. Additionally, there are certain other federal funding programs that, although not specifically aimed at barrier removal, might be used for such a purpose. Two such potential funding sources are Community Development funds pursuant to the Community Development Act (42 U.S.C. § 5301 et seq.) and Revenue Sharing funds pursuant to the State and Local Fiscal Assistance Act of 1972, as amended in 1976. In regard to the latter, 31 U.S.C. § 1242 specifically provides that recipients of revenue-sharing funds are prohibited from discriminating against handicapped persons; in addition to funding possibility, therefore, this section provides another legal mandate for physical accessibility.

E.   FEDERAL AGENCY ENFORCEMENT

1.   Transbus

The debate about the feasibility of an accessible city bus was ended in 1977 by a decision of the Secretary of Transportation to require all new vehicles purchased with

Urban Mass Transportation Administration funds to meet "Transbus" specifications. As virtually all urban transportation systems currently in operation are heavily subsidized by federal dollars, the impact of this decision was enormous.

It is important to note that when the Transbus concept was first conceived, accommodation of the needs of physically handicapped was only one of several goals sought to be accomplished. Conservation of energy through encouraging mass ridership and increasing competition among bus manufacturers were important incentives in redesigning urban buses.

DECISION OF BROCK ADAMS, SECRETARY OF TRANSPORTATION, TO MANDATE
TRANSBUS

May 19, 1977

The question before me is whether to mandate or encourage the acquisition of a low-floor, ramped bus ("Transbus") by all local transit authorities seeking federal assistance for the purchase of standard-size mass transit buses, after a certain date.

* * *

In 1971, the Urban Mass Transportation Administration ("UMTA") of the Department of Transportation ("DOT") initiated a major research project to develop an improved transit bus that would attract mass ridership, be accessible to those elderly and handicapped persons for whom the high floors and stairs of current buses provide serious obstacles and encourage continued competition among the manufacturers of transit buses. UMTA enlisted the aid of the three major domestic bus manufacturers, AM General, General Motors and the Flxible Co. (a wholly-owned subsidiary of Rohr Industries), to supply prototypes of such a bus for testing. Prototypes were built by all three manufacturers, tested by UMTA contractors and demonstrated in actual service in four cities. This process enabled the development of draft specifications for production of Transbus.

* * *

After carefully weighing the data and views submitted by manufacturers, the American Public Transit Association ("APTA"), individual transit authorities, groups representing the elderly and handicapped and others, I have decided, for the reasons stated below, to mandate Transbus. This mandate will take the form of requiring the use of a Transbus specification for all standard-size buses acquired with UMTA assistance. The mandate will apply to all procurements containing vehicle specifications approved by UMTA, issued for bid after September 30, 1979. The specifications already developed after consultation with APTA and others will be used with some minor modifications. The specifications include a requirement for a stationary floor height of not more than 22 inches, for an effective floor height including a kneeling feature of not more than 18 inches, and for a ramp for boarding and exiting.

* * *

Section 16 of the UMT Act, section 504 of the Rehabilitation Act and other statutory provisions have resulted in a number of lawsuits brought by elderly and handicapped persons. Although DOT has generally been successful in that litigation, litigation success alone provides no reason to avoid or defer a federal mandate of technological improvements as they become available, especially when, as here, those improvements significantly advance the mass transportation interests of all persons, including the elderly and handicapped, and when the improvements are quite unlikely to be introduced without a federal mandate.

* * *

A review of the statutes that guide this decision suggests strongly that any inclination to postpone a mandate further would thwart the intent of the Congress. A review of recent litigation suggests equally strongly that the courts are also not prepared to countenance needless delay in making urban mass transit vehicles accessible to the elderly and handicapped.

Even if the Congressional and judicial concerns were not as clear as they are, I believe it is my responsibility to insure to the extent feasible that no segment of our population is needlessly denied access to public transportation. It is now within our technological capability to insure that elderly and handicapped persons are accorded access to urban mass transit buses. This access is fundamental to the ability of such persons to lead independent and productive lives. In my view, a decision assuring that access could have been made some years ago.

DISABLED IN ACTION OF PENNSYLVANIA, INC. v. COLEMAN

United States District Court for the Eastern District of Pennsylvania, 1978
448 F.Supp. 109

BECHTLE, District Judge.

The above-named plaintiffs brought this action on June 17, 1976, against the defendants, on behalf of the class of all mobile disabled and elderly persons who are denied ready access to, and effective use of, federally financed mass transportation by reason of the physical and structural barriers in the design of public transit equipment.

Plaintiffs' (hereinafter "Disabled") claims are based upon the Urban Mass Transportation Act ("UMTA"), 49 U.S.C. § 1601 *et seq.*; the Federal-Aid Highway Acts, 23 U.S.C. § 101 *et seq.;* the Rehabilitation Act of 1973, 29 U.S.C. § 794; the Commerce Clause, Article I § 8 cl. 3, United States Constitution; the Privileges and Immunities Clause, Article IV § 2 cl. 1, United States Constitution; and the First and Fifth Amendments to the United States Constitution. Specifically, Disabled alleges that the statutory and constitutional provisions upon which their claims are based require that federal funds allocated to local transportation authorities be used only to purchase "Transbus," a low-floor, wide-door, ramped model bus, and that the Secretary has not complied with this mandate. Disabled requests injunctive and declaratory relief in the form of a Court Order declaring Disabled's interpretation of the statutory and constitutional provisions to be correct and enjoining the Secretary from refusing to comply with these provisions. The jurisdiction of this Court is invoked pursuant to 28 U.S.C. §§ 1361, 1332 and 1343(4).

The Secretary filed a motion to dismiss the complaint or, in the alternative, for summary judgment, pursuant to Fed.R. Civ.P. 12(b)(6) and 56 respectively. The Secretary contends that the statutes are not mandatory but merely state a policy that "special efforts" should be used to make mass transportation services available to the elderly and the handicapped, and that it is solely within the discretion of the Secretary to determine the means by which that policy is to be implemented.

In January, 1977, while that motion and other motions filed by the plaintiffs were still pending, William T. Coleman, Jr., was replaced as Secretary of Transportation by Brock Adams ("Adams"). On May 19, 1977, Adams initiated a major policy change by issuing his decision to mandate a low-floor, wide-door, ramped model bus. See Decision of Brock Adams, Secretary of Transportation, To Mandate Transbus, Policy Statement, May 19, 1977. That decision requires that all standard-size buses procured by local transit authorities with the assistance of federal funds conform to required specifications after September 30, 1979. Regulations implementing this policy were promulgated and published in the Federal Register on September 23, 1977. See 49 C.F.R. Part 609.15(a)–(c).

Subsequent to the issuance of Adams' policy, a show cause hearing, convened upon the Court's motion, was held before this Court on June 6, 1977, on the issue of whether the Secretary's policy rendered the controversy moot. Shortly after the hearing, Disabled filed a Fed.R.Civ.P. 56 motion for summary judgment on the issue of whether the statutes upon which their claims were based required that UMTA funds be disbursed only for the purchase of Transbus. In addition, Disabled argued that the controversy was not moot, because Adams was a temporary political appointee and, as such, his policy decisions were not binding upon his successors. The Secretary responded by arguing that his decision to mandate a low-floor, wide-door, ramped model bus rendered the controversy moot, because he has required implementation of the precise vehicle specifications demanded by the plaintiffs.

Before turning to the merits of the motions pending before this Court, we must determine whether Disabled's claims are rendered moot by the Secretary's decision to mandate a low-floor, wide-door, ramped bus. For the reasons stated below, we hold that Disabled's action is moot.

It is well settled that federal courts are courts of limited jurisdiction. Judicial power to adjudicate a claim is dependent not only upon a statutory or constitutional basis for that jurisdiction, but also upon the existence of a live case or controversy. Article III, United States Constitution; *Mills* v. *Green,* 159 U.S. 651, 653, 16 S.Ct. 132, 40 L.Ed. 293 (1895); *DeFunis* v. *Odegaard,* 416 U.S. 312, 317, 94 S.Ct. 1704, 40 L.Ed.2d 164 (1974). By assuring that the issues raised before the Court are concrete, ripe and adversarial, the case or controversy requirements insures that federal courts will not exceed their limited jurisdiction by rendering advisory, premature or unwarranted opinions, or by encroaching upon the constitutional authority of the other branches of the Federal Government. Where events have occurred to render a controversy insubstantial, or one not admitting of specific relief through a decree of a conclusive character, the controversy is moot; that is, the controversy is no longer live and is inappropriate for judicial determination. In the instant case, it is clear that the controversy between these parties is no longer live because the Secretary has promulgated regulations which, while not identical to Disabled's requested relief, are so nearly identical as to fulfill plaintiffs' objective. The regulations have been published in the Federal Register pursuant to 5 U.S.C. § 552 and, therefore, have the full force and effect of law. *United States* v. *Green,* 344 F.Supp. 474, 476 (E.D.Pa. 1972). Further, we have no reason to believe that Adams' policy was not undertaken in good faith; nor do we have reason to believe that Adams' decision will not be respected by his successors, or that the prior policy will be reinstated, particularly since the manufacturers of transit buses are now engaged in the complicated, time-consuming and costly process of "tooling up" in order to comply with the new regulations by September 30, 1979. In conclusion, we find that there is no live case or controversy before us and that this case is moot. Inasmuch as the issues raised in Disabled's complaint are moot for the reasons herein stated, the complaint will be dismissed.

An appropriate Order will be entered.

NOTES

1. The "Transbus Group" (plaintiffs in *Disabled in Action* v. *Coleman*) was a coalition of various local and national associations organized to support the interests of elderly and handicapped citizens. The legal strategy employed in *DIA* varied significantly from previous suits that had sought to compel accessibility. While earlier cases had concentrated mainly on forcing local officials to purchase accessible vehicles, primary targets in *DIA* were federal authorities who funded such purchases.

As the federal share of all new buses is 80% of the total cost, by allowing federal funds to be released only for accessible buses, accessibility of transit systems nationwide would be practically ensured.

2. Since the Transbus mandate, several possible delays in implementation have been encountered. The major bus manufacturers have claimed that the expenses they will incur in retooling their factories will not be offset by the profits earned from the new bus. The producers of the rear axle designed especially for Transbus have reported delays in production, thus threatening the September 30, 1979 deadline. The culmination of such problems has been that one by one all the American bus manufacturers have dropped out of the bidding on the first government procurement. The impact of this development on the Transbus specifications and timetables remains to be seen.

3. During the interim period before the introduction of Transbus, Secretary Adams stated that

> ... [E]xisting policy ... should be continued. That policy is based on requirements that all manufacturers offer optional equipment (e.g., lifts) for loading wheelchair-bound and other handicapped passengers, and that local transit authorities must either purchase accessible buses, or provide special services suitable for transporting elderly and handicapped passengers.[c]

Several disputes have arisen during this period concerning the use of separate transit systems to transport handicapped persons. The issue is whether such systems meet the "special services" requirement of the U.S. Department of Transportation's interim policy.

In *Vanko* v. *Finley*, 440 F.Supp. 656 (N.D.Ohio 1977), the court extensively examined one such special service known as Community Responsive Transit (CRT). CRT is typical of most special service systems, providing door-to-door operations on a demand responsive basis. Although the court found the system to not yet be fully operable (it offered no peak-hour service to those persons confined to wheelchairs), it

---

[c]Decision of Brock Adams, Secretary of Transportation, to Mandate Transbus, May 19, 1977, at 11.

held that the defendants were in compliance with the Department of Transportation requirements.

The opinion does not consider many of the criticisms levied at the separate system concept. Primarily, opponents argue that separate systems merely serve to further segregate handicapped people from the rest of society. Other attacks have centered on the inconvenience of such systems, severely limited operating hours, and excessive expense. See, generally, Reed, G., "Equal Access to Mass Transportation for the Handicapped," 9 *Transportation Law Journal* 167 (1977).

The ramifications of the Transbus decision are likely to affect the entire realm of transportation. Encouraged by their success in the Transbus litigation, advocates of the rights of disabled individuals are turning their attention to various other modes of transportation.

Presently, much of the transportation industry is engaged in evaluating its policies concerning handicapped travelers. The prohibitive cost of litigation and the recent Congressional enactments concerning transportation barriers provide great incentive to design and implement accessible systems. For example, Amtrak, the nation's passenger rail system, has begun to replace its older, inaccessible cars with models that comfortably accommodate the needs of the disabled passenger. Many transporters currently provide special services to handicapped individuals who notify them, in advance of their intended departure date, of their particular needs. See, for example, Amtrak, *Access Amtrak: A Guide to Amtrak Services for Elderly and Handicapped Travelers* (May, 1978), and Trans World Airlines, Inc., *Consumer Information About Air Travel for the Handicapped* (November, 1976).

5. The federal regulations in regard to Transbus are codified at 49 CFR § 609.15(a) *et seq.*

2. The Architectural and Transportation Barriers Compliance Board

Section 502 of the Rehabilitation Act of 1973 (P.L. 93-112), as Amended by the Rehabilitation, Comprehensive Services, and Developmental Disabilities Amendments of 1978 (P.L. 95-602)

29 U.S.C. 792

(a)(1) There is established within the Federal Government the Architectural and Transportation Barriers Compliance Board (hereinafter referred to as the 'Board') which shall be composed as follows:

(A) Eleven members shall be appointed by the President from among members of the general public of whom five shall be handicapped individuals.

(B) The remaining members shall be the heads of each of the following departments or agencies (or their designees whose positions are executive level IV or higher):

(i) Department of Health, Education and Welfare.
(ii) Department of Transportation.
(iii) Department of Housing and Urban Development.
(iv) Department of Labor.

    (v)   Department of the Interior.

   (vi)   Department of Defense.

  (vii)   Department of Justice.

 (viii)   General Services Administration.

   (ix)   Veterans' Administration.

    (x). United States Postal Service.

The President shall appoint the first Chairman of such Board who shall serve for a term of not more than two years; thereafter, the Chairman shall be elected by a vote of a majority of the Board for a term of one year.

    (2)   The term of office of each appointed member of the Board shall be 3 years; except that (i) the members first taking office shall serve, as designated by the President at the time of appointment, four for a term of one year, four for a term of two years, and three for a term of three years, and (ii) any member appointed to fill a vacancy shall serve for the remainder of the term for which his predecessor was appointed.

    (3)   If any appointed member of the Board becomes a Federal employee, such member may continue as a member of the Board for not longer than the sixty-day period beginning on the date he becomes such an employee.

    (4)   No individual appointed under paragraph (1)(A) of this subsection who has served as a member of the Board may be reappointed to the Board more than once unless such individual has not served on the Board for a period of two years prior to the effective date of such individual's appointment.

    (5)(A)   Members of the Board who are not regular full-time employees of the United States shall, while serving on the business of the Board, be entitled to receive compensation at rates fixed by the President, but not to exceed the daily rate prescribed for GS-18 under section 5332 of title 5, United States Code, including traveltime, for each day they are engaged in the performance of their duties as members of the Board; and shall be entitled to reimbursement for travel, subsistence, and other necessary expenses incurred by them in carrying out their duties under this section.

    (B)   Members of the Board who are employed by the Federal Government shall serve without compensation, but shall be reimbursed for travel, subsistence, and other necessary expenses incurred by them in carrying out their duties under this section.

    (b)   It shall be the function of the Board to:

    (1)   insure compliance with the standards prescribed pursuant to the Act of August 12, 1968, commonly known as the Architectural Barriers Act of 1968 (including the application of that Act to the United States Postal Service) including but not limited to enforcing all standards under that Act, and insuring that all waivers and modifications of standards are based upon findings of fact and are not inconsistent with provisions of such Act and this section;

    (2)   investigate and examine alternative approaches to the architectural, transportation, communication, and attitudinal barriers confronting handicapped individuals, particularly with respect to telecommunication devices, public buildings and monuments, parks and parklands, public transportation (including air, water, and

surface transportation whether interstate, foreign, intrastate, or local), and residential and institutional housing; (3) determine what measures are being taken by Federal, State, and local governments and by other public or nonprofit agencies to eliminate the barriers described in clause (2) of this subsection; (4) promote the use of the International Accessibility Symbol in all public facilities that are in compliance with the standards prescribed by the Administrator of the General Services Administration, the Secretary of Defense, and the Secretary of Housing and Urban Development pursuant to the Architectural Barriers Act of 1968; (5) make to the President and to Congress reports which shall describe in detail the results to its investigations under clauses (2) and (3) of this subsection; (6) make to the President and to the Congress such recommendations for legislation and administration as it deems necessary or desirable to eliminate the barriers described in clause (2) of this subsection; (7) establish minimum guidelines and requirements for the standards issued pursuant to the Act of August 12, 1968, as amended, commonly known as the Architectural Barriers Act of 1968; and (8) insure that public conveyances including rolling stock, are readily accessible to, and usable by, physically handicapped persons.

(c) The Board shall also (1)(A) determine how and to what extent transportation barriers impede the mobility of handicapped individuals and aged handicapped individuals and consider ways in which travel expenses in connection with transportation to and from work for handicapped individuals can be met or subsidized when such individuals are unable to use mass transit systems or need special equipment in private transportation, and (B) consider the housing needs of handicapped individuals; (2) determine what measures are being taken, especially by public and other nonprofit agencies and groups having an interest in and a capacity to deal with such problems, (A) to eliminate barriers from public transportation systems (including vehicles used in such systems), and to prevent their incorporation in new or expanded transportation systems and (B) to make housing available and accessible to handicapped individuals or to meet sheltered housing needs; and (3) prepare plans and proposals for such further actions as may be necessary to the goals of adequate transportation and housing for handicapped individuals, including proposals for bringing together in a cooperative effort, agencies, organizations, and groups already working toward such goals or whose cooperation is essential to effective and comprehensive action.

(d)(1) In carrying out its functions under this Act, the Board shall, directly or through grants to public or private nonprofit organizations, or contracts with private nonprofit or for profit organizations carry out its functions under subsections (b) and (c) of this section, and shall conduct investigations, hold public hearings, and issue such orders as it deems necessary to insure compliance with the provisions of the Acts cited in subsection (b).

Except as provided in paragraph (3) of subsection (e), the provisions of subchapter II of chapter 5, and chapter 7 of title 5, United States Code, shall apply to procedures under this section, and an order of compliance issued by the Board shall be a final order for purposes of judicial review. Any such order affecting any Federal department, agency, or instrumentality of the United States shall be final and binding on such department, agency, or instrumentality. An order of compliance may include the withholding or suspension of Federal funds with respect to any building or public conveyance or rolling stock found not to be in compliance with standards enforced under this section. Pursuant to chapter 7 of title 5, United States Code, any complainant or participant in a proceeding under this subsection may obtain review of a final order issued in such proceeding.

(2)   The executive director is authorized, at the direction of the Board—

(A)   to bring a civil action in any appropriate United States district court to enforce, in whole or in part, any final order of the Board under this subsection; and

(B)   to intervene, appear, and participate, or to appear as *amicus curiae,* in any court of the United States or in any court of a State in civil actions which related to this section or to the Architectural Barriers Act of 1968.

Except as provided in section 518(a) of title 28, United States Code, relating to litigation before the Supreme Court, the executive director may appear for and represent the Board in any civil litigation brought under this section.

(3)   The Board, in consultation and coordination with other concerned Federal departments and agencies and agencies within the Department of Health, Education, and Welfare, shall develop standards and provide appropriate technical assistance to any public or private activity, person, or entity affected by regulations prescribed pursuant to this title with respect to overcoming architectural, transportation, and communication barriers. Any funds appropriated to any such department or agency for the purpose of providing such assistance may be transferred to the Board for the purpose of carrying out this paragraph. The Board may arrange to carry out its responsibilities under this paragraph through such other departments and agencies for such periods as the Board determines is appropriate. In carrying out its technical assistance responsibilities under this paragraph, the Board shall establish a procedure to insure separation of its compliance and technical assistance responsibilities under this section.

(e)(1)   There shall be appointed by the Board an executive director and such other professional and clerical personnel as are necessary to carry out its functions under this Act. The Board is authorized to appoint as many hearing examiners as are necessary for proceedings required to be conducted under this section. The provisions applicable to hearing examiners appointed under section 3105 of title 5, United States Code, shall apply to hearing examiners appointed under this subsection.

(2)   The Executive Director shall exercise general supervision over all personnel employed by the Board (other than hearing examiners and their assistants). The Executive Director shall have final authority on behalf of the Board, with respect to the investigation of alleged noncompliance in the issuance of formal complaints before the Board, and shall have such other duties as the Board may prescribe.

(3)   For the purpose of this section, an order of compliance issued by a hearing examiner shall be deemed to be an order of the Board and shall be the final order for the purpose of judicial review.

(f)   The departments or agencies specified in subsection (a) of this section shall make available to the Board such technical, administrative, or other assistance as it may require to carry out its functions under this section, and the Board may appoint such other advisers, technical experts, and consultants as it deems necessary to assist it in carrying out its functions under this section. Special advisory and technical experts and consultants appointed pursuant to this subsection shall, while performing their functions under this section, be entitled to receive compensation at rates fixed by the Secretary, but not exceeding the daily pay rate, for a person employed as a GS-18 under section 5332 of title 45, United States Code, including traveltime, and while serving away from their homes or regular places of business they may be allowed travel expenses, including per diem in lieu of subsistence, as authorized by section 5703 of such title 5 for persons in the Government service employed intermittently.

(g) The Board shall, at the end of each fiscal year, report its activities during the preceding fiscal year to the Congress. Such report shall include an assessment of the extent of compliance with the Acts cited in subsection (b) of this section, along with a description and analysis of investigations made and actions taken by the Board, and the reports and recommendations described in clauses (5) and (6) of subsection (b) of this section. The Board shall prepare two final reports of its activities under subsection (c). One such report shall be on its activities in the field of transportation barriers to handicapped individuals, and the other such report shall be on its activities in the field of the housing needs of handicapped individuals. The Board shall, not later than September 30, 1975, submit each such report, together with its recommendations, to the President and the Congress. The Board shall also prepare for such submission an interim report of its activities in each such field within 18 months after the date of enactment of this Act.

(h)(1) Within one year following the enactment of this subsection, the Board shall submit to the President and the Congress a report containing an assessment of the amounts required to be expended by States and by political subdivisions thereof to provide handicapped individuals with full access to all programs and activities receiving Federal assistance.

(2) The Board may make grants to, or enter into contracts with, public or private organizations to carry out its duties under subsections (b) and (c). The Board may also make grants to any designated State unit for the purpose of conducting studies to provide the cost assessments required by paragraph (1). Before including in such report the findings of any study conducted for the Board under a grant or contract to provide the Board with such cost assessments, the Board shall take all necessary steps to validate the accuracy of such findings.

(i) There are authorized to be appropriated for the purpose of carrying out the duties and functions of the Board under this section such sums as may be necessary for each fiscal year ending before October 1, 1982, but in no event shall the amount appropriated for any one fiscal year exceed $3,000,000.

NOTES

1. Some changes made by the 1978 amendments include an addition to the Board's authority of public conveyances and rolling stock, coverage of the United States Postal Service, authority over "communication" barriers, the authority to commence a civil action for enforcement of its orders, and the option of intervening in lawsuits involving the Architectural Barriers Act of 1968. It is too early to gauge the effect of these amendments on the Board's operation, but it is clear that Congress intended to give the Board broad and strong authority in enforcing architectural and transportation barriers measures.

Some of the activities of the Board under its previous mandate have been described as follows:

> The Architectural and Transportation Barriers Compliance Board (A&TBCB), created by Congress in 1973, provides important federal leadership in making the man-made environment functional for all people. The board was established primarily to ensure compliance with the Architectural Barriers Act of 1968 (Public Law 90-480). But since its establishment the board's role has grown significantly. . . .
>
> Under its present authority, the A&TBCB is charged with assuring the accessibility of all buildings and facilities constructed, leased, or altered for the federal government or with the use of certain federal funds to persons with physical handicaps. Not all government buildings and facilities are covered by P.L. 90-480, but the Executive Director of the board, Robert M. Johnson, estimates nearly a half million buildings and facilities do fall within the A&TBCB's jurisdiction.
>
> Thus, the A&TBCB faces a massive task in trying to enforce the law. Up to the present, the board's primary mode of enforcement has been to respond to complaints it receives from the public. General Counsel Charles Goldman points with pride to an 80–85 percent rate of amicable resolution of the complaints the board receives. Because of increased public awareness and the growing realization that the board means business, the number of complaints is rapidly growing.
>
> Between July 1, 1975, and September 30, 1976, the board received 53 complaints. In the fiscal year ending September 30, 1977, 100 complaints had been filed. By June 30 of this year [1978] 96 complaints had reached the board. By the end of this fiscal year, one board spokesman acknowledged, the total could easily exceed 150.
>
> Executive Director Johnson speaks of the necessity of moving beyond the so-called "complaint responsive mode," expanding the enforcement efforts of the board to include reviews of existing facilities and of plans for new ones. The board is also currently launching a major public awareness campaign, "Access America," which will include televised messages dramatically illustrating the problems of architectural and attitudinal barriers.
>
> The board's compliance division is stepping up its prosecution of cases. In the past year, according to Johnson, four major citations have been served. The board has claimed its first major victory recently in the Union Station National Visitors' Center decision. A federal administrative law judge ordered the Department of the Interior to make Union Station fully accessible to all visitors. The board will monitor compliance with this order.
>
> New Modes of Compliance
>
> This fall [1978] the board will initiate a series of directed field reviews which will involve surveying facilities in ten major cities across the country. Johnson views this program as the most important initiative that the board could have undertaken at this point. Six of the nine member agencies on the board have voted to provide the board with staff from their regional offices to assist them. The board will also enlist the aid of handicapped consumers in the review.
>
> After the review, the board will follow up its findings with the agencies involved and assist them in developing implementation plans for remedying violations. The board will also be developing and testing a new field-review survey instrument which it aims to make generally available to advocacy organizations and interested citizens for use in their own communities.
>
> Another major project currently in the early stages of development is a decentralized compliance system throughout the federal bureaucracy.[d]

---

[d]National Center for Law and the Handicapped, "Federal Leadership in Removing Architectural Barriers," July/August *Amicus* 33 (1978).

2. The A&TBCB regulations regarding its enforcement procedures are codified at 36 CFR Part 1150.

ADDITIONAL READING

Note, "Abroad in the Land: Legal Strategies to Effectuate the Rights of the Physically Disabled," 61 *Geo. L. J.* 1501 (1973).

Achtenberg, J., " 'Crips' Unite to Enforce Symbolic Laws: Legal Aid for the Disabled: An Overview," 4 *U. San Fernando Valley L. Rev.* 161 (1975).

Reed, G., "Equal Access to Mass Transportation for the Handicapped," 9 *Transp. L. J.* 167 (1977).

Note, "The Forgotten Minority: The Physically Disabled and Improving Their Physical Environment," 48 *Chi.-Kent L. Rev.* 215 (1971).

Farber, A. J., "The Handicapped Plead for Entrance—Will Anyone Answer?" 64 *Ky. L. J.* 99 (1975).

Achtenberg, J., "Law and the Physically Disabled: An Update with Constitutional Implications," 8 *S.W.U.L. Rev.* 847 (1976).

Note, "Mass Transportation for the Handicapped and the Elderly," 1976 *Det. Coll. L. Rev.* 277 (1976).

tenBroek, J., "The Right to Live in the World: The Disabled in the Law of Torts," 54 *Cal. L. Rev.* 841 (1966).

5

FREEDOM OF CHOICE: COMPETENCY AND GUARDIANSHIP

Susan P. Leviton

A. INTRODUCTION

THE ONLY FREEDOM WHICH DESERVES THE NAME is that of pursuing our own good in our own way, so long as we do not attempt to deprive others of theirs, or impede their efforts to obtain it. Each is the proper guardian of his own health, whether bodily, or mental and spiritual. Mankind are greater gainers by suffering each other to live as seems good to themselves than by compelling each to live as seems good to the rest (John Stuart Mill, *On Liberty,* 12–13 (Castell, ed.)).

Whether this freedom is called "self-determination," "liberty," "the right to pursuit of happiness," or "freedom of choice," it has long occupied an honored place in American law. United States citizens have come to take for granted the fact that we may chart our individual courses, make our own decisions, and put our ideas into action. The right to make choices and to exercise personal preferences is close to the heart of the traditions of individual liberty upon which our system of government is founded.

However, elderly persons and individuals with mental handicaps or severe physical handicaps have frequently been denied the opportunity to exercise their freedom of choice. Through guardianship proceedings authorized by state laws, the decision-making ability of these persons has often been divested from them and assigned to persons appointed to be their guardians. Thereafter, decisions are made by the guardian on behalf of the "ward." The legally appointed guardian is placed in the same position relative to his ward as a parent occupies in relation to his or her minor child. Because the ward is viewed as being incompetent to manage his or her own affairs, the law grants the guardian both the responsibility and authority to take care of the ward.

Because the notion of competency can be applied to many different and separate aspects of life, a person can be competent in one area while simultaneously being incompetent in another. For example, a person might be fully capable of managing his or her daily life but not have the requisite competency skills to manage a large estate or securities investments. A handicapped or elderly individual might exhibit an ability to lead an otherwise normal life in the community but be unable to fully attend to nutritional, medical, or other personal needs.

Unfortunately, until recently, guardianship laws have tended to be an all-or-nothing proposition; they have required that a person be declared either totally competent or totally incompetent. A person who exhibited an inability to cope in one particular area and who was, therefore, judicially determined to be incompetent, lost all authority to make decisions or to exercise rights in all other areas as well. Until a subsequent judicial decision determined that the person had regained competence, only his or her guardian could make economic, legal, and personal choices for his or her "ward." Under the guise of protecting the ward, these guardianship proceedings actually deprived these persons of all their rights, the opportunity to exercise their unimpaired faculties, and consequently almost every semblance of human dignity. Guardianship practices in this country have borne out the often quoted warning of former Supreme Court Justice Brandeis:

> Experience should teach us to be most on our guard to protect liberty when the government's purposes are beneficent. . . . The greatest dangers to liberty lurk in insidious encroachment by men of zeal, well-meaning but without understanding (*Olmstead v. United States*, 277 U.S. 438, 479 (1928) (Brandeis, J., dissenting)).

The modern trend—which appears more in line with constitutional guarantees—is toward a system known as "limited guardianship." The concept of limited guardianship permits a court to declare a particular person to be incompetent for a specific purpose and to appoint a guardian to act to protect his or her interests. Even though the person is incompetent with regard to the particular matters involved in the determination of incompetence, he or she retains the right to make decisions and exercise authority in all other areas.

Another approach to incompetency, which is even more progressive than limited guardianship, practically sidesteps the guardianship process altogether by setting up systems of supportive services for elderly and handicapped individuals. These support services provide special assistance to these people in the area(s) in which their competence is lacking. For example, instead of appointing a guardian for a person who is unable to manage financial matters, a contractual arrangement might be worked out wherein some person or agency would assist in the individual's financial management on a temporary basis, while simultaneously providing training on monetary matters so that the client might eventually learn to manage his or her own finances. Likewise, instead of having an elderly person declared incompetent and placed in a nursing home, sufficient supportive services, such as food preparation, medical attention, and housekeeping, might be arranged so that the person could continue to live at home in the community.

B. THE RIGHTS AT STAKE

1. An Overview

HORSTMAN, P., "PROTECTIVE SERVICES FOR THE ELDERLY: THE LIMITS OF PARENS
PATRIAE"

40 Mo. L. Rev. *215, 231–235 (1975)*

Protective Services

III. Guardianship Proceedings

A. What Is at Stake?

For the individual, guardianship results in a deprivation of personal rights and
civil liberties which is devastating. The adult who is found to be in need of guardianship is reduced to the status of a child in the eyes of the law. Although there are
individual differences between states, most statutes deprive the ward of the right to buy
or sell property, to contract, to sue and be sued, to make gifts, to write checks, and
generally to engage in financial transactions of any kind. The ward is also generally
deprived of the right to vote, to marry, to operate a motor vehicle, and to consent to or
refuse medical treatment.

It may be difficult to underestimate the psychological impact of depriving an
individual of the right to manage his own property as he sees fit. Surrogate management of one's finances has been described as "the kind of intervention [which] is a
basic deprivation of a right cherished in a free society: the right for an individual to
self-determination."[63] For an elderly person struggling to maintain his independence
and self-esteem in the face of forced inactivity due to mandatory retirement, the loss of
control over assets accumulated during a working lifetime may be a critical blow to the
individual's sense of integrity. The right to "acquire, enjoy, own and dispose of
property" has received judicial recognition as a fundamental attribute of citizenship;
"an essential pre-condition to the realization of other basic civil rights and liberties."[64]

> The right to enjoy property without unlawful deprivation, no less than the right to speak
> or the right to travel, is in truth a "personal" right. ... In fact, a fundamental inter-
> dependence exists between the personal right to liberty and the personal right in prop-
> erty.[65]

In addition to the loss of his right to dispose of his property and enjoy his wealth
according to his own judgment, the ward stands to lose his personal liberty and his
freedom to associate with persons of his own choice. The deprivation of these fundamental rights can occur in three ways.

First, guardianship of the person often gives the guardian the power to determine the ward's place of residence. This means that the guardian can place the ward,

---

[63]Alexander, G., and Lewin, T., *The Aged and the Need for Surrogate Management* 2 (1972).

[64]*Lynch* v. *Household Finance Corp.*, 405 U.S. 538, 545 (1972).

[65]*Id.* at 552.

against his will, in a private board and care home, nursing home, or convalescent hospital and authorize the institutional facility to require him to stay. In some states this power allows the guardian to commit the ward involuntarily to a state mental hospital without recourse to the formal statutory hospitalization procedures.

Second, in some jurisdictions the concept of "voluntary admission" to state mental hospitals is worded so that it includes admission of a ward by his guardian.

Finally, although guardianship and involuntary hospitalization serve different purposes and concern different legal issues, they share a common terminology. Incompetency, or *non compos mentis,* is often used in place of mental illness. Both are used interchangeably with terms such as "insanity" and "lunacy." In a few states, hospitalization and incompetency are completely merged so that an order for hospitalization automatically constitutes a finding of incompetency despite the fact that many mentally ill persons are perfectly capable of signing and endorsing checks, completing tax returns, and generally managing a great many personal and financial affairs while undergoing a course of treatment. Similarly, many persons may need assistance in managing their personal or financial affairs, but may not need involuntary confinement in a mental hospital. The fact that confusion persists between guardianship and hospitalization in so many states means that a ward found unable to manage his affairs for purposes of appointing a guardian runs a substantial risk that the incompetency determination will be used subsequently as *prima facie* evidence of insanity for purposes of involuntary confinement.

Assuming that an elderly ward is institutionalized under any of these possibilities, his detention is likely to be not only indeterminate but permanent. Because of the widely held belief that senility is an incurable disease, an atmosphere of "therapeutic nihilism" surrounds medical treatment of institutionalized aged persons. As a result, most institutionalized elderly are doomed to receive only custodial care.

Finally, in addition to the loss of personal and economic rights, the ward bears the stigma of having been judged to be of unsound mind. The stigma of incompetency has received judicial recognition as a basic interference with fundamental personal rights. In *Dale* v. *Hahn,*[77] the Court of Appeals for the Second Circuit discussed the importance of stigmatization in the context of a challenge to New York's *ex parte* procedure for appointing surrogate property managers for those alleged to be mentally incompetent:

> Although the plaintiff requests recovery of money alleged to have been illegally spent by the [guardian], any right she may have to the money is not the critical interest sought to be protected. The important ones are, rather, those affected by the declaration that she was incompetent to handle her own affairs. The stigma of incompetency, the implication that she has some kind of mental deficiency, with attendant untrustworthiness and irresponsibility, and the consequences to her reputation and her normal human relationships with others in her community involve more than a property right, and are sufficient to support jurisdiction under § 1343.[78]

---

[77]440 F.2d 633 (2d Cir. 1971).

[78]*Id.* at 636.

NOTES

1.   While the Horstman article deals with elderly persons and guardianship resulting from mental illness, most of the observations apply with equal validity to guardianship on account of mental retardation or other handicapping conditions.

2.   In accord with the *Dale* v. *Hahn* ruling that guardianship proceedings result in stigmatization, is the ruling in *McAuliffe* v. *Carlson,* 377 F.Supp. 896 (D.Conn. 1974), cert. denied, 427 U.S. 911 (1976), where the court held that notice and an opportunity to be heard were constitutionally required before appointment of a conservator, because such proceedings result in an individual being "officially branded with the stigma of being unable to manage his affairs," *id.* at 905.

3.   In *Schutte* v. *Schutte,* 86 W. Va. 701, 104 S.E. 108 (1920), overruled on other grounds, 202 S.E.2d (W.Va. 1974), the Supreme Court of Appeals of West Virginia discussed the significant liberty interest at stake in an incompetency determination:

> An adjudication of insanity immediately and directly works a restraint upon liberty. It raises a presumption of incapacity to make contracts, which hampers and restrains the person so adjudged. Being unable to transact business as a normal man, his estate is charged with the expenses and hazards of committee management, and is deprived of the benefit of his own business judgment, ability, and management. Deprived of the opportunity to enlarge his estate by his industry and capacity, he and those dependent upon him reduce it by their living and other expenses. But, aside from all this, liberty, full and complete liberty, is a right of the very highest nature. It stands next in order to life itself. The Constitution guarantees and safeguards it. An adjudication of insanity is a partial deprivation of it (*Id.* at 104 S.E. 110).

2.   The Concept of Consent

In general, except in the legitimate exercise of governmental authority, one individual may not intrude upon the person or prerogatives of another except with the consent of the latter, or, in the case of minors, with the consent of the individual's parents. This principle is a logical corollary of the right to freedom of choice and self-determination, inherent in the concept of liberty guaranteed by the United States Constitution.

> Consent has been defined as:

> . . . an act of reason, accompanied with deliberation, the mind weighing as in a balance the good or evil on each side. It means voluntary agreement by a person in the possession and exercise of sufficient mentality to make an intelligent choice to do something proposed by another (*Gray* v. *Grunnagle,* 423 Pa. 144, 223 A.2d 663, 669 (1966)). [citations omitted]

Consent has three important components: it must be knowing, voluntary, and competent (*Kaimowitz* v. *Department of Mental Health for State of Michigan,* see pp. 808–824, below). The requirement that an individual's consent be knowing means that sufficient information must be provided concerning the subject matter for which consent is sought so that the individual can exercise self-determination and meaningful decision whether or not to consent. The withholding, by the person seeking consent, of any information that might reasonably be thought to be material to the decision is generally considered to invalidate consent. Considerable case law in this regard has developed in the area of consent to medical treatment. See, e.g., *Canterbury* v.

Spence, 464 F.2d 772 (D.C.Cir. 1972) *cert. denied* 409 U.S. 1064 (1972); *Cobbs* v. *Grant,* 8 Cal.3d 229, 502 P.2d 1, 104 Cal.Rptr. 505 (1972). See pp. 756–765, below. Inasmuch as comprehension of the information provided is the vital goal, the method of disclosure can be almost equally as important a consideration as the substantive content. See generally, *Consent Handbook,* American Association on Mental Deficiency, Special Publication No. 3 (1977).

In addition to being knowing, consent must also be voluntary. Voluntariness in the context of consent requires that the person giving or withholding consent must be "so situated as to be able to exercise free power of choice without the intervention of any element of force, fraud, deceit, duress, over-reaching, or other ulterior form of constraint of coercion"; this is the definition used in the Nuremberg Code, which is set forth in *United States* v. *Karl Brandt: Trial of War Criminals before the Nuremberg Military Tribunals,* Volumes 142, "The Medical Case," U.S. Govt. Printing Office (1948); see *Kaimowitz* v. *Department of Mental Health for State of Michigan,* at p. 808, below.

The third requirement, that consent be competent, is in some ways the most problematic of the three components of consent. "Competency" is used differently in numerous legal contexts; one study found over 100 separate legal uses of the term (Mezer, R., and Rheingold, P., "Mental Capacity and Incompetency: A Psycholegal Problem," 118 *Am. J. Psychiatry* 827 (1962)). For example, competency may be defined with respect to: 1) the person's age (those under the age of majority being legally incompetent to make various legal decisions); 2) specific situations (standards being different for determining competency to stand trial, to enter into a contract, or to make a valid will); and 3) the person's physical or mental capacity (the impairment of which can lead to a judicial declaration of incompetency and appointment of a substitute decision maker).

In guardianship proceedings, the state, through its *parens patriae* powers, may limit an individual's exercise of self-determination by means of a judicial declaration of incompetency and the appointment of a guardian to assume decision-making responsibility. While terminology varies widely from state to state, with terms such as "incapacitated" or "disabled" being substituted for "incompetent," and "guardians" being variously called "conservators," "committees," or "curators," every state has such a process.

In its most general sense, a guardian can be defined as "a person lawfully invested with the power, and charged with the duty, of taking care of the person and managing the property and rights of another person, who, for some peculiarity of status, or defect of age, understanding, or self-control, is considered incapable of administering his own affairs" (*Black's Law Dictionary,* 834 (4th ed. 1968)).

Thus, guardianship is a legal mechanism for substitute decision making; it sets up a "legal relationship whose essential purpose is to replace the disabled individual's legal authority to make personal decisions in his or her own self-interest. . ." (*Guardianship for Mentally Retarded Persons: An AAMD Policy Statement,* 1975 C-4).

Parents are the "natural guardians" of their minor children; care and guidance is provided by the parent until the child reaches the age of majority and gains full legal capacity. Until reaching majority, the child is subject to decisions made by the parent regarding the child's personal life, activities, and conduct. According to statutes in every state, however, an adult may, by official proceedings, be placed under a guardianship which approximates part or all of the control held by the parent over the minor child.

ADDITIONAL READING

Brakel, S., and Rock, R., "Incompetency, Guardianship, and Restoration," *The Mentally Disabled and the Law,* American Bar Foundation (1971).

Kindred, M., "Guardianship and Limitations Upon Capacity," *The Mentally Retarded Citizen and the Law,* The President's Committee on Mental Retardation, 62-87 (1976).

Alexander, G., "On Being Imposed Upon by Artful or Designing Persons—The California Experience with the Involuntary Placement of the Aged," 14 *San Diego L. Rev.* 1083 (1977).

Chambers, D., "Alternatives to Civil Commitment of the Mentally Ill: Practical Guides and Constitutional Imperatives," 70 *Michigan L. Rev.* 1107 (1972).

Cohen, B., Oosterhout, B., and Leviton, S., "Tailoring Guardianship to the Needs of Mentally Handicapped Citizens," 6 *Md. L. Forum* 91 (1976).

Horstman, P., "Protective Service for the Elderly: The Limits of *Parens Patriae,*" 40 *Missouri L. Rev.* 215 (1975).

Regan, J., "Protective Services for the Elderly: Civil Commitment, Guardianship and Alternatives," 13 *Wm. & Mary L. Rev.* 569 (1972).

Regan, J., and Springer, G., *Protective Services for the Elderly: A Working Paper,* U.S. Senate Special Committee on Aging, 95th Cong., 1st Sess. (1977).

C. HISTORICAL SOURCES OF GUARDIANSHIP

COHEN, B., OOSTERHOUT, B., AND LEVITON, S., "TAILORING GUARDIANSHIP TO THE NEEDS OF MENTALLY HANDICAPPED CITIZENS"

6 Md. L. Forum *91, 91-93 (1976)*

The Historical Basis and Development of Guardianship Laws

In ancient Rome in 449 B.C., references were made to the mentally disabled in the Twelve Tables of Rome. The mere fact that an individual did not act like other people served as justification for relatives assuming full control of his person and his goods. No judicial decree was required.

By the time of Justinian, the courts had become involved in guardianship to a limited extent. Upon the death of the person who exercised control over a disabled person, the magistrate designated a "curator." The curator was usually a relative appointed in the will of the person who had previously exercised control over the disabled person. Guardianship was suspended during lucid moments of the ward. However, no new proceedings were required when the disability reappeared; the former guardianship became automatically operative. Testaments made by the disabled person during lucid moments were valid.

The guardians' control over the ward's goods was much more limited than it is today. The guardian was unable to sell or transfer the real property of the ward, to make a gift in his name, or to liberate his slaves. To insure honesty, the law required the guardian to account to either the former ward or his heirs when guardianship ended. Roman law placed greater stress on protection of the property of the ward than on protection of his person.

> Although the ward's property has always been well cared for, his body, depending upon the temper of the times, has at worst been subjected to tortures designed to exorcise the spirits possessing it, and at best been cared for privately by friends and relatives.[26]

In medieval England, it was the duty of the lord of the manor to protect the person and property of the "insane." Although he was required to protect their personal interests, the main reason for guardianship was to prevent the mentally disabled from becoming public burdens and from spending all of their assets to the detriment of their heirs.

In the late thirteenth century, the king was given the rights and duties of wardship by the statute of De Praerogativa Regis.

> The King . . . as the political father and guardian of his kingdom, has the protection of all his subjects, and of their lands and goods, and he is bound, in a more peculiar manner, to take care of those who, by reason of their imbecility and want of understanding, are incapable of taking care of themselves.[30]

The mentally disabled, or "insane," were divided into two categories, the "idiot" and the "lunatic." All right and title to property of the "idiot" or mentally retarded went to the king, who could retain the profits from the land after providing the "idiot" with necessities. Upon the "idiot's" death, title to the land was returned to the "idiot's" heirs. Guardianship of the "lunatic" or the mentally ill person was not so profitable for the king. The ward's property was to be used only for his support, and was to be returned to him upon his recovery or to his heirs upon his death.

By the early seventeenth century, the king's authority as guardian of the mentally handicapped was designated in a "sign manual" to the Chancellor. The designation afforded the mentally handicapped procedural safeguards. Before the court of chancery obtained jurisdiction over the person or estate of an "idiot" or a "lunatic," an inquisition by a jury of twelve men must have found the person to be *non compos mentis*. Four types of individuals were included in this term: 1) the idiot or natural fool; 2) he who was of good and sound memory, but who by the visitation of God has lost it; 3) the lunatic, who was sometimes lucid and sometimes *non compos mentis;* and 4) he who by his own acts deprived himself of reason, such as the drunkard. If an inquisition was held and

> . . . if an incompetent was determined by the jury to be a lunatic, the chancellor committed him to the care of some friend, who received an allowance with which to care for him. The incompetent's heir was generally made the manager of the estate, although,

---

[26]Horstman, P., "Protective Services for the Elderly: The Limits of *Parens Patriae*," 40 *Mo. L. Rev.* 215, 219-20 (1975).

[30]Kittrie, N., *The Right to Be Different: Deviance and Enforced Therapy* 59 (1971).

according to Blackstone, "to prevent sinister practices," he was not given the custody of the incompetent. For the custody of the estate the heir was responsible to the court of chancery, to the recovered lunatic, or to his administrator.[39]

However, the safeguard of the inquisition by jury had only limited application because only those with sufficient funds could afford such a proceeding.

The Chancellor was given custody of the person of the disabled as well as of his land, but there is no indication that public money was used for this purpose. Rather, the protection of the person consisted of caring for his needs out of the proceeds from his lands.

In colonial America, responsibility for the care of incompetents was originally given to the family. Those without families were subjected to the same fate as the itinerant poor: they wandered from town to town, begging. Gradually, the community became involved in the welfare of the incompetents and towns paid relatives and, later, other interested parties to care for the disabled. However, the institution of support payments reflected concern for the plight of the family rather than for that of the disabled person.

Ironically, American law concerning the guardianship of the mentally handicapped became more like English law after the Revolutionary War.

> [C]ourts of equity, applying English common law, or acting under constitutional provisions or statutes, exercised a modified form of *parens patriae* jurisdiction over the persons and property of the mentally incompetent to assure that those unable to care for themselves were protected from harm.[47]

As in England, an elaborate set of customs, rules, and standards developed for the protection of the ward's property, whereas protection of the person remained secondary. Many of these rules were necessitated by the disabled person's inability to contract. However, statutes of several states provide that the contract of an incompetent is void and cannot be enforced by the "incompetent" against the "healthy" party. In some states, such protection is denied if it injures the other party to the contract. Thus, guardians protect both the incompetent person's property interest as well as society's interest in certainty and finality in commercial transactions.

While the guardian of the property has many duties such as conserving the estate, managing assets, and protecting society by keeping the ward from becoming a public charge, "a strong motivation for the use of a guardian is the resolution of the legal plight posed by the incompetent's inability to act in a legal sense and the imperative necessity that such action should be taken."[51] The appointment of a guardian of the property serves to protect the ward from wasting his assets, to protect the ward from the imposition of unscrupulous persons, and to allow commercial activities to proceed unhindered.

> With this background, it is understandable that the development of the law was primarily in terms of protection of property, and that few guidelines were developed with respect

---

[39][Brakel, S., and Rock, R., *The Mentally Disabled and the Law* (1971)] at 3–4.

[47]*Supra,* note 26 at 219.

[51][Allen, R., Ferster, E., and Weihofen, H., *Mental Impairment and Legal Incompetency* 2 (1968)] at 71.

to the guardian's duties toward the ward as a person. It was evidently assumed that the guardian would have his ward's welfare at heart and would see to it that he was adequately cared for.[52]

NOTES

1.   A case often cited as one of the earliest judicial discussions of the concept of guardianship is *Beverly's Case,* 4 Co.Rep. 123b, 16 Eng.Rul.Cas. 702 (1603). While that decision includes a lengthy discussion of the status of "lunatics" and involved the participation of the legendary Lord Coke, it is a ponderous and confusing opinion which would provide a difficult exercise for a Latin scholar and is therefore not included here. For additional information about the early development of guardianship in England, see Blackstone, 1 *Commentaries,* Ch. 8, § 18, 302–307 (1765) (Lewis, W., ed, pp. 270–273, 1897); Blackstone, 3 *Commentaries,* Ch. 27, § 2, p. 427 (1765) (Lewis, W., ed., pp. 1385–1897); W. Holdsworth, 1 *A History of English Law* 473–476 (7th ed. 1956).

2.   In *Hawaii* v. *Standard Oil Co. of California,* 405 U.S. 251 (1972), the United States Supreme Court declared:

> The concept of *parens patriae* is derived from the English constitutional system. As the system developed from its feudal beginnings, the King retained certain duties and powers, which were referred to as the "royal prerogative." . . . These powers and duties were said to be exercised by the King in his capacity as "father of the country." Traditionally, the term was used to refer to the King's power as guardian of persons under legal disabilities to act for themselves. For example, Blackstone refers to the sovereign or his representative as "the general guardian of all infants, idiots, and lunatics," and as the superintendent of "all charitable uses in the kingdom." In the United States, the "royal prerogative" and the "parens patriae" function of the King passed to the States. [Citations and footnotes omitted.] (*Id.* at 257.)

Actually the Supreme Court's historical summary is something of an oversimplification. As the Cohen, Oosterhout, and Leviton article makes clear, the custody of "idiots" and "lunatics" has shifted to a number of different forums in the course of history. Originally owned by the lord of the manor, persons *non compos mentis* then came under the care of the King of England, who eventually delegated this authority to the Chancery; after the American Revolution this responsibility, in the United States, came to reside with the people, who, having joined together to form the states, acted through their state legislatures to delegate the guardianship power to particular courts in each state.

For other judicial synopses of the history of guardianship, see *Hamilton* v. *Traber,* 78 Md. 26, 29–31, 27 A. 229, 230–31 (1893); *Witt* v. *Heyen,* 114 Kan. 869, 221 P. 262, 264–265 (1923); *In re Easton,* 214 Md. 176, 181, 133 A.2d 441 (1957).

3.   In the United States, guardianship is now almost entirely governed by state statutes. 43 Fed.Reg. 11328, 11345-51 (1978).

---

[52]*Id.* at 3.

D.   STANDARDS FOR DETERMINING INCOMPETENCY

1.   Statutory Standards

Guardianship proceedings are governed by the standards set out in the guardianship statutes in each state. A survey of laws in the 50 states and the District of Columbia has shown that, despite differences in scope and language, nearly all guardianship statutes have a similar two-component formula for determining incompetency; see 43 Fed.Reg. 11328, 11345-51 (1978). The first part of the statutory test is a "status" component, i.e., the existence of some defective mental or physical condition; the second is a "functional" component—a substantive standard involving a functional disability resulting from the "status" component.

A typical statutory incompetency standard is that found in Ohio law. An "incompetent" is defined as:

> . . . any person who by reason of advanced age, improvidence, or mental or physical disability or infirmity, chronic alcoholism, mental retardation, or mental illness, is incapable of taking proper care of himself or his property or fails to provide for his family or other persons for whom he is charged by law to provide, or any person confined to a penal institution within this state (Ohio Rev. Code Ann. § 2111.01(D) (Supp. 1978)).

The standard set forth in the Uniform Probate Code broadens the scope of "incapacitated person" to include any person who is impaired by any cause:

> . . . "incapacitated person" means any person who is impaired by reason of mental illness, mental deficiency, physical illness or disability, advanced age, chronic use of drugs, chronic intoxication, or other cause (except minority) to the extent that he lacks sufficient understanding or capacity to make or communicate responsible decisions concerning his person . . . (Uniform Probate Code § 5-101(1)).

This standard has been adopted by many states; see, e.g., Ariz. Rev. Stat. § 14-5301 (1974); Idaho Code § 15-5-101 (Supp. 1978); Kan. Stat. § 59-3002(1) (1976); Me. Rev. Stat. Tit. 18 § 3601 (1975); Mont. Rev. Codes Ann. § 91A-5-101(1) (1974); Neb. Rev. Stat § 30-2601(1) (1975); N.M. Stat. Ann. § 38-4-14 (1978); N.D. Cent. Code § 30.1-26-91(1) (Supp. 1975); 20 Pa. C.S.A. § 5501 (1974); Utah Code Ann. § 75-1-201(18) (1978).

However, these standards provide little direction to the courts, and in most cases the decision as to whether an individual is "incapacitated" will depend on the subjective views of the court as to whether the alleged "incapacitated" person's decisions are "responsible."

IN RE KEISER

Supreme Court of Nebraska, 1925
113 Neb. 645, 204 N.W. 394

EVANS, J.

Harry Keiser, son of Levi Keiser, filed in the county court of Saunders county a petition, alleging that Levi Keiser, his father, was 79 years of age, and the owner of notes and securities in the sum of $40,000; that the parent, Levi Keiser, had fallen into the hands of a designing woman; that by reason of extreme old age and other causes Levi Keiser was mentally incompetent to have charge of his estate or manage his property, and that he was wasting his estate, and if permitted to so continue would be reduced to want and will become a county charge; and the petitioner prayed that a guardian be appointed over his estate. Notice of the time and place of the hearing on the petition was served upon Levi Keiser and hearing had on February 15, 1925. A general demurrer was filed to paragraphs No. 4 and No. 5 of the petition, which was overruled. On February 19, 1925, after a hearing, Levi Keiser was found by the county judge to be mentally incompetent, and Eli Keiser, his brother, was appointed guardian of the person and estate of Levi Keiser. From this order and judgment of the county court, Levi Keiser appealed to the district court, and said cause was tried in the district court, the petition filed therein alleging substantially the same facts as that filed in the court below. The appellant demurred to the fourth, fifth and sixth paragraphs of the petition. The demurrer was overruled and the case was tried to the court without the intervention of a jury. The court found:

> That by reason of extreme age, or other causes, the said Levi Keiser is incompetent and unable to care for his person or to have charge or control of his property and estate, and that it is for the best interests of all concerned that a guardian be appointed for the purpose of caring for the person and property and estate of said Levi Keiser.
>
> The court further finds that the guardian, heretofore appointed by the county court, was properly appointed, and that the decision of said county court and the appointment of said guardian ought to be approved by this court.
>
> It is therefore ordered, adjudged and decreed that the decision and appointment of the said county court of Saunders county, Nebraska, be and the same hereby is, approved, and the said Eli Keiser is appointed guardian of the person and property and estate of the said Levi Keiser.
>
> It is further ordered and decreed that the said guardian be, and he hereby is, ordered and directed not to remove the said Levi Keiser from the county of Saunders, nor from his home therein, nor to restrain him of his personal liberty, until the further order of the court.

From this judgment Levi Keiser has appealed to this court.

* * *

It is urged by the appellant that the fact that Levi Keiser is 79 years old is no evidence that he is mentally incompetent to transact his ordinary business affairs. He also insists that the fact that Levi Keiser loaned money to Mrs. Buell under the circumstances and conditions present in this case is not evidence of incompetency. It may be conceded that, were there no other evidence of incompetency than the age of Mr. Keiser and the loan to Mrs. Buell, it would not support a finding of mental incapacity, but the record is not so lacking or circumscribed.

Old age and failure of memory do not, of themselves, establish incompetency to care for ordinary business affairs. *Speer* v. *Speer,* 146 Iowa 6, 123 N.W. 176, 27 L.R.A. (N.S.) 294, 140 Am.St.Rep. 268. The fact that a man is 79 years old, and, by reason of his feeble condition, has not sufficient strength of mind to manage his business with ordinary care and prudence, does not warrant the appointment of a guardian under the provisions of section 1590, Comp. St. 1922, which provides for the appointment of a guardian of the property for a person of unsound mind.

No set rule can be enunciated which will be a safe criterion in all cases. It is not sufficient that incompetency alone is established, for it may well be, even where incompetency exists, that the situation and surroundings of the incompetent are such that no necessity exists for the appointment of a guardian, and that no good purpose would be served thereby. The incapacity of a person, which, within the statute, will authorize the appointment of a guardian, is a question of fact in each case for the trial court, whose finding thereon will not ordinarily be disturbed. *Goddard* v. *Treat,* 83 Conn. 516, 77 A. 959.

While the scope of the examination rests in the sound discretion of the court, the examination should be limited to inquiries which have for their object the finding and determination of the mental condition of the subject of the inquiry. 37 C. J. 640, § 443; *Alvord* v. *Alvord,* 109 Iowa, 113, 80 N.W. 306. It has been held that in making a test as to mental incapacity the same test should be applied as in suits to avoid deeds and wills. *Leatherman* v. *Leatherman,* 82 W. Va. 748, 97 S.E. 294. But the present proceeding is under a statute, one of whose purposes is, indeed its chief purpose is, to prevent the necessity of such actions; and, while each individual is entitled to control his own property, the legislative intent was to prevent its dissipation in litigation over contracts secured by improper persons through improper means and to save to the owners of such property that which age and disease have made them unable and incapable to save for and to themselves.

The appellant complains that the court permitted nonexpert witnesses to give opinions as to the mental capacity of Levi Keiser without having first laid a proper foundation for the same, and avers that so doing constituted prejudicial error. Where a case is tried to the court without a jury, upon review thereof in this court it will be presumed that the trial court in arriving at its decision considered only competent and material evidence. And "this court will not reverse the judgment in a case tried to the court without a jury merely because of the admission of improper evidence." *Lunney* v. *Healey,* 56 Neb. 313, 76 N.W. 558, 44 L.R.A. 593.

The descriptive words, "mentally incompetent," "incompetent," and "incapable," as used in sections 1589, 1590, Comp. St. 1922, mean any one who, though not insane, is, by reason of old age, disease, weakness of mind, or from any other cause or causes, unable or incapable, unassisted, of properly taking care of himself or managing his property, and by reason thereof would be liable to be deceived or imposed upon by artful or designing persons. Mental incompetency or incapacity is established when there is found to exist an essential privation of reasoning faculties, or when a person is incapable of understanding and acting with discretion in the ordinary affairs of life. Where a person has insufficient mental capacity for the just protection of his property and his mental condition is such that he is guided by the will of others instead of his own in its disposition, a guardian should be appointed. *Lang* v. *Lang,* 157 Iowa 300, 135 N.W. 604. In a proceeding for the appointment of a guardian for alleged incompetency because incapable of caring for his property, where the person is a party to the proceeding and has not been adjudged insane, his admissions, declarations, and showing of facts inconsistent with mental soundness are admissible as substantive evidence on the issue of sanity. *Conway* v. *Murphy,* 135 Iowa 171, 112 N.W. 764.

" 'Sanity' and 'competency to manage an estate' are not synonymous terms. A man may be sane in the sense that it is not necessary to incarcerate him in an asylum and yet be incompetent to manage an estate even though he be not a spendthrift or a drunkard." *Guardianship of Farr,* 169 Wis. 451, 171 N.W. 951. See, also, *Robinson v. VanCamp,* 79 Ind.App. 382, 135 N.E. 580.

The record has been carefully examined, and the court is convinced that, in consequence of the character, extent, and kind of property of which the estate consists, the finding of the trial court—"that by reason of extreme age, or other causes, the said Levi Keiser is incompetent and unable to care for his person or to have charge or control of his property and estate, and that it is for the best interests of all concerned that a guardian be appointed for the purpose of caring for the person and property and estate of said Levi Keiser"—is fully sustained by the evidence.

A careful consideration of sections 1576-1621, art. 6, c. 16, Comp. St. 1922, leads the court to the conclusion that it was not the legislative intent to at any time deprive an individual of his right to liberty of action, and that under sections 1589, 1590, 1591, Comp. St. 1922, it was the intent, in a proper case, to vest authority in the court to appoint a guardian of either the person or estate, or of both, as the circumstances of the particular case require.

There is, however, an entire lack of evidence that Levi Keiser is in such condition as to be a menace either to himself or to others, and the provision in the judgment of the trial court—"It is further ordered and decreed that said guardian be, and he hereby is, ordered and directed not to remove the said Levi Keiser from the county of Saunders, nor from his home therein, nor to restrain him of his personal liberty, until the further order of this court"—is right and proper, and should be and is approved, and he should be left in his present family relations uninterfered with in the engagement of his liberty.

This court further finds that Eli Keiser, who is appointed as guardian, has interests which conflict, or are liable to conflict, with those of the estate of Levi Keiser, and he should not have been appointed as guardian of the person and estate of said Levi Keiser, and that a disinterested person and one competent to properly care for Levi Keiser's estate should be appointed in his stead.

Section 9151, Comp. St. 1922, provides:

> When a judgment or final order shall be reversed either in whole or in part, in the Supreme Court, the court reversing the same shall proceed to render such judgment as the court below should have rendered, or remand the cause to the court below for such judgment.

As the decision in this action has been modified in so far as the person of the guardian is concerned, and as both parties in this litigation in proceedings herein have expressed confidence in Hugo A. Wiggenhorn, the said Hugo A. Wiggenhorn, is hereby appointed guardian of the person and estate of Levi Keiser under the terms and conditions of this judgment, and the statute with reference thereto, with directions that he appear in the county court of Saunders county and take the oath of office and give the bond required by law, the same to be approved by the county judge of said county.

The decision of the trial court is modified accordingly and the cause remanded for further proceedings in accordance with this opinion.

Modified and remanded.

NOTE

Scrutinize the standards for incompetency applied by the *Kaiser* court. Can you suggest any more concrete criteria?

IN RE WARNER'S ESTATE

Supreme Court of Nebraska, 1939
137 Neb. 25, 288 N.W. 39

EBERLY, Justice.

Robert Richardson and Hazel Richardson filed in the county court of Polk county a petition, alleging that "Leo M. Warner, an inhabitant of and residing in Polk county in the state of Nebraska, is mentally incompetent to have the charge and management of his property"; that said incompetent person is possessed of personal property situated in Polk county of the value of about $4,500 and is also the owner of an interest in real estate situated within the state of Nebraska of the value of about $300; that said incompetent person has minor children dependent upon him for support, and it is necessary for the welfare of said incompetent person and his dependent children that a guardian be appointed for the purpose of taking charge of the property, etc. The petition also sets forth that petitioners are relatives of said incompetent person, being a nephew and a niece of him, and prays for the appointment of E. C. Nordlund as such guardian. Notice of hearing on this petition was served on Leo M. Warner, Eva B. Warner, Floyd M. Warner, Dean M. Warner and Herbert K. Richardson. A demurrer was thereupon filed to said petition by Leo M. Warner, challenging the capacity of the plaintiffs to sue, the jurisdiction of the county court to hear the proceeding, and the sufficiency of the petition to state a cause of action. Thereupon Leo M. Warner filed an answer which carried forward the challenge to the capacity of plaintiffs to sue and to the jurisdiction of the county court, and denied generally the allegations of the petition. On August 16, 1937, being the date to which the hearing on said matter was continued by consent and agreement of parties, the county court overruled the demurrer of Leo M. Warner, also adjudged that "due and legal service has been had on all parties herein as provided by law, and that the facts set out and alleged in the petition filed herein are true and that said Leo M. Warner is mentally incompetent to have the charge and management of his property," etc. Further, the county court appointed E. C. Nordlund as guardian of said Leo M. Warner. In connection with this judgment there appears a stipulation that service of process was lawfully obtained as provided by law upon Leo M. Warner, the alleged incompetent, herein, and the next of kin of said Leo M. Warner. E. C. Nordlund thereupon qualified as such guardian and gave his official bond which was duly approved on August 26, 1937.

Leo M. Warner appealed from the judgment so entered, and on October 6, 1937, petitioners Robert Richardson and Hazel Richardson filed in this cause in the district court for Polk county, Nebraska, their petition on appeal which contained the essential averments originally set forth in the petition filed by them in the county court of Polk county, Nebraska. To this petition on appeal, Leo M. Warner answered by a general denial. The issues thus made up were submitted by the district court to a jury, which, after hearing the evidence, returned as their findings and verdict "That Leo M.

Warner is now incompetent to have charge and management of his property." Thereupon Leo M. Warner filed his motion for a new trial which was by the district court overruled, and thereupon a judgment was entered for petitioners as prayed. This judgment recites, in part, viz.:

> Now, on this 14th day of July, 1938, this matter came on for hearing upon said motion for new trial and for a consideration of the advisory verdict of the jury and after due consideration, the court finds that said motion for new trial should be overruled, and an order and decree entered herein in accordance with the advisory verdict returned by the jury in said matter; further, the court finds that the allegations set forth in the petition herein are true, and finds generally for the petitioners; further the court finds from the evidence submitted that the said Leo M. Warner is now incompetent to have charge and management of his property, and that the appeal herein should not be sustained, and guardianship affirmed, and the case remanded to the county court for further proceedings.
>
> It is therefore, ordered, adjudged and decreed by the court, that the motion for new trial filed herein by Leo M. Warner be, and the same is hereby overruled; that Leo Warner is now incompetent to have the care and management of his property and estate; that he should have a guardian to manage and handle his property and estate, and that the appeal in said guardianship matter to this court be not sustained, and that the guardianship findings and decree of the county court should be sustained and the same is hereby affirmed and sustained and said case is hereby remanded to the county court for further proceedings.

From this judgment, Leo M. Warner appeals.

* * *

In determining the sufficiency of the evidence to support the findings and judgment of the district court, appealed from, there are certain facts as to which no serious conflict is to be found in the proof. The defendant was 43 years of age. He had inherited approximately $5,000 in cash, of which he was about to come into possession. He is, and was, without doubt a moron, and his present degree of intelligence and mental competency has existed and remained unchanged for more than twenty years past. The question in fact is not whether the defendant is of impaired mentality, but the degree of mental impairment was for determination by the trial court. On this subject two expert "medical" witnesses testified in behalf of the defendant, and without substantial disagreement classify his degree of mental competency as the intelligence of a child between ten and twelve years of age. The evidence as to the determinative tests is that Warner was unable to perform those of a twelve year old child, but was able to successfully carry out the test for the next grade thereunder. These experts, on the basis of their test and observation, testify to the opinion that the defendant is not mentally incompetent to have the charge and management of his property. "It is obvious, however, that the opinions of even medical experts, though worthy of the most careful consideration, and respectful attention, and to be weighed with other testimony in reaching a conclusion, cannot and ought not solely to control the court or jury in the opinion they are to pronounce on the facts before them." Woerner, *American Law of Guardianship*, 410.

In addition, as lay witnesses, we have relatives and close acquaintances of the defendant, who, in testifying detail facts and circumstances relating to the conduct and life of defendant, on the basis of which they testify to opinions that the defendant is mentally competent to have charge and management of his property.

Opposed to this proof, we have the evidence of members of his father's family, and others, who, likewise from the basis of observation, which the situation in which they lived and contact with the defendant accorded them, testify to the opinion that the defendant is mentally incompetent to have charge and management of his property. The facts testified to by certain of these witnesses tend to support the conclusion that the defendant was never competent to, and did not, transact the important business transactions arising during his life; that so long as his father lived he transacted most of the defendant's important transactions for him; that finally, in the year 1929, defendant's mother, and his brothers and sisters, requested Dr. Frank W. Warner, a brother of the defendant, to handle the business and property of Leo M. Warner, the defendant. Circumstances appearing in the record indicate that Dr. Warner complied with these requests, and undertook the duties contemplated thereby. The record shows that it was at this time that the petition for the appointment of Dr. Frank W. Warner as his guardian was filed by the defendant, the signed consent of Dr. Warner to such appointment being indorsed thereon. It is further disclosed by the record that Dr. Warner duly qualified and continued to serve as such guardian until all moneys and personal property then belonging to the ward and coming into his possession as guardian had been disposed of as provided by law and the orders of said court, whereupon his resignation as such guardian was presented to and accepted by the county court, and he was thereupon on June 29, 1936, discharged as such. However, it appears that this order of the county court of Polk county neither expressly nor by implication in any manner changed or modified its determination as to the mental incompetency of defendant as necessarily made and determined in its order of April 15, 1929.

However, the conclusiveness of this evidence need not be determined. So considered, it is clear that the presiding judge in the district court accepted the testimony given in behalf of the plaintiffs and rejected the testimony offered in behalf of the defendant. The trial judge heard the testimony of Leo M. Warner and of the witnesses testifying in his behalf, and also the witnesses testifying for the petitioners. The demeanor of defendant's witnesses was necessarily observed by him, as well as of those who testified adversely to the defendant. He accepted as true and correct the testimony of plaintiffs' witnesses and similarly rejected the testimony in behalf of the defendant. The trial judge's opportunity for thus ascertaining the truth was greater than that afforded the members of this tribunal.

In consideration of the entire record, we are impressed with the view that this case was correctly determined. The judgment of the district court is, therefore, in all things, affirmed.

SIMMONS, Chief Justice (dissenting).

*   *   *

All persons are presumed to be sane and competent. An individual is entitled to the control of his own property unless good cause is shown for denying that control to him. *Keiser* v. *Keiser*, 113 Neb. 645, 204 N.W. 394. The burden of proof was upon the plaintiffs to establish that the defendant was "mentally incompetent to have the charge and management of his property." Comp.St. 1929, sec.38-201. Woerner, *American Law of Guardianship*, 408, sec. 124. *In re Phillips*, 158 Mich. 155, 122 N.W. 554.

The Nebraska statute and the Michigan statute are in almost identical language. This court has often cited and followed the Michigan court in interpreting our guardianship act. Mental incompetency must be established. "The statute does not say merely 'incompetent,' but 'mentally incompetent.' It does not refer to persons who are sane, but not, perhaps, as wise or intelligent as some other persons. It applies to those whose minds is so affected as to have lost control of itself to such a degree as to deprive the person afflicted of sane and normal action." *In re Guardianship of Storick*, 64 Mich. 685, 31 N.W. 582, 583. Here it is noted that the plaintiffs' witnesses were not limited by their questions to the mental competency or incompetency of the defendant, but were asked merely as to their opinion of defendant's competency.

The power, vested in the courts, to place a guardian over a person or his property should not be exercised except in cases that clearly require that action. 32 C.J. 632; *In re Guardianship of Wilson*, 23 Ohio App. 390, 155 N.E. 654; *McCammon* v. *Cunningham*, 108 Ind. 545, 9 N.E. 455; *In re Bryden's Estate*, 211 Pa. 633, 61 A. 250.

It was early held in Michigan: "The fact that a man is unable to provide comfortable and suitable maintenance for his family, even when coupled with the fact that he makes foolish bargains and squanders all he earns, is not made by either statute a reason why he should have a guardian appointed over him. If it were, a goodly number of people would be under guardianship. . . . The power of appointment of a guardian by the probate court is derived from the statute, and, in order to obtain jurisdiction in such cases, the statute must be strictly pursued." *Partello* v. *Holton*, 79 Mich. 372, 44 N.W. 619, 620. See *North* v. *Joslin*, 59 Mich. 624, 26 N.W. 810; *In re Guardianship of Bassett*, 68 Mich. 348, 36 N.W. 97; *In re Guardianship of Storick*, 64 Mich. 685, 31 N.W. 582.

* * *

The real cause for the bringing of this proceeding is the desire of plaintiffs to aid their father in the collection of an alleged claim against the defendant. Guardianship proceedings are not intended to be a substitute for attachment or proceedings in aid of execution. Courts have repeatedly condemned the bringing of proceedings of this character by expectant heirs, for the purpose of conserving an estate for their inheritance. This proceeding presents a situation far more subject to condemnation. The plaintiffs herein are dominated by the selfish interest of aiding their father in the collection of a claim, rather than the unselfish interest of friends having the welfare of the defendant uppermost in their minds. Nowhere in this record is there any evidence indicating that these plaintiffs have ever been concerned about the defendant or his welfare.

* * *

> Each case involving the guardianship of an [alleged] incompetent person must, of necessity, stand or fall upon the circumstances and evidence shown and the conditions surrounding the transaction. (*In re Guardianship of Blochowitz*, 135 Neb. 163, 280 N.W. 438, 441.)

After a careful reading of this entire record in the light of the circumstances and conditions therein disclosed, I am convinced that the appointment of a guardian for the person and property of the defendant is not justified and is not authorized by the statute under which this proceeding was had.

In my opinion the judgment of the district court should be reversed and the case dismissed.

NOTES

1. In other portions of his dissenting opinion, which are not included here, Chief Justice Simmons marshals much of the evidence presented at trial in *Warner's Estate,* including the testimony of several friends and relatives and two medical doctors, which tends to indicate that Leo Warner was capable of managing his own affairs.

2. Interpretation of the often vague standards contained in guardianship statutes necessarily involves considerable discretion on the part of the trial court. In borderline cases, such as *In re Warner's Estate,* the subjective opinion of the trial judge becomes all-important. A court using a standard such as the Uniform Probate Code's "responsible decisions," can label an individual incompetent if the court simply disagrees with the substance of his decisions. This is particularly apparent in cases concerning guardianship for the purpose of overturning an adult's refusal to consent to a medical procedure; a judge's opinion may well depend on what he or she would do in such a situation rather than on a consideration of the individual's right to freedom of choice; see, e.g., Friedman, P., "Legal Regulation of Applied Behavior Analysis in Mental Institutions and Prisons," 17 *Ariz. L. Rev.* 39, 78-80 (1975); see also Chapter 8, this volume.

Some commentators have proposed that standards for determining incompetency should not be based on the reasonableness or rationality of an individual's decisions; they have suggested, rather, that the inquiry should go simply to whether the person can hear a question and can answer it either affirmatively or negatively. As long as a valid response is given, such decisions would be honored. *Id.* at 78-80. *Cf. Wyatt* v. *Aderholt,* 368 F.Supp. 1383-1385 (M.D.Ala. 1974), pp. 904-908, below, where the court held that the standard for determining whether an incompetent resident of a state institution could consent to sterilization was whether the resident could form, without coercion, a genuine desire to be sterilized. If so, the procedure was to be performed.

2. The Role of Medical Testimony

In recent years, criticism has been directed at the improper reliance upon medical opinions so frequently demonstrated in determinations of incompetency. Although incompetency is a legal question, in practice it is often treated as a medical question to be answered by medical experts. For example, a 2-year study of incompetency hearings, including a field study of over 600 cases covering a 10-year period in New York, resulted in the conclusion that "[i]n practice the medical standard becomes the primary, if not the sole, basis for adjudicating incompetency" (Alexander, G., and Lewin, T., *The Aged and the Need for a Surrogate Management,* 25 (1972)). The authors noted that in the incompetency hearings they studied:

> No specific inquiry is made into the way the particular aberrational condition affects the subject's ability to manage his financial resources. . . . [and] Not one transcript examined nor medical report studied revealed any attempt by the physician to detail the manner in which the patient's capacity to manage his estate had been affected by the underlying condition.
>
> * * *
>
> There is . . . a medical definition which often becomes the sole factor in adjudicating incompetency. When this occurs, the determination of incompetency is abrogated from the judiciary to the medical profession. Worse, the psychiatric determination is usually stated in conclusionary terms based more frequently on medical or psychiatric symptoms than upon how much in fact these symptoms affect the person's legal status and ability to manage property (*Id.* at 24).

Thus, all too often, the labeling of an individual as mentally deficient by the examining physician serves as the sole criterion for a determination of incompetency and the appointment of a guardian; a functional analysis (concentrating on the individual's demonstrated abilities rather than, for example, the results of standard intelligence tests) is glossed over, if not ignored completely. Yet many authorities are highly skeptical of the validity of psychological, psychiatric diagnostic procedures and their ability to determine competency; see Ennis, B., and Litwack, T., "Psychiatry and the Presumption of Expertise: Flipping Coins in the Courtroom," 62 *Cal. L. Rev.* 693 (1974); *O'Connor* v. *Donaldson,* 422 U.S. 563, 579 (1975) (Burger, C.J., concurring) ("The Court appropriately takes notice of the uncertainties of psychiatric diagnosis. . . .").

An example of this distrust for medical testimony can be gleaned from the appellate court's decision in *In re Waite's Guardianship,* 97 P.2d 238, 239 (Supreme Court of California, 1939). In summarizing the proceeding before the lower court, the court stated:

> On August 15, 1938, Pearl Stewart, daughter of the alleged incompetent, filed a petition praying for the issuance of letters of guardianship of the person and estate of appellant, aged 78. At the hearing two doctors, appointed by the trial court, were called by the respondent and testified. Upon the conclusion of the doctors' evidence the court having been informed by counsel for respondent that there were eight lay witnesses in the matter, said: "I am prepared to make the order in this matter right now, and I am relying on the testimony of the doctors . . . I don't want to hear any lay witnesses."
>
> Counsel for appellant requested permission of the court to call appellant as a witness. The court replied: "I don't want to hear from her." Counsel for appellant then called appellant to the stand and offered her to be sworn. The court said: "If you have any medical testimony I will be glad to hear it, but I don't want to hear from the lady. I don't know anything personally about her mental condition."
>
> The court thereupon made the decree appointing Pearl Stewart, the daughter, guardian of the person, and Crocker First National Bank, guardian of the estate (*Id.* at 239).

The court then went on to discuss the invalidity of the doctors' determinations that the allegedly incompetent person "lacked judgment":

> The second ground of appeal relates to the sufficiency of evidence to prove incompetence. The testimony of the doctors, in so far as it was based upon their observation of appellant, was entirely favorable to her. They testified that she was in fine physical

condition and was very well preserved for her age; that she was clear mentally and that her memory was very clear as to transactions occurring over a period of four or five years previous to the examination; that she knew the nature of the transactions in which she engaged, and understood the nature, status and title of her property; that she knew who her relatives were, and gave intelligent answers to questions concerning them.

The doctors examined appellant separately. Each testified to certain facts related to them by appellant which they refer to in their testimony as her "past history," and each of the doctors gave these facts as the basis for his conclusion relative to appellant's competency. The facts so related are in substance as follows:

At the time of the hearing appellant was 78 years old. Her second husband had died about 3 years previously leaving her $31,000. At the age of 76 she married her third husband, aged 45. She lived with him about two months and the marriage and subsequent divorce cost her about $4,000. Appellant had always wanted to live on a ranch, and about one month before the hearing she purchased a ranch in Dublin canyon, where she resided at the time of the hearing. She paid $8,000 for the ranch and stocked it with cattle for which she paid $850. She gave a one-half interest in the ranch and the income therefrom to a man under an arrangement whereby the latter would take care of the cattle, do all the work on the ranch, and serve her as chauffeur. At the time of the hearing she was dissatisfied with the ranch and wanted to get rid of it.

One doctor testified that these facts showed "a serious defect in judgment insofar as the handling of her affairs is concerned," and stated that he thought she was liable to be imposed upon or deceived by artful or designing persons. The other doctor testified that "considering her recent past history" he believed "that she is over credulous and has shown a lack of judgment" and that her marriage to a man of 45 "is a subnormality" and shows "intelligence defect."

This testimony is inadequate to support the order. The opinions of the doctors as to her "lack of judgment" and "intelligence defect" are to be tested by a consideration of the facts from which those opinions are derived; and if those facts do not justify the conclusions, the opinions are arbitrary, and without substantial value as evidence. There was no evidence that the price paid for the ranch was in excess of its real value, or that it was a bad investment. The fact that appellant may have been disappointed in her hope for happiness in her third marriage to a man much younger than herself could hardly be considered substantial evidence of incompetency. The arrangement which appellant made with a man to manage and care for her ranch and act as her chauffeur in return for the half interest in the ranch might indicate poor business judgment, but such conclusion does not necessarily follow. Moreover, there must be something more than poor business judgment to establish incompetency. As the court remarked in *Estate of Watson,* 176 Cal. 342, 345, 168 P. 341, 343, speaking of the alleged incompetent: "She was the owner of the property. It was her right to manage it as she pleased, either personally or through agents of her choice, and to dispose of it as she saw fit, unless her mental faculties were impaired to such an extent as to make her unable to properly manage and take care of it or to render her liable to imposition by 'artful or designing persons'."

In our opinion the finding of incompetency is not supported by any substantial evidence.

The decree and order are reversed (*Id.* at 240).

At least one state values medical opinion so highly that it provides for a quasi-judicial commission composed of two physicians and one attorney to hear testimony and decide whether the individual before it requires a guardian, Ga. Code Ann. § 49-604.1(b)-(d) (Supp. 1979).

Recently, however, other states have given specific emphasis to the need to evaluate functional factors. California, for example, provides in its guardianship statute that:

... the phrase "incompetent person," "incompetent," or "conservatee" shall mean a legal, not a medical disability and shall be measured by functional inabilities. It shall be construed to mean or refer to any adult person who, in the case of guardianship of the person, is unable properly to provide for his own personal needs for physical health, food, clothing or shelter, and, in the case of guardianship of the estate, is substantially unable to manage his own financial resources. "Substantial inability" shall not be evidenced solely by isolated incidents of negligence or improvidence (Cal. Prob. Code § 1460 (West Supp. 1979).

In re Guardianship of Pickles

District Court of Appeals of Florida, First District, 1965
170 S.2d 603

Rawls, Judge.

Upon the petition of her mother, an examining committee ... was convened ... for the purpose of inquiring into the competency of Muriel Pickles. On April 14, 1964, this committee, ... determined that she was incompetent "by reason of mental incompetency, to-wit: mental disease; that same is acute; that she has no particular hallucinations; that she is of the age of 29 and her propensities were that she leaves home for several days at a time; and that she does not require mechanical restraint to prevent her from self-injury or violence to others." The county judge after considering this report and receiving extensive testimony adjudicated Muriel Pickles mentally incompetent but did not order commitment. She filed notice of appeal from said order on the same date.

The sole point presented by appellant on this appeal is that the evidence was insufficient to support the adjudication of incompetency.

Appellant's history, as developed by the testimony of her parents and the medical experts, discloses: Muriel Pickles, age 29, was one of 9 children of Joe and Jeanette Pickles of Havana, Florida. In high school she was a cheer leader, played basketball, and was elected homecoming queen. She went to Washington for two years where she worked for a congressman, for the un-American Activities Committee, and for the F.B.I. When she failed to write home for a three months' period, her family after several telephone calls located her in a home for pregnant girls. Her father sent her money for her medical expenses and for the trip home. During the next four years she and her baby—a boy, now 6 years old—lived at her parents' home in Havana, Florida. A part of that time she worked for the State Road Department where she got into trouble, apparently with the credit union. Rather than be fired or demoted she went to work for the Florida Legislature and later for a Tallahassee attorney. About that time she had several small checks [$2.00 to $5.00 to $10.00] bounce due to insufficient funds. She then moved to Naples where she worked for an insurance company. When caught embezzling funds ($960 to $1,960) from petty cash, she contended that her boss also took money from that source without signing slips. She was released in the care of her parents with the understanding her father would make restitution in monthly installments. She has earned as much as $345.00 per month when employed, but has been living at home, unemployed, for the last 4 months. She leaves home for several days at a time without informing her family of her plans. On occasions they have found her staying with a friend in Havana. Her mother cares for her small son during these absences. Muriel thinks her parents are always reminding her of her mistakes. Her parents, who have been told by several of Muriel's employers that she needs help, feel that they impose no restrictions on her, that any mention they make of her past mistakes is in the nature of helping her so she will not repeat them in the future, and that she is irresponsible to the extent she absents herself from home leaving the care of her child to her mother. They feel that if she moves away from their home she will get into more trouble and the financial burden of her "mistakes" is more than they are able to afford. They want her to have medical treatment if she needs it.

The lay member of the examining committee testified that he talked to Muriel's father and mother at which time they "briefed me on the situation" and that Muriel when asked if she would have herself committed, replied, "No." Upon cross examination, he stated that he read the statement the doctors gave and according to his understanding of Muriel's behavior she was endangering her health and the child's in that she was neglecting the child. He felt that Muriel needs advice.

One of the medical doctors who has practiced for 50 years (specializing in obstetrics) testified that he had observed Muriel Pickles, that he was the family physician and that he had known her for a long time. In response to the court's question, "Is it your opinion she is in need of psychiatric help?" this doctor testified that her past history as related by her parents indicates that she needs psychiatric treatment. His only other testimony on direct examination was that he concurred in the other examining physician's tentative diagnosis. On cross examination, this doctor stated that Muriel came to his office voluntarily, that he talked to her parents procuring a history from them prior to her visit, and that he didn't ask Muriel any questions. In response to the question, "The report here shows the tentative diagnosis of schizophrenia. Would you define?" the doctor answered, "I think she needs psychiatric treatment." He further testified, "She was schizophrenic from history—the way she was doing," and the next answer to a question concerning mental diseases was, "I am not familiar with schizophrenia; not a psychiatrist." He then states that the symptoms displayed by a schizophrenic are, "They run away from home—different things." His basis for concurring in the other doctor's diagnosis of schizophrenia was from the family history related to him of her actions in leaving home. He further testified that Muriel was not in any way dangerous to herself or anyone else; that he did not classify her as being insane.

It is interesting to note that after the testimony was taken of those two members of the examining committee and of a doctor produced on behalf of Muriel, the judge advised Muriel's attorney that he was going to continue the hearing, he would be glad to discuss the matter, and in the event "nothing is worked out," he would like to have the other examining doctor's testimony. Muriel was left on her own as far as liberty was concerned until a final disposition was made of the matter.

On April 22, 1964, the hearing was reconvened to receive the testimony of the remaining member of the examining committee, a general practicing surgeon of 28 years. In his opinion the patient exhibited signs of schizophrenia though he could not classify the type because to do so is very difficult and requires a long period of observation.

Upon cross examination the doctor testified that he had no special training in the field of psychiatry or psychology; that schizophrenia is commonly called split-personality; that Muriel was not paranoid and had no hallucinations; that he did not think she is a true psychotic; that she does not suffer from alcoholism or depression and does not have any history of violence; and that he did not think there is any danger in her harming anyone else.

The medical doctor produced on behalf of Muriel testified that he had practiced 2½ years in the United States Army, 1½ years at Florida State Hospital, and 16 years in Tallahassee, Florida; that he had an extensive interview with Muriel at which time she gave him her entire history telling a very straightforward story of sequence of events showing reason and logic; that she now realized when she was getting into trouble; that he did not believe that the problems of getting into trouble per se indicate insanity; that he had gotten into trouble and didn't know anyone who hadn't gotten into trouble; that he did not believe that Muriel is psychotic; that any mental disease she suffered was in a minor degree; that the key to the whole mental problem is what is normal; that a savage would be considered normal in Africa; that in his opinion she was not insane in either a legal or medical sense; that she does need counseling and guidance and this could probably be handled best on an out-patient basis; and that she knew the consequences of her acts. At this point the court asked the following questions:

Q   Doctor, in view of these things that she has been involved in from time to time since she got out of school, and later trouble that she had down the state, and assuming that she did have trouble with the law, with reference to bad checks that she gave, do you still think that she is able to take care of herself and stay out of trouble, leading a normal life, in view of all those circumstances?

A   Judge, I cannot answer that question if she is capable of staying out of trouble.

Q   If she was confined to Florida State Hospital, they would want to know if she was capable of leading a normal life—she had been committed and they would know she was subject to be released—they would be concerned.

* * *

A   A lot of people are concerned. It will keep her out of trouble for that period of time; whether she is capable of managing her own affairs—many people get into trouble—they are not incompetent.

Q   In view of her case, do you feel that she is in need of psychiatric treatment?

A   She is in need of counseling.

Q   That is the thing we are concerned about; whether she is in need of psychiatric treatment. You don't think she is in need of psychiatric treatment?

A   No—not by a person who limits himself to psychiatry only.

Q   What type of treatment do you feel she is in need of?

A   Counseling and guidance would be a help.

Q   What type of treatment?

A   Someone who understands a little more about human nature—somebody to talk to her.

Q   You are getting back to psychiatric treatment when you say the treatment she needs is somebody to talk to her—if you can limit that to doctors—is there any other type of treatment?

A   Yes, every doctor of gynecology, obstetrics—does some degree of it.

Q   Do you think that type of doctor could be of help to her?

A   Yes, I do.

Q   You have talked to her on two occasions?

A   Yes.

Q In view of your observations, the conversations you had, you feel it would be a mistake to commit her?

A Yes, I don't feel she fulfills legal requirements for commitment.

Q The legal requirements—that is not up to you—what I want you to tell me is whether or not her condition is such as to require treatment. The legal requirement—I don't think that is the question. Whether she needs psychiatric help is what I am concerned about.

A She needs it; but to say she needs it by a psychiatrist, that is not a necessity.

Q If she can get it otherwise—

A Judge, to be frank, I don't think she would be benefited by state institution. She does not get that individual care.

Q Are you familiar with the treatment she would get if committed?

A I spent a year and a half on the staff.

THE COURT: Thank you very much, doctor. Mr. Toney, I'm going to follow the findings and reports of the doctors and I'm going to adjudge her incompetent. I'm not going to commit her this time, if there is a possibility that she and her parents might work out something that would be more satisfactory to her and to them than going to Florida State Hospital. I understand they have been talking about it, but I don't think anything has been done except making conversation, so far. If they work out something so she can come on home and look after the child and get treatment outside of the Florida State Hospital, it's all right if they work that out, and that's entirely up to them.

In ancient times the law that governed mentally disabled persons took the form of taboos and tribal customs. Until the Golden Age of Greece the prevailing explanation for mental disabilities was that the afflicted person was possessed of demons, and the chief method of treatment was exorcising the demon from such person. Hippocrates (460–370 B.C.), the father of medicine, and the Greek physicians and philosophers who followed him recognized mental disabilities as natural phenomena and attempted to classify them. Roman law held that mentally disabled persons were legally incapable of agreeing to marriage or entering into contracts, and that once a guardian was appointed, the ward lost all legal capacity. As English jurisprudence developed, the legal incapacity of mental incompetents was recognized. In the early 17th century, Lord Coke, in *Beverly's* case, expounded the law of insanity and listed four types of persons included in the generic term *non compos mentis* as:

1. The idiot or natural fool;
2. He who was of good and sound memory and by the visitation of God has lost it;
3   Lunatics, those who are sometimes lucid and sometimes *non compos mentis;*
4   Those who by their own acts deprive themselves of reason, as the drunkard.

At early common law, the lord of the fee was endowed with the custody and care of insane persons and other incompetents. Subsequently, such power became vested in the king as *parens patriae.* So, after the Revolution the power became vested in the states, or the people thereof, upon two grounds; first, the duty to protect the community from the acts of those who are not under the guidance of reason; and, secondly, the state's duty to protect them as a class incapable of protecting themselves.

Florida initially provided for judicial commitment of insane persons in 1856. As early as 1906 competency proceedings were commenced by a petition, followed by an examination of the alleged incompetent by a court-appointed examining committee, and concluded by an adjudication. The General Statutes, 1906, provided:

§ 1200—When it is supposed that a person, resident of this State, is insane, either non compos mentis or sufficiently devoid of reason to be incapable of self control a petition signed by five reputable citizens, . . . setting forth that he or she is to each of the petitioners personally known and that their knowledge of the mental condition of the subject is sufficient to justify the belief that he or she is insane, and asking that examination be instituted. . . .

§ 1203—On receiving the report of the examining committee, the county judge . . . shall examine the same; and if satisfied therefrom that the person examined and reported is insane within the meaning of this act, he the said judge shall so adjudge . . . [and order commitment to the State Hospital]. Provided, When the proceedings reported by the said committee show the alleged insanity is chronic, or produced by epilepsy or senility and that the person does not require confinement or mechanical restraint to prevent self injury or violence to others, but that he or she is indigent, the county judge . . . shall adjudge and decree that the person is incurably insane . . . [and order that such person be delivered to a responsible person for care and custody or to the county to receive the care and maintenance provided by law for paupers.]

Florida Statutes 1945, provided:

§ 394.20—Whenever any person within this state is believed to be incompetent by reason of sickness, drunkenness, excessive use of drugs, insanity, or other mental or physical condition, so that he is incapable of caring for himself or managing his property, or is likely to dissipate or lose his property or become the victim of designing persons, or inflict harm on himself or others, application by written petition, under oath, may be made to the county judge. . . .

§ 394.22(1)—If the judge, from the report of the examining committee and from the evidence introduced at the hearing, finds that the person under investigation is incompetent, mentally or physically or both, he shall so adjudge, and his judgment shall set forth the nature and extent of the incompetency; but, if he finds that such person is not incompetent, he shall dismiss the cause and discharge said person.

§ 394.22(3)—Whenever any person who had been adjudged mentally incompetent requires confinement or restraint to prevent self-injury or violence to others, the said judge shall direct that such person be forthwith delivered to the superintendent of the Florida state hospital. . . .

As to the beliefs necessary for the petition, Florida Statutes 1963, § 394.22(1), F.S.A. contains the identical language quoted above from § 394.20 of the 1945 statutes except it adds the words "mental illness" prior to the word "sickness." The 1945 wording of the section relating to the judgment was carried forward verbatim in the 1963 statutes and the commitment provisions are in substance the same. From 1906 to the present date the examining committee is required to be composed of one intelligent citizen and two practicing physicians. Also carried forward to the present date is the 1945 statutory presumption that one adjudged either physically or mentally incompetent is incapable, during the duration of such incompetency, of managing his own affairs or making any gift, contract or instrument in writing which is binding on him or his estate.

The word "insanity" is well known to be a legal and not a medical term. Though frequently used in the early laws governing incompetency proceedings, it was never defined for that purpose. In spite of the refinement in terminology appearing in the 1945 law wherein words such as "mental illness," "mental incompetency" and the like were substituted for "insanity," our courts have referred to persons adjudicated incompetent under Chapter 394 as being insane. It should be noted that a different procedure is provided by § 917.01 for adjudication of insanity of criminal defendants and that this statute has, since its enactment, used the word "insanity."

*   *   *

Although the early Florida cases recognized that adjudication of insanity for hospital purposes was a condition distinguishable from insanity for criminal purposes, the recent cases have obliterated this distinction at least in so far as ability to stand trial is concerned. If for no other reason, the far reaching effects of those recent criminal decisions lead us to the conclusion that extreme care should be exercised in adjudicating one incompetent, particularly since the words "insanity," "incompetency" and "mental illness" have not yet been defined by Chapter 394.

The Draft Act for the Hospitalization of the Mentally Ill[8] was published in 1952 by the National Institute of Mental Health, Federal Security Agency, as a guide for states in revising their commitment statutes. This Act defines "mentally ill" as "substantial impairment of mental health by psychiatric or other disease" which is broader language than the term "insane." The words "mentally ill" as used in the Act have been construed by text writers to include all persons who should receive medical or psychiatric treatment. The Draft Act authorizes, but does not create a right to, hospitalization for all persons mentally ill. Its objectives are:

> (a) To make hospitalization readily obtainable by those mentally ill persons who voluntarily seek it and create a psychological atmosphere in which such hospitalization will be sought.
> (b) To create procedures for the involuntary hospitalization of the mentally ill which will not be harmful to the mentally ill person; with special reference to the problems of serving personal notice on the individual who is mentally ill and requiring him to make a personal appearance during the involuntary hospitalization procedures.
> (c) To secure for the individual who is mentally ill maximum protection of his civil rights or liberties.
> (d) To secure by law, to the person who is mentally ill, directly or indirectly, some elements of proper medical care.

The proposed provisions contained in the Draft Act have been endorsed by members of the medical profession and the bar; however, our legislature has not seen fit to enact such a measure and even though we might consider the overall objectives of said Act—which would require the state to provide medical treatment for all persons suffering from mental illness—to be commendable, it is not a function of the court to usurp this clear legislative responsibility under the guise of interpreting the law.[9] In the absence of legislation similar to the Draft Act the determinative question is not whether

---

[8]*The George Washington Law Review,* Vol. 19 (1950–51), pp. 512–516.

[9]"Mental patients now occupy one half of the hospital beds in the country. One out of every 18 persons in the United States is suffering from some form of mental illness, and it is estimated that one out of every ten persons will need psychiatric care at some time in his life. See Parren, One out of Ten, *This Week,* Nov. 7, 1946, p. 5; Statistics Pertinent to Psychiatry in the United States, Report No. 7, G.A.P., March, 1949; Bowman, Presidential Address, 103 *Am.J. Psychiatry* 1 (1946); Barton, Hospital Services for the Mentally Ill, 286 *Annals* 107 (1953)." 31 *North Carolina Law Review,* Hospitalization of the Mentally Ill, 1952–53, p. 274, Footnote 2.

the person is suffering from a mental illness, is in need of psychiatric treatment, is in need of counseling, is staying out of trouble, or is leading a normal life. The pertinent question presented to the judge in cases such as this is whether the alleged incompetent is suffering from a mental illness to such an extent that he is incapable of caring for himself, or managing his property or is likely to dissipate or lose his property or become the victim of designing persons. There is a glaring absence of such proof in this record.

That the trial judge applied erroneous principles of law in the instant cause is apparent from the questions propounded by him to the examining doctors. The sum and substance of his inquiry was: "Does Muriel need psychiatric treatment?" Such might well be the principal point of inquiry if the legislature of Florida sees fit to enact the principal provisions of the Draft Act. The examining doctors concluded that Muriel exhibited signs and symptoms of schizophrenia, but could not classify type for to do so would require a long period of time.[10]

Maloy in his treatise entitled Nervous and Mental Diseases quotes Obernoff as stating:

> ". . . As time went on everyone recognized that the borderline . . . between schizophrenia and the neuroses (nervous diseases) is a fine one, that probably everyone is a bit schizoid as well as neurotic, and that it is the degree of constancy that determines whether the patient becomes schizophrenic in the pathologic (pertaining to disease) sense. The normal person has transitory schizoid episodes. The deduction from the above is, first, that in borderline cases—in cases in which there is not yet a preponderance of universally accepted symptoms of dementia praecox, there is often present a possibility of error in diagnosis; second, that much is yet to be learned about the disease; and third, that many persons apparently normal sitting in judgment in a case of insanity may not be entirely sound in mind themselves."

Thus, it is apparent that a diagnosis of schizophrenia standing by itself (which is not classified as to type) is insufficient to support an adjudication of incompetency within the purview of Florida Statutes 394.22, F.S.A. Weighing the evidence presented to the trial judge in light of the foregoing principles of law, we are compelled to conclude that he applied erroneous legal concepts in deciding that Muriel Pickles was incompetent as contemplated by Florida Statutes 394.22, F.S.A.

No question of bad motive on anyone's part is demonstrated in this proceeding. The concern of the trial judge and the examining committee has obviously been directed toward assisting Appellant. It is apparent that Appellant's parents have "walked the long mile" in trying to aid her when she has gotten into trouble. She admits to having passed worthless checks and embezzling funds which resulted in her seeking assistance from her parents. It is likewise apparent that Appellant has violated the mores of conduct regarded as normal by the present day standards of society. We do not condone these derelictions on Appellant's part; however, the proofs submitted herein do not constitute sufficient grounds for adjudicating a person to be incompetent.

---

[10]One doctor testified that the three types of schizophrenia are simple; hebrephrenic and paranoid. That simple is a disparity between emotions and ideas and reality; in the hebrephrenic they are usually more withdrawn from society and will often not move for long periods of time; paranoid which involves hallucinations could be eliminated; and that Muriel was probably borderline between simple and hebrephrenic.

As stated by the doctor who testified in behalf of Appellant, "Many people get into trouble—they are not incompetent."

A person under restraint of his liberty is entitled to liberation where reasonable doubt exists as to his mental condition. An adjudication of incompetency is a partial deprivation of it. The contents of this record fail to support the adjudication of incompetence, so the cause is reversed with directions to dismiss the petition.

Reversed.

STURGIS, Chief Judge and WIGGINTON, J., concur.

NOTES

1. The trial court in the *Pickles* case clearly was confused about the differences between the standard for committing an individual to a state mental hospital and the standard for determining incompetency. Using the Florida statutory scheme, the court could only have committed Muriel Pickles on a finding that she required confinement or restraint to prevent self-injury or violence to others. On appeal, the court did little to clear up the confusion; after presenting a long discussion as to the need of institutional care, it determined that the lower court was in error because Ms. Pickles did not meet the statutory definition of incompetence.

The confusion and merger of these two standards is in many cases carried over into statutory provisions. Although many states provide explicitly that commitment to a state hospital for the mentally ill or retarded raises no presumption of incompetency, e.g., Conn. Gen. Stat. Ann. § 17-206b (West 1975), other states are silent on the matter, e.g., Del. Code Ann., Title 16, §§ 121-5142 (1974), and still others create such presumptions, e.g., Ind. Code Ann., § 29-1-18-20 (Burns 1972).

Some statutes have created presumptions in certain instances but not in others; for example, until recently, Hawaii's statute provided that no presumption was to arise from commitment of an individual to an institution for the mentally ill. However, any mentally retarded person committed to the state training school and hospital automatically comes under the legal guardianship of the Director of Health and remains under guardianship until discharged absolutely from the state school and hospital, Haw. Rev. Stat. §§ 3-34-34 to 57 (1976).

The Wisconsin guardianship statute provides that commitment is not an adjudication of incompetency, but it does raise a rebuttable presumption of incompetency while the patient is under the jurisdiction of hospital authorities, Wisc. Stat. Ann. § 51.0051 (West 1957). Indiana's statutory scheme, on the other hand, provides that, in most situations, commitment to a hospital for the insane will be equivalent to a prior adjudication of incompetency for the purpose of appointing a guardian of the person, of the estate, or both, Ind. Code Ann. § 29-1-18-20 (Burns 1972).

This merger of the standards for determining guardianship and commitment is found not only in statutes but also in practice. Individuals committed to state institutions often are presumed incompetent. The opposite is also true; individuals who are determined "incompetent" often spend at least some time institutionalized. One extensive study reported that there was a remarkably high correlation between findings of incompetency and subsequent institutionalization:

... [V]ery few people in the entire population studied who were declared incompetent did not manage to spend at least a portion of their time in a psychiatric ward. The conclusion is obvious. Not only is a person found to be incompetent bound to be deprived of his right to manage his property, but is very likely to lose his liberty in the process. (Alexander, G., and Lewin, J., Hearings on Legal Problems Affecting Older Americans Before the Special Comm. on Aging, United States Senate, 91st Cong., 2d Sess. 12 (1970).)

This direct loss of freedom as a result of guardianship determinations is confirmed by a study conducted in San Diego, which concluded that despite an attempt to keep persons in the community, legal intervention through incompetency proceedings caused higher rates of institutionalization than otherwise would have occurred (Horowitz, G., and Estes, C., *Protective Services for the Aged* (1971)). This concept is discussed thoroughly in Horstman, P., "Protective Services for the Elderly: The Limits of *Parens Patriae*," 40 *Mo L. Rev.* 215 (1975) (see also pp. 523–524).

2. The confusion between incompetency and commitment standards discussed in note 1, above, is exacerbated by the number of interrelated subissues considered by the courts in such cases. For example, in determining whether or not the defendant was incompetent, the trial and appellate courts in *Pickles* considered: 1) whether Muriel Pickles had gotten into trouble or deviated from "normal" behavior patterns, 2) whether she was in need of some kind of help, 3) whether she needed counseling and guidance, 4) whether she was in need of psychiatric treatment, 5) whether her mental condition fit into any recognized category of mental disease, 6) whether she needed residential confinement, 7) whether she was insane, and 8) whether she was likely to injure herself or others. Which of these were appropriate for consideration in a competency case under the Florida statutes?

3. Notice the specification, at the end of the *Pickles* opinion of "beyond a reasonable doubt" as the appropriate standard of proof. This holding was subsequently overruled in *In re Beverly*, 342 S.2d 481, 488 (Fla. 1977), which held that "clear and convincing evidence" was the appropriate standard.

E. CONSTITUTIONAL CHALLENGES

Schafer v. Haller

Supreme Court of Ohio, 1923
108 Ohio St. 322, 140 N.E. 517

On the 12th day of June, 1922, an application was filed in the probate court of Crawford county for the appointment of a guardian for Valentine Schafer, the application alleging "that the said Valentine Schafer is incompetent and by reason thereof is incapable of taking care of or preserving his property." Such proceedings were had thereon that upon the 1st day of July, 1922, Valentine Schafer was adjudged an incompetent by the probate court, and on July 5 letters of guardianship were issued. On July 31, 1922, Valentine Schafer filed in the probate court an application for an order terminating such guardianship, averring that:

If he in fact lost reason at the time, or prior thereto, of the appointment of said guardian, J. W. Haller, herein, which said Valentine Schafer denies, said Valentine Schafer avers he is restored to reason, and further avers that letters of such said guardianship have been improperly issued, and that as to such said guardian an entry ought to go upon the journal of court terminating such said guardianship.

This application was heard in the probate court, and such proceedings had hereon that on the 25th day of August, 1922, the termination of the guardianship was denied. An appeal was prosecuted to the court of common pleas, hearing thereon had, and the application refused. Error was prosecuted to the Court of Appeals, which court made the following entry:

The court, being fully advised in the premises and on consideration thereof, find the plaintiff in error to be competent mentally, but physically incompetent, to care for his property, and that there is no reversible error in the record of the said proceedings and judgment. . . .

The Court of Appeals thereupon affirmed the judgment of the court of common pleas and remanded the cause for execution.

ROBINSON, J. The application of the plaintiff in error for a termination of the guardianship was made under section 11010, General Code, which reads:

When the probate judge is satisfied that an idiot, imbecile, or lunatic, or a person as to whom guardianship has been granted as such, is restored to reason, or that letters of guardianship have been improperly issued, he shall make an entry upon the journal that such guardianship terminate.

It will be observed that this section authorizes the probate judge not only to terminate a guardianship, when the person over whom guardianship has been granted is restored to reason, but also to terminate the guardianship when letters of guardianship have been improperly issued, and, since all power of the probate court with reference to the appointment of guardians is conferred by statute, the question as to this proceeding being a collateral attack upon the judgment appointing the guardian is disposed of by the express provision of section 11010, *supra,* giving to the probate court jurisdiction to terminate a guardianship where "letters of guardianship have been improperly issued."

The Court of Appeals in its review upon error of the application to terminate the guardianship found that the judgment of the court of common pleas upon the question of the mental incompetency of Valentine Schafer was against the weight of the evidence, and affirmatively found "the plaintiff in error to be competent mentally," and thereupon affirmed the judgment of the court of common pleas upon the ground that he was competent mentally, but incompetent physically, to care for his property. The petition in error here, in the light of the journal entry of the Court of Appeals, brings to this court the questions:

(1) Whether section 10989, General Code, authorizes the probate court to appoint a guardian for a person who is mentally competent, but physically incompetent?

(2) If it does so authorize the appointment of a guardian for a person mentally competent, and physically incompetent, has the Legislature the power to so provide?

Section 10989 reads, in part:

> Upon satisfactory proof that a person resident of the county, or having legal settlement in any township thereof, is an idiot or imbecile, or lunatic, or an incompetent by reason of advanced age or mental or physical disability or infirmity, the probate court shall appoint a guardian for such person.

In the discharge of its obligation to so interpret each enactment of the Legislature as to make it conform to the provisions of the Constitution of the state and federal government, this court has endeavored to construe section 10989, General Code, so as to qualify the word "incompetent" by the word "mentally"; but by reason of the fact that the Legislature has made its own classification of persons subject to guardianship under this provision, and, in addition to idiots, imbeciles, and lunatics, has made a general classification under the comprehensive term "incompetent," and has furnished its own definition of the word "incompetent," by declaring such to be a person "incompetent by reason of advanced age," "incompetent by reason of . . . mental . . . disability or infirmity," "incompetent by reason of . . . physical disability or infirmity," and has distinguished between mental incompetency and physical incompetency, and made each a ground for the appointment of a guardian, this court cannot by any process, other than by an arbitrary disregard of the language of the section itself, arrive at the conclusion that the Legislature did not intend to make a person suffering from a physical disability alone an incompetent within the provisions of this section. The majority of the court being of that opinion, the court is confronted with the second question propounded above.

The practice of the state exercising a paternal supervision over the property of persons mentally incompetent to exercise such supervision for themselves has existed in some form or other since the foundation of government among men. Without going into a history of the various forms of guardianship which have prevailed in the various jurisdictions of the world, it is sufficient to say that, in so far as we have been able to discover, the guardianship of property has always and everywhere been confined to the guardianship of the property of persons mentally incapable of managing such property—incapable either by reason of infancy or by reason of lack or impairment of intellect; the theory being that the acquisition of property constitutes an act of the will, that a person acquires property either by the exercise of his own will to dominate exclusively an animate or inanimate object, which is under the domination of no person, and thereby subjects such object to his will, and therefore makes such object his property, or, by the exercise of his will in conjunction with the exercise of the will of the person who already dominates such object, receives a transfer of such domination from the person who theretofore exercised such domination, and that, where a person either by reason of his infancy has not attained the power to exercise his will, or by reason of a defect from birth never has and never can have the will to exercise, or by reason of accident or disease has lost the power to exercise his will, the state, in the exercise of its sovereignty, supplies to such through the medium of a guardian the mental attribute which such person has not yet attained, will never have, or has for the time being lost.

Blackstone has described property as the "sole and despotic domination which one man claims and exercises over the external things of the world, in total exclusion of the right of any other individual in the universe.'' *Blackstone's Commentaries,* book 2, c. 1, p. 2. While this definition, in the light of present-day situations, would necessarily have to be rather liberally construed, it states the essential characteristic of property. Woerner in his American Law of Administration (2d Ed.) § 1, states:

> My property is that which is mine. That only is mine which I acquire, hold, and dispose of by my will. It is my will which determines the acquisition of a thing by me, whether originally, by reducing to possession, and thus making my property that which was no one's property before, or by contract, by which a thing becomes mine through the concurrence of my will with that of its former owner.

And in section 4 he states:

> Property, then, is the realization of the free will of a person, the external sphere of his freedom. As such, it partakes of, and is clothed with, the dignity and inviolability of the person. The things which constitute property can have no rights, for they have no will; and will alone, or the person in which it has its abode and vehicle, can be the subject of right and of its correlative, duty. The law recognizes and deals with property only in so far as it recognizes and deals with the will of the owner, realized or externalized therein.

In section 3 he states:

> Alienability is of the essence of property; an infringement of my right or power to alienate my property is therefore a limitation upon my free will, and to that extent a violation of my personal liberty, because my free will finds realization in property. The infraction of my personal freedom is precisely the same if a limitation is put upon my power to alienate property as if I were prevented from acquiring, or from holding or using it. The limitation would in either case deprive me of my power to contract, and thus destroy my liberty.

It thus follows that the function of the state in exercising a guardianship over the property of one of its defective subjects, whether defective by reason of age, birth, accident, or disease, arises out of the fact that such defective is lacking in the power to exercise his will, which we have come to term "mental capacity to manage," and not out of lack of physical ability to care for, control, develop, and utilize.

The existence of the power to exercise the will, the mental capacity to manage, implies the ability to employ or secure some one physically able to perform the tasks set, and if the power to exercise the will, the mental capacity to manage, exists, that function can be performed as well by a person physically incapacitated as by a guardian, for it is not contemplated by section 10989, General Code, that the guardian shall perform the physical labor necessary for the utilization and enjoyment of property, but that out of the proceeds of the estate of the ward such physical labor shall be employed; and, since a ward "competent mentally, but physically incompetent," possesses the mental capacity to manage, and therefore the mental capacity to employ or secure some one possessing physical capacity to carry out his will, all reason for the substitution for his mental capacity to manage of the mental capacity of a guardian to manage disappears.

Section 1, art. 1, of the Constitution of Ohio, guarantees to all persons within its borders: "Certain inalienable rights, among which are those of enjoying and defending life and liberty, acquiring, possessing, and protecting property."

There being no sound reason for the provision of section 10989, General Code, that makes physical disability or infirmity a ground for the appointment of a guardian of the property of a person mentally competent, but physically incompetent, the provision is an unwarranted abridgment of the liberty of such person, and an unwarranted abridgment of his right to acquire, possess and protect property, and therefore in violation of section 1, art.1, of the Constitution.

Judgment reversed.

MARSHALL, C. J., and WANAMAKER, JONES, MATTHIAS, DAY, and ALLEN, JJ., concur.

NOTES

1. *Schafer* v. *Haller* was distinguished in *In re Guardianship of Schmidt,* 221 Or. 535, 352 P.2d 152 (1960). In *Schmidt* the statute challenged as unconstitutional declared:

> "Incompetent" includes every person who is, by reason of old age, disease, weakness of mind or from any other cause, unable unassisted to properly manage and take care of himself or his property, and by reason thereof would be likely to be deceived or imposed upon by artful or designing persons (ORS 126.005(2)).

The court concluded that the *Schafer* v. *Haller* precedent was not applicable:

> In Oregon not only must physical disability or mental incompetence or other cause be shown to authorize guardianship, but it must also appear that he is incapable of conducting his own affairs, as that term has been previously construed, and further that he is unable unassisted to properly manage and take care of himself or his property and by reason thereof would be deceived or imposed upon by artful or designing persons. . . . Thus, the Oregon statutes do not proceed on the theory of physical disability alone, but there are additional requirements as above stated. In view of these, it is our opinion that such statutes are constitutional (*Id.* at 154).

2. As of 1978, only 21 states mentioned physical illness or disability as a ground for the appointment of a guardian in incompetency adjudications, see 43 Fed.Reg. 11328, 11350 (1978), although several other states include catch-all provisions (e.g., "and other causes") in their statutes, *id.* at 11349, 11350.

3. The response of Ohio lawmakers to the *Schafer* decision was to amend the law to require that if a person is incompetent due to physical disability the disabled individual must consent to the appointment of a guardian; furthermore, the disabled individual can choose the person to be appointed as long as the nominee is found by the court to be suitable, Ohio Rev. Code Ann., § 2111.02 (Page 1976).

VECCHIONE V. WOHLGEMUTH

United States District Court for the Eastern District of Pennsylvania, 1974
377 F.Supp. 1361, cert. denied 434 U.S. 943 (1977)
EDWARD R. BECKER, District Judge.

I.   Preliminary Statement

This is a civil rights case, arising under 42 U.S.C. § 1983. It deals with the right of patients confined in state mental hospitals in Pennsylvania to control and manage their own property as against: (1) the right of the Commonwealth to summarily seize and control it for the duration of the hospitalization, without prior notice or hearing on the issue of the patient's competency to control that property; and (2) the right of the Commonwealth to appropriate part of the patient's property in satisfaction of the cost of care and maintenance, without prior or subsequent hearing on the correctness of the Commonwealth's assessment.

The case arises within the framework of sections 424 and 501 of the Pennsylvania Mental Health and Mental Retardation Act of 1966 (Act), 50 P.S. §§ 4424 and 4501. Section 501 provides that persons receiving diagnosis, treatment, care and rehabilitation at state mental hospitals are responsible for all costs thereof. Section 424 provides that, as to all persons who are not adjudged incompetent, civilly admitted or committed to a state mental hospital, the revenue agent at the hospital shall, without application to any court, seize any and all possessory property and present entitlements payable to such persons, manage them and appropriate from them for the cost of such person's care and maintenance as assessed by the revenue agent under § 501 of the Act. On the other hand, as to all persons who are adjudged incompetent, § 424 requires the revenue agent to turn over all money or property of such persons to their guardians with a full and certified accounting. Payment of any monies to the Commonwealth in satisfaction of its § 501 claims out of the estates of those adjudged incompetent persons must be preceded by prior notice and prior judicial hearing and approval, by virtue of the Incompetents' Estates Act of 1955, 50 P.S. § 3101 et seq. In addition, § 424 requires the Commonwealth to initiate proceedings under the Incompetents' Estates Act of 1955 for appointment of a guardian of the estate, if none exists already, of any patient with assets in excess of $2,500 at the time of their admission to the mental institution. However, patients with $2,500 or less do not receive such an opportunity to have their assets protected by a guardian or court under the Incompetents' Estates Act of 1955.

Plaintiff contends that § 424 of the Act creates two classes of civilly admitted or committed patients for purposes of Due Process safeguards. One class, composed of all patients who have not been adjudged incompetent, is denied any prior notice or hearing before the Commonwealth takes control of those patients' assets and appropriates part of such assets to satisfy § 501 claims. Another class, composed of adjudged incompetent patients, is afforded both prior notice and hearing before the Commonwealth can seize control of their funds and appropriate them to satisfy § 501 assessments. Section 424 further separates these two classes by requiring the Commonwealth to seek, under the Incompetents' Estates Act of 1955, the appointment of a guardian for patients with assets in excess of $2,500, thereby augmenting the latter class. As to those patients with less than $2,500, however, the Commonwealth does not have to give them the benefit of notice or an opportunity for a hearing on whether they are incompetent, so these patients generally have no guardian or court to protect their assets, thus relegating them to the former, disadvantaged class.

Ironically, while these patients with more than $2,500 of assets receive prior notice and a hearing before being adjudged incompetent, if they are declared competent at such a hearing, the Commonwealth can then act under § 424 to take control of and appropriate their funds without any further notice or hearing. Plaintiff submits that there is no legitimate state interest in differentiating between these two classes of patients and that the statutory classification offends the Equal Protection Clause of the Fourteenth Amendment. Plaintiff's second claim is that, to the extent that these statutes fail to provide prior notice and prior opportunity for full and fair hearing before taking control of and/or appropriating a mental patient's funds for payment of the Commonwealth's claims, they are invalid as contrary to the Due Process Clause of the Fourteenth Amendment.

Plaintiff Elvira Vecchione was, at the time that this action was brought, a patient at the Philadelphia State Hospital at Byberry (Byberry). She had not been declared incompetent and her assets were less than $2,500. Plaintiff sued in her own behalf and in behalf of all mental patients who are *sui juris* or are non-adjudged incompetent persons with assets less than $2,500 and who are civilly admitted or committed to Pennsylvania State hospitals for observation, diagnosis, care and treatment, and subject to §§ 424 and 501 of the Act. In the prayer of her complaint, plaintiff sought declaratory and injunctive relief and also restitution of the sums withheld by the revenue agent. Since the action sought to enjoin enforcement by a state officer of statutes of statewide application, a three-judge court was constituted.

On March 2, 1973, the District Court, sitting alone, and pursuant to a stipulation of the parties, ordered that temporary relief be afforded plaintiff until the case could be determined by the three-judge court. Following a pretrial conference, the parties agreed that, with the exception of the testimony of two psychiatrists, the case could be determined on a stipulated record. A stipulation of facts was thereupon filed in which the defendants admitted the allegations contained in virtually all the paragraphs of plaintiff's complaint. For the hearing, plaintiff submitted an extensive brief upon the law. The Commonwealth submitted no brief, either before or after trial. For the reasons which follow, we agree with plaintiff's contentions that the provisions of § 424 in question offend the Equal Protection Clause and that as to the disadvantaged class, § 424 of the Act violates procedural Due Process guarantees of the Fourteenth Amendment. Accordingly, the permanent relief requested by plaintiff will be granted.

*   *   *

B. The Statute as Applied to Plaintiff

The plaintiff was confined at Byberry from October 29, 1971, to April 16, 1973. The Commonwealth concedes that she was at all times during her confinement competent to manage her financial affairs. Yet, by virtue of the statute, defendant Shoemaker is required to apply half of the plaintiff's money to maintain a petty cash reserve fund for each patient of up to $500, and uses the other half and any funds in excess of the $500 reserve to pay for the assessed costs, without prior adjudication of liability or attachment proceedings of any kind. In terms of the plaintiff's property, defendant Shoemaker, without notice and hearing or explanation, acting pursuant to §§ 424 and 501, summarily seized and appropriated $1,253.85 of her Social Security OASDI benefits to pay the alleged debt incurred by her for her care and treatment at Byberry. In the same manner, the Commonwealth seized control of an additional $1,356.63 of her Social Security OASDI benefits, and interest thereon, and deprived her of control thereof until her discharge. This $1,356.63 was turned over to plaintiff as follows: $332.39 was returned in cash at the time of discharge; $766.64 was spent by plaintiff from her petty cash fund as authorized by her attending physician over the course of her hospitalization, and, pursuant to this Court's Temporary Restraining Order, $257.60 was returned to plaintiff after she had established a permanent residence at 2024 Green Street, Philadelphia, Pa. in May 1973.

Under 50 P.S. §§ 4501 and 4424, the Commonwealth did not afford plaintiff the opportunity to challenge the validity and amount of the underlying indebtedness at any time prior or subsequent to appropriation of monies for alleged patient indebtedness for care. Under Pennsylvania law and defendants' procedures authorized by §§ 424 and 501 of the Act, defendants are not required to afford plaintiff a subsequent opportunity for hearing, final determination of liability and restoration of her property; in fact, the Commonwealth is not obligated to initiate court action or make an accounting of any kind to plaintiff or to the court at any time. On the other hand, adjudged incompetent patients and non-adjudged incompetent patients with property and present entitlements in excess of $2,500 were afforded both prior notice and hearing on the correctness of assessments for hospital care.

Plaintiff contends that she was deprived of procedural due process by the appropriation and application of her funds to the Commonwealth's claim without notice and hearing. Her claim is buttressed by her enumeration of the defenses which she would interpose to the Commonwealth's claim, but which she had no opportunity to assert because of the operation of the Act. While we do not need to reach a judgment on the merits of these defenses, we note that plaintiff has not received any hearing or opportunity to raise these contentions in a challenge to the Commonwealth's assessment against her for the cost of her hospitalization care and maintenance. These defenses include the following:

(a) Plaintiff alleges that imposition of any liability upon her would impose an undue financial and psychological hardship upon her, and accordingly would be excused, modified or abated under § 504 of the Act,[9] and under *Commonwealth* v. *Heiser*, 95 *Montg.Cy.L.R.* 152 (Montg.C.P.1972).

(b) Absent a knowing voluntary and intelligent assignment of Social Security OASDI benefits by the plaintiff, of which there was none, she alleges that such benefits are under the express terms of 42 U.S.C. § 407 insulated from claims of creditors, including the state as provider of services. *See Philpott* v. *Essex County Welfare Board*, 409 U.S. 413, 93 S.Ct. 590, 34 L.Ed.2d 608 (1973). *Accord, In re Algier's Estate*, 43 Pa.D. & C.2d 351 (Chester Cy.O.C. 1967).

---

[9]50 P.S. § 4504 provides in relevant part:

[T]he secretary . . . shall have the power . . . to abate, modify, compromise or discharge the [501] liability so imposed provided:

(1) He is satisfied that the imposition of such liability would: (i) result in the loss of financial payments or other benefits from any public or private source which a mentally disabled person would receive, would be eligible to receive or which would be expended on his behalf except for such liability, or (ii) result in a substantial hardship upon the mentally disabled person, a person owing a legal duty to support such person or the family of either, or (iii) result in a greater financial burden upon the people of the Commonwealth, or (iv) create such a financial burden upon such mentally disabled person as to nullify the results of care, treatment, service or other benefits afforded to such person under any provision of this act.

(c) Plaintiff alleges that throughout her hospitalization Byberry afforded her less than constitutionally required treatment under *Wyatt* v. *Stickney,* 344 F.Supp. 387 (M.D.Ala. 1972), thereby prolonging her hospitalization and the costs therefor or warranting that she not have been committed at all.[10] Alternatively, plaintiff contends that the value of her care, on a *quantum meruit* basis or otherwise, was less than the value of her benefits appropriated by the Commonwealth. To support this contention, plaintiff notes that, until enjoined by Temporary Restraining Order dated March 2, 1973, the Commonwealth continued to appropriate at least 50% of plaintiff's Social Security OASDI benefits, despite the fact that from January 19, 1973, plaintiff no longer required hospitalization.

(d) Throughout the period that plaintiff resided at Byberry, in order to feel active and useful, she performed maintenance and housekeeping work consisting principally of making 16 beds per day and occasionally mopping floors for one to two hours per day, seven days per week, despite the efforts of defendants and their agents and employees to discourage plaintiff from performing any work because of her heart condition. Given a due process hearing, plaintiff would assert an offsetting claim for the value of this work performed by her which benefited the Commonwealth, under § 504 of the Act, as interpreted by *Estate of MacKnight,* 58 Pa.D. & C.2d 794 (Phila.O.C. en ban, 1972) (Consent Decree). *See also Downs* v. *Dept. of Public Welfare,* 368 F.Supp. 454 Civil No. 73-1246 (E.D.Pa. filed May 7, 1974) (consent decree ordering Commonwealth as of Dec. 7, 1974, to pay patients for work which benefits mental institution).

C. The Competency of Plaintiff and Other Mental Patients to Handle Their Own Finances

In addition to appropriating plaintiff's assets, the Commonwealth also took control of them under 50 P.S. § 4424. This provision allows the Commonwealth to entirely divest plaintiff throughout her hospitalization of control of her own personal property and entitlements, except for small amounts which it granted or withheld at the discretion of the defendants herein and their officers and agents.

Throughout the period of her hospitalization, plaintiff was and she still remains *sui juris.* Defendants concede that plaintiff was and is competent to handle her own funds. At the hearing, two psychiatrists, with impressive qualifications in the field of treating mental patients, testified that mental patients like plaintiff, in general, are no less able to handle their own assets than the population at large. The psychiatrists acknowledged that for a brief period of a few days after patients are admitted to a mental institution, a large percentage of them may be in an acute or traumatic stage that would prevent them from handling their own funds during that brief period. This situation is analogous to the incapacity of a nonmental patient, such as an accident victim, who may not be able to manage his own funds for a period while his injury is acute. But the experts opined that such a brief incapacity should not be grounds for indefinitely denying such mental or nonmental patients control over their assets.

---

[10]Plaintiff concedes that the duration of her hospitalization was prolonged in part by the unavailability of an aftercare placement facility deemed suitable for her by Byberry.

The psychiatrists also testified that depriving mental patients of any control and responsibility over their own funds would tend to prolong a person's stay in a mental hospital, while giving them such control and responsibility is therapeutic. Plaintiff, in her brief, and these doctors referred to numerous studies to support these contentions. *See* Hearings Before the Subcomm. on Constitutional Rights of the Sen. Comm. on the Judiciary, 87th Cong. 1st Sess. 1961; Allen, Ferster and Weihofen, *Mental Impairment and Legal Incompetency* (Prentice-Hall, 1968); *The Mentally Disabled and the Law*, Lindman (ed.) (Chicago, 1961); Greenblatt, York and Brown, *From Custodial to Therapeutic Patient Care in Mental Hospitals* (Russell Sage Foundation, 1955); Williams, "Money and the Therapeutic Process," 18 *Canada's Mental Health* 20 (1970); Cummings and Cummings, *Ego and Milieu* (Prentice-Hall, 1962). The medical judgment that mental patients are not prima facie incapable of handling their own financial affairs is apparently so well-established that on November 4, 1971, the Board of Directors of the National Association for Mental Health adopted a "Position Statement on Civil Rights of Mental Patients" which read at item 3:

> The fact that institutional care is required should not in and of itself create a status of incompetency either by operation of law or administrative practice. Admission to a service or treatment program should not give rise to a presumption of inability to manage one's affairs or exercise jural and civil rights.

At the hearing, the Court pressed the Commonwealth as to its position concerning the validity of these treatises and of the expert testimony elicited. Counsel for the Commonwealth responded that the Commonwealth accepted the view that "mental patients are, barring an adjudication of incompetency, capable of managing their financial affairs." [Partial Transcript at 58.] In light of the impressive and uncontested evidence on this point and the Commonwealth's significant concession, we reject the existence of any *presumption* that mental patients, including plaintiff, are less capable of handling their assets than the public at large.

III.   Discussion

A.   The Equal Protection Claim

Under the rubric of the Equal Protection Clause, the Supreme Court has repeatedly held that statutory schemes may treat classes of citizens differently only if the statutory classifications are rationally related to the purpose of the statute.

*   *   *

The Pennsylvania statute and collection practice challenged herein fails to meet this minimal rationality standard of equal protection. Section 424 establishes two classes of civilly admitted or committed mental patients. The first consists of all patients adjudged incompetent by a court of appropriate jurisdiction. The second class consists of all patients not adjudged incompetent. As noted, since under § 424(4), the Commonwealth must initiate proceedings under the Incompetents' Estates Act of 1955 to seek a guardian for all patients with assets in excess of $2,500, the first class is thus augmented, although if such patients are not adjudged incompetent, then they fall into the second, disadvantaged class, which also perforce includes those with assets less than $2,500. As to the first class, payment to the Commonwealth out of each incompetent's estate must, by force of Pennsylvania law governing administration of incompetents' estates, be preceded by notice to all interested parties and by judicial hearing and approval. As to the second class (in which plaintiff finds herself), §§ 424 and 501 expressly authorize defendants to summarily deprive this class of patients of custody and control of their property and apply it to pay hospital costs without prior or subsequent notice and hearing as to any patient indebtedness or the availability of patient property in satisfaction thereof.

The Commonwealth has pointed to no rational basis, not even revenue raising, for classifying mental patients in this manner for any purpose set forth in the Act. In fact, when viewed in light of § 504(a) of the Act, which is calculated to alleviate the harsh economic and psychological consequences to indigent mental patients of strict imposition of § 501 costs, the practices authorized by §§ 424(1) and 501 appear counter-productive and internally inconsistent with the goals of the Act. More affluent incompetent mental patients would presumably be better able to afford the costs under § 501 and would therefore be a great source of income. Maximizing the right of such persons to resist imposition of liability, while minimizing the rights of all others seems arbitrary and capricious.

Under the statutory scheme, the Commonwealth is able to summarily seize and appropriate assets of a patient not adjudged incompetent, while having to provide notice and opportunity for a hearing to a patient adjudged incompetent, but whose financial interests are protected by a guardian or a court under the Incompetents' Estates Act of 1955. Such a differentiation allows the Commonwealth to exercise stronger creditor's rights against competent patients than as against incompetent patients, without any regard to the liability or financial capability of these patients to meet their obligations. Furthermore, in view of our rejection of any presumption that mental patients are less capable of handling their assets than the public at large, it is arbitrary to treat those who are not adjudged incompetent as if they were not able to handle their own funds, and those who are adjudged incompetent as if they were, since the Commonwealth must then deal with a guardian or court under the Incompetents' Estates Act of 1955.

*　*　*

In sum, we find that the classification of patients in state hospitals under § 424 is irrational, arbitrary and so wholly unrelated to any purpose of the law in which the classification is made that it is impermissible on its face under the Equal Protection Clause of the Fourteenth Amendment to the United States Constitution and 42 U.S.C. § 1983.

B. The Procedural Due Process Claim

Although we have addressed plaintiff's equal protection claim first, reflection reveals that her equal protection claim is essentially a claim for due process, since the invidious classification deprived plaintiff of any notice or opportunity for a hearing before or after the Commonwealth took control of and appropriated plaintiff's assets. We find that, in addition to violating the Equal Protection Clause, provisions of section 424 of the Act are also unconstitutional because they fail to provide the procedural due process required by the Fourteenth Amendment.

*　*　*

In the instant case, property rights entitled to constitutional protection are at stake. As in the case of the welfare benefits involved in *Goldberg* v. *Kelly,* 397 U.S. 254, 90 S.Ct. 1011, 25 L.Ed.2d 287 (1970), and the driver's license involved in *Bell* v. *Burson,* 402 U.S. 535, 91 S.Ct. 1586, 29 L.Ed.2d 90 (1971), the Social Security benefits or other income patients receive and which defendants have intercepted and appropriated under §§ 424 and 501 of the Act are a matter of statutory entitlement to plaintiff, and thus are property within the meaning of the Due Process Clause. *Goldberg* v. *Kelly, supra,* 397 U.S. at 262, 90 S.Ct. 1011. Moreover, defendants' practice of taking custody and control of all monies in addition to the funds appropriated by the Commonwealth deprives plaintiff of her rights to use of her property. *Cf. Fuentes* v. *Shevin,* 407 U.S. 67 at 86, 92 S.Ct. 1983, 32 L.Ed.2d 556 (1972). *See also Sniadach* v. *Family Finance Corp.,* 395 U.S. at 342, 89 S.Ct. 1820 (Harlan, J. concurring).

* * *

Analogous to the instant case is *Dale* v. *Hahn,* 486 F.2d 76 (2d Cir. 1973), aff'g Unreported District Court Order, on remand from 440 F.2d 633 (2d Cir. 1971), wherein New York's failure to provide adequate notice prior to the appointment of a committee to receive and disburse plaintiff's assets was challenged as violative of the Due Process Clause and of 42 U.S.C. § 1983. The *Dale* court was faced with the circumstance that a patient was not adequately notified of the pendency of a judicial proceeding in which the state declared her incompetent and suspended her right to possession, use and control of her property. In the instant case, the state does not even provide a judicial hearing, let alone notice thereof. *A fortiori* the practice assailed herein must be set aside as violative of the Due Process Clause.

At oral argument the Commonwealth attempted to justify its practice of taking custody of plaintiff's property before its right to appropriate the property can be judicially established, on the theory that there is an immediate threat of destruction, loss or mismanagement of the sought-after property by this type of plaintiff. The Commonwealth argument must fail for two reasons. The first problem with the Commonwealth's argument is that even if the Commonwealth's practice was generally justifiable under the facts, the statutes in question are not sufficiently narrowly drawn to track their alleged purpose. A similar type of class presumption was raised and rejected in *Fuentes* v. *Shevin, supra,* with respect to the entire population of debtors there subject to prejudgment replevin. The statutes assailed herein, as in *Fuentes,* are not drawn to meet the "unusual condition" of an immediate risk of loss or destruction posed by certain individuals, but are aimed at an entire undifferentiated population. *See also Lebowitz* v. *Forbes Leasing & Finance Corp.,* 326 F.Supp. 1335, 1349 (E.D.Pa. 1971), aff'd 456 F.2d 979 (3d Cir.), cert. denied, 409 U.S. 843, 93 S.Ct. 42, 34 L.Ed.2d 82 (1972).

The second and even more fundamental problem with the Commonwealth's attempted justification of the statutes involved is that its factual underpinning, i.e., that mental patients are presumptively incapable of handling their own funds, has been stripped by the Record in this case. If there were a necessary correlation between hospitalization and incompetency, the statutes could perhaps be justified. However, in our findings of fact we have rejected the Commonwealth's hypothesis that mental patients may be presumed less competent to handle their own assets than the public at large. Hence there is no legitimate justification for the Commonwealth's interference with plaintiff's custody and control of her property without an adjudication that she was incompetent to manage it. Defendants concede, and we have found, that plaintiff was entirely competent to manage her affairs throughout her hospitalization and up to the present time. Moreover, the Commonwealth's own statutes reject the automatic correlation between hospitalization and incompetency. If the Commonwealth's hypothesis that all mental patients present an immediate risk of loss or destruction of property were in fact true, all mental patients could be adjudged legally incompetent. Pennsylvania's Incompetents' Estates Act of 1955, however, requires not just evidence of mental illness, but of three factors: (1) mismanagement, (2) mental illness, *and* (3) a causal nexus between the two. *In re Streda's Estate,* 12 Pa.D. & C.2d 523 (Del.Cy.O.C. 1957).

In view of our conclusion that § 424, read in conjunction with § 501, of the Act offends the equal protection and due process clauses of the Fourteenth Amendment to the United States Constitution in the general context of this case, relief must be granted as requested by the plaintiff.

NOTES

1. As a result of *Vecchione* the Pennsylvania Department of Justice was required within 6 months to file roughly 7,100 guardianship petitions to determine if the mentally ill or mentally retarded patients were competent to handle their own money. At these hearings counsel to represent the allegedly disabled individuals was to be provided.

However, as of August 30, 1978, 179 hearings had been held and 179 patients had been declared incompetent to handle their property. Of the 179 patients who were declared incompetent, the vast majority, if not all, did not appear and were unrepresented (Pennsylvania Legal Service Memorandum, dated 9/1/78, ''Training on *Vecchione* v. *Wohlgemuth* Hearings''). See pp. 591–594, below, for a discussion of the importance of counsel and the presence of the alleged incompetent individual at guardianship hearings.

2. Several recent suits have been brought challenging statutory incompetency standards on constitutional grounds that they are vague and overbroad. The arguments made were that: 1) the statutes fail to give fair warning of what particular conduct or behavior will subject the individual to a loss of rights, and 2) there is an absence of standards restricting the discretion of governmental authority of courts in applying the law. See Horstman, P., ''Protective Services for the Elderly: The Limits of *Parens Patriae,*'' 40 *Mo. L. Rev.* 215, 259 (1975). See, also, *Schultz* v. *Borradaile,* Civ. No. 74-40123 (E.D.Mich., filed October 12, 1974) (three-judge court in its memorandum opinion and order dated August 8, 1978 abstained because of comity considerations); *Kay* v. *Rhodes,* No. C77-48 (N.D.Ohio, filed November 14, 1977) (on March 2, 1978 the federal district court abstained).

F.   TYPES OF GUARDIANSHIP

While all types of statutory guardianship share the same basis—the legal sanctioning of substitute decision making—there are a number of possible methods or mechanisms for achieving such goals. Some guardianship statutes have remained essentially unchanged since .the 1800s; see, e.g., Ala. Code §§ 26-2-40 to 54 (1975); Comment, "North Carolina Guardianship Laws: The Need for Change," 54 *N.C. L. Rev.* 389, 389 (1976). In other states, however, there has been a growing movement to increase the variety of guardianship options in conformance with modern trends of care, support, and respect for the rights of disabled persons. This section examines the range of guardianship models, from the most extreme example, general guardianship, to the more benign types of "limited" guardianship and other less drastic approaches.

1.   General Guardianship

The traditional approach of guardianship involves an all-or-nothing proposition. An individual is either found totally competent to manage his affairs or else found totally incompetent; if he is adjudicated incompetent, a general guardian will be appointed to take over total control of virtually every area of decision making in the incompetent person's life; see, e.g., Regan, J., "Protective Services for the Elderly: Commitment, Guardianship, and Alternatives," 13 *Wm. & Mary L. Rev.* 569, 607 (1972). As the court observed in *Modlich* v. *Jennings,* 244 Mass. 183, 138 N.E. 897 (1923), "the guardian has not only control of the property, but also custody of the person, of his ward. . . ."

For all practical purposes, the ward under a general guardianship is in the same position relative to his guardian as an unemancipated child is to his or her parent. The general declaration of incompetency serves to strip the ward of his or her ability to make binding decisions; society looks instead to the decision of the guardian to determine the wishes of the ward. Among the significant rights of the ward affected by this transfer of authority to the guardian are the right to contract (see Chapter 10), the right to vote (see Chapter 11), the right to consent to medical treatment (see Chapter 8), the right to marry (see Chapter 9), and the right to choose one's place of residence; in fact, almost no personal or property rights are left untouched by the imposition of a general guardianship.

2.   Guardianship of the Person

Provisions for the appointment of a guardian to manage the personal affairs of an incompetent individual are found in the laws of every state. While such provisions are sometimes kept distinct from other types of guardianship, e.g., Md. Est. & Trusts Code Ann. § 13-201(a) (Cum.Supp. 1977) (guardianship of property); Md. Est. & Trusts Code Ann. § 13-705 (Cum.Supp. 1978) (guardianship of person), it is quite common to find a single statutory provision that authorizes the appointment of a guardian of the person, a guardian of the property, or a guardian of both; see, e.g., Del. Code, Tit. 13, § 3914(a) (Supp. 1977). In a few states, guardianship statutes only authorize the appointment of a general guardian; see, e.g., Ala. Code, § 26-2-40 (1975).

The linkage of personal guardianship with guardianship of property is an outgrowth of the traditional guardianship scheme, which determined the need for a guardian based on a disabled person's inability to manage his estate. Many statutory distinctions between guardianship of the property and the person have not been successfully carried over into actual practice. The unfortunate result is that a guardian of the person *and* property is all too often appointed, when a showing of need for a guardian of the property alone has been demonstrated; a superfluous request in the petition asking for a dual guardianship is frequently the cause of such "overprotection" by courts; see, e.g., Note, "Conservatorship of the Person in Illinois: The Forgotten Protective Service for Incompetent Citizens," 1977 *Univ. of Ill. L. F.* 1113 (1977). An Illinois circuit court judge is reported to have said that he often includes a personal guardianship in the final order as a "precaution" even though the petitioner may not have requested such appointment; *id.* at 1114, n. 6. The appointment of a personal guardian in this manner reveals an incorrect assumption that an individual's need for personal supervision must necessarily accompany a need for supervision of his finances; see, *Guardianship and Protective Services . . . A Report of the Nat'l Council on Aging* 81 (Lehmann, V., and Mathiasen, G., eds., 1963).

While many guardianship cases have resulted in the appointment of just a guardian of the property, surprisingly few can be found in which only guardianship of the person has been imposed. With the exception of requests to the court for consent to medical treatment, e.g., *In re Estate of Brooks,* 32 Ill.2d 361, 205 N.E.2d 435 (1965) (see generally, Chapter 8), almost no cases can be found dealing with the issue of guardianship of the person separate and distinct from the issue of guardianship of the property (Allen, R., Ferster, E., and Weihofen, H., *Mental Impairment and Legal Incompetency* 95 (1968)).

A typical guardianship of the person statute requires a showing that the allegedly incompetent person is unable to care for himself and is therefore in need of personal supervision; see, e.g., Md. Est. & Trusts Code Ann. § 13-705(b) (Cum.Supp. 1978).

In *Raymond* v. *Lawrence,* 86 Minn. 310, 90 N.W. 769 (1902), a case involving a guardianship over a woman described as "nearly 75 years of age, suffering from paralysis, and constantly increasing senile dementia," the Supreme Court of Minnesota outlined the scope of authority of the woman's personal guardians:

> Until removed by the court having original jurisdiction in such cases, these guardians are the custodians of the incompetent, and can care for and control her in any reasonable manner. They may designate the persons in whose immediate charge she shall be, . . . and may insist upon the observance of reasonable rules and regulations conducive to her health and comfort (*Id.* at 770).

Nonetheless, the court asserted that there were limits to the power of a guardian:

> The welfare of the ward is the chief matter to be considered,—not the wishes of the relatives, nor the convenience of the guardian. . . . And a court of chancery has full and complete jurisdiction over the persons and estates of infants and all others laboring under legal disability, as well as their guardians, trustees, or other custodians (*Id.* at 770).

Unfortunately, however, this judicial authority to oversee the performance of guardians, to countermand decisions against the interest of the ward, and to remove guardians who do not live up to their duties is only rarely exercised; see, e.g., Allen, R., Ferster, E., and Weihofen, H., *Mental Impairment and Legal Incompetency* 96 (1968); Brakel, S., and Rock, R., *The Mentally Disabled and the Law* Table 8.3 at 280–292 (1971).

3. Guardian of the Property

Historically, the focus of guardianship law was on preservation of the estates of mentally unsound persons, and this focus remains to a great extent in present-day application of guardianship. As the court in *State* v. *England,* 328 S.W.2d 732, 738 (Mo. 1959) stated, "The public has an interest . . . in guardianship proceedings for various reasons, one of them being that it is to the interest of the public that the estate of the proposed ward be not squandered."

Every state has a statutory basis for the judicial appointment of a guardian to administer the property and financial affairs of incompetent persons, although the standards by which appointment will be made vary in coverage, procedure, and nomenclature from state to state. The terms "committee," "curator," and, especially, "conservator" are in some statutes in place of the "guardian of the property" or "guardian of the estate." See Brakel, S., and Rock, R., *The Mentally Disabled and the Law* Table 8.1 (1971) at 266–272 for a state-by-state survey of standards. In general, a substitute decision maker will be appointed to control the finances of an individual who, by reason of mental, physical, and/or moral defect, is unable to manage his or her property.

Statutes in this area range from all-inclusive provisions (combining, for example, the mentally retarded, mentally ill, drug addicts, physically disabled, and those subject to excessive "gaming, idleness, and debauchery of any kind"), e.g., R.I. Gen. Laws § 33-15-8 (1969), to specific provisions for elderly or mentally retarded persons.

In re Bryden's Estate

Supreme Court of Pennsylvania, 1905
211 Pa. 633, 61 A. 250

The following is the opinion of the court below (Freas, P. J.):

"The petitioners are five of the seven children of Elizabeth Bryden, and they ask for the appointment of a guardian for the estate of their mother on the ground that 'she has become so weak in mind that she is unable to take care of her property, and in consequence thereof is liable to dissipate or lose the same, and to become the victim of designing persons.' Her estate consists of a house and lot in which she lives, worth $6,500, and bonds amounting to $42,000, yielding an annual income of about $2,075. These bonds are in the possession of W. L. Watson, vice president of the First National Bank of Pittston, who reinvests the funds as the bonds mature, and collects the interest, which latter he deposits in cash in the bank to the credit of Mrs. Bryden. The money is drawn out of the bank by checks signed by Agnes Bryden, her daughter, who holds a power of attorney from her mother, authorizing her so to do.

"The entire income has lately been expended, and in addition the sum of $1,200 was spent, which money came from a mortgage not in Mr. Watson's care. Otherwise the principal has not been encroached upon. Mrs. Bryden lives in her own home with her only unmarried child, Agnes, who is about thirty-five years old. The mother is perfectly satisfied with her daughter's services, and the disinterested witnesses say she has faithfully cared for her mother. For the past four years Mrs. Bryden has been in ill health, and the services of a nurse were necessary, whose pay is $12 per week and her board. She keeps a servant at $3 per week, and pays $18 per month for the care of a horse. Agnes does the buying, runs the household, pays the bills, and assists in the care of her mother. She has also doctor and drug bills, household expenses, taxes, insurance, and the usual expenses incident to keeping alive and owning property. A little figuring will show that $2,075 per year is not too much with which to pay these necessary expenses. The $1,200 obtained from the mortgage were spent in these ways: Mrs. Bryden presented Agnes with a horse and harness costing $650, and she had a trap repaired at a cost of $100. These are used by the mother as well as the daughter. She also gave Agnes a diamond pendant worth $175, and paid $50 and $75 for repairs to a sealskin coat given Agnes by her father in his lifetime. Her house was afire, and she spent more money in repairs than she got from the insurance company. Agnes took trips with her mother, and two trips alone to New York City. She also gave $120 to her son Alexander. It is insisted by the petitioners that the expenditure of the $1,200 is evidence of a disposition to dissipate or lose the estate, and that she may become the victim of designing persons. The real causes of this proceeding are the gift of the horse and pendant to Agnes, and the failure of other children to obtain money from their mother. That she should discriminate in favor of her only unmarried child, who lives with her and cares for her, is not surprising or unnatural. While the horse was a gift to Agnes, yet its use and enjoyment are as much the mother's. It is her plain duty under the circumstances to dress her daughter, and we see nothing extravagant in paying for the repairs of a coat given the daughter by her father. We have left, then, the gift of the pendant, and we need not say that a mother seventy-six years old, worth $48,500, may buy her daughter a piece of jewelry worth $175 without being thought a victim of a designing person. Under any view of the case, this woman has not lived extravagantly, nor has she dissipated her estate.

"But while thus considering her expenditures, we must not lose sight of the basic principle involved, as laid down in *Lines* v. *Lines*, 142 Pa. 149, 21 Atl. 809, 24 Am. St. Rep. 487, that a man may do what he pleases with his personal estate during his life. He may even beggar himself and his family if he chooses to commit such an act of folly. When he dies, and then only, do the rights of his heirs attach to his estate. The act of June 19, 1901 (P.L. 574), has not changed the law in this respect one iota. Before an estate can be taken from the owner and transferred to a guardian, it must be established that the respondent is so weak in mind that he is unable to take care of his property, and in consequence thereof is liable to dissipate or lose the same, and to become the victim of designing persons. The act is for the protection of the respondent, and is not intended to prevent the owner of an estate from doing with his own what he pleases, in order that his children may inherit a greater amount. Nor is favoritism of one child over another evidence that the respondent is a victim of a designing person, for a parent may make such distribution among his children as he may see fit, either during life, or by will after his death, so long as it is the free and conscious act of a sane mind. Applications of this nature are not to be encouraged, and should not be granted except in a clear case. As is declared in *Hoffman's Estate,* 209 Pa. 357, 58 Atl. 665, it is a dangerous statute, easily capable of abuse by designing relatives to accomplish the very wrong intended to be guarded against, and therefore to be administered by the courts with the utmost caution and conservatism. It is the policy of our law to allow an owner to manage his own estate, and it can be taken from him only for his own personal good, and not because his children think they, or some one for them, can manage it to better advantage.

"The respondent is very far from being so weak in mind that she is unable to take care of her property. She appeared in court under the most trying circumstances a person can be subjected to, and seemed to possess the mind and memory usually found in persons of her age, and all disinterested witnesses were of this opinion. She allows her securities to remain in the hands of Mr. Watson, where they have been for twelve years, and who is well qualified to execute the trust. In fact, if this court appointed a guardian, Watson would be selected, as the friend of the respondent best qualified for the position. The estate cannot be converted without his knowledge or consent, and in case of danger he would be the first to give the alarm. All that can reasonably be expected of a woman seventy-six years old, in the management of her estate, is the selection of a competent and trustworthy agent, and this she has done. The court could do no more.

"And now, October 15, 1904, the petition is refused."

Argued before MITCHELL, C. J., and BROWN, MESTREZAT, POTTER, and ELKIN, JJ.

PER CURIAM. This is a very clear case of attempt by children to take their mother's property out of her control, not in her interest, but in their own, and is an illustration of the dangers of the statute referred to in *Hoffman's Estate,* 209 Pa. 357, 58 Atl. 665.

The decree is affirmed on the opinion of the court below.

NOTES

1. As the court observes in *Bryden,* the heirs of an allegedly incompetent person often institute guardianship of the property proceedings to conserve their inheritance rather than to protect the owner of the property; see, e.g., Comment, "An Assessment of the Pennsylvania Estate Guardianship Incompetency Standard," 124 *U. Pa. L. Rev.* 1048 (1976); R.I. Gen. Law §§ 33-15-8 (1969). Such misuse of guardianship laws is far from uncommon and sometimes extends to petitions filed by state hospital administrators anxious to prevent dissipation of the assets of patients.

2. A guardian of the property is an agent of the court and as such is answerable to it for the judicious use of the ward's funds. Usual duties include all aspects of property management, making contracts for the ward, and representing the ward in legal proceedings. Although statutory duties vary from state to state, almost all jurisdictions require that a bond be posted by the guardian and that periodic accounts reflecting the financial status of the estate be filed.

At common law, the discretionary powers of the guardian were rather limited; court approval was required prior to most transactions, such as investments, sales of property, and compromise of legal claims. Statutory provisions in some states, e.g.,

Md. Est. & Trusts Code Ann. § 13-213 (1974); Uniform Probate Code § 5-424(c), have greatly expanded the discretionary power of guardians, with the result that property management is more efficient than under the common law scheme. The guardian remains answerable to the courts, however, for breach of the fiduciary duty. By retaining the requirement of periodic reports to be made to the court of transactions by the guardian, it is felt that accountability can be preserved without the expense and delay of court approval for all transactions.

4. Temporary Guardian

Pursuant to statutes in a number of states, e.g., Me. Rev. Stat., Tit. 18, § 3630 (1978); R.I. Gen. Laws §§ 33-15-10 to 33-15-12 (1969); Wis. Stat. § 880.15 (West 1978), a court may appoint a temporary guardian of the person and/or of the estate of an individual alleged to be incompetent or disabled. While the procedural elements of such statutes vary considerably from state to state, it may be said generally that, under such statutes, the courts are given much more discretion to forego normal due process procedural prerequisites than is the case in the appointment of "permanent" guardians.

An example of the broad discretion given the court can be found in a Minnesota statute:

> Upon a showing of necessity or expediency, the court with or without notice may appoint a special guardian or conservator of the person or estate or both of any person [who is subject to general guardianship], whether a petition for general guardianship or conservatorship has been filed or not. There shall be no appeal from any order appointing or refusing to appoint a special guardian or conservator. A special guardian or conservator of the person shall have charge of the person of the ward or conservatee. A special guardian or conservator of the estate shall collect the assets and conserve the estate, unless his powers are limited by the court in the order of appointment and in the letters to the performance of specified acts. Upon a showing of necessity or expediency, the court with or without notice may expressly confer upon a special guardian or conservator power to perform any or all acts in the administration of the guardianship or conservatorship, not exceeding the powers conferred by law upon general guardians or conservators (Minn. Stat. Ann. § 525.591 (1975)).

The judicial proceedings in temporary guardianship cases may be purely perfunctory. For example, in a Nevada case, *In re Chamberlin,* No. 78-148 (Second Judicial District Court, Washoe Cty., Nev., Jan. 9, 1978), temporary and permanent guardianship proceedings were initiated against a 68-year-old man by his landlady; the Petition for Appointment of Guardian was filed on January 9, 1978, at 3:42 p.m. The proposed ward, Mr. Chamberlin, received no notice of the proceedings; he was not represented by counsel, and he had no opportunity to appear at the hearing. At 3:49 p.m., 7 minutes after the petition was filed, Mr. Chamberlin was adjudicated incompetent for a period not to exceed 6 months and the petitioner was appointed temporary guardian of the estate. An accompanying formality, a letter of temporary guardianship was issued 6 minutes after the filing of the order. In all, Chamberlin was deprived of his right to control his property in a mere 13 minutes. The landlady waited, however, until the following day to submit and obtain the judge's approval of her motion for an order that Mr. Chamberlin's savings account in the amount of $18,000 be transferred to her account. See *Chamberlin* v. *Bowen,* Civ. No. R-78-0096 BRT (D.Nev., filed May 30, 1978) for a federal court challenge to the legality of the aforesaid proceedings.

The usefulness of temporary guardianship is seen in situations that require a quick decision to protect life or property. In evaluating the propriety of such procedures, the necessity of quick action must be balanced against the loss of substantial rights, frequently without the benefit of even minimal due process.

McKINSTRY v. DEWEY

Supreme Court of Iowa, 1921
192 Iowa 753, 185 N.W. 565

FAVILLE, J. From the record before us, it appears that on the 10th day of May, 1921, one Charley McKinstry presented . . . in chambers, a petition praying that he, the said Charley McKinstry, be apppointed temporary guardian of the person and estate of the petitioner herein; that at said time the said respondent entered an order upon said petition appointing the said Charley McKinstry temporary guardian of the property of the said John McKinstry.

* * *

Said petition does not appear to have been filed in the office of the clerk of the district court of Washington county, Iowa, at said time, nor had any notice of the said hearing before the respondent as judge of said court, or of the commencement of said action in the district court of Washington county, Iowa, been had upon the petitioner. Petitioner brings this action in this court by certiorari to review the action of the respondent as judge of said district court in making said order, appointing a temporary guardian of the property of the petitioner without any notice whatever being given to the petitioner of said proceedings.

The sole question for our determination is whether or not, under the statutes of this state, a judge of the district court, upon presentation of a petition of this character, can legally appoint a temporary guardian of the person and property of an alleged incompetent, without any notice being given to such person of the application for the appointment of said temporary guardian.

Section 225 of the Code provides that the district court shall have jurisdiction "to appoint guardians of the persons and property of all persons resident in the county subject to guardianship."

Section 3219 of the Code provides for the appointment of a guardian for a person of unsound mind and that the said proceedings shall be by a petition, verified by affidavit, and presented to the district court of the county of which the alleged incompetent is an inhabitant.

Section 3220 of the Code provides:

> Such petition shall set forth, as particularly as may be, the facts upon which the application is based, and shall be answered as in other ordinary actions, all the rules of which shall govern so far as applicable and not otherwise provided in this chapter. The applicant shall be plaintiff and the other party defendant, and either party may have a trial by jury. The petition may be presented to the judge, who may appoint a temporary guardian.

The proceedings in the instant case were had under the last sentence in said section. The question for our determination is whether or not, in proceedings under the authority conferred by said section 3220, the judge may appoint a temporary guardian upon the mere presentation of the petition, without requiring the appearance of the defendant in said action or the service of any notice on said defendant of said proceedings. The section is broad in its terms and requires that the proceedings in court shall conform as nearly as may be to actions by ordinary proceedings in this state. This would require the service of an original notice within proper time before the defendant would be required to answer in the district court. In the trial in the district court, by the terms of this statute, a jury may be required. But granting that such notice is essential to the final determination and trial of the question involved, and to the appointment of a permanent guardian, we are still confronted with the question as to whether or not, under this statute, the power conferred upon the judge to appoint a temporary guardian upon presentation of the petition confers the power so to do without any notice to the defendant in the action of said application for the appointment of a temporary guardian. The proceeding for the appointment of a guardian, who is an inhabitant of the county, under this statute, is a proceeding in personam. *Raher* v. *Raher,* 150 Iowa 511, 129 N.W. 494, 35 L.R.A. (N.S.) 292, Ann. Cas. 1912D. 680; *Holly* v. *Holly,* 157 Iowa 584, 138 N.W. 445.

It cannot be disputed that by such order of appointment, the defendant in such an action could be deprived of his liberty by the guardian and could likewise be deprived of all management, control, and use of his property by the temporary guardian. Can this be done upon the presentation of a verified petition to a judge and without any notice whatever to the party who is thus placed under temporary guardianship? This identical question does not appear to have been before us for determination.

* * *

In proceedings like those under consideration in the instant case, the object is, not the care and confinement of a lunatic in the state hospital for the insane, but solely the appointment of a guardian of the person or property of one alleged to be incompetent. Under the statute, the petition may be presented to the judge by any person. No proof is required by affidavits, or otherwise, beyond the verified averments of the petition, unless, on his own motion, the judge may require other proof.

In *Chase* v. *Hathaway,* 14 Mass. 222, the Supreme Judicial Court of Massachusetts, in 1817, discussed the question. This was a case wherein the judge of the probate court appointed a guardian for an alleged non compos without notice. The language of the court is pertinent to a situation similar to the one in the case at bar. The court said:

> There being no provision in the statute for notice to the party who is alleged to be incompetent, by reason of insanity, to manage his estate, it seems that the judge of probate did not think such notice essential to his proceedings. But we are of the opinion that, notwithstanding the silence of the statute, no decree of a probate court, so materially affecting the rights of property and the person, can be valid, unless the party to be affected has had an opportunity to be heard in defense of his rights.
>
> It is a fundamental principle of justice, essential to every free government, that every citizen shall be maintained in the enjoyment of his liberty and property, unless he has forfeited them by the standing laws of the community, and has had opportunity to

answer such charges as, according to those laws, will justify a forfeiture or suspension of them.

[The court goes on to cite cases from Alabama, Illinois, Indiana, Kentucky, Connecticut, Maine, Kansas, Vermont, Colorado, West Virginia, and Tennessee that have held that notice of temporary guardianship proceedings is required irrespective of statutory provisions which indicate that no such notice is necessary.]

It is contended by the counsel for respondent that the statute in question has been in the Code for many years and it has been the universal custom and practice of judges throughout the state during all of that time to appoint temporary guardians upon the presentation of a petition and without any notice. A similar situation arose and a similar argument was presented to the Supreme Court of Missouri in *Hunt* v. *Searcy*, 167 Mo. 158, 67 S.W. 206, in which the court said:

> It is too clear for argument that this qualification and attempted authority for depriving the accused of his liberty or property without notice violates both the state and federal Constitutions, and does not constitute "due process of law." But one reason can be suggested for not serving the person to be tried with notice, and that is that, as he is insane, a notice to him would be useless and meaningless. This argument begs the question; for the issue to be tried is whether he is insane or not, and to fail to give him notice for this reason is to forestall the very purpose of the inquest. But even if he be a raving maniac, he can appear by attorney or through his friends, and see that a proper person is appointed guardian, or that a proper care is given to his property and to his person. . . . It will not do to say that, in the 37 years that these provisions not requiring notice have been on the statute books, no instance is recorded of any sane person being so adjudged and deprived of his liberty or property, and that instances of such outrages are found only in highly colored and improbable stories in works of fiction. . . . It would be a travesty upon justice, worthy to be dramatized, to hold that a sane man is entitled to notice before his liberty or property can be taken from him, but that this can be done in a probate court in a proceeding to declare the person so as to be treated to be insane, or to declare that the protection of the Constitution does not extend to a person who is charged to be insane, and that upon such an ex parte charge, in an ex parte proceeding, his liberty and property can be taken . . . from him.

With little conflict, the authorities sustain the general propositions announced in the foregoing cases in actions of this kind. We cannot, of course, in this proceeding, review the facts alleged in the petition presented to respondent. It presents the not altogether unusual situation of a man of advanced years, who has been twice married and has children by both marriages. One son, it appears, has been unfortunate financially, and the father has apparently favored him by large assistance. The alleged incompetent appears to own and manage a large farm and to have property worth $200,000. Without any notice, or any appearance in his behalf, this man has been summarily placed under guardianship and his entire property turned over to a guardian. As before stated, we cannot and do not pass upon the question of the advisability, necessity, or propriety of having a guardian appointed for the person or property of the petitioner. We are constrained to hold, however, that such appointment cannot legally be made in any case until after notice to the alleged incompetent and until he has a right to be heard in his own behalf.

The basic guaranty of our fundamental law is that no man shall be deprived of life, liberty, or property without the due process of law. This is of the very genius of our institutions. It has come down to us from the days of the Magna Charta. It is among our choice heritages. It should not be lightly cast aside, even under a claim of necessity. If such proceedings can be had without any notice, the door is opened wide for the machinations of the designing or the malicious. Under such a rule, no citizen can rest in security of either person or property, for utterly unbeknown to him and without opportunity to be heard, he may suddenly discover that he has been placed under guardianship as an incompetent, and his property turned over to a conservator. Such a rule is repulsive to our American ideals of justice, and antagonistic to the fundamental rights guaranteed to the individual citizen. It would contravene those essential principles which a liberty-loving and law-respecting people cherish and hold most sacred. It is argued by counsel that the appointment of guardians in such cases, without notice, has been a universal custom in this state. If such be the case, "it is a custom more honored in the breach than in the observance." Neither age nor custom can make valid that which is essentially and fundamentally wrong.

This case is an original proceeding in certiorari to test the legality of the action of the respondent, as judge, in appointing a guardian of the property of the petitioner, without any notice of the proceedings being had on petitioner. Limiting our decision expressly to that question, we hold that the respondent, as judge, acted illegally in appointing a guardian for the property of the petitioner without reasonable notice to petitioner of said proceedings.

Said appointment is therefore void, and the order complained of is annulled.

EVANS, C. J., and STEVENS and ARTHUR, JJ., concur.

NOTE

McKinstry v. *Dewey* is illustrative of the fact that many courts are reluctant to make important decisions without any opportunity for direct input from the affected party, even when a need for precipitous action is alleged. One proposal would attempt to alleviate this concern for hearing the ward's "side of the story" by calling for a court-appointed "visitor" to interview the proposed ward and report back to the court prior to any decision. See Uniform Probate Code §§ 5-303(b) and 5-308. A visitor is defined as "a person who is trained in law, nursing or social work and is an officer, employee, or special appointee of the court with no personal interest in the proceedings" (*Id.* at § 5-308). If the situation indicated a need for a hearing with more substantial due process provisions, the court could proceed accordingly. Does such a proposal satisfy due process requirements?

Another alternative to the appointment of a temporary guardian is for the trial judge to make the necessary emergency decisions pending a guardianship hearing preceded by full notice. See, e.g., Uniform Probate Code § 5-310.

5. Modern Approaches: Limited Guardianship, Public Guardianship, Protective Services

In recent years there has been a growing impetus for eliminating some of the archaic aspects of guardianship law. Increased concern for protecting the civil rights of handicapped and elderly citizens has led to the enactment of laws that moderate the harshness of the traditional guardianship schemes.

The most glaring defect of traditional guardianship is the all-or-nothing nature of its application, resulting in social and legal stigmata for the ward. Few individuals are disabled in regard to all functions and activities, and yet there is no middle ground between overprotection and no protection at all. Consequently, the families and friends of disabled persons often are understandably reluctant to petition for a declaration of incompetency and the appointment of a general guardian; see, e.g., Hodgson, R., "Guardianship of Mentally Retarded Persons: Three Approaches to a Long Neglected Problem," 37 *Albany L. Rev.* 407 (1973).

Some of the principles on which reforms have been based are summarized in the findings of a legislative committee of the General Assembly of Pennsylvania. While dealing specifically with mentally retarded people these concepts are relevant to all persons subject to guardianship:

(1) There are varying degrees of mental retardation. Although mentally retarded, an individual may have sufficient ability to attend to himself and his personal affairs. For such persons the institution of guardianship must not be invoked.

(2) Mentally retarded persons must be assumed to have full human and legal rights and privileges. The mere fact of retardation must not be in and of itself sufficient to remove rights by appointment of a guardian or otherwise.

(3) Merely because a mentally retarded person is in need of various forms of assistance does not mean a guardian is required. In addition to the institution of formal guardianship, parallel services, such as personal counseling, should be available to retarded individuals who may not require formal guardianship if appropriate guidance and advice is provided on a continuing basis.

(4) Mere intellectual ability or disability is an inadequate determinant as to the necessity for guardianship, as intellect does not necessarily correspond to social adaptation. Determination of the need for guardianship must be a process considering both intelligence and functioning ability. Behavior is the crucial determinant.

(5) An adult is presumed legally capable of directing his or her personal life unless a court determines otherwise through guardianship proceedings.

(6) In those instances in which the retarded person is unable to manage himself or his personal affairs, a suitably designated guardianship program must be arranged.

(7) Guardianship of a mentally retarded person should be viewed positively as a means of implementing rights and opportunities with as much participation by the retarded ward in all decisions as is practical. The underlying goal of a guardian should be to do everything possible to help the retarded ward be self-sufficient in all respects.

(8) The guardianship program must be flexible, permitting adaptation to the specific needs of the particular retarded person. A guardianship relationship must be subject to revision as the needs of the person change.

(9) Mentally retarded persons must be allowed freedom—the maximum freedom consistent with their abilities, even freedom to make their own mistakes. Guardianship must be designed to fully utilize the retarded person's abilities and capabilities. *Limited guardianship with the scope of the guardianship specified in the judicial order is preferred.*

(10) The guardian's role as advisor and personal advocate of the mentally retarded ward must transcend the role as manager of the estate. *The welfare of the retarded person, not of the estate, must determine the legal and social provisions.* (Subcommittee Report on House Bill 1516 to the Judiciary Committee of the House of Representatives, Pa., Sept. 1974.)

a. Limited Guardianship. One relatively simple revision of guardianship laws, which has gained increasing acceptance in recent years, is the inclusion of statutory language requiring a limited guardianship if warranted by the circumstances of a case; see, e.g., Va. Code § 37.1-128.1 (1976); Md. Est. & Trusts Code Ann. §§ 13-706 to 710 (Cum.Supp. 1977); Conn. Gen. Stat. Ann. § 45.78(c) (Supp. 1978); N.Y. Surr. Ct. Proc. Act, § 1751 (McKinney's Supp. 1978). Washington's statute is a good example of this trend:

> The superior court for each county shall have power to appoint limited guardians for the persons and estates, or either thereof, of disabled persons, who by reason of their disability have need for protection and assistance, but who cannot be found to be fully incompetent, upon investigation [by the court or any agency jointly designated by the mental health board and mental retardation board (or county social service administrative board where applicable) of the county where such person resides]. After considering all evidence presented as a result of such investigation, the court shall impose, by order, only such specific limitations and disabilities on a disabled person to be placed under a limited guardianship as the court finds necessary for such person's protection and assistance. A person shall not be presumed to be incompetent nor shall a person lose any legal rights or suffer any legal disabilities as the result of being placed under a limited guardianship, except as to those rights and disabilities specifically set forth in the court order establishing such a limited guardianship. In addition, the court order shall state the period of time for which it shall be applicable. (Wash. Rev. Code Ann. § 11.88.010(2) (Supp. 1978)).

The effect of most limited guardianship provisions is to reduce the social stigma and legal disability traditionally attached to guardianship. In general, these statutes provide that courts will base the removal of specific decision-making powers on relevant and material evidence showing that the ward is unable to exercise such rights. By limiting the guardian's powers, emphasis is placed on encouraging self-sufficiency in the ward and eliminating his unnecessary dependency on others.

Even limited guardianship has drawbacks, however, when it is used for individuals who, although disabled, are capable of making their own choices. By eliminating the harsh aspects of general guardianship laws, the appointment of substitute decision makers for "borderline" cases is made more attractive to relatives and professional service providers.

Another problem with the limited guardianship formula is that courts will still be tempted to "overprotect." Unless there is a zealous advocate arguing for the rights of the disabled person, it is probable that courts will continue to provide petitioning parties with a range of powers as broad as they request.

Board of Regents State Universities v. Davis

Supreme Court of California, In Bank
14 C.3d 33, 533 P.2d 1047, 120 Cal.Rptr. 407

Tobriner, Justice.

Plaintiff Board of Regents State Universities, State of Wisconsin, appeals from a judgment on the pleadings in defendant's favor in an action to collect from the estate of a former conservatee, now deceased, a claim for $150,000. The question presented is whether the imposition of a conservatorship without a finding of incompetency deprives the conservatee of the capacity to contract. We conclude that, subject to the limitations of Probate Code section 1858, it does not.

On August 25, 1967, defendant Ralph Davis, Jr., petitioned for appointment as conservator of the estate of Ralph Davis, Sr. The petition alleged that Davis, Sr., was over the age of 80 and unable properly to care for his property, a sizable estate with a net worth of $1.8 million. The court appointed defendant as a temporary conservator, and on October 25, 1967, named a committee of five, including defendant, as permanent conservators. The temporary conservatorship continued until the court issued letters of conservatorship for the five committee members on January 15, 1968. The petition did not allege, nor did the court find, that Davis, Sr., was either insane or incompetent.

Davis, Sr., was a graduate and former director of the Wisconsin Mining School, now the Wisconsin State University–Platteville. On January 6, 1968, he attended a stadium fund raising dinner in Platteville, Wisconsin, at which time he signed a written agreement pledging $150,000 on a matching basis, for construction of a stadium for his alma mater. Thereupon the university, unaware that Davis, Sr., was a conservatee, widely publicized the pledge in order to solicit matching contributions.

On September 10, 1968, the conservators filed in the probate court a petition for an order to show cause why the conservators should not be instructed to rescind the pledge, but, on September 21, 1968, before the petition could be heard, Davis, Sr., died. The court appointed defendant as executor of the estate. Representing the Wisconsin State University–Platteville, plaintiff filed a claim in probate for $150,000, and upon defendant's rejection of the claim, commenced the present action.

Defendant filed a demurrer to plaintiff's complaint, contending in part that the mere existence of a conservatorship deprived the deceased conservatee of the capacity to enter into a pledge agreement. The trial court overruled the demurrer; defendant then moved for judgment on the pleadings on the ground that the complaint failed to state a cause of action for the reasons set forth in the demurrer. The trial court denied that motion. Defendant then renewed his motion for judgment on the pleadings, alleging that the Court of Appeal's decision in *Place* v. *Trent* [3] (1972) 27 Cal.App.3d 526, 103 Cal.Rptr. 841, filed August 29, 1972, after denial of the original motion, required the court to grant the motion. The trial court granted the renewed motion, entering judgment on the pleadings in favor of defendant.

Prior to 1957, a petition for guardianship presented the only procedure available for a party to assume administration of the estate of an adult unable to manage his affairs (Prob.Code, div. 4). Except in the case of minors, a guardianship requires both allegation and proof of the insanity or incompetency of the proposed ward. (Prob. Code, § 1460.) A ward under a guardianship lacks the capacity to enter into a contract (*Hellman Commercial T. & S. Bk.* v. *Alden* (1929) 206 Cal. 592, 608–609, 275 P. 794).

Believing that the stigma of the label "incompetent" discouraged persons unable to conduct their affairs from seeking appointment of a guardian, the State Bar of

---

[3] In *Place* v. *Trent, supra,* the court held void a conveyance of property from a conservatee to her nephew by deed of gift. The court rejected the argument that lack of a finding of incompetency on the part of the conservatee left her with full capacity to contract; the court reasoned that because guardianships and conservatorships were designed to serve the same purposes, the conservatee, like the ward, lacked capacity to contract even if the conservatee had not been adjudicated incompetent.

California recommended, and the Legislature established, the new protective relationship of conservatorship. These efforts resulted in 1957 in the addition to the Probate Code of a fifth division, consisting of sections 1701 through 2207 (Stats.1957, ch. 1902, § 1) establishing probate conservatorships.

The legislative history[5] indicates that both the State Bar and the Senate Judiciary Committee intended that the new relationship achieve two major objectives. The first was the establishment of the conservatorship as an alternative to guardianship to avoid, as we have noted, the "stigma" of the label "incompetency." In such a situation a conservator is merely another linguistic designation for a guardian.

The second objective of the new statute was to extend its embrace to those who would otherwise find themselves without legal protection. The Legislature achieved this objective by providing that the court could appoint a conservator for a person who was neither insane nor incompetent, but who, for a variety of other reasons, needed direction in the management of his affairs. Thus, clearly, the Legislature designed the conservatorship statute to cover a much more extensive category of eligible persons than the more limited guardianship law.

In view of the fact that the Legislature sought to accomplish by its conservatorship structure both the avoidance of the stigma of incompetency and the inclusion of a wider class, we must decide whether the Legislature intended that the conservatee who had not been adjudicated incompetent should nevertheless lose his capacity to enter into a contract. Although *Place* v. *Trent, supra*, 27 Cal.App.3d 526, 103 Cal.Rptr. 841, held that in this respect the conservatee could not be distinguished from the ward in his inability to contract, we do not believe that the legislative history confirms this identity. As we shall show, this court has recognized a distinction between conservatee

---

[5]While the conservatorship bill was pending in the Legislature an analysis in the State Bar Journal commented: "This bill would add a new division to the Probate Code, creating and defining the office of conservator and the concept of conservatorship. Conservatorships would be an alternative to guardianships in some instances and would provide the benefits of a conservator in certain others wherein guardianships are not now permissible. Many elderly or ill persons are reluctant to ask that a guardian be appointed to conduct their affairs because of the label of 'incompetent' which attaches to them under the present law. The proposed legislation, by eliminating all reference to 'incompetency,' seeks to overcome this reluctance. Various changes from guardianship proceedings are also made in procedure...." (Mull & Farley, 1957 Legislative Progress (1957) 32 *State Bar J.* 13, 23.)

In its report to the Senate the Senate Judiciary Committee distinguished conservatorships from guardianships in the following language:

The State Bar explained the purpose of the bill, as introduced, as follows:

Conservatorship

Senate Bill No. 1045 would add an entirely new division (Division 5) to the Probate Code, creating and defining the office of conservator and the concept of conservatorship. Conservatorships would be an alternative to guardianships in certain instances and would provide the benefits of a conservator in certain others wherein guardianships are not now permissible.

(1) Purpose ... there are in California today a great many people whose affairs should be given the protection of a guardianship but for whom such protection has not been sought. The proposed legislation, by calling the person requiring assistance a "conservatee," and the person appointed by the court to assist him a "conservator," and by eliminating all references of "incompetency" seeks to overcome the reluctance to use the protection which should be available under the law.... (1 Sen.J.Appendix (1957 reg. sess.) p. 487.) The Senate committee's report then proceeded to outline some but not all of the many differences between the statutory scheme for guardians and that for conservators. (*Id* at pp. 487–488.)

See also Lord, Conservatorship v. Guardianship (1975), 33 *L.A. Bar Bull.* 5.

and ward; furthermore, we shall point out that section 1858 expressly upholds the conservatee's limited power to contract and, finally, that the Lanterman-Petris-Short Act (Welf. & Inst. Code, § 5000 et seq.) likewise recognizes such restricted power of the conservatee.

In our past treatment of the present problem we have linked the incapacity to contract under Civil Code section 40 with an adjudication of incompetency. Thus in *Hellman Commercial T. & S. Bk.* v. *Alden, supra,* 206 Cal. 592, 275 P. 794, we held that a ward's incapacity to contract stems from Civil Code section 40 which reads, as amended, in pertinent part, "Subject to Sections 1561 and 1910 of the Probate Code, and subject to Part I (Commencing with Section 5000) of Division 5 of the Welfare and Institutions Code after his incapacity has been judicially determined, a person of unsound mind can make no conveyance or other contract, nor delegate any power or waive any right, until his restoration to capacity. . . ." As we explained, when "a court has regularly adjudged one to be incompetent, he thereby becomes incapable of making a valid contract, and it is deemed to be void, not because he is unable, unassisted, to properly care for his property, or lacked understanding of the nature and effect of the particular transaction, but because the decree of incompetency is notice to the world of his incapacity to make a valid contract." (206 Cal. at p. 604, 275 P. at p. 799.)

Hellman has accordingly determined that an adjudication of *incompetency* presupposes a lack of capacity to understand the nature and effect of a contract. (206 Cal. at p. 605, 275 P. 794.) Noting that Code of Civil Procedure section 1764 authorizes a court to appoint a guardian for a person who is either insane or incompetent, the *Hellman* court concluded that such an appointment is an adequate adjudication of incompetency, and hence also of incapacity under Civil Code section 40. (206 Cal. at pp. 604–605, 275 P. 794.)

The argument that a conservatee lacks capacity to contract would necessarily, if it has any statutory source at all, stem from Civil Code section 40. Yet, inasmuch as *Hellman* holds that it is the finding of *incompetency* that serves notice of a person's incapacity under Civil Code section 40, conservatees who have *not* been adjudged incompetent should not be bound by that section's proscriptions.

The fact that a conservatee has at least a limited power to contract is further evidenced by the 1963 amendment to section 1858 (Stats.1963, ch. 1549, p. 3132, § 1), which provides in part that "The conservator shall pay debts incurred by the conservatee during the conservatorship for the necessaries of life. . . . The conservator shall pay any other debts incurred by the conservatee during the conservatorship only if they appear to be such as a reasonably prudent person might incur." This section quite clearly indicates that a conservatee retains power to contract, subject to the conservator's right to disaffirm unreasonable contracts other than those involving the purchase of necessaries which cannot be disaffirmed. This section also provides that if the conservator entertains any doubt as to the propriety of the debt he may petition the court for instructions. If all contracts of a conservatee, like those of a ward, were void, the protections of amended section 1858 would be totally unnecessary.

Although defendant attacks this interpretation by urging that the term "debts" in section 1858 should be construed to include only liability for "nonconsensual" debts such as tort and quasi-contractual obligations, we believe that such a construction of the statute is strained. Nothing supports the hypothesis that the Legislature intended so abnormal a restriction of a commonly used word.

The Lanterman-Petris-Short Act (Welf. & Inst.Code, § 5000 et seq.) also manifests the Legislature's recognition that conservatees retain a limited capacity to contract under probate conservatorships. Dealing with the mentally disordered person and chronic alcoholic, this act provides that such an individual may be placed under a conservatorship identical to those set forth in the Probate Code for conservatorships. (Welf. & Inst.Code, § 5350.) Implicitly recognizing a conservatee's right to contract, section 5357 provides that all conservators appointed under the act shall have all the general powers possessed by probate conservators and such additional powers, if any, that a court could grant under probate conservatorships. The section also provides: "The report[14] shall also recommend for or against the imposition of each of the following disabilities on the proposed conservatee: . . . (b) The right to enter into contracts. The officer may recommend against a person having the right to enter specified types of transactions or transactions in excess of specified money amounts."

If all conservatees were already presumed incapable of contracting, clearly this provision would be inappropriate. The provision cannot properly be read to mean, as defendant suggests, that a conservatee only retains a right to contract under sections 1861 (allowances) and 1910 (wages), which the court under the Lanterman-Petris-Short Act can then limit and restrict. This interpretation cannot stand because the court, under sections 1861 and 1910, already retains the discretion to limit and restrict the conservatee's right to dispose of those funds, if any. . . . Thus the only natural interpretation of Welfare and Institutions Code section 5357 is that the conservatee does, indeed, have some right to contract, which is defined pursuant to the Probate Code, and that under the Lanterman-Petris-Short Act this right may not be totally obliterated but only restricted by explicit judicial declaration.

Finally, we do not accept defendant's contentions that recognition of the conservatee's right to contract will frustrate the purposes of the Conservatorship Act and render unmanageable the administration of conservatorships. The fact that two persons co-manage property does not necessarily mean that the property thereby becomes unmanageable. Many types of relationships are premised upon co-management. (E.g., tenancy in common, joint tenancy, community property.) In some situations, in fact, the conservator will more likely play the role of supervisor rather than co-manager as in the case of a conservatee, not adjudged an incompetent, who has entered into reasonable contracts. The Legislature surely accepted the fact of co-management when it determined that a conservatee cannot totally be deprived of the right to contract.

Nor will our affirmation of the power of the conservatee to contract or convey property, subject to supervision and review by the probate court, defeat the primary purpose of the conservatorship, i.e., a means to enable a competent person legally to assist the conservatee in the management of his property. (*Conservatorship of Steward* (1969) 276 Cal.App.2d 211, 214, 80 Cal.Rptr. 738.) Since the transfer of property and the incurrence of contracts undertaken by the conservatee remain subject to supervision

---

[14]Before the court can authorize a conservatorship under this act, an officer must conduct a conservatorship investigation and issue a report pursuant thereto. (Welf. & Inst.Code, §§ 5352, 5356.)

and review by the probate court (§§ 1858, 1862), the conservatee retains the protection of the conservatorship.

In sum the scheme provides for a flexible and adequate protective relationship that enables the competent conservatee who for some reason is unable properly to care for his property, to enter into a valid contract, upon the condition that it "appear to be such as a reasonably prudent person might incur." If a proposed conservator harbors reservations about the proposed conservatee's competency he may simply ask the court to render a specific finding that the conservatee is a person "for whom a guardian could be appointed" in order that this conservatee, like a ward, be incapable of contracting. (§ 1751.) On the other hand, if a proposed conservatee is competent, no reason compels a total abolition of his right to contract. We therefore disapprove language in *Place* v. *Trent, supra,* to the effect that a conservatee is necessarily incapable of making a valid contract.

Conservatorship is a modern legal mechanism conceived to meet a realistic human desire to avoid the stigma of incompetency; the courts should permit its plenary use, unimpaired by the debilitating interpretation that strips the competent conservatee of the limited power to contract.

The judgment is reversed. The case is remanded to the superior court with instructions to set aside its order granting the motion for judgment on the pleadings.

WRIGHT, C. J., and McCOMB, MOSK, SULLIVAN, CLARK and RICHARDSON, JJ., concur.

NOTES

1. To what other legal rights of the conservatee could the reasoning of the *Davis* court apply?

2. In regard to the right to enter into contracts generally, see Chapter 10, this volume.

3. If Mr. Davis was competent enough to handle a transaction involving $150,000, is there a need for a conservator at all?

b. Public Guardianship. A number of states have created public guardianship systems which allow designated state or local government officials to accept guardianship appointments, e.g., Ariz. Rev. Stat. 14-5601 (1975); Cal. Welf. & Inst. Code §§ 8000–8015 (West 1972); Del. Code, Tit. 12, § 3991 (Cum.Supp. 1978); Me. Rev. Stat., Tit. 18, §§ 3621, 3638 (1973). Although some statutes mandate that the public guardian be appointed only as a last resort if no private individual can be found, e.g., Me. Rev. Stat., Tit. 18, § 3621 (1973), other states use the office to provide services to a broad range of disabled and dependent persons, e.g., Cal. Welf. & Inst. Code § 8006 (West 1972); Cal. Health & Safety Code § 416 (West Supp. 1978) (guardianship over certain developmentally disabled persons).

Praised by some commentators as a means of providing free or low cost guardianship services to the poor and to individuals without friends or concerned relatives (see U.S. Senate Special Comm. on Aging, 95th Cong., 1st Sess., *Protective Services for the Elderly: A Working Paper* 40–42 (1977), which contains a Model Public Guardianship Act at Appendix 3, p. 111), public guardianship has also generated considerable adverse criticism. The chief complaints concern the lack of personal attention to the ward and the conflict of interest that exists when a government service provider acts as guardian; see Hodgson, R., "Guardianship of Mentally Retarded Persons: Three Approaches to a Long Neglected Problem," 37 *Albany L. Rev.* 407, 421 (1973). In addition, some reports indicate that one of the major "services" provided to the public wards is the initiation of civil commitment proceedings; see Hodgson, R., *supra,* at 432; Mitchell, A., "Involuntary Guardianship for Incompetents: A Strategy for Legal Services Advocates," 12 *Clearinghouse Rev.* 451, 463 (Dec. 1978).

In re Guardianship of Raymond C.

Court of Appeals of California, 1977
72 Cal.App.3d 417, 140 Cal.Rptr. 133

Christian, Associate Justice.

These appeals are from orders appointing the director of the department of health guardian of the persons of appellants, who are mentally disabled persons.

Appellants contend that the appointment of the Director of Health as guardian of their persons, under section 416 of the Health and Safety Code, deprives them and other developmentally disabled persons similarly situated of the protection the relationship is presumed to provide because a conflict of interest is created. Appellants contend that the appointment of the Director of Health as their guardian reduces the guardian-ward relationship to a mere legal fiction.

Appellants concede that as developmentally disabled persons as defined in section 38003, subdivision (h), of the Health and Safety Code, they are in need of a guardian. Appellants point out that they presently reside in state institutions administered by the Director of Health, and that they are eligible for the services of the regional centers which are funded and controlled by the Director of Health. Appellants argue that inherent in this relationship is a potential conflict between the interests of appellants and the interests of their guardian, such that the interest of appellants cannot be adequately protected. They argue that the appointment of the State Director of Health as their guardian fails to provide them with the impartial agent necessary to protect their right to privacy, their right to refuse unnecessary medical or surgical treatment (see Welf. & Inst. Code, § 7518), their right to receive effective treatment, and other civil rights accorded to wards or mentally disordered persons. (See Prob. Code, § 1461.5; Health & Saf.Code, §§ 416.23, 38110 [repealed Stats.1976, c. 1368, § 1; see now § 38223]; see also Health & Saf. Code, §§ 38002, 38004, 38009.1, 38223 [added Stats.1976, c. 1364, 1368, effective Jan. 1, 1977].) According to appellants, the director's role as guardian of appellants and as protector of their rights and interests is in potential conflict with the director's role as manager of the state mental hospital system. But appellants' argument is contrary to the express provisions of the applicable statute. Section 416 of the Health and Safety Code provides as follows:

> The Director of Health may be appointed as either guardian or conservator of the person and estate, or person or estate, of any developmentally disabled person, who is either of the following:
> (1) Eligible for the services of a regional center.
> (2) A patient in any state hospital, and who was admitted or committed to such hospital from a county served by a regional center.

(See Health & Saf.Code, § 38150 [renumbered and amended by Stats.1976, c. 1373, § 8; now § 38500]; see also 58 Ops.Cal.Atty.Gen. 688 [1975].) There are two methods by which the director may be appointed guardian of a developmentally disabled person: One method is through nomination by a parent, relative or friend of the developmentally disabled person, or through nomination by a prior guardian, or through nomination by the developmentally disabled person himself. (See Health & Saf.Code, § 416.5.) The second method by which the Director of Health may become guardian is by the director's making direct application to the court for appointment. (See Health & Saf.Code, § 416.6; 58 Ops.Cal.Atty.Gen. 688, 690 [1975].)

Section 416.16 of the Health and Safety Code provides that, upon his appointment, the Director of Health shall have the same powers and duties as those established for guardians in the Guardianship Act (see Prob.Code, § 1400 *et seq.*). When acting as guardian of the person of a developmentally disabled person, the Director of Health is directed to maintain close contact with the developmentally disabled person, to "act as a wise parent would act in caring for his developmentally disabled child" and to "permit and encourage maximum self-reliance on the part of the developmentally disabled person under his protection." (Health & Saf.Code, § 416.17.) The statutory duty of the director as guardian is thus to act in the best interests of the disabled ward. The designation of a public agency to undertake the responsibilities of guardianship of developmentally disabled persons is a matter for legislative determination, in the absence of a pertinent constitutional restriction.

Affirmed.

CALDECOTT, P. J., and RATTIGAN, J., concur.

NOTE

Criticism of the various public guardianship systems centers mostly on the deficiencies of a bureaucratic system and on the lack of accountability to which public guardians are held. Both of these weaknesses are compounded when, as in California, the public guardian is also the provider of services.

Ideally, guardianship provides personalized individual care to a ward who is dependent on others for help in decision making. When the guardian is a large bureaucratic system, this relationship is impossible. Even if the nominal guardian is the top-ranking official in an agency, the actual work is handled by a constantly shifting body of caseworkers, who are more likely than not burdened with a large number of clients. The head of the Office of the Public Guardian in Los Angeles County has testified that his deputies spend an average of 2 hours per case annually (*Public Hearing on House Resolution 106: A Review of California's Programs for the Mentally Disabled before the Permanent Subcomm. on Mental Health and Developmental Disabilities* (Nov. 7, 1977)).

Accountability to the court and to concerned friends and relatives may be extremely limited. The Minnesota statute, for example, calls for an annual review of "the physical, mental and social progress of every ward," but there is no right of anyone outside the department to contest the findings in such reports and no need to send it to the court or any other outside body (Minn. Stat. Ann. § 252A.16 (1979)).

The conflict of interest problem complained of in the *Raymond C.* case is a serious drawback to many public guardianship schemes.

In re Burley

Circuit Court for Prince George's County, Maryland, 1978
Case No. E-3936, June 5, 1978

Mason, Judge.

This cause having been heard upon petition of Mildred Burley at a hearing at which George Burley was present and represented by counsel, and it having been found by the Court that George Burley, an adult male, 26 years of age, lacks sufficient understanding or capacity to make or communicate responsible decisions concerning his person because of mental retardation and a neurological disorder manifested by seizures, and it having been agreed to by all parties and found by this Court that George Burley is disabled within the meaning of Maryland Estate & Trusts Article 13-704, and as George Burley is now a voluntarily committed patient at Spring Grove Hospital Center in Catonsville, Maryland, and as no less restrictive form of intervention is available consistent with George Burley's welfare and safety, and that the Maryland Department of Health and Mental Hygiene is best qualified to provide service and/or serve as guardian of the person of George Burley, it is therefore this 5th day of June, 1978, by the Circuit Court for Prince George's County,

ORDERED; That the Secretary of the Maryland Department of Health and Mental Hygiene shall provide or contract for the provision of a day program at Melwood Horticultural Training Center, Inc., Upper Marlboro, Maryland, and for the provision of socialization skills, and it is further

ORDERED; The Secretary of the Maryland Department of Health & Mental Hygiene arrange and pay for any transportation necessary for George Burley to travel on a daily basis between Spring Grove Center and the day program which he attends, and it is further

ORDERED; That the Secretary of the Maryland Department of Health & Mental Hygiene arrange and pay for lunch costs incidental to George Burley's attendance at such a program, and it is further

ORDERED; That the Secretary of the Maryland Department of Health & Mental Hygiene be empowered to consent and arrange for all medical care necessary to control George Burley's seizure disorder; to treat his myopia; to treat his gingival hypertrophy; and to treat the mild edema of his lower extremities; and to treat the tineal infection of his trunk; and it is further

ORDERED; That the Secretary of the Maryland Department of Health & Mental Hygiene monitor on a regular basis all such medical care provided to George Burley, and it is further

ORDERED; that the determination by the Court that George Burley is a disabled person does not modify any of his civil rights, may not be the basis for his involuntary commitment to a mental facility and does not grant to the Prince George's County Department of Social Services any powers with regard to George Burley except those specifically stated in this Order.

NOTE

Notwithstanding the possible conflict of interest problems, public guardianship statutes may provide a mechanism for mandating that public agencies provide community services for adult handicapped individuals. Although P.L. 94-142, the Education for All Handicapped Children's Act, requires that children receive appropriate services in the least restrictive environment, see pp. 278–293, above, in most states there is no similar requirement that state agencies provide services so that adult handicapped individuals can live in the community. One mechanism for achieving this goal is to file petitions for public guardianship and recommend to the court that public agencies be appointed as guardians who would then be responsible for providing the needed services in the least restrictive environment. This approach, illustrated in *Burley,* permits the development of court orders tailored to meet the specific needs of the particular handicapped individual.

     c. Protective Services and Emergency Intervention. If guardianship of disabled persons is to be avoided, there must be an effective means of providing services to meet the special needs of the handicapped and the elderly on a voluntary basis. The use of involuntary intervention on behalf of such individuals should be as limited in duration and scope as possible. A number of states have incorporated these concepts in "adult protective services" statutes. See, generally, U.S. Senate Special Comm. on Aging, 95th Cong., 1st Sess., *Protective Services for the Elderly: A Working Paper* (1977). (A Model Protective Services Act is set out at 56-74.) See, e.g., Colo. Rev. Stat. § 26-3-101 to 112 (Supp. 1978); Wis. Stat. § 55.001-07 (Supp. 1979).

     A comprehensive example of such a statute is provided by Chapter 23 of Title 14 of the Tenn. Code Ann., entitled "Protective Services for Elderly Persons." Section 14-2301 declares:

> Legislative intent and purpose.   It shall be the responsibility of the state of Tennessee to develop and to encourage the provision of protective services for elderly persons residing in the state in need of such services.

Section 14-2302 defines certain terms and includes the following:

> (b) The words "elderly person in need of protective services" shall mean any elderly person unable to perform or obtain for himself services which are necessary to maintain his mental and physical health.
> (c) The words "services which are necessary to maintain mental and physical health" shall include, but shall not be limited to the provision of medical care for physical and mental health needs, assistance in personal hygiene, food, clothing, adequately heated and ventilated shelter, protection from health and safety hazards, foster care, day care, protection from physical mistreatment, and transportation necessary to secure any of the above-stated needs; provided that the words "services which are necessary to maintain mental and physical health" shall not include taking the elderly person into physical custody without his consent, except as provided in § 14-2306 and in title 33 of this Code.
> (d) The words "protective services" shall mean services which are necessary to maintain mental and physical health and which an elderly person is unable to perform or obtain for himself.

Sections 14-2303 and 2304 provide for reporting needy elderly persons and the duty of the State Department of Human Services upon receipt of such report.

Section 14-2305 provides for furnishing protective services to consenting elderly persons and concludes as follows:

> (c) If an elderly person does not consent to the receipt of protective services, or if he withdraws his consent, the services shall be terminated, unless the department determines that the elderly person lacks capacity to consent, in which case it may seek court authorization to provide protective services pursuant to § 14-2306.

Section 14-2306(a) provides:

> If the department determines that an elderly person who is in need of protective services is in imminent danger of death if he does not receive protective services and lacks capacity to consent to protective services, then the department may file a complaint with the chancery court for an order authorizing the provision of protective services necessary to prevent imminent death. The chancellor shall hear the complaint ahead of any other business then pending in court or in chambers. This order may include the designation of an individual or organization to be responsible for the personal welfare of the elderly person and for consenting to protective services in his behalf. The complaint must allege specific facts sufficient to show that the elderly person is in imminent danger of death if he does not receive protective services and lacks capacity to consent to protective services.
>
> The chancellor, prior to entering the order, must find that the elderly person is in imminent danger of death if he does not receive protective services and lacks capacity to consent to protective services.
>
> Within five (5) days of entering an order pursuant to this section, the court shall hold a hearing on the merits. If such a hearing is not held within such time, the order authorizing the provision of protective services shall be dissolved.
>
> The elderly person must receive at least forty-eight (48) hours' notice of the hearing. He has a right to be present and represented by counsel at the hearing. If the elderly person is indigent, or in the determination of the chancellor, lacks capacity to waive the right to counsel, then the court shall appoint counsel. If the elderly person is indigent, the cost of representation by counsel shall be borne by the state.
>
> At this hearing, the chancellor may find that the elderly person is in imminent danger of death if he does not receive protective services and lacks capacity to consent to protective services. If the chancellor finds that the elderly person is not in imminent danger of death if he does not receive protective services or that the elderly person does not lack capacity to consent to protective services, then the original order shall be dissolved.
>
> Protective services necessary to prevent imminent death authorized by order pursuant to this section may include taking the elderly person into physical custody in the home or in a medical or nursing care facility, provided that the court finds that such custody is for the purpose of medical examination and treatment necessary to prevent imminent death or protection from physical mistreatment necessary to prevent imminent death and provided that the court specifically authorizes such custody in its order. If the court authorizes such custody in its order, the court shall review its decree at least every six (6) months to determine whether the prerequisites for custody continue to exist.

In *State Dept. of Human Services* v. *Northern,* 563 S.W.2d 197 (Tenn.App. 1978), these Tennessee provisions were used as a basis for providing emergency intervention in a case involving a 72-year-old woman who had refused medical treatment for her gangrenous feet (see Chapter 8, this volume). Such intervention is, in effect, a temporary guardianship of the person for the purpose of consenting to services. After the danger of death is past, the individual immediately and automatically reacquires full freedom of choice.

Disabled and elderly persons are the groups most likely to be affected by such programs. The danger inherent in these systems is that excessively independent and eccentric individuals can be placed under involuntary "protection" because of their resistance to the intrusions of overzealous officials into their lives. The failure to conform to community norms can easily be construed in terms of mental incapacity and used as validation for a restriction of freedom.

There is also danger that protective services legislation can be used to increase the involuntary placement of individuals in nursing homes or other custodial facilities. Consequently, the disabled and elderly, through the guise of "protective services," can end up being institutionalized. As one commentator stated in regard to elderly persons, although the statement applies equally to handicapped people:

> . . . the elderly who are beneficiaries of social services may be at an even higher risk of injury or death. When the elderly receive that attention, this may mean that the social workers and courts will put the client in an institution where both the enjoyment and length of life are curtailed. In addition to a shortened life, confinement in an institution usually means loss of self-esteem, of freedom, and of useful activity (U.S. Senate Special Comm. on Aging, 95th Cong., 1st Sess., *Protective Services for the Elderly: A Working Paper* 7 (1977)).

d. Other Alternatives

i.   *Court Authorization of Specific Transactions*   Just as emergency intervention by a court in certain medical situations may obviate the need for a guardian of the person, so may guardianship of the property be avoided by a statutory provision allowing a court to authorize a specific financial transaction.

Under one such law, a court having jurisdiction under the standards set out in the guardianship of the property provision:

> without appointing a guardian, may authorize or direct a transaction with respect to the property, service, or care arrangement of the . . . disabled person. These transactions include but are not limited to (1) payment, delivery, deposit, or retention of funds or property; (2) sale, mortgage, lease, or any other transfer of property; (3) purchase of contracts for an annuity, life care, training, or education; or (4) any other transaction described in [the section enumerating the powers of a fiduciary] (Md. Est. & Trusts Code Ann. § 13.204 (1974)).

See Uniform Probate Code § 5-409(a).

Under such a provision a person thought to be lacking in the capacity to contract need not come under a full guardianship simply to make possible a valid financial transfer.

ii.   *Substitute Payee*   Several federal statutes authorize federal agencies to make an administrative determination of incompetency for the purpose of appointing a substitute payee to receive and manage benefits paid by the agency; see, e.g., 42 U.S.C. § 405(j) (1976) (Social Security Administration); 38 U.S.C. § 3202-03 (1976) (Veterans' Administration); 37 U.S.C. § 601-04 (1970) (Department of Defense); 45 U.S.C. § 288 (1972) (Railroad Retirement Board); 5 U.S.C. § 8345(e) (Supp. 1979)

Civil Services). The basis for the determination of incompetency is the beneficiary's inability to manage the funds due him or her, and it has no effect on legal competence or the right to manage any funds other than payments from the agency.

While this system has the advantage of its simplicity and low cost in comparison to guardianship litigation, these same factors may warrant criticism on constitutional grounds. A major defect is the lack of notice and a hearing on the issue of competency. In addition, the criteria used in determining when a substitute payee should be named are often vague and overly broad.

For a case in which a lower court was ruled to have committed reversible error in ordering a general guardianship established in proceedings for the appointment of a substitute payee (although termed a "guardian" under the state law) for Veterans' Administration benefits, see *In re Vaell's Estate,* 322 P.2d 579 (Cal.App. 1958). See, also, Allen, R., Ferster, E., and Weihofen, H., *Mental Impairment and Legal Incompetency* 84 (1968); U.S. Senate Special Comm. on Aging, 95th Cong., 1st Sess., *Protective Services for the Elderly: A Working Paper* 45 (1977).

   iii. *Power of Attorney and Trusts*   The simplest and least expensive means of authorizing one person to manage the financial affairs of another is to create a power of attorney. If permitted by statute, such a document can be used to transfer legal authority to sign documents and conduct transactions from a disabled individual to a trusted relative or associate who has been designated before the onset of disability.

The use of power of attorney in anticipation of future disability is often an effective means of bypassing the need for an estate guardian; see *In re Bryden's Estate,* pp. 565–567, above. Inasmuch as competency is required at the time such arrangements are made, power of attorney is more suited to an individual whose ability to manage financial affairs is deteriorating than to persons with permanent handicapping conditions. Under common law, a power of attorney was terminated by the onset of disability; see Stiller, S., and Redden, R., "Statutory Reform in the Administration of Estates of Maryland Decedents, Minors and Incompetents," 29 *Md. L. Rev.* 85, 121 (1969). Statutory provisions can solve this by providing that a power of attorney may be drafted so that it will either continue or take effect after the principal becomes disabled; see, e.g., Uniform Probate Code §§ 5-501 and 502. See, also, Legal Research and Services for the Elderly and National Council of Senior Citizens, *Legislative Approaches to the Problems of the Elderly: A Handbook of Model State Statutes,* 157 (1971) (Model Special Power of Attorney for Small Property Interests Act). In drafting such arrangements, phrases like "This power of attorney shall not be affected by disability of the principal," or "This power of attorney shall become effective upon the disability of the principal" should be included.

Trust arrangements can also be used effectively for financial management on behalf of a broad range of disabled persons. For example, testamentary gifts to mentally retarded individuals may be made in trust so that the management of such funds will not precipitate guardianship proceedings; moreover, such an arrangement might be effective evidence in guardianship hearings that appointment is unnecessary. See Hodgson, R., "Guardianship of Mentally Retarded Persons: Three Approaches to a Long Neglected Problem," 37 *Albany L. Rev.* 407, 425-28 (1973) for a discussion of the various "retardate trusts" that have been established by private citizens' groups to meet the needs of mentally retarded beneficiaries. See, also, U.S. Senate Special Comm. on Aging, 95th Cong., 1st Sess., *Protective Services for the Elderly: A Working Paper* 46 (1977). The major shortcoming of this type of financial or property arrangement is that the management costs of administering a trust can be very high and thus are often not an effective mechanism for low or middle income individuals.

G. THE GUARDIANSHIP PROCEEDING

Guardians are appointed in a civil proceeding based upon the state's role as *parens patriae*. In the past, guardianship has frequently been considered a benevolent action by the petitioning party and the state. For these reasons, courts have assumed that relaxed and informal procedures are legally permissible and, in fact, beneficial to the emotional welfare of the alleged incompetent person. This attitude was typified in *In re Prokosch's Guardianship*, 128 Minn. 324, 151 N.W. 130, 132 (1915), when the court stated:

> In the determination of the question whether the appointment of a guardian of an alleged incompetent person is proper and necessary, the court is not controlled by the ordinary forms of procedure regulating the trial of actions at law. . . . It is not adversary in nature, but rather one by the state in its character of parens patriae; and the manner and method of determining the facts, when jurisdiction has once vested in the court as required by law, rests in its sound judgment and discretion, controlled, of course, by the general rules of judicial procedure. [citations omitted]

See, also, Allen, R., Ferster, E., and Weihofen, H., *Mental Impairment and Legal Incompetency* 87 (1968).

This paternalistic attitude toward due process safeguards in guardianship proceedings should be contrasted with sentiments such as that expressed by the United States Supreme Court in *In re Gault,* 387 U.S. 1, 20 (1967):

> Due process of law is the primary and indispensable foundation of individual freedom. It is the basic and essential term in the social compact which defines the rights of the individual and delimits the powers which the state may exercise.

Although the Supreme Court has not yet considered the extent to which procedural safeguards must be required in guardianship proceedings, it is clear from its decisions defining the rights of juveniles and of persons subject to commitment in mental institutions that, when an individual is subject to loss of property or liberty, certain procedural safeguards must be followed.

The determination of the appropriate procedure due an individual is dependent on the particular situation and the importance of the rights involved; see *Morrissey* v. *Brewer,* 408 U.S. 471, 481 (1972). A strong case can be made that in guardianship proceedings the rights involved are fundamental and the deprivation total. As the Supreme Court of New Hampshire has stated:

> A person who is legally declared incompetent is substantially deprived of liberty. An incompetent person is reduced to the status of a child and cannot dispose of his property or determine his place of residence. He cannot give his informed consent to medical treatment (*In re Albert Gamble,* 78-082, 78-142 (Supreme Court of New Hampshire, November 15, 1978)).

This section examines some of the important facets of procedural due process that may be pertinent in the context of guardianship proceedings.

1. Notice and Hearing

DALE v. HAHN

United States Court of Appeals for the Second Circuit, 1973
486 F.2d 76, cert. denied, sub nom., Dale v. Miller, 419 U.S. 826 (1974)

TIMBERS, Circuit Judge:

These cross-appeals are from an order entered May 7, 1973 in the Southern District of New York, which (1) held that the 1962 state court order declaring plaintiff-appellee-appellant Rita Hooper Dale ("appellee") to be incompetent and appointing a committee to manage her affairs was null and void *ab initio;* and (2) directed the return to appellee by defendants-appellants-appellees ("appellants") of the sum of $2,152.35, plus interest from July 24, 1962, representing expenditures, other than payments to the New York State Department of Mental Hygiene, made by the committees from her estate.

The primary issue raised on appeal is whether the district court's finding that appellee had not been adequately notified of the committee-appointment proceeding was clearly erroneous. We hold that it was not. We affirm.

I

In 1951, appellee was involuntarily committed to a state mental hospital where she remained until 1967. In 1962, allegedly due to appellee's failure to pay the New York State Department of Mental Hygiene for services and treatment provided her, the hospital director filed a petition in the New York Supreme Court, Bronx County, which sought an order declaring appellee incompetent and appointing a committee to manage her affairs. No hearing was held. On July 24, 1962, the petition was granted. Appellant Hahn was appointed as the committee. Upon the court's acceptance of Hahn's resignation in 1966 and the settlement of his account, defendant Pious was appointed as the successor committee pursuant to the same procedure. On April 18, 1967, appellee was discharged from the hospital. She subsequently was declared competent to manage her own affairs.

During the tenure of the committees, almost $8,000 of appellee's assets was expended, of which $5,686.16 was paid to the Department of Mental Hygiene. The remainder went for expenses which appellee allegedly would not have incurred had she been permitted to manage her own affairs.

In 1969, appellee commenced in the Southern District of New York a class action challenging the constitutionality of N.Y. Mental Hygiene Law § 102 (McKinney 1971) on the ground that its provision for the appointment of a committee to manage the affairs of an incompetent, without first affording to the incompetent notice of the proceedings and an opportunity to be heard in opposition, violated the due process clause of the Fourteenth Amendment. Declaratory and injunctive relief was sought, together with the return of all sums expended by the allegedly unlawful committees. On March 26, 1970, Judge Cooper denied the motion to convene a three-judge court and dismissed the complaint. 311 F.Supp. 1293 (S.D.N.Y. 1970). On appeal, we affirmed the denial of the motion for a three-judge court and the determination that the class action was inappropriate; but we reversed the dismissal of the complaint and remanded for the purpose, inter alia, of determining the adequacy of the notice given to appellee of the committee-appointment proceedings. 440 F.2d 633 (2d Cir. 1971).

On remand, Judge Knapp held the notice to have been inadequate. In an oral finding of fact made at the conclusion of the trial, he found that the testimony of appellee and John C. Miller (the state's process server), both of whom were credited as "truthful" witnesses, indicated either that appellee had not been served with notice of the proceeding at all, or that "it was handed to her in circumstances where its meaning did not get through to her." Either of these situations, the court held, would satisfy appellee's burden of establishing that she was not provided with adequate notice. In its written memorandum and order that followed, the court held that our 1971 decision precluded appellee from asserting that she could recover sums paid to the Department of Mental Hygiene by the first committee, and further that she "has offered no reason why the amounts paid to the hospital by her second committee should be treated any differently." That order is now challenged on appeal by both sides. Appellants contend that the finding of inadequate notice was erroneous. Appellee objects to the limitation of recovery to payments other than those to the Department of Mental Hygiene.

II

As stated above, the district court did not determine whether appellee was or was not physically served with notice of the committee-appointment proceeding. Rather, the finding was to the effect that, assuming arguendo that appellee actually had been served, under the circumstances of her incompetency such notice was inadequate.

The premise underlying that finding is that there may be situations in which physical service of process will not constitute adequate notice. We are satisfied that such a premise is supported by the cases.

The landmark case dealing with the question of constitutional sufficiency of notice, *Mullane* v. *Central Hanover Bank & Trust Co.*, 339 U.S. 306 (1950), while distinguishable on its facts, nevertheless does have a direct bearing here. In *Mullane,* the Court held that notice by publication was inadequate to inform known beneficiaries of a common trust fund of the proposed judicial settlement of certain accounts by the trustee. In so holding, the Court stated the critical due process requirement as follows:

> An elementary and fundamental requirement of due process in any proceeding which is to be accorded finality is notice reasonably calculated, under all the circumstances, to apprise interested parties of the pendency of the action and afford them an opportunity to present their objections.
>
> [W]hen notice is a person's due, process which is a mere gesture is not due process. The means employed must be such as one desirous of actually informing the [person] might reasonably adopt to accomplish it. . . . 339 U.S. at 314-15 [citations omitted].

The New York state courts likewise have recognized the importance of the particular circumstances of a case in assessing the constitutional adequacy of notice. One court summarized the rule as permitting a finding of inadequacy where "the circumstances [are] such as to show that the [recipient] did not come into actual possession of the papers and that his attention was not drawn to their character, or that he had not willfully ignored them and refused to ascertain their nature for the purpose of evading service." *Heller* v. *Levinson,* 166 App.Div. 673, 674, 152 N.Y.S. 35, 36 (1st Dept. 1915). See *In re Barbara,* 14 Misc.2d 223, 226-27, 180 N.Y.S.2d 924, 928 (Sup.Ct., Tioga Co., 1958), *aff'd,* 7 App.Div.2d 340, 183 N.Y.S.2d 147 (3d Dept. 1959). This rule has been held to require the vacating of an order where, despite undisputed personal written notice of an impending judgment of foreclosure, the recipient's "advanced age and lack of experience and understanding" were such as to lull her "into a false state of security." *Brown* v. *Giesecke,* 40 App.Div.2d 1009, 338 N.Y.S.2d 967, 969 (2d Dept. 1972). See also *In re Coates,* 9 N.Y.2d 242, 251-53, 173 N.E. 2d 797, 802-03, 213 N.Y.S.2d 74, 81-82 (1961), *appeal dismissed sub nom. Coates* v. *Walters,* 368 U.S. 34 (1961).

The decision below was in accord with those principles.[8] The state was not serving notice on an ordinary party in a civil suit; on the contrary, it was dealing with a person committed to a state mental hospital as an incompetent—a fact necessarily known to the state in light of the very nature of the proceeding. The district court found that the notice given was not reasonably calculated under the circumstances to apprise appellee of the fact that a substantial interest was involved. We hold that finding to have been permissible as a matter of law, and on the record before us it was not clearly erroneous. . . .

NOTES

1. In *Covey* v. *Town of Somers,* 351 U.S. 141, 146 (1956), the Court, citing *Mullane* v. *Central Hanover Bank and Trust Co.,* 339 U.S. 306 (1950), asserted that "the means employed [to serve constitutionally adequate notice] must be such as one desirous of actually informing the [defendant] might reasonably adopt to accomplish it." In that case a "known incompetent" was a defendant in a foreclosure of tax lien cases; the court decided that compliance with the otherwise valid notice requirement was insufficient for someone known to lack a normal understanding of the nature of the proceedings. *Id.* at 146.

2. In contrast to other legal proceedings, most guardianship hearings are preceded by rather minimal notice, generally consisting of a copy of the petition and notice of the time and place of the hearing; in some jurisdictions, only time and place of the hearing are required, e.g., Ariz. Rev. Stat. § 14-5309(b) (1975). The allegedly incompetent person is rarely alerted to the serious legal and personal implications of guardianship and the importance of obtaining counsel and preparing a defense. If the petition merely

---

[8]*Chaloner* v. *Sherman,* 242 U.S. 455 (1917), does not compel a different conclusion. There, damages were sought by a person adjudged to be an incompetent for the withholding of his property by a committee appointed under New York law. Plaintiff alleged that the applicable statute was unconstitutional because there was no express requirement of notice and an opportunity to be heard at the committee appointment proceeding. The Supreme Court's affirmance of the order directing a verdict in favor of the defendant committee was based on the finding that plaintiff had received constitutionally adequate notice at every stage and that the failure to oppose the petition was therefore not open to collateral attack. 242 U.S. at 461.

parrots the language contained in the statute, the individual may not be made aware of the specific facts underlying the petition.

Considering the substantial deprivation of rights that results from an adjudication of incompetency (including, in some states, the possibility of involuntary hospitalization), notice similar to that being required in civil commitment proceedings should be mandated; see Horstman, P., "Protective Services for the Elderly" 40 *Mo. L. Rev.* 215, 240 (1975). Such a standard was rejected, however, in *Rud* v. *Dahl,* No. 77-2052, 77C-2361 (7th Cir.N.D.Ill. June 5, 1978).

3. The rights to notice and hearing may be waived; see *State of Indiana* v. *Vigo Circuit Court,* 240 Ind. 168, 162 N.E.2d 614 (1959). Can an "incompetent" person, alleged to be in need of guardianship, give a valid waiver?

4. Rhode Island's statute specifically provides that, if the physician at the mental hospital certifies that in his own opinion service of the notice of an application for the appointment of a guardian will be injurious to the patient's mental health, no notice will be served on the patient (R.I. Gen. Law § 33-15-9 (Supp. 1970)).

5. California has implemented statutory reform of notice requirements to correct the inadequacies of past practices. California now requires that notice be sufficient to:

> ... inform the alleged incompetent person as to the nature and purpose of the guardianship proceeding, that the appointment of a guardian for his person and estate or person or estate is a legal adjudication of his incompetence, the effect of such an adjudication on his basic rights, the identity of the person who has been nominated as his guardian, that he has a right to oppose such proceedings, to have the matter tried by jury, and to be represented by legal counsel if he chooses (Cal. Prob. Code § 1461.5 (West Supp. 1977)).

2. Right to Counsel and Guardian *ad Litem*

In every jurisdiction an individual for whom guardianship is sought has a right to retain counsel, e.g., Ala. Code, Tit. 21, § 15 (1958); Alaska Stat. § 13.26.105(b) (1974); Ariz. Rev. Stat. § 14-5303 (1975); Ark. Stat. Ann. § 57-620 (1971); Cal. Prob. Code § 1461 (West Supp. 1979); Del. Code, Tit. 12, § 3914(b) (Supp. 1978); Fla. Stat. Ann. § 744.331(4) (West Supp. 1979); 1976 Haw. Sess. Laws § 5-303(b); Idaho Code § 15-5-303(b) (Supp. 1979); Kan. Stat. § 59-3010(A)(3) (1976); Minn. Stat. Ann. § 252A.09 (West Supp. 1979); N.M. Stat. Ann. § 32-3-1 (1953); N.Y. Mental Hyg. Law § 78.03(e) (McKinney 1978); N.D. Cent. Code § 30.1-28-03(2) (Supp. 1976); Ohio Rev. Code Ann. § 2111.02 (Page 1976); Okla. Stat. Ann., Tit. 43A, § 54.1 (West Supp. 1978); Or. Rev. Stat. § 126.103 (Supp. 1978); R.I. Gen. Laws § 33-15-9 (1970); Tenn. Code Ann. § 33-313 (Supp. 1978); Tex. Prob. Code Ann., Tit. 9, § 417 (1956); Wash. Rev. Code Ann. § 11.88.045 (Supp. 1978); W.Va. Code § 27-11-1(b) (Supp. 1978); Wis. Stat. Ann. § 880.33(2) (West Supp. 1979); and Wyo. Stat. § 3-29.5(b) (Supp. 1975).

Because of the traditional notion that guardianship is not an adversarial process, however, few states have guaranteed this right by providing for court appointment of counsel for those not represented; see Brakel, S., and Rock, R., *The Mentally Disabled and the Law,* 280-288 (Table 8.3) (1971). Notice and an opportunity to be heard may be of little value to a disabled and allegedly incompetent person if he or she is without the assistance of counsel; hearings in such cases may become, in effect, *ex parte*.

Because the guardianship proceedings may result in the loss of the individual's fundamental rights and restrict his or her personal liberty, an analogy may be made to the requirement of counsel in juvenile and civil commitment proceedings. In juvenile court cases, the Supreme Court has stated that a child whose liberty is in question:

> ... needs the assistance of counsel to cope with problems of law, to make skilled inquiry into the facts, to insist upon the regularity of the proceedings, and to ascertain whether he has a defense and to prepare and submit it (*In re Gault,* 387 U.S. 1, 36 (1967)).

In *Heryford* v. *Parker,* 396 F.2d 393 (10th Cir. 1968), a case concerning the involuntary commitment of a mentally retarded individual to a state hospital, the court declared:

> [L]ike *Gault,* and of utmost importance, we have a situation in which the liberty of an individual is at stake, and we think the reasoning in *Gault* emphatically applies. It matters not whether the proceedings be labeled "civil" or "criminal" or whether the subject matter be mental instability or juvenile delinquency. It is the likelihood of involuntary incarceration—whether for punishment as an adult for a crime, rehabilitation as a juvenile for delinquency, or treatment and training as a feeble-minded or mental incompetent—which commands observance of the constitutional safeguards of due process. Where, as in both proceedings for juveniles and mentally deficient persons, the state undertakes to act in *parens patriae,* it has the inescapable duty to vouchsafe due process, and this necessarily includes the duty to see that a subject of an involuntary commitment proceedings is afforded the opportunity to the guiding hand of legal counsel at every step of the proceedings, unless effectively waived by one authorized to act in his behalf (*Id.* at 396).

The principles outlined in *Gault* and *Heryford* v. *Parker* would seem manifestly applicable in the context of guardianship proceedings, and, therefore, the right to counsel would be constitutionally mandated. In such proceedings, however, at least one court has reached a contrary result, *Rud* v. *Dahl,* No. 77-2052, 77-C2361 (7th Cir.N.D.Ill. June 5, 1978).

Several states provide for the discretionary or mandatory appointment of a guardian *ad litem* in guardianship cases; e.g., Ind. Code Ann. § 29-1-18-14 (Supp. 1978) (discretionary); Alaska Stat. § 13.26.105(b) (1974) (mandatory).

While the functions of a guardian *ad litem* are similar in some respect to those of counsel for the alleged incompetent person, they are by no means identical. The guardian *ad litem* is an individual appointed by the court to look after the best interests of a disabled party, whether plaintiff or defendant. While the guardian *ad litem* is expected to take an adversary role when required, he or she is often viewed as a neutral fact finder, working on behalf of the court as much as the proposed ward (Allen, R., Ferster, E., and Weihofen, H., *Mental Impairment and Legal Incompetency* 89 (1968)). See, e.g., *Mazza* v. *Pechacek,* 233 F.2d 666 (D.C.Cir. 1956). This nonadversarial role is described in *Aho* v. *Rhodes,* 39 N.Y.2d 241, 383 N.Y.S.2d 285, 288, 347 N.E.2d 647, 650-651 (1976), where the court observed:

> [A] guardian *ad litem* may of necessity be obligated to act contrary to the desires of the incompetent and to adopt a position adverse to that urged by his ward. In the discharge of his objective responsibility the guardian [*ad litem*] may conclude that the best interest of the incompetent [ward] would not be served by prosecuting an appeal . . . [T]he wishes of the ward will be relevant but not determinative.

It is apparent, therefore, that the right to counsel will not necessarily be satisfied by the appointment of a guardian *ad litem,* nor vice versa.

Several states have made statutory reforms that mandate the representation by counsel of allegedly incompetent persons in guardianship hearings, e.g., Cal. Prob. Code § 1461 (1977); Md. Est. & Trusts Code Ann. § 13-705(d) (Cum.Supp. 1977). And old assumptions about the benevolence and protective aspects of guardianship are being challenged by commentators; see, e.g., Comment, "The Disguised Oppression of Involuntary Guardianship: Have the Elderly Freedom to Spend?" 73 *Yale L.J.* 676 (1964); Horstman, P., "Protective Services for the Elderly: The Limits of *Parens Patriae*" 40 *Mo. L. Rev.* 215 (1975). The definite trend seems to be toward affording persons facing an adjudication of incompetency with the vital services of counsel and of a guardian *ad litem* at all phases of this judicial process.

3. Presence of the Allegedly Incompetent Person at the Hearing

Most state statutes allow for the alleged incompetent persons to be present at the guardianship hearing, and, in those states where the right to be present is not mentioned, it is generally assumed (Brakel, S., and Rock, R., *The Mentally Disabled and the Law,* 280-292 (1971)). See *In re Propst,* 144 N.C. 563, 57 S.E. 342 (1907), where the court refused to honor a guardian's decision to dispose of certain property because the ward had not had an opportunity to appear at the guardianship proceeding. The court's rationale was that "frequently persons falling within the class called 'idiots' are so near on the shadowy border line that nothing but personal examination will enable the jury or court to pass intelligently upon their capacity to attend to their business" (*Id.* at 344).

In reality, however, very few prospective wards are ever in attendance at their hearings, because in most states (45 states and the District of Columbia) the court may dispense with the individuals' attendance for "medical reasons" or if the "best interests" of the alleged incompetent person would be served thereby (Horstman, P., "Protective Services for the Elderly: The Limits of *Parens Patriae*" 40 *Mo. L. Rev.* 215 (1975)). The National Senior Citizens Law Center studied all guardianships filed in Los Angeles County Central District for a 1-year period (July 1, 1973 to June 30, 1974). In 84.2% of the cases the only persons present at the adjudication were the judge, the petitioner, and the petitioner's attorney (*Id.* at 235-236). As a result, incompetency proceedings resemble *ex parte* administrative determinations more than they resemble adversary hearings. The testimony of the alleged incompetent should serve as extremely important evidence of his mental and physical condition for the judge or jury to observe first hand. The fact that the individual is so often not present serves to thwart this line of investigation and, if anything, allows the court to presume the "incompetency" of the individual by implication.

Such practices open the proceeding to particular abuse if the petitioning party causes the absence of the alleged incompetent by submitting certification to the effect that an appearance would not be in the best interests of the proposed ward. When combined with a lack of representation by counsel, this absence renders the outcome of the proceeding a foregone conclusion. California has attempted to correct this situation by authorizing the court to appoint a court investigator to personally interview the proposed ward anytime an affidavit or certificate is filed with the court alleging that the proposed ward is unable to attend the hearing. Cal. Prob. Code § 1461.1 (West Supp. 1979) states:

> Upon receipt of the affidavit or certificate attesting to the proposed ward's inability to attend the hearing, the court shall appoint a court investigator to personally interview the proposed ward and to inform him as to the contents of the citation, the nature, purpose and effect of the proceeding, and of his right to oppose the proceeding, attend the hearing, have the matter tried by jury and be represented by counsel. The investigator shall also determine whether it appears that the proposed ward is unable to attend the hearing, whether the proposed ward wishes to contest the establishment of the guardianship, whether the proposed ward wishes to be represented by counsel, and if so, whether the proposed ward has retained counsel, and if not, the name of an attorney the proposed ward wishes to retain.
>
> The court investigator shall report his findings, including the proposed ward's express statement concerning representation by counsel, in writing, to the court at least five days before the date set for hearing.
>
> As used in this chapter, a "court investigator" or "investigator" is a person trained in law who is an officer or special appointee of the court with no personal or other beneficial interest in the proceedings.

4. Trial by Jury

WARD v. BOOTH

United States Court of Appeals for the Ninth Circuit, 1952
197 F.2d 963

POPE, Circuit Judge.

A judge of the Circuit Court of the First Judicial Circuit of the Territory of Hawaii, sitting in chambers in probate upon the hearing of a petition for the appointment of a guardian of the estate of Hattie Kulamanu Ward, alleged to be incompetent, made an order in accordance with the prayer of the petition appointing Hawaiian Trust Company, Limited, guardian of the estate of the named incompetent.

After the appointed guardian had qualified, Lucy K. Ward, one of the appellants here, a sister of the alleged incompetent, who had appeared and been represented by counsel in the original guardianship proceedings, describing herself as "next of friend of Hattie Kulamanu Ward," moved the court for an order appointing her as "next of friend" of the claimed incompetent, for the purpose of moving for the vacation of the appointment or the removal of the Trust Company as guardian. The motion was presented to another judge of the same court, *ex parte,* and an order appointing Lucy K. Ward as such "next of friend" was made. Thereupon Lucy K. Ward, describing herself as sister, attorney-in-fact, and next friend of Hattie Kulamanu Ward, moved to vacate the order appointing the Trust Company as guardian, to remove the guardian, and to hold further hearings respecting the issues raised by the petition for the appointment of a guardian.

The judge who made the order appointing Lucy K. Ward as next friend, granted a temporary restraining order, without notice, restraining the Trust Company, as such guardian, from voting the stock belonging to said estate in Victoria Ward, Ltd., at the annual meeting of its stockholders. The restraining order was accompanied by an order to show cause directed to the Trust Company and to the other two sisters of the alleged incompetent who had filed the original petition for the appointment of a guardian, requiring them to appear and show cause why the order appointing the guardian should not be vacated or the guardian removed.

Upon return to the order to show cause the matter came on for hearing before the judge who made the original appointment, who thereupon vacated both the order appointing Lucy K. Ward as next friend of the alleged incompetent, and the restraining order; denied the motion for removal of the guardian, and assessed counsel fees against Lucy K. Ward.

Lucy K. Ward and Kathleen V. Ward, another sister, sued out a writ of error to the Supreme Court of Hawaii to review both the order appointing the guardian and the order denying vacation or removal. Lucy K. Ward, describing herself as "next of friend" appealed from the last named order, and both review proceedings were consolidated in the Supreme Court. From the judgment and decree of that court affirming the orders of the circuit judge sitting in probate, the appellants have brought this appeal asserting (1) that it presents a case involving the Constitution of the United States, and (2) that the case below is a civil case where the value in controversy exceeds $5000 exclusive of interest and costs.

The principal claim that the case involves the Constitution of the United States is based upon the appellant's assertion, first made in the Supreme Court of the Territory, that under the requirements of the Fifth and Seventh Amendments, the appellants and the alleged incompetent were entitled to a jury trial upon the issues presented by the original petition for the appointment of a guardian.

The provision for the appointment of a guardian of the estate of an insane person (including "every idiot, non-compos, lunatic and distracted person" Rev. Laws Hawaii 1945, § 12508) is made by § 12509, Revised Laws of Hawaii 1945. In its decision the Supreme Court of Hawaii held that this section "clearly permits a probate judge in guardianship proceedings 'after a full hearing' to adjudge an alleged incompetent to be insane and to appoint 'a guardian of his person or estate or both' without the intervention of a jury."

It is argued that a jury trial was required here because of the requirement of the Seventh Amendment that "In Suits at common law, where the value in controversy shall exceed twenty dollars, the right of trial by jury shall be preserved. . . ." We agree with the conclusion arrived at by the Supreme Court of the Territory, and ably expounded in its opinion, that the proceedings here in question bear no resemblance to the "Suits at common law" referred to in the Seventh Amendment.

It has been pointed out that prior to the adoption of the Constitution and under the ancient English practice, the Lord Chancellor, as the delegate of the King to conduct insanity proceedings, was wont to issue a writ *de lunatico inquirendo* under which a jury was summoned to determine the question of sanity. *Sporza* v. *German Savings Bank,* 192 N.Y. 8, 84 N.E. 406, 408; 1 Blackstone, pp. 303, 305. Our attention is called to a number of decisions by state courts holding that under the provisions of some state constitutions the question of a person's insanity must be tried to a jury. . . . The state courts have arrived at divergent views with respect to the meaning of their own constitutional provisions. Those upon which appellants have relied have merely construed constitutional provisions similar to those in New York and New Jersey as comprehending that the ancient practice whereby the Lord Chancellor required trial by jury in proceedings to determine a person's insanity, or some subsequent statutory provision of a similar nature which was in effect in the particular state when the constitution in question was adopted must be continued and followed.

But there is a substantial difference between such state constitutional provisions and the Seventh Amendment, for the latter has application only to "Suits at common law." We are unable to perceive any such resemblance as would require the classification of the special proceedings here involved as "Suits at common law." The Seventh Amendment more nearly resembles the provision of the Wisconsin State Constitution which was considered in *Gaston* v. *Babcock,* 6 Wis. 503, and which states that "The right of trial by jury shall remain inviolate, and shall extend to all cases at law." The court there held that a proceeding for the appointment of a guardian for an insane person was not a case at law, and hence a jury trial was not required by the Wisconsin provision. It is to be noted also that the Seventh Amendment refers to "Suits at common law, where the value in controversy shall exceed twenty dollars," etc. In a proceeding such as the one here involved, it cannot strictly be said that there is any value in controversy. The matter in controversy is the question of the competence or incompetence of the person named, and while the result of such a determination may affect extensive property holdings, it cannot be said that the issue to be tried is one where there is any "value in controversy."

We think that the language of the Seventh Amendment is thus not aptly descriptive of the proceedings here. The only statement of any federal court which appellants have undertaken to cite in support of their position is that of the District Court for the Eastern Division of Kentucky, in *Hager* v. *Pacific Mutual Life Insurance Co.,* 43 F.Supp. 22, 26 (E.D. Kentucky 1942). There, however, the brief statement of the judge that "I do not believe that under our Federal and State Constitutions a person can be declared incompetent and have his property taken out of his hand or be placed in confinement without the intervention of a jury . . ." is predicated in part upon the court's view of the state constitution. The language does not indicate whether, in referring to the federal Constitution, he had in mind the Fifth or seventh Amendment, or some other provision. We cannot regard that case as persuasive authority here.

As for the contention that failure to provide trial by jury violates the Fifth Amendment, this is wholly without merit. *Montana Co.* v. *St. Louis Mining & Milling Co.,* 152 U.S. 160, 171, 14 S.Ct. 506, 38 L.Ed. 398 (1893).

[The remainder of the opinion, which discusses other claims of procedural impropriety, is omitted.]

NOTE

While *Ward* v. *Booth* indicates that there may not be any constitutional right to trial by jury in a guardianship proceeding (accord, *In re Easton,* 214 Md. 176, 133 A.2d 441 (1957); see U.S. Senate Special Comm. on Aging, 95th Cong., 1st Sess., *Protective Services for the Elderly: A Working Paper* 39 (1977)), many jurisdictions recognize such a right by statute. See Brakel, S., and Rock, R., *The Mentally Disabled and the Law,* 280-288 (1971); generally, Annot., 33 ALR2d 1145 (1954). In nearly half of the states a jury trial is optional, e.g., Alaska Stat. § 13.26.105(b) (1974); Cal. Prob. Code § 1461 (West Supp. 1979); D.C. Code § 21-1107 (1973); Ill. Ann. Stat., Ch. 3, § 117(c) (Smith-Hurd Supp. 1978); Ind. Code § 29-1-18-19 (Supp. 1978); Iowa Code § 633.555 (1975); Kan. Stat. Ann. § 59-3013 (1976); N.J. Stat. Ann. § 3A: 6-35 (West 1953); N.M. Stat. Ann. § 32-3-1 (1953); N.Y. Mental Hyg. Law § 78.03(e) (McKinney 1978); N.C. Gen. Stat. § 35-2 (1976); Okla. Stat., Tit. 43A, § 54.1 (1976); 20 Pa. Cons. Stat. Ann. § 5511 (Purdon 1975); Tex. Prob. Code Ann., Arts. 115, 417 (Vernon 1956); Va. Code § 37.1-128.02 (1976); Wash. Rev. Code § 11.88.045 (Supp. 1978); Wis. Stat. § 880 33(2) (1979); and Wyo. Stat. § 3-29.6 (Supp. 1975) (jury trial at court's discretion). In at least two states a jury trial is mandatory in a proceeding for a guardianship of the person; Ala. Code, Tit. 21, § 13 (1958); Ky. Rev. Stat. § 387.220(1) (1978).

Trial by jury often does not occur even when permitted, however, not only because this right can be waived by the allegedly incompetent person but because some statutes provide for a presumption of a waiver of a jury trial if a jury trial is not expressly requested; see Allen, R., Ferster, E., and Weihofen, H., *Mental Impairment and Legal Incompetency* 84 (1968).

5. Standard of Proof

In most civil proceedings, findings are based on a "preponderance of the evidence." The use of this standard has been justified on the ground that, when only monetary interests are involved, it is "no more serious . . . for there to be an erroneous verdict in the defendant's favor than for there to be an erroneous verdict in the plaintiff's favor" (*In re Winship,* 397 U.S. 358, 371 (1970) (Harlan, J., concurring)). When more is at stake than mere economic considerations of a civil proceeding, however, courts frequently impose standards of proof higher than preponderance of the evidence; see, e.g., *Woodby* v. *Immigration and Naturalization Service,* 385 U.S. 276 (1966); Combs, H., "Burden of Proof and Vagueness in Civil Commitment Proceedings," 2 *Am. J. Crim. Law* 47, 59-63 (1973); Note, "Commitment and Release Standards and Procedures: Uniform Treatment for the Mentally Ill," 41 *U. Chi. L. Rev.* 285 (1974).

The similarities between an incompetency adjudication and a civil commitment where a strict standard is applied, indicate that a standard of mere preponderance of the evidence may not meet the requirements of due process. Some courts, e.g., *Mills* v. *Neubert,* 250 Wis. 401, 27 N.W.2d 375 (1947), have held that proof of incompetency must be "clear and convincing." In a recent case, *In re Estate of Roulet,* 23 Cal.3d 346, 152 Cal.Rptr. 425 (1979), the Supreme Court of California held that, in circumstances where a conservator had the authority to commit a conservatee to a state hospital for up to one year, the conservatorship had to be determined on a standard of "beyond a reasonable doubt."

6. Hearsay Evidence

In guardianship incompetency hearings, hearsay evidence is frequently admitted in the form of letters from physicians. The doctor will certify that the potential ward's attendance at the hearing would be detrimental or he will certify that the proposed ward is "incompetent," "insane," or "unable to care for himself." The problem with this . . . is that although incompetency is theoretically a legal disability which should be measured by functional inabilities (to care for oneself, manage money, etc.), it has become largely a medical disability measured in medical terms. As a result, a physician's expert medical opinion as to the potential ward's mental incompetence is more often than not determinative of the legal issue as well (Horstman, P., "Protective Services for the Elderly: The Limits of *Paren Patriae*" 40 *Mo. L. Rev.* 215, 252 (1975)).

Although unwarranted reliance on medical opinion may be problematic in any event, particular harm results when the opinion takes the form of hearsay. An opportunity to confront and cross-examine the witness is essential in contesting the allegations of incompetency. Quite often, however, the medical evidence takes the form of a printed affidavit in which blanks have been filled out with the name and infirmity of the alleged incompetent. The meager information contained on this type of "physician's certification of incompetence" can be fully explained only through testimony in court.

In civil commitment proceedings, the use of hearsay has been held to violate the patient's constitutional rights. The court in *Lessard* v. *Schmidt,* 349 F.Supp. 1078 (E.D.Wis. 1972); *vacated and remanded* 414 U.S. 473 (1973); 379 F.Supp. 1376 (E.D.Wis. 1974); *vacated and remanded* 421 U.S. 957 (1975); 413 F.Supp. 1318 (E.D.Wis. 1976) (prior judgment reinstated), observed:

Where standard exclusionary rules forbid the admission of evidence, no sound policy reasons exist for admitting such evidence in an involuntary mental commitment hearing. Indeed, as noted throughout this opinion, the seriousness of the deprivation of liberty and the consequences which follow an adjudication of mental illness make imperative strict adherence to the rules of evidence generally applicable to other proceedings in which an individual's liberty is in jeopardy. As Justice Brandeis noted in an often quoted statement: "Experience should teach us to be most on our guard to protect liberty when the government's purposes are beneficent. . . . The greatest dangers to liberty lurk in insidious encroachment by men of zeal, well-meaning but without understanding" *Olmstead* v. *United States,* 277 U.S. 438, 479 (1928) (Brandeis, J., dissenting). (*Id.* at 349 F.Supp. 1103.)

Arguably, such concerns apply with equal validity to the context of guardianship proceedings.

6

FREEDOM FROM RESIDENTIAL CONFINEMENT

Robert L. Burgdorf, Jr.

A. THE NATURE OF INSTITUTIONS

IN RE D.

Family Court of Richmond County, New York, 1972
70 Misc.2d 953, 335 N.Y.S.2d 638, 649–651

RALPH E. CORY, Judge.

[The court held that as a Family Court it had no jurisdiction over petitions filed by the Richmond County Society for the Prevention of Cruelty to Children on behalf of children at the Willowbrook State School]

Although this court has no jurisdiction under the present statutes, it cannot help but express its feelings regarding the horrible conditions at Willowbrook as documented in over 300 pages of minutes of the week-long hearings held in the early part of this year and made a part of the petition. See *Minutes Willowbrook Hearings,* January 31, 1972–February 4, 1972.

Such conditions are a blot on the conscience of New York State. The shocking apathy of the public was rudely awakened by the newspaper and other media, spotlighting the dreadful conditions at Willowbrook where the most helpless and defenseless of our citizens were left living "on a thread of life, human vegetables rotting in inadequate warehouses," the living among the dead, the dead among the living.

The glory seekers have drained all the publicity out of Willowbrook for their own selfish purposes and have long since fled the scene. The ghosts of apathy are again returning, but there is light and hope in the encircling gloom.

As Winston Churchill so eloquently and truthfully said, "The mills of the Gods grind but they grind exceedingly slow." It is to be hoped that the Legislative and Executive branches of the State government will remedy the sub-human conditions at Willowbrook by providing sufficient funds to operate such institutions as Willowbrook or phase them out altogether for smaller, more personal institutions or provide foster care in family units where possible, as is done in cases involving neglect.

Also important is more specific legislation as to what judicial review is available and in which courts, to correct wrongful conditions such as arose at Willowbrook and to prevent a multiplicity of lawsuits and fragmentation of the existing court system. It is self evident from a perusal of the minutes that the Board of Visitors whose membership consists of well-meaning persons cannot do an effective job since it reports to the Executive Branch of government. Under present law the Department of Mental Hygiene sets down its own policy, conducts its own investigation and in effect is prosecutor, judge and jury within its own domain. It was shocking to read in the minutes about the Director of Willowbrook pleading with the Commissioner of Mental Hygiene for more money to properly run the institution only to be informed there was none and that staff and budget cuts had to be made—a budget gap of some 27 million dollars and an attrition in staff resulting therefrom of some 900 persons for an institution of over 5,000 people. The resulting conditions at Willowbrook were not only appalling but frightful.

No one is above the law, not even the sovereign state of New York and its Department of Mental Hygiene. Yet in all fairness, if they do not receive necessary funds to operate institutions such as Willowbrook, how can they be faulted when their appeals fall on deaf ears and result in despondent exercises in futility. Mentally retarded children suffering from neglect caused more by acts of omission rather than commission cannot wait for budgets to be balanced or funds found for their care. They may be dead tomorrow.

The time for rhetoric, excuses and regret has long since passed. The correction of conditions of children at institutions such as Willowbrook revealed in the hearings and in the present petitions is of immediate importance. Otherwise, we are heading for an irretrievable breakdown not only in justice but in basic humaneness.

The time for more hearings has also long since passed. Otherwise, the hearings already concluded become a fiction and "no fiction can destroy constitutional guarantees." *Sharkey* v. *Thurston,* 268 N.Y. 123, 126, 196 N.E. 766, 767.

The application of such constitutional guarantees for each child at Willowbrook so that his full potential no matter how limited can be obtained, should be the newest mission of the law. The right to life, liberty and the pursuit of happiness is not reserved to the healthy, able-bodied children and adults. It applies with even more force and intent to the helpless, the physically handicapped, the mentally retarded, the mentally defective and the most unfortunate of children such as those at Willowbrook. Only then can we say: "... The walls that are laid in darkness may laugh to the kiss of the sun. ... "

BURGDORF, M., AND BURGDORF, R., "A HISTORY OF UNEQUAL TREATMENT: THE QUALIFICATIONS OF HANDICAPPED PERSONS AS A 'SUSPECT CLASS' UNDER THE EQUAL PROTECTION CLAUSE"

15 Santa Clara Lawyer *855, 889–891 (1976)*

Let us now examine the structure and operation of those facilities to discover what life in a contemporary institution is like.

First, consider the physical plant and thus the lifestyle dictated by the architecture of a state institution. Typically, the buildings were designed as monuments, as public relations endeavors; they were built for the convenience of the staff, the architect, and the community, but never for that of the residents. One observer has chronicled some of the dehumanizing conditions characteristic of today's state institutions:[224]

a. A fence or wall surrounding an entire building or even an entire facility.

b. Barred windows and more sophisticated but equally effective reinforced window screens (so-called security screening).

c. Locked living units. In the case of children or physically handicapped persons, door knobs may be set high above reach. These restrictive access mechanisms permit staff to perceive the facility as "open" even though it is actually locked.

d. Caretaker stations providing maximum visual control over resident areas, while minimizing staff involvement. The glass-enclosed nursing station is a classical example.

e. Segregation of the sexes. Such segregation becomes an absurd practice with infants and children, as well as the aged.

f. Large dormitory sleeping quarters, with no (or only low) partitions between beds. Lights may burn even at night to facilitate supervision.

g. Bedrooms lacking doors. Where doors exist they almost always contain peepholes, or "Judas-windows."

h. Toilets and showers lacking partitions, curtains or doors. Bathing facilities are frequently designed for the efficient cleansing of a large number of residents by a small number of caretakers: slabs, hoses and mass showers are used rather than installations conducive to self-cleaning.

i. Often no place to store one's personal possessions. Even if there are such places, frequently they are under lock and key and inaccessible to the resident. The use of personalized clothing is denied; clothes are supplied from a common pool.

j. Beds or bed stalls are designed to be picked up and immersed in cleansing solution in their entirety.

k. Walls and floors made of a material that is virtually impossible to "deface," scratch, soil or stain. Entire rooms can be hosed down as in a zoo. Often living units have drains in the floors.

l. "Segregated" staff lounges to which caretakers withdraw for meals and coffee, heightening the "we-they" attitude of supervision and control.

Residents of institutions usually face these oppressive surroundings for a lifetime, because institutionalization is a deadend proposition. Few residents are ever released. The Stockholm Symposium of 1967 found that the practice is to "institutionalize and throw away the key."[225] The Symposium also commented on the degenerative effect the institutional environment has upon individual development.[226]

---

[224][Wolfensberger, W., "The Origin and Nature of Our Institutional Models," in *Changing Patterns in Residential Services for the Mentally Retarded* 59 (Kugel, R., and Wolfensberger, W., eds., 1969)] at 72-77.

[225]See Schoenfeld, "Human Rights for the Mentally Retarded: Their Recognition by the Providers of Service," 4 *Human Rights* 31, 46 (1974), *citing International League of Societies for the Mentally Handicapped, Legislative Aspects of Mental Retardation, Conclusions of the Stockholm Symposium III* 3 (c), (d), (e) (1967).

[226]*Id.* at 39.

A description of the physical plant of an average institution reveals that these facilities are little more than prisons. Listing the standard architectural and operational restrictions, however, does not begin to cover the violations of individual rights and freedoms. Not only is segregation of the sexes prevalent, but segregation from families, normal society and peer groups is also a product of institutionalization. Inmates are deprived of social touchstones which most of us take for granted: stores, bus stops, the neighborhood church, the Burger King, the football stadium. Restrictions are imposed with respect to visitors and use of the phone, while censorship of incoming and outgoing mail is common.

NOTES

1. In *Wyatt* v. *Stickney,* 334 F.Supp. 1341, 1343–1344 (M.D.Ala. 1971), the court described the conditions at Bryce Hospital, a state institution for mentally ill persons:

> In the matters presented to this Court by the parties, there seem to be three fundamental conditions for adequate and effective treatment programs in public mental institutions. These three fundamental conditions are: (1) a humane psychological and physical environment, (2) qualified staff in numbers sufficient to administer adequate treatment and (3) individualized treatment plans. The report filed by defendants with this Court, as well as the reports and objections of other parties who have studied the conditions at Bryce Hospital, demonstrates rather conclusively that the hospital is deficient in all three of these fundamental respects.
>
> The psychological and physical environment problems are, in some instances, interrelated. For example, the dormitories are barn-like structures with no privacy for the patients. For most patients there is not even a space provided which he can think of as his own. The toilets in restrooms seldom have partitions between them. These are dehumanizing factors which degenerate the patients' self-esteem. Also contributing to the poor psychological environment are the shoddy wearing apparel furnished the patients, the non-therapeutic work assigned to patients (mostly compulsory, uncompensated housekeeping chores), and the degrading and humilitating admissions procedure which creates in the patient an impression of the hospital as a prison or as a "crazy house." Other conditions which render the physical environment at Bryce critically substandard are extreme ventilation problems, fire and other emergency hazards, and overcrowding caused to some degree by poor utilization of space. In addition, the quality of the food served the patients is inferior. Only fifty cents per patient per day is spent for food, and sanitation procedures with regard to the preparation and service of food, commonly recognized as basic health practices and utilized at other such hospitals, are not followed at Bryce.
>
> The second fundamental condition needed for effective treatment is a qualified and numerically sufficient staff. It is clear from the reports of Bryce's expert consultants that Bryce is wholly deficient in this area, both as regards its professional staff and its nonprofessional staff. More psychiatrists, Doctor of Philosophy level psychologists and qualified Medical Doctors are not only a medical but are also a constitutional necessity in this public institution. Special staff is needed to place the custodial patients still residing at Bryce. Although, as *Rouse* v. *Cameron,* 125 U.S. App.D.C. 366, 373 F.2d 451 (1966) points out, contact with the nonprofessional staff should be therapeutic, very little of this therapeutic value is realized at Bryce. The nonprofessional staff is poorly trained; nurses aides, for example, are required to have only a tenth grade education. Also there is no effective "in-service" training program for, or even any regular supervision over, the nonprofessional staff. The nonprofessionals are spread very thinly; thus, they are overworked, creating not only an inadequate situation for the patients but

extreme stresses for individual aides. Both Bryce consultants agree with amici and plaintiffs that additional aides and activities therapists are a necessity.

The third necessary condition for an effective treatment program is individualized treatment plans. Bryce is also deficient in this area. Although every patient has been classified as to treatability, the records made on each patient are inadequate. Minimum medical standards require that periodic inquiries be made into the needs of the patients with a view toward providing suitable treatment for them. Yet, at Bryce the records evidence no notations of mental change. They consist generally only of notations of the times and amounts of drugs given and participation in the Patient Operated Program, the Token Economy Program or the Level Program. Bryce's own consultant advises that treatment is geared primarily to housekeeping functions. The three main programs which have been implemented motivate the patients to some activity and do effect some degree of socialization, but at a minimum level. What programs there are do not yet seem to be operating effectively, partly because of the untrained staff members supervising them.

All the objections raised by amici and by plaintiffs generally are supported by the reports of Bryce's consultants. There seems to be a consensus of opinion among the experts that the treatment program at Bryce Hospital continues to be wholly inadequate.

In a companion order, the *Wyatt* court described the conditions at Partlow State School and Hospital, an Alabama institution for mentally retarded people:

The Court's conclusion, compelled by the evidence, is unmistakably clear. Put simply, conditions at Partlow are grossly substandard. Testimony presented by plaintiffs and amici has depicted hazardous and deplorable inadequacies in the institution's operation. Commendably, defendants have offered no rebuttal. At the close of the testimony, the Court, having been impressed by the urgency of the situation, issued an interim emergency order "to protect the lives and well-being of the residents of Partlow." In that order, the Court found that:

"The evidence . . . has vividly and undisputedly portrayed Partlow State School and Hospital as a warehousing institution which, because of its atmosphere of psychological and physical deprivation, is wholly incapable of furnishing [habilitation] to the mentally retarded and is conducive only to the deterioration and the debilitation of the residents. The evidence has reflected further that safety and sanitary conditions at Partlow are sub-standard to the point of endangering the health and lives of those residing there, that the wards are grossly understaffed, rendering even simple custodial care impossible, and that overcrowding remains a dangerous problem often leading to serious accidents, some of which have resulted in deaths of residents." *Wyatt* v. *Stickney*, March 2, 1972. (Unreported Interim Order.) (*Wyatt* v. *Stickney*, 344 F.Supp. 387, 391 (M.D.Ala. 1972).

The court also discussed some of the expert testimony in the case:

The most comprehensive testimony on the conditions currently prevailing at Partlow was elicited from Dr. Philip Roos, the Executive Director for the National Association for Retarded Children. Dr. Roos inspected Partlow over a two-day period and testified as to his subjective evaluation of the institution. In concluding his testimony, Dr. Roos summarized as follows:

" . . . I feel that the institution and its programs as now conceived are incapable of providing habilitation of the residents. Incarceration, certainly for most of the residents, would I feel have adverse consequences; would tend to develop behaviors which would interfere with successful community functioning. I would anticipate to find stagnation or deterioration in physical, intellectual, and social spheres. The conditions at Partlow today are generally dehumanizing, fostering deviancy, generating self-fulfilling prophecy of parasitism and helplessness. The conditions I would say are hazardous to psychological integrity, to health, and in some cases even to life. The administration, the physical plants, the programs, and the institution's articulation with the community and with the consumers reflect destructive models of mental retardation. They hark back to decades ago when the retarded were misperceived as being sick, as being threats to society, or as being subhuman organisms. The new concepts in the field of mental retardation are unfortunately not reflected in Partlow as we see it today—concepts such as normalization, developmental model in orientation toward mental retardation, the thrust of consumer involvement, the trend toward community orientation and decentralization of services; none of these are clearly in evidence in the facility today" (*Id.* at 391, n. 7).

Another nationally known expert in mental retardation, Dr. Gunnar Dybwad, testified regarding the deteriorative effects of institutionalization:

I think if you walk through Partlow, you can see it; you can see the effect—the people who begin to become involved in eccentric mannerisms, the rocking back and forth, peculiar behavior mechanisms, the people who sit in a semi-stupor in a place, without any activity, the people who slowly deteriorate and turn to the simple elements of human behavior. . . . I can assure you that this kind of behavior is due to neglect and is not an outcome of the mental retardation, itself. . . . In other words, it is a deterioration. I would further now add to this from my own observations, but not at Partlow that we have ample documentation in this country that individuals who come to institutions and can walk stop walking, who come to institutions and can talk will stop talking, who come to institutions and can feed themselves will stop feeding themselves; in other words, in many other ways, a steady process of deterioration.[a]

A most frightening aspect of the experts' testimony in *Wyatt* was their observation that, although the conditions in Alabama institutions were bad, they were "no worse than those in many of our largest and richest states." *Ibid.*[a] This conclusion has been borne out in subsequent lawsuits which have brought about the disclosure of similar conditions in large institutions in other parts of the country; see, e.g., *NYSARC, Inc.* v. *Rockefeller,* 357 F.Supp. 752, 755–757 (E.D.N.Y. 1973); *Welsch* v. *Likins,* 373 F.Supp. 487 (D.Minn. 1974); *Halderman* v. *Pennhurst,* 446 F.Supp. 1295, 1302–1310 (E.D.Pa. 1977).

2. Descriptions of the realities of daily life in an institution can be found in both popular and professional literature; e.g., Goffman, E., *Asylums* (1961); Ferleger, D., "Loosing the Chains: In-Hospital Civil Liberties of Mental Patients," 13 *Santa Clara Lawyer* 447 (1973); Blatt, B., and Kaplan, F., *Christmas in Purgatory: A. Photographic Essay on Mental Retardation* (1966); Wolfensberger, W., *The Origin and Nature of Our Institutional Models* (1975); Kesey, K., *One Flew Over the Cuckoo's Nest* (1962); Rivera, G. *Willowbrook: A Report on How It Is and Why It Doesn't Have to Be That Way* (1972); Herr, S., "Civil Rights, Uncivil Asylums and the Retarded," 43 *Cincinnati L. Rev.* 679 (1974); Blatt, B., *Exodus from Pandemonium* (1970); Donaldson, K., *Insanity Inside Out* (1976); Rosenhan, D., "On Being Sane in Insane Places," 179 *Science* 250 (1973), reprinted 13 *Santa Clara Lawyer* 379 (1973); and Barry, A., *Bellevue Is a State of Mind* (1971). One authority has given this metaphoric overview of his impression of such conditions: "Scratch an institution and pus oozes" (Blatt, B., *Exodus from Pandemonium* 158 (1970)).

---

[a]See Mental Health Law Project, *Basic Rights of the Mentally Handicapped* 12 (1973).

An affidavit submitted by expert witness Linda Glenn in the *NYSARC* suit capsulized the situation she saw at Willowbrook State School:

> All the residents were lined up like cattle, either along the walls, in front of the TV set, which was on the ceiling, or on mats in the corners piled on top of each other. The staff was apparently without concern about the activities the residents are involved in, about the programs that will assist them in becoming more independent, or about individualization of care. In several of the wards in this building all the staff were sitting watching television and paying no attention to the residents, even though the residents were in dangerous positions, e.g., falling out of the side of their chairs or with their heads caught in the stairs. The atmosphere again, was one of hopelessness, and I saw no effort to create even limited programs for these residents.[b]

The history of residential institutions and how they came to be what they are today has been examined in the Burgdorf article, *id.* at 883–889, and by several other authorities, e.g., Wolfensberger, W., *op. cit.;* Goffman, E., *op. cit.;* Deutsch, A., *The Mentally Ill in America: A History of Their Care and Treatment from Colonial Times* (2d ed. 1949); Herr, S., *op. cit.* at 694–700. See also, *Employees* v. *Missouri Public Health Department*, 411 U.S. 279, 284 n. 2 (1973), quoting Rothman, D., *The Discovery of the Asylum* 130 (1971). One scholar has noted some of the residual effects of the historical development of institutions in America:

> The complementary goals of isolation and segregation are still pursued today. Old institutions are still being enlarged; and despite the fact that normalizing community services have been shown to be less expensive than institutional services, new institutions are still being built for upwards of 1,000 residents at a capital cost per resident, for example, of $24,000 in Illinois, $30,000 in Missouri, $35,000 in New York, and even more. This continued expansion of uneconomic institutional services can only be interpreted as an expression of the desire on the part of society and those responsible for the delivery of services to continue to segregate and dehumanize mentally retarded individuals. Institutions are still omnibus in purpose, and lack rational admitting criteria, intellectualized lipservice notwithstanding. Institutions are still placed in inappropriate isolated locations, and even the most expensive ones are still dehumanizing.[c]

B. RATIONALE FOR CONFINEMENT

JACKSON v. INDIANA

Supreme Court of the United States, 1972
406 U.S. 715

MR. JUSTICE BLACKMUN delivered the opinion of the Court.

We are here concerned with the constitutionality of certain aspects of Indiana's system for pretrial commitment of one accused of crime.

Petitioner, Theon Jackson, is a mentally defective deaf mute with a mental level

---

[b]Affidavit of Linda Glenn, June 26, 1972, para. 8(c), quoted in Herr, S., *op. cit.* at 688 n. 46.

[c]Affidavit of W. Wolfensberger, p. 8, *Maryland Ass'n. for Retarded Children* v. *Maryland*, Civil No. 72-733-M (Md. Cir. Ct., Baltimore Cty., filed April 9, 1974), quoted in Herr, S., *op. cit.* at 699.

of a pre-school child. He cannot read, write, or otherwise communicate except through limited sign language. In May 1968, at age 27, he was charged in the Criminal Court of Marion County, Indiana, with separate robberies of two women. The offenses were alleged to have occurred the preceding July. The first involved property (a purse and its contents) of the value of four dollars. The second concerned five dollars in money. The record sheds no light on these charges since, upon receipt of not-guilty pleas from Jackson, the trial court set in motion the Indiana procedures for determining his competency to stand trial. Ind. Ann. Stat. § 9-1706a (Supp. 1971), now Ind. Code 35-5-3-2 (1971).

As the statute requires, the court appointed two psychiatrists to examine Jackson. A competency hearing was subsequently held at which petitioner was represented by counsel. The court received the examining doctors' joint written report and oral testimony from them and from a deaf-school interpreter through whom they had attempted to communicate with petitioner. The report concluded that Jackson's almost nonexistent communication skill, together with his lack of hearing and his mental deficiency, left him unable to understand the nature of the charges against him or to participate in his defense. One doctor testified that it was extremely unlikely that petitioner could ever learn to read or write and questioned whether petitioner even had the ability to develop any proficiency in sign language. He believed that the interpreter had not been able to communicate with petitioner to any great extent and testified that petitioner's "prognosis appears rather dim." The other doctor testified that even if Jackson were not a deaf mute, he would be incompetent to stand trial, and doubted whether petitioner had sufficient intelligence ever to develop the necessary communication skills. The interpreter testified that Indiana had no facilities that could help someone as badly off as Jackson to learn minimal communication skills.

On this evidence, the trial court found that Jackson "lack[ed] comprehension sufficient to make his defense," § 9-1706a, and ordered him committed to the Indiana Department of Mental Health until such time as that Department should certify to the court that "the defendant is sane."

Petitioner's counsel then filed a motion for a new trial, contending that there was no evidence that Jackson was "insane," or that he would ever attain a status which the court might regard as "sane" in the sense of competency to stand trial. Counsel argued that Jackson's commitment under these circumstances amounted to a "life sentence" without his ever having been convicted of a crime, and that the commitment therefore deprived Jackson of his Fourteenth Amendment rights to due process and equal protection, and constituted cruel and unusual punishment under the Eighth Amendment made applicable to the States through the Fourteenth. The trial court denied the motion. On appeal the Supreme Court of Indiana affirmed, with one judge dissenting. 253 Ind. 487, 255 N.E.2d 515 (1970). Rehearing was denied, with two judges dissenting. We granted certiorari, 401 U.S. 973 (1971).

For the reasons set forth below, we conclude that, on the record before us, Indiana cannot constitutionally commit the petitioner for an indefinite period simply on account of his incompetency to stand trial on the charges filed against him. Accordingly, we reverse.

I   Indiana Commitment Procedures

Section 9-1706a contains both the procedural and substantive requirements for pretrial commitment of incompetent criminal defendants in Indiana. If at any time before submission of the case to the court or jury the trial judge has "reasonable ground" to believe the defendant "to be insane," he must appoint two examining physicians and schedule a competency hearing. The hearing is to the court alone, without a jury. The examining physicians' testimony and "other evidence" may be adduced on the issue of incompetency. If the court finds the defendant "has not comprehension sufficient to understand the proceedings and make his defense," trial is delayed or continued and the defendant is remanded to the state department of mental health to be confined in an "appropriate psychiatric institution." The section further provides that "[w]henever the defendant shall become sane" the superintendent of the institution shall certify that fact to the court, and the court shall order him brought on to trial. The court may also make such an order *sua sponte*. There is no statutory provision for periodic review of the defendant's condition by either the court or mental health authorities. Section 9-1706a by its terms does not accord the defendant any right to counsel at the competency hearing or otherwise describe the nature of the hearing; but Jackson was represented by counsel who cross-examined the testifying doctors carefully and called witnesses on behalf of the petitioner-defendant.

Petitioner's central contention is that the State, in seeking in effect to commit him to a mental institution indefinitely, should have been required to invoke the standards and procedures of Ind. Ann. Stat. § 22-1907, now Ind. Code 16-15-1-3 (1971), governing commitment of "feeble-minded" persons. That section provides that upon application of a "reputable citizen of the county" and accompanying certificate of a reputable physician that a person is "feeble-minded and is *not insane* or epileptic" (emphasis supplied), a circuit court judge shall appoint two physicians to examine such person. After notice, a hearing is held at which the patient is entitled to be represented by counsel. If the judge determines that the individual is indeed "feeble-minded," he enters an order of commitment and directs the clerk of the court to apply for the person's admission "to the superintendent of the institution for feeble-minded persons located in the district in which said county is situated." A person committed under this section may be released "at any time," provided that "in the judgment of the superintendent, the mental and physical condition of the patient justifies it." § 22-1814, now Ind. Code 16-15-4-12 (1971). The statutes do not define either "feeble-mindedness" or "insanity" as used in § 22-1907. But a statute establishing a special institution for care of such persons, § 22-1801, refers to the duty of the State to provide care for its citizens who are "feeble-minded, and are therefore unable properly to care for themselves." These provisions evidently afford the State a vehicle for commitment of persons in need of custodial care who are "not insane" and therefore do not qualify as "mentally ill" under the State's general involuntary civil commitment scheme. See §§ 22-1201 to 22-1256, now Ind. Code 16-14-9-1 to 16-14-9-31, 16-13-2-9 to 16-13-2-10, 35-5-3-4, 16-14-14-1 to 16-14-14-19, and 16-14-15-5, 16-14-15-1, and 16-14-19-1 (1971).

Scant attention was paid this general civil commitment law by the Indiana courts in the present case. An understanding of it, however, is essential to a full airing of the equal protection claims raised by petitioner. Section 22-1201 (1) defines a "mentally ill person" as one who

> is afflicted with a psychiatric disorder which substantially impairs his mental health; and, because of such psychiatric disorder, requires care, treatment, training or detention in the interest of the welfare of such person or the welfare of others of the community in which such person resides.

Section 22-1201 (2) defines a "psychiatric disorder" to be any mental illness or disease, including any mental deficiency, epilepsy, alcoholism, or drug addiction. Other sections specify procedures for involuntary commitment of "mentally ill" persons that are substantially similar to those for commitment of the feeble-minded. For example, a citizen's sworn statement and the statement of a physician are required. § 22-1212. The circuit court judge, the applicant, and the physician then consult to formulate a treatment plan. § 22-1213. Notice to the individual is required, § 22-1216, and he is examined by two physicians, § 22-1215. There are provisions for temporary commitment. A hearing is held before a judge on the issue of mental illness. §§ 22-1209, 22-1216, 22-1217. The individual has a right of appeal. § 22-1210. An individual adjudged mentally ill under these sections is remanded to the department of mental health for assignment to an appropriate institution. § 22-1209. Discharge is in the discretion of the superintendent of the particular institution to which the person is assigned, § 22-1223; Official Opinion No. 54, Opinions of the Attorney General of Indiana, Dec. 30, 1966. The individual, however, remains within the court's custody, and release can therefore be revoked upon a hearing. *Ibid.*

II Equal Protection

Because the evidence established little likelihood of improvement in petitioner's condition, he argues that commitment under § 9-1706a in his case amounted to a commitment for life. This deprived him of equal protection, he contends, because, absent the criminal charges pending against him, the State would have had to proceed under other statutes generally applicable to all other citizens: either the commitment procedures for feeble-minded persons, or those for mentally ill persons. He argues that under these other statutes (1) the decision whether to commit would have been made according to a different standard, (2) if commitment were warranted, applicable standards for release would have been more lenient, (3) if committed under § 22-1907, he could have been assigned to a special institution affording appropriate care, and (4) he would then have been entitled to certain privileges not now available to him.

In *Baxstrom* v. *Herold,* 383 U.S. 107 (1966), the Court held that a state prisoner civilly committed at the end of his prison sentence on the finding of a surrogate was denied equal protection when he was deprived of a jury trial that the State made generally available to all other persons civilly committed. Rejecting the State's argument that Baxstrom's conviction and sentence constituted adequate justification for the difference in procedures, the Court said that "there is no conceivable basis for distinguishing the commitment of a person who is nearing the end of a penal term from all other civil commitments." 383 U.S., at 111–112; see *United States ex rel. Schuster*

v. *Herold,* 410 F.2d 1071 (CA2), cert. denied, 396 U.S. 847 (1969). The Court also held that Baxstrom was denied equal protection by commitment to an institution maintained by the state corrections department for ''dangerously mentally ill'' persons, without a judicial determination of his ''dangerous propensities'' afforded all others so committed.

If criminal conviction and imposition of sentence are insufficient to justify less procedural and substantive protection against indefinite commitment than that generally available to all others, the mere filing of criminal charges surely cannot suffice. This was the precise holding of the Massachusetts Court in *Commonwealth* v. *Druken,* 356 Mass. 503, 507, 254 N.E.2d 779, 781 (1969). The *Baxstrom* principle also has been extended to commitment following an insanity acquittal, *Bolton* v. *Harris,* 130 U.S.App.D.C. 1, 395 F.2d 642 (1968); *Cameron* v. *Mullen,* 128 U.S.App.D.C. 235, 387 F.2d 193 (1967); *People* v. *Lally,* 19 N.Y.2d 27, 224 N.E.2d 87 (1966), and to commitment in lieu of sentence following conviction as a sex offender. *Humphrey* v. *Cady,* 405 U.S. 504 (1972).

Respondent argues, however, that because the record fails to establish affirmatively that Jackson will never improve, his commitment ''until sane'' is not really an indeterminate one. It is only temporary, pending possible change in his condition. Thus, presumably, it cannot be judged against commitments under other state statutes that are truly indeterminate. The State relies on the lack of ''exactitude'' with which psychiatry can predict the future course of mental illness, and on the Court's decision in what is claimed to be ''a fact situation similar to the case at hand'' in *Greenwood* v. *United States,* 350 U.S. 366 (1956).

Were the State's factual premise that Jackson's commitment is only temporary a valid one, this might well be a different case. But the record does not support that premise. One of the doctors testified that in his view Jackson would be unable to acquire the substantially improved communication skills that would be necessary for him to participate in any defense. The prognosis for petitioner's developing such skills, he testified, appeared ''rather dim.'' In answer to a question whether Jackson would ever be able to comprehend the charges or participate in his defense, even after commitment and treatment, the doctor said, ''I doubt it, I don't believe so.'' The other psychiatrist testified that even if Jackson were able to develop such skills, he would *still* be unable to comprehend the proceedings or aid counsel due to his mental deficiency. The interpreter, a supervising teacher at the state school for the deaf, said that he would not be able to serve as an interpreter for Jackson or aid him in participating in a trial, and that the State had no facilities that could, ''after a length of time,'' aid Jackson in so participating. The court also heard petitioner's mother testify that Jackson already had undergone rudimentary out-patient training in communications skills from the deaf and dumb school in Indianapolis over a period of three years without noticeable success. There is nothing in the record that even points to any possibility that Jackson's present condition can be remedied at any future time.

Nor does *Greenwood,* which concerned the constitutional validity of 18 U.S.C. §§ 4244 to 4248, lend support to respondent's position. That decision, addressing the ''narrow constitutional issue raised by the order of commitment in the circumstances of this case,'' 350 U.S., at 375, upheld the Federal Government's constitutional authority to commit an individual found by the District Court to be "insane," incompetent to stand trial on outstanding criminal charges, and probably dangerous to the safety of the officers, property, or other interests of the United States. The *Greenwood* Court construed the federal statutes to deal "comprehensively" with defendants "who are insane or mentally incompetent to stand trial," and not merely with "the problem of temporary mental disorder." 350 U.S., at 373. Though Greenwood's prospects for improvement were slim, the Court held that "in the situation before us," where the District Court had made an explicit finding of dangerousness, that fact alone "does not defeat federal power to make this initial commitment." 350 U.S., at 375. No issue of equal protection was raised or decided. See Petitioner's Brief, No. 460, O.T. 1955, pp. 2, 7–9. It is clear that the Government's substantive power to commit on the particular findings made in that case was the sole question there decided. 350 U.S., at 376.

We note also that neither the Indiana statute nor state practice makes the likelihood of the defendant's improvement a relevant factor. The State did not seek to make any such showing, and the record clearly establishes that the chances of Jackson's ever meeting the competency standards of § 9-1706a are at best minimal, if not nonexistent. The record also rebuts any contention that the commitment could contribute to Jackson's improvement. Jackson's § 9-1706a commitment is permanent in practical effect.

We therefore must turn to the question whether, because of the pendency of the criminal charges that triggered the State's invocation of § 9-1706a, Jackson was deprived of substantial rights to which he would have been entitled under either of the other two state commitment statutes. *Baxstrom* held that the State cannot withhold from a few the procedural protections or the substantive requirements for commitment that are available to all others. In this case commitment procedures under all three statutes appear substantially similar: notice, examination by two doctors, and a full judicial hearing at which the individual is represented by counsel and can cross-examine witnesses and introduce evidence. Under each of the three statutes, the commitment determination is made by the court alone, and appellate review is available.

In contrast, however, what the State must show to commit a defendant under § 9-1706a, and the circumstances under which an individual so committed may be released, are substantially different from the standards under the other two statutes.

Under § 9-1706a, the State needed to show only Jackson's inability to stand trial. We are unable to say that, on the record before us, Indiana could have civilly committed him as mentally ill under § 22-1209 or committed him as feeble-minded under § 22-1907. The former requires at least (1) a showing of mental illness and (2) a showing that the individual is in need of "care, treatment, training or detention." § 22-1201 (1). Whether Jackson's mental deficiency would meet the first test is unclear; neither examining physician addressed himself to this. Furthermore, it is problematical whether commitment for "treatment" or "training" would be appropriate since the record establishes that none is available for Jackson's condition at any state institution. The record also fails to establish that Jackson is in need of custodial care or "detention." He has been employed at times, and there is no evidence that the care he long received at home has become inadequate. The statute appears to require an independent showing of dangerousness ("requires ... detention in the interest of the welfare of such person or . . . others . . . ''). Insofar as it may require such a showing, the pending criminal charges are insufficient to establish it, and no other supporting evidence was introduced. For the same reasons, we cannot say that this record would support a feeble-mindedness commitment under § 22-1907 on the ground that Jackson is ''unable properly to care for [himself].'' § 22-1801.

More important, an individual committed as feeble-minded is eligible for release when his condition ''justifies it,'' § 22-1814, and an individual civilly committed as mentally ill when the ''superintendent or administrator shall discharge such person, or [when] cured of such illness.'' § 22-1223 (emphasis supplied). Thus, in either case release is appropriate when the individual no longer requires the custodial care or treatment or detention that occasioned the commitment, or when the department of mental health believes release would be in his best interests. The evidence available concerning Jackson's past employment and home care strongly suggests that under these standards he might be eligible for release at almost any time, even if he did not improve. On the other hand, by the terms of his present § 9-1706a commitment, he will not be entitled to release at all, absent an unlikely substantial change for the better in his condition.

Baxstrom did not deal with the standard for release, but its rationale is applicable here. The harm to the individual is just as great if the State, without reasonable justification, can apply standards making his commitment a permanent one when standards generally applicable to all others afford him a substantial opportunity for early release.

As we noted above, we cannot conclude that pending criminal charges provide a greater justification for different treatment than conviction and sentence. Consequently, we hold that by subjecting Jackson to a more lenient commitment standard and to a more stringent standard of release than those generally applicable to all others not charged with offenses, and by thus condemning him in effect to permanent institutionalization without the showing required for commitment or the opportunity for release afforded by § 22-1209 or § 22-1907, Indiana deprived petitioner of equal protection of the laws under the Fourteenth Amendment.

III   Due Process

For reasons closely related to those discussed in Part II above, we also hold that Indiana's indefinite commitment of a criminal defendant solely on account of his incompetency to stand trial does not square with the Fourteenth Amendment's guarantee of due process.

A.   *The Federal System.* In the federal criminal system, the constitutional issue posed here has not been encountered precisely because the federal statutes have been construed to require that a mentally incompetent defendant must also be found ''dangerous'' before he can be committed indefinitely. But the decisions have uniformly articulated the constitutional problems compelling this statutory interpretation.

The federal statute, 18 U.S.C. §§ 4244 to 4246, is not dissimilar to the Indiana law. It provides that a defendant found incompetent to stand trial may be committed ''until the accused shall be mentally competent to stand trial or until the pending charges against him are disposed of according to law.'' § 4246. Section 4247, applicable on its face only to convicted criminals whose federal sentences are about to expire, permits commitment if the prisoner is (1) "insane or mentally incompetent" and (2) "will probably endanger the safety of the officers, the property, or other interests of the United States, and . . . suitable arrangements for the custody and care of the prisoner are not otherwise available," that is, in a state facility. See *Greenwood* v. *United States,* 350 U.S., at 373–374. One committed under this section, however, is entitled to release when any of the three conditions no longer obtains, "whichever event shall first occur." § 4248. Thus, a person committed under § 4247 must be released when he no longer is "dangerous."

In *Greenwood,* the Court upheld the pretrial commitment of a defendant who met all three conditions of § 4247, even though there was little likelihood that he would ever become competent to stand trial. Since Greenwood had not yet stood trial, his commitment was ostensibly under § 4244. By the related release provision, § 4246, he could not have been released until he became competent. But the District Court had in fact applied § 4247, and found specifically that Greenwood would be dangerous if not committed. This Court approved that approach, holding § 4247 applicable before trial as well as to those about to be released from sentence. 350 U.S., at 374. Accordingly, Greenwood was entitled to release when no longer dangerous, § 4248, even if he did not become competent to stand trial and thus did not meet the requirement of § 4246. Under these circumstances, the Court found the commitment constitutional.

Since *Greenwood,* federal courts without exception have found improper any straightforward application of §§ 4244 and 4246 to a defendant whose chance of attaining competency to stand trial is slim, thus effecting an indefinite commitment on the ground of incompetency alone. *United States* v. *Curry,* 410 F.2d 1372 (C.A.4 1969); *United States* v. *Walker,* 335 F.Supp. 705 (N.D.Cal. 1971); *Cook* v. *Ciccone,* 312 F.Supp. 822 (W.D.Mo. 1970); *United States* v. *Jackson,* 306 F. Supp. 4 (N.D.Cal. 1969); *Maurietta* v. *Ciccone,* 305 F.Supp. 775 (W.D.Mo. 1969). See *In re Harmon,* 425 F.2d 916 (C.A.1 1970); *United States* v. *Klein,* 325 F.2d 283 (C.A.2 1963); *Martin* v. *Settle,* 192 F.Supp. 156 (W.D.Mo. 1961); *Royal* v. *Settle,* 192 F.Supp. 176 (W.D.Mo. 1959). The holding in each of these cases was grounded in an expressed substantial doubt that §§ 4244 and 4246 could survive constitutional scrutiny if interpreted to authorize indefinite commitment.

These decisions have imposed a "rule of reasonableness" upon §§ 4244 and 4246. Without a finding of dangerousness, one committed thereunder can be held only for a "reasonable period of time" necessary to determine whether there is a substantial chance of his attaining the capacity to stand trial in the foreseeable future. If the chances are slight, or if the defendant does not in fact improve, then he must be released or granted a §§4247–4248 hearing.

B. *The States.* Some States[10] appear to commit indefinitely a defendant found incompetent to stand trial until he recovers competency. Other States require a

---

[10]Cal. Penal Code §§ 1370, 1371 (1970); Conn. Gen. Stat. Rev. § 54–40 (c) (1958); Minn. Stat. Ann. § 631.18 (Supp. 1972–1973); N. J. Rev. Stat. § 2A:163–2 (1971); Ohio Rev. Code Ann. §§ 2945.37 and 2945.38 (1954); Wis. Stat. Ann. § 971.14 (1971). See Note, "Incompetency to Stand Trial," 81 *Harv. L. Rev.* 454 (1967).

finding of dangerousness to support such a commitment[11] or provide forms of parole.[12] New York has recently enacted legislation mandating release of incompetent defendants charged with misdemeanors after 90 days of commitment, and release and dismissal of charges against those accused of felonies after they have been committed for two-thirds of the maximum potential prison sentence.[13] The practice of automatic commitment with release conditioned solely upon attainment of competence has been decried on both policy and constitutional grounds.[14] Recommendations for changes made by commentators and study committees have included incorporation into pretrial commitment procedures of the equivalent of the federal "rule of reason," a requirement of a finding of dangerousness or of full-scale civil commitment, periodic review by court or mental health administrative personnel of the defendant's condition and progress, and provisions for ultimately dropping charges if the defendant does not improve.[15] One source of this criticism is undoubtedly the empirical data available which tend to show that many defendants committed before trial are never tried, and that those defendants committed pursuant to ordinary civil proceedings are, on the average, released sooner than defendants automatically committed solely on account of their incapacity to stand trial.[16] Related to these statistics are substantial doubts about whether the rationale for pretrial commitment—that care or treatment will aid the accused in attaining competency—is empirically valid given the state of most of our mental institutions.[17] However, very few courts appear to have addressed the problem directly in the state context.

In *United States ex rel. Wolfersdorf* v. *Johnston,* 317 F.Supp. 66 (S.D.N.Y) 1970), an 86-year-old defendant committed for nearly 20 years as incompetent to stand trial on state murder and kidnaping charges applied for federal *habeas corpus.* He had been found "not dangerous," and suitable for civil commitment. The District Court granted relief. It held that petitioner's incarceration in an institution for the criminally insane constituted cruel and unusual punishment, and that the "shocking circumstances" of his commitment violated the Due Process Clause. The court quoted approvingly the language of *Cook* v. *Ciccone,* 312 F.Supp., at 824, concerning the

---

[11]Iowa Code Ann. § 783.3 (Supp. 1972); Okla. Stat. Ann., Tit. 22, § 1167 (1958); S.D. Comp. Laws Ann. § 23-38-6 (1967).

[12]Mich. Comp. Laws Ann. § 767.27a (8) (1967); Ore. Rev. Stat. § 426.300 (1) (1971); Wis. Stat. Ann. § 51.21 (6) (Supp. 1972).

[13]N. Y. Crim. Proc. Law § 730.50 (1971); see also Ill. Rev. Stat., c. 38, § 104-3 (c) (1971).

[14]Foote, "A Comment on Pre-Trial Commitment of Criminal Defendants," 108 *U. Pa. L. Rev.* 832 (1960); Note, "Incompetency to Stand Trial," 81 *Harv. L. Rev.* 454-456, 471-472 (1967); N.Y. Report 91-107.

[15]Judicial Conference of the District of Columbia Circuit, Report of the Committee on Problems Connected with Mental Examination of the Accused in Criminal Cases, Before Trial 49-52, 54-58, 133-146 (1965) (hereafter D.C. Report); N.Y. Report 73-124; Note, *supra,* 81 *Harv. L. Rev.,* at 471-473.

[16]See Matthews, *Mental Disability and the Criminal Law* 138-140 (American Bar Foundation 1970); Morris, "The Confusion of Confinement Syndrome: An Analysis of the Confinement of Mentally Ill Criminals and Ex-Criminals by the Department of Correction of the State of New York," 17 *Buffalo L. Rev.* 651 (1968); McGarry & Bendt, "Criminal vs. Civil Commitment of Psychotic Offenders: A Seven-Year Follow-Up," 125 *Am. J. Psychiatry* 1387, 1391 (1969); D.C. Report 50-52.

[17]Note, *supra,* 81 *Harv. L. Rev.,* at 472-473; American Bar Foundation, *The Mentally Disabled and the Law* 415-418 (rev. ed. 1971) (hereafter ABF Study); N.Y. Report 72-77, 102-105, 186-190.

"substantial injustice in keeping an unconvicted person in . . . custody to await trial where it is plainly evident his mental condition will not permit trial within a reasonable period of time."

In a 1970 case virtually indistinguishable from the one before us, the Illinois Supreme Court granted relief to an illiterate deaf mute who had been indicted for murder four years previously but found incompetent to stand trial on account of his inability to communicate, and committed. *People ex rel. Myers* v. *Briggs*, 46 Ill.2d 281, 263 N.E.2d 109 (1970). The institution where petitioner was confined had determined, "[I]t now appears that [petitioner] will never acquire the necessary communication skills needed to participate and cooperate in his trial." Petitioner, however, was found to be functioning at a "nearly normal level of performance in areas other than communication." The State contended petitioner should not be released until his competency was restored. The Illinois Supreme Court disagreed. It held:

> This court is of the opinion that this defendant, handicapped as he is and facing an indefinite commitment because of the pending indictment against him, should be given an opportunity to obtain a trial to determine whether or not he is guilty as charged or should be released. *Id.*, at 288, 263 N.E.2d, at 113.

C.   *This Case.* Respondent relies heavily on *Greenwood* to support Jackson's commitment. That decision is distinguishable. It upheld only the initial commitment without considering directly its duration or the standards for release. It justified the commitment by treating it as if accomplished under allied statutory provisions relating directly to the individual's "insanity" and society's interest in his indefinite commitment, factors not considered in Jackson's case. And it sustained commitment only upon the finding of dangerousness. As Part A, *supra,* shows, all these elements subsequently have been held not simply sufficient, but necessary, to sustain a commitment like the one involved here.

The States have traditionally exercised broad power to commit persons found to be mentally ill.[18] The substantive limitations on the exercise of this power and the procedures for invoking it vary drastically among the States.[19] The particular fashion in which the power is exercised—for instance, through various forms of civil commitment, defective delinquency laws, sexual psychopath laws, commitment of persons acquitted by reason of insanity—reflects different combinations of distinct bases for commitment sought to be vindicated.[20] The bases that have been articulated include dangerousness to self, dangerousness to others, and the need for care or treatment or training.[21] Considering the number of persons affected,[22] it is perhaps remarkable that

---

[18]See generally ABF Study 34–59.

[19]*Id.*, at 36–49. The ABF Study shows that in nine States the sole criterion for involuntary commitment is dangerousness to self or others; in 18 other States the patient's need for care or treatment was an alternative basis; the latter was the sole basis in six additional States; a few States had no statutory criteria at all, presumably leaving the determination to judicial discretion.

[20]See Note, "Civil Restraint, Mental Illness, and the Right to Treatment," 77 *Yale L. J.* 87 (1967).

[21]See Note, "Civil Commitment of the Mentally Ill: Theories and Procedures," 79 *Harv. L. Rev.* 1288, 1289–1297 (1966).

[22]In 1961, it was estimated that 90% of the approximately 800,000 patients in mental hospitals in this country had been involuntarily committed. Hearings on Constitutional Rights of the Mentally Ill before the

the substantive constitutional limitations on this power have not been more frequently litigated.

We need not address these broad questions here. It is clear that Jackson's commitment rests on proceedings that did not purport to bring into play, indeed did not even consider relevant, *any* of the articulated bases for exercise of Indiana's power of indefinite commitment. The state statutes contain at least two alternative methods for invoking this power. But Jackson was not afforded any "formal commitment proceedings addressed to [his] ability to function in society,"[24] or to society's interest in his restraint, or to the State's ability to aid him in attaining competency through custodial care or compulsory treatment, the ostensible purpose of the commitment. At the least, due process requires that the nature and duration of commitment bear some reasonable relation to the purpose for which the individual is committed.

We hold, consequently, that a person charged by a State with a criminal offense who is committed solely on account of his incapacity to proceed to trial cannot be held more than the reasonable period of time necessary to determine whether there is a substantial probability that he will attain that capacity in the foreseeable future. If it is determined that this is not the case, then the State must either institute the customary civil commitment proceeding that would be required to commit indefinitely any other citizen, or release the defendant. Furthermore, even if it is determined that the defendant probably soon will be able to stand trial, his continued commitment must be justified by progress toward that goal. In light of differing state facilities and procedures and a lack of evidence in this record, we do not think it appropriate for us to attempt to prescribe arbitrary time limits. We note, however, that petitioner Jackson has now been confined for three and one-half years on a record that sufficiently establishes the lack of a substantial probability that he will ever be able to participate fully in a trial.

These conclusions make it unnecessary for us to reach petitioner's Eighth-Fourteenth Amendment claim.

IV   Disposition of the Charges

Petitioner also urges that fundamental fairness requires that the charges against him now be dismissed. The thrust of his argument is that the record amply establishes his lack of criminal responsibility at the time the crimes are alleged to have been committed. The Indiana court did not discuss this question. Apparently it believed that by reason of Jackson's incompetency commitment the State was entitled to hold the charges pending indefinitely. On this record, Jackson's claim is a substantial one. For a number of reasons, however, we believe the issue is not sufficiently ripe for ultimate decision by us at this time.

Subcommittee on Constitutional Rights of the Senate Committee on the Judiciary, 87th Cong., 1st Sess., pt. 1, pp. 11, 43 (1961). Although later U.S. Census Bureau data for 1969 show a resident patient population almost 50% lower, other data from the U.S. Department of Health, Education, and Welfare estimate annual admissions to institutions to be almost equal to the patient population at any one time, about 380,000 persons per annum. See ABF Study xv.

[24] *In re Harmon,* 425 F.2d 916, 918 (C.A.1 1970).

A. Petitioner argues that he has already made out a complete insanity defense. Jackson's criminal responsibility at the time of the alleged offenses, however, is a distinct issue from his competency to stand trial. The competency hearing below was not directed to criminal responsibility, and evidence relevant to it was presented only incidentally. Thus, in any event, we would have to remand for further consideration of Jackson's condition in the light of Indiana's law of criminal responsibility.

B. Dismissal of charges against an incompetent accused has usually been thought to be justified on grounds not squarely presented here: particularly, the Sixth-Fourteenth Amendment right to a speedy trial,[27] or the denial of due process inherent in holding pending criminal charges indefinitely over the head of one who will never have a chance to prove his innocence.[28] Jackson did not present the Sixth-Fourteenth Amendment issue to the state courts. Nor did the highest state court rule on the due process issue, if indeed it was presented to that court in precisely the above-described form. We think, in light of our holdings in Parts II and III, that the Indiana courts should have the first opportunity to determine these issues.

C. Both courts and commentators have noted the desirability of permitting some proceedings to go forward despite the defendant's incompetency.[29] For instance, § 4.06 (3) of the Model Penal Code would permit an incompetent accused's attorney to contest any issue "susceptible of fair determination prior to trial and without the personal participation of the defendant." An alternative draft of § 4.06 (4) of the Model Penal Code would also permit an evidentiary hearing at which certain defenses, not including lack of criminal responsibility, could be raised by defense counsel on the basis of which the court might quash the indictment. Some States have statutory provisions permitting pretrial motions to be made or even allowing the incompetent defendant a trial at which to establish his innocence, without permitting a conviction.[30] We do not read this Court's previous decisions to preclude the States from allowing, at a minimum, an incompetent defendant to raise certain defenses such as insufficiency of the indictment, or make certain pretrial motions through counsel. Of course, if the Indiana courts conclude that Jackson was almost certainly not capable of criminal responsibility when the offenses were committed, dismissal of the charges might be warranted. But even if this is not the case, Jackson may have other good defenses that could sustain dismissal or acquittal and that might now be asserted. We do not know if

---

[27] *People ex rel. Myers* v. *Briggs,* 46 Ill.2d 281, 287–288, 263 N.E.2d 109, 112–113 (1970); *United States ex rel. Wolfersdorf* v. *Johnston,* 317 F.Supp. 66, 68 (S.D.N.Y. 1970); *United States* v. *Jackson,* 306 F.Supp. 4, 6 (N.D.Cal. 1969); see Foote, *supra,* n. 14, at 838–839; D.C. Report 145–146 (Recommendation No. 16).

[28] See cases cited in n. 27; N.Y. Report 119–121 (Recommendation No. 15); D.C. Report 52–53; Model Penal Code § 4.06 (2) (Proposed Official Draft 1962).

[29] *People ex rel. Myers* v. *Briggs, supra,* at 288, 263 N.E.2d, at 113; *Neely* v. *Hogan,* 62 Misc.2d 1056, 310 N.Y.S.2d 63 (1970); N.Y. Report 115–123 (Recommendation No. 13); D.C. Report 143–144 (Recommendation No. 15); Foote, *supra,* n. 14, at 841–845; Model Penal Code § 4.06 (alternative subsections 3, 4) (Proposed Official Draft 1962); ABF Study 423.

[30] Wis. Stat. Ann. § 971.14 (6) (1971); N.Y. Crim. Proc. Law § 730.60 (5) (1971); Mass. Gen. Laws, c. 123, § 17 (Supp. 1972); Mont. Rev. Code Ann. § 95–506 (c) (1969); Md. Ann. Code, Art. 59, § 24(a) (1972). See *Reg.* v. *Roberts,* [1953] 3 W.L.R. 178, [1953] 2 All.E.R. 340 (Devlin, J.).

Indiana would approve procedures such as those mentioned here, but these possibilities will be open on remand.

Reversed and remanded.

MR. JUSTICE POWELL and MR. JUSTICE REHNQUIST took no part in the consideration or decision of this case.

NOTES

1. Although the *Jackson* case arose from a criminal context, it includes much discussion of the justifications asserted by the states for the practice of involuntary civil commitment. Few Supreme Court decisions prior to *Jackson* dealt with the issue of civil commitment at all, and those few were like *Jackson* in that they considered it only as a comparative standard for the evaluation of practices of institutionalization arising from criminal charges or convictions. See, e.g., *Greenwood* v. *United States*, 350 U.S. 366 (1956); *Lynch* v. *Overholser*, 369 U.S. 705 (1962); *Baxstrom* v. *Herold*, 383 U.S. 107 (1966); *Specht* v. *Patterson*, 386 U.S. 605 (1967).

Less than 3 months before its decision in *Jackson*, the Supreme Court presented some perspectives on civil commitment in its opinion in *Humphrey* v. *Cady*, 405 U.S. 504 (1972), a case involving the commitment for an indefinite period of a person convicted of a sexual offense. In a significant paragraph of the opinion, the Court declared:

> Since 1880, Wisconsin has relied on a jury to decide whether to confine a person for compulsory psychiatric treatment. Like most, if not all, other States with similar legislation, Wisconsin conditions such confinement not solely on the medical judgment that the defendant is mentally ill and treatable, but also on the social and legal judgment that his potential for doing harm, to himself or to others, is great enough to justify such a massive curtailment of liberty. In making this determination, the jury serves the critical function of introducing into the process a lay judgment, reflecting values generally held in the community, concerning the kinds of potential harm that justify the State in confining a person for compulsory treatment. (*Id.* at 509.)

Since *Jackson*, there have been, as we shall see, some Supreme Court decisions dealing more directly with the subject of civil commitment. By and large, however, the *Jackson* court was quite accurate in its observation that "it is . . . remarkable that the substantive constitutional limitations on this power have not been more frequently litigated."

2. Shortly after the *Jackson* decision, the Court had another occasion to apply its principle that "due process requires that the nature and duration of commitment bear some reasonable relation to the purpose for which the individual is committed." *McNeil* v. *Director, Patuxent Institution*, 407 U.S. 245 (1972), involved a convicted felon who was referred, under an *ex parte* order, to Patuxent Institution for an indefinite term. The Court declared:

> [R]espondent contends that petitioner has been committed merely for observation, and that a commitment for observation need not be surrounded by the procedural safeguards (such as an adversary hearing) that are appropriate for a final determination. . . . Were the commitment for observation limited in duration to a brief period, the argument might have some force. But petitioner has been committed "for observation"

for six years, and on respondent's theory of his confinement there is no reason to believe it likely that he will ever be released. A confinement that is in fact indeterminate cannot rest on procedures designed to authorize a brief period of observation. (*Id.* at 249.)

3. The Illinois case of *People ex rel. Myers* v. *Briggs*, discussed in the *Jackson* opinion, has been popularized in a book, *Dummy*, by Ernest Tidyman (1974).

O'CONNOR v. DONALDSON

Supreme Court of the United States, 1975
422 U.S. 563

Mr. JUSTICE STEWART delivered the opinion of the Court.

The respondent, Kenneth Donaldson, was civilly committed to confinement as a mental patient in the Florida State Hospital at Chattahoochee in January of 1957. He was kept in custody there against his will for nearly 15 years. The petitioner, Dr. J. B. O'Connor, was the hospital's superintendent during most of this period. Throughout his confinement Donaldson repeatedly, but unsuccessfully, demanded his release, claiming that he was dangerous to no one, that he was not mentally ill, and that, at any rate, the hospital was not providing treatment for his supposed illness. Finally, in February of 1971, Donaldson brought this lawsuit under 42 U.S.C. § 1983, in the United States District Court for the Northern District of Florida, alleging that O'Connor, and other members of the hospital staff, named as defendants, had intentionally and maliciously deprived him of his constitutional right to liberty. After a four-day trial, the jury returned a verdict assessing both compensatory and punitive damages against O'Connor and a codefendant. The Court of Appeals for the Fifth Circuit affirmed the judgment, 493 F.2d 507. We granted O'Connor's petition for certiorari, 419 U.S. 894, 95 S.Ct. 171, 42 L.Ed.2d 138 because of the important constitutional questions seemingly presented.

I

Donaldson's commitment was initiated by his father, who thought that his son was suffering from "delusions." After hearings before a county judge of Pinellas County, Florida, Donaldson was found to be suffering from "paranoid schizophrenia" and was committed for "care, maintenance, and treatment" pursuant to Florida statutory provisions that have since been repealed. The state law was less than clear in specifying the grounds necessary for commitment, and the record is scanty as to Donaldson's condition at the time of the judicial hearing. These matters are, however, irrelevant, for this case involves no challenge to the initial commitment, but is focused, instead, upon the nearly 15 years of confinement that followed.

The evidence at the trial showed that the hospital staff had the power to release a patient, not dangerous to himself or others, even if he remained mentally ill and had been lawfully committed. Despite many requests, O'Connor refused to allow that power to be exercised in Donaldson's case. At the trial, O'Connor indicated that he had believed that Donaldson would have been unable to make a "successful adjustment outside the institution," but could not recall the basis for that conclusion. O'Connor retired as superintendent shortly before this suit was filed. A few months thereafter, and before the trial, Donaldson secured his release and a judicial restoration of competency, with the support of the hospital staff.

The testimony at the trial demonstrated, without contradiction, that Donaldson had posed no danger to others during his long confinement, or indeed at any point in his life. O'Connor himself conceded that he had no personal or secondhand knowledge that Donaldson had ever committed a dangerous act. There was no evidence that Donaldson had ever been suicidal or been thought likely to inflict injury upon himself. One of O'Connor's codefendants acknowledged that Donaldson could have earned his own living outside the hospital. He had done so for some 14 years before his commitment, and immediately upon his release he secured a responsible job in hotel administration.

Furthermore, Donaldson's frequent requests for release had been supported by responsible persons willing to provide him any care he might need on release. In 1963, for example, a representative of Helping Hands, Inc., a halfway house for mental patients, wrote O'Connor asking him to release Donaldson to its care. The request was accompanied by a supporting letter from the Minneapolis Clinic of Psychiatry and Neurology, which a codefendant conceded was a "good clinic." O'Connor rejected the offer, replying that Donaldson could be released only to his parents. That rule was apparently of O'Connor's own making. At the time, Donaldson was 55 years old, and, as O'Connor knew, Donaldson's parents were too elderly and infirm to take responsibility for him. Moreover, in his continuing correspondence with Donaldson's parents, O'Connor never informed them of the Helping Hands offer. In addition, on four separate occasions between 1964 and 1968, John Lembcke, a college classmate of Donaldson's and a longtime family friend, asked O'Connor to release Donaldson to his care. On each occasion O'Connor refused. The record shows that Lembcke was a serious and responsible person, who was willing and able to assume responsibility for Donaldson's welfare.

The evidence showed that Donaldson's confinement was a simple regime of enforced custodial care, not a program designed to alleviate or cure his supposed illness. Numerous witnesses, including one of O'Connor's codefendants, testified that Donaldson had received nothing but custodial care while at the hospital. O'Connor described Donaldson's treatment as "milieu therapy." But witnesses from the hospital staff conceded that, in the context of this case, "milieu therapy" was a euphemism for confinement in the "milieu" of a mental hospital. For substantial periods, Donaldson was simply kept in a large room that housed 60 patients, many of whom were under criminal commitment. Donaldson's requests for ground privileges, occupational training, and an opportunity to discuss his case with O'Connor or other staff members were repeatedly denied.

At the trial, O'Connor's principal defense was that he had acted in good faith and was therefore immune from any liability for monetary damages. His position, in short, was that state law, which he had believed valid, had authorized indefinite custodial confinement of the "sick," even if they were not given treatment and their release could harm no one.

The trial judge instructed the members of the jury that they should find that O'Connor had violated Donaldson's constitutional right to liberty if they found that he had

> confined [Donaldson] against his will, knowing that he was not mentally ill or dangerous or knowing that if mentally ill he was not receiving treatment for his mental illness.
>
> * * *
>
> Now the purpose of involuntary hospitalization is treatment and not mere custodial care or punishment if a patient is not a danger to himself or others. Without such treatment there is no justification from a constitutional standpoint for continued confinement unless you should also find that [Donaldson] was dangerous either to himself or others.[6]

The trial judge further instructed the jury that O'Connor was immune from damages if he

> reasonably believed in good faith that detention of [Donaldson] was proper for the length of time he was so confined. . . .
>
> However, mere good intentions which do not give rise to a reasonable belief that detention is lawfully required cannot justify [Donaldson's] confinement in the Florida State Hospital.

---

[6]The District Court defined treatment as follows:

"You are instructed that a person who is involuntary civilly committed to a mental hospital does have a constitutional right to receive such treatment *as will give him a realistic opportunity to be cured or to improve his mental condition.*" [Emphasis added.] O'Connor argues that this statement suggests that a mental patient has a right to treatment even if confined by reason of dangerousness to himself or others. But this is to take the above paragraph out of context, for it is bracketed by paragraphs making clear the trial judge's theory that treatment is constitutionally required only if mental illness alone, rather than danger to self or others, is the reason for confinement. If O'Connor had thought the instructions ambiguous on this point, he could have objected to them and requested a clarification. He did not do so. We accordingly have no occasion here to decide whether persons committed on grounds of dangerousness enjoy a "right to treatment."

In pertinent part, the instructions read as follows:

"The Plaintiff claims in brief that throughout the period of his hospitalization he was not mentally ill or dangerous to himself or others, and claims further that if he was mentally ill, or if Defendants believed he was mentally ill, Defendants withheld from him the treatment necessary to improve his mental condition.

"The Defendants claim, in brief, that Plaintiff's detention was legal and proper, or if his detention was not legal and proper, it was the result of mistake, without malicious intent.

* * *

"In order to prove his claim under the Civil Rights Act, the burden is upon the Plaintiff in this case to establish by a preponderance of the evidence in this case the following facts:

"That the Defendants confined Plaintiff against his will, knowing that he was not mentally ill or dangerous or knowing that if mentally ill he was not receiving treatment for his mental illness.

* * *

"[T]hat the Defendants' acts and conduct deprived the Plaintiff of his Federal Constitutional right not to be denied or deprived of his liberty without due process of law as that phrase is defined and explained in these instructions. . . .

* * *

"You are instructed that a person who is involuntarily civilly committed to a mental hospital does have a constitutional right to receive such treatment as will give him a realistic opportunity to be cured or to improve his mental condition.

"Now the purpose of involuntary hospitalization is treatment and not mere custodial care or punishment if a patient is not a danger to himself or others. Without such treatment there is no justification from a constitutional stand-point for continued confinement unless you should also find that the Plaintiff was dangerous either to himself or others."

The jury returned a verdict for Donaldson against O'Connor and a codefendant, and awarded damages of $38,500, including $10,000 in punitive damages.[7]

The Court of Appeals affirmed the judgment of the District Court in a broad opinion dealing with "the far-reaching question whether the Fourteenth Amendment guarantees a right to treatment to persons involuntarily civilly committed to state mental hospitals." 493 F.2d, at 509. The appellate court held that when, as in Donaldson's case, the rationale for confinement is that the patient is in need of treatment, the Constitution requires that minimally adequate treatment in fact be provided. *Id.*, at 521. The court further expressed the view that, regardless of the grounds for involuntary civil commitment, a person confined against his will at a state mental institution has "a constitutional right to receive such individual treatment as will give him a reasonable opportunity to be cured or to improve his mental condition." *Id.*, at 520. Conversely, the court's opinion implied that it is constitutionally permissible for a State to confine a mentally ill person against his will in order to treat his illness, regardless of whether his illness renders him dangerous to himself or others. See *id.*, at 522–527.

II

We have concluded that the difficult issues of constitutional law dealt with by the Court of Appeals are not presented by this case in its present posture. Specifically, there is no reason now to decide whether mentally ill persons dangerous to themselves or to others have a right to treatment upon compulsory confinement by the State, or whether the State may compulsorily confine a nondangerous, mentally ill individual for the purpose of treatment. As we view it, this case raises a single, relatively simple, but nonetheless important question concerning every man's constitutional right to liberty.

The jury found that Donaldson was neither dangerous to himself nor dangerous to others, and also found that, if mentally ill, Donaldson had not received treatment.[8] That verdict, based on abundant evidence, makes the issue before the Court a narrow one. We need not decide whether, when, or by what procedures, a mentally ill person may be confined by the State on any of the grounds which, under contemporary statutes, are generally advanced to justify involuntary confinement of such a person— to prevent injury to the public, to ensure his own survival or safety,[9] or to alleviate or

---

[7]The trial judge had instructed that punitive damages should be awarded only if "the act or omission of the Defendant or Defendants which proximately caused injury to the Plaintiff was maliciously or wantonly or oppressively done."

[8]Given the jury instructions, see n. 6 *supra,* it is possible that the jury went so far as to find that O'Connor knew not only that Donaldson was harmless to himself and others but also that he was not mentally ill at all. If it so found, the jury was permitted by the instructions to rule against O'Connor regardless of the nature of the "treatment" provided. If we were to construe the jury's verdict in that fashion, there would remain no substantial issue in this case: That a wholly sane and innocent person has a constitutional right not to be physically confined by the State when his freedom will pose a danger neither to himself nor to others cannot be seriously doubted.

[9]The judge's instructions used the phrase "dangerous to himself." Of course, even if there is no foreseeable risk of self-injury or suicide, a person is literally "dangerous to himself" if for physical or other reasons he is helpless to avoid the hazards of freedom either through his own efforts or with the aid of willing family members or friends. While it might be argued that the judge's instructions could have been more detailed on this point, O'Connor raised no objection to them, presumably because the evidence clearly showed that Donaldson was not "dangerous to himself" however broadly that phrase might be defined.

cure his illness. See *Jackson* v. *Indiana,* 406 U.S. 715, 736–737, 92 S.Ct. 1845, 1857–1858, 32 L.Ed.2d 435; *Humphrey* v. *Cady,* 405 U.S. 504, 509, 92 S.Ct. 1048, 1052, 31 L.Ed.2d 394. For the jury found that none of the above grounds for continued confinement was present in Donaldson's case.[10]

Given the jury's findings, what was left as justification for keeping Donaldson in continued confinement? The fact that state law may have authorized confinement of the harmless mentally ill does not itself establish a constitutionally adequate purpose for the confinement. See *Jackson* v. *Indiana, supra,* 406 U.S., at 720–723, 92 S.Ct., at 1849–1851; *McNeil* v. *Director, Patuxent Institution,* 407 U.S. 245, 248–250, 92 S.Ct. 2083, 2086–2087, 32 L.Ed.2d 719. Nor is it enough that Donaldson's original confinement was founded upon a constitutionally adequate basis, if in fact it was, because even if his involuntary confinement was initially permissible, it could not constitutionally continue after that basis no longer existed. *Jackson* v. *Indiana, supra,* 406 U.S., at 738, 92 S.Ct., at 1858; *McNeil* v. *Director, Patuxent Institution, supra.*

A finding of "mental illness" alone cannot justify a State's locking a person up against his will and keeping him indefinitely in simple custodial confinement. Assuming that that term can be given a reasonably precise content and that the "mentally ill" can be identified with reasonable accuracy, there is still no constitutional basis for confining such persons involuntarily if they are dangerous to no one and can live safely in freedom.

May the State confine the mentally ill merely to ensure them a living standard superior to that they enjoy in the private community? That the State has a proper interest in providing care and assistance to the unfortunate goes without saying. But the mere presence of mental illness does not disqualify a person from preferring his home to the comforts of an institution. Moreover, while the State may arguably confine a person to save him from harm, incarceration is rarely if ever a necessary condition for raising the living standards of those capable of surviving safely in freedom, on their own or with the help of family or friends. See *Shelton* v. *Tucker,* 364 U.S. 479, 488–490, 81 S.Ct. 247, 252–253, 5 L.Ed.2d 231.

May the State fence in the harmless mentally ill solely to save its citizens from exposure to those whose ways are different? One might as well ask if the State, to avoid public unease, could incarcerate all who are physically unattractive or socially eccentric. Mere public intolerance or animosity cannot constitutionally justify the deprivation of a person's physical liberty. See *e.g., Cohen* v. *California,* 403 U.S. 15, 24–26, 91 S.Ct. 1780, 1787–1789, 29 L.Ed.2d 284; *Coates* v. *City of Cincinnati,* 402 U.S.

---

[10] O'Connor argues that, despite the jury's verdict, the Court must assume that Donaldson was receiving treatment sufficient to justify his confinement, because the adequacy of treatment is a "nonjusticiable" question that must be left to the discretion of the psychiatric profession. That argument is unpersuasive. Where "treatment" is the sole asserted ground for depriving a person of liberty, it is plainly unacceptable to suggest that the courts are powerless to determine whether the asserted ground is present. See *Jackson* v. *Indiana, supra.* Neither party objected to the jury instruction defining treatment. There is, accordingly, no occasion in this case to decide whether the provision of treatment, standing alone, can ever constitutionally justify involuntary confinement or, if it can, how much or what kind of treatment would suffice for that purpose. In its present posture this case involves not involuntary treatment but simply involuntary custodial confinement.

611, 615, 91 S.Ct. 1686, 1689, 29 L.Ed.2d 214; *Street* v. *New York,* 394 U.S. 576, 592, 89 S.Ct. 1354, 1365-1366, 22 L.Ed.2d 572; *cf. United States Dept. of Agric.* v. *Moreno,* 413 U.S. 528, 534, 93 S.Ct. 2821, 2825-2826, 37 L.Ed.2d 782.

In short, a State cannot constitutionally confine without more a nondangerous individual who is capable of surviving safely in freedom by himself or with the help of willing and responsible family members or friends. Since the jury found, upon ample evidence, that O'Connor, as an agent of the State, knowingly did so confine Donaldson, it properly concluded that O'Connor violated Donaldson's constitutional right to freedom.

III

O'Connor contends that in any event he should not be held personally liable for monetary damages because his decisions were made in "good faith." Specifically, O'Connor argues that he was acting pursuant to state law which, he believed, authorized confinement of the mentally ill even when their release would not compromise their safety or constitute a danger to others, and that he could not reasonably have been expected to know that the state law as he understood it was constitutionally invalid. A proposed instruction to this effect was rejected by the District Court.

The District Court did instruct the jury, without objection, that monetary damages could not be assessed against O'Connor if he had believed reasonably and in good faith that Donaldson's continued confinement was "proper," and that punitive damages could be awarded only if O'Connor had acted "maliciously or wantonly or oppressively." The Court of Appeals approved those instructions. But that court did not consider whether it was error for the trial judge to refuse the additional instruction concerning O'Connor's claimed reliance on state law as authorization for Donaldson's continued confinement. Further, neither the District Court nor the Court of Appeals acted with the benefit of this Court's most recent decision on the scope of the qualified immunity possessed by state officials under 42 U.S.C. § 1983. *Wood* v. *Strickland,* 420 U.S. 308, 95 S.Ct. 992, 43 L.Ed.2d 214.

Under that decision, the relevant question for the jury is whether O'Connor "knew or reasonably should have known that the action he took within his sphere of official responsibility would violate the constitutional rights of [Donaldson], or if he took the action with the malicious intention to cause a deprivation of constitutional rights or other injury to [Donaldson]." *Id.,* 420 U.S. 322, 95 S.Ct. 1001. See also *Scheuer* v. *Rhodes,* 416 U.S. 232, 247-248, 94 S.Ct. 1683, 1692, 40 L.Ed.2d 90; *Wood* v. *Strickland, supra,* 420 U.S. at 330, 95 S.Ct. at 1005 (opinion of Powell, J.). For purposes of this question, an official has, of course, no duty to anticipate unforseeable constitutional developments. *Wood* v. *Strickland, supra,* 420 U.S. at 322, 95 S.Ct. at 1001.

Accordingly, we vacate the judgment of the Court of Appeals and remand the case to enable that court to consider, in light of *Wood* v. *Strickland,* whether the District Judge's failure to instruct with regard to the effect of O'Connor's claimed reliance on state law rendered inadequate the instructions as to O'Connor's liability for compensatory and punitive damages.[12]

It is so ordered.

Vacated and remanded.

Mr. Chief Justice Burger, concurring.

Although I join the Court's opinion and judgment in this case, it seems to me that several factors merit more emphasis than it gives them. I therefore add the following remarks.

I

With respect to the remand to the Court of Appeals on the issue of official immunity,[1] it seems to me not entirely irrelevant that there was substantial evidence that Donaldson consistently refused treatment that was offered to him, claiming that he was not mentally ill and needed no treatment.[2] The Court appropriately takes notice of the uncertainties of psychiatric diagnosis and therapy, and the reported cases are replete with evidence of the divergence of medical opinion in this vexing area. E.g., Greenwood v. United States, 350 U.S. 366, 375, 76 S.Ct. 410, 415, 100 L.Ed. 412 (1957). See also Drope v. Missouri, 420 U.S. 162, 95 S.Ct. 896, 43 L.Ed.2d 103 (1975). Nonetheless, one of the few areas of agreement among behavioral specialists is that an uncooperative patient cannot benefit from therapy and that the first step in effective treatment is acknowledgement by the patient that he is suffering from an abnormal condition. See e.g., Katz, "The Right to Treatment—An Enchanting Legal Fiction?" 36 U.Chi.L.Rev. 755, 768–769 (1969). Donaldson's adamant refusal to do so should be taken into account in considering petitioner's good-faith defense.

Perhaps more important to the issue of immunity is a factor referred to only obliquely in the Court's opinion. On numerous occasions during the period of his confinement Donaldson unsuccessfully sought release in the Florida courts; indeed, the last of these proceedings was terminated only a few months prior to the bringing of this action. See Donaldson v. O'Connor, 234 So.2d 114 (Fla. 1969), cert. denied, 400 U.S.

---

[12]Upon remand, the Court of Appeals is to consider only the question whether O'Connor is to be held liable for monetary damages for violating Donaldson's constitutional right to liberty. The jury found, on substantial evidence and under adequate instructions, that O'Connor deprived Donaldson, who was dangerous neither to himself nor to others and was provided no treatment, of the constitutional right to liberty. Cf. n. 8, supra. That finding needs no further consideration. If the Court of Appeals holds that a remand to the District Court is necessary, the only issue to be determined in that court will be whether O'Connor is immune from liability for monetary damages.

Of necessity our decision vacating the judgment of the Court of Appeals deprives that court's opinion of precedential effect, leaving this Court's opinion and judgment as the sole law of the case. See United States v. Munsingwear, 340 U.S. 36, 71 S.Ct. 104, 95 L.Ed. 36.

[1]I have difficulty understanding how the issue of immunity can be resolved on this record and hence it is very likely a new trial may be required; if that is the case I would hope these sensitive and important issues would have the benefit of more effective presentation and articulation on behalf of petitioner.

[2]The Court's reference to "milieu therapy," ante, at 569 may be construed as disparaging that concept. True, it is capable of being used simply to cloak official indifference, but the reality is that some mental abnormalities respond to no known treatment. Also some mental patients respond, as do persons suffering from a variety of physiological ailments, to what is loosely called "milieu treatment," i.e., keeping them comfortable, well-nourished, and in a protected environment. It is not for us to say in the baffling field of psychiatry that "milieu therapy" is always a pretense.

869, 91 S.Ct. 104, 27 L.Ed.2d 109 (1970). Whatever the reasons for the state courts' repeated denials of relief, and regardless of whether they correctly resolved the issue tendered to them, petitioner and the other members of the medical staff at Florida State Hospital would surely have been justified in considering each such judicial decision as an approval of continued confinement and an independent intervening reason for continuing Donaldson's confinement. Thus, this fact is inescapably related to the issue of immunity and must be considered by the Court of Appeals on remand and, if a new trial is ordered, by the District Court.[3]

II

As the Court points out, *ante,* at 2491 n. 6, the District Court instructed the jury in part that ''a person who is involuntarily civilly committed to a mental hospital does have a *constitutional* right to receive such treatment as will give him a realistic opportunity to be cured,'' (emphasis added) and the Court of Appeals unequivocally approved this phrase, standing alone, as a correct statement of the law. *O'Connor* v. *Donaldson,* 493 F.2d 507, 520 (CA5 1974). The Court's opinion plainly gives no approval to that holding and makes clear that it binds neither the parties to this case nor the courts of the Fifth Circuit. See *ante,* at 2495 n. 12. Moreover, in light of its importance for future litigation in this area, it should be emphasized that the Court of Appeals' analysis has no basis in the decisions of this Court.

A

There can be no doubt that involuntary commitment to a mental hospital, like involuntary confinement of an individual for any reason, is a deprivation of liberty which the State cannot accomplish without due process of law. *Specht* v. *Patterson,* 386 U.S., at 608, 87 S.Ct., at 1211. *Cf. In re Gault,* 387 U.S. 1, 12–13, 87 S.Ct. 1428, 1435–1436, 18 L.Ed.2d 527 (1967). Commitment must be justified on the basis of a legitimate state interest, and the reasons for committing a particular individual must be established in an appropriate proceeding. Equally important, confinement must cease when those reasons no longer exist. See *McNeil* v. *Director, Patuxent Institution,* 407 U.S., at 249–250, 92 S.Ct., at 2086–2087; *Jackson* v. *Indiana,* 406 U.S., at 738, 92 S.Ct., at 1858.

The Court of Appeals purported to be applying these principles in developing the first of its theories supporting a constitutional right to treatment. It first identified what it perceived to be the traditional bases for civil commitment—physical dangerousness to oneself or others, or a need for treatment—and stated:

> [W]here, as in Donaldson's case, the rationale for confinement is the *''parens patriae''* rationale that the patient is in need of treatment, the due process clause requires that minimally adequate treatment be in fact provided . . . ''To deprive any citizen of his or her liberty upon the altruistic theory that the confinement is for humane therapeutic reasons and then fail to provide adequate treatment violates the very fundamentals of due process.'' 493 F.2d, at 521.

---

[3]That petitioner's counsel failed to raise this issue is not a reason why it should not be considered with respect to immunity in light of the Court's holding that the defense was preserved for appellate review.

The Court of Appeals did not explain its conclusion that the rationale for respondent's commitment was that he needed treatment. The Florida statutes in effect during the period of his confinement did not require that a person who had been adjudicated incompetent and ordered committed either be provided with psychiatric treatment or released, and there was no such condition in respondent's order of commitment. *Cf. Rouse* v. *Cameron,* 125 U.S.App.D.C. 366, 373 F.2d 451 (1966). More important, the instructions which the Court of Appeals read as establishing an absolute constitutional right to treatment did not require the jury to make any findings regarding the specific reasons for respondent's confinement or to focus upon any rights he may have had under state law. Thus, the premise of the Court of Appeals' first theory must have been that, at least with respect to persons who are not physically dangerous, a State has no power to confine the mentally ill except for the purpose of providing them with treatment.

That proposition is surely not descriptive of the power traditionally exercised by the States in this area. Historically, and for a considerable period of time, subsidized custodial care in private foster homes or boarding houses was the most benign form of care provided incompetent or mentally ill persons for whom the States assumed responsibility. Until well into the 19th century the vast majority of such persons were simply restrained in poorhouses, almshouses, or jails. See A. Deutsch, *The Mentally Ill in America* 38–54, 114–131 (2d ed. 1949). The few States that established institutions for the mentally ill during this early period were concerned primarily with providing a more humane place of confinement and only secondarily with "curing" the persons sent there. See *id.,* at 98–113.

As the trend toward state care of the mentally ill expanded, eventually leading to the present statutory schemes for protecting such persons, the dual functions of institutionalization continued to be recognized. While one of the goals of this movement was to provide medical treatment to those who could benefit from it, it was acknowledged that this could not be done in all cases and that there was a large range of mental illness for which no known "cure" existed. In time, providing places for the custodial confinement of the so-called "dependent insane" again emerged as the major goal of the State's programs in this area and continued to be so well into this century. See *id.,* at 228–271; D. Rothman, *The Discovery of the Asylum* 264–295 (1971).

In short, the idea that States may not confine the mentally ill except for the purpose of providing them with treatment is of very recent origin, and there is no historical basis for imposing such a limitation on state power. Analysis of the sources of the civil commitment power likewise lends no support to that notion. There can be little doubt that in the exercise of its police power a State may confine individuals solely to protect society from the dangers of significant antisocial acts or communicable disease. *Cf. Minnesota ex rel. Pearson* v. *Probate Court of Ramsey County,* 309 U.S. 270, 60 S.Ct. 523, 84 L.Ed. 744 (1940); *Jacobson* v. *Massachusetts,* 197 U.S. 11, 25–29, 25 S.Ct. 358, 360–362, 49 L.Ed. 643 (1905). Additionally, the States are vested with the historic *parens patriae* power, including the duty to protect "persons under legal disabilities to act for themselves." *Hawaii* v. *Standard Oil Co.,* 405 U.S. 251, 257, 92 S.Ct. 885, 888, 31 L.Ed.2d 184 (1972). See also *Mormon Church* v. *United States,* 136 U.S. 1, 56–58, 10 S.Ct. 792, 807–808, 34 L.Ed. 478 (1890). The classic example of this role is when a State undertakes to act as " 'the general guardian of all infants, idiots, and lunatics.' " *Hawaii* v. *Standard Oil Co., supra,* quoting 3 W. Blackstone, *Commentaries* * 47.

Of course, an inevitable consequence of exercising the *parens patriae* power is that the ward's personal freedom will be substantially restrained, whether a guardian is appointed to control his property, he is placed in the custody of a private third party, or committed to an institution. Thus, however the power is implemented, due process requires that it not be invoked indiscriminately. At a minimum, a particular scheme for protection of the mentally ill must rest upon a legislative determination that it is compatible with the best interests of the affected class and that its members are unable to act for themselves. *Cf. Mormon Church* v. *United States, supra.* Moreover, the use of alternative forms of protection may be motivated by different considerations, and the justifications for one may not be invoked to rationalize another. Cf. *Jackson* v. *Indiana,* 406 U.S., at 737–738, 92 S.Ct., at 1857–1858. See also American Bar Foundation, *The Mentally Disabled and the Law,* 254–255 (S. Brakel & R. Rock ed. 1971).

However, the existence of some due process limitations on the *parens patriae* power does not justify the further conclusion that it may be exercised to confine a mentally ill person only if the purpose of the confinement is treatment. Despite many recent advances in medical knowledge, it remains a stubborn fact that there are many forms of mental illness which are not understood, some which are untreatable in the sense that no effective therapy has yet been discovered for them, and that rates of "cure" are generally low. See Schwitzgebel, "The Right to Effective Mental Treatment," 62 *Calif.L.Rev.* 936, 941–948 (1974). There can be little responsible debate regarding "the uncertainty of diagnosis in this field and the tentativeness of professional judgment." *Greenwood* v. *United States,* 350 U.S. 366, 375, 76 S.Ct. 410, 415, 100 L.Ed. 412 (1957). See also Ennis and Litwack, "Psychiatry and the Presumption of Expertise: Flipping Coins in the Courtroom," 62 *Calif.L.Rev.* 693, 697–719 (1974).[5] Similarly, as previously observed, it is universally recognized as fundamental to effective therapy that the patient acknowledge his illness and cooperate with those attempting to give treatment; yet the failure of a large proportion of mentally ill persons to do so is a common phenomenon. See Katz, *supra,* 36 *U.Chi.L.Rev.,* at 768–769 (1969). It may be that some persons in either of these categories,[6] and there may be others, are unable to function in society and will suffer real harm to themselves unless provided with care in a sheltered environment. See, *e.g., Lake* v. *Cameron,* 124 U.S.App.D.C. 264, 270–271, 364 F.2d 657, 663–664 (1966) (dissenting opinion). At the very least, I am not able to say that a state legislature is powerless to make that kind of judgment. See *Greenwood* v. *United States, supra.*

---

[5] Indeed, there is considerable debate concerning the threshold questions of what constitutes "mental disease" and "treatment." See Szasz, "The Right to Health," 57 *Geo.L.J.* 734 (1969).

[6] Indeed, respondent may have shared both of these characteristics. His illness, paranoid schizophrenia, is notoriously unsusceptible to treatment, see Livermore, Malmquist, and Meehl, "On the Justifications for Civil Commitment," 117 *U.Pa.L.Rev.* 75, 93 & n. 52 (1968), and the reports of the Florida State Hospital Staff which were introduced into evidence expressed the view that he was unwilling to acknowledge his illness and generally uncooperative.

B

Alternatively, it has been argued that a Fourteenth Amendment right to treatment for involuntarily confined mental patients derives from the fact that many of the safeguards of the criminal process are not present in civil commitment. The Court of Appeals described this theory as follows:

> [A] due process right to treatment is based on the principle that when the three central limitations on the government's power to detain—that detention be in retribution for a specific offense; that it be limited to a fixed term; and that it be permitted after a proceeding where the fundamental procedural safeguards are observed—are absent, there must be a *quid pro quo* extended by the government to justify confinement. And the *quid pro quo* most commonly recognized is the provision of rehabilitative treatment. 493 F.2d, at 522.

To the extent that this theory may be read to permit a State to confine an individual simply because it is willing to provide treatment, regardless of the subject's ability to function in society, it raises the gravest of constitutional problems, and I have no doubt the Court of Appeals would agree on this score. As a justification for a constitutional right to such treatment, the *quid pro quo* theory suffers from equally serious defects.

It is too well established to require extended discussion that due process is not an inflexible concept. Rather, its requirements are determined in particular instances by identifying and accommodating the interests of the individual and society. See, *e.g.*, *Morrissey* v. *Brewer*, 408 U.S. 471, 480–484, 92 S.Ct. 2593, 2599–2602, 33 L.Ed.2d 484 (1972); *McNeil* v. *Director, Patuxent Institution*, 407 U.S., at 249–250, 92 S.Ct., at 2086–2087; *McKeiver* v. *Pennsylvania*, 403 U.S. 528, 545–555, 91 S.Ct. 1976, 1986–1991, 29 L.Ed.2d 647 (1971). Where claims that the State is acting in the best interests of an individual are said to justify reduced procedural and substantive safeguards, this Court's decisions require that they be "candidly appraised." *In re Gault*, 387 U.S., at 21, 27–29, 87 S.Ct., at 1440, 1443–1445. However, in so doing judges are not free to read their private notions of public policy or public health into the Constitution. *Olsen* v. *Nebraska ex rel. Western Reference & Bond Ass'n*, 313 U.S. 236, 246–247, 61 S.Ct. 862, 865–866, 85 L.Ed. 1305 (1941).

The *quid pro quo* theory is a sharp departure from, and cannot coexist with, these due process principles. As an initial matter, the theory presupposes that essentially the same interests are involved in every situation where a State seeks to confine an individual; that assumption, however, is incorrect. It is elementary that the justification for the criminal process and the unique deprivation of liberty which it can impose requires that it be invoked only for commission of a specific offense prohibited by legislative enactment. See *Powell* v. *Texas*, 392 U.S. 514, 541–544, 88 S.Ct. 2145, 2158–2160, 20 L.Ed.2d 1254 (1968) (opinion of Black, J.). But it would be incongruous to apply the same limitation when quarantine is imposed by the State to protect the public from a highly communicable disease. See *Jacobson* v. *Massachusetts*, 197 U.S., at 29–30, 25 S.Ct., at 362–363.

A more troublesome feature of the *quid pro quo* theory is that it elevates a concern for essentially procedural safeguards into a new substantive constitutional right.[8] Rather than inquiring whether strict standards of proof or periodic redetermination of a patient's condition are required in civil confinement, the theory accepts the absence of such safeguards but insists that the State provide benefits which, in the view of a court, are adequate "compensation" for confinement. In light of the wide divergence of medical opinion regarding the diagnosis of and proper therapy for mental abnormalities, that prospect is especially troubling in this area and cannot be squared with the principle that "courts may not substitute for the judgments of legislators their own understanding of the public welfare, but must instead concern themselves with the validity of the methods which the legislature has selected." *In re Gault,* 387 U.S., at 71, 87 S.Ct., at 1466 (opinion of Harlan, J.). Of course, questions regarding the adequacy of procedure and the power of a State to continue particular confinements are ultimately for the courts, aided by expert opinion to the extent that is found helpful. But I am not persuaded that we should abandon the traditional limitations on the scope of judicial review.

C

In sum, I cannot accept the reasoning of the Court of Appeals and can discern no other basis for equating an involuntarily committed mental patient's unquestioned constitutional right not to be confined without due process of law with a constitutional right to *treatment*. Given the present state of medical knowledge regarding abnormal human behavior and its treatment, few things would be more fraught with peril than to irrevocably condition a State's power to protect the mentally ill upon the providing of "such treatment as will give [them] a realistic opportunity to be cured." Nor can I accept the theory that a State may lawfully confine an individual thought to need treatment and justify that deprivation of liberty solely by providing some treatment. Our concepts of due process would not tolerate such a "trade-off." Because the Court of Appeals' analysis could be read as authorizing those results, it should not be followed.

NOTES

1. The "right to treatment" concept, relied upon by the Court of Appeals, sidestepped by the majority opinion of the Supreme Court, and blasted by Chief Justice Burger, was succinctly summarized in *Wyatt* v. *Stickney,* 325 F.Supp. 781, 785 M.D.Ala. 1971), aff'd in relevant part sub nom *Wyatt* v. *Aderholt,* 503 F.2d 1305 (5th Cir. 1974):

> To deprive any citizen of his or her liberty upon the altruistic theory that the confinement is for humane therapeutic reasons and then fail to provide adequate treatment violates the very fundamentals of due process.

The first articulation of this theory is generally credited to Dr. Morton Birnbaum, who in an article in the American Bar Association Journal in 1960, proposed that

---

[8]Even advocates of a right to treatment have criticized the *quid pro quo* theory on this ground. *E.g.,* Note, "Developments in the Law—Civil Commitment of the Mentally Ill," 87 *Harv.L.Rev.* 1190, 1325, n. 39 (1974).

... the courts under their traditional powers to protect the constitutional rights of our citizens begin to consider the problem of whether or not a person who has been institutionalized solely because he is sufficiently mentally ill to require institutionalization for care and treatment so that he may regain his health, and therefore his liberty, as soon as possible; that the courts do this by means of recognizing and enforcing the right to treatment; and, that the courts do this, independent of any action by any legislature, as a necessary and overdue development of our concept of due process of law.[d]

In 1966, Birnbaum's concept was accepted in *Rouse* v. *Cameron,* 373 F.2d 451, 453 (D.C.Cir. 1966), where the court ruled that a Washington, D.C., statute mandated treatment for those persons committed to a public hospital because of mental illness and added that failure to provide such treatment could raise constitutional questions. Subsequently, the right to treatment rationale was embraced by a number of courts; e.g., *Wyatt* v. *Aderholt,* 503 F.2d 1305, 1315 (5th Cir. 1974); *Welsch* v. *Likins,* 373 F.Supp. 487 (D.Minn. 1974), aff'd in part and vacated and remanded in part, 550 F.2d 1122 (8th Cir. 1977); *Davis* v. *Watkins,* 384 F.Supp. 1196, 1197 (N.D.Ohio 1974); *Nelson* v. *Heyne,* 491 F.2d 352, 358 (7th Cir. 1974), cert. denied 417 U.S. 976 (1974) (juvenile institution); *Nason* v. *Superintendent of Bridgewater State Hosp.,* 353 Mass. 604, 233 N.E.2d 908, 913–914 (1968). See also *Saville* v. *Treadway,* 404 F.Supp. 430, 433 (M.D.Tenn. 1974).

In the *Wyatt* case, the district court ruled that a treatment program had three fundamental elements: "(1) a humane psychological and physical environment, (2) qualified staff in numbers sufficient to administer adequate treatment, and (3) individualized treatment plans (*Wyatt* v. *Stickney,* 344 F.Supp. 373, 375 (M.D.Ala. 1972)), and it went into great detail in specifying how these three elements were to be fulfilled. Thus, the court developed two comprehensive and detailed sets of standards, one labeled "Minimum Constitutional Standards for Adequate Treatment of the Mentally Ill," *id.* at 379–386, and one entitled "Minimum Constitutional Standards for Adequate Habilitation of the Mentally Retarded," *id.* at 395–407. (The distinction between habilitation and treatment is discussed in *Halderman* v. *Pennhurst State School and Hospital,* 446 F.Supp. 1295, 1314 (E.D.Pa. 1977), pp. 661–697, below.)

Legal scholars have devoted much attention to the right to treatment; e.g., Burgdorf, M., and Burgdorf, R., "A History of Unequal Treatment: The Qualifications of Handicapped Persons as a 'Suspect Class' Under the Equal Protection Clause," 15 *Santa Clara Lawyer* 855, 891–895 (1975); Herr, S., "Civil Rights, Uncivil Asylums and the Retarded," 43 *Cin.L.Rev.* 679, 729–741 (1974); "Symposium—The Right to Treatment," 57 *Geo.L.J.* 673 (1969); Bazelon, D., "Implementing the Right to Treatment," 36 *U.Chi.L.Rev.* 742 (1969); Birnbaum, M., "Some Remarks on 'The Right to Treatment'," 23 *Ala.L.Rev.* 623 (1971); Note, "The Nascent Right to Treatment," 53 *Va.L.Rev.* 1134 (1969); Case Comment, "*Wyatt* v. *Stickney* and the Right of Civilly Committed Mental Patients to Adequate Treatment," 86 *Harv.L.Rev.* 1282 (1973); Note, "The Wyatt Case: Implementation of a Judicial Decree Ordering Institutional Change," 84 *Yale L.J.* 1338 (1975). The doctrinal development of the right to treatment is also examined in some detail in the

---

[d]Birnbaum, M., "The Right to Treatment," 46 *A.B.A.J.* 499 (1960).

Court of Appeals opinion in *Donaldson, Donaldson* v. *O'Connor*, 493 F.2d 507, 519–525 (5th Cir. 1974), and in *Halderman* v. *Pennhurst State School and Hospital, supra,* see pp. 679–686, below.

In spite of Chief Justice Burger's misgivings, courts have continued to find a constitutional right to treatment subsequent to *O'Connor* v. *Donaldson;* e.g., *Gary W.* v. *State of La.,* 437 F.Supp. 1209 (E.D.La. 1976); *Halderman* v. *Pennhurst State School and Hospital, supra,* pp. 661–697, below; *Woe* v. *Mathews,* 408 F.Supp. 419, 429 (E.D.N.Y. 1976), remanded in part, dismissed in part sub nom. *Woe* v. *Weinberger,* 556 F.2d 563 (2d Cir. 1977); *McRedmond* v. *Wilson,* 533 F.2d 757 (2d Cir. 1976) (institutionalized juveniles). See also, *Scott* v. *Plante,* 532 F.2d 939, 947 (1976).

The importance of the right to treatment as a basis for litigation in this area has been waning, not because of lack of receptivity by the courts, but rather because of a recognition by many advocates that the right to treatment does not go to the heart of the issues raised by institutionalization.

> While the *Wyatt* case attempted to remedy the inhumane conditions in Alabama institutions, it did not deal with the underlying problem: the *existence* of segregated facilities. The formulation of elaborate standards for recordkeeping, staffing ratios, living conditions and disciplinary policies implies the necessity for the existence of such institutions. *Wyatt* never confronted the basic issue of whether any large-scale, geographically remote, fulltime residential institution *could* beneficially affect the lives of its residents.
> There is fear among many mental health and mental retardation professionals that simply improving the conditions at residential institutions for the handicapped will guarantee their continued existence.[e]

For the more modern approaches to tackling the problem institutions, see part D of this chapter.

2.   Is Chief Justice Burger's opinion a dissent in concurring clothing? With what portions of the majority holding does he agree? With what parts does he disagree?

3.   An alternative approach to improving conditions within institutions has been the enunciation by some courts of a "right to protection from harm," *New York St. Assn. for Retarded Children, Inc.* v. *Rockefeller,* 357 F.Supp. 752, 764–765 (E.D.N.Y. 1973); *Welsch* v. *Likins,* 373 F.Supp. 487, 502–503 (D.Minn. 1974), vacated on other grounds, 550 F.2d 1122 (8th Cir. 1977); *Wuori* v. *Zitnay,* Civil Action N. 75-80 S.D. (D.Me. July 21, 1978); or of a right to a "safe and humane environment," *Harper* v. *Cserr,* 544 F.2d 1121, 1124 (1st Cir. 1976); *Goodman* v. *Parwatikar,* 570 F.2d 801, 804–805 (8th Cir. 1978). These rights are based upon a theory that institution residents are entitled to be treated no worse than convicted criminals and are grounded in the cruel and unusual punishment proscription of the Eighth Amendment and in the Due Process and Equal Protection clauses of the Fourteenth Amendment. These theories suffer, however, the same shortcoming mentioned above in Note 1 in regard to the

---

[e]Burgdorf, M., and Burgdorf, R. "A History of Unequal Treatment: The Qualifications of Handicapped Persons as a 'Suspect Class' Under the Equal Protection Clause," 15 Santa Clara Lawyer 894 (1975).

right to treatment, in that they address the superficial improvement of the physical conditions in the institution without addressing the underlying question of whether it is appropriate to confine people in such institutions at all.

4. Eventually, Mr. Donaldson did recover monetary damages in the amount of $20,000 plus attorneys' fees, *Donaldson v. O'Connor*, 454 F.Supp. 311 (N.D.Fla. 1978), in compensation for the 15 years of liberty of which he was deprived. He subsequently wrote a book about his confinement and battle for freedom; Donaldson, K., *Insanity Inside Out* (1976).

ADDINGTON v. STATE OF TEXAS

Supreme Court of the United States, 1979
——*U.S.*——, 47 U.S.L.W. 4473 (Apr. 30, 1979)

Mr. Chief Justice BURGER delivered the opinion of the Court.

The question in this case is what standard of proof is required by the Fourteenth Amendment to the Constitution in a civil proceeding brought under state law to commit an individual involuntarily for an indefinite period to a state mental hospital.

I

On seven occasions between 1969 and 1975 appellant was committed temporarily, Texas Mental Health Code Ann., Art. 5547-31-39 (Vernon), to various Texas state mental hospitals and was committed for indefinite periods, *id.*, at 5547-40-57, to Austin State Hospital on three different occasions. On December 18, 1975, when appellant was arrested on a misdemeanor charge of "assault by threat" against his mother, the county and state mental health authorities therefore were well aware of his history of mental and emotional difficulties.

Appellant's mother filed a petition for his indefinite commitment in accordance with Texas law. The county psychiatric examiner interviewed appellant while in custody and after the interview issued a Certificate of Medical Examination for Mental Illness. In the Certificate, the examiner stated his opinion that appellant was "mentally ill and require[d] hospitalization in a mental hospital." Art. 5547-42.

Appellant retained counsel and a trial was held before a jury to determine in accord with the statute:

> (1) whether the proposed patient is mentally ill, and if so
> (2) whether he requires hospitalization in a mental hospital for his own welfare and protection or the protection of others, and if so
> (3) whether he is mentally incompetent. Art. 5547-51.

The trial on these issues extended over six days.

The State offered evidence that appellant suffered from serious delusions, that he often had threatened to injure both of his parents and others, that he had been involved in several assaultive episodes while hospitalized and that he had caused substantial property damage both at his own apartment and at his parents' home. From these undisputed facts, two psychiatrists, who qualified as experts, expressed opinions that appellant suffered from psychotic schizophrenia and that he had paranoid tendencies. They also expressed medical opinions that appellant was probably dangerous both to himself and to others. They explained that appellant required hospitalization in a closed area to treat his condition because in the past he had refused to attend out-patient treatment programs and had escaped several times from mental hospitals.

Appellant did not contest the factual assertions made by the State's witnesses; indeed, he conceded that he suffered from a mental illness. What appellant attempted to show was that there was no substantial basis for concluding that he was probably dangerous to himself or others.

The trial judge submitted the case to the jury with the instructions in the form of two questions:

> 1) Based on clear, unequivocal and convincing evidence, is Frank O'Neal Addington mentally ill?
> 2) Based on clear, unequivocal and convincing evidence, does Frank O'Neal Addington require hospitalization in a mental hospital for his own welfare and protection or the protection of others?''

Appellant objected to these instructions on several grounds, including the trial court's refusal to employ the ''beyond a reasonable doubt'' standard of proof.

The jury found that appellant was mentally ill and that he required hospitalization for his own or others' welfare. the trial court then entered an order committing appellant as a patient to Austin State Hospital for an indefinite period.

Appellant appealed that order to the Texas Court of Civil Appeals, arguing, among other things, that the standards for commitment violated his substantive due process rights and that any standard of proof for commitment less than that required for criminal convictions, i.e., beyond a reasonable doubt, violated his procedural due process rights. The Court of Civil Appeals agreed with appellant on the standard of proof issue and reversed the judgment of the trial court. Because of its treatment of the standard of proof, that court did not consider any of the other issues raised in the appeal.

On appeal, the Texas Supreme Court reversed the Court of Civil Appeals' decision. In so holding the supreme court relied primarily upon its previous decision in State v. Turner, 556 S.W.2d 563 (Tex.), cert. denied, 435 U.S. 929 (1977).

In Turner, the Texas Supreme Court held that a ''preponderance of the evidence'' standard of proof in a civil commitment proceeding satisfied due process. The court declined to adopt the criminal law standard of ''beyond a reasonable doubt'' primarily because it questioned whether the State could prove by that exacting standard that a particular person would or would not be dangerous in the future. It also distinguished a civil commitment from a criminal conviction by noting that under Texas law the mentally ill patient has the right to treatment, periodic review of his condition and immediate release when no longer deemed to be a danger to himself or others. Finally, the Turner court rejected the ''clear and convincing'' evidence standard because under Texas rules of procedure juries could be instructed only under a beyond a reasonable doubt or a preponderance standard of proof.

Reaffirming Turner, the Texas Supreme Court in this case concluded that the trial court's instruction to the jury, although not in conformity with the legal requirements, had benefited appellant, and hence the error was harmless. Accordingly, the court reinstated the judgment of the trial court.

We noted probable jurisdiction. 435 U.S. 967. After oral argument it became clear that no challenge to the constitutionality of any Texas statute was presented. Under 28 U.S.C. § 1257 (2) no appeal is authorized; accordingly, construing the papers filed as a petition for a writ of certiorari, we now grant the petition.

II

The function of a standard of proof, as that concept is embodied in the Due Process Clause and in the realm of factfinding, is to "instruct the fact finder concerning the degree of confidence our society thinks he should have in the correctness of factual conclusions for a particular type of adjudication." *In re Winship,* 397 U.S. 358, 370 (1970) (Harlan, J., concurring). The standard serves to allocate the risk of error between the litigants and to indicate the relative importance attached to the ultimate decision.

Generally speaking the evolution of this area of the law has produced across a continuum three standards or levels of proof for different types of cases. At one end of the spectrum is the typical civil case involving a monetary dispute between private parties. Since society has a minimal concern with the outcome of such private suits, plaintiff's burden of proof is a mere preponderance of the evidence. The litigants thus share the risk of error in roughly equal fashion.

In a criminal case, on the other hand, the interests of the defendant are of such magnitude that historically and without any explicit constitutional requirement they have been protected by standards of proof designed to exclude as nearly as possible the likelihood of an erroneous judgment. In the administration of criminal justice our society imposes almost the entire risk of error upon itself. This is accomplished by requiring under the Due Process Clause that the state prove the guilt of an accused beyond a reasonable doubt. *In re Winship,* 397 U.S. 358 (1970).

The intermediate standard, which usually employs some combination of the words "clear," "cogent," "unequivocal," and "convincing," is less commonly used, but, nonetheless "is no stranger to the civil law." *Woodby* v. *INS,* 385 U.S. 276, 285 (1967). See also McCormick, Evidence § 320 (1954); 9 Wigmore, Evidence § 2498 (3d ed. 1940). One typical use of the standard is in civil cases involving allegations of a fraud or some other quasi-criminal wrongdoing by the defendant. The interests at stake in those cases are deemed to be more substantial than mere loss of money and some jurisdictions accordingly reduce the risk to the defendant of having his reputation tarnished erroneously by increasing the plaintiff's burden of proof. Similarly, this Court has used the "clear, unequivocal and convincing" standard of proof to protect particularly important individual interests in various civil cases. See, e.g., *Woodby* v. *INS, supra,* at 285 (deportation); *Chaunt* v. *United States,* 364 U.S. 350, 353 (1960) (denaturalization); *Schneiderman* v. *United States,* 320 U.S. 118, 125, 159 (1943) (denaturalization).

Candor suggests that, to a degree, efforts to analyze what lay jurors understand concerning the differences among these three tests or the nuances of a judge's instructions on the law may well be largely an academic exercise; there are no directly relevant empirical studies. Indeed, the ultimate truth as to how the standards of proof affect decision making may well be unknowable, given that factfinding is a process shared by countless thousands of individuals throughout the country. We probably can assume no more than that the difference between a preponderance of the evidence and proof beyond a reasonable doubt probably is better understood than either of them in relation to the intermediate standard of clear and convincing evidence. Nonetheless, even if the particular standard-of-proof catch-words do not always make a great difference in a particular case, adopting a "standard of proof is more than an empty semantic exercise." *Tippett* v. *Maryland,* 436 F.2d 1153, 1166 (C.A.4 1971) (Sobeloff, J., concurring and dissenting), cert. dismissed *sub nom. Murel* v. *Baltimore City Criminal Court,* 407 U.S. 355 (1972). In cases involving individual rights, whether criminal or civil, "the standard of proof at a minimum reflects the value society places on individual liberty." *Ibid.*

III

In considering what standard should govern in a civil commitment proceeding, we must assess both the extent of the individual's interest in not being involuntarily confined indefinitely and the state's interest in committing the emotionally disturbed under a particular standard of proof. Moreover, we must be mindful that the function of legal process is to minimize the risk of erroneous decisions. See *Mathews* v. *Eldridge,* 424 U.S. 319, 335 (1976); *Speiser* v. *Randall,* 357 U.S. 513, 525–526 (1958).

A

This Court repeatedly has recognized that civil commitment for any purpose constitutes a significant deprivation of liberty that requires due process protection. See, *e.g., Jackson* v. *Indiana,* 406 U.S. 715 (1972); *Humphrey* v. *Cady,* 405 U.S. 504 (1972); *In re Gault,* 387 U.S. 1 (1967); *Specht* v. *Patterson,* 386 U.S. 605 (1967). Moreover, it is indisputable that involuntary commitment to a mental hospital after a finding of probable dangerousness to self or others can engender adverse social consequences to the individual. Whether we label this phenomena "stigma" or choose to call it something else is less important than that we recognize that it can occur and that it can have a very significant impact on the individual.

The state has a legitimate interest under its *parens patriae* powers in providing care to its citizens who are unable because of emotional disorders to care for themselves; the state also has authority under its police power to protect the community from the dangerous tendencies of some who are mentally ill. Under the Texas Mental Health Code, however, the State has no interest in confining individuals involuntarily if they are not mentally ill or if they do not pose some danger to themselves or others. Since the preponderance standard creates the risk of increasing the number of individuals erroneously committed, it is at least unclear to what extent, if any, the state's interests are furthered by using a preponderance standard in such commitment proceedings.

The expanding concern of society with problems of mental disorders is reflected in the fact that in recent years many states have enacted statutes designed to protect the rights of the mentally ill. However, only one state by statute permits involuntary commitment by a mere preponderance of the evidence, Miss. Code Ann. § 41-21-75, and Texas is the only state where a court has concluded that the preponderance of the evidence standard satisfies due process. We attribute this not to any lack of concern in those states, but rather to a belief that the varying standards tend to produce comparable results. As we noted earlier, however, standards of proof are important for their symbolic meaning as well as for their practical effect.

At one time or another every person exhibits some abnormal behavior which might be perceived by some as symptomatic of a mental or emotional disorder, but which is in fact within a range of conduct that is generally acceptable. Obviously such behavior is no basis for compelled treatment and surely none for confinement. However, there is the possible risk that a factfinder might decide to commit an individual based solely on a few isolated instances of unusual conduct. Loss of liberty calls for a showing that the individual suffers from something more serious than is demonstrated by idiosyncratic behavior. Increasing the burden of proof is one way to impress the factfinder with the importance of the decision and thereby perhaps to reduce the chances that inappropriate commitments will be ordered.

The individual should not be asked to share equally with society the risk of error when the possible injury to the individual is significantly greater than any possible harm to the state. We conclude that the individual's interest in the outcome of a civil commitment proceeding is of such weight and gravity that due process requires the state to justify confinement by proof more substantial than a mere preponderance of the evidence.

B

Appellant urges the Court to hold that due process requires use of the criminal law's standard of proof—"beyond a reasonable doubt." He argues that the rationale of the *Winship* holding that the criminal law standard of proof was required in a delinquency proceeding applies with equal force to a civil commitment proceeding.

In *Winship,* against the background of a gradual assimilation of juvenile proceedings into traditional criminal prosecutions, we declined to allow the state's "civil labels and good intentions" to "obviate the need for criminal due process safeguards in juvenile courts." 397 U.S., at 365–366. The Court saw no controlling difference in loss of liberty and stigma between a conviction for an adult and a delinquency adjudication for a juvenile. *Winship* recognized that the basic issue—whether the individual in fact committed a criminal act—was the same in both proceedings. There being no meaningful distinctions between the two proceedings, we required the state to prove the juvenile's act and intent beyond a reasonable doubt.

There are significant reasons why different standards of proof are called for in civil commitment proceedings as opposed to criminal prosecutions. In a civil commitment state power is not exercised in a punitive sense.[4] Unlike the delinquency proceeding in *Winship,* a civil commitment proceeding can in no sense be equated to a criminal prosecution. Cf. *Woodby* v. *INS, supra,* at 284–285.

In addition, the "beyond a reasonable doubt" standard historically has been

---

[4] The State of Texas confines only for the purpose of providing care designed to treat the individual. As the Texas Supreme Court said in *State* v. *Turner,* 556 S. W. 2d 563, 566 (1977): "The involuntary mental patient is entitled to treatment, to periodic and recurrent review of his mental condition, and to release at such time as he no longer presents a danger to himself and others."

reserved for criminal cases. This unique standard of proof, not prescribed or defined in the Constitution, is regarded as a critical part of the ''moral force of the criminal law,'' 397 U.S., at 364, and we should hesitate to apply it too broadly or casually in noncriminal cases. Cf. *ibid.*

The heavy standard applied in criminal cases manifests our concern that the risk of error to the individual must be minimized even at the risk that some who are guilty might go free. *Patterson* v. *New York,* 432 U.S. 198, 208 (1977). The full force of that idea does not apply to a civil commitment. It may be true that an erroneous commitment is sometimes as undesirable as an erroneous conviction, 5 Wigmore § 1400. However, even though an erroneous confinement should be avoided in the first instance, the layers of professional review and observation of the patient's condition, and the concern of family and friends generally will provide continuous opportunities for an erroneous commitment to be corrected. Moreover, it is not true that the release of a genuinely mentally ill person is no worse for the individual than the failure to convict the guilty. One who is suffering from a debilitating mental illness and in need of treatment is neither wholly at liberty nor free of stigma. See Chodoff, ''The Case for Involuntary Hospitalization of the Mentally Ill,'' 133 *Am. J. Psychiatry* 496, 498 (1976); Schwartz et al., ''Psychiatric Labeling and the Rehabilitation of the Mental Patient,'' 31 *Arch. Gen. Psychiatry* 329, 335 (1974). It cannot be said, therefore, that it is much better for a mentally ill person to ''go free'' than for a mentally normal person to be committed.

Finally, the initial inquiry in a civil commitment proceeding is very different from the central issue in either a delinquency proceeding or a criminal prosecution. In the latter cases the basic issue is a straightforward factual question—did the accused commit the act alleged. There may be factual issues to resolve in a commitment proceeding, but the factual aspects represent only the beginning of the inquiry. Whether the individual is mentally ill and dangerous to either himself or others and is in need of confined therapy turns on the *meaning* of the facts which must be interpreted by expert psychiatrists and psychologists. Given the lack of certainty and the fallibility of psychiatric diagnosis, there is a serious question as to whether a state could ever prove beyond a reasonable doubt that an individual is both mentally ill and likely to be dangerous. See *O'Connor* v. *Donaldson,* 422 U.S. 563, 584 (1976) (concurring opinion); *Blocker* v. *United States,* 110 U.S. App.D.C. 41, 288 F.2d 853, 860–861 (1961) (concurring opinion). See also *Tippett* v. *Maryland,* 436 F.2d 1153, 1165 (C.A.4 1973) (Sobeloff, J., concurring and dissenting), cert. dismissed *Sub nom. Murel* v. *Baltimore City Criminal Court,* 407 U.S. 355 (1974); Note, ''Civil Commitment of the Mentally Ill.: Theories and Procedures,'' 79 *Harv.L.Rev.* 1288, 1291 (1968); Note, ''Due Process and the Development of ''Criminal'' Safeguards in Civil Commitment Adjudications,'' 42 *Ford.L.Rev.* 611, 624 (1974).

The subtleties and nuances of psychiatric diagnosis render certainties virtually beyond reach in most situations. The reasonable doubt standard of criminal law functions in its realm because there the standard is addressed to specific, knowable facts. Psychiatric diagnosis, in contrast, is to a large extent based on medical ''impressions'' drawn from subjective analysis and filtered through the experience of the diagnostician. This process often makes it very difficult for the expert physician to offer definite conclusions about any particular patient. Within the medical discipline, the traditional standard for "factfinding" is a "reasonable medical certainty." If a trained psychiatrist has difficulty with the categorical "beyond a reasonable doubt" standard, the untrained lay juror—or indeed even a trained judge—who is required to rely upon expert opinion could be forced by the criminal law standard of proof to reject commitment for many patients desperately in need of institutionalized psychiatric care. See Note, 42 *Ford.L.Rev.*, at 624. Such "freedom" for a mentally ill person would be purchased at a high price.

That practical considerations may limit a constitutionally based burden of proof is demonstrated by the reasonable doubt standard, which is a compromise between what is possible to prove and what protects the rights of the individual. If the state was required to guarantee error-free convictions, it would be required to prove guilt beyond all doubt. However, "[d]ue process does not require that every conceivable step be taken, at whatever cost, to eliminate the possibility of convicting an innocent person." *Patterson* v. *New York,* 432 U.S. 197, 208 (1977). Nor should the state be required to employ a standard of proof that may completely undercut its efforts to further the legitimate interests of both the state and the patient that are served by civil commitments.

That some states have chosen—either legislatively or judicially—to adopt the criminal law standard[5] gives no assurance that the more stringent standard of proof is needed or is even adaptable to the needs of all states. The essence of federalism is that states must be free to develop a variety of solutions to problems and not be forced into a common, uniform mold. As the substantive standards for civil commitment may vary from state to state, procedures must be allowed to vary so long as they meet the constitutional minimum. See Monahan & Wexler, "A Definite Maybe: Proof and Probability in Civil Commitment," 2 *Law & Human Behavior* 49, 53–54 (1978); Share, "The Standard of Proof in Involuntary Civil Commitment Proceedings," 1977 *Det. Coll. L. Rev.* 209, 210. We conclude that it is unnecessary to require states to apply the strict, criminal standard.

C

Having concluded that the preponderance standard falls short of meeting the demands of due process and that the reasonable doubt standard is not required, we turn to a middle level of burden of proof that strikes a fair balance between the rights of the individual and the legitimate concerns of the state. We note that 20 states, most by statute, employ the standard of "clear and convincing" evidence;[6] three states use

---

[5]Haw. Rev. Stat. § 334-60 (4) (I); Idaho Code § 66-329 (i); Kan. Stat. Ann. § 59-2917; Mont. Rev. Codes Ann. § 38-1305 (7); Okla. Stat. Tit. 43A, § 54.1 (C); Ore. Rev. Stat. § 426.130; Utah Code Ann. § 64-7-36 (6); Wis. Stat. § 51.20 (14)(e); *Superintendent of Worcester State Hospital* v. *Hagberg,* ____Mass. ____, 372 N.E.2d 242 (1978); *Proctor* v. *Butler,* 380 A.2d 673 (N.H. 1977); *In re Hodges,* 325 A.2d 605 (D.C. 1974); *Lausche* v. *Comm'r of Public Welfare,* 302 Minn. 65, 225 N.W.2d 366 (1974), cert. denied, 420 U.S. 993 (1975). See also *In re J. W.,* 44 N.J.Super. 216, 130 A.2d 64 (App. Div.), cert. denied 24 N.J. 465, 132 A.2d 558 (1957); *Danton* v. *Commonwealth,* 383 S.W.2d 681 (Ky. 1964) (dicta).

[6]Ariz. Rev. Stat. Ann. § 36-540; Colo. Rev. Stat. § 27-10-111(1); Conn. Gen. Stat. § 17-178(c); Del. Code, Tit. 16, § 5010(2); Ga. Code § 88-501(a); Ill. Rev. Stat. ch. 91½, § 3-808; Iowa Code § 229.12; La. Rev. Stat. Ann., Tit. 28, § 55E (West); Me. Rev. Stat. Ann. Tit. 34, § 2334(5)(A)(1); Mich. Stat. Ann.,

"clear, *cogent,* and convincing" evidence;[7] and two states require "clear, *un-equivocal* and convincing" evidence.[8]

In *Woodby* v. *INS,* 385 U.S. 276 (1967), dealing with deportation and *Schneiderman* v. *United States,* 320 U.S. 118, 125, 159 (1943), dealing with denaturalization, the Court held that "clear, unequivocal and convincing" evidence was the appropriate standard of proof. The term "unequivocal," taken by itself, means proof that admits of no doubt,[9] a burden approximating, if not exceeding, that used in criminal cases. The issues in *Schneiderman* and *Woodby* were basically factual and therefore susceptible of objective proof and the consequences to the individual were unusually drastic—loss of citizenship and expulsion from the United States.

We have concluded that the reasonable doubt standard is inappropriate in civil commitment proceedings because, given the uncertainties of psychiatric diagnosis, it may impose a burden the state cannot meet and thereby erect an unreasonable barrier to needed medical treatment. Similarly, we conclude that use of the term "unequivocal" is not constitutionally required, although the states are free to use that standard. To meet due process demands, the standard has to inform the factfinder that the proof must be greater than the preponderance of the evidence standard applicable to other categories of civil cases.

We noted earlier that the trial court employed the standard of "clear, unequivocal and convincing" evidence in appellant's commitment hearing before a jury. That instruction was constitutionally adequate. However, determination of the precise burden equal to or greater than the "clear and convincing" standard which we hold is required to meet due process guarantees is a matter of state law which we leave to the Texas Supreme Court. Accordingly, we remand the case for further proceedings not inconsistent with this opinion.

Vacated and remanded.

Mr. Justice POWELL took no part in the consideration or decision of this case.

NOTES

1. Although *Addington* is, on its face, concerned with the issue of the proper evidentiary standard, does it provide any precedential expressions as to what justifications for commitment are constitutionally adequate? Has Chief Justice Burger changed his views since he authored his concurring opinion in *Donaldson?*

2. What implications do the Court's observations about the uncertainty of psychiatric testimony have in regard to the insanity defense in criminal cases? Conversely, if the state can prove, beyond a reasonable doubt, that a defendant in a criminal case is not

---

§ 14.800 (465); Neg. Rev. Stat. § 83-1035; N. M. Stat. Ann. § 34-2A-11C; N. D. Cent. Code § 25-03.1-19; Ohio Rev. Code Ann. § 5122.15(B); Pa. Cons. Stat. Tit. 50, § 7304(f); S. C. Code § 44-17-580; S. D. Comp. Laws Ann. § 27A-9-18; Vt. Stat. Ann. Tit. 18, § 7616(b); Md. Dept. of Health & Mental Hygiene Reg. 10.04.03G; *In re Beverly,* 342 So.2d 481 (Fla. 1977).

[7]N. C. Gen. Stat. § 122-58.7(i); Wash. Rev. Code § 71.05.310; *State ex rel. Hawks* v. *Lazaro,* 202 S.E.2d 109 (W. Va. 1974).

[8]Ala. Code, Tit. 22, § 52-10(a); Tenn. Code Ann. § 33-604(d).

[9]See *Webster's Third New International Dictionary* 2494 (1969).

insane, which it must do to overcome an insanity defense, why can it not prove beyond a reasonable doubt that a person for whom commitment is sought is mentally ill?

C. PROCEDURAL PREREQUISITES TO INSTITUTIONALIZATION

HERYFORD v. PARKER

United States Court of Appeals for the Tenth Circuit, 1968
396 F.2d 393

Before MURRAH, Chief Judge, HILL and SETH, Circuit Judges.
MURRAH, Chief Judge.

This case was first before us on denial of a writ of habeas corpus sought by a mother as natural guardian in behalf of her mentally deficient son. The complaint was that the son was committed to the Wyoming State Training School for feeble-minded and epileptic under applicable Wyoming statutes without due process and particularly that he was denied his right to counsel and confrontation. We remanded to determine whether in view of *In the Matter of the Application of Gault, etc.*, 387 U.S. 1, 87 S.Ct. 1428, 18 L.Ed.2d 527, the patient had a constitutional right to counsel, and if so, whether his mother as natural guardian could and did waive it. 10 Cir., 379 F.2d 556. On remand the writ was granted and the State of Wyoming brings this appeal. We affirm.

The background and undisputed facts are that in 1946, when Charles Parker was about nine years of age, his mother requested the County Attorney to institute proceedings for commitment of Charles to the Wyoming Training School for feeble-minded and epileptic. The Wyoming Statutory procedure, i.e., see 9-444 thru 9-449, Wyo.Stat., provides that commitment of the feeble-minded and epileptic may be initiated by application of a relative or guardian or the prosecuting attorney on a form subscribed to under oath which states that the applicant verily believes that the proposed patient is a fit subject for care, treatment and training in the school and asks that the subject be brought before the District Court for examination and commitment; that if the subject be a minor without parent or guardian, the Judge shall appoint a guardian *ad litem* to represent him. The statute further provides that the application shall be accompanied by a written history of the proposed patient certified under oath by an examining physician in which he answers prescribed questions touching suitability of the subject for admission to the school. The court shall, upon receipt of the application and history, cause the proposed patient to be examined by a physician and psychologist separately, and each shall certify that the subject is fit for care, treatment and training at the school. Provision is made for a hearing on the application pursuant to notice before a judge of the District Court, and it becomes the duty of the County and Prosecuting Attorney to "appear and prosecute the application on behalf of the state." § 9-449. The applicant, at least one examiner and the patient (unless his presence would be injurious to him) shall be present, and the court is authorized to require any other person to appear and testify. The application, history and certificates of suitability by the two doctors are expressly made a part of the evidence in the case, and the statute pertinently provides that the proposed patient "may be represented by counsel." § 9-449. A jury may be demanded, and if it is found that the patient should be committed, the judge may forthwith order commitment.

Pursuant to this procedure, and at the instance of the mother, the application for Parker's commitment was signed by the County Attorney, and a hearing was conducted at which the prosecuting attorney, the certifying psychologist and the mother as natural guardian were all present. While the certifying physician did not appear, both his and the certifying psychologist's certificates of suitability were admitted into evidence. At no time during the hearing was Charles Parker represented by retained or appointed counsel, nor was he represented by a court appointed guardian *ad litem*. Parker was found to be a fit subject and was committed to the training school where he remained continually until 1963, at which time he was released to the custody of his parents. In 1965, against the wishes of his parents, he was returned to the training school where he remains to this day.

Subsequent to Parker's return to the school, this federal habeas corpus proceedings was instituted alleging that he had been denied his constitutional right to counsel and confrontation in the proceedings pursuant to which he was originally confined in the training school. On remand the trial judge held that in view of *Gault*, Parker was constitutionally entitled to the assistance of counsel in the original commitment proceedings, and that while his mother as natural guardian could have waived his rights, she did not expressly do so.

In the posture in which the case comes to us on this appeal the constitutionality of the Wyoming statute as according due process is not directly in issue. The state apparently takes the position, as indeed it must, that the standards for due process erected in *Gault* are not the same as required in civil proceedings such as these. The argument seems to be that the nature of the proceedings in *Gault* is easily distinguishable from ours in that *Gault* was concerned with commitment for correction or rehabilitation of juveniles, while our proceedings are concerned solely with civil commitment for teaching and training the mentally deficient.

It is true that *Gault* involved procedures for adjudging a juvenile offender "Delinquent" and committing him to a state institution. The query was whether he is entitled to the same Fourteenth Amendment due process procedures required to deprive an adult of his freedom for the commission of a crime. The effect of the decision was to place both juveniles and adults on the same Fourteenth Amendment due process footing. Mr. Justice Fortas reasoned that, "It is of no constitutional consequence . . . that the institution to which [a juvenile] is committed is called an Industrial School. The fact of the matter is that however euphemistic the title, a 'receiving home' or an 'industrial school' for juveniles is an institution of confinement in which the child is incarcerated for a greater or lesser time. His world becomes a 'building with whitewashed walls, regimented routine and institutional hours . . . '." The overriding consideration of the court was that in either case the determination carried with it the "awesome prospect of incarceration in a state institution." The court concluded that in these circumstances the Due Process Clause of the Fourteenth Amendment entitles the child to the fundamental right of representation by counsel, confrontation and cross-examination.

We do not have the distinction between the procedures used to commit juveniles and adults as in *Gault*. But, like *Gault*, and of utmost importance, we have a

situation in which the liberty of an individual is at stake, and we think the reasoning in
Gault emphatically applies. It matters not whether the proceedings be labeled "civil"
or "criminal" or whether the subject matter be mental instability or juvenile delinquency. It is the likelihood of involuntary incarceration—whether for punishment as an
adult for a crime, rehabilitation as a juvenile for delinquency, or treatment and training
as a feeble-minded or mental incompetent—which commands observance of the constitutional safeguards of due process. Where, as in both proceedings for juveniles and
mentally deficient persons, the state undertakes to act in *parens patriae,* it has the
inescapable duty to vouchsafe due process, and this necessarily includes the duty to see
that a subject of an involuntary commitment proceedings is afforded the opportunity to
the guiding hand of legal counsel at every step of the proceedings, unless effectively
waived by one authorized to act in his behalf. Certainly, this duty is not discharged
when, as here, the prosecuting attory undertakes to "prosecute the application [for
commitment] on behalf of the state," and the proposed patient is not otherwise represented by counsel. *In re Custody of a Minor,* 102 U.S.App.D.C. 94, 250 F.2d 419;
Kent v. *United States,* 383 U.S. 541, 86 S.Ct. 1045, 16 L.Ed.2d 84; *McDaniel* v.
Shea, 108 U.S.App.D.C. 15, 278 F.2d 460; *Dooling* v. *Overholser,* 100
U.S.App.D.C. 247, 243 F.2d 825; *Shioutakon* v. *District of Columbia,* 98 U.S.
App.D.C. 371, 236 F.2d 666; Anno. 87 A.L.R.2d 950. Nor is it sufficient that the
Wyoming statute permissively provides that the proposed patient "may be represented
by counsel." Fourteenth Amendment due process requires that the infirm person, or
one acting in his behalf, be fully advised of his rights and accorded each of them unless
knowingly and understandingly waived.

We recognize, as did the court in *Gault* that special problems may arise with
respect to the effective waiver of rights by minors and mentally deficient persons. But,
we need not decide here whether Parker's mother as natural guardian, having set into
motion the commitment machinery, represented such conflicting interests that she
could not effectively waive her son's right to counsel, for we agree with the trial court,
no one seems to dispute, and it is sufficient to affirmance that there was no express
attempt to waive such right.

This brings us to the question of the retroactivity of the Fourteenth Amendment
due process standards recognized for the first time in Gault and made applicable to
situations like ours. The crux of the state's argument seems to be that there is nothing in
the principles announced in Gault to warrant retroactivity and its application in collateral proceedings would result in wholesale release of immates in the Wyoming institutions and like institutions all over the country.

Retroactivity of a rule establishing a new standard for Fourteenth Amendment
due process is not automatic. Nor does it have case-by-case application. Rather, as we
read the case law as epitomized in *Stovall* v. *Deno,* 388 U.S. 293, 297, 87 S.Ct. 1967,
18 L.Ed.2d 1199, and *Reck* v. *Pate,* 367 U.S. 433, 81 S.Ct. 1541, 6 L.Ed.2d 948,
retroactivity depends upon a pragmatic balancing of the public interests against the
gravity of the right involved. Thus, if the rule or newly established standard goes to the
very integrity of the fact finding process by which liberty is taken—as where the
accused was convicted without benefit of counsel, i.e., see *Gideon* v. *Wainwright,*
372 U.S. 335, 83 S.Ct. 792, 9 L.Ed.2d 799, or upon a coerced confession, i.e., see

Jackson v. *Denno,* 378 U.S. 368, 84 S.Ct. 1774, 12 L.Ed.2d 908, or was denied an appeal because of his poverty, i.e., see *Griffin* v. *People of State of Illinois,* 351 U.S. 12, [additional citations omitted]—retroactivity should be accorded even though it may result in wholesale consideration of the standards by which factual determinations were made.

In our case the fundamental right to counsel is involved and failure to have counsel at every step of the proceedings may result in indefinite and oblivious confinement and work shameful injustice. Indeed, the expressed concern lest retroactivity in cases like these result in wholesale release from confinement in mental institutions is a compelling reason for the desirability, if not necessity, for retroactivity in our case.

Affirmed.

NOTES

1. Although the court's ruling that due process applies to the commitment proceedings seems straightforward, at least one state court decision prior to *Heryford* and prior to *In re Gault* had reached an opposite conclusion. In *Prochaska* v. *Brinegar,* 251 Iowa 834, 102 N.W.2d 870 (1960), a habeus corpus challenge to a patient's confinement in a mental hospital, the Supreme Court of Iowa engaged in the following remarkable reasoning:

> It must be kept in mind that Appellant is not charged with a crime and is not so incarcerated. He is being restrained of his liberty in that he is not free to come and go at will but such restraint is not in the way of punishment, but for his own protection and welfare as well as for the benefit of society. Such loss of liberty is not such liberty as is within the meaning of the constitutional provision that "no person shall be deprived of life, liberty or property without due process of law." (*Id.* at 102 N.W.2d 872.)

Are there two types of liberty—one of which is constitutionally protected and the other of which is not?

2. One of the questions held not to be at issue in the factual situation in *Heryford*—whether parents can effectively waive the procedural due process rights of their children for whom commitment is sought—has been the subject of much subsequent litigation. See, e.g., *Bartley* v. *Kremens,* 402 F.Supp., 1039 (E.D.Pa. 1975), vacated on procedural grounds, 431 U.S. 119 (1977), opinion reinstated sub nom. *Institutionalized Juveniles* v. *Secretary of Public Welfare,* 459 F.Supp. 30 (E.D.Pa. 1978); *Saville* v. *Treadway,* 404 F.Supp. 430 (M.D.Tenn. 1974); *J.L.* v. *Parham,* 412 F.Supp. 112 (M.D.Ga. 1976), prob. jur. noted, 431 U.S. 936 (1977); *New York State Association for Retarded Children* v. *Rockefeller,* 357 F.Supp. 752, 762 (E.D.N.Y. 1973); *Horacek* v. *Exon,* 357 F.Supp. 71 (D.Neb. 1973), Memorandum and Order of June 4, 1974, p. 1; *In re Roger S.,* 19 Cal.3d 921, 141 Cal.Rptr. 298, 569 P.2d 1286 (1977).

Thus far, these courts have ruled uniformly that, because of potential conflicts of interest between parents and child in regard to commitment, parents may not make a waiver of the child's due process rights. See Murdock, C., "Civil Rights of the Mentally Retarded: Some Critical Issues," 47 *Notre Dame Lawyer* 133, 140–144 (1972), for a discussion of some of the societal pressures that influence parents to institutionalize their mentally handicapped children. It is such pressures, concerns, and interests of parents that can result in a "fundamental conflict of interest between a parent who is ready to avoid the responsibility of caring for an abnormal child and the best interest of the child." *New York State Association for Retarded Children* v. *Carey, supra* at 762. See generally, Ellis, J., "Volunteering Children: Parental Commitment of Minors to Mental Institutions," 62 *Cal.L.Rev.* 840 (1974); Herr, S., "Civil Rights, Uncivil Asylums and the Retarded," 43 *Cincinnati L. Rev.* 679, 709–725 (1974).

LYNCH v. BAXLEY

United States District Court for the Middle District of Alabama, Northern Division,
1974
386 F.Supp. 378

Before RIVES, Circuit Judge, and JOHNSON and VARNER, District Judges.

JOHNSON, District Judge:

The named plaintiff and intervening plaintiff,[1] suing on their own behalf and as representatives of a class composed of persons who are now, or who may be, involuntarily civilly committed in Alabama, seek to have three statutes[2] authorizing

---

[1]Plaintiff Jean P. Lynch is presently incarcerated in Bryce Hospital pursuant to an involuntary commitment order. Leave to intervene was granted to Jesse M. Hughes, whose handwritten petition to this Court alleged that he was in imminent danger of being involuntarily committed by the Probate Judge of Clarke County. Although Mr. Hughes was released rather than committed upon the recommendation of the former Commissioner of Mental Health, Dr. Stonewall Stickney, intervening plaintiff believes that his "admittedly eccentric habits" render him continually vulnerable to involuntary commitment under Alabama's statutory procedures.

[2]Ala. Code, tit. 15, § 432 (1958), provides:

> Any insane person who is at large and not under the control, restraint, or management of any person may be taken into custody or arrested by any officer or person and carried immediately to the probate judge of the county, who shall issue a mittimus or commitment of such insane person either to the county jail or the Alabama state hospitals until inquisition proceedings may be had as to such person so confined. Thereafter the person so confined shall abide by the decree or order of the inquisition proceedings. When such person is brought before the probate judge, if the judge shall be satisfied that the person brought before him is not insane, he may direct the discharge of such person from custody and arrest and decline to institute the proceedings of lunacy. But if the judge of probate be satisfied that such person is insane, or if he has a reasonable doubt as to his sanity, he shall have the person or persons so bringing the alleged insane person before him to institute the inquisition proceedings of lunacy as is now provided by law.

Ala. Code, tit. 45, § 208 (1958), provides in relevant part:

> When a relative, friend, or other party interested desires to place a person as a patient in one of the state hospitals, he shall apply to the judge of probate of the county in which the person resides, and the judge of probate, without delay, shall investigate the case, by examining witnesses, or not, as he sees fit, and, if he is reasonably convinced that the case is a suitable one, he shall make application to the superintendent at Tuscaloosa for his, or her admission, and shall accompany his application with as full and as explicit answers as possible to the following interrogatories describing the case. . . .

Ala. Code, tit. 45, § 210 (1958), provides in relevant part:

> When informed by the superintendent that the person can be received as a patient, the judge of probate shall examine witnesses, at least one of whom shall be a physician, and fully investigate the facts of the case, either with or without a jury, and either with or without the presence in court of the person, the grade of whose mental disqualification is under investigation, according to his discretion; and if the judge, or the jury, as the case may be, believe that the person is sufficiently defective

involuntary commitment declared unconstitutional on their face and as applied and to have their enforcement enjoined.

This action arises under the Fourteenth Amendment to the Constitution of the United States. Plaintiffs invoke the jurisdiction of this Court pursuant to 42 U.S.C. § 1983 and 28 U.S.C § 1343(3).

The defendants are the Attorney General of the State of Alabama; the Commissioner of the Department of Mental Health of the State of Alabama; and the Probate Judges of Montgomery County, Alabama, and Clarke County, Alabama, individually and as representatives of all other judges of probate in the State of Alabama.

Because an injunction was sought against statutes of statewide application whose constitutionality was at issue, plaintiffs requested that a three-judge court be convened. A survey of the pertinent case law indicated that the complaint raised a substantial constitutional question, *Ex parte Poresky,* 290 U.S. 30, 54 S.Ct. 3, 78 L.Ed. 152, (1933), but that the defense of the constitutionality of the statutes was neither frivolous nor foreclosed by prior decisions of the United States Supreme Court, *Bailey* v. *Patterson,* 369 U.S. 31, 82 S.Ct. 549, 7 L.Ed.2d 512 (1962). Consequently, a three-judge court was constituted pursuant to the requirements of 28 U.S.C. §§ 2281 and 2284.

The case is submitted upon the pleadings, briefs, stipulations, and documentary evidence. All parties are in agreement that the Due Process Clause of the Fourteenth Amendment applies to involuntary commitment proceedings, *Specht* v. *Patterson,* 386 U.S. 605, 608, 87 S.Ct. 1209, 18 L.Ed.2d 326 (1967); *Donaldson* v. *O'Connor,* 493 F.2d 507, 520 (5th Cir. 1974), and that certain minimal constitutional standards and safeguards must be observed throughout the commitment process. Whereas plaintiffs argue that the statutes in question are unconstitutional both on their face and as applied, defendants maintain that they are constitutional on their face but concede that they may have been applied unconstitutionally in some cases. There being substantial controversy concerning the specific minimal standards and safeguards mandated by the Due Process Clause, the parties in this case join in requesting this Court to determine those constitutionally required standards and safeguards.

I

From the pleadings and stipulations in this case, it appears that plaintiff Jean P. Lynch, a resident of Montgomery County, was arrested by the Montgomery County Sheriff's Department on November 2, 1973, pursuant to a warrant issued that date by the defendant Probate Judge of Montgomery County under the authority of Ala. Code, tit. 15, § 432 (1958). Said warrant was sworn out by one Theresa Lynch, daughter of the named plaintiff, who averred that plaintiff "is at large and not under the control, restraint or management of any person, and that she is not able to restrain or manage said person, and that it is necessary for his [sic] own and the public good that she be

---

mentally to be sent as a patient to a hospital for insane persons, the judge of probate shall make two copies of a certificate of mental disqualification, one copy of which shall be filed in his office and the other he shall send with the patient to the hospital. . . .

restrained and an inquisition proceedings had to determine whether or not she should be committed to an insane hospital.''

On the same day the warrant was issued, inquiry was made by the probate court as to the availability of facilities at Bryce Hospital for the accommodation of plaintiff, who was at that time confined in the Montgomery County Jail. Also on the same day an order was issued by the probate judge directing the Sheriff to summon six (6) jurors at 2:00 p.m. that day to determine whether ''the said Jean P. Lynch is so deficient mentally that she should be committed to an insane hospital.'' At the appointed time, a hearing was held, and the jury returned a verdict that plaintiff was ''sufficiently defective mentally to be sent as a patient to a hospital for insane persons.'' It is undisputed that plaintiff was not present at the hearing, that she was not represented by counsel, and that she was not advised of any right to the presence of counsel and the appointment of counsel if indigent. On November 6, 1973, plaintiff was ordered committed to Bryce Hospital by the defendant Probate Judge of Montgomery County under the authority of Ala.Code, tit. 45, §§ 208 and 211. Plaintiff remains at this date an involuntary patient in Bryce Hospital.

The parties have entered into the following stipulations regarding the procedures ordinarily followed in the course of involuntary civil commitments in Alabama:

1. The individual who is the subject of the commitment proceeding is given no notice of hearing, is not present during the hearing, is not informed of his/her right to counsel, and is not appointed counsel if indigent.
2. The defendant Probate Judge of Montgomery County, as well as certain other judges of probate, empanels a jury composed of six (6) persons to determine if the subject of an involuntary commitment proceeding should be committed to a state mental hospital.
3. The defendant Probate Judge of Clarke County, as well as certain other judges of probate, does not empanel a jury in civil commitment proceedings.
4. The only standard which is charged to the jury (if there is a jury) and which is applied by the trier of fact (judge or jury) is that contained in Ala.Code, tit. 45, § 205:

> A person shall be adjudged insane who has been found by a proper court sufficiently deficient or defective mentally to require that, for his own or others' welfare, he be moved to the insane hospital for restraint, care and treatment.

II

This action is properly maintainable as a Rule 23(b)(2) class action because defendants are alleged to have taken action or refused to take action with respect to the plaintiff class as a whole, and final relief of an injunctive and a declaratory nature, settling the legality of the behavior with respect to the class as a whole, is appropriate. See Advisory Committee Note to Rule 23(b)(2). As a practical matter, it is immaterial that certain potential class members may be satisfied with their present status and indifferent as to the constitutionality of the statutes herein attacked. If the statutes are declared unconstitutional, all those similarly situated will be equally affected. The fact that each member of the class is subject to the same deprivation of constitutional rights as the representative parties is sufficient to fulfill the representation requirements of Rule 23(a)(3) and (4). *Sullivan* v. *Houston Independent School District,* 307 F.Supp. 1328, 1338 (S.D.Tex. 1969). Thus, assuming, as the dissent does, that there may be members of the class who would not benefit by the *effect* of a declaration of the unconstitutionality of Alabama's civil commitment statutes, this is not determinative of plaintiffs' representative status. *Davy* v. *Sullivan,* 354 F.Supp. 1320, 1326 (M.D.Ala. 1973).

III

This Court concludes from the evidence presented that the named plaintiff and members of the class she represents have been involuntarily civilly committed to Bryce and Searcy Hospitals as a result of proceedings and procedures which do not comport with the minimum requirements of the Due Process Clause of the Fourteenth Amendment. *Specht* v. *Patterson, supra.*

We further conclude and declare that Ala.Code, tit. 15, § 432 (1958), which provides for emergency detention in the county jail or state mental hospitals, and Ala.Code, tit. 45 § 210 (1958), which outlines certain procedures for involuntary commitment to such hospitals, are unconstitutional on their face because they purport to authorize *ex parte* and summary deprivation of liberty without any of the rudimentary protections long recognized as required by the due process of law. Unlike our dissenting brother, we find it unnecessary to reach the question of whether these particular statutes might be saved by excising from them certain constitutionally offensive words and phrases. On the contrary, we are compelled to hold each violative of the Fourteenth Amendment on account of the absence of the substantial procedural protections constitutionally required, as well as because of the offending provisions present in the statutes.

While recognizing that Ala.Code, tit. 45, § 208 (1958), like the other statutes herein attacked, may have been applied unconstitutionally on occasion, we perceive no facial infirmity with respect to Title 45, Section 208, nor anything constitutionally offensive with respect to the authority therein conferred upon the probate judges of Alabama.

IV

This Court shall now proceed to act forth those standards and safeguards which, at a minimum, the Due Process Clause requires for the protection of persons whose liberty is placed in jeopardy as a consequence of their becoming the subjects of civil commitment proceedings against their will.

Due to the wording of the commitment statutes in question and the practices and procedures followed by the probate judges of Alabama in involuntary commitment proceedings, all Alabama probate court commitments are to be presumed involuntary unless and until there has been a judicial determination in an adversary proceeding during which the person proposed to be committed is represented by counsel, that the commitment is in fact a voluntary one, knowingly and intelligently consented to by the person to be committed. In the absence of any such judicial determination, the commitment proceedings are involuntary as a matter of law and must comply with the following minimum standards:

(A) Emergency detention

It cannot be seriously doubted that the state may on occasion have a compelling interest in the emergency detention of those who theaten immediate and serious violence to themselves or others. Since the interests of these emergency detainees in retaining their liberty and avoiding unwarranted civil commitment are comparable to the interests of persons accused of criminal offenses in retaining their liberty and avoiding wrongful incarceration, the burden on the state to justify the emergency detention must be similarly heavy. As one means of assuring that persons accused of crimes are not held in custody and involuntarily deprived of their liberty without a showing of probable cause to believe that they have committed punishable offenses, it is generally required that such persons be brought before a judicial officer without unnecessary delay after arrest to determine whether they are being detained on probable cause. Rule 5, Federal Rules of Criminal Procedure; *McNabb* v. *United States,* 318 U.S. 332, 343–344, 63 S.Ct. 608, 87 L.Ed. 819 (1943); *Brown* v. *Fauntleroy,* 143 U.S.App.D.C. 116, 442 F.2d 838, 839 (1971). Likewise, in the situation here, where a person said to be mentally ill and dangerous is involuntarily detained, he must be given a hearing within a reasonable time to test whether the detention is based upon probable cause to believe that confinement is necessary under constitutionally proper standards for commitment. *In re Barnard,* 147 U.S.App.D.C. 302, 455 F.2d 1370, 1374 (1971); *Lessard* v. *Schmidt,* 349 F.Supp. 1078, 1090–1091 (E.D.Wis. 1972), vacated and remanded 414 U.S. 473, 94 S.Ct. 713, 38 L.Ed.2d 661 (1974); *Fhagen* v. *Miller,* 306 F.Supp. 634, 638 (S.D.N.Y. 1969).

Emergency detention without a hearing on its appropriateness and necessity can be justified only for the length of time required to arrange a probable cause hearing before the probate judge or other judicial officer empowered by law to commit persons to Alabama mental institutions. *Lessard* v. *Schmidt,* 349 F.Supp. at 1091. In no event may such detention in the absence of a probable cause hearing exceed seven (7) days from the date of the initial detention.

Due process does not require that the probable cause hearing be characterized by the formality of the proceedings for final adjudication of commitment; neither does it require that each and every constitutional protection required in the subsequent proceedings be accorded. At the very least, however, due process does require that the hearing be preceded by adequate notice informing the person (or his counsel) of the factual grounds upon which the proposed commitment is predicated and the reasons for the necessity of confinement: that the person be represented by counsel, appointed if necessary; and that the person proposed to be committed be present at the hearing unless his presence is waived by counsel and approved by the court after an adversary hearing at the conclusion of which the court judicially finds and determines that the detainee is so mentally or physically ill as to be incapable of attending the probable cause hearing.

Just as emergency detention is justified only until a probable cause hearing can be conducted, temporary detention following a finding of probable cause to believe that confinement is necessary can be justified only for the length of time required to arrange a full hearing on the need for commitment. Due process requires that such hearing be held within a reasonable time following initial detention, but in no event sooner than will permit adequate preparation of the case by counsel or later than thirty (30) days from the date of the initial detention.

(B) Formal commitment proceedings

(1) *Notice.* Due process requires that notice be given of the hearing to be held on the necessity for commitment "sufficiently in advance of scheduled court proceedings so that reasonable opportunity to prepare will be afforded." *In re Gault,* 387 U.S. 1, 33, 87 S.Ct. 1428, 1446, 18 L.Ed.2d 527 (1967); *Lessard* v. *Schmidt,* 349 F.Supp. at 1092. Such notice should include the date, time, and place of the hearing; a clear statement of the purpose of the proceedings and the possible consequences to the subject thereof; the alleged factual basis for the proposed commitment; and a statement of the legal standard upon which commitment is authorized.

(2) *Presence of the person proposed to be committed.* Due process requires the presence of the person proposed to be involuntarily committed at all judicial proceedings conducted for that purpose, *Specht* v. *Patterson,* 386 U.S. at 610, 87 S.Ct. 1209, unless the right has been knowingly and intelligently waived by such person or by adversary counsel acting in his behalf and for good cause shown. Waiver by the person to be committed in his own behalf is valid only upon acceptance by the court following a judicial determination that he understands his rights and is competent to waive them. Waiver by counsel in his client's behalf is valid only upon approval by the court after an adversary hearing at the conclusion of which the court judicially finds and determines that the person proposed to be committed is so mentally or physically ill as to be incapable of attending such proceedings.

The right to be present at the hearing necessarily includes the right to participate therein to the extent of the subject's ability. Due process is not accorded by a hearing in which the individual, though physically present, has no meaningful opportunity to participate because of incapacity caused by excessive or inappropriate medication. *Lessard* v. *Schmidt,* 349 F.Supp. at 1092.

(3) *Right to counsel.* The subject of an involuntary civil commitment proceeding has the right to the effective assistance of counsel at all significant stages[5] of the commitment process. *Heryford* v. *Parker,* 396 F.2d 393, 396 (10th Cir. 1968); *Lessard* v. *Schmidt,* 349 F.Supp. at 1099; *Dixon* v. *Attorney General of Commonwealth of Pennsylvania,* 325 F.Supp. 966, 974 (M.D.Pa. 1971). Further, he has the right to be advised of his right to counsel, *In re Gault,* 387 U.S. at 42, 87 S.Ct. 1428, and to the appointment of counsel if indigent. *Lessard* v. *Schmidt,* 349 F.Supp. at

---

[5] By "significant stages" we should be understood to mean all judicial proceedings and any other official proceedings at which a decision is, or can be, made which may result in a detrimental change in the conditions of the subject's liberty. The right to counsel does not, however, extend to preliminary information-gathering stages, such as psychiatric interviews, where custodial decisions are not made. It is generally agreed that the examination stage is most effectively conducted according to the directions of the examining physician and that the presence of counsel, unless specifically invited by the physician, might unduly interfere with the objective evaluation of the patient's mental condition. *Lessard* v. *Schmidt,* 349 F.Supp. at 1100.

1097; *Dixon* v. *Attorney General,* 325 F.Supp. at 974. Counsel must be made available far enough in advance of the final commitment hearing to ensure adequate opportunity for preparation. In order to aid counsel in the effective presentation of his client's interests, the names of the examining physicians and all others who may testify in support of the petition to commit must be made available to counsel in advance of the hearing, and he must be afforded a reasonable opportunity to inspect any documents and records pertaining to the case. *Sarzen* v. *Gaughan,* 489 F.2d at 1085, 1086.

The right to counsel is a right to representative counsel occupying a traditional adversarial role. Where state law requires or permits the appointment of a guardian *ad litem,* such appointment shall be deemed to satisfy the constitutional right to counsel if, but only if, the appointed guardian is a licensed attorney and occupies a truly adversary position. To the extent that these conditions are fulfilled, this Court perceives no difference between a guardian *ad litem* and other appointed counsel.

(4) *Requisite findings to support an order of commitment.* It has long been recognized in this country that the involuntary confinement of the mentally ill is justified only under certain specific circumstances where conduct is threatened with which the state has the obligation to deal:

> [T]he right to restrain an insane person of his liberty is found in that great law of humanity, which makes it necessary to confine those whose going at large would be dangerous to themselves or others. . . . And the necessity which creates the law, creates the limitation of the law. The questions must then arise in each particular case, whether a patient's own safety, or that of others, requires that he should be restrained for a certain time, and whether restraint is necessary for his restoration or will be conducive thereto. The restraint can continue as long as the necessity continues. This is the limitation, and the proper limitation. Matter of Josiah Oakes, 8 Law Rep. 123, 125 (Supreme Judicial Court of Massachusetts, 1845).

Like the Massachusetts Court—and more recently—the Supreme Court of the United States has indicated that the "massive curtailment of liberty," *Humphrey* v. *Cady,* 405 U.S. 504, 509, 92 S.Ct. 1048, 31 L.Ed.2d 394 (1972), occasioned by involuntary civil commitment is permissible only in those situations in which threatened or actual behavior is of a nature which the state may legitimately control: specifically, where the conduct resulting from mental illness poses a serious threat of substantial harm to self or to others. In *Humphrey* v. *Cady,* the court interpreted a Wisconsin statute authorizing involuntary civil commitment of a "proper subject for custody and treatment" as requiring a "social and legal judgment that [the mentally ill individual's] potential for doing harm, to himself or to others, is great enough to justify such a massive curtailment of liberty." *Id.* And in *Jackson* v. *Indiana,* 406 U.S. 715, 728, 92 S.Ct. 1845, 1853, 32 L.Ed.2d 435 (1972), the court construed a statute authorizing detention "in the interest of the welfare of such person or . . . others. . . . " to require an independent showing of dangerousness. See also *Donaldson* v. *O'Connor,* 493 F.2d 507, 520 (5th Cir. 1974).

Because the power of the state to curtail the liberty of a citizen not convicted of a crime, but believed to be suffering from a mental illness, is thus limited, it must follow that an involuntary commitment order must be based upon specific findings sufficient to bring the subject of the proceedings within the limited sphere of legitimate governmental concern. Accordingly, each order of involuntary commitment shall be supported by the following minimum findings made by the fact-finder upon the basis of the evidence introduced at the commitment hearing:

(a) The person to be committed is mentally ill.

(b) The person to be committed poses a real and present threat of substantial harm to himself or to others. *Dixon* v. *Attorney General*, 325 F.Supp. at 974.

Although dangerousness to self and dangerousness to others are frequently considered together, it is clear that they actually represent quite different state interests. Commitment on account of dangerousness to others serves the police power, while commitment for dangerousness to self partakes of the *parens patriae* notion that the state is the ultimate guardian of those of its citizens who are incapable of caring for their own interests. See *In re Ballay*, 157 U.S.App.D.C. 59, 482 F.2d 648, 658 (1973). Valid exercise of the *parens patriae* power presumes an incapability to manage one's affairs that approximates, if it is not identical with, legal incompetence to act. Consequently, in order to deprive a person alleged to be a danger to himself alone of the right to choose between treatment and liberty, the state must first demonstrate that, because of his mental illness, he lacks the capacity to weigh for himself the risks of freedom and the benefits of hospitalization.

A finding of dangerousness indicates the likelihood that the person to be committed will inflict serious harm on himself or on others. In the case of dangerousness to others, this threat of harm comprehends the positive infliction of injury—ordinarily physical injury, but possibly emotional injury as well. In the case of dangerousness to self, both the threat of physical injury and discernible physical neglect may warrant a finding of dangerousness. Although he does not threaten actual violence to himself, a person may be properly commitable under the dangerousness standard if it can be shown that he is mentally ill, that his mental illness manifests itself in neglect or refusal to care for himself, that such neglect or refusal poses a real and present threat of substantial harm to his well-being, and that he is incompetent to determine for himself whether treatment for his mental illness would be desirable.

(c) The danger posed by the person to be committed has been evidenced by a recent overt act. Due process requires that the need for confinement be based upon a substantial likelihood that dangerous behavior will be engaged in unless restraints are applied. While the actual assessment of the likelihood of danger calls for an exercise of medical judgment, the sufficiency of the evidence to support such a determination is fundamentally a legal question. A mere expectancy that danger-productive behavior might be engaged in does not rise to the level of legal significance when the consequence of such an evaluation is involuntary confinement. To confine a citizen against his will because he is likely to be dangerous in the future, it must be shown that he has actually been dangerous in the recent past and that such danger was manifested by an overt act, attempt or threat to do substantial harm to himself or to another. *Lessard* v. *Schmidt*, 349 F.Supp. at 1093; *Cross* v. *Harris*, 135 U.S.App.D.C. 259, 418 F.2d 1095, 1102 (1969); cf. *Millard* v. *Harris*, 406 F.2d at 973.

(d) There is treatment available for the illness diagnosed. Because patients involuntarily committed through non-criminal proceedings "unquestionably have a constitutional right to receive such individual treatment as will give each of them a realistic opportunity to be cured or to improve his or her mental condition," *Wyatt* v. *Stickney*, 325 F.Supp. 781, 784 (M.D.Ala. 1971), affirmed sub nom., *Wyatt* v. *Aderholt*, 503 F.2d 1305, No. 72-2634 (5th Cir. 1974); *Donaldson* v. *O'Connor*, 493 F.2d 507, 527 (5th Cir. 1974), the fact-finder must ascertain the existence and availability of a treatment program for the illness suffered by the person whose commitment is sought.

An exception to this general requirement of due process is recognized in the case of a presently and seriously dangerous person for whose illness there is no known cure or treatment. In such instances, the state may well have an obligation under the police power to restrain the liberty of the threatening individual, even though his condition is not amenable to any currently available treatment. Since the involuntary commitment of an untreatable person is an exception to the general due process requirement that treatment be available and afforded, the committing court must make a finding, based upon clear and convincing evidence, that confinement even without a proposed treatment program is necessary for the safety and well-being of the community and of the person to be committed. Such orders of commitment, when granted, shall provide that, should treatment for the patient's illness become available at any time during the period of his confinement, such treatment shall be made available to him immediately.

(5) *The proposed commitment is the least restrictive alternative necessary and available for the person's illness.* In addition to the findings which are required to be made by the fact-finder, the state, acting through the probate court or whichever of its agents designates the place of confinement, shall have the burden of demonstrating that the proposed commitment is to the least restrictive environment consistent with the needs of the person to be committed. *Welsch* v. *Likins*, 373 F.Supp. 487, 502 (D.Minn. 1974); *cf. Covington* v. *Harris*, 136 U.S.App.D.C. 35, 419 F.2d 617, 623 (1969); *Wyatt* v. *Stickney*, 344 F.Supp. 373, 379 (M.D.Ala. 1972), affirmed sub nom., *Wyatt* v. *Aderholt*, 503 F.2d 1305, No. 72-2634 (5th Cir. 1974). This duty of investigation and burden of persuasion derive from the general and well-recognized principle that " . . . even though the governmental purpose be legitimate and substantial, that purpose cannot be pursued by means that broadly stifle fundamental personal liberties when the end can be more narrowly achieved." *Shelton* v. *Tucker*, 364 U.S. 479, 488, 81 S.Ct. 247, 252, 5 L.Ed.2d 231 (1960).

Specifically, the state, which knows or has the means of knowing the available alternatives, must bear the burden of proving what alternatives are available, what alternatives were investigated, and why the investigated alternatives were not deemed suitable. *Lessard* v. *Schmidt*, 349 F.Supp. at 1096.

Moreover, it should be pointed out that due process does not preclude, and indeed may require, commitment of a person suffering from a mental illness to an environment other than full-time confinement in Bryce or Searcy Hospital. Possible alternatives include voluntary or court-ordered out-patient treatment, day treatment in the hospital, night treatment in the hospital, placement in a private hospital, placement in the custody of a willing and responsible relative or friend, placement in a nursing home, referral to a community health clinic, home health aide services, and prescribed medication.

(6) *Standard of proof.*   The standard of proof required to be adduced in an adjudicatory proceeding is "the kind of question which has traditionally been left to the judiciary to resolve . . . " *Woodby* v. *Immigration Service,* 385 U.S. 276, 284, 87 S.Ct. 483, 487, 17 L.Ed.2d 362 (1966). Its function, as pointed out by Mr. Justice Harlan, concurring in *In re Winship,* is "to instruct the fact-finder concerning the degree.of confidence our society thinks he should have in the correctness of factual conclusions for a particular type of adjudication." 397 U.S. 358, 370, 90 S.Ct. 1068, 1076, 25 L.Ed.2d 368 (1970). It is "more than an empty semantic exercise; it reflects the value society places on individual liberty." *Tippett* v. *State of Maryland,* 436 F.2d 1153, 1166 (4th Cir. 1971), Sobeloff, J., concurring in part and dissenting in part, cert. dismissed as improvidently granted, sub nom. *Murel* v. *Baltimore City Criminal Court,* 407 U.S. 355, 92 S.Ct. 2091, 32 L.Ed.2d 791 (1972).

The degree of confidence demanded of any judicial determination reflects in part the significance of the interests to be affected thereby. It cannot be doubted that the interests of those facing civil commitment proceedings are of the most serious nature:

> The destruction of an individual's personal freedoms effected by civil commitment is scarcely less total than that effected by confinement in a penitentiary. Indeed, civil commitment, because it is for an indefinite term, may in some ways involve a more serious abridgement of personal freedom than imprisonment for commission of a crime usually does. Civil commitment involves stigmatizing the affected individuals, and the stigma attached, though in theory less severe than the stigma attached to criminal conviction, may in reality be as severe, or more so. *Donaldson* v. *O'Connor,* 493 F.2d 507, 520 (5th Cir. 1974).

Because the stigmatization and loss of liberty attendant upon forced confinement are of the most profound consequence to the individual affected, due process demands that he be subjected to such disabilities only if the necessity for his commitment is proved by evidence having the highest degree of certitude reasonably attainable in view of the nature of the matter at issue. In a civil commitment proceeding, the questions involved are the primarily subjective ones of the subject's mental condition and the likelihood that he will be dangerous in the future. Such subjective determinations cannot ordinarily be made with the same degree of certainty that might be achieved where purely objective facts and occurrences are at issue. Consequently, the trier of fact must be persuaded by clear, unequivocal, and convincing evidence that the subject of the hearing is in need of confinement under the minimum standards for commitment herein enumerated. No greater margin for error can be tolerated as to either the underlying facts or the ultimate conclusion.[12] *Tippett* v. *State of Maryland,*

---

[12]We reject defendants' assertion that the preponderance of the evidence standard is controlling, with the observation that a civil commitment proceeding, where liberty is at stake, is significantly different from the unusal civil proceeding where the stakes are ordinarily economic and where "we view it as no more serious in general for there to be an erroneous verdict in the defendant's favor than for there to be an erroneous verdict in the plaintiff's favor." *In re Winship,* 397 U.S. at 371, 90 S.Ct. at 1076; *Woodby* v. *Immigration Service, supra.*

We also reject as demanding a degree of proof virtually unattainable at this stage in the development of psychiatric medicine plaintiffs' contention that due process requires proof beyond a reasonable doubt. While we agree in principle with the conclusion in *In re Winship* that proof beyond a reasonable doubt is *supra* 436 F.2d at 1165–1166 (Sobeloff, J.); *Dixon* v. *Attorney General*, 325 F.Supp. at 974.

(7) *Conduct of the commitment hearing.* Due process requires that the subject of an involuntary commitment proceeding, whether civil or criminal, be given the opportunity to offer evidence in his own behalf. *Specht* v. *Patterson*, 386 U.S. at 610, 87 S.Ct. 1209. "The right to offer the testimony of witnesses, and to compel their attendance, if necessary, is in plain terms the right to present a defense. . . . This right is a fundamental element of due process of law." *Washington* v. *Texas*, 388 U.S. 14, 19, 87 S.Ct. 1920, 1923, 18 L.Ed.2d 1019 (1967).

Due process likewise requires that the subject of a commitment hearing have the opportunity to be confronted with and to cross-examine the witnesses testifying in support of commitment. *Specht* v. *Patterson*, 386 U.S. at 610, 87 S.Ct. 1209; *Millard* v. *Harris*, 406 F.2d at 973. Holding the commitment hearing in the absence of the person proposed to be committed shall not be deemed an abridgement of his rights of confrontation and cross-examination if, but only if, there has been a prior judicial determination, after an adversary hearing at which he was represented by counsel, that he is so mentally or physically ill as to be incapable of attending the hearing.

The privilege against self-incrimination, which can be claimed "in any proceeding, be it criminal or civil, administrative or judicial, investigatory or adjudicatory," *Murphy* v. *Waterfront Commission*, 378 U.S. 52, 94, 84 S.Ct. 1594, 1611, 12 L.Ed.2d 678 (1964), White, J., concurring; *In re Gault*, 387 U.S. at 49–50, 87 S.Ct. 1428, is fully applicable at all stages of the civil commitment process, including the psychiatric interviews. See *Millard* v. *Harris*, 406 F.2d at 973. It protects any disclosures which the subject may reasonably believe could be used in a criminal prosecution or which could lead to other evidence that might be so used. *Murphy* v. *Waterfront Commission, supra.*

As we have noted repeatedly, the gravity of the consequences flowing from adjudication of the need for commitment compels the application of procedural safeguards comparable in most instances to those required in criminal proceedings. At the very least, due process requires that the rules of evidence applicable to other judicial proceedings be followed in involuntary commitment proceedings. *Lessard* v. *Schmidt*, 349 F.Supp. at 1103. In particular, if hearsay evidence would be excluded from other proceedings, it should be excluded from commitment hearings as well. See *In re Gault*, 387 U.S. at 11, n. 7, 87 S.Ct. 1428.

(8) *Trial by jury.* It has been generally assumed that there is no common law right to trial by jury in traditionally equitable probate court proceedings. *McKeiver* v. *Pennsylvania*, 403 U.S. 528, 543, 91 S.Ct. 1976, 29 L.Ed.2d 647 (1971); *Hanks* v. *Hanks*, 281 Ala. 92, 97, 199 So.2d 169 (1967); *Ex parte Floyd*, 250 Ala. 154, 33 So.2d 340 (1948). Moreover, the Supreme Court of the United States has held that trial

---

constitutionally necessary where interests of "immense importance" are at stake, 387 U.S. at 363, 90 S.Ct. 1068, we nevertheless find that reasoning inapplicable to a situation such as this where the ultimate determination of the need for commitment must of necessity be based upon subjective conclusions and predictions, albeit derived from underlying objective facts. *Contra: In re Ballay*, 157 U.S.App.D.C. 59, 482 F.2d 648; *Lessard* v. *Schmidt*, 349 F.Supp. at 1095.

by jury is neither a necessary element of the "fundamental fairness" guaranteed litigants by the Due Process Clause, nor an essential component of accurate fact-finding. *McKeiver* v. *Pennsylvania, supra*. Plaintiffs have cited no case, and independent research has disclosed no case, holding that trial by jury is constitutionally required in civil commitment proceedings.

Although there may be no such constitutional right, we believe that in most, if not all, instances a jury is desirable. Involuntary confinement is premised

> . . . not solely on the medical judgment that the defendant is mentally ill and treatable, but also on the social and legal judgment that his potential for doing harm, to himself or to others, is great enough to justify such a massive curtailment of liberty. In making this determination, the jury serves the critical function of introducing into the process a lay judgment, reflecting values generally held in the community, concerning the kinds of potential harm that justify the State in confining a person for compulsory treatment. *Humphrey* v. *Cady*, 405 U.S. at 509, 92 S.Ct. at 1052.

It is not enough, however, to say that the right to trial by jury is not in itself an absolute constitutional right. That argument was emphatically rejected by the Supreme Court when it said that the question of whether

> . . . summarily denying Rachel Brawner access to the site of her former employment violated the requirements of the Due Process Clause of the Fifth Amendment . . . cannot be answered by easy assertion that, because she had no constitutional right to be there in the first place, she was not deprived of liberty or property by the Superintendent's action. "One may not have a constitutional right to go to Baghdad, but the Government may not prohibit one from going there unless by means consonant with due process of law." *Cafeteria & Restaurant Workers Union* v. *McElroy*, 367 U.S. 886, 894, 81 S.Ct. 1743, 1748, 6 L.Ed.2d 1230 (1961), quoting *Homer* v. *Richmond*, 110 U.S.App.D.C. 226, 229, 292 F.2d 719, 722 (1961); *Dixon* v. *Alabama State Board of Education*, 294 F.2d 150, 156 (5th Cir. 1961).

To the extent, then, that Ala. Code. tit. 45, § 210 (1958) permits the exercise of an unbridled discretion by the probate judge in determining whether to empanel or not to empanel a jury, the statute violates the Due Process Clause of the Fourteenth Amendment.

There is a statutory right to trial by jury on the demand of a person *confined* as insane who prosecutes a writ of habeas corpus to determine the issue of his sanity. Ala.Code, tit. 15, § 3 (1958); *Phillips* v. *Giles*, 287 Ala. 469, 475, 252 So.2d 624, 629 (1971). The State of Alabama, having thus granted the right in some cases, may not deny it in others except on the basis of a rational distinction. *Humphrey* v. *Cady*, 405 U.S. at 512, 92 S.Ct. 1048; *Baxstrom* v. *Herold*, 383 U.S. 107, 110-111, 86 S.Ct. 760, 15 L.Ed.2d 620 (1966); *Gomez* v. *Miller*, 337 F.Supp. 386, 391 (S.D.N.Y. 1971). We can perceive no rational basis upon which the state can predicate a decision to grant jury determinations as of right to persons already deprived of their liberty, stigmatized by institutionalization, and removed from their relationships in the community, while denying the same right to persons whose continued freedom, good name, and ongoing associations are at stake. We, therefore, hold that basing the right to a jury determination of the need for commitment on the essentially irrelevant factor of present confinement violates the Equal Protection Clause of the Fourteenth Amendment.

We further hold that, if juries are used in civil commitment proceedings, equal protection requires that all commitment juries throughout the state perform the same function: if the jury is the fact-finder in some jurisdictions, it must be the fact-finder in all jurisdictions.

Plaintiffs maintain that a jury of twelve persons is constitutionally required. It is well settled that, as far as the Sixth Amendment is concerned, the states are left free to prescribe the precise number that shall constitute a jury. *Williams* v. *Florida,* 399 U.S. 78, 103, 90 S.Ct. 1893, 26 L.Ed.2d 446 (1970). Similarly, in the context of the Seventh Amendment, the Supreme Court has declined to hold that twelve members is a substantive aspect of the right to trial by jury. *Colgrove* v. *Battin,* 413 U.S. 149, 157, 93 S.Ct. 2448, 37 L.Ed.2d 522 (1973). A claim of the right to a jury of twelve is equally unavailing under Section 11 of the Alabama Constitution of 1901, for the Supreme Court of Alabama has recently indicated that jury composed of six members "would be clearly constitutional" if the right to trial by jury exists, as in this situation, solely by legislative grace. *Gilbreath* v. *Wallace,* 292 Ala. 267, 292 So.2d 651, 652 (1974).

(9) *Record of proceedings.* A full record of the commitment proceedings, including findings adequate for review, shall be compiled and maintained by the probate court. *Specht* v. *Patterson,* 386 U.S. at 610, 87 S.Ct. 1209.

(10) *Waiver of rights.* The knowing and intelligent waiver of constitutional safeguards required in involuntary commitment proceedings is acceptable, provided that the waiver is made by counsel with the informed consent of the subject and with the approval of the court. When a waiver is proposed by counsel, but the subject is deemed incapable of giving his informed consent after appropriate inquiry and finding of facts, the court may approve such waiver for good cause shown.

Finally, we wish to emphasize that our purpose is not to impose unnecessary restrictions or procedural requirements upon the authorities charged with the care and treatment of Alabama's mentally ill. It is not our intention that the treatment of any mentally ill resident of Alabama's mental institutions be disrupted. And, contrary to the assumption made by our dissenting brother, we neither contemplate nor order that the state release from its care and custody any persons presently confined in state mental hospitals who are unable to care and provide for themselves. Such persons over whom the state has heretofore assumed a significant custodial relationship, but who are not proper subjects for commitment to state mental hospitals under the standards herein set forth, shall be permitted to remain where they are presently confined if they so choose after being informed of the available alternatives. Those patients not electing to remain and unable by reason of their physical or mental condition to be released from care entirely shall be transferred to custodial facilities appropriate for the care and treatment of their particular infirmities.

The evidence presented to the Court in this case reflects, as we have herein outlined, that several thousand Alabama citizens are now suffering a "massive curtailment of liberty" by confinement in the state's mental institutions pursuant to court proceedings that were conducted and decrees that were entered in flagrant disregard of the substantial constitutional rights of those committed and now confined. We do, therefore, require, first, that all future involuntary commitments to any of Alabama's mental institutions fully comport with the requirements of procedural and substantive due process and, second, that all patients previously committed in violation of their constitutional rights and who remain committed in Alabama's mental institutions either: (a) be released therefrom; (b) be permitted to remain if they so choose and if they are incapable of caring for themselves; (c) be transferred to appropriate facilities designed for the care and treatment of their particular infirmities; or (d) be afforded, in accordance with the requirements of this opinion and the order to be entered herein, new hearings attended by the full panoply of constitutional rights to which these citizens were initially entitled but of which they were deprived.

A formal judgment will be entered accordingly.

[The dissenting opinion of VARNER, District Judge, is omitted.]

NOTES

1. Other decisions, which like *Lynch* v. *Baxley* have set out a list of due process procedural prerequisites to commitment, include: *Dixon* v. *Attorney General of Commonwealth of Pennsylvania,* 325 F.Supp. 966 (M.D.Pa. 1971); *Bell* v. *Wayne County General Hospital,* 384 F.Supp. 1085 (E.D.Mich. 1974); *State ex rel. Hawks* v. *Lazaro,* 202 S.E.2d 109 (W.Va. 1974); *Schneider* v. *Radack* (1st Judicial Circuit Ct., Yankton Cty., S.D., May 9, 1974); *Kendall* v. *True,* C.A. No. C 74-64 L(A) (W.D.Ky., Feb. 26, 1975); *Suzuki* v. *Quiesenberry,* 411 F.Supp. 1113 (D.Hawaii 1976); *Lessard* v. *Schmidt,* 349 F.Supp. 1078 (E.D.Wis. 1972, vacated and remanded on other grounds, 414 U.S. 473 (1974), redecided, 413 F.Supp. 1318 (E.D.Wis. 1976). The procedures prescribed in these cases are substantially the same as those required in *Lynch.* Cf. *French* v. *Blackburn,* 428 F.Supp. 1351 (M.D.N.C. 1977).

There are also a number of decisions that have considered only one or another of the procedural aspects of a constitutionally adequate commitment proceeding; e.g., 1) notice and hearing: *State ex rel. Fuller* v. *Mullinax,* 364 Mo. 858, 269 S.W.2d 72 (1954); *In re Buttonow,* 23 N.Y.2d 385, 297 N.Y.S.2d 97 (1968); *Anderson* v. *Solomon,* 315 F.Supp. 1192 (D.Md. 1970); *Souder* v. *Watson,* 413 F.Supp. 711 (M.D.Pa 1976); *Evans* v. *Paderick,* 443 F.Supp. 583 (E.D.Va. 1977); cf. *State of Missouri* v. *Kee,* 510 S.W.2d 477 (Mo. 1974); 2) right to counsel: *In re Sippy,* 97 A.2d 455 (Mun.App.D.C. 1953); *State of Oregon* v. *Collman,* 9 Or.App. 476, 497 P.2d 1233 (1972); *In re Fisher,* 39 Oh.St.2d 71, 68 Oh.Op.2d 12, 313 N.E.2d 851 (1974); *Heryford* v. *Parker,* above at pp. 640–643; cf. *U.S.* v. *Snow,* 219 F.Supp. 417 (S.D.N.Y. 1963); 3) jury trial: *Gomez* v. *Miller,* 341 F.Supp. 323 (S.D.N.Y. 1972); *Quesnell* v. *State of Washington,* 83 Wash.2d 224, 517 P.2d 568 (1974); 4) the right to a transcript or record of the proceedings: *In re Barnard,* 455 F.2d 1370 (D.C. Cir. 1971); *State of Oregon* v. *Collman,* 9 Or.App. 476, 497 P.2d 1233 (1972); *Shuman* v. *State of Florida,* 358 So.2d 1333 (Fla. 1978); and 5) inadmissibility of hearsay evidence: *Denton* v. *Commonwealth of Kentucky,* 383 S.W.2d 681 (Ky. 1964).

2. Several cases have held that stringent procedural safeguards are not required for emergency or temporary commitments; e.g., *Logan* v. *Arafeh,* 346 F.Supp. 1265 (D.Conn. 1972), affirmed sub nom., *Briggs* v. *Arafeh,* 411 U.S. 911 (1973); *Fhagen* v. *Miller,* 29 N.Y.2d 348, 328 N.Y.S.2d 393, 278 N.E.2d 615 (1972), cert. denied,

409 U.S. 845 (1972); *Coll* v. *Hyland,* 411 F.Supp. 905 (D.N.J. 1976). How long is "temporary"? How does the *Lynch* court answer this question?

3. *Lessard* v. *Schmidt,* 349 F.Supp. 1078 (E.D.Wis. 1972); vacated and remanded on other grounds, 414 U.S. 473 (1974), redecided, 379 F.Supp. 1376 (E.D.Wis. 1974), vacated and remanded on other grounds, 421 U.S. 957 (1975), redecided 413 F.Supp. 1318 (E.D.Wis. 1976), relied upon heavily by the *Lynch* v. *Baxley* court is a comprehensive and scholarly decision on the question of constitutionally adequate procedures for involuntary commitment. It is also an example of admirable judicial persistence, for on two separate occasions the United States Supreme Court has side-stepped the weighty substantive issues involved and has vacated and remanded the case on procedural grounds, and, on each such occasion, the lower court, after remedying the supposed procedural deficiencies, has reinstated its original decision. Notable features of the *Lessard* opinion are a discussion of the historical sources of commitment laws and a thorough examination of legal precedent dealing with the requirements of due process in the context of commitment.

One very significant conclusion of the *Lessard* court was its holding that, in order to justify the deprivation of an individual's liberty, there is required to be a finding of "dangerousness" to self or others, *id.* at 349 F.Supp. 1093. The court elaborated:

> Although attempts to predict future conduct are always difficult, and confinement based upon such a prediction must always be viewed with suspicion, we believe civil confinement can be justified in some cases if the proper burden of proof is satisfied and dangerousness is based upon a finding of a recent overt act, attempt or threat to do substantial harm to oneself or another. *Ibid.*

This requirement that dangerousness to self or others be proved by "a recent overt act, attempt or threat to do substantial harm" is an important doctrinal contribution by the *Lessard* court and one that has had an impact on subsequent decisions, including *Lynch* v. *Baxley.*

In a footnote, the Lessard court added an interesting observation:

> Even an overt attempt to substantially harm oneself cannot be the basis for commitment unless the person is found to be 1) mentally ill and 2) in immediate danger at the time of the hearing of doing further harm to oneself. The considerations which permit society to detain those who because of mental illness are likely to harm others do not necessarily apply to potential harm to oneself.
>
> Furthermore, to say that attempted suicide must always be the product of an irrational mind would seem to imply that no one could be punished for murder or its attempt. Yet we have always believed that persons are capable of rationally making the decision to intentionally take another person's life. *Id.* at 1093–1094, ftnote 24.

Was the *Lessard* court recognizing a "right to commit suicide"?

Another important feature of the *Lessard* holding, also followed in *Lynch* v. *Baxley,* was the concept of the least restrictive alternative:

> Perhaps the most basic and fundamental right is the right to be free from un-wanted restraint. It seems clear, then, that persons suffering from the condition of being mentally ill, but who are not alleged to have committed any crime, cannot be totally deprived of their liberty if there are less drastic means for achieving the same basic goal.

... We believe that the person recommending full-time involuntary hospitalization must bear the burden of proving (1) what alternatives are available; (2) what alternatives were investigated; and (3) why the investigated alternatives were not deemed suitable. These alternatives include voluntary or court-ordered outpatient treatment, day treatment in a hospital, night treatment in hospital, placement in the custody of a friend or relative, placement in a nursing home, referral to a community mental health clinic, and home health aide services. *Id.* at 1096.

The implications of this concept are considered further in section D of this chapter, pp. 661–701, below, but the *Lessard* decision is one of the earliest and most specific statements of the responsibilities of persons seeking commitment to provide less restrictive alternatives to long term institutionalization.

ADDINGTON v. STATE OF TEXAS

Supreme Court of the United States, 1979
_____U.S. _____, 47 U.S.L.W. 4473 (Apr. 30, 1979)
See pp. 632–639, above.

NOTES

1. While the Supreme Court's decision in *Addington* settles the dispute as to what standard of proof is the minimum constitutional requirement in commitment cases, does the Court's opinion make it clear *what* must be proved by clear and convincing evidence? Under the Texas commitment statute at issue in *Addington,* a showing of mental illness and the need for "hospitalization in a mental hospital for his own welfare and protection or the protection of others" were required. Yet, several times in the course of its opinion, the Court refers to a finding of probable dangerousness to self or others. Is the Court adopting the standard of "dangerousness" as enunciated in *Lynch* v. *Baxley* and *Lessard* v. *Schmidt*? Cf. Chief Justice Burger's concurring opinion in *O'Connor* v. *Donaldson,* pp. 624–629, above.

The *Addington* Court rejects the reasonable doubt standard because it concludes that proof of mental illness can not attain such a level of certainty. Is such a conclusion also true with regard to dangerousness? The *Lynch* and *Lessard* courts required that proof of dangerousness be based upon an overt act, threat, or attempt. Could these be proved beyond a reasonable doubt? How feasible would it be to have differing evidentiary standards for showing mental illness and for showing dangerousness? Is it inconsistent with the Court's language in *Addington* to insist that the overt act, threat, or attempt requirement is necessary for proving dangerousness?

For a discussion of the unreliability of psychiatric predictions of dangerousness, see Ennis, B., and Litwack, J., "Psychiatry and the Presumption of Expertise: Flipping Coins in the Courtroom," 62 *Cal.L.Rev.* 693, 711–716 (1974).

2. In *Goldy* v. *Beal,* 429 F.Supp. 640 (M.D.Pa. 1976), a Pennsylvania statute providing for the involuntary and indefinite commitment of persons "in need of care and treatment" because of their "mental disability," 50 Pa. Stats. Section 4406 (1966), was struck down as unconstitutionally vague. How different is this language from the statute considered in *Addington*? In light of this vagueness problem, would it be possible to draft a constitutional commitment statute that implements the sentiments

expressed in Chief Justice Burger's concurring opinion in *O'Connor* v. *Donaldson*, pp. 624–629 above? Cf. *In re Alexander*, 336 F.Supp. 1305 (D.D.C. 1972), where the court held that a statutory standard for involuntary commitment that required that one "be likely to injure himself or others" was not unconstitutionally vague.

3. For an examination of many of the procedural aspects of commitment statutes, see Comment, "Pennsylvania's Commitment: The Mental Health Procedures Act," 50 *Temple L. Q.* 1035 (1977).

4. The procedural safeguards required in involuntary commitment proceedings are generally considered unnecessary in situations where a person commits himself or herself voluntarily. However, as one study has shown, see Gilboy, J., and Schmidt, J., "'Voluntary' Hospitalization of the Mentally Ill," 66 *N.W.U.L. Rev.* 429 (1971), the bulk of "voluntary" admissions are not truly voluntary at all, and patients are frequently induced to sign admission papers by the threat that involuntary commitment proceedings will be initiated if they do not. In light of such evidence, should full due process safeguards be applied to "voluntary" commitments? Compare this problem with that of children "voluntarily" committed by their parents, see note 2 on p. 643 above.

5. The importance of strict procedural safeguards and commitment standards is highlighted whenever one encounters one of the not very rare horror stories about the confinement of people in residential institutions for any number of inappropriate and often absurd reasons. Persons have been involuntarily committed for permissive sexual behavior, see, e.g., Herr, S., "Civil Rights, Uncivil Asylums and the Retarded," 43 *Cincinnati L. Rev.* 679, 703 ftnt. 121 (1974); for leaving a university against parents' wishes, e.g., *Maniaci* v. *Marquette University*, 50 Wis.2d 287, 184 N.W.2d 168 (1971); for being a "hippie," e.g. *In re Sealy*, 218 So.2d 765 (Fla.App. 1969); and for deviating from sterotypes of appropriate behavior for females, see, e.g., Roth, R., and Lerner, J., "Sex-Based Discrimination in the Mental Institutionalization of Women," 62 *Cal.L.Rev.* 789 (1974). In one case, a woman from a non–English-speaking family was taken to a District of Columbia institution for mentally retarded people because she was suffering from typhoid fever. Subsequently, because of her poor command of English, staff members did not acquiesce to her requests for release nor give credence to her claims that she was being inappropriately confined; they labeled her "moderately retarded." The woman was finally released in 1978—some 45 years after her original confinement. Stevens, J., "Confined 45 Years, Woman Rejoins Family," *The Pittsburgh Press* (Oct. 29, 1978). In another instance, a man charged with attempted rape was sent to an institution for a "sanity investigation"; he was finally released 38 years later. See, Torrey, E. F., *The Death of Psychiatry* 88 (1974). And, in many instances, individuals with normal or above average intelligence have been confined in mental retardation facilities because they happened to be victims of cerebral palsy, epilepsy, deafness, or some other condition not affecting intelligence. See, e.g., Herr, S., *op. cit.* at 703, ftnt. 121; see note 4 on p. 121 (GH), above. See, generally, Ennis, B., *Prisoners of Psychiatry: Mental Patients, Psychiatrists, and the Law* (1972).

D. ALTERNATIVES TO INSTITUTIONALIZATION

HALDERMAN v. PENNHURST STATE SCHOOL AND HOSPITAL

United States District Court for the Eastern District of Pennsylvania, 1978
446 F.Supp. 1295

Index

OPINION

RAYMOND J. BRODERICK, District Judge.

This is a class action in which the named plaintiffs are either residents or former residents of Pennhurst State School and Hospital, now known as Pennhurst Center ("Pennhurst"), an institution owned and operated by the Commonwealth of Pennsylvania, located in Spring City, Pennsylvania. These plaintiffs are all retarded persons, or their representatives, who claim injury based on violations of certain state[1] and federal[2] statutes as well as violations of certain constitutional rights[3] in connection with their institutionalization at Pennhurst. The plaintiffs seek both damages and broad equitable relief including the closing of Pennhurst, and mandating that the defendants provide them with education, training and care in their respective communities. "Habilitation" is the term of art used to refer to that education, training and care required by retarded individuals to reach their maximum development.

This matter was tried before the Court, sitting without a jury, over a period of

---

[1]50 P.S. §§4101 *et seq.,* 4507, 4509.

[2]29 U.S.C. § 794; 42 U.S.C. §§ 1983, 1986, 6010.

[3]First, Eighth, Ninth, and Fourteenth Amendments to the United States Constitution.

thirty-two days, testimony being limited solely to the issue of liability. In connection therewith, the Court makes the following findings of fact and conclusions of law:

Mental retardation, by definition, is an impairment in learning capacity and adaptive behavior[4] (Roos, N.T. 1-86). Retardation is wholly distinct from mental illness. Retarded individuals, just as other members of society, may suffer from mental illness. Mental retardation is primarily an educational problem and not a disease which can be cured through drugs or treatment. However, with proper habilitation, the level of functioning of every retarded person may be improved (Glenn, N.T. 5-186).[5]

The incidence of mental retardation is about 3% in the general population. There are four basic levels of mental retardation: (1) mild (IQ 52-69) which comprises 89% of the mentally retarded population; (2) moderate (IQ 36-51) which comprises 6% of the mentally retarded population; (3) severe (IQ 20-35) which in conjunction with (4) profound (IQ less than 20) comprises 5% of the mentally retarded population (Roos, N.T. 1-89, 1-90).

Pennhurst, as an institution for the retarded, was on trial. Recent years have witnessed an assault upon such institutions.[6] At issue is whether the residents at Pennhurst have been the victims of violations of their statutory or constitutional rights; specifically whether Pennhurst as an institution has been violating the statutory or constitutional rights of its retarded residents in failing to provide them with minimally adequate education, training and care.

History is replete with misunderstanding and mistreatment of the retarded. As Wolf Wolfensberger points out in *The Origin and Nature of Our Institutional Models* 3 (1975):

> It is chastening to recall that the retarded in American history were long grouped with other types of deviant groups. In early America, the Puritans looked with suspicion on any deviation from behavioral norms, and irregular conduct was often explained in terms of the supernatural, such as witchcraft. There is reason to believe that retarded individuals were hanged and burned on this suspicion. Later in New England, records show that lunatics, "distracted" persons, people who were *non compos mentis,* and those who had "fits" were all classed together, perhaps with vagabonds and paupers thrown in.... Connecticut's first house of correction in 1722 was for rogues, vagabonds, the idle, beggars, fortune tellers, diviners, musicians, runaways, drunkards, prostitutes, pilferers, brawlers—and the mentally afflicted.... As late as about 1820, the retarded, together with other dependent deviant groups such as aged paupers, the sick poor, or the mentally distracted were publicly "sold" ("bid off") to the *lowest* bidder, i.e., bound over to the person who offered to take responsibility for them for the lowest amount of public support....
>
> The 10th (1880) U.S. census first combined "defectives," "dependents," and "delinquents" for reporting purposes. The Public Health Service combined "criminals, defectives, and delinquents" as late as the 1920's.

---

[4]Intelligence is generally measured through intelligence quotient tests (IQ), while ability to deal with social environment is measured through social quotient tests.

[5]An individual may be functioning at a retarded level due to lack of education and/or training, and once supplied with that education and/or training, may be removed from the ranks of the retarded.

[6]*See, e.g.,* Mason & Menolascino, "The Right to Treatment for Mentally Retarded Citizens: An Evolving Legal and Scientific Interface," 10 *Creighton L.Rev.* 124 (1976) [hereinafter cited as Mason & Menolascino].

The National Conference on Charities and Correction, between about 1875 and 1920, often grouped the idiotic, imbecilic and feeble-minded with the deaf, dumb, blind, epileptic, insane, delinquent and offenders into one general class of "defectives." Few of us today are aware of the fact that the more contemporary term "mental defective" was coined to distinguish the retarded from these other "defectives," and it is no coincidence that many state institutions were for both the retarded and the epileptic. During the "indictment period," discussed later, an incredible range of deviances were associated with retardation; indeed, they were seen to be caused by it: illness, physical impediments; poverty; vagrancy; unemployment; alcoholism; sex offenses of various types, including prostitution and illegitimacy; crime; mental illness; and epilepsy. All these were called the "degeneracies."

Institutions for a number of "deviant" groups were founded in the United States in the mid-nineteenth century for the purpose of making the deviant less deviant. They were originally relatively small centers, often located within the community, in which intensive training could be concentrated on the deviants. Their emphasis was on education; they were viewed as temporary boarding schools, geared toward returning the individuals to their family or living group once appropriate skills were learned. By the late nineteenth century, however, these schools were replaced by asylums isolated from the community, where instead of providing the individual with the education and training necessary to return to the community, they provided the protection and care it was thought that these individuals required. The asylum grew to be viewed as a permanent residential facility for the deviant. In the more progressive states, the retarded received their own facilities separated from other "deviant" groups. With this concept came increased isolation and increased size permitting little time for habilitation. *See generally*, W. Wolfensberger, *supra* at 24–56. Pennhurst was the product of this era.[7]

I. Procedural History

This action was commenced in May, 1974. On November 26, 1976, it was certified by the Court as a class action, with the plaintiff class of retarded persons defined as:

> All persons who as of May 30, 1974, and at any time subsequent, have been or may become residents of Pennhurst State School and Hospital. The members of the class are persons resident at Pennhurst State School and Hospital, persons residing in Bucks, Chester, Delaware, Montgomery and Philadelphia Counties who are on a waiting list for placement at Pennhurst State School and Hospital, and persons residing in Bucks, Chester, Delaware, Montgomery and Philadelphia Counties, who, because of the unavailability of alternate services in the community, may be placed at the Pennhurst State School and Hospital.

On February 4, 1977, by agreement of the parties, we entered an Order trifurcating the trial. This Order reads, in pertinent, part, as follows:

---

[7]From 1860 to 1960 there had been a marked increase in the number of mentally retarded individuals residing in our nation's institutions. Since 1966, this number has been decreasing. In 1966, 99 out of every 100,000 mentally retarded individuals were institutionalized. By 1976, that number had dropped to 71 out of every 100,000. In 1976, 154,000 mentally retarded individuals were residing in state public institutions, 32,000 were in hospitals for the mentally ill and 32,000 were in private institutions of various kinds (Roos, N.T. 1–92, 1–93).

Said trial will be bifurcated—the first phase limited solely to the issue of liability. At such time as the Court issues its findings of fact and conclusions of law thereafter, a date shall be set for the second phase of the trial—to determine what relief, if any, a federal court can and should grant in this situation. At the conclusion of the second phase of the trial, a date shall be set for the third phase of the trial, if one is deemed necessary,—to determine damages due Plaintiffs.

The first phase of his non-jury trial began on April 18, 1977 and ended on June 13, 1977, occupying thirty-two court days.

II. The Parties

The original complaint in this action was filed as a class action by Terri Lee Halderman, a retarded individual who had been admitted to Pennhurst on the application of her parents pursuant to 50 P.S. § 4402[8] in 1966. On July 29, 1974, the first amended complaint was filed, adding as name plaintiffs seven other retarded individuals[9] who had been admitted to Pennhurst upon the application of their parents. The amended complaint also added as a plaintiff the Parents and Family Association of Pennhurst representing 200 parents of retarded residents at Pennhurst. The Association was organized in 1967 to protect the rights of retarded citizens at Pennhurst and other institutions. (First amended complaint at 4.)

On January 17, 1975, the Court granted the United States of America leave to intervene as a party plaintiff.[10] On November 12, 1975, the Court, without opposition, granted leave to intervene to the Pennsylvania Association for Retarded Citizens ("PARC") and four retarded individuals,[11] three of whom were court committed to

---

[8]50 P.S. § 4402 provides:

    (a) Application for voluntary admission to a facility for examination, treatment and care may be made by:

    (1) Any person over eighteen years of age.

    (2) A parent, guardian or individual standing *in loco parentis* to the person to be admitted, if such person is eighteen years of age or younger.

    (b) When an application is made, the director of the facility shall cause an examination to be made. If it is determined that the person named in the application is in need of care or observation, he may be admitted.

    (c) Except where application for admission has been made under the provisions of section 402(a)(2) and the person admitted is still eighteen years of age or younger, any person voluntarily admitted shall be free to withdraw at any time. Where application has been made under the provisions of section 402(a)(2), only the applicant or his successor shall be free to withdraw the admitted person so long as the admitted person is eighteen years of age or younger.

    (d) Each admission under the provisions of this section shall be reviewed at least annually by a committee, appointed by the director from the professional staff of the facility wherein the person is admitted, to determine whether continued care is necessary. Said committee shall make written recommendations to the director which shall be filed at the facility and be open to inspection and review by the department and such other persons as the secretary by regulation may permit.

Where the admission is under the provisions of section 402(a)(2), the person admitted shall be informed at least each sixty days of the voluntary nature of his status at the facility.

[9]Larry Taylor, Kenny Taylor, Robert Sobetsky, Theresa Sobetsky, Nancy Beth Bowman, Linda Taub, and George Sorotos.

[10]On November 29, 1976, we denied defendants' motion to dismiss the United States for lack of standing. Defendants' attempt to mandamus this Court to dismiss the United States failed. *Beal* v. *Broderick* (3d Cir. 1976), cert. denied, 431 U.S. 933, 97 S.Ct. 2641, 53 L.Ed.2d 250 (1977).

[11]Jo Suzanne Moskowitz, Robert Hight, David Preusch, and Charles DiNolfi.

Pennhurst pursuant to 50 P.S. § 4406[12] or an earlier statute. PARC is a non-profit corporation which was founded in 1950 (Schmidt, N.T. 14-108) and has member chapters in fifty-seven of Pennsylvania's sixty-seven counties; its purpose being to advance the interest of retarded persons in Pennsylvania. The members of PARC include parents, other relatives, guardians, and next friends of persons residing at Pennhurst, and those in jeopardy of residing there.

Defendants are: Pennhurst; the Pennsylvania Department of Public Welfare; various state and county[13] officials responsible for supervising the Commonwealth's and the counties' retardation programs; and the superintendent and various employees of Pennhurst.

III.   Education, Training and Care (Habilitation) Afforded the Retarded at Pennhurst

Pennhurst, a residential institution for the retarded, was founded in 1908. It is owned and operated by the Commonwealth of Pennsylvania, and is located in Spring City, Pennsylvania about 30 miles from Philadelphia. Since its founding in 1908, the institution has been overcrowded and understaffed. (PARC Exhibit 40, R. Smilovitz, Pennhurst in Perspective: Purpose, Programs, Possibilities.) The present resident population is approximately 1,230, reduced from a high of nearly 4,000 in the early 1960's (Youngberg, N.T. 22-123). Its staff numbers approximately 1,500. All parties concede that the institution has undergone tremendous improvement since the 1950's when, at

---

[12]50 P.S. § 4406 provides:

(a)   Whenever a person is believed to be mentally disabled, and in need of care or treatment by reason of such mental disability, and examination of such person has been made by a physician or physicians, or for any reason the examination of such person cannot be made, a petition may be presented to the court of common pleas of the county in which a person resides or is, for his immediate examination or commitment to an appropriate facility for examination, observation and diagnosis.

(1)   The petition may be made by a relative, guardian, friend, individual standing *in loco parentis* or by the executive officer or an authorized agent of a governmental or recognized nonprofit health and welfare organization or agency or any responsible person.

(2)   The petition shall set forth the facts upon which the petitioner bases his belief of mental disability and the efforts made to secure examination of the person by a physician.

(3)   Said court upon consideration of such petition shall: (i) issue a warrant requiring that such person be brought before said court; (ii) fix a date for a hearing which shall be as soon as the warrant is executed, and (iii) notify the parties in interest.

(4)   After hearing, said court may: (i) order an immediate examination by two physicians appointed by said court, or (ii) order the commitment of the person believed to be mentally disabled, to a facility for a period not exceeding ten days for the purpose of examination. If the examination can be accomplished by partial hospitalization said court may so direct.

(b)   If, upon examination, it is determined that such person is in need of care at a facility, the examining physicians or director, as the case may be, shall immediately report to said court which may order the commitment of such person for care and treatment.

In its order of commitment, said court may permit partial hospitalization or outpatient care, or if at any time thereafter the director shall determine such partial hospitalization or outpatient care to be beneficial to the person so committed, the same may be permitted by said court upon application by the director.

The court in *Goldy* v. *Beal*, 429 F.Supp. 640 (M.D.Pa. 1976) (three-judge court) found this statute unconstitutionally vague with respect to the commitment of mentally ill persons. Pennsylvania's procedure for the involuntary commitment of mentally ill persons is now found in 50 P.S. §§ 7301-7306. The constitutionality of § 4406 as it applies to the retarded is not challenged in this litigation.

[13]Representing Bucks, Chester, Delaware, Montgomery and Philadelphia Counties.

best, the residents' treatment could be described as "warehousing." Even with these improvements, it was admitted by the defendants that Pennhurst does not presently meet minimum standards for the habilitation of its residents (Rice, N.T. 26-24; Youngberg, Deposition at 22-31).[14]

Approximately half of the residents at Pennhurst have been admitted upon application of their parents or guardians, while the other half have been committed by a court (Youngberg, N.T. 22-122). No distinction is made in the services extended to either group. The average[15] resident age at Pennhurst is 36, and the average stay at the institution is 21 years. Forty-three percent of the residents have had no family contact within the last three years.[16] Seventy-four percent of the residents are severely to profoundly retarded.[17] The average resident has had one psychological evaluation every three years and one vocational adjustment service report every 10 years. Those residents who have had more than one Vineland examination (measuring social quotient) during their residency at the institution, have, on the basis of this test, shown a decline rather than an increase in social skills while at Pennhurst (they declined an average of 7.542 points during their residence at Pennhurst, a loss of .596 points per year).[18]

At its best, Pennhurst is typical of large residential state institutions for the retarded.[19] These institutions are the most isolated and restrictive settings in which to treat the retarded (Lancaster-Gaye, N.T. 4-79). Pennhurst is almost totally impersonal (*Id.*, N.T. 4-71). Its residents have no privacy (Roos, N.T. 1-149)—they sleep in large, overcrowded wards (Youngberg, Deposition at 22), spend their waking hours together in large day rooms and eat in a large group setting (Clements, N.T. 2-57,

---

[14]Pennhurst must satisfy both federal and state licensing standards to qualify for federal medical assistance (Title XIX funds), standards which Dr. Youngberg and Dr. Rice equated with minimally acceptable professional standards (Rice, N.T. 27-57; Youngberg, Deposition at 27). Both the individual and the area in which he or she resides must be certified in order for the institution to qualify for funds. At Pennhurst only 16 out of 40 living areas have been certified, though a majority of these areas have deficiencies. The deficiencies have either been waived, or Pennhurst has filed plans for correcting the deficiencies (Pool, N.T. 18-27, 28-28). Five hundred fourteen residents live on these 16 wards and are eligible for funding. Another 600 Pennhurst residents would be eligible were they to reside on a certified ward (*Id.*, N.T. 17-209).

To meet medical assistance living standards, the population of Pennhurst must be reduced to 850 residents. In addition, $1,028,327 is being expended to correct Life Safety Code violations—the completion date of this project is December 31, 1977 (the project was awarded in December, 1975, with an original completion date of April, 1977).

To meet medical assistance care standards, Pennsylvania is planning to expend an additional $2,367,500 (Rice, N.T. 26-6). The institution is presently in jeopardy of losing its current certification if the waivers it presently has, contingent on repairs being made, are withdrawn (*Id.*, at 26-13, 26-14).

[15]The statistics set forth in this paragraph are taken from a systematic sampling of 10% of the resident population at Pennhurst (PARC Exhibit 48).

[16]It is unclear what percentage of the residents have family members still living.

[17]See text following note 5, *supra.*

[18]It appears that the Vineland has an inherent bias against retarded individuals from age ten through twenty-five, in that social quotients over this period, as measured by the Vineland, have a tendency to decline (Hare, N.T. 8-195, 8-196). This phenomena ceases once the individual reaches the age of twenty-five (*Id.* N.T. 8-203). An analysis of those Pennhurst residents who had received at least two Vineland examinations since their twenty-fifth birthday showed an average regression of 2.3 points (*Id.*, N.T. 9-16).

[19]Dr. Gunnar Dybwad, who has visited institutions for the retarded in 49 states testified that Pennhurst was in the bottom category of the large residential state institutions for the retarded (N.T. 7-62).

2-71, 2-72). They must conform to the schedule of the institution which allows for no individual flexibility. Thus, for example, all residents on Unit 7[20] go to bed between 8:00 and 8:30 p.m., are awakened and taken to the toilet at 12:00–12:30 a.m. and return to sleep until 5:30 a.m. when they are awakened for the day (Barton, Deposition at 21-26, 33-34; Roos, N.T. 1-50), which begins with being toileted and then having to wait for a 7:00 a.m. breakfast.

A. Staffing

On the whole, the staff at Pennhurst appears to be dedicated and trying hard to cope with the inadequacies of the institution (Hersh, N.T. 13-130).[21] Many of the problems at Pennhurst result from overcrowding and understaffing.[22] As professionals leave the staff, they are often not replaced, their jobs being turned over to direct care staff; thus, in the last two years nineteen professionals have left the staff without being replaced (Roos, N.T. 1-153). Nearly every witness who testified concerning Pennhurst stated that it was grossly understaffed to adequately habilitate the residents. None of the standard reference sources now generally used by professionals in the field of mental retardation define the qualifications and minimal numbers of mental retardation professionals necessary to provide minimally adequate programs of habilitation. (Clements Report at 6). However, the court in *Wyatt* v. *Stickney*, 344 F.Supp. 387 (N.D.Ala. 1972), attempted to provide such guidelines. A comparison of the *Wyatt* ratios to those at Pennhurst in 1975[23] reveals:

		Wyatt Standards	Pennhurst
a.	Psychologists	23	23
b.	Social Workers	40	6
c.	Vocational Therapists	5	4
d.	Recreation Therapists	23	0
e.	Occupational Therapists	18	10
f.	Registered Nurses	95	54
g.	Physicians	7	6
h.	Physical Therapists	14	2
i.	Speech and Hearing Therapists	14	9
j.	Dentists	7	4
k.	Chaplains	7	4
l.	Teachers[24]	51	8

(Clements, N.T. 2-26, 2-27.)

---

[20]Pennhurst is organized around the unit system and is composed of nine units, representing various levels of educational and behavioral development and physical handicap (United States of America Exhibit 10).

[21]As defendants themselves have expressed it: "The staff at Pennhurst is a dedicated lot with precious little to work with." Commonwealth Defendants' Post-Trial Proposed Findings of Fact and Legal Arguments at 5.

[22]In his budget proposal for fiscal year 1977–78, Superintendent Youngberg requested 23 additional ward clerks, 1 additional unit secretary and 717 mental retardation aides (Youngberg, Deposition at 42).

[23]There was no testimony that these ratios have changed dramatically in the intervening two years, though 19 professional positions have been eliminated since Dr. Clements' tour of Pennhurst (Roos, N.T. 1-153).

[24]In 1975, 206 school age residents were enrolled in the school program operated by IU teachers. There teachers were excluded from the calculation.

No psychologists are on duty at Pennhurst at night or over the weekend, thus, if a resident has an emotional crisis, he or she may go without treatment until the next morning or until the weekend is over (Riznyk, N.T. 17-182). Moreover, routine housekeeping services are not available during evenings and weekends, thus it is common to find urine and feces on ward floors over these periods (Smith, Deposition at 41; Roos, N.T. 1-158).

B. Habilitation at Pennhurst

All parties to this litigation are in agreement that Pennhurst as an institution is inappropriate and inadequate for the habilitation of the retarded. It is also admitted that the inadequacies in programming at Pennhurst are directly attributable to staff short- ages. Residents' records commonly contain a notation that they would benefit from specific types of programming. However, such programming has, for the most part, been unavailable to the individual because of staff shortages (Foster, Deposition at 42; DeAngelis, N.T. 16-49). The average resident receives only 1½ hours of programming per weekday and no programming on weekends (Thurman, N.T. 14-60; DeAngelis, N.T. 16-31). No one, except those in school, gets more than 3½ to 4 hours per day. If one factors out those programs which are not considered beneficial, the average drops to about fifteen minutes per day (Thurman, N.T. 14-60).[25] Some residents receive no programming due to their extreme hyperactivity, medical problems, or their own refusal of treatment (DeAngelis, N.T. 16-32; Cooper, N.T. 29-46). Some individuals have not been accepted into occupational therapy, since only group programs are available and they require individual attention. Some Pennhurst residents have been dropped from existing programs due to lack of progress and motivation. The record indicates that the residents at Pennhurst are made to fit into existing programs, and that the programs are not altered to fit the needs of the individuals. Further, it appears that an individual's motivation and not his or her needs determine whether the resident continues with the program (Hare, N.T. 8-180, 8-181.)[26]

Residents are referred to special programs at Pennhurst, but often, due to staff shortages, placements are not made (DeAngelis, N.T. 16-40, 16-41). Almost every

---

[25]For example, the programming for residents on Unit 8, the unit in which the most aggressive residents reside, includes several hours per day during which the residents watch TV. Mr. Pirmann the Director of the unit, testified that this was to increase the residents' attention span and to teach them to sit and tolerate the presence of others (N.T. 19-104, 19-105). "Programming" such as this appears to be primarily for the convenience of the staff, rather than for the benefit of the residents (Thurman, N.T. 14-68).

[26]George Sorotos, a named plaintiff, was enrolled in speech therapy at the end of 1972. At that time, he was unable to communicate, and his program was designed to develop his communicative skills. Though initially he made progress, he soon plateaued. In August, 1973, he was switched to a manual communication program. This continued for six months, again with some initial success. During each program, he was self-abusive, which the staff attributed to frustration. He was never able to use these skills for communica- tion. George Sorotos was terminated from all speech activity because the director of the speech and hearing department determined that her time would be better spent with other residents with whom she could accomplish more (Riggott, N.T. 20-160 to 20-164). Thus, since George Sorotos did not respond well and was self-abusive, he was denied speech therapy, a skill essential for his habilitation.

Similarly, plaintiff Terri Lee Halderman was initially included in speech therapy, but because of abusive tendencies, both to herself and to others, she was dropped from the program (Id., N.T. 20-164 to 20-166).

service offered at Pennhurst has a long waiting list (Foster, Deposition at 42). For example, as of April 15, 1977, there were 511 residents on the referral list for occupational therapy (Hilker, N.T. 20-43). While 50-60 Pennhurst residents have wheelchairs which have been individually adapted to meet the individual's needs, 75-100 residents need such adaptions (Fekula, N.T. 20-99). The consequences for the resident not having his or her wheelchair adapted are especially grave, including: (1) loss of vital functions; (2) severe muscular contractions; and (3) loss of ability to be programmed. (*Id.* N.T. 20-101). While over 300 residents at the institution have hearing impairments, only 51 have been fitted with hearing aids. There are 106 residents on the waiting list for speech therapy, and nearly every resident at Pennhurst could benefit from some type of communication programming. (Riggot, N.T. 20-155).[27] Three to four hundred residents presently need physical therapy to prevent physical deterioration, however, only 143 are receiving this therapy (Rossi, Deposition at 12, 22).[28]

Pennhurst has established a communication center for 22 non-verbal individuals, but the institution has approximately 300 non-verbal residents. In theory, the residents in the communication center spend their day in classes learning signing (*i.e.,* sign language skills), academics, and self-care skills. However, when there is only minimal staff coverage, classes are not offered since the staff is totally occupied with custodial tasks. During the month of April, 1977, there were 5 days during which there was minimal coverage on the first shift (7:00 a.m.–4:00 p.m.); 25 days of minimal coverage on the second shift (4:00 p.m.–11:00 p.m.); and thirty days of minimal coverage on the third shift (11:00 p.m.–7:00 a.m.)—on five of these days during the third shift, there was less than minimum staff coverage (Nelson, N.T. 21-23, 21-24).

Not only is the programming at Pennhurst inadequate to meet minimum professional standards (Rice, Deposition at 179, 180), but so are the evaluations performed on the residents to determine what is required to adequately habilitate the individual. None of the residents at Pennhurst had a full multi-discipline assessment as of January, 1977 (PARC Exhibit 53; Flueck, N.T. 4-9). Twenty and six-tenths percent of the residents have not received a limited multi-discipline assessment since January, 1975, and those assessments which have been made are generally limited to psychological, speech and hearing skills and are rarely concerned with vocational or self-care skills (Hare, N.T. 8-165, 8-166). Proper habilitation cannot be provided to retarded persons unless those responsible for providing such programs are aware of the individual's needs.

Defendants have not made "full exit plans," *i.e.,* plans delineating: (1) a place for each individual to live outside of Pennhurst; (2) the daily activity necessary for each individual living outside Pennhurst; (3) necessary support services; and (4) the person

---

[27]Some residents have been on the waiting list for at least 3½ years (Nelson, N.T. 21-27).

[28]Pennhurst does an especially inadequate job for those with motor disabilities. Dr. Lancaster-Gaye, an expert in, among other things, the management of services for severely disabled persons (N.T. 4-69), toured the institution in March, 1977 and reported that young retarded individuals who suffered from cerebral palsy were sitting on the floor in positions which would lead to physical deterioration. He stated that these individuals were receiving little physical therapy and that without such therapy, the muscles in the limbs of these youths would contract and become useless (N.T. 4-74, 4-75).

who would be responsible, for any Pennhurst resident.[29] Such plans are very important in planning for the resident's eventual return to the community from the institution.

Defendants have also failed to make full "program plans," i.e., plans containing: (1) identification of long and short term goals; (2) specification of the conditions under which the individual might achieve these goals; and (3) specification of the criteria to evaluate the individual's mastery of the goals, for Pennhurst residents.[30]

The record keeping at Pennhurst is also below acceptable minimum standards (Clements, N.T. 2-22). Adequate record keeping is essential for proper habilitation of the residents.[31] Without such records, the staff will not know what the individual is already able to do, what type of care he or she should be receiving, and how to evaluate progress made by the individual. (Id.)

Pennsylvania's immediate plans for Pennhurst call for a reduction of the population at the institution to 850[32] and to provide, by July 1, 1978, 2½ hours of programming per resident per day. Dr. Rice, the Commissioner of Mental Retardation for Southeast Pennsylvania felt that such programming would fulfill the minimum requirements to qualify for medical assistance (i.e., federal financing). However, he knew of no other set of standards which would consider this level of programming minimally acceptable, and personally did not feel that it was adequate (N.T. 27-78). As a matter of practice, the Department of Mental Retardation for the Southeast Region will not approve a community living arrangement for a mentally retarded individual unless it provides for programming of at least five and one-half hours per day (Rice, N.T. 27-80).

C. Restraints at Pennhurst

At Pennhurst, restraints are used as control measures in lieu of adequate staffing[33] (Clements, N.T. 2-82, 2-84; Roos, N.T. 1-135; Sprague, N.T. 3-44; Hersh, N.T. 13-153, Foster, Deposition at 81). This is not to say that restraints should never be used in the habilitation of the retarded. When an individual's aggressive behavior interferes with his or her ability to take advantage of other programming which the individual should receive, or poses a physical threat to him or herself and others it may

[29] Sixty and eight-tenths percent of the residents had no mention of the community or of an exit plan in their files, and those that had some indication that the individual's eventual exit from the institution had been considered, never specified the type of placement which would be required nor who would be responsible for the individual (Hare, N.T. 8-167).

[30] Twenty-eight and nine-tenths percent had no program plan. Those that did have some plan rarely had a precise statement of goals and objectives (Hare, N.T. 8-166).

[31] An individual's record should contain: (1) a current comprehensive evaluation of the individual; (2) a list of short and long term goals for the individual; (3) a specific plan outlining the procedures to accomplish these goals. The program should also provide for on-going monitoring, periodic re-evaluations of the individual, and periodic modifications of the objectives and procedures to reflect the findings of the re-evaluations (Roos, N.T. 1-115, 1-116).

[32] Decreasing the population to 850 is contingent on an increase in funds appropriated by the Pennsylvania legislature, along with an ambitious placement program—unfortunately much of this placement is from one institution (Pennhurst) to other institutions rather than to the community.

[33] Restraints can be either physical or chemical. The physical restraints range from placing the individual into a seclusion room to binding the person's hands or ankles with muffs or poseys, and binding the individual to a bed or a chair. Chemical restraints are usually psychotropic (i.e., tranquilizing) drugs.

be proper to restrain that person. Soon, it is hoped, once the individual has benefited from the other programming, the restraint will not be needed (Clements, N.T. 2-86). It is generally conceded that most, if not all, outbursts of violence by the retarded can be prevented by adequate programming.

Seclusion rooms[34] have been used to punish aggressive behavior. One eighteen year old individual spent six consecutive days in seclusion in 1974 for assaulting a Down's Syndrome resident (Lowrie, N.T. 5-6, 5-7). In 1975, a committee was formed to investigate the use of seclusion rooms at Pennhurst. It recommended that seclusion rooms, if they were to be used at all, should be limited to medical emergencies and should not be utilized for punishment (Lowrie, N.T. 5-5). Seclusion rooms are still in use at Pennhurst (M. Conley, N.T. 16-150; Boyle, N.T. 17-72, 17-73; L. Miller, N.T. 77-102; Malone, N.T. 17-140, 17-141; Lowrie, N.T. 5-71); though the incidence of their use is less than it was in years past. There is now a policy that seclusion rooms be used only for medical emergency, when a resident becomes extremely abusive, and no other alternative will control the individual. One-to-one interaction with staff members is often effective in calming the resident and stopping this maladaptive behavior. However, since normally the wards are, at best, minimally staffed, there frequently is not a staff person who can be spared to participate in this intensive interaction (Lowrie, N.T. 5-9; Miller, N.T. 17-122). Thus, seclusion is often necessary only because there is insufficient staff. (Lowrie, N.T. 4-131).[35]

Often physical restraints are also used due to staff shortages. An extreme example is a female resident who, during the month of June 1976, was in a physical restraint for 651 hours 5 minutes; for the month of August, 1976, was in physical restraints for 720 hours; during September, 1976, was in physical restraints for 674 hours 20 minutes; and during the month of October, 1976, was in physical restraints for 647 hours 5 minutes (Matthews, Deposition at 64-68). This resident was extremely self-destructive—she totally blinded herself. She was not enrolled in occupational therapy until early 1977. Once initiated, her programming has apparently been quite successful, and she is now able to be out of restraints for as much as four hours per day (Foster, N.T. 23-43). Had this programming been initiated earlier, her self-inflicted injuries might have been avoided or at least lessened.

Physical restraints are potentially physically harmful and can create conditions in which physical injuries are more likely to occur (Clements, N.T. 2-87; Hirst, N.T. 7-131; Roos, N.T. 1-166),[36] and prevent residents from learning or exercising self-care skills (Clements, N.T. 2-87).

---

[34]The seclusion rooms at Pennhurst are small rooms generally with one window and one door. The walls are masonry, the floors either tile or terrazzo—both hard surfaces. None of the rooms are padded. Many have exposed radiators, and other potentials for danger to the resident placed within it (Youngberg, Deposition at 69; Lowrie, N.T. 4-183 to 4-190).

[35]One young male resident had a tendency to run away from the institution. When he was given one-to-one interaction with staff, he would not attempt to run away. When the program of one-to-one interaction was dropped due to staff shortages, he again began running away. He was warned that he would be put on a locked ward if his behavior continued, and he became abusive to staff. As a result of this behavior, he was put into a seclusion room (Foster, N.T. 22-44 to 22-46).

[36]In 1972, an eleven year old child strangled to death when tied to a chair in "soft" restraints (Lowrie, N.T. 4-133–4-135).

Psychotropic drugs at Pennhurst are often used for control and not for treatment, and the rate of drug use on some of the units is extraordinarily high (Hersh, N.T. 13-153).[37] Dr. Sprague, an expert in psychopharmacology,[38] testifying on behalf of the United States, conducted a survey of 39 residents at Pennhurst, a group which he considered to be statistically representative of the residents at Pennhurst. He found that 51% of the group were receiving psychotropic drugs, 35% of the group were receiving anti-convulsant medication, and 40% were receiving two or more psychotropic drugs at one time (N.T. 3-36). In comparison with similar institutions throughout the country, Dr. Sprague stated that these percentages were very high, though he said that some institutions administer comparable levels.[39]

Dr. Sprague also found that Pennhurst residents on drugs were inadequately monitored. Without monitoring, one cannot determine whether the drug has been effective and whether it should be continued. Dr. Sprague found that in only 29% of the cases in which a drug was administered were its effects on the individual evaluated (N.T. 3-45). He further testified that the drug practice at Pennhurst does not meet minimally professional standards and is physically hazardous to the residents (N.T. 3-55, 3-90).

One of the side effects of the use of psychotropic medication is that it may make the individual receiving it lethargic—so much so that the recipient may fall asleep during school, or during other times when activities and/or programming are being attempted (Lowrie, N.T. 5-22). Other hazardous side effects of these drugs include hypersensitivity to sunlight; ataxia (inability to maintain balance and gait); and gingival hyperplasia (gum tissue condition marked by inflammation, bleeding and increased growth) (Hedson, Deposition at 59-61). Thus, the administration of such drugs actually impedes the habilitation of the resident, especially when used as a control rather than a habilitation device.

D. Deterioration and Abuse of the Residents at Pennhurst

The physical environment at Pennhurst is hazardous to the residents, both physically and psychologically (Clements, N.T. 2-59). There is often excrement and urine on ward floors (Roos, N.T. 1-158; Smith, Deposition at 41), and the living areas do not meet minimal professional standards for cleanliness (Youngberg, Deposition at 24). Outbreaks of pinworms and infectious disease are common (M. Conley, N.T. 16-193; Lowrie, N.T. 4-153; Hedson, Deposition at 122). As Superintendent Youngberg noted:

---

[37]Until March, 1977, Pennhurst had no written policy against the use of PRN orders (*"pro re nata"* or "as needed") for restraints or seclusion. In its most extreme form, a doctor would prescribe a restraint or seclusion for a patient to be administered in the discretion of a direct care aide or a nurse (Boyle, N.T. 17-93, 17-94). At best, the doctor would be called prior to administration of the drug, but he or she seldom personally visited the resident either before or shortly after the medication or physical restraint was administered (Boyle, Deposition at 22).

[38]"Psychopharmacology" is the area of study dealing with prescription medicines that are prescribed for mind alteration for behavior control (Sprague, N.T. 3-12, 3-13).

[39]Dr. Sprague testified that at a state institution in Georgia serving the most severely retarded individuals, only 25% of the residents were on drugs (N.T. 3-38).

There is not adequate space for [the residents. The living areas do] not provide privacy for those persons who can handle privacy. There does not seem to be adequate activity areas or program areas or even general activity areas within the general living area or even adequate activity program areas away from the home living area (Deposition at 23).

The environment at Pennhurst is not only not conducive to learning new skills, but it is so poor that it contributes to losing skills already learned[40] (Clements, N.T. 2-59). For example, Pennhurst has a toilet training program, but one who has successfully completed the program may not be able to practice the newly learned skill, and is therefore likely to lose it (Clement, N.T. 2-36, 2-37). Moreover, most toilet areas do not have towels, soap or toilet paper,[41] and the bathroom facilities are often filthy and in a state of disrepair. Obnoxious odors and excessive noise permeate the atmosphere at Pennhurst. Such conditions are not conducive to habilitation (Dybwad, N.T. 7-52). Moreover, the noise level in the day rooms is often so high that many residents simply stop speaking (Clements, N.T. 2-59).

Meals are eaten in a large group setting. Staff supervision is at a minimum, and residents are often free to steal food from other residents—which results in some residents not getting enough to eat (Clements, N.T. 2-73). Obviously, diet control in such an environment is almost impossible.

Injuries to residents by other residents, and through self-abuse, are common. For example, on January 8, 1975, one individual bit off three-quarters of the earlobe and part of the outer ear of another resident while the second resident was alseep (Matthews, Deposition at 83). About this same period, one resident pushed a second to the floor, resulting in the death of the second resident (Barton, Deposition at 67, 68). Such resident abuse of residents continues. In January, 1977 alone, there were 833 minor and 25 major injuries reported[42] (Youngberg, Deposition at 83).

In addition, there is some staff abuse of residents. In 1976, one resident was raped by a staff person (Ruddick, N.T. 3-115 to 3-117); one resident was badly bruised when a staff person hit him with a set of keys (Barton, Deposition at 40); another resident was thrown several feet across a room by a staff person (Ruddick, N.T. 3-113; Caranfa, N.T. 12-79); and one resident was hit by a staff person with a shackle belt (Bowman, N.T. 13-83; Pirmann, N.T. 19-94). On each occasion, an investigation was conducted and the staff person responsible was suspended and/or terminated (Ruddick, N.T. 3-114; Bowman, N.T. 13-82, 13-83, 13-84; Pirmann, N.T. 19-94).

Many of the residents have suffered physical deterioration and intellectual and behavioral regression during their residency at Pennhurst. Terri Lee Halderman, the original plaintiff in this action, was admitted to Pennhurst in 1966 when she was twelve years of age. During her eleven years at Pennhurst, as a result of attacks and accidents,

---

[40]A survey conducted by Dr. Betty Hare revealed that 34% of the individuals in the group surveyed had some notation of regression in their records (PARC Exhibit 53, Hare, N.T. 8-167). Those "skills" which are learned at Pennhurst are often antisocial (Roos, N.T. 1-139; Clements, N.T. 2-84).

[41]Direct care aides testified that there was no soap or towels in the toilet areas because when placed there, the residents stuffed them down the toilets (Roy, N.T. 15-108). These same aides also testified, however, that no programming had been conducted to try to negate this behavior (Id., N.T. 15-127).

[42]This figure includes injuries due to self-abuse and to accidents.

she has lost several teeth and suffered a fractured jaw, fractured fingers, a fractured toe and numerous lacerations, cuts, scratches and bites .[43] Prior to her admission to Pennhurst, Terri Lee could say "dadda," "mamma," "noynoy" (no), "baba" (goodby) and "nana" (grandmother). She no longer speaks (Halderman, N.T. 9-69, 9-71, 9-78, 9-87, 9-88).

Plaintiff Charles DiNolfi was admitted to Pennhurst when he was nine years old; he is now forty-five and has resided at the institution continually except for short stays at White Haven State School and Hospital (Hunsicker, N.T. 9-39). Dorothy Hunsicker, his sister, testified that whenever she or her family visited him, Mr. DiNolfi had some type of bandage on. (Id.) Twenty-six years ago, while at Pennhurst, Mr. DiNolfi lost an eye. A Pennhurst physician told Ms. Hunsicker that Mr. DiNolfi slipped while taking a shower, and hit the spigot with his eye. The sight in his remaining eye has been impaired due to injury. (Id., N.T. 9-46, 9-47). He has only a few teeth remaining and his nose has been battered. (Id., N.T. 9-41).

Plaintiffs Robert and Theresa Sobetsky were admitted to Pennhurst on November 29, 1971.[44] They were placed on extremely overcrowded wards where beds were placed in the aisles. Robert was never assigned to a particular bed (Sobetsky, N.T. 9-145, 9-146). During his residency at Pennhurst, Robert Sobetsky suffered from bruises, bites, scratches, welts and he smelled of urine. (Id., N.T. 9-147, 9-148). His record shows a number of reported injuries, some of which, though labeled minor injuries, represented bruises that were three to five inches in length (Id., 9-151, 9-152). Theresa also suffered such injuries (Id., N.T. 9-148).

Plaintiff Robert Hight, born in 1965, was admitted to Pennhurst in September, 1974. He was placed on a ward with forty-five other residents. His parents visited him two and one-half weeks after his admission and found that he was badly bruised, his mouth was cut, he was heavily drugged and did not recognize his mother. On this visit, the Hights observed twenty-five residents walking the ward naked, others were only partially dressed. During this short period of time, Robert had lost skills that he had possessed prior to his admission. The Hights promptly removed Robert from the institution, Mrs. Hight commenting that she "wouldn't leave a dog in conditions like that" (N.T. 11-22, 11-23).

Plaintiff George Sorotos entered Pennhurst in 1970 at the age of seven. In the seven years that George has been at Pennhurst, his former foster mother, Marion Caranfa,[45] testified that in her weekly visits to Pennhurst there have been only four occasions when George was not injured (N.T. 12-63). During this period, he has suffered from numerous reported injuries, including bites, scratches, black eyes and loss of teeth. In addition, Mrs. Caranfa testified that she recently observed what appeared to be cigarette burns on George's chest (N.T. 12-65).

---

[43]Terri Lee Halderman's medical records contain a listing of over forty reported injuries.

[44]Since January, 1976, they have been residing at Woodhaven, a Pennsylvania institution for the mentally retarded run by Temple University.

[45]The Caranfas were made George Sorotos' foster parents when he was six weeks old. Sometime after he entered Pennhurst, the agency which had supervision over George removed them as his foster parents. They still consider him as one of their family and have continued their visits (Caranfa, N.T. 12-62, 12-105).

Plaintiffs Larry and Kenny Taylor entered Pennhurst on February 28, 1961. In the early 1970's, Mrs. Taylor questioned the staff about the medication being given to Larry. He was very lethargic, falling asleep at school and barely able to walk (Taylor, N.T. 13-24). The physician in charge of Larry's unit, checked Larry's medical record and found that he was on dilantin, a drug used to control epileptic seizures. Mrs. Taylor testified that Larry had had only one seizure that she knew of and that had been when he was a baby. Larry was removed from dilantin and placed on mellaril, a psychotropic drug. This, too, made him lethargic (*Id.*, N.T. 13-26 to 13-28). Larry and Kenny were transferred to Woodhaven in 1975 where Mrs. Taylor testified that Larry does not receive any psychotropic medication, and is able to walk independently (*Id.*, N.T. 13-32). Larry was often injured while at Pennhurst; on one occasion, he was hospitalized for two weeks because of head and face injuries he received as a result of a beating by another resident (*Id.*, N.T. 13-30). Kenny, too, suffered serious injuries while at Pennhurst (*Id.*, 13-29).

Plaintiff Nancy Beth Bowman entered Pennhurst at the age of ten in 1961. She was placed on a large ward which had sixty-five residents and often only two child-care aides in attendance (Bowman, N.T. 13-71; Pirmann, N.T. 19-89). During her residency at Pennhurst she developed maladaptive behavior, *i.e.*, biting and pushing (Bowman, *Id.*) As a result of this maladaptive behavior she has been placed in seclusion for days at a time (*Id.*, N.T. 13-71). While at Pennhurst, she has lost teeth, been badly bruised and has been abused by the staff (*Id.*, N.T. 13-72, 13-73, 13-81). When asked about her present physical condition Nancy Beth's mother replied, ''Nancy Beth will be scarred for the rest of her life'' (*Id.*, N.T. 13-94).

Plaintiff Linda Taub, who is blind in addition to being retarded, was admitted to Pennhurst in 1966 at the age of fifteen. According to her father, during her nine year residency at Pennhurst Linda received only custodial care and she experienced regression rather than growth (Taub, N.T. 2-170). Time on the ward was spent sitting and rocking, with few activities (*Id.*, N.T. 2-155). During one of their visits in 1968, Linda's parents found Linda, a person capable of walking, strapped to a wheelchair by a straightjacket. A staff member explained that by strapping her into the chair, they would know exactly where Linda was (*Id.*, N.T. 2-152, 2-153). While at the institution, Linda was badly bruised and scarred (*Id.*, N.T. 2-164).

E. Voluntariness

Approximately 21 of the 45 living units at Pennhurst are locked (Matthews, Deposition at 34) to prevent individuals from leaving their living units (Uphold, Deposition at 139). Those individuals over the age of 18 who have been ''voluntarily'' admitted to Pennhurst are theoretically free to leave the institution at any time (Allen, N.T. 21-185). Those admitted on the petition of their parents are informed by their caseworker when they reach the age of 18 that they do not have to remain at Pennhurst. If the residents state that they wish to leave the institution and the staff determines that there is no place for them in the community, or believes that the individuals are not ready to go into the community, the staff will petition the courts to have the individuals committed to the institution by a court (*Id.*, N.T. 21-186, 21-205). Furthermore, those residents who either do not understand their alternatives, or are physically unable to indicate that they wish to leave Pennhurst, will be deemed to have consented to their continued placement at the institution (*Id.*, N.T. 21-210). Thus, the notion of voluntariness in connection with admission as well as in connection with the right to leave Pennhurst is an illusory concept. Few if any residents now have, nor did they have at the time of their admission, any adequate alternative to their institutionalization. As a practical matter, Pennhurst was and is their only alternative.[46]

F. Community Services in the Five County Area

Since the early 1960's there has been a distinct humanistic renaissance, replete with the acceptance of the theory of normalization for the habilitation of the retarded. Mason & Menolascino, *supra* note 6, at 136. The principles of normalization are an outgrowth of studies showing that those in large institutions suffered from apathy, stunted growth and loss in IQ, and that the smaller the living unit on which the retarded individual lived, the higher the level of behavioral functioning shown by the individual (Roos, N.T. 1-96 to 1-104). Under the principles of normalization, the retarded individual is treated as much like the non-retarded person as possible (*Id.*, N.T. 1-106, 1-107). The basic tenet of normalization is that a person responds according to the way he or she is treated (Glenn, N.T. 5-186, 5-187). The thrust of habilitation through normalization is the remediation of the delayed learning process so as to develop the maximum growth potential by the acquisition of self-help, language, personal, social, educational, vocational and recreation skills. Mason & Menolascino, *supra* note 6, at 139-140. The older theories of habilitating the retarded stressed protecting the individual, and were characterized by little expectation of growth. Given this lack of expectation, the individual rarely exhibited growth. However, once removed from depressing, restrictive routines, the retarded have been able to accomplish a great deal (Dybwad, N.T. 7-160).[47]

The environment at Pennhurst is not conducive to normalization. It does not reflect society. It is separate and isolated from society and represents group rather than family living (Hirst, N.T. 7-124). The principles of normalization have been accepted by the administration of Pennhurst and by the Department of Public Welfare, which is responsible for the administration of programs for the retarded in the five county area (Youngberg, N.T. 22-171; Rice, N.T. 26-43 to 26-45; Bilyew, N.T. 24-13; Hirst, N.T. 7-120), and the current intention of the Department of Public Welfare is to transfer all residents from Pennhurst by the early 1980's (Rice, N.T. 28-48).

The five county area (Bucks, Chester, Delaware, Montgomery and Philadelphia) has some community facilities providing for the education, training and care of the retarded covering all ages of retardation, including the profoundly retarded with multiple handicaps (Girardeau, N.T. 4-140, 4-141). These community facilities have

---

[46]Nearly all the parents of Pennhurst residents who testified stated that they placed their children in Pennhurst only as a last resort, and had there been community facilities or aid programs, their children would not have been placed at Pennhurst (Sobetsky, N.T. 9-142; Hight, N.T. 11-21).

[47]Mrs. Grace Auerback testified concerning the changes she has observed in her son, Sid, since his transfer from Pennhurst into a community home in 1973. While at Pennhurst, he was subdued and never talked; now, she testified, you cannot stop him. He is now able to cook, work and keep his own bank account. She testified that Sid had learned more in the last 3½ years while in the community than he had in the 38 years that he had resided at Pennhurst (N.T. 8-47, 8-48, 8-49, 8-51).

been an outgrowth of the acceptance of the principle of normalization and the rejection of institutions such as Pennhurst in connection with the habilitation of the retarded.

Many individuals now living at Pennhurst could be moved immediately into the community and would be able to cope with little or no supervision (Settle, N.T. 6-126; Hirst, N.T. 7-116). All the parties in this litigation are in agreement that given appropriate community facilities, all the residents at Pennhurst, even the most profoundly retarded with multiple handicaps, should be living in the community (Dybwad, N.T. 7-68).

The primary limiting factor in the transfer of Pennhurst residents to community facilities has been the failure of the Commonwealth and its subdivisions to provide sufficient living units, vocational and day care facilities and other support services at the community level. Since fiscal year 1972, only 186 Pennhurst residents have been transferred from the institution directly into community living units (Bilyew, N.T. 24-50); although 176 others were transferred from Pennhurst to other institutions during 1974 and 1975 (Clark, N.T. 21-170).

In November, 1970, Act 256 was signed by the Governor of Pennsylvania. This legislation appropriated twenty-one million dollars for the purpose of planning, designing and constructing community facilities which would enable 900 Pennhurst residents to be transferred to the community. In 1971, the McDowell report was prepared at a cost of $68,000. It detailed the programs and services needed to support the 900 Pennhurst residents in the community and provided a blueprint for the implementation of the Act (Samuels, N.T. 23-9, 23-10, 23-55). Though seven years have passed since the Act was signed, few of the facilities have become operational. The Department of Public Welfare now expects this program to be completed by 1980 (*Id.*, N.T. 23-44). Over eighteen million dollars of this fund remains unspent but is allocated to building these facilities (Stipulation, N.T. 7-97). As of April 25, 1977, however, only 37 Pennhurst residents have directly benefited from the Act (Samuels, N.T. 23-80).

Comparable facilities in the community are generally less expensive than large isolated state institutions. Services can be purchased at regular rates, rather than at rates which must be paid to attract individuals to work in a setting like Pennhurst (Conley, N.T. 11-107). The cost of running Pennhurst in 1976 was $27.8 million dollars, or $60 per resident per day. (*Id.*, N.T. 12-28). This does not include the fair rental value of the buildings at Pennhurst (estimated at $3–$4 per resident per day) (*Id.*, N.T. 11-114). The statewide cost of community living arrangements in Pennsylvania for 1976 was $17.64 per individual per day (PARC Exhibit 63, 64). Program services, which ⅓ of mentally retarded individuals would need, average approximately $10 per individual per day (Conley, N.T. 11-116, 11-117). Moreover, keeping the retarded individual in the community makes it possible for him or her to get employment. Eighty-five percent of the mentally retarded can be employed; though not all are capable of competitive employment (Settle, N.T. 7-4). The lifetime earnings of a mildly retarded individual often exceeds $500,000 (Conley, N.T. 12-21). For those with an IQ between 25 and 50, 45% of men and 12% of women earn about 20% of the average wage (*Id.*, N.T. 12-31). When the retarded can work, the amount of financial support which society must provide decreases and the individuals may benefit society with the taxes they pay. Furthermore, the investment per individual at Pennhurst is primarily for warehousing and not for the individual's well-being or future planning, as is the case with community facilities (*Id.*, N.T. 11-23, 11-24).

G. County Participation

The counties presently have a financial incentive to send their retarded to Pennhurst rather than provide them with habilitation within the community. When a retarded individual is placed in a state institution, such as Pennhurst, the Commonwealth pays 100% of the costs incurred in the habitation of the individual. However, if the individual receives services within the community, the county must provide 10% of the funds necessary to provide some of the services.

Every mentally retarded individual within the Commonwealth is assigned to a Base Service Unit (BSU) which is the county unit responsible for arranging community and institutional placements and for coordinating services for the individual (Rice, N.T. 25-67). Pennhurst residents are assigned to a BSU either on the basis of where they resided prior to admission to the institution, or where their family presently resides. Almost all of the parents of Pennhurst residents who testified stated that they had little or no contact with their child's BSU (Hunsicker, N.T. 9-49; Taylor, N.T. 13-30). The BSU's are invited to attend their residents' annual program review, but almost never do (Roy, N.T. 15-134; Hare, N.T. 8-176). The BSU's often fail to investigate the least restrictive alternative for the retarded individual under their charge. Placement at Pennhurst is often the only alternative presented to the committing judge at court commitment proceedings.[48]

The BSU's have been doing little to prepare Pennhurst residents to leave Pennhurst. Although the Pennsylvania Department of Public Welfare, Pennhurst staff and county officials are in complete agreement that the residents of Pennhurst should be transferred as soon as practicable to appropriate community facilities, apparently no one has taken the initiative to accomplish this objective (Hersh, N.T. 13-136).

The five county defendants are not in compliance with the Commonwealth's Community Living Arrangement (CLA) policy that at least 50% of the residents for these living facilities must be drawn from institutions. In contrast to other regions in the state, the counties which Pennhurst serves have a lower percentage of CLA residents drawn from institutions than from the community (Knowlton, Deposition at 52).

IV. The Merits

This case concerns the constitutional and statutory rights of retarded persons institutionalized at Pennhurst. Our discussion herein pertains to the retarded, individuals who, because of circumstances beyond their control, are unable to function at the same educational and behavioral levels as the rest of society. It concerns solely the retarded and not persons who are mentally or emotionally ill. These are individuals who have not broken any laws, carry no contagious disease and are not in any way a

---

[48]One Philadelphia BSU made a referral to Pennhurst for a child it had decided needed a structured environment with one-to-one interaction, even though it knew that the individual would not receive such individualized treatment at Pennhurst (Cooper, N.T. 29-74).

danger to society. If anyone is in need of training, education and care, they are. At issue is whether the Commonwealth's system of incarcerating the retarded in an institution known as Pennhurst in any way violates their constitutional or statutory rights.

Having concluded the trial phase of the liability portion of this litigation, it has become apparent that by and large the parties share the same goals: all desire to improve the education, training and care provided the retarded in Pennsylvania and believe that Pennhurst should be closed and that all the residents should be educated, trained and cared for in the community. All agree that institutions such as Pennhurst are inappropriate and inadequate for the habilitation of the retarded. Defendants agree with plaintiffs' contention that the habilitation provided Pennhurst residents does not meet minimally acceptable professional standards. The Commonwealth in recent years has been attempting to upgrade Pennhurst and the education, training and care provided therein to its retarded residents. Moreover, the Pennsylvania Department of Public Welfare's current plans call for the transfer of all Pennhurst residents from the institution into the community (though perhaps temporarily into other institutions) by the early 1980's. Defendants contend, however, that they are neither constitutionally nor statutorily mandated to make these transfers or to upgrade the care, education and training provided at Pennhurst. It is their position that no constitutional or statutory rights have been violated. We disagree. Moreover, defendants' plans to upgrade and eventually close Pennhurst have little, if any, bearing on the issue of whether the statutory or constitutional rights of Pennhurst's retarded residents have been, or are being, violated. As the court in *Welsch* v. *Likins*, 373 F.Supp. 487, 498 (D.Minn. 1974), aff'd in part, vacated and remanded in part, 550 F.2d 1122 (8th Cir. 1977), stated:

> good faith is not at issue here. "[R]ather the issue is of the protection of the constitutional rights" of the residents. . . . It does not suffice, therefore, to show that conditions have been upgraded at [the institution], that the situation will continue to improve in the future, and that even more achievements would be forthcoming were it not for the restrictions imposed by the legislature. It is the Court's duty, under the Constitution, to assure that every resident of [the institution] receives at least minimally adequate care and treatment consonant with the full and true meaning of the due process clause.

A.   Constitutional Right to Minimally Adequate Habilitation

The Supreme Court has not as yet stated that the retarded have a constitutional right to habilitation. It has, however, discussed the right to treatment of the mentally ill. *O'Connor* v. *Donaldson*, 422 U.S. 563, 95 S.Ct. 2486, 45 L.Ed.2d 396 (1975). Donaldson had been civilly committed to a state mental hospital in 1957 and had remained there involuntarily for nearly fifteen years. Repeatedly, but without success, he had demanded his release, contending that he was neither dangerous nor mentally ill, and that even if he were mentally ill, that he should be released since the hospital had not provided him with treatment for his illness. The *Donaldson* holding is very narrow: "a State cannot constitutionally confine without more a nondangerous individual who is capable of surviving safely in freedom by himself or with the help of willing and responsible family members or friends." *Id*. at 576, 95 S.Ct. at 2494.

Donaldson allegedly was suffering from "paranoid schizophrenia," *id*. at 565,

95 S.Ct. 2486, and was not retarded. When dealing with the retarded, the concern is for "habilitation" rather than for "treatment."[49]

> The use of the concept "habilitation" instead of "treatment" in the context of mental retardation reflects an awareness that "mental illness" is not synonymous with "mental retardation." Mental illness concerns an inability to cope with one's environment regardless of intellectual level. Mental illness can occur at any stage of life while mental retardation is considered to be a developmental disability beginning in the early years.

Mason & Menolascino, *supra* note 6, at 147 n. 72 (1976). Although we are convinced that the concept of "habilitation" for the retarded and "treatment" for the mentally and emotionally ill are separate and distinct concepts which should never be confused, in dealing with the question of the right of the retarded to adequate habilitation one must consider, to the extent applicable, those cases which deal with the right to treatment of the mentally ill.[50]

A great deal of scholarly and judicial attention has been focused on the question of a constitutional right to treatment and habilitation since Dr. Morton Birnbaum's seminal work, *The Right to Treatment*, 46 A.B.A.J. 499 (1960).[51]

Rouse v. *Cameron*, 125 U.S.App.D.C. 366, 373 F.2d 451 (1966), was one of the first federal cases to deal with the right to treatment. Rouse had been involuntarily committed to a mental hospital following his acquittal by reason of insanity of a misdemeanor for which the maximum term of imprisonment was one year. Rouse filed

---

[49]Often, those courts which have dealt with mentally ill and retarded individuals have blurred the issues involved. The "right to treatment" is frequently used in conjunction with the retarded, when in fact, these individuals are not in need of medical treatment, but of education and training. In part, this blurring is due to the fact that some of the cases involved several facilities, some for the retarded and some for the mentally ill, *see, e.g., Wyatt* v. *Stickney*, 325 F.Supp. 781 (M.D.Ala. 1971) (mentally ill), 344 F.Supp. 387 (M.D.Ala. 1972) (retarded), and others involved a single facility serving both retarded and mentally ill individuals, *see, e.g., Davis* v. *Watkins*, 384 F.Supp. 1196 (N.D.Ohio 1974).

[50]Of course, as the Supreme Court has noted, "careful attention must be paid to the differences between mentally ill and mentally retarded.... " *Kremens* v. *Bartley*, 431 U.S. 119, 135, 97 S.Ct. 1709, 1718, 52 L.Ed.2d 184 (1977). However, as one court has noted: "[i]n the context of the right to appropriate care for people civilly confined to public mental institutions, no viable distinction can be made between the mentally ill and the mentally retarded." *Wyatt* v. *Stickney*, 344 F.Supp. 387, 390 (M.D.Ala. 1972), aff'd in part, rev'd in part and remanded in part sub nom. *Wyatt* v. *Aderholt*, 503 F.2d 1305 (5th Cir. 1974).

[51]Dr. Birnbaum wrote:

> It is proposed ... that the courts under their traditional powers to protect the constitutional rights of our citizens begin to consider the problem of whether or not a person who has been institutionalized solely because he is sufficently mentally ill to require institutionalization for care and treatment actually does receive adequate medical treatment so that he may regain his health, and therefore his liberty, as soon as possible; that the courts do this by means of recognizing and enforcing the right to treatment; and, that the courts do this independent of any action by any legislature, as necessary and overdue development of our present concept of due process of law. 46 A.B.A.J. at 503.

See, e.g.: Mason & Menolascino, *supra* note 6; "Developments in the Law—Civil Commitment of the Mentally Ill," 87 *Harv.L.Rev.* 1190 (1974); Herr, "Civil Rights, Uncivil Asylums and the Retarded," 43 *Cin.L.Rev.* 679 (1974); Drake, "Enforcing the Right to Treatment: *Wyatt* v. *Stickney*, 10 Amer. *Crim.L.Rev.* 587 (1972); Case Comment, "*Wyatt* v. *Stickney* and the Right of Civilly Committed Mental Patients to Adequate Treatment," 86 *Harv.L.Rev.* 1282 (1973); Note, "The *Wyatt* Case: Implementation of a Judicial Decree Ordering Institutional Change," 84 *Yale L.J.* 1338 (1975); Hoffman and Dunn, "Beyond *Rouse* and *Wyatt*: An Administrative-Law Model for Expanding and Implementing the Mental Patient's Right to Treatment," 61 *Va.L.Rev.* 297 (1975).

a petition for habeas corpus which the district court denied, contending that he had a right to be released if he was not accorded adequate treatment. Although the Circuit Court reversed on the basis of a District of Columbia statute, Chief Judge Bazelon stated that "involuntary confinement" without treatment is 'shocking'," *id.* 125 U.S.App.D.C. at 370, 373 F.2d at 455, and noted that the purpose of involuntary hospitalization is treatment and not punishment. *Id.* 125 U.S.App.D.C. at 367, 373 F.2d at 452. He pointed out that a statute which provides for the mandatory commitment of an individual acquitted of a criminal offense by reason of insanity is permissible only because of its "humane therapeutic goals," and concluded that if treatment were not required under the statute, the statute might violate the Due Process, Equal Protection and Cruel and Unusual Punishment Clauses of the Constitution. *Id.* 125 U.S.App.D.C. at 368, 373 F.2d at 453.

Civil Commitment entails a "massive curtailment of liberty." *Humphrey* v. *Cady,* 405 U.S. 504, 509, 92 S.Ct. 1048, 31 L.Ed.2d 394 (1972). The only permissible justifications for committing the mentally ill are: (1) danger to the individual, (2) danger to others, and (3) need for treatment. *Jackson* v. *Indiana,* 406 U.S. 715, 737, 92 S.Ct. 1845, 32 L.Ed.2d 435 (1972); *Wyatt* v. *Aderholt,* 503 F.2d 1305, 1312 (5th Cir. 1974). Although this Court entertains serious doubts as to whether retarded individuals should ever be subjected to "commitment," there is no doubt that under the present case law, the only possible justification for committing the retarded to an institution such as Pennhurst is to provide them with habilitation, *i.e.,* education, training and care. Failure to provide adequate habilitation may well mean commitment for the life of the retarded individual. *Welsch* v. *Likins,* 373 F.Supp. 487, 497 (D. Minn. 1974), aff'd in part and vacated and remanded in part, 550 F.2d 1122 (8th Cir. 1977). In fact, at Pennhurst the average residency is twenty-one years.

Moreover, as the Court stated in *Jackson* v. *Indiana,* 406 U.S. at 738, 92 S.Ct. at 1858, "[a]t the least, due process requires that the nature and duration of commitment bear some reasonable relation to the purposes for which the individual is committed." Since the only justifiable purpose for the commitment of the retarded is habilitation, if habilitation is not provided, the nature of the commitment bears no reasonable relation to its purpose and the individual's due process rights have been violated. *Wyatt* v. *Aderholt,* 503 F.2d 1305, 1312 (5th Cir. 1974); *Donaldson* v. *O'Connor,* 493 F.2d 507, 521 (5th Cir. 1974), vacated, 422 U.S. 563, 95 S.Ct. 2486, 45 L.Ed.2d 396 (1975).[52]

---

[52]As heretofore pointed out, the Supreme Court's decision in *Donaldson* was very narrow; the Court did not pass upon the issue of the right to treatment or habilitation. The Court vacated the Fifth Circuit's broad holding and stated: "[o]f necessity our decision vacating the judgment of the Court of Appeals deprives that court's opinion of precedential effect, leaving this Court's opinion and judgment as the sole law of the case." 422 U.S. 563, 577 n. 12, 95 S.Ct. 2486, 2495, 45 L.Ed.2d 396 (1975). Prior to the Supreme Court's decision, the Fifth Circuit rendered a second right to treatment decision which relied heavily on its *Donaldson* opinion, *Wyatt* v. *Aderholt,* 503 F.2d 1305 (5th Cir. 1974), which like *Donaldson* was authored by Judge Wisdom. At least one commentator suggests "that *Wyatt* is still good law, thus leaving the right to treatment issue where it was before." "Without More": A Constitutional Right to Treatment?" 22 *Loyola L.Rev.* 373, 383 (1976). In support of this proposition, it should be noted that four days after deciding *Donaldson,* the Supreme Court denied *certiorari* in yet another Fifth Circuit right to treatment case. *The Department of Human Resources of the State of Georgia* v. *Burnham,* 422 U.S. 1057, 95 S.Ct. 2680, 45 L.Ed.2d 709 (1975). In *Burnham,* the district court had found that there was no constitutional right to

In *Robinson* v. *California*, 370 U.S. 660, 82 S.Ct. 1417, 8 L.Ed.2d 758 (1962), the Supreme Court held that incarceration solely on the basis of an individual's status constitutes cruel and unusual punishment. (Robinson was convicted of being a narcotics addict.) As was pointed out in *Welsch:*

> because plaintiffs [retarded individuals] have not been guilty of any criminal offenses against society, treatment is the only constitutionally permissible purpose of their confinement, regardless of procedural protections under the governing civil commitment statute. . . . This argument rests upon the Eighth and Fourteenth Amendments, relying principally upon the Supreme Court's decision in *Robinson* v. *California.* . . . The plaintiffs in the instant action are not criminals; they are victims of uncontrollable "status."
>
> If they are subject to "detention for mere illness—without a curative program," . . . plaintiffs will be within the ambit of the *Robinson* proscription.

373 F.Supp. at 496. Thus, commitment of the retarded can withstand constitutional scrutiny only when it is coupled with minimally adequate habilitation. *See United States* v. *Jackson,* 179 (U.S.App.D.C. 375, 385, 553 F.2d 109, 119 (1976).

Of the federal courts which have considered the right to habilitation issue in connection with involuntarily committed retarded individuals and the right to treatment of involuntarily committed mentally or emotionally ill individuals, only two reported cases have been called to our attention which denied the existence of such a constitutional right: *Burnham* v. *Department of Public Health of the State of Georgia,* 349 F.Supp. 1335 (N.D.Ga. 1972), and *New York State Ass'n for Retarded Children, Inc.* v. *Rockefeller,* 357 F.Supp. 752 (E.D.N.Y. 1973). *Burnham* was reversed by the Fifth Circuit, 503 F.2d 1319 (5th Cir. 1974), cert. denied, 422 U.S. 1057, 95 S.Ct. 2680, 45 L.Ed.2d 709 (1975), and the *Rockefeller* court, in approving a consent decree in that action appeared to be questioning its earlier finding of no constitutional right to treatment:

> Somewhat different legal rubrics have been employed in [the *Donaldson,* Wyatt line of] cases—"protection from harm" in this case and "right to treatment" and "need for care" in others. It appears that there is no bright line separating these standards. In the present posture of this case, there is no need for the court to re-examine the constitutional standard properly applicable to Willowbrook's residents. The relief which the parties agreed to will advance the very rights enunciated in the case law since this court's 1973 ruling.

New York State Ass'n for Retarded Children, Inc. v. *Carey,* 393 F.Supp. 715, 719 (E.D.N.Y. 1975).

The other courts which have examined the issue have all found a constitutional right to treatment or habilitation. *See, e.g., Wyatt* v. *Aderholt,* 503 F.2d 1305 (5th Cir. 1974); *Donaldson* v. *O'Connor,* 493 F.2d 507 (5th Cir. 1974), vacated 422 U.S. 563, 95 S.Ct. 2486, 45 L.Ed.2d 396 (1975); *Gary W.* v. *Louisiana,* 437 F. Supp. 1209 at 1219, (E.D.La.), modified, October 28, 1976 (involuntarily committed retarded chil-

---

treatment. 349 F.Supp. 1335 (N.D.Ga. 1972). The Fifth Circuit reversed on the basis of its *Donaldson* and *Aderholt* decisions. 503 F.2d 1319 (5th Cir. 1974). Even though the Supreme Court had vacated the *Donaldson* decision only four days before, it denied *certiorari* in *Burnham,* apparently allowing *Aderholt,* with its holding of a constitutional right to treatment to remain as the law of the Fifth Circuit.

dren have a constitutional right "to a program of treatment that affords the individual a reasonable chance to acquire and maintain those life skills that enable him to cope as effectively as his own capacities permit with the demands of his own person and of his environment and to raise the level of his physical, mental and social efficiency"); *Woe* v. *Mathews*, 408 F.Supp. 419, 429 (E.D.N.Y. 1976), remanded in part, dismissed in part sub· nom. *Woe* v. *Weinberger*, 556 F.2d 563 (2d Cir. 1977) ("[a]s a tentative formulation it would seem encumbent upon the State as confiner . . . to employ whatever means are necessary, including such care and treatment as are reasonably possible in the circumstances of the case, to promote the speedy release and return to liberty of the person confined."); *Davis* v. *Watkins*, 384 F.Supp. 1196, 1197 (N.D.Ohio 1974) (the court, dealing with a state facility apparently serving both mentally ill and retarded individuals held that "the State, upon committing an individual 'until he regains his sanity', incurs a responsibility to provide such care as is reasonably calculated to achieve that goal."); *Saville* v. *Treadway*, 404 F.Supp. 430 (M.D.Tenn. 1974) (three-judge court), consent agreement approved, 404 F.Supp. 433 (retarded individuals in state institutions have right to habilitative services); *Welsch* v. *Likins*, 373 F.Supp. 487 (D.Minn. 1974), aff'd in part and vacated and remanded in part, 550 F.2d 1122 (8th Cir. 1977) (retarded individuals involuntarily committed to state institutions have a constitutional right to treatment).

The Third Circuit has not yet decided the right to treatment or habilitation question. However, in *Scott* v. *Plante*, 532 F.2d 939, 947 (1976) it reversed a district court's F.R.Civ.P. 12(b)(6) dismissal of a right to treatment claim by an involuntarily committed mentally ill patient, stating:

> The Supreme Court did not reach the issue in *O'Connor* v. *Donaldson, supra.* Nor has this court considered it. It is not the kind of issue, however, which we should attempt to resolve definitively on the record that is before us. . . . It suffices for present purposes to say that it does not appear to a certainty that Scott would be entitled to no relief on his right to treatment claim under any state of facts he could prove in support of that claim. Thus, a Rule 12(b)(6) dismissal was improper.[53]

We hold that when a state involuntarily commits retarded persons, it must provide them with such habilitation as will afford them a reasonable opportunity to acquire and maintain those life skills necessary to cope as effectively as their capacities permit. *See Gary W.* v. *Louisiana*, 437 F.Supp. 1209 at 1219, (E.D.La.), modified,

---

[53]The constitutional right to treatment and habilitation has been extended to include other classes of involuntarily committed non-criminal offenders. *See, e.g., McRedmond* v. *Wilson*, 533 F.2d 757 (2d Cir. 1976) (wayward juveniles who have been institutionalized have a constitutional right to treatment); *Nelson* v. *Heyne*, 491 F.2d 352, 358 (7th Cir.), cert. denied, 417 U.S. 976, 94 S.Ct. 3183, 41 L.Ed.2d 1146 (1974) (juveniles who were involuntarily committed—one-third for non-criminal offenses—to a correctional institution have a constitutional right to rehabilitative treatment); *Pena* v. *New York State Division for Youth*, 419 F.Supp. 203, 207 (S.D.N.Y. 1976) ("this court finds that the detention of a youth under a juvenile justice system *absent provision for the rehabilitative treatment of such youth* is a violation of due process rights guaranteed under the Fourteenth Amendment."); *see also, Morgan* v. *Sproat*, 432 F.Supp. 1130, 1136 (S.D.Miss. 1977); *Morales* v. *Turman*, 383 F.Supp. 53, 124 (E.D.Tex. 1974), rev'd on other grounds, 535 F.2d 864 (5th Cir. 1976), judgment of Court of Appeals rev'd and remanded, 430 U.S. 322, 97 S.Ct. 1189, 51 L.Ed.2d 368 (1977); *Inmates of Boys' Training School* v. *Affleck*, 346 F.Supp. 1354, 1372 (D.R.I. 1972); *Stachulak* v. *Coughlin*, 364 F.Supp. 686 (N.D.Ill. 1973); and *Martarella* v. *Kelley*, 349 F.Supp. 575, 600 (S.D.N.Y. 1972).

October 28, 1976. On the basis of the evidence presented in these proceedings, we find that the retarded residents of Pennhurst have not received, and are not receiving, minimally adequate habilitation. Furthermore, on the basis of this record we find that minimally adequate habilitation cannot be provided in an institution such as Pennhurst. As the Court has heretofore found, Pennhurst does not provide an atmosphere conducive to normalization which is so vital to the retarded if they are to be given the opportunity to acquire, maintain and improve their life skills. Pennhurst provides confinement and isolation, the antithesis of habilitation. We found that Pennhurst has produced regression and in many instances destroyed life skills possessed by its retarded residents at the time of their admission.[54] We are inclined to agree with the following comments of Mason & Menolascino, *supra* note 6, at 156–7 (footnotes omitted):

> Although *Wyatt* and *Welsch* are significant in their recognition of the principles of normalization and the developmental model for the factual foundation of their formulation of the constitutional right to habilitation, their approach can be considered only the rudimentary beginning. The logic of normalization and the developmental model which *Wyatt* and *Welsch* recognized suggests full implementation of habilitation can only be achieved in a non-institutional setting. Institutions, by their very structure—a closed and segregated society founded on obsolete custodial models—can rarely normalize and habilitate the mentally retarded citizen to the extent of community programs created and modeled upon the normalization and developmental approach components of habilitation. Neither *Wyatt* nor *Welsch* fully implemented the right to habilitation in that they failed to challenge the very existence of the institution. Consequently, the two institutional characteristics most antithetical to the application of the normalization principle remain intact: segregation from the community and the total sheltering of retarded citizens in all spheres of their lives.

We wish to make it clear that our finding that the retarded at Pennhurst are being deprived of their constitutional right to minimally adequate habilitation is not limited to those residents who were court committed. Nearly fifty percent of the residents at Pennhurst did not go through court commitment procedures. They have been, and are being, deprived of minimally adequate habilitation to the same extent as those who were court committed. Moreover, as we have heretofore found, voluntariness in connection with admission and exit from Pennhurst is an illusory concept. The record in this case shows that Pennhurst residents had no practical alternative at the time of their admission and at the present time, they have no place else to go.

No constitutional mandate has been called to our attention which would require a state to provide habilitation for its retarded citizens. However, whenever a state accepts retarded individuals into its facilities, it cannot create or maintain those facilities in a manner which deprives those individuals of the basic necessities of life. In the case of the retarded, this constitutes an obligation to provide them with minimally adequate habilitation. *See Welsch* v. *Likins,* 550 F.2d 1122, 1132 (8th Cir.

---

[54]There has been no evidence introduced that any of the plaintiffs were committed to Pennhurst because they posed a danger to society, and, thus, we are not faced with that issue in this case. Moreover, as we have heretofore pointed out, the retarded pose no danger of physical harm to society. Retarded individuals who suffer from emotional and mental problems may pose a danger to society; however, these are due to mental and emotional problems which do not come within the purview of this opinion.

1977); *Nelson* v. *Heyne,* 491 F.2d 352, 360 (7th Cir.), cert. denied, 417 U.S. 976, 94 S.Ct. 3183, 41 L.Ed.2d 1146 (1974); *Vanderzeil* v. *Hudspeth,* No. J76-262(R) at 6 (S.D.Miss., filed February 11, 1977).

Once admitted to a state facility, the residents have a constitutional right to be provided with minimally adequate habilitation under the least restrictive conditions consistent with the purpose of the commitment. *Eubanks* v. *Clarke,* 434 F.Supp. 1022, 1028, (E.D.Pa. 1977); *J. L.* v. *Parham,* 412 F.Supp. 112, 139 (M.D.Ga. 1976) (three-judge court), appeal pending 431 U.S. 936, 97 S.Ct. 2647, 53 L.Ed.2d 253 (1977); *Gary W.* v. *Louisiana,* 437 F.Supp. 1209, (E.D.La.), modified, October 28, 1976; *Woe* v. *Mathews,* 408 F.Supp. 419, 428 (E.D.N.Y. 1976), remanded in part, dismissed in part sub nom. *Woe* v. *Weinberger,* 556 F.2d 563 (2d Cir. 1977); *Suzuki* v. *Quisenberry,* 411 F.Supp. 1113, 1132-33 (D.Hawaii 1976); *Lynch* v. *Baxley,* 386 F.Supp. 378, 392 (M.D.Ala. 1974); *Davis* v. *Watkins,* 384 F.Supp. 1196, 1206 (N.D.Ohio 1974); *Saville* v. *Treadway,* 404 F.Supp. 430, 437 (M.D.Tenn. 1974); *Welsch* v. *Likins,* 373 F.Supp. 487, 502 (D.Minn. 1974), aff'd in part and vacated and remanded in part, 550 F.2d 1122 (8th Cir. 1977); *Morales* v. *Turman,* 383 F.Supp. 53, 124 (E.D.Tex. 1974), rev'd on other grounds, 535 F.2d 864 (5th Cir. 1976), judgment of Court of Appeals rev'd and remanded, 430 U.S. 322, 97 S.Ct. 1189, 51 L.Ed.2d 368 (1977); *Wyatt* v. *Stickney,* 344 F.Supp. 387 (M.D.Ala. 1972), aff'd in part, remanded in part and decision reserved in part sub nom. *Wyatt* v. *Aderholt,* 503 F.2d 1305 (5th Cir. 1974); *Lessard* v. *Schmidt,* 349 F.Supp. 1078, 1096 (E.D.Wis. 1972) (three-judge court), vacated and remanded on other grounds, 414 U.S. 473, 94 S.Ct. 713, 38 L.Ed.2d 661 (1974); *Dixon* v. *Attorney General of the Commonwealth of Pennsylvania,* 325 F.Supp. 966, 973-4 (M.D.Pa. 1971) (consent decree), *but see Patton* v. *Dumpson,* 425 F.Supp. 621, 624 (S.D.N.Y. 1977).[55]

The right to minimally adequate habilitation in the least restrictive alternative stems from the Supreme Court's decision in *Shelton* v. *Tucker,* 364 U.S. 479, 81 S.Ct. 247, 5 L.Ed.2d 231 (1960), in which the Court, addressing itself to the question of permissible abridgment of constitutional liberties, stated:

> even though the governmental purpose be legitimate and substantial, that purpose cannot be pursued by means that broadly stifle fundamental personal liberties when the end can be more narrowly achieved. The breadth of legislative abridgment must be viewed in the light of less drastic means for achieving the same basic purpose.

---

[55]The *Patton* court was troubled by the fact that in *Sanchez* v. *New Mexico,* 396 U.S. 276, 90 S.Ct. 588, 24 L.Ed.2d 469 (1970), the Supreme Court dismissed an appeal from a case which had rejected the least restrictive alternative for "want of a substantial federal question." For the precedential effect of a summary dismissal for want of a substantial federal question *see Mandel* v. *Bradley,* 432 U.S. 173, 97 S.Ct. 2238, 2240, 53 L.Ed.2d 199 (1977) ("Summary actions, however . . . should not be understood as breaking new ground but as applying principles established by prior decisions to the particular facts involved.") Moreover, the constitutional right to treatment and habilitation is a newly developed area of the law. Nearly all of the federal cases dealing with a constitutional right to treatment for mentally ill individuals and a constitutional right to habilitation for retarded individuals have arisen since *Sanchez. See, e.g., O'Connor* v. *Donaldson,* 422 U.S. 563, 95 S.Ct. 2486, 45 L.Ed.2d 396 (1975); *Wyatt* v. *Aderholt,* 503 F.Supp. 1305 (5th Cir. 1974); *Welsch* v. *Likins,* 373 F.Supp. 487 (D.Minn. 1974), aff'd in part and vacated and remanded in part, 550 F.2d 1122 (8th Cir. 1977). We feel that when the Court next examines the issue, it will find that there is such a constitutional right. *See Welsch,* 373 F.Supp. at 501-2; *Lynch,* 386 F.Supp. at 392. *See also,* "Developments in the Law—Civil Commitment of the Mentally Ill," 87 *Harv.L.Rev.* 1190, 1247-8 (1974).

All admissions to state facilities, be it through court commitment, or otherwise, entail an infringement on fundamental rights and freedoms. *See Eubanks* v. *Clarke,* 434 F.Supp. 1022, 1028, (E.D.Pa. 1977). Because of this, due process demands that if a state undertakes the habilitation of a retarded person, it must do so in the least restrictive setting consistent with that individual's habilitative needs. As we have heretofore pointed out, isolation and confinement are counter-productive in the habilitation of the retarded. Furthermore, since the law recognizes that habilitation other than in the least restrictive setting is a violation of one's constitutional rights, there is no question that Pennhurst, as an institution for the retarded, should be regarded as a monumental example of unconstitutionality with respect to the habilitation of the retarded.[56] The Commonwealth and its subdivisions have a constitutional duty to explore and provide the least stringent practicable alternatives to confinement of retarded individuals at Pennhurst. *Welsch* v. *Likins,* 373 F.Supp. 487, 502 (D.Minn. 1974), aff'd in part and vacated and remanded in part, 550 F.2d 1122 (8th Cir. 1977). On the basis of this record, we find that the Commonwealth and its subdivisions did not fulfill and are not fulfilling this constitutional obligation with respect to the retarded at Pennhurst.

B. Constitutional Right to be Free from Harm

The retarded at Pennhurst have been physically abused. Lack of adequate supervision has produced an atmosphere of danger to the residents. Occasionally, there have been incidents of staff abuse of residents, including rape and beatings. Hundreds of injuries, both major and minor, are reported every month.

Residents of state institutions for the retarded have both an Eighth and Fourteenth Amendment right to freedom from harm. *Spence* v. *Staras,* 507 F.2d 554, 557 (7th Cir. 1974); *Romeo* v. *Youngberg,* No. 76-3429 at 3 (E.D.Pa., filed June 6, 1977); *Welsch* v. *Likins,* 373 F.Supp. 487, 502-3 (D.Minn. 1974), aff'd in part and vacated and remanded in part, 550 F.2d 1122 (8th Cir. 1977); *New York State Association for Retarded Children, Inc.* v. *Rockefeller,* 357 F.Supp. 752, 764 (E.D.N.Y. 1973). Defendants have argued that the recent Supreme Court decision, *Ingraham* v. *Wright,* 430 U.S. 651, 97 S.Ct. 1401, 51 L.Ed.2d 711 (1977), limits the applicability of the Eighth Amendment to those convicted of crimes. *Ingraham* held that the use of corporal punishment in public schools did not violate the student's Eighth Amendment rights. *Id.* 97 S.Ct. at 1409. In reaching this result, the Court reasoned:

> The schoolchild has little need for the protection of the Eighth Amendment. Though attendance may not always be voluntary, the public school remains an open institution. Except perhaps when very young, the child is not physically restrained from leaving school during school hours; and at the end of the school day, the child is invariably free to return home. Even while at school, the child brings with him the support of family and

---

[56]Moreover, habilitation in the least restrictive setting answers one of Chief Justice Burger's concerns, expressed in his concurrence in *Donaldson,* with respect to a constitutional right to treatment. His concern is that a state constitutionally might be able to justify indiscriminate confinement of individuals merely by providing treatment. *O'Connor* v. *Donaldson,* 422 U.S. 563, 589, 95 S.Ct. 2486, 45 L.Ed.2d 396 (1975). Since a state cannot constitutionally confine an individual in other than the least restrictive setting consistent with that individual's habilitative needs, it cannot confine a retarded person in a Pennhurst-like institution if that individual could benefit from habilitation in a less restrictive setting.

friends and is rarely apart from teachers and other pupils who may witness and protest any instances of mistreatment.

The openness of the public school and its supervision by the community afford significant safeguards agains the kinds of abuses from which the Eighth Amendment protects the prisoner. In virtually every community where corporal punishment is permitted in the schools, these safeguards are reinforced by the legal constraints of the common law. Public schoolteachers and administrators are privileged at common law to inflict only such corporal punishment as is reasonably necessary for the proper education and discipline of the child; any punishment going beyond the privilege may result in both civil and criminal liability. . . . As long as the schools are open to public scrutiny, there is no reason to believe that the common law constraints will not effectively remedy and deter excess such as those alleged in this case.

Id. 97 S.Ct. at 1412 (footnote omitted). The retarded at Pennhurst have none of these safeguards. Due to their own handicaps, few of the retarded are in a position to aid or protect their fellow residents, or to complain about their own treatment. Pennhurst is isolated and segregated from the community. The residents are not free to leave at the end of the day. In addition, few, if any, of the physically abusive incidents at Pennhurst were committed as disciplinary measures. Furthermore, the *Ingraham* Court specifically reserved the question of the availability of the Eighth Amendment to individuals confined in "mental" institutions. *Id*. 97 S.Ct. at 1411 n. 37.

As stated by Judge Judd in *New York Association for Retarded Children, Inc.* v. *Rockefeller*, 357 F.Supp. 752, 764-5 (E.D.N.Y. 1973);

> Since Willowbrook [an institution for the retarded] residents are for the most part confined behind locked gates, and are held without the possibility of a meaningful waiver of their right to freedom they must be entitled to at least the same living conditions as prisoners. . . . One of the basic rights of a person in confinement is protection from assaults by fellow immates or by staff. . . . Another is the correction of conditions which violate "basic standards of human decency."

On the basis of the evidence in this record, we find that the constitutional right to be free from harm of the retarded residents at Pennhurst has been violated.

C. Constitutional Right to Non-Discriminatory Habilitation

In a three-judge decision emanating from this court, *Pennsylvania Association for Retarded Children* v. *Commonwealth of Pennsylvania*, 343 F.Supp. 279 (E.D.Pa. 1972), it was legally recognized for the first time that the retarded had a constitutional right pursuant to the Equal Protection Clause of the Fourteenth Amendment to receive at least as much education and training as was being afforded by the Commonwealth to others.

As stated by Professor Burt in "Beyond the Right to Habilitation," in *The Mentally Retarded Citizen and the Law* 425-32 (1976):

> The *PARC* theory can and should mean that any state program that segregates mentally retarded citizens as such from others is highly suspect and that courts will require states to treat mentally retarded persons indistinguishably from others, except in ways that are both very limited and very clearly beneficial to the individual. By this test, segregation of the mentally retarded in a remote large-scale institution could never pass constitutional muster. . . .
> [E]xisting large-scale geographically remote institutions cannot by their nature provide adequate programs to remedy the intellectual and emotional shortcoming and the galling

social stigma that led the retarded residents to these institutions. If this evidence is fully marshaled in litigation, courts can . . . rule that present patterns of state segregation of retarded persons for "habilitation" or "educational" purposes are impermissible. Courts can . . . force states to close the Partlows and Willowbrooks and, even more important, to require alternative programs for mentally retarded persons which treat them as indistinguishably as possible from other persons. . . . A powerful case can thus be mounted that courts should command states to use extraordinary effort to avoid institutionalizing retarded citizens. By this analysis, *Wyatt* clearly was wrong in failing to address directly the adequacy of community alternatives to geographically remote residential institutional care. In this analysis, the adequacy of in-community resources is not an afterthought. It is central to the inquiry into whether separate treatment for the mentally retarded person is not inherently unequal just as racially segregated education was found inherently unequal in *Brown* v. *Board of Education.*

In this record, the evidence has been "fully marshaled" and we find that the confinement and isolation of the retarded in the institution called Pennhurst is segregation in a facility that clearly is separate and *not* equal. We are convinced that the same equal protection principles enunciated by the court in *Pennsylvania Association of Retarded Children* v. *Commonwealth of Pennsylvania,* 343 F.Supp. 279 (E.D.Pa. 1972), prohibit the segregation of the retarded in an isolated institution such as Pennhurst where habilitation does not measure up to minimally adequate standards. As we have heretofore discussed in this opinion, the retarded at Pennhurst have been segregated in an institution in which they have been and are being denied minimally adequate habilitation. Thus, on the basis of this record we find that the retarded at Pennhurst have been and presently are being denied their Equal Protection Rights as guaranteed by the Fourteenth Amendment to the Constitution.

D. *Pennsylvania Statutory Right to Minimally Adequate Habilitation*

The question has also been presented to the Court as to whether the residents at Pennhurst have a statutory right to minimally adequate habilitation. 50 P.S. § 4201 provides in pertinent part:

> The department [of public welfare] shall have power, and its duty shall be:
> (1) To assure within the State the availability and equitable provision of adequate mental health and mental retardation services for all persons who need them. . . .

This statute was first interpreted in *In Re: Joyce Z., a minor child* No. 2035-69 (Common Pleas, Allegheny County, filed March 31, 1975). Joyce Z.'s caseworker petitioned the court, pursuant to 50 P.S. § 4406,[57] to commit Joyce to a state facility for care and treatment. The caseworker suggested Western State School and Hospital as a proper facility for Joyce's commitment. A commitment hearing was held at which all the witnesses, including the superintendent of the institution itself, testified that Joyce would not receive adequate treatment at Western State School and Hospital. *Id.* at 9. In fact, the Commissioner of Mental Retardation for the Department of Welfare, Western Region, testified that if Joyce were placed in the institution, the regression which she was presently experiencing would continue because she would not be able to interact with staff due to staff shortages. *Id.* at 4. In its opinion the court, in construing 50 P.S. § 4201, stated:

---

[57] *See supra* note 12.

These are brave words. We mean to see that the State, acting through the Department of Public Welfare, abides by them.

Joyce has a right to life given to her by the Constitution of the United States; *she has a right to treatment given to her by the Mental Health and Mental Retardation Act of Pennsylvania;* this court may order that course of treatment best suited to meet Joyce's needs.

Id. at 10-11 [Emphasis supplied.]

It is abundantly clear that the Mental Health and Mental Retardation Act, 50 P.S. §§ 4201 *et seq.,* grants to the retarded in Pennsylvania the statutory right to minimally adequate habilitation. *See Eubanks* v. *Clarke,* 434 F.Supp. 1022, 1027 (E.D.Pa. 1977); *In Re Joyce Z.*[58] Furthermore, it is equally clear that the Commonwealth and the counties have been charged under the Act with the responsibility of providing such minimally adequate habilitation to the retarded. The Act envisions

a comprehensive cooperative State-county (or multi-county) program for the care, treatment and rehabilitation of persons who are . . . mentally retarded. . . . The State, through the Department of Welfare, is responsible for the overall supervision and control of the program to assure the availability of and equitable provision for adequate . . . mental retardation facilities, and the counties, separately or in concert, are assigned responsibilities as to particular programs. *Hoolick* v. *Retreat State Hospital,* 24 Pa.Cmwlth. 218, 221–22, 354 A.2d 609, 611 (1976). *See also,* 50 P.S. § 4201(8).[59]

On the basis of this record, we find that both the Commonwealth and the counties have violated their statutory obligation to provide minimally adequate habilitation to the retarded residents at Pennhurst. In particular, the Commonwealth has violated its statutory mandate to supervise and control the program of minimally adequate habilitation to these individuals.

E.   Federal Statutory Right to Non-Discriminatory Habilitation

The question has also been presented whether Section 504 of the Rehabilitation Act of 1973, 29 U.S.C. § 794, grants federal statutory rights to the retarded residents at Pennhurst which have been violated. Section 504 provides:

No otherwise qualified handicapped individual in the United States, as defined in section 706(6) of this title, shall, solely by reason of his handicap, be excluded from the participation in, be denied the benefits of, or be subjected to discrimination under any program or activity receiving Federal financial assistance.

There is no question that the retarded are "handicapped individuals" within the meaning of the Act, 42 Fed.Reg. 22678; *cf. Rhode Island Society for Autistic Children* v. *Board of Regents for Education for the State of Rhode Island,* No. 5081 at 8 (D.R.I., filed August 1, 1975), nor is there any question that Pennhurst is a "program or activity receiving Federal financial assistance."

In enacting Section 504 of the Rehabilitation Act of 1973, Congress has in effect codified the constitutional right to equal protection. Section 504 was originally

---

[58] *Cf. Janet D.* v. *Carros,* 240 Pa.Super. 291, 362 A.2d 1060 (1976) (Juvenile Court Act, 11 P.S. §§ 50-101 *et seq.,* provides civilly committed juveniles a right to treatment).

[59] The counties also have the power to establish "[a]ny other service or program designed to prevent . . . the necessity of admitting or committing the mentally disabled to a facility." 50 P.S. § 4301(e)(3).

introduced in 1971–72 as a bill to include the handicapped in the Civil Rights Act of 1964. Introducing the bill in the Senate on January 20, 1972, Senator Humphrey, its primary sponsor there, said:

> I introduce . . . a bill . . . to insure equal opportunities for the handicapped by prohibiting needless discrimination in programs receiving Federal financial assistance. . . . The time has come when we can no longer tolerate the invisibility of the handicapped in America. . . . I am calling for public attention to three-fourths of the Nation's institutionalized mentally retarded, who live in public and private residential facilities which are more than 50 years old, functionally inadequate, and designed simply to isolate these persons from society. . . . These people have the right to live, to work to the best of their ability—to know the dignity to which every human being is entitled. But too often we keep children, whom we regard as "different" or a "disturbing influence," out of our schools and community activities altogether. . . . Where is the cost-effectiveness in consigning them to . . . "terminal" care in an institution?
>
> These are people who can and must be helped to help themselves. That this is their constitutional right is clearly affirmed in a number of recent decisions in various judicial jurisdictions.

118 Cong. Rec. 525 (1972).

In view of our finding that the Equal Protection Clause of the Fourteenth Amendment prohibits the segregation of the retarded in an isolated institution such as Pennhurst where the habilitation provided the retarded does not meet minimally adequate standards, consistency requires that we find that the Pennhurst residents' federal statutory right to habilitation in a non-discriminatory manner has been violated. See *Mattie T. v. Charles E. Holladay,* No. DC 75-31-S (N.D.Miss., filed July 20, 1977). We hold that Section 504 confers a private right of action; that it imposes affirmative obligations on state and local governmental officials and that under Section 504 unnecessarily separate and minimally inadequate services are discriminatory and unlawful. *Lloyd* v. *Regional Transportation Authority,* 548 F.2d 1277 (7th Cir. 1977); *Barnes* v. *Converse College,* 436 F.Supp. 635 (D.S.C., filed July 12, 1977); *Gurmankin* v. *Costanzo,* 411 F.Supp. 982 (E.D.Pa. 1976) aff'd, 556 F.2d 184 (3d Cir. 1977); 42 Fed.Reg. 22687 (1977); *cf. Lau* v. *Nichols,* 414 U.S. 563, 94 S.Ct. 786, 39 L.Ed.2d 1 (1974). On the basis of this record, we find that the rights of the retarded at Pennhurst under Section 504 of the Rehabilitation Act of 1973 have been and are being violated.

V. Liability of the Individual Defendants

Plaintiffs Terri Lee Halderman, Larry Taylor, Kenny Taylor, Robert Sobetsky, Theresa Sobetsky, Nancy Beth Bowman, George Sorotos, and Linda Taub[60] are retarded individuals who resided at Pennhurst. They seek monetary damages for injuries received while at the institution from the following defendants: Frank S. Beal (Secretary of the Pennsylvania Department of Public Welfare); Stanley Meyers (Deputy Secretary for Mental Retardation, Pennsylvania Department of Public Welfare); Helen Wohlgemuth (former Secretary of the Pennsylvania Department of Public Welfare);

---

[60]Mr. Taub testified that neither he nor his daughter, Linda, seek monetary damages despite the allegation in the complaint to the contrary.

Aldo Colautti (Executive Deputy Secretary, Pennsylvania Department of Public Welfare); Wilbur Hobbs (Deputy Secretary for Southeastern Region, Pennsylvania Department of Public Welfare); Russell Rice, Jr. (Commissioner of Mental Retardation for Southeastern Region, Pennsylvania Department of Public Welfare); C. Duane Youngberg (Superintendent of Pennhurst); Robert Smilovitz (former Assistant Superintendent of Pennsylvania); Joseph Foster (Assistant Superintendent of Pennhurst); Margaret Green (employee at Pennhurst); Betty Uphold (a supervisor on Unit 9 at Pennhurst); Alice Barton (a supervisor on Unit 7 at Pennhurst); P. E. (Pauline) Klick (charge aid on Unit 7 at Pennhurst); Dr. Parocca (a former Pennhurst physician) and Helen Francis (Director of Nursing at Pennhurst).

As the Court heretofore found, these plaintiffs did suffer serious injury during their residence at Pennhurst. However, there was no evidence introduced at trial that any one of the above named defendants was, in any way, personally involved with the physical abuses inflicted upon these residents. To the contrary, the evidence shows that the defendants acted in the utmost good faith and that they did not know nor reasonably should have known that the actions which they took, or failed to take, within the sphere of their official responsibilities were in any way violative of the rights of the retarded residents at Pennhurst. For the most part, the evidence showed that those affiliated with the administration of Pennhurst were dedicated and sincere in their efforts to habilitate the retarded who came within the sphere of their supervision. They apparently took every means available to them to reduce the incidents of abuse and injury, but were constantly faced with staff shortages. In addition, as we have already found, the administration at Pennhurst was saddled with an institution which by its very nature produced an atmosphere conducive to injury. The Court, therefore, finds that the defendants have met their burden of convincing us by a preponderance of the evidence that they are entitled to the good faith immunity from damages afforded to such officials in connection with the injuries suffered by the named plaintiffs. *O'Connor* v. *Donaldson*, 422 U.S. 563, 576–77, 95 S.Ct. 2486, 45 L.Ed.2d 396 (1975); *Wood* v. *Strickland,* 420 U.S. 308, 95 S.Ct. 992, 43 L.Ed.2d 214 (1975); *Thompson* v. *Burke,* 556 F.2d 231, 239–40 (3d Cir. 1977); *Skehan* v. *Board of Trustees of Bloomsburg State College,* 538 F.2d 53, 59-62 (3d Cir. 1976). We find that the individual defendants are dedicated professionals in the field of retardation who were given very little with which to accomplish the habilitation of the retarded at Pennhurst.

Accordingly, we find that there is no basis for awarding monetary damages in this case.

VI. Conclusion

This opinion is in lieu of Findings of Fact and Conclusions of Law, pursuant to Rule 52(a) of the Federal Rules of Civil Procedure. As we have attempted to make clear, our Findings and Conclusions pertain solely to the retarded at Pennhurst.

For the reasons heretofore enunciated, the Court finds that the retarded at Pennhurst have been and are presently being denied certain constitutional and statutory rights in connection with their institutionalization at Pennhurst.

In an Order filed this date, we have scheduled a hearing for Friday, January 6, 1978 at 9:00 a.m. in Courtroom 10-B of this United States Courthouse, 601 Market

Street, Philadelphia, Pennsylvania for the purpose of determining the appropriate relief to be granted.

ON INJUNCTIVE RELIEF

In an opinion filed on December 23, 1977, this Court made findings of fact and conclusions of law in this matter. Upon its findings, the Court held that the constitutional and statutory rights of the retarded at Pennhurst State School and Hospital ("Pennhurst") had been and are being violated. Some of the determinations made by the Court in its opinion were:

1. That when a state institutionalizes individuals because they are retarded, the United States Constitution (Eighth and Fourteenth Amendments) and the laws of Pennsylvania (50 P.S. §§ 4101 *et seq.*) require the state to provide such minimally adequate habilitation as will afford a reasonable opportunity for them to acquire and maintain such life skills as are necessary to enable them to cope as effectively as their capacities permit.

2. That the Rehabilitation Act of 1973, 29 U.S.C. § 794, grants rights to the retarded residents of Pennhurst, which rights have been and are being violated.

3. That the retarded at Pennhurst are not receiving minimally adequate habilitation and that such minimally adequate habilitation cannot be provided at Pennhurst because it does not provide an atmosphere conducive to normalization, which the experts all agree is vital to the minimally adequate habilitation of the retarded.

Having concluded the liability phase of this litigation, we must now determine the appropriate relief. In view of the Court's finding that institutionalization at Pennhurst is not conducive to normalization, which is vital to the habilitation of the retarded, our Order must provide that immediate steps be taken to remove the retarded residents from Pennhurst. Great caution and care must be exercised, however, to make certain that each and every retarded resident who is moved from Pennhurst can be accommodated in a community facility which will provide minimally adequate habilitation. Furthermore, the Court's Order shall not be construed to limit in any manner the use of the Pennhurst facilities from any other purpose in the future.

A hearing was held on January 6, 1978, at which the Court requested that the parties meet and attempt to agree upon a Court Order which would be acceptable to all the litigants. After meeting, the parties informed the Court that they had been unable to agree and would never be able to agree. The Court then directed that the parties submit proposed Orders detailing their views as to the appropriate relief for the Court to grant together with a memorandum pointing out what they considered unacceptable in their opponent's proposed Order.

The Order submitted by the Commonwealth defendants contained a plan which was essentially the same plan introduced by them at the trial in May, 1977. As was pointed out in this Court's opinion, the Commonwealth defendants agreed that the retarded should be removed from Pennhurst and readily admitted that the only reason that the litigation was necessary was because they wished to accomplish the closing of Pennhurst as a residence for the retarded, pursuant to their own schedule which was vague and indefinite.

A final hearing was held on January 16, 1978, at which time the parties informed the Court that they did not intend to introduce any additional evidence. All the parties agreed that the record in this case contained all the evidence necessary for the Court to formulate its Order.

Accordingly, we shall this date enter an Order of judgment in favor of the plaintiffs and against the defendants, and shall mandate the appropriate injunctive relief necessary to remedy the constitutional and statutory violations which the Court in its Opinion of December 23, 1977 found are being suffered by the retarded residents at Pennhurst.

ORDER

AND NOW, this 17th day of March, 1978, pursuant to findings of fact and conclusions of law made by the Court in an Opinion filed December 23, 1977, it is hereby ORDERED that judgment is entered in favor of the plaintiffs and against the defendants, and injunctive relief is ORDERED as follows:

1. Commonwealth and county defendants, their successors, and their officers, agents, servants, employees, attorneys and all persons in active concert or participation with them are permanently enjoined to provide suitable community living arrangements for the retarded residents of Pennhurst, and those retarded persons on its waiting list, together with such community services as are necessary to provide them with minimally adequate habilitation until such time as the retarded individual is no longer in need of such living arrangement and/or community service.

2. Commonwealth and county defendants, as aforesaid, are permanently enjoined to develop and to provide a written individualized program plan, formulated in accordance with professional standards (Opinion, page 25; Roos N.T. 1–115, 1–116, Hare N.T. 8–168) to each member of plaintiff class, to provide to each an individualized habilitation program, to provide annual periodic review thereof and the opportunity to each member of plaintiff class and to his or her next friend to be heard thereon.

3. Commonwealth and county defendants, as aforesaid, are permanently enjoined to provide all necessary and proper monitoring mechanisms to assure that community living arrangements and other community services of the necessary quantity and quality are provided and maintained.

4. Commonwealth and county defendants, as aforesaid, are permanently enjoined to implement with dispatch Act 256 of the 1970 Pennsylvania General Assembly, the specific schedule to be set by further Order of this Court upon recommendation of the Master as set forth in paragraph 6(a) below.

5. The Court, on the basis of nine weeks' testimony in this case and the submissions of all parties, finds that the implementation of this Order will be impossible without the appointment of a Special Master, and, therefore, pursuant to Rule 53, Fed.R.Civ.P., and in the exercise of the Court's equitable powers, the Court shall appoint a Special Master with the power and duty to plan, organize, direct, supervise and monitor the implementation of this and any further Orders of the Court. Commonwealth and county defendants, their successors, officers, agents, servants, employees, attorneys and all persons in active concert or participation with them shall provide the Master with access to all premises, records, documents and personnel and residents and with every other cooperation and service necessary to the discharge of the Master's duties and shall make available to the Master all professional and other resources of the

Department of Public Welfare, the Pennhurst State School and Hospital, the County Offices of Mental Retardation and the Base Service Units as may be necessary to execute this Court's Orders.

6. The Special Master shall prepare and present to this Court for its approval and Order a Plan of Implementation which shall include the following:

(a) A plan specifying the quantity and type of community living arrangements and other community services necessary for the habilitation of all plaintiffs in the least separate, most integrated, least restrictive community setting, taking into account the existing community services in the five county area and including, by county, specification of the residential, program and staffing patterns necessary, the delineation of responsibility for their creation and maintenance, their funding and a specified time frame for their provision.

(b) A report specifying resources, procedures, and a schedule for individual evaluations and the formulation of individual exit and community program plans required for the habilitation of each member of plaintiff class and for their periodic review.

(c) A plan for the recruitment, hiring and training of a sufficient number of qualified community staff to be detailed to each Base Service Unit to manage the preparation of individual exit and community program plans for each member of plaintiff class and upon completion of such plans to assist in the execution of the responsibility to create, develop, maintain, and monitor the community living arrangements and other services required.

(d) A plan for the creation, development and maintenance of mechanisms to monitor a system of community services to assure that community living arrangements and other community services of the necessary quality and quantity are continuously provided to retarded persons in the least separate, most integrated, least restrictive community setting, which plan shall include but shall not be limited to the provision of friend-advocates to assist in the protection of the rights of each member of plaintiff class.

(e) A plan to provide retarded people, members of the class, with continuing information concerning the effect and the implementation of the Court's decision, concerning the plans to provide all necessary community living arrangements and other community services to them and any other general or specific information regarding the conditions necessary to habilitation of retarded persons and to provide for consultation with them.

(f) A plan to provide parents and family of the members of the class with continuing information concerning the effect and the implementation of the Court's decision, concerning the plans to provide all necessary community living arrangements and other community services to their relative and any other general or specific information regarding the conditions necessary to habilitation of retarded persons and to provide for consultation with them.

(g) A plan to provide opportunities for alternative employment to each employee of Pennhurst State School and Hospital, including employment in community programs and otherwise.

7. Within not more than sixty (60) days after appointment, the Master shall file with this Court the reports required at paragraphs 6(a) and (b) above and 11 below. A hearing will then be scheduled by the Court within fifteen (15) days from the date of their filing. Following the adoption of any plan by Order of the Court, it shall be implemented forthwith.

8. The Master shall engage such staff of his or her own as he or she finds necessary, subject to the approval of the Court. The Master and his or her staff shall be compensated by commonwealth defendants at a rate to be set by the Court; the expenses of the mastership shall be borne by the commonwealth defendants. The Master shall promptly submit to the Court a form of Order with respect to these matters.

9. County defendants, as aforesaid, are hereby enjoined from recommending or in any way counselling that any individual be committed to Pennhurst, and from petitioning for the commitment of any individual to Pennhurst, and from advancing in any way any application for admission to Pennhurst, and are herewith enjoined from participating in any program or activity in connection with the placement in the future or commitment in the future of any retarded person at Pennhurst.

10. Commonwealth defendants, as aforesaid, are hereby enjoined from recommending or in any way counselling that any individual be committed to Pennhurst, and from petitioning for the commitment of any individual to Pennhurst, and from advancing in any way any application for admission to Pennhurst, and are herewith enjoined from participating in any program or activity in connection with the placement in the future or commitment in the future of any retarded person at Pennhurst. Commonwealth defendants are further enjoined from providing a residence and/or habilitation at Pennhurst to any retarded person who is not as of this date a resident at Pennhurst.

11. The Special Master, as aforesaid, shall prepare and present to the Court for its Order a plan for the interim operation of Pennhurst pending its prompt replacement by community living arrangements and other community services. The plan shall address, but need not be limited to, the matters referenced in paragraphs 12–19 below, any other condition at Pennhurst which threatens the life, safety or well-being of any Pennhurst resident, and measures to assure that the interim operation of Pennhurst, including all activities therein, contributes to the prompt provision of services in the community necessary to the habilitation of each Pennhurst resident.

12. Commonwealth defendants are hereby mandated to take every precaution to prevent the physical or psychological abuse, neglect or mistreatment of any Pennhurst resident. Each and every alleged incident of abuse, neglect or mistreatment shall be promptly investigated. The manner and mechanisms of such investigations shall be developed and established by the plan referenced in paragraph 11.

13. Commonwealth defendants are hereby enjoined to exert the maximum effort in enforcing the following Department of Public Welfare regulations on the "Use of Restraints in Treating Patients/Residents" and "Personnel Rules and Institutional Policy on Acts of Abuse Against Patients/Residents" (promulgated in 7 Pennsylvania Bulletin 3199 (October 29, 1977)) which include *inter alia* the following requirements:

a. That mechanical restraints controlling involuntary movement or lack of muscular control due to organic conditions be employed only as part of an individual program plan, upon a finding of the program team trained in the use of such restraints, and only when necessary to 1) prevent injury to self or others, or 2) promote normative body positioning and physical functioning.

b. That restraints shall be used to control acute or episodic, aggressive behavior only when a resident is acting in such a manner as to be a clear and present danger to self or others and only when less restrictive measures and techniques have been proven to be less effective.

c. That mechanical restraints may be used only upon the order of a qualified mental retardation professional for a period not to exceed two hours; that the resident must be checked every fifteen minutes and must be examined by a physician before the initial order is renewed.

d. That chemical restraints may be administered only upon the order of a physician.

e. That seclusion (practice of placing a resident alone in a locked room) is prohibited in all cases except where it is apparent that there exists a clear and present danger to the resident, other residents or staff and all other less restrictive methods have failed or have been deemed inappropriate. (Title XIX-ICF-MR 249.13 and State Agency Letter No. 77-30 issued December 14, 1977.)

f. That individual program plans shall require and document that all possible attempts be made at preventing assaultive behavior by positive, constructive intervention.

g. That acts of abuse by employees directed at residents are absolutely prohibited and are cause for disciplinary action including dismissal.

h. That an abusive act is any action which may cause or causes physical or emotional harm or injury and includes any wilful action which violates the regulations on use of restraints.

14. Commonwealth defendants are hereby enjoined from:

(a) Administering excessive or unnecessary medications to class members;

(b) Using medication as punishment, for the convenience of the staff, as a substitute for programming, or in quantities that interfere with a Pennhurst resident's functioning;

(c) Failing to ensure that only appropriately trained staff are allowed to administer drugs to residents;

(d) Failing to provide training programs to staff who administer drugs to residents. The nature of such training programs, and the qualifications to be required of staff members who administer drugs to residents shall be established in the plan;

(e) Administering drugs to residents on a p.r.n. basis. Written policies and procedures governing the safe administration and handling of medications shall be established pursuant to guidelines developed in the plan;

(f) Failing to monitor and to provide for at least monthly reviews by a physician of each resident's medications.

15. Commonwealth defendants are enjoined from failing to provide a program of medical and health related services for residents which provides accessibility, quality and continuity of care for physical illness or injury. The plan of implementation shall develop and establish detailed standards for the provision of adequate medical and health related services to residents.

16. Commonwealth defendants are hereby enjoined from failing to provide individualized adaptive wheelchairs to each physically handicapped resident who needs

them. Each and every individual resident shall be immediately evaluated to ascertain the need for such equipment.

17. Commonwealth defendants are hereby enjoined from feeding any resident in the supine position or in any position less than the maximum upright position consistent with their capabilities and handicaps.

18. Commonwealth defendants are hereby enjoined from denying any resident programmed activities as punishment.

19. Commonwealth defendants are enjoined to take every precaution to keep every Pennhurst building currently housing residents clean, odorless and insect-free at all times.

20. All bulletins, memoranda, directives of official policy issued by the defendants in connection with the implementation of this Court's Order, shall, upon issuance, be sent to counsel for each of the plaintiffs.

21. Jurisdiction is retained by this Court until further Order.

NOTES

1. The *Pennhurst* decision obviously brings together almost all of the legal theories that have been applied to the problem of inhumane residential institutions. It also breaks some new doctrinal ground in finding a "constitutional right to non-discriminatory habilitation." But the most progressive aspect of the opinion is the use of all these legal theories not to merely improve conditions and programs at Pennhurst but rather to mandate deinstitutionalization of the residents out of Pennhurst and into community alternatives. During the sixth week of trial in *Halderman,* Judge Broderick was quoted as having asked one of the expert witnesses, "Would you agree with the other witnesses I've heard that it is time to sound the death knell for institutions for the retarded?" Ferleger, D., "The Future of Institutions for Retarded Citizens," *Mental Retardation and the Law,* 28 (July, 1978). As the cases cited in Judge Broderick's opinion make clear, *Halderman* was not the first decision to rely upon the concept of least restrictive alternatives, but it was the first to follow the concept to its logical conclusion—sounding the death knell for large inhumane institutions and forcing state officials to provide services to mentally retarded people in local communities.

2. The *Pennhurst* ruling was made possible by the development of models and working examples of community alternatives for serving handicapped people. Some of the pioneering work in this area grew out of programs in Omaha, Nebraska, and a few other innovative efforts in other parts of the country. See, e.g., President's Committee on Mental Retardation, *Changing Patterns in Residential Services for the Mentally Retarded* (Kugel, R., and Shearer, A., eds. 1976); Wolfensberger, W., *Normalization: The Principle of Normalization in Human Services,* (1972). Federal support of the community alternatives concept has been described in a report of the General Accounting Office:

> In 1963 President Kennedy proposed and the Congress approved two major Federal grant programs aimed at developing community services and facilities needed to shift the place of care away from State institutions. At that time there were more than 680,000 mentally disabled persons in public institutions. The President's special message to the Congress, which cited deplorable conditions in institutions and the Nation's

limited ability to treat the mentally disabled in or out of the institutions, called for a bold new approach to the problems of mental disability. Three major objectives were included in the approach; they were (1) to seek out the causes of mental illness and mental retardation and eradicate them, (2) to strengthen the underlying resources of knowledge and skilled manpower needed by the Nation to attack mental disability, and (3) to strengthen and improve the program and facilities serving the mentally disabled, with emphasis on developing community-based services. The President stated that the new mental health program would make it possible, within a decade or two, to reduce the numbers of mentally ill persons in institutions by 50 percent or more. No specific numbers were cited for reducing the institutionalized mentally retarded population.

The resulting Mental Retardation Facilities and Community Mental Health Centers Construction Act of 1963 (42 U.S.C. 2689) became the basis for a major part of the Federal Government's involvement in deinstitutionalization. In subsequent years, other Federal programs, such as Medicaid, Supplemental Security Income (SSI), Vocational Rehabilitation, and Developmental Disabilities, have been initiated or changed to make it possible for more mentally disabled persons to live and be treated in their communities.

The deinstitutionalization effort was further enhanced in November 1971 when President Nixon established, as a national goal, the return of one-third of the over 200,000 mentally retarded persons in public institutions to useful lives in the community. He also called upon the Department of Justice to strengthen the assurance of full legal rights for the retarded and called upon the Department of Housing and Urban Development (HUD) to assist in the development of special housing arrangements to help retarded persons live independently in the community. In October 1974, President Ford issued a statement in support of the November 1971 goal.[f]

The result in *Pennhurst* was based upon strong evidence presented to the court regarding the negative effects of large-scale institutions in contrast to the advantages of programs in the community:

> The court's ruling was based on the testimony of fourteen experts that not one of the 1200 people at Pennhurst needed to be there for habilitation, that they could all be accommodated in small-scale community homes with services in integrated, community settings, that this was so because the development of retarded people, especially severely and profoundly retarded people, requires individualized interaction, and that such individualization was systematically impossible in large remote institutions, but possible, and even likely, in small, integrated community settings. The court also had in front of it three studies confirming that the necessary individualized relationships flourish in small group settings but wither in institutional settings.[g]

Moreover, as the court noted in its opinion, community programs are preferable to large institutions upon purely cost-benefit grounds; it is cheaper for a state to provide community-based alternatives to institutions. See, e.g., Comptroller General of the United States, *Returning the Mentally Disabled to the Community: Government Needs to Do More* 5-7; Conley, R., *The Economics of Mental Retardation* (1973); Murphy, J., and Datel, W., "A Cost-Benefit Analysis of Community Versus Institutional Living," 27 *Hospital and Community Psychiatry* 165 (Mar., 1976).

---

[f]Comptroller General of the United States, *Returning the Mentally Disabled to the Community: Government Needs to Do More* 3-4 (1977).

[g]Laski, F., "Right to Services in the Community: Implications of the Pennhurst Case," 5 *Health Law Project Library Bulletin* 1, 2 (May, 1978).

3.   The results of the deinstitutionalization movement have not all been totally positive. In a few instances, the banner of deinstitutionalization has been waved for institutional release programs, which turned out to be little more than the "dumping" of
residents out of an institution, with no arrangements made for appropriate housing or
pgorams in the community. Mental patients have been summarily taken from institutions and sent to fend for themselves in the community, where they often wind up in
substandard nursing homes and run down "welfare" hotels—what *Newsweek*
magazine has called "miniature snake pits" (Clark, M., "The New Snake Pits,"
Newsweek 93,94 (May 15, 1978).

Fear that institutions will be closed or phased out without the development of
adequate community alternatives has been a major factor resulting in resistance to
deinstitutionalization. In its injunctive relief, the *Pennhurst* court has sought to ensure
that no resident be moved except to a community-based alternative where appropriate
habilitation programs are available. The Pennhurst experiment is being closely watched
to see if the phasing out of a large institution can be accomplished without the dumping
of residents into communities unprepared or unwilling to provide needed services or
programs.

Awareness of the two-edged sword of deinstitutionalization has been recognized in a carefully worded position statement by the National Association for Retarded
Citizens:

ISSUE: PLACEMENT IN A RESIDENTIAL FACILITY
   The lack of alternatives within a community, the limited availability of service
monies, and the perception of a retarded person as having fewer needs than the ordinary
citizen, have all contributed to many inappropriate residential placements.
   The problem of dehumanization may occur in all types of community programs and
residential facilities. Too often, in an attempt to move an individual from a large
residential facility back into a community setting, the safeguards necessary to ensure that
the needs of the individual are in fact being adequately met have not always been
established.
POSITION:
   The retarded individual has a right to receive services in the least restrictive environment capable of meeting the person's developmental needs. The placement of an individual in any particular residential setting must be based on that individual's needs at
that point in time. Every effort must be made to meet the retarded person's needs
through generic resources of the community rather than resorting to a routine residential
placement. The individual retarded person, as well as parents or guardians, should
participate in the selection of an appropriate residential alternative. Depending upon the
individual's ability to communicate opinions or wishes, his or her choice should be
given priority in making long-range decisions about where he or she is to live. No
individual should be admitted to a facility which is unable to meet his or her particular
needs. Prior to admission the prospective resident should have a comprehensive evaluation, covering physical, emotional, social and cognitive factors, conducted by an interdisciplinary team. The interdisciplinary team has a responsibility to involve parents or
guardians to the maximum extent possible. Only when it is determined by a team review
that the individual will benefit more appropriately from institutional programs should
institutional placement be considered.
   Each resident who is not actively represented by a parent, guardian or friend should
have a citizen volunteer advocate in order to ensure the resident's rights and welfare. No
resident should be represented solely by a person who is an employee of the residential
service agency.

In considering individual needs for a residential service, it must be remembered that adults usually have a need to live separately from their parents in the least restrictive environment suitable to their current level of independence.

When a resident is ready to transfer from one type of residential facility to a different type, adequate resources and services for meeting his or her needs must be available. Responsibility for the supervision of persons who have returned to independent or semi-independent community living should not be relinquished by the residential facility until assistance is assured from an accountable source (agency). The less restrictive placement must guarantee programs of equal or greater quality than the residential facility from which the individual came.[h]

4.   While most of the legal principles and precedents are very adequately discussed in the *Pennhurst* opinion, persons interested in additional perspectives on some of the doctrinal development preceding *Pennhurst* may wish to examine the lengthy opinions in two of the cases upon which the *Pennhurst* court most heavily relied: *Welsch* v. *Likins*, 373 F.Supp. 487 (D.Minn. 1974), affirmed in part 550 F.2d 1122 (8th Cir. 1977); and *Gary W.* v. *State of La.*, 437 F.Supp. 1209 (E.D.La. 1976).

5.   One of the few potential legal theories dealing with the problems of institutionalization with which the *Pennhurst* court did not deal is 42 U.S.C. Section 6010, section 111 of the Developmental Disabilities Assistance and Bill of Rights Act as amended. This section provides:

Congress makes the following findings respecting the rights of persons with developmental disabilities:

(1)   Persons with developmental disabilities have a right to appropriate treatment, services, and habilitation for such disabilities.

(2)   The treatment, services, and habilitation for a person with developmental disabilities should be designed to maximize the developmental potential of the person and should be provided in the setting that is least restrictive of the person's personal liberty.

(3)   The Federal Government and the States both have an obligation to assure that public funds are not provided to any institutional or other residential program for persons with developmental disabilities that—

(A)   does not provide treatment, services, and habilitation which is appropriate to the needs of such persons; or

(B)   does not meet the following minimum standards;

(i)   Provision of a nourishing, well-balanced daily diet to the persons with developmental disabilities being served by the program.

(ii)   Provision to such persons of appropriate and sufficient medical and dental services.

(iii)   Prohibition of the use of physical restraint on such persons unless absolutely necessary and prohibition of the use of such restraint as a punishment or as a substitute for a habilitation program.

(iv)   Prohibition on the excessive use of chemical restraints on such persons and the use of such restraints as punishment or as a substitute for a habilitation program or in quantities that interfere with services, treatment, or habilitation for such persons.

(v)   Permission for close relatives of such persons to visit them at reasonable hours without prior notice.

(vi)   Compliance with adequate fire and safety standards as may be promulgated by the Secretary.

---

[h]National Association for Retarded Citizens, *Residential Services: Position Statements of the National Association for Retarded Citizens* 6-7 (1976).

(4)   All programs for persons with developmental disabilities should meet standards which are designed to assure the most favorable possible outcome for those served, and—

(A)   in the case of residential programs serving persons in need of comprehensive, health-related, habilitative, or rehabilitative services, which are at least equivalent to those standards applicable to intermediate care facilities for the mentally retarded promulgated in regulations of the Secretary on January 17, 1974 (39 Fed. Reg. pt. II), as appropriate when taking into account the size of the institutions and the service delivery arrangements of the facilities of the programs;

(B)   in the case of other residential programs for persons with developmental disabilities, which assure that care is appropriate to the needs of the persons being served by such programs, assure that the persons admitted to facilities of such programs are persons whose needs can be met through services provided by such facilities, and assure that the facilities under such programs provide for the humane care of the residents of the facilities, are sanitary, and protect their rights; and

(C)   in the case of nonresidential programs, which assure the care provided by such programs is appropriate to the persons served by the programs.

The rights of persons with developmental disabilities described in findings made in this section are in addition to any constitutional or other rights otherwise afforded to all persons.

At least one federal court has held that the requirements of § 6010 may be enforced by a private right of action, *Naughton* v. *Bevilacqua,* 458 F.Supp. 610 (D.R.I. 1978). The impact of this section on the practices of state institutions is as yet largely unmeasured, but it seems to hold significant potential.

6.   The defendants in *Pennhurst* were held to be protected by good faith immunity from monetary damages claims by the plaintiffs. This result should be contrasted with *O'Connor* v. *Donaldson,* pp. 618–629, above, where the plaintiff was held entitled to an award of damages. In a number of other circumstances, institution officials have been held liable for monetary damages arising from the improper performance of their duties: *Wheeler* v. *Glass,* 473 F.2d 983 (7th Cir. 1973) (cruel and unusual punishment in using extreme disciplinary measures on residents); *Goodman* v. *Parwatikar,* 570 F.2d 801 (8th Cir. 1978) (confinement without treatment; injury by beating from other patient); *Winters* v. *Miller,* 446 F.2d 65 (2d Cir. 1971), cert. denied 404 U.S. 985 (1971) (forced medication of mentally competent, Christian Scientist patient); *Shattuck* v. *State,* 166 Misc. 271, 2 N.Y.S.2d 353 (1938) (negligence in permitting escape of mentally retarded boy who subsequently lost legs due to freezing); see generally, Annotations, 38 A.L.R.3d 699; 70 A.L.R.2d 347. Cf. *Eanes* v. *United States,* 407 F.2d 823 (4th Cir. 1969) (no liability for injuries caused by patient released under "open door" policy). Recently, in *Naughton* v. *Bevilacqua,* Note 5, above, a federal court has ruled that a claim of good faith immunity may be overcome if a plaintiff can prove that an institution official administered a medication with potentially serious side effects not for any ostensible habilitative purpose but rather as a deliberate method of controlling a patient's behavior. What other circumstances might vitiate the presumed "good faith" of institution personnel?

7

HOUSING AND ZONING RESTRICTIONS

Alice K. Nelson and Robert L. Burgdorf, Jr.

The impetus toward deinstitutionalization, as discussed in the preceding chapter and the more generalized trend toward normalization of handicapped persons into the mainstream of American society have given rise to a need for additional housing alternatives for handicapped individuals. While the cohabiting male-female couple, with or without children, and, to a slightly lesser extent, the single person living alone can be considered the traditional societal norm, such living arrangements may not be appropriate for individuals with particular handicapping conditions, or may be appropriate only after a period of residence in some intermediate alternative where necessary skills and practices can be learned. For these reasons, a whole gamut of less-than-institutional living alternatives are called for. While broad-based implementation has been woefully lacking, theorists and programmers have developed a number of models and operating examples of such residential arrangements. Some of the more common alternatives are halfway houses, cooperative apartments, cluster apartments, group homes, foster homes, family care programs, sheltered care facilities, foster communities, long term medical care facilities, and crisis centers. See, e.g., Goldmeir, J., "Community Residential Facilities for Former Mental Patients: A Review," 1 *Psychosocial Rehab. J.* No. 4, p. 1 (1977); President's Committee on Mental Retardation, *Changing Patterns in Residential Services for the Mentally Retarded* (Kugel, R., and Wolfensberger, W., eds., 1969).

In addition to their size, a major difference between these modern residential alternatives and the traditional residential institution is that they are located in and integrated into the community, as opposed to being in an isolated rural or industrial setting. This need for proximity to the community has sometimes proved an impediment to the establishment of such residences when there has been opposition to the location of such a program in particular neighborhoods. Misinformation, fears, and prejudices have sometimes given rise to fierce opposition to a proposed residential alternative for handicapped people. The tone and substance of such attitudes are exemplified in the allegations contained in a complaint filed by neighbors seeking to prevent the location of a school for mentally retarded children in the Village of Pelham Manor in Westchester County, New York:

... that the presence of defendant's pupils at its school or institution and in the village will of necessity cause close and intimate contact between said mental defectives and plaintiffs and plaintiffs' children and that such daily contact and the action and mannerisms of said mental defectives will have a profound, deleterious, depressing effect upon the minds, hearts, emotions and nervous systems of plaintiffs and particularly of plaintiffs' children and that plaintiffs' health and the health of plaintiffs' children will thereby be impaired; that the presence of these numerous mental defectives in the midst of such a highly residential section of the village of Pelham Manor and their close and intimate contact with the average normal child of plaintiffs will unfortunately and of necessity give rise to many unpleasant incidents upon the public streets and thoroughfares of the village between them and plaintiffs' children whereby breaches of the peace will or may be occasioned and plaintiffs will be thereby harassed and annoyed and will become embroiled and involved in endless litigation both of a civil and criminal nature; that the value of plaintiffs' real and personal property and their health, safety and welfare will be adversely affected, and that plaintiffs will suffer and will continue to suffer irreparable damage and diminution in the value of their properties. *Rogers* v. *Association for the Help of Retarded Children,* 308 N.Y. 126, 123 N.E.2d 806, 807–808 (1954).

Studies have shown that fears of lowered property values and increased crime rates are unfounded; see, e.g., Thomas, J., "An Overview of Washington State's Group Homes for Developmentally Disabled Persons," *Group Homes for the Mentally Retarded* (Sigelman, C., ed., 1973); Knowles, E., and Baba, R., *The Social Impact of Group Homes: A Study of Small Residential Services in First Residential Areas,* Green Bay Planning Commission (1973); Lauber, D., and Bangs, F., *Zoning for Family and Group Care Facilities,* Report No. 300, Chicago: American Society of Planning Officials (1974). Likewise, evidence tends to indicate that once such facilities are located in a neighborhood they tend to be accepted by the neighbors; see, e.g., Mamula, R., and Newman, N., *Community Placement of the Mentally Retarded: A Handbook for Community Agencies and Social Work Practitioners* 59-60 (1973). Nonetheless, unenlightened opposition, such as that exhibited by the plaintiffs in the *Rogers* case, has sometimes persisted. This chapter examines some of the means by which those hostile to housing alternatives for handicapped people have sought to prevent such facilities from being developed in their communities.

A. ZONING RESTRICTIONS

In *Euclid* v. *Ambler Realty Co.,* 272 U.S. 365 (1926), the United States Supreme Court gave constitutional approval to local land use regulation through zoning as a legitimate exercise of the police power. The Court indicated that local zoning ordinances would be upheld unless they were "clearly arbitrary and unreasonable, having no substantial relation to the public health, safety, morals, or general welfare." *Id.* at 395. This holding has been reaffirmed as recently as 1978 when the Court declared:

this Court has recognized, in a number of settings, that States and cities may enact land use restrictions or controls to enhance the quality of life by preserving the character and desirable aesthetic features of a city ... *Penn Central Transportation Company* v. *City of New York,* 438 U.S. 104, 129 (1978).

The authority to regulate land use is most often exercised by local government entities, usually through the enactment of zoning ordinances which divide the jurisdiction into distinct areas designated for various categories of residential, business, and other uses. Frequently, a zoning board, planning agency, or other administrative body is authorized to enforce and modify the zoning restrictions.

1. Single Family Residential Property

LITTLE NECK COMMUNITY ASSOCIATION V. WORKING ORGANIZATION FOR RETARDED CHILDREN

Supreme Court of New York, Appellate Division, Second Judicial Department, 1976
52 App.Div.2d 90, 383 N.Y.S.2d 364

Before HOPKINS, Acting P. J., and LATHAM, CHRIST, TITONE and HAWKINS, JJ.
TITONE, Justice.

In this action, plaintiffs, a number of property owners and their community organization, seek to enjoin the respondent Working Organization for Retarded Children (WORC) from using a one-family residence as a group home for mentally retarded children. The subject premises which WORC contracted to purchase, and to which it acquired title during the pendency of this action, is located in a one-family residential zone in Little Neck, Queens.

In granting WORC's motion for summary judgment, the Special Term held that the proposed group home was a permitted use in a single-family residential zone since its future occupants will constitute a "family" within the definition of that term set forth in the New York City Zoning Resolution. That resolution defines a "family" as: "Not more than four unrelated persons occupying a dwelling, living together and maintaining a common household" (N.Y.City Zoning Resolution, § 12–10). Thus, the focal issue is whether a group home for retarded children constitutes a "family" within the purview of the New York City Zoning Resolution.

The respondent WORC, a not-for-profit corporation, approved by the New York State Department of Social Welfare, is authorized to operate a "group home" program for mentally retarded children (see Social Services Law, § 374-c). As set forth in the Social Services Law, a "group home" is "a facility for the care and maintenance of not less than seven, nor more than twelve children, who are at least five years of age" (Social Services Law, § 371, subd. 17). The rules of the Department of Social Welfare set forth extensive requirements with which the operator of the group home must comply in order to receive operating certification. It is noteworthy that the rules specify that the "group home shall be in *an appropriate neighborhood and so located that it is readily accessible to religious, school and recreational facilities and other community resources"* (18 NYCRR 11.3[d][1] [emphasis supplied]).

In *City of White Plains* v. *Ferraioli*, 34 N.Y.2d 300, 357 N.Y.S.2d 449, 313 N.E.2d 756, Abbott House, a not-for-profit membership corporation licensed by the New York State Department of Social Welfare to care for neglected and abandoned children, sought to operate a group home for 10 foster children in an "R-2" single-family residential zone pursuant to the identical statutory authority involved herein. The city sought to enforce its zoning ordinance and to enjoin use of the single-family house purchased for this purpose, contending that the group home was not a single-family use, but either a philanthropic institution, allowed only by special permit, or a boarding house, wholly excluded from an "R-2" zone. The Court of Appeals stated that the narrow issue was whether the "group home," consisting of a married couple and their two children, together with 10 foster children, qualified as a single "family" unit, under the ordinance. The ordinance defined a "family" as "one or more persons limited to the spouse, parents, grandparents, grandchildren, sons, daughters, brothers or sisters of the owner or the tenant or of the owner's spouse or tenant's spouse living together as a single housekeeping unit with kitchen facilities."

The unanimous court concluded that the group home was a family for the purpose of a zoning ordinance. It observed that (pp. 304–306, 357 N.Y.S.2d pp. 452–453, 313 N.E.2d p. 758):

> It is significant that the group home is structured as a single housekeeping unit and is, to all outward appearances, a relatively normal, stable and permanent family unit, with which the community is properly concerned.
>
> * * *
>
> The group home is not, for purposes of a zoning ordinance, a temporary living arrangement as would be a group of college students sharing a house and commuting to a nearby school (cf. *Village of Belle Terre* v. *Boraas,* 416 U.S. 1, 94 S.Ct. 1536, 39 L.Ed.2d 797). . . . The group home is a permanent arrangement and akin to a traditional family, which also may be sundered by death, divorce, or emancipation of the young. Neither the foster parents nor the children are to be shifted about; the intention is that they remain and develop ties in the community. The purpose is to emulate the traditional family and not to introduce a different "life-style." . . . .
>
> So long as the group home bears the generic character of a family unit as a relatively permanent household, and is not a framework for transients or transient living. it conforms to the purpose of the ordinance. . . . Moreover, in no sense is the group home an institutional arrangement, which would be another matter. Indeed, the purpose of the group home is to be quite the contrary of an institution and to be a home like other homes.

The appellants contend that the present case may be distinguished from *Ferraioli* since the children who will occupy the proposed group home are retarded. They assert that the proposed group home will resemble a mini-institution because the childrens' handicap will necessitate special care, that their retardation will inhibit them from interacting (among themselves) as people in a normal family do and that they will be unable to participate in normal activities with the community at large. While professing to be sympathetic to the plight of these unfortunate children, the appellants nevertheless suggest that the proposed group home should be located in a residential zone other than one restricted to single-family homes. They also suggest that retarded children are not denied access to single-family residential zones since they are free to live in such zones with their natural parents.

WORC contends that it has the right to locate the "State-created" family known as a group home in a single-family residential zone. It argues that, notwithstanding the fact that the children residing therein will suffer from mental retardation, the proposed group home will possess the same attributes as a conventional family, including permanency, community participation and life-style. It further asserts that certain modifications of the New York City Building Code relating to the structural requirements of group homes explicitly recognizes this fact. In addition, WORC contends that the definitional test has nothing to do with the normalcy of the occupants of a group home; if it were precluded from locating its proposed home in a single-family residential zone because of the retardation of the children, then the mentally retarded would be denied equal protection of the laws simply because of their affliction.

The term "family" is subject to numerous definitions in zoning ordinances. Courts have often been called upon to determine whether a "family" exists in the context of a particular situation (see Ann., 172 A.L.R. 1172). It is our opinion that a group home for mentally retarded children constitutes a family for the purposes of a zoning ordinance. Our decision is based primarily upon the fact that a group home which is organized pursuant to the Social Services Law is specifically designed to emulate in appearance a reasonably sized biological unitary family. "Zoning is intended to control types of housing and living and not genetic or intimate internal family relations of human beings" (*City of White Plains* v. *Ferraioli, supra,* 34 N.Y.2d p. 305, 357 N.Y.S.2d p. 452, 313 N.E.2d p. 758). Although a municipality may exercise its police power to enact single-family residential zones segregated from multiple dwelling houses (see, e.g., *Baddour* v. *City of Long Beach,* 279 N.Y. 167, 18 N.E.2d 18), we are not persuaded that the proposed group home will, in and of itself, alter the quality of life or the character of the neighborhood which a single-family residential zone is specifically designed to protect and enhance.

The proposed group home will neither provide accommodations for transients nor introduce a life-style which is repugnant to traditional family values (cf. *Village of Belle Terre* v. *Boraas,* 416 U.S. 1, 94 S.Ct. 1536, 39 L.Ed.2d 797). Rather, it will provide retarded children with a stable environment in a setting in which they will have a real opportunity to develop to their full potential. Furthermore, we see no effect upon this status if the house parents are provided on a rotating basis.

We are fully aware that mental retardation involves a mental disability and that the State has traditionally provided services to the mentally disabled, and particularly the mentally retarded, in the role of *parens patriae.* Institutionalization has been the traditional means of accommodating and caring for the mentally retarded (see Mental Hygiene Law, § 7.15). However, the recent trend has been toward the establishment of community residence programs for the mentally disabled, including mentally retarded children (see, e.g., Mental Hygiene Law, § 1.05, subds. 18, 24; § 13.01, eff. Apr. 1, 1976). Indeed, the regulations of the Department of Mental Hygiene recognize the State's continued interest in these individuals and require certification of the group home for retarded children to indicate compliance with its regulations as well as with those of the Department of Social Welfare (14 NYCRR 86.4[b]). This procedure is consistent with the recognition that retarded children have special needs related to their handicap and that the provider of services to these children must be subject to regulatory oversight. However, this fact does not alter our expressed view that a group home for mentally retarded children constitutes a family for the purposes of a zoning ordinance. Although WORC will provide services to children who would otherwise be subject to institutionalization, the services will be provided in a noninstitutional environment.

Assuming, *arguendo,* that a group home for retarded children does not constitute a family, we would nevertheless conclude that the proposed home is a permitted use as of right. The New York City Zoning Resolution provides that, except in certain community districts, a health related facility, as defined by the New York State Hospital Code, is a permitted use as of right in a single-family residential zone (N.Y.City Zoning Resolution, § 22-13). A "health related facility" includes, *inter alia,* a facility providing lodging, board and social and physical care to six or more residents (10 NYCRR 700.2[a][4]). In view of the fact that the regulations of the Department of Mental Hygiene treat the group home as a residential facility for the mentally disabled, it falls within the definitional category of a health related facility. Since the property WORC has purchased is located in Community District 11 in Queens, and as that district is not subject to special permit requirements, the proposed group home would be a permitted use even if we were not to conclude that it falls within the definitional category of a family (see N.Y. City Zoning Resolution, § 74-903).

In view of the above, we need not reach any other issue. Accordingly, the order of the Special Term should be affirmed. The order of this court enjoining WORC from making structural changes in the house is hereby vacated.

Order of the Supreme Court, Queens County, dated September 23, 1975, affirmed, with $50 costs and disbursements, and the stay contained in the order of this court, dated October 29, 1975, is hereby vacated.

Hopkins, Acting P. J., and Latham, Christ and Hawkins, JJ., concur.

NOTES

1. *Driscoll* v. *Goldberg,* Case No. 73 C.A. 59 (7th District Court of Appeals, Mahoning Cty., Ohio, Apr. 9, 1974), dealt with a proposed group home for 11 mentally retarded children which was challenged by neighbors as being in violation of a single-family dwelling provision of the Youngstown, Ohio, zoning ordinance. "Family" was defined as "One or more persons occupying the premises and living as a single housekeeping unit, as distinguished from a group occupying a boarding house, lodging house, club, fraternity, or hotel." *Id.* at 3. The court looked at the interpretation of this provision within the following perspective:

> At the outset we note that zoning ordinances are in derogation of the common law right to the full and free use of one's property. As to the constitutionality of zoning there can be no doubt, but Ohio courts have long held that the imposition of restrictions on the use of property by ordinance or statute are to be strictly construed and their scope cannot be extended to include limitations not clearly prescribed. *Id.* at 3-4.

The court concluded that the proposed group home fit within the definition of a family:

> ... the purpose of the house is to create a family atmosphere in every respect possible. Meals will be prepared and served by the house parents, the children will be housed according to sex in their separate bedrooms, separate bath facilities will be available to each sex. During the day they will be bussed to a school or a job training facility. Recreation facilities will be available in a basement playroom. In the summer months, when not in residence at the home, the children will attend a summer camp.

We can see no difference in the intended use than that of a family group comprised of a father and mother and eleven natural children. *Id.* at 5-6.

Shortly before the *Driscoll* decision, a Connecticut court had reached the same conclusion under an almost identical zoning ordinance. In *Oliver* v. *Zoning Commission of Town of Chester*, 31 Conn.Sup. 197, 326 A.2d 841 (1974), a proposed group home for nine mentally retarded adults was held to constitute a permitted single-family use. Said the court, "It is not the mutual relationship between the occupants of the dwelling, but its use 'as a single housekeeping unit' that controls, and that is what is contemplated . . . " *Id.* at 326 A.2d 845.

In 1977, a community residence for eight mentally retarded women was held to be permissible in a residential "A" zoning district reserved for single-family dwellings, *Incorp. Village of Freeport* v. *Association for Help of Retarded Children*, 94 Misc. 2d 1048, 406 N.Y.S.2d 221 (1977). The court declared:

> Such a "community residence" bears the generic character of a family unit as a rela-tively stable and permanent household and is consonant with the lifestyle intended for a family-oriented neighborhood, and thus conforms to the purpose of the village zoning ordinance. *Id.* at 406 N.Y.S.2d 223.

Prior to *Little Neck, Driscoll, Freeport,* and *Oliver,* a Wisconsin court had ruled, in *Browndale International Limited* v. *Board of Adjustment for County of Dane,* 60 Wis.2d 182, 208 N.W.2d 121 (1973), cert. denied 416 U.S. 936 (1974), that a group home for emotionally disturbed children was not a single-family dwelling. The *Browndale* situation was unusual, however, in that 1) the group home was a profit-making venture, 2) the home was the first of six such group homes that were to be established on the same site, and 3) there was much additional evidence that the staffing and operation of the group home would make it differ significantly from other homes in the area. The result in *Browndale* is a useful monition that the structure, location, and operating procedures of residential alternatives for handicapped persons should be designed with an eye toward conforming to the neighborhood and its normal uses.

2. The case of *Village of Belle Terre* v. *Boraas,* 416 U.S. 1 (1974), referred to in *Little Neck,* is a well known decision often discussed in law school "Property" courses. In *Boraas,* the Supreme Court ruled that six university students sharing a house did not constitute a "family" within the meaning of a zoning ordinance. The provision at issue in *Boraas* was not susceptible to a broad reading as in *Little Neck* since it limited the definition of "family" to persons related by blood, adoption, or marriage, or to not more than two unrelated persons living together as a single house-keeping unit. The students challenged the ordinance as unconstitutional but the Su-preme Court did not agree, ruling that no fundamental right was at stake and that the ordinance bore "a rational relationship to a permissible state objective," *id.* at 8. The Court declared:

> A quiet place where yards are wide, people few, and motor vehicles restricted are legitimate guidelines in a land use project addressed to family needs. . . . The police power is not confined to elimination of filth, stench, and unhealthy places. It is ample to

lay out zones where family values, youth values, and the blessings of quiet seclusion, and clean air make the area a sanctuary for people. *Id.* at 9.

Based upon such a rationale, the Court held that it was legitimate for the Village of Belle Terre to prohibit more than two unrelated persons from living together.

The *Boraas* decision should be contrasted with the early Supreme Court decision in *Seattle Trust Co.* v. *Roberge,* 278 U.S. 116 (1928), which struck down a Seattle zoning ordinance that permitted a "philanthropic home for children or for old people" in a particular district only with the written consent of the owners of two-thirds of the property within four hundred feet of the proposed building, *id.* at 118. The Court held that such a requirement was violative of due process because it was unnecessarily and unreasonably restrictive in light of the fact that the proposed home for indigent, elderly persons had not been shown "to work any injury, inconvenience, or annoyance to the community, the district or any person." *Id.* at 122.

Since the *Boraas* ruling, the Supreme Court has decided another zoning case, *Moore* v. *City of East Cleveland,* 431 U.S. 494 (1977). In *Moore* the Court held unconstitutional a Cleveland, Ohio, ordinance under which a grandmother was being prosecuted for allowing her grandson to live with her. The Court reasoned that such a restrictive definition of "family" invaded the right of family privacy and therefore had to be measured under a stricter standard of review than was applicable in *Boraas. Id.* at 499. Under such a standard, found the Court, there were not sufficient governmental goals to justify the ordinance. *Id.* at 500.

In light of the *Roberge, Boraas,* and *Moore* precedents, if the group home at issue in *Little Neck* could not have fit within the ordinance's definition of family, could a constitutional challenge have been successfully mounted against the ordinance?

3. *City of White Plains* v. *Ferraioli,* 34 N.Y.2d 300, 313 N.E.2d 756, 357 N.Y.S.2d 449 (1974), which was held to be controlling in *Little Neck,* not only ruled that a group home for abandoned and neglected children fit within the definition of "family," but indicated that there were limits upon the restrictiveness with which the term *family* could be defined by ordinance:

> In short, an ordinance may restrict a residential zone to occupancy by stable families occupying single-family homes, but neither by express provision nor construction may it limit the definition of family to exclude a household which in every but a biological sense is a single family. The minimal arrangement to meet the test of a zoning provision, as this one, is a group headed by a householder caring for a reasonable number of children as one would be likely to find in a biologically unitary family. *Id.* at 357 N.Y.S.2d 453.

Although the *Ferraioli* case did not involve a facility for handicapped persons *per se,* the *Little Neck* case is illustrative of the fact that the principles of *Ferraioli* are applicable in such contexts. There are a number of other decisions that, like *Ferraioli,* have held a variety of group living arrangements to constitute permissible single-family dwelling usages; e.g., *Missionaries of Our Lady of La Salette* v. *Village of Whitefish Bay,* 267 Wis. 609, 66 N.W.2d 627 (1954) (house for priests and brothers); *Robertson* v. *Western Baptist Hospital,* 267 S.W.2d 395 (Ky.App. 1954) (home for 20 nurses); *Carroll* v. *City of Miami Beach,* 198 So.2d 643 (Fla.App. 1967) (house for religious novices under direction of a mother superior); *State ex rel. Ellis* v. *Liddle,* 520 S.W.2d 644 (Mo.App. 1975) (home for juvenile boys); *YWCA of Summit* v. *Board of Adjustment,* 134 N.J.Super. 384, 341 A.2d 356 (1975) (group home for adolescent girls); *Group House of Port Washington* v. *Bd. of Zoning and Appeals,* 45 N.Y.2d 266, 380 N.E.2d 207, 408 N.Y.S.2d 377 (1978) (group home for foster children). There are also a few cases reaching a contrary result; e.g., *Planning and Zoning Comm'n* v. *Synanon Foundation, Inc.,* 153 Conn. 305, 216 A.2d 442 (1966) (home for up to 34 unrelated people); *Newark* v. *Johnson,* 70 N.J.Super. 381, 175 A.2d 500 (1961) (home for children who were wards of State Board of Child Welfare).

For cases in which zoning ordinances that sought to exclude certain family-like residential facilities from residential areas have been declared unconstitutional, see, e.g., *Village of University Heights* v. *Cleveland Jewish Orphans' Home,* 20 F.2d 743 (6th Cir. 1927) (orphanage); *Women's Kansas City St. Andrew Society* v. *Kansas City, Mo.,* 58 F.2d 593 (8th Cir. 1932) (home for elderly women); Buckingham v. *City of Dayton, Ohio,* Civil No. 4504 (S.D.Ohio, Feb. 20, 1974) (communal living arrangement).

In this regard, see especially *Berger* v. *State,* 71 N.J. 206, 364 A.2d 993, 1001–1004 (1976) (foster home for multihandicapped preschool children) (see pp. 722–726, below).

4.   In regard to the determination, near the end of the *Little Neck* decision, that the proposed group home would constitute a permissible use as a "health related facility," see section 2, below.

2.   Other Permissible Uses

SCHONNING V. PEOPLE'S CHURCH HOME, INC.

Superior Court of Worcester, Massachusetts, 1977
Civil Action No. 7188, Jan. 28, 1977

JOHN H. MEAGHER, Associate Justice.

The plaintiff in this action alleges a violation of the zoning ordinances of the City of Worcester in that the defendant is operating a facility at 41 Randolph Road, Worcester, in violation of the RS7 zoning requirements.

People's Church Home, Inc., is a non-profit operation. The application described the program [as] assessing the needs of children. The Worcester Ordinance permits educational uses under Section B Use Regulations, Section 6, school, college or other educational institution not conducted as a gainful business. The People's Church Home, Inc., has a provisional, existing and valid license from the Massachusetts Office of Children for the operation of said facility.

Thd defendant operates the facility under a contract with the Massachusetts Department of Mental Health; this contract is its primary source of funds for the operation of the facility. The program is called CLEAT, which signifies Community Living Education Aiding Teams. The purpose of the program is the continued education and training of certain selected emotionally disturbed adolescents, directed to it from the Worcester State Hospital. These are adolescents whose problems are emotional and behavioral, such as persons with socializing problems, skill deficits with others such as withdrawal and depression, or who may be borderline retarded cases or who have basic living skill deficits or who may have family conflicts. The program does not serve moderate or severely retarded youngsters, delinquents or those with typically anti-social, psychopathic and acting-out behavior.

The Massachusetts Department of Mental Health has a "Normalization" policy by which it seeks to deinstitutionalize persons under its supervision so as to return them to society. As part of this "Normalization" program, small community residential group care facilities under the supervision of the Department of Mental Health are established, and the Department retains supervision of such programs in accordance with its regulations and standards of care.

At the facility at 41 Randolph Road the residents have a daily educational program designed to educate and train the residents in basic self-help skills, daily living skills such as improvement in personal hygiene and self-care skills, meal preparation, cooking, cleaning, basic household chores, money management, shopping, responsibility for chore completion, getting along with others, use of public transportation facilities, safety education in home, group therapy and tutoring as needed in reading and mathematics.

At the facility there is a resident manager and his wife from Sunday night at 6 p.m. to Friday at 5 p.m., and a relief manager and his wife from Friday at 5 p.m. to Sunday at 6 p.m. These are persons with college degrees. The resident manager is a candidate for a Ph.D degree and has been a consultant to the Town of Shrewsbury Schools; his wife has a college degree with practice teaching as part of her college course.

41 Randolph Road was previously used for a rest home for the elderly with application made for its present use in 1975.

The instruction and training given to the residents at the group care facility at 41 Randolph Road is a dominantly-educational purpose within the meaning of G.L.Ch. 40A, paragraph 2. The goal is to prepare the children to live independently in the community without institutional assistance.

The educational purpose is public in that it is owned by a non-profit organization; its principal funding is from public sources and the selection of persons for admission is done by a public agency.

I FIND that according to the decision in *Mount Hermon Boys School* v. *Gill*, 145 Mass. 139, the facility at 41 Randolph Road is encompassed in the definition of educational purposes and that it does not violate the Zoning Ordinances of the City of Worcester.

Let judgment enter dismissing the complaint.

NOTES

1. In *Mount Hermon Boys' School* v. *Town of Gill*, 145 Mass. 139, 13 N.E. 354 (1887), relied upon in *Schonning*, the Supreme Judicial Court of Massachusetts held that a boarding school's use of a farm on its grounds constituted a use of the land for educational purposes. The Court posited a very expansive concept of education:

Education is a broad and comprehensive term. It has been defined as "the process of developing and training the powers and capabilities of human beings." To educate, according to one of Webster's definitions, is "to prepare and fit for any calling or business, or for activity and usefulness in life." Education may be particularly directed to either the mental, moral, or physical powers and faculties, but in its broadest and best sense it relates to them all. *Id.* at 145 Mass. 146, 13 N.E. 357.

If the group care facility in *Schonning* had contemplated that the resident children would go to the public schools during the day, could it still have qualified as an educational institution under the *Mount Hermon* formulation? What types of programs and activities might have lent support to such a contention?

These questions were addressed by another Massachusetts court in *Dynamic Action Residence Enterprises, Inc.* v. *Board of Appeals of Town of Mashpee,* No. 36049 (Superior Ct., Barnstable, Mass., Feb. 3, 1977), less than a week after the *Schonning* decision. The "group home/settlement house" of Dynamic Action Residence Enterprises (DARE) had qualified as an educational facility permissible in a residential zone, as long as it had provided on-grounds academic instruction. In 1974, however, DARE ceased its on-grounds educational program and began to send its residents to the public schools. The Town of Mashpee took the position that DARE had ceased to serve an educational purpose and could thereafter operate only pursuant to a special permit, which it granted for a 2-year period and then refused to renew. The court observed:

> The program at DARE, aside from the elimination of basic academic instruction, has not changed signficantly since the fall of 1972. DARE provides a structured environment in which residents learn basic social and living skills, receive counselling and develop academic and vocational interests. Residents earn increased privileges as they accomplish personal goals established through individual counselling. The upkeep of DARE grounds and all household and cooking chores are the responsibility of the residents.
>
> One-to-one tutoring in academic subjects is conducted on DARE premises by teachers employed in the Falmouth public schools and by counsellors employed by DARE. Individual and group counselling is conducted at DARE by a professsional clinical psychologist and by DARE staff. Other activities conducted at DARE include pottery, gardening, painting, woodworking, auto mechanics, outdoor skills, sports, cooking, personal hygiene and household chores.
>
> Although most of the DARE program would perhaps be provided by a good parent, DARE is more than a home. The young people at DARE come from homes that for one reason or another did not alleviate their emotional and/or educational difficulties. The special needs of DARE residents require more treatment than they would receive in foster-homes. DARE's program is designed to meet residents' needs and prepare them to return to their families or re-enter the community on their own. *Id.* at 7-8.

Relying upon the *Mount Hermon* case and other broad interpretations of education in Massachusetts law, the court concluded:

> Under these definitions of education, DARE, Inc., is an educational purpose. DARE residents require education in basic community and living skills as well as purely academic areas. The DARE program fulfills this broad educational need and thus promotes fuller individual development of young people who have had difficulties both at home and at school.

In addition to the broad view taken in case law, the policies of deinstitutionalization and normalization, now being implemented by the Departments of Mental Health, Youth Services and Education, require a broad view of the term "education." G.L. c. 40A, s. 3, must be construed to protect programs like DARE, which are carrying out state policy, from exclusion by towns such as Mashpee. If towns were permitted to restrict and prohibit DARE-type facilities it would totally frustrate the state's explicit policy of treating people with special needs in the community. *Id.* at 9-10.

2. In *Stoller* v. *Board of Zoning and Appeals,* 40 A.D.2d 867, 337 N.Y.S.2d 946 (1972), a Human Resources School for handicapped persons, which included a light manufacturing plant where handicapped workers were employed, sought to expand its facilities and parking lot onto residential property. The court upheld a decision of the zoning board that such a use was for an educational purpose and was permitted in a residential zone:

> Concededly, a light manufacturing plant employing handicapped persons is located on the subject property. However, it is evident that this commercial enterprise is but a singular means used in the overall training and placement of handicapped individuals. The Human Resources School, the lessee of the entire tract, is, in fact, operating the entire compound solely for eleemosynary and educational purposes. In short, we consider this to be an entire educational complex of which the manufacturing plant is but one integral part. *Id.* at 337 N.Y.S.2d 948.

3. An early federal circuit court decision, *Village of University Heights* v. *Cleveland Jewish Orphans' Home,* 20 F.2d 743 (6th Cir. 1927), held that, since schools were permitted within a residential zone, it was unreasonable to prohibit the operation of an orphanage in such zone. The court ruled that the impact on the community of an orphanage was so similar to that of a private school as to make differentiation of the two uses unreasonable. To what other types of uses might such a rationale apply?

CRIST V. BISHOP

Supreme Court of Utah, 1974
520 P.2d 196

CROCKETT, Justice:

Defendants seek reversal of a decree of the district court which directed them to honor a permit previously issued authorizing the plaintiffs to establish and operate "The Provo Canyon School" northeast of Provo in Utah County.

Plaintiffs had previously made an abortive attempt to establish a similar school in Mapleton. After the failure of that attempt, they acquired a building and about four acres of the land, which had been used as a country club, to convert into this school. On January 8, 1973, the Utah County Planning Department issued a permit. On January 25, protesting property owners in the area filed an appeal to the Board of Adjustment. Pursuant to notice and hearing thereon the board agreed with the contention of the protestants: that the plaintiffs' institution was not a "school" within the meaning of the county ordinance and ordered the permit revoked. Plaintiffs filed this action in the district court to challenge that order. After a plenary trial, including an inspection of the institution, the court found that it was a "school" and directed the defendants to honor the previously issued permit.

Commendably the parties are in agreement in identifying the issue involved here as: whether the institution known as "The Provo Canyon School" as established and operated by the plaintiffs is a "school" within the meaning of that term as used in the zoning ordinance of Utah County.

The ordinance authorizes in this zone buildings, structures, and uses of land:

* * *

C.   Schools, churches, public parks and playgrounds, arboretums, public buildings. . . .

The argument of the defendants is that although plaintiffs' establishment has some of the attributes of a "school," it "has an additional and paramount purpose that far transcends school attributes" so that it cannot properly be so characterized, but is in reality a detention and correctional institution. In support of this they point out that plaintiffs' advertising is designed to attract maladjusted boys with mental or emotional problems, who need detention and control in connection with their education and training; that they will take "failing students in a fantasy world," or who are "adversely influenced by drugs," boys with "brain damage," with "schizophrenia symptoms." Plaintiffs' school offers "residential treatment with a therapeutically designed round-the-clock living program" including "medical care," "psychiatry," and "professional discipline," along with other aspects of education. It is shown that during past operations the plaintiffs have found it necessary in some instances to use forcible restraints such as chains and manacles on some of the boys and/or keep them in locked rooms to detain them.

We agree that it is not the name used that determines the character of an institution, but this is to be ascertained from what it actually consists of and its method of operation. The term "school" is a generic one which has numerous meanings. As a noun, it is used to denote various types of institutions of learning, or specialized schools within such institutions; and in a broader sense, to symptoms of thought, or of doctrine, philosophy, music or the arts; and also to denote certain groups of fish, or animals, or people; and as a verb in the sense of, to teach, train or control; and also as an adjective to so characterize many of the nouns.

The foregoing is said to show how versatile and various some words can be in their meanings, and to demonstrate the wisdom and the necessity of the rule applicable here: That where there is doubt or uncertainty as to the meaning of terms, they should be analyzed in the light of the total context of the ordinance (or statute or instrument); and also in relation to the purpose, and the background circumstances, in which they are used.

The soundness of this doctrine is illustrated by cases cited and relied on by the defendants themselves. For example, they cite *In the Matter of Townsend*[5] for the proposition that a special school for nurses was held not to be a "school" as that term is generally used in statutes. The issue arose under a New York law which prohibited the issuance of liquor licenses for locations within 200 feet of a schoolhouse. Inasmuch as it was shown that the age of the nurses was 23 years and over, it was reasoned that

---

[5]195 N.Y. 214, 88 N.E. 41.

this was not the type of school intended to be protected by the statute, but rather elementary and intermediate schools attended by children and youth. Similarly, the case of *Granger* v. *Lorenzen*,[6] also relied on by defendants, involved a statutory prohibition of saloons within given distances from "schools." The institution in question was a business college for adults.

In the case of *Devereux Foundation*[7] the ordinance which permitted buildings for educational and religious uses had a provision specifically excluding cemeteries, hospital, homes, sanitarium, correctional institution or structure or other place for accommodating the insane or other persons mentally deficient, weak or abnormal. The court found that the school in question came within the quoted exclusion, which was a valid exercise of the zoning prerogative.

It will thus be seen that the cases referred to are not in discord, but rather are in harmony, with the idea of looking to the context, the background and the purpose in which the term "school" is used in order to determine the meaning and intent of the ordinance. In accord with that doctrine and more closely analogous to our case is *Wiltwyck School, etc.* v. *Hill*.[8] The institution was a special one for the care and instruction of delinquent, neglected and maladjusted boys, who were referred there because of their failure to get along in society, and where many needed special discipline and psychiatric care. A challenge was made similar to that urged here: That it was not a "school" within the meaning of the zoning ordinance. Upon a lucid discussion of the terms: education, training and school, as applying even to the maladjusted, delinquent and mentally handicapped, the court concluded that their education and training came within the meaning of "school" where there was no qualification or limitation upon that term.

Looking at the circumstances shown in our case in the light of what has been said above, we think it was reasonable and proper for the trial court to take the view that the meaning of "schools" as used in the ordinance in question was in the sense it is most commonly used and understood in that locality: institutions for education and training. The requisites of such a school are: some physical facility, teachers, a curriculum for study or training, and students who are the objective thereof. If these requisites are met, the status of the institution is not changed because of variation in methods of teaching or of training, or of discipline or control. These are all present in greater or lesser degree in practically all schools; and they may vary greatly without preventing one from being properly so characterized.

In regard to the point upon which the defendants place special emphasis: that because of elements of forcible restraint and severe methods of discipline, this is in reality a detention and correctional institution: there is this very significant difference: the boys are sent to this school by a voluntary choice of their parents; and they can similarly be withdrawn. There is not, nor can there be, any absolute right of detention in the sense there is public penal or correctional institutions.

---

[6]28 S.D. 295, 133 N.W. 259.
[7]351 Pa. 478, 41 A.2d 744.
[8]11 N.Y.2d 182, 227 N.Y.S.2d 655, 182 N.E.2d 268.

Consistent with what has been said, it is our opinion that the trial court was justified in concluding that the plaintiffs' institution is a "school" within the meaning of that term as used in the zoning ordinance of Utah County, and in ordering defendants to honor the permit heretofore issued.

Affirmed. No costs awarded.

CALLISTER, C. J., and ELLETT and TUCKETT, JJ., concur.

HENRIOD, Justice (dissenting):

Appeal from a judgment directing the zoning authority to grant a permit to allow a "school" for boys,—described in a predecessor decision of ours, of similar import,[1] as a "detention place" for 26 wayward boys, including drug addicts from ages 12 through 17, and to afford them such training and "schooling" as "would be proper,"—basing our decision apparently on a technical procedural rule, but obviously because the people of Mapleton did not feel safe to have a "school," as we said, inhabited by wayward boys,—drug addicts and otherwise.

The main opinion completely has ignored private property rights. It says, in effect, that you may put a "school" for incorrigibles or those having violent or homicidal tendencies next door to an erstwhile law-abiding citizen who certainly would not have purchased his property had he anticipated the action of not the zoning authorities that turned it down, but the courts that overruled them, or by the interpretation this court would place on the word "school," in the common connotation.

It seems to me that this is no "school" in its commonly employed sense, but a "correctional institution for actual or potential criminals," who, even if rehabilitated, will be replaced by the same type of actual or potential criminals, *ad infinitum.* One wonders how the members of this court would react by way of fear for themselves or their children, if the institution, subject of this litigation, were established near *their* homes, or what kind of equitable reaction they would enjoy, if by such establishment, of such institution, where the main opinion concedes there is the use of chains, shackles and maximum security measures by isolation in locked rooms to restrain these unfortunate but nonetheless dangerous misfits,—where the net result obviously would be to depreciate the value of such homes to a figure much less than previous sales value, and possibly to utter worthlessness to such members.

I am of the opinion that the revocation of the plaintiffs' permit by the Planning Board, better equipped than the District, or this Court, to determine whether admitted conditions of danger, detention of incorrigibles, the use of chains and locked rooms therefor, is a "school" in the commonly accepted meaning thereof,—particularly when such conditions and facts do not relate at all to a "school," but perfectly describe and justify need for a "jail" instead.

Everyone concedes that one of the state prison's primary purposes is to rehabilitate, but I would venture the speculation that not even the wildest of social softies would dub that institution a "school." The main opinion's logic and conclusion would seem to justify the removal of the Utah State Prison from the Point of the Mountain to Penrose Drive or in between the Governor's Mansion and the nearby church house.

---

[1] *Crist* v. *Mapleton City,* 28 Utah 2d 7, 497 P.2d 633.

I am of the opinion this case should be reversed with instructions to re-instate the Planning Board's rejection of the permit.

NOTES

1. While one might question the use of "chains and manacles" in any modern program for juveniles, whether it be educational or penal, how much does the use of such techniques support the contention of the dissenting judge that the proposed land use was a correctional institution? Could a more open and normalized program be acceptable in a residential zone while a more confining and regressive model might not? Can a determination of the character of a facility for zoning purposes be based upon the instructional or disciplinary philosophy it embraces?

2. The land at issue in *Crist* had formerly been used as a country club. What would you expect the reaction of neighbors to be to the proposed change of use for the land? Should planners of schools or residential alternatives for handicapped people consider the previous uses of property as a factor in assessing likely community acceptance of such a facility?

3. The case of *In re Application of Devereux*, 351 Pa. 478, 41 A.2d 744 (1945), discussed in *Crist*, is an interesting, albeit probably obsolete, precedent. The Devereux School's plans to build a dormitory adjoining its school for children with psychological or psychiatric disorders was held a violation of an Easttown Township, Pa., zoning ordinance. The unusual ordinance provided that in an "A residence district" a building might be used, *inter alia*, for an "educational or religious use, including dormitory of an educational institution, but excluding cemeteries, hospital, homes, sanitarium, correctional institution or structure or other place for accommodating the insane or other persons mentally deficient, weak or abnormal." *Id.* at 41 A.2d 745. The court upheld the legality and application of this blatantly discriminatory provision:

> The Foundation contends that this interpretation creates an invalid discrimination between a dormitory of this school and those of other schools, public and private, all of which probably contain some pupils who are mentally retarded or deficient. But as Mr. Justice Holmes so frequently pointed out, most of the distinctions of the law are distinctions of degree, and there is a marked practical difference, justifying a legal differentiation, between the dormitory of a school all of whose occupants are, from the standpoint of mentality, of the problem type which it is the very purpose and function of the institution to serve, and the dormitory of a school in which only a negligible percentage of the occupants are mentally sub-normal. *Id.* at 41 A.2d 746.

In contrast to *Devereux* and, like *Crist*, more indicative of modern judicial approaches, is *Wiltwyck School for Boys, Inc.* v. *Hill*, 11 N.Y.2d 182, 227 N.Y.S.2d 655 (1962), also discussed in *Crist*. In *Wiltwyck*, a school for emotionally disturbed boys was proposed in a residential zone in Yorktown, New York. The local building inspector and the zoning board ruled that the proposed use of the property was not permissible in a residential area. The evidence indicated that the residential program at the Wiltwyck School was to be provided in conjunction with an educational program offered by the New York City school system:

> Supplementing this instruction and care, Wiltwyck provides a counseling service from the close of the daily school session until bedtime, as well as in week-end, holiday and

vacation periods, in the form of athletic, social, cultural, musical and normal boarding-school type of activities, plus medical care. Its children engage in competition with neighborhood baseball, basketball and softball "little leagues," give musical performances at Tanglewood Music Circle and Carnegie Hall, attend art exhibits, Shakespearean plays, concerts and dances. *Id.* at 11 N.Y.2d 192, 227 N.Y.S.2d 660.

The court held that such a program constituted a permissible educational use:

> We are therefore of the opinion—as was Judge Kleinfeld below—that in thus operating closely with the New York City Board of Education in a common school enterprise, and in carrying out the educational functions of the State, Wiltwyck School for Boys is a school within the unqualified language of the Yorktown ordinance, and that it was arbitrary and unreasonable to hold otherwise. *Id.* at 11 N.Y.2d 193, 227 N.Y.S.2d 661.

UNITED CEREBRAL PALSY ASSOCIATION V. ZONING BOARD OF ADJUSTMENT

Supreme Court of Pennsylvania, 1955
382 Pa. 67, 114 A.2d 331

Before STERN, C. J., and STEARNE, JONES, BELL, CHIDSEY, MUSMANNO and ARNOLD, JJ.

HORACE STERN, Chief Justice.

The Overbrook Farms Club, an association of neighborhood residents, objects, on this appeal, to the grant by the court below of a use registration permit for a residence at 6020 Overbrook Avenue, Philadelphia, to be occupied by a group of young men physically handicapped by cerebral palsy.

The United Cerebral Palsy Association of Philadelphia and Vicinity applied to the Zoning Division of the Philadelphia Department of Licenses and Inspection for the use registration permit in question. The project of the Association is to establish a residence, presently for ten, possibly later for twenty, members of a group ranging in age from 18 to 35, who have formed themselves into an organization called the "Pioneers." They do not require nursing or custodial care and no medical treatment of any kind will be administered to them on the premises. They are of normal mentality but they suffer in common from the disability visited upon them by their affliction. They will assist in the running of the household. Their reason for associating in a habitation where they will live, dine and sleep is because they presently lack suitable home environments. Many of them are regularly employed and self-supporting.

The property at 6020 Overbrook Avenue is a large stone residence of ten bedrooms. It is situated in spacious and well-planted grounds. It has an elevator, commodious kitchen facilities, a greenhouse and a four-car garage. Portions of the accessory buildings will probably be used for vocational training, handicraft, horticulture and recreational activities for members of the group.

The property for which the use registration permit was requested is in an "A" residential district. The Zoning Division denied the application, and, on appeal to the Zoning Board, that tribunal likewise held that the permit should not be granted nor a variance allowed. The Court of Common Pleas, however, reversed the order of the Board and granted the use registration permit. The present appeal from that order is by the Overbrook Farms Club which intervened in the original proceedings.

The Philadelphia Zoning Ordinance of August 10, 1933, listed, among the specific uses permitted in a "A" residential district, club houses, schools and dormitories. Also permitted were hospitals, sanitaria, eleemosynary and public institutions (other than correctional), but there was a provision that buildings for such uses should be located at least 75 feet from any adjoining lot or lots. It was because of this requirement that the Zoning Board rejected plaintiff's application because it held that the proposed use of the building for which the permit was requested was that of a sanitarium, and, as it had side yards of only 25 feet and 45 feet and a rear yard of 10 feet in width it did not meet the 75 foot requirement.

In *Walker* v. *Zoning Board of Adjustment,* 380 Pa. 228, 110 A.2d 414, decided after the action of the Zoning Board in the present case, we held that the use of premises for a school for physically handicapped children suffering from cerebral palsy did not constitute a sanitarium. We there pointed out that a sanitarium is a health station or retreat,—an institution for the recuperation and treatment of persons suffering from physical or mental disorders, whereas the institution in that case was not designed to give, nor did it give, any treatment to its students for physical illness. The same ruling applies to the present case since here also there is to be no medical or other treatment for the cure or amelioration of the disease with which these young men are afflicted; none of the attributes of a sanitarium, much less of a hospital, are present. It is true that plaintiff's operations are dependent to some extent on charitable support, but the phrase "eleemosynary and public institutions" must be construed to mean, under the rule of *ejusdem generis,* institutions of the nature of hospitals or sanitaria; this is obvious from the fact that there could not exist any valid reason for a 75 foot requirement in the case of such institutions as churches, schools, colleges, universities, convents, dormitories, libraries, art galleries and public museums, all of which are permitted in an "A" residential district and any or all of which might be eleemosynary or public institutions. It is clear, therefore, that the Board erred in rejecting the application for the permit because of the 75 foot requirement applicable to sanitaria and eleemosynary institutions.

We are of opinion that the court below correctly concluded that plaintiff was entitled to the grant of its requested permit as a "club house," or "dormitory," or both. Those terms are not defined in the ordinance and presumably are used in the broadest possible sense since restrictions imposed by zoning ordinances must be strictly construed: *Appeal of Lord,* 368 Pa. 121, 126, 81 A.2d 533, 535; *Appeal of Medinger,* 377 Pa. 217, 221, 104 A.2d 118, 120; *Shapiro* v. *Zoning Board of Adjustment,* 377 Pa. 621, 628, 105 A.2d 299, 302. A "club," of which there are many different types, is, in substance, merely an organization or association of persons who meet or live together for the purpose of social intercourse or some other common object such as the pursuit of literature, science, politics or good fellowship; see *D.B.S. Building Association* v. *City of Erie,* 177 Pa.Super. 487, 111 A.2d 367; *Pollock* v. *Borough of Pottstown,* 68 Montg. Co. Law Rep'r 340. A "dormitory" is defined by Webster as "a sleeping room, or a building containing a series of sleeping rooms." While the organization of the "Pioneers" may not follow some of the conventional practices and the formal methods of association usually employed by "clubs," but which it might, if deemed necessary, readily adopt, it is in essence a club composed of persons pursuing a common object and bound together by common ties. Nor is the combination of club and dormitory an unusual one since sleeping quarters, dining and recreational activities are quite ordinary adjuncts to club houses. As a club, or as a dormitory, or as both combined, the proposed use of plaintiff's property qualifies for admission into this "A" residential district: cf. *Overbrook Farms Club* v. *Philadelphia Zoning Board of Adjustment,* 351 Pa. 77, 40 A.2d 423. It is therefore unnecessary to consider whether, as plaintiff contends, it should in any event be entitled to a variance from the strict application of the 75 foot provision even if it were held to be a sanitarium.

Appellants urge as an additional objection to the grant of the permit that the ordinance requires of all buildings in an "A" residential district that the minimum depth of the rear yard should be 25 feet whereas the rear yard of plaintiff's property has a depth of only 10 feet. As a matter of fact the distance from the building to the lot in the rear is 77 feet but it appears that there are two accessory structures, a garage and a greenhouse, which are only 10 feet from the back line of the lot. Plaintiff, relying upon Section 2(18) (c) of the ordinance,* contends that the measurement in this regard should be made to the rear line not from the accessory buildings but from the main building. Be that as it may, plaintiff points out that the garage and the greenhouse were constructed long before the Zoning Ordinance was enacted, would therefore constitute a legal nonconforming use as to rear yard requirements, and accordingly are protected by a provision in the ordinance to the effect that any building or the use of any building existing at the time of the passage of the ordinance that does not conform in use, height, location, size or bulk with the regulations of the district in which it is located, shall be considered a non-conforming building or use, and may continue such use in its present location.

The order is affirmed at the cost of appellants.

NOTES

1.   In *Walker* v. *Zoning Board of Adjustment,* 380 Pa. 228, 110 A.2d 414 (1955), discussed in the *UCPA* decision, the same appellant, Overbrook Farms Club, was equally unsuccessful in preventing the establishment of a school for pupils with cerebral palsy. In the circumstances of that case, the facility was held to constitute a school, rather than a sanitarium as the appellant contended.

Another alternative to the *UCPA* approach of finding a facility to constitute a clubhouse or a dormitory, and to the *Walker/Crist* line of cases which concluded that the facilities at issue qualified as schools, is found in *La Salle National Bank* v. *The Thresholds,* 27 Ill.App.3d 635, 327 N.E.2d 22 (1975), where, in a well reasoned opinion, a program to assist persons recovering from mental or emotional illness to reestablish themselves in the community was held to be a "philanthropic or eleemosynary" use permissible in a residential zone. The potential ramification of such a theory, approved in a case where "eleemosynary" was ruled equivalent to "charity," *id.* at 327 N.E.2d 28, could be a tremendous boon to planners of facilities and residential alternatives for handicapped people.

---

*"Rear yard" is there defined as "A yard of the full width of the lot, located between the extreme rear line of *the building* and the extreme rear line of the lot. . . . "

Still another approach possible under some zoning ordinances is to have a residential facility for handicapped persons declared to be a boarding or rooming house. In *Ganim* v. *Village of New York Mills,* 75 Misc.2d 653, 347 N.Y.W.2d 372 (1973), a "family care" program for mentally ill patients operated by a state hospital was held to be a boarding or rooming house use permitted in a residential zone.

2. The courts have been somewhat more favorable in zoning challenges to programs and facilities serving handicapped persons than they have been to programs of a more "correctional" nature. See, for example, *Arkansas Release Guidance Foundation* v. *Hummel,* 245 Ark. 953, 435 S.W.2d 774 (1969), in which a "halfway house" for rehabilitation of convicted felons was held not to constitute an "institution of educational, religious or philanthropic nature." A clubhouse perhaps?

3. State Preemption and Immunity

BERGER v. STATE

Supreme Court of New Jersey, 1976
71 N.J. 206, 364 A.2d 993

MOUNTAIN, J.

This case presents the question of whether a group home for multi-handicapped, pre-school children must cease its operation either because of restrictive covenants in deeds of record or because of zoning provisions limiting the area to single family dwellings.

By deed dated July 9, 1973 William and Florence A. Graessle conveyed their premises in the Borough of Mantoloking as a gift to the New Jersey State Department of Institutions and Agencies. The deed specified that the premises, on which were located a well-maintained, 12 room ocean-front house and three-car garage, were to be known as the Graewill House and were to be devoted exclusively to the care of disadvantaged pre-school children under the age of nine. If the property were not so used, it would revert to the grantors. Moreover, the deed specified that the conveyance was subject to easements, covenants and restrictions of record as well as to the Borough's zoning provisions.

Pursuant to these conditions, the State formulated plans to utilize the property. The State intended that 8 to 12 multi-handicapped, pre-school children, most of whom would be wards of the State, would reside in the home with a married couple having 22 years of experience as foster parents. This arrangement would enable the children, who would otherwise be confined to hospitals, to grow and develop in a family environment. Supportive services would be provided by an educational specialist, two para-professionals, a cook-housekeeper and a maintenance man, none of whom would reside on the premises.

The children would neither attend local public schools nor participate in local community programs such as the Little League. Rather, most of their activities including school instruction, as well as play, training and physical therapy sessions, would take place at Graewill House. Their length of stay in the home, to be determined by individual progress, was anticipated to average between 12 and 18 months. Ultimately, it was hoped that the children, having learned adequately to cope with their individual handicaps, would be able either to return to their own homes or be placed in adoptive or foster homes.

In formulating these plans, the State also engaged in negotiations with the Mayor and Borough Attorney of Mantoloking and conducted a public meeting attended by concerned residents of the municipality. Ultimately, in the fall of 1973, the State agreed to execute a binding agreement with the Borough, which was to provide, among other things, that no more than 12 children and the appropriate staff would reside at Graewill House at any one time, that the State would maintain the structure to conform with the appearance of the neighborhood, and that a community advisory committee would be established to participate in the implementation of the project. This agreement was to be effective for a period of fifteen years. The record is not clear as to whether such an agreement was actually executed and delivered.

Four couples owning property either adjacent or in close proximity to the Graessle premises instituted this action on October 30, 1973 to restrain the use of the facility proposed by the State. Named as defendants were the State of New Jersey, Maurice G. Kott, Acting Commissioner of the Department of Institutions and Agencies, William and Florence A. Graessle, and the Borough of Mantoloking. Plaintiffs predicated their challenge on two bases: first, that the intended use of the Graessle premises would constitute a clear violation of the negative reciprocal covenants contained in deeds of record establishing a neighborhood scheme of single family residences, and second, that the proposed use would contravene Mantoloking's zoning ordinance restricting the area to single family dwellings.

Plaintiffs' application for a preliminary injunction was denied on November 29, 1973. At approximately the same time, the State officially began using Graewill House to care for handicapped children in the manner set forth above, a use which presently continues. Cross motions for summary judgment were made by the parties, culminating in a decision rendered July 26, 1974 denying plaintiffs' motion and granting summary judgment to defendants. The trial court's decision was based upon findings that the restrictive covenants regulated only the type of structure, not the occupancy or use of the premises, and that in any event the house was being used as a dwelling. It was also held that the zoning ordinance was invalid and that the State enjoyed immunity from its provisions. We certified plaintiffs' appeal prior to argument in the Appellate Division. 68 N.J. 175, 343 A.2d 463 (1975). For reasons hereinafter set forth we affirm.

[The court's discussion of the issue of restrictive covenants is omitted here but is examined at p. 746, below.]

The other basis for plaintiffs' attack is that the use of the Graessle premises as a group-care home violates the zoning ordinance of the Borough of Mantoloking, which provides for only two zones within the municipality, a business zone and a residential zone. The latter zone, which encompasses 95% of the land of the Borough and includes the Graessle tract, is restricted to "single family dwellings," defined as "detached building[s] designed for, or occupied exclusively by, one family in one dwelling unit." "Family" is defined as

> one person living alone or two or more persons related by blood, marriage or adoption and living together as a single unit in one house or within one curtilage and under one

head (pater or mater familias); domestic servants, one companion, one housekeeper and occasional nonpaying guests may be included but no other person.

It is readily apparent that the residents of Graewill House do not constitute a family as defined by the above quoted section of the ordinance. We are, however, for reasons discussed below, unable to accept plaintiffs' argument that the operation of Graewill House should therefore be enjoined.

Initially, it should be noted that state agencies are generally immune from the zoning ordinance provisions of a municipality. *Rutgers* v. *Piluso,* 60 N.J. 142, 153, 286 A.2d 697 (1972). *See generally,* 2 Anderson, *American Law of Zoning* § 9.06 (1968); Note, "Governmental Immunity from Local Zoning Ordinances," 84 *Harv.L.Rev.* 869 (1971). While there are no precise criteria by which to determine the existence or scope of such immunity, we have recognized that the test is basically one of legislative intent—i.e., whether the Legislature intended the particular governmental unit to be immune with respect to the particular enterprise. As we indicated in *Rutgers* v. *Piluso, supra,* legislative intent is to be gleaned from a number of factors, including "the nature and scope of the instrumentality seeking immunity, the kind of function or land use involved, the extent of the public interest to be served thereby, the effect local land use regulation would have upon the enterprise concerned and the impact upon legitimate local interests." 60 N.J. at 153, 286 A.2d at 702. Consideration of these factors in the instant case compels the conclusion that the State is immune from the Mantoloking zoning ordinance.

The Department of Institutions and Agencies, a principal department in the executive branch of the State government, is entrusted with the responsibility of providing care for children whose needs cannot be adequately met in their own homes. See N.J.S.A. 30:4C-1 *et seq.* To advance the public policy of providing adequate care and supervision for dependent children, the Legislature has proscribed discrimination in zoning regulations as between children in a conventional family setting and children in a group home—defined as any single family dwelling used in the placement of 12 or fewer children and recognized as such by the Department of Institutions and Agencies. N.J.S.A. 30:4C-2(m); 30:4C-26; 40:55-33.2. From these enactments, it is clear that the Legislature intended to immunize the Department of Institutions and Agencies from the operation of local zoning provisions which prohibit the establishment of a group home.

Additional considerations buttress our conclusion that the State is immune in the instant case. The use of the Graessle premises as a residence for a group functioning as a family entity substantially effectuates the purposes of the zoning provision sought to be enforced. Moreover, it furthers the public interest of providing quality care for handicapped children. Finally, the impact of Graewill House on legitimate local interests is slight when compared with the beneficial goals sought to be accomplished. Indeed, it is consonant with, not destructive of, the residential nature of the community. All of these factors unite to convince us that the Mantoloking zoning provisions cannot frustrate the State's operations of Graewill.

It is fundamental, however, that any assertion of immunity must be reasonable so as not "to arbitrarily override all important legitimate local interests." *Rutgers* v. *Piluso, supra,* 60 N.J. at 153, 286 A.2d at 703; *Township of Washington* v. *Village of*

Ridgewood, 26 N.J. 578, 584–86, 141 A.2d 308 (1958). Plaintiffs assert that the failure of the State to consider the objections of the community prior to establishing Graewill illustrates its unreasonableness. To support their position they rely on *Long Branch Division of United Civic & Taxpayers Org.* v. *Cowan,* 119 N.J.Super. 306, 291 A.2d 381 (App.Div.), certif. den. 62 N.J. 86, 299 A.2d 84 (1972), wherein the Appellate Division held that the State Department of Health was immune from local zoning provisions thus permitting the establishment of a residential narcotic rehabilitation and treatment center in a residential zone of Long Branch. Nevertheless, the court took cognizance of the widespread opposition registered by the community with respect to the site selection and remanded the matter for a hearing on the issue of whether the Department had acted unreasonably or arbitrarily in selecting the location of the center.

We are not persuaded that the instant case merits the same disposition. We see nothing to suggest that the State acted arbitrarily in deciding to utilize the Graessle premises as a residential home for handicapped children, a use which is markedly different from a drug treatment center. The State negotiated with officials of Mantoloking to assure that Graewill House would continue to be compatible in appearance with the neighborhood and met with concerned residents of the town. The fact that many of the residents voiced opposition to Graewill House does not, in and of itself, mean that the State acted unreasonably in proceeding with its plans. Rather, the reasonableness of its action must be evaluated in terms of the effect Graewill has on the surrounding area. We find nothing to convince us that Graewill has such a detrimental effect as to warrant judicial interference, and have no difficulty in concluding that the State, acting reasonably, is immune from the Mantoloking zoning provisions restricting single family dwellings to persons related by blood, marriage or adoption.

That Graewill has been established as a group home gives rise to an equally compelling reason for one finding the zoning restriction to be without effect. Municipalities must look to legislation to determine the scope of their zoning powers. These are as comprehensive or as restrictive as the relevant statutes determine. The New Jersey Legislature has expressly prohibited municipalities from discriminating in their zoning ordinances governing single family dwellings between children residing therein by virtue of their relationship by blood, marriage or adoption and children residing therein by virtue of their placement in a group home. N.J.S.A. 30:4C-26; 40:55-33.2.[2] *See also YWCA* v. *Board of Adjustment of City of Summit,* 134 N.J.Super.

---

[2]The recently enacted Municipal Land Use Law, N.J.S.A 40:55D-1 *et seq.,* L1975, c. 291, § 53(c) continues to prohibit zoning discrimination against children placed in group homes. This section provides as follows:

> No zoning ordinance shall, by any of its provisions or by any regulation adopted in accordance therewith discriminate between children who are members of families by reason of their relationship by blood, marriage or adoption, and foster children placed with such families in a dwelling by the Division of Youth and Family Services in the Department of Institutions and Agencies or a duly incorporated child care agency and children placed pursuant to law in single family dwellings known as group homes. As used in this section, the term "group home" means and includes any single family dwelling used in the placement of children pursuant to law recognized as a group home by the Department of Institutions and Agencies in accordance with rules and regulations adopted by the Commissioner of Institutions and Agencies provided, however, that no group home shall contain more than 12 children.

384, 389–90, 341 A.2d 356 (Law Div. 1975), aff'd, 141 N.J.Super. 315, 358 A.2d 211 (App.Div. 1976). These two statutes were each amended to confirm and clarify the status of group homes for children as being single family units. This clearly evidences the Legislature's desire to accord the same protections to children placed in group homes as had been previously extended to foster children. Moreover, it may be interpreted as indicative of the Legislature's position that the zoning enabling act was not designed to empower municipalities to restrict a family to those biologically or legally related. *Kirsch Holding Co. v. Borough of Manasquan,* 59 N.J. 241, 251, 281 A.2d 513 (1971). In summary, the Legislature has defined "group home" to include the kind of dwelling arrangement we are considering here, and has further declared that any municipal effort to treat such an arrangement as in any way different than a biological family unit will result in a declaration of invalidity.

Plaintiffs also contend that neither N.J.S.A. 30:4C-26 nor 40:55-33.2 validates the use of the Graessle premises as Graewill House because it is not being used as either a foster or group home. Plaintiffs seem to perceive Graewill as a non-residential facility in a single family residential area. While it may differ from the conventional foster or group home in that the children do not become active participants in the community and do require educational and medical services within the home, this is hardly sufficient to justify plaintiffs' characterization of Graewill. It is, both in essence and in operation, a family home and fully within the meaning of group homes as defined in the applicable legislation. As such, it is clear that N.J.S.A. 30:4C-26 and 40:55-33.2 invalidate so much of Mantoloking's zoning ordinance as restricts single family dwellings exclusively to persons related by blood, marriage or adoption.

* * *

It is our judgment that Graewill House need not cease its operation; that it violates neither restrictive covenants of record, nor the Borough's zoning provisions, the latter, to the extent indicated above, having been held invalid. Accordingly all forms of relief sought by plaintiffs are denied.

Judgment is affirmed.

For affirmance:

Chief Justice Hughes and Justices Mountain, Sullivan, Pashman and Schreiber—5.

For reversal: Judge Conford—1.

[The dissenting opinion of Judge Conford is omitted.]

NOTES

1. A ruling quite similar to *Berger* was made in *Village of Walbridge* v. *State of Ohio,* Case No. 78-CIV-37 (Ct. of Common Pleas of Wood Cty., Ohio, July 11, 1978), where the Village of Walbridge sued to enjoin the State of Ohio, the Ohio Department of Mental Health and Retardation, and the Wood County Board of Mental Retardation from establishing a "family home" for mentally retarded individuals on state-owned property. In holding that the Village's complaint should be dismissed for failure to state a claim upon which relief could be granted, the court observed:

> The plaintiff in its complaint states that the defendants intend to operate a "family home" for retarded individuals on property purchased and owned by the state. The

plaintiff also asserts that such a use by the defendants would violate its "single family" zoning ordinance. It is undisputed that the land involved was purchased by the state and is owned by the State of Ohio. It is also undisputed that the State, through its instrumentalities or agencies, intended to use the property for the purpose of establishing, maintaining and operating a "family home" for mentally retarded individuals.

It has been recognized by the Supreme Court of Ohio that when Ohio appropriates real estate, whether through purchase or condemnation, such exercise of appropriation is an exercise in its eminent domain power. *Norfolk and Western R. Co.* v. *Gale,* 119 Ohio St. 110, 162 N.E. 385 (1928), app. dism'd., 278 U.S. 571. In the instant case, the state's purchase of the real estate in question was an exercise of the state's eminent domain power. Further, when the state exercises its eminent domain powers, it is not subject to local zoning ordinances. *State ex rel. Ohio Turnpike Commission* v. *Allen,* 158 Ohio St. 168, 107 N.E.2d. 345 (1952). See also Ohio Attorney General Opinion No. 77-051. Therefore, the Court finds that as to the plaintiff's first cause of action set forth in its complaint, the plaintiff has not alleged a set of facts which state a claim upon which relief can be granted.

In the plaintiff's second cause of action, the plaintiff asserts that the creation, maintenance and operation of the proposed "family home" would be detrimental to the health, safety and welfare of neighboring villagers and, therefore, would constitute a nuisance from which the plaintiff should be granted injunctive relief. As set forth above, the State of Ohio acquired the real estate in question through the exercise of its eminent domain powers. The Supreme Court of Ohio stated in paragraph number four of its syllabus in *Toledo Disposal Co.* v. *State,* 89 Ohio St. 230, 106 N.E. 6 (1914):

> "A public nuisance arises out of the violation of public rights or the doing of unlawful acts: and if the legislature, by a law passed within its legislative power, authorizes an act to be done which, in the absence of statute, would be a public nuisance, such act ceases to be legally a nuisance so far as the public is concerned."

> Also see *Clabaugh* v. *Harriss,* 27 Ohio Misc. 153 (Franklin Co. C.P. 1971). Ohio Revised Code Section 5123.18 specifically authorizes the creation and operation of a "family home" as here in question. Therefore, even if the village established that the "family home" was a nuisance, the creation and operation of the family home has been authorized by the state's legislature which is a complete defense to the charge of maintaining a public nuisance. Therefore, the Court finds that as to the plaintiff's second cause of action set forth in its complaint, the plaintiff has not alleged a set of facts upon which state a claim upon which relief can be granted. *Id.* at 5-6.

Another Ohio decision reaching the same result is *Boyd* v. *Gateways to Better Living, Inc.,* Case No. 73 CI 531 (Ct. of Common Pleas of Mahoning Cty., Ohio, June 24, 1974), where the defendants, who proposed to establish a residential facility for ambulatory mentally retarded children, were held to be immune from City of Youngstown Zoning Ordinances which would have prohibited the facility's location at the chosen site.

2.   In *City of Temple Terrace* v. *Hillsborough Association for Retarded Citizens, Inc.,* 322 So.2d 571 (Fla.App. 1975), aff'd. 332 So.2d 610 (Fla. 1976), the City of Temple Terrace filed suit to enjoin the operation of a short term respite care facility for mentally retarded persons in a single-family residential zone. The facility was run by the Hillsborough Association for Retarded Citizens pursuant to a contract with the Division of Retardation, Department of Health and Rehabilitative Services of the State of Florida. The trial court held that the respite care facility was exempt from the zoning restrictions:

After the taking of testimony, the court entered a judgment in which it found that even though the use of the premises was contrary to the city's single family residential zoning ordinance, the ordinance could not be enforced against the operation of the facility. The court reasoned that when it was performing respite care services for the retarded, the Association stood in the shoes of the State of Florida and, as such, was not subject to municipal zoning ordinances. *Id.* at 322 So.2d 573.

The Court of Appeals and the Supreme Court of Florida, however, held that such reasoning was too simplistic. These courts declared that there were several alternative tests that could be applied to determine the extent to which state agencies (or those acting in their stead) are subject to municipal zoning ordinances: a Superior Sovereign Test, a Governmental Proprietary Test, a Power of Eminent Domain Test, and a Balancing of Interests Test. *Id.* at 322 So.2d 576–579. All but the last of these tests tended to give priority to the activities and determinations of state agencies. The appellate court and the Supreme Court of Florida held that the Balancing of Interests Test was the more modern and preferable standard:

> ... we believe that it presents the fairest method by which this type of case can be decided. It permits a case by case determination which takes into consideration all of the factors which may properly influence the result.
> The old tests were adopted at a time when state government was much smaller. The myriad of agencies now conducting the functions of the state have necessarily resulted in a diminution of centralized control. The decision of a person administering an outlying function of a state agency with respect to the site where this function should be performed is not necessarily any better than the decision of the local authorities on the subject of land use. The adoption of the balancing of interests test will compel governmental agencies to make more responsible land-use decisions by forcing them to consider the feasibility of other sites for the facility as well as alternative methods of making the use of the proposed site less detrimental to the local zoning scheme. *Id.* at 322 So.2d 578–579, adopted by Supreme Court of Florida at 332 So.2d 610, 612.

Accordingly, the case was remanded to the trial court for a determination under the Balancing of Interests Test. *Id.* at 332 So.2d 613.

How would the application of such a standard have affected the outcome of the *Berger* case?

3. In a portion of the *Berger* decision not included here, the court indicated that, if the local zoning ordinance had not been overridden by the state statutes, the restrictive definition of "family" would have been constitutionally invalid. *Id.* at 364 A.2d 1001–1004.

Conners v. New York State Association of Retarded Children, Inc.

Supreme Court of New York, Special Term, Rensselaer County, 1975
82 Misc.2d 861, 370 N.Y.S.2d 474

A. Franklin Mahoney, Justice.

In this action for a permanent injunction, plaintiff seeks an Order preliminarily enjoining and restraining the defendants from using premises known as 54 Maple Avenue, in the City of Troy, New York, heretofore purchased by the New York State Department of Mental Hygiene and leased to the New York State Association of Retarded Children, Inc., Rensselaer County Chapter, for use as a halfway house or hostel for the mentally retarded. The defendant, New York State Department of Mental Hygiene, has made a cross motion for judgment dismissing the complaint upon the grounds that the Court lacks jurisdiction of the person of the defendant and the subject matter of the action and upon the ground that the complaint fails to state a cause of action. The claim that the Court has no jurisdiction of the subject matter of the action and of the person of the defendant Mental Hygiene Department (CPLR 3211, subd. [a], pars. 2 and 8), is without merit and denied.

The plaintiff herein is an owner of premises as tenant by the entirety which are in close proximity to the subject premises which the defendants are presently using as a hostel or home for mentally retarded adults. The subject property is situated in an R-2 residential district in the City of Troy in which the proposed use by the defendants is not permitted. The defendants have not nor do they intend to make any application to the City's zoning authorities for approval of the use, it being their position that said use is in furtherance of a governmental purpose and is thereby immunized and exempt from local zoning ordinances. The plaintiff contends that said use by the defendants will cause substantial injury to the value of her property and of the properties of other persons similarly situated and, further, that such use is incompatible with the residential character of the street, and denegrates aesthetic and property values of residences located not only on Maple Avenue but in the remainder of the R-2 residential zone. The gravamen of the complaint is that the present and contemplated use violates the zoning ordinance of the City of Troy and is thereby illegal and void.

The issue raises the ancient dichotomy of distinguishing between governmental and proprietary functions of state and local governments. Section 1.03 of Article 1 of the Mental Hygiene Law states that "The protection and promotion of the mental health of the people of the state and the prevention of mental illness, mental retardation . . . are matters of public concern. The state and local government shall share responsibility . . . for developing plans, programs and services for the care, treatment and rehabilitation of the mentally retarded, . . . " Next, Section 11.01 of Article 11 of the Mental Hygiene Law, entitled "Declaration of purpose," states that "This article is designed to enable and encourage local governments to develop in the community preventive, rehabilitative, and treatment services offering continuity of care; to improve and to expand existing community programs for the mentally ill, the mentally retarded, . . . whose conditions, . . . are associated with mental disabilities, . . . ; to plan for the integration of community, regional, and state services and facilities for the mentally disabled; . . . " In furtherance of the aforedescribed statutory state purpose to aid the mentally ill, Section 11.33 of Article 11 of the Mental Hygiene Law states that "The commissioner shall have the power to operate or cause to be operated community residential facilities as hostels for the mentally disabled. . . . "

Clearly, the purchase of the premises at 54 Maple Avenue in the City of Troy and the leasing of the same by the State to the local chapter of the State Association of Retarded Children was in furtherance of a legitimate State purpose and the operation of the subject premises is governmental in nature and thereby exempt from the provisions of the zoning ordinance of the City of Troy. (*Town of Mamaroneck* v. *County of Westchester*, 22 A.D.2d 143, 255 N.Y.S.2d 290, affd. 16 N.Y.2d 940, 264 N.Y.S.2d 925, 212 N.E.2d 442; *City of Rochester* v. *Town of Rush*, 67 Misc.2d 328,

324 N.Y.S.2d 201, affd. 37 A.D.2d 795, 324 N.Y.S.2d 888; *Abbott House* v. *Village of Tarrytown,* 34 A.D.2d 821, 822, 312 N.Y.S.2d 841, 843; *Matter of Wiltwyck School for Boys* v. *Hill,* 11 N.Y.2d 182, 227 N.Y.S.2d 655, 182 N.E.2d 268). The governmental nature of the subject premises is not altered or changed or made proprietary merely because the residents pay for services, all or in part, by their own resources. (14 NYCRR 111.5[a][5][7], 111.8[b][2]). A use is governmental if it is created pursuant to a duty imposed upon the sovereign to provide for the well-being and health of a community. It is non-arguable that the State, in cooperation with local communities, has a duty to provide for the unfortunate among us and, in furtherance of that duty, to declare that duty as a purpose and to move affirmatively to implement that goal. In my view, therefore, the "retarded home" at 54 Maple Avenue is authorized under the afore-cited Articles of the Mental Hygiene Law and its use is exempt from the provisions of the local zoning ordinance. (*Matter of Moore et al.* v. *Nowakowski et al. of the City of Syracuse,* 46 A.D.2d 996, 361 N.Y.S.2d 795[1]; *City of White Plains* v. *Ferraioli,* 34 N.Y.2d 300, 357 N.Y.S.2d 449, 313 N.E.2d 756).

It does not follow, however, that because a use is governmental in nature and thereby less restricted than a proprietary use, that the sovereign can arbitrarily select a site in any community for the operation of the facility in furtherance of the governmental purpose. As Judge Jones noted in *People* v. *Renaissance Project,* 36 N.Y.2d 65, 69, 364 N.Y.S.2d 885, 887, 324 N.E.2d 355, 357, ". . . it does not follow, of course, that the promoters of every worthwhile community project thereby, *ipso facto,* become entitled to set their project down in any location of their choosing in any municipality they may select." The sovereign must act reasonably and rationally under the circumstances so that the governmental purpose may be achieved with the least amount of invasion or diminution of private rights. The State, in cooperation with the local community, is not absolutely free to locate any governmental use in any location without a showing that less objectionable means are not available. Herein, as in (*People* v. *Renaissance Project, supra*) the record is barren of any evidentiary proof that the subject use could not be carried out in any other location in the City of Troy. There is nothing before this Court that would aid it in determining whether the defendants acted arbitrarily or capriciously in the purchase and use of the property and that due consideration was not given to the character of the neighborhood and that less objectionable methods of accomplishing the same result could have been found. While "It is the settled policy of the courts not to review the exercise of discretion by public officials in the enforcement of State statutes, in the absence of a clear violation of some constitutional mandate" (*Gaynor* v. *Rockefeller,* 15 N.Y.2d 120, 131, 256 N.Y.S.2d 584, 592, 204 N.E.2d 627, 632) Article 78 review is always available to determine, based upon a proper evidentiary showing, if the affirmative act was beyond the parameters of reason and without a rational basis. The record before me fails to disclose the considerations of the defendants that caused them to purchase and place in use as a hostel the premises at 54 Maple Avenue and I am, therefore, unable to review the reasoning or rationale of the defendants that caused them to act as they did. Next, I cannot alter the form of the action, since it challenged the acts of the defendants on the ground that they were without warrant of authority to open the hostel, as it is proper in form. (§ 103[c] CPLR). I can, however, reserve to the plaintiff herein the right to

review by an Article 78 proceeding the considerations employed by the defendants in the
purchase and dedication of the premises located at 54 Maple Avenue in the City of Troy.

The application for a preliminary injunction is denied. The cross motion to
dismiss the verified complaint for a permanent injunction on the ground it fails to state
a cause of action (CPLR 3211) is granted, without prejudice to the plaintiff's commencement of an Article 78 proceeding to review the acts of the defendants, if the
plaintiff so elects within the time limited for the commencement of such a proceeding.

NOTE

The concept of state preemption or immunity from local zoning ordinances has been
applied in situations other than facilities for handicapped people. In *Abbott House* v.
Village of Tarrytown, 34 A.D.2d 821, 312 N.Y.S.2d 841 (1970), a boarding home for
neglected and abandoned children was held to be exempt from a restrictive zoning
ordinance. The court declared:

> It is clear that this Zoning Ordinance has the effect of totally thwarting the State's policy,
> as expressed in its Constitution and Social Service Law, of providing for neglected
> children. We are therefore of the opinion that the Tarrytown Zoning Ordinance, insofar
> as it conflicts and hinders an overriding State Law and policy favoring the care of
> neglected and abandoned children, is void as exceeding the authority vested in the
> Village of Tarrytown. *Id.* at 312 N.Y.S.2d 843.

The *Abbott House* ruling has been followed in *Unitarian Universalist Church
of Central Nassau* v. *Shorten,* 63 Misc.2d 978, 314 N.Y.S.2d 66 (1970), and in
Nowack v. *Department of Audit and Control,* 72 Misc.2d 518, 338 N.Y.S.2d 52
(1973). In *Shorten,* it was held that, because of a state policy favoring day care centers,
a local zoning ordinance was invalid insofar as it prohibited the operation of a day care
center approved by the State Department of Social Services. In *Nowack,* the Division
of Youth of the Executive Department of the State of New York, which sought to
establish a youth center in a residential district, was held to be exempt from local
zoning ordinances in light of a state policy favoring such youth centers.

Can a purely private agency claim exemption from zoning ordinances because
its facility would further some recognized public policy? How much state involvement
is necessary?

4. Special Situations and Zoning Variations

EAST HOUSE CORPORATION v. RIKER

Supreme Court of New York, Monroe County, 1973
72 Misc.2d 823, 339 N.Y.S.2d 511

EMMETT J. SCHNEPP, Justice.

This article 78 proceeding reviews a decision of the Zoning Board of Appeals of
the City of Rochester denying the application for a special exception to use premises in
an R-3 district at 109 Dartmouth Street, Rochester, New York, as a half-way house for
mentally restored persons. Petitioner is a non-profit corporation supported by public
funds and private contributions. It acquired this property in 1967 and for some time
prior to the application used the premises for this purpose without zoning approval,

because of the erroneous issuance of a certificate of occupancy. It conducts a similar function in the immediate neighborhood at 155 Dartmouth Street, which is located in an R-2 zone, a higher use district. Economies were effected in operational costs due to the use of the same staff and other facilities at both sites.

On May 16, 1972 respondents approved the use of 155 Dartmouth Street for this purpose as a special exception by a 4-2 vote. Thereafter petitioner was notified by the Zoning Administrator of the City that the operation of a half-way house at 109 Dartmouth Street required authorization as a special exception. Its application was denied on August 24, 1972 by a 2-2 vote. The board members voting against the applications were the same in both cases.

The facts presented in connection with the within application were substantially the same as those submitted for 155 Dartmouth Street. Under the ordinance an R-3 district is described as "walk up apartment uses" and the principle [sic] uses are those permitted in an R-2 district, plus multiple and row dwellings for any number of families, subject to certain conditions. Certain special exception uses permitted in an R-3 district are excluded in an R-2 district.

In either district a convalescent home, not less than twenty feet distance from any other lot, may be authorized under the zoning ordinance of the City of Rochester as a special exception upon approval of the board (Section 115-27 B), "... if it is found that such use will not be injurious to the contiguous or surrounding property and that the spirit of the ordinance shall be observed and substantial justice done. The board may impose such conditions and safeguards as are appropriate under this chapter." (Section 115-87 B).

Section 115-6 of the Ordinance defines a special exception as a "use not usually or ordinarily permitted within a district which may be authorized by the Board provided such use will serve public convenience and welfare in accordance with general or specific conditions and safeguards therein contained and any additional conditions and safeguards which may be imposed by the Board to protect the appropriate use of neighboring property."

Both the board members who approved the application and those who disapproved it made findings. The approving members adopted to 109 Dartmouth Street the findings made in connection with the approval of the application for 155 Dartmouth Street. This included a finding that the use is essentially residential in character and in keeping with the appearance of the neighborhood, with no external manifestations of institutional use and that the general character of the neighborhood is "heterogeneous, having multiple dwellings, single-family dwellings, and institutional uses existing in close proximity to the property in question." The two board members, who voted against the application, found that the use would increase the density over the present allowable use by four people and would be the fourth "... institutional use" "... within one or two blocks." They further found that a concentration of such uses "... causes a loss of residential uses" "... envisioned by the R-3 zoning," and that as more units are converted to institutional uses the "... less that remain to form a solid nucleus of R-3 permitted principal uses."

A special exception is a use authorized by a zoning ordinance under stated conditions and is in compliance with rather than in variance of the ordinance. The granting of a special exception is allowable when the facts and circumstances specified in the Ordinance upon which the exception is permitted are found to exist. The power to grant or withhold these permits is limited by standards sufficient to contain the discretion of the board and provide the courts with a reasonable basis for judicial review of the board's decision. The standard here is the injury to the contiguous and surrounding property and the observance of the spirit of the ordinance. The gist of the findings, which resulted in a denial of the application, relate to increased occupancy, the number of such institutions in the area and the affect such institutions have on what is termed "... permitted uses...." These conclusory statements find no substantiation in the record. There is no finding whatever as to the injurious affect [sic] of the use on surrounding property. In considering the number of such uses within the "... one or two blocks area," described, no consideration whatever was given to the entire zoning district in which the subject property is located. The question as to how many uses of this type will develop in the area or the number of institutional uses is a matter for the concern of the legislative body in framing the ordinance. This type of use is permitted and within the spirit of the ordinance. The findings of the board in granting the approval of 155 Dartmouth Street, which were utilized by the two board members who approved the application, were established by the evidence before the board in this proceeding and these findings are relevant to what the board may consider on these applications, and there is no significant reason to differentiate between the two applications.

The purpose of the petitioner is to use the premises as a convalescent home, a permitted use as a special exception under certain conditions. The findings of those board members whose vote resulted in a denial of the application amounts to opposition to the expressed intent of the ordinance to permit this use in this zone. The proposed use is lawful and the findings which resulted in the denial of the application are without support in the evidence, are erroneous and arbitrary and are annulled. (*In the Matter of Grand Chapter Phi Sigma Kappa v. Grosberg et al., Zoning Board of Appeals of City of Troy*, 30 A.D.2d 887, 291 N.Y.S.2d 606.) Accordingly it is directed that the special exception permit be issued to petitioner to use the premises at 109 Dartmouth Street as a half-way house for mentally restored persons in accordance with its application therefore, and the action of the board is reversed, annulled and set aside.

NOTES

1.   Special exceptions have been used in many circumstances to obtain approval for facilities for handicapped persons in zones where they would otherwise have been prohibited. In *City of Evanston v. Ridgeview House, Inc.*, 64 Ill.2d 40, 349 N.E.2d 399 (1976), a sheltered care home facility for mentally retarded persons and former residents of mental health facilities was held entitled to a special use permit even though the city ordinance that granted approval of the special use had added as a condition "that persons suffering from mental retardation or mental disorders apt to make them a burden to the other residents or to the surrounding neighborhood shall not be permitted to reside in the sheltered care facility." *Id.* at 349 N.E.2d 402. In *School Lane Hills, Inc. v. East Hempfield Township Zoning Hearing Board*, 336 A.2d 901 (Pa. Cmwlth., 1975), the court upheld a special exception for a child development

center for mentally retarded persons in a residential section, and indicated that an Easter Seal rehabilitation center for physically handicapped persons would be eligible for such an exception if, upon remand to the trial court, it could be shown to be educational in nature, a finding which the record to that point did not support. In *In re Gilden's Appeal*, 406 Pa. 484, 178 A.2d 562 (1962), a school for exceptional children was held to be permitted in a residential district by special exception as an "educational institution." In *Hazel Wilson Hotel Corp.* v. *City of Chicago*, 17 Ill.App.3d 415, 308 N.E.2d 372 (1974), the court ordered that a special use permit be issued in regard to a sheltered care home for mental health clients.

It should be noted that the distinction between special exceptions, which require the specific approval of the zoning agency, and permissible uses, which require no approval, depends upon the wording of the zoning ordinance at issue. Thus, in many jurisdictions, educational uses are permitted within residential zones, while in other locales they are denominated special exceptions.

2. In *Unteed* v. *Lehman*, 77 Ohio L.Abs. 353, 150 N.E.2d 509 (1957), the court held that no special permit was required for a rooming house for mentally retarded former residents of the Columbus State School because it did not constitute a "sanitarium" for which a permit was required. The opinion contained an admirable expression of judicial sentiment concerning appropriate public attitudes toward such facilities:

> This Court would like to say further that it is the responsibility of the public at large not to ignore the problems which exist and which may in many instances not touch them except indirectly, but to accept the responsibility to provide, so far as possible, an environment so that all people might have an opportunity to live a healthy normal existence and not to wash their hands of the problems that exist such as is contained in this case, as well as many others. It is time that we take a sensible view toward the social problems which come from an increased urban population and not to put the burden upon certain public servants alone for the solution of all people in a democracy and that the one thing that each of us should strive for above all, in our duty to others, is to see that all people are adequately furnished with the facilities which will provide them with the type of an environment which will help them to lead happy and normal lives. Let us remember that with longevity becoming a common thing, if each of us lives long enough, mental retardation and senility may be our lot, so we can see that the problem here presented is one to be solved and not ignored. *Id.* at 150 N.E.2d 514.

City Planning Commission of Greensburg v. Threshold, Inc.

Commonwealth Court of Pennsylvania, 1974
12 Pa.Cmwlth. 104, 315 A.2d 311

Before Bowman, President Judge, and Kramer, Wilkinson, Mercer, Rogers and Blatt, JJ.

Opinion

Blatt, Judge.

Threshold, Inc. (Threshold), applied to the Planning Commission of the City of Greensburg (City) for a conditional use permit for the operation of a transitory living service, Threshold having been established to provide such a facility for the County mental health and mental retardation program. After conducting several hearings, the

Planning Commission voted 3-3 to recommend the proposed use to the City Council. The application for the conditional use when submitted to the City Council, however, was unanimously rejected. Threshold then appealed to the Court of Common Pleas of Westmoreland County, which held a full hearing on the matter, made a view of the property in question and held that the application should be approved.

Section 603 of the Municipalities Planning Code, 53 P.S. § 10603, provides that zoning ordinances may contain: "Provisions for conditional uses to be allowed or denied by the governing body after recommendations by the planning agency, pursuant to express standards and criteria set forth in the ordinances. . . . " The City has provided certain categories of conditional uses in Section 1601 of its zoning ordinance, which are:

1. Uses publicly operated or traditionally affected with a public interest;
2. Uses entirely private in character, but of such an unusual nature that their operation may give rise to unique problems with respect to their impact upon neighboring property or public facilities;
3   Developments, either public or private, consisting of a multiplicity of units or uses, controlled and planned as a single entity.

If a use fits within the above categories, Section 1603 of the zoning ordinance provides further guidelines, as follows:

General Standards. The following findings shall be used as guidelines by the Commission and the Council in acting upon conditional use applications:

1. That the establishment, maintenance, or operation of the conditional use will not be detrimental to or endanger the public health, safety, morals, comfort, or general welfare.
2. That the conditional use will not be injurious to the use and enjoyment of other properties in the immediate vicinity for the purposes already permitted, nor substantially diminish and impair property values within the neighborhood.
3. That the establishment of the conditional use will not impede the normal and orderly development and improvement of the surrounding property for uses permitted in the district.
4. That adequate utilities, access roads, drainage, and/or necessary facilities have been or are being provided.
5. That adequate measures have been or will be taken to provide ingress and egress so designed as to minimize traffic congestion in the public streets.

In applying for a conditional use, we believe that the applicant carries the burden of proving that his proposed use is one permitted as a conditional use by the applicable zoning ordinance and that he has complied with all reasonable standards established by that ordinance. When such proofs have been established, however, the burden of going forward with the evidence and establishing that the proposed conditional use does not meet the standards of the ordinance shifts to the objecting party. There is little difference in this regard between applications for a conditional use and a special exception, although the legislative body does retain the right to define differing standards for each.

In the instant case, it would appear that Threshold did establish its proposed use to be one which was permitted as a conditional use by the appropriate city ordinance. Even if the proposed use is a boarding house, as argued by the City, the requirements of category (2) would seem to have been met. As to the further standards set out by the ordinance, the lower court clearly set forth in its opinion the substantial evidence which Threshold presented as to each. The objectors, on the other hand, presented little evidence to rebut this extensive expert testimony. In fact, the court below found "that the plaintiff has produced such an overwhelming case in its behalf to the extent that the testimony in favor of the plaintiff far outweighs the testimony presented on behalf of the defendant."

We must agree with the lower court that Threshold clearly carried its burden of proving that it met the standards for a conditional use as set out in the zoning ordinance. The lower court also found, we believe correctly, that the objectors failed to meet their burden of rebutting this evidence, and that Threshold was thus entitled to the permit for a conditional use.

The City has contended that this action by the lower court usurps the functions of the Planning Commission and the City Council. We cannot agree. The City Council has the option of determining whether or not it wishes to include conditional uses as part of its zoning ordinance, and, if it does, what standards must be met if such uses are to be permitted. Thereafter, the function of the Planning Commission and the City Council is to determine whether or not a proposed conditional use meets the requirements of the ordinance, but, in so doing they may not arbitrarily reject an application which clearly meets such standards and which has not been shown to be a danger to the public health, safety or welfare.

For the above reasons therefore, we must affirm the order of the court below.

NOTES

1. It appears that the phrase "conditional uses" simply refers to special exceptions to which statements of conditions can be attached.

2. Almost indistinguishable from special exceptions and conditional uses are "variances" that are permitted under many zoning ordinances. In *Kunzler* v. *Hoffman,* 48 N.J. 277, 225 A.2d 321 (1966), a local Board of Adjustment granted a variance permitting, if a list of conditions were met, the construction of a hospital for emotionally disturbed adults and children in a residential neighborhood. Pursuant to New Jersey statutes, a variance could be granted in situations where the following findings were made:

> (1) that the variance "can be granted without substantial detriment to the public good and will not substantially impair the intent and purpose of the zone plan and zoning ordinance"; and (2) that "special reasons" exist for the granting of such a variance. *Id.* at 225 A.2d 325.

In light of the Board of Adjustment's findings that such hospitals were urgently needed and would render substantial benefit to the community, and that the proposed hospital would not pose a threat to life, person, or property of adjoining residences nor would impair the purposes of the overall zoning plan, the Supreme Court of New Jersey held that the grant of variance was appropriate.

3. Even though a particular land use is not in conformance with the requirements for the zone in which it is located, it may be permissible if it is a continuation of a prior

nonconforming use. Thus, in *Rogers* v. *Ass'n for the Help of Retarded Children,* 308 N.Y. 126, 123 N.E.2d 806 (1954), a residential facility and school for mentally retarded children was held to be permitted, although in violation of a local zoning ordinance, because it was a continuation of a nonconforming use by the predecessor in title as a convalescent home and school for children with cardiac disorders.

Likewise, in *Kastendike* v. *Baltimore Ass'n for Retarded Children,* 297 A.2d 745 (Md.App. 1972), a home for mentally retarded adults was held to be permitted in a residential zone as a continuation of a nonconforming use by the predecessors in title, who operated a nursing home on the premises. In the absence of express language so indicating, the court held that it would not interpret the zoning ordinance to have a retroactive impact. *Id.* at 297 A.2d 749.

4. Of course, if a proposed property use is not in conformance with the uses specified for the zone in which it is located, the most direct course would be to simply have the property rezoned. However, even if the hurdles of community attitudes and zoning inertia can be overcome, there may be some problem with the legal concept of "spot zoning." In *Schubach* v. *Silver,* 461 Pa. 366, 336 A.2d 328 (1975), for example, the Pine Hill Home, Inc., succeeded in having a plot of land reclassified from residential to commercial in order to permit it to establish a nursing home facility for multiply handicapped children. This rezoning was challenged by neighbors as unconstitutional spot zoning. Indeed, in an earlier related action, *Schubach* v. *Zoning Board of Adjustment,* 440 Pa. 249, 270 A.2d 397 (1970), the Pine Hill Home's attempt to obtain a special certificate to permit the establishment of the nursing home was frustrated when the Supreme Court of Pennsylvania held that the special certificate constituted a classic case of spot zoning, and declared:

> It is well-settled that 'an ordinance cannot create an "island" of more or less restricted use within a district zoned for a different use or uses, where there are no differentiating relevant factors between the "island" and the district.... Thus, singling out of one lot or a small area for different treatment from that accorded to similar surrounding land indistinguishable from it in character, for the economic benefit of the owner of that lot or to his economic detriment, is invalid "spot" zoning.' *Id.* at 440 Pa. 253–254, 270 A.2d 399.

In the later case, however, the same court held that the rezoning was not "spot zoning" because some adjacent property had been simultaneously reclassified as commercial, the rezoned property fronted on other commercial land, and the property was ill suited for residential use. *Id.* at 336 A.2d 337. Thus the court ruled that the rezoning was appropriate as a "natural extension" of the already existing commercial use. *Ibid.*

5. Legislative Action

STATE EX REL. THELEN V. CITY OF MISSOULA

Supreme Court of Montana, 1975
543 P.2d 173

JOHN C. HARRISON, Justice.

This is an original proceeding brought by property owners of the city of Missoula praying that an alternative writ of prohibition issue directing the city of Missoula to restrain from further interference in the sale of their residence and in the establishment of a home for the developmentally disabled in a one-family residential zone.

Relators are residents of the city of Missoula and owners under a contract for deed of a residence in that city. The property is located in a zone classified by the city as R-I, one-family residential district. The zoning classification, as set forth in section 32.93 of the code of the city of Missoula, allows uses of the premises as follows: "Any use permitted in RR-I." Such uses are set out in section 32-9.8 of the code of the city of Missoula as:

(a) One-family dwelling.
(b) Parks and Playgrounds.

The applicable definition of "family" is contained in section 32-2 of the code of the city of Missoula, and provides:

> One or more persons related by blood, adoption, or marriage, exclusive of household servants, living and cooking together as a single housekeeping unit, or not more than two persons though not related by blood, adoption or marriage, living and cooking together as a single housekeeping unit shall be deemed to constitute a family.

Relators desire to sell their residence and received an offer from the Missoula Developmentally Disabled Community Homes Council, a nonprofit organization, which intends to use the home for not more than 8 developmentally disabled persons. Because the property was located in an R-I area, the matter was taken before the Missoula city council to see what action it would take in view of the fact that the Montana legislature in 1974 amended Title 11, Cities and Towns, Chapter 27, Building Regulations-Zoning Commission sections providing for community residential facilities. Sections 11-2702.1 and 11-2702.2, R.C.M.1947, now exempt homes for the developmentally disabled from the provisions of local zoning ordinances. They provide:

> 11-2702.1. *Community residential facility–defined.* "Community residential facility" means (1) a group, foster, or other home specifically provided as a place of residence for developmentally disabled or handicapped persons who do not require nursing care, or (2) a district youth guidance home established pursuant to section 10-1103, or (3) a halfway house operated in accordance with regulations of the department of health and environmental sciences for the rehabilitation of alcoholics or drug dependent persons.
> 11-2702.2. *Foster, boarding homes, community residential facilities considered residential.* A foster or boarding home operated under the provision of sections 10-520 through 10-523, or community residential facility serving eight (8) or fewer persons, is considered a residential use of property for purposes of zoning if the home provides care on a twenty-four (24) hour a day basis.
> The homes are a permitted use in all residential zones, including, but not limited to, residential zones for single-family dwellings. Nothing in this paragraph shall be construed to prohibit a city or county from requiring a conditional use permit in order to maintain a home pursuant to the provisions of this paragraph; provided such home is licensed by the department of health and environmental sciences and the department of social and rehabilitation services. Any safety or sanitary regulation of the department or any other agency of the state or political subdivision thereof which is not applicable to residential occupancies in general may not be applied to a community residential facility serving eight (8) or fewer persons.

Hearings were held before a special committee of the city council and the council. Both proponents and opponents for allowing the sale to the nonprofit group were represented. The final action by the city council directed the city attorney to file an action testing the amendments to the state zoning law exempting homes for the developmentally disabled. The consensus of the city council was that while it did not oppose laudable objectives of the legislation, the purpose of the law suit was to challenge the state's taking over city zoning; zoning under the law theretofore had been a locally controlled function that should be left at the local level.

Thereafter the city of Missoula filed an action against relators entitled *City of Missoula v. Joe R. Thelen and G. Barbara Thelen, his wife, and Susan K. Browder,* seeking an order to permanently enjoin and prohibit relators, their successors and assigns, from residence use of said premises by more than one family. In addition, the city filed a lis pendens notice preventing the consummation of the sale by relators, as well as preventing the future use of the home as a group home for the developmentally disabled.

Three issues are pertinent in this proceeding:

1. Are relators entitled to have this Court assume original jurisdiction in this cause?
2. Are relators exempt from the city zoning power, classification and definition of a one-family residence district?
3. Are sections 11-2702.2, 71-2001, 71-2004, 71-2401 through 71-2414, and 80-2607 through 80-2610, R.C.M. 1947, relating to establishment, operation and appropriation for group home facilities constitutional within the purview of the United States Constitution and the 1972 Montana Constitution?

For the purposes of this opinion we will combine the first two issues. Relators argue that recourse to the district court and subsequent appellate channels will not afford them adequate relief in that the final disposition of the issue presented by their petition affects the validity of the buy-sell agreement entered into between relators and the Missoula Developmentally Disabled Community Homes Council; that the city has repeatedly stated it intended to bring the issue to this Court to establish judicial precedent; and that reaching a supreme court decision through appellate channels will unreasonably delay the sale of the residence, the construction of a new residence planned by relators with proceeds of the sale, and the eventual use of the residence as a group residence within the statutes of this state.

Respondent city argues that relators are attempting to short circuit the district court process and this Court is asked to act in a vacuum, alleging that relators who now claim urgency, have made no effort to bring the matter to trial in the district court and have thereby denied this Court a factual determination that could be properly disposed of by this Court on appeal. Respondent cites and relies on this Court's holding in *State ex rel. Kober & Kyriss v. District Court,* 147 Mont. 116, 117, 410 P.2d 945, 946, where this Court held:

> In view of the provisions of the Montana Rules of Appellate Civil Procedure for the expeditious handling of appeals we are not inclined to issue writs of supervisory control as a method of shortcut appeal, except under the most extenuating circum-

stances which we need not attempt to catalog. In this cause no such circumstances appear.

Looking to the quoted language, we ask what, if any, are the extenuating circumstances here that would warrant intervention of this Court at this time? First, relators, with their buy-sell agreement, are unable to sell their property due to the lawsuit filed by respondent city and the lis pendens notice. Second, a zoning regulation of respondent city that has been neutralized by an act of the legislature. Third, the provisions of Article XII, Section 3(3), 1972 Montana Constitution which provides:

> The legislature shall provide such economic assistance and social rehabilitative services as may be necessary for those inhabitants who, by reason of age, infirmities, or misfortune may have need for the aid of society.

We find such extenuating circumstances warrant this Court's intervention in this cause.

While we recognize respondent city's arguments as to the desirability of maintaining local government control of zoning regulations in its city, there is no question that the power of the legislature over the city in this matter is supreme. The legislature can give the cities of this state the power to regulate through zoning commissions, and the legislature can take it away. Respondent's remedy lies not in this Court, but in the legislature. This Court in *State* v. *Holmes,* 100 Mont. 256, 274, 47 P.2d 624, 629, said:

> ... The powers granted to a municipal corporation are of two classes. "The first including those which are legislative, public or governmental, and import sovereignty; the second are those which are proprietary or quasi private, conferred, for the private advantage of the inhabitants and of the city itself as a legal person." [Citing cases] ...
>
> As to the first class of powers of a city enumerated above, the power of the Legislature is supreme except as limited by express constitutional prohibitions. ... "

This Court in *State ex rel. Griffin* v. *City of Butte,* 151 Mont. 546, 548, 445 P.2d 739, 740, quoting from *Leischner* v. *Knight,* (City of Billings), 135 Mont. 109, 112, 337 P.2d 359, said:

> It is well-settled law in this state that cities have only those powers granted them by statute or which are necessarily implied as adjuncts to powers granted by statute. This court has repeatedly stated that "unless a power is vested in the municipality by express law [or by necessary implication therefrom], the presumption is against the exercise by the city of any such power. *State ex rel. Great Falls Housing Authority* v. *City of Great Falls,* 110 Mont. 318, 328, 100 P.2d 915, 921.

In the instant case, while respondent city may well have acted within the power granted it by the legislature in adopting its "one-family" criteria for zoning, that power was modified by later legislative language and respondent city should have revised its zoning regulations to meet the legislative requirements.

That the legislature has power to modify or withdraw various powers given a municipality has long been recognized in Montana. This Court noted in *Stephens* v. *City of Great Falls,* 119 Mont. 368, 371, 175 P.2d 408, 410:

> There is no principle of law better established than that a city has no power, except such as is conferred upon it by Legislative grant, either directly or by necessary

implication. [Citations] Resting as it does upon legislative grants the legislative branch of the government may, at its pleasure, modify or withdraw the power so granted. "It may, if it chooses, repeal any charter or any law under which municipalities may be created, and destroy any municipal corporation at its will and pleasure." [Citation].

Montana's legislature having determined that the constitutional rights of the developmentally disabled to live and develop within our community structure as a family unit, rather than that they be segregated in isolated institutions, is paramount to the zoning regulations of any city it becomes our duty to recognize and implement such legislative action.

Respondent city argues that a recent opinion of the United States Supreme Court, *Village of Belle Terre* v. *Boraas,* 416 U.S. 1, 94 S.Ct. 1536, 39 L.Ed.2d 797, 804, affirms the constitutionality of an ordinance defining "family" which is for all practical purposes identical to the provisions of section 32-2 of the Missoula city code defining "family."

We do not so view it. *Village of Belle Terre* is an entirely different factual situation and is unrelated to state legislation that is focused on the carrying out of new constitutional mandates. There, the city of *Belle Terre* had an ordinance similar to Missoula's restricting land use to one-family dwellings and prohibiting the occupancy of a dwelling by more than two unrelated persons as a "family." Plaintiffs in that case, the owners of a house, were charged with violating the ordinance due to the fact that three of six college students rented the house. Plaintiffs argued that the ordinance violated equal protection rights and rights of association, travel and privacy. The district court upheld the constitutionality of the ordinance, the circuit court reversed, and the United States Supreme Court in an opinion authored by Mr. Justice Douglas, reversed the circuit court.

Mr. Justice Douglas gave as the Court's reasons for finding the ordinance constitutional the fact that the ordinance (a) was not aimed at transients and thus did not violate any right of interstate travel, (b) involved no procedural disparity inflicted on some but not on others, (c) involved no fundamental constitutional right, such as the right of association and privacy, and (d) was reasonable and bore a rational relationship to a permissible state objective, thus not violative of equal protection. Viewing our fact situation in the instant case, we find the *Village of Belle Terre* case inapplicable particularly in the criteria of the opinion set forth under (c).

Here, the Montana legislature adopted a new policy as applied to the developmentally disabled in an effort to implement a new constitutional mandate, and in so doing it was furthering a permissible state objective. Mr. Justice Douglas noted in *Village of Belle Terre* that every line drawn by a legislature leaves something out that might well have been included, but notes, however that that exercise of discretion is a legislative, not a judicial, function. Justice Douglas then quotes the language of Mr. Justice Holmes in his dissenting opinion in *Louisville Gas Co.* v. *Coleman,* 277 U.S. 32, 41, 48 S.Ct. 423, 426, 72 L.Ed. 770:

> "When a legal distinction is determined, as no one doubts that it may be, between night and day, childhood and maturity, or any other extremes, a point has to be fixed or a line has to be drawn, or gradually picked out by successive decisions, to mark where the change takes place. Looked at by itself without regard to the necessity behind

it the line or point seems arbitrary. It might as well or nearly as well be a little more to one side or the other. But when it is seen that a line or point there must be, and that there is no mathematical or logical way of fixing it precisely, the decision of the Legislature must be accepted unless we can say that it is very wide of any reasonable mark.''

Under the facts of the instant case, we uphold the legislative acts providing for community residential facilities for developmentally disabled in all residential zones, including, but not limited to, residential zones for one-family dwellings.

Let the writ issue. Attorney fees are set in the amount of $2,000.00.

JAMES T. HARRISON, C. J., and DALY and CASTLES, JJ., concur.

NOTES

Given the proper legislative climate, the effort to enact a statute such as that in *Thelen* may prove to be a most effective means for avoiding zoning hassles. An increasing number of states have passed such laws; see, e.g., Cal. Welf. and Inst. Code Sections 5115 and 5116; Mich. Stats. Ann. 5.2961 (16a) (1) and (2); and 5.2933(2) (1) and (2).

ADDITIONAL READING

Comment, "Exclusionary Zoning and Its Effects on Group Homes in Areas Zoned for Single-Family Dwellings," 24 *Kan.L.Rev.* 677 (1976).

Comment, "Exclusion of the Mentally Handicapped: Housing the Non-Traditional Family," 7 *U.Cal.Davis L.Rev.* 150 (1974).

Jensen, T., "From Belle Terre to East Cleveland: Zoning, the Family, and the Right of Privacy," 13 *Fam.L.Q.* 1 (1979).

Lippincott, M., "'A Sanctuary for People': Strategies for Overcoming Zoning Restrictions on Community Homes for Retarded Persons," 31 *Stanford L.Rev.* 767 (1979).

Mental Health Law Project, Combatting Exclusionary Zoning: The Right of Handicapped People to Live in the Community (1979).

Mooney, R., and Burgdorf, M., *Zoning and the Handicapped: Position Paper,* National Center for Law and the Handicapped (1974).

Hopperton, R., *Zoning for Community Homes: Handbook for Local Legislative Change,* Law Reform Project, Ohio State University (1975).

Chandler, J., and Ross, S., "Zoning Restrictions and the Right to Live in the Community," Chapter 11 of *The Mentally Retarded Citizen and the Law* 306 (Kindred, M., Cohen, J., Penrod, D., and Shaffer, T., eds., 1976).

Smith, J., and Millemann, M., "Group Homes in Maryland," 5 *Md.L.Forum* 89 (1976).

Annotations, 71 A.L.R.3d 693 and 84 A.L.R.3d 1187.

B. OTHER HOUSING BARRIERS

BELLARMINE HILLS ASSOCIATION v. THE RESIDENTIAL SYSTEMS CO.

Court of Appeals of Michigan, 1978
No. 77-3989, July 1, 1978

Before: BASHARA, P. J., and M. J. KELLY and ALLEN, JJ.

BASHARA, P. J.

Defendants appeal from a summary judgment granted to plaintiff. That judgment permanently enjoined defendants from using a certain residence for treatment of six or less mentally retarded children. Treatment was rendered under an arrangement whereby six or fewer retarded children would live with a resident foster parent.

Plaintiff is an incorporated association of home-owners having their residences in the same subdivision as the foster care facility. The subdivision is comprised entirely of single-family residences, one of which is leased by defendant Residential Systems from defendant Hopping. Residential Systems is a charitable organization, within the meaning of the Internal Revenue Code, that locates and leases residential property for the operation of foster care facilities for mentally retarded children.

The facility with which this litigation is concerned is licensed by the Department of Social Services pursuant to the child care organizations act. At the time this action was initiated, four mentally retarded children and one foster parent lived in the residence on a permanent basis. Other personnel would visit the home during the day to render care and treatment to the children. The children also attend special classes at the local public schools.

At such time as a child has sufficiently responded to treatment that he can return to the care of his parents, his residency at the facility terminates, and another child is assigned to the home by the Department of Social Services. Two additional children were scheduled to be assigned to the residence by the Department when this suit commenced. That assignment is being held in abeyance pending the resolution of this controversy.

All property in the subdivision is subject to a restrictive covenant limiting the type of structures built thereon to single-family residences.[3] Plaintiff alleged that defendants' use of the property was in violation of that covenant. The theory underlying that allegation was that six mentally retarded children residing with a foster parent for the purpose of receiving care and treatment of their affliction does not constitute a family as that term is used in the covenant.

Both parties moved for summary judgment. Each claimed that there was no genuine issue of material fact, and that the legal definition of family entitled them to prevail as a matter of law.

Defendants maintain that the judgment for plaintiff is erroneous, because the

---

[3]In pertinent part, the restrictive covenant provides as follows:

"RESIDENTIAL LOTS: All lots in said subdivision shall be known and described as residential lots. No structure shall be erected, altered, placed or permitted to remain on any residential lots other than one single private family dwelling with attached private garage for not less than two (2) cars, except as herein otherwise provided. . . . "

restrictive covenant controls only the type of structure that may be constructed, not the use and occupancy of the property. Further, defendants contend that the trial court erred in defining "family" to preclude defendants' use of the property as violative of the covenant, and that such result is contrary to this state's declared public policy.

Unquestionably, promoting the development and maintenance of quality programs and facilities for the care and treatment of the mentally handicapped is a settled public policy of our state. That policy has both a constitutional[4] and legislative[5] foundation. But we must also recognize that restrictive covenants may constitute valuable property rights. *Kaplan* v. *City of Huntington Woods*, 357 Mich. 612, 617; 99 N.W.2d 514 (1959), *Monroe* v. *Menke*, 314 Mich. 268, 273; 22 N.W.2d 369 (1946). Further, it has been the policy of our judiciary to protect property owners who have complied with the restrictions from violations of the covenants by others. *Wood* v. *Blancke*, 304 Mich. 283, 287–88; 8 N.W.2d 67 (1943).

Where restrictive covenants describe the character of permissible structures to be erected upon the property, they also contemplate that use and occupancy of the property shall be commensurately restricted. *Bassett Building Co* v. *Jehovah Evangelical Lutheran Church*, 371 Mich. 459, 463; 124 N.W.2d 236 (1963), *Wood* v. *Blancke, supra*. Covenants of restriction, especially those pertaining to residential use, preserve not only monetary value, but aesthetic characteristics considered to be essential constituents of a family environment. Consequently, failure to give complete effect to restrictive covenants in accordance with their import works a great injustice to the property owners. *Wood, supra*.

---

[4]*See* Const. 1963, art. 8, § 8, which provides:

"Institutions, programs and services for the care, treatment, education or rehabilitation of those inhabitants who are physically, mentally or otherwise seriously handicapped shall always be fostered and supported."

This section expanded the scope of the prior constitutional language, which was thought to be excessively restrictive, given the advances achieved in mental and physical treatment methodology. The revised language was intended to impart more expansive concepts into its meaning so as to avoid limiting treatment programs to those purely institutional in character. See Convention Comment reported at 2 M.C.L., p. 500.

[5]Of particular pertinence to the type of facility operated by defendants are the provisions of § 16a of 1943 P.A. 183 and 184, and § 36 of 1921 P.A. 207, all added by 1976 P.A. 394, § 1. Identically phrased, those sections denominate such facilities as residential uses for purposes of county, municipal, or township zoning, stating as follows:

"(1)   As used in this section, "state licensed residential facility" means a structure constructed for residential purposes that is licensed by the state pursuant to Act No. 287 of the Public Acts of 1972, as amended, being sections 331.681 to 331.694 of the Michigan Compiled Laws, or Act No. 116 of the Public Acts of 1973, as amended, being sections 722.111 to 722.128 of the Michigan Compiled Laws, which provides resident services for 6 or less persons under 24-hour supervision or care for persons in need of that supervision or care.

"(2)   In order to implement the policy of this state that persons in need of community residential care shall not be excluded by zoning from the benefits of normal residential surroundings, a state licensed residential facility providing supervision or care, or both, to 6 or less persons shall be considered a residential use of property for the purposes of zoning and a permitted use in all residential zones, including those zoned for single family dwellings, and shall not be subject to a special use or conditional use permit or procedure different from those required for other dwellings of similar density in the same zone." M.C.L. 125.216a(1), (2), 125.286a(1), (2), 125.583b(1), (2); M.S.A. 5.2961(16a) (1), (2), 5.2963(16a) (1), (2), 5.2933 (2) (1), (2).

In the case under review, as the trail court correctly held, the property is restricted to single-family use. As a result, the foregoing public policies confront one another in contest, with the legal concept of "family" resting at the fulcrum of determination.

Concerned with the legal definition of family, our Supreme Court, in the seminal case of *Carmichael* v. *Northwestern Mutual Benefit Association*, 51 Mich. 494; 16 N.W. 871 (1883), stated:

> Now this word "family," contained in the statute, is an expression of great flexibility. It is applied in many ways. It may mean the husband and wife having no children and living alone together, or it may mean children, or wife and children, or blood relatives, or any group constituting a distinct domestic or social body. It is often used to denote a small select corps attached to an army chief, and has even been extended to whole sects, as in the case of the Shakers. *Id.* at 496.

Our examination of subsequent cases and authority from other jurisdictions discloses no more specific definition of the term. Rather, the word family denotes a concept, the application of which is dependent upon the basis of affiliation of the group being analyzed juxtaposed with the public policies invoked by the particular circumstances of the case being reviewed.

For example, in *Carmichael* the Court construed family to encompass an unmarried man residing with an unrelated young woman so as to entitle her to the benefits from his life insurance policy. The Court observed that the man and girl had lived together since her early youth, and that he considered and cared for her as a daughter. Apparently, the Court perceived the man's voluntarily offered support and care for the child as a relationship favored by public policy.

That relationship was compared and contrasted by the Court with the situation presented in *Mutual Benefit Association of Michigan* v. *Hoyt*, 46 Mich. 473; 9 N.W. 497 (1881). In that case, the plaintiff attempted to secure the benefits from the decedent's life insurance policy. Although he resided with decedent, the Court found that he was endeavoring to obtain a financial advantage from the decedent's ailing health by acquiring insurance under which plaintiff named himself as beneficiary and paid the premiums. As noted by the *Carmichael* Court, the transaction was tainted by fraud and bad faith and was to be discouraged as a matter of public policy. *Id.* at 496. Consequently, the relationship in *Hoyt* was found not to come within the meaning ascribed to "family."

Similarly, the term family has been interpreted so as to give effect to the public policy of discouraging meritricious relationships. *McDonald* v. *Kelly Coal Co*, 335 Mich. 325; 55 N.W.2d 851 (1952). But the religious affiliation between clergymen is perceived as a basis favored by public policy so as to constitute a single family use of property within the meaning of a restrictive covenant. *Boston-Edison Protective Association* v. *Paulist Fathers, Inc.*, 306 Mich. 253; 10 N.W.2d 847 (1943). On the other hand, such a favored basis of affiliation does not inhere in the operation of a boarding house[6] or a college fraternity house.[7]

---

[6]*Nerrerter* v. *Little*, 258 Mich. 462; 243 N.W. 25 (1932).

[7]*Seeley* v. *Phi Sigma Delta House Corp*, 245 Mich. 252; 222 N.W. 180 (1928).

The basis of affiliation in the case under consideration is the mutual need of the children for expert treatment of their mental retardation. We have previously noted the momentous public policy supporting that endeavor. Defendants have afforded treatment to the children in an atmosphere that enables them to retain the benefits of residing in a household, instead of an institution. Further, parents of mentally retarded children may be encouraged to seek professional care for their children, knowing that they will reside in a home-like environment in lieu of being "institutionalized."

In analyzing a similar facility to discern the existence of family characteristics, the Court of Appeals of New York observed:

> It is significant that the group home is structured as a single housekeeping unit and is, to all outward appearances, a relatively normal, stable, and permanent family unit, with which the community is properly concerned.
>
> The group home is not, for purposes of a zoning ordinance, a temporary living arrangement as would be a group of college students sharing a house and commuting to a nearby school (cf. *Village of Belle Terre* v. *Boraas,* 416 U.S. 1, 94 S.Ct. 1536, 39 L.Ed.2d 797 [1974]). Every year or so, different college students would come to take the place of those before them. There would be none of the permanency of community that characterizes a residential neighborhood of private homes. Nor is it like the so-called "commune" style of living. The group home is a permanent arrangement and akin to a traditional family, which also may be sundered by death, divorce, or emancipation of the young. Neither the foster parents nor the children are to be shifted about; the intention is that they remain and develop ties in the community. The purpose is to emulate the traditional family and not to introduce a different "life style." *City of White Plains* v. *Ferraioli,* 34 N.Y.2d 300, 304–05; 313 N.E.2d 756, 758; 357 N.Y.S.2d 449, 452 (1974).

The group in the instant case has those family characteristics described in *Ferraioli.* Indeed, the licensing legislation restricts the number of persons to be assigned to such facilities with the apparent intent being to impart, to the extent possible, a family image to the group.[8] The associational nexus of the group clearly occupies a favored position in our state's public policy.

Accordingly, we are constrained by the foregoing principles to conclude that the children and foster parent in this case constitute a family, as perceived in the eyes of the law. Therefore, the defendants are entitled as a matter of law to a judgment dismissing the plaintiff's action.

Reversed. No costs, this being a public question.

NOTE

The *Bellarmine Hills* decision illustrates that the language of restrictive covenants may be subject to the same interpretational analysis that is applied to zoning provisions. A similar approach was taken in construing the language of restrictive covenants in deeds of record in *Berger* v. *State,* 71 N.J. 206, 364 A.2d 993, 996–999 (1976) (see pp. 722–726, above). The *Berger* court held that a group home for multihandicapped preschool children did not violate restrictive covenants which provided that the property could be used only for "one dwelling house" per lot. *Id.* at 364 A.2d 996–997.

---

[8]See M.C.L. 722.111, *et seq;* M.S.A. 25.358(11), *et seq.,* and note 5 *supra.*

The court ruled that such restrictive covenants should be strictly construed, that the language of the covenant did not specify *one-family* residences, that, even if the covenant were construed to require private residential living and single-family residences, the group home at issue satisfied these requirements. *Id.* at 997–998.

The nature of a restrictive covenant is, however, different from a zoning restriction in some respects; the fact that restrictive covenants result from voluntary agreements of parties to a private transaction distinguishes them from zoning ordinances, which are an exercise of governmental authority under the police power. *Seaton* v. *Clifford*, 24 Cal.App.3d 46, 100 Cal.Rptr. 779 (1972), manifests some of the ramifications of this difference in origin. The *Seaton* court found that a particular home for mentally retarded men operated as a "business" in violation of restrictive covenants applicable to the property where the home was located. *Id.* at 100 Cal.Rptr. 781–782. Notwithstanding that California had enacted a statute defining such homes as "residential" for zoning purposes, the court ruled that the restrictive covenants were enforceable, and that, while the statute might "operate as shield to the operator of such a facility as against the attempted enforcement of its zoning regulations by a municipality, such an artificial and arbitrary attempt by the state at redefinition of terms cannot impair private contractual and property rights." *Id.* at 782. The court indicated further that, if the state found it necessary to do so, it had the power to circumvent such restrictive covenants in particular cases by exercising its power of eminent domain to provide facilities for mentally retarded people. *Id.* at 782.

STONER V. MILLER

United States District Court for the Eastern District of New York, 1974
377 F.Supp. 177

BRUCHHAUSEN, District Judge.

This is a class action, brought pursuant to Rule 23 of the Federal Rules of Civil Procedure. It is a civil rights suit, which seeks injunctive and declaratory relief, pursuant to 28 U.S.C. Sections 1651, 2201, 2202, and 42 U.S.C. § 1983.

The plaintiffs challenge the constitutionality of certain sections of Ordinance No. 1195/1973 promulgated by the City of Long Beach. It is entitled:

> Ordinance Amending the Municipal Code of the City of Long Beach Regulating the Operation, Occupancy and Life Safety of Hotels, Boarding and Rooming Houses.

The suit does not challenge the authority of Long Beach to enact legislation, the purpose of which is for the health, safety, and welfare of its inhabitants. It challenges the exercise of that power, concerning sections 5-705, 5-706, portions of 5-710, 5-715 and 5-718 of the ordinance. In substance, the sections challenged relate to the registration of the mentally ill. Those patients requiring continuous medical or psychiatric services shall not be registered; that such services shall not be provided by the proprietor; that in the event such services are required, they shall be purchased by the resident, that an interview with the prospective residents is required to determine if the facility can meet their needs; that certain personal records shall be maintained for any person registered and remaining in excess of fifteen days.

Section 5-706 provides for the termination of the occupancy, and Section 5-718 provides for penalties for violation of any of the provisions of this ordinance.

Subsequent to the filing of the complaint, motions on behalf of The Mental Health Association of New York and Bronx Counties, American Psychiatric Association, National Association For Mental Health, New York State Committee of The National Association for Mental Health, National Council of Community Mental Health Centers were made to intervene as plaintiffs or to appear as *amicus curiae*.

The Attorney General of the State of New York and the United States of America moved for an order granting leave to appear as amicus curiae in support of the plaintiffs' position.

The Court denies the motions for intervention, however, leave is granted to all parties to appear as *amicus curiae*.

It is alleged that the plaintiffs, Amelia Stoner and Patrick O'Neill are presently residing in the hotels in Long Beach. The plaintiffs, Jean Denerstein, Gladys Di-Grande, and Pauline Sarlon are currently patients of a state hospital for the mentally ill, and upon release therefrom in the near future, desire to reside in Long Beach. They all require some psychiatric treatment, with the exception of Thomas J. Keane who requires continuous medical services. Furthermore, the plaintiffs, Amelia Stoner, Patrick O'Neill and Thomas J. Keane are subject to eviction, and the plaintiffs, Jean Denerstein, Gladys DiGrande, and Pauline Sarlon are precluded from registering within Long Beach, pursuant to this ordinance.

The plaintiffs seek injunctive and declaratory relief. The defendant seeks an order that the plaintiffs are not proper parties to maintain this class action and/or for an order dismissing the complaint on the ground that the complaint fails to state a claim against the defendant.

The position of the defendant is untenable.

In *Eisen* v. *Carlisle & Jacquelin,* 391 F.2d 555, at page 563 (Cir. 2), the Court held in part:

> ... Indeed, we hold that the new rule should be given a liberal rather than a restrictive interpretation, *Escott* v. *Barchris Construction Corp.,* 340 F.2d 731, 733 (2d Cir. 1965), cert. denied 382 U.S. 816, 86 S.Ct. 37, 15 L.Ed.2d 63 (1966), and that the dismissal in limine of a particular proceeding as not a proper class action is justified only by a clear showing to that effect and after a proper appraisal of all the factors enumerated on the face of the rule itself.

Rule 23(a) provides that a class action may be maintained only if (1) the class is so numerous that joinder of all members is impracticable. It is well settled that no specified number of plaintiffs is required to maintain a class action. Here, it is alleged (1) that from 1,000 to 1,800 persons are involved who may be affected by this ordinance; (2) there are questions of law or fact common to the class. Here the members either face eviction or are to be excluded pursuant to an alleged unconstitutional ordinance of Long Beach; (3) the claims or defenses of the representative parties are typical of the claims or defenses of the class. The members again are subject to eviction or exclusion, pursuant to this ordinance. The claim in the case at bar is based upon the identical legal theory; (4) the representative parties will fairly and adequately protect the interest of the class. It is uncontradicted that counsel are well qualified and that the litigants are not involved in a collusive suit.

The Court after reviewing all of the factors rules that this suit is a proper class action.

The Court now considers whether there is an "actual controversy" a requirement imposed by the express terms of the Federal Declaratory Judgment Act, 28 U.S.C. § 2201. In the case at bar, although Long Beach has not enforced the ordinance under attack, the dispute is real and the Court is obliged to consider the actual controversy that presently exists. It is immaterial that the ordinance has not been enforced. See *Steffel* v. *Thompson,* opinion announced March 20, 1974, 415 U.S. 452, 94 S.Ct. 1209, 39 L.Ed.2d 505, 42 L.W. 4357. The declaratory judgment action is, therefore, proper and maintainable.

The Court rules that the sections of the ordinance challenged are unconstitutional.

It is apparent that this ordinance can effectively frustrate the movement towards deinstitutionalization in the treatment of the mentally ill, also, the issues herein bear directly upon the rights of citizens who are mentally ill to be treated in the least restrictive setting appropriate to their needs, and upon the right of such persons to choose their own places of residence, without unreasonable governmental interference. The State of New York, pursuant to the Mental Hygiene Law, McKinney's Consol.Laws, c. 27 has begun to discharge non-violent patients from state hospitals. The social workers are attempting to place these patients in hotels best suited for their needs. In the case at bar, the individual plaintiffs are either residents of Long Beach or desire to become residents of Long Beach. However, because of this ordinance, the plaintiffs are not able to register or are subject to eviction from these hotels because of their mental health problems. A reading of the ordinance indicates clearly that it is exclusionary in nature, and, therefore, a restriction on a citizen's right to travel.

In *Cole* v. *Housing Authority of City of Newport,* 1 Cir., 435 F.2d 807, at page 808 the Court held in part:

> Plaintiffs assert that the two year durational requirement violates their rights under the Equal Protection clause of the Fourteenth Amendment . . . , which impinges upon their constitutional right to travel without serving any legitimate or compelling interest of the Authority. *Shapiro* v. *Thompson,* 394 U.S. 618, 89 S.Ct. 1322, 22 L.Ed.2d 600. . . .

The Court further held at page 809:

> The Supreme Court has clearly indicated that the right to travel is a fundamental personal right that can be impinged only if to do so is necessary to promote a compelling governmental interest. *Shapiro, supra* at 634.

The Court in *Cole, supra,* struck down a residency requirement as in the *Shapiro* case. It held that the requirement impinged on the right to travel and was not justified by a compelling state interest. It is immaterial whether travel is interstate or intrastate. See *King* v. *New Rochelle Municipal Housing Authority,* 442 F.2d 646 (2d Cir. 1971) adopting the reasoning in *Cole, supra.* In the case at bar the municipality has failed to show any compelling governmental interest to abridge the plaintiffs' right to travel. See also *Memorial Hospital, et al.* v. *Maricopa County, et al.*, decided by the United States Supreme Court, February 26, 1974, 415 U.S. 250, 94 S.Ct. 1076, 39 L.Ed.2d 306, 42 L.W. 4277.

In *Village of Belle Terre, et al.* v. *Boraas*, decided April 1, 1974, 416 U.S. 1, 94 S.Ct. 1536, 39 L.Ed.2d 797 the Supreme Court upheld a village ordinance, restricting the use of the land to one-family dwellings which define the word family to mean one or more persons related by blood, adoption, or marriage, or not more than two unrelated persons, living and cooking together as a single housekeeping unit. The Court upheld the ordinance and held since it was not aimed at transients and involves no procedural disparity inflicted on some but not on others or deprivation of any "fundamental" right—meets that constitutional standard and must be upheld as valid land-use legislation addressed to family needs. *Berman* v. *Parker*, 348 U.S. 26, 75 S.Ct. 98, 99 L.Ed. 27. In the case at bar, the ordinance is to prevent the ingress of outsiders into Long Beach. *Cole* v. *Housing Authority of City of Newport, supra.*

The ordinance is further objectionable in that it invades one's absolute right of privacy. Section 5-710 requires the hotel staff to maintain specified records of residents who intend to remain registered in excess of fifteen days. It is now well settled that a citizen's right to privacy is fundamental. *Griswold* v. *Connecticut*, 381 U.S. 479, 85 S.Ct. 1678, 14 L.Ed.2d 510; *Eisenstadt* v. *Baird*, 405 U.S. 438, 92 S.Ct. 1029, 31 L.Ed.2d 349; *Roe* v. *Ingraham*, 480 F.2d 102 (2d Cir. 1973).

Finally, the ordinance is vague. Subsection (b) of 5-705 fails to establish any clear registration procedure, fails to define the term continuous, fails to define which residents are referred to, and fails to define when a resident may become dangerous. The sub-section also fails to define when a resident's action becomes "so disturbing" that may affect other residents.

The Court concludes that the sections attacked are unconstitutional, and the defendant is enjoined from enforcing said sections of the ordinance.

Settle order on five (5) days' notice.

NOTES

1. *Stoner* is one of the few judicial decisions reaching the merits of constitutional claims by handicapped persons in regard to housing rights. While the ordinance at issue in *Stoner* is quite unusual, the constitutional analysis of the court may be applicable to other instances where state or local officials create unnecessary barriers to the obtaining of suitable housing by handicapped persons.

Difficulties sometimes arise in trying to bring residential facilities for handicapped persons into compliance with local fire, housing, and licensing codes. Under many such codes, facilities for handicapped residents are not categorized with other ordinary residential uses and may be subjected to more elaborate requirements. Thus, for example, a group home in an average residential neighborhood may be mandated to have external fire escapes, a sprinkler system, fire extinguishers, and fire alarm boxes. Such requirements are frequently premised upon humanitarian impulses to protect "helpless" persons, and are often prompted by local tragedies, such as fires at large nursing homes where many patients could not be evacuated in time. Such elaborate protective standards, however, are often at odds with principles of normalization, which would seek to have a residential alternative for handicapped persons be as much like the neighboring private homes as possible. Moreover, the exorbitant costs of alterations necessary to bring a building into compliance with strict code and ordinance requirements may make the use of otherwise suitable existing structures economically unfeasible. To what extent might such stringent local code and licensing provisions, and their vigorous enforcement by local officials, be susceptible to challenge under constitutional theories espoused in *Stoner* v. *Miller*?

2.   There is a multitude of federal programs, many of which are administered by the United States Department of Housing and Urban Development, that have some relevance to housing opportunities for handicapped persons. Most such programs are covered by the nondiscrimination on the basis of handicap mandate of section 504 of the Rehabilitation Act of 1973, 29 U.S.C. § 794 (see generally, pp. 194–213, above). HUD has proposed regulations that specify how it will enforce this nondiscrimination requirement; see 43 Fed. Reg. p. 16652 (April 19, 1978).

One major federal housing program administered by HUD to which some handicapped people have sought access is the Section 8 Housing Program. Under Section 8 of the United States Housing Act of 1937, as amended by the Housing and Community Development Act of 1974 and the Housing Authorization Act of 1976, 42 U.S.C. Section 1437(f), federal funds are provided through local housing authorities for the purpose of enabling lower income persons to obtain decent, safe, and sanitary housing. This is accomplished, *inter alia,* by promoting rental to eligible applicants of existing housing units that meet program standards. Accordingly, HUD provides funds to local housing agencies which are responsible for determining whether individual owners and their units comply with federal, state, and local program requirements, for contracting with rental unit owners for participation in the program, and for making rent supplement payments to owners pursuant to these contracts.

If they meet the income standards and other eligibility requirements, there is no reason why handicapped persons should not participate in these Section 8 programs on an equal basis with other applicants. Yet owners and operators of Section 8 housing have in some instances disapproved the application of a physically or mentally handicapped person for such housing, or have failed to make the housing units accessible to and fully usable by handicapped people. In at least one case, a handicapped person has gone to court to challenge the denial of Section 8 housing as a violation of Section 504 and of the due process clause; see, *La Marche* v. *Gatewood Associates,* CA 77-0332 (D.R.I., filed June 1, 1977). Similar lawsuits are likely to be filed in attempts to make the Section 8 programs around the country available to eligible handicapped applicants.

Another important federal housing program, announced by HUD on June 15, 1978, is an $18 million demonstration housing program to benefit people with chronic mental illness, HUD News Release No. 78-190 (June 15, 1978).

3.   A few states have statutes that prohibit discrimination against handicapped persons in the area of housing. For example, Cal. Civil Code Section 54.1(b)(1) provides:

> Blind persons, visually handicapped persons, deaf persons, and other physically disabled persons shall be entitled to full and equal access, as other members of the general public, to all housing accommodations offered for rent, lease, or compensation in this

state, subject to the conditions and limitations established by law, or state or federal regulation, and applicable alike to all persons.

And in *Portner* v. *James,* No. 239969 (Mun.Ct. of Cal., Berkeley-Albany Judicial District, filed August 5, 1977), a severely disabled person confined to a wheelchair filed suit under this provision to challenge a landlord's refusal to rent an apartment to him.

4. A very useful "how-to" book that includes examples of model housing programs around the country, information on financing, practical guidelines about selecting a housing site and adapting existing buildings, and a bibliography is Thompson, M., *Housing for the Handicapped and Disabled: A Guide for Local Action,* The National Association of Housing and Redevelopment Officials (1977).

8

EQUAL ACCESS TO MEDICAL SERVICES

Elizabeth E. Hogue

A. INTRODUCTION

THE INCREASING SOPHISTICATION AND COMPLEXITY of modern medical science have brought with them increased public concern over issues of access to medical services, informed consent, refusal of medical services, and access to medical records. These issues affect all segments of the population, but they raise special problems for handicapped persons. Individuals with particular handicapping conditions may have greater needs for temporary or ongoing medical care and therapy than the average person. Questions about ability to make an informed decision whether or not to accept medical treatment are often raised in cases where an individual is considered to have a mental disability.

And because many handicapped persons have a continuing need for medical services, access to medical records is often crucial in determining the quality and progress of the treatment programs they receive. This chapter focuses upon various legal issues that have emerged in relation to the access of handicapped persons to medical services.

B. DENIAL TO HANDICAPPED PERSONS OF MEDICAL TREATMENT AVAILABLE TO OTHERS

While medical intervention may be of critical importance in ameliorating or undoing some of the functional limitations resulting from handicapping conditions (see, for example, the discussion of the medical procedures and rehabilitative measures provided to the severely handicapped child involved in the *In re G.H.* case at p. 121n.4, above) or even in maintaining the very life of a handicapped person, handicapped persons often encounter a variety of difficulties as they attempt to gain access to medical services.

In addition to transportation problems which may make it difficult for handicapped persons to get to doctors' offices, clinics, hospitals, and other medical facilities (see generally Chapter 6), handicapped patients often encounter discriminatory attitudes on the part of the medical personnel themselves. In *Lyons* v. *Grether*, 239

S.E.2d 103 (Va. 1977), for example, a blind woman arrived at a physician's office for an appointment for treatment of a vaginal infection. She was told that the physician would not treat her unless her guide dog was removed from the waiting room. When the woman insisted that her guide dog remain with her, the physician "evicted" her, her son, and her dog from his waiting room, refused to treat her condition, and failed to assist her in finding other medical attention. In her damage suit against the doctor, the Supreme Court of Virginia ruled that the woman had a cause of action for breach of the physician's duty to treat her and for violation of her rights under Virginia's White Cane Act to have a guide dog accompany her in places to which the general public is invited.

While such situations might prompt many handicapped people simply to find another physician rather than to go the litigative route chosen by the plaintiff in *Lyons* v. *Grether,* in other circumstances such options are not available, and the handicapped patient may be totally helpless and at the mercy of the medical professionals. One type of such cases, which periodically generate a good deal of publicity, concerns medical treatment for severely handicapped newborns. For example, in 1971, the *Washington Post* ran the following story:

> For 15 days—until he starved to death—the newborn infant lay in a bassinet in a back corner of the nursery at the Johns Hopkins University Hospital. A sign said, "Nothing by mouth."
>
> The baby's life could have been saved by a simple operation to correct the intestinal blockage that kept him from digesting any food.
>
> But because he was born mongoloid, the parents refused to give the hospital permission to operate. And without that permission, the doctors said they had no legal right to perform the operation.[a]

It has been estimated that on a national level several thousand severely handicapped newborns are probably left to die each year ("Defective Babies Left to Die, Doctors Testify," United Press International News article, June 11, 1974).

Maine Medical Center v. Houle

Superior Court, Cumberland, Maine, 1974
Civil Action Docket No. 74-145, February 14, 1974

The complaint herein seeks the intervention of the court between the parents of a newborn child and the hospital and attending physician concerning parental decision as to the future course of treatment. The existence of the child herein gives the court equitable jurisdiction to fulfill the responsibility of government in its character as *parens patriae* to care for infants and protect them from neglect. This power has been historically exercised by courts of chancery, and the existence of statutory jurisdiction in the Probate Court and District Court does not divest this court of its equity powers.

The testimony herein indicates that a male child was born to the defendants on February 9, 1974 at the Maine Medical Center. Medical examination by the hospital staff revealed the absence of a left eye, a rudimentary left ear with no ear canal, a malformed left thumb and a tracheal esophageal fistula. The latter condition prevented the ingestion of nourishment, necessitated intravenous feeding and allowed the entry of

---

[a] "Doctors Ponder Ethics of Letting Mongoloid Die," *The Washington Post,* Oct. 15, 1971, p. A1.

fluids into the infant's lungs leading to the development of pneumonia and other complications. The recommended medical treatment was surgical repair of the tracheal esophageal fistula to allow normal feeding and respiration. Prior to February 11, 1974, the child's father directed the attending physician not to conduct surgical repair of the fistula and to cease intravenous feeding.

By Temporary Restraining Order issued *ex parte* on February 11, 1974, this court authorized the continuance of such measures as might be medically dictated to maintain said child in a stable and viable condition and restrained the defendants from issuing any orders, which, in the opinion of the attending physician, would be injurious to the current medical situation of said child.

In the interim the child's condition has deteriorated. Periods of apnea have necessitated the use of a bag breathing device to artificially sustain respiration. Several convulsive seizures of unknown cause have occurred. Medications administered include gentimycin for the treatment of pneumonia and phenobarbitol to control convulsive seizures. Further medical evaluation indicates the lack of response of the right eye to light stimuli, the existence of some non-fused vertebrae and the virtual certainty of some brain damage resulting from anoxia. The most recent developments have caused the attending physician to form the opinion that all life supporting measures should be withdrawn. The doctor is further of the opinion that without surgical correction of the tracheal esophageal fistula the child will certainly die and that with surgical correction the child can survive but with some degree of permanent brain damage.

The court heard further testimony concerning the present posture of the mother's emotional condition and attitude toward the future survival of the child. Without disparaging the seriousness of the emotional impact upon the parents and without ignoring the difficulties which this court's decision may cause in the future, it is the firm opinion of this court that questions of permanent custody, maintenance and further care of the child are for the moment legally irrelevant.

Quite literally the court must make a decision concerning the life or death of a new born infant. Recent decisions concerning the right of the state to intervene with the medical and moral judgments of a prospective parent and attending physician may have cast doubts upon the legal rights of an unborn child; but at the moment of live birth there does exist a human being entitled to the fullest protection of the law. The most basic right enjoyed by every human being is the right to life itself.

Where the condition of a child does not involve serious risk of life and where treatment involves a considerable risk, parents as the natural guardians have a considerable degree of discretion and the courts ought not intervene. The measures proposed in this case are not in any sense heroic measures except for the doctor's opinion that probable brain damage has rendered life not worth preserving. Were it his opinion that life itself could not be preserved, heroic measures ought not be required. However, the doctor's qualitative evaluation of the value of the life to be preserved is not legally within the scope of his expertise.

In the court's opinion the issue before the court is not the prospective quality of the life to be preserved, but the medical feasibility of the proposed treatment compared with the almost certain risk of death should treatment be withheld. Being satisfied that corrective surgery is medically necessary and medically feasible, the court finds that the defendants herein have no right to withhold such treatment and that to do so constitutes neglect in the legal sense. Therefore, the court will authorize the guardian *ad litem* to consent to the surgical correction of the tracheal esophageal fistula and such other normal life supportive measures as may be medically required in the immediate future. It is further ordered that Respondents are hereby enjoined until further order of this court from issuing any orders to Petitioners or their employees which, in the opinion of the attending physicians or surgeons would be injurious to the medical condition of the child.

The court will retain jurisdiction for the purpose of determining any further measures that may be required to be taken and eventually for the purpose of determining the future custody of the child should the court determine that it is appropriate to do so.

NOTES

1.   Should the court have considered the potential quality of Baby Houle's life before making a decision? As a matter of fact, can members of the medical profession accurately predict the potential for a productive, independent life for any newborn?

2.   The court's only recognition of Baby Houle's parents' position is one broad, fleeting reference to the "emotional impact upon the parents" and "difficulties which this court's decision may cause in the future." What is the parents' position in both legal and practical terms?

3.   For other cases involving court intervention to require medical treatment for handicapped newborns, see *In re Baby Girl Obernauer*, Juvenile and Domestic Relations Court of Morris County, N.J., Order Relating to Protective Services, Dec. 22, 1970; *In re Teague*, Circuit Court, Baltimore City, filed Dec. 4, 1974, Equity No. 104/212/81886.

4.   For a detailed discussion of the legal issues raised in such cases, see Robertson, J., "Involuntary Euthanasia of Defective Newborns: A Legal Analysis," 27 *Stan. L. Rev.* 213-269 (1975).

C.   INFORMED CONSENT

1.   The Legal Doctrine

CANTERBURY v. SPENCE

United States Court of Appeals for the District of Columbia Circuit, 1972
464 F.2d 772, cert. den., 409 U.S. 1064 (1972)

SPOTTSWOOD W. ROBINSON, III, Circuit Judge:

This appeal is from a judgment entered in the District Court on verdicts directed for the two appellees at the conclusion of plaintiff-appellant Canterbury's case in chief. His action sought damages for personal injuries allegedly sustained as a result of an operation negligently performed by appellee Spence, a negligent failure by Dr. Spence to disclose a risk of serious disability inherent in the operation, and negligent postoperative care by appellee Washington Hospital Center. On close examination of the record, we find evidence which required submission of these issues to the jury. We accordingly reverse the judgment as to each appellee and remand the case to the District Court for a new trial.

I

The record we review tells a depressing tale. A youth troubled only by back pain submitted to an operation without being informed of a risk of paralysis incidental thereto. A day after the operation he fell from his hospital bed after having been left without assistance while voiding. A few hours after the fall, the lower half of his body was paralyzed, and he had to be operated on again. Despite extensive medical care, he has never been what he was before. Instead of the back pain, even years later, he hobbled about on crutches, a victim of paralysis of the bowels and urinary incontinence.

* * *

III

Suits charging failure by a physician adequately to disclose the risks and alternatives of proposed treatment are not innovations in American law. They date back a good half-century, and in the last decade they have multiplied rapidly. There is, nonetheless, disagreement among the courts and the commentators on many major questions, and there is no precedent of our own directly in point. For the tools enabling resolution of the issues on this appeal, we are forced to begin at first principles.

The root premise is the concept, fundamental in American jurisprudence, that "[e]very human being of adult years and sound mind has a right to determine what shall be done with his own body. . . ."[12] True consent to what happens to one's self is the informed exercise of a choice, and that entails an opportunity to evaluate knowledgeably the options available and the risks attendant upon each. The average patient has little or no understanding of the medical arts, and ordinarily has only his physician to whom he can look for enlightenment with which to reach an intelligent decision. From these almost axiomatic considerations springs the need, and in turn the requirement, of a reasonable divulgence by physician to patient to make such a decision possible.

A physician is under a duty to treat his patient skillfully but proficiency in diagnosis and therapy is not the full measure of his responsibility. The cases demonstrate that the physician is under an obligation to communicate specific information to the patient when the exigencies of reasonable care call for it. Due care may require a physician perceiving symptoms of bodily abnormality to alert the patient to the condition. It may call upon the physician confronting an ailment which does not respond to his ministrations to inform the patient thereof. It may command the physician to

---

[12] *Schloendorff* v. *Society of New York Hospital,* 211 N.Y. 125, 105 N.E. 92, 93 (1914). See also *Natanson* v. *Kline,* 186 Kan. 393, 350 P.2d 1093, 1104 (1960), clarified. 187 Kan. 186, 354 P.2d 670 (1960); W. Prosser, Torts § 18 at 102 (3d ed. 1964); Restatement of Torts § 49 (1934).

instruct the patient as to any limitations to be presently observed for his own welfare, and as to any precautionary therapy he should seek in the future. It may oblige the physician to advise the patient of the need for or desirability of any alternative treatment promising greater benefit than that being pursued. Just as plainly, due care normally demands that the physician warn the patient of any risks to his well-being which contemplated therapy may involve.

The context in which the duty of risk-disclosure arises is invariably the occasion for decision as to whether a particular treatment procedure is to be undertaken. To the physician, whose training enables a self-satisfying evaluation, the answer may seem clear, but it is the prerogative of the patient, not the physician, to determine for himself the direction in which his interests seem to lie. To enable the patient to chart his course understandably, some familiarity with the therapeutic alternatives and their hazards becomes essential.

A reasonable revelation in these respects is not only a necessity but, as we see it, is as much a matter of the physician's duty. It is a duty to warn of the dangers lurking in the proposed treatment, and that is surely a facet of due care. It is, too, a duty to impart information which the patient has every right to expect. The patient's reliance upon the physician is a trust of the kind which traditionally has exacted obligations beyond those associated with arms-length transactions. His dependence upon the physician for information affecting his well-being, in terms of contemplated treatment, is well-nigh abject. As earlier noted, long before the instant litigation arose, courts had recognized that the physician had the responsibility of satisfying the vital informational needs of the patient. More recently, we ourselves have found "in the fiducial qualities of [the physician-patient] relationship the physician's duty to reveal to the patient that which in his best interests it is important that he should know."[30] We now find, as a part of the physician's overall obligation to the patient, a similar duty of reasonable disclosure of the choices with respect to proposed therapy and the dangers inherently and potentially involved.

This disclosure requirement, on analysis, reflects much more of a change in doctrinal emphasis than a substantive addition to malpractice law. It is well established that the physician must seek and secure his patient's consent before commencing an operation or other course of treatment. It is also clear that the consent, to be efficacious, must be free from imposition upon the patient. It is the settled rule that therapy not authorized by the patient may amount to a tort—a common law battery—by the physician. And it is evident that it is normally impossible to obtain a consent worthy of the name unless the physician first elucidates the options and the perils for the patient's edification. Thus the physician has long borne a duty, on pain of liability for unauthorized treatment, to make adequate disclosure to the patient. The evolution of the obligation to communicate for the patient's benefit as well as the physician's protection has hardly involved an extraordinary restructuring of the law.

---

[30]*Emmett* v. *Eastern Dispensary and Cas. Hosp.*, 130 U.S.App.D.C. 50, 54, 396 F.2d 931 (1967). See also Swan, "The California Law of Malpractice of Physicians, Surgeons, and Dentists," 33 *Cal. L. Rev.* 248, 251 (1945).

IV

Duty to disclose has gained recognition in a large number of American jurisdictions, but more largely on a different rationale. The majority of courts dealing with the problem have made the duty depend on whether it was the custom of physicians practicing in the community to make the particular disclosure to the patient. If so, the physician may be held liable for an unreasonable and injurious failure to divulge, but there can be no recovery unless the omission forsakes a practice prevalent in the profession. We agree that the physician's noncompliance with a professional custom to reveal, like any other departure from prevailing medical practice, may give rise to liability to the patient. We do not agree that the patient's cause of action is dependent upon the existence and nonperformance of a relevant professional tradition.

There are, in our view, formidable obstacles to acceptance of the notion that the physician's obligation to disclose is either germinated or limited by medical practice. To begin with, the reality of any discernible custom reflecting a professional consensus on communication of option and risk information to patients is open to serious doubt. We sense the danger that what in fact is no custom at all may be taken as an affirmative custom to maintain silence, and that physician-witnesses to the so-called custom may state merely their personal opinions as to what they or others would do under given conditions. We cannot gloss over the inconsistency between reliance on a general practice respecting divulgence and, on the other hand, realization that the myriad of variables among patients makes each case so different that its omission can rationally be justified only by the effect of its individual circumstances. Nor can we ignore the fact that to bind the disclosure obligation to medical usage is to arrogate the decision on revelation to the physician alone. Respect for the patient's right of self-determination on particular therapy demands a standard set by law for physicians rather than one which physicians may or may not impose upon themselves.

More fundamentally, the majority rule overlooks the graduation of reasonable-care demands in Anglo-American jurisprudence and the position of professional custom in the hierarchy. The caliber of the performance exacted by the reasonable-care standard varies between the professional and non-professional worlds, and so also the role of professional custom. "With but few exceptions," we recently declared, "society demands that everyone under a duty to use care observe minimally a general standard."[48] "Familiarly expressed judicially," we added, "the yardstick is that degree of care which a reasonably prudent person would have exercised under the same or similar circumstances."[49] "Beyond this," however, we emphasized, "the law requires those engaging in activities requiring unique knowledge and ability to give a performance commensurate with the undertaking."[50] Thus physicians treating the sick must perform at higher levels than non-physicians in order to meet the reasonable care standard in its special application to physicians[51]—"that degree of care and skill

---

[48]*Washington Hosp. Center* v. *Butler*, 127 U.S.App.D.C. 379, 383, 384 F.2d 331, 335 (1967).
[49]*Id.*
[50]*Id.*
[51]*Id.*

ordinarily exercised by the profession in [the physician's] own or similar localities."[52] And practices adopted by the profession have indispensable value as evidence tending to establish just what that degree of care and skill is.[53]

We have admonished, however, that "[t]he special medical standards[54] are but adaptations of the general standard to a group who are required to act as reasonable men possessing their medical talents presumably would."[55] There is, by the same token, no basis for operation of the special medical standard where the physician's activity does not bring his medical knowledge and skills peculiarly into play. And where the challenge to the physician's conduct is not to be gauged by the special standard, it follows that medical custom cannot furnish the test of its propriety, whatever its relevance under the proper test may be. The decision to unveil the patient's condition and the chances as to remediation, as we shall see, is ofttimes a non-medical judgment and, if so, is a decision outside the ambit of the special standard. Where that is the situation, professional custom hardly furnishes the legal criterion for measuring the physician's responsibility to reasonably inform his patient of the options and the hazards as to treatment.

The majority rule, moreover, is at war with our prior holdings that a showing of medical practice, however probative, does not fix the standard governing recovery for medical malpractice. Prevailing medical practice, we have maintained, has evidentiary value in determinations as to what the specific criteria measuring challenged professional conduct are and whether they have been met, but does not itself define the standard. That has been our position in treatment cases, where the physician's performance is ordinarily to be adjudicated by the special medical standard of due care. We see no logic in a different rule for nondisclosure cases, where the governing standard is much more largely divorced from professional considerations. And surely in nondisclosure cases the factfinder is not invariably functioning in an area of such technical complexity that it must be bound to medical custom as an inexorable application of the community standard of reasonable care.

Thus we distinguished, for purposes of duty to disclose, the special- and general-standard aspects of the physician-patient relationship. When medical judgment enters the picture and for that reason the special standard controls, prevailing medical practice must be given its just due. In all other instances, however, the general standard exacting ordinary care applies, and that standard is set by law. In sum, the physician's duty to disclose is governed by the same legal principles applicable to others in comparable situations, with modifications only to the extent that medical judgment enters the picture. We hold that the standard measuring performance of that duty by physicians, as by others, is conduct which is reasonable under the circumstances.

---

[52]*Rodgers* v. *Lawson*, 83 U.S.App.D.C. at 282, 170 F.2d at 158. See also *Brown* v. *Keaveny*, 117 U.S.App.D.C. at 118, 326 F.2d at 661; *Quick* v. *Thurston*, 110 U.S.App.D.C. at 171, 290 F.2d at 362.

[53]E.g., *Washington Hosp. Center* v. *Butler*, *supra*, note 48, 127 U.S.App.D.C. at 383, 384 F.2d at 335.

[54]*Id.* at 383 ns. 10-12, 384 F.2d at 335 ns. 10-12.

[55]*Id.* at 384 n. 15, 384 F.2d at 336 n. 15.

V

Once the circumstances give rise to a duty on the physician's part to inform his patient, the next inquiry is the scope of the disclosure the physician is legally obliged to make. The courts have frequently confronted this problem but no uniform standard defining the adequacy of the divulgence emerges from the decisions. Some have said "full" disclosure, a norm we are unwilling to adopt literally. It seems obviously prohibitive and unrealistic to expect physicians to discuss with their patients every risk of proposed treatment—no matter how small or remote—and generally unnecessary from the patient's viewpoint as well. Indeed, the cases speaking in terms of "full" disclosure appear to envision something less than total disclosure, leaving unanswered the question of just how much.

The larger number of courts, as might be expected, have applied tests framed with reference to prevailing fashion within the medical profession. Some have measured the disclosure by "good medical practice," others by what a reasonable practitioner would have bared under the circumstances, and still others by what medical custom in the community would demand. We have explored this rather considerable body of law but are unprepared to follow it. The duty to disclose, we have reasoned, arises from phenomena apart from medical custom and practice. The latter, we think, should no more establish the scope of the duty than its existence. Any definition of scope in terms purely of a professional standard is at odds with the patient's prerogative to decide on projected therapy himself. That prerogative, we have said, is at the very foundation of the duty to disclose, and both the patient's right to know and the physician's correlative obligation to tell him are diluted to the extent that its compass is dictated by the medical profession.

In our view, the patient's right of self-decision shapes the boundaries of the duty to reveal. That right can be effectively exercised only if the patient possesses enough information to enable an intelligent choice. The scope of the physician's communications to the patient, then, must be measured by the patient's need, and that need is the information material to the decision. Thus the test for determining whether a particular peril must be divulged is its materiality to the patient's decision: all risks potentially affecting the decision must be unmasked. And to safeguard the patient's interest in achieving his own determination on treatment, the law must itself set the standard for adequate disclosure.

Optimally for the patient, exposure of a risk would be mandatory whenever the patient would deem it significant to his decision, either singly or in combination with other risks. Such a requirement, however, would summon the physician to second-guess the patient, whose ideas on materiality could hardly be known to the physician. That would make an undue demand upon medical practitioners, whose conduct, like that of others, is to be measured in terms of reasonableness. Consonantly with orthodox negligence doctrine, the physician's liability for nondisclosure is to be determined on the basis of foresight, not hindsight; no less than any other aspect of negligence, the issue on nondisclosure must be approached from the viewpoint of the reasonableness of the physician's divulgence in terms of what he knows or should know to be the patient's informational needs. If, but only if, the fact-finder can say that the physician's communication was unreasonably inadequate is an imposition of liability legally or morally justified.

Of necessity, the content of the disclosure rests in the first instance with the physician. Ordinarily it is only he who is in position to identify particular dangers; always he must make a judgment, in terms of materiality, as to whether and to what extent revelation to the patient is called for. He cannot know with complete exactitude what the patient would consider important to his decision, but on the basis of his medical training and experience he can sense how the average, reasonable patient expectably would react. Indeed, with knowledge of, or ability to learn, his patient's background and current condition, he is in a position superior to that of most others—attorneys, for example—who are called upon to make judgments on pain of liability in damages for unreasonable miscalculation.

From these considerations we derive the breadth of the disclosure of risks legally to be required. The scope of the standard is not subjective as to either the physician or the patient; it remains objective with due regard for the patient's informational needs and with suitable leeway for the physician's situation. In broad outline, we agree that "[a] risk is thus material when a reasonable person, in what the physician knows or should know to be the patient's position, would be likely to attach significance to the risk or cluster of risks in deciding whether or not to forego the proposed therapy."[84]

The topics importantly demanding a communication of information are the inherent and potential hazards of the proposed treatment, the alternatives to that treatment, if any, and the results likely if the patient remains untreated. The factors contributing significance to the dangerousness of a medical technique are, of course, the incidence of injury and the degree of the harm threatened. A very small chance of death or serious disablement may well be significant; a potential disability which dramatically outweighs the potential benefit of the therapy or the detriments of the existing malady may summons discussion with the patient.

There is no bright line separating the significant from the insignificant; the answer in any case must abide a rule of reason. Some dangers—infection, for example—are inherent in any operation; there is no obligation to communicate those of which persons of average sophistication are aware. Even more clearly, the physician bears no responsibility for discussion of hazards the patient has already discovered, or those having no apparent materiality to patients' decision on therapy. The disclosure doctrine, like others marking lines between permissible and impermissible behavior in medical practice, is in essence a requirement of conduct prudent under the circumstances. Whenever nondisclosure of particular risk information is open to debate by reasonable-minded men, the issue is for the finder of the facts.

VI

Two exceptions to the general rule of disclosure have been noted by the courts. Each is in the nature of a physician's privilege not to disclose, and the reasoning

---

[84][Waltz and Scheuneman, "Informed Consent to Therapy," 64 *Nw.U.L.Rev.* 628, 639-40 (1970)] at 640.

underlying them is appealing. Each, indeed, is but a recognition that, as important as is the patient's right to know, it is greatly outweighed by the magnitudinous circumstances giving rise to the privilege. The first comes into play when the patient is unconscious or otherwise incapable of consenting, and harm from a failure to treat is imminent and outweighs any harm threatened by the proposed treatment. When a genuine emergency of that sort arises, it is settled that the impracticality of conferring with the patient dispenses with need for it. Even in situations of that character the physician should, as current law requires, attempt to secure a relative's consent if possible. But if time is too short to accommodate discussion, obviously the physician should proceed with the treatment.

The second exception obtains when risk-disclosure poses such a threat of detriment to the patient as to become unfeasible or contraindicated from a medical point of view. It is recognized that patients occasionally become so ill or emotionally distraught on disclosure as to foreclose a rational decision, or complicate or hinder the treatment, or perhaps even pose psychological damage to the patient. Where that is so, the cases have generally held that the physician is armed with a privilege to keep the information from the patient, and we think it clear that portents of that type may justify the physician in action he deems medically warranted. The critical inquiry is whether the physician responded to a sound medical judgment that communication of the risk information would present a threat to the patient's well-being.

The physician's privilege to withhold information for therapeutic reasons must be carefully circumscribed, however, for otherwise it might devour the disclosure rule itself. The privilege does not accept the paternalistic notion that the physician may remain silent simply because divulgence might prompt the patient to forego therapy the physician feels the patient really needs. That attitude presumes instability or perversity for even the normal patient, and runs counter to the foundation principle that the patient should and ordinarily can make the choice for himself. Nor does the privilege contemplate operation save where the patient's reaction to risk information, as reasonably foreseen by the physician, is menacing. And even in a situation of that kind, disclosure to a close relative with a view to securing consent to the proposed treatment may be the only alternative open to the physician.

VII

No more than breach of any other legal duty does nonfulfillment of the physician's obligation to disclose alone establish liability to the patient. An unrevealed risk that should have been made known must materialize, for otherwise the omission, however unpardonable, is legally without consequence. Occurrence of the risk must be harmful to the patient, for negligence unrelated to injury is nonactionable. And, as in malpractice actions generally, there must be a causal relationship between the physician's failure to adequately divulge and damage to the patient.

A causal connection exists when, but only when, disclosure of significant risks incidental to treatment would have resulted in a decision against it. The patient obviously has no complaint if he would have submitted to the therapy notwithstanding awareness that the risk was one of its perils. On the other hand, the very purpose of the disclosure rule is to protect the patient against consequences which, if known, he would have avoided by foregoing the treatment. The more difficult question is whether the factual issue on causality calls for an objective or a subjective determination.

It has been assumed that the issue is to be resolved according to whether the factfinder believes the patient's testimony that he would not have agreed to the treatment if he had known of the danger which later ripened into injury. We think a technique which ties the factual conclusion on causation simply to the assessment of the patient's credibility is unsatisfactory. To be sure, the objective of risk-disclosure is preservation of the patient's interest in intelligent self-choice on proposed treatment, a matter the patient is free to decide for any reason that appeals to him. When, prior to commencement of therapy, the patient is sufficiently informed on risks and he exercises his choice, it may truly be said that he did exactly what he wanted to do. But when causality is explored at a post-injury trial with a professedly uninformed patient, the question whether he actually would have turned the treatment down if he had known the risks is purely hypothetical: "Viewed from the point at which he had to decide, would the patient have decided differently had he known something he did not know?"[107] And the answer which the patient supplies hardly represents more than a guess, perhaps tinged by the circumstance that the uncommunicated hazard has in fact materialized.

In our view, this method of dealing with the issue on causation comes in second-best. It places the physician in jeopardy of the patient's hindsight and bitterness. It places the factfinder in the position of deciding whether a speculative answer to a hypothetical question is to be credited. It calls for a subjective determination solely on testimony of a patient-witness shadowed by the occurrence of the undisclosed risk.

Better it is, we believe, to resolve the causality issue on an objective basis: in terms of what a prudent person in the patient's position would have decided if suitably informed of all perils bearing significance. If adequate disclosure could reasonably be expected to have caused that person to decline the treatment because of the revelation of the kind of risk or danger that resulted in harm, causation is shown, but otherwise not. The patient's testimony is relevant on that score of course but it would not threaten to dominate the findings. And since that testimony would probably be appraised congruently with the factfinder's belief in its reasonableness, the case for a wholly objective standard for passing on causation is strengthened. Such a standard would in any event ease the fact-finding process and better assure the truth as its product.

VIII

In the context of trial of a suit claiming inadequate disclosure of risk information by a physician, the patient has the burden of going forward with evidence tending to establish *prima facie* the essential elements of the cause of action, and ultimately the burden of proof—the risk of nonpersuasion—on those elements. These are normal impositions upon moving litigants, and no reason why they should not attach in nondisclosure cases is apparent. The burden of going forward with evidence pertaining to a privilege not to disclose, however, rests properly upon the physician. This is not only because the patient has made out a *prima facie* case before an issue on privilege is

---

[107]Waltz and Scheuneman, "Informed Consent to Therapy," 64 *Nw.U.L.Rev.* 628, 647 (1970).

reached, but also because any evidence bearing on the privilege is usually in the hands of the physician alone. Requiring him to open the proof on privilege is consistent with judicial policy laying such a burden on the party who seeks shelter from an exception to a general rule and who is more likely to have possession of the facts.

As in much malpractice litigation, recovery in nondisclosure lawsuits has hinged upon the patient's ability to prove through expert testimony that the physician's performance departed from medical custom. This is not surprising since, as we have pointed out, the majority of American jurisdictions have limited the patient's right to know to whatever boon can be found in medical practice. We have already discussed our disagreement with the majority rationale. We now delineate our view on the need for expert testimony in nondisclosure cases.

There are obviously important roles for medical testimony in such cases, and some roles which only medical evidence can fill. Experts are ordinarily indispensable to identify and elucidate for the factfinder the risks of therapy and the consequences of leaving existing maladies untreated. They are normally needed on issues as to the cause of any injury or disability suffered by the patient and, where privileges are asserted, as to the existence of any emergency claimed and the nature and seriousness of any impact upon the patient from risk-disclosure. Save for relative infrequent instances where questions of this type are resolvable wholly within the realm of ordinary human knowledge and experience, the need for the expert is clear.

The guiding consideration our decisions distill, however, is that medical facts are for medical experts and other facts are for any witnesses—expert or not—having sufficient knowledge and capacity to testify to them. It is evident that many of the issues typically involved in nondisclosure cases do not reside peculiarly within the medical domain. Lay witness testimony can competently establish a physician's failure to disclose particular risk information, the patient's lack of knowledge of the risk, and the adverse consequences following the treatment. Experts are unnecessary to a showing of the materiality of risk to a patient's decision on treatment, or to the reasonably expectable effect of risk disclosure on the decision. These conspicuous examples of permissible uses of nonexpert testimony illustrate the relative freedom of broad areas of the legal problem of risk nondisclosure from the demands for expert testimony that shackle plaintiffs' other types of medical malpractice litigation.

NOTES

1. *Canterbury* v. *Spence* has set the tone for many subsequent decisions dealing with the requirement of informed consent. See, e.g., *Sawyer* v. *Methodist Hospital*, 522 F.2d 1102 (6th Cir. 1975); *Betesh* v. *United States*, 400 F.Supp. 238 (D.D.C. 1974); *Bowers* v. *Garfield*, 382 F.Supp. 503 (E.D.Pa. 1974); *Cobbs* v. *Grant*, 8 Cal.3d 229, 502 P.2d 1, 104 Cal. Rptr. 505 (1972); *Wilkinson* v. *Vesey*, 110 R.I. 606, 295 A.2d 676 (1972). Extensive analysis of the *Canterbury* case and its impact on subsequent legal decisions can be found in Meisel, A., "The Expansion of Liability for Medical Accidents: From Negligence to Strict Liability by Way of Informed Consent," 56 *Neb. L. Rev.* 51, 93–113 (1977).

2. Robinson, G., and Merav, A., "Informed Consent: Recall by Patients Tested Postoperatively," 22 *Annals of Thoracic Surgery* 209 (1976), describes a study of the

meaningfulness of informed consent. In carefully constructed, but informal sessions with patients one or two days before surgery, the elements of informed consent were systematically covered in considerable detail. Between 4 and 6 months after surgery, 20 patients were selected for reinterview to determine the capacity of each individual to recall the details of his or her informed consent interview. Each selected patient convalesced uneventfully after a satisfactory postoperative course. Otherwise, patient selection was totally random. Ages ranged between 35 and 66 years, with a mean age of 52 years. Nine of the 20 selected had undergone surgery for atherosclerotic heart disease. The remaining 11 patients had been operated upon for acquired vascular heart disease.

At the reinterview each category of consent was reviewed twice to determine the patient's ability to recall. Findings indicated generally poor retention in all categories of informed consent information. Even with the influence of suggestion and a point-by-point review of every item covered in the original interview, patients could remember only 42% of the items that had been covered in the informed consent interview. Each of the 20 patients failed to recall major parts of the interview. Sixteen of the 20 patients positively denied that certain major items had been discussed at all. What effect, if any, should these findings have on decisions like *Canterbury* v. *Spence?*

3. For a discussion of the elements of consent generally, see pp. 525–527, above.

4. Unlike typical narrowly framed judicial decisions, the *Canterbury* v. *Spence* opinion is a broad treatise on the subject of informed consent. For further information about some of the legal generalities summarized in the text of the decision, reference should be made to the extensive block citations that were addended as footnotes, not included herein, to the *Canterbury* opinion.

2. Application to Handicapped Persons

a. Elective Corrective Surgery

IN RE WEBERLIST

Supreme Court of New York, Special Term, New York County, Part 2, 1974
79 Misc.2d 753, 360 N.Y.S.2d 783

SIDNEY H. ASCH, Justice:

This proceeding concerns Eugene Weberlist, a mentally retarded resident of Manhattan Developmental Services ("MDS"). A petition has been filed by the Director of MDS requesting an order to show cause why MDS should not arrange for treatment and surgery for Eugene.

Eugene Weberlist was born January 18, 1952 at Lenox Hill Hospital. His twin died within 44 minutes of birth, and his parents were advised that he would probably also die soon thereafter. Eugene was born hydrocephalic, with a cleft palate and webbed fingers and toes. He remained at Lenox Hill Hospital but did not die. After eight and one-half months, the hospital requested his discharge.

His parents, Eugene and Grace Harley Weberlist, had one normal child at home who had already been told that Eugene had died. Therefore, the parents requested an alternative and placement at Willowbrook State School which was arranged on March 26, 1953, through court certification. His parents remained in contact with Willowbrook though they did not visit him. In 1967, and again in 1968, his mother was contacted and paid for special shoes that Eugene needed. Letters sent to the family in 1969 were returned "addressee unknown." In 1970, Patient Resources tried to locate the family but were unable to do so. No further contact with the family has been made and their whereabouts are considered unknown.

On October 4, 1973, Eugene was transferred to MDS and was admitted upon a non-objecting application signed by the Director of the institution.

Eugene's condition was diagnosed as severe mental retardation associated with diseases and conditions due to unknown prenatal influence, hydrocephalus, congenital, Binet IQ approximately 20. He is unable to speak, but he does make sounds similar to words such as "yes" and "no." He is well-behaved, cooperative and understands simple commands which he is able to follow. He has most self-help skills and is able to function in his apartment within the institution. However, he is very shy and tends to stay alone, which may be a reaction to his physical appearance. Eugene does not have the ability to understand and would not be able to consent to the treatment and surgery.

Proposed treatments would include dental work and hand surgery, surgery for the cleft palate and jaw, and intracranial surgery for facial restoration.

At a conference at New York University School of Medicine on January 14, 1974, attended by a representative of the Mental Health Information Service, the Plastic Surgery Unit stated that such surgery was feasible, necessary and could be beneficial. It was noted that without such surgery Eugene would remain in an institution for his entire life. However, with this surgery, he would have the potential to be educable or at least trainable and, with a changed appearance, possess the ability to live a more normal life outside of an institution. A discussion of the risks involved indicated that they were very low. Possible advantages highly outweighed any small risks involved.

In reviewing the records and the proposed procedures, the Mental Health Information Service found no reason to object to a judge's order permitting the requested treatment and surgery.

A guardian *ad litem* has been appointed, since no person with a close family relationship could be located to consent to the proposed surgery. The guardian *ad litem* visited Eugene at MDS. He met also with the physician in charge of Eugene. The guardian *ad litem* observed his ward and confirmed that the latter appeared to be suffering from the various physical conditions already discussed. The guardian recommended that the court authorize the performance of the surgery requested in the petition with the condition, however, that following each surgical procedure, an opportunity be given to the Mental Health Information Service of the First Department to determine whether the patient has responded to the surgery and is physically able to withstand the next procedure to be undertaken.

If this were an emergency life-saving situation, it would be unnecessary to entertain the petition since the hospital could take the full responsibility for the course of treatment necessary under the circumstances without need for judicial authority. (See, *In re Nemser,* 51 Misc.2d 616, 622, 273 N.Y.S.2d 624, 629; *Application of*

Georgetown College, 118 U.S.App.D.C. 90, 331 F.2d 1000.) But this is not such a case. It cannot be found by this Court that such surgery is of an emergency nature or necessary to save Eugene's life. The affidavit of Dr. J. M. Converse in support of the petition does nothing more than claim that the projected treatment and surgery "may in due time enable him to contribute his part for earning a living instead of remaining all his life in custodial care. . . ."

Under its police powers, a State may exert its coercive force on an individual if he represents a significant danger to other persons or to society. The authority of the State to dictate compulsory medical procedures, however, is usually sanctioned by the doctrine of *parens patriae,* rather than its police power (*Jacobson* v. *Commonwealth,* 197 U.S. 11, 25 S.Ct. 358, 49 L.Ed. 643; see also, *Prince* v. *Commonwealth,* 321 U.S. 158, 166–167, 64 S.Ct. 438, 88 L.Ed. 645; Hershey, Compulsory Personal Health Measure Legislation, 84 Pub. Health Reps. 341–352 [1969]). The rationale of *parens patriae* is that the State must intervene in order to protect an individual who is not able to make decisions in his own best interest. The decision to exercise the power of *parens patriae* must reflect the welfare of society, as a whole, but mainly it must balance the individual's right to be free from interference against the individual's need to be treated, if treatment would in fact be in his best interest. Because of the variables, the question of whether this power should be exercised in a given situation is quite difficult. (See *Cude* v. *State,* 237 Ark. 927, 377 S.W.2d 816; *Mannis* v. *State,* 240 Ark. 42, 398 S.W.2d 206; Note, "Compulsory Medical Treatment and the Free Exercise of Religion," 42 *Ind.L.J.* 386 [1967]; John and Peterson, "Legal Status of Christian Science Treatment," 10 *Med.Trial Tech.Q.* 13 [1963]; How, "Religion, Medicine and Law," 3 *Can.B.J.* 365 [1960]; Note, "Compulsory Medical Treatment: The State's Interest Re-Evaluated," 51 *Minn.L.Rev.* 293 [1966].)

"The issue . . . is whether it is justifiable, and under what circumstances, to radically alter the nature of the individual" (P. London, quoted in The Hastings Center Report, May, 1973, p. 9). Courts have been reluctant to authorize surgical intervention in a "nonemergency" situation where the individual is under a disability. (*In re Seiferth,* 309 N.Y. 80, 127 N.E.2d 820; *In re Tuttendario,* 21 Pa.Dist. 561; *In re Hudson,* 13 Wash.2d 673, 126 P.2d 765; *In re Green,* 452 Pa. 373, 307 A.2d 279; *In re Sampson,* 65 Misc.2d 658, 317 N.Y.S.2d 641, aff'd 37 A.D.2d 668, 323 N.Y.S.2d 253, aff'd per curiam, 29 N.Y.2d 900, 328 N.Y.S.2d 686, 278 N.E.2d 918; *In re Rotkowitz,* 175 Misc. 948, 950, 25 N.Y.S.2d 624, 626; *In re D,* 70 Misc.2d 953, 335 N.Y.S.2d 638; *In re Comm'r of Social Services,* 72 Misc.2d 428, 339 N.Y.S.2d 89; *State* v. *Perricone,* 37 N.J. 463, 181 A.2d 751; *In re Carstairs,* Dom.Rel.Ct., 115 N.Y.S.2d 314; Note, 30 A.L.R.2d 1138 [1953]; Note, "Court-Ordered Non-Emergency Care for Infants," 18 *Clev.-Mar.L.Rev.* 296 [1969]; Zaremski, "Blood Transfusions and Elective Surgery," 23 *Cleveland State L.Rev.,* Spring, 1974, p. 231.)

The Court is faced with the possibility that the ward may simply serve as an object for experimentation. Organized concern with the threat of human experimentation can be dated back to the so-called Nuremberg Code of 1946. (See, e.g., "Symposium on Ethical Aspects of Experimentation with Human Subjects," 98 *Daedalus* 219, *et seq.* [1969]; Freund, "Ethical Problems in Human Experimentation," 273

New Engl.J.Med. 687 [1967]; Curran and Beecher, "Experimentation in Children," 10 *J.A.M.A.* 77 [1969]; Lasagna, "Special Subjects in Human Experimentation," 98 *Daedalus* 449 [1969]; Note, "Experimentation on Human Beings," 20 *Stan.L.Rev.* 99 [1967]; Rules and Regulations of the U.S. Dept. of Health, Education and Welfare in the Protection of Human Subjects, effective July 1, 1974.) It may well be that: "Human experimentation has been a part of medical science since it gained the title of 'science' some centuries ago. There are still physicians who insist that all medical treatment is still experimental" (Curran and Shapiro, *Law, Medicine and Forensic Science* [Second Edition, 1970] p. 887), but the critical factor in this case is its beneficial potential for Eugene Weberlist.

Ordinarily, this Court would be constrained to follow the philosophy expressed by Mr. Justice Brandeis in *Olmstead* v. *United States,* 277 U.S. 438, at 478, 48 S.Ct. 564, at 572, 72 L.Ed. 944 (1928):

> The makers of our Constitution... sought to protect Americans in their beliefs, their thoughts, their emotions and their sensations. They conferred, as against the government, the right to be let alone—the most comprehensive of rights and the right most valued by civilized men.

In this case, the Court must decide what its ward would choose, if he were in a position to make a sound judgment. Certainly, he would pick the chance for a fuller participation in life rather than a rejection of his potential as a more fully endowed human being. The Court does not know what the future holds in store for its unfortunate ward—whether the treatment will be successful. But the most humble of us is entitled to the promise of the Declaration of Independence for "Life, Liberty and the Pursuit of Happiness." We owe the respondent that opportunity and accordingly, the Court authorizes the proposed medical intervention.

NOTES

1. The court's declaration that it "must decide what its ward would choose, if he were in a position to make a sound judgment," is a succinct description of the substitute judgment doctrine, whereby a court exercises the rights of informed consent on behalf of an individual considered incompetent to give legally valid consent.

2. For a discussion of the relationship between consent, competency, and guardianship, see pp. 521–550, above.

3. The *Weberlist* court touched upon the need to protect persons considered incompetent from being used as guinea pigs for medical experimentation. The legal and ethical constraints surrounding the use of human subjects for experimentation have received a considerable amount of attention from legal and medical commentators. In addition to the authorities cited in *Weberlist,* are the following two informative sources: Katz, J., *Experimentation with Human Beings* (1972) and Fletcher, J., "Human Experimentation—Ethics in the Consent Situation," *Medical Progress and the Law* 60 (Hairghurst, C., ed., 1969). A good summary of specific case law in this area, along with a discussion of general principles and legal issues raised by experimentation, is found in Chapter 6, "Legal Perspectives," of the *Report and Recommendations of the National Commission for the Protection of Human Subjects of Biomedical and Be-*

havioral Research, 43 Fed.Reg. 11328, 11345–11351 (Mar. 17, 1978). The U.S. Department of Health, Education, and Welfare has issued "Proposed Regulations on Research Involving Those Institutionalized as Mentally Disabled," 43 Fed.Reg. 53950 (Nov. 17, 1978), which would control most federally funded experimentation.

4. A tragedy of the *Weberlist* case is that the New York authorities did not seek to have the corrective medical procedures performed until Eugene Weberlist was 22 years old. The psychological and developmental damage engendered by such delay seems apparent.

b. Lifesaving or Life-Prolonging Measures

Maine Medical Center v. Houle

See pp. 754–756, above.

Superintendent of Belchertown v. Saikewicz

Supreme Judicial Court of Massachusetts, Hampshire, 1977
____ Mass. ____, 370 N.E.2d 417

Before Hennessey, C. J., and Braucher, Kaplan, Wilkins and Liacos, JJ. Liacos, Justice.

On April 26, 1976, William E. Jones, superintendent of the Belchertown State School (a facility of the Massachusetts Department of Mental Health), and Paul R. Rogers, a staff attorney at the school, petitioned the Probate Court for Hampshire County for the appointment of a guardian of Joseph Saikewicz, a resident of the State school. Simultaneously they filed a motion for the immediate appointment of a guardian *ad litem,* with authority to make the necessary decisions concerning the care and treatment of Saikewicz, who was suffering with acute myeloblastic monocytic leukemia. The petition alleged that Saikewicz was a mentally retarded person in urgent need of medical treatment and that he was a person with disability incapable of giving informed consent for such treatment.

On May 5, 1976, the probate judge appointed a guardian *ad litem.* On May 6, 1976, the guardian *ad litem* filed a report with the court. The guardian *ad litem*'s report indicated that Saikewicz's illness was an incurable one, and that although chemotherapy was the medically indicated course of treatment it would cause Saikewicz significant adverse side effects and discomfort. The guardian *ad litem* concluded that these factors, as well as the inability of the ward to understand the treatment to which he would be subjected and the fear and pain he would suffer as a result, outweighed the limited prospect of any benefit from such treatment, namely, the possibility of some uncertain but limited extension of life. He therefore recommended "that not treating Mr. Saikewicz would be in his best interests."

A hearing on the report was held on May 13, 1976. Present were the petitioners and the guardian *ad litem.* The record before us does not indicate whether a guardian for Saikewicz was ever appointed. After hearing the evidence, the judge entered findings of fact and an order that in essence agreed with the recommendation of the guardian *ad litem.* The decision of the judge appears to be based in part on the testimony of Saikewicz's two attending physicians who recommended against chemotherapy. The judge then reported to the Appeals Court the two questions set forth in the margin.[2] An application for direct appellate review was allowed by this court. On July 9, 1976, this court issued an order answering the questions reported in the affirmative with the notation "rescript and opinion . . . will follow."[3] We now issue that opinion.

I

The judge below found that Joseph Saikewicz, at the time the matter arose, was sixty-seven years old, with an IQ of ten and a mental age of approximately two years and eight months. He was profoundly mentally retarded. The record discloses that, apart from his leukemic condition, Saikewicz enjoyed generally good health. He was physically strong and well built, nutritionally nourished, and ambulatory. He was not, however, able to communicate verbally—resorting to gestures and grunts to make his wishes known to others and responding only to gestures or physical contacts. In the course of treatment for various medical conditions arising during Saikewicz's residency at the school, he had been unable to respond intelligibly to inquiries such as whether he was experiencing pain. It was the opinion of a consulting psychologist, not contested by the other experts relied on by the judge below, that Saikewicz was not aware of dangers and was disoriented outside his immediate environment. As a result of his condition, Saikewicz had lived in State institutions since 1923 and had resided at the Belchertown State School since 1928. Two of his sisters, the only members of his family who could be located, were notified of his condition and of the hearing, but they preferred not to attend or otherwise become involved.

On April 19, 1976, Saikewicz was diagnosed as suffering from acute myeloblastic monocytic leukemia. Leukemia is a disease of the blood. It arises when organs of the body produce an excessive number of white blood cells as well as other abnormal cellular structures, in particular undeveloped and immature white cells. Along with these symptoms in the composition of the blood the disease is accompanied by enlargement of the organs which produce the cells, e.g., the spleen, lymph glands, and bone marrow. The disease tends to cause internal bleeding and weakness, and, in the acute form, severe anemia and high susceptibility to infection. *Attorneys' Dictionary of Medicine* L-37-38 (1977). The particular form of the disease present in this case, acute myeloblastic monocytic leukemia, is so defined because the particular cells which

---

[2] "(1) Does the Probate Court under its general or any special jurisdiction have the authority to order, in circumstances it deems appropriate, the withholding of medical treatment from a person even though such withholding of treatment might contribute to a shortening of the life of such person?

"(2) On the facts reported in this case, is the Court correct in ordering that no treatment be administered to said JOSEPH SAIKEWICZ now or at any time for his condition of acute myeloblastic monocytic leukemia except by further order of the Court?"

[3] After briefly reviewing the facts of the case, we stated in that order: "Upon consideration, based upon the findings of the probate judge, we answer the first question in the affirmative, and a majority of the Court answer the second question in the affirmative. However, we emphasize that upon receiving evidence of a significant change either in the medical condition of Saikewicz or in the medical treatment available to him for successful treatment of his condition, the probate judge may issue a further order."

increase are the myeloblasts, the youngest form of a cell which at maturity is known as the granulocytes. *Id.* at M-138. The disease is invariably fatal.

Chemotherapy, as was testified to at the hearing in the Probate Court, involves the administration of drugs over several weeks, the purpose of which is to kill the leukemia cells. This treatment unfortunately affects normal cells as well. One expert testified that the end result, in effect, is to destroy the living vitality of the bone marrow. Because of this effect, the patient becomes very anemic and may bleed or suffer infections—a condition which requires a number of blood transfusions. In this sense, the patient immediately becomes much "sicker" with the commencement of chemotherapy, and there is a possibility that infections during the initial period of severe anemia will prove fatal. Moreover, while most patients survive chemotherapy, remission of the leukemia is achieved in only thirty to fifty percent of the cases. Remission is meant here as a temporary return to normal as measured by clinical and laboratory means. If remission does occur, it typically lasts for between two and thirteen months although longer periods of remission are possible. Estimates of the effectiveness of chemotherapy are complicated in cases, such as the one presented here, in which the patient's age becomes a factor. According to the medical testimony before the court below, persons over age sixty have more difficulty tolerating chemotherapy and the treatment is likely to be less successful than in younger patients. This prognosis may be compared with the doctors' estimates that, left untreated, a patient in Saikewicz's condition would live for a matter of weeks or, perhaps, several months. According to the testimony, a decision to allow the disease to run its natural course would not result in pain for the patient, and death would probably come without discomfort.

An important facet of the chemotherapy process, to which the judge below directed careful attention, is the problem of serious adverse side effects caused by the treating drugs. Among these side effects are severe nausea, bladder irritation, numbness and tingling of the extremities, and loss of hair. The bladder irritation can be avoided, however, if the patient drinks fluids, and the nausea can be treated by drugs. It was the opinion of the guardian *ad litem,* as well as the doctors who testified before the probate judge, that most people elect to suffer the side effects of chemotherapy rather than to allow their leukemia to run its natural course.

Drawing on the evidence before him, including the testimony of the medical experts and the report of the guardian *ad litem,* the probate judge issued detailed findings with regard to the costs and benefits of allowing Saikewicz to undergo chemotherapy. The judge's findings are reproduced in part here because of the importance of clearly delimiting the issues presented in this case. The judge below found:

> 5. That the majority of persons suffering from leukemia who are faced with a choice of receiving or foregoing such chemotherapy, and who are able to make an informed judgment thereon, choose to receive treatment in spite of its toxic side effects and risks of failure.
> 6. That such toxic side effects of chemotherapy include pain and discomfort, depressed bone marrow, pronounced anemia, increased chance of infection, possible bladder irritation, and possible loss of hair.
> 7. That administration of such chemotherapy requires cooperation from the patient

over several weeks of time, which cooperation said JOSEPH SAIKEWICZ is unable to give due to his profound retardation.[5]

8. That, considering the age and general state of health of said JOSEPH SAIKEWICZ, there is only a 30–40 percent chance that chemotherapy will produce a remission of said leukemia, which remission would probably be for a period of time of from 2 to 13 months, but that said chemotherapy will certainly not completely cure such leukemia.

9. That if such chemotherapy is to be administered at all it should be administered immediately, inasmuch as the risks involved will increase and the chances of successfully bringing about remission will decrease as time goes by.

10. That, at present, said JOSEPH SAIKEWICZ's leukemia condition is stable and is not deteriorating.

11. That said JOSEPH SAIKEWICZ is not now in pain and will probably die within a matter of weeks or months a relatively painless death due to the leukemia unless other factors should intervene to themselves cause death.

12. That it is impossible to predict how long said JOSEPH SAIKEWICZ will probably live without chemotherapy or how long he will probably live with chemotherapy, but it is to a very high degree medically likely that he will die sooner without treatment than with it.

Balancing these various factors, the judge concluded that the following considerations weighed *against* administering chemotherapy to Saikewicz: "(1) his age, (2) his inability to cooperate with the treatment, (3) probable adverse side effects of treatment, (4) low chance of producing remission, (5) the certainty that treatment will cause immediate suffering, and (6) the quality of life possible for him even if the treatment does bring about remission."

The following considerations were determined to weigh in *favor* of chemotherapy: "(1) the chance that his life may be lengthened thereby, and (2) the fact that most people in his situation when given a chance to do so elect to take the gamble of treatment."

Concluding that, in this case, the negative factors of treatment exceeded the benefits, the probate judge ordered on May 13, 1976, that no treatment be administered to Saikewicz for his condition of acute myeloblastic monocytic leukemia except by further order of the court. The judge further ordered that all reasonable and necessary supportive measures be taken, medical or otherwise, to safeguard the well-being of Saikewicz in all other respects and to reduce as far as possible any suffering or discomfort which he might experience.

It is within this factual context that we issued our order of July 9, 1976.

Saikewicz died on September 4, 1976, at the Belchertown State School hospital. Death was due to bronchial pneumonia, a complication of the leukemia. Saikewicz died without pain or discomfort.

---

[5]There was testimony as to the importance of having the full cooperation of the patient during the initial weeks of the chemotherapy process as well as during follow-up visits. For example, the evidence was that it would be necessary to administer drugs intravenously for extended periods of time—twelve or twenty-four hours a day for up to five days. The inability of Saikewicz to comprehend the purpose of the treatment, combined with his physical strength, led the doctors to testify that Saikewicz would probably have to be restrained to prevent him from tampering with the intravenous devices. Such forcible restraint could, in addition to increasing the patient's discomfort, lead to complications such as pneumonia.

II

We recognize at the outset that this case presents novel issues of fundamental importance that should not be resolved by mechanical reliance on legal doctrine. Our task of establishing a framework in the law on which the activities of health care personnel and other persons can find support is furthered by seeking the collective guidance of those in health care, moral ethics, philosophy, and other disciplines. Our attempt to bring such insights to bear in the legal context has been advanced by the diligent efforts of the guardian *ad litem* and the probate judge, as well as the excellent briefs of the parties and amici curiae. As thus illuminated, the principal areas of determination are:

A. The nature of the right of any person, competent or incompetent, to decline potentially life-prolonging treatment.

B. The legal standards that control the course of decision whether or not potentially life-prolonging, but not life-saving, treatment should be administered to a person who is not competent to make the choice.

C. The procedures that must be followed in arriving at that decision.

For reasons we develop in the body of this opinion, it becomes apparent that the questions to be discussed in the first two areas are closely interrelated. We take the view that the substantive rights of the competent and the incompetent person are the same in regard to the right to decline potentially life-prolonging treatment. The factors which distinguish the two types of persons are found only in the area of how the State should approach the preservation and implementation of the rights of an incompetent person and in the procedures necessary to that process of preservation and implementation. We treat the matter in the sequence above stated because we think it helpful to set forth our views on (A) what the rights of all persons in this area are and (B) the issue of how an incompetent person is to be afforded the status in law of a competent person with respect to such rights. Only then can we proceed to (C) the particular procedures to be followed to ensure the rights of the incompetent person.

A

1. It has been said that "[t]he law always lags behind the most advanced thinking in every area. It must wait until the theologians and the moral leaders and events have created some common ground, some consensus." Burger, "The Law and Medical Advances," 67 *Annals Internal Med. Supp.* 7, 15, 17 (1967), quoted in Elkinton, "The Dying Patient, the Doctor, and the Law," 13 *Vill.L.Rev.* 740 (1968). We therefore think it advisable to consider the framework of medical ethics which influences a doctor's decision as to how to deal with the terminally ill patient. While these considerations are not controlling, they ought to be considered for the insights they give us.

Advances in medical science have given doctors greater control over the time and nature of death. Chemotherapy is, as evident from our previous discussion, one of these advances. Prior to the development of such new techniques the physician perceived his duty as that of making every conceivable effort to prolong life. On the other hand, the context in which such an ethos prevailed did not provide the range of options available to the physician today in terms of taking steps to postpone death irrespective of the effect on the patient. With the development of the new techniques, serious questions as to what may constitute acting in the best interests of the patient have arisen.

The nature of the choice has become more difficult because physicians have begun to realize that in many cases the effect of using extraordinary measures to prolong life is to "only prolong suffering, isolate the family from their loved one at a time when they may be close at hand or result in economic ruin for the family." Lewis, "Machine Medicine and Its Relation to the Fatally Ill," 206 *J.A.M.A.* 387 (1968).

Recognition of these factors led the Supreme Court of New Jersey to observe "that physicians distinguish between curing the ill and comforting and easing the dying; that they refuse to treat the curable as if they were dying or ought to die, and that they have sometimes refused to treat the hopeless and dying as if they were curable." *In re Quinlan*, 70 N.J. 10, 47, 355 A.2d 647, 667 (1976).

The essence of this distinction in defining the medical role is to draw the sometimes subtle distinction between those situations in which the withholding of extraordinary measures may be viewed as allowing the disease to take its natural course and those in which the same actions may be deemed to have been the cause of death. See Elkinton, *supra* at 743. Recent literature suggests that health care institutions are drawing such a distinction, at least with regard to respecting the decision of competent patients to refuse such measures. Rabkin, Gillerman, and Rice, "Orders Not to Resuscitate," 293 *N.E.J. of Med.* 364 (1976). Cf. Beecher, "Ethical Problems Created by the Hopelessly Unconscious Patient," 278 *N.E.J. of Med.* 1425 (1968).

The current state of medical ethics in this area is expressed by one commentator who states that: "we should not use *extraordinary* means of prolonging life or its semblance when, after careful consideration, consultation and the application of the most well conceived therapy it becomes apparent that there is no hope for the recovery of the patient. Recovery should not be defined simply as the ability to remain alive; it should mean life without intolerable suffering." *Lewis, supra.* See Collins, "Limits of Medical Responsibility in Prolonging Life," 206 *J.A.M.A.* 389 (1968); Williamson, "Life or Death—Whose Decision?" 197 *J.A.M.A.* 793 (1966).

Our decision in this case is consistent with the current medical ethos in this area.

2. There is implicit recognition in the law of the Commonwealth, as elsewhere, that a person has a strong interest in being free from nonconsensual invasion of his bodily integrity. *Thibault* v. *Lalumiere*, 318 Mass. 72, 60 N.E.2d 349 (1945). *Commonwealth* v. *Clark*, 2 Metc. 23 (1840). *Union Pac. Ry.* v. *Botsford*, 141 U.S. 250, 251, 11 S.Ct. 1000, 35 L.Ed. 734 (1891). In short, the law recognizes the individual interest in preserving "the inviolability of his person." *Pratt* v. *Davis*, 118 Ill.App. 161, 166 (1905), aff'd, 224 Ill. 300, 79 N.E. 562 (1906). One means by which the law has developed in a manner consistent with the protection of this interest is through the development of the doctrine of informed consent. While the doctrine to the extent it may justify recovery in tort for the breach of a physician's duty has not been formally recognized by this court, *Schroeder* v. *Lawrence*, — Mass. —, 359 N.E.2d 1301 (1977); see *Baird* v. *Attorney Gen.*, — Mass. —, 360 N.E.2d 288

(1977); *Reddington* v. *Clayman,* 334 Mass. 244, 134 N.E.2d 920 (1956); G.L. c. 112, § 12F, it is one of widespread recognition. Capron, "Informed Consent in Catastrophic Disease Research and Treatment," 123 *U.Pa.L.Rev.* 340, 365 (1974); Cantor, "A Patient's Decision to Decline Life-Saving Medical Treatment: Bodily Integrity Versus the Preservation of Life," 26 *Rutgers L.Rev.* 228, 236-238 (1973). W. Prosser, Torts § 18 (4th ed. 1971). As previously suggested, one of the foundations of the doctrine is that it protects the patient's status as a human being. Capron, *supra* at 366-367.

Of even broader import, but arising from the same regard for human dignity and self-determination, is the unwritten constitutional right of privacy found in the penumbra of specific guaranties of the Bill of Rights. *Griswold* v. *Connecticut,* 381 U.S. 479, 484, 85 S.Ct. 328, 13 L.Ed.2d 339 (1965). As this constitutional guaranty reaches out to protect the freedom of a woman to terminate pregnancy under certain conditions, *Roe* v. *Wade,* 410 U.S. 113, 153, 93 S.Ct. 705, 35 L.Ed.2d 147 (1973), so it encompasses the right of a patient to preserve his or her right to privacy against unwanted infringements of bodily integrity in appropriate circumstances. *In re Quinlan, supra* 70 N.J. at 38-39, 355 A.2d 647. In the case of a person incompetent to assert this constitutional right of privacy, it may be asserted by that person's guardian in conformance with the standards and procedures set forth in sections II(B) and II(C) of this opinion. See *Quinlan* at 39, 355 A.2d 647.

3. The question when the circumstances are appropriate for the exercise of this privacy right depends on the proper identification of State interests. It is not surprising that courts have, in the course of investigating State interests in various medical contexts and under various formulations of the individual rights involved, reached differing views on the nature and the extent of State interests. We have undertaken a survey of some of the leading cases to help in identifying the range of State interests potentially applicable to cases of medical intervention.

In a number of cases, no applicable State interest, or combination of such interests, was found sufficient to outweigh the individual's interests in exercising the choice of refusing medical treatment. To this effect are *Erickson* v. *Dilgard,* 44 Misc.2d 27, 252 N.Y.S.2d 705 (N.Y.Sup.Ct. 1962) (scheme of liberty puts highest priority on free individual choice); *In re Estate of Brooks,* 32 Ill.2d 361, 205 N.E.2d 435 (1965) (patient may elect to pursue religious beliefs by refusing life-saving blood transfusion provided the decision did not endanger public health, safety or morals); see *In re Osborne,* 294 A.2d 372 (D.C.App. 1972); *Holmes* v. *Silver Cross Hosp. of Joliet, Ill.,* 340 F.Supp. 125 (D.Ill. 1972); Byrn, Compulsory Lifesaving Treatment for the Competent Adult, 44 Fordham L.Rev. 1 (1975). See also *In re Guardianship of Pescinski,* 67 Wis.2d 4, 226 N.W.2d 180 (1975).

Subordination of State interests to individual interests has not been universal, however. In a leading case, *Application of the President & Directors of Georgetown College, Inc.,* 118 U.S.App.D.C. 80, 331 F.2d 1000, cert. denied, 377 U.S. 978, 84 S.Ct. 1883, 12 L.Ed.2d 746 (1964), a hospital sought permission to perform a blood transfusion necessary to save the patient's life where the person was unwilling to consent due to religious beliefs. The court held that it had the power to allow the action to be taken despite the previously expressed contrary sentiments of the patient. The court justified its decision by reasoning that its purpose was to protect three State interests, the protection of which was viewed as having greater import than the individual right: (1) the State interest in preventing suicide, (2) a *parens patriae* interest in protecting the patient's minor children from "abandonment" by their parent, and (3) the protection of the medical profession's desire to act affirmatively to save life without fear of civil liability. In *John F. Kennedy Memorial Hosp.* v. *Heston*, 58 N.J. 576, 279 A.2d 670 (1971), a case involving a fact situation similar to *Georgetown*, the New Jersey Supreme Court also allowed a transfusion. It based its decision on *Georgetown*, as well as its prior decisions. See *Raleigh Fitkin-Paul Morgan Memorial Hosp.* v. *Anderson*, 42 N.J. 421, 201 A.2d 537, cert. denied, 377 U.S. 985, 84 S.Ct. 1894, 12 L.Ed.2d 1032 (1964);[8] *State* v. *Perricone*, 37 N.J. 463, 181 A.2d 751, cert. denied, 371 U.S. 890, 83 S.Ct. 189, 9 L.Ed.2d 124 (1962). The New Jersey court held that the State's paramount interest in preserving life and the hospital's interest in fully caring for a patient under its custody and control outweighed the individual decision to decline the necessary measures. See *United States* v. *George*, 239 F.Supp. 752 (D.Conn. 1965); *Long Island Jewish-Hillside Medical Center* v. *Levitt*, 73 Misc.2d 395, 342 N.Y.S.2d 356 (N.Y.Sup.Ct. 1973); *In re Sampson*, 65 Misc.2d 658, 317 N.Y.S.2d 641 (Fam.Ct. 1970), aff'd 37 App.Div.2d 668, 323 N.Y.S.2d 253 (1971), aff'd per curiam, 29 N.Y.2d 900, 328 N.Y.S.2d 686, 278 N.E.2d 918 (1972); *In re Weberlist*, 79 Misc.2d 753, 360 N.Y.S.2d 783 (N.Y.Sup.Ct. 1974); *In re Karwath*, 199 N.W.2d 147 (Iowa 1972).

   This survey of recent decisions involving the difficult question of the right of an individual to refuse medical intervention or treatment indicates that a relatively concise statement of countervailing State interests may be made. As distilled from the cases, the State has claimed interest in: (1) the preservation of life; (2) the protection of the interests of innocent third parties; (3) the prevention of suicide; and (4) maintaining the ethical integrity of the medical profession.

   It is clear that the most significant of the asserted State interests is that of the preservation of human life. Recognition of such an interest, however, does not necessarily resolve the problem where the affliction or disease clearly indicates that life will soon, and inevitably, be extinguished. The interest of the State in prolonging a life must be reconciled with the interest of an individual to reject the traumatic cost of that prolongation. There is a substantial distinction in the State's insistence that human life be saved where the affliction is curable, as opposed to the State interest where, as here, the issue is not whether but when, for how long, and at what cost to the individual that life may be briefly extended. Even if we assume that the State has an additional interest in seeing to it that individual decisions on the prolongation of life do not in any way tend to "cheapen" the value which is placed in the concept of living, see *Roe* v. *Wade, supra,* we believe it is not inconsistent to recognize a right to decline medical treatment in a situation of incurable illness. The constitutional right to privacy, as we conceive it, is an expression of the sanctity of individual free choice and self-determination as fundamental constituents of life. The value of life as so perceived is

---

[8] While *Quinlan* would seem to limit the effect of these decisions, the opinion therein does not make clear the extent to which this is so.

lessened not by a decision to refuse treatment, but by the failure to allow a competent human being the right of choice.

A second interest of considerable magnitude, which the State may have some interest in asserting, is that of protecting third parties, particularly minor children, from the emotional and financial damage which may occur as a result of the decision of a competent adult to refuse life-saving or life-prolonging treatment. Thus, in *Holmes* v. *Silver Cross Hosp. of Joliet, Ill.,* 340 F.Supp. 125 (D.Ill. 1972), the court held that, while the State's interest in preserving an individual's life was not sufficient, by itself, to outweigh the individual's interest in the exercise of free choice, the possible impact on minor children would be a factor which might have a critical effect on the outcome of the balancing process. Similarly, in the *Georgetown* case the court held that one of the interests requiring protection was that of the minor child in order to avoid the effect of "abandonment" on that child as a result of the parent's decision to refuse the necessary medical measures. See Byrn, *supra* at 33; *United States* v. *George, supra.* We need not reach this aspect of claimed State interest as it is not an issue on the facts of this case.

The last State interest requiring discussion is that of the maintenance of the ethical integrity of the medical profession as well as allowing hospitals the full opportunity to care for people under their control. See *Georgetown, supra; United States* v. *George, supra; John F. Kennedy Memorial Hosp.* v. *Heston, supra.* The force and impact of this interest is lessened by the prevailing medical ethical standards, see Byrn, *supra* at 31. Prevailing medical ethical practice does not, without exception, demand that all efforts toward life prolongation be made in all circumstances. Rather, as indicated in *Quinlan,* the prevailing ethical practice seems to be to recognize that the dying are more often in need of comfort than treatment. Recognition of the right to refuse necessary treatment in appropriate circumstances is consistent with existing medical mores; such a doctrine does not threaten either the integrity of the medical profession, the proper role of hospitals in caring for such patients or the State's interest in protecting the same. It is not necessary to deny a right of self-determination to a patient in order to recognize the interests of doctors, hospitals, and medical personnel in attendance on the patient. Also, if the doctrines of informed consent and right of privacy have as their foundations the right to bodily integrity, see *Union Pac. Ry.* v. *Botsford,* 141 U.S. 250, 11 S.Ct. 1000, 35 L.Ed. 734 (1891), and control of one's own fate, then those rights are superior to the institutional considerations.

Applying the considerations discussed in this subsection to the decision made by the probate judge in the circumstances of the case before us, we are satisfied that his decision was consistent with a proper balancing of applicable State and individual interests. Two of the four categories of State interests that we have identified, the protection of third parties and the prevention of suicide, are inapplicable to this case. The third, involving the protection of the ethical integrity of the medical profession, was satisfied on two grounds. The probate judge's decision was in accord with the testimony of the attending physicians of the patient. The decision is in accord with the generally accepted views of the medical profession, as set forth in this opinion. The fourth State interest—the preservation of life—has been viewed with proper regard for the heavy physical and emotional burdens on the patient if a vigorous regimen of drug therapy were to be imposed to effect a brief and uncertain delay in the natural process of death. To be balanced against these State interests was the individual's interest in the freedom to choose to reject, or refuse to consent to, intrusions of his bodily integrity and privacy. We cannot say that the facts of this case required a result contrary to that reached by the probate judge with regard to the right of any person, competent or incompetent, to be spared the deleterious consequences of life-prolonging treatment. We therefore turn to consider the unique considerations arising in this case by virtue of the patient's inability to appreciate his predicament and articulate his desires.

B

The question what legal standards govern the decision whether to administer potentially life-prolonging treatment to an incompetent person encompasses two distinct and important subissues. First, does a choice exist? That is, is it the unvarying responsibility of the State to order medical treatment in all circumstances involving the care of an incompetent person? Second, if a choice does exist under certain conditions, what considerations enter into the decision-making process?

We think that principles of equality and respect for all individuals require the conclusion that a choice exists. For reasons discussed at some length in subsection A, *supra*, we recognize a general right in all persons to refuse medical treatment in appropriate circumstances. The recognition of that right must extend to the case of an incompetent, as well as a competent, patient because the value of human dignity extends to both.

This is not to deny that the State has a traditional power and responsibility, under the doctrine of *parens patriae*, to care for and protect the "best interests" of the incompetent person. Indeed, the existence of this power and responsibility has impelled a number of courts to hold that the "best interests" of such a person mandate an unvarying responsibility by the courts to order necessary medical treatment for an incompetent person facing an immediate and severe danger to life. *Application of the President & Directors of Georgetown College, Inc.*, 118 U.S.App.D.C. 80, 331 F.2d 1000, cert. denied, 377 U.S. 978, 84 S.Ct. 1883, 12 L.Ed.2d 746 (1964). *Long Island Jewish-Hillside Medical Center* v. *Levitt*, 73 Misc.2d 395, 342 N.Y.S.2d 356 (N.Y.Sup.Ct. 1973). Cf. *In re Weberlist*, 79 Misc.2d 753, 360 N.Y.S.2d 783 (N.Y.Sup.Ct. 1974). Whatever the merits of such a policy where life-saving treatment is available—a situation unfortunately not presented by this case—a more flexible view of the "best interests" of the incompetent patient is not precluded under other conditions. For example, other courts have refused to take it on themselves to order certain forms of treatment or therapy which are not immediately required although concededly beneficial to the innocent person. *In re CFB*, 497 S.W.2d 831 (Mo.App. 1973). *Green's Appeal*, 448 Pa. 338, 292 A.2d 387 (1972). *In re Frank*, 41 Wash.2d 294, 248 P.2d 553 (1952). Cf. *In re Rotkowitz*, 175 Misc. 948, 25 N.Y.S.2d 624 (N.Y.Dom.Rel.Ct. 1941); *Mitchell* v. *Davis*, 205 S.W.2d 812 (Tex.App. 1947). While some of these cases involved children who might eventually be competent to make the necessary decisions without judicial interference, it is also clear that the additional period of waiting might make the task of correction more difficult. See, e.g., *In re Frank, supra*. These cases stand for the proposition that, even in the exercise of the *parens patriae* power, there must be respect for the bodily integrity of the child or respect for the rational decision of those parties, usually the parents, who for one reason or another are seeking to protect the bodily integrity or other personal interest of the child. See *In re Hudson*, 13 Wash.2d 673, 126 P.2d 765 (1942).

The "best interests" of an incompetent person are not necessarily served by imposing on such persons results not mandated as to competent persons similarly situated. It does not advance the interest of the State or the ward to treat the ward as a person of lesser status or dignity than others. To protect the incompetent person within its power, the State must recognize the dignity and worth of such a person and afford to that person the same panoply of rights and choices it recognizes in competent persons. If a competent person faced with death may choose to decline treatment which not only will not cure the person but which substantially may increase suffering in exchange for a possible yet brief prolongation of life, then it cannot be said that it is always in the "best interests" of the ward to require submission to such treatment. Nor do statistical factors indicating that a majority of competent persons similarly situated choose treatment resolve the issue. The significant decisions of life are more complex than statistical determinations. Individual choice is determined not by the vote of the majority but by the complexities of the singular situation viewed from the unique perspective of the person called on to make the decision. To presume that the incompetent person must always be subjected to what many rational and intelligent persons may decline is to downgrade the status of the incompetent person by placing a lesser value on his intrinsic human worth and vitality.

The trend in the law has been to give incompetent persons the same rights as other individuals. *Boyd* v. *Registrars of Voters of Belchertown*, 368 Mass. —, 334 N.E.2d 629 (1975). Recognition of this principle of equality requires understanding that in certain circumstances it may be appropriate for a court to consent to the withholding of treatment from an incompetent individual. This leads us to the question of how the right of an incompetent person to decline treatment might best be exercised so as to give the fullest possible expression to the character and circumstances of that individual.

The problem of decision-making presented in this case is one of first impression before this court, and we know of no decision in other jurisdictions squarely on point. The well publicized decision of the New Jersey Supreme Court in *In re Quinlan*, 70 N.J. 10, 355 A.2d 647 (1976), provides a helpful starting point for analysis, however.

Karen Ann Quinlan, then age twenty-one, stopped breathing for reasons not clearly identified for at least two fifteen-minute periods on the night of April 15, 1975. As a result, this formerly healthy individual suffered severe brain damage to the extent that medical experts characterized her as being in a "chronic persistent vegetative state." *Id.* at 24, 355 A.2d 647. Although her brain was capable of a certain degree of primitive reflex-level functioning, she had no cognitive function or awareness of her surroundings. Karen Quinlan did not, however, exhibit any of the signs of "brain death" as identified by the Ad Hoc Committee of the Harvard Medical School. She was thus "alive" under controlling legal and medical standards. *Id.* at 25, 355 A.2d 647. Nonetheless, it was the opinion of the experts and conclusion of the court that there was no reasonable possibility that she would ever be restored to cognitive or sapient life. *Id.* at 26, 355 A.2d 647. Her breathing was assisted by a respirator, without which the experts believed she could not survive. It was for the purpose of getting authority to order the disconnection. of the respirator that Quinlan's father petitioned the lower New Jersey court.

The Supreme Court of New Jersey, in a unanimous opinion authored by Chief Justice Hughes, held that the father, as guardian, could, subject to certain qualifications, exercise his daughter's right to privacy by authorizing removal of the artificial life-support systems. *Id.* at 55, 355 A.2d 647. The court thus recognized that the preservation of the personal right to privacy against bodily intrusions, not exercisable directly due to the incompetence of the right-holder, depended on its indirect exercise by one acting on behalf of the incompetent person. The exposition by the New Jersey court of the principle of substituted judgment, and of the legal standards that were to be applied by the guardian in making this decision, bears repetition here.

> If a putative decision by Karen to permit this non-cognitive, vegetative existence to terminate by natural forces is regarded as a valuable incident of her right of privacy, as we believe it to be, then it should not be discarded solely on the basis that her condition prevents her conscious exercise of the choice. The only practical way to prevent destruction of the right is to *permit the guardian and family of Karen to render their best judgment,* subject to the qualifications [regarding consultation with attending physicians and hospital "Ethics Committee"] hereinafter stated, as to *whether she would exercise it in these circumstances.* If their conclusion is in the affirmative this decision should be accepted by a society the overwhelming majority of whose members would, we think, in similar circumstances, exercise such a choice in the same way for themselves or for those closest to them. It is for this reason that we determine that Karen's right of privacy may be asserted in her behalf, in this respect, by her guardian and family under the particular circumstances presented by this record [emphasis supplied]. *Id.* at 41-42, 355 A.2d 647.

The court's observation that most people in like circumstances would choose a natural death does not, we believe, detract from or modify the central concern that the guardian's decision conform, to the extent possible, to the decision that would have been made by Karen Quinlan herself. Evidence that most people would or would not act in a certain way is certainly an important consideration in attempting to ascertain the predilections of any individual, but care must be taken, as in any analogy, to ensure that operative factors are similar or at least to take notice of the dissimilarities. With this in mind, it is profitable to compare the situations presented in the *Quinlan* case and the case presently before us. Karen Quinlan, subsequent to her accident, was totally incapable of knowing or appreciating life, was physically debilitated, and was pathetically reliant on sophisticated machinery to nourish and clean her body. Any other person suffering from similar massive brain damage would be in a similar state of total incapacity, and thus it is not unreasonable to give weight to a supposed general, and widespread, response to the situation.

Karen Quinlan's situation, however, must be distinguished from that of Joseph Saikewicz. Saikewicz was profoundly mentally retarded. His mental state was a cognitive one but limited in his capacity to comprehend and communicate. Evidence that most people choose to accept the rigors of chemotherapy has no direct bearing on the likely choice that Joseph Saikewicz would have made. Unlike most people, Saikewicz had no capacity to understand his present situation or his prognosis. The guardian *ad litem* gave expression to this important distinction in coming to grips with this "most troubling aspect" of withholding treatment from Saikewicz: "If he is treated with toxic drugs he will be involuntarily immersed in a state of painful suffering, the reason for which he will never understand. Patients who request treatment know the risks involved and can appreciate the painful side-effects when they arrive. They know the reason for the pain and their hope makes it tolerable." To make a worthwhile comparison, one would have to ask whether a majority of people would choose chemotherapy if they were told merely that something outside of their previous experience was going to be done to them, that this something would cause them pain and discomfort, that they would be removed to strange surroundings and possibly restrained for extended periods of time, and that the advantages of this course of action were measured by concepts of time and mortality beyond their ability to comprehend.

To put the above discussion in proper perspective, we realize that an inquiry into what a majority of people would do in circumstances that truly were similar assumes an objective viewpoint not far removed from a "reasonable person" inquiry. While we recognize the value of this kind of indirect evidence, we should make it plain that the primary test is subjective in nature—that is, the goal is to determine with as much accuracy as possible the wants and needs of the individual involved.[15] This may or may not conform to what is thought wise or prudent by most people. The problems of arriving at an accurate substituted judgment in matters of life and death vary greatly in degree, if not in kind, in different circumstances. For example, the responsibility of Karen Quinlan's father to act as she would have wanted could be discharged by drawing on many years of what was apparently an affectionate and close relationship. In contrast, Joseph Saikewicz was profoundly retarded and noncommunicative his entire life, which was spent largely in the highly restrictive atmosphere of an institution. While it may thus be necessary to rely to a greater degree on objective criteria, such as the supposed inability of profoundly retarded persons to conceptualize or fear death, the effort to bring the substituted judgment into step with the values and desires of the affected individual must not, and need not, be abandoned.

The "substituted judgment" standard which we have described commends itself simply because of its straightforward respect for the integrity and autonomy of the individual. We need not, however, ignore the substantial pedigree that accompanies this phrase. The doctrine of substituted judgment had its origin over 150 years ago in

---

[15] In arriving at a philosophical rationale in support of a theory of substituted judgment in the context of organ transplants from incompetent persons, Professor Robertson of the University of Wisconsin Law School argued that "maintaining the integrity of the person means that we act toward him 'as we have reason to believe [he] would choose for [himself] if [he] were [capable] of reason and deciding rationally.' It does not provide a license to impute to him preferences he never had or to ignore previous preferences. . . . If preferences are unknown, we must act with respect to the preferences a reasonable, competent person in the incompetent's situation would have." Robertson, "Organ Donations by Incompetents and the Substituted Judgment Doctrine," 76 *Colum. L. Rev.* 48, 63 (1976), quoting J. Rawls, A Theory of Justice 209 (1971). In this way, the "free choice and moral dignity" of the incompetent person would be recognized. "Even if we were mistaken in ascertaining his preferences, the person [if he somehow became competent] could still agree that he had been fairly treated, if we had a good reason for thinking he would have made the choices imputed to him." Robertson, *supra* at 63.

the area of the administration of the estate of an incompetent person. *Ex parte Whitbread in re Hinde, a Lunatic,* 35 Eng. Rep. 878 (1816). The doctrine was utilized to authorize a gift from the estate of an incompetent person to an individual when the incompetent owed no duty of support. The English court accomplished this purpose by substituting itself as nearly as possible for the incompetent, and acting on the same motives and considerations as would have moved him. *City Bank Farmers Trust Co.* v. *McGowan,* 323 U.S. 594, 599, 65 S.Ct. 496, 89 L.Ed. 483 (1945). In essence, the doctrine in its original inception called on the court to "don the mental mantle of the incompetent." *In re Carson,* 39 Misc.2d 544, 545, 241 N.Y.S.2d 288, 289 (N.Y.Sup.Ct. 1962). Cf. *Strange* v. *Powers,* 358 Mass. 126, 260 N.E.2d 704 (1970).

In modern times the doctrine of substituted judgment has been applied as a vehicle of decision in cases more analogous to the situation presented in this case. In a leading decision on this point, *Strunk* v. *Strunk,* 445 S.W.2d 145 (Ky.Ct.App. 1969), the court held that a court of equity had the power to permit removal of a kidney from an incompetent donor for purposes of effectuating a transplant. The court concluded that, due to the nature of their relationship, both parties would benefit from the completion of the procedure, and hence the court could presume that the prospective donor would, if competent, assent to the procedure. Accord, *Hart* v. *Brown,* 29 Conn.Supp. 368, 289 A.2d 386 (1972). But see *In re Guardianship of Pescinski,* 67 Wis.2d 4, 226 N.W.2d 180 (1975). See generally Baron and others, "Life Organ and Tissue Transplants from Minor Donors in Massachusetts," 55 *B.U.L.Rev.* 159 (1975).

With this historical perspective, we now reiterate the substituted judgment doctrine as we apply it in the instant case. We believe that both the guardian *ad litem* in his recommendation and the judge in his decision should have attempted (as they did) to ascertain the incompetent person's actual interests and preferences. In short, the decision in cases such as this should be that which would be made by the incompetent person, if that person were competent, but taking into account the present and future incompetency of the individual as one of the factors which would necessarily enter into the decision-making process of the competent person. Having recognized the right of a competent person to make for himself the same decision as the court made in this case, the question is, do the facts on the record support the proposition that Saikewicz himself would have made the decision under the standard set forth? We believe they do.

The two factors considered by the probate judge to weigh in favor of administering chemotherapy were: (1) the fact that most people elect chemotherapy and (2) the chance of a longer life. Both are appropriate indicators of what Saikewicz himself would have wanted, provided that due allowance is taken for this individual's present and future incompetency. We have already discussed the perspective this brings to the fact that most people choose to undergo chemotherapy. With regard to the second factor, the chance of a longer life carries the same weight for Saikewicz as for any other person, the value of life under the law having no relation to intelligence or social position. Intertwined with this consideration is the hope that a cure, temporary or permanent, will be discovered during the period of extra weeks or months potentially made available by chemotherapy. The guardian *ad litem* investigated this possibility and found no reason to hope for a dramatic breakthrough in the time frame relevant to the decision.

The probate judge identified six factors weighing against administration of chemotherapy. Four of these—Saikewicz's age,[17] the probable side effects of treatment, the low chance of producing remission, and the certainty that treatment will cause immediate suffering—were clearly established by the medical testimony to be considerations that any individual would weigh carefully. A fifth factor—Saikewicz's inability to cooperate with the treatment—introduces those considerations that are unique to this individual and which therefore are essential to the proper exercise of substituted judgment. The judge heard testimony that Saikewicz would have no comprehension of the reasons for the severe disruption of his formerly secure and stable environment occasioned by the chemotherapy. He therefore would experience fear without the understanding from which other patients draw strength. The inability to anticipate and prepare for the severe side effects of the drugs leaves room only for confusion and disorientation. The possibility that such a naturally uncooperative patient would have to be physically restrained to allow the slow intravenous administration of drugs could only compound his pain and fear, as well as possibly jeopardize the ability of his body to withstand the toxic effects of the drugs.

The sixth factor identified by the judge as weighing against chemotherapy was "the quality of life possible for him even if the treatment does bring about remission." To the extent that this formulation equates the value of life with any measure of the quality of life, we firmly reject it. A reading of the entire record clearly reveals, however, the judge's concern that special care be taken to respect the dignity and worth of Saikewicz's life precisely because of his vulnerable position. The judge, as well as all the parties, were keenly aware that the supposed ability of Saikewicz, by virtue of his mental retardation, to appreciate or experience life had no place in the decision before them. Rather than reading the judge's formulation in a manner that demeans the value of the life of one who is mentally retarded, the vague, and perhaps ill-chosen, term "quality of life" should be understood as a reference to the continuing state of pain and disorientation precipitated by the chemotherapy treatment. Viewing the term in this manner, together with the other factors properly considered by the judge, we are satisfied that the decision to withhold treatment from Saikewicz was based on a regard for his actual interests and preferences and that the facts supported this decision.

C

We turn now to a consideration of the procedures appropriate for reaching a decision where a person allegedly incompetent is in a position in which a decision as to the giving or withholding of life-prolonging treatment must be made. As a preliminary matter, we briefly inquire into the powers of the Probate Court in this context.

The Probate Court is a court of superior and general jurisdiction. G.L. c. 215, § 2. *Wilder* v. *Orcutt,* 257 Mass. 100, 153 N.E. 332 (1926). The Probate Court is given equity jurisdiction by statute. G.L. c. 215, § 6. It has been given the specific grant of equitable powers to act in all matters relating to guardianship. G.L. c. 215, § 6.

---

[17]This factor is relevant because of the medical evidence in the record that people of Saikewicz's age do not tolerate the chemotherapy as well as younger people and that the chance of a remission is decreased. Age is irrelevant, of course, to the question of the value or quality of life.

Buckingham v. *Alden,* 315 Mass. 383, 387, 53 N.E.2d 101 (1944). The Probate Court has the power to appoint a guardian for a retarded person. G.L. c. 201, § 6A. It may also appoint a temporary guardian of such a person where immediate action is required. G.L. c. 201, § 14. Additionally, the Probate Court may appoint a guardian *ad litem* whenever the court believes it necessary to protect the interests of a person in a proceeding before it. *Buckingham* v. *Alden, supra.* This power is inherent in the court even apart from statutory authorization, and its exercise at times becomes necessary for the proper function of the court. *Lynde* v. *Vose,* 326 Mass. 621, 96 N.E.2d 172 (1951). *Buckingham* v. *Alden, supra.*

In dealing with matters concerning a person properly under the court's protective jurisdiction, "[t]he court's action . . . is not limited by any narrow bounds, but it is empowered to stretch forth its arm in whatever direction its aid and protection may be needed. . . ." *In re Quinlan,* 70 N.J. 10, 45, 355 A.2d 647, 666 (1976), quoting from 27 Am.Jur.2d Equity § 69 (1966). In essence the powers of the court to act in the best interests of a person under its jurisdiction, *Petition of the Dep't of Pub. Welfare to Dispense with Consent to Adoption,* — Mass. —, 358 N.E.2d 794 (1976); must be broad and flexible enough "to afford whatever relief may be necessary to protect his interests." *Strunk* v. *Strunk,* 445 S.W.2d 145, 147 (Ky.Ct.App. 1969), quoting from 27 Am.Jur.2d Equity § 69, at 592 (1966). The Probate Court is the proper forum in which to determine the need for the appointment of a guardian or a guardian *ad litem.* It is also the proper tribunal to determine the best interests of a ward.

In this case, a ward of a State institution was discovered to have an invariably fatal illness, the only effective—in the sense of life-prolonging—treatment for which involved serious and painful intrusions on the patient's body. While an emergency existed with regard to taking action to begin treatment, it was not a case in which immediate action was required. Nor was this a case in which life-saving, as distinguished from life-prolonging, procedures were available. Because the individual involved was thought to be incompetent to make the necessary decisions, the officials of the State institutions properly initiated proceedings in the Probate Court.

The course of proceedings in such a case is readily determined by reference to the applicable statutes. The first step is to petition the court for the appointment of a guardian. (G.L. c. 201, § 6A) or a temporary guardian (G.L. c. 201, § 14). The decision under which of these two provisions to proceed will be determined by the circumstances of the case, that is, whether the exigencies of the situation allow time to comply with the seven-day notice requirement prior to the hearing on the appointment of a guardian. G.L. c. 201, §§ 6A, 7. If appointment of a temporary guardian is sought, the probate judge will make such orders regarding notice as he deems appropriate. G.L. c. 201, § 14. At the hearing on the appointment of a guardian or temporary guardian, the issues before the court are (1) whether the person involved is mentally retarded within the meaning of the statute (G.L. c. 201, § 6A) and (2), if the person is mentally retarded, who shall be appointed guardian. *Id.* As an aid to the judge in reaching these two decisions, it will often be desirable to appoint a guardian *ad litem, sua sponte* or on motion, to represent the interests of the person. Moreover, we think it appropriate, and highly desirable, in cases such as the one before us to charge the guardian *ad litem* with an additional responsibility to be discharged if there is a finding of incompetency. This will be the responsibility of presenting to the judge, after as thorough an investigation as time will permit, all reasonable arguments in favor of administering treatment to prolong the life of the individual involved. This will ensure that all viewpoints and alternatives will be aggressively pursued and examined at the subsequent hearing where it will be determined whether treatment should or should not be allowed. The report of the guardian or temporary guardian will, of course, also be available to the judge at this hearing on the ultimate issue of treatment. Should the probate judge then be satisfied that the incompetent individual would, as determined by the standards previously set forth, have chosen to forego potentially life-prolonging treatment, the judge shall issue the appropriate order. If the judge is not so persuaded, or finds that the interests of the State require it, then treatment shall be ordered.

Commensurate with the powers of the Probate Court already described, the probate judge may, at any step in these proceedings, avail himself or herself of the additional advice or knowledge of any person or group. We note here that many health care institutions have developed medical ethics committees or panels to consider many of the issues touched on here. Consideration of the findings and advice of such groups as well as the testimony of the attending physicians and other medical experts ordinarily would be of great assistance to a probate judge faced with such a difficult decision. We believe it desirable for a judge to consider such views wherever available and useful to the court. We do not believe, however, that this option should be transformed by us into a required procedure. We take a dim view of any attempt to shift the ultimate decision-making responsibility away from the duly established courts of proper jurisdiction to any committee, panel or group, ad hoc or permanent. Thus, we reject the approach adopted by the New Jersey Supreme Court in the *Quinlan* case of entrusting the decision whether to continue artificial life support to the patient's guardian, family, attending doctors, and hospital "ethics committee." 70 N.J. at 55, 355 A.2d 647, 671. One rationale for such a delegation was expressed by the lower court judge in the *Quinlan* case, and quoted by the New Jersey Supreme Court: "The nature, extent and duration of care by societal standards is the responsibility of a physician. The morality and conscience of our society places this responsibility in the hands of the physician. What justification is there to remove it from the control of the medical profession and place it in the hands of the courts?" *Id.* at 44, 355 A.2d at 665. For its part, the New Jersey Supreme Court concluded that "a practice of applying to a court to confirm such decisions would generally be inappropriate, not only because that would be a gratuitous encroachment upon the medical profession's field of competence, but because it would be impossibly cumbersome. Such a requirement is distinguishable from the judicial overview traditionally required in other matters such as the adjudication and commitment of mental incompetents. This is not to say that in the case of an otherwise justiciable controversy access to the courts would be foreclosed; we speak rather of a general practice and procedure." *Id.* at 50, 355 A.2d at 669.

We do not view the judicial resolution of this most difficult and awesome question—whether potentially life-prolonging treatment should be withheld from a person incapable of making his own decision—as constituting a "gratuitous encroachment" on the domain of medical expertise. Rather, such questions of life and death seem to us to require the process of detached but passionate investigation and decision that forms the ideal on which the judicial branch of government was created. Achieving this ideal is our responsibility and that of the lower court, and is not to be entrusted to any other group purporting to represent the "morality and conscience of our society," no matter how highly motivated or impressively constituted.

III

Finding no State interest sufficient to counterbalance a patient's decision to decline life-prolonging medical treatment in the circumstances of this case, we conclude that the patient's right to privacy and self-determination is entitled to enforcement. Because of this conclusion, and in view of the position of equality of an incompetent person in Joseph Saikewicz's position, we conclude that the probate judge acted appropriately in this case. For these reasons we issued our order of July 9, 1976, and responded as we did to the questions of the probate judge.

NOTES

1. What are the major differences between the *Saikewicz* decision and the *In re Quinlan* opinion discussed in *Saikewicz?* Which result is based upon sounder legal reasoning? Which result is better as a matter of policy? Compare the advantages and disadvantages of hospital ethics committees with those of courts in serving as the decision makers in such cases?

2. What arguments can be made in favor of invoking all lifesaving or significantly life-prolonging measures for persons unable to decide for themselves?

3. In the *Houle* case, medical procedures were ordered undertaken in an effort to save the handicapped child's life, while in *Saikewicz* chemotherapy was withheld. Are these results inconsistent?

4. One of the factors which the court says weighs against treatment for Mr. Saikewicz is the fact that because of his mental impairment he will not understand the reason for and nature of the proposed treatment, understanding which can make suffering meaningful. Is this a valid factor for consideration in such a case? What are the dangers raised by this reasoning? Would the same considerations apply to small children who would be unable to understand the purpose for and pain resulting from life-prolonging treatment?

LANE V. CANDURA

Appeals Court of Massachusetts, Middlesex, 1978
____ Mass. ____, 376 N.E.2d 1232

BY THE COURT.

This case concerns a 77-year-old widow, Mrs. Rosaria Candura, of Arlington, who is presently a patient at the Symmes Hospital in Arlington suffering from gangrene in the right foot and lower leg. Her attending physicians recommended in April that the leg be amputated without delay. After some vacillation, she refused to consent to the operation, and she persists in that refusal. Her daughter, Grace R. Lane of Medford, filed a petition in the Probate Court for Middlesex County seeking appointment of herself as temporary guardian with authority to consent to the operation on behalf of her mother. An order and a judgment were entered in the Probate Court to that effect, from which the guardian *ad litem* appointed to represent Mrs. Candura has appealed.

We hold that Mrs. Candura has the right under the law to refuse to submit either to medical treatment or a surgical operation, that on the evidence and findings in this case the decision is one that she may determine for herself, and that therefore her leg may not be amputated unless she consents to that course of action.

The right of a person in most circumstances to decline treatment is clearly recognized in the important recent case of *Superintendent of Belchertown State Sch.* v. *Saikewicz,* — Mass. — – —, 370 N.E.2d 417 (1977). "The constitutional right to privacy, as we conceive it, is an expression of the sanctity of individual free choice and self-determination as fundamental constituents of life. The value of life as so perceived is lessened not by a decision to refuse treatment, but by the failure to allow a competent human being the right of choice." *Id.* at —, 370 N.E.2d at 426. Although the *Saikewicz* case also recognizes certain countervailing interests of the State which may in some cases outweigh the right of a competent individual to refuse life-saving or life-prolonging treatment, the case before us does not involve factors which would bring it within those lines of cases and thus warrant a court's overriding the will of a competent person.

The principal question arising on the record before us, therefore, is whether Mrs. Candura has the legally requisite competence of mind and will to make the choice for herself. We look first to the findings of fact made by the judge who heard the testimony, including that of Mrs. Candura herself. His decision does not include a clear-cut finding that Mrs. Candura lacks the requisite legal competence. The nearest approach to such a finding is contained in the following passage from his decision:

> It is fair to conclude—without necessarily finding that the ward is mentally ill for all purposes—that she is incapable of making a rational and competent choice to undergo or reject the proposed surgery to her right leg. To this extent, at least, her behavior is irrational. She has closed her mind to the entire issue to the extent that the Court cannot conclude that her decision to reject further treatment is rational and informed. . . . In the absence of substantial evidence that the ward has come to her current position as a result of a rational process after careful consideration of the medical alternatives, the Court finds that her confused mental condition resulting from her underlying senility and depression warrants the exercise of the jurisdiction of this Court and the application of a substitute choice for the ward as enunciated in the [*Saikewicz*] case. . . .

In context, the quoted passage means only that, given some indications of a degree of senility and confusion on some subjects, the judge was not satisfied that Mrs. Candura arrived at her decision in a rational manner, i.e., "after careful consideration of the medical alternatives." We do not think that the passage can be construed as a finding of legal incompetence, and we do not think that the evidence in the case would have warranted such a finding.

The facts found by the judge or established by uncontradicted evidence are as follows. Mrs. Candura was born in Italy, emigrated to the United States in 1918, was married, and had a daughter and three sons. She lost her husband in 1976 and has been depressed and unhappy since that time. Her relationship with her children is marked by a considerable degree of conflict. She lived in her own home until her hospitalization in

November, 1977. In 1974 she had an infection in a toe on her right foot which became gangrenous. It was discovered at that time that she was diabetic. The toe was amputated. In 1977 she bruised her right leg while getting into a bus. The bruise developed into gangrene which resulted in an operation in November, 1977, in which a portion of her right foot was amputated. At that time an arterial bypass was done to decrease the likelihood that gangrene would recur. She went from the hospital to a rehabilitation center, where she remained until April. She then returned to the hospital and was found to have gangrene in the remainder of the foot. She originally agreed to amputation of the leg, but she withdrew her consent on the morning scheduled for the operation. She was discharged on April 21 and went to her daughter's home but returned to the Symmes Hospital after a few days. Around May 9, responding to the persuasion of a doctor who has known Mrs. Candura for many years, she consented to the operation, but soon thereafter she reiterated her refusal. She has discussed with some persons the reasons for her decision: that she has been unhappy since the death of her husband; that she does not wish to be a burden to her children; that she does not believe that the operation will cure her; that she does not wish to live as an invalid or in a nursing home; and that she does not fear death but welcomes it. She is discouraged by the failure of the earlier operations to arrest the advance of the gangrene. She tends to be stubborn and somewhat irascible. In her own testimony before the judge she expressed a desire to get well but indicated that she was resigned to death and was adamantly against the operation. Her testimony (corroborated by that of several of the witnesses) showed that she is lucid on some matters and confused on others. Her train of thought sometimes wanders. Her conception of time is distorted. She is hostile to certain doctors. She is on occasion defensive and sometimes combative in her responses to questioning. But she has exhibited a high degree of awareness and acuity when responding to questions concerning the proposed operation. She has made it clear that she does not wish to have the operation even though that decision will in all likelihood lead shortly to her death. We find no indication in any of the testimony that that is not a choice with full appreciation of the consequences. The most that is shown is that the decision involves strong, emotional factors, that she does not choose to discuss the decision with certain persons, and that occasionally her resolve against giving consent weakens.

We start with the proposition that, in a proceeding for the appointment of a guardian under G. L. c. 201, § 6A or § 14 (permanent and temporary guardianships, respectively), the burden is on the petitioner to prove that the proposed ward is incompetent. *Willett* v. *Willett,* 333 Mass. 323, 324, 130 N.E.2d 582 (1955). A person is presumed to be competent unless shown by the evidence not to be competent. *Howe* v. *Howe,* 99 Mass. 88, 98-99 (1868). See *Wright* v. *Wright,* 139 Mass. 177, 182, 29 N.E. 380 (1885). Such evidence is lacking in this case. We recognize that Dr. Kelley, one of two psychiatrists who testified, did state that in his opinion Mrs. Candura was incompetent to make a rational choice whether to consent to the operation. His opinion appears to have been based upon (1) his inference from her unwillingness to discuss the problem with him that she was unable to face up to the problem or to understand that her refusal constituted a choice; (2) his characterization of "an unwilling[ness], for whatever reason, to consent to life saving treatment . . . as suicidal;" and (3) a possibility, not established by evidence as a reasonable probability, that her mind might be impaired by toxicity caused by the gangrenous condition. His testimony, read closely, and in the context of the questions put to him, indicates that his opinion is not one of incompetency in the legal sense, but rather that her ability to make a rational choice (by which he means the *medically* rational choice) is impaired by the confusion existing in her mind by virtue of her consideration of irrational and emotional factors.

A careful analysis of the evidence in this case, including the superficially conflicting psychiatric testimony, indicates that there is no real conflict as to the underlying facts. Certainly, the evidence presents no issue of credibility. The principal question is whether the facts established by the evidence justify a conclusion of legal incompetence. The panel are unanimous in the opinion that they do not.

The decision of the judge, as well as the opinion of Dr. Kelley, predicates the necessity for the appointment of a guardian chiefly on the irrationality (in medical terms) of Mrs. Candura's decision to reject the amputation. Until she changed her original decision and withdrew her consent to the amputation, her competence was not questioned. But the irrationality of her decision does not justify a conclusion that Mrs. Candura is incompetent in the legal sense. The law protects her right to make her own decision to accept or reject treatment, whether that decision is wise or unwise. Compare *In re Estate of Brooks*, 32 Ill.2d 361, 205 N.E.2d 435 (1965).[7]

Similarly, the fact that she has vacillated in her resolve not to submit to the operation does not justify a conclusion that her capacity to make the decision is impaired to the point of legal incompetence. Indeed, her reaction may be readily understandable in the light of her prior surgical experience and the prospect of living the remainder of her life nonambulatory. Senile symptoms, in the abstract, may, of course, justify a finding of incompetence, but the inquiry must be more particular. What is lacking in this case is evidence that Mrs. Candura's areas of forgetfulness and confusion cause, or relate in any way to, impairment of her ability to understand that in rejecting the amputation she is, in effect, choosing death over life. This is not a case, therefore, like *In the Matter of Northern*, Tenn.App. (1978), in which the ward elected both to live and to reject an amputation operation, not appreciating that she must choose. Rather, this case is like *In the Matter of Quackenbush*, 156 N.J.Super. 282, 383 A.2d 785 (Morris County Ct. 1978), in which an elderly person, although subject (like Mrs. Candura) to fluctuations in mental lucidity and to occasional losses of his train of thought, was held to be competent to reject a proposed operation to amputate gangrenous legs because he was capable of appreciating the nature and consequences of his decision. See generally *In re Osborne*, 294 A.2d 372 (D.C. 1972) (guardianship to consent to blood transfusion denied); *In re Melideo*, 88 Misc.2d 974, 390 N.Y.S.2d 523 (1976) (court permission for blood transfusion denied); *In re Yetter*, 62 Pa.D. &

---

[7]In that case the court stated: "Even though we may consider appellant's beliefs unwise, foolish or ridiculous, in the absence of an overriding danger to society we may not permit interference therewith in the form of a conservatorship established in the waning hours of her life for the sole purpose of compelling her to accept medical treatment forbidden by her religious principles, and previously refused by her with full knowledge of the probable consequences." 32 Ill. at 373, 205 N.E.2d at 412. See *People* v. *Preveleta*, 74 Cal.App.3rd 936, 947–948, 141 Cal. Rptr. 764, 769–770 (1977) [Ct.App. 1977]. See also Burger, J., dissenting in *Application of President and Directors of Georgetown College, Inc.*, 118 U.S.App.D.C. 90, 97, 331 F.2d 1010, 1017 (1964).

C.2d 619 (1973) (guardianship to consent to biopsy and surgical removal of possible breast cancer denied, notwithstanding patient's delusions on some subjects). Contrast *Matter of Schiller,* 148 N.J.Super. 168, 372 A.2d 360 (1977), and *Application of L. I. Jewish-Hillside Medical Center,* 73 Misc.2d 395, 342 N.Y.S.2d 356 (1973), both amputation cases in which the patient was held to be incompetent.

Mrs. Candura's decision may be regarded by most as unfortunate, but on the record in this case it is not the uninformed decision of a person incapable of appreciating the nature and consequences of her act. We cannot anticipate whether she will reconsider and will consent to the operation, but we are all of the opinion that the operation may not be forced on her against her will.

The order appointing a temporary guardian and the judgment authorizing the temporary guardian to consent to the operation are reversed, and a new judgment is to enter dismissing the petition.

So ordered.

NOTES

1. What argument can be framed that an otherwise competent individual who refuses life-saving medical treatment thereby becomes incompetent? What public policies would be served by such a principle? What values would be sacrificed?

2. Another well publicized offspring of the *Saikewicz* decision is *In re Custody of a Minor,* ____ Mass. ____, 379 N.E.2d 1053 (1978), in which the court approved an order directing the administration, over the parents' objection, of chemotherapy to treat leukemia in a small boy. Unlike *Saikewicz,* the proposed treatment in *Custody of a Minor* was not a temporary, stop-gap measure:

> The expert testimony established that, in the child's case, chemotherapy was more than a brief means of prolonging life—it offered the child a substantial hope for cure. . . . The judge's order is supported by the physician's judgment that the child's life can be saved with chemotherapy (*Id.* at 379 N.E.2d 1067).

3. In *In re Vasko,* 238 A.D. 128, 263 N.Y.S. 552 (1933), the Appellate Division of the Supreme Court of New York reviewed an order of a Children's Court judge that authorized eye surgery upon a 2-year-old child despite the parents' refusal to give consent. Relying upon the testimony of a court-appointed physician at the lower court proceeding, the Appellate Division concurred with the conclusions of the judge:

> The report of the doctor's examination confirmed the hospital's eye clinic's diagnosis, and was to the effect that the eye is now permanently blind; that the growth is probably of a malignant nature, and will increase in size until it fills the eyeball, will then burst through it and protrude between the lids; that in all probability, if left to nature, it will follow the optic nerve into the brain, and "there is no doubt the child will die of it." This is indeed a tragic prospect for this child if left unaided by the surgeon's skill. In the opinion of the doctor, the child has an excellent chance of living if operated upon. He testified that statistics show a cure in something like 50 per cent of the cases.
>
> Medicine and surgery are not exact sciences, and the result of an operation may not be foretold with accuracy. Decision must be made, and the parents persist in their refusal to consent. Children come into the world helpless, subject to all the ills to which flesh is heir. They are entitled to the benefit of all laws made for their protection—whether

affecting their property, their personal rights, or their persons—by the Legislature, the sovereign power of the state. The learned court has acted in this case not only in strict compliance with the law, but with scrupulous care and moderation and upon ample and competent proof. His discretion should not be disturbed (*Id.* at 263 N.Y.S. 555-556).

c. Organ Donations

LITTLE v. LITTLE
Court of Civil Appeals of Texas, San Antonio, 1979
576 S.W.2d 493

OPINION

CADENA, Chief Justice

Anne Little, who has been adjudged incompetent, appeals through her attorney *ad litem* from an order of the probate court of Guadalupe County authorizing her mother and guardian, Margaret Little, to consent to a surgical procedure involving the removal of a kidney from Anne's body for the purpose of transplanting such kidney into the body of Anne's younger brother, Stephen, who is suffering from endstage renal disease.

On August 8, 1978, Anne, then aged 14, was declared to be of unsound mind and her mother, appellee here, was appointed guardian of the person and of the estate of Anne. No effort was made to proceed under the Limited Guardianship provisions of the Probate Code which make possible the appointment of a guardian without requiring a finding of mental incompetency. Tex.Prob.Code Ann. § 130A (Vernon Supp. 1978-1979). One week later, on August 15, 1978, the guardian filed this application for an order authorizing the transplant operation. The guardian, after alleging the nature of Stephen's illness and the fact that a kidney transplant is the only acceptable medical alternative to continued dialysis treatment for Stephen, pointed out that Anne is the only living related donor with acceptable matching characteristics and that permitting Anne to donate her kidney to her brother would be in Anne's best interest and would result in "great and tangible" benefits to her. The guardian added that the operation would present no threat to Anne's life and that "to the best of her ability and comprehension" Anne desires to donate her kidney to her brother and would do so if she were competent to make such decision.

The attorney *ad litem* appointed by the court to represent Anne's interests filed an answer opposing the operation and the authorization sought by the guardian on the ground that there was no constitutional or statutory provision empowering the probate court to authorize removal of an incompetent's kidney for the purpose of benefiting a person other than the incompetent. In this case this court has had the benefit of extremely helpful briefs by counsel for the guardian and the attorney *ad litem* as well as an extensively researched *amicus* brief filed by Advocacy, Incorporated, a nonprofit federally funded corporation dedicated to the protection of the rights of "developmentally disabled Texans." The brief filed by *amicus* in this case truly deserves the designation as a gesture by a "friend of the court"; it expresses no opinion on the question of whether the judgment of the probate court in this case should be affirmed or reversed, but limits itself to an effort to insure that this court be furnished with as much relevant information as possible.

The general rule in this State is that a minor cannot consent to medical or surgical treatment. No claim is here made that this case comes within the statutory exceptions to this rule. See Tex.Fam.Code Ann. § 35.03 (Vernon 1975). Persons adjudged to be mentally incompetent share the same disability to consent to medical or surgical treatment. See 45 Tex.Jur.2d, *Physicians and Other Healers* § 101 (1963). Parents whose parental rights have not been terminated and managing conservators of minors are authorized to consent to medical and surgical treatment of minors. Tex.Fam.Code Ann. §§ 12.04(6), 14.02(b)(5). The guardian of a mentally incompetent person has the same powers and duties as does the managing conservator of a minor. *In re Guardianship of Henson*, 551 S.W.2d 136 (Tex.Civ.App.—Corpus Christi 1977, writ ref'd n.r.e.). Significantly, however, for our purposes, this power of parents, managing conservators and guardians to consent to surgical intrusions upon the person of the minor or ward is limited to the power to consent to medical "treatment." See Tex.Fam.Code Ann. § 12.04(6) (Vernon Supp. 1978–1979); Tex.Prob. Code Ann. § 229 (Vernon 1956); *In re Guardianship of Henson*, 551 S.W.2d 136 (Tex.Civ.App.—Corpus Christi 1977, writ ref'd n.r.e.). Even ascribing to the word "treatment" its broadest definition, it is, nevertheless, limited to "the steps taken to effect a cure of an injury or disease . . . including examination and diagnosis as well as application of remedies." Black's Law Dictionary 1673 (rev. 4th ed. 1968).

We cannot accept the guardian's argument that a donor nephrectomy constitutes medical treatment for the donor. In this case the ward's mental incompetency results from the fact that she suffers from Down's Syndrome, often called "mongolism," which is caused by a "specific chromosomal abnormality which occurs most frequently as an unpredictable non-disjunction of autosome 21" or, less frequently, "as the Mendelian transmission of a translocated portion of autosome 21." See President's Comm. on Mental Retardation, Mental Retardation: Past and Present, at 149 (1977). Since the guardian does not contend that removal of a kidney is a medically acceptable method of curing or treating Down's Syndrome, Family Code Sections 12.04(6) and 14.02(b)(5) are inapplicable. We think it is clear that the medical procedure authorized by the probate court in this case constitutes "treatment" of the ward's brother, Stephen, and that the proposed medical procedure has as its purpose curing, remedying or ameliorating the condition of the proposed donee of the ward's kidney. The fact that the proposed surgical procedure cannot be classified as medical treatment of the ward in this case is made apparent by the medical testimony that a donor nephrectomy is medically acceptable, generally, only if the donor is in good health. All of the testimony in this case stresses the fact that the ward is being considered as a donor only because she is in good health and there are no signs of the upper respiratory problems and hypertension frequently associated with mongolism.

Our legislature has not specifically addressed the problem of organ transplants in cases where the proposed donor is a minor or a non-resident mental incompetent who is incapable of giving legally adequate consent to the surgical invasion of his body. The Anatomical Gift Act deals exclusively with anatomical gifts to take effect upon the death of the donor and limits such donations by living persons to those who have testamentary capacity under the Probate Code, although it does provide for gifts of bodies, or parts of bodies, of deceased persons by specified survivors. Tex.Rev.Civ.Stat.Ann. art. 4590-2 (Vernon 1976).

We are not persuaded by the guardian's argument that the Mentally Retarded Persons Act of 1977 can be construed as a legislative recognition of the right of a minor or mental incompetent to participate as a donor in an organ transplant operation. Tex.Rev.Civ.Stat.Ann. art. 5547-300 (Vernon Supp. 1978-1979). Subchapter E, section 24(c) of that statute expressly prohibits the Texas Department of Mental Health and Mental Retardation from performing unusually hazardous treatment procedures, experimental research, nontherapeutic surgery for experimental research or organ transplantations on residents of state institutions for the mentally retarded. The guardian contends that the legislature, by enacting such restrictions on the Department, must have acted on the belief that the Department, absent such prohibition, would have the authority to engage in these prohibited activities. The guardian further infers that since the statute imposes no restrictions on donations of organs by "non-resident" incompetents, the legislature must therefore have intended to permit the donation of organs by such non-residents.

We reject guardian's argument as being untenable. If guardian's theory of statutory construction is adopted a court would have to hold that a guardian or court can consent to the performance of unusually dangerous nontherapeutic surgery on a non-resident ward, which may have no benefit to the ward. We think that section 24(c) can be explained as reflecting legislative familiarity with widespread reports, whether true or not, regarding exploitation of "residents" of governmental institutions who are unwilling or less than fully informed participants in programs sought to be justified as attempts to achieve medical or scientific "progress." Further, we cannot logically construe section 24(c) as permitting transplants on non-residents while rejecting such interpretation as to experimental nontherapeutic surgery or other highly dangerous experimental medical procedures.

The guardian relies heavily on the decision of the Kentucky Court in *Strunk* v. *Strunk*, 445 S.W.2d 145 (Ky. 1969). In that case, the proposed donee of the kidney was suffering from endstage renal disease, as is Stephen in the case before us, and, again, like Stephen, he was being kept alive by hemodialysis, which consists of filtering the blood of the afflicted person through an external artificial kidney. The donee's brother in *Strunk* was an institutionalized ward of the state who had an I.Q. of about 35, was tested and was found highly compatible as the donor of the required kidney. The "committee" of the incompetent (analogous to a guardian under the Texas law), who was the mother of both the incompetent and the victim of the renal disease, petitioned the court for authority to consent to the transplant, using the kidney of the incompetent. The court, by a 4-3 decision, authorized the transplant, apparently relying on four grounds:

(1) The power of equity to provide for others from the estate of an incompetent, as the incompetent himself would do if not disabled, applies to matters of "personal affairs" as well as to matters of property. This doctrine of "substituted judgment" is broad enough to encompass "all matters touching on the well-being of the ward," including the donation of a kidney for his psychological benefit. 445 S.W.2d at 148;

(2) Psychiatric testimony supported the conclusion that the operation would be beneficial to the incompetent because his brother's death would be psychologically detrimental. The court was also apparently impressed by the argument of *amicus*, the

Kentucky Department of Mental Health, which pointed out that mental defectives have a need for close intimacy and that since the defective identified with his ill brother and the family, the sick brother's life was vital to the incompetent's well-being. *Amicus* also argued that the incompetent's awareness that he could play a vital role in easing familial tensions would generate feelings of guilt if the incompetent failed to act and his brother died. *Id.* at 146-47;

(3) The chance of a successful kidney transplant is greatly increased where donor and donee are genetically related. *Id.* at 148;

(4) The operation involved only minimal risk to the donor. *Id.* at 148-49.

No useful purpose would be served by detailing the evidence in this case. We will merely say that the evidence before us closely parallels that on which the Kentucky court relied in *Strunk*. Additionally, there was medical testimony in this case that, for purposes of a kidney transplant, the ward and Stephen were a perfect "match," and that the use of any other member of the family or a non-related donor would significantly lessen the chances for a successful transplant. The undisputed testimony here also established that the chances of obtaining a suitable kidney from a cadaver were extremely remote.

Judicial approval for intra-family transplants from incompetent donors has been granted in most cases. Robertson, *Organ Donations by Incompetents and the Substituted Judgment Doctrine,* 76 Colum.L.Rev. 48, 53 (1976). In at least two cases, however, courts have refused to authorize transplants from incompetent donors. *Lausier* v. *Pescinski,* 67 Wis.2d 4, 226 N.W.2d 180 (1975); *In re Richardson,* 284 So.2d 185 (La.Ct.App.), *cert. denied,* 284 So.2d 338 (La. 1973). In *Lausier,* the court justified its refusal to authorize a transplant by noting the absence of specific statutory authority and calling attention to Wisconsin decisions denying the power of a guardian to make gifts from the estate of his ward. However, the following language in the opinion is, perhaps, significant:

> An incompetent particularly should have his own interests protected. Certainly no advantage should be taken of him. In the absence of real consent on his part, and in a situation where no benefit to him has been established, we fail to find any authority for the county court, or this court, to approve this operation.

226 N.W.2d at 182. The lone dissenter brushed aside "benefit" to the incompetent as "pretty thin soup on which to base a decision as to whether or not the donee is to be permitted to live," but would have permitted the transplant by applying the substituted judgment doctrine's standard which would make the decision turn on what the donor would do if he were competent, concluding that in all probability the incompetent would consent because for him "it would be a short period of discomfort which would not affect his ability either to enjoy life or his longevity." *Id.* at 182-83. The dissenter did not choose to explain how ignoring benefits to the incompetent while speculating as to the choice the donor would make if competent would result in a "thicker soup."

In *Richardson,* the Louisiana court, in refusing to authorize the operation, pointed out that the facts in *Strunk,* "particularly the conclusion relative to the 'best interest' of the incompetent, are not similar to the facts in the instant case...." 284 So.2d at 187. The court also pointed out that under Louisiana law a guardian is prohibited from making any donations of the ward's property.

Since our law affords this unqualified protection against intrusion into a comparatively mere property right, it is inconceivable to us that it affords less protection to a minor's right to be free in his person from bodily intrusion to the extent of loss of an organ unless such loss be in the best interest of the minor.

Id. The court then noted that such statement and its conclusion were "restricted to the facts of the present case."

The substituted judgment doctrine was apparently first applied in 1816 by Lord Eldon. Its stated purpose was to authorize gifts from an incompetent's estate to persons to whom the incompetent owed no duty of support. *Ex parte Whitebread,* 35 Eng.Rep. 878. The doctrine is based on the principle that a court will not refuse to act if it is probable that the incompetent would have taken the same action had he been normal. The doctrine requires that the court "substitute itself as nearly as may be for the incompetent and to act upon the same motives and considerations as would have moved" the incompetent. *City Bank Farmers Trust Co.* v. *McGowan,* 323 U.S. 594, 599, 65 S.Ct. 496, 498, 89 L.Ed. 483 (1945).

The substituted judgment doctrine has been adopted in some jurisdictions and rejected in others. See Comment, *Gifts by Guardians: Texas Rejects Substitution of Judgment Doctrine,* 19 Baylor L.Rev. 411, 418-30 (1967). In Texas, it has been held that the guardian of the estate of an incompetent lacks the power to make a gift from the estate of the ward, even though the evidence establishes that the ward, if competent, would have made such a gift. *In re Guardianship of Estate of Neal,* 406 S.W.2d 496 (Tex.Civ.App.—Houston [1st Dist.]), *writ ref'd n.r.e. per curiam,* 407 S.W.2d 770 (Tex. 1966). Significantly, in refusing the application for writ of error, the Supreme Court expressly approved the holding of the Court of Civil Appeals that the proposed gift did not satisfy the requirements of the Probate Code and that "the probate court is without power to authorize the same even though it appears (1) that the ward, if competent, would make the gift, and (2) that a prudent man owning and managing the ward's estate would make the gift." 407 S.W.2d at 771. The purpose of the gift to the residuary legatees under the ward's will was to minimize estate taxes which would become due upon the death of the ward, and the trial court found that the proposed gift, if permitted, would reduce estate taxes by a minimum of $240,000.00. The evidence showed that prior to the onset of her incompetence, the ward had made gifts to the proposed donees totaling approximately $2,500,000.00 and that such gifts were at least partially motivated by a desire to minimize estate taxes by reducing the size of her estate. Subsequent to the *Neal* decision the Probate Code was amended to permit a guardian to make gifts from the ward's estate under certain circumstances for the purpose of minimizing estate taxes. Tex.Prob.Code Ann. § 230(b)(2) (Vernon Supp. 1978-1979).

It is clear in transplant cases that courts, whether they use the term "substituted judgment" or not, will consider the benefits to the donor as a basis for permitting an incompetent to donate an organ. Although in *Strunk* the Kentucky Court discussed the substituted judgment doctrine in some detail, the conclusion of the majority there was based on the benefits that the incompetent donor would derive, rather than on the theory that the incompetent would have consented to the transplant if he were competent. We adopt this approach. As already pointed out, the courts in *Lausier* and

Richardson, in refusing to approve the transplant operations on the basis of the substituted judgment doctrine, pointed to the lack of evidence showing that the incompetent donors would realize benefits from the operations. In *Neal,* the case which is frequently referred to as rejecting the substituted judgment doctrine in Texas, the detailed findings of fact by the trial court made no mention of any benefit to the person of the incompetent, as distinguished from benefit to the estate of the ward—a benefit which would not be realized until after the death of the ward. The Supreme Court's approval of the civil appeals holding in *Neal* does no more than assert that a gift of the ward's property is not authorized merely because it is established that the ward, if competent, would make the gift and that a prudent man owning and managing the estate would make the gift. Thus, there is no Texas case holding that an action by a guardian is unauthorized where the ward, if competent, would so act, and such action would result in benefits to the ward which he would enjoy during his lifetime.

We do not assert that the evidence in this case is sufficient to establish that Anne has the mental capacity to fully understand the concept of death. The suggestion, accepted in *Strunk,* that an incompetent potential donor would be subjected to feelings of guilt if his sibling died because the transplant did not take place may also, perhaps, be taken with a grain of salt. But the testimony in this case conclusively establishes the existence of a close relationship between Anne and Stephen, a genuine concern by each for the welfare of the other and, at the very least, an awareness by Anne of the nature of Stephen's plight and an awareness of the fact that she is in a position to ameliorate Stephen's burden. Assuming that Anne is incapable of understanding the nature of death, there is ample evidence to the effect that she understands the concept of absence and that she is unhappy on the occasions when Stephen must leave home for hours when he journeys to San Antonio for dialysis. It may be conceded that the state of development of the behavioral arts is such that the testimony of psychiatrists and psychologists must still be classified as speculative, but, as of today, that has not been accepted as justifying a judicial rejection of the value of such testimony. Indeed, on the basis of such speculative testimony, citizens are deprived of their freedom so that they may be treated for mental illness, and in criminal prosecutions persons are condemned to death on the basis of psychiatric testimony concerning their propensity to engage in certain types of conduct in the future.

Nor is it fair to say that the evidence concerning "psychological" benefits to Anne consists merely of testimony as to the prevention of detrimental effects which she may suffer if Stephen dies. The testimony is not limited to the prevention of sadness. There is uncontradicted testimony relating to increased happiness. Studies of persons who have donated kidneys reveal resulting positive benefits such as heightened self-esteem, enhanced status in the family, renewed meaning in life, and other positive feelings including transcendental or peak experiences flowing from their gift of life to another. Robertson, *supra,* 76 Colum.L.Rev. at 68; Arrow, *Gifts and Exchanges,* 1 Philos. & Public Affairs 343 (1972); Fellner, *Organ Donation—For Whose Sake?,* 79 Annals of Internal Medicine 589 (1973). The record before us indicates that Anne is capable of experiencing such an increase in personal welfare from donating her kidney.

The medical experts who testified in this case conceded that Anne would experience pain and discomfort, but they all referred to it as minimal, and there is evidence that Anne has a high pain threshold. There is, however, the possibility that Anne, because of her limited intellectual development, may be less able to understand the transplant procedures or to adapt to the unfamiliar surroundings of a hospital, so that her ordeal may be more burdensome than that of a normal adult. We must assume that all of these possibilities were carefully weighed by the trial judge, who had the opportunity to observe Anne and to hear her unsworn answers to questions, some of which were suggested by the court.

The circumstances of this case may be fairly summarized as follows:

(1) The parents and guardian of Anne consent to the kidney donation by Anne;

(2) Although Anne's statement that she was willing to donate her kidney to her brother cannot be realistically viewed as a knowing consent, there is no evidence indicating that she has been subjected to family pressure and the trial judge took the precaution, at the close of the testimony and before he announced his decision, of requesting and obtaining a physical and psychological evaluation of Anne;

(3) The evidence establishes that without a transplant Stephen will, at the very least, suffer severe and progressive deterioration, and that there are no medically preferable alternatives to a kidney transplant for Stephen;

(4) The dangers of the operation are minimal. Since she is in good health, the risks to Anne are small, and there is evidence that she will not suffer psychological harm;

(5) The evidence establishes that neither long-term dialysis nor a cadaver transplant or transplant from other living donors is medically acceptable;

(6) Stephen will probably benefit substantially from the transplant, and the risk to him from the operation, including long-term risks, are medically acceptable;

(7) The trial court's decision to authorize the operation was made only after a full judicial proceeding in which the interests of Anne were championed by an attorney *ad litem,* appointed by the court. The attorney *ad litem* has assumed an adversarial role, asserting the child's interest in not being a donor and vigorously questioning the power of the court to authorize the operation. This is not a case where the attorney *ad litem* assumed a purely passive role, participating in the hearing merely to rubber-stamp the guardian's decision while giving to the proceedings the outward appearance of compliance with due process requirements.

Given the presence of all the factors and circumstances outlined above, and limiting our decision to such facts and circumstances, we conclude that the trial court did not exceed its authority by authorizing the participation of Anne in the kidney transplant as a donor, since there is strong evidence to the effect that she will receive substantial psychological benefits from such participation. Nothing in this opinion is to be construed as being applicable to a situation where the proposed donee is not a parent or sibling of the incompetent.

We consider it proper and judicious to suggest that the problem of organ donations by incompetents can be more effectively addressed by the legislature, whose members can promulgate standards based on expert medical, psychiatric and psychological information, as well as testimony and experience of social workers which is not readily available to the judiciary. While we believe that the limited nature of our decision in this case will prevent the exploitation of minors and mental incompetents, we acknowledge that legislators are better qualified to conduct the necessary investigations which will yield a system of rules to adequately protect minors and other incompetents from exploitation without denying them such benefits as competent adults may derive from the organ-donating experience.

The judgment of the trial court is affirmed.

NOTES

1. *Little* v. *Little* is a very recent example of judicial attitudes on the issue of kidney donations by substitute judgment. In light of *Strunk* v. *Strunk, Lausier* v. *Pescinski,* and *In re Richardson* discussed in *Little,* does the *Little* case suggest any modern trend in such cases, or does each case rise or fall on its own facts and circumstances?

2. Since all minors in such situations are incompetent to give valid informed consent to kidney donation surgery, why do the legal issues raised in *Little, Lausier, Strunk,* and *Richardson* rarely come to the courts in cases involving nonhandicapped children as potential donors? Is a value judgment being made regarding the relative worth of handicapped persons?

3. For an extensive discussion of these and other organ donation cases, see Robertson, J., "Organ Donations by Incompetents and the Substituted Judgment Doctrine," 76 *Colum. L. Rev.* 48 (1976).

d. Electroconvulsive Therapy, Psychosurgery, and Nonconsensual Drug Therapy

NEW YORK CITY HEALTH & HOSP. CORP. v. STEIN

Supreme Court of New York, Special Term, New York County, Part I, 1972
70 Misc.2d 944, 335 N.Y.S.2d 461

ABRAHAM J. GELLINOFF, Justice:

This is an application by the New York City Health and Hospitals Corporation, and the Associate Director of Bellevue Hospital, for an order authorizing the psychiatric staff of Bellevue Hospital to administer electroshock therapy to a patient Paula Stein, the respondent herein. Mrs. Stein has objected to this treatment, and refuses to give her consent to it.

This Court, on July 11, 1972, after a hearing conducted at Bellevue Hospital, concluded that respondent was mentally ill; accordingly this Court issued an order authorizing the retention of the patient for care and treatment [Mental Hygiene Law, § 72]. Therefore, the psychiatric staff at Bellevue Hospital, and any other hospital to which the patient may be transferred, is now free to carry out whatever course of treatment they deem advisable, including electroshock therapy, regardless of the patient's consent and without the necessity of prior judicial approval.

However, petitioners have commendably chosen to proceed in accordance with the spirit of the new recodification of the Mental Hygiene Law, Section 15.03, effective January 1, 1973, which provides that, "subject to the regulations of the commissioner [of the department of mental hygiene], the director of a facility shall require . . . consent for . . . shock treatment.'' Although the statute is silent as to whose consent is required, and no regulations by the Commissioner in this regard have been brought to the Court's attention, the new statute presumably requires the consent of the patient himself, provided he possesses the mental capacity to knowingly consent or withhold his consent, or, in the absence of such mental capacity, the consent of the closest relative, or guardian of the person, if there be any, or, where necessary, of the Court [see, *Anonymous* v. *State,* 17 A.D.2d 495, 236 N.Y.S.2d 88 (3rd Dept. 1963)]. In this case, the patient's mother has given her consent, for, seeking only the health of her daughter, she has consented to the doctors doing whatever they believe might help her. The patient herself, however, continues in her refusal to consent.

Petitioners are reluctant to proceed with the electroshock therapy on the consent of the mother only, and assert that consent of the patient herself should be dispensed with herein, on the ground that she is incompetent to make a reasoned decision, and that the Court should authorize petitioners to administer such electroshock therapy despite the patient's non-consent.

Electroshock therapy is a technique by which a current of from 70 to 130 volts of electricity is permitted to flow through the patient's brain, causing a convulsion equivalent to an epileptic seizure. This form of treatment is the subject of great controversy within the psychiatric profession, both as to its efficacy, and as to its dangers. It has been known to aid significantly in the cure of the mentally ill, as well as to cause such other ailments as pulmonary edema, bone fractures, and, in exceedingly rare instances, even death.

In a case such as this, where the determination may be critical to the future health and life of a patient suffering from mental disorder, a court, not blessed with omniscience, must tread cautiously. It must consider both the benefits to be derived if its decision is correct, and also the costs of error. It must make what the late Mr. Justice Harlan described as ''a very fundamental assessment of the comparative social [and in this case personal] costs of erroneous factual determinations'' [*In Re Winship,* 397 U.S. 358, 370, 90 S.Ct. 1068, 1075, 25 L.Ed.2d 368 (1970) (concurring opinion)]. On the one hand is the possibility of harm, conceivably even fatal harm, serving no useful purpose, if the Court erroneously permits the treatment. On the other hand is the fear of petitioners' staff that ''if this treatment is not undertaken and completed the patient's condition will be significantly impaired to the extent of possible irreversibility.''

The choice is hardly a simple one. But since obviously the greatest suffering from an incorrect decision will be borne by respondent herself, the Court must permit her refusal to be determinative unless the evidence is sufficient to convince the Court that she lacks the mental capacity to knowingly consent or withhold her consent.

The evidence adduced at the hearing on this application has left the issue far from conclusively resolved. Eminent and learned psychiatric specialists have testified before the Court—both as to respondent's capacity to know and understand the nature and extent of her illness and the consequences of her refusal to consent to electroshock treatment, as well as to the desirability of electroshock treatment in her circumstances—and have reached different conclusions. All of the witnesses are agreed that respondent suffers from schizophrenia which is chronic, probably undifferentiated, with tendencies for acute flare-ups. And almost all are agreed that she continues to require psychiatric treatment within a structured environment. But there is a sharp dispute as to what form that treatment should take.

The doctors produced by petitioner testified that, since respondent did not respond to conventional psychopharmacological treatment, and in view of her marked improvement after two electroshock treatments, electroshock treatment is the treatment of choice for her condition, and that respondent "is not now nor was she during any period of her hospitalization able to make a rational judgment about any treatment she might require."

On the other hand, the independent psychiatrists permitted by this court to examine respondent [Judiciary Law, § 35(3)] have concluded that "she has the mental competence to consent or withhold consent for her treatment and to participate with her physicians in the choice of appropriate treatment modalities." Moreover, they conclude, "electro-convulsive therapy is not clinically indicated"—urging instead the use of drugs such as phenothiazines.

From all of the evidence before the Court, as well as from its own observations of respondent, the Court has concluded that she is sufficiently mentally ill to require further retention. However, that determination does not imply that she lacks the mental capacity to knowingly consent or withhold her consent to electroshock therapy. After considering all the evidence, including the Court's own conversations with respondent in open court in the presence of all the doctors, the Court concludes that respondent does have the mental capacity to know and understand whether she wishes to consent to electroshock therapy. It does not matter whether this Court would agree with her judgment; it is enough that she is capable of making a decision, however unfortunate that decision may prove to be. It is her own well-being that is at stake, and, giving effect to the spirit of Mental Hygiene Law, Section 15.03 (effective January 1, 1973), she must be permitted to consent or withhold her consent.

The application is accordingly denied.

NOTES

1.   Is the court's ultimate holding in the *Stein* case consistent with its observation early in the opinion that the hospital is free to carry out electroshock therapy or any other treatment without the mentally ill patient's consent or prior judicial approval? Is not the holding in *Stein* premised upon the principle that even a person committed as mentally ill to a facility can have sufficient mental capacity to make a binding decision as to whether or not to undergo electroconvulsive therapy?

2.   In *Anonymous* v. *State,* 17 A.D.2d 495, 236 N.Y.S.2d 88 (1963), mentioned in *Stein,* another New York court had upheld a father's written consent to the performance of shock therapy on his adult mentally ill son. The court declared that

> . . . absent an emergency the consent of a parent to the performance of an operation on a minor child is required. Analogy dictates . . . that he is authorized to speak in behalf of a mentally ill adult for whom no committee of the person has been appointed (*Id.* at 236 N.Y.S.2d 90).

Is this adequate analysis of the legal issues in the context of electroshock? The current validity of the *Anonymous* reasoning is doubtful in light of subsequent decisions; see, e.g., *Price* v. *Sheppard,* below; *Aden* v. *Younger,* pp. 824–837, below; *Wyatt* v. *Stickney,* discussed at p. 838n.3, below.

3. Statutes in some states mandate that consent be sought from patients for whom electroconvulsive therapy is prescribed, e.g., Cal. Welf. and Inst'ns. Code §§ 5325 (f) and (g) (West Supp. 1977); N.Y. Mental Hygiene Law § 15.03(b)(4) (1975); Wash. Rev. Code Ann. § 71.05.370(7) (1975). See *Aden* v. *Younger,* pp. 824–837, below.

PRICE v. SHEPPARD

Supreme Court of Minnesota, 1976
239 N.W.2d 905

Considered and decided by the court en banc.

Yetka, Justice.

This appeal from a summary judgment entered in the Ramsey County District Court involves an action against the medical director of the Minnesota Security Hospital at St. Peter, Dr. Charles G. Sheppard, for (1) assault and battery, and (2) violation of plaintiff Dwight Price's civil rights under 42 U.S.C.A. § 1983. The claims arise out of the administration of a series of 20 electroshock treatments, given against the express wishes of plaintiff Willa Mae Price, Dwight's mother and natural guardian, while Dwight, a minor, was under involuntary commitment in the Minnesota Security Hospital at St. Peter.

Defendant's motion for summary judgment on Count I, alleging assault and battery, was granted March 22, 1974, based on the court's ruling that the defendant, acting in his official capacity, was immune from suit. Summary judgment was also granted on Count IV, alleging violation of Dwight's civil rights, on November 29, 1974. The court ruled that the electroshock treatments were neither cruel and unusual punishment under the Eighth Amendment of the United States Constitution, nor a violation of Dwight's right to privacy. We affirm.

Dwight Price was committed to the Hastings State Hospital September 8, 1971, by order of the Ramsey County Probate Court, which found Dwight to be "mentally ill–inebriate." The commitment petition was brought by Dwight's mother, Willa Mae Price, apparently in order to secure treatment for Dwight for a developing drug and alcohol problem. Several attempts at voluntary treatment, prior to the commitment proceedings, had proved unsuccessful.

Shortly after being admitted to Hastings, Dwight allegedly attempted to strangle one of the hospital staff. Because Hastings was not equipped to handle dangerous patients, Dwight was transferred to the Security Hospital at St. Peter on September 11, 1971.

Dwight's condition, upon his admission at St. Peter, was diagnosed as simple schizophrenia. He was treated with tranquilizing and antidepressant medications, but apparently failed to respond and continued to be aggressive and assaultive to the staff and other patients. For this reason, Dr. Sheppard prescribed electroshock therapy.

He sought Mrs. Price's consent to administer the electroshock treatments. Through her attorney Mrs. Price arranged for an independent medical examination by Dr. William Chalgren, a Mankato psychiatrist, for the purpose of determining the advisability of the proposed treatment. Dr. Chalgren examined Dwight November 27, 1971, and recommended that drug treatment continue but that if Dwight did not respond favorably, electroshock treatment be given.

Dr. Chalgren's recommendations were followed by the staff at St. Peter, but Dwight's condition did not improve. Accordingly, on December 22, 1971, without the consent of Mrs. Price, electroshock therapy began and was continued to February 11, 1972. Dwight was released from St. Peter June 19, 1972.

The issues raised on this appeal are:

(1) Does the administration of electroshock therapy to an involuntarily committed minor patient of a state mental hospital, without the consent of the minor's guardian, violate his rights (a) to be free from cruel and unusual punishment, and (b) of privacy?

(2) Is a state official entitled to immunity from an action for damages for acts performed by him in good faith and which he could not reasonably have known would violate the constitutional rights of another?

1. We do not agree with the claim that the electroshock therapy was cruel and unusual punishment for the reason that the record does not suggest, nor have plaintiffs demonstrated, how those treatments, under the circumstances of this case, can be regarded as "punishment." While plaintiffs are certainly correct in the statement that the characterization of electroshock therapy by defendant as "treatment" does not insulate it from Eighth Amendment scrutiny, that alone does not establish that the treatments were "punishment."

The Supreme Court's decision in *Trop* v. *Dulles,* 356 U.S. 86, 78 S.Ct. 590, 2 L.Ed.2d 630 (1958), involving the question of whether a law which provided for loss of United States citizenship upon conviction of desertion from the military violated the Eighth Amendment, is instructive.

> ... In deciding whether or not a law is penal, this Court has generally based its determination upon the purpose of the statute. If the statute imposes a disability for the purposes of punishment—that is, to reprimand the wrongdoer, to deter others, etc.—it has been considered penal. But a statute has been considered nonpenal if it imposes a disability, not to punish, but to accomplish some other legitimate governmental purpose. The court has recognized that any statute decreeing some adversity as a consequence of certain conduct may have both a penal and a nonpenal effect. The controlling nature of such statutes normally depends on the evident purpose of the legislature. The point may be illustrated by the situation of an ordinary felon. A person who commits a bank robbery, for instance, loses his right to liberty and often his right to vote. If, in the exercise of the power to protect banks, both sanctions were imposed for the purpose of punishing bank robbers, the statutes authorizing both disabilities would be penal. But because the purpose of the latter statute is to designate a reasonable ground of eligibility for voting, this law is sustained as a nonpenal exercise of the power to regulate the franchise. (356 U.S. 96, 78 S.Ct. 595, 2 L.Ed.2d 639.)

Applying the *Trop* rationale, if the electroshock treatments given the minor plaintiff served legitimate purpose rather than deterrence or reprimand, the Eighth Amendment claim must fail. Cf. *Knecht* v. *Gillman,* 488 F.2d 1136, 1138 (8 Cir. 1973).

It is difficult to perceive, on the record before the court, how the electroshock therapy administered to the plaintiff could be regarded as anything but treatment. The purpose of Dwight's presence in the state's mental hospital system was not to reprimand him or deter him from certain behavior but rather for the treatment of his mental problems and developing chemical dependency. Moreover, the decision to administer electroshock therapy was not triggered by any single incident nor did it involve an isolated treatment, both of which would be more characteristic of punishment. Rather, the decision to administer a series of 20 treatments over a substantial period of time was made after other forms of treatment failed to show any curative effect on Dwight's condition, diagnosed as schizophrenia.

The circumstances of this case are simply unlike those presented in *Knecht* v. *Gillman, supra*. Inmates of the Iowa Security Medical Facility, confined there for examination, diagnosis, and treatment of mental disorders, for minor violations of hospital protocol, were given injections of a drug which caused the inmate to vomit for 15 minutes to an hour. Although characterized as aversive therapy, the apparent purpose of administering the drug in response to a violation of protocol was to reprimand the inmate.

In *Inmates of Boys' Training School* v. *Afflect*, 346 F.Supp. 1354 (D.R.I. 1972), also cited by plaintiffs in support of their claim, the retributive nature of the challenged conduct is even more clear. For committing infractions of the institution's rules, inmates of a juvenile corrections institution were isolated in cold, dark cells containing only a toilet and mattress. Finally, in *Vann* v. *Scott*, 467 F.2d 1235 (7 Cir. 1972), cited by plaintiffs, the court did not decide whether the incarceration of runaway juveniles was punishment but on the contrary indicated that under some circumstances, where it served the purpose of safeguarding the lives and welfare of juveniles, it would not be. Cf. *Robinson* v. *California*, 370 U.S. 660, 82 S.Ct. 1417, 8 L.Ed.2d 758 (1962).

Under the circumstances of this case, where electroshock therapy involving multiple treatments over a substantial period of time was prescribed for an involuntarily committed patient of a state mental hospital who had failed to respond to other forms of treatment, we hold that the administration of such electroshock treatments, absent the effective consent of the patient or his guardian, is not cruel or unusual punishment.

2. Plaintiffs' second claimed violation of the minor's civil rights—the right of privacy—is more troublesome, primarily because that emerging right is currently so ill-defined. While its origins are said to date back to the late nineteenth century, its birth as an independent constitutional right, clearly denominated as such, is generally regarded as coming in *Griswold* v. *Connecticut*, 381 U.S. 479, 85 S.Ct. 1678, 14 L.Ed.2d 510 (1965), where the court overturned a statute prohibiting the use of contraceptives by married couples.

The right has since served as the basis of decisions striking down a Georgia statute prohibiting possession of obscene materials in one's home, *Stanley* v. *Georgia*, 394 U.S. 557, 89 S.Ct. 1243, 22 L.Ed.2d 542 (1969); extending the *Griswold* ruling to include unmarried individuals, *Eisenstadt* v. *Baird*, 405 U.S. 438, 92 S.Ct. 1029, 31 L.Ed.2d 349 (1972); and overturning a Texas statute prohibiting abortions, *Roe* v. *Wade*, 410 U.S. 113, 93 S.Ct. 705, 35 L.Ed.2d 147 (1973). The right remains, however, an extremely amorphous one.

We recognize that it is far too early in the evolution of the right of privacy to offer any single definition or rule of what the right entails. Only its broadest contours have been sketched. We do feel, however, because of the importance of that emerging right, it is appropriate for us, at this time, to set forth more than our bare conclusion that the right of privacy is or is not involved.

At the core of the privacy decisions, in our judgment, is the concept of personal autonomy—the notion that the Constitution reserves to the individual, free of governmental intrusion, certain fundamental decisions about how he or she will conduct his or her life. Like other constitutional rights, however, this right is not an absolute one and must give way to certain interests of the state, the balance turning on the impact of the decision on the life of the individual. As the impact increases, so must the importance of the state's interest. Some decisions, we assume, will be of little consequence to the individual and a showing of a legitimate state interest will justify its intrusion; other decisions, on the other hand, will be of such major consequence that only the most compelling state interest will justify the intrusion.

But once justified, the extent of the state's intrusion is not unlimited. It must also appear that the means utilized to serve the state's interest are necessary and reasonable, or, in other words, in light of alternative means, the least intrusive.

To summarize, our understanding of at least one aspect of the privacy decisions to date is that where the state proposes to intrude into a fundamental decision affecting the conduct of an individual's life, in order to justify that intrusion, it must first demonstrate a legitimate and important state interest. The sufficiency of the interest will be directly dependent on the impact of the decision on the individual's life. And secondly, the means it intends to utilize in serving that interest must, in light of the alternatives, be the least intrusive.

The question in the case before us is whether the state, consistent with Dwight Price's right of privacy, can assume the decision of whether Dwight, an involuntarily committed mental patient, will undergo psychiatric treatment. We observe that the more fundamental decision, whether he was to undergo hospitalization, was assumed by the state at the commitment proceeding, the validity of which is not contested.

The impact of the decision on the individual is unquestionably great, for the result is the alteration of the patient's personality. The state's interest in assuming the decision is in acting as *parens patriae,* fulfilling its duty to protect the well-being of its citizens who are incapable of so acting for themselves. Under the circumstances of this case, that interest can be articulated as the need for the state to assume the decision-making role regarding the psychiatric treatment for one who, presumptively, based on the fact of commitment on the ground of mental illness, is unable to *rationally* do so for himself. If that interest of the state is sufficiently important to deprive an individual of his physical liberty, it would seem to follow that it would be sufficiently important for the state to assume the treatment decision. We hold that it is.

Under the *parens patriae* rationale, an individual may be committed when he lacks capacity to make a rational decision concerning hospitalization, and the treatment or custodial care available would be beneficial enough to outweigh the deprivations which commitment would impose on him. Inherent in an adjudication that an individual should be committed under the state's *parens patriae* power is the decision that he can be forced to accept the treatments found to be in his best interest; it would be incongruous if an individual who lacks capacity to make a treatment decision could frustrate the very justification for the state's action by refusing such treatments. Note, *Developments in the Law—Civil Commitment of the Mentally Ill,* 87 Harv.L.Rev. 1190, 1344 (1974).

The more important question, we believe, involved in the state's assumption of the treatment decision is the necessity and reasonableness of the means utilized by the state in treating an involuntarily committed patient. The techniques generally available to treat psychological disorders range in degree of severity and coerciveness from the least intrusive forms such as milieu therapy (behavior changes produced by manipulation of the patient's environment) and psychoanalysis, to drug, aversion, or electroconvulsive therapy, and ultimately to psychosurgery. Some of these techniques require the voluntary participation of the patient in order to be effective, while others can be effective when involuntarily imposed. As the techniques increase in severity, so do the risks of serious and long-lasting psychological or neurological damage.

Whether the administration of electroshock treatments, one of the most intrusive forms of treatment, was necessary and reasonable in the treatment of Dwight Price is a question we cannot reach. We believe, and so hold, that whatever the answer to that question may be, on the record before us the defendant is immune from liability under 42 U.S.C.A. § 1983.

The Supreme Court has recently considered the qualified immunity possessed by state officials acting in their official capacity, *O'Connor* v. *Donaldson, 422* U.S. 563, 95 S.Ct. 2486, 45 L.Ed.2d 396 (1975); *Wood* v. *Strickland,* 420 U.S. 308, 95 S.Ct. 992, 43 L.Ed.2d 214 (1975); *Scheuer* v. *Rhodes,* 416 U.S. 232, 94 S.Ct. 1683, 40 L.Ed.2d 90 (1974). In *O'Connor,* the court summarized the nature of that immunity:

> . . . [T]he relevant question for the jury is whether [the state official] "knew or reasonably should have known that the action he took within his sphere of official responsibility would violate the constitutional rights of [the plaintiff], or if he took the action with the malicious intention to cause a deprivation of constitutional rights or other injury to [the plaintiff]." . . . [*Wood* v. *Strickland,* 420 U.S. 322, 95 S.Ct. 1001, 43 L.Ed.2d 225.] For purposes of this question, an official has, of course, no duty to anticipate unforeseeable constitutional developments. [Citations omitted.]

It seems abundantly clear, given the vagueness of the constitutional right of privacy, that the defendant could not reasonably have known that the administration of electroshock treatments to Dwight Price violated a "clearly established" constitutional right. *Wood* v. *Strickland,* 420 U.S. 322, 95 S.Ct. 1001, 43 L.Ed.2d 225.

Moreover, it is evident from the record that the defendant acted without malice and in good faith. Less intrusive means of treatment were employed by the defendant for a period of 3 months without success. Dwight continued to be assaultive and for that reason required confinement to his room most of the time, a circumstance which the defendant believed was a substantial obstacle to recovery and which could be corrected by electroshock. He followed the recommendation of the plaintiff's own doctor and continued the less intrusive forms of treatment for a further period before commencing the electroshock treatments. Proper medical procedures were followed in administering the treatments, and their administration did not contravene any state statute or regulation. In short, measured by accepted conduct at that time, the defendant's actions were proper.

Because the potential impact of the more intrusive forms of treatment is so great, we are reluctant in those cases where the patient or guardian refuse their consent, to leave the imposition of the more intrusive forms of treatment solely within the discretion of medical personnel at our state hospitals. For that reason, we adopt the following procedure for future cases:

(1) If the patient is incompetent to give consent or refuses consent or his guardian other than persons responsible for his commitment also refuses his consent, before more intrusive forms of treatment may be utilized, the medical director of the state hospital must petition the probate division of the county court in the county in which the hospital is located for an order authorizing the prescribed treatment;

(2) the court shall appoint a guardian *ad litem* to represent the interests of the patient;

(3) in an adversary proceeding, pursuant to the petition, the court shall determine the necessity and reasonableness of the prescribed treatment.

In making that determination the court should balance the patient's need for treatment against the intrusiveness of the prescribed treatment. Factors which should be considered are (1) the extent and duration of changes in behavior patterns and mental activity effected by the treatment, (2) the risks of adverse side effects, (3) the experimental nature of the treatment, (4) its acceptance by the medical community of this state, (5) the extent of intrusion into the patient's body and the pain connected with the treatment, and (6) the patient's ability to competently determine for himself whether the treatment is desirable.

We cannot draw a clear line between the more intrusive forms of treatment requiring this procedural hearing and those which do not. Certainly this procedure is not intended to apply to the use of mild tranquilizers or those therapies requiring the cooperation of the patient. On the other hand, given current medical practice, this procedure must be followed where psychosurgery or electroshock therapy is proposed.

Affirmed.

NOTES

1. Where does the court get the authority to promulgate standards and procedures for electroshock cases in the future? Is this an arrogation of a legislative function?

2. The known side effects of electroshock therapy include memory loss:

> ECT affects the memory for events experienced before the seizure . . . and for those experienced after it. . . . It has been convincingly shown by many investigators . . . that ECT affects retention and not learning [citations omitted] and that long-term memory is more affected than short-term memory.[b]

It is also widely argued that ECT causes damage to the brain. One authority has commented:

---

[b]Dornbush, R., and Williams, M., "Memory & ECT," in *Psychobiology of Convulsive Therapy,* 199, 201 (Fink, M., Kety, S., McGaugh, J., and Williams, T., eds., 1974).

At the termination of a course of ECT under the best circumstances, you are left with an acute insult to the brain, leaving an individual confused, disoriented without judgment, in which his emotion level may be quite disorganized, in which it is virtually impossible to obtain any intelligent responses to any kind of testing, and in which if one measures the electrical activity of the brain at that time, there isn't any question that there's been an injury.[c]

Does this information affect your opinion of the decisions in *Price* v. *Sheppard* and *Stein?*

Kaimowitz v. Michigan Department of Mental Health

Circuit Court of Wayne County, Michigan, 1973
No. 73-19434-AW (July 10, 1973), reported in 2 Prison L. Rptr. 433 (1973),
summarized in 42 U.S.L.W. 2063 (July 31, 1973)

Before Gilmore, Bowles and O'Hair, JJ. This case came to this Court originally on a complaint for a Writ of Habeas Corpus brought by Plaintiff Kaimowitz on behalf of John Doe and the Medical Committee for Human Rights, alleging that John Doe was being illegally detained in the Lafayette Clinic for the purpose of experimental psychotherapy.

John Doe had been committed by the Kalamazoo County Circuit Court on January 11, 1955, to the Ionia State Hospital as a Criminal Sexual Psychopath, without a trial of criminal charges, under the terms of the then existing Criminal Sexual Psychopathic law. He had been charged with the murder and subsequent rape of a student nurse at the Kalamazoo State Hospital while he was confined there as a mental patient.

In 1972, Drs. Ernst Rodin and Jacques Gottlieb of the Lafayette Clinic, a facility of the Michigan Department of Mental Health, had filed a proposal "For the Study of Treatment of Uncontrollable Aggression."

This was funded by the Legislature of the State of Michigan for the fiscal year 1972. After more than 17 years at the Ionia State Hospital, John Doe was transferred to the Lafayette Clinic in November of 1972 as a suitable research subject for the Clinic's study of uncontrollable aggression.

Under the terms of the study, 24 criminal sexual psychopaths in the State's mental health system were to be subjects of experiment. The experiment was to compare the effects of surgery on the amygdaloid portion of the limbic system of the brain with the effect of the drug cyproterone acetate on the male hormone flow. The comparison was intended to show which, if either, could be used in controlling aggression of males in an institutional setting, and to afford lasting permanent relief from such aggression to the patient.

Substantial difficulties were encountered in locating a suitable patient population for the surgical procedures and a matched controlled group for the treatment by the anti-androgen drug. As a matter of fact, it was concluded that John Doe was the only known appropriate candidate available within the state mental health system for the surgical experiment.

---

[c]Interview, Grimm, ABC News Closeup, "Madness and Medicine," May 26, 1977, transcript at 20.

John Doe signed an "informed consent" form to become an experimental subject prior to his transfer from the Ionia State Hospital.[5] He had obtained signatures from his parents giving consent for the experimental and innovative surgical procedures to be performed on his brain, and two separate three-man review committees were established by Dr. Rodin to review the scientific worthiness of the study and the validity of the consent obtained from Doe.

The Scientific Review Committee, headed by Dr. Elliot Luby, approved of the procedure, and the Human Rights Review Committee, consisting of Ralph Slovenko, a Professor of Law and Psychiatry at Wayne State University, Monsignor Clifford Sawher, and Frank Moran, a Certified Public Accountant, gave their approval to the procedure.

Even though no experimental subjects were found to be available in the state mental health system other than John Doe, Dr. Rodin prepared to proceed with the equipment on Doe, and depth electrodes were to be inserted into his brain, on or about January 15, 1973.

Early in January, 1973, Plaintiff Kaimowitz became aware of the work being contemplated on John Doe and made his concern known to the Detroit Free Press. Considerable newspaper publicity ensued and this action was filed shortly thereafter.

With the rush of publicity on the filing of the original suit, funds for the research project were stopped by Dr. Gordon Yudashkin, Director of the Department of Mental Health, and the investigators, Drs. Gottlieb and Rodin, dropped their plans to pursue the research set out in the proposal. They reaffirmed at trial, however, their belief in the scientific, medical and ethical soundness of the proposal.

Upon the request of counsel, a Three-Judge Court was empanelled, Judges John

---

[5]The complete "Informed Consent" form signed by John Doe is as follows:

"Since conventional treatment efforts over a period of several years have not enabled me to control my outbursts of rage and anti-social behavior, I submit an application to be a subject in a research project which offers me a form of effective therapy. This therapy is based upon the idea that episodes of anti-social rage and sexuality might be triggered by a disturbance in certain portions of my brain. I understand that in order to be certain that a significant brain disturbance exists, which might relate to my anti-social behavior, an initial operation will have to be performed. This procedure consists of placing fine wires into my brain, which will record the electrical activity from those structures which play a part in anger and sexuality. These electrical waves can then be studied to determine the presence of an abnormality.

"In addition electrical stimulation with weak currents passed through these wires will be done in order to find out if one or several points in the brain can trigger my episodes of violence or unlawful sexuality. In other words this stimulation may cause me to want to commit an aggressive or sexual act, but every effort will be made to have a sufficient number of people present to control me. If the brain disturbance is limited to a small area, I understand that the investigators will destroy this part of my brain with an electrical current. If the abnormality comes from a larger part of my brain, I agree that it should be surgically removed, if the doctors determine that it can be done so, without the risk of side effects. Should the electrical activity from the parts of my brain into which the wires have been placed reveal that there is no significant abnormality, the wires will simply be withdrawn.

"I realize that any operation on the brain carries a number of risks which may be slight, but could be potentially serious. These risks include infection, bleeding, temporary or permanent weakness or paralysis of one or more of my legs or arms, difficulties with speech and thinking, as well as the ability to feel, touch, pain and temperature. Under extraordinary circumstances, it is also possible that I might not survive the operation.

"Fully aware of the risks detailed in the paragraphs above, I authorize the physicians of Lafayette Clinic and Providence Hospital to perform the procedures as outlined above."

D. O'Hair and George E. Bowles joining Judge Horace W. Gilmore. Dean Francis A. Allen and Prof. Robert A. Burt of the University of Michigan Law School were appointed as counsel for John Doe.

Approximately the same time *Amicus Curiae,* the American Orthopsychiatric Society, sought to enter the case with the right to offer testimony. This was granted by the Court.

Three ultimate issues were framed for consideration by the Court. The first related to the constitutionality of the detention of Doe. The full statement of the second and third questions, to which this Opinion is addressed, are set forth in the text below.

The first issue relating to the constitutionality of the detention of John Doe was considered by the Court, and on March 23, 1973, an Opinion was rendered by the Court holding the detention unconstitutional. Subsequently, after hearing testimony of John Doe's present condition, the Court directed his release.

In the meantime, since it appeared unlikely that no project would go forward because of the withdrawal of approval by Dr. Yudashkin, the Court raised the question as to whether the rest of the case had become moot. . . . The Court held [in a separate opinion] that even though the original experimentation program was terminated, there was nothing that would prevent it from being instituted again in the near future, and therefore the matter was ripe for declaratory judgment.

The facts concerning the original experiment and the involvement of John Doe were to be considered by the Court as illustrative in determining whether legally adequate consent could be obtained from adults involuntarily confined in the state mental health system for experimental or innovative procedures on the brain to ameliorate behavior, and, if it could be, whether the State should allow such experimentation on human subjects to proceed.

The two issues framed for decision in this declaratory judgment action are as follows:

1. After failure of established therapies, may an adult or a legally appointed guardian, if the adult is involuntarily detained, at a facility within the jurisdiction of the State Department of Mental Health give legally adequate consent to an innovative or experimental surgical procedure on the brain, if there is demonstrable physical abnormality of the brain, and the procedure is designed to ameliorate behavior, which is either personally tormenting to the patient, or so profoundly disruptive that the patient cannot safely live, or live with others?

2. If the answer to the above is yes, then is it legal in this State to undertake an innovative or experimental surgical procedure on the brain of an adult who is involuntarily detained at a facility within the jurisdiction of the State Department of Mental Health, if there is demonstrable physical abnormality of the brain, and the procedure is designed to ameliorate behavior, which is either personally tormenting to the patient, or so profoundly disruptive that the patient cannot safely live, or live with others?

Throughout this Opinion, the Court will use the term psychosurgery to describe the proposed innovative or experimental surgical procedure defined in the questions for consideration by the Court.

At least two definitions of psychosurgery have been furnished the Court. Dr. Bertram S. Brown, Director of the National Institute of Mental Health, defined the erm as follows in his prepared statement before the United States Senate Subcommittee on health of the Committee on Labor and Public Welfare on February 23, 1973:

> Psychosurgery can best be defined as a surgical removal or destruction of brain tissue or the cutting of brain tissue to disconnect one part of the brain from another, with the intent of altering the behavior, even though there may be no direct evidence of structural disease or damage to the brain.

Dr. Peter Breggin, a witness at the trial, defined psychosurgery as the destruction of normal brain tissue for the control of emotions or behavior; or the destruction of abnormal brain tissue for the control of emotions or behavior, where the abnormal tissue has not been shown to be the cause of the emotions or behavior in question.

The psychosurgery involved in this litigation is a sub-class, narrower than that defined by Dr. Brown. The proposed psychosurgery we are concerned with encompasses only experimental psychosurgery where there are demonstrable physical abnormalities in the brain. Therefore, temporal lobectomy, an established therapy for relief of clearly diagnosed epilepsy is not involved, nor are accepted neurological surgical procedures, for example, operations for Parkinsonism, or operations for the removal of tumors or the relief of stroke.

We start with the indisputable medical fact that no significant activity in the brain occurs in isolation without correlated activity in other parts of the brain. As the level of complexity of human behavior increases, so does the degree of interaction and integration. Dr. Ayub Ommaya, a witness in the case, illustrated this through the phenomenon of vision. Pure visual sensation is one of the functions highly localized in the occipital lobe in the back of the brain. However, vision in its broader sense, such as the ability to recognize a face, does not depend upon this area of the brain alone. It requires the integration of that small part of the brain with the rest of the brain. Memory mechanisms interact with the visual sensation to permit the recognition of the face. Dr. Ommaya pointed out that the more we know about brain function, the more we realize with certainty that many functions are highly integrated, even for relatively simple activity.

It is clear from the record in this case that the understanding of the limbic system of the brain and its function is very limited. Practically every witness and exhibit established how little is known of the relationship of the limbic system to human behavior, in the absence of some clearly defined clinical disease such as epilepsy. Drs. Mark, Sweet and Ervin have noted repeatedly the primitive state of our understanding of the amygdala, for example, remarking that it is an area made up of nine to fourteen different nuclear structures, with many functions, some of which are competitive with others. They state that there are not even reliable guesses as to the functional location of some of the nuclei.[11]

The testimony showed that any physical intervention in the brain must always be approached with extreme caution. Brain surgery is always irreversible in the sense that any intrusion into the brain destroys the brain cells and such cells do not regener-

---

[11] .Mark, Sweet and Ervin, 'The Effect of Amygdalotomy on Violent Behavior in Patients with Temporal Lobe Epilepsy," in Hitchcock, Ed., *Psycho-Surgery: Second International Conference* (Thomas Pub. 1972), 135 at 153.

ate. Dr. Ommaya testified that in the absence of well defined pathological signs, such as blood clots pressing on the brain due to trauma, or tumor in the brain, brain surgery is viewed as a treatment of last resort.

The record in this case demonstrates that animal experimentation and non-intrusive human experimentation have not been exhausted in determining and studying brain function. Any experimentation on the human brain, especially when it involves an intrusive, irreversible procedure in a non life-threatening situation, should be undertaken with extreme caution, and then only when answers cannot be obtained from animal experimentation and from non-intrusive human experimentation.

Psychosurgery should never be undertaken upon involuntarily committed populations, when there is a high-risk low-benefit ratio as demonstrated in this case. This is because of the impossibility of obtaining truly informed consent from such populations. The reasons such informed consent cannot be obtained are set forth in detail subsequently in this Opinion.

There is widespread concern about violence. Personal violence, whether in a domestic setting or reflected in street violence, tends to increase. Violence in group confrontations appears to have culminated in the late 60's but still invites study and suggested solutions. Violence, personal and group, has engaged the criminal law courts and the correctional systems, and has inspired the appointment of national commissions. The late President Lyndon B. Johnson convened a commission on violence under the chairmanship of Dr. Milton Eisenhower. It was a commission that had fifty consultants representing various fields of law, sociology, criminology, history, government, social psychiatry, and social psychology. Conspicuous by their absence were any professionals concerned with the human brain. It is not surprising, then, that of recent date, there has been theorizing as to violence and the brain, and just over two years ago, Frank Ervin, a psychiatrist, and Vernon H. Mark, a neurosurgeon, wrote *Violence and the Brain*[12] detailing the application of brain surgery to problems of violent behavior.

Problems of violence are not strangers to this Court. Over many years we have studied personal and group violence in a court context. Nor are we unconcerned about the tragedies growing out of personal or group confrontations. Deep-seated public concern begets an impatient desire for miracle solutions. And necessarily, we deal here not only with legal and medical issues, but with ethical and social issues as well.

Is brain function related to abnormal aggressive behavior? This, fundamentally, is what the case is about. But, one cannot segment or simplify that which is inherently complex. As Vernon H. Mark has written, "Moral values are social concerns, not medical ones, in any presently recognized sense."[13]

Violent behavior not associated with brain disease should not be dealt with surgically. At best, neurosurgery rightfully should concern itself with medical problems and not the behavior problems of a social etiology.

The Court does not in any way desire to impede medical progress. We are much

---

[12]Mark and Ervin, *Violence and the Brain* (Harper and Row, 1970).

[13]Mark, "Brain Surgery in Aggressive Epileptics," *The Hastings Center Report*, Vol. 3, No. 1 (February, 1973).

concerned with violence and the possible effect of brain disease on violence. Much research on the brain is necessary and must be carried on, but when it takes the form of psychosurgery, it cannot be undertaken on involuntarily detained populations. Other avenues of research must be utilized and developed.

Although extensive psychosurgery has been performed in the United States and throughout the world in recent years to attempt change of objectionable behavior, there is no medically recognized syndrome for aggression and objectionable behavior associated with nonorganic brain abnormality.

The psychosurgery that has been done has in varying degrees blunted emotions and reduced spontaneous behavior. Dr. V. Balasubramaniam, a leading psychosurgeon, has characterized psychosurgery as "sedative neurosurgery," a procedure by which patients are made quiet and manageable.[14] The amygdalotomy, for example, has been used to calm hyperactive children, to make retarded children more manageable in institutions, to blunt the emotions of people with depression, and to attempt to make schizophrenics more manageable.[15]

As pointed out above, psychosurgery is clearly experimental, poses substantial danger to research subjects, and carries substantial unknown risks. There is no persuasive showing on this record that the type of psychosurgery we are concerned with would necessarily confer any substantial benefit on research subjects or significantly increase the body of scientific knowledge by providing answers to problems of deviant behavior.

The dangers of such surgery are undisputed. Though it may be urged, as did some of the witnesses in this case, that the incidents of morbidity and mortality are low from the procedures, all agree dangers are involved, and the benefits to the patient are uncertain.

Absent a clearly defined medical syndrome, nothing pinpoints the exact location in the brain of the cause of undesirable behavior so as to enable a surgeon to make a lesion, remove that portion of the brain, and thus affect undesirable behavior.

Psychosurgery flattens emotional responses, leads to lack of abstract reasoning ability, leads to a loss of capacity for new learning and causes general sedation and apathy. It can lead to impairment of memory, and in some instances unexpected responses to psychosurgery are observed. It has been found, for example, that heightened rage reaction can follow surgical intervention on the amygdala, just as placidity can.

It was unanimously agreed by all witnesses that psychosurgery does not, given the present state of the art, provide any assurance that a dangerously violent person can be restored to the community.

---

[14]See Defendant's Exhibit 38, Sedative Neurosurgery by V. Balasubramaniam, T. S. Kanaka, P. V. Ramanuman, and B. Ramuaurthi, 53 *Journal of the Indian Medical Association,* No. 8, page 377 (1969).

[15]The classical lobotomy of which thousands were performed in the 1940's and 1950's is very rarely used these days. The development of drug therapy pretty well did away with the classical lobotomy. Follow-up studies showed that the lobotomy procedure was overused and caused a great deal of damage to the persons who were subjected to it. A general bleaching of the personality occurred and the operations were associated with loss of drive and concentration. Dr. Brown in his testimony before the United States Senate, *supra,* page 9, stated: "No responsible scientist today would condone a classical lobotomy operation."

Simply stated, on this record there is no scientific basis for establishing that the removal or destruction of an area of the limbic brain would have any direct therapeutic effect in controlling aggressivity or improving tormenting personal behavior, absent the showing of a well defined clinical syndrome such as epilepsy.

To advance scientific knowledge, it is true that doctors may desire to experiment on human beings, but the need for scientific inquiry must be reconciled with the inviolability which our society provides for a person's mind and body. Under a free government, one of a person's greatest rights is the right to inviolability of his person, and it is axiomatic that this right necessarily forbids the physician or surgeon from violating, without permission, the bodily integrity of his patient.[18]

Generally, individuals are allowed free choice about whether to undergo experimental medical procedures. But the State has the power to modify this free choice concerning experimental medical procedures when it cannot be freely given, or when the result would be contrary to public policy. For example, it is obvious that a person may not consent to acts that will constitute murder, manslaughter, or mayhem upon himself. In short, there are times when the State for good reason should withhold a person's ability to consent to certain medical procedures.

It is elementary tort law that consent is the mechanism by which the patient grants the physician the power to act, and which protects the patient against unauthorized invasions of his person. This requirement protects one of society's most fundamental values, the inviolability of the individual. An operation performed upon a patient without his informed consent is the tort of battery, and a doctor and a hospital have no right to impose compulsory medical treatment against the patient's will. These elementary statements of tort law need no citation.

Jay Katz, in his outstanding book *Experimentation with Human Beings* (Russell Sage Foundation, N.Y. (1972)) points out on page 523 that the concept of informed consent has been accepted as a cardinal principle for judging the propriety of research with human beings.

He points out that in the experimental setting, informed consent serves multiple purposes. He states (pages 523 and 524):

> ... Most clearly, requiring informed consent serves society's desire to respect each individual's autonomy, and his right to make choices concerning his own life.
>
> Second, providing a subject with information about an experiment will encourage him to be an active partner and the process may also increase the rationality of the experimentation process.
>
> Third, securing informed consent protects the experimentation process by encouraging the investigator to question the value of the proposed project and the adequacy of the measures he has taken to protect subjects, by reducing civil and criminal liability for nonnegligent injury to the subjects, and by diminishing adverse public reaction to an experiment.
>
> Finally, informed consent may serve the function of increasing society's awareness about human research. . . .

---

[18]See the language of the late Justice Cardozo in *Schloendorff* v. *Society of New York Hospitals,* 211 N.Y. 125, 105 N.E. 92, 93 (1914), where he said, "Every human being of adult years or sound mind has a right to determine what shall be done with his own body. . . ."

It is obvious that there must be close scrutiny of the adequacy of the consent when an experiment, as in this case, is dangerous, intrusive, irreversible, and of uncertain benefit to the patient and society.

Counsel for Drs. Rodin and Gottlieb argues that anyone who has ever been treated by a doctor for any relatively serious illness is likely to acknowledge that a competent doctor can get almost any patient to consent to almost anything. Counsel claims this is true because patients do not want to make decisions about complex medical matters and because there is the general problem of avoiding decision making in stress situations, characteristic of all human beings.

He further argues that a patient is always under duress when hospitalized and that in a hospital or institutional setting there is no such thing as a volunteer. Dr. Ingelfinger in Volume 287, page 466, of the *New England Journal of Medicine* (August 31, 1972) states:

> ... The process of obtaining "informed consent" with all its regulations and conditions, is no more than an elaborate ritual, a device that when the subject is uneducated and uncomprehending, confers no more than the semblance of propriety on human experimentation. The subject's only real protection, the public as well as the medical profession must recognize, depends on the conscience and compassion of the investigator and his peers.

Everything defendants' counsel argues militates against the obtaining of informed consent from involuntarily detained mental patients. If, as he argues, truly informed consent cannot be given for regular surgical procedures by noninstitutionalized persons, then certainly an adequate informed consent cannot be given by the involuntarily detained mental patient.

We do not agree that a truly informed consent cannot be given for a regular surgical procedure by a patient, institutionalized or not. The law has long recognized that such valid consent can be given. But we do hold that informed consent cannot be given by an involuntarily detained mental patient for experimental psychosurgery for the reasons set forth below.

The Michigan Supreme Court has considered in a tort case the problems of experimentation with humans. In *Fortner* v. *Koch,* 272 Mich. 273, 261 N.W. 762 (1935), the issued turned on whether the doctor had taken proper diagnostic steps before prescribing an experimental treatment for cancer. Discussing medical experimentation, the Court said at page 282:

> We recognize the fact that if the general practice of medicine and surgery is to progress, there must be a certain amount of experimentation carried on; but such experiments must be done with the knowledge and consent of the patient or those responsible for him, *and must not* vary too radically from the accepted method of procedure. [Emphasis added.]

This means that the physician cannot experiment without restraint or restriction. He must consider first of all the welfare of his patient. This concept is universally accepted by the medical profession, the legal profession, and responsible persons who have thought and written on the matter.

Furthermore, he must weigh the risk to the patient against the benefit to be obtained by trying something new. The risk-benefit ratio is an important ratio in considering any experimental surgery upon a human being. The risk must always be relatively low, in the non life-threatening situation to justify human experimentation.

Informed consent is a requirement of variable demands. Being certain that a patient has consented adequately to an operation, for example, is much more important when doctors are going to undertake an experimental, dangerous, and intrusive procedure than, for example, when they are going to remove an appendix. When a procedure is experimental, dangerous, and intrusive, special safeguards are necessary. The risk-benefit ratio must be carefully considered, and the question of consent thoroughly explored.

To be legally adequate, a subject's informed consent must be competent, knowing and voluntary.

In considering consent for experimentation, the ten principles known as the Nuremberg code give guidance. They are found in the Judgment of the Court in *United States* v. *Karl Brandt.*[21]

There the Court said:

> ... Certain basic principles must be observed in order to satisfy moral, ethical and legal concepts:
>
> 1. The voluntary consent of the human subject is absolutely essential.
>
> This means that the person involved should have legal capacity to give consent; should be so situated as to be able to exercise free power of choice, without the intervention of any element of force, fraud, deceit, duress, overreaching, or other ulterior form of constraint or coercion; and should have sufficient knowledge and comprehension of the elements of the subject matter involved as to enable him to make an understanding and enlightened decision. This latter element requires that before the acceptance of an affirmative decision by the experimental subject, there should be made known to him the nature, duration and purpose of the experiment; the method and means by which it is to be conducted; all inconveniences and hazards reasonably to be expected; and the effects upon his health or person which may possibly come from his participation in the experiment.
>
> The duty and responsibility for ascertaining the quality of the consent rests upon each individual who initiates, directs, or engages in the experiment. It is a personal duty and responsibility which may not be delegated to another with impunity.
>
> 2. The experiment should be such as to yield fruitful results for the good of society unprocurable by other methods or means of study and not random and unnecessary in nature.
>
> 3. The experiment should be so designed and based on the results of animal experimentation and a knowledge of the natural history of the disease or other problem under study that the anticipated results will justify the performance of the experiment.
>
> 4. The experiment should be so conducted as to avoid all unnecessary physical and mental suffering and injury.
>
> 5. No experiment should be conducted where there is an *a priori* reason to believe that death or disabling injury will occur; except, perhaps, in those experiments where the experimental physicians also serve as subjects.
>
> 6. The degree of risk to be taken should never exceed that determined by the humanitarian importance of the problem to be solved by the experiment.

---

[21]*Trial of War Criminals before the Nuremberg Military Tribunals.* Volume 1 and 2. "The Medical Case," Washington, D.C.; U.S. Government Printing Office (1948) reprinted in *Experimentation with Human Beings,* by Katz (Russell Sage Foundation (1972)) page 305.

7. Proper preparations should be made and adequate facilities to protect the experimental subject against even remote possibilities of injury, disability, or death.

8. The experiment should be conducted only by scientifically qualified persons. The highest degree of skill and care should be required through all stages of the experiment of those who conduct or engage in the experiment.

9. During the course of the experiment the human subject should be at liberty to bring the experiment to an end if he has reached the physical or mental state where continuation of the experiment seems to him to be impossible.

10. During the course of the experiment the scientist in charge must be prepared to terminate the experiment at any stage, if he has probable cause to believe, in the exercise of the good faith, superior skill, and careful judgment required of him that a continuation of the experiment is likely to result in injury, disability, or death to the experimental subject.

In the Nuremberg Judgment, the elements of what must guide us in decision are found. The involuntarily detained mental patient must have legal capacity to give consent. He must be so situated as to be able to exercise free power of choice without any element of force, fraud, deceit, duress, overreaching, or other ulterior form of restraint or coercion. He must have sufficient knowledge and comprehension of the subject matter to enable him to make an understanding decision. The decision must be a totally voluntary one on his part.

We must first look to the competency of the involuntarily detained mental patient to consent. Competency requires the ability of the subject to understand rationally the nature of the procedure, its risks, and other relevant information. The standard governing required disclosure by a doctor is what a reasonable patient needs to know in order to make an intelligent decision. See Waltz and Scheunenman, "Informed Consent Therapy," 64 *Northwestern Law Review* 628 (1969).

Although an involuntarily detained mental patient may have a sufficient I.Q. to intellectually comprehend his circumstances (in Dr. Rodin's experiment, a person was required to have at least an I.Q. of 80), the very nature of his incarceration diminishes the capacity to consent to psychosurgery. He is particularly vulnerable as a result of his mental condition, the deprivation stemming from involuntary confinement and the effects of the phenomenon of "institutionalization."

The very moving testimony of John Doe in the instant case establishes this beyond any doubt. The fact of institutional confinement has special force in undermining the capacity of the mental patient to make a competent decision on this issue, even though he be intellectually competent to do so. In the routine of institutional life, most decisions are made for patients. For example, John Doe testified how extraordinary it was for him to be approached by Dr. Yudashkin about the possible submission to psychosurgery, and how unusual it was to be consulted by a physician about his preference.

Institutionalization tends to strip the individual of the support which permits him to maintain his sense of self-worth and the value of his own physical and mental integrity. An involuntarily confined mental patient clearly has diminished capacity for making a decision about irreversible experimental psychosurgery.

Equally great problems are found when the involuntarily detained mental patient is incompetent, and consent is sought from a guardian or parent. Although guardian or parental consent may be legally adequate when arising out of traditional circumstances, it is legally ineffective in the psychosurgery situation. The guardian or parent cannot do that which the patient, absent a guardian, would be legally unable to do.

The second element of an informed consent is knowledge of the risk involved and the procedures to be undertaken. It was obvious from the record made in this case that the facts surrounding experimental brain surgery are profoundly uncertain, and the lack of knowledge on the subject makes a knowledgeable consent to psychosurgery literally impossible.

We turn now to the third element of an informed consent, that of voluntariness. It is obvious that the most important thing to a large number of involuntarily detained mental patients incarcerated for an unknown length of time, is freedom.

The Nuremberg standards require that the experimental subjects be so situated as to exercise free power of choice without the intervention of any element of force, fraud, deceit, duress, overreaching, or other ulterior form of constraint or coercion. It is impossible for an involuntarily detained mental patient to be free of ulterior forms of restraint or coercion when his very release from the institution may depend upon his cooperating with the institutional authorities and giving consent to experimental surgery.

The privileges of an involuntarily detained patient and the rights he exercises in the institution are within the control of the institutional authorities. As was pointed out in the testimony of John Doe, such minor things as the right to have a lamp in his room, or the right to have ground privileges to go for a picnic with his family assumed major proportions. For 17 years he lived completely under the control of the hospital. Nearly every important aspect of his life was decided without any opportunity on his part to participate in the decision-making process.

The involuntarily detained mental patient is in an inherently coercive atmosphere even though no direct pressures may be placed upon him. He finds himself stripped of customary amenities and defenses. Free movement is restricted. He becomes a part of communal living subject to the control of the institutional authorities.

As pointed out in the testimony in this case, John Doe consented to this psychosurgery partly because of his effort to show the doctors in the hospital that he was a cooperative patient. Even Dr. Yudashkin, in his testimony, pointed out that involuntarily confined patients tend to tell their doctors what the patient thinks these people want to hear.

The inherently coercive atmosphere to which the involuntarily detained mental patient is subjected has bearing upon the voluntariness of his consent. This was pointed up graphically by Dr. Watson in his testimony (page 67, April 4). There he was asked if there was any significant difference between the kinds of coercion that exist in an open hospital setting and the kinds of coercion that exist on involuntarily detained patients in a state mental institution.

Dr. Watson answered in this way:

> There is an enormous difference. My perception of the patients at Ionia is that they are willing almost to try anything to somehow or other improve their lot, which is—you know—not bad. It is just plain normal—you know—that kind of desire. Again, that pressure—again—I don't like to use the word "coercion" because it implies a kind of

deliberateness and that is not what we are talking about—the pressure to accede is perhaps the more accurate way, I think—the pressure is perhaps so severe that it probably ought to cause us to not be willing to permit experimentation that has questionable gain and high risk from the standpoint of the patient's posture, which is, you see, the formula that I mentioned we hashed out in our Human Use Committee.

Involuntarily confined mental patients live in an inherently coercive institutional environment. Indirect and subtle psychological coercion has profound effect upon the patient population. Involuntarily confined patients cannot reason as equals with the doctors and administrators over whether they should undergo psychosurgery. They are not able to voluntarily give informed consent because of the inherent inequality in their position.[23]

It has been argued by defendants that because 13 criminal sexual psychopaths in the Ionia State Hospital wrote a letter indicating they did not want to be subjects of psychosurgery, that consent can be obtained and that the arguments about coercive pressure are not valid.

The Court does not feel that this necessarily follows. There is no showing of the circumstances under which the refusal of these thirteen patients was obtained, and there is no showing whatever that any effort was made to obtain the consent of these patients for such experimentation.

The fact that thirteen patients unilaterally wrote a letter saying they did not want to be subjects of psychosurgery is irrelevant to the question of whether they can consent to that which they are legally precluded from doing.

The law has always been meticulous in scrutinizing inequality in bargaining power and the possibility of undue influence in commercial fields and in the law of wills. It also has been most careful in excluding from criminal cases confessions where there was no clear showing of their completely voluntary nature after full understanding of the consequences. No lesser standard can apply to involuntarily detained mental patients.

The keystone to any intrusion upon the body of a person must be full, adequate and informed consent. The integrity of the individual must be protected from invasion into his body and personality not voluntarily agreed to. Consent is not an idle or symbolic act; it is a fundamental requirement for the protection of the individual's integrity.

---

[23]It should be emphasized that once John Doe was released in this case and returned to the community he withdrew all consent to the performance of the proposed experiment. His withdrawal of consent under these circumstances should be compared with his response on January 12, 1973, to questions placed to him by Prof. Slovenko, one of the members of the Human Rights Committee. These answers are part of Exhibit 22 and were given after extensive publicity about this case, and while John Doe was in Lafayette Clinic waiting the implantation of depth electrodes. The significant questions and answers are as follows:

"1. Would you seek psychosurgery if you were not confined to an institution?
"A. Yes, if after testing this showed it would be of help.
"2. Do you believe that psychosurgery is a way to obtain your release from the institution?
"A. No, but it would be a step in obtaining my release. It is like any other therapy or program to help persons to function again.
"3. Would you seek psychosurgery if there were other ways to obtain your release?
"A. Yes. If psychosurgery were the only means of helping my physical problem after a period of testing."

We therefore conclude that involuntarily detained mental patients cannot give informed and adequate consent to experimental psychosurgical procedures on the brain.

The three basic elements of informed consent—competency, knowledge, and voluntariness—cannot be ascertained with a degree of reliability warranting resort to use of such an invasive procedure.[25]

To this point, the Court's central concern has primarily been the ability of an involuntarily detained mental patient to give a factually informed, legally adequate consent to psychosurgery. However, there are also compelling constitutional considerations that preclude the involuntarily detained mental patient from giving effective consent to this type of surgery.

We deal here with State action in view of the fact the question relates to involuntarily detained mental patients who are confined because of the action of the State.

Initially, we consider the application of the First Amendment to the problem before the Court, recognizing that when the State's interest is in conflict with the Federal Constitution, the State's interest, even though declared by statute or court rule, must give way. See *NAACP* v. *Button,* 371 U.S. 415 (1963) and *United Transportation Workers' Union* v. *State Bar of Michigan,* 401 U.S. 576 (1971).

A person's mental processes, the communication of ideas, and the generation of ideas, come within the ambit of the First Amendment. To the extent that the First Amendment protects the dissemination of ideas and the expression of thoughts, it equally must protect the individual's right to generate ideas.

As Justice Cardozo pointed out:

> We are free only if we know, and so in proportion to our knowledge. There is no freedom without choice, and there is no choice without knowledge,—or none that is not illusory. Implicit, therefore, in the very notion of liberty is the liberty of the mind to absorb and to beget.... The mind is in chains when it is without the opportunity to choose. One may argue, if one please, that opportunity to choice is more an evil than a good. One is guilty of a contradiction if one says that the opportunity can be denied, and liberty subsist. At the root of all liberty is the liberty to know....
>
> Experimentation there may be in many things of deep concern, but not in setting boundaries to thought, for thought freely communicated is the indispensable condition of intelligent experimentation, the one test of its validity. (Cardozo, "The Paradoxes of Legal Science," *Columbia University Lectures,* reprinted in *Selected Writings of Benjamin Nathan Cardozo* (Fallon Publications (1947), pages 317 and 318.))

Justice Holmes expressed the basic theory of the First Amendment in *Abrams* v. *United States,* 250 U.S. 616, 630 (1919) when he said:

> ... The ultimate good desired is better reached by free trade in ideas—that the best test of truth is the power of the thought to get itself accepted in the competition of the market, and that truth is the only ground upon which their wishes safely can be carried

---

[25]It should be noted that Dr. Vernon H. Mark, a leading psychosurgeon, states that psychosurgery should not be performed on prisoners who are epileptic because of the problem of obtaining adequate consent. He states in *Brain Surgery in Aggressive Epileptics, the Hastings Center Report,* Vol. 3, No. 1 (February, 1973): "Prison inmates suffering from epilepsy should receive only medical treatment. Surgical therapy should not be carried out because of the difficulty of obtaining informed consent."

out. That at any rate is the theory of our Constitution. . . . We should be eternally vigilant against attempts to check expressions of opinion that we loathe and believe to be fraught with death, unless they so imminently threaten immediate interference with the lawful and pressing purposes of the law that an immediate check is required to save the country. . . .

Justice Brandeis in *Whitney* v. *California,* 274 U.S. 357, 375 (1927), put it this way:

> Those who won our independence believed that the final end of the State was to make men free to value their faculties; and that in its government the deliberative force should prevail over the arbitrary. . . . They believed that freedom to think as you will and to speak as you think are means indispensable to the discovery and spread of political truth; that without free speech and assembly discussion would be futile; that with them, discussion affords ordinarily adequate protection against the dissemination of noxious doctrine; that the greatest menace to freedom is an inert people; that public discussion is a political duty; and that this should be a fundamental principle of the American government. . . .

Thomas Emerson, a distinguished writer on the First Amendment, stated this in ''Toward a General Theory of the First Amendment,'' 72 *Yale Law Journal* 877, 895 (1963):

> The function of the legal process is not only to provide a means whereby a society shapes and controls the behavior of its individual members in the interests of the whole. It also supplies one of the principal methods by which a society controls itself, limiting its own powers in the interests of the individual. The role of the law here is to mark the guide and line between the sphere of social power, organized in the form of the state, and the area of private right. The legal problems involved in maintaining a system of free expression fall largely into this realm. In essence, legal support for such a society involves the protection of individual rights against interference or unwarranted control by the government. More specifically, the legal structure must provide:
>
> 1. Protection of the individual's right to freedom of expression against interference by the government in its efforts to achieve other social objectives or to advance its own interests. . . .
>
> 3. Restriction of the government in so far as the government itself participates in the system of expression.
>
> All these requirements involved control over the state. The use of law to achieve this kind of control has been one of the central concerns of freedom-seeking societies over the ages. Legal recognition of individual rights, enforced through the legal processes, has become the core of free society.

In *Stanley* v. *Georgia*, 394 U.S. 557 (1969), the Supreme Court once again addressed the free dissemination of ideas. It said at pages 565–66:

> Our whole constitutional heritage rebels at the thought of giving government the power to control men's minds. . . . Whatever the power of the state to control dissemination of ideas inimical to public morality, it cannot constitutionally premise legislation on the desirability of controlling a person's private thoughts.

Freedom of speech and expression, and the right of all men to disseminate ideas, popular or unpopular, are fundamental to ordered liberty. Government has no power or right to control men's minds, thoughts, and expressions. This is the command of the First Amendment. And we adhere to it in holding that an involuntarily detained mental patient may not consent to experimental psychosurgery.

For, if the First Amendment protects the freedom to express ideas, it necessarily follows that it must protect the freedom to generate ideas. Without the latter protection, the former is meaningless.

Experimental psychosurgery, which is irreversible and intrusive, often leads to the blunting of emotions, the deadening of memory, the reduction of affect, and limits the ability to generate new ideas. Its potential for injury to the creativity of the individual is great, and can impinge upon the right of the individual to be free from interference with his mental processes.

The State's interest in performing psychosurgery and the legal ability of the involuntarily detained mental patient to give consent must bow to the First Amendment, which protects the generation and free flow of ideas from unwarranted interference with one's mental processes.

To allow an involuntarily detained mental patient to consent to the type of psychosurgery proposed in this case, and to permit the State to perform it, would be to condone State action in violation of basic First Amendment rights of such patients, because impairing the power to generate ideas inhibits the full dissemination of ideas.

There is no showing in this case that the State has met its burden of demonstrating such a compelling State interest in the use of experimental psychosurgery on involuntarily detained mental patients to overcome its proscription by the First Amendment of the United States Constitution.

In recent years, the Supreme Court of the United States has developed a constitutional concept of right of privacy, relying upon the First, Fifth and Fourteenth Amendments. It was found in the marital bed in *Griswold* v. *Conn.* 381 U.S. 479 (1962); in the right to view obscenity in the privacy of one's home in *Stanley* v. *Georgia*, 394 U.S. 557 (1969); and in the right of a woman to control her own body by determining whether she wishes to terminate a pregnancy in *Roe* v. *Wade,* 41 L.W. 4213 (1973).

The concept was also recognized in the case of a prison inmate subjected to shock treatment and an experimental drug without his consent in *Mackey* v. *Procunier,* 477 F.2d 877 (9th Cir. 1973).

In that case, the 9th Circuit noted that the District Court had treated the action as a malpractice claim and had dismissed it. The 9th Circuit reversed, saying, *inter alia:*

> It is asserted in memoranda that the staff at Vacaville is engaged in medical and psychiatric experimentation with "aversion treatment" of criminal offenders, including the use of succinycholine on fully conscious patients. It is emphasized the plaintiff was subject to experimentation without consent.
>
> Proof of such matters could, in our judgment, raise serious constitutional questions respecting cruel and unusual punishment or *impermissible tinkering with the mental processes.* (Citing Stanley among other cases.) In our judgment it was error to dismiss the case without ascertaining at least the extent to which such charges can be substantiated. [Emphasis added.]

Much of the rationale for the developing constitutional concept of right to privacy is found in Justice Brandeis' famous dissent in *Olmstead* v. *United States,* 277

U.S. 438 (1928), at 478, where he said:

> The makers of our Constitution undertook to secure conditions favorable to the pursuit of happiness. They recognized the significance of man's spiritual nature, of his feelings and of his intellect. They knew that only a part of the pain, pleasure, and satisfaction of life are to be found in material things. They sought to protect Americans in their beliefs, their thoughts, their emotions and their sensations. They conferred, as against the Government, the right to be let alone—the most comprehensive of rights and the right most valued by civilized men.

There is no privacy more deserving of constitutional protection than that of one's mind. As pointed out by the Court in *Huguez* v. *United States*, 406 F.2d 366 (1968), at page 382, footnote 84:

> . . . Nor are the intimate internal areas of the physical habitation of mind and soul any less deserving of precious preservation from unwarranted and forcible intrusion than are the intimate internal areas of the physical habitation of wife and family. Is not the sanctity of the body even more important, and therefore, more to be honored in its protection than the sanctity of the home? . . .

Intrusion into one's intellect, when one is involuntarily detained and subject to the control of institutional authorities, is an intrusion into one's constitutionally protected right of privacy. If one is not protected in his thoughts, behavior, personality and identity, then the right of privacy becomes meaningless.

Before a State can violate one's constitutionally protected right of privacy and obtain a valid consent for experimental psychosurgery on involuntarily detained mental patients, a compelling State interest must be shown. None has been shown here.

To hold that the right of privacy prevents laws against dissemination of contraceptive material as in *Griswold* v. *Connecticut (supra),* or the right to view obscenity in the privacy of one's home as in *Stanley* v. *Georgia (supra),* but that it does not extend to the physical intrusion in an experimental manner upon the brain of an involuntarily detained mental patient is to denigrate the right. In the hierarchy of values, it is more important to protect one's mental processes than to protect even the privacy of the marital bed. To authorize an involuntarily detained mental patient to consent to experimental psychosurgery would be to fail to recognize and follow the mandates of the Supreme Court of the United States, which has constitutionally protected the privacy of body and mind.

Counsel for John Doe has argued persuasively that the use of the psychosurgery proposed in the instant case would constitute cruel and unusual punishment and should be barred under the Eighth Amendment. A determination of this issue is not necessary to decision, because of the many other legal and constitutional reasons for holding that the involuntarily detained mental patient may not give an informed and valid consent to experimental psychosurgery. We therefore do not pass on the issue of whether the psychosurgery proposed in this case constitutes cruel and unusual punishment within the meaning of the Eighth Amendment.

For the reasons given, we conclude that the answer to question number one posed for decision is no.

In reaching this conclusion, we emphasize two things.

First, the conclusion is based upon the state of the knowledge as of the time of the writing of this Opinion. When the state of medical knowledge develops to the extent that the type of psychosurgical intervention proposed here becomes an accepted neurosurgical procedure and is no longer experimental, it is possible, with appropriate review mechanisms, that involuntarily detained mental patients could consent to such an operation.

Second, we specifically hold that an involuntarily detained mental patient today can give adequate consent to accepted neurosurgical procedures.

In view of the fact we have answered the first question in the negative, it is not necessary to proceed to a consideration of the second question, although we cannot refrain from noting that had the answer to the first question been yes, serious constitutional problems would have arisen with reference to the second question.

NOTES

1. Would the rationale of the court in *Kaimowitz* preclude the use of experimental surgical techniques in an attempt to correct an imminently fatal medical condition of an institutionalized person? What is the scope of medical procedures to which the principles of *Kaimowitz* should be applied?

2. In light of the "inherently coercive atmosphere to which the involuntarily detained mental patient is subjected," can an involuntarily committed individual give valid informed consent to anything? Compare *New York City Health & Hosp. Corp. v. Stein,* at pp. 799–801, above.

3. The *Kaimowitz* case has been the subject of extensive discussion in a "Symposium on Psychosurgery," 54 *B.U.L. Rev.* 215 (1974).

ADEN v. YOUNGER

Court of Appeals of California, Fourth District, Division 1, 1976
57 Cal.App.3d 662, 129 Cal.Rptr. 535

GERALD BROWN, Presiding Justice.

Petitioners Jane Doe and Betty Roe are mentally ill. Doe has had electroconvulsive therapy (ECT) and may need further voluntary treatments. Roe wants a surgical "Multiple target procedure," or psychosurgery. Petitioner Aden, a licensed California physician, is certified by the American Board of Psychiatry and Neurology as a specialist in the treatment of psychiatric illnesses. Dr. Aden is Jane Doe's attending physician. Dr. Brown, who is a California licensed surgeon and physician, is Betty Roe's treating physician and surgeon. He specializes in neurosurgery and is a member of the American Board of Neurological Surgeons and the American College of Surgeons. Petitioner Campbell is a licensed California physician and surgeon, with a specialty in neurology and psychiatry for over 30 years, but he is not certified by the American Board of Psychiatry and Neurology.

The Attorney General, the Director of Health, and the Board of Medical Examiners are respondents.

The law involved in this petition is part of the Lanterman-Petris-Short Act

(Welf. & Inst.Code §§ 5000-5404.1).[1] The law changes conditions under which psychosurgery and shock treatment can be performed. The changes applicable to persons involuntarily detained and persons voluntarily admitted to state hospitals, private mental institutions, county psychiatric hospitals and certain mentally retarded persons, are:

Psychosurgery: (§§ 5325, 5326, 5326.3.)

Patients have the right to refuse psychosurgery and the professional person in charge of the facility may not deny them that right. If a patient refuses consent, it must be entered on the record.

If a patient wants psychosurgery, then the conditions for performing such surgery include:

(a) The patient must give written informed consent, dated, witnessed and entered in his record. The consent may be withdrawn at any time. An oral explanation by the doctor is necessary.

(b) The patient must have capacity to consent.

(c) A relative, guardian or conservator to a responsible relative, guardian or conservator.

(d) The reasons for surgery must be in the patient's treatment record, other treatments must be exhausted and surgery must be critically needed.

(e) Three appointed physicians (two board-certified psychiatrists or neurosurgeons) must examine the patient and unanimously agree with the treating physician's determinations and that the patient has capacity to consent. There must be a 72-hour wait after the patient's written consent before surgery.

Shock Treatment: (§ 5326.4.)

If the treating physician feels shock treatments are necessary, he must give an extensive oral explanation to the patient and his relative, guardian, or conservator.

Shock treatments shall be performed only after:

(a) The patient gives written informed consent.

(b) The patient has capacity to consent.

(c) A relative, guardian or conservator has been given a thorough oral explanation.

(d) "Adequate documentation" has been entered in the patient's record. All other treatments have been exhausted and the treatment is critically needed.

(e) There has been a review by three appointed physicians (two board-certified) who agree with the treating physician that the patient has capacity to consent.

If the patient does not have the capacity to consent, shock treatments can be given if conditions (c), (d) and (e) are met.

No shock treatments may be given if the patient is able to give informed consent and refuses.

The bill also provides for civil penalties of $10,000 or license revocation of doctors who violate these sections (§ 5326.5).

---

[1] All references to statutes are to the Welfare and Institutions Code unless otherwise stated.

Petitioners assert the changes are unconstitutional in certain respects and want a peremptory writ of mandate permanently preventing respondents from enforcing the amendments.

Original jurisdiction in this Court is proper. The Supreme Court and the Court of Appeal may take original jurisdiction in cases of mandamus, prohibition or certiorari. (Cal.Const., art. 6, § 10.) However, California Rules of Court, Rule 56(a)(1) requires:

> If the petition might lawfully have been made to a lower court in the first instance, it shall set forth the circumstances which ... render it proper that the writ should issue originally from the reviewing court. ...

Thus, exceptional circumstances must be shown before a reviewing court will take jurisdiction, such as issue of great public import and the necessity for prompt resolution of those issues (*Ramirez* v. *Brown*, 9 Cal.3d 199, 202-203, 107 Cal.Rptr. 137, 507 P.2d 1345; *Jolicoeur* v. *Mihaly*, 5 Cal.3d 565, 570, 96 Cal.Rptr. 697, 488 P.2d 1, fn. 1 & 2; *San Francisco Unified School Dist.* v. *Johnson*, 3 Cal.3d 937, 944, 92 Cal.Rptr. 309, 479 P.2d 669; *State Board of Equalization* v. *Watson*, 68 Cal.2d 307, 66 Cal.Rptr. 377, 437 P.2d 761; *County of Sacramento* v. *Hickman*, 66 Cal.2d 841, 59 Cal.Rptr. 609, 428 P.2d 593). In the present proceeding, the constitutionality of a state-wide law is challenged; and the rights of mental patients are dramatically affected by delaying a dispositive decision of this legislation's constitutionality. The case is proper for this Court to exercise original jurisdiction (see *Villa* v. *Hall*, 6 Cal.3d 227, 98 Cal.Rptr. 460, 490 P.2d 1148, vacated 406 U.S. 965, 92 S.Ct. 2407, 32 L.Ed.2d 664, subs. opn. 7 Cal.3d 926, 103 Cal.Rptr. 863; 500 P.2d 887; *Mooney* v. *Pickett*, 4 Cal.3d 669, 674-675, 94 Cal.Rptr. 279, 483 P.2d 1231; Witkin, *Cal.Proc.*, 2d ed. Extraordinary Writs, 1975 Supp., pp. 57-58). The use of a writ of mandate to prohibit the enforcement of an illegal statute is proper where prohibition would not lie.

Respondents contend there are issues of fact to be resolved and evidence must be taken on various aspects of the treatments, for example, whether there are sufficient psychiatrists available for review committees and the influence of the consultation procedures on the doctor-patient relationship.

These matters, however, are not necessary facts. The writ challenges the Legislature-dictated changes in how a patient may *consent* to the psychosurgery and shock therapy, not the efficacy of the treatments.

Perhaps the most striking feature of authorities (and case law) in the area dealt with by this legislation is they are quite uniform in acknowledging that the processes by which electroconvulsive therapy and psychosurgery induce therapeutic effects are not fully understood. The two modes of treatment are quite different in several aspects and their relevant characteristics will be considered briefly and separately.

Psychosurgery, as defined in section 5325(g), as amended, includes those operations "referred to as lobotomy, psychiatric surgery, and behavioral surgery. ..." Instructive and persuasive in this area is the case of *Kaimowitz* v. *Department of Mental Health for the State of Michigan*, 2 Prison L.Rptr. p. 433, which does not appear to be reported in an official report. We utilize it as a secondary authority, the citation of which is not prohibited by California Rules of Court, Rule 977, prohibiting citation of California cases not certified for publication in the California official reports.

The distinctive feature of such psychosurgical procedures is the destruction, removal, or disconnection of brain tissue in order to modify or control "thoughts, feelings, actions, or behavior" when the tissue is normal or when there is no evidence any abnormality has caused the behavioral disorder. Psychosurgery is also distinguished from "shock" therapy by its *experimental* nature. Psychosurgery is an irreversible alteration of the brain and its functions that presents serious risks to patients, some of which risks are unknown. The court in *Kaimowitz, supra,* at page 475 concluded that the dangers of such surgery are undisputed. Such a procedure often leads to "the blunting of emotions, the deadening of memory, the reduction of affect, and limits the ability to generate new ideas." (*Kaimowitz, supra,* at p. 478.)

"Shock" treatment, more accurately termed "electroconvulsive therapy" (ECT), is the name given to a group of therapies which involves passing electrical currents through the brain in order to induce convulsions. The therapeutic effects of ECT are generally believed to be obtained by the seizure produced by the stimulation of the central nervous system. The risks attending such treatment have been greatly reduced by the use of muscle relaxants and general anesthetics, which greatly reduce the body convulsions that led to bone fractures in the past. The mechanism by which ECT confers its benefits is still unknown, but two facts stand out in almost every discussion of the treatment: first, ECT does relieve symptoms of certain mental illnesses, most notably acute depression, and is widely recognized therapy for obtaining remission of those symptoms; second, ECT has several adverse effects, including memory loss and intellectual disorientation. The extent of memory loss and the risk of permanent memory loss are not fully known or agreed upon, but the fact of memory loss is not questioned. The risk of other adverse effects is possible, since the procedure is still so little understood. Those possible risks include permanent brain damage in the local area of the electrodes and a slowing of brain waves. The outstanding features of ECT, then, are the acknowledged benefits in the treatment of certain illnesses, and the intrusive and possibly hazardous character of the treatment.

The petitioners, and *amici curiae* in support of the petition for writ of mandate, rest their attack on the amended and added Welfare & Institutions Code sections on several asserted constitutional infirmities: They allege denial of equal protection under the Fourteenth Amendment because of unreasonable classifications of mental patients. They allege the prescribed statutory disclosure to patients of "all of the possible risks and possible side effects" conflicts with the standard set for informed consent in *Cobbs* v. *Grant,* 8 Cal.3d 229, 245-246, 104 Cal.Rptr. 505, 502 P.2d 1, that there need not be disclosure of risks if the patient does not want to know and a limited disclosure if the patient would be so seriously upset he could not "dispassionately weigh the risks of refusing to undergo the recommended treatment"; the procedures for informing the patient so he may consent, and the procedures for obtaining review board approval of the proposed therapy are said to violate due process because the language is unconstitutionally vague. The changes are said to violate substantive and procedural due process because the patient's constitutional rights of privacy, freedom of thought, and access to adequate medical treatment are infringed upon without adequate procedural safeguards or sufficient relation to a compelling state interest.

A. Equal Protection

Petitioners' equal protection arguments are without merit. Regulation of intrusive and possibly hazardous forms of medical treatments is a proper exercise of the state's police power. Public health and safety protection in the field of medical practice is an acknowledged, legitimate function of the police power. Licensing of physicians (Bus. & Prof.Code § 2000 *et seq.*), regulation of conditions within medical treatment facilities (Health & Saf. Code § 1400 *et seq.;* Welf. & Inst.Code § 7000 *et seq.*), and regulation of drug administration (Health & Saf.Code § 11000 *et seq.*), are examples of the proper exercise of this power (see *Blinder* v. *Division of Narcotic Enforcement,* 25 Cal.App.3d 174, 181-182, 101 Cal.Rptr. 635). The provisions of the Lanterman-Petris-Short Act "demonstrate the concern of the Legislature that the *patient's* rights receive full protection at all times" (*Thorn* v. *Superior Court,* 1 Cal.3d 666, 673-674, 83 Cal.Rptr. 600, 605, 464 P.2d 56, 61). [Emphasis added.] The added and amended law is an extension of the protection of those rights and must be viewed as more than the mere regulation of medical procedures for the public health and safety.

The equal protection clause of the Fourteenth Amendment is a limitation on the police power. The Legislature may make a reasonable classification of persons and other activities and pass special legislation applying to certain classes, if the classification is not arbitrary and is based on some difference in the classes having a substantial relation to a legitimate object to be accomplished (*Brown* v. *Merlo,* 8 Cal.3d 855, 861, 106 Cal.Rptr. 388, 506 P.2d 212). The objective of the challenged law is to insure certain medical procedures are not performed on unwilling patients. The classifications that single out mental patients and two specific procedures are rationally related to that objective.

Mental patients are distinct from other ill patients in two special circumstances. First, their competence to accede to treatment is more questionable than that of other patients. Mental patients' incompetence may not be presumed solely by their hospitalization (§ 5331), but it is common knowledge mentally ill persons are more likely to lack the ability to understand the nature of a medical procedure and appreciate its risks. Second, their ability to voluntarily accept treatment is questionable. The impossibility of an involuntarily detained person voluntarily giving informed consent to these medical procedures is fully treated in *Kaimowitz* v. *Department of Mental Health for the State of Michigan, supra,* 2 Prison L.Rptr. at p. 477 and *Wyatt* v. *Hardin* (Civ. Action No. 3195-N [M.D.Ala. Feb. 28, 1975]) *supra.* "Voluntary" patients, newly included within the protection of the "Patients' Bill of Rights" (§ 5325) are susceptible to many of the pressures placed on involuntary patients. The Legislature's inclusion of these "voluntary" patients recognizes the fact the "voluntary" label is a creation of the Legislature, and often only means the patient did not formally protest hospitalization. These circumstances make the separate treatment of mental patients clearly rationally related to the objective of insuring their rights to refuse treatment. The special regulation of psychosurgery and ECT is also a reasonable classification because these procedures, associated with *mental* illness, present a great danger of violating the patient's rights.

Petitioners and *amici* in support of the petition assert section 5326.4 conflicts with California law and violates patients' constitutional rights as declared in *Cobbs* v. *Grant, supra,* 8 Cal.3d 229. Petitioners object to the requirement "[a]ll of the possible risks and possible side effects to the patient should he consent" to ECT, be disclosed to the patient as an element of the "informed consent" necessary before treatment. Petitioners do not object to the almost identical language of section 5326.3 referring to the elements of informed consent for psychosurgery. Petitioners rely on *Cobbs* v. *Grant, supra,* 8 Cal.3d 229, 104 Cal.Rptr. 505, 502 P.2d 1, contending that decision gives patients the right to *refuse* information.

The court in *Cobbs* was concerned with the patient's right to express an informed consent before medical treatment. The petitioners rely on language which concerns a doctor's defenses to tort actions for battery or negligence. In the context of a malpractice suit, the patient's request to be left uninformed would be a defense to the doctor's nondisclosure. The court also said the *only* time a patient should be "denied the opportunity to weigh the risks" is

> ... where it is evident he cannot evaluate the data, as for example, where there is an emergency or the patient is a child or incompetent. (*Cobbs* v. *Grant*, 8 Cal.3d 229, 243, 104 Cal.Rptr. 505, 514, 502 P.2d 1, 10.)

Thus, a patient's request to be left uninformed may provide a doctor a defense to a tort action, but it does not *obligate* or constitutionally coerce the doctor into acceding to the patient's wishes. The Legislature has determined ECT and psychosurgery are such intrusive and hazardous procedures that informed consent is a mandatory prerequisite to treatment. *Cobbs* v. *Grant, supra,* 8 Cal.3d 229, 104 Cal.Rptr. 505, 502 P.2d 1, does not prevent such a determination; it provides that, except in the instances of simple procedures, or where the patient is incompetent to make a decision, there is a right to full information. The right to fully informed consent protects the patient's constitutional rights. (See *Kaimowitz* v. *Department of Mental Health for the State of Michigan, supra,* 2 Prison L.Rptr. p. 477; see also *New York City Health & Hosp. Corp.* v. *Stein,* 70 Misc.2d 944, 335 N.Y.S.2d 461, 464.)

B. Vagueness

'[A] statute which either forbids or requires the doing of an act in terms so vague that men of common intelligence must necessarily guess at its meaning and differ as to its application violates the first essential of due process of law.' (*Connally* v. *General Construction Co.* ... 269 U.S. 385, 391, 46 S.Ct. 126, 127, 70 L.Ed. 322; ...) (*People* v. *Barksdale*, 8 Cal.3d 320, 327, 105 Cal.Rptr. 1, 6, 503 P.2d 257, 260.)

Petitioners contend various provisions of the new statute are so ambiguous they cannot be constitutionally enforced: first, the terms "private mental institution," "psychosurgery" and "shock treatment" (§ 5325); second, the terms of sections 5326.3(c) and 5326.4(3) which establish elements of informed consent; and third, the terms of sections 5326.3(d) and 5326.4(d) which refer to the criteria for approval by a review committee.

> Where the requisite certainty is not apparent on the face of the statute the deficiency may be satisfied by "common understanding and practices" [citations] "or from any demonstrably established technical or common law meaning of the language in question" [citation]. (*People* v. *Barksdale*, 8 Cal.3d 320, 327, 105 Cal.Rptr. 1, 6, 503 P.2d 257, 260.)

Contrary to petitioners' contentions "psychosurgery" and "shock treatment" have established technical meanings. The meaning of "psychosurgery" is evident on the *face* of the statute. It clearly does not refer to surgical procedures other than those used for modification of behavior, thought, or feelings, in the treatment of mental illnesses. "Shock treatment" is an inexact term since it refers to the characteristics of "shock" rather than "convulsion," which is the primary feature of that form of treatment. It is clear, however, the Legislature intended to include electroconvulsive therapy (ECT) within the term "shock treatment" and did not intend to include "defibrillation of the heart" which is not associated with the treatment of mental disorders. It is less clear whether convulsive therapies based on drug-induced convulsions are properly included within the term. "Shock treatment" does not necessarily include all convulsive therapies, although the intention of the Legislature to so include them may be inferred from their similarity to ECT in almost every respect. Because certain drug therapies are referred to as insulin "shock" therapies, it is reasonable to conclude "shock treatment" is not restricted to ECT, and includes both insulin coma therapy and other drug-induced convulsion therapies.

The term "private mental institution" means "acute psychiatric hospital" (Health & Saf.Code § 1250(b)), which provides for the care of persons referred to an institution under Division 5 and Division 6 of the Welfare & Institutions Code. An institution does not become a "mental institution" merely by providing psychiatric services under Health and Safety Code section 1255(e). In addition to its meaning set out in the statute, the term is also commonly understood.

The contention the subsections of sections 5326.3 and 5326.4, requiring explanations of all of the possible risks, possible side effects, and the degree of uncertainty of the benefits and hazards associated with the procedure, are void for vagueness is also unmeritorious. Whatever may be the wisdom of such a strict standard of disclosure, the statutory language calls for a full explanation to the patient of all relevant information. Thus, the requirement of all possible risks and possible side effects must be read to mean the disclosure of all risks and side effects thought to be associated with these procedures. As the court's opinion in *People* v. *Barksdale, supra,* 8 Cal.3d 320, 328, 105 Cal.Rptr. 1, 503 P.2d 257, makes clear, "risk" is a sufficiently well-defined term, and even "substantial risk" is not unconstitutionally vague. *Barksdale* objects to language using a degree of impairment as a standard. Describing the uncertainty of results in terms of degree is a far cry from determining the degree of harm which is meant by "gravely impair."

Petitioners' final concern is with the requirements of sections 5326.3 and 5326.4 that the treating physician give "adequate documentation" of the reasons for the procedure and determine "all other appropriate treatment modalities have been exhausted and . . . this mode of treatment is critically needed for the welfare of the patient." "Adequate documentation" is documentation of sufficient facts for a review committee to make independent determinations on the basis of the record. Mere conclusory statements may not be used as a basis for concurrence. "Appropriate modalities" are any forms of treatment medically appropriate for a *particular* patient with a *particular* condition. Alternative forms of treatment have been "exhausted" when they have been tried and found insufficient. The legislative intent is to make the more radical procedures the treatments of "last resort" and to require medically appropriate alternative therapies be attempted first. Every possible form of therapy need not actually be used on a patient, because not all forms will be considered appropriate for that patient. This is a purely medical determination, which is within a doctor's professional judgment.

There is, however, one criterion which is so imprecise this Court is compelled to conclude it as impermissibly vague: the requirement a procedure be "critically" needed for the patient's welfare. While the "welfare" of a patient is arguably imprecise, it encompasses the patient's physical well-being, psychological health, ability to function in his society, and ability to attain happiness—a broad range of interests to be considered and protected. The requirement a procedure be "critically" needed for the patient's welfare, however, provides no guide to the degree of need required.

In *People* v. *Barksdale, supra*, 8 Cal.3d 320, 105 Cal.Rptr. 1, 503 P.2d 257, the court considered the California Therapeutic Abortion Act, and specifically the language concerning the criteria for approval of an abortion. The most frequently used ground of approval was "[a] substantial risk that continuance of the pregnancy would gravely impair" the health of the mother (Health & Saf.Code § 25951, subd. (c)(1). The court said it was unable to ascertain the "degree of impairment" that would "gravely impair" a prospective abortee's health. For similar reasons, this Court cannot ascertain what degree of need is required by a "critical" need.

"Critically" means "in a critical manner." "Critical" means "crucial, decisive"; "in or approaching a crisis"; "of doubtful issue: attended by risk or uncertainty" (Webster's 3d *New Internat. Dict.*, unabridged). "Critical" is also defined as "fraught with danger or risk; perilous" (*Am. Heritage Dict. of the Eng. Lang.*, W. Morris, ed., 1969). A patient with acute depression and suicidal tendencies would come within the standard if the form of treatment were essential to protect his life. But what of the patient who does not have self-destructive tendencies and is completely dysfunctional psychologically? Does an inability to remain employed or married qualify as a "critical" condition? Must there be a danger of deterioration, or is a stable condition of severe psychosis critical? If all other forms of appropriate therapies have been attempted, has a "critical" need for ECT or psychosurgery been established?

It seems probable the legislative intent was to require a compelling need for these forms of treatment beyond the mere existence of a behavioral or mental disorder. There seems to be a tacit assumption by the Legislature the cure is sometimes more harmful than the disease, and only the most dangerous and harmful conditions should be so treated. Some persons of "common intelligence" may agree an assessment of impending injury, absent prompt treatment, gives rise to a critical need. Others of like intelligence may demand considerably more, or somewhat less. We conclude on its face the "critically needed" criterion is impermissibly vague.

C. Due Process

The regulation of ECT and psychosurgery is a legitimate exercise of the state's inherent police power. The state has an interest in seeing that these procedures, like other medical procedures, are performed under circumstances insuring maximum safety for the patient. These two procedures are not identical in their effect on the patient, nor in their acceptance by the medical community, and may be regulated in different ways and to differing extents. The state has an interest in protecting patients from unwarranted, unreasonable and unconsented-to invasions of body and mind. Arrayed against these legitimate state interests are equally valid considerations of rights of privacy, freedom of speech and thought, and the right to medical treatment.

Petitioners contend the right of privacy is broad enough to include the selection of, and consent to, medical procedures. Although the Constitution does not explicitly mention the right of personal privacy, it has been found in the First, Third, Fourth, Fifth, Ninth and Fourteenth Amendments, and in the penumbra of the Bill of Rights. "[But] only personal rights that can be deemed 'fundamental' . . . are included in this guarantee of personal privacy" (*Roe* v. *Wade,* 410 U.S. 113, 152, 158, 93 S.Ct. 705, 726, 35 L.Ed.2d 147). Those fundamental rights include activities relating to marriage (*Loving* v. *Commonwealth of Virginia,* 388 U.S. 1, 87 S.Ct. 1817, 18 L.Ed.2d 1010); procreation (*Skinner* v. *State of Oklahoma,* 316 U.S. 535, 62 S.Ct. 1110, 86 L.Ed. 1655); contraception (*Eisenstadt* v. *Baird,* 405 U.S. 438, 92 S.Ct. 1029, 31 L.Ed.2d 349); family relationships (*Prince* v. *Commonwealth of Massachusetts,* 321 U.S. 158, 64 S.Ct. 438, 88 L.Ed. 645); and child rearing and education (*Pierce* v. *Society of the Sisters of the Holy Name, etc.,* 268 U.S. 510, 45 S.Ct. 571, 69 L.Ed. 1070; *Meyer* v. *State of Nebraska,* 262 U.S. 390, 43 S.Ct. 625, 67 L.Ed. 1042; *Roe* v. *Wade, supra,* 410 U.S. 113, 152-153, 93 S.Ct. 705, 35 L.Ed.2d 147). While the decision to terminate a pregnancy is includable within those "fundamental" rights as an activity closely related to the above activities, we need not decide whether the decision to undergo medical treatment is deserving of constitutional protection in and of itself (*cf. Roe* v. *Wade, supra,* 410 U.S. 113, 209-221, 95 S.Ct. 705, 35 L.Ed.2d 147), because the right to privacy so clearly includes privacy of the mind.

The right to be free in the exercise of one's own thoughts is essential to the exercise of other constitutionally guaranteed rights. First Amendment rights of free speech would mean little if the state were to control thought. "Our whole constitutional heritage rebels at the thought of giving government the power to control men's minds. . . ." (*Stanley* v. *Georgia,* 394 U.S. 557, 565-566, 89 S.Ct. 1243, 1248, 22 L.Ed.2d 542). Here the state has sought to control neither what is thought by mental patients, nor how they think. Rather, the state is attempting to regulate the use of procedures which touch upon thought processes in significant ways, with neither the intention nor the effect of regulating thought processes, *per se.* Yet despite the lack of any showing the state has attempted to regulate freedom of thought, this legislation may diminish this right. If so, the legislation can only be sustained by showing (1) it is necessary to further a "compelling state interest" and (2) the least drastic means has been employed to further those interests (*Roe* v. *Wade, supra,* 410 U.S. 113, 155, 93 S.Ct. 705, 35 L.Ed.2d 147).

Freedom of thought is intimately touched upon by any regulation of procedures affecting thought and feelings. In an effort to protect freedom of thought, the state has put procedural and substantive obstacles in the path of those who both need and desire certain forms of treatment, and in that way their freedom of thought remains impaired because they cannot get treatment. The means of alleviating mental disorders generate their own kinds of fear and misunderstanding. This attitude touches our public affairs; the fact of treatment alone may impair our confidence in people of unquestioned talent and industry. Psychosurgery and (ECT) are viewed, rightly or wrongly, as drastic, radical forms of treatment compared to psychotherapy or drug therapy, and indicative of more severe illness. Public exposure, or even disclosure to limited numbers of government representatives, may have a chilling effect on patients' efforts to undergo these treatments, thereby restricting their freedom of thought. Some patients will be denied treatment as a natural and intended result of this legislation. Although the reasons for such denials may be the patients' own best interests, such regulation must be justified by a compelling state interest.

As previously explained, there are three changes because of the new legislation: First, voluntary patients as well as institutionalized mentally retarded persons are included within the mental patients' Bill of Rights of the Lanterman-Petris-Short Act. This change recognizes the fact that "voluntary" and "involuntary" labels do not always indicate the voluntariness of a specific patient. Second, the denial of patients' rights for good cause (§ 5326) was made inapplicable to psychosurgery and "shock treatment" by requiring the informed consent of the patient prior to treatment. To this end, the Legislature defined the contents of informed consent. The purpose was to insure consent was competent, informed, and voluntary. Third, a review procedure was established to determine the patient's competence and the necessity and appropriateness of the proposed treatment. The review procedure was also established to approve the administration of "shock treatment" to patients who were found incompetent to give or withhold consent.

Additionally, the new law requires informing a "responsible relative," as well as the patient, of the risks of treatment to obtain informed consent (§ 5326.3). In order to control abuse of denials of patients' rights, a system of reporting is established by section 5326.

Thus, the state's interests, as expressed in the challenged law, may be summarized as the protection of the right to refuse treatment and the prevention of unnecessary administration of hazardous and intrusive treatments. The test of the constitutionality of these provisions will be whether each of them furthers a compelling state interest and is necessary to accomplish the purpose.

The provision that a "responsible relative" be informed of the eight items constituting "informed consent" before the treatment be administered is a violation of the patient's right of privacy and the right to confidentiality established by section 5328. The disclosure of the nature and seriousness of the patient's disorder is a clear infringement of the patient's right of privacy and no countervailing state interest is apparent. Because no standing to assert the patient's rights is granted to the relative, it is doubtful this disclosure furthers the protection of patients' rights or prevents unnecessary treatment. Thus, the requirement of such disclosure is an unconstitutional invasion of the patient's right to privacy.

The establishment of a reporting system seeking to control possible abuses of patients' rights would be a clear invasion of the patients' privacy if the patients' identities were disclosed. The state has a valid interest in the prevention of denials of patients' rights without good cause, and such a reporting system is a reasonable means of achieving that end. To further that end, it must be possible to identify which patients' rights are denied, both to correct individual wrongs and to correct general patterns of abuse. Thus, the report to the Director of Health must provide for identification of individual treatment records, as in section 5326. Although such reports are to be made available to members of the state Legislature, or a member of the county board of supervisors, under the new procedure, those people need not be able to identify individual patients. No report may disclose a patient's identity other than by a code which refers to the patient's treatment record. Members of the Legislature and members of the county boards of supervisors are able to request information pertaining to a denial of rights in such treatment records, but they are not to be permitted to learn the patient's identity or to acquire information other than that pertaining to a denial of rights.

Information in a treatment record about the denial of rights to a patient is also available to the individual patient, his attorney, conservator, or guardian. The disclosure of such information is a limited infringement upon the patient's right to privacy, but it is also one of the most effective possible remedies to abuses. Because only information pertaining to a denial of rights is permitted, and those most likely to assert the patient's rights are the recipients of the information, we interpret that provision of section 5326 as a constitutionally permissible limited infringement on the confidentiality of a patient's identity.

Sections 5326.3 and 5326.4, listing items of information that must be orally explained to the patient in order to get his informed consent before treatment, constitute a minimal invasion of privacy. An oral explanation only invades the patient's privacy to the extent the treating physician would not otherwise be in possession of such information. The information is not recorded in the patient's record and is not made available to any review committee. The explanation does insure the patient gives consent in a knowing, intelligent, and voluntary manner. The state's interest in protecting the patient's right to refuse treatment could not be accomplished by any measure short of such disclosure, and the procedure is constitutional.

The most difficult aspects of this legislation involve the mandatory review of proposed treatments by a review committee. As discussed above, the two forms of treatment are distinct and may be regulated to differing degrees. An analysis of the review procedures involved in each form of treatment will be considered separately.

Consent to psychosurgery is regulated and applied differently to three groups of patients: incompetent, involuntary, and all others. The state's interest in protecting patients from unconsented-to and unnecessary administrations of psychosurgery clearly justifies a review procedure which insures the competence of the patient and the truly voluntary nature of his consent. The incompetent patient is incapable of consenting to such a procedure, and the state's interest in protecting him from such procedures fully justifies the attendant invasion of privacy. Although there are substantial problems of procedural due process involved, a review of a patient's competence by a review committee is constitutional where, as here, there is reason to suspect incompetence.

The involuntary patient presents the dilemma of either prohibiting the administration of psychosurgery to such patients (see *Kaimowitz* v. *Department of Mental Health for the State of Michigan, supra,* 2 Prison L.Rptr. 433), or providing for a substitute decision-making process (see *Wyatt* v. *Stickney,* D.C., 344 F.Supp. 373). Because the voluntariness of such a patient's consent can never be adequately confirmed, the establishment of a review committee to make the treatment decision for the patient is justified by the state's compelling interest in preventing involuntary administration of psychosurgery.

The substantive review of proposed treatments for competent and voluntary patients is a different problem. Once the competency of the patient and voluntariness of the consent is confirmed, what interest of the state can justify the substitution of the review committee's decision for that of the patient and his physician?

The hazardous, experimental nature of psychosurgery is a legitimate reason for the state to regulate its use as a treatment of last resort. Requiring unanimity by the review committee insures each approved treatment is an appropriate use of an experimental procedure. The importance of assuring that consents to psychosurgery be voluntarily given by informed, competent mental patients, plus the need to regulate an experimental procedure, justify the Legislature's decision to remove these considerations from the sole discretion of the treating physician. There are sound reasons why the treating physician's assessment of his patient's competency and voluntariness may not always be objective, and he may not necessarily be the best or most objective judge of how appropriate an experimental procedure would be. Because the consequences to the patient of such a procedure are so serious, and the effects he may suffer are so intrusive and irreversible, tort damages are totally inadequate. The need for some form of restraint is a sufficiently compelling state interest to justify the attendant invasion of the patient's right to privacy. That right to privacy is not absolute (*Roe* v. *Wade, supra,* 410 U.S. 113, 154-155, 93 S.Ct. 705, 35 L.Ed.2d 147) and must give way to appropriate regulation.

The new regulatory scheme as it applies to "shock treatment" is almost identical to the regulatory system for psychosurgery. As previously noted, the oral explanation to the patient required by section 5326.4 is constitutional. The review procedures of section 5326.3, as applied to involuntary or incompetent patients, function the same as those under section 5326.4, and the review is also constitutional. These procedures for involuntary patients provide for a substitute decision-making process because of the difficulty of acquiring a truly voluntary consent to such a procedure (see *Kaimowitz, supra,* and *Wyatt* v. *Stickney, supra,* 344 F.Supp. 373). In the case of incompetent patients, the substitute decision-making process permits the use of this form of treatment for patients who cannot consent for themselves. These applications of section 5326.4 are constitutional for the reasons previously discussed.

The thorny question in section 5326.4 concerns the application of the review system to voluntary competent patients. As already noted, the state has a compelling interest in assuring the competency and voluntariness of patients who undergo this form of treatment. To this end, the review system is compatible with due process. However, once the competency of a voluntary patient has been confirmed, and the truly voluntary nature of his consent is determined, the state has little excuse to invoke the substitute decision-making process. "Shock treatment," or more precisely ECT, is not an experimental procedure, nor are its hazards as serious as those of psychosurgery. Petitioners' reliance on *Doe* v. *Bolton,* 410 U.S. 179, 93 S.Ct. 739, 35 L.Ed.2d 201 is well-founded. Where informed consent is adequately insured, there is no justification for infringing upon the patient's right to privacy in selecting and consenting to the treatment. The state has varied interests which are served by the regulation of ECT, but these interests are not served where the patient and his physician are the best judges of the patient's health, safety and welfare.

Therefore, insofar as section 5326.4 applies to competent and voluntary patients who have given competent, voluntary and informed consent, it is unconstitutional. Substantive review is proper for involuntary or incompetent patients because there is a need for a substitute decision-maker. Any possible need which exists for the voluntary and competent patient cannot prevail in the face of the serious infringement to the patient's right to privacy as guaranteed by *Roe* v. *Wade, supra,* 410 U.S. 113, 93 S.Ct. 705, 35 L.Ed.2d 147 and *Doe* v. *Bolton, supra,* 410 U.S. 179, 93 S.Ct. 739, 35 L.Ed.2d 201.

Petitioners and *amici* also assert the new legislation denies procedural due process because it denies substantive rights without adequate procedural safeguards.

> The fundamental requirement of due process is an opportunity to be heard upon such notice and proceedings as are adequate to safeguard the right for which the constitutional protection is invoked. (*Anderson Nat. Bank* v. *Luckett,* 321 U.S. 233, 246 [64 S.Ct. 599, 606, 88 L.Ed. 692].)

The new procedures provide an inadequate hearing for patients on the issues of competency and voluntariness, and for these reasons are found lacking in procedural due process.

Relying upon *Jacobson* v. *Massachusetts,* 197 U.S. 11, 25 S.Ct. 358, 49 L.Ed. 643, petitioners also assert a constitutional right to care for one's own health is unconstitutionally invaded by the new procedure. We reject the notion the case recognizes any such fundamental right. The court deciding *Jacobson* held the vaccination of citizens against smallpox is a valid exercise of the state's police power. Petitioners also unmeritoriously assert a constitutional right to medical treatment (*Rouse* v. *Cameron,* 125 U.S.App.D.C. 366, 373 F.2d 451). Where this right is concerned, due process requires only that the state, once it has institutionalized a person for the purpose of treatment, provide reasonable treatment or release the person (see *Wyatt* v. *Aderholt,* 5 Cir., 503 F.2d 1305, 1312-1314). In the present case, any denial of treatment is tantamount to a finding that that particular form of treatment is not reasonable. It is not a denial of any or all treatment.

Petitioners contend the requirement two members of the review committee be certified constitutes an unconstitutional infringement upon the doctor-patient relationship as guaranteed by *Doe* v. *Bolton, supra,* 410 U.S. 179, 93 S.Ct. 739, 35 L.Ed.2d

201. *Doe* struck down the requirement that hospitals in which abortions were to be performed must be accredited by the Joint Commission on Accreditation of Hospitals, as violating the Fourteenth Amendment, because the accreditation requirement was not based on differences "reasonably related to the purposes of the Act in which it is found" (*Morey* v. *Doud*, 354 U.S. 457, 465, 77 S.Ct. 1344, 1350, 1 L.Ed.2d 1485). Here, the board certification is based on the fact the treatment procedures are hazardous and intrusive in a way other procedures are not. Furthermore, psychosurgery is considered experimental. These treatment aspects call for a higher level of competence and training where the physician must exercise his judgment in place of the patient's. The requirement is constitutional.

Conclusion

The validity of section 5326 except for references to sections 5325(f) and 5326.4 is not challenged. With the exception of section 5325(g), the unchallenged portions of section 5326 and the remainder of section 5325 were enacted before the objectionable amendments. They list patient rights, require the list to be posted, regulate the denial of those rights, and provide for release of information. They do not relate to the conditions for allowing psychosurgery or shock treatment, and can stand alone. Section 5325(g) defines psychosurgery for the purpose of disallowing the procedure when the patient refuses, which is a valid legislative purpose under the police power, a result which is unaffected by our declaration other sections are unconstitutional.

Section 5326 is constitutional when the references to section 5325(f) and 5326.4 are excised.

Section 5326.3 is unconstitutionally vague insofar as the criterion for treatment is "critically needed for the welfare of the patient"; the requirement of informing a "responsible relative" is an unconstitutional invasion of the patient's right to privacy; and the failure to provide for adequate notice of hearing is a denial of procedural due process.

Section 5326.4 has the same constitutional infirmities as section 5326.3, and, in addition, is unconstitutional because it subjects the decision of competent, voluntary patients to substantive review.

To excise the constitutionally infirm provisions from sections 5326.3 and 5326.4 would involve a wholesale rewriting of those sections, a task not properly undertaken by a court (*People* v. *Stevenson*, 58 Cal.2d 794, 798, 26 Cal.Rptr. 297, 376 P.2d 297). We thus hold sections 5326.3 and 5326.4 are unconstitutional in their entirety.

Section 5326.5 fails because it is a penalty provision dependent on sections 5326.3 and 5326.4 (*People* v. *Stevenson*, *supra*, 58 Cal.2d 794, 798, 26 Cal.Rptr. 297, 376 P.2d 297).

For the reasons stated, we declare the reference to sections 5325(f) and 5326.4 in section 5326, sections 5326.3, 5326.4 and 5326.5 invalid.

Accordingly, let a peremptory writ of mandate issue.

AULT and CALOGNE, JJ., concur.

NOTES

1.   The statutory provision dealing with the involvement of a "responsible relative," which was struck down by the *Aden* v. *Younger* court, is exemplary of a belief, held by many medical personnel, that relatives have a say in the treatment of patients. As the decision indicates, except for formally appointed guardians, the views or consent of relatives have little legal relevance to treatment decisions in such instances. Cf. *Anonymous* v. *State,* discussed in n. 2 on p. 801, above.

2.   The extensive statutory safeguards at issue in *Aden* v. *Younger* are perhaps the result of previous abuses of electroshock and psychosurgery in California as documented in *Farber* v. *Olkon,* 40 C.2d 503, 254 P.2d 520 (1953). The unfortunate plaintiff in *Farber* was a patient whose condition was diagnosed as "chronic schizophrenia with hebephrenic and paranoid features with progressive mental deterioration," 254 P.2d at 521. With the consent of the patient's father, a lobotomy was performed upon him. Some 2 months after the lobotomy, he was subjected to electroshock treatment. He emerged from the electroshock therapy with fractures of both femur bones, which resulted in permanent deformations of both hips. To add legal insult to grievous mental and physical injury, the Supreme Court of California held that the electroshock procedures had been performed with due care and that, therefore, the harm inflicted upon the plaintiff gave rise to no cause of action in tort.

3.   The comprehensive standards for treatment of mentally ill patients established in *Wyatt* v. *Stickney,* 344 F.Supp. 373 (M.D.Ala. 1971) (see p. 630, above) included the following:

> 9. Patients have a right not to be subjected to treatment procedures such as lobotomy, electro-convulsive treatment, adversive reinforcement conditioning or other unusual or hazardous treatment procedures without their express and informed consent after consultation with counsel or interested party of the patient's choice (*Id.* at 380).

This provision should be contrasted with the comparable *Wyatt* standards for Alabama's institutions for mentally retarded persons:

> 24. Behavior modification programs involving the use of noxious or aversive stimuli shall be reviewed and approved by the institution's Human Rights Committee and shall be conducted only with the express and informed consent of the affected resident, if the resident is able to give such consent, and of his guardian or next of kin, after opportunities for consultation with independent specialists and with legal counsel. Such behavior modification programs shall be conducted only under the supervision of and in the presence of a Qualified Mental Retardation Professional who has had proper training in such techniques.
>
> 25. Electric shock devices shall be considered a research technique for the purpose of these standards. Such devices shall only be used in extraordinary circumstances to prevent self-mutilation leading to repeated and possibly permanent physical damage to the resident and only after alternative techniques have failed. The use of such devices shall be subject to the conditions prescribed in Standard 24, *supra,* and Standard 29, *infra,* and shall be used only under the direct and specific order of the superintendent.
>
> * * *
>
> 29. Residents shall have a right not to be subjected to experimental research without the express and informed consent of the resident, if the resident is able to give such consent, and of his guardian or next of kin, after opportunities for consultation with

independent specialists and with legal counsel. Such proposed research shall first have been reviewed and approved by the institution's Human Rights Committee before such consent shall be sought. Prior to such approval the institution's Human Rights Committee shall determine that such research complies with the principles of the Statement on the Use of Human Subjects for Research of the American Association on Mental Deficiency and with the principles for research involving human subjects required by the United States Department of Health, Education and Welfare for projects supported by that agency (*Wyatt* v. *Stickney,* 344 F.Supp. 387, 400-402 (M.D.Ala. 1971)).

Why are the standards for mentally retarded residents different from those for mentally ill persons? Is there a legal basis for permitting next of kin to give informed consent on behalf of a mentally retarded adult? Cf. *Kaimowitz* v. *Michigan Department of Mental Health,* pp. 808–824, above.

KNECHT v. GILLMAN

United States Court of Appeals for the Eighth Circuit, 1973
488 F.2d 1136

Before HEANEY, ROSS and STEPHENSON, Circuit Judges.

ROSS, Circuit Judge.

This is an action by Gary Knecht and Ronald Stevenson, both in the custody of the State of Iowa, against officials of that state, under 42 U.S.C. § 1983. Their complaint alleged that they had been subjected to injections of the drug apomorphine at the Iowa Security Medical Facility (ISMF) without their consent and that the use of said drug by the defendants constituted cruel and unusual punishment in violation of the eighth amendment. The trial court dismissed their complaint for injunctive relief. We reverse with directions to enjoin the defendants from further use of the drug except pursuant to specific guidelines hereinafter set forth.

After this case was filed in the district court, an order was entered assigning the case to the United States Magistrate for an evidentiary hearing pursuant to Rule 53 of the Federal Rules of Civil Procedure. This hearing was conducted by the magistrate who later filed his "Report and Recommendation" which included a summary of all of the evidence, findings and recommendations to the trial court. He recommended that the complaint be dismissed but that, if the drug was to be used in the future at ISMF, certain precautionary steps be taken in administering the drug and in employing the help of inmate aides. The trial court then gave the parties ten days within which to file objections to the report and recommendations pursuant to Rule 53(e)(2) of Federal Rules of Civil Procedure. Knecht and Stevenson filed their objections seeking clarification of two factual findings of fact. They objected to the recommendations of the magistrate and again requested that the trial court enjoin the injections of apomorphine into nonconsenting inmates. They also requested that the court incorporate the magistrate's recommendation, regarding the future use of inmate aides, into the court's order. The trial court dismissed the complaint and did not adopt the recommendations of the magistrate concerning the administration of apomorphine in the future.

* * *

The summary of the evidence contained in the report of the magistrate showed that apomorphine had been administered at ISMF for some time prior to the hearing as "aversive stimuli" in the treatment of inmates with behavior problems. The drug was administered by intra-muscular injection by a nurse after an inmate had violated the behavior protocol established for him by the staff. Dr. Loeffelholz testified that the drug could be injected for such pieces of behavior as not getting up, for giving cigarettes against orders, for talking, for swearing, or for lying. Other inmates or members of the staff would report on these violations of the protocol and the injection would be given by the nurse without the nurse or any doctor having personally observed the violation and without specific authorization of the doctor.

When it was determined to administer the drug, the inmate was taken to a room near the nurses' station which contained only a water closet and there given the injection. He was then exercised and within about fifteen minutes he began vomiting. The vomiting lasted from fifteen minutes to an hour. There is also a temporary cardiovascular effect which involves some change in blood pressure and "in the heart." This aversion type "therapy" is based on "Pavlovian conditioning."

The record is not clear as to whether or not the drug was always used with the initial consent of the inmate. It has apparently been administered in a few instances in the past without obtaining written consent of the inmate and once the consent is given, withdrawal thereof was not permitted. Apparently, at the time of trial apomorphine was not being used unless the inmate signed an initial consent, but there is no indication that the authorities now permit an inmate to withdraw his consent once it is given. Neither is there any indication in the record that the procedure has been changed to require the prior approval of a physician each time the drug is administered. Likewise there is no indication that there has been any change in the procedure which permits the administration of the drug upon reports of fellow inmates despite a recommendation by the magistrate that this practice should be avoided.

The testimony relating to the medical acceptability of this treatment is not conclusive. Dr. Steven Fox of the University of Iowa testified that behavior modification by aversive stimuli is "highly questionable technique" and that only a 20% to 50% success is claimed. He stated that it is not being used elsewhere to his knowledge and that its use is really punishment worse than a controlled beating since the one administering the drug can't control it after it is administered.

On the other hand, Dr. Loeffelholz of the ISMF staff testified that there had been a 50% to 60% effect in modifying behavior by the use of apomorphine at ISMF. There is no evidence that the drug is used at any other inmate medical facility in any other state.

The Iowa Security Medical Facility is established by Section 223.1, Code of Iowa, 1973. It is an institution for persons displaying evidence of mental illness or psychological disorders and requiring diagnostic services and treatment in a security setting. The patients admitted to the facility may originate from the following sources:

> 1) residents of any institution under the jurisdiction of the department of social services;
> 2) commitments by the courts as mentally incompetent to stand trial under Chapter 783 of the Iowa Code;
> 3) referrals by the court for psychological diagnosis and recommendations as part of the pretrial or presentence procedure or determination of mental competency to stand trial;

4) mentally ill prisoners from county and city jails for diagnosis, evaluation, or treatment.

Section 223.4, Code of Iowa, 1973.

Those transferred from institutions where they were committed pursuant to civil statutes or those who were committed by order of the court prior to conviction, suffer a compromise of their procedural rights in the process of the transfer to ISMF. The constitutional justification of this compromise of procedure is that the purpose of commitment is treatment, not punishment. Cf. *McKeiver* v. *Pennsylvania,* 403 U.S. 528, 552, 91 S.Ct. 1976, 29 L.Ed.2d 647 (White, J., concurring) (1971); *Sas* v. *Maryland,* 334 F.2d 506, 509 (4th Cir. 1964). Beyond this justification for treatment is the clear command of the statutes that the purpose of confinement at ISMF is not penal in nature, but rather one of examination, diagnosis and treatment. Naturally, examination and diagnosis, by their very definition, do not encompass the administration of drugs. Thus, when that course of conduct is taken with respect to any particular patient, he is the recipient of treatment.

The use of apomorphine, then, can be justified, only if it can be said to be treatment. Based upon the testimony adduced at the hearing and the findings made by the magistrate and adopted by the trial court, it is not possible to say that the use of apomorphine is a recognized and acceptable medical practice in institutions such as ISMF. Neither can we say, however, that its use on inmates who knowingly and intelligently consent to the treatment, should be prohibited on a medical or a legal basis. The authorities who testified at the evidentiary hearing indicate that some form of consent is now obtained prior to this treatment. The only question then is whether, under the eighth amendment, its use should be prohibited absent such consent; and if so what procedure must be followed to prevent abuses in the treatment procedures and to make certain the consent is knowingly and intelligently made.

At the outset we note that the mere characterization of an act as "treatment" does not insulate it from eighth amendment scrutiny. In *Trop* v. *Dulles,* 356 U.S. 86, 95, 78 S.Ct. 590, 2 L.Ed. 2d 630 (1958), the Supreme Court stated that the legislative classification of a statute is not conclusive in determining whether there had been a violation of the eighth amendment. Instead, the Court examined the statute by an "inquiry directed to substance," reasoning that "even a clear legislative classification of a statute as 'nonpenal' would not alter the fundamental nature of a plainly penal statute." *Trop* v. *Dulles, supra,* 356 U.S. at 95, 78 S.Ct. at 595.

Other courts have examined nonpenal statutes in the manner suggested by the Supreme Court in *Trop.* The contention that a state's incarceration of runaway juveniles could not violate the eighth amendment because the statute did not authorize any punishment of juveniles was struck down in *Vann* v. *Scott,* 467 F.2d 1235, 1240 (7th Cir. 1972):

> Whatever the State does with the child is done in the name of rehabilitation. Since—the argument runs—by definition the treatment is not "punishment," it obviously cannot be "cruel and unusual punishment." But neither the label which a State places on its own conduct, nor even the legitimacy of its motivation, can avoid the applicability of the

Federal Constitution. We have no doubt that well intentioned attempts to rehabilitate a child could, in extreme circumstances, constitute cruel and unusual punishment proscribed by the Eighth Amendment.

The absence of criminal incarceration did not prohibit a federal court from entertaining an eighth amendment claim to test the conditions of confinement in a boys' training school:

> The fact that juveniles are *in theory* not punished, but merely confined for rehabilitative purposes, does not preclude operation of the Eighth Amendment. The reality of confinement in Annex B is that it is punishment.

Inmates of the Boys' Training School v. *Affleck,* 346 F.Supp. 1354, 1366 (D.R.I. 1972).

Such findings of cruel and unusual punishment have been sustained with respect to the death penalty, penal incarceration for status, civil commitment for status without treatment, striprooms and solitary confinements, tranquilizing drugs, and corporeal punishment for prisoners. However, any such determination rests on the facts of a particular case.

Here we have a situation in which an inmate may be subjected to a morphine base drug which induces vomiting for an extended period of time. Whether it is called "aversive stimuli" or punishment, the act of forcing someone to vomit for a fifteen minute period for committing some minor breach of the rules can only be regarded as cruel and unusual unless the treatment is being administered to a patient who knowingly and intelligently has consented to it. To hold otherwise would be to ignore what each of us has learned from sad experience—that vomiting (especially in the presence of others) is a painful and debilitating experience. The use of this unproven drug for this purpose on an involuntary basis is, in our opinion, cruel and unusual punishment prohibited by the eighth amendment.

We turn then to the question of how best to prevent abuse in the treatment procedures of consenting participants and how to make certain that the consent is knowingly and intelligently given. 42 U.S.C. § 1983 does not specify the scope of judicial relief available in an action successfully sustained under its terms. Yet this fact does not limit the courts in framing appropriate relief. Its counterpart, 42 U.S.C. § 1982, is likewise framed only in declaratory terms, but the Supreme Court has held that a federal court is not thereby precluded from fashioning an effective equitable remedy. *Jones* v. *Alfred H. Mayer Co.,* 392 U.S. 409, 414 n.13, 88 S.Ct. 2186, 20 L.Ed.2d 1189 (1968). The substantive scope of relief available is a matter of the equitable powers of the federal courts. Accordingly, courts have exercised broad remedial power in civil rights actions.

* * *

In this case the trial court should enjoin the use of apomorphine in the treatment of inmates at the ISMF except when the following conditions are complied with:

1. A written consent must be obtained from the inmate specifying the nature of the treatment, a written description of the purpose, risks and effects of treatment, and advising the inmate of his right to terminate the consent at any time. This consent

must include a certification by a physician that the patient has read and understands all of the terms of the consent and that the inmate is mentally competent to
understand fully all of the provisions thereof and give his consent thereto.

2.   The consent may be revoked at any time after it is given and if an inmate orally
expresses an intention to revoke it to any member of the staff, a revocation form
shall be provided for his signature at once.

3.   Each apomorphine injection shall be individually authorized by a doctor and be
administered by a doctor, or by a nurse. It shall be authorized in each instance only
upon information based on the personal observation of a member of the professional staff. Information from inmates or inmate aides of the observation of behavior in violation of an inmate's protocol shall not be sufficient to warrant such
authorization.

The judgment of the district court is reversed with directions to grant the
injunction under the terms hereinbefore set forth.

STEPHENSON, Circuit Judge.

I concur with the result.

NOTES

1.   Are the procedural prerequisites set out by the court applicable to all kinds of
medical treatment, or is the court particularly concerned because the treatment consists
of aversive conditioning or because it involves injection of a drug?

2.   Are the safeguards outlined in *Knecht* v. *Gillman* adequate for use in the context
of psychosurgery or electroshock?

SCOTT v. PLANTE

United States Court of Appeals for the Third Circuit, 1976
532 F.2d 939, 945-947

Before SEITZ, Chief Judge, and GIBBONS and ROSENN, Circuit Judges.
OPINION OF THE COURT
GIBBONS, Circuit Judge.

[The Plaintiff, Allen B. Scott, described as "a long time resident of Trenton
State Hospital, a psychiatric hospital to which New Jersey has customarily committed
persons charged with a crime but unable to stand trial or acquitted by reason of
insanity," filed a series of *pro se* complaints alleging a variety of claims against an
array of defendants. The district court had disposed of these claims either by dismissal
for insufficiency or by granting summary judgment to defendants. The Court of Appeals
held that several of these dispositions were erroneous. Only the portion of the court's
opinion dealing with the plaintiff's involuntary medication claim is included here.]

I. The Involuntary Medication Claim

Scott never saw, and hence could never respond to, the affidavits filed in
support of the Attorney General's motion for summary judgment on the involuntary
medication claim. Our examination of Dr. Saexinger's affidavit discloses that Scott has

received Thorazine, Compazine, Mellaril, Vesprin and Trilafon.[8] (Saexinger affidavit at 2, 4.) But neither Dr. Saexinger's nor Frances McRoberts' affidavit responds to Scott's allegation that he has been given drugs without his consent or that of a guardian. Thus, for present purposes we must take Scott's assertion as true, and we can affirm the award of summary judgment only if we conclude, as the district court did, that an allegation of the involuntary administration of psychotherapeutic substances does not state a cause of action under 42 U.S.C. § 1983 and the fourteenth amendment.

The district court made reference to N.J.S.A. 30:4-7.2, which requires notice to and a request for consent from a parent or guardian before treatment can be given to an incompetent inmate of a New Jersey mental institution, and suggested that if the statute was violated there might be a cause of action under the New Jersey Tort Claims Act. See N.J.S.A. 59:1-1 et seq. Certainly, absent an emergency, unconsented to medical treatment is a tort. E.g., Winters v. Miller, 446 F.2d 65, 68 (2d Cir.), cert. denied, 404 U.S. 985, 92 S.Ct. 450, 30 L.Ed.2d 369 (1971); Dunham v. Wright, 423 F.2d 940 (3d Cir. 1970). The district court concluded, however, that it was inconceivable that the involuntary administration of psychotherapeutic substances could also establish a constitutional deprivation. We cannot agree with this conclusion, for existing case law points to at least three[9] conceivable constitutional deprivations that may accompany the involuntary administration of such substances by state officers acting under color of state law to inmates confined in a state institution. There is no need at this point in the proceedings to define with precision the particular source of Scott's constitutional deprivation.[10] It is sufficient to recognize that the involuntary administration of drugs which affect mental processes, if it occurred, could amount, under an appropriate set of facts, to an interference with Scott's rights under the first amendment. See Mackey v. Procunier, 477 F.2d 877 (9th Cir. 1973); Kaimowitz v. Dep't of Mental Health, Civ. No. 73-19434-AW (Mich.Cir.Ct., Wayne County, July 10, 1973). Moreover, on this record we must assume that Scott, though perhaps properly committable, has never been adjudicated an incompetent who is incapable of giving an informed consent to medical treatment. Under these circumstances due process would

---

[8] It is beyond the scope of this opinion to discuss all the medical effects of these drugs. See generally Goodman & Gillman, Pharmacological Basis of Therapeutics (4th ed. 1970). Thorazine, and to a lesser extent Compazine, have been described as producing a dazed condition, engendering apathy and slowing the thought process. See Ferleger, "Loosing the Chains: In-Hospital Civil Liberties of Mental Patients," 13 Santa Clara Law. 447, 470 n. 72 (1973), citing Goodman and Gillman, supra. Potential side effects of Thorazine are said to include interference with ejaculation, menstrual changes, drowsiness, rashes, euphoria, enlargement of the breasts, convulsions and Parkinsonism. See Note, "Conditioning and Other Technologies Used to 'Treat?' 'Rehabilitate?' 'Demolish?' Prisoners and Mental Patients," 45 S.Cal.L.Rev. 616 (1972).

[9] A possible fourth constitutional deprivation might include invasion of the inmate's right to bodily privacy which has been adumbrated in various Supreme Court decisions. See, e.g., Roe v. Wade, 410 U.S. 113, 152–53, 93 S.Ct. 705, 35 L.Ed.2d 147 (1973) (brief history of the development of the right); "Developments in the Law–Civil Commitment of the Mentally Ill," 87 Harv.L.Rev. 1190, 1195–96n. 12(1974) (hereinafter Developments in the Law–Civil Commitment); Note, "On Privacy: Constitutional Protection for Personal Liberty," 48 N.Y.U.L.Rev. 670 (1973). The scope of such a right, however, remains ill-defined.

[10] See generally Schwartz, "In the Name of Treatment: Autonomy, Civil Commitment and the Right to Refuse Treatment," 50 Notre Dame Law. 808 (1975); Comment, "Advances in Mental Health: A Case for the Right to Refuse Treatment," 48 Temp.L.Q. 354 (1975).

require, in the absence of an emergency, that some form of notice and opportunity to be heard be given to Scott or to someone standing *in loco parentis* to him before he could be subjected to such treatment. Finally, under certain conditions, Scott's claim may raise an eighth amendment issue respecting cruel and unusual punishment. *See Knecht* v. *Gillman*, 488 F.2d 1136 (8th Cir. 1973); *Mackey* v. *Procunier, supra* at 878.

While the record in this case is inadequate for assessment of the merits of these possible constitutional deprivations, we conclude that the district court's summary dismissal of Scott's involuntary medication claim was improper.

NOTES

1.   Other decisions holding that involuntary administration of drugs can amount to a constitutional deprivation include:

a.   *Nelson* v. *Heyne*, 355 F.Supp. 451 (N.D.Ind. 1972), cert denied 417 U.S. 976 (1973). The court ruled that administration of "major tranquilizing drugs" to control excited behavior at the Indiana Boys' School was "shocking to the conscience and a violation of the Plaintiffs' Eighth and Fourteenth Amendment rights," *id.* at 455.

b.   *Mackey* v. *Procunier*, 477 F.2d 877 (9th Cir. 1973). The Court of Appeals reversed a district court's dismissal of a state prisoner's complaint, and held that a claim that the prisoner had received, without his consent, a "fright drug" at a state medical facility was a sufficient allegation of a violation of the right to freedom from cruel and unusual punishment under the Eighth Amendment and also of the right to be free from "impermissible tinkering with the mental processes," *id.* at 878.

c.   *Souder* v. *McGuire*, 423 F.Supp. 830 (M.D.Pa. 1976). The court upheld against defendants' motion to dismiss the claim of a former inmate at a state hospital for the criminally insane that he and other inmates had been forcibly treated with psychotropic (mind-affecting) drugs. The court ruled that involuntary administration of drugs having a painful or frightening effect can amount to cruel and unusual punishment and may also constitute "an unwarranted governmental intrusion into the patient's thought processes in violation of his constitutional right to privacy," *id.* at 832.

2.   In *In re Fussa*, File No. 66110 (Prob. Ct., Cty. of Hennepin, Minnesota, June 4, 1976), hospital officials petitioned the court for a hearing, pursuant to *Price* v. *Sheppard* pp. 802–807, above), to determine the legal propriety of administering intramuscular Prolixin to an involuntarily committed mental patient. Characterizing Prolixin as "an anti-psychotic medication both generally accepted and frequently prescribed by the practicing psychiatric medical community," Order at p. 2, the court held that the hospital had the authority to administer the proposed treatment without specific court authorization, and dismissed the petition for a hearing as unnecessary. In a Memorandum accompanying its Order, the court declared:

> The proposed form of therapy and treatment with Prolixin is a commonly accepted and generally prescribed procedure by the practicing medical community, similar to injections of Penicillin. There is, therefore, no need in the present case to convene a

hearing to formalize considerations concerning changes in behavior patterns, risks of adverse side effects, or the consideration of any experimental nature of the treatment. To conduct formal hearings in such cases of commonly employed medical practice transfers all discretionary functions of carrying out a proper treatment program from the hospital staff where it belongs, to the courts.

It would require a parade of medical witnesses from distant state hospitals through this Court every time there is objection to medical treatment. In every case where medication is refused, matters of medical professional discipline would, of necessity, become belabored, delayed and obscured in the costly and frequent transfer process to the legal forum. Treatment would be needlessly costly, delayed, and in many cases, completely frustrated.

It appears to this Court that the relief sought by the petitioner herein is neither required by the meaning and intent of the rule in *Price* v. *Sheppard,* nor should it be appropriate precedent to hold hearings in such cases by which this court should encumber future practice in this forum without further and more specific clarification of such rule by the Supreme Court. If the drug is claimed to be harmful to this individual, or there is an allergic reaction, then, of course, treatment of this kind should be terminated, and this Court would not hesitate in such event to hear the matter and determine the merits of such a claim. Where psycho-surgery or electroshock therapy is proposed, we, of course, have a different procedure, in which cases, the Court clearly must proceed with a hearing (Memorandum at pp. 1-2).

Is this rationale valid? What are the limits of its applicability?

Alleging that Prolixin alters personality and moods over a sustained period of time, is a powerful antiemetic, and can have dangerous side effects, Paul Fussa appealed the probate court's decision to the Minnesota Supreme Court, Joint Petition for Writ of Prohibition and Writ of Mandamus, June 7, 1976. This appeal was denied by the Minnesota Supreme Court on June 14, 1976, *In re Fussa,* No. 46912 (Minn., June 14, 1976).

Is the relevant question in such cases the nature of the proposed treatment or the competency of the patient to make a meaningful choice to give or withhold consent regarding treatment decisions? In reference to the reasoning expressed by the probate court in *Fussa,* should not a patient have the right to turn down even widely accepted treatments such as penicillin?

ADDITIONAL READING

Plotkin, R., "Limiting the Therapeutic Orgy: Mental Patients' Rights to Refuse Treatment," 72 *Nw.U.L. Rev.* 461 (1977).

Note, "Regulation of Electroconvulsive Therapy," 75 *Mich. L. Rev.* 363 (1976).

Note, "Legislative Control of Shock Therapy," 9 *U. San Francisco L. Rev.* 738 (1975).

Peters, J., and Lee, J., "Psychosurgery: A Case for Regulation," 1978 *Det. Col. L. Rev.* 383 (1978).

Comment, "Psychosurgery: The Rights of Patients," 23 *Loy. Law Rev.* 1007 (1977).

Sitnick, S., "Major Tranquilizers in Prison: Drug Therapy and the Unconsenting Inmate," 11 *Williamette L. J.* 378 (1975).

Wexler, D., "Mental Health Law and the Movement Toward Voluntary Treatment," 62 *Cal. L. Rev.* 671 (1974).

D.   ACCESS TO MEDICAL INFORMATION

1.   By the Patient or the Patient's Representative

GAERTNER v. STATE

Supreme Court of Michigan, 1971
385 Mich. 49, 187 N.W.2d 429

Before the Entire Bench.

WILLIAMS, Justice.

This case involves the question whether a State hospital may lawfully bar the legal representative of a patient from access to that patient's hospital records on the basis of MCLA 600.2157 (MSA 27A.2157) making those records confidential. The Attorney General contends for non-access to such records as a protection to hospital physicians against loss of licensure, suit or prosecution for violation of the aforesaid statutory provisions.

Plaintiff, a guardian of a mentally incompetent minor, successfully sought to enjoin the State of Michigan and its agents from interfering with her general access to medical records reflecting treatment of her ward as an in-patient at the Lapeer State Home and Training School and the Fort Custer State Home and Training School for the period from 1959 to 1968. The plaintiff's attorney first requested access to the records in April, 1968, from the Fort Custer State Home and Training School in whose possession the records now are. He submitted with the request a waiver of the physician-patient privilege signed by the plaintiff. The request was referred to the Department of Mental Health which in turn referred it to the office of the Attorney General. Upon the advice of the Attorney General, the request was denied.

The trial court granted an injunction prohibiting the "State of Michigan, its officers, agents and employees and those acting in concert therewith . . . from interfering with or denying plaintiff the right to examine, inspect and copy the hospital records of Sharon Gaertner" (the plaintiff's mentally incompetent ward). The Court of Appeals affirmed, 24 Mich. App. 503, 180 N.W.2d 308. From the decision of the Court of Appeals, the Sate of Michigan, represented by the Attorney General, appeals to this Court.

MCLA 600.2157 (MSA 27A.2157) reads as follows:

> No person duly authorized to practice medicine or surgery shall be allowed to disclose any information which he may have acquired in attending any patient in his professional character, and which information was necessary to enable him to prescribe for such patient as a physician, or to do any act for him as a surgeon: Provided, however, That in case such patient shall bring an action against any defendant to recover for any personal injuries, or for any malpractice, if such plaintiff shall produce any physician as a witness in his own behalf, who has treated him for such injury, or for any disease or condition, with reference to which such malpractice is alleged, he shall be deemed to have waived the privilege hereinbefore provided for, as to any or all other physicians, who may have treated him for such injuries, disease or condition: Provided further, That after the decease of such patient, in a contest upon the question of admitting the will of such patient to probate, the heirs at law of such patient, whether proponents or contestants of his will, shall be deemed to be personal representatives of such deceased patient for the purpose of waiving the privilege hereinbefore created.

The purpose of this statute is to protect the confidential nature of the physician-patient relationship. In *Schechet* v. *Kesten*, 372 Mich. 346, 351, 126 N.W.2d 718, 721 (1964), this Court said of the statute:

> ... It prohibits the physician from disclosing, in the course of any action wherein his patient or patients are not involved and do not consent, even the names of such noninvolved patients.

The privilege of confidentiality belongs to the patient; it can be waived only by the patient. *Schechet* v. *Kesten, supra.* In *Storrs* v. *Scougale,* 48 Mich. 387, 395, 12 N.W. 502, 505 (1882), this Court by Justice Cooley said of this privilege of confidentiality:

> ... a privilege is guarded which does not belong to him [the physician] but to his patient, and which continues indefinitely, and can be waived by no one but the patient himself.

The remaining question is whether the guardian for the mental incompetent in this case can act for his ward. The mentally incompetent ward cannot act for himself, and the law will not leave him helpless. For example, MCLA 704.2 (MSA 27.3178[252]) which governs the relationship of a fiduciary to those persons for whom he is empowered to act provides in pertinent part as follows:

> ... no facts or knowledge pertaining to their property in his hands or to their affairs shall be disclosed by the fiduciary in any manner except with the consent of the cestui, heir, devisee, legatee, beneficiary or ward: Provided, however, That such consent may be given by the fiduciary of a minor or incompetent, in behalf of such minor or incompetent. . . .

This Court therefore holds that a State hospital may not lawfully deny the guardian of an incompetent minor access to the records of his ward on the basis of MCLA 600.2157 (MSA 27A.2157). The physician-patient privilege is the privilege of the patient. The guardian can legally act for his mentally incompetent ward who cannot act for himself.

In his brief (p. 13), the Attorney General has made a valid point that in the case of the mentally ill:

> ... it is often the medical duty of a psychiatrist to withhold from patients the contents of medical records to the extent that such records contain family confidences, disclosures of past behavior or medical predictions of possible future recurrences of bizarre or disturbed behavior or other disclosures certain to upset the patient severely.

There is nothing in this case to indicate that the records of the plaintiff's ward are of that character. Suffice it to say that upon a proper showing courts may take appropriate action in the future to suppress such portions of mental patients' records as necessary to adequately protect those patients, otherwise the patient or his lawful representative shall have access to all of the patient's hospital records.

Furthermore physicians and hospitals may protect patients and themselves by requiring, as the Court of Appeals allowed, the execution of "a valid consent and waiver of the privilege" before exposing a patient's record.

* * *

Affirmed.

T. M. KAVANAGH, C. J., and BLACK, ADAMS, BRENNAN, T. G. KAVANAGH and SWAINSON, JJ., concur.

NOTES

1. Consider the procedure outlined by the *Gaertner* court to govern those situations in which some portion of medical records legitimately needs to be suppressed. What are the advantages and disadvantages of such a process?

2. Cases in accord with the *Gaertner* holding that the privilege of confidentiality is no bar to access to medical records by the patient or the patient's representative include: *Bush* v. *Kallen*, 123 N.J.Super. 175, 302 A.2d 142 (1973); *Thomas* v. *State*, 94 N.Y.S.2d 770 (1950); and *In re Greenberg's Estate*, 89 N.Y.S.2d 807 (1949).

GOTKIN v. MILLER
United States Court of Appeals for the Second Circuit, 1975
514 F.2d 125

Before HAYS and FEINBERG, Circuit Judges, and HOLDEN, District Judge.

HAYS, Circuit Judge:

Janet Gotkin, a former mental patient, and her husband Paul brought an action in the United States District Court for the Eastern District of New York under 42 U.S.C. § 1983 and 28 U.S.C. § 1343 (1970) seeking to have Mrs. Gotkin's records at Brooklyn State Hospital, Long Island Jewish-Hillside Medical Center, and Gracie Square Hospital made available to her. Judge Travia granted summary judgment in favor of the defendants. He held that the plaintiffs had failed to demonstrate that they had a constitutional right to inspect and copy Mrs. Gotkin's records. *Gotkin* v. *Miller*, 379 F.Supp. 859 (E.D.N.Y. 1974). We affirm.

I

The facts are essentially undisputed. Between 1962 and 1970 Janet Gotkin was voluntarily hospitalized on several occasions mainly because of a series of suicide attempts. She has not received treatment since September, 1970. In April, 1973, the Gotkins contracted to write a book about Janet's experiences. In order to verify her recollections of various incidents, she wrote to three hospitals at which she had been a patient asking them to send her copies of her records. Brooklyn State Hospital and Long Island Jewish-Hillside Medical Center refused her request,[2] and Gracie Square Hospital did not respond.

---

[2]Long Island Jewish-Hillside Medical Center offered to release Mrs. Gotkin's records to her physician, but no request for such a release was made. Mrs. Gotkin did not attempt to obtain her records from the other hospitals through her physician, although the hospitals claim that their policy is to release records to a physician designated by the patient. The hospitals explain that they prefer to release records to a designated physician rather than to the patient himself because 1) medical records are often unintelligible to the layman, 2) the revelation of certain information could be detrimental to the individual's current well-being, and 3) the records often contain references to other individuals who might be harmed by disclosure. See New York State Department of Mental Hygiene, Department Policy Manual § 2932 (1974). The designated physician is expected to withhold material which might be harmful to the patient or third parties. Cf. Part IV, *infra*.

The Gotkins then filed suit against the directors of the three hospitals and the New York State Commissioner of Mental Hygiene, alleging that the policies of the hospitals against granting requests such as Mrs. Gotkin's violated the rights of former mental patients under the First, Fourth, Ninth, and Fourteenth Amendments of the United States Constitution. The complaint demanded declaratory and injunctive relief in favor of the Gotkins and all others similarly situated. The court granted the defendants' motion for summary judgment. It held that Paul Gotkin was not a proper plaintiff because he was not a former mental patient and had not requested access to his or his wife's records. 379 F.Supp. at 862. As to Janet Gotkin and other members of her purported class, the court held that former mental patients have no First Amendment right to receive information contained in their hospital records, 379 F.Supp. at 862-63; that the Fourth Amendment prohibition of unreasonable searches and seizures is inapplicable, *id.* 379 F.Supp. at 863; that plaintiffs enjoy no right of privacy entitling them to their records for purposes of publishing a book, *id.*; and that plaintiffs had not been deprived of "liberty" or "property" protected by the due process clause of the Fourteenth Amendment, *id.* 379 F.Supp. at 864-68.

II

Appellants' main argument on this appeal is that the refusal by the hospitals to allow former mental patients to inspect their records deprives the patients of property without due process of law. We can find no basis for the proposition that mental patients have a constitutionally protected property interest in the direct and unrestricted access to their records which the appellants demand.

In *Board of Regents of State Colleges* v. *Roth*, 408 U.S. 564, 92 S.Ct. 2701, 33 L.Ed.2d 548 (1972), the Supreme Court held that the Fourteenth Amendment is not an independent source of property rights. *Id.* 408 U.S. at 577, 92 S.Ct. 2709. The due process clause protects only those property interests already acquired as a result of "existing rules or understandings that stem from an independent source such as state law—rules or understandings that secure certain benefits and that support claims of entitlement to those benefits." *Id.*

In an attempt to satisfy the *Roth* criteria, appellants argue that under New York case law, patients have a property interest in their hospital records. However, none of the cases cited by appellants indicates that patients have a right to unrestricted access to their records. The majority of the cited cases hold simply that under the discovery provisions of New York law, patients are entitled to a court order granting them access to their records for purposes of litigation. See *Application of Weiss*, 208 Misc. 1010, 147 N.Y.S.2d 455 (Sup.Ct. 1955); *In re Greenberg's Estate*, 196 Misc. 809, 89 N.Y.S.2d 807 (Sup.Ct. 1949); *Hoyt* v. *Cornwall Hospital*, 169 Misc. 361, 6 N.Y.S.2d 1014 (Sup.Ct. 1938); *Application of Warrington*, 105 N.Y.S.2d 925 (Ct.Cl. 1950) (mem.); *Thomas* v. *State*, 197 Misc. 288, 94 N.Y.S.2d 770 (Ct.Cl. 1950).

Appellants argue that these cases must be interpreted as establishing a general property right because in several instances courts ordered the hospitals to produce records even though no action had yet been filed. See, e.g., *Application of Weiss*, *supra; In re Greenberg's Estate*, *supra.* However, appellants fail to note that under New York law, discovery may be ordered by a court even before an action is commenced. N.Y.C. P.L.R. § 3102(c) (McKinney 1970) (previously N.Y.C.P.A. § 295). The court orders in *Weiss, Greenberg,* and *Hoyt* were explicitly founded on that provision.

Appellants claim that other New York cases grant patients access to their records regardless of pending or proposed litigation. In *Sosa* v. *Lincoln Hospital,* 190 Misc. 448, 74 N.Y.S.2d 184 (Sup.Ct. 1947) the court did allow access while discounting the possibility of litigation. However, the decision was based on a New York City Charter provision, not applicable here, which granted all taxpayers free access to city records. In *Glazer* v. *Department of Hospitals,* 2 Misc.2d 207, 155 N.Y.S.2d 414 (Sup.Ct. 1956), the court ordered records produced under Article 78 of the Civil Practice Act (now N.Y.C.P.L.R. § 7801 *et seq.* (McKinney 1963)) rather than under the discovery provisions. However, the plaintiff claimed that she needed her records for purposes of a suit she had brought, and the court based its decision on the arbitrariness of the hospital's policy of refusing to release records to patients involved in litigation unless they assigned the proceeds of their actions to the hospital and to certain unnamed physicians. See 155 N.Y.S.2d at 417.

The only New York decision cited by the parties which deals directly with the question of whether a patient has a property interest in his records is *In re Culbertson's Will,* 57 Misc.2d 391, 292 N.Y.S.2d 806 (Surr.Ct. 1968). In that case the court held that the records were the property of the physician but that a provision in a doctor's will calling for the destruction of his records would not be enforced because it violated public policy. *Culbertson* is consistent with the cases cited by the appellants. All of them indicate that patients have certain rights in their records short of the absolute property right to unrestricted access which the appellants are claiming here.

New York statutory law also establishes that while patients may exercise a considerable degree of control over their records, they do not have the right to demand direct access to them. Under § 15.13 of the Mental Hygiene Law (McKinney's Consol.Laws, c. 27, Supp. 1974), records may not be released to third parties without the consent of the patient, except in certain enumerated situations. Section 17 of the Public Health Law (McKinney's Consol.Laws, c. 45, Supp. 1974) provides for the release of medical records to a hospital or physician designated by the patient. These sections indicate the existence of substantial limitations on the right of access claimed by appellants. We therefore hold that the Fourteenth Amendment does not support appellants' claim that former mental patients have a constitutionally protected, unrestricted property right directly to inspect and copy their hospital records.

III

Appellants also argue that the hospitals' policy violates the Fourteenth Amendment because it deprives former mental patients of liberty without due process of law. They claim that since the policy against unrestricted disclosure is in part based on the fear that such disclosure could have an adverse effect on the patient, see note 2 *supra,* the refusal by the hospitals to grant Mrs. Gotkin access to her records stigmatizes her as mentally ill, although she is now sane and competent.

We agree that the due process clause applies not only when one's physical liberty is threatened but also "[w]here a person's good name, reputation, honor, or integrity is at stake.'' *Wisconsin* v. *Constantineau,* 400 U.S. 433, 437, 91 S.Ct. 507, 510, 27 L.Ed.2d 515 (1971), quoted in *Board of Regents of State Colleges* v. *Roth, supra* 408 U.S. at 573, 92 S.Ct. 2701. However, the contention that Mrs. Gotkin is being stigmatized by the hospitals is without merit. No one has branded her as mentally ill or otherwise incompetent. Compare *Wisconsin* v. *Constantineau, supra* 400 U.S. at 437, 91 S.Ct. 507; *Lombard* v. *Board of Education,* 502 F.2d 631, 637 (2d Cir. 1974). Mrs. Gotkin has no valid claim of deprivation of liberty under the Fourteenth Amendment.

Nor do we find merit in appellants' contention that the hospitals' refusal to disclose Mrs. Gotkin's records violated her right to privacy and control over her own body. This is not a case such as *Canterbury* v. *Spence,* 150 U.S. App.D.C. 263, 464 F.2d 772, cert. denied, 409 U.S. 1064, 93 S.Ct. 560, 34 L.Ed.2d 518 (1972), cited by appellants, in which a physician allegedly failed to disclose the risks which were involved in the course of treatment which he had prescribed. Mrs. Gotkin is not undergoing or contemplating treatment. She alleges that she wants the records to help her in the publication of her book, not to evaluate her medical condition. No serious interest in privacy or control over one's body is at issue.

We also find no merit in the argument that the Fourth Amendment guarantee against unreasonable searches and seizures is relevant to this case. See 379 F.Supp. at 863.

IV

Finally, appellants argue that summary judgment should not have been granted because material issues of fact are still at issue. They contest the claims of the hospitals that patients may obtain access to their records through a designated physician. Appellants also argue that even if such a policy is followed, it is not needed to protect patients or third parties, as the hospitals contend.

We agree with the district court that the defendants were entitled to summary judgment regardless of the outcome of these factual disputes. See 379 F.Supp. at 868-69. Plaintiffs in this action sought nothing short of unrestricted, direct access to Mrs. Gotkin's records. See note 2 *supra.* They failed to establish a constitutional basis for this claim, and it was therefore unnecessary for the district court to judge the wisdom of the hospitals' screening procedures or to decide if those procedures were properly administered.

Affirmed.

NOTES

1. Although the court held that there was no right to direct and unrestricted access to one's records, what circumstances might have induced it to find a cognizable right of access for particular purposes?

2. From a strategy viewpoint, was the factual situation in *Gotkin* a good one for litigating the right of access to medical records?

3. What options are available to the Gotkins to obtain the desired records in spite of the court decision?

4.   Who owns the medical record? the physician? the hospital? the patient? If the answer is more than one of these, what are the property interests of each?

2. By Third Parties

IN RE S.W.

Court of Appeal of California, Second District, Division 4, 1978
79 Cal.App.3d 719, 145 Cal.Rptr. 143

FILES, Presiding Justice.

Rosemary W. appeals from a judgment made November 2, 1976, declaring her two sons to be dependent children of the court pursuant to Welfare and Institutions Code section 600, subdivisions (a) and (d) (now Welf. & Inst.Code, § 300, subdivisions (a) and (d)), and determining that custody should be given to someone other than a parent.

The legal issue requiring discussion is the admissibility of the records of Central City Community Mental Health Facility relating to the mother's treatment as an outpatient. Her counsel's objection, based upon the psychotherapist-patient privilege defined in section 1012 of the Evidence Code, was overruled upon the theory that Welfare and Institutions Code section 5328, subdivision (f) (a part of the Lanterman-Petris-Short Act, under which the treatment was provided), authorized the use of those records in evidence. We have concluded that section 5328 does not override the privilege; and that the trial court erred in refusing to consider whether the records were privileged under the Evidence Code; but the error does not require a reversal because other evidence compelled the decision to make the children dependents of the court.

The pertinent language of Welfare and Institutions Code section 5328 is as follows: "All information and records obtained in the course of providing services under Division 5 (commencing with Section 5000), Division 6 (commencing with Section 6000), or Division 7 (commencing with Section 7000), to either voluntary or involuntary recipients of services shall be confidential. Information and records may be disclosed only: "... (f) To the courts, as necessary to the administration of justice. ..."

This portion of the Lanterman-Petris-Short Act is a general prohibition against disclosure of information, subject to defined exceptions. The confidentiality imposed by this act goes beyond matter which is protected by any of the privileges established in the Evidence Code. For example, a record showing only that a person had entered a facility for treatment or evaluation under the Act would probably not contain privileged matter, but its disclosure could bring embarrassment or more serious consequences to the individual involved. One of the purposes of section 5328 is to avoid that kind of undesired publicity. (See *County of Riverside* v. *Superior Court* (1974) 42 Cal.App.3d 478, 481, 116 Cal.Rptr. 886.)

The listing of exceptions to that general policy does not make admissible in a court proceeding records which are inadmissible under the rules established by the Evidence Code. Subsection (f) excepts necessary court use from the general prohibition of section 5328, but it does not authorize a court to order disclosure of matter which the Evidence Code makes privileged.

The juvenile court received the records of the Central City Community Mental Health Facility relating to Rosemary W. as a single item. It is apparent that some documents in that file reflect privileged matter. Whether other portions were admissible in evidence depended upon circumstances not explored in the trial court. But for the trial court's erroneous interpretation of section 5328, counsel for Mrs. W. would have had the opportunity to assume the burden of showing that the records to which he objected were privileged. (See Evid.Code, § 405; *San Diego Professional Assn.* v. *Superior Court* (1962) 58 Cal.2d 194, 199, 23 Cal.Rptr. 384, 373 P.2d 448; *Dwelly* v. *McReynolds* (1936) 6 Cal.2d 128, 131, 56 P.2d 1232.)

The county counsel urges us to hold that the hospital records, if privileged under the Evidence Code, should be held admissible in this kind of proceeding because of the overriding importance of protecting children against ill or incapacitated parents. But counsel does not point to any statute which would arguably support such a rule. We have already pointed out that Welfare and Institutions Code section 5328 states a limitation on disclosure, not a ground for admissibility of evidence. Sections 5328.1 through 5328.9 provide authorization for disclosure under specified circumstances, but none relates to the admission of evidence in juvenile court trials. Evidence Code sections 996-1007 list exceptions to the physician-patient privilege, and sections 1016-1026 give the exceptions to the psychotherapist-patient privilege. But none of those are applicable here.

The tension between the individual's need for privacy and society's need for the ascertainment of truth appears whenever a privilege is defined or interpreted. (See Com., Law Rev. Comm. following Evid. Code, § 910; *In re Lifschutz* (1970) 2 Cal.3d 415, 422, 85 Cal.Rptr. 829, 467 P.2d 557.) When a parent is afflicted with an illness or disability which may affect the welfare of the child, the confidentiality of communication with a therapist may encourage the parent to seek treatment, and may permit a kind of treatment otherwise impossible. Moreover, as the record of this case illustrates, a case for judicial protection of minor children may be made without exposing privileged communications. We must assume the Legislature weighed these considerations in defining the scope of the relevant privileges. Counsel have not shown any basis, statutory or otherwise, for an implied exception in cases of dependent children.

Other evidence received at the trial showed without conflict that Mrs. W. lacked the capacity to care for her two sons, aged 14 and 3 respectively. The father's location was unknown, and the household consisted of the mother and the two boys. The 14-year-old testified that his mother had drunk herself into insensibility 40 to 50 times in the immediately preceding 3 months. He had been absent from high school 79 days in the 1975–1976 school year, mostly from February on. The 3-year-old was an active youngster, who required the attention of an older person, and who would miss his meals unless the older boy provided them.

A close family friend and two cousins of Mrs. W. corroborated the fact that the mother's drinking had seriously impaired her ability to care for the children. Her problem had existed for several years. Mrs. W. had received treatment both at

Camarillo and at Metropolitan Hospital "numbers of times." A grandmother had lived in the home until her death in 1975. There had been a homemaker looking after the family until February 1976, when Mrs. W. falsely accused her of abusing the 3-year-old, and the homemaker left.

Mrs. W. took the witness stand to explain that the night she had locked out her 14-year-old son she did not know he was outside. She had called the police because she thought a burglar was on the porch. No other defense evidence was offered.

The evidence, putting aside the hospital records, strongly supports the finding of the juvenile court that the two boys lacked a parent exercising or capable of exercising adequate care and control, and that the mother's home was an unfit place by reason of the mother's behavior. Whether the truancy of the older boy was due to the conditions in the home, as the boy testified, or due to his own inclinations, as counsel for the mother suggests, the need for change is manifest.

It is not reasonably probable that a retrial on this kind of record would result in a different finding. A reversal of the judgment is not required.

The order appealed from is affirmed.

KINGSLEY and JEFFERSON, JJ., concur.

NOTES

1. The court observes that the existence of a privilege creates a tension between the individual's need for privacy and society's need for the ascertainment of the truth. In what circumstances might the latter triumph?

2. *Roe* v. *Ingraham,* 480 F.2d 102 (2d Cir. 1973), involved a constitutional challenge by a group of patients and doctors to a New York statute that provided for the central filing of information (including names and addresses) about all prescriptions written for certain potentially addictive drugs. The justification offered for this statute was that it enabled the state to readily detect abuses, such as patients' obtaining contemporaneous prescriptions from several doctors, overprescription by doctors, and thefts or forgeries of prescriptions, which increase addiction, and illicit traffic in such drugs. The district court had dismissed the complaints alleging constitutional defects in the statutory scheme. The Court of Appeals, while observing that the "right to privacy in matters such as those here at issue surely is not absolute," *id.* at 108, reversed the order of dismissal by the district court. The plaintiffs had contended that the abuses sought to be curbed could be adequately controlled without central filing, or by central filing without the patients' names, and that the added efficiency was not worth the price in terms of risk of disclosure. The Court of Appeals held that a determination on this issue would have to await evidence regarding the measures implemented by the state health officials to ensure that confidentiality of the information was in fact being adequately safeguarded:

> . . . we do not believe that . . . the complaint could properly have been dismissed without further exploration of the degree of need for central filing including the patients' names on the one hand, and the adequacy of the provisions to protect against malicious or careless disclosure on the other (*Id.* at 109).

3. A major exception to the physician-patient or psychotherapist-patient privilege emerged in 1974 when the Supreme Court of California recognized a legal "duty to warn":

> When a doctor or a psychotherapist, in the exercise of his professional skill and knowledge, determines, or should determine, that a warning is essential to avert danger arising from the medical or psychological condition of his patient, he incurs a legal obligation to give that warning (*Tarasoff* v. *Regents of University of California,* 118 Cal.Rptr. 129, 529 P.2d 553 (1974)).

The *Tarasoff* case was a damage suit filed by parents of a murdered girl against, *inter alia,* a psychologist to whom the killer had confided his intention to kill the girl. The court held that the psychologist was not protected from liability by the psychotherapist-patient privilege:

> We conclude that the public policy favoring protection of the confidential character of patient-psychotherapist communications must yield in instances in which disclosure is essential to avert danger to others. The protective privilege ends where the public peril begins.
>
> Our current crowded and computerized society compels the interdependence of its members. In this risk-infested society we can hardly tolerate the further exposure to danger that would result from a concealed knowledge of the therapist that his patient was lethal. If in the exercise of reasonable care the therapist can warn the endangered party or those who can reasonably be expected to notify him, we see no sufficient societal interest that would protect and justify concealment. The containment of such risks lies in the public interest (*Id.* at 529 P.2d 561).

Compare the exception to the psychotherapist-patient privilege in *Tarasoff* to the attorneys' Code of Professional Responsibility, which apparently allows an attorney to reveal contemplation of future crime by the client. In what circumstances are these exceptions to the psychiatrist-patient privilege and the attorney-client privilege justified?

9

PROCREATION, MARRIAGE, AND RAISING CHILDREN

Nancy B. Shuger

SEXUAL, MARITAL AND PARENTAL RIGHTS are close to the heart of the constitutionally guaranteed liberty that Americans take as their birthright. Yet there have been, and continue to be, drastic intrusions upon these very personal rights of many handicapped citizens. This chapter deals with the legal framework surrounding the rights to procreate, marry, and raise children.

A. PROCREATION

1. The Right at Stake

Skinner v. *Oklahoma,* 316 U.S. 535 (1942) dealt with a constitutional challenge to an Oklahoma statute providing for the sterilization of "habitual criminals." In *Skinner,* the statute was to be applied to a man convicted of stealing chickens—larceny under Oklahoma law, *id.* at 537. The Supreme Court noted that this crime was virtually indistinguishable from the nonfelonious crime of embezzlement to which, under Oklahoma law, the sterilization penalty did not apply, *id.* at 538–539. The Court, therefore, examined the validity of the Oklahoma sterilization statute under the equal protection clause of the Fourteenth Amendment.

The Court noted that an equal protection challenge to a sterilization statute had been labeled "the usual last resort of constitutional arguments" in *Buck* v. *Bell,* 274 U.S. 200, 208 (1927) (see pp. 875–877, below), *id.* at 539. Ultimately, however, the *Skinner* Court rejected the reasoning that had prevailed in *Buck* v. *Bell*:

> We are dealing here with legislation which involves one of the basic civil rights of man. Marriage and procreation are fundamental to the very existence and survival of the race. The power to sterilize, if exercised, may have subtle, far-reaching and devastating effects. In evil or reckless hands it can cause races or types which are inimical to the dominant group to wither and disappear. There is no redemption for the individual whom the law touches. Any experiment which the State conducts is to his irreparable injury. He is forever deprived of a basic liberty. We mention these matters not to

reexamine the scope of the police power of the States. We advert to them merely in emphasis of our view that strict scrutiny of the classification which a State makes in a sterilization law is essential, lest unwittingly, or otherwise, invidious discriminations are made against groups or types of individuals in violation of the constitutional guaranty of just and equal laws. The guaranty of "equal protection of the laws is a pledge of the protection of equal laws." *Yick Wo* v. *Hopkins,* 118 U.S. 356, 369. When the law lays an unequal hand on those who have committed intrinsically the same quality of offense and sterilizes one and not the other, it has made as invidious a discrimination as if it had selected a particular race or nationality for oppressive treatment. *Yick Wo* v. *Hopkins, supra; Gaines* v. *Canada,* 305 U.S. 337. Sterilization of those who have thrice committed grand larceny, with immunity for those who are embezzlers, is a clear, pointed, unmistakable discrimination. Oklahoma makes no attempt to say that he who commits larceny by trespass or trick or fraud has biologically inheritable traits which he who commits embezzlement lacks. Oklahoma's line between larceny by fraud and embezzlement is determined, as we have noted, "with reference to the time when the fraudulent intent to convert the property to the taker's own use" arises. *Riley* v. *State, supra,* 64 Okla. Cr. at p. 189, 78 P.2d p. 715. We have not the slightest basis for inferring that that line has any significance in eugenics, nor that the inheritability of criminal traits follows the neat legal distinctions which the law has marked between those two offenses. In terms of fines and imprisonment, the crimes of larceny and embezzlement rate the same under the Oklahoma code. Only when it comes to sterilization are the pains and penalties of the law different. The equal protection clause would indeed be a formula of empty words if such conspicuously artificial lines could be drawn. See *Smith* v. *Wayne Probate Judge,* 231 Mich. 409, 420–421, 204 N.W. 140. In *Buck* v. *Bell, supra,* the Virginia statute was upheld though it applied only to feeble-minded persons in institutions of the State. But it was pointed out that "so far as the operations enable those who otherwise must be kept confined to be returned to the world, and thus open the asylum to others, the equality aimed at will be more nearly reached." 274 U.S. p. 208. Here there is no such saving feature. Embezzlers are forever free. Those who steal or take in other ways are not. If such a classification were permitted, the technical common law concept of a "trespass" (Bishop, Criminal Law, 9th ed., vol. 1, §§ 566, 567) based on distinctions which are "very largely dependent upon history for explanation" (Holmes, *The Common Law,* p. 73) could readily become a rule of human genetics (*Id.* at 541–542).

Although *Skinner* was the second Supreme Court case to consider sterilization (*Buck* v. *Bell,* below at 875–877, was the first), it represented the first time that the Supreme Court elevated procreation to a fundamental constitutional right. Well before *Skinner* was decided, however, a long line of Supreme Court cases consistently had acknowledged a right to privacy of one's person either as within the liberty interest protected by the Fourth and Fourteenth Amendments or as an essential part of our common law heritage. See *Union Pacific Railway Co.* v. *Botsford,* 141 U.S. 250, 251 (1891) ("the right of every individual to the possession and control of his own person"); *Jacobson* v. *Massachusetts,* 197 U.S. 11, 29 (1905) ("a sphere within which the individual may assert the supremacy of his own will and rightfully dispute the authority of any human government"); *Meyer* v. *Nebraska,* 262 U.S. 390, 399 (1923) ("freedom from bodily restraint"); *Olmstead* v. *United States,* 277 U.S. 438, 478 (1928) (Brandeis, J., dissenting) ("the right to be let alone").

NOTES

1.   Was *Skinner* merely a logical extension of the right to privacy or a departure from it that established the right to procreate as having an independent constitutional basis?

Does *Skinner* locate the source of this right in the Fourteenth Amendment or in a liberty based upon natural law outside the specific guarantees of the United States Constitution?

2. For more discussion of the import of the "strict scrutiny" standard versus the "rational basis" test, see pp. 91–92 n.5, above.

2. Historical Sources of Deprivation of the Right to Procreate

BURGDORF, R. AND BURGDORF, M., "THE WICKED WITCH IS ALMOST DEAD: *BUCK v. BELL* AND THE STERILIZATION OF HANDICAPPED PERSONS" *50* Temple L.Q. *995, 997–1000 (1977)*

* * *

American sterilization laws had their origin in the science of eugenics, the discipline which deals with the improvement of hereditary qualities. The term "eugenics," which is derived from the Greek word meaning "good birth," was coined in the 1880's by Sir Francis Galton, who defined it as "the study of agencies under social control that may improve or impair . . . future generations either physically or mentally." The concept of selective breeding to improve the human race had been proposed as early as Plato's *Republic* and has been advocated by numerous social philosophers at various times in history. The supporters of human hereditary improvement were further bolstered in the middle of the nineteenth century by the work of Charles Darwin and Gregor Mendel regarding evolution and heredity.

The Social Darwinism of the last decades of the nineteenth century gave rise to a eugenics movement which reached its peak in the United States around the 1920's, but which has persisted in recent times. The movement was marked by the flourishing of a belief that the prevalence of mental and physical disabilities was the root of almost all social problems, and by a fear that the occurrence of such disabilities was increasing rapidly in modern civilization. The spread of such ideas was fueled by notable studies such as those of the family trees of the Jukes and the Kallikaks which revealed generation after generation of defective, degenerate, and criminal persons. Acceptance of the necessity for scientific control of human heredity was widespread, and many thinkers warned that the spreading of handicapping conditions through heredity was the single most important problem facing American society. The tenor of such outcries was epitomized in the language of a law review note which called for a sterilization statute in the state of Kentucky:

> Since time immemorial, the criminal and defective have been the "cancer of society." Strong, intelligent, useful families are becoming smaller and smaller; while irresponsible, diseased, defective families are becoming larger. The result can only be race degeneration. To prevent this race suicide we must prevent the socially inadequate persons from propagating their kind, i.e., the feebleminded, epileptic, insane, criminal, diseased, and others.[21]

As an outgrowth of such sentiments, the eugenics movement generated various proposals for dealing with the ostensible problem of the propagation of degeneracy.

---

[21]Note, "A Sterilization Statute for Kentucky," 23 *Ky. L.J.* 168, 168 (1934).

These proposed solutions included euthanasia, prohibitions on marriage of defective persons, outlawing sexual intercourse with defective persons, segregation of defective persons, and compulsory sterilization. In considering many such proposals in its 1912 report, the Eugenics Section of the American [Cattle] Breeders Association, which later became the American Eugenics Society and played a major role in directing the course of eugenic propaganda in the United States, concluded that only two solutions were practical: sterilization procedures and segregation of those defective persons capable of reproduction.

Sterilization for eugenic purposes only became practically feasible at the end of the nineteenth century. Prior to the 1890's, the only surgical method available for producing sterility was castration,[27] a procedure which was usually considered too radical because it was medically dangerous, caused undesirable changes in secondary sexual characteristics, and was widely regarded as morally unacceptable. In the middle of the 1890's, F. Hoyt Pilcher, Superintendent of the Winfield Kansas State Home for the Feebleminded, castrated forty-four boys and fourteen girls, but adverse public sentiment soon caused a cessation of this activity. Near the end of the nineteenth century, however, Dr. Harry C. Sharpe of the Indiana State Reformatory developed a relatively simple method for the sterilization of males called vasectomy. At about the same time, French and Swiss doctors perfected the now-standard method of sterilizing females, salpingectomy—the cutting or removal of the fallopian tubes. Eugenics advocates were quick to take advantage of this new technology and a number of physicians began to perform involuntary sterilization operations notwithstanding the fact that they had no legal authority to do so. Dr. Sharpe reportedly put his innovative surgery into practice by performing sterilizations on some six or seven hundred boys at the Indiana reformatory. Similarly, superintendents of institutions in several states apparently engaged in secret sterilizations of mentally retarded people.

The history of legislation dealing with eugenic sterilizations began in 1897 when a bill authorizing such operations was introduced in the Michigan legislature. It has been suggested that the Michigan bill failed to pass because forced sterilization for eugenic purposes was a concept alien to American legal ideals. Eight years later, the legislature of Pennsylvania passed a sterilization statute, which was vetoed by the Governor. In 1907, however, Indiana, the home state of Dr. Sharpe, enacted the nation's first sterilization law. The Indiana statute applied to inmates of state institutions who were confirmed criminals, idiots, imbeciles, or rapists. By 1910 Washington, California, and Connecticut had followed Indiana's lead and enacted sterilization measures. The next decade witnessed the passage of sterilization statutes in fourteen additional states and by 1930 the total number of such statutes had swelled to twenty-eight. In 1922 eugenicists published a Model Eugenic Sterilization Law which proposed to eliminate through sterilization a broad range of defects: the law provided for sterilization of persons who were feebleminded, insane, criminalistic, epileptic, inebriate, diseased, blind, deaf, deformed, and dependent.

---

[27]Castration is used here in its broad sense to include sterilization of females by removal of the ovaries—spaying—as well as removal of the testicles of males—gelding.

SMITH V. BOARD OF EXAMINERS OF FEEBLE-MINDED

Supreme Court of New Jersey, 1913
85 N.J.L. 46, 88 A. 963

Certiorari to Court of Common Pleas, Somerset County.

The Board of Examiners of Feeble-Minded ordered that an effective operation for the prevention of procreation be performed upon Alice Smith, and she brings certiorari. Order set aside.

The order brought up by this writ of certiorari is as follows:

> The Board of Examiners of Feeble-Minded (including idiots, imbeciles, and morons), Epileptics, Criminals and other Defectives, together with David F. Weeks, the chief physician of the New Jersey State Village for Epileptics, having, on the 31st day of May, 1912, regularly convened at the Administration Building at the New Jersey State Village for Epileptics (according to the provisions of chapter 190, p. 353, of the Laws of 1911, Statutes of the State of New Jersey), and at that time, in the presence of Azariah M. Beekman, counsel regularly appointed to represent Alice Smith, an inmate of said village, committed thereto on August 19, 1902, by Alfred F. Skinner, judge of the court of common pleas of Essex county, application for the appointment of said counsel having been made to and the appointment having been made, previous to the holding of said hearing, by the judge of the court of common pleas of the county of Somerset, in which county the institution in which the said Alice Smith is an inmate is located, having examined into the mental and physical condition of the said Alice Smith, do find and declare her to be an epileptic person within the meaning of the said act, and the said board, together with the chief physician of said institution, having unanimously found in the case of said Alice Smith that procreation by her is inadvisable, and that there is no probability that the condition of said Alice Smith, so examined, will improve to such an extent as to render procreation by said Alice Smith advisable:

> It is therefore, on this the 31st day of May, nineteen hundred and twelve, ordered that the operation of salpingectomy, as the most effective operation for the prevention of procreation, be performed upon the said Alice Smith in accordance with the motion at said hearing unanimously adopted.

The pertinent parts of the statute under which this order was made are as follows:

> An act to authorize and provide for the sterilization of feeble-minded (including idiots, imbeciles and morons), epileptics, rapists, certain criminals and other defectives. (P.L. 1911, p. 353.)

> Whereas, heredity plays a most important part in the transmission of feeble-mindedness, epilepsy, criminal tendencies and other defects:

> Be it enacted by the Senate and General Assembly of the State of New Jersey:

> 1. Immediately after the passage of this act, the Governor shall appoint by and with the advice of the Senate, a surgeon and a neurologist, each of recognized ability, one for a term of three (3) years and one for a term of five (5) years, their successors each to be appointed for the full term of five years, who in conjunction with the commissioner of charities and corrections shall be known as and is hereby created the "Board of Examiners of Feeble-Minded (including idiots, imbeciles and morons), Epileptics, Criminals and other Defectives," whose duty it shall be, to examine into the mental and physical condition of the feeble-minded, epileptic, certain criminal and other defective inmates confined in the several reformatories, charitable and penal institutions in the counties and state.

> 2. The criminals who shall come within the operation of this law shall be those who have been convicted of the crime of rape, or of such succession of offenses against the

criminal law as in the opinion of this board of examiners shall be deemed to be sufficient evidence of confirmed criminal tendencies.

3. Upon application of the superintendent or other administrative officer of any institution in which such inmates are or may be confined, or upon its own motions, the said Board of Examiners may call a meeting to take evidence and examine into the mental and physical condition of such inmates confined as aforesaid, and if said Board of Examiners, in conjunction with the chief physician of the institution, unanimously find that procreation is inadvisable, and that there is no probability that the condition of such inmate so examined shall improve to such an extent as to render procreation by such inmate advisable, it shall be lawful to perform such operation for the prevention of procreation as shall be decided by said Board of Examiners to be most effective, and thereupon it shall and may be lawful for any surgeon qualified under the laws of this state, under the direction of the chief physician of said institution, to perform such operation.

Argued June term, 1913, before GARRISON, TRENCHARD, and MINTURN, JJ.

GARRISON, J. (after stating the facts as above). The question propounded is whether or not the statute under which the order now before us was made is a valid exercise of the police power. The statute, it will be observed, applies also to criminals, in which aspect it does not now concern us, since the prosecutrix is an epileptic, an unfortunate person, but not a criminal.

The order is made by the Board of Examiners provided by the act of April 21, 1911 (P.L. p. 353). Briefly stated, the order, after reciting that Alice Smith is an epileptic inmate of a state charitable institution, that procreation by her is inadvisable, and that there is no probability that her condition will improve to such an extent as to render procreation by her advisable, orders that the operation of salpingectomy be performed upon the said Alice Smith.

Salpingectomy is the incision or excision of the Fallopian tube, i.e., either cutting it off or cutting it out. The Fallopian tube is an essential part of the female reproductive system, and consists of a narrow conduit, some four inches in length, that extends on each side of a woman's body from the base of the womb to the ovary upon that side. These three organs—i.e., the ovary, the Fallopian tube, and the uterus— are all concerned in normal childbearing, the relation between them being that the unfecundated ovum which is periodically produced in the ovary passes down through the Fallopian tube into the body of the uterus, where, if fecundation by the male seed takes place, or has taken place, the embryo is formed and developed into the fetus or unborn child.

The statute is broad enough to authorize an operation for the removal of any one of these three organs essential to procreation. These organs are in pairs on either side of the body, excepting the uterus, which is a single organ lying deep in the pelvis back of the bladder. The operation of salpingectomy, therefore, to be effective, must be performed on both sides of the body, and hence is in effect two operations, both requiring deepseated surgery, under profound and prolonged anaesthesia, and hence involving all of the dangers to life incident thereto, whether arising from the anaesthetic, from surgical shock, or from the inflammation or infection incident to surgical interference with the peritoneal cavity. These ordinary incidents and dangers of such an operation are not lessened where the operation is not sought by the patient, but must be performed upon her by force, at least to the extent of the production of such anaesthesia as shall completely destroy all liberty of will or action. The order is addressed to no one, and is silent as to the person by whom this operation is to be performed, and the statute likewise is silent upon this subject excepting that when an order is made, "thereupon it shall be and may be lawful for any surgeon qualified under the laws of this state, under the direction of the chief physician of said institution to perform such operation."

The prosecutrix falls within the classification of the statute in that she is an inmate of the State Village for Epileptics, a state charitable institution, "the objects of which," as stated in the act creating it, are "to secure the humane, curative, scientific and economical care and treatment of Epilepsy." 4 Comp. Stat. p. 4961.

The prosecutrix has been an inmate of this charity since 1902, and for the five years last past she has had no attack of the disease. From this statement of the facts it is clear that the order with which we have to deal threatens possibly the life, and certainly the liberty, of the prosecutrix in a manner forbidden by both the state and federal Constitutions, unless such order is a valid exercise of the police power. The question thus presented is therefore not one of those constitutional questions that are primarily addressed to the Legislature, but a purely legal question as to the due exercise of the police power, which is always a matter for determination by the courts.

This power, stated as broadly as the argument in support of the order requires, is the exercise by the Legislature of a state of its inherent sovereignty to enact and enforce whatever regulations are in its judgment demanded for the welfare of society at large in order to secure or to guard its order, safety, health, or morals. The general limitation of such power to which the prosecutrix must appeal is that under our system of government the artificial enhancement of the public welfare by the forceable suppression of the constitutional rights of the individual is inadmissible.

Somewhere between these two fundamental propositions the exercise of the police power in the present case must fall, and its assignment to the former rather than to the latter involves consequences of the greatest magnitude. For while the case in hand raises the very important and novel question whether it is one of the attributes of government to essay the theoretical improvement of society by destroying the function of procreation in certain of its members who are not malefactors against its laws, it is evident that the decision of that question carries with it certain logical consequences, having far-reaching results. For the feeble-minded and epileptics are not the only persons in the community whose elimination as undesirable citizens would, or might in the judgment of the Legislature, be a distinct benefit to society. If the enforced sterility of this class be a legitimate exercise of governmental power, a wide field of legislative activity and duty is thrown open to which it would be difficult to assign a legal limit.

If in the present case we decide that such a power exists in the case of epileptics, the doctrine we shall have enunciated cannot stop there. For epilepsy is not the only disease by which the welfare of society at large is injuriously affected, indeed, not being communicable by contagion or otherwise, it lacks some of the gravest dangers that attend upon such diseases, as pulmonary consumption or communicable syphilis. So that it would seem to be a logical necessity that, if the Legislature may, under the police power, theoretically benefit the next generation by the sterilization of the epileptics of this, it both may and should pursue the like course with respect to the other diseases mentioned, with the additional gain to society thereby arising from the protection of the present generation from contagion or contamination. Even when these and many other diseases that might be named have been included, the limits of logical necessity have, by no means, been reached.

There are other things besides physical or mental diseases that may render persons undesirable citizens, or might do so in the opinion of a majority of a prevailing Legislature. Racial differences, for instance, might afford a basis for such an opinion in communities where that question is unfortunately a permanent and paramount issue. Even beyond all such considerations it might be logically consistent to bring the philosophic theory of Malthus to bear upon the police power to the end that the tendency of population to outgrow its means of subsistence should be counteracted by surgical interference of the sort we are now considering.

Evidently the large and underlying question is, How far is government constitutionally justified in the theoretical betterment of society by means of the surgical sterilization of certain of its unoffending, but undesirable, members? If some, but by no means all, of these illustrations are fanciful, they still serve their purpose of indicating why we place the decision of the present case upon a ground that has no such logical results or untoward consequences.

Such a ground is presented by the classification upon which the present statute is based, which is of such a nature that the persons included within it are not afforded the equal protection of the laws under the fourteenth amendment of the Constitution of the United States, which provides that "no state shall deny to any person within its jurisdiction the equal protection of the laws." Under this provision it has been uniformly held that a state statute that bears solely upon a class of persons selected by it must not only bear alike upon all the individuals of such class, but that the class as a whole must bear some reasonable relation to the legislation thus solely affecting the individuals that compose it.

"It is apparent," said Mr. Justice Brewer in *Gulf, Colorado, etc., R. R. Co.* v. *Ellis,* 165 U.S. 150, 17 Sup.Ct. 255, 41 L.Ed. 666, after a review of many cases, "that the mere fact of classification is not sufficient to relieve a statute from the reach of the equality clause of the fourteenth amendment, and that in all cases it must appear, not only that a classification has been made, but also that it is one based upon some reasonable ground—some difference which bears a just and proper relation to the attempted classification—and is not a mere arbitrary selection."

This summarizes a mass of cases that might be cited.

Turning our attention now to the classification on which the present statute is based, and laying aside criminals and persons confined in penal institutions with which we have no present concern, it will be seen that—as to epileptics, with which alone we have to do—the force of the statute falls wholly upon such epileptics as are "inmates confined in the several charitable institutions in the counties and state." It must be apparent that the class thus selected is singularly narrow when the broad purpose of the statute and the avowed object sought to be accomplished by it are considered. The objection, however, is not that the class is small as compared with the magnitude of the purpose in view, which is nothing less than the artificial improvement of society at large, but that it is singularly inept for the accomplishment of that purpose in this respect, *viz.,* that if such object requires the sterilization of the class so selected, then *a fortiorari* does it require the sterilization of the vastly greater class who are not protected from procreation by their confinement in state or county institutions.

The broad class to which the legislative remedy is normally applicable is that of epileptics; i.e., all epileptics. Now, epilepsy, if not, as some authorities contend, mainly a disease of the well to do and overfed, is at least one that affects all ranks of society, the rich as well as the poor. If it be conceded, for the sake of argument, that the Legislature may select one of these broadly defined classes—i.e., the poor—and may legislate solely with reference to this class, it is evident that, by the further sub-classification of the poor into those who are and those who are not inmates in public charitable institutions, a principle of selection is adopted that bears no reasonable relation to the proposed scheme for the artificial betterment of society. For not only will society at large be just as injuriously affected by the procreation of epileptics who are not confined in such institutions as it will be by the procreation of those who are so confined, but the former vastly outnumber the latter, and are, in the nature of things, vastly more exposed to the temptation and opportunity of procreation, which indeed in cases of those confined in a presumably well-conducted public institution is reduced practically to nil.

The particular vice, therefore, of the present classification is not so much that it creates a subclassification, based upon no reasonable basis, as that having thereby arbitrarily created two classes, it applies the statutory remedy to that one of those classes to which it has the least, and in no event a sole, application, and to which indeed upon the presumption of the proper management of our public institutions it has no application at all. When we consider that such statutory scheme necessarily involves a suppression of personal liberty and a possible menace to the life of the individual who must submit to it, it is not asking too much that an artificial regulation of society that involves these constitutional rights of some of its members shall be accomplished, if at all, by a statute that does not deny to the persons injuriously affected the equal protection of the laws guaranteed by the federal Constitution.

The suggestion that the classification might be sufficient if the scheme of the statute were to turn the sterilized inmates of such public institutes loose upon the community, and thereby to effect a saving of expense to the public, is not deserving of serious consideration. The palpable inhumanity and immorality of such a scheme forbids us to impute it to an enlightened Legislature that evidently enacted the present statute for a worthy social end, upon the merits of which our present decision upon strictly legal lines is in no sense to be regarded as a reflection.

The conclusion we have reached is that without regard to the power of the state to subject its citizens to surgical operations that shall render procreation by them impossible the present statute is invalid, in that it denies to the prosecutrix of this writ the equal protection of the laws to which, under the Constitution of the United States, she is entitled.

The order brought up by this writ is set aside.

NOTES

1. While holding that the power had been improperly exercised in the New Jersey statute, the court gives a good definition of the legal basis asserted for the enactment of compulsory sterilization measures—the police power of the state: "the exercise by the Legislature of a state of its inherent sovereignty to enact and enforce whatever regulations are in its judgment demanded for the welfare of society at large in order to secure or to guard its order, safety, health, or morals."

2. *Smith* v. *Board of Examiners of Feeble-Minded* is exemplary of a pattern in the first quarter of this century whereby the legislative surge to authorize eugenic sterilizations was frustrated by the courts. Prior to 1925, all eugenic sterilization statutes that reached the courts were declared unconstitutional (Ferster, E., "Eliminating the Unfit—Is Sterilization the Answer?" 27 *Oh. St. L.J.* 591, 593 (1966)). Some of these state sterilization laws were struck down as cruel and unusual punishment, e.g., *Mickle* v. *Henrichs,* 262 F. 687, 690–691 (D.Nev. 1918); *Davis* v. *Berry,* 216 F. 413, 416–417 (S.D.Ia. 1914), reversed sub nom. *Berry* v. *Davis,* 242 U.S. 468 (1917). Others were invalidated under the due process clause, e.g., *Williams* v. *Smith,* 190 Ind. 526, 528, 131 N.E. 2, 2 (1921), or, as in *Smith* v. *Board of Examiners,* as violative of equal protection, e.g., Haynes v. *Lapeer Circuit Judge,* 201 Mich. 138, 145, 166 N.W. 938, 941 (1918); *Osborn* v. *Thomson,* 103 Misc. 23, 35, 169 N.Y.S. 638, 644 (Sup. Ct.), aff'd., 185 App.Div. 902, 171 N.Y.S. 1094 (1918). And in one case, a sterilization statute was held to constitute a "bill of attainder," *Davis* v. *Berry,* 216 F. 413, 419 (S.D.Ia. 1914).

3. Beliefs expressed in *Smith* v. *Board of Examiners* that epilepsy is primarily hereditary, and that it is beneficial to confine persons with epilepsy in residential institutions, have, of course, long been disproved and discarded.

Smith v. Command

Supreme Court of Michigan, 1925
231 Mich. 409, 204 N.W. 140

McDonald, C. J.   Willie Smith is 16 years of age. He was duly adjudged to be feeble-minded by the probate court of Wayne county, and is now confined in the State Home at Lapeer. His father, with the consent of the mother, filed a petition under Act 285, Public Acts of 1923, to have him sterilized. The proceedings resulted in an order by the court appointing a competent physician to treat the plaintiff by X-ray or by vasectomy, or by other treatment that may be least dangerous to life, in order to render him incapable of procreation. To secure a reversal of this order, the plaintiff brings certiorari.

The purpose of the act as expressed in its title is "to authorize the sterilization of mentally defective persons." Mentally defective persons are deemed to include idiots, imbeciles, and the feeble-minded, but not the insane. When one of this class has been adjudged mentally defective by a court of competent jurisdiction, application may be made to have him treated so that he may be incapable of procreation. Upon filing the application, the court is required to fix a day for hearing, to cause a 10 days' notice thereof to be given, to appoint a guardian *ad litem,* and to name three reputable physicians to examine into the mental condition of the defective with a view to obtaining their opinions as to whether he should be dealt with under the act. At the hearing, which may be by the court alone or by the court and a jury, full evidence is required to be taken in writing as to the mental and physical condition of the defective and as to his personal history. After such hearing, the court may make an order for treatment or operation to render the defective incapable of procreation whenever it shall be found:

> 1 (a) That the said defective manifests sexual inclinations which make it probable that he will procreate children unless he be closely confined or be rendered incapable of procreation; (b) that children procreated by said adjudged defective will have an inherited tendency to mental defectiveness; and (c) that there is no probability that the condition of said person will improve so that his or her children will not have the inherited tendency aforesaid; or
> 2 (a) That said defective manifests sexual inclinations which make it probable that he will procreate children unless he be closely confined, or be rendered incapable of procreation; and (b) That he would not be able to support and care for his children, if any, and such children would probably become public charges by reason of his own mental defectiveness.

The question presented for our consideration is whether this act is a valid exercise of police power within the limitations of the Constitution.

It is first urged by counsel for the plaintiff that the act is an unreasonable, arbitrary, and unnecessary interference with the fundamental rights and privileges of individuals, that its effect upon the person or upon the public welfare is experimental, and that courts cannot sustain it as a valid exercise of police power until science or experience has demonstrated its reasonableness.

Biological science has definitely demonstrated that feeble-mindedness is hereditary. The English Royal Commission of 1904 took the testimony of all the noted experts of England on the subject of mental diseases. The consensus of opinion thus gathered was that feeble-mindedness, if not accidental, is hereditary. It would not be advisable to extend this opinion by repeating the testimony of these eminent biological and medical experts. We may content ourselves with quoting from Dr. A. F. Tredgold, one of the greatest authorities on feeble-mindedness, who, after reviewing the findings of the Royal Commission, says:

> It is quite clear, therefore, that there is now an overwhelming body of evidence from those qualified by experience to express an opinion on this matter, to the effect that in the great majority of cases of amentia (feeble-mindedness) the condition is due to innate or germinal causes, and that it is transmissible (Mental Deficiency Edition of 1916 by Dr. A. F. Tredgold).

To the same effect are the opinions of many notable biological students in this country. In the Trend of the Human Race, by Samuel J. Holmes of the University of California, it is said:

> The fact that defective mentality is strongly transmitted is established beyond the possibility of sane objection, and the particularly disastrous results that are pretty sure to follow from the mating of two mentally defectives have certainly been made sufficiently impressive by the work of recent investigators.

From this and a great quantity of other evidence to which we will not here refer, it definitely appears that science has demonstrated to a reasonable degree of certainty that feeble-mindedness is hereditary. This fact, now well known with its alarming results, presents a social and economic problem of grave importance. It is known by conservative estimate that there are at least 20,000 recognized feeble-minded persons in the state of Michigan—eight times as many as can be segregated in state institutions. The Michigan Home and Training School at Lapeer is full to overflowing with these unfortunates, and hundreds of others are on the waiting lists. That they are a serious menace to society no one will question.

In view of these facts, what are the legal rights of this class of citizens as to the procreation of children? It is true that the right to beget children is a natural and constitutional right, but it is equally true that no citizen has any rights superior to the common welfare. Acting for the public good, the state, in the exercise of its police powers, may always impose reasonable restrictions upon the natural and constitutional rights of its citizens. Measured by its injurious effect upon society, what right has any citizen or class of citizens to beget children with an inherited tendency to crime, feeble-mindedness, idiocy, or imbecility? This is the right for which Willie Smith is here contending. It is a right which this statute, enacted for the common welfare, denies to him. The facts and conditions which we have here related were all before the Michigan Legislature. Under the existing circumstances it was not only its undoubted right, but it was its duty, to enact some legislation that would protect the people and preserve the race from the known effects of the procreation of children by the feeble-minded, the idiots, and the imbeciles.

Thus far we have been attempting to show that this statute, measured by the purpose for which it was enacted and the conditions which warranted it, and justified by the findings of biological science, is a proper and reasonable exercise of the police power of the state. The next question that naturally follows is whether the means provided by the statute to carry out its object are so cruel, inhuman, unreasonable, and oppressive that the Legislature has no constitutional right to enforce them.

It is claimed that the statute violates section 15, art. 2, of the Constitution, which provides that "cruel or unusual punishment shall not be inflicted." The only purpose of this constitutional provision is to place a limitation on the power of the Legislature in fixing punishment for crimes. There is no element of punishment involved in the sterilization of feeble-minded persons. In this respect it is analogous to compulsory vaccination. Both are nonpunitive. It is therefore plainly apparent that the constitutional inhibition against cruel or unusual punishment has no application to the surgical treatment of feeble-minded persons. It has reference only to punishments inflicted after convictions of crimes.

* * *

But the methods provided by the statute to accomplish its purpose are not cruel or inhuman. It requires treatment by X-rays or the operation of vasectomy on males or salpingectomy on females, or other treatment as may be least dangerous to life. These operations are the least radical known to medical science. None of them require the removal of any of the organs or sex glands; the result being accomplished by a severance of the sex germ-carrying ducts. The operation does not destroy sexual

desires or capacity for sexual intercourse, but renders procreation impossible. In Penal
and Reformatory Institutions, vol. 2, prepared for the Eighth International Prison
Congress, Russell Sage Foundation, Dr. Sharp, surgeon of the Reformatory at Jeffer-
sonville, Ind., speaking of vasectomy, says:

> This operation is indeed very simple and easy to perform. I do it without administer-
> ing an anesthetic, either general or local. It requires about three minutes' time to perform
> the operation, and the subject returns to his work immediately, suffering no inconve-
> nience, and is in no way impaired for the pursuit of life, liberty, and happiness, but is
> effectively sterilized. I have been doing this operation for over nine years. I have 456
> cases that have afforded splendid opportunity for postoperative observation, and I have
> never seen any unfavorable symptoms. After observing nearly 500 males, in whom I
> have severed the vas deferens, I am prepared to state that there is not only a diminution
> of the muscular and nervous fatigue, resulting from muscular exertion, but also a
> lessening of fatigue sensation and a decided increase of well-being. I have observed
> splendid results in cases of neurasthenia.

By another authority it is said:

> Vasectomy is a very simple operation, which is accompanied by very little shock, and
> may be performed without an anesthetic, although most surgeons advise that it be done
> under local anesthesia. Its pain without an anesthetic has been compared by men who
> were vasectomized to that experienced in the extraction of a tooth.

Salpingectomy is recommended as the best available method for the sterilization of females. It is a more serious operation than vasectomy, but is safely and
effectively performed by the skillful surgeon. Surgical Treatment (Warbasse) vol.
3, p. 429.

As to the X-ray treatment, Dr. Arthur C. Christie, president of the American
Roentgen Ray Society, says that: "No physiological dangers accompany the proper
application of X-rays for effecting sterility."

It is clearly apparent, therefore, that the methods provided by the statute for
carrying out its purpose are not unreasonable, cruel, or oppressive, and that the results
are beneficial both to the subject and to society.

It is further urged by counsel that the statute makes an unconstitutional
classification, that it excepts the insane, that it does not apply to all mental defectives,
and thus denies to the class upon which it is intended to operate their constitutional
right to equal protection of the laws. In discussing this question, we will follow the
order in which the classification is made by the statute. Section 7 makes two separate
and distinct divisions to which the act is made applicable.

> 1 (a) That the said defective manifests sexual inclinations which make it probable that
> he will procreate children unless he be closely confined, or be rendered incapable of
> procreation; (b) that children procreated by said adjudged defective will have an inher-
> ited tendency to mental defectiveness; and (c) that there is no probability that the
> condition of said person will improve so that his or her children will not have the
> inherited tendency aforesaid.
> 2 (a) That said defective manifests sexual inclinations which make it probable that he
> will procreate children unless he be closely confined, or be rendered incapable of
> procreation; and (b) that he would not be able to support and care for his children, if any,
> and such children would probably become public charges by reason of his own mental
> defectiveness.

> It is elementary that legislation which, in carrying out a public purpose for the common good, is limited by reasonable and justifiable differentiation to a distinct type or class of persons is not for that reason unconstitutional because class legislation, if germane to the object of the enactment, and made uniform in its operation upon all persons of the class to which it naturally applies; but, if it fails to include and affect alike all persons of the same class and extends immunities or privileges to one portion and denies them to others of like kind, by unreasonable or arbitrary subclassification, it comes within the constitutional prohibition against class legislation. (*Haynes* v. *Lapeer Circuit Judge*, 201 Mich. 138, 166 N.W. 938, L.R.A. 1918D, 233.)

Applying the tests announced by Mr. Justice Steere to the first division of the classification, it would seem clear that it is not unconstitutional as class legislation. It is germane to the object of the enactment, the common good. It is made uniform upon all persons of the class to which it naturally applies. It is a reasonable classification because it applies to a class of feeble-minded persons who are a menace to the public welfare. In making this classification the Legislature did not carve a class out of a class, but took a natural class of defectives whose children will have an inherited tendency to feeble-mindedness. It is as reasonable and no more class legislation than the compulsory vaccination of those who have been exposed to smallpox. The feeble-minded include distinct types of which the imbeciles and idiots are lower orders. The Legislature took one of these natural classes and applied the law to all members alike. The insane do not belong in this class, and there are apparent good and substantial reasons why the Legislature differentiated between them. While we do not know, of course, what the Legislature had in mind, it is reasonable to suppose that they knew that the insane have less of the sexual impulses than the feeble-minded, and that biological science has not so definitely demonstrated their inheritable tendencies. We think the classification made in the first division of section 7 of the statute is not arbitrary or unreasonable, and that in this respect it does not offend the constitutional provision which gives to every person equal protection of the laws.

The second division of the classification in section 7 presents a different situation. It brings within the operation of the law only those of the feeble-minded class who are unable to support any children they might have, and whose children probably will become public charges by reason thereof. The evident purpose of the Legislature in enacting the second division was to protect the public from being required to support the children of mentally defective persons. In attempting to do so, an element inconsistent with the beneficial purpose of the statute was introduced. It is not germane to the object of the enactment as expressed in its title. It carves a class out of a class. In that it does not apply to those of the class who may be financially able to support their children, it is not made applicable alike to all members of the class. We think that it is subject to the constitutional objection discussed by Justice Steere in *Haynes* v. *Lapeer Circuit Judge, supra,* and by Justice Sharpe in *Peninsular Stove* v. *Burton,* 220 Mich. 284, 189 N.W. 880.

As the first division of section 7 is a complete classification in itself, its constitutionality is not in any way affected by that of the second.

Nor does this statute violate the "due process of law" clause of the Constitution. It requires ample notice of the time and place of hearing by personal service, not only on the alleged defective, but upon the prosecuting attorney of the county, upon the relatives, father, mother, wife, or child of the defective, or upon the person with whom he resides, or at whose house he may be; and, in case no relatives can be found, service is required upon a guardian *ad litem* appointed by the court to receive such notice and to represent the defective at the hearing. Regular proceedings are followed, and opportunities to defend with the right of appeal are provided. Nothing further is required by the "due process of law" clause of the Constitution.

* * *

Our attention is called to the recorded decisions of other states where sterilization laws have been held to be unconstitutional. In most of them there was a plain and unreasonable violation of constitutional rights. But an examination of these cases will show that the great weight of authority supports the right of the state in the exercise of its police power to enact reasonable legislation for the sexual sterilization of certain natural classes of mental defectives and degenerates. In examining the recorded decisions of other jurisdictions, we have read the sterilization statutes of ten states. In most of them the matter of determining whether a defective shall be dealt with under the act is left to an administrative officer or board. In the Michigan statute that matter is left to court procedure and judicial determination, aided by the expert knowledge of three competent physicians. The distinguishing feature of our statute is found in these provisions, and in the safeguards which it throws around those of the class who have not the inherited tendencies which bring them within the operation of the law. It provides for a jury trial and the right of appeal. It requires all testimony to be taken in writing and a complete record made, so that it may be reviewed.

In the operation of this statute the only serious question, as we view it, is whether the fact that defective mentality is of such a character and due to such causes that children, procreated by a person so afflicted, will have an inherited tendency to mental defectiveness, can be determined with reasonable certainty. Primarily this question was for the Legislature, and they have answered it in the affirmative by the enactment of the statute.

* * *

That feeble-mindedness is hereditary in certain cases, there can be no doubt. While a difference of opinion undoubtedly exists as to whether the condition of feeble-mindedness in a particular person is such that it is reasonably certain his children will, or will not, be affected thereby, we are of the opinion that the weight of authority, as evidenced by scientific writings and reports, is convincing that it may be so determined. We can at least say that we are not convinced to the contrary "beyond rational doubt."

In comparison, our statute is much more reasonable and conservative than the laws of other states. Yet those states, with less perfect laws on the subject, have found that in their practical working out they have been satisfactorily beneficial both to the person and to society. California, a pioneer state in the matter of sexual sterilization, during the period between 1907 and 1921 sterilized 2,558 persons. During the same period, under the various statutes, a total of 3,233 persons were sterilized in the United States. Of these, 1,853 were males operated on by vasectomy, and 1,380 were females operated on by salpingectomy. See Laughlin's Statistical Summary in ''Eugenical Sterilization in the United States.'' These statistics are referred to in refutation of the claim that our law is an experiment.

The Michigan statute is not perfect. Undoubtedly time and experience will bring changes in many of its workable features. But it is expressive of a state policy apparently based on the growing belief that, due to the alarming increase in the number of degenerates, criminals, feeble-minded, and insane, our race is facing the greatest peril of all time. Whether this belief is well founded is not for this court to say. Unless for the soundest constitutional reasons, it is our duty to sustain the policy which the state has adopted. As we before have said, it is no valid objection that it imposes reasonable restraints upon natural and constitutional rights. It is an historic fact that every forward step in the progress of the race is marked by an interference with individual liberties.

Except as to the second division of section 7, this statute, should be sustained as a reasonable exercise of the police powers of the state within the limitations of the Constitution.

While sustaining the statute as a valid exercise of the police power vested in the Legislature, we are of the opinion that the order made by the defendant should be set aside because the statutory proceedings were not followed. The return to the writ states that all of the records and proceedings in the probate court are fully set forth in the petition for the writ. The calendar entries are annexed. The petition to the probate court was filed on December 29, 1923. The physicians were at that time appointed, and an order fixing January 24th for hearing was made. On that day the certificates of the physicians were filed and the hearing continued until February 14th, on which day the petition was ''heard and submitted.'' On April 14th, a month thereafter, Mr. Butzil was appointed guardian *ad litem*. On the 19th he filed objections to the making of the order for sterilization. It was made on April 21st.

There was no such substantial compliance with the statute as conferred jurisdiction upon the court to make the order. It contains specific provisions as to the procedure in such cases. When the petition is filed, an order of hearing shall be made and served as directed in section 4. A copy must be served on the guardian *ad litem*. Clearly, the guardian must be appointed when the order of hearing is made.

There is no provision for the filing of certificates made by the physicians. The procedure is in no way similar to that provided for on petitions to commit to an insane asylum. 1 Comp. Laws 1915, § 1325. Section 5 provides that:

> The court shall cause the defective to be examined by three reputable physicians . . . with a view to obtaining the opinion of said physicians on the question whether the adjudged defective should be dealt with under the terms of this act.

The intent is clear that the physicians shall appear in court at the hearing and submit to an examination by the court, the prosecuting attorney, the guardian or other person upon whom notice has been served. The certificates filed in this case are simply statements in the language of the statute that the facts are present which the court must find to warrant the making of the order. It is not for the physicians to determine the question before the court. While, of course, they may express their opinions concerning it, the reasons for such opinions should be inquired into in order that the court may, after due consideration thereof and of the other proof submitted, as provided for in section 6, determine whether the person examined should be dealt with under the terms of the act. Section 6 reads:

> The court shall take full evidence in writing at the hearing as to the mental and physical condition of the adjudged defective and the history of his case.

No witnesses were examined. This provision is mandatory, and must be complied with. No more important duty devolves on a probate judge than that imposed on him under this act. The responsibility of determining that a surgical operation shall be performed on a human being who is mentally defective "for his own welfare or the welfare of the community" rests upon him, and it may properly be discharged by him only on the most painstaking and thorough investigation of the facts disclosed upon the hearing.

The requirements of the statute above referred to are jurisdictional, and no valid order can be made without a substantial compliance with them.

It follows that the order made will be vacated and set aside.

MOORE, STEERE and SHARPE, JJ., concurred with McDONALD, C. J.

NOTES

1.   In a dissenting opinion joined in by two of his brethren, Justice Wiest went to great length to vent his outrage at the approval by the majority of the concept of eugenic sterilization. In a rambling but provocative opinion, he attacked the Michigan sterilization scheme philosophically, scientifically, and legally. Some notable excerpts from his rhetorical tirade include:

> When pity and mercy and humanitarianism are subordinated to utilitarian considerations, and power of the state is employed to destroy the virility of unfortunate human beings rather than their segregation and treatment toward recovery or amelioration, we as a people invite atavism to the state of mind evidenced in Sparta, ancient Rome, and the Dark Ages, where individuality counted for naught against the mere animal breeding of human beings for purposes of the state or tribe.
>
> > *   *   *
>
> Poor old Archidamus ran contrary to the Spartan breeding idea, and was fined for having married a diminutive wife. Diodorus Siculus, in his history, stated that in Ceylon: "Those that are lame, or have any other weakness or informity of body (according to the severe law of their country) are put to death." Book 2, chapter 4.
>
> And he gives the reason why the "Troglodites" were all of sound and strong bodies: "All the Troglodites are circumcised like the Egyptians, except those who by reason of some accident are called cripples; for these only, of all those that inhabit these streights, have from their infancy that member (which in others is only circumcised) wholly cut off with a razor."
>
> He said they killed the aged and made it lawful to put to death any that became lame or seized with any desperate and incurable distemper. "For they count it the highest and greatest offense for any one to love his life when he is able to do nothing worth living. And therefore all the Troglodites are of sound bodies and of a strong and healthful age, none exceeding three score." (Of course!) Book 3, chapter 2.
>
> Law 3, table 4, Twelve Tables of Rome, provided: "If a father has a child born, which is monstrously deformed, let him kill him immediately."

This inhuman law was evidently deemed eugenistically essential to the welfare of the Roman Republic. It was eugenics, in infancy, bent on the survival of the fittest.

We shudder at the cruelty of the ancients, practiced upon the helpless, the deformed, and the aged, and some who shuddered are inclined to revert to old time cruelties because sugar-coated with a scientific name and heralded as a new thing under the sun. The subject of eugenics is as old as history, and there runs a suspicion that one prime purpose was to save bother and expense (at 204 N.W. 147.)

We have found no case in the books holding that in a Christian civilization it is neither cruel nor unusual to emasculate the feeble-minded. It has remained for the civilization of the twentieth century to write such a law upon the statute book. Even savages have had more consideration for idiots. (*Id.* at 149.)

My Brother states that biological science has definitely demonstrated that feeble-mindedness is hereditary. To understand this asserted law of heredity it seems necessary to enter upon a study of the origin of some of the many theories it seeks to carry out. This heralded revelation of heredity, in its modern acceptation by some, lay sealed until an Austrian monk, in experimenting with high vine and low vine peas in 1865, it is said, solved the riddle, and even then the great medical profession did not recognize the significance of his pastime, until 1900, and he died with praises unsung, but his old garden is now a mecca for disciples, and his praise is raised in season and out, and his little idea has spread and been amplified by theories of his followers, to the unraveling of mysteries, even to the imagined finding of the reason for the fall of nations. This poor monk, however, would not recognize his discovery in its present Gargantuan proportions. (*Id.* at 149.)

Without conceding the desirability of improving the human race by mutilation of the generative organs of idiots, imbeciles, and the feeble-minded, is there power to so legislate without violation of constitutional guarantees relative to the bodily integrity of persons? This statute is far-reaching; it goes beyond the probable apprehension of the members of the legislative body enacting it. If one breeds a fool, is the idea to sterilize the fool and also the breeders for fear they may repeat? If the feeble-minded breeds a normal, then is the idea to sterilize him because, under the theory of heredity, such progeny may throw back? If the purpose is to prevent operation of the defective germ plasm, that plasm must be looked for in all carriers thereof. Short or long reasoning on the subject leads to rejection of the whole scheme.

* * *

It would reach the blind, deaf and dumb, insane, tubercular by heredity (if there is any such thing), syphilitic by heredity and acquirement, and the medical disciple would revel in a very saturnalia of asexualization.

* * *

If this law is held valid, then the measure of power of asexualization has not yet been marked, and classes may be added, and tyranny expanded. This law violates the Constitution and inherent rights, transcends legislative power, imposes cruel and unusual mutilations upon some citizens, while constituting the like treatment of all others a crime, thereby depriving some of the equal protection of the law, and is void. (*Id.* at 152-153.)

The majority's admission that "the right to beget children is a natural and constitutional right," and the dissent's reference to a constitutional guarantee of bodily integrity are particularly noteworthy. In 1891, the United States Supreme Court had spoken of "the right of every individual to the possession and control of his own person," *Union Pacific Railway Co.* v. *Botsford,* 141 U.S. 250, 251 (1891). Are these concepts precursors of the fundamental constitutional rights of procreation and privacy as subsequently expounded in *Skinner* v. *Oklahoma?*

2.   The majority opinion makes an amazing assertion that "it is no valid objection that it imposes reasonable constraints upon natural and constitutional rights. It is an historic fact that every forward step in the progress of the race is marked by an interference with individual liberties," at 204 N.W. 145. Under this historical analysis, the Magna Charta, Declaration of Independence, United States Constitution, and Bill of Rights must surely be seen as steps backward.

3.   The *Smith* v. *Command* court assumes, in the absence of any evidence on the issue, that "feeble-minded" persons have more sexual impulses than insane persons. This myth of the exaggerated sexuality of mentally retarded persons has been a persistent one despite its lack of scientific basis in fact. Although sexuality plays an important role in the lives of mentally retarded persons, as it does in the lives of others, the modern consensus is that mentally retarded persons have, on the average, slightly less sex drive than other persons.

4.   Although the court held part of the Michigan statute invalid under equal protection analysis, and although it held that the statutory procedures had not been followed in the facts of the case before it, the *Smith* v. *Command* decision has the dubious distinction of being the first judicial opinion upholding a eugenic sterilization measure.

5.   What exactly was the court's reasoning for declaring the second division of the statute unconstitutional?

BUCK V. BELL

Supreme Court of the United States, 1927
274 U.S. 200

MR. JUSTICE HOLMES delivered the opinion of the Court.

This is a writ of error to review a judgment of the Supreme Court of Appeals of the State of Virginia, affirming a judgment of the Circuit Court of Amherst County, by which the defendant in error, the superintendent of the State Colony for Epileptics and Feeble Minded, was ordered to perform the operation of salpingectomy upon Carrie Buck, the plaintiff in error, for the purpose of making her sterile. 143 Va. 310. The case comes here upon the contention that the statute authorizing the judgment is void under the Fourteenth Amendment as denying to the plaintiff in error due process of law and the equal protection of the laws.

Carrie Buck is a feeble minded white woman who was committed to the State Colony above mentioned in due form. She is the daughter of a feeble minded mother in the same institution, and the mother of an illegitimate feeble minded child. She was eighteen years old at the time of the trial of her case in the Circuit Court, in the latter part of 1924. An Act of Virginia, approved March 20, 1924, recites that the health of the patient and the welfare of society may be promoted in certain cases by the sterilization of mental defectives, under careful safeguard, etc.; that the sterilization may be effected in males by vasectomy and in females by salpingectomy, without serious pain or substantial danger to life; that the Commonwealth is supporting in various institutions many defective persons who if now discharged would become a menace but if incapable of procreating might be discharged with safety and become self-supporting with benefit to themselves and to society; and that experience has shown that heredity plays an important part in the transmission of insanity, imbecility, etc. The statute then enacts that whenever the superintendent of certain institutions including the above named State Colony shall be of opinion that it is for the best interests of the patients and of society that an inmate under his care should be sexually sterilized, he may have the operation performed upon any patient afflicted with hereditary forms of insanity, imbecility, etc., on complying with the very careful provisions by which the act protects the patients from possible abuse.

The superintendent first presents a petition to the special board of directors of his hospital or colony, stating the facts and the grounds for his opinion, verified by affidavit. Notice of the petition and of the time and place of the hearing in the institution is to be served upon the inmate, and also upon his guardian, and if there is no guardian the superintendent is to apply to the Circuit Court of the County to appoint one. If the inmate is a minor notice also is to be given to his parents if any with a copy of the petition. The board is to see to it that the inmate may attend the hearings if desired by him or his guardian. The evidence is all to be reduced to writing, and after the board has made its order for or against the operation, the superintendent, or the inmate, or his guardian, may appeal to the Circuit Court of the County. The Circuit Court may consider the record of the board and the evidence before it and such other admissible evidence as may be offered, and may affirm, revise, or reverse the order of the board and enter such order as it deems just. Finally any party may apply to the Supreme Court of Appeals, which, if it grants the appeal, is to hear the case upon the record of the trial in the Circuit Court and may enter such order as it thinks the Circuit Court should have entered. There can be no doubt that so far as procedure is concerned the rights of the patient are most carefully considered, and as every step in this case was taken in scrupulous compliance with the statute and after months of observation, there is no doubt that in that respect the plaintiff in error has had due process of law.

The attack is not upon the procedure but upon the substantive law. It seems to be contended that in no circumstances could such an order be justified. It certainly is contended that the order cannot be justified upon the existing grounds. The judgment finds the facts that have been recited and that Carrie Buck "is the probable potential parent of socially inadequate offspring, likewise afflicted, that she may be sexually sterilized without detriment to her general health and that her welfare and that of society will be promoted by her sterilization," and thereupon makes the order. In view of the general declarations of the legislature and the specific findings of the Court, obviously we cannot say as matter of law that the grounds do not exist, and if they exist they justify the result. We have seen more than once that the public welfare may call upon the best citizens for their lives. It would be strange if it could not call upon those who already sap the strength of the State for these lesser sacrifices, often not felt to be such by those concerned, in order to prevent our being swamped with incompetence. It is better for all the world, if instead of waiting to execute degenerate offspring for crime, or to let them starve for their imbecility, society can prevent those who are manifestly unfit from continuing their kind. The principle that sustains compulsory vaccination is broad enough to cover cutting the Fallopian tubes. *Jacobson* v. *Massachusetts,* 197 U.S. 11. Three generations of imbeciles are enough.

But, it is said, however it might be if this reasoning were applied generally, it fails when it is confined to the small number who are in the institutions named and is not applied to the multitudes outside. It is the usual last resort of constitutional arguments to point out shortcomings of this sort. But the answer is that the law does all that is needed when it does all that it can, indicates a policy, applies it to all within the lines, and seeks to bring within the lines all similarly situated so far and so fast as its means allow. Of course so far as the operations enable those who otherwise must be kept confined to be returned to the world, and thus open the asylum to others, the equality aimed at will be more nearly reached.

Judgment affirmed.

MR. JUSTICE BUTLER dissents.

NOTES

1.   In regard to the factual underpinnings of *Buck* v. *Bell,* one article has observed:

> There is general agreement that Justice Holmes was incorrect in his presumptions of fact concerning Carrie Buck. His phrase "three generations of imbeciles" is based upon the supposition that Carrie's mother and Carrie's infant daughter were both imbeciles. Subsequent investigation has revealed, however, that neither the mother nor Carrie's child were, in fact, imbeciles. A sociologist who delved into the evidence concerning Carrie Buck's mother reported that she was only mildly mentally retarded which, under the terminology employed in the 1920's, would have qualified her, at worst, as a moron and not an imbecile. Moreover, it was reported that Carrie's baby, the supposed third generation imbecile, was not mentally retarded at all. The daughter was only one month old at the time she was cavalierly labeled mentally defective by a Red Cross nurse. The child died in 1932 of measles, but by that time she had completed the second grade of school where she had demonstrated her mental normality and, indeed, was reported to be very bright.[a]

2.   In resolving the constitutional issues of the case in the last two paragraphs, did Justice Holmes adequately address the equal protection and due process analysis involved? In arguments before the Court, the attorney for Carrie Buck asserted "her constitutional right of bodily integrity," 274 U.S. at 201, and "[t]he inherent right of mankind to go through life without mutilation of organs of generation," *id.* at 202. Did Justice Holmes make any rejoinder to these assertions? Cf. *Skinner* v. *Oklahoma,* pp. 857–858, above.

3.   Justice Holmes analogized the situation in *Buck* v. *Bell* to compulsory smallpox vaccination and to the conscription of soldiers during wartime. Is either of these analogies sound?

4.   Justice Holmes viewed the plaintiff's equal protection claim with derision, calling it "the usual last resort of constitutional arguments." How does this characterization square with the fact that equal protection challenges to compulsory sterilization statutes had prevailed in three state supreme courts prior to *Buck* v. *Bell: Smith* v. *Board of Examiners of Feeble-Minded,* pp. 861–865, above; *Haynes* v. *Lapeer Circuit Judge,* 201 Mich. 138, 166 N.W. 938 (1918); *Osborn* v. *Thomson,* 185 App.Div. 902, 171 N.Y.S. 1094, aff'g. *In re Thomson,* 103 Misc. 23, 169 N.Y.S. 638 (1918)?

---

[a]Burgdorf, R., and Burgdorf, M., "The Wicked Witch Is Almost Dead: *Buck* v. *Bell* and the Sterilization of Handicapped Persons," 50 *Temple L.J.* 995, 1006-1007 (1977).

5.   Legal commentators have subjected the Supreme Court's holding in *Buck* v. *Bell* to frequent and severe criticism over the years; e.g., Ferster, E., "Eliminating the Unfit—Is Sterilization the Answer?" 27 *Ohio St. L.J.* 591, 617 (1966); Gest, J., "Eugenic Sterilization: Justice Holmes v. Natural Law," 23 *Temple L.J.* 306 (1950); Kindregan, C., "Sixty Years of Compulsory Eugenic Sterilization: 'Three Generations of Imbeciles' and the Constitution of the United States," 43 *Chi.-Kent L. Rev.* 123, 134-135, 143 (1966); Murdock, C., "Sterilization of the Retarded: A Problem or a Solution?" 62 *Cal. L. Rev.* 917, 921-922 (1974); O'Hara, J., and Sanks, H., "Eugenic Sterilization," 45 *Geo. L.J.* 20, 29-32 (1956); Note, "The Individual and the Involuntary Sterilization Laws, 1966," 31 *Albany L. Rev.* 97, 102 (1967).

6.   With phrases like "socially inadequate offspring," the need "to prevent our being swamped with incompetence," and the idea that "[i]t is better for all the world, if instead of waiting to execute degenerate offspring for crime, or to let them starve for their imbecility, society can prevent those who are manifestly unfit from continuing their kind," 274 U.S. at 207, the *Buck* v. *Bell* opinion is, like *Smith* v. *Command,* pp. 866–873, above, and even some of the reasoning in *Smith* v. *Board of Examiners of Feeble-Minded,* pp. 861–865, above, premised upon the beliefs of the eugenics movement (see pp. 859–860, above). For a discussion of the disrepute into which these eugenics theories have subsequently fallen, see pp. 880–883, below.

7.   For a discussion of the obsolescence and negative connotations of terms like "imbecile" and "feeble-minded" and other terminology employed in *Buck* v. *Bell* and in the two *Smith* cases, see Chapter 1, this volume.

ADDITIONAL READING

Bligh, R., "Sterilization and Mental Retardation," 51 *A.B.A.J.* 1059 (1965).
Murdock, C., "Sterilization of the Retarded: A Problem or a Solution?" 62 *Cal. L. Rev.* 917 (1974).
O'Hara, J., and Sanks, H., "Eugenic Sterilization," 45 *Geo. L.J.* 20 (1956).
Vukowich, W., "The Dawning of the Brave New World—Legal, Ethical and Social Issues of Eugenics," 1971 *U. Ill. L. Forum* 189 (1971).
Wolfensberger, W., *The Origin and Nature of Our Institutional Models* (1975).

3.   Developments in Constitutional Law and Eugenics after *Buck* v. *Bell*

a.   The Fundamental Right to Personal Privacy

SKINNER V. OKLAHOMA
See pp. 857–858, above.

NOTES

1.   Although a right to privacy had been acknowledged in earlier Supreme Court decisions, see p. 858, above, the *Skinner* opinion was the first to recognize that privacy in the context of procreation was a fundamental constitutional right meriting strict scrutiny under the equal protection clause. Despite the fact that the *Skinner* decision cites *Buck* v. *Bell* without overturning it, does not the advance in constitu-

tional theory regarding procreation in *Skinner* undermine the jurisprudential basis of *Buck* v. *Bell?* Dean Charles Murdock has outlined this contention:

> Although *Buck* has never been explicitly overruled, the Court's reasoning would almost certainly be inadequate today. Its holding rests on a standard of review, rational basis, which affords challenged legislation an almost insurmountable presumption of validity. At one time nearly the exclusive test in equal protection cases, rational basis is today only one of several standards used by the Court in deciding fourteenth amendment issues. Since 1942 equal protection analysis has included a "strict scrutiny" test reserved for classifications affecting "fundamental interests" or involving "suspect criteria." Additionally, the Court has most recently employed a "means-focused" review or balancing approach in a few cases.
>
> Due process analysis today has similar diversity. Where legislation touches upon fundamental interests the statute must not be unnecessarily broad, nor effect an irrebuttable presumption, and must use the least burdensome means available. As will be seen, the right to procreate is among the fundamental interests that trigger more active review under modern interpretations of the equal protection and due process clauses. In short, the rational basis reasoning of *Buck*, sufficient in 1926, would be anachronistic today.[b]

2. The history of the right to privacy was summarized by the Supreme Court in *Roe* v. *Wade,* 410 U.S. 113 (1973), which dealt with the authority of states to prohibit abortions. The court declared:

> The Constitution does not explicitly mention any right of privacy. In a line of decisions, however, going back perhaps as far as *Union Pacific R. Co.* v. *Botsford,* 141 U.S. 250, 251 (1891), the Court has recognized that a right of personal privacy, or a guarantee of certain areas or zones of privacy, does exist under the Constitution. In varying contexts, the Court or individual Justices have, indeed, found at least the roots of that right in the First Amendment, *Stanley* v. *Georgia,* 394 U.S. 557, 564 (1969); in the Fourth and Fifth Amendments, *Terry* v. *Ohio,* 392 U.S. 1, 8-9 (1968), *Katz* v. *United States,* 389 U.S. 347, 350 (1967), *Boyd* v. *United States,* 116 U.S. 616 (1886), see *Olmstead* v. *United States,* 277 U.S. 438, 478 (1928) (Brandeis, J., dissenting); in the penumbra of the Bill of Rights, *Griswold* v. *Connecticut* 381 U.S. at 484-485; in the Ninth Amendment, *id.,* at 486 (Goldberg, J., concurring); or in the concept of liberty guaranteed by the first section of the Fourteenth Amendment, see *Meyer* v. *Nebraska,* 262 U.S. 390, 399 (1923). These decisions make it clear that only personal rights that can be deemed "fundamental" or "implicit in the concept of ordered liberty," *Palko* v. *Connecticut,* 302 U.S. 319, 325 (1937), are included in this guarantee of personal privacy. They also make it clear that the right has some extension to activities relating to marriage, *Loving* v. *Virginia,* 388 U.S. 1, 12 (1967); procreation, *Skinner* v. *Oklahoma,* 316 U.S. 535, 541-542 (1942); contraception, *Eisenstadt* v. *Baird,* 405 U.S., at 453-454; *id.,* at 460, 463-465 (White, J., concurring in result); family relationships, *Prince* v. *Massachusetts,* 321 U.S. 158, 166 (1944); and child rearing and education, *Pierce* v. *Society of Sisters,* 268 U.S. 510, 535 (1925), *Meyer* v. *Nebraska, supra.*
>
> This right of privacy, whether it be founded in the Fourteenth Amendment's concept of personal liberty and restrictions upon state action, as we feel it is, or, as the District Court determined, in the Ninth Amendment's reservation of rights to the people, is broad enough to encompass a woman's decision whether or not to terminate her pregnancy (*Id.* at 152-153).

---

[b]Murdock, C., "Sterilization of the Retarded: A Problem or a Solution?" 62 *Cal. L. Rev.* 917, 921-922 (1974).

The import of *Skinner* in recognizing the right of privacy in regard to procreation as a fundamental constitutional right necessitating strict judicial scrutiny is reinforced by its citation with approval for such a holding in *Roe* and in many of the cases cited therein, e.g., *Eisenstadt* v. *Baird, Griswold* v. *Connecticut,* and *Stanley* v. *Georgia.*

3. The close link between privacy and procreation was demonstrated by the Supreme Court in *Eisenstadt* v. *Baird,* 405 U.S. 438, 453 (1972), where the Court declared: "If the right of privacy means anything, it is the right of the *individual,* married or single, to be free from unwarranted governmental intrusion into matters so fundamentally affecting a person as the decision whether to bear or beget a child."

ADDITIONAL READING

Clark, R., "Constitutional Sources of the Penumbral Right to Privacy," 19 *Villanova L. Rev.* 833 (1974).

Gunther, G., "Foreword: In Search of Evolving Doctrine on a Changing Court: A Model for a Newer Equal Protection," 86 *Harv. L. Rev.* 1, 12 (1972).

Heymann, P., and Barzelay, D., "The Forest and the Trees: *Roe* v. *Wade* and Its Critics," 53 *B.U. L. Rev.* 765 (1973).

Note, "Fundamental Personal Rights: Another Approach to Equal Protection," 40 *U. Chi. L. Rev.* 807 (1973).

Note, "On Privacy: Constitutional Protection for Personal Liberty," 48 *N.Y.U. L. Rev.* 670 (1973).

Parker, R., "A Definition of Privacy," 27 *Rutgers L. Rev.* 275 (1974).

Tribe, L., "Forward: Toward a Model of Roles in the Due Process of Life and Law," 87 *Harv. L. Rev.* 1 (1973).

Tussman, J., and tenBroek, J., "The Equal Protection of the Laws," 37 *Cal. L. Rev.* 341 (1949).

b. Eugenics Reexamined

Extracts from Committee of the American Neurological Association, Eugenical Sterilization (1936)

Quoted in Ferster, E., "Eliminating the Unfit—Is Sterilization the Answer?" 27 Ohio St. L.J. *591, 602-603 (1966)*

1. There is nothing to indicate that mental disease and mental defect are increasing, and from this standpoint there is no evidence of a biological deterioration of the race. 2. The reputedly high fecundity of the mentally defective groups ... is a myth based on the assumption that those who are low in the cultural scale are also mentally and biologically defective. 3. Any law concerning sterilization ... under the present state of knowledge (of heredity) should be voluntary ... rather than compulsory. 4. Nothing in the acceptance of heredity as a factor in the genesis of any condition considered by this report excludes the environmental agencies of life as equally potent, and in many instances as even more effective.

COMMITTEE TO STUDY CONTRACEPTIVE PRACTICES AND RELATED PROBLEMS,
AMERICAN MEDICAL ASSOCIATION PROCEEDINGS 54, MAY 1937

Quoted in Ferster, E., "Eliminating the Unfit—Is Sterilization the Answer?" 27 Ohio
St. L.J. *591, 603 (1966)*

Our present knowledge regarding human heredity is so limited that there appears to be very little scientific basis to justify limitation of conception for eugenic reasons. . . .

Note, "Human Sterilization," 35 *Iowa L. Rev.* 251, 254 (1950).

Just as it was once the belief that tuberculosis and cancer were inherited, so the first exponents of sterilization thought to rid the nation of future criminals by sterilizing those living. That notion has generally dissipated, though a few criminal traits are still believed to have a hereditary basis. Belief in the influence of heredity in other classifications, for example, in most forms of insanity and epilepsy, has been decreasing. Doubts as to the inheritance of feeble-mindedness, thought to be the cornerstone of all mental heredity, are increasing. The laws developed by Mendel in his experimentation with peas cannot be bodily transplanted into the world of human beings. The variables of the characteristic-carrying genes cannot be catalogued to permit scientific determination of just which recessive trait or traits have combined to produce a subnormal individual. The "unit particle rule" cannot be applied to human beings. According to the present trend in scientific thought, feeble-mindedness, insanity, epilepsy, and the like are the result of interaction between heredity and environment, with the latter probably being more influential. Whether a child born of a certain parent will inherit a tendency found in the parent has proved difficult to determine and perhaps impossible with respect to some traits. Often two feeble-minded parents bear children of normal intelligence, and it has been estimated that 89 per cent of all feeble-minded children come from normal parentage.

MURDOCK, C., "STERILIZATION OF THE RETARDED: A PROBLEM OR A SOLUTION?"
62 Cal. L. Rev. *917, 924-927 (1974)*

Eugenics as a Basis for Sterilization

Like the statute considered in *Buck* v. *Bell,* most statutes authorizing involuntary sterilization of the retarded are premised upon a eugenic purpose: preventing the birth of children who will inherit genetic defects. Not all retardation, however, is genetically based. In fact, three different bases are discernible: purely genetic, both genetic and environmental, and purely environmental.

Two examples of the first type are Down's syndrome and Tay-Sachs disease. Down's syndrome is characterized by an extra chromosome and is transmitted, if at all, by a dominant gene. Tay-Sachs disease, on the other hand, is transmitted by a recessive gene. Despite this difference, a sterilization program designed to reduce the incidence of either form of retardation would require sterilizing many more normal than retarded persons. In cases of Down's syndrome the defective gene is rarely inherited by the parents; it is usually a mutation of the mother's genes associated with advancing age.

The mutation itself does not produce retardation in the mother but only in a child; that is, the carrier usually is not retarded and therefore not identifiable on that basis. With Tay-Sachs disease, on the other hand, the affected child usually dies before puberty. Preventing this form of retardation, therefore, would require sterilizing persons who carry the recessive gene but remain unafflicted by the disability.

In other cases the defect, though genetic, requires the influence of environmental factors to produce retardation. For example, galactosemia will cause retardation only in children who are fed milk, since the hereditary defect does not itself cause retardation but only prevents metabolism of milk sugar. Similarly, diet is a factor in causing retardation from phenylketonuria (PKU), and a controlled diet may lessen or avert the retardation which otherwise accompanies this genetic condition. Where retardation results from these and similar combinations of genetic and environmental factors, identifying the relevant environmental factors and controlling them is all that is necessary to avoid retardation.

Finally, retardation may result solely from environmental factors. Trauma can cause brain injury and retardation. Moreover, some retardation formerly thought to be hereditary is now known to result from an impoverished intellectual or emotional environment that deprives children of the stimulation necessary for mental growth and development.

These non-genetic causes of retardation reveal the obvious weaknesses of eugenic justification for sterilizing the retarded. Sterilization is inapposite where the retardation results solely from environmental factors; moreover, retardation dependent upon both genetic and environmental factors can, at least in some cases, be prevented by means less onerous than sterilization.

But even retardation resulting solely from inheritance of defective genes cannot be greatly reduced by sterilizing only the retarded, for eighty to ninety percent of retarded offspring are born to normal parents. Although this figure reflects the effects of mutation and environmental factors, it also suggests the significance of recessive genes in causing inheritable retardation. A recessive gene, such as is involved in Tay-Sachs disease, causes retardation only in persons who are homozygous; that is, only when both genes governing the characteristic are defective will the child be retarded. If a person affected by retardation caused by recessive genes marries a non-carrier, their children will be heterozygous; that is, they will carry the gene but not manifest the trait. In future generations, the gene may be lost (where no child of the carrier receives the deleterious gene, but instead the dominant, normal gene) or transmitted in a heterozygous state, or coupled with a matching recessive gene. Only in the last case will the descendant manifest the characteristics of retardation.

Thus, the child of a recessively retarded parent will be affected by the same form of retardation only if the other parent also carries the defective gene. If the other parent is heterozygous, there is a 50 percent chance that the child will be retarded. If the other parent is homozygous, the probability of retardation increases to certainty. On the other hand, two heterozygous parents, both of whom will appear normal, have a 25 percent chance of conceiving an affected child.

By contrast, where retardation is attributable to a dominant gene, as in Down's syndrome, the risk of retardation in children of a retarded parent is 50 percent. Since the retarded parent carries at least one defective gene and since it is dominant, the gene and hence retardation will appear statistically in at least half the offspring.

The significance of these percentages is plain. In cases of retardation due to recessive genes, the retardation of a prospective parent is only one factor in determining the risk of retarded offspring. The presence of a recessive gene in the other parent is necessary. to create any risk of retardation in the children. Only where the defective gene is dominant can future retardation properly be presumed statistically.

Yet sterilization statutes aimed at reducing inherited retardation continue to apply to broad classes of retarded persons without regard to the dominant or recessive character of the defective gene or to the fact that only certain forms of retardation are genetic at all. Such legislation may be constitutionally defective for both under- and over-inclusiveness.

Statutes authorizing sterilization only of the retarded may be under-inclusive because normal carriers far outnumber retarded carriers. A truly effective program of eugenics would require sterilization of all those who carry the defective gene, not just those who manifest its traits. As one author concluded: "It has been estimated that the carriers are from 10 to 30 times more numerous than the affected persons. [A thorough program of eugenics] would involve the sterilization of . . . at least 10% of the population."

Statutes that apply to all retarded persons may also be over-inclusive because some forms of retardation are not caused by defective genes. Moreover, only dominant genes pose a substantial risk of retardation if just one parent is a carrier. Hence, a statute premised on eugenics risks invalidation for over-inclusiveness unless it limits sterilization to only those retarded persons who carry a dominant defective gene.

NOTES

1.   The eugenics movement was in vogue for a relatively short period of time. From the early 1930s onward, modern scientific studies began to challenge and undermine the eugenicist's theories that mental retardation, epilepsy, insanity, and other traits are hereditary. As the eugenics movement has waned, so has the prevalence of, and the justification for, involuntary sterilizations.

2.   Based on developments in constitutional law and in scientific knowledge about heredity, would the Supreme Court be likely to decide *Buck* v. *Bell* today as it did in 1927?

ADDITIONAL READING

Burgdorf, R., and Burgdorf, M., "The Wicked Witch Is Almost Dead: *Buck* v. *Bell* and the Sterilization of Handicapped Persons," 50 *Temple L.J.* 995 (1977).
Ferster, E., "Eliminating the Unfit—Is Sterilization the Answer?" 27 *Ohio St. L.J.* 591 (1966).
Gest, J., "Eugenic Sterilization: Justice Holmes v. Natural Law," 23 *Temple L.J.* 306 (1950).
Kindregan, C., "Sixty Years of Compulsory Eugenic Sterilization: 'Three Generations of Imbeciles' and the Constitution of the United States," 43 *Chi.-Kent L. Rev.* 123 (1966).

The Mentally Disabled and the Law 211-12 (rev. ed., Brakel, S., and Rock, R., eds., 1971).

Note, "Eugenic Sterilization—A Scientific Analysis," 46 *Denver L.J.* 631 at 643–644 (1969).

Note, "The Individual and the Involuntary Sterilization Laws: 1966" 31 *Albany L. Rev.* 97 (1967).

Pitts, J., "Sexual Sterilization: A New Rationale?" 26 *Ark. L. Rev.* 353, 356-357 (1972).

Wald, P., "Basic Personal and Civil Rights," in *The Mentally Retarded Citizen and the Law* 11 (Kindred, M., ed., 1976).

4. Modern Legal Approaches to the Sterilization of Handicapped Persons

a. Statutory Validity

North Carolina Association for Retarded Children (NCARC) v. State of North Carolina

*United States District Court for the Middle District
of North Carolina, Raleigh Division, 1976
420 F.Supp. 451*

Before Craven, Circuit Judge, Larkins, Chief District Judge, and Dupree, District Judge.

Craven, Circuit Judge:

What is now before this three-judge court is a piece of a much more ambitious lawsuit that involves the whole panoply of constitutional rights of mentally retarded persons in North Carolina. Because the legislature of North Carolina has changed or repealed most of the statutes relating to the treatment, training, and education of retarded children, we have concluded that all such questions presented by the pleadings should be severed from the issue relating to the constitutionality of the sterilization statute as applied to mentally retarded persons. We have retained only the latter, and have remanded all other questions to a single judge of the Eastern District of North Carolina for decision.

I

Based upon the pleadings and documents received in evidence or judicially noticed, and upon the depositions and the live testimony heard at Wilmington, North Carolina, we make the following ultimate findings of fact:

1. The statute under attack is N.C.Gen.Stat. §§ 35-36 through -50, entitled Article 7, Sterilization of Persons Mentally Ill and Mentally Retarded. Plaintiffs attack its constitutionality as applied and applicable to mentally retarded persons.

2. As defined by the American Association of Mental Deficiency, mental retardation refers to significantly subaverage general intellectual functioning existing concurrently with defects in adaptive behavior and manifested during the developmental period.

3. Another section of the same North Carolina Chapter defines mental defective as follows:

A "mental defective" shall mean a person who is not mentally ill but whose mental development is so retarded that he has not acquired enough self-control, judgment, and discretion to manage himself and his affairs, and for whose own welfare or that of others, supervision, guidance, care, or control is necessary or advisable. The term shall be construed to include "feeble-minded," "idiot," and "imbecile." N.C.Gen.Stat. § 35-1.1.

4. Sterilization is a drastic procedure, almost impossible to reverse in females and difficult and uncertain to reverse in males, that is intended to be permanent and prevent procreation. It is not, medically speaking, a dangerous procedure.

5. Most competent geneticists now reject social Darwinism and doubt the premise implicit in Mr. Justice Holmes' incantation that ". . . three generations of imbeciles is enough." But however doubtful is the efficacy of sterilization to improve the quality of the human race, there is substantial medical opinion that it may be occasionally desirable and indicated. Not even Dr. Clements, who testified for the United States and expressed strongly his general disapproval of sterilization for the mentally retarded, would go so far as to say that in an extreme case he would not use an involuntary sterilization statute if available. We think it a fair statement, from the expert testimony we have heard and read, to say that the best opinion presently is that rarely would a competent doctor recommend involuntary sterilization—but that he might do so in an extreme case. As a corollary to that proposition, it is also fair to say, we think, that prevalent medical opinion views with distaste even voluntary[2] sterilization for the mentally retarded and is inclined to sanction it only as a last resort and in relatively extreme cases. In short, the medical and genetical experts are no longer sold on sterilization to benefit either retarded patients or the future of the Republic.

6. The statute under attack became effective January 1, 1975. Since that time, only one resident of a North Carolina mental retardation center has undergone sterilization pursuant to the statutory procedure.

7. Between June 1970 and April 1974, 23 sterilizations were performed upon residents of North Carolina's mental retardation centers pursuant to the provisions of the preceding statute. Viewed over a longer time span, there has been a diminishing frequency in use of the sterilization procedure, reflecting, we think, diminishing confidence of medical doctors in its efficacy for any purpose except to prevent conception. That it will do.

8. Mental retardation is a difficult, complex phenomenon. The nature of retardation, its causes and effects are not susceptible to facile generalizations. The problem in this litigation is compounded in that the plaintiff class is very broadly defined, and includes all mentally retarded persons in North Carolina, regardless of their ages, the causes of their retardation, the degree of their intellectual, mental and social capabilities, their prospects for future growth and development.

9. Some general propositions nevertheless must be regarded as established by the evidence in this case. We emphasize that the following statements do *not* apply to all or even a majority of the plaintiff class. All, however, are true with respect to at least some members of the class:

---

[2]Because mentally retarded persons are often highly suggestible, to say it is "voluntary" may mean only that the retardee has been talked into it without even necessarily understanding it.

(a) Mental retardation in some cases has as its cause an identifiable genetic defect. Under some circumstances it is within the capability of modern medical and genetical science to establish that the genetic defect is inheritable and that there is a significant probability or substantial likelihood that the offspring of a mentally defective parent would also be retarded.

(b) Mental retardation in some cases can be traced to an environment which blocks or shrinks the mental and intellectual development of a child. Under some circumstances it is within the capability of modern medical and sociological science to determine that a mentally retarded parent or parents would be incapable of providing offspring with an environment in which a child could reasonably be expected to develop in a normal manner. As a corollary to this proposition, it is in some cases possible to predict with substantial accuracy that a mentally retarded person would be incapable of discharging the responsibilities of parenthood.

(c) While mentally retarded persons may be entitled to express themselves sexually, it can in some cases be determined that a mentally defective person does not understand or cannot appreciate the natural consequences of sexual activity. It can, likewise, be determined in some cases that the conception of a child is neither the intention nor the expectation of the sexually active mental retardate.

(d) Some mentally retarded persons who are sexually active may not want children. While many sexually active retarded persons are capable of employing various methods of birth control effectively, some are incapable of effective voluntary contraception.

(e) In rare and unusual cases, it can be medically determined that involuntary sterilization is in the best interests of either the mentally retarded person or the State or both.

II

The statute is applicable to persons "mentally ill" or "mentally retarded," but we are here concerned only with those provisions which relate to mentally retarded persons.

The statute authorizes both voluntary and involuntary sterilizations. It applies to mentally defective persons housed in state institutions and those who are not patients in state institutions. In the case of a patient who is confined in a state institution, the person in charge of the sterilization procedure is the director of the institution. For retarded persons not in state institutions, the key official is the county director of Social Services. The appropriate state or county official is authorized by the statute to petition the state district court for the sterilization of the mentally retarded person when it "may be considered in the best interest of the mental, moral, or physical improvement" of the retarded person, "or for the public good." The sterilization operation, whether voluntary or involuntary, is paid for by the State or the county in which the retarded person lives.

The statute expressly provides that sterilization operations shall only be performed by qualified, licensed North Carolina physicians and then only pursuant to an order issued by an appropriate state court. If the person to be sterilized wishes to select his own physician, he may do so but must then pay for the costs and expenses of the operation. Otherwise the physician is selected by the "petitioner," i.e., the director of the institution or the county director of Social Services.

Section 35-39 makes it the *duty* of the petitioner to institute sterilization proceedings under the following circumstances:

(1) when he feels that sterilization is in the best interests of the mental, moral or physical improvement of the retarded person,

(2) when he feels that sterilization is in the best interests of the public at large,

(3) when, in his opinion, the retarded person "would be likely, unless sterilized, to procreate a child or children who would have a tendency to serious physical, mental, or nervous disease or deficiency; or, because of a physical, mental, or nervous disease or deficiency which is not likely to materially improve, the person would be unable to care for a child or children."

(4) when the next of kin or legal guardian of the retarded person requests that he file the petition.

We conclude that subparagraph 4 of Section 39 is irrational and irreconcilable with the first three subparagraphs. The first three paragraphs make out a complete and sensible scheme: that the public servant concern himself *either* with the best interest of the retarded person *or* the best interest of the public, or both, *and* that he act to begin the procedure *only* when in his opinion the retarded person would either likely procreate a defective child or would himself be unable to care for his own child or children. All of this makes sense. The fourth subparagraph does not. Instead, it grants to the retarded person's next of kin or legal guardian the power of a tyrant: for any reason, or for no reason at all, he *may require* an otherwise responsible public servant to initiate the procedure. This he may do without reference to any standard and without regard to the public interest or the interest of the retarded person. We think such confidence in *all* next of kin and *all* legal guardians is misplaced, and that the unstated premises of competency to decide to force initiation of the proceeding and never failing fidelity to the interest of the retarded person are invalid. We hold this subsection four unconstitutional as an arbitrary and capricious delegation of unbridled power and a correspondingly irrational withdrawal of responsibility sensibly placed upon the director of the institution or the county director of Social Services by the other three coherent and compatible subparagraphs.

Written into § 35-39 are two fundamental but unarticulated premises. First, the statute presumes that it is possible in some cases to determine that the retarded person has a genetic defect which likely would be inherited by his children. Secondly, the statute presumes that some persons may be so severely retarded that they would be unable to properly care for a child should they conceive one. As determined in the findings of fact, *supra,* we are of the opinion that in some cases, rare though they may be, these two general presumptions inherent in the statute are valid.

The petition which is filed with the district court is required to contain information from which the district court will be able to make appropriate findings of fact and conclusions of law regarding the propriety of the requested sterilization operation. The petition must contain the results of psychological or psychiatric testing which support the petitioner's assertion that the retarded person is subject to the statute and must contain any statement by an examining physician which indicates "any known contra indication to the requested surgical procedure.'' The petition also requires the written consent or objection of the legal guardian or next of kin of the retarded person, and if there is none provides for appointment of a guardian *ad litem* ''who *shall* make investigation and report to the court. . . .'' The petition ''should also contain the consent or objection of the person upon whom the sterilization operation is to be performed.'' If the mentally retarded person is incapable of giving his consent or registering his objection, the petitioner must certify to the court that the procedure has been explained to the person.

A copy of the petition filed with the district court must be served upon the retarded person and his legal or natural guardian or a guardian ad litem or next of kin at least 20 days prior to the hearing on the petition. The district court is also authorized to conduct an investigation in certain circumstances.

After the petition is filed and upon appropriate notice to the retarded person and upon his request, a hearing will be held in the district court without a jury. Unless the retarded person or his representative objects, the hearing may be conducted without witnesses and the judge may enter judgment. If a hearing is requested and the retarded person does desire the appearance of witnesses, he is entitled to present evidence in his own behalf. The retarded person is likewise guaranteed the right to cross-examine witnesses who testify in support of the petition. Before the district court judge may enter an order requiring that the operation be performed, he must make the findings of fact required by § 35-43, which amounts to a judicial determination that the allegations contained in the petition are true.

We construe this Section 43 to mean that the judge must find that the subject is likely to engage in sexual activity without utilizing contraceptive devices and is therefore likely to impregnate or become impregnated. We derive that meaning from the clause of the statute saying ''. . . because the person would be likely, unless sterilized, to procreate a child or children. . . .'' Although the phrase is not contained in the prior clause, it must have been the sense of the legislature to require only that which is necessary, and unless sexual activity and inability or unwillingness to utilize contraception is indicated by the evidence, there would be no occasion for resort to sterilization.

If the retarded person is dissatisfied with the outcome in the district court, an appeal as of right is available to the superior court for a trial de novo before a jury. The result in the superior court may be appealed through the normal appellate channels to the North Carolina Court of Appeals and to the North Carolina Supreme Court.

Section 35-45 establishes the retarded person's right to counsel and assures that this right must be protected ''at all stages of the proceedings provided for herein.'' The statute provides for ''*Miranda*-type'' advice to the retarded person of entitlement to counsel at the time notice of the petition is given. Moreover, ''this information shall be given in language and in a manner calculated to insure, insofar as such is possible in view of the individual's capability to comprehend it, that the recipient understands the entitlement.'' The retarded person is entitled to retain counsel, or, in the case of indigency, an attorney must be appointed.

The remaining sections of the statute govern the sterilization procedure after the court order has been entered, and presumably, affirmed, if appealed.

Other provisions of North Carolina law, which apply to civil proceedings generally, must also be regarded as applicable to proceedings under the sterilization statute. N.C.Gen.Stat. § 8-59 provides that the retarded person would have the ability to subpoena witnesses in his own behalf for proceedings before the district court. *See also* Rule 45, N.C. Rules of Civil Procedure, N.C.Gen.Stat. 1A-1. N.C.Gen.Stat. § 7A-198 provides for the reporting of all cases in the district court unless waived by consent of all parties, and N.C.Gen.Stat. § 7A-95 provides for similar reporting in the superior court. N.C.Gen.Stat. § 1-288 makes a transcript of the proceedings available to the retarded person, even if he is unable to pay the expense.

The statute does not contain any statement of the petitioner's burden of proof. But the North Carolina Supreme Court, in *In re Sterilization of Moore*, 289 N.C. 95, 221 S.E.2d 307 (1976), announced that "in keeping with the intent of the General Assembly, clearly expressed throughout the article, that the rights of the individual must be fully protected, we hold that the evidence must be *clear, strong and convincing* before such an order may be entered." [Emphasis added.]

III

The United States as intervenor and the original plaintiff urge that we hold Article 7 of Chapter 35 of the North Carolina General Statutes unconstitutional insofar as it provides for sterilization of mentally retarded persons.

* * *

We hold that the legislative classification of mentally retarded persons is neither arbitrary nor capricious, but rests upon respectable medical knowledge and opinion that such persons are in fact different from the general population and may rationally be accorded different treatment for their benefit and the benefit of the public. Moreover, the classification is itself narrowed as to impact so that, as we interpret it, only mentally retarded persons who are sexually active, and unwilling or incapable of controlling procreation by other contraceptive means, *and* who are found to be likely to procreate a defective child, *or* who would be unable because of the degree of retardation to be able to care for a child, may be sterilized. The legislative dual purpose—to prevent the birth of a defective child or the birth of a nondefective child that cannot be cared for by its parent—reflects a compelling state interest and the classification rests upon a difference having a fair and substantial relation to the object of the legislation and does not, therefore, violate the Equal Protection Clause of the Fourteenth Amendment of the Constitution of the United States. *Cf. Stanton* v. *Stanton,* 421 U.S. 7, 14, 95 S.Ct. 1373, 43 L.Ed.2d 688 (1975).

The traditional equal protection test is invidious discrimination. *Williamson* v. *Lee Optical Co.,* 343 U.S. 483, 489, 75 S.Ct. 461, 99 L.Ed. 563 (1955). Indeed the Supreme Court has often gone so far as to justify setting aside legislative classifications "only if no grounds can be conceived to justify them." *McGowan* v. *United States,* 366 U.S. 420, 426, 81 S.Ct. 1101, 6 L.Ed.2d 393 (1961); *Schilb* v. *Kuebel,* 404 U.S. 357, 364, 92 S.Ct. 479, 484, 30 L.Ed.2d 502 (1971). But the Court has also said that a statutory classification based upon suspect criteria or affecting fundamental rights will encounter equal protection difficulties unless justified by a compelling governmental interest. *Shapiro* v. *Thompson,* 394 U.S. 618, 634, 638, 89 S.Ct. 1322, 22 L.Ed.2d 600 (1969) (*Schilb* v. *Kuebel,* 404 U.S. 357, 365, 92 S.Ct. 479, 484, 30 L.Ed.2d 502

(1971)). We think that all mentally retarded persons are sufficiently different from the general population to justify classification for some purposes without meeting the compelling governmental interest test. But we also think that the right to procreate is a fundamental one and that under equal protection challenge sterilization cannot be ordered short of demonstrating a compelling governmental interest. *Eisenstadt* v. *Baird,* 405 U.S. 438, 92 S.Ct. 1029, 31 L.Ed.2d 349 (1972).

We hold that the statute is not overly broad. Although it permits initiation of the sterilization procedure against any and all members of the class, it does *not* contemplate that all members of the class will be sterilized. Nor is the standard of selection so vague that it cannot be comprehended and applied. As we have made clear in our findings of fact, we are convinced that competent medical doctors and geneticists can predict in some cases with reasonable accuracy the likelihood of birth of a defective child and also the likelihood of whether the parent will be able to care for his child. The burden of proof put upon the petitioner by the North Carolina Supreme Court that the evidence must be clear, strong and convincing strongly protects against predictive error and should effectively limit application of the statute to those members of the class within the stated legislative purpose. Failure to prove predictability would require, of course, denial of an order authorizing sterilization.

For the reasons stated by Mr. Justice Moore for the Supreme Court of North Carolina, we hold that the statute is procedurally adequate to survive challenge under the Due Process Clause of the Fourteenth Amendment.

Finally we consider briefly the contention that the statute is invalid as a matter of "substantive" due process. We agree with the United States that the right to procreate is a fundamental right, *Eisenstadt* v. *Baird,* 405 U.S. 438, 92 S.Ct. 1029, 31 L.Ed.2d 349 (1972); *Skinner* v. *Oklahoma,* 316 U.S. 535, 62 S.Ct. 1110, 86 L.Ed.2d 1655 (1942). As such it is protected by the Fourteenth Amendment's concept of personal autonomy and perhaps by other specific Amendments within the Bill of Rights. *See Roe* v. *Wade,* 410 U.S. 113, 93 S.Ct. 705, 35 L.Ed.2d 147 (1973). The due process test of constitutionality of a statute that infringes upon a fundamental right is more than the ordinary one of a rational relationship to a valid state objective. To sustain this statute against substantive due process challenge it must be found that the state's interest is "compelling." We interpret Article 7 as narrowly drawn to express only the legitimate State interest of preventing the birth of a defective child or the birth of a nondefective child that cannot be cared for by its parent, and that so viewed, the State's interest rises to the dignity of a compelling one. It would be otherwise had the State presumed to enact and implement that *all* mentally retarded persons should be sterilized. That is *not* the thrust of the statute.

By way of summary we hold that the entire statutory scheme embraced in Article 7 of Chapter 35, §§ 36-50, is constitutional except for subparagraph four of § 39. We construe the statute to mean that a sterilization procedure may be initiated only by the director of the institution in which the retarded person resides or by the county director of social services. We further construe the statute to mean (§ 43) that before an order of sterilization can be entered, there must be a finding from evidence that is clear, strong and convincing that the subject is likely to engage in sexual activity without using contraceptive devices and that either a defective child is likely to be born or a child born that cannot be cared for by its parent. So construed, the statute is valid.

An appropriate judgment will be entered in accordance with this opinion.

NOTES

1.   Notice that Judge Craven rejects the premises of social Darwinism implicit in the *Buck* opinion. He also characterizes contemporary medical opinion as viewing with distaste sterilization of mentally retarded persons. This viewpoint is widely accepted; see, e.g., "Sterilization of Persons Who Are Mentally Retarded," an official statement of the American Association on Mental Deficiency, approved by the AAMD Executive Committee March 8, 1974, Guideline IIIA.

2.   Scrutinize the *NCARC* court's equal protection analysis. Does the court properly apply the strict scrutiny test? Does it examine whether there is a compelling reason justifying the sterilization of the specific class of persons affected by the state? Would the compelling interests asserted by the court provide a rationale for sterilizing all persons likely to be unfit parents or to transmit hereditary defects, regardless of whether they are mentally retarded? The court indicates that the classification *mentally retarded persons* is "neither arbitrary nor capricious" because mentally retarded people "are in fact different from the general population and may rationally be accorded different treatment," at p. 889, above. Is this compelling state interest analysis? Is the question of difference from the general population the determinative consideration?

3.   Was the court's substantial redrafting of the North Carolina statute a proper judicial function? Would the court have upheld the statute if it had not construed it narrowly? How would the *NCARC* court rule on the statute upheld in *Buck* v. *Bell*? How would the present Supreme Court decide *NCARC*?

4.   Between 1940 and 1970, the only decision relying upon *Buck* v. *Bell* to uphold the constitutionality of an involuntary sterilization statute was *In re Cavitt,* 182 Neb. 712, 157 N.W.2d 171, *reh. denied,* 183 Neb. 243, 159 N.W.2d 566 (1968), *prob. juris noted sub nom. Cavitt* v. *Nebraska,* 393 U.S. 1078, *vacated as moot,* 396 U.S. 996 (1969). The *Cavitt* decision was based upon a three-judge majority, with four justices dissenting. This odd situation was the result of a Nebraska constitutional provision requiring the concurrence of five justices to hold a legislative act unconstitutional.

The Nebraska sterilization statute at issue in *Cavitt* gave broad powers to a "Board of Examiners of Mental Deficients" to order sterilization to be performed upon residents of Nebraska's institution for mentally retarded people whenever the patient was mentally deficient, "apparently capable of bearing offspring," and, in the Board's opinion, should be sterilized as a condition of parole or discharge from the institution, 182 Neb. at 713-714, 157 N.W.2d at 174. In spite of the apparent constitutional difficulties of such a broad and vague power of sterilization, the *Cavitt* court upheld the Nebraska scheme in reliance upon *Buck* v. *Bell,* and observed:

> It can hardly be disputed that the right of a woman to bear and the right of a man to beget children is a natural and constitutional right, nor can it be successfully disputed

that no citizen has any rights that are superior to the common welfare. Acting for the public good, the state, in the exercise of its police power, may impose reasonable restrictions upon the natural and constitutional rights of its citizens. Measured by its injurious effect upon society, the state may limit a class of citizens in its right to bear or beget children with an inherited tendency to mental deficiency, including feeblemindedness, idiocy, or imbecility. It is the function of the Legislature, and its duty as well, to enact appropriate legislation to protect the public and preserve the race from the known effects of the procreation of mentally deficient children by the mentally deficient (*Id.* at 157 N.W.2d 175).

The Supreme Court of the United States noted probable jurisdiction over *Cavitt* but dismissed it when the Nebraska legislature repealed the compulsory portion of the sterilization statute, thus mooting the case. Did the Court's acceptance of the appeal indicate a willingness to reconsider the ruling in *Buck* v. *Bell?*

The *Cavitt* court was willing to infer a tendency toward sexual impropriety because "[i]t is an established fact that mental deficiency accelerates sexual impulses and any tendencies toward crime to a harmful degree," *id.* at 719, 157 N.W.2d at 177. In regard to this myth, see note 3 on p. 875, above.

The court indicated, as an alternative justification for approving the sterilization measure, that the statute was not truly compulsory, but operates only as a prerequisite to release from the state institution, *id.* at 720, 157 N.W.2d at 177. Upon motion for rehearing, this view was reiterated even more bluntly by the court:

> The order does not require her sterilization. It does provide, in accordance with the statute, that she shall not be released unless she is sterilized. The choice is hers (183 Neb. at 247, 159 N.W.2d at 568).

Was dissenting Justice Smith on the mark when he labeled this contention "the fictive option of sterilization or life imprisonment," 182 Neb. at 723, 157 N.W.2d at 179?

Other anomalies and shortcomings of the *Cavitt* decision are discussed in Burgdorf, R., and Burgdorf, M., "The Wicked Witch Is Almost Dead: *Buck* v. *Bell* and the Sterilization of Handicapped Persons," 50 *Temple L.Q.* 995, 1016-1020 (1977).

5.   Prior to *NCARC,* the North Carolina sterilization statute had been ruled constitutionally valid by the state supreme court in *In re Sterilization of Moore,* 289 N.C. 95, 221 S.E.2d 307 (1976). In upholding the statute against an equal protection challenge, the *Moore* court declared: "We have found no case that holds that sterilization of all mentally ill or retarded persons denies equal protection.... Since the North Carolina law applies to all those named in the statute, these statutes ... do not violate the equal protection clauses of the United States Constitution or the Constitution of North Carolina," at 221 S.E.2d 313-314. The *NCARC* court, however, in also upholding the statute to equal protection challenge, declared that "[i]t would be otherwise had the State presumed to enact and implement that *all* mentally retarded persons should be sterilized. That is *not* the thrust of the statute," at p. 890, above. Can these holdings be reconciled? Is either totally adequate?

For an extensive discussion and criticism of the *Moore* decision, including the court's use of the rational basis test under equal protection, see Gauvey, S., and

Shuger, N., "The Permissibility of Involuntary Sterilization under the *Parens Patriae* and Police Power Authority of the State,'' 6 *Md. L. Forum* 109 (1976).

6. Twenty-two states currently regulate involuntary sterilization of various categories of individuals by statute: Ariz. Rev. Stat. Ann. §§ 36-532 to -544 (1974); Ark. Stat. Ann. §§ 59-501 to -502 (1971 Repl. Vol.); Cal. Penal Code Ann. § 2670 (Deering 1970); Conn. Gen. Stat. Ann. § 17-19 (1975); Del. Code Ann. 16, § 5701-05 (1975); Idaho Code §§ 39-3901 to 3910 (Supp. 1975); Ind. Ann. Stat. §§ 16-13-13-1 to -6, 16-13-14-1 to -5 (1973); Iowa Code Ann. § 145.9 (1972); Me. Rev. Stat. Ann. §§ 34-2461 to -2468 (1964); Mich. Stat. Ann. § 14.381-.390 (1969); Minn. Stat. Ann. § 256.07 (1971); Miss. Code Ann. §§ 41-45-1 to -19 (1973); Mont. Rev. Code Ann. §§ 38-601 to -08 (1947); N.C. Gen. Stat. § 35-36 to -50 (1975 Cum. Supp.); N.H. Rev. Stat. Ann. §§ 174:1 to :14 (1964); Okla. Stat. Ann., Tit. 43A, § 341-46 (1951); Ore. Rev. Stat. §§ 436.010 to -.150 (1973 Repl. Vol.); S.C. Code Ann. §§ 44-47-10 to -100 (1962); Utah Code Ann. §§ 64-10-1 to -14 (1953); Va. Code Ann. § 37.1-156-71 (1970 Repl. Vol.); Wash. Rev. Code Ann. § 9.92.100 (1961); W. Va. Code Ann. § 27-16-1 (Cum. Supp. 1975).

ADDITIONAL READING

Baker, J., "Sexual Sterilization—Constitutional Validity of Involuntary Sterilization and Consent Determinative of Voluntariness," 40 *Mo. L. Rev.* 509 (1975).

Comment, "Eugenic Sterilization Statutes: A Constitutional Re-evaluation," 14 *J. Family Law* 280 (1975).

Comment, "Sterilization of Mental Defectives: Compulsion and Consent," 27 *Baylor L. Rev.* 174 (1975).

Gauvey, S., and Shuger, N., "The Permissibility of Involuntary Sterilization under the *Parens Patriae* and Police Power Authority of the State: *In re Sterilization of Moore,"* 6 *Md. L. Forum* 109 (1976).

Burgdorf, R., and Burgdorf, M., "The Wicked Witch Is Almost Dead: *Buck* v. *Bell* and the Sterilization of Handicapped Persons," 50 *Temple L. Q.* 995 (1977).

Ghent, J., "Validity of Statutes Authorizing Asexualization or Sterilization of Criminals or Mental Defectives," 53 A.L.R.3d 960.

Murdock, C., "Sterilization of the Retarded: A Problem or a Solution?" 62 *Cal. L. Rev.* 917 (1974).

Note, "Rights of Mentally Ill Involuntary Sterilization—Analysis of Recent Statutes," 78 *W.Va. L. Rev.* 131 (1975).

Paul, "The Sterilization of Mentally Retarded Persons: The Issues and Conflicts," 3 *Family Planning/Population Reporter* 96 (1974).

Price and Burt, "Sterilization, State Action and the Concept of Consent," *Law and Psychology Rev.* (Spring, 1975).

Ruthman, R., "The Individual and the Involuntary Sterilization Laws, 1966" 31 *Albany L. Rev.* 97 (1967).

Special Report, "Society's Right to Sterilize: What Are the Limits?" 2 *Amicus* (Feb. 1977).

b. In the Absence of a Statute

Frazier v. Levi

Court of Civil Appeals of Texas, Houston, First District, 1969

440 S.W.2d 393

Peden, Justice.

Application filed by the guardian of the person and estate of a mentally incompetent ward seeking an order authorizing an operation which would render the ward sexually sterile. There is no medical or physical necessity for the operation sought by the guardian; the application is based on social and economic grounds only.

When this cause was filed by the guardian in the County Court, a guardian *ad litem* was duly appointed for the ward; he filed on the ward's behalf an exception in the nature of a general demurrer, asserting that under Texas law there are no grounds upon which the application could be granted; this exception was sustained. The guardian declined to amend her petition, and her application was ordered dismissed.

She appealed from the dismissal order to the District Court, where her application was submitted on the same pleadings as in the County Court. The District Judge also sustained the ward's exception and dismissed the case; the guardian has perfected her appeal to this Court from that order of dismissal.

In her points of error the guardian alleges that the courts below erred 1) in ruling that there are no legal grounds in Texas upon which the application for sexual sterilization could be granted, 2) in sustaining the ward's exception in the nature of a general demurrer to the guardian's pleading and 3) in dismissing the guardian's application for sexual sterilization of a ward. This seems to be a case of first impression in Texas.

The trial courts' decisions were based on the pleadings as a matter of law, so we will consider as true the allegations in the guardian's application. In it she pleaded that she is the aged mother of the ward, is in poor health and is unable to stand the physical, financial or emotional strain of caring for any more children of the ward. She and her husband are already providing for the ward and the ward's two children, both of whom are mentally retarded. The ward, age 34, has the mentality of about a six year old, is sexually promiscuous, unable to support or take care of herself or her children, but is in good physical health. No medical reason for her sexual sterilization exists, and the officials of John Sealy Hospital in Galveston have refused to have such an operation performed on the ward without the court's approval.

We overrule appellant's points of error.

As a mentally incompetent person, the ward lacks the mental capacity to consent to the operation or to oppose it. Her legal rights are to be carefully protected and must not be taken from her without due process of law even though her natural mother and guardian feels that the operation would benefit all.

> Power with respect to the care and custody of persons of unsound mind and the possession and control of their estates are vested in the state, or the people thereof, the exercise of which power the people may delegate to the courts by constitutional or statutory provision. Insane persons are considered as wards of the state; and the state as *parens patriae* is under a special duty to protect them and their property as a class incapable of protecting themselves, as well as to protect the public from the acts of those

who are not under the guidance of reason. Within constitutional limitations, the state may enact statutory provisions for the protection of such persons, which provisions must have reasonable regard for the rights of persons and property, and must be liberally construed to the end that their purpose may be effectuated. An insane person cannot be deprived of his legal rights otherwise than in the manner expressly provided by the statute, . . . (44 C.J.S. Insane Persons § 3, p. 48.)

That statutory or constitutional authority is needed to authorize the courts to approve and order such an operation is not doubted and, indeed, is not questioned by the guardian in this case. Instead, she urges that the authority of the County Court to issue the order sought is contained in Article 5, Section 16 of the Texas Constitution, Vernon's Ann.St., whereby the County Court is given the general jurisdiction of a Probate Court to appoint guardians of persons *non compos mentis* and transact all business appertaining to them; also in Section 36 of the Probate Code, V.A.T.S., which provides in part: "It shall be the duty of the judge of each county court to use reasonable diligence to see that personal representatives of estates being administered under orders of the court, guardians of the persons of wards, and other officers of the court, perform the duties enjoined upon them by law pertaining to such estates and wards," and in Section 229 of the Probate Code: "The guardian of the person is entitled to the charge and control of the person of the ward, and the care of his support and education, and his duties shall correspond with his rights. It is the duty of the guardian of the person of a minor to take care of the person of such minor, to treat him humanely, and to see that he is properly educated; and, if necessary for his support, to see that he learns a trade or adopts a useful profession."

We do not find in such provisions authority for the court to order the operation, and find no such authority in any other provision of the Texas Constitution or statutes.

> Although the authorities are not in complete accord, generally the courts have sustained as valid legislation providing for the sterilization of certain types of convicted criminals, criminally insane persons, and feeble-minded persons. Sterilization statutes have been held to be a valid exercise of the police power, and not unconstitutional as being in contravention of the constitutional guaranty of life, liberty, and the pursuit of happiness, or of the prohibition against cruel and unusual punishment, or as being a delegation of judicial power to an executive board, or as denying equal protection. Nor do they violate due process of law where proper notice is given followed by a hearing in which all interested parties may be heard. Moreover, a statute providing for sterilization of feeble-minded persons is not rendered invalid by failure to provide what courts shall have jurisdiction of such cases, if the court is sufficiently indicated by general provisions of the act, nor is such a statute rendered invalid by a constitutional provision that institutions for the feeble-minded shall always be fostered and supported. There is, however, authority that sterilization statutes are unconstitutional because sterilization constitutes cruel and unusual punishment.
>
> Other cases have held sterilization statutes invalid because they constitute unconstitutional class legislation, because they deny due process in failing to provide for notice to, and hearing of, the person whose sterilization is proposed, and because they violate the equal protection clause.
>
> It is essential to a valid order for the sterilization of a mental defective that there be a substantial compliance with the jurisdictional requirements of the statute, such as, that physicians appear before a court and be examined and that a guardian ad litem be appointed within the time specified by the statute (41 Am.Jur.2d 570-1, Incompetent Persons, § 32.)

Section 32 of the Probate Code states: "The rights, powers and duties of executors, administrators, and guardians shall be governed by the principles of the common law, when the same do not conflict with the provisions of the statutes of this State."

> It will be noted that this section of the Probate Code by its silence denies by implication the exercise by the Probate Court of equitable powers. But even if the words, "principles of the common law," are construed to include equitable powers, this section of the code does not grant to the court common law powers, but merely provides that the rights, powers and duties of executors, administrators, and guardians shall be governed by the principles of the common law, when the same do not conflict with the provisions of the statutes of this State. (*In re Guardianship of Estate of Neal,* 406 S.W.2d 496 (Houston Civ.App., 1966, writ ref., n. r. e.).)

Any order authorizing the operation proposed by the appellant would be in excess of the power delegated by the statutes of Texas and would be invalid.

The judgment of the Trial Court is affirmed.

HOLMES v. POWERS

Court of Appeals of Kentucky, 1969
439 S.W.2d 579

PALMORE, Judge.

This, to say the least, is an unusual case. The appellants, county health officer and local medical society of Whitley County, seek a declaratory judgment to the effect that they can sterilize the appellee, a 35-year-old unmarried woman who is mentally retarded and has two illegitimate children (one of whom also is retarded), without civil or criminal liability to themselves. They appeal from an adjudication that they "cannot legally perform a sexual sterilization operation upon the defendant because the defendant is not mentally competent to grant permission and there is no legal authority providing for the granting of such permission in any manner."

There simply is no escape from the conclusion reached by the trial court. If, as alleged and proved, the appellee is in fact mentally incompetent, she does not have legal capacity to consent to anything. Nor, at her age, does the law give her parents any control of her person or property. It may be (though we do not decide) that a legally constituted committee could exercise such a choice, but there has been no inquest and there is no committee. The guardian *ad litem* has, of course, only the power to defend, which he has done. And neither by statute nor from the common law does any court of this state have authority to fill the void.

The judgment is affirmed.

All concur.

IN RE LAMBERT

Probate Court for Davidson County, Tennessee, 1976
No. 61156, March 1, 1976

LUTON, Probate Judge.

By the Petition to Establish Guardianship for Medical Consent, filed by Mrs. Etta E. Lambert, mother of Gloria Sue Lambert, it is sought to have petitioner appointed guardian of her said child and to have the Court empower petitioner, as such guardian, to consent to a hysterectomy or alternative form of sterilization operation to be performed on her said child.

A guardian *ad litem* was appointed for said Gloria Sue Lambert and the cause was heard by the Court upon the pleadings, testimony of the petitioner adduced orally before the Court, Interrogatories and Answer of Dr. John Zelenik, oral arguments and briefs filed by counsel for petitioner and by the guardian *ad litem,* together with the entire record.

Since the hearing, Gloria Sue Lambert has attained the age of eighteen years. This would not, in the opinion of the Court, affect the proceedings herein other than to change the designation of the petitioner, upon the Court's finding that an appointment is proper, from that of guardian to conservator.

Gloria Sue Lambert, because of her condition of mental deficiency, is unable to adequately handle her personal affairs or to make rational personal decisions. According to the Petition, petitioner believes it to be for the manifest best interest of Gloria Sue that she have a hysterectomy or an alternative form of sterilization operation performed on her person, said Gloria Sue being unaware of the logical consequences of sexual intercourse while possessing normal desires for same and being psychologically and physically ill equipped to give birth to a child and act in any capacity as a mother to a child. The Petition further alleges that prior to any hysterectomy or other form of sterilization being performed by a hospital, either actual informed consent to such an operation or, in the absence of such consent, a court order must be obtained.

Dr. Zelenik, Acting Chairman, Department of Obstetrics and Gynecology, Vanderbilt University School of Medicine, says that Gloria Sue has been treated in the Vanderbilt Gynecology Clinic at varying times during 1974 with progestational agents in an effort to reduce the bleeding with her periods and the intermenstrual bleeding; that this has met with varying success; that the recommendation for this surgery is not because of this patient's gynecological problem; that, if this patient were mentally competent, he would under no circumstances recommend a sterilizing procedure; that the recommended procedure is not primarily for the purpose of sterilization, although that is one of the objectives to be achieved; that the other objective is to relieve the mother of Gloria Sue of the management problem on her daughter so that she does not have to be continually changing pads, changing bed sheets, and, in other ways having to care for the menstrual secretions of a patient who is not able to take care of these on her own; that, stimulated by their ovarian hormones, these unfortunate persons tend to be attracted to men and are easy prey for a sexual relationship if they are not continuously watched; that while sterilization would take care of the problem of pregnancy, her menstrual problem perhaps requires more extensive surgery.

Brief of petitioner insists that the relief herein sought should be granted under the doctrine of substituted judgment. Cases are cited, including Tennessee cases, wherein this doctrine has been applied in dealing with the property of persons unable to make decisions for themselves. Apparently there are no Tennessee cases dealing with the precise question here presented, that is, the jurisdiction of this Court to authorize this petitioner as conservator of her daughter to consent to the hysterectomy operation on her daughter.

Petitioner cites the case of *Strunk* v. *Strunk,* 445 S.W.2d 145, wherein the Kentucky Court of Appeals, after finding that it was in the interest of the incompetent to keep his brother alive and that the risk of surgery to the incompetent would be small, ordered removal of the incompetent's kidney to transplant into his brother. It was the judgment of the Court that the incompetent would have wanted to save his brother's life. This judgment was substituted for the void of judgment on the part of the incompetent.

Petitioner cites a Wisconsin case holding contrary to the *Strunk* decision.

Petitioner cites the cases generally dealing with situations in which medical care was ordered over the objection of parents of children, such as needed blood transfusions, deformed foot operation rendered necessary by polio and similar cases. Petitioner further calls attention to the cases where the Court has ordered surgery for adults over their objections.

No case is cited by petitioner which specifically rules in the manner here desired by petitioner.

In the brief filed by the guardian *ad litem,* it is pointed out that Tennessee has a sterilization statute, T.C.A. Section 53-4608, which makes it lawful for any physician or surgeon licensed in this state when so requested by any person eighteen years of age or over, or less than eighteen years of age if legally married, to perform upon such person a surgical interruption of the vas deferens or Fallopian tubes, as the case may be, provided a request in writing is made by such person prior to the performance of such surgical operation and provided further that prior to or at the time of such request, a full and reasonable medical explanation is given by such physician or surgeon to such person as to the meaning and consequence of such operation. Apparently there is no legislation in Tennessee which gives a court jurisdiction to authorize the performance of the operation here suggested upon persons not competent to make a decision for themselves.

The brief filed by the guardian *ad litem* points out that the cases cited in petitioner's brief dealing with life or death situations do not apply here because this is no life or death situation.

The guardian *ad litem* further points out that petitioner's brief is in error in insisting that under a Tennessee case cited in petitioner's brief, the Court would not refuse to do for the benefit of a lunatic that which it is probable the lunatic himself would have done. The guardian *ad litem* points out Dr. Zelenik's testimony that, if Gloria Sue were a normal person mentally with the same gynecological problems as she has, he would not recommend the surgery which he recommends here.

The guardian *ad litem's* brief further cites several cases dealing with the problem here at hand. The case of *A.L.* v. *G.R.H.,* 325 N.E.2d 501, is an Indiana case wherein a mother sought to have her fifteen-year-old son who had an I.Q. seven points below the normal range, permanently sterilized under the common law attributes of the parent-child relationship. The Indiana Court of Appeals refused the permanent sterilization since the desire to do so emanated not from any lifesaving necessity but from a desire to prevent the child from fathering children. The Court recognized the problems of impregnation of females with whom the fifteen-year-old was associating but held that the law simply does not allow it.

The Court said:

> In considering the fact at hand, it should be first noted that we are not dealing with a legislative enactment permitting sterilizations without consent where certain conditions exist.
>
> Secondly, the facts do not bring the case within the framework of those decisions holding either that the parents may consent on behalf of the child to medical services necessary for the child, or where the state may intervene over the parents' wishes to rescue the child from parental neglect or to save its life.
>
> Permanent sterilization as here proposed is a different matter. Its desirability emanates not from any lifesaving necessities. Rather, its sole purpose is to prevent the capability of fathering children.
>
> We believe the common law does not invest parents with such power over their children even though they sincerely believe the child's adulthood would benefit therefrom. This result has been reached most recently in *In Interest of M.K.R.* (1974), Mo., 515 S.W.2d 467, and *In re Kemp's Estate* (1974), 43 Cal.App.3d 758, 118 Cal. Rptr. 64, where the courts of Missouri and California held that their respective juvenile statutes making general provision for the welfare of children were insufficient to confer jurisdiction to authorize the sterilization of retarded girls in the absence of specific sterilization legislation. See, also, *Wade* v. *Bethesda* (S.D.Ohio 1973), 356 F.Supp. 380; *Frazier* v. *Levi* (1969), Tex.Civ.App., 440 S.W.2d 393; *Holmes* v. *Powers* (1969), Ky., 439 S.W.2d 579."

In the case of *In re Kemp's Estate,* cited in the above quote from the Indiana case, the California Appellate Court, in holding that the Probate Court did not have jurisdiction to order sterilization because there was not any express statutory authority, said:

> Although the probate court in exercising its jurisdiction in guardianship matters may be said to have powers analogous to those of chancery, it has been stated that the probate court has no general equity jurisdiction. (*Security-First National Bank* v. *Superior Court* (1934) 1 Cal.2d 749, 757, 37 P.2d 69.) Its jurisdiction is limited in that it has "only those powers which are granted by statute and such incidental powers, legal and equitable, as enable it to exercise the powers granted." (*Estate of Muhammad* (1971) 16 Cal.App.3d 726, 731, 94 Cal. Rptr. 856, 859.) Assuming that under the reasoning of the *Reynolds* case, the probate court in the exercise of its continuing jurisdiction over a guardianship has authority by virtue of Probate Code section 1400 to issue instructions providing for the mental and physical welfare of an incompetent person, it must be determined whether a judgment of a probate court ordering a sterilization operation to be performed upon the person of an incompetent is within the limits of such jurisdiction. The trial judge in the instant case found authority for his order "in the exercise of its residual chancery powers under the provisions of California Probate Code section 1400." Appellants contend that if such a power exists, it does not extend to involuntary sterilization.
>
> There does not appear to be any case law in California supporting the proposition that a probate court may order the sterilization of a mentally incompetent ward. There is no statute in California which specifically confers such authority upon the probate court. The Welfare and Institutions Code does provide for the sterilization of certain mentally disordered or mentally retarded persons, but only after the individual has been committed to a state mental hospital and only under specified conditions. (Welf. & Inst. Code section 7254.)

In the case of *In the Interest of M.K.R.,* 515 S.W.2d 467, cited in the above quotation from the Indiana case, the Missouri Supreme Court held that a Juvenile Court could not authorize sterilization under a juvenile code section providing that the practice was as in equity in the absence of specific legislation conferring jurisdiction.

In the case of *Wade* v. *Bethesda Hospital,* 356 F.Supp. 380, the Court held that a Probate Judge was not entitled to judicial immunity in ordering a feeble-minded girl to submit to sterilization where the Judge acted in the absence of jurisdiction.

In the case of *Frazier* v. *Levi,* 440 S.W.2d 393, the Texas Court of Civil Appeals held that a Probate Court does not have jurisdiction to authorize sterilization of a thirty-four-year-old sexually promiscuous ward because of a lack of statutory authority. Said case cites *44 C.J.S., Insane Persons,* Section 3, Page 48, in quoting as follows: "An insane person can not be deprived of his legal rights otherwise than in the manner expressly provided by the statute. . . ."

In the case of *Holmes* v. *Powers,* 439 S.W.2d 579, the Kentucky Court of Appeals held that the parents of a thirty-five-year-old unmarried female could not consent to sterilization; that perhaps a committee could do so.

The County (Probate) Courts of Tennessee are recognized by the Constitution but they possess no judicial jurisdiction other than that conferred by statute. T.C.A. Sections 16-701 *et seq.; Dick* v. *Dick,* 223 Tenn. 228; *Linnville* v. *Darby,* 60 Tenn. 306; *Brewer* v. *Griggs,* 10 Tenn.App. 378.

No statutory power given to this Court to authorize the operation here desired has been cited to the attention of the Court by counsel nor has the Court been able to find any such statutory authority or jurisdiction.

It is, therefore, the conclusion of the Court that this Court does not have the jurisdiction or authority to empower the petitioner to have the operation here requested and, therefore, the Petition should be dismissed at the cost of the petitioner.

NOTES

1. In *In re M.K.R.,* 515 S.W.2d 467 (Mo. 1974), referred to in *In re Lambert,* the Supreme Court of Missouri declared:

> The courts are not faced in this case with a prayer for a judgment authorizing ordinary medical treatment, or radical surgery necessary to preserve the life of a child; we are faced with a request for sanction by the state of what no doubt is a routine operation which would irreversibly deny to a human being a fundamental right, the right to bear or beget a child. Jurisdiction of the juvenile court to exercise the awesome power of denying that right may not be inferred from the general language of the sections of the code to which we have referred. Such jurisdiction may be conferred only by specific statute.
>
> Whatever might be the merits of permanently depriving this child of this right, the juvenile court may not do so without statutory authority—authority which provides guidelines and adequate legal safeguards determined by the people's elected representatives to be necessary after full consideration of the constitutional rights of the individual and the general welfare of the people. (at 515 S.W.2d 470-471.)

2. The *Lambert* opinion provides a fairly comprehensive summary of *In re Kemp's Estate,* 43 Cal.App.3d 758, 118 Cal. Rptr. 64 (1974), and other case law in this area. In the absence of specific statutory authorization, state courts consistently have refused to infer the existence of such power from limited juvenile court acts, from more general

probate statutes, or even from the general powers of an equity court where sterilization has been sought as being in the best interest of the handicapped person.

3.   Assuming a statute existed that granted jurisdiction and that accorded procedural due process and equal protection of the laws, should sterilization have been authorized under the circumstances presented by the *Frazier, Holmes,* and *Lambert* cases? What factors would each court need to consider in making this decision? In one modern case, which considered the merits of an involuntary sterilization, the court declined to authorize it. In *In re Anderson,* Civ.No. 5-67-1648 (Dave County Ct., Branch 1 Wis., Nov., 1974) (reported in Mental Retardation and the Law, 22-23, June, 1975), a father, as temporary guardian, sought permission to consent to sterilization of his 19-year-old daughter. The *Anderson* court, finding that dispute existed as to whether sterilization would be in the woman's best interest denied the petition, holding:

1.   It was totally correct for the temporary guardian to petition the court, since regardless of the medical necessity that may be involved or what may be perceived as the best interests of the ward, authorization to sterilize should only come from a court after a full evidentiary hearing.
2.   Before sterilization should be authorized, a court must be satisfied:
    a.   That the procedure is a medical necessity or in the best interests of the ward;
    b.   That all the less drastic alternatives have been investigated, and;
    c.   That all the less drastic alternatives are unsuitable.
3.   Although there is evidence that sterilization is in the best interests of the ward, the guardian *ad litem* disagreed. Any doubts about such matters should be resolved against sterilization.
4.   There are less drastic alternatives which should be explored by the guardian.

Do the criteria set forth by the *Anderson* court give any guidance as to how the above-mentioned cases should be decided on the merits?

4.   Can the best interests of a mentally handicapped person who is unable to understand the nature and consequences of sterilization and to communicate his or her opinion ever be determined objectively? Would sterilization of a mentally handicapped person ever be in his or her best interests if those interests cannot be determined objectively? Do the opinions in *Superintendent of Belchertown State School* v. *Saikewicz,* pp. 770–787, *supra,* in *Little* v. *Little,* pp. 792–799, *supra,* and *In re Quinlan,* pp. 780–781, *supra,* indicate a judicial willingness to consider provision of controversial therapies like sterilization where the patient himself is unable to give or withhold informed consent? Does the "substitute judgment doctrine" employed in those opinions provide a criterion that can be applied to decision making in such a sterilization case?

A.L. v. G.R.H.

Court of Appeals of Indiana, Third District, 1975
325 N.E.2d 501 cert. denied 425 U.S. 936

GARRARD, Judge.

A.L. filed a complaint for declaratory judgment seeking declaration of her right under the common law attributes of the parent-child relationship to have her son, G.R.H., sterilized.

The boy, age fifteen, had suffered brain damage as the result of being struck by an automobile during his early childhood.

Expert testimony indicated that at the time of trial he had an I.Q. of 83. This was described as seven points below the normal range and in the "dull" or "border-line" area. Retarded ranges were assertedly below 70. It was stated that the boy had benefited substantially from the special education program in which he was enrolled and that he appeared capable of further improvement. (His I.Q. two years before the action had tested at 65.) It was the opinion of the experts that he would be capable of earning his own livelihood either in specially supervised work or in entry-level jobs in the general marketplace.

His mental disability would not be transmittable to his offspring. In addition, he had exhibited no behavior from which a propensity to force his attentions on others might be inferred. It was the opinion of his psychiatrist that it was unlikely that G.R.H. would initiate antisocial activity, although his residual brain damage might render him more susceptible to being led into such activities. It was the expert's opinion that G.R.H. was sufficiently intelligent to understand what was involved in sterilization and to participate in the decision-making process.

On the other hand, the evidence showed the boy had become interested in girls, that he wanted to date, and liked to kiss. Furthermore, it was shown that most of his female social contact was with other children from his special education classes. It is thus urged that if he impregnates a female, the great likelihood is that it will be one of these retarded or handicapped children.

The evidence at trial did not describe the proposed surgery, except to identify it as a vasectomy. However, from the positions taken by the parties, we are justified in assuming the operation would be simple, virtually painless and irreversible. It would leave G.R.H. unimpaired in his physical ability to have intercourse although he would be rendered permanently sterile.

The trial court denied the mother's right to secure the operation, and this appeal follows.

At the outset, we thank counsel for their excellent efforts in representing a seriously concerned parent and in providing the guardian *ad litem* defense of the child's interest.

In considering the facts at hand, it should be first noted that we are not dealing with a legislative enactment permitting sterilizations without consent where certain conditions exist.

Secondly, the facts do not bring the case within the framework of those decisions holding either that the parents may consent on behalf of the child to medical services necessary for the child, or where the state may intervene over the parents' wishes to rescue the child from parental neglect or to save its life.

Permanent sterilization as here proposed is a different matter. Its desirability emanates not from any life-saving necessities. Rather, its sole purpose is to prevent the capability of fathering children.

We believe the common law does not invest parents with such power over their children even though they sincerely believe the child's adulthood would benefit therefrom. This result has been reached most recently in *In Interest of M.K.R.* (1974), Mo.,

515 S.W.2d 467, and *In re Kemp's Estate* (1974), 43 Cal.App.3d 758, 118 Cal.Rptr. 64, where the courts of Missouri and California held that their respective juvenile statutes making general provision for the welfare of children were insufficient to confer jurisdiction to authorize the sterilization of retarded girls in the absence of specific sterilization legislation. See, also, *Wade* v. *Bethesda* (S.D.Ohio 1973), 356 F.Supp. 380; *Frazier* v. *Levi* (1969), Tex.Civ.App., 440 S.W.2d 393; *Holmes* v. *Powers* (1968), Ky., 439 S.W.2d 579.

The trial court correctly denied the requested relief.

Affirmed.

STATON, P. J., and HOFFMAN, J., concur.

NOTES

1. What is the basis of Judge Garrard's decision?

2. The *A.L.* court's rejection of parents' power to authorize their children's sterilization was unequivocal. Other courts' decisions have been consistent with this conclusion. The *Holmes* court recognized that parents of a mentally handicapped adult lacked authority *qua* parents to authorize sterilization. See p. 896, *supra*. The *NCARC* court refused to confer upon the next of kin or guardian of a mentally retarded person a duty to initiate sterilization proceedings. See pp. 884–891, *supra*. These decisions cast considerable doubt upon the power of parents or guardians to consent to the sterilization of their children or wards, in the absence of medical necessity. Is this judicial trend more or less protective of the legal rights of handicapped people?

3. The foregoing cases indicate that a judicial order authorizing a sterilization is invalid in the absence of a statute specifically giving the court such power. If a judge erroneously made such an unauthorized order, it would presumably be struck down on appeal. But what if a judge orders a sterilization and it is performed before access can be had to the appellate courts? Can the judge be held liable for damages for acting beyond the scope of his jurisdiction? In *Wade* v. *Bethesda Hospital,* 337 F.Supp. 671 (S.D.Ohio, 1971), an Ohio judge had ordered the sterilization of an allegedly mentally retarded girl. Upon turning 21 and marrying, the girl filed a damage action against the judge, the doctor who performed the operation, the hospital where it was performed, and the social workers and welfare workers who recommended the surgery. The defendant judge moved to dismiss the complaint on the ground that he was protected by judicial immunity. The federal court held that judicial immunity did not apply, observing: "There is no statute in Ohio which authorizes a judge to order sterilization for any purpose. Nor has this court been able to discover any judicial precedent for such an order in the absence of a specific statute," at 337 F.Supp. 673-674.

In *Stump* v. *Sparkman,* 435 U.S. 349 (1978), *reh. denied* 436 U.S. 957, however, the Supreme Court has apparently foreclosed such damage suits against judges. The Court upheld the claim of an Indiana judge to judicial immunity even though he had approved, without a hearing, the sterilization of a 15-year-old, possibly "somewhat mentally retarded" girl, who was told that she was having her appendix removed. The Court interpreted the scope of judicial immunity to be extremely broad: "A judge will not be deprived of immunity because the action he took was in error, was done maliciously, or was in excess of his authority . . . ,' at 435 U.S. 356.

4. A novel result was reached in *Ruby* v. *Massey,* Civ.No. H-76-315 (D.Conn., Summary Judgment, May 16, 1978), where the court held that it was a violation of equal protection for the state of Connecticut not to have provided some means by which parents of three mentally retarded girls (ages 12, 13, and 15) could have their daughters sterilized by hysterectomy. The court was apparently under the misimpression that nonhandicapped minors or their parents can consent to sterilization. Thus, it was concluded that denial of such a right to handicapped minors would be a denial of equal treatment. While the sentiment is admirable, its application seems absurd in this situation. The children's rights might more properly have been realized by protecting them from hysterectomies to the same degree that nonhandicapped children are protected from such irreversible destruction of their procreative processes. What if, however, the plaintiffs in *Ruby* v. *Massey* had been mentally retarded adults?

ADDITIONAL READING

Gauvey, S., and Shuger, N., "The Permissibility of Involuntary Sterilization under the *Parens Patriae* and Police Power Authority of the State: *In re Sterilization of Moore,*" 6 *Md. L. Forum* 109 (1976).

Note, "Courts—Scope of Authority—Sterilization of Mental Defectives," 61 *Mich. L. Rev.* 1359 (1963).

Robertson, J., "Organ Donations by Incompetents and the Substituted Judgment Doctrine," 76 *Colum. L. Rev.* 48 (1976).

Trenkner, T. R., "Jurisdiction of Court to Permit Sterilization of Mentally Defective Persons in Absence of Specific Statutory Authority," 74 A.L.R.3d 1210.

Brand, G., "The Discipline of Judges," 46 *A.B.A.J.* 1315 (1960).

Brazier, M., "Judicial Immunity and the Independence of the Judiciary," *Public Law* 397, Winter (1976).

Kates, D., "Immunity of State Judges under the Federal Civil Rights Acts: *Pierson* v. *Ray* Reconsidered," 65 *Nev. U. L. Rev.* 615 (1970).

Note, "Immunity of Federal and State Judges from Civil Suit—Time for a Qualified Immunity?" 27 *Case West. Res. L. Rev.* 727 (1977).

Note, "Liability of Judicial Officers Under Section 1983," 79 *Yale L.J.* 322 (1969).

McCormack, W., and Kirkpatrick, L., "Immunities of State Officials under Section 1983," 8 *Rutgers-Camden L.J.* 65 (1976).

Miller, F., "Discipline of Judges," 50 *Mich. L. Rev.* 737 (1952).

b. Under *Parens Patriae*

WYATT v. ADERHOLT

United States District Court for the Middle District of Alabama, Northern Division,
1973
368 F.Supp. 1382

OPINION AND ORDER
PER CURIAM.

The plaintiffs filed on July 25, 1973 a document styled "Amended Complaint or alternatively Motion for Further Relief," in which they prayed for an injunction enjoining the enforcement of the following statute of the State of Alabama:

> § 243. *Treatment of inmates prescribed by assistant.*—The assistant with the advice and consent of the superintendent shall prescribe for the treatment of the inmates of the home, and if after consultation with the superintendent, they deem it advisable they are hereby authorized and empowered to sterilize any inmate. (Tit. 45, Code of Ala., Recomp. 1958.)

Pursuant to 28 U.S.C. § 2281, this three-judge court was appointed to decide whether an injunction should be granted restraining the enforcement of that statute.

The defendants insist that they have never relied on that statute as authorization for performing sterilization operations, and the uncontradicted evidence so shows.

The position taken by the United States is indicated by footnote 6 to its brief:

> The fact that defendants contend, and the evidence tends to show, that the challenged statute has not been used as a basis for sterilization of Partlow residents raises a question as to whether, without an imminent threat of enforcement, the constitutionality of a State statute may be adjudicated, or its enforcement enjoined, by a Federal court. *Poe* v. *Ullman*, 367 U.S. 497 [81 S.Ct. 1752, 6 L.Ed.2d 989] (1961). However, the instant case presents special circumstances which would distinguish it from the factual situation in *Poe*. Members of the plaintiff class are confined at Partlow; sterilizations are being performed, at a gradually increasing rate; and though it is claimed that the statute is not the basis for the Partlow procedures, no other authority is cited. Moreover, in requesting the Court to promulgate standards which must be followed in future sterilizations, the plaintiffs in effect are seeking to enjoin the operation of the challenged statute, since the proposed standards and the statute are necessarily in conflict.

An injunction is not necessary, but by way of extreme precaution to protect the inmates of Partlow State School and Hospital, we do formally declare that the statute is clearly and obviously unconstitutional. The sterilization *vel non* of mentally retarded inmates cannot be left to the unfettered discretion of any two officials or individuals. Further, the statute contains no provision for notice, hearing or any other procedural safeguard. *Cf. Buck* v. *Bell,* 1927, 274 U.S. 200, 207, 47 S.Ct. 584, 71 L.Ed. 1000; *In re Opinion of the Justices,* 230 Ala. 543, 162 So. 123.

With this declaration of the unconstitutionality of the Alabama statute, the three-judge court has performed its essential function. It is therefore ordered and adjudged that the three-judge district court be and the same is hereby dissolved.

WYATT v. ADERHOLT

United States District Court for the Middle District of Alabama, Northern Division,
1974
368 F.Supp. 1383

ORDER

JOHNSON, Chief Judge.

On December 20, 1973, the three-judge court in *Wyatt* v. *Aderholt,* D.C., 368 F.Supp. 1382, declared that Tit. 45, § 243, Code of Alabama, is unconstitutional. As a consequence of that action, the three-judge feature of this case is now complete and that court has been dissolved. However, since it appears that sterilization continues to be performed in certain instances by the state health authorities, it is necessary that this

Court promulgate adequate standards and procedural safeguards to insure that all future sterilizations be performed only where the full panoply of constitutional protections has been accorded to the individuals involved. Accordingly, it is ordered that the following standards be and they are hereby adopted and ordered implemented from this date for the sterilization of mentally retarded residents of the state retardation facilities:

1. (a) "Sterilization," as used in these standards, means any medical or surgical operation or procedure which results in a patient's permanent inability to reproduce.

(b) A determination that a proposed sterilization is in the best interest of a resident, as referred to in these standards, must include a determination that no temporary measure for birth control or contraception will adequately meet the needs of such resident, and shall not be made on the basis of institutional convenience or purely administrative considerations.

2. No resident who has not attained the chronological age of 21 years shall be sterilized except in cases of medical necessity as determined in accordance with the procedures set forth below. No other resident shall be sterilized except in accordance with procedures set forth below.

3. No resident shall be sterilized unless such resident has consented in writing to such sterilization. Except as set forth below, such consent must be informed, in that it is (a) based upon an understanding of the nature and consequences of sterilization, (b) given by a person competent to make such a decision, and (c) wholly voluntary and free from any coercion, express or implied. It shall be the responsibility of the Director of the Partlow State School (with the assistance of employees or officials designated by him) to provide the resident with complete information concerning the nature and consequences of sterilization, to assist the resident in comprehending such information, and to identify any barriers to such comprehension.

4. The Director shall prepare a report evaluating the resident's understanding of the proposed sterilization and describing the steps taken to inform the resident of the nature and consequences of sterilization. If the resident has been determined by a court of competent jurisdiction to be legally incompetent, or if the Director cannot certify without reservation that the resident understands the nature and consequences of sterilization, the sterilization shall not be performed unless (a) the Director sets forth reasonable grounds for believing that such sterilization is in the best interest of the resident; (b) the Review Committee described below approves such sterilization; and (c) it is determined by a court of competent jurisdiction that such sterilization is in the best interest of the resident.

5. No sterilization shall be performed without the prior approval of a Review Committee formed in accordance with this paragraph. The Review Committee shall consist of five members, and shall be selected by the Partlow Human Rights Committee and approved by the Court. The members shall be so selected that the Committee will be competent to deal with the medical, legal, social, and ethical issues involved in sterilization; to this end, at least one member shall be a licensed physician, at least one shall be a licensed attorney, at least two shall be women, at least two shall be minority group members, and at least one shall be a resident of the Partlow State School (the foregoing categories are not mutually exclusive). No member shall be an officer,

employee, or agent of the Partlow State School, nor may any member be otherwise involved in the proposed sterilization.

Any fees or costs incurred by reason of services performed by the Review Committee, including reasonable fees for the physician and the attorney, shall be paid by the Alabama Department of Mental Health upon a certification of reasonableness by the Partlow Human Rights Committee.

6. Prior to approving the proposed sterilization of any resident, the Review Committee shall:

(a) Review appropriate medical, social, and psychological information concerning the resident, including the report of the Director prepared pursuant to paragraph 4;

(b) Interview the resident to be sterilized;

(c) Interview concerned individuals, relatives, and others who in its judgment will contribute pertinent information;

(d) Determine whether the resident has given his or her informed consent to the sterilization, or, if the resident is legally incompetent or the Director cannot certify without reservation that the resident understands the nature and consequences of sterilization, whether the resident has formed, without coercion, a genuine desire to be sterilized. In making such determination, the Review Committee shall take into consideration, *inter alia*, the report prepared by the Director pursuant to paragraph 4 and the interview required by paragraph 6(b).

(e) Determine whether the proposed sterilization is in the best interest of the resident.

If the Review Committee does not reach an affirmative determination as to the matters set forth in paragraphs 6(d) and (e), it shall not approve the proposed sterilization. Any doubts as to such matters shall be resolved against proceeding with sterilization.

7. Residents shall be represented throughout all the procedures described above by legal counsel appointed by the Review Committee from a list of such counsel drawn up by the Partlow Human Rights Committee and approved by the Court. Such counsel shall, *inter alia*, ensure that all considerations militating against the proposed sterilization have been adequately explored and resolved. No such counsel shall be an officer, employee, or agent of the Partlow State School, nor may such counsel be otherwise involved in the proposed sterilization.

8. The Review Committee shall maintain written records of its determinations and the reasons therefor, with supporting documentation. Such records shall be available for examination by the Partlow Human Rights Committee, the Court, and counsel of record in this cause. The Review Committee shall report in writing at least monthly to the Human Rights Committee, the Court, and counsel of record in this cause as to the number and nature of sterilizations approved and disapproved, the procedures employed in approving or disapproving such sterilizations, the reason for determining that such sterilizations were in the best interest of the residents involved, the number and nature of proposed sterilizations referred to courts of competent jurisdiction, and all other relevant information. The identity of residents sterilized or to be sterilized shall not be disclosed in such reports.

9. There shall be no coercion in any form with regard to sterilization of any resident. Consent to sterilization shall not be made a condition for receiving any form of public assistance, nor may it be a prerequisite for any other health or social service, or for admission to or release from the Partlow State School. Any individual having knowledge of coercion of any resident with regard to sterilization shall immediately bring such matter to the attention of the Partlow Human Rights Committee, the Court, or counsel of record in this cause.

It is further ordered that the defendants, their agents, employees and those acting in concert with them be and each is hereby enjoined from failing to implement the standards hereinabove set out for the sterilization of mentally retarded residents of the Alabama retardation facilities.

NOTES

1. While *Buck* v. *Bell* and its progeny were based upon the "police power" of the state and sought to justify compulsory sterilization as necessary to protect the health, safety, and morals of other citizens from the supposed hazard of handicapped people procreating, the *Wyatt* v. *Aderholt* procedures are grounded upon the notion of the "best interests" of the affected individual. This latter legal basis, whereby the state acts as "father-protector" on behalf of citizens, is frequently called the *parens patriae* power of the state. *Parens patriae* has prevailed over the police power as the legal theory justifying sterilization in most modern judicial decisions.

2. As in the *NCARC* case above, the *Wyatt* v. *Aderholt* sterilization determinations were part of a broader legal action. For discussion of other aspects of the *Wyatt* case, see Chapter 6, pp. 629–630.

3. How workable are the *Wyatt* procedures?

4. Just as the *NCARC* court narrowed the scope of the state's police power to sterilize mentally retarded persons, so did Judge Johnson restrict substantially the state's *parens patriae* power to authorize involuntary sterilization. Note that under the *Wyatt* standards a minor may not be sterilized except in cases of medical necessity. Also, under the *Wyatt* standards adult residents factually incapable of giving informed consent or adjudicated incompetent may be considered for sterilization if, *inter alia,* they can form, without coercion, a genuine desire to be sterilized. Assuming this provision was intended to limit the number of such residents who could be sterilized, is it adequate to prohibit the abuse it was meant to prevent?

5. Can institutionalized mentally retarded persons ever give consent to sterilization that is truly knowing, competent, and voluntary?

c. Federal Regulation of Sterilizations

RELF v. WEINBERGER

United States Court of Appeals for the District of Columbia Circuit, 1977
565 F.2d 722

Before DANAHER, Senior Circuit Judge, and McGOWAN and TAMM, Circuit Judges.

Opinion PER CURIAM.

PER CURIAM:

The appeals before us derive from proceedings in the District Court involving challenges to Department of Health, Education, and Welfare regulations covering sterilizations financed by HEW agencies in support of family planning services. By reason of representations made to us by HEW at the time the case was taken under submission, it is for decisional purposes in a somewhat unusual posture, posing a substantial question as to its current justiciability. How that has come about is apparent only from a recounting of the chronology of this litigation in some detail.

I

One of the two complaints in the District Court was filed on July 31, 1973 (five individual women plaintiffs), and the other (National Welfare Rights Organization, plaintiff) on February 6, 1974. In the period between those two dates, HEW had no regulations relating to sterilization in effect, but it initiated and completed rule making proceedings under the Administrative Procedure Act resulting in regulations issued on the latter date. These regulations became the focus of attack in both complaints, it being asserted that they suffered from constitutional deficiencies as well as lack of statutory authorization. The merits of these claims came before the District Court on cross-motions for summary judgment. HEW having honored the Court's request that the effective date of the regulations be deferred until March 18, 1974, the Court issued its decision on March 15, 1974. *Relf, et al.* v. *Weinberger,* 372 F.Supp. 1196.

The District Court, consolidating the two actions for all purposes, declared that the relevant statutes do not authorize federal funding for the sterilization of any person who (1) has been judicially declared mentally incompetent, or (2) is in fact legally incompetent under the applicable state laws to give informed and binding consent to such an operation because of age or mental capacity; and it permanently enjoined HEW from providing federal funds for this purpose.

The Court next declared that the regulations in issue are "arbitrary and unreasonable" in authorizing the use of federal funds for sterilizing a legally competent person without requiring that he be advised prior to the solicitation or receipt of his consent that no benefits under any federally funded programs may be terminated or withheld by reason of his refusal to consent, and without requiring that such advice be prominently displayed at the top of the consent form; and the Court directed HEW promptly to amend its regulations to bring them into conformity with the Court's order.

HEW's first response to the Court's action was to issue, effective April 18, 1974, what it termed "interim regulations" relating to persons legally competent to consent to sterilizations. 39 Fed.Reg. 13872-73, 13887-88 (1974). These regulations not only complied with the Court's order but were accompanied by the continuation by HEW of a moratorium on federal funding of all non-emergency sterilizations of persons under 21 or mentally incompetent, thereby imposing greater restrictions on the use of federal funds for sterilization than those ordered by the Court. As will appear hereinafter, these are the regulations—and the only regulations—which have been in effect from that day to this, and are currently being observed by HEW.

HEW also, on May 13, 1974, appealed the District Court's order of March 15, as did both the Relf plaintiffs and NWRO. While these appeals were pending, HEW undertook to revise the regulations issued February 6, 1974; and, on July 24, 1974, revisions were approved by the Secretary, as was a further revision on September 3, 1974. Promulgation of the regulations as so altered was deferred pending resolution of the litigation. In a letter to the District Court dated January 3, 1975, signed by all of the parties to the appeals, it was stated that the regulations as revised were satisfactory to the parties, who sought, under the procedure prescribed by this court in *Smith* v. *Pollin,* 90 U.S.App.D.C. 178, 194 F.2d 349 (1952), "to propose modifications, consented to by all parties," to the final decree entered by the District Court on March 15, 1974. Appended to this letter was a copy of the revised regulations, as well as a suggested order modifying the Court's decree; and the parties requested an opportunity to appear before the Court in conference or hearing to accomplish the agreed accommodation of the law suit.

The District Court orally advised the parties that it would not consider the proposed modifications. Subsequently HEW moved this court in the pending appeal that the District Court's decree, modified to reflect the revised regulations, be summarily affirmed. The other parties to the appeal moved for summary affirmance without modification. A motions division of this court on April 21, 1975, denied both motions without prejudice, and remanded the record to the District Court for consideration of the proposed modifications. In its remanding order, the court noted that, since the modifications would entail a reversal of part of the decree appealed from, it could not consider such a course in the absence of a statement of the Court's reasons for accepting or rejecting the proposed regulations.

On October 22, 1975, the District Court made its disposition of the remand. *Relf, et al.* v. *Mathews,* 403 F.Supp. 1235. It entered an order rejecting the proposed modifications as "inappropriate and not in the public interest" for the reasons set forth in its accompanying memorandum. In that memorandum, however, the Court characterized the modifications as having been first proposed to the Court of Appeals, and as designed to substitute a universal federal standard of voluntariness which, under various conditions and procedures, will permit federal funding of sterilization of persons 18 or over even when such persons are otherwise incompetent because of age or mental condition under state standards. The Court said that, when the case was before it earlier and prior to the entry of its March 15 order, HEW "never proposed a federal standard governing voluntariness." Because of the limited purposes of the remand and the retention of jurisdiction by this court, the District Court conceived that it had "no authority to do more than approve or disapprove the precise modifications proposed and cannot fashion alternative solutions." In rejecting the modifications, the Court noted, among other things, that

> A regulation establishing a federal standard for voluntary sterilization should be considered through the rulemaking process, after publication in the *Federal Register,* so that it will ultimately be fashioned with due regard for the views of the states and interested sectors of the community. The modifications proposed have not been subject to this process.

The Court concluded its discussion of the proposed modifications by asserting that "the present procedural difficulties can be surmounted only after the appeal has run its course;'' and concluded by saying that

> [I]n the event of affirmance there is nothing to prevent defendants' publishing proposed rules for establishing a workable federal standard. After an appropriate rule-making proceeding and decision, the Court could consider modifying its Order and would have the benefit of extensive data that would be generated in the rule-making proceeding reflecting experience under the Order as drawn.

On the day that these appeals were orally argued in this court, counsel for HEW delivered a letter to the Clerk, stating that he had been advised by HEW the preceding day that it ''intends to institute rule making proceedings, under the Administrative Procedure Act, with regard to regulations governing the federal funding of family planning sterilizations. It is my understanding that proposed regulations will be published in the Federal Register, and interested persons will have the opportunity to submit comments.'' The letter went on to state that counsel had also been informed that ''while the precise terms of the proposed regulations have not yet been finally determined, they will be similar to the terms of the proposed regulations set forth in the Appendix at 375-420.'' Counsel's letter concluded by noting that the District Court's injunction was still before the court and that, ''while it remains in effect, the Secretary may not promulgate any regulations that violate its terms.'' At the oral argument itself, counsel for the Government called the court's attention to this letter, and also represented that, until new regulations were promulgated at the conclusion of rule making proceedings, the interim regulations would continue in effect.

After the case was taken under submission, counsel for HEW, on February 1, 1977, wrote a further letter to the Clerk of this court stating that ''the Secretary does not intend to institute rulemaking proceedings until these appeals have been decided. We believe it inadvisable to commence rulemaking proceedings while the extent of the Secretary's statutory authority is in doubt and while the Secretary remains under an injunction.''

II

The circumstances that now exist by reason of the foregoing seem to us to be as follows: The regulations promulgated February 6, 1974, after rule making, and which never became effective by reason of HEW's deference to the District Court's request, have been withdrawn by HEW. The same is true of the revisions of those regulations made without rule making, which were first tendered to the District Court by all parties as part of a settlement effort, and which were later presented to this court as the basis of a motion by HEW to affirm the District Court's decree with modifications.

The interim regulations are now in effect, as they have been since they were issued without rule making on April 18, 1974, and as they will be until new regulations are arrived at after rule making. Those regulations, as noted above, conform to the District Court's order of March 15, 1974, and indeed are more restrictive than that order requires.

In this state of affairs, appellant National Welfare Rights Organization asserts in its brief that because it ''has no present objection to the District Court's March 15, 1974 order nor to its October 22, 1975 order following remand ... NWRO's cross-appeal may be deemed withdrawn.'' The *Relf* appellants in their brief (filed before oral argument) continue to seek reversal of the District Court's order of March 15, 1974, insofar as it finds no statutory authority for federal funding of the sterilization of persons legally incompetent to give consent under applicable state laws because of age. They urge that a federal minimum age standard of 18 should be adopted; and that HEW should be required to develop stricter voluntariness safeguards for persons between 18 and 21 than for those over 21.

The HEW appellants profess agreement with the basic principle enunciated by the District Court—that under the federal statute authorizing the use of federal funds for "voluntary" family planning, "federally assisted family planning sterilizations are permissible only with the voluntary, knowing and uncoerced consent of individuals competent to give such consent." They assert that voluntariness is to be determined by a federal standard and not solely by reference to state law; and that the Court erred in its insistence upon the latter.[3] They argue that the regulations promulgated on February 6, 1974 after rule making, as modified by the revisions approved by the Secretary on July 24 and September 3, 1974, constitute an allowable federal standard under the statute, and one which is reasonable in its terms.

It is apparent that the contentions we are called upon to resolve relate to regulations, both as initially formulated and as proposed to be revised, which no longer have any official status. They have never actually become effective, and HEW now has represented to this court that it has no purpose to make them so, even absent the compulsions of the District Court's injunction. It has signified, instead, that it intends to issue a new notice of rule making under the Administrative Procedure Act, at the conclusion of which it will promulgate comprehensive regulations for the federal funding of sterilizations. Until that event the interim regulations will continue to be followed.

The interim regulations have not been challenged as such, either in the District Court or here. Far from violating the District Court's injunction, they are more restrictive than the District Court required. The District Court itself, in its memorandum on remand, has disclaimed the absolute rejection by it of any federal standard of voluntariness, but rather has urged the utility of a new rule making proceeding in the formulation of a federal standard, in order that such a standard "will ultimately be fashioned with due regard for the views of the states and interested sectors of the community," a process to which, it was careful to remark, the modifications had not been subjected.

In this state of affairs we think that this litigation is wanting in the vitality appropriate for resolution by us of the legal questions presented, or indeed necessitated by the constitutional demands of Article III. Accordingly, we find this controversy to

---

[3]Where federal funds are authorized by Congress to be expended for sterilizations which are voluntary in nature, the question of what constitutes voluntariness in this context would appear to be one of federal law. In formulating standards for this purpose, it is surely true that state legal requirements cannot be controlling by their own force. A federal standard may still of course, to the extent the federal agency devising the standard finds wise or helpful, take note of state law and utilize available state legal mechanisms in designing and effectuating the federal standard. But how a federal statute is to be implemented remains a matter as to which federal law is supreme, and the agency charged by Congress with implementation is not bound to shape its concept of voluntariness to the contours of state law. *See generally Planned Parenthood of Central Missouri* v. *Danforth,* 428 U.S. 52, 96 S.Ct. 2831, 49 L.Ed.2d 788 (1976); *Wyatt* v. *Aderholt,* 368 F.Supp. 1383, 1384 (M.D.Ala. 1974).

have been mooted by HEW's withdrawal of its reliance upon and sponsorship of the product of the rule making proceeding resulting in the promulgation of regulations on February 6, 1974, and its declared purpose to initiate a new rule making leading to the promulgation of a new set of regulations.

The orders of the District Court before us for review are vacated, *United States* v. *Munsingwear, Inc.*, 340 U.S. 36, 71 S.Ct. 104, 95 L.Ed. 36 (1950), and the case is remanded to the District Court with directions to dismiss the complaints.

IT IS SO ORDERED.

REGULATIONS OF DEPARTMENT OF HEALTH, EDUCATION, AND WELFARE REGARDING FEDERAL FUNDING OF STERILIZATIONS

43 Fed. Reg. 52146, 52165-52168 (Nov. 8, 1978), 42 C.F.R. §§ 50.201-50.210
Subpart B of 42 CFR Part 50 is revised to read as follows:

Subpart B—Sterilization of Persons in
Federally Assisted Family Planning Projects

Sec.
50.201   Applicability.
50.202   Definitions.
50.203   Sterilization of a mentally competent individual aged 21 or older.
50.204   Informed consent requirement.
50.205   Consent form requirements.
50.206   Sterilization of a mentally incompetent individual or an institutionalized individual.
50.207   Sterilization by hysterectomy.
50.208   Program or project requirements.
50.209   Use of Federal financial assistance.
50.210   Review of regulation.
Appendix: Required consent form.
AUTHORITY: Sec. 215, Public Health Service Act, as amended (42 U.S.C. 216).

Subpart B—Sterilization of Persons in
Federally Assisted Family Planning
Projects

§ 50.201   Applicability.
The provisions of this subpart are applicable to programs or projects for health services which are supported in whole or in part by Federal financial assistance, whether by grant or contract, administered by the Public Health Service.

§ 50.202   Definitions.
As used in this subpart:
"Arrange for" means to make arrangements (other than mere referral of an individual to, or the mere making of an appointment for him or her with, another health care provider) for the performance of a medical procedure on an individual by a health care provider other than the program or project.

"Hysterectomy" means a medical procedure or operation for the purpose of removing the uterus.

"Institutionalized individual" means an individual who is (1) involuntarily confined or detained, under a civil or criminal statute, in a correctional or rehabilitative facility, including a mental hospital or other facility for the care and treatment of mental illness, or (2) confined, under a voluntary commitment, in a mental hospital or other facility for the care and treatment of mental illness.

"Mentally incompetent individual" means an individual who has been declared mentally incompetent by a Federal, State, or local court of competent jurisdiction for any purpose unless he or she has been declared competent for purposes which include the ability to consent to sterilization.

"Public Health Service" means the Health Services Administration, Health Resources Administration, National Institutes of Health, Center for Disease Control, Alcohol, Drug Abuse and Mental Health Administration and all of their constituent agencies.

The "Secretary" means the Secretary of Health, Education, and Welfare and any other officer or employee of the Department of Health, Education, and Welfare to whom the authority involved has been delegated.

"Sterilization" means any medical procedure, treatment, or operation for the purpose of rendering an individual permanently incapable of reproducing.

§ 50.203   Sterilization of a mentally competent individual aged 21 or older.

Programs or projects to which this subpart applies shall perform or arrange for the performance of sterilization of an individual only if the following requirements have been met:

(a) The individual is at least 21 years old at the time consent is obtained.

(b) The individual is not a mentally incompetent individual.

(c) The individual has voluntarily given his or her informed consent in accordance with the procedures of § 50.204 of this subpart.

(d) At least 30 days but not more than 180 days have passed between the date of informed consent and the date of the sterilization, except in the case of premature delivery or emergency abdominal surgery. An individual may consent to be sterilized at the time of premature delivery or emergency abdominal surgery, if at least 72 hours have passed after he or she gave informed consent to sterilization. In the case of premature delivery, the informed consent must have been given at least 30 days before the expected date of delivery.

§ 50.204   Informed consent requirement.

Informed consent does not exist unless a consent form is completed voluntarily and in accordance with all the requirements of this section and § 50.205 of this subpart.

(a) A person who obtains informed consent for a sterilization procedure must offer to answer any questions the individual to be sterilized may have concerning the procedure, provide a copy of the consent form, and provide orally all of the following information or advice to the individual who is to be sterilized:

(1) Advice that the individual is free to withhold or withdraw consent to the procedure any time before the sterilization without affecting his or her right to future

care or treatment and without loss or withdrawal of any federally funded program benefits to which the individual might be otherwise entitled:

(2) A description of available alternative methods of family planning and birth control;

(3) Advice that the sterilization procedure is considered to be irreversible;

(4) A thorough explanation of the specific sterilization procedure to be performed;

(5) A full description of the discomforts and risks that may accompany or follow the performing of the procedure, including an explanation of the type and possible effects of any anesthetic to be used;

(6) A full description of the benefits or advantages that may be expected as a result of the sterilization; and

(7) Advice that the sterilization will not be performed for at least 30 days except under the circumstances specified in § 50.203(d) of this subpart.

(b) An interpreter must be provided to assist the individual to be sterilized if he or she does not understand the language used on the consent form or the language used by the person obtaining the consent.

(c) Suitable arrangements must be made to insure that the information specified in paragraph (a) of this section is effectively communicated to any individual to be sterilized who is blind, deaf or otherwise handicapped.

(d) A witness chosen by the individual to be sterilized may be present when consent is obtained.

(e) Informed consent may not be obtained while the individual to be sterilized is:

(1) In labor or childbirth;

(2) Seeking to obtain or obtaining an abortion; or

(3) Under the influence of alcohol or other substances that affect the individual's state of awareness.

(f) Any requirement of State and local law for obtaining consent, except one of spousal consent, must be followed.

§ 50.205   Consent form requirements.

(a) *Required consent form.* The consent form appended to this subpart or another consent form approved by the Secretary must be used.

(b) *Required signatures.* The consent form must be signed and dated by:

(1) The individual to be sterilized; and

(2) The interpreter, if one is provided; and

(3) The person who obtains the consent; and

(4) The physician who will perform the sterilization procedure.

(c) *Required certifications.* (1) The person obtaining the consent must certify by signing the consent form that: (i) before the individual to be sterilized signed the consent form, he or she advised the individual to be sterilized that no Federal benefits may be withdrawn because of the decision not to be sterilized, (ii) he or she explained orally the requirements for informed consent as set forth on the consent form, and (iii) to the best of his or her knowledge and belief, the individual to be sterilized appeared mentally competent and knowingly and voluntarily consented to be sterilized.

(2) The physician performing the sterilization must certify by signing the consent form, that: (i) shortly before the performance of the sterilization, he or she advised the individual to be sterilized that no Federal benefits may be withdrawn because of the decision not to be sterilized, (ii) he or she explained orally the requirements for informed consent as set forth on the consent form, and (iii) to the best of his or her knowledge and belief, the individual to be sterilized appeared mentally competent and knowingly and voluntarily consented to be sterilized. Except in the case of premature delivery or emergency abdominal surgery, the physician must further certify that at least 30 days have passed between the date of the individual's signature on the consent form and the date upon which the sterilization was performed. If premature delivery occurs or emergency abdominal surgery is required within the 30-day period, the physician must certify that the sterilization was performed less than 30 days but not less than 72 hours after the date of the individual's signature on the consent form because of premature delivery or emergency abdominal surgery, as applicable. In the case of premature delivery, the physician must also state the expected date of delivery. In the case of emergency abdominal surgery, the physician must describe the emergency.

(3) If an interpreter is provided, the interpreter must certify that he or she translated the information and advice presented orally, read the consent form and explained its contents and to the best of the interpreter's knowledge and belief, the individual to be sterilized understood what the interpreter told him or her.

§ 50.206   Sterilization of a mentally incompetent individual or of an institutionalized individual.

Programs or projects to which this subpart applies shall not perform or arrange for the performance of a sterilization of any mentally incompetent individual or institutionalized individual.

§ 50.207   Sterilization by hysterectomy.

(a) Programs or projects to which this subpart applies shall not perform or arrange for the performance of any hysterectomy solely for the purpose of rendering an individual permanently incapable of reproducing or where, if there is more than one purpose to the procedure, the hysterectomy would not be performed but for the purpose of rendering the individual permanently incapable of reproducing.

(b) Programs or projects to which this subpart applies may perform or arrange for the performance of a hysterectomy not covered by paragraph (a) of this section only if:

(1) The person who secures the authorization to perform the hysterectomy has informed the individual and her representative, if any, orally and in writing, that the hysterectomy will render her permanently incapable of reproducing; and

(2) The individual or her representative, if any, has signed a written acknowledgment of receipt of that information.

§ 50.208   Program or project requirements.

(a) A program or project must, with respect to any sterilization procedure or hysterectomy it performs or arranges, meet all requirements of this subpart.

(b) The program or project shall maintain sufficient records and documentation to assure compliance with these regulations, and must retain such data for at least 3 years.

(c) The program or project shall submit other reports as required and when requested by the Secretary.

§ 50.209   Use of Federal financial assistance.

(a) Federal financial assistance administered by the Public Health Service may not be used for expenditures for sterilization procedures unless the consent form appended to this section or another form approved by the Secretary is used.

(b) A program or project shall not use Federal financial assistance for any sterilization or hysterectomy without first receiving documentation showing that the requirements of this subpart have been met. Documentation includes consent forms, and acknowledgments of receipt of hysterectomy information.

§ 50.210   Review of regulation.

The Secretary will request public comment on the operation of the provisions of this subpart not later than 3 years after their effective date.

[The Appendix, consisting of Required Consent Forms and two pamphlets—one for women and one for men—providing general information about birth control and sterilization procedures, is omitted.]

NOTES

1.   Informed consent of the patient of his or her legal guardian is generally required before a health practitioner may administer any medical procedure including sterilization. For further discussion of this requirement see Chapter 8, pp. 756–766.

2.   At every major stage during the *Relf* litigation the courts were adamant that, because of the irreversibility of the sterilization procedure, the constitutional right involved, and the congressional mandate involved, voluntariness by the prospective patient must be required before federal financing of sterilization could be authorized. Was the district court correct that minority and diminished mental capacity are factors that preclude a prospective patient from giving informed consent to sterilization? Should federal financing of sterilization for minors and for mentally handicapped persons be allowed for those who can give informed consent to the procedure? Is such a requirement constitutionally mandated to prevent discrimination against such minors or mentally handicapped people. Could such a requirement be implemented? What procedural safeguards would be necessary to prevent abuse?

3.   Pending issuance of the final H.E.W. regulations, the courts have wrestled with whether it is constitutional to deny federal financing for sterilizations of children and mentally handicapped people. Compare *Voe* v. *Califano,* 434 F.Supp. 1058 (D.Conn. 1977) (upholding the temporary H.E.W. regulation prohibiting funding although plaintiff was 20 years old, fully emancipated under state law, and had given informed consent), with *Douglas* v. *Holloman,* Civ.No. 76 Civ. 6 (S.D.N.Y. filed January 5, 1976) (challenging *inter alia* the constitutionality of the federal ban on funding sterilizations for persons under 21 or mentally handicapped).

4.   The H.E.W. regulations on federal financing of sterilizations require *inter alia* that the individual be at least 21 years old and able to give informed consent. H.E.W. also considered but rejected the possibility of permitting funding for those individuals able to give informed consent even if previously adjudicated incompetent under state law. Would such a regulation be within the scope of H.E.W.'s authority?

5.   A typical state statute on voluntary sterilization by minors is Ann. Code of Md., Art 43, § 135 (1977 Supp.):

> (a) A minor shall have the same capacity to consent to medical treatment as an adult if one or more of the following apply:
>
> * * *
>
> (2) The minor seeks treatment or advice concerning venereal disease, pregnancy or *contraception not amounting to sterilization*. [emphasis supplied]

What is the legislative intent underlying such a statute?

6.   In view of the judicial trend not to allow parents and guardians to consent to a child's sterilization (see pp. 894–904, *supra*), the developing federal policy to deny federal funding for those unable to give informed consent because of age or mental condition, and the legislative trend to prohibit minors from consenting to their own sterilization, what should an attorney advise a parent or guardian who seeks to sterilize a mentally handicapped person? What factors should be considered in furnishing such advice?

B.   MARRIAGE

1.   The Right at Stake

The status of the institution of marriage in our society was outlined by the United States Supreme Court as long ago as 1888. In *Maynard* v. *Hill,* 125 U.S. 190 (1888), the Court declared:

> Marriage, as creating the most important relation in life, as having more to do with the morals and civilization of a people than any other institution, has always been subject to the control of the legislature. That body prescribes the age at which parties may contract to marry, the procedure or form essential to constitute marriage, the duties and obligations it creates, its effects upon the property rights of both, present and prospective, and the acts which may constitute grounds for its dissolution (*Id.* at 205).

And further:

> It is also to be observed that, whilst marriage is often termed by text writers and in decisions of courts as a civil contract—generally to indicate that it must be founded upon the agreement of the parties, and does not require any religious ceremony for its solemnization—it is something more than a mere contract. The consent of the parties is of course essential to its existence, but when the contract to marry is executed by the marriage, a relation between the parties is created which they cannot change. Other contracts may be modified, restricted, or enlarged, or entirely released upon the consent of the parties. Not so with marriage. The relation once formed, the law steps in and holds the parties to various obligations and liabilities. It is an institution, in the maintenance of which in its purity the public is deeply interested, for it is the foundation of the

family and of society, without which there would be neither civilization nor progress (*Id.* at 210-211).

In *Meyer* v. *Nebraska,* 262 U.S. 390 (1923), the Court listed the right to marry as part of the "liberty" guaranteed under the Fourteenth Amendment and as one of "those privileges long recognized at common law as essential to the orderly pursuit of happiness by free men," *id.* at 399.

In *Loving* v. *Virginia,* 388 U.S. 1 (1967), the Court struck down a Virginia statute prohibiting racial intermarriage and declared:

> These statutes also deprive the Lovings of liberty without due process of law in violation of the Due Process Clause of the Fourteenth Amendment. The freedom to marry has long been recognized as one of the vital personal rights essential to the orderly pursuit of happiness by free men.
>
> Marriage is one of the "basic civil rights of man," fundamental to our very existence and survival. *Skinner* v. *Oklahoma,* 316 U.S. 535, 541 (1942). See also *Maynard* v. *Hill,* 125 U.S. 190 (1888). To deny this fundamental freedom on so unsupportable a basis as the racial classifications embodied in these statutes, classifications so directly subversive of the principle of equality at the heart of the Fourteenth Amendment, is surely to deprive all the State's citizens of liberty without due process of law. The Fourteenth Amendment requires that the freedom of choice to marry not be restricted by invidious racial discriminations. Under our Constitution, the freedom to marry, or not marry, a person of another race resides with the individual and cannot be infringed by the State (*Id.* at 12).

The status of the right to marry as a fundamental constitutional right has been further underscored in other cases; see, e.g. *Skinner* v. *Oklahoma,* pp. 857–858, *supra,* and *Roe* v. *Wade,* p. 879n.2, *supra.*

When read together, the Supreme Court cases concerning marriage make it clear that the right to marry is fundamental under our Constitution, and, although it may be subject to regulation under the police power of the state, restrictions placed upon the right must be narrowly drawn and justified by a compelling state interest.

2. Regulation under the Police Power of the Fundamental Right to Marry: Protecting Society from the Marriage of Handicapped People

The Supreme Court very early endorsed the right of the state to regulate the marriage and divorce of its citizens as a proper function of the police power in supervising the public health and morals of its citizens, *Fensterwald* v. *Burk,* 129 Md. 131, 98 A. 358, rehearing denied, 248 U.S. 592 (1918). *See also,* Annot. 3 A.L.R. 1568 (1919). For many years this authority under the police power has been used by various states to protect society from the supposed danger to public health, safety, and morals posed by permitting certain handicapped people to marry.

GOULD v. GOULD

Supreme Court of Errors of Connecticut, 1905
78 Conn. 242, 61 A. 604

BALDWIN, J. In 1895 a statute was enacted of which the first section reads as follows: "No man or woman, either of whom is epileptic, imbecile, or feeble-minded, shall intermarry, or live together as husband and wife, when the woman is under forty-five years of age. Any person violating or attempting to violate any of the provisions of this section shall be imprisoned in the state prison not less than three years." Pub. Acts 1895, p. 667, c. 325. Cf. Gen. St. 1902, § 1354. In 1899 the plaintiff, at the age of 22, married the defendant, who was an epileptic. In 1903 a child was born, issue of the marriage, and soon afterwards the plaintiff, then first learning of the statute mentioned, left the defendant, and brought this suit for a divorce or a decree that the marriage was null and void. In her complaint she alleged that the defendant, though an epileptic, falsely and fraudulently concealed this fact from her, and represented that he had never had epilepsy; in consequence of which representations she, believing them to be true, had been induced to enter the contract of marriage. On the trial in this court, no argument was submitted in behalf of the defendant. The proper disposition of a cause of this character is, however, a matter of public concern, in the interest of society, and we feel bound to examine such considerations in support of the judgment appealed from as he might have urged, had he been represented by counsel. *Allen* v. *Allen,* 73 Conn. 54, 55, 46 Atl. 242, 49 L.R.A. 142, 84 Am. St. Rep. 135.

Was the statute a valid act of legislation? It forbade the marriage of certain classes of persons under any circumstances. One of these, only, it is now necessary to consider—that of epileptics. The provisions of the act of 1895 were separable with respect to the different classes of persons with whom it deals, and, so far as this action is concerned, it is enough if it can be supported as to marriages contracted after its enactment by those in the condition of the defendant. Pub. Acts 1895, p. 667, c. 325. The Constitution of this state (preamble and article 1, § 1) guaranties to its people equality under the law in the rights to "life, liberty, and the pursuit of happiness." *State* v. *Conlon,* 65 Conn. 478, 489-491, 33 Atl. 519, 31 L.R.A. 55, 48 Am. St. Rep. 227. One of these is the right to contract marriage, but it is a right that can only be exercised under such reasonable conditions as the Legislature may see fit to impose. It is not possessed by those below a certain age. It is denied to those who stand within certain degrees of kinship. The mode of celebrating it is prescribed in strict and exclusive terms. Gen. St. 1902, § 4538. The universal prohibition in all civilized countries of marriages between near kindred proceeds in part from the established fact that the issue of such marriages are often, though by no means always, of an inferior type of physical or mental development. That epilepsy is a disease of a peculiarly serious and revolting character, tending to weaken mental force, and often descending from parent to child, or entailing upon the offspring of the sufferer some other grave form of nervous malady, is a matter of common knowledge, of which courts will take judicial notice. *State* v. *Main,* 69 Conn. 123, 135, 37 Atl. 80, 36 L.R.A. 623, 61 Am.St.Rep. 30. One mode of guarding against the perpetuation of epilepsy obviously is to forbid sexual intercourse with those afflicted by it, and to preclude such opportunities for sexual intercourse as marriage furnishes. To impose such a restriction upon the right to contract marriage, if not intrinsically unreasonable, is no invasion of the equality of all men before the law, if it applies equally to all, under the same circumstances, who belong to a certain class of persons, which class can reasonably be regarded as one requiring special legislation either for their protection or for the protection from them of the community at large. It cannot be pronounced by the judiciary to be intrinsically unreasonable if it should be regarded as a determination by the General Assembly that a law of this kind is necessary for the preservation of public health, and if there are substantial grounds for believing that such determination is supported by the facts upon which it is apparent that it was based. *Holden* v. *Hardy,* 169 U.S. 366, 398, 18 Sup.Ct. 383, 42 L.Ed. 780; *Bissell* v. *Davison,* 65 Conn. 183, 192, 32 Atl. 348, 29 L.R.A. 251. There can be no doubt as to the opinion of the General Assembly, nor as to its resting on substantial foundations. The class of persons to whom the statute applies is not one arbitrarily formed to suit its purpose. It is certain and definite. It is a class capable of endangering the health of families and adding greatly to the sum of human suffering. Between the members of this class there is no discrimination, and the prohibitions of the statute cease to operate when, by the attainment of a certain age by one of those whom it affects, the occasion for the restriction is deemed to become less imperative. While Connecticut was the pioneer in this country with respect to legislation of this character, it no longer stands alone. Michigan, Minnesota, Kansas, and Ohio have, since 1895, acted in the same direction. 2 Howard on Matrimonial Institutions, 400, 479, 480; Sess. Laws Ohio, 1904, p. 83. Laws of this kind may be regarded as an expression of the conviction of modern society that disease is largely preventable by proper precautions, and that it is not unjust in certain cases to require the observation of these, even at the cost of narrowing what in former days was regarded as the proper domain of individual right. It follows that the statute in question was not invalid, as respects marriages contracted by epileptics, after it took effect.

The next question which presents itself is whether the marriage of the plaintiff was void. A contract for any matter or thing against the prohibition of a statute is treated as void, although the statute does not declare it to be so, if such contract be relied on in any action as the foundation of the right of recovery. *Preston* v. *Bacon,* 4 Conn. 471, 480; *Finn* v. *Donahue,* 35 Conn. 216. But a contract of marriage is *sui generis.* It is simply introductory to the creation of a status, and what that status is the law determines. A contract executed in contravention of law may yet establish a status which the law will recognize, and, if one of the contracting parties were innocent of any intention to violate the law, may recognize as carrying with it in his favor the same rights and duties as if the contract had been entirely unexceptionable. *In re Grimley,* 137 U. S. 147, 152, 153, 11 Sup.Ct. 54, 34 L.Ed. 636. The common law of England followed the canon law in regarding a marriage once lawfully entered into as dissoluble only by an extraordinary act of the sovereign power. It followed the canon law also in holding marriages entered into by those under canonical disabilities to be voidable by the spiritual courts, and held them to be voidable only. They were therefore esteemed valid for all civil purposes, unless a sentence of nullity were pronounced during the life of both parties. Glanville, book 3, c. 17; Kenn's Case, 7 Rep. 42. On the other hand, there were certain fundamental disabilities, depending not on the canon law, but on universal or municipal law, which might render a marriage void *ab initio*; such as a prior marriage of either party, a want of age sufficient to give capacity to consent, and a want at any age of the necessary mental capacity. 1 Blackstone's Comm. 434-439. In the Revision of 1702 the General Assembly of this state prohibited marriages between those within certain degrees of kinship, and also the celebration of marriages without the publication of banns, and, in case of minors, without the consent of the parent or guardian, or before one not having due authority. In case of a violation of the prohibition first mentioned the marriage was expressly declared to be null and void. For a violation of the others a pecuniary forfeiture was prescribed. Rev. 1702, p. 74. In 1717 bigamous marriages were declared to be null and void, and those between parties under the age of consent. Questions soon arose as to whether the marriages celebrated in contravention of the prohibition of the statute of 1702 could be treated as valid. That they could be if the only objection was the want of the consent of parent or guardian, or a failure to publish the banns, was generally conceded; but it was seriously questioned if one could be upheld which was celebrated before a person not duly authorized. To settle this point a provision was introduced into the Revision of 1821, following in part Lord Hardwicke's act of 1753, expressly declaring such a marriage to be void. Rev. 1821, pp. 316, 318, note; Gen. St. 1902, § 4538. The act of 1895 did not (and Gen. St. 1902, § 1354, does not) make such a declaration with reference to the marriage of an epileptic. It contented itself with imposing criminal penalties. It inferentially sanctioned, in case of such a marriage, the living together of the parties "as husband and wife" after the latter arrived at the age of 45. The omission to declare the marriage to be void is made doubly significant by the fact that such a declaration is found embodied in two of the other statutory prohibitions (Gen. St. 1902, §§ 4534, 4538), and not in a third (section 4535). It may well be that the General Assembly were no more inclined to bastardize the issue of the marriage of an epileptic than that of a minor married without parental consent. We therefore conclude that the Legislature intended to leave the effect of a marriage contracted in violation of the act of 1895 to be determined by the general principles of the common law. These lead to the conclusion that it is dissoluble, rather than void.

The common law, however, held that, when a marriage was avoided on account of canonical disabilities, it must be by a decree of nullity which pronounced it void *ab initio*. This doctrine rested on the theory of the Roman Catholic Church that, if a marriage were once contracted under its sanction, it acquired a sacramental character, and was indissoluble by human authority. A spiritual court could adjudge that two parties, though apparently married, never really were. No court could dissolve what was in fact a marriage for any cause. No such theory was ever recognized in the laws of Connecticut. Divorces have been freely granted from the first, and since 1667 one of the causes has been "fraudulent contract." This was judicially defined more than a century ago as a fraud entering into the substance of the marriage relation, preceding it, "and such a one as rendered the marriage unlawful *ab initio*, as consanguinity, corporal imbecility, and the like; in which case the law looks upon the marriage as null and void, being contracted in fraudem legis, and decrees a separation a vinculo matrimonii." *Benton* v. *Benton*, 1 Day, 111, 114. The words quoted were taken from 3 Blackstone's Commentaries, 94, and accurately describe the original theory, as to divorce, of English law. That theory, however, is hardly consonant with the divorce statutes of this state. . . .

The memorandum of decision filed by the court below shows that it felt bound by the decision in *Benton* v. *Benton* to rule that the cause of divorce claimed by the plaintiff did not come within the scope of the term "fraudulent contract," because it was not one rendering the marriage void *ab initio*. This ground is untenable. The fraud which makes the contract of marriage fraudulent, as that word is used in the statute of divorce, is a fraud in law and upon the law. Such a fraud is accomplished whenever a person enters into that contract knowing that he is incapable of sexual intercourse, and yet, in order to induce the marriage, designedly and deceitfully concealing that fact from the other party, who is ignorant of it, and has no reason to suppose it to exist. Whether such incapacity proceeds from a physical or a merely legal cause is immaterial. The prohibition of the act of 1895 fastened upon the defendant an incapacity, which, if unknown to the plaintiff, and by him fraudulently concealed from her with the purpose thereby to induce a marriage, made his contract of marriage, in the eye of the law, fraudulent. Whether, on such a state of facts, he could ask for a divorce, or would be precluded from thus taking advantage of his own wrong, we have no occasion to determine. The plaintiff could. The superior court has power to pass a decree of divorce from the bonds of matrimony in favor of a party to a marriage, not an epileptic, who has been tricked into it by the other party, who was an epileptic, through his fraud in inducing a belief that he was legally and physically competent to enter into the marital relation and fulfill all its duties, when he knew that he was not. *Guilford* v. *Oxford*, 9 Conn. 321, 328; *Ferris* v. *Ferris*, 8 Conn. 166.

Whether the facts found by the court were sufficient to support a judgment in her favor we do not think it necessary or proper to determine upon the present record. The finding was prepared under a misconception of the law, which naturally made it less full and precise on certain points than it would otherwise have been, and the case is of such a character that a rehearing will best serve the interests of justice.

There is error, and a new trial is ordered.

NOTES

1.   The basic holding of *Gould* v. *Gould* is succinctly summarized in the concurring opinion of Justice Hamersley:

> At the time of this marriage each of the parties was able to perform the ordinary mutual obligations involved in marriage. Each was capable of giving the assent requisite to a valid marriage. The act does not declare either party to be incapable of marriage, but recognizes the ability of each to marry another person, as well as to marry each other. Persons such as the plaintiff and defendant, after the passage of the act, remained as such persons ever before had been, capable of intermarriage; but the act punishes them for an exercise of this capacity at the time or under the circumstances mentioned—that is, while the man is subject to the disease or before the woman attains the statutory age. The motives that may have suggested this legislation cannot be affirmed. Its origin and history, as shown by public records and files, would indicate that a controlling motive may have been the hope of restraining an unnecessary increase of the helpless persons who are a charge upon the state through severe punishment of sexual intercourse with paupers and other dependent persons (at 61A.608).

However:

> We hold that it is legally possible, under the allegations of facts in support of the application for a divorce as contained in the second count of the complaint, to prove a state of facts that will justify a divorce on the ground of "fraudulent contract" (*Id.* at 609).

2.   The "matters of common knowledge," of which the court takes judicial notice, concerning the nature, causes, effects, and inheritability of epilepsy, are, of course, all obsolete and totally inaccurate. For additional information about epilepsy, see Chapter 1, Section E4.

3.   What is the significance of the fact that the 1895 Connecticut statute applied only to women under 45 years of age? What public policy was the court seeking to further in construing the statute?

4.   The void/voidable distinction discussed by the *Gould* court concerns a question presented in nearly every case concerning a marriage whose validity is questioned because of the mental capacity of one of the partners. At common law and by statute in many states until recently, marriage of a person lacking mental capacity under applicable law was void *ab initio,* was subject to collateral attack, and might be declared invalid in any proceeding in which the question arose and required no annulment decree to establish its invalidity. Where the rule has been changed by statute, such a marriage is merely voidable, i.e., not subject to collateral attack, and valid until set aside in a proper proceeding for that purpose. See, 55 C.J.S. § 12, Marriage, "Mental Capacity." Which rule better allows people to exercise their constitutional right to marry?

E.P. MARRIAGE LICENSE

Orphans' Court of Philadelphia County,
Pennsylvania, 1957
8 District and County Reports 2d 598

LEFEVER and SHOYER, JJ., May 23, 1957.—It appears from the statements of E. P., the male applicant in the pending application for marriage license, that he is an epileptic. Mr. MacDonnell, assistant orphans' court clerk, pursuant to section 9 of The Marriage Law of August 22, 1953, P.L. 1344, 48 PS §§ 1-1, *et seq.,* refused to issue the license and certified the matter to this court. Thereafter, a full hearing and a supplemental hearing were held.

Section 5 of The Marriage Law of 1953, *inter alia,* provides:

> No license shall be issued by any clerk of the orphans' court . . .
> (e) If either of the applicants is an *epileptic,* or is or has been, within five years preceding the time of the application, *an inmate of an institution for epileptics,* weak-minded, insane, or persons of unsound mind, unless a judge of the orphans' court shall decide that it is for the best interest of such applicant and the general public to issue the license, and shall authorize the clerk of the orphans' court to issue the license. [Italics supplied.]

There are no reported decisions in Pennsylvania with regard to granting to an epileptic a license to marry under The Marriage Law of 1953. This application presents an important problem because there are today between 800,000 and 1,500,000 epileptics in the United States, and a proportionate share of them in Pennsylvania.

From ancient times epilepsy has been considered loathsome and wicked. When a person had it, he was described as being "possessed of the devil." One of the best descriptions of this theory of epilepsy appears in the Bible. There are old tales to the effect that it was considered wise to put the head of a person suffering convulsions into the furnace to burn the devil out of his body. Epileptics were kept segregated, were abhorred and even feared.

The visual unpleasantness of an epileptic seizure tends to prompt a superstitious reaction in the observer and a desire to avoid contact with epileptics; it stigmatizes the disease. Consequently, employees sometimes refuse to work beside an epileptic and certain parents object to an epileptic child's attending school with their children. Such has been the prejudice against epilepsy that many states by statute have absolutely prohibited the marriage of an epileptic. Pennsylvania had such a statute. Section 3 of the Act of June 24, 1913, P.L. 1013, provided that: "No license to marry shall be issued where either of the contracting parties is an . . . epileptic. . . ."

Epilepsy may manifest itself as grand mal, or petit mal. In grand mal, the epileptic is subject to convulsive seizures with the customary prostration, unconsciousness, foaming at the mouth, biting of tongue and lips, etc. These seizures may occur as frequently as a half dozen times daily or as infrequently as once a year. Frequent grand mal seizures may cause brain deterioration. There is much less likelihood of convulsive seizures in petit mal, although the patient "may black out but not show outward signs of seizure" and the possibility of brain deterioration is minimal. Petit mal is less apt to be transmissible.

Epilepsy may be either acquired or idiopathic. The acquired type may be brought on by various known factors, namely, brain injury, intracranial tumors, chemical and metabolic disorder, infections of the nervous system such as encephalitis, hypertension and diabetes. Many persons, who have an acquired type of epilepsy, go through life without any overt signs of the malady. "Idiopathic" or "essential" epilepsy encompasses all other cases which may or may not be definable, *viz.*, congenital, inheritable or epilepsy springing from no known cause; it is a "catch all" in a field of medical science which is still in the pioneer stages. The proportion of idiopathic cases decreases as knowledge of the causes of epilepsy places more cases in the acquired category.

"There is no positive answer" as to whether "epilepsy is transmissible." Many physicians are of the present opinion that epilepsy is not *inheritable,* although a predisposition to the disorder may be inherited, as a recessive trait. The tendency to convulsions among descendants of patients who have had attacks is about one in forty. The children of parents having "idiopathic" seizures are about five times as likely to have attacks as children of apparently normal parents. However, the likelihood of occurrence of grand mal in the epileptic's issue is greater, particularly where the epilepsy is idiopathic; but the modern view is that the transmissibility does not follow an exact Mendelian or genetic pattern. Consideration must also be given to the fact that "carriers" outnumber those who have exhibited seizures, by a ratio of ten to one. A marriage of two carriers may produce offspring with a greater tendency to seizures than offspring of a marriage between one person who has had seizures and one who is completely free of the malady. Yet, there is no practicable way for either the applicant for a marriage license or the issuing official to detect this latent condition.

Happily, all forms of epilepsy usually respond to modern medication. The customary treatment is a combination of barbiturates with dilantin, tridione, mesantoin or other recently developed anticonvulsants. Ordinarily where the epileptic responds to one of these drugs, there is likelihood that other of the drugs will be efficacious when a tolerance develops to the first drug. However, there are certain cases of epilepsy which do not respond to these drugs. In such cases, eventual brain deterioration is common, and the prognosis is guarded at best. By use of anticonvulsants, over 50 percent of those subject to seizure gain complete control, while another 30 percent have fewer seizures. Still others respond to surgery. Therefore, the group which does not respond to any treatment is small, and epilepsy remains a disabling disorder in less than 20 percent of cases.[6]

Marriage produces problems. However, many married epileptics are free from care and worry, do hard work and are as well controlled as people who are not married.

It would seem that certain epileptics should not be permitted to marry, *viz.,* those who show mental deterioration, those whom medicine is unable to control, and those whose family history is studded with epileptics. Others should probably be granted a marriage license, especially where the applicant has ''acquired'' epilepsy, where the seizures are controlled by medication, and where there is no family history of epilepsy. In between is the great borderline group. Each such case depends upon its own facts as to whether ''. . . it is for the best interest of such applicant and the general public to issue the license.''

In deciding each case, attention should be given, *inter alia,* to the following factors:

1. The likelihood of transmissibility of epilepsy to the issue of the applicants.
2. The likelihood of brain deterioration on the part of the epileptic.
3. The effect of marriage on the epileptic.
4. The physical and emotional condition of the other applicant and what is the reasonable likelihood of this ability to adjust to, and live in a married status with, the epileptic.

In the instant case, the epileptic male applicant is 29 years of age. He has suffered an eye condition, known as nystagmus, since birth. This makes it difficult for him to focus his eyes. However, he can distinguish objects, walk without a cane or other aid and even read print either with the aid of a magnifying glass or with the book held very close to his eyes. Nevertheless, his visual disability is sufficiently serious that he is receiving a blind pension of $60 a month.

When E.P. was 12 years of age, he suffered his first convulsive seizure. He had been shoveling snow in the bright sunshine when he suddenly fell to the ground, striking his head. Dr. Michael O. Grassi, the medical expert, was of the opinion that the striking of his head was the *result* of the seizure and not the *cause.* Therefore, it would seem that E.P.'s epilepsy is idiopathic.

---

[6]''Epilepsy and the Law,'' by Dr. Howard D. Fabing and Dean Roscoe L. Barrow (1956), pages 1 and 2.

E.P. has suffered epileptic attacks since that time. At first they were quite frequent. However, he presently undergoes only two or three attacks a year. Customarily, he receives a warning at least 15 minutes before a ''spell'' and can take precautions to forestall an attack or protect against injury to himself or others during a convulsion. His present medication consists of daily doses of barbiturates and tridione. Electroencephalograms of E.P. were recorded, both when he was under his usual medication, and also when he had desisted from the medication for several days. The significant finding was: ''The electroencephalogram indicates that the condition is being kept under control by the medication.'' Dr. Grassi testified that E.P. ''can be kept well under control with mesantoin and tridione and dilantin. I am not saying that we can close the door, but because of his response to the medication he should be fairly free from any seizures.'' He doubted that the epilepsy would be transmitted to E.P.'s issue, but conceded that there was a possibility of such transmissibility. He was of the opinion that there would be no brain deterioration in this case, provided that E.P. remained under a physician's care, regularly took his medication, and occasional psychotherapy. He stated that E.P. may ''be employed in whatever field he might try to excel in. I think he could live a very normal life. . . . I don't think there is any likelihood that he would wind up in an institution.''

E.P. conducted himself with poise, frankness and calm dignity on the witness stand. He appears to be a well adjusted and well educated man, a student in a Catholic theological seminary for several years, and, more recently, a student at LaSalle College, where he is presently a member of the junior class. It appears to the hearing judges that E.P. has met his afflictions with fortitude, understanding and equanimity, and that he will be able to adjust to the problems of matrimony without undue stress or untoward emotional upset which would superinduce more frequent epileptic attacks. Dr. Grassi was of the definite and unequivocal opinion that it is in the best interests not only of the applicant, but of the general public to issue the license.

The female applicant is 26 years of age, attractive and personable. She seemed more emotional and less self-contained than E.P. However, after listening to the lengthy and detailed testimony of Dr. Grassi as to the concomitants of epilepsy, including possible transmissibility of the disease to her children and the chance that E.P. might suffer some brain deterioration, she forthrightly and unconditionally reaffirmed her desire to marry E.P.

Since the family is the basic unit of society, limitation of the epileptic's right to marry may constitute a formidable obstacle to his adjustment. Fear that legal sanctions may be invoked against marriage increases the epileptic's tension. The resulting maladjustment may add a substantial obstacle to the successful treatment of the epileptic. Moreover, laws prohibiting marriage may sacrifice strong moral and ethical values in the society which imposes such sanctions. Furthermore, there appears to be no relationship between mental ability and epilepsy.[10]

---

[10] ''One might as well claim a relationship between genius and epilepsy as between mental defect and epilepsy. Among the great men of history who are reputed to have been epileptic are Buddha, Socrates, Alexander the Great, Julius Caesar, Mohammed, Peter the Great, and Napoleon Bonaparte. The fact is that

This court, in *F.A. Marriage License,* 4 D. & C. 2d 1, granted a license where the female applicant had been treated for schizophrenia. We concluded in that case: "This is a borderline case and we confess that we are beset with doubts. However, life at its very best is uncertain. Probably in a strictly disciplined society persons of defective mentality would be deprived of the blessings of matrimony. This, however, is an imperfect world. It is difficult to foretell the unhappy consequences which might result from our refusing to issue a marriage license in this case. . . ."

This, too, is a borderline case, not free from doubt. However, the hearing judges entertain less doubt here than in the cited case. Life indeed is uncertain. It is probably far better that we cannot foresee the future. However, in this case, it appears that the dangers flowing from E.P.'s epilepsy are not overawing, that there is no history of epilepsy in his family, that he is responding magnificently to medical treatment, that the four factors mentioned *supra* in this case favor the marriage and that "it is for the best interests of such applicant and the general public to issue the license."

Accordingly, we enter the following *Decree*

And now, to wit, May 23, 1957, the clerk is directed forthwith to issue a marriage license to the applicants.

NOTES

1. What tests would the Supreme Court use today in interpreting the statutes construed in *Gould* and *E.P. Marriage License?* In view of the language quoted from the *F.A. Marriage License* case, see pp. 929–933, below, what would be the likely result if a case like *Gould* were before the Supreme Court today?

2. A review of state statutes indicates that epilepsy has been deleted as a prohibition to marriage in an increasing number of states which previously included it in their legislation. See Brakel, S., and Rock, R., *The Mentally Disabled and the Law,* 227 (1971).

EXAMPLES OF STATE STATUTES

Rev. Codes Montana §§ 48-104 and 105 (1947) (repealed by Sec. 45, Ch. 536, Laws of 1975, effective Jan. 1, 1976):

> 48-104　Certain marriages voidable. If either party to a marriage be incapable from physical causes of entering into the marriage state, or if the consent of either be obtained by fraud or force, the marriage is voidable.
> 48-105　Incompetency of parties to marriages between . . . persons, either of whom is feeble-minded, are incestuous and void from the beginning. . . .

Ky. Rev. Stats. Ann. 402.020 (1969):

---

there is no relationship between epilepsy and either idiocy or genius. An epileptic may possess other infirmities or he may be richly endowed. If an epileptic also happens to be mentally defective, the eugenic law would be applied because of the mental defect even if the eugenic law were rendered inapplicable to epileptics. In the ordinary case, the good qualities far outweigh the person's epilepsy. It should be remembered, moreover, that the application of eugenic laws to those epileptics who are richly endowed may prevent persons of the highest intelligence and who are possessed of unusual gifts from marrying and transmitting their potentialities to succeeding generations."

Marriage is prohibited and void:
(1) With an idiot or lunatic;

*   *   *

Rev. Code Wash. Ann. Title 26 § 26.04.030, as amended by laws 1st Extra
Session 1973, Ch. 154 § 27 (1976 Pocket Part):

> No marriage shall take place between two persons in which one or both, is a common
> drunkard, habitual criminal, imbecile, feeble-minded person, idiot or insane person, or
> person who has theretofore been afflicted with hereditary insanity, or who is afflicted
> with pulmonary tuberculosis in its advanced stages, or any contagious venereal disease,
> shall hereafter intermarry or marry any other person within this state unless it is estab-
> lished that procreation is not possible by the couple intending to marry.

F.A. MARRIAGE LICENSE

Orphans' Court of Philadelphia County,
Pennsylvania, 1955
4 District and County Reports 2d 1

KLEIN, P. J., and LEFEVER, J., May 19, 1955.—Application for a marriage
license was filed by the applicants on April 30, 1955. It appears from the statements
made by the female applicant (herein referred to as F.A.), that she was a mental patient
in St. Mary's Hospital, Philadelphia, for a period of two months in 1951.

Mr. MacDonnell, assistant orphans' court clerk, pursuant to the provisions of
section 9 of The Marriage Law of August 22, 1953, P.L. 1344, 48 PS § 1, *et seq.,*
refused to issue the license and certified the matter to this court for hearing.

This is the first time that this court has been asked to construe the provisions of
the new marriage law, pertaining to the issuance of a marriage license to a person who
has been afflicted with mental illness within a period of five years prior to the date of
application for the license.

For years the marriage statutes of this Commonwealth had lacked clarity and
had been out of adjustment with advances in medical science and our changing approaches to social problems.

* * *

The discovery of new drugs has dramatically reduced the ill effects of epilepsy.
Enlightened medical opinion now regards the absolute bar to marriage of epileptics as
harsh, unjust, and unnecessary. Tremendous strides have also been made in the care of
the mentally ill, resulting in cures in many cases and substantial improvements in
others. It is now possible for some of these people to marry without serious risk to
themselves, their spouses, their offspring, or the community generally.

The Marriage Law of 1953 recognized these advances in medicine, and in
a large measure, corrected these long existing, entrenched deficiencies in our marriage laws.

The uncertainty with respect to officials who are permitted to solemnize marriages has been removed. Section 13 of the act designates with particularity the persons
in whom such authority is now vested.

The judges of the orphans' courts now have jurisdiction, under certain designated circumstances, to decide that the spouse of an applicant is a presumed decedent.

For a discussion of this phase of the new marriage law see the companion opinion (which was drafted contemporaneously with this, although filed two days later), *viz., Application for Marriage License of Magdalene Pest and Josef Kolesnik,* 4 D. & C. 2d 12.

The provisions of the old law, which forbade the issuance of a license to a person who "is an imbecile, . . . of unsound mind, or under guardianship as a person of unsound mind," has been substantially reenacted in the new act.[5] However, the absolute prohibition against the issuance of a marriage license to an epileptic has been repealed. Under the 1953 statute a marriage license may be issued to a person who is suffering from epilepsy or who has been, within five years preceding the time of the application, an inmate of an institution for epileptics, but only if authorized by a judge of the orphans' court.[5] Likewise, if the applicant has been an inmate of an institution "for weak-minded, insane or persons of unsound mind" within five years preceding the time of the application, the license may be issued only if authorized by a judge of the orphans' court.

The legislature has thus placed a great social responsibility on the orphans' court. It is our duty to determine whether "it is for the best interest of such applicant and the general public to issue the license." Yet, the statute contains no criteria, standards or rules for determining this fact; and no definition of crucial terms used in the statute. This is perhaps necessary, for the broad discretion vested in the courts, will enable them, in true common-law tradition, to progress with the advances of science in this difficult and inexact field of law and medicine and decide each case on its own facts.

A vast, hazy shadowland exists between mental health and mental illness. The gradations of abnormalities are as varied and diffused as the merging colors of the rainbow. The most illustrious and respected psychiatrists often disagree radically in their opinions with respect to the sanity of an individual.

The following extract from the Encyclopaedia Britannica, vol. 12, p. 383 (14th ed.) points up the difficulty very sharply:

"INSANITY. This term ordinarily connotes more or less severe unsoundness of mind. Though its loose usage is almost synonymous with mental disease, scientifically the term should only be applied to the mental condition of an individual who, through socially inefficient conduct, has to be placed under supervision and control. The mind is the mechanism by means of which we adapt adequately to our environment and when, through its derangement, conduct is exhibited which the community looks upon as evidence of disease and as implying irresponsibility, the individual concerned is said to be insane and the law steps in to certify him as such. Strictly speaking, then, insanity

---

[5] "Section 5. Restrictions on the Issue of Marriage License.—No license to marry shall be issued by any clerk of the orphans' court: . . .

"(d) If either of the applicants for a license is weak-minded, insane, of unsound mind, or is under guardianship as a person of unsound mind.

"(e) If either of the applicants is an epileptic, or is or has been, within five years preceding the time of application, an inmate of an institution for epileptics, weak-minded, insane, or persons of unsound mind, unless a judge of the orphans' court shall decide that it is for the best interest of such applicant and the general public to issue the license, and shall authorize the clerk of the orphans' court to issue the license."

is really a social and legal term and not medical. Mental illness is a broad concept which may include very efficient members of society. No satisfactory definition can therefore be arrived at, since it would be necessary to define what we mean by sanity, which would involve us in equal difficulties.''

The phrase ''an inmate of an institution for weak-minded, insane, or persons of unsound mind'' is, likewise, subject to interpretation. Institutions for the insane are no longer regarded merely as places in which persons of unsound mind are confined as custodial cases to rid the general public of their troublesome presence. Today, great progress is being made toward curing the mentally sick and the establishments in which they are housed are usually called ''hospitals.'' In fact, many general hospitals have departments set aside for the care of the mentally sick. Furthermore, in present day usage the word ''inmate'' has been generally replaced by the more charitable word ''patient.'' The language of the statute is general, but we believe that the legislature intended to include all cases in which the applicant has been hospitalized for treatment of some form of mental illness or deficiency in any mental institution, including a general hospital which conducts a department for the care of the mentally sick.

Basically, the problem which confronts us is one for the medical profession. A diagnosis by judicial decree should not be made except with the advice, and upon the recommendation of, trained psychiatrists.

The statute does not in so many words state that an applicant who has been in a mental institution must be cured permanently at the time the application is made. However, because the issuance of a license to a person who is weak-minded, insane or of unsound mind is absolutely prohibited by the statute, the legislature must have intended that a license is to be issued only to a person who has been completely cured of his mental illness or whose condition has so improved that he can be expected to lead a normal life and to take his place in society without serious risk to himself or to the community generally.

Leading members of the medical profession freely admit that the science of caring for the mentally ill is in its infancy. Much research and investigation has been undertaken recently which has resulted in tremendously enhancing the chances of curing or, at least, improving the condition of persons suffering from mental sickness.

It seems clear that under no circumstances should a marriage license be issued to persons having a mental deficiency of severe degree, e.g., an idiot or imbecile. It is also apparent that persons suffering irremedial brain injury, or deteriorating organic brain syndromes which are of progressive or irreversible nature, e.g., senile dementia, should not be permitted to marry.

On the other hand, many persons who are unable to cope with the intense pressures of the modern age, suffer what is commonly designated as ''mental break-downs'' and are institutionalized. Most of these people respond favorably to therapy; many are completely cured. These obviously are the persons whom the legislature intended to benefit primarily and furnish no serious problem when they apply for marriage licenses.

The real difficulties arise with respect to persons who suffer moderate mental deficiency or who have been hospitalized because of the more serious mental illnesses, such as manic-depressive psychosis, schizophrenia (dementia praecox), post-partum psychosis, and involutional melancholia. Although many of these cases are completely hopeless, a great number show marked improvement under modern therapy, such as shock treatment, psychotherapy, and the use of newly discovered drugs. Some of these persons are able to leave the mental hospitals and, at least temporarily, take their places in society as useful citizens. Some apparently have complete remission from their malady. Whether they have recovered sufficiently to assume the responsibilities of marriage presents an extremely delicate question.

No general rule can be handed down. Each case is *sui generis* and must be decided upon its own facts. The discretion vested in the orphans' court must be carefully exercised in order to protect not only the applicants and their issue, but the general public as well.

Three preliminary requirements seem to be indicated in every case before a license should issue: (1) Full disclosure must be made to both applicants of all of the details of the case history of the applicant who has been mentally afflicted; (2) the court must be satisfied that such applicant has recovered sufficiently to adjust normally to the problems of everyday living, particularly those arising from the marriage relationship, and (3) the court must be reasonably assured that if children are born of the marriage, such children will be normal, healthy children, free from the taint of mental illness or deficiency.

With these principles in mind, let us examine the factual situation existing in the present case.

No question is raised concerning the sanity of the male applicant. He was present at the hearing, fully cognizant of the history of F.A.'s mental sickness, and is, nevertheless, not only willing, but eager, to marry her.

F.A. is 30 years of age. She was graduated from a Catholic parochial grade school and attended Little Flower High School for two years. She left school when she was about 17 years old and took a job in a hosiery mill, "sewing on piece-work." She continued in the hosiery industry until, apparently, the pressure of "piece-work" caused her to have a mental breakdown. She was hospitalized at St. Mary's Hospital in Philadelphia for a period of eight weeks with a diagnosis of dementia praecox. While in the hospital she received a full course of electric shock treatments, following which she received treatments as an out-patient until December 1953, when she was pronounced well. It appears, further, from the testimony that since her discharge from the hospital she has managed the household of her invalid sister satisfactorily and efficiently and has given no evidence of any recurrence of her malady.

Dr. William L. Long, the physician who treated F.A., was the principal witness in her behalf. Dr. Long has specialized in neuropsychiatry since 1928 and is well and favorably known to the court. He is chief neuropsychiatrist at St. Mary's Hospital, and is on the psychiatric staff at Nazareth Hospital, Doctor's Hospital, and the Philadelphia General Hospital. Dr. Long examined F.A. shortly before the date of the hearing. He testified: "I am satisfied that she is fully recovered from her illness and I think she now has a well-adjusted emotional life."

He testified further that, in his opinion, if she had children they would be normal. He recommended that the marriage license be issued.

Following the hearing, at the request of the hearing judges, F.A. was examined by Dr. Nicholas G. Frignito, neuropsychiatrist for the Municipal Court of Philadelphia. Dr. Frignito filed a written report in which he made a diagnosis of dementia praecox (recovered normal intelligence). This report concluded with the opinion that F.A. is now recovered from her mental illness and is competent to marry.

After a careful study of the record in this case we make the following findings of fact:

1. That St. Mary's Hospital, Philadelphia, is an institution for persons who are insane or of unsound mind, within the purview of The Marriage Law of 1953;

2. That F.A. was an inmate of the mental department of that institution from April 16, 1951, to June 16, 1951;

3. That F.A. was an out-patient of the mental department of that institution from June 1951 until December 1953, when she was discharged as cured;

4. That F.A. is not at this time weak-minded, insane, or a person of unsound mind;

5. That the male applicant is fully aware of the entire history of F.A.'s mental illness, and

6. That there is no compelling evidence that children, if any, born of this marriage will be mentally deficient or predisposed to mental illness.

This is a borderline case and we confess that we are beset with doubts. However, life at its very best is uncertain. Probably in a strictly disciplined society persons of defective mentality would be deprived of the blessings of matrimony. This, however, is an imperfect world. It is difficult to foretell the unhappy consequences which might result from our refusing to issue a marriage license in this case in view of the fact that the marriage banns have been posted, and all of the arrangements for the marriage have been made. The applicants are obviously in love with each other. If they cannot be married in this State, they may be tempted to live together without the benefit of marriage, or to seek a marriage license in another State where the restrictions are less stringent. Under all of the existing circumstances, we are of the opinion that it is for the best interest of the applicants and the general public to issue the marriage license.

Accordingly, we enter the following *Decree*

And now, May 19, 1955, the clerk of the court is directed forthwith to issue a marriage license to the applicants.

NOTES

1. The recently repealed Montana statute, and the statutes currently in effect in Kentucky, Pennsylvania, and Washington, typify contemporary restrictions upon the constitutional right to marry based upon mental handicap. For a compilation of all current statutory provisions affecting the right of mentally disabled persons to marry, see Appendix to Note, "The Right of the Mentally Disabled to Marry: A Statutory Evaluation," 15 *J. Fam. L.* 463, 487 (1976-77). Note that the statutes excerpted above describe various mental conditions with antiquated and vague terminology without defining the terms employed, e.g., "idiot" (Ky., Wash.); "insane" (Pa., Wash.); "weak-minded" (Pa.); "feeble-minded" (Mont., Wash.). Do these statutes satisfy

procedural due process? Substantive due process? Equal protection? How would the Supreme Court be likely to construe them today?

2.   Note that the Kentucky and Montana statutes preserve the void/voidable distinction found in the 1895 Connecticut statute at issue in *Gould*.

3.   The Washington statutory prohibition does not apply if "it is established that procreation is not possible by the couple intending to marry." What public policy is this provision designed to accomplish? Is it any different from similar language found in the 1895 Connecticut statute? Who bears the burden under this statute of proving that procreation is not possible? Who should bear this burden? Is such a burden constitutional?

4.   Section 48-104 of the Montana Statute provides that a marriage is voidable if either party is "incapable from physical causes of entering into the marriage state." What does this language mean? What legitimate state interest is such a provision designed to accomplish?

5.   Note the commingling of the police power and *parens patriae* power of the state in Section 5(e) of the Pennsylvania statute. Does the *parens patriae* authority of the state permit it to restrict the ability of individuals to marry? Should the state be able to restrict the ability of an individual to marry based on prior institutionalization for mental illness or retardation? What is the source of the state's authority to act in this regard? Is such a restriction constitutional? Under the Pennsylvania scheme have sufficient standards been delegated by the legislature to the orphans' court for it to interpret this statute within the limits of the Constitution?

6.   Should the *F.A.* court have allowed a marriage license to be issued to F.A. if she had been unable to demonstrate that she had been cured of her mental illness?

7.   What evidence should the *F.A.* court have considered sufficiently compelling to show that children born of the marriage would be mentally deficient or predisposed to mental illness? Can this test be constitutionally met? Who should bear the burden on this point?

3. The Capacity to Marry

Larson v. Larson

Appellate Court of Illinois, Second District,
Second Division, 1963
42 Ill.App.2d 467, 192 N.E.2d 594

Crow, Presiding Justice.

This is an appeal by the plaintiff, Sidney F. Larson, from a decree dismissing a suit for want of equity on a complaint for annulment of a marriage between the plaintiff and the defendant, Myrtle Larson. The complaint, so far as material, alleged that a marriage was entered into between the plaintiff and the defendant in Sycamore, Illinois, on March 21, 1950; at the time of the marriage and for some time prior thereto, the defendant was and continues to be of unsound mind, so as to be incapable of understanding a contract of marriage; and soon after the marriage the defendant was committed to Elgin State Hospital and still is a patient there.

* * *

When the celebration of a marriage is shown, the contract of marriage, the capacity of the parties, and, in fact, everything necessary to the validity of the marriage, in the absence of proof to the contrary, will be presumed; the burden of proof was upon the plaintiff to show the marriage was invalid; to enable a party legally to contract a marriage he or she must be capable of understanding the nature of the act: *Flynn et al.* v. *Troesch et al.* (1940) 373 Ill. 275, 26 N.E.2d 91. When a marriage is shown the law raises a strong presumption in favor of its validity, and the burden is upon the party objecting thereto to prove such facts and circumstances as necessarily establish its invalidity; there is no clear dividing line between competency and incompetency, and each case must be judged by its own peculiar facts; the parties must have sufficient mental capacity to enter into the status, but proof of lack of mental capacity must be clear and definite; if the party possesses sufficient mental capacity to understand the nature, effect, duties, and obligations of the marriage contract into which he or she is entering, the marriage contract is binding, as long as they are otherwise legally competent to enter into the relation: *Ertel* v. *Ertel* (1942) 313 Ill.App. 326, 40 N.E.2d 85. A marriage contract will be invalidated by the want of consent of capable persons; it requires the mutual consent of two persons of sound mind, and if at the time one is mentally incapable of giving an intelligent consent to what is done, with an understanding of the obligations assumed, the solemnization is a mere idle ceremony,—they must be capable of entering understandingly into the relation: *Hagenson* v. *Hagenson et al.* (1913) 258 Ill. 197, 101 N.E. 606. It is impossible to prescribe a definite rule by which the mental condition as to sanity or insanity in regard to a marriage can in every case be tested; the question is not altogether of brain quantity or quality in the abstract, but whether the mind could and did act rationally regarding the precise thing in contemplation,—marriage,—and the particular marriage in dispute,—not whether his or her conduct was wise, but whether it proceeded from a mind sane as respects the particular thing done: *Cf. Orchardson* v. *Cofield et al.* (1897) 171 Ill. 14, 49 N.E. 197, 40 L.R.A. 256; *Cf. Pyott* v. *Pyott et al.* (1899) 90 Ill.App. 210.

The decree here is not contrary to the manifest weight of the evidence or to the law. Prior to and at the time of the marriage the plaintiff noticed nothing abnormal about the defendant. There is no evidence that any of the unusual things she thought and did some months after the marriage had also occurred prior to and at the time of the marriage. Her first commitment to Elgin State Hospital was in 1952, more than two years after the marriage. In 1954 she was found to have recovered and was restored to all her civil rights. She got along good for awhile thereafter. Her second commitment was in 1956, more than four and one-half years after the marriage. The plaintiff continued to live regularly with the defendant as husband and wife except for such times as she was actually physically confined at the Hospital.

* * *

The plaintiff has not satisfied the burden of proving, clearly and definitely, that the defendant was an "insane person" at the particular time of this marriage, March

21, 1950,—that she was at that time incapable of understanding the nature of the act, that she had insufficient mental capacity to enter into the status and understand the nature, effect, duties, and obligations of the marriage contract, that she was mentally incapable of giving an intelligent understanding consent, or that her mind could not and did not act rationally regarding the precise thing in contemplation, marriage, and this particular marriage in dispute.

The decree is correct and it will be affirmed.

Affirmed.

WRIGHT and SPIVEY, JJ., concur.

HOMAN v. HOMAN
Supreme Court of Nebraska, 1967
181 Neb. 259, 147 N.W.2d 630

Heard before WHITE, C. J., and CARTER, SPENCER, BOSLAUGH, BROWER, SMITH and McCOWN, JJ.

BOSLAUGH, Justice.

This is an action to annul a marriage between Eugene J. Homan and Lucille Homan, the defendant. Although the action is brought by a guardian and next friend, Eugene J. Homan will be referred to as the plaintiff. The trial court found that the marriage was valid and dismissed the action. The guardian has appealed.

The petition alleged that the ward was mentally incompetent at the time of the marriage. By statute a marriage is void "when either party is insane or an idiot at the time of marriage, and the term idiot shall include all persons who from whatever cause are mentally incompetent to enter into the marriage relation." Section 42-103, R.S.Supp., 1965.

A marriage contract will not be declared void for mental incapacity to enter into it unless there existed at the time of the marriage such a want of understanding as to render the party incapable of assenting thereto. *Fischer* v. *Adams,* 151 Neb. 512, 38 N.W.2d 337. Mere weakness or imbecility of mind is not sufficient to void a contract of marriage unless there be such a mental defect as to prevent the party from comprehending the nature of the contract and from giving his free and intelligent consent to it.

Absolute inability to contract, insanity, or idiocy will void a marriage, but mere weakness of mind will not unless it produces a derangement sufficient to avoid all contracts by destroying the power to consent. *Aldrich* v. *Steen,* 71 Neb. 33, 98 N.W.2d 445; *Adams* v. *Scott,* 93 Neb. 537, 141 N.W. 148. A marriage is valid if the party has sufficient capacity to understand the nature of the contract and the obligations and responsibilities it creates. *Fischer* v. *Adams, supra; Kutch* v. *Kutch,* 88 Neb. 114, 129 N.W. 169.

The plaintiff has a history of mental illness and mental deficiency. When he was 5 years old he was ill with scarlet fever and encephalitis which resulted in a permanent impairment of his mental ability. In December 1950, the plaintiff was treated for schizophrenia. Treatment for this condition continued through 1958 but there is no evidence that the plaintiff received any treatment for this condition between 1958 and 1963. The plaintiff attended Immaculate Conception Grade School in

Omaha, Nebraska, and completed 3 years of high school. He was then employed as a laborer by Goodwill Industries and later by Armour & Company.

The plaintiff first met the defendant in 1959. They commenced keeping company and approximately 3 months later the plaintiff proposed marriage. The marriage took place about 6 months later on February 27, 1960. The plaintiff was then 29 years of age.

During the courtship the plaintiff made plans to purchase a house and saved a part of his earnings for the downpayment. A property was selected, a mortgage negotiated, and the purchase completed. The parties moved into their first home a week after the ceremony. In March 1962, the parties traded this home for a larger property.

In 1963 the plaintiff was sent home from his employment with instructions to obtain medical treatment. The plaintiff consulted a physician, was referred to a psychiatrist, and was hospitalized.

At the time of the trial the plaintiff was on leave from the hospital. He was living with his parents in Omaha and working part time. The defendant last saw the plaintiff in August 1964. He was placed under guardianship in October 1964. The plaintiff did not attend the trial and, apparently, did not know of the action or the trial.

A marriage is presumed valid, and the burden of proof is upon the party seeking annulment. *Adams* v. *Scott, supra*. To succeed in this action it was necessary for the guardian to establish that the plaintiff was mentally incompetent on February 27, 1960.

The plaintiff suffers from a mental impairment that is the result of a childhood illness. This condition is permanent and existed at the time of the marriage. The guardian produced the testimony of the psychiatrist who had treated the plaintiff prior to the marriage. This witness testified that the plaintiff had a mental age of approximately 11 years; an intelligence quotient of between 69 and 75; and that the plaintiff would be classified as a high-grade moron. This witness further testified that, in his opinion, the plaintiff would have an inadequate or superficial understanding of the responsibilities of marriage.

The defendant testified at length concerning her acquaintance and relationship with the plaintiff from the time of their first meeting in 1959 until the hospitalization of the plaintiff in 1963. This evidence contradicts that of the guardian and tends to prove that the plaintiff had a sufficient understanding of the marriage relationship and its obligations and responsibilities. During this time the plaintiff was steadily employed as a maintenance and custodial worker, managed his finances, purchased two properties, and had a reasonably normal life. The evidence supports an inference that the marriage would have continued without difficulty if the plaintiff's mental illness had not recurred in 1963.

Although the plaintiff suffered from schizophrenia prior to the marriage and again in 1963, the evidence shows that this illness was in remission at the time of the marriage and was not a disabling factor at that time. Although handicapped mentally, the plaintiff had sufficient ability to transact business and the capacity to enter into the marriage on February 27, 1960.

The marriage in this case may have been unwise or unfortunate, but it was not void. The judgment of the district court is correct and it is affirmed.

Affirmed.

NOTES

1. In *Beddow* v. *Beddow*, 257 S.W.2d 45 (Ky. 1952) the Court of Appeals of Kentucky had to determine the validity of the marriage of two Kentucky residents, one of whom was alleged to be "an idiot or a lunatic," who had gone to the state of Mississippi to have their marriage performed. The marriage would have been void under Kentucky law prohibiting marriage with "an idiot or lunatic," but in Mississippi the marriage would have been voidable only. Kentucky had a statute which specified that Kentucky would recognize the validity of a marriage if valid in the state where solemnized. The *Beddow* court, however, ruled that this statutory requirement of recognition of foreign marriages was "but a statement of the common law rule of *lex loci contractus* as it relates to marriages," *id.* at 47, and held that there was an exception to it if a marriage was against the public policy of a state, *ibid.* The court then declared:

> We next have to determine whether or not the marriage of an idiot or a lunatic is against the public policy of this State. In *Jenkins* v. *Jenkins' Heirs,* 2 Dana 102, 32 Ky. 102, Chief Justice Robertson said: "A person of unsound mind—an idiot, for example, is, as to all intellectual purposes, dead; and such a thing, destitute of intellectual light and life, is as incapable as a dead body of being a husband or a wife in a legal, rational or moral sense."
>
> At common law, such a marriage was void. 35 Am.Jur.P. 247, Sec. 107, Marriage: *Jenkins* v. *Jenkins' Heirs, supra.*
>
> A proper concern for the institution of marriage impels our conclusion that the marriage of an idiot or a lunatic violates the fundamental public policy of this State. The capacity to enter into a marriage contract does not require sufficient mental capacity to exercise clear reason, discernment and sound judgment. We may say in passing that some of the marriages this Court has been called upon to untangle would indicate a complete absence of these qualities. However, the thought of marriage by one who is devoid of reason, or whose mind is so beclouded by insanity as to be incapable of understanding the nature of such a contract, is abhorrent. Such a marriage should be regarded as a farce (*Id.* at 48).

Contrast the court's attitude in *Beddow* with that of the courts' in *Larson* and *Homan*.

2. The approaches taken by the *Beddow, Larson,* and *Homan* courts to the question of what degree of mental capacity is required to make a marriage valid are typical of judicial approaches to the problem. What is the test employed by these courts? What public policies underlie it? Are these policies legitimate state interests? Does the formulation that "a person has sufficient mental capacity to marriage if he or she understands the nature and obligations of the marriage contract" really assist the courts in such cases? Does this formulation lend itself to anything more precise than subjective interpretation by the courts? Does such a test satisfy the requirements of procedural due process? Substantive due process? Equal protection? Can you suggest a more objective criterion?

3. Is the capacity to enter into a marriage contract different from the capacity to contract generally?

4. Effect of Prior Adjudication of Insanity or Incompetency

GELLERT V. BUSMAN'S ADMINISTRATOR

Court of Appeals of Kentucky, 1931
239 Ky. 328, 39 S.W.2d 511

CLAY, J.

Jessie M. Busman, who was married to George Busman on January 5, 1924, died intestate a resident of Louisville on February 22, 1928, survived by her husband and one son, Frank C. Gellert, the issue of a former marriage. At the time of her death, she and her husband had a joint savings account of $4,775. The Louisville Trust Company was appointed administrator of her estate. Thereafter Frank Gellert brought this suit against the administrator for a settlement of his mother's estate. He charged in substance that his mother was a lunatic at the time of her marriage to Busman, and that the marriage was void under section 2097, Kentucky Statutes, which prohibits marriage with an idiot or lunatic. For this reason he alleged that Busman was not entitled to any portion of Mrs. Busman's property, and asserted title in himself to the whole of the joint savings account, to certain furniture of the estimated value of $2,000, and to an Oakland automobile of the value of $1,100. Issue was joined between Gellert and George Busman, and on final hearing the chancellor upheld the marriage and adjudged that Busman was entitled to one-half of the joint savings account, and that, after the payment of the debts of Mrs. Busman, the remaining one-half should be equally divided between George Busman and Frank C. Gellert.

* * *

The first question to be determined is whether Mrs. Busman was insane at the time of her marriage. The evidence may be summarized as follows: Some time in the year 1920 Mrs. Busman fell in love with a young man by the name of Anderson. In the year 1921 she was accompanied by Anderson to Michigan, and was seriously injured in an automobile accident there. As the result of the accident her limbs were severely burned. After the accident, Anderson appears to have changed his affections to another. Whether due to this fact or the accident, or both combined, Mrs. Busman's mind was seriously affected. She became very nervous, and could not sleep except under the influence of opiates. In the fall of 1922 she became insane. In October of that year she was taken to the Beechhurst Sanatorium, where she became so violent that it was necessary to put her under physical restraint. On December 12, 1922, she was adjudged insane in an inquest proceeding in the Jefferson circuit court, and was then committed to the asylum at Lakeland. For a while after her commitment she did not know any one. She then began to improve, and on February 23, 1923, she was paroled in the care of her son, the appellant, with the understanding that she would be returned if her mental condition made it necessary. Appellant says that he knew at the time that his mother was not well, but that she begged to be taken home, and he secured her parole thinking it would benefit her. Appellant and the mother of Mrs. Busman both say that after the parole she was nervous and easily excited, and would have frequent crying spells. They also say that she required her husband to get up as early as 3 o'clock to take her automobile riding. In addition to this evidence, Dr. L.W. Neblett, who treated Mrs. Busman at the time she was committed to the sanatorium, Dr. Louis

W. Eckles, examining surgeon of the United States government and for the criminal court of Jefferson county, Dr. R.C. Anderson, who was also an examiner for the United States government and for the Jefferson circuit court in sanity cases, Dr. George F. Simpson, a general practitioner of more than 40 years' experience, and Drs. B.A. Moore and W.T. Baker, prominent physicians, all testified that, in their opinion, Mrs. Busman was suffering from dementia praecox or melancholia, a form of insanity for which there was practically no cure, and that she was insane at all times from 1922 until the time of her death.

On the other hand, several physicians, who had specialized in the diagnosis and treatment of mental disorders, gave it as their opinion that the decedent had a functional rather than an organic disturbance, which was not of a permanent nature, but responded to treatment, and expressed the view that she was not insane at the time of her marriage. Sam Bloch, who ran a lunch counter, testified that the decedent worked for him, that she was very capable, and that she had always appeared to be a normal person. Dr. Leon Abraham, who operated a pharmacy at First and Broadway, in Louisville, and who employed the decedent for a number of years, testified that she always did her work well, and that he never at any time saw anything wrong with her mind. In addition to this, numerous persons, who were associated with decedent in her work, or who were patrons of the establishment where she worked, all swore to her efficiency, and to the fact that they never saw anything abnormal in her conduct. It further appears that she was a careful industrious business woman, and, though inclined to save her income, made frequent contributions to the support of her mother and occasional presents to her son.

In determining whether one has mental capacity sufficient to contract a valid marriage, the test usually applied is whether there is a capacity to understand the nature of the contract and the duties and responsibilities which it creates. *Note to Roether* v. *Roether*, 28 A.L.R. 631, on page 641. If the case turned wholly on the expert testimony, there would be more or less doubt in its solution, but the testimony of the employers of the decedent and of those who associated with her daily is most persuasive of her sanity. A woman who takes in roomers, performs her duties as a wife, engages in outside business, and conducts it to the satisfaction of her employers and their patrons, without exhibiting further evidence of unsoundness of mind than a few occasional tears, is certainly capable of understanding the nature of the marriage contract and the duties and responsibilities which it creates. Especially is this true where, after contracting the marriage, she shows her appreciation and understanding of the relationship by performing in a satisfactory manner all the duties that the relationship imposes. On the whole we conclude that, whatever be the rule as between the two presumptions, the one arising from the judgment of insanity, and the other in favor of the validity of the marriage, the evidence is such as to leave no doubt that Mrs. Busman was not insane at the time of her marriage.

At the time of her death the savings account belonged to Mrs. Busman and her husband. There being no contract or survivorship, one-half of it belonged to her estate and one-half of it to Mr. Busman. On her death he was entitled to his half, and the one-half of her one-half after the payment of her debts. Section 2132, Kentucky Statutes. It follows that the judgment with respect to this item was correct.

[The remainder of the opinion, dealing with ownership of other property, is omitted.]

NOTES

1. In *Johnson* v. *Johnson,* 8 N.W.2d 620 (Minn. 1943), the Supreme Court of Minnesota upheld the determination of the lower court that a 77-year-old man did have the requisite mental capacity to enter into a marriage, notwithstanding that he had been adjudicated incompetent and had a guardian of his estate and person appointed. The court declared:

> 1. A person under guardianship is conclusively presumed to be incompetent to make a valid contract or disposition of his property. "This rule is based upon convenience and necessity, for the protection of the guardian, and to enable him to properly discharge his duties as such." *Thorpe* v. *Hanscom,* 64 Minn. 201, 205, 66 N.W. 1.
>
> 2. When the reason for the rule ceases the rule does not apply. Convenience and necessity of the guardian extend only to those acts which he is authorized to do on behalf of the ward, such as managing and controlling his property and his estate. The guardian's authority does not extend to the marriage of his ward. *Banker* v. *Banker,* 63 N.Y. 409. The appointment of a guardian disables the alleged incompetent only from making contracts which relate to his estate, but not other kinds of contracts. One who has been adjudged an incompetent may contract a valid marriage if he has in fact sufficient mental capacity for that purpose [citation omitted].
>
> An adjudication of incompetency by the probate court is evidence, but not conclusive, in any litigation to prove the mental condition of the alleged incompetent at the time the judgment was rendered or at any past time during which the judgment finds the person to be incompetent [citation omitted]. In a particular case the question of mental competency to contract marriage is a fact question. So it was here. (*Id.* at 622.)

2. Should an adjudication of insanity prior to marriage (as in *Gellert*) or an adjudication of incompetency and appointment of a guardian prior to marriage (as in *Johnson*) be relevant in determining a person's mental capacity to marry? If so, how should such a fact be considered by the court considering the validity of the marriage?

3. Are the tests for capacity to marry employed by the courts in *Gellert,* and in *Johnson,* pp. 941–946, *infra,* any more precise than the formulations employed by the *Beddow, Larson,* and *Homan* courts?

4. *Gellert, supra,* and *Johnson, infra,* pp. 941–946, indicate that the mental capacity to marry must exist only at the time the marriage is entered into. It need not exist after that point for the marriage still to be valid.

5. The Presumption of Validity

JOHNSON v. JOHNSON

Supreme Court of North Dakota, 1960
104 N.W.2d 8

DOUGLAS B. HEEN, District Judge.

The plaintiff, Bennie O. Johnson, by Duane Davis, his guardian, brought this action for annulment of marriage on the grounds that plaintiff, at the time of marriage to defendant, was feeble-minded, a common drunkard and afflicted with a contagious disease, all or any of which, it is alleged, would prevent his marriage under the laws of this state.

The district court, after hearing the evidence, found that plaintiff at the time of marriage was of unsound mind and was incompetent to the extent that he did not understand the duties and obligations of the marriage relationship. The defendant has appealed from such judgment and demands a trial *de novo* in this court.

The evidence establishes that plaintiff, Bennie O. Johnson, was previously married and that his wife died in January 1952. Prior to her death, plaintiff and his then wife visited in Canada, and while on such trip made the acquaintanceship of a Mrs. Speirs. Following the death of his first wife, plaintiff in the summer of 1953 again made a trip to Canada and renewed such acquaintanceship, which ripened to the extent that Mrs. Speirs made visits to North Dakota to visit plaintiff. It appears that plaintiff was addicted to the use of intoxicating liquor, and in May 1955 entered a hospital for treatment of delirium tremens and a liver condition, remaining in the hospital until June 22, 1955, when he entered the State Hospital and there remained under treatment and observation until July 11, 1955, when he was released or paroled to his attorney, Cyrus Lyche. Mr. Lyche arranged for plaintiff to enter a private mental hospital in Minnesota, and on or about July 12, 1955, plaintiff entered the latter hospital as a patient, and was released therefrom about September 9, 1955.

During plaintiff's stay at the Minnesota hospital, he received medical and psychiatric care, and for much of this time Mrs. Speirs stayed near the hospital. Certain other of plaintiff's relatives also visited him during this confinement.

While such a patient, on August 31, 1955, plaintiff secured a Minnesota marriage license, naming himself and Winnifred Speirs, the defendant herein, as principal parties.

After leaving the Minnesota hospital about September 9, 1955, the plaintiff, Mrs. Speirs and Mr. Lyche began the return trip to North Dakota, stopping en route for plaintiff to give a specimen for a blood test for social disease.

Prior to release from the Minnesota hospital, certain interested relatives filed a petition for the appointment of a guardian of the person and property of plaintiff, and a hearing on such petition was set by the county court for September 30, 1955. On September 16, 1955, plaintiff and defendant were married at Detroit Lakes, Minnesota. Following such marriage, and on the same day, the parties went to Fargo, North Dakota, where the services of an attorney, Mr. J. Gerald Nilles, was secured and an interview had for preparation and purpose of opposing the petition for guardianship. Apparently several interviews between plaintiff and Mr. Nilles took place prior to the guardianship hearing on September 30, 1955, at which date evidence was received by the county court, and the hearing continued until October 7, 1955, when further proof was adduced. On October 19, 1955, the county court issued its order dismissing petition for appointment of guardian for Bennie O. Johnson, and finding "that he is of sound mind; that he is competent to manage his own property and affairs; that it is not necessary or convenient that a guardian be appointed either for the person or of the estate of the said Bennie O. Johnson."

It appears that plaintiff and defendant lived together for a short time, although the evidence is not clear in this respect, and the parties then separated. The record contains charges and countercharges with respect to such separation, and it appears that plaintiff at one time commenced an action for divorce which was discontinued. Upon petition, a guardian, Duane Davis, was appointed for plaintiff on March 28, 1957, and the present action was instituted on April 1, 1957, which resulted in judgment for plaintiff, decreeing annulment of the marriage.

In this State, the formalities of the marriage relationship are wholly regulated and controlled by statute. Section 14-0301 NDRC 1943 provides that,

> Marriage is a personal relation arising out of a civil contract to which the consent of the parties is essential. The marriage relation shall be entered into, maintained, annulled, or dissolved only as provided by law.

See *Schumacher* v. *Great Northern Ry. Co.,* 23 N.D. 231, 136 N.W. 85.

The consent contemplated by the terms of the above statute is a then present assent, freely, voluntarily and understandingly given, representing a mutual intention of marital relationship by competent contracting parties. For a general discussion, see 35 Am.Jur., Marriage, Section 20, page 192 *et seq.*; 55 C.J.S. Marriage § 18b, p. 840 *et seq.*

It is a general rule that marriage is regarded with favor by the law and such proposition is subscribed to in North Dakota. *Woodward* v. *Blake,* 38 N.D. 38, 164 N.W. 156, L.R.A.1918A, 88.

In North Dakota the presumption, by statute, is "That a man and woman deporting themselves as husband and wife have entered into a lawful contract of marriage." Section 31-1103, subd. 30 NDRC 1943.

Where a marriage in fact has been proved, a presumption arises that such marriage is in all things valid. 34 A.L.R. 464 and 77 A.L.R. 730. And further, it is held, almost universal in application, that a person who has contracted a marriage is presumed to be mentally capable of legally contracting the marriage relationship. The burden of overcoming such presumption is upon the party attacking the validity of the marriage. 28 A.L.R. 652 and authorities there cited. 35 Am.Jur., Marriage, Section 113, page 251; 55 C.J.S. Marriage, § 58a, p. 937. While a presumption is not evidence of a fact and is not conclusive, yet presumptions are indulged in to supply the place of facts. *Starkenberg* v. *North Dakota Workmen's Compensation Bureau,* 73 N.D. 234, 13 N.W.2d 395.

A presumption is a rule of law, the office of which is to place the burden of going forward with the proof upon the party contesting the validity of the marriage, and as stated in *In re Drake's Estate,* 150 Neb. 568, 35 N.W.2d 417, 423, a presumption takes the place of evidence,

> ... unless and until evidence appears to overcome or rebut it, and when evidence sufficient in quality appears to rebut it the presumption disappears and thereafter the determination of the issues depends upon the evidence with the requirement as in other civil actions that the party having the affirmative of the issue involved in order to succeed shall sustain his position by a preponderance of the evidence.

*　　*　　*

Under the laws of this State:

> A marriage may be annulled by an action in the district court to obtain a decree of nullity for any of the following causes existing at the time of the marriage: . . .
> 3. That either party was of unsound mind, unless such party, after coming to reason, freely cohabited with the other as husband or wife; . . . . (Section 14-0401 NDRC 1943.)

Section 14-0307 NDRC 1943 provides:

> Marriage by a woman under the age of forty-five years or by a man of any age, unless he marries a woman over the age of forty-five years, is prohibited if such man or woman is a common drunkard, . . . an imbecile, a feeble minded person, an idiot, an insane person, . . . or a person afflicted . . . with any contagious venereal disease.

* * *

It is established in this State, that although marriage of those persons designated in Section 14-0307, *supra,* is prohibited, yet a marriage contracted by those persons is rendered merely voidable and not void. *First National Bank in Grand Forks* v. *North Dakota Workmen's Compensation Bureau, supra.* Only in the instances of incestuous marriage, or marriage by a person having a former husband or wife while such former marriage was then in force, is the marriage a nullity. *Michels* v. *Fennell,* 15 N.D. 188, 107 N.W. 53; *First National Bank in Grand Forks* v. *North Dakota Workmen's Compensation Bureau,* 68 N.W.2d 661.

The questioned marriage of the parties to this action, being voidable, must be directly attacked under an applicable statute. Such a direct attack upon the marriage in question has been made by the plaintiff pursuant to the annulment statute as above set forth.

At this point it should be noted that this is the second appearance of the parties in this Court and after long and bitter litigation the record is replete with recriminatory charges and statements which have no bearing upon the merits of this legal action. The issue here for determination is not the methods or character, good, bad or indifferent of the defendant wife or of other interested parties, nor whether the marriage in question in the opinion of relatives or others was hasty or ill advised, as common experience indicates that such many times is the wont of the human race, but rather the critical inquiry is whether Bennie O. Johnson, at the very date of such marriage, was of unsound mind thereby lacking sufficient mental capacity to contract a valid marriage; whether he as alleged in the complaint, was feeble-minded, was a common drunkard and afflicted with a contagious disease.

Examination of authorities discloses that there is no precise definition of the term "unsound mind," as employed by Section 14-0401, *supra,* and the difficulty of formulating a comprehensive definition long has been recognized. In a very early case, *Elzey* v. *Elzey,* 1857, 1 Houst., Del., 308, the following language was used which is appropriate to the case at hand:

> It would be dangerous, perhaps, as well as difficult to prescribe the precise degree of mental vigor, soundness, and capacity essential to the validity of such engagement; which, after all, in many cases, depends more on sentiments of mutual esteem, attachment, and affection, which the weakest may feel as well as the strongest intellects, than on the exercise of a clear, unclouded reason, or sound judgment, or intelligent discern-

ment and discrimination, and in which it differs in a very important respect from all other contracts.

While there has been a hesitancy on the part of the courts to judicially define the phrase "unsound mind," it is established that such term has reference to the mental capacity of the parties at the very moment of inception of the marriage contract. Ordinarily, lack of mental capacity, which renders a party incapable of entering into a valid marriage contract, must be such that it deprives him of the ability to understand the objects of marriage, its ensuing duties and undertakings, its responsibilities and relationship. There is a general agreement of the authorities that the terms "unsound mind" and "lack of mental capacity" carry greater import than eccentricity or mere weakness of mind or dullness of intellect. 28 A.L.R. 635 and cited authorities; 55 C.J.S. Marriage § 12, p. 824, and cited authorities; 35 Am.Jur., Marriage, Sections 17-18, page 189, *et seq.*

In 28 A.L.R. 635 we find an informative digest and compilation of authorities dealing with mental capacity to marry, wherein it is authoritatively stated that there is no ". . . general comprehensive test for determining the degree of mental capacity required to contract marriage . . . ," and this Court is of the opinion that the following criterion is the better rule:

> It seems that the best accepted test as to whether there is a mental capacity sufficient to contract a valid marriage, is whether there is a capacity to understand the nature of the contract and the duties and responsibilities which it creates. (28 A.L.R. 641; *Dunphy* v. *Dunphy,* 161 Cal. 380, 119 P. 512, 38 L.R.A., N.S., 818; *Kutch* v. *Kutch,* 88 Neb. 114, 129 N.W. 169),

and such issue must be resolved by the ascertained and established facts in each case. In this connection an action for annulment is predicated upon, and pertinent inquiry must be directed to, some ground existing at the very time of the marriage, *Kawabata* v. *Kawabata,* 48 N.D. 1160, 189 N.W. 237; *First National Bank in Grand Forks* v. *North Dakota Workmen's Compensation Bureau, supra,* and the burden of proof is upon the party attacking the validity of the marriage to prove such ground by clear, convincing and satisfactory evidence.

The scope of trial inquiry is set forth in 2 Wigmore on Evidence, 3rd Edition, Section 233, as follows:

> Courts are today universally agreed that both prior and subsequent mental condition, within some limits, are receivable for consideration; stress being always properly laid on the truth that these conditions are merely evidential towards ascertaining the mental condition at the precise time of the act in issue. There seems to be no agreed definition of the limit of time which such prior or subsequent condition is to be considered, and in the nature of things no definition is possible. The circumstances of each case must furnish the varying criterion, and the determination of the trial judge ought to be allowed to control.

Evidence of previous or subsequent mental condition, whether opinion or otherwise, is admissible only insofar as it may throw light on mental capacity at the precise moment of marriage.

* * *

During the trial of the instant action, defendant's counsel moved that judicial notice be taken of the guardianship proceedings of September 30, 1955, which resulted in the issuance of an order of the county court finding and determining sound mind and mental competency on the part of Johnson two weeks subsequent to the questioned marriage. Such order as duly issued by the county court in the exercise of its jurisdiction is entitled and accorded full recognition in view of Section 27-0739, *supra*. While such order is not *res judicata* nor a conclusive adjudication of plaintiff's mental capacity at the very time of prior actual marriage, nevertheless, such order was properly admissible for consideration as probative evidence of such mental capacity at the time in question, to be considered with all other evidence of the case [citations omitted].

The order of the county court is not conclusive as to the plaintiff's mental capacity. Tests judicially applied for a determination of incompetency in guardianship matters differ markedly from those applied for the determination of mental capacity to contract a marriage.

It frequently has been held in other jurisdictions, that a person even though under guardianship as an incompetent may have in fact sufficient mental capacity to validly contract marriage.

* * *

After a careful consideration and review of the entire record, we conclude that the ascertained and established evidence falls far short of proving a lack of requisite mental capacity to contract a valid marriage at the date thereof on the part of Bennie O. Johnson. The evidence however, does affirmatively establish that Bennie O. Johnson at the date of the marriage in question did possess sufficient mental capacity to validly contract such marriage, and that the marriage is not prohibited by any laws of this state.

* * *

Upon the entire record, the judgment of the District Court granting and decreeing unto plaintiff an annulment of marriage must be in all things reversed.

The judgment is reversed and the case remanded with directions to enter a judgment in favor of the defendant for dismissal of the action.

Sathre, C. J., and Morris, Burke and Teigen, JJ., concur.

Strutz, J., deeming himself disqualified, did not participate, Honorable Douglas B. Heen, one of the Judges of the Second Judicial District, sitting in his stead.

NOTE

Johnson, pp. 941–946, *supra, Larson,* pp. 934–936, *supra,* and *Homan,* pp. 936–937, *supra,* indicate that courts generally will presume a marriage valid unless it can be shown otherwise. What public policy does such a presumption advance? Does such a policy adequately protect the rights of handicapped persons to marry?

ADDITIONAL READING

Allen, Ferster, E., and Weihofen, H., *Mental Impairment and Legal Incompetency* (1968).

Andron, L, and Strum, M. L., "Is 'I Do' in the Repertoire of the Retarded?" 11 *M.R. Jour.* 31 (Feb. 1973).

Anno. "Mental Capacity to Marry," 82 *A.L.R.*2d 1040.

Bass, M., "Marriage for the Mentally Deficient," 2 *M.R.* 198 (Aug. 1964).

Bass, M., "Marriage, Parenthood, and Prevention of Pregnancy for the Mentally Deficient," 11 *Eugenics Quarterly* 96 (1964).

Bass, M., "Outline of Workshops—Marriage and Parenthood in Sexual Rights and Responsibilities of the Mentally Retarded," in *Proceedings of the Conference of the American Association on Mental Deficiency,* Region IX 136-37 (Bass, M., ed., rev. ed., 1975).

Brakel, S., and Rock, R., eds., *The Mentally Disabled and the Law,* 2nd ed. (1971).

55 C.J.S. § 12 "Marriage: Mental Capacity."

Calamari, J., and Perillo, J., "The Mentally Infirm" in *Contracts* 2nd ed., Ch. 8B (1977).

Carnahan, W., "Rights to Love, Marry and Bear Children, to Vote, Hold Property, Have a Job and Go to Court," *Legal Rights of the Mentally Handicapped,* Vol. 2, 1015 (1973).

Frotheringham, J., "The Concept of Social Competence as Applied to Marriage and Child Care in Those Classified as Mentally Retarded," 104 *C.M.A.J.* 813 (1971).

Fuller, C. "Washington's Statutory Restrictions on Marriage: Ripe for Legislative Review," 12 *Gonzaga L.R.* 403 (1977).

Note, "The Right of the Mentally Disabled to Marry: A Statutory Evaluation," 15 *J. Fam. L.* 463 (1976-77).

Mattinson, J., *Marriage and Mental Handicap* (1970).

Mickelson, P., "The Feeble-minded Parent: A Study of 90 Family Cases," 51 *Am. J. Ment. Defic.* 644 (1947).

C. RAISING CHILDREN

1. The Right at Stake

The constitutional status of the right to raise one's children is well settled. In *Ginsberg* v. *New York,* 390 U.S. 629 (1968), the Supreme Court observed:

> [C]onstitutional interpretation has consistently recognized that the parents' claim to authority in their own household to direct the rearing of their children is basic in the structure of our society (*Id.* at 639).

The fundamental nature of parental rights was further emphasized in *Wisconsin* v. *Yoder,* 406 U.S. 205 (1971):

> The history and culture of Western civilization reflect a strong tradition of parental concern for the nurture and upbringing of their children. This primary role of the parents in the upbringing of their children is now established beyond debate as an enduring American tradition (*Id.* at 232).

And in *Stanley* v. *Illinois,* 405 U.S. 645 (1972), the Supreme Court declared:

> The private interest here, that of a man in the children he has sired and raised, undeniably warrants deference and, absent of a powerful countervailing interest, protection. It is plain that the interest of a parent in the companionship, care, custody, and management of his or her children "come[s] to this Court with a momentum for respect lacking when appeal is made to liberties which derive merely from shifting economic arrangements." *Kovacs* v. *Cooper,* 336 U.S. 77, 95 (1949) (Frankfurter, J., concurring).
>
> The Court has frequently emphasized the importance of the family. The rights to conceive and to raise one's children have been deemed "essential," *Meyer* v. *Nebraska,* 262 U.S. 390, 399 (1923), "basic civil rights of man," *Skinner* v. *Oklahoma,* 316 U.S. 535, 541 (1942), and "[r]ights far more precious . . . than property rights," *May* v. *Anderson,* 345 U.S. 528, 533 (1953).
>
> * * *
>
> The integrity of the family unit has found protection in the Due Process Clause of the Fourteenth Amendment, *Meyer* v. *Nebraska, supra,* at 399, the Equal Protection Clause of the Fourteenth Amendment, *Skinner* v. *Oklahoma, supra,* at 541, and the Ninth Amendment, *Griswold* v. *Connecticut,* 381 U.S. 479, 496 (1965) (Goldberg, J., concurring). (*Id.* at 651.)

More recently, in *Quilloin* v. *Walcott,* 434 U.S. 246 (1978), a case dealing with the constitutionality of denying the father of an illegitimate child a voice in consenting to the adoption of the child, the Court underscored the fundamental status of parental rights:

> We have recognized on numerous occasions that the relationship between parent and child is constitutionally protected [citations omitted]. It is cardinal with us that "the custody, care and nurture of the child resides first in the parents, whose primary function and freedom include preparation for obligations the state can neither supply nor hinder." *Prince* v. *Massachusetts,* 321 U.S. 158, 166 (1944). And it is now firmly established that "freedom of personal choice in matters of . . . family life is one of the liberties protected by the Due Process Clause of the Fourteenth Amendment." *Cleveland Board of Education* v. *LaFleur,* 414 U.S. 632, 639-640 (1974). (*Id.* at 255.)

As we shall see, however, the status of the right to raise one's children as a fundamental constitutional right has not prevented this right from being denied to many handicapped parents. For, while parental rights are natural and fundamental, they are not absolute.

> To be sure, the power of the parents . . . may be subject to limitation . . . if it appears that parental decisions will jeopardize the health or safety of the child, or have a potential for significant social burdens. *Wisconsin* v. *Yoder,* 406 U.S. 205, 233-234 (1971).

Under their *parens patriae* power, states have claimed the authority to protect the "best interests" of children by imposing limitations upon parental rights and, in extreme situations, such as child abuse and neglect, by severing the parental rights entirely. In such situations, difficult issues are raised that involve the weighing of the basic, fundamental rights of parents against the welfare of the child.

2.   *Parens Patriae*, **Handicaps, and Parental Unfitness**

a.   **Proceedings and Factual Considerations**

STATE *ex rel.* PAUL v. DEPARTMENT OF PUBLIC WELFARE

Court of Appeals of Louisiana, Third Circuit, 1965
170 So.2d 549

EN BANC.

HOOD, Judge.

This is a habeas corpus proceeding instituted by Mildred Paul to obtain the custody of her infant child, Timothy Paul, who by order of court has been placed in the care and control of the Louisiana Department of Public Welfare. The suit was instituted against the Department of Public Welfare and against Carl Smith, chief probation officer of Rapides Parish, Louisiana. After a hearing, judgment was rendered rejecting plaintiff's demands, and plaintiff has appealed.

Plaintiff is a 35-year-old unmarried white woman. The child whose custody is being sought was born on March 3, 1964, at the Huey P. Long Charity Hospital in Pineville, Louisiana. A few days after the child was born plaintiff was summoned to appear at a hearing scheduled to be held in the juvenile court for Rapides Parish, Louisiana, to determine her right to the custody of the child. Following that hearing, judgment was rendered by the juvenile court on March 17, 1964, placing the custody of the child temporarily with the Department of Public Welfare of the State of Louisiana. The child has been in the custody of the Department of Public Welfare continuously since that time.

This habeas corpus proceeding was instituted on July 27, 1964. A hearing was held in due course, and judgment was rendered by the trial court on August 24, 1964, decreeing ''that the rule be recalled and that the judgment of March 17, 1964 remain unchanged.'' The trial judge assigned as reasons for that decree that ''the best interest of the child would be served by leaving him in the custody of the Department of Public Welfare as the petitioner cannot properly care for the child.''

Plaintiff contends that she is mentally and physically able to care for the child, and that the trial court erred in rejecting her demands for custody. Defendants contend that plaintiff is not mentally capable of caring for the child, and that it would be detrimental to the child to return him to the custody of the plaintiff.

The evidence shows that plaintiff is in good physical health. She has a congenital motor speech defect, however, which is of such a nature that it is impossible for her to speak words or to communicate orally with anyone other than her mother, who has learned to understand what plaintiff is trying to say. Plaintiff has a very low level of intelligence, having an I.Q. of about 45 and a mental age of about 7.3 years. The experts in psychology who examined her classify her as either a low-grade moron or a high-grade imbecile. Although plaintiff testified that she went to the seventh grade in school, she is unable to read and write, other than to sign her name, and it is clear from the evidence that she would not be able to qualify for the seventh grade in any ordinary school.

Plaintiff lives in a small house with her 72-year-old mother and with two of her sisters, and both of these sisters have a lower level of intelligence than does plaintiff. Her older sister, who is 44 years of age, suffered polio while a young child and has been paralyzed on her left side since that time. This sister also has a speech defect similar to that of plaintiff, and she has an I.Q. of 31 and a mental age of between 2.8 and 4.7 years. She is definitely an imbecile. Plaintiff's younger sister is 31 years of age, and she has an I.Q. of 34 and a mental age of 5.8 years. The mother is classified as mentally dull, but she has a higher intelligence quotient than any of the daughters.

The house in which these four adults live is a small, three-room, unpainted frame house, located in a wooded rural area about 14 or 15 miles from the city of Alexandria, which they rent for $10.00 per month. The house is equipped with gas and electricity, but the water which they need is supplied by a pump located outside the house with a rubber hose leading from this pump into the building, and water is obtained inside the house by operating a nozzle on the end of this hose. The furniture or appliances in the house include four double beds, an electric washing machine, a woodstove and a gas stove. The evidence indicates that in spite of their mental limitations, plaintiff and the other occupants of the house keep the house in a fairly clean and orderly condition, and that plaintiff generally dresses neatly.

Prior to the time plaintiff moved to this home, about four years ago, she lived with her parents and other members of the family near Columbia, Louisiana. While living there she was required by her father to work in the fields from early hours in the morning until late at night. The family apparently lived in poverty, and plaintiff had no opportunity to go anywhere. Psychologists and lay witnesses indicate that she is able to perform work in a field, such as picking vegetables and fruits, hoeing cotton and other similar types of work, without supervision. She also is able to cook and to can or preserve fruits and vegetables. She unquestionably loves the child and wants to obtain custody of it.

Neither plaintiff nor any of the other occupants of the house are employed, and they have no income or means of support other than the assistance which is given to them by the Department of Public Welfare. Although plaintiff may be capable of performing work of some menial type, none of the other members of the household are capable of holding any type of employment at all.

Dr. Ralph Ware, a psychiatrist employed at Central Louisiana State Hospital, examined plaintiff on two occasions, once shortly before the child was born and a second time after the birth of the child. Although he did not test her I.Q., he concluded that "she is a borderline mentally defected" person. He testified that she walks well, handles her hands well, knows the time of day, knows the difference between hot and cold, knows the day of the week, and she can perform common ordinary tasks at home well, such as cleaning, cooking, canning, bathing and dressing. In his opinion, plaintiff could handle the bringing up of this child. He feels there would be no danger to the child, and that plaintiff "would do the best she could" to raise him. He concedes that plaintiff could not teach the child to speak, that she could not help him with his school lessons, and that the environment is not good, but he feels that plaintiff can take care of the physical needs of the child, and that she can provide a mother's love.

Dr. Robert H. Cassell, chief of psychological services at Pinecrest State

School, examined plaintiff and her two sisters on January 13, 1963. He feels that plaintiff can give the child love and affection, and could care for it as long as only routine care is required. In his opinion, however, plaintiff would not be able to function if something of a non-routine nature occurred. She, for instance, could not determine when the child was sick, what is dangerous and what is not dangerous, or when the child should be taken to a doctor. He thinks the probability of plaintiff being able to nurse and raise her child are poor. He feels that she might routinely nurse the baby with a bottle, but he has great concern as to whether she would be able to cope with an emergency.

Mr. Bernard Phelps, a psychologist who is serving as psychological assistant at Pinecrest State School, examined plaintiff on January 13, 1964. He feels very strongly that plaintiff is mentally incapable of taking care of the child. He testified that awarding custody of the child to plaintiff would result in "utter havoc for the child's concern, for the parent's concern, and some question as to the survival of the infant."

The lay evidence is conflicting as to whether plaintiff is or is not able to care for the child. Four neighbors or acquaintances of plaintiff testified to the effect that plaintiff is able to count money, that she dresses neatly, that she does not conduct herself in a disorderly manner, and that the home is kept reasonably clean. One of these witnesses stated that she feels that plaintiff is able to care for a child, and that she would have no hesitancy in leaving her own grandchild under plaintiff's care. A children's case worker for the Department of Public Welfare testified that the child is presently being cared for in a foster home provided by the Department of Public Welfare and that he is receiving good treatment. She also stated that the child has a tendency to upper respiratory infection, that he has been sick frequently, that it has been necessary to have him treated by a pediatrician, and that the child was hospitalized for four days on one occasion. A welfare visitor, who is employed by the Department of Public Welfare and who has visited in the home, expressed the opinion that plaintiff is not able to care for the child, and that the child is in need of protection because of the environment and the mental limitation of the mother.

On this evidence, together with the testimony of plaintiff and of her mother (plaintiff's testimony being interpreted by her mother), the trial judge rejected plaintiff's demands.

The law is settled that a mother has a right to the custody of her child as against third persons, but that this right must yield to the superior right of the state to deprive her of such custody in the event she is morally, mentally or otherwise unfit or incapable of caring for the child, or the welfare of the child requires it. [Citations omitted.]

The love of a mother for her child is one of the most powerful of human emotions, and in custody cases it is a most important factor to consider in determining what is best for the child's welfare. The mere fact that the defendants may be better able than the mother, financially and otherwise, to take care of the child does not warrant the court in refusing to recognize the right of the mother to the custody of her child. *State ex rel. Monroe* v. *Ford,* 164 La. 149, 113 So. 798. In a contest between a mother and a third person for the custody of a child, the mother is entitled to obtain custody unless it is shown that she is morally, mentally or otherwise unfit or incapable of caring for the child, or that for some other reason it would be detrimental to the child's health, safety or welfare to place him under the care of the mother. *State ex rel. Sevier* v. *Sevier, et al.*, 141 La. 60, 74 So. 630; and *State* v. *Miller, supra*.

The burden, of course, is on those resisting the parent's demand for custody to show that the latter is disqualified or unfit to have the custody, that the parent is incapable of caring for the child, or that it would be detrimental to the child's welfare to place him under the care of the parent [citations omitted].

Although the natural parent's right to the custody of his or her child is superior to that of another relative or stranger, courts should and will consider the mental health of the parent along with other factors in arriving at a custody award best serving the welfare of the child. [Citations omitted].

*   *   *

In matters involving the custody of children, we particularly give great weight to the findings of the trial judge and we are reluctant to reverse his conclusions, because he has had an opportunity to observe the persons who are claiming the custody and the witnesses who testified at the trial [citations omitted].

The evidence in the instant suit convinces us that plaintiff loves her child and would be able to provide him with routine physical care. The evidence also establishes, however, that she would not be able to provide some of the training which the child must have, such as the ability to speak, or to properly care for him in case of sickness or emergencies. It would be unrealistic, of course, to assume that no illness or emergencies would occur in the raising of a child. The evidence also indicates to us that the home environment, with two mentally retarded adults besides the mother living in the same small house, would be detrimental to the physical, moral and mental welfare of the child.

Under the facts presented in the instant suit we must agree with the trial judge that plaintiff is not able, primarily because of her mental limitations, to care for the child, and that the welfare and best interest of the child would be served by allowing him to remain in the custody and care of the defendants.

We know that the plaintiff in this case loves her child, and we assume that in spite of her limitations she will experience the deep heartache which must accompany a judgment of this kind. It is with considerable regret, therefore, that we find it necessary to reject her demands. A judgment involving custody, however, is always revocable where conditions warrant its modification. If there should be a substantial improvement in plaintiff's ability to care for the child and in the home environment, then it may be that in subsequent proper proceedings a modification of the judgment will be justified.

For the reasons herein set out, the judgment appealed from is affirmed. All costs of this appeal are assessed to plaintiff appellant.

Affirmed.

Tate, Judge (concurring).

The majority opinion has fairly stated the surrounding facts concerning the serious problem before the court: Should a mother of low intelligence be deprived of her child because a more favorable environment might produce a better chance of favorable development for the child?

However, I must frankly state that, based on the transcript of evidence alone, I think it would be manifestly wrong to deprive this mother of her child, were the child still with the mother.

The mother is a healthy and clean young woman of 35, who keeps house, cooks for her sisters, and manages her shopping and other normal activities of life. She has no vicious or immoral habits, and aside from the birth of this illegitimate child apparently has lived a respectable life. While it sounds bad to say that she is a low-grade moron with an IQ of 45-50, on the other hand the evidence indicates that there are many, many low-grade morons living normal lives in paying jobs—that a person of such a capacity has the ability to care for herself, to take care of children (in fact, the State Colony uses low-grade morons to take care of retarded children left there), and to fend for themselves in the routine activities of life. Perhaps for a lay person a more accurate impression of the mother's mental capacity is conveyed by the classification of her under another accepted psychologic scale, as "borderline mentally defected," Tr. 56, or one with "moderate mental deficiency," Tr. 57.

The testimony of the mother herself at the trial is sensible and straightforward and seems to corroborate the testimony of an examining psychiatrist (Dr. Ware) that the mother has good judgment.

A further complication here, however, is that the mother and additionally her two sisters have a speech defect. (This no doubt gave social workers casually observing her an impression of greater mental deficiency than was justified.) The trial court apparently gave this speech defect great weight, as its questioning was concerned with whether this might not handicap the development of normal speech in the child, and how could these moronic parents and guardians help the child with homework, or provide a normal social growth for the child.

All these are undoubtedly matters of great concern. It is difficult not to agree that a better environment for the child could be provided than the mother's home. But this is not the legal question: for the mother's paramount right to custody must be respected unless such would be detrimental to the child's health, safety, or welfare.

In America, unlike in communistic or other totalitarian countries, the state's function is not all-powerfully to rearrange families and take control of children just because some social workers (however well-intentioned) feel it might be better. The right of parents to their own children comes from God, not the state. In the absence of abandonment of this right by the parent, or active detriment to the child, the state just simply cannot disrupt the God-created relationship of parent and child.

Because parents are poor or stupid or have speech defects, can be no reason by themselves to take a child from its mother. It may well be that a given child might have had a better chance in life had it been born in a different home, but that again by itself does not give the state the power to deprive a mother of her child.

The evidence is very strong in favor of the mother's ability to take care of the child suitably in accordance with their station of life. Four neighbors very much familiar with the mother and her home are positive to this effect, as is the only psychiatrist testifying, a Dr. Ware employed at the state mental hospital.

The chief of psychological services there, a Ph.D. psychologist, Dr. Cassell, was of the contrary opinion; but based only on the idea that in emergencies of a non-routine nature the mother might not function properly, or might not recognize serious illness. This very fair expert witness also stated frankly, "there is no question in my mind that this kind of person can give love and affection [to children] and there is no argument as to that."

The other evidence of maternal incapacity is, to me, almost weightless: a welfare worker who worked a month or so with the mother when she was pregnant and visited her four to six times, Tr. 95 (after the welfare department had *already* determined the child should be removed from the mother despite her desire to keep the child); a psychologist who tested the sister (*not* the mother), but who incidentally saw the mother for a matter of twenty minutes (Tr. 129) while she was in a waiting room (this was the witness who testified as to the "utter havoc for the child's welfare" posed by the mother's custody! Tr. 130); some welfare department case reports, hearsay (and anonymous hearsay at that), concerning the unfavorable environment—which are refuted by the only sworn evidence in the record, the testimony of the four neighbors.

No reported case in Louisiana, nor elsewhere so far as I have been able to ascertain, has yet held that a person of low intelligence but capable of taking care of herself and her child (for this sums up what a borderline defective or a low-grade moron is) should be deprived of custody of her child on account of that low intelligence. Nor has any decision yet held that a parent with a speech defect cannot retain custody of her child because the child's ability to learn to speak might be impaired. For instance, *State ex rel. Mouton* v. *Williams,* 222 La. 457, 62 So.2d 641, relied upon by the majority, held that the mother might be deprived of custody of the child because of a mental condition; but the mental condition there involved was a manic-depressive psychosis. It was the possibility of homicidal tendencies or physical harm to the child or the child's subjection to severe physical, mental, and emotional strain that concerned the court there. 62 So.2d 642.

And there is another factor that has disturbed me.

Here, the child has been taken from its family and placed in a foster boarding home which boards other welfare children in return for subsistence payments by the welfare department. There is no evidence whatsoever as to the child's individual capacities or possible defects, and perhaps none is possible at such an early age.

But, picturing the child as a normal middle-class child, we have assumed that any environment at all is better than that which the loving mother can afford this baby boy. But what if the child is of the same physical and mental class as its mother? Is it really better to board it out with strangers caring for it and other children for compensation, than to leave such a child in the only home in the whole wide world in which mother-love will recognize the miraculous wonder that God has breathed life and a soul and a need to love and to be loved into this misshapen clay? In which mother-love will see this retarded child, not as a creature to be boarded in return for pay, but as a wonderful being and the shining center of its tiny, family world in which it is warmly loved?

And even though the baby boy might be normal, he may indeed have better social development going through life as a paid boarder in the welfare's foster homes in which he is put as he proceeds towards adulthood (for he cannot be adopted without the mother's consent); but can we be truly certain that we have without doubt done the best thing for the child's welfare by sentencing him to an emotionally empty life, a waif without family, not harbored within the cherished security of the love of his own mother and of his own family?

Another disturbing factor is that before the child was even born, social workers, no doubt well-intentioned, had decided that the baby should be removed from its mother after its birth despite her objections. Immediately after birth, the child was taken, and at a custody hearing at which the mother did not appear (in effect, an *ex parte* hearing), on the apparent basis of hearsay case reports of a social worker (which the sworn evidence of neighbors at the trial refutes, the only uncontradicted sworn first-hand evidence in the record). We do not have an instance where the mother had custody of the child and was unable to take care of it; the child was taken from the mother immediately after birth, on fears that the mother might not be able to care properly for her child, before the mother had a chance to prove her capacity or incapacity to take care of her own child.

But this is the dilemma in which the courts are placed: We know (from hearsay evidence to this effect of a social worker) that the infant is adjusted and in good health in its present environment. We have the testimony of a respected and apparently fair psychologist witness (Dr. Cassell) that he does not think the mother's intelligence is sufficient in case of emergencies to take care of her child. Despite expert medical testimony (Dr. Ware), contrary to these forebodings, the strong testimony of neighbors to the contrary, and also the more or less common sense impression from the testimony that this mother should at least have been given a chance to care for her child and would probably have been able to do so successfully—yet we are faced with the fait accompli that the child *is* doing well in its present environment, and *might* not do so as well and *might* even be endangered (if an emergency illness arose) if returned to its mother's care.

On these narrow grounds just stated, and also because the trial court which saw and heard the witnesses might have some reason to discount the testimony favorable to the mother which reads so strongly in the transcript, I concur for the present in the dismissal of the mother's claim for the return of her child.

NOTE

How do the factual matters discussed in Judge Tate's concurring opinion square with the holding of the majority? Does Judge Tate's reliance upon the fact that the child is already in an environment other than the home of his mother and is doing well in that environment provide sufficient justification for his concurrence in the result reached in the majority opinion? If a child is wrongly taken from a parent, should the fact that the child is happy or well adjusted in the improperly obtained placement be grounds for not returning the child to the natural parent?

IN RE MCDONALD

Supreme Court of Iowa, 1972
201 N.W.2d 447

This matter was heard and determined by the full bench.
MASON, Justice.
This is an appeal from an order of the municipal court of the city of Davenport

sitting as the juvenile court of Scott County terminating the relationship of parent and child existing between David McDonald, father and Diane McDonald, mother, and their twin daughters, Joyce and Melissa McDonald. The parents challenge sufficiency of the evidence to support the order.

A Scott County juvenile probation officer had filed a petition seeking termination of the relationship in which it was alleged the relationship should be terminated in that the parents are unfit by reasons of conduct found by the court likely to be detrimental to the physical or mental health or morals of children as defined in section 232.41(2)(d) and for the further reason that following an adjudication of dependency, March 3, 1969, reasonable efforts under the direction of the court had failed to correct the conditions leading to the termination. Section 232.41(2)(e).

Termination of the relationship between the parents and a child is controlled in this factual situation by sections 232.41 through 232.50, The Code.

Section 232.41 provides in part:

> When relationship changed. The court may upon petition terminate the relationship between parent and child:
> 1. . . .
> 2. If the court finds that one or more of the following conditions exist:
> a. . . .
> b. . . .
> c. . . .
> d. That the parents are unfit by reasons of debauchery, intoxication, habitual use of narcotic drugs, repeated lewd and lascivious behavior, or other conduct found by the court likely to be detrimental to the physical or mental health or morals of the child.
> e. That following an adjudication of neglect or dependency, reasonable efforts under the direction of the court have failed to correct the conditions leading to the termination.

The court appointed an attorney to represent the parents at the hearing required by section 232.44. He has continued to represent them on their appeal to this court. Separate counsel was also appointed to represent the children at the hearing. He takes no part in this appeal. The hearing commenced June 24, 1970 was adjourned until July 22 and concluded on that day. Findings of fact were filed August 8 and decree August 10.

The court, after summarizing the evidence produced at the hearing, noted in its findings of fact that the evidence compelled a finding "that Diane McDonald, primarily because of her very low IQ, is simply not able to give to these twins the proper care and attention, including but not limited to the stimulation which the twins need and to which they responded almost immediately when placed in the foster homes. Nor is there any reasonable probability that Diane McDonald would be able to substantially improve her past performance with the twins, should they continue for a further period even as long as a year, in foster care. The Court is reluctantly convinced that because of this mother's very low IQ she could never adequately take the proper care of these twins or at least provide them with the stimulation in her home that they must have to grow and develop into normal, healthy children. Unfortunately, although David McDonald is able to do considerably better, the best interests of the twins requires a termination as to him as well."

The court concluded,

2. That the relationship now existing between David McDonald, father, and Diane McDonald, mother, and Joyce McDonald and Melissa McDonald, children, should be terminated because the parents are unfit by reason of conduct found by the Court to be detrimental to the physical and mental health of said children, as defined in section 232.41(2)(d). . . .

3. That the relationship now existing between David McDonald, father, and Diane McDonald, mother, and Joyce McDonald and Melissa McDonald, children should be terminated because following an adjudication of dependency on March 3, 1969, reasonable efforts under the direction of the Court have failed to correct the conditions leading to such findings, as provided in section 232.41(2)(e).

* * *

As a witness David repeatedly expressed a desire to have the twins returned to him and his wife. He testified he had had experience in bathing and feeding his mother's small children and declared a willingness to help with the children in the evenings after coming home from work.

He told of an arrangement made with a 25-year-old lady who lives across the hall from his apartment to help take care of the twins and the third child born to this marriage for the first few months in order to get the children on schedule and assist his wife and teach her how to care for the children in the event the children were returned to the McDonald home. This lady had two small children of her own, the older being approximately two and a half years. She and her husband were separated. Whether she is in the process of seeking dissolution is not clear from the record. He felt he could pay her $15 a week from his wages.

David said he had also made arrangements before the children were taken to the foster homes through General Housekeeping to send a lady in from 7 a.m. until he arrived home in the evenings to coach his wife and give her child care training but when the twins were placed in foster homes this did not materialize.

* * *

Although there has been considerable improvement in Diane's ability to keep house, there still remained at the time of the termination hearing held more than two years after the birth of the twins a serious doubt as to Diane's ability to cope with the situation requiring guidance and to perform those things a mother must do in raising children.

As noted in the quoted portion of its findings, the juvenile court was "reluctantly convinced that because of this mother's very low I.Q. she could never adequately take the proper care of these twins or at least provide them with the stimulation in her home that they must have to grow and develop into normal healthy children." There is substantial evidence to support this finding. [Three witnesses] expressed doubt as to Diane's ability to perform the functions of a mother because of her very low IQ.

Since there is no reasonable probability Diane would be able to substantially improve her past performance in caring for the children, the longer they remain in foster homes the more difficult adoption will become.

By the time this opinion is filed the twins will be four and half years old. They should have proper guidance and a healthy mental atmosphere from those who have their custody. *In re Augustus,* 158 N.W.2d at 629, and authorities cited.

When the twins were seen in May before the hearing they appeared to be normal children in all respects, mentally and physically.

II. This court has repeatedly stated that in matters of this kind the primary consideration is the welfare and best interests of the child. While there is a presumption that the best interests of the child will be served by leaving it with its parents, this is not conclusive. The State, as *parens patriae,* has the duty to see that every child within its borders receives proper care and treatment. *Re Interest of Morrison Children v. State,* 259 Iowa at 311, 144 N.W.2d at 103 and *In re Interest of Yardley,* 260 Iowa at 268, 149 N.W.2d at 167-168.

In equity matters, such as this, where our review is *de novo* it is our responsibility to review the facts as well as the law and adjudicate rights anew on those propositions properly presented, provided issue has been raised and error, if any, preserved in the course of the trial court's proceedings. *Rouse v. Rouse,* 174 N.W.2d 660, 666 (Iowa 1970). Therefore, we conclude, as did the juvenile court, that the best interests of the twins require termination of the relationship existing between David McDonald, father, and Diane McDonald, mother, and Joyce and Melissa McDonald, children.

The case is therefore

Affirmed.

All Justices concur, except LeGrand, J., who takes no part.

NOTES

1.   In summarizing the evidence presented at trial, the court observed:

> David had been given the Wechsler Adult Intelligence Scale January 21, 1965 and recorded a full scale IQ of 74. David had quit school in the eleventh grade. Diane had been tested September 21, 1964 and her full scale score IQ was 47. We are not told about her background except that she came from "a very cruel and immoral home" (at 201 N.W.2d 449).

Notice that David's IQ score, although below average, is in the "normal" range.

2.   Both the *Paul* and *McDonald* decisions rested largely upon the presumption that people with low intelligence quotients cannot provide adequate parental care. Is evidence of mental deficiency and inability to care for the child in each case sufficient to justify the result reached by the court? What is the "best interest" test relied upon by each court? Does it provide a constitutionally valid basis for decision in such cases?

3.   Many medical and psychiatric authorities would dispute the presumption that influenced the *Paul* and *McDonald* cases, i.e., that mentally retarded parents cannot rear children adequately. See Frotheringham, "The Concept of Social Competence as Applied to Marriage and Child Care in Those Classified as Mentally Retarded," 104 *C.M.A.J.* 813, 816 (1971); and Kanner, L., *A Miniature Textbook of Feeblemindedness* 4-5 (1949). One practitioner has observed:

> In my 20 years of psychiatric work with thousands of children and their parents, I have seen percentually at least as many "intelligent" adults unfit to rear their offspring as I have seen such "feebleminded" adults. I have—and many others have—come to

the conclusion that, to a large extent independent of the I.Q., fitness for parenthood is determined by emotional involvements and relationships.[c]

The relationship between mental retardation and fitness for parenthood is discussed in Murdock, C., "Sterilization of the Retarded: A Problem or a Solution?" 62 *Cal. L. Rev.* 917, 928-932 (1974). The author concludes: "Lack of fitness for parenthood is not characteristic of all retarded persons, nor is this disability limited only to the retarded." *Id.* at 932.

4. *State ex rel. Paul* was an appeal from a habeas corpus proceeding, while *In re McDonald* was an appeal from a juvenile court proceeding. Should the posture in which each case was tendered make a difference in the outcome? Is it of any significance that Mildred Paul's child had been taken from her before she had any practical opportunity to begin caring for the child?

5. The statute interpreted in *In re McDonald* is typical of legislation found in many states. Although it lacks any specific provision for termination of parental rights based upon the parent's inability to care for a child because of mental deficiency, it was used for that purpose.

6. *State* v. *McMaster,* 486 P.2d 567 (Oreg. 1971), involved a proceeding to terminate the parental rights of parents who were alleged to be "unfit by reason of conduct or condition seriously detrimental to the child," *id.* at 568. Although upholding the legality of such a standard of parental unfitness, the Supreme Court of Oregon held that the standard was not met by the evidence in the case:

> We are of the opinion that the state of the McMaster family is duplicated in hundred of thousands of American families,—transiency and incapacity, poverty and instability. The witness was undoubtedly correct when he stated that living in the McMaster's household would not "allow this child to maximize her potential." However, we do not believe the legislature contemplated that parental rights could be terminated because the natural parents are unable to furnish surroundings which would enable the child to grow up as we would desire all children to do. When the legislature used the phrase, "seriously detrimental to the child," we believe that they had in mind a more serious and uncommon detriment than that caused by the conduct of parents such as the McMasters. The best interests of the child are paramount; however, the courts cannot sever the McMaster's parental rights when many thousands of children are being raised under basically the same circumstances as this child. The legislature had in mind conduct substantially departing from the norm and unfortunately for our children the McMaster's conduct is not such a departure (*Id.* at 572-573).

Is this an accurate appraisal of the state of parenthood in modern America?

To what extent were the courts in *McDonald* and *Paul* influenced by concerns articulated by the *McMaster* court? Should material or intellectual impoverishment of the home environment be a factor in determining whether parental rights should be terminated? If the state may not institutionalize a person, thereby depriving him of his right to liberty in order to improve his standard of living, *O'Connor* v. *Donaldson, supra,* pp. 618-629, may the state terminate parental rights, thereby depriving the parent of his right to raise his child, for the same purpose?

---

[c]Bligh, R., "Sterilization and Mental Retardation," 51 *A.B.A.J.* 1059, 1062 (1965).

Lewis v. Davis

Superior Court of Chatham County, Georgia, 1974
No. D-26437, July 19, 1974

Judge Cheatham.

Plaintiff, the mother of an infant born on April 19, 1974, filed a petition for habeas corpus against defendant seeking custody of said infant. Defendants had previously obtained temporary custody of the infant by virtue of an *ex parte* order under the Juvenile Code.

At the hearing defendants admitted that they had not conformed to all the technical requirements of Georgia Code § 24A-1401 and § 24A-1701, but took the position that the habeas corpus petition opens up the question of whether or not the plaintiff mother is legally fit to have custody of the child, and if not, what disposition should be made of the infant.

I agree that the question on habeas corpus is, first, whether or not the natural parent is a fit parent and qualified to have custody of the infant and, if not, who or what agency of government should have custody. For this reason, the oversight of defendant in complying with the aforesaid Code Sections is immaterial.

The evidence in the case indicated that the plaintiff is sixteen years old, is marginally mentally retarded, and became the mother of a child born out of wedlock while under foster care with the Department of Family and Children Services of the Department of Human Resources of the State of Georgia. The infant was taken from the possession of the mother shortly after the birth of the child by an *ex parte* order. Defendants maintain that the mother is not capable of properly caring for the child without the supportive care and training of the Department of Family and Children Services. Defendants further maintain that if custody of the child is given to the mother, that small financial resources will be available to the mother, whereas, on the other hand, if custody is given to the Department of Family and Children services, considerable additional funds would be available. Defendants further maintain that they have placed the infant with the mother and for all intents and purposes she has full possession of the child if not legal custody, and that it would be in the best interest of the child to place custody of the infant formally with the Department of Family and Children Services.

The evidence further indicated that plaintiff has been an attentive mother to the child and has been receptive to training given to date by the Department, and the probability of her becoming an adequate mother to care for the child with continued training and supervision for an unspecified period of time is good.

Several witnesses expressed the opinion that if this mother were not under foster care, she would not have the resources, training, and capabilities at present to adequately care for the child, and that it would be to the best interest of the child under those circumstances to have custody taken from the mother and placed in the Department or elsewhere.

The Court is faced with the dilemma of a mother who becomes qualified in that capacity because of the supportive services of the Department of Family and Children Services and not because of her own present state of development.

However, I am of the opinion that the facts must be taken as they exist and not what they might be had the mother been living under other circumstances. The facts are that the mother is in the custody of the Department of Family and Children Services and that she is in a home setting now in which both she and the child are receiving adequate care. Further, the mother is adequately performing under the present controlled circumstances and will probably remain in the care of the Department for several years.

Under the circumstances, I am of the opinion that insufficient facts have been shown to permit the Court to deprive the mother of formal legal custody of the child.

IT IS, THEREFORE, CONSIDERED, ORDERED, AND ADJUDGED that plaintiff's petition for habeas corpus be granted and that the custody of the infant child aforesaid be and the same is hereby placed in plaintiff, Minnie Lee Lewis.

NOTES

1. In *Lewis* the factor or borderline retardation was evident, as it was in *McDonald* and *Paul, supra*. However, the *Lewis* court's order rests upon the premise that custody will remain in the natural parent unless sufficient facts can be established to prove that the parent is unfit because of mental deficiency. Is this the same premise that formed the basis of Judge Tate's concurring opinion in *Paul, supra?*

2. If Minnie Lewis had not been receiving supportive services from the Department of Family and Children Services, would custody of her child have been returned to her?

3. Before reaching their decisions which terminated the parent-child relationship, should the *Paul* and *McDonald* courts have been compelled to find that adequate parental care could not have been provided even with supportive services like those available to Minnie Lewis?

PEOPLE IN INTEREST OF M.A. v. P.A.

Colorado Court of Appeals, 1974
529 P.2d 333

STERNBERG, Judge.

An order of the district court terminated the parental rights of a mother, P.A., in her eight-year-old son, M.A. She appeals. We reverse and remand for further findings consistent with the views hereinafter set forth.

Hospital reports and social histories were used as evidence by agreement of the parties. They showed both that the mother had a history of mental and emotional disorders requiring hospitalization on several occasions, and that the child had been neglected. Based upon this evidence, a decree adjudicating M.A. to be "dependent and neglected" was entered by the district court on June 14, 1972. M.A. was taken from his mother and placed in a foster home. P.A. began receiving treatment at the Colorado State Hospital. Thereafter, on February 21, 1973, the court severed the parental ties.

No question has been raised about, and no appeal taken from the determination adjudicating M.A. to be a dependent and neglected child as defined by 1967 Perm. Supp., C.R.S.1963, 22-1-3(19). Rather, P.A. focuses her attack on the termination proceeding and urges that it was the duty of the court to balance the rights of the parent and child, that it is the duty of the courts and the Department of Social Services to provide supportive services for the mother before terminating her rights in the child, and that the court did not have before it sufficient facts to justify termination of parental rights.

The statute under which the rights were terminated, 1967 Perm.Supp., C.R.S.1963, 22-3-11(2)(a), provides that a decree terminating parental rights may be entered when the court determines it to be in the best interest and welfare of the child. Balanced against that portion of the children's code, however, is 1967 Perm.Supp., C.R.S.1963, 22-1-2, which codifies the policy of the state in reference to preservation of the family and protection of the home as follows:

> 1(a) The general assembly hereby declares that the purposes of this chapter are:
>
> (b) To secure for each child, subject to these provisions, such care and guidance, preferably in his own home, as will best serve his welfare and the interests of society;
>
> (c) To preserve and strengthen family ties whenever possible, including improvement of the home environment;
>
> (d) To remove a child from the custody of his parents only when his welfare and safety or protection of the public would otherwise be endangered. . . .''

P.A. argues that the facts of this case show the need for an exception to the statutory direction to consider the best interests and welfare of the child as being controlling. If a parent is mentally incompetent to care for her child, respondent would require the courts to give more weight to the parent's interest in the child than is accorded to the interests of the child itself, and, before permitting a termination of such a parent's rights, she would place the burden on the state to provide supportive services to the parent. This argument is based on the statutory language which states that the purpose of the children's code is to ''strengthen family ties whenever possible, including improvement of the home environment.'' We cannot, even if we were so inclined, enunciate such an amendment to the statute.

In People in Interest of K.S. and M.S., Colo.App., 515 P.2d 130, this court set forth specific guidelines providing that parental rights should be terminated only where:

> [T]here is a history of severe and continuous neglect by the parent . . . a substantial probability of future deprivation, and . . . under no reasonable circumstances can the welfare of the child be served by a continuation of the legal relationship of the child with that parent.

These guidelines were approved by the Supreme Court in *In re People in Interest of M.M.,* Colo., 520 P.2d 128. In that case the court stated:

> To determine that the best interests and welfare of a dependent or neglected child would be served by a termination of parental rights, the trial court must find that the condition which resulted in the determination that the child is dependent and neglected will in all probability continue into the future. Further, the court must find that under no reasonable circumstances can the welfare of the child be served by a continuation of the parent-child relationship. This second test requires the court to explore and specifically eliminate alternative remedies.

The only findings made by the trial court at the time of the dependency hearing, and the later termination proceeding, related to the best interest of the child. As the basis for this determination, however, the trial court must follow the guidelines and make the findings required by *In Re People in Interest of M.M., supra,* and *People in Interest of K.S. and M.S., supra.*

Since the court did not make the required findings, and since the trial judge is deceased, the cause is remanded for a new trial on the issue of termination of parental rights.

ENOCH and PIERCE, JJ., concur.

NOTE

The *M.A.* court refuses to require the state Department of Social Services to provide supportive services to parents before seeking a termination of parental rights. Yet, the court requires the lower courts to "explore and specifically eliminate alternative remedies." Is there a meaningful difference between the two?

IN RE APPEAL IN PIMA COUNTY, JUVENILE ACTION NO. S-111

Court of Appeals of Arizona, Division 2, 1975
25 Ariz.App. 380, 543 P.2d 809

KRUCKER, Judge.

A juvenile court order severing the parental relationship between a mother and child is the subject of this appeal taken by the mother.

A.R.S. Sec. 8-533 includes as grounds for termination of the parent-child relationship (1) that the parent has neglected the child and (2) that the parent is unable to discharge the parental responsibilities because of mental illness or mental deficiency and there are reasonable grounds to believe that the condition will continue for a prolonged indeterminate period. The juvenile court found that these two grounds for termination existed and ordered severance. The mother now challenges the sufficiency of the evidence to support the court's findings.

* * *

The right to custody and control of one's children is a fundamental one. *Stanley v. Illinois,* 405 U.S. 645, 92 S.Ct. 1208, 31 L.Ed.2d 551 (1972); *Appeal in Pima County, Juvenile Action No. J-46735 v. Howard,* 112 Ariz. 170, 540 P.2d 642 (1975). We recently pointed out that severance of the parent-child relationship is a serious matter and should not be considered a panacea: rather, it should be resorted to only when concerted effort to preserve the relationship fails. *See, Arizona State Dept. of Economic Security v. Mahoney,* 24 Ariz.App. 534, 540 P.2d 153 (1975). In *Caruso v. Superior Court,* 100 Ariz. 167, 412 P.2d 463 (1966), it was held that a parent's right to his child could only be overcome by a showing of unfitness.

We are of the opinion that severance of the relationship between this mother and her child was at this juncture erroneous. We are not bound to accept the lower court's findings of fact when, as here, we are definitely and firmly convinced, on the basis of all the evidence, that a mistake has been committed. *Wackerman* v. *Wackerman,* 16 Ariz.App. 382, 493 P.2d 928 (1972).

* * *

As to the mother's "mental illness," i.e., schizophrenia, the evidence pertaining thereto is primarily the testimony of Dr. Maccabe, whose opinion in July, 1974, that he saw little basis for recovery, was based on 1973 testing of the mother, the therapist's evaluation, and his brief contacts with her on three or four occasions from April, 1972 to July, 1974, for the purpose of evaluating the effects of medication. He admitted that schizophrenia is curable and that if the status quo was maintained, the mother could have help. It is apparent, however, that his recommendation of severance was colored by his opinion that the best interests of the child would thereby be served. He pointed out that the most beneficial environment for a child is with parents who are emotionally and socially stable and that there are many such parents. On the other hand, the later psychological testing in 1975 was the basis for the clinical psychologist's opinion that the mother was not schizophrenic. Furthermore, apart from the 1972 incidents that caused the mother to realize she had a problem and resulted in her seeking help, there is no evidence that her "instability" in fact caused harm to the child. It is at least arguable that the repeated suggestions that she voluntarily relinquish the child for adoption may have contributed to such "instability."

The evidence reflects that despite her emotional problems, the mother attempted to secure various jobs and was moderately successful in maintaining them. True, the duration of her various jobs was not extended. But this is not an unusual situation in our society today. Further, at the time of the severance hearing the mother's employment status and living situation had stabilized for a period of several months. She was apparently making an effort to supply "the stable environment" which had been recommended. Whether she was motivated solely by the fear of losing her child as a result of the impending severance hearing is not material. As we said in *Hyatt* v. *Hyatt,* 24 Ariz.App. 170, 536 P.2d 1062 (1975):

> The most telling evidence was the testimony . . . that he had not had the opportunity to observe how Roberta could care for her son after her recovery. No one has been able to make this observation.
>
> The state and its courts should do everything in their power to keep the family together and not destroy it. . . . If, for some reason, there is difficulty encountered . . . , agencies are available which can give the family the needed support while preserving its unity. There are many families in which one parent is incapacitated or only one parent is living, but this does not justify the leviathan power of the state to descend upon it and snatch away a child. (536 P.2d at 1068-69.)

The subject child had not been with his mother since June of 1973, and the only time he spent with her from that time until the date of the hearing had been the "visitation" time allowed by D.E.S. It is true that the mother acquiesced in the foster home placement and did not actively seek to have the child returned to her. However, it is apparent that during this period she was trying to achieve the goals delineated by the therapist and consistently refused to relinquish her child for adoption. She periodically made progress and then regressed, according to the therapist, who had established lifestyle guidelines for her. No attempt was ever made to allow the mother to assume parental responsibility with support of assistance in the form of counseling, psychotherapy and medication.

Under these circumstances, we cannot agree with the juvenile court's finding that she was unable to discharge parental responsibilities because of mental illness and there were reasonable grounds to believe that the condition would continue for a prolonged indeterminate period of time. In fact, the record reflects reluctance to maintain the status quo with a view to preserving the mother-child relationship because it would be better for the child to be placed in an adoptive home. This is not the controlling criterion in deciding whether or not to terminate the relationship. *In re Adoption of Smith,* 229 Or. 277, 366 P.2d 875 (1961). We agree with the following statement of the Oregon Supreme Court in *State* v. *McMaster,* 259 Or. 291, 486 P.2d 567 (1971):

> 1. . . . [W]e do not believe the legislature contemplated that parental rights could be terminated because the natural parents are unable to furnish surroundings which would enable the child to grow up as we would desire all children to do. (486 P.2d at 572.)

* * *

We also do not agree with the finding of the trial court that the mother had neglected the child. The expression "neglect" has no fixed meaning; its meaning varies as the context of circumstances changes. *In re Pima County Juvenile Action No. J-31853,* 18 Ariz.App. 219, 501 P.2d 395 (1972). A.R.S. Sec. 8-531(9) defines the term "neglected" for purposes of Art. 2:

> "Neglected" used with respect to a child refers to a situation in which the child lacks proper parental care necessary for his health, morals and well-being.

Thus we see that neglect is defined primarily in terms of parental conduct. The definitions of neglect offered by legal scholars are similar. For example, Professor Sanford Katz states that "child neglect connotes a parent's conduct, usually thought of in terms of passive behavior, that results in a failure to provide for the child's needs as defined by the preferred values of the community." S. Katz, *When Parents Fail,* 1971, at 22. Professor Katz is of the opinion that the absence of precise standards for state intervention is a necessity:

> . . . neglect statutes recognize that 'neglectful' behavior can also vary, and thus cannot be easily or specifically defined. . . . The broad neglect statutes allow judges to examine each situation on its own facts. (*Id.* at 64.)

What is proper parental care? In 1870, in a highly controversial decision, *People ex rel. O'Connell* v. *Turner,* 55 Ill. 280 (1870), the Supreme Court of Illinois declared unconstitutional an 1867 statute providing for commitment to reform schools for children between the ages 6 and 16 "who are destitute of proper parental care, and growing up in mendicancy, ignorance, idleness, or vice." The court saw the provision as encroaching too deeply into the constitutionally protected rights of a parent to raise his child as he sees fit:

> What is proper parental care? The best and kindest parents would differ, in the attempt to solve the question. No two scarcely agree; and when we consider the watchful supervision, which is so unremitting over the domestic affairs of others, the conclusion

is forced upon us, that there is not a child in the land who could not be proved, by two or more witnesses, to be in this sad condition. . . . Before any abridgement of the right [to custody], gross misconduct or almost total unfitness on the part of the parent, should be clearly proved. (55 Ill. at 283-85.)

We have recognized that parents enjoy a constitutional right with regard to raising their children and that a child has a right to be with his natural parents, *Hernandez* v. *State ex rel. Department of Economic Security,* 23 Ariz.App. 32, 530 P.2d 389 (1975). We are of the opinion that termination of the parent-child relationship on the grounds of neglect requires a showing of serious harm to the child, be it physical, mental, or "moral." *See,* Wald, State Intervention on Behalf of "Neglected" Children: A Search for Realistic Standards, 27 *Stan.L.Rev.* 985 (1975); Note, "Child Neglect: Due Process for the Parents," 70 *Col.L.Rev.* 465 (1970).

The sum and substance of the evidence presented here as to lack of proper parental care is that the mother's "lifestyle," if allowed to continue, would be detrimental to the child and that he deserves a more stable environment. The mother, when she sought help at the Southern Arizona Mental Health Center, did not manifest unconcern for her child's well-being, but rather the contrary. From the time she agreed to foster home placement in 1973, she has had no opportunity to demonstrate her ability to privide "proper parental care." To deprive her of her right to raise her child and concomitantly to deprive her child of the love and affection of his natural mother, on this meager showing, we cannot sanction. In effect, we would be punishing her for trying to improve her situation emotionally and physically so that she could take care of her child. Whether or not she is ready and able to resume custody of her child is a question we do not answer. We merely hold that the evidence did not warrant termination of the parent-child relationship.

Reversed.

Howard, C. J., concurring.

Hathaway, Judge (specially concurring).

I concur with the result reached by the majority, but I do not agree with all their reasons nor with their analysis of the record.

The court faced a dilemma in dealing with the competing interest of attempting to retain the family unit intact and taking the time necessary to determine whether this was possible, contrasted with the desirability of a prompt adoption placement. Resolving the problem by providing a permanent and stable home was, of course, the court's aim. Both results may be achieved with a little more time. I am not persuaded from the record that an adequate effort was put forth to retain, repair and strengthen the family unit, thus my concurrence in the result.

NOTES

1. Like mentally retarded parents, those suffering from mental illness often are presumed by courts to be unable to provide adequate care for their children.

2. In *Matter of Appeal in Pima County,* where parental rights were not terminated, the court noted that no attempt was ever made to allow the mother to assume parental

responsibility with supportive assistance in the form of counseling, psychotherapy, and medication. This approach of requiring the state agencies to put forth an adequate effort "to retain, repair, and strengthen the family unit" was the basis for Judge Hathaway's concurring opinion.

3. *People in Interest of K.S.*, 515 P.2d 130 (Colo. 1973) provides some guidelines for statutory interpretation in cases involving termination of parental rights:

> [T]ermination of parental rights, so called, severs permanently, not only the rights and obligations of the parent relative to the child, but those of the child as well. The child loses the right of support and maintenance, for which he may thereafter be dependent upon society; the right to inherit; and all other rights inherent in the legal parent-child relationship, not just for the period during which he is subject to the code, but forever. No degree of rehabilitation by the parent or achievement by the child can restore the relationship.
>
> *   *   *
>
> Many state legislatures have provided guidelines for the courts by limiting termination of parental rights to statutorily defined, extreme situations. Wis. Stat. § 48.40 (1971); see Kan. Stat. Ann. § 38-826 (1972 Supp.).
>
> Where the legislatures have failed to provide clear guidelines, the courts have attempted to supply classifications in compliance with a perceived legislative intention to limit termination of parental rights to special cases.
>
> *   *   *
>
> We believe that the legislation was enacted with an understanding and appreciation of the societal interest in maintaining and protecting the natural parents' interests in the child, and those of the child in the parent, absent parental acts or omissions sufficiently harmful to the child to mandate a forfeiture of those rights. It is our view that parental rights are personal between each parent and child and that termination following a determination of dependency and neglect should result only where there is a history of severe and continuous neglect by the particular parent whose rights are sought to be terminated, a substantial probability of future deprivation, and a determination that under *no* reasonable circumstances can the welfare of the child be served by a continuation of the legal relationship of the child with that parent (*Id.* at 132-133).

b.   Constitutional Validity

IN RE WILLIAM L.

Supreme Court of Pennsylvania, 1978
477 Pa. 322, 383 A.2d 1228

Before EAGEN, C. J., and O'BRIEN, ROBERTS, POMEROY, NIX and MANDERINO, JJ.

OPINION OF THE COURT.

ROBERTS, Justice.

These are appeals from final decrees of the Orphans' Court Division of the Court of Common Pleas of Lycoming County terminating the parental rights of appellant Gladys B. to her daughter Judith Denise B. and of appellant Marjorie L. to her three sons William L., Mark L., and Frank L. Appellee, in both appeals, is Lycoming County Children's Services [Children's Services]. The parental rights of both appellants were terminated pursuant to section 311(2) of the Adoption Act of 1970.[2] In addition to challenging the sufficiency of the evidence to support the decrees entered in their respective cases, both appellants claim that section 311(2) is vague, in violation of the due process clause of the fourteenth amendment. They also assert that section 311(2), as applied to them, deprives them of their interest in maintaining their parental relationships protected by the first, ninth, and fourteenth amendments to the United States Constitution. Because of the substantial similarity of these claims, we agreed to hear and decide the two cases together. We affirm in both appeals.

I.   SECTION 311(2) OF THE 1970 ADOPTION ACT IS NEITHER UNCONSTITUTION-ALLY VAGUE NOR VIOLATIVE OF SUBSTANTIVE DUE PROCESS AND MAY CONSTITUTION-ALLY BE APPLIED TO TERMINATE APPELLANTS'S PARENTAL RIGHTS.

Every presumption is in favor of the constitutionality of legislative acts, Statutory Construction Act of 1972, 1 Pa. C.S. § 1922(3) (Supp.1977), and statutes are to be construed whenever possible to uphold their constitutionality. *Bentman* v. *Seventh Ward Democratic Executive Committee,* 421 Pa. 188, 218 A.2d 261 (1966). "Courts may not declare a statute unconstitutional 'unless it *clearly, palpably,* and *plainly* violates the Constitution.' " *Tosto* v. *Pennsylvania Nursing Home Loan Agency,* 460 Pa. 1, 16, 331 A.2d 198, 205 (1975), quoting *Daly* v. *Hemphill,* 411 Pa. 263, 271, 191 A.2d 835, 840 (1963). Appellants' constitutional challenges do not meet this stringent burden.

Appellants both assert that section 311(2) of the Adoption Act is unconstitutional unless given a narrowing interpretation precluding its application to terminate their respective parental rights. They assert that parents have a fundamental interest in continued association with their children protected by the United States Constitution. They contend that section 311(2) violates this interest unless interpreted to require two showings before parental rights may be terminated: (1) that the parent has demonstrated a "high and substantial degree of misconduct"; and (2) that the child, while in the parent's custody, has suffered substantial physical or mental harm because of the absence of a basic need such as food, clothing, shelter, or medical care. Appellants contend that, absent such a narrow interpretation, the phrase "has caused the child to be without essential parental care, control, or subsistence necessary for his physical or mental well-being" in section 311(2) is unconstitutionally vague because it is susceptible to arbitrary enforcement and fails to give adequate notice to parents of the conduct required of them. We do not agree. Section 311(2) is not unconstitutionally vague and may constitutionally be applied to terminate parental rights where, as here, the record establishes "the repeated and continued incapacity" of a parent to provide the child with the "essential parental care, control, or subsistence necessary for his physical or mental well-being."

---

[2]Act of July 24, 1970, P.L. 620, § 311(2), 1 P.S. § 311(2) (Supp. 1977). Section 311(2), for which there was no corollary provision in the previous Adoption Act, authorizes termination of parental rights when:

> The repeated and continued incapacity, abuse, neglect, or refusal of the parent has caused the child to be without essential parental care, control, or subsistence necessary for his physical or mental well-being and the conditions and causes of the incapacity, abuse, neglect, or refusal cannot or will not be remedied by the parent.

A. Section 311(2) is not unconstitutionally vague because the language of the section and the decisions of this Court interpreting section 311(2) provide sufficiently precise guidelines to ensure reasonable notice and proper application.

Vague statutes may offend the Constitution in three ways: (1) they may trap the innocent by failing to give a person of ordinary intelligence reasonable opportunity to know what is prohibited so that he may act accordingly; (2) they may result in arbitrary and discriminatory enforcement in the absence of explicit guidelines for their application, and (3) where they implicate first amendment freedoms, they may inhibit constitutionally protected activity. *Grayned* v. *City of Rockford,* 408 U.S. 104, 108-09, 92 S.Ct. 2294, 2298-99, 33 L.Ed.2d 222 (1972). Appellants argue that the language "has caused the child to be without essential parental care, control, or subsistence necessary for his physical or mental well-being" in section 311(2) presents all three dangers. See *Alsager* v. *District Court of Polk City, Iowa,* 406 F.Supp. 10 (S.D.Iowa 1975), aff'd in part, 545 F.2d 1137 (8th Cir. 1976).

Considering first the question of notice, we believe appellants misperceive the nature of section 311(2). Unlike the typical statute attacked on vagueness grounds, section 311(2) does not prohibit or regulate any particular conduct. Section 311(2) is concerned only with the welfare of children whose essential needs have not been met, and whose parent cannot or will not meet those needs in the future. In the instant cases, the basis for termination is several years of demonstrated parental incapacity, which does not involve parental misconduct. When a statute attaches consequences to parental incapacity, a requirement that the statute "give a person of ordinary intelligence fair notice that his contemplated conduct is forbidden by the statute," *United States* v. *Harriss,* 347 U.S. 612, 617, 74 S.Ct. 808, 812, 98 L.Ed. 989 (1954), serves no purpose, because the statute applies only to a parent incapable of conforming conduct to avoid the effect of the statute.

Of course, the other bases for termination relate to parental neglect, abuse, or refusal to meet the child's essential needs and thus involve parental misconduct. Section 311(2), however, requires that, before parental rights may be terminated, the court must find that the "conditions and causes of the incapacity, abuse, neglect, or refusal cannot or will not be remedied by the parent." 1 P.S. § 311(2) (Supp.1977). This requirement excludes the possibility that parental rights will be terminated because of insufficient notice, since the parent's inability or unwillingness to meet the child's essential needs must be affirmatively demonstrated. The requirement that parental conduct resulting in termination of parental rights be irremediable negates appellants' notice argument.[5]

---

[5]When termination is sought on the basis of parental conduct causing the child to be without essential parental care, the requirement that the conduct be shown to be irremediable could be met rarely, if ever, absent evidence that the deficiencies in parental conduct had been identified, and the parent was nonetheless unwilling or unable to modify the conduct to remedy the situation. Moreover, because of the Commonwealth's commitment to the preservation of the family, when termination is sought by an agency, a normal element of the agency's proof will be that services have been made available to the parent to help remedy the causes of removal and have proved unavailing. See *Adoption of R.I.,* 468 Pa. 287, 295 n.9, 361 A.2d 294, 298 n.9 (1976). We need not decide whether such a showing is required in light of the Commonwealth's public policy, since it is clear that both appellants have received years of assistance from Children's Services and related public agencies.

Second, section 311(2) does not create the potential for arbitrary and discriminatory enforcement. The language of section 311(2) is broad and speaks in general terms, as do most statutes concerned with neglect. However, our strong policy protecting the family from unwarranted state intrusion protects against arbitrary or discriminatory applications of section 311(2).

When the child is in the home, this on-going relationship will not be disturbed except upon a showing by clear and convincing evidence that removal is "clearly necessary." *Adoption of R.I.*, 468 Pa. 287, 294, 361 A.2d 294, 297 (1976); *Interest of Larue*, 244 Pa.Super. 218, 366 A.2d 1271, 1275 (1976). It is not enough to justify termination of parental rights under section 311(2) to demonstrate that the home is "submarginal" and likely to result in a "cultural deprivation." *In re Geiger*, 459 Pa. 636, 640, 331 A.2d 172, 174 (1975). These decisions render agency officials powerless to remove a child from parental care and control absent a clear showing that the child either has been subjected to abuse or suffered serious harm, or that the threat of such harm is real and substantial and cannot be alleviated by means less drastic than removal.

Often, as in these appeals, the question of whether to terminate parental rights arises long after the unity of the family has been disrupted by separation of the child from the parent. Marjorie L's three sons have been in foster care since 1971; Gladys B's daughter Judith has been in foster care since 1974. Extended relegation of a child to the care of others as a result of parental incapacity or neglect is relevant in determining whether the child has been without essential parental care or control. See *Rothstein* v. *Lutheran Social Services of Wisconsin and Upper Michigan*, 405 U.S. 1051, 92 S.Ct. 1488, 31 L.Ed.2d 786 (1972); cf. *In re Smith's Adoption*, 412 Pa. 501, 194 A.2d 919 (1963) (that natural mother allowed foster parents to meet child's physical and mental needs for over a year was relevant to termination of parental rights). A stable family relationship is "necessary for [a child's] physical or mental well-being." "Continuity of parental affection and care provides the cornerstone for the child's sense of self worth and security; parental discipline and example develop the wellsprings of values and ideals." Note, In the Child's Best Interests: Rights of the Natural Parents in Child Placement Proceedings, 51 N.Y.U.L.Rev. 446, 450 (1976). The essential need of a child for close and continuous association with a parent or parent-figure is well recognized in psychological literature. See sources cited in *id.* at 449-51.

Accordingly, when a child has been placed in foster care, a parent has an affirmative duty to work towards the return of the child. See *Involuntary Termination of Parental Rights of S.C.B. and K.T.*, 474 Pa. 615, 379 A.2d 535 (1977); *Appeal of Diane B.*, 456 Pa. 429, 321 A.2d 618 (1974). However, even when there has been a long separation occasioned by parental neglect or incapacity, termination of parental rights will not be ordered if there is a reasonable possibility that the causes and conditions which have led to the separation can be remedied and the family restored. *Jones Appeal*, 449 Pa. 543, 297 A.2d 117 (1972), demonstrates our deference to this requirement. There, although the mother was an accomplice to sexual abuse of her daughter, we refused to terminate her parental rights because the evidence did not establish that the causes or conditions leading to the abuse could not be remedied. *Id.* at 548, 297 A.2d at 120.

The language of section 311(2) does not admit of an interpretation permitting termination of parental rights based upon personal preferences or speculative concepts of proper child rearing. The needs of the child unmet by the parent must be "essential" and "necessary" to his "physical or mental well-being." In addition, the evidence must establish that the causes and conditions of the deprivation "cannot or will not be remedied."

We conclude that the demanding standards of section 311(2), together with the Legislature's and this Court's strong policy of restraint from interfering with the family, sufficiently protect against the arbitrary and discriminatory application of section 311(2).

Similarly, even assuming that decisions affecting private family concerns implicate first amendment values, see *Griswold* v. *Connecticut,* 381 U.S. 479, 485, 85 S.Ct. 1678, 1682, 14 L.Ed.2d 510 (1965), we must reject appellants' argument that the language of section 311(2) may have a "chilling" effect on protected parental conduct. The decisions of this Court interpreting section 311(2) protect parental conduct which does not deprive the child of its essential needs. See *In re Geiger, supra.* However, parental misconduct which deprives the child of essential needs is not protected by the Constitution. Mr. Chief Justice Burger, writing for the Court, stated in *Wisconsin* v. *Yoder:* "To be sure, the power of the parent even when linked to a free exercise claim, may be subject to limitation . . . if it appears that parental decisions will jeopardize the health or safety of the child, or have a potential for significant social burdens." 406 U.S. 205, 233-34, 92 S.Ct. 1526, 1542, 32 L.Ed.2d 15 (1972). Section 311(2) and our decisions are sufficiently clear to avoid any significant possibility a parent would be inhibited from engaging in protected conduct not constituting deprivation of essential needs of the child.

B.   Section 311(2) does not violate substantive due process rights because a state may constitutionally intervene to terminate parental rights when a natural parent's continued incapacity causes the child to be without essential parental care.

Appellants argue that the application of section 311(2) to terminate their respective parental rights, in the absence of a showing of "high and substantial misconduct" and that their children, while in their custody, had ever suffered substantial physical or mental harm, violates their constitutionally protected interest in mutual association with their children. We do not agree.

There is no doubt that the Constitution protects the family against certain intrusions by the state. *Meyer* v. *Nebraska,* 262 U.S. 390, 43 S.Ct. 625, 67 L.Ed. 1042 (1923), generally considered the seminal case recognizing constitutional protection of family concerns, invalidated a statute which prohibited teaching young children any language other than English because the statute unreasonably infringed upon the liberty interest, protected by the fourteenth amendment, of parents, teachers, and children. Noting that the contours of the liberty interest guaranteed by the fourteenth amendment had never been exactly defined, the Court stated: "Without doubt, it denotes not merely freedom from bodily restraint but also the right of the individual to . . . marry, establish a home, and bring up children. . . ." *Id.* at 399, 43 S.Ct. at 626. Accord, *Pierce* v. *Society of Sisters,* 268 U.S. 510, 45 S.Ct. 571, 69 L.Ed. 1070 (1925) (striking down a statute requiring that all children attend public schools). In

Prince v. *Massachusetts,* 321 U.S. 158, 64 S.Ct. 438, 88 L.Ed. 645 (1944), the Court recognized that:

> It is cardinal with us that the custody, care and nurture of the child reside first in the parents, whose primary function and freedom include preparation for obligations the state can neither supply nor hinder [citing *Pierce*]. And it is in recognition of this that these decisions [*Pierce* and *Meyer*] have respected the private realm of family life which the state cannot enter.

Id. at 166, 64 S.Ct. at 442.

The continued vitality of the principle that there is a "private realm of family life which the state cannot enter" cannot be questioned. Just last term the United States Supreme Court stated that "when the government intrudes on choices concerning family living arrangements, this Court must examine carefully the importance of the governmental interests advanced and the extent to which they are served by the challenged regulation." *Moore* v. *City of East Cleveland, Ohio,* 431 U.S. 494, 499, 97 S.Ct. 1932, 1936, 52 L.Ed.2d 531 (1977) (plurality opinion). See also *Smith* v. *Organization of Foster Families for Equality and Reform,* 431 U.S. 816, 829, 97 S.Ct. 2094, 2109, 53 L.Ed.2d 14 (1977); *Cleveland Board of Education* v. *LaFleur,* 414 U.S. 632, 639-40, 94 S.Ct. 791, 796, 39 L.Ed.2d 52 (1974) ("This Court has long recognized that freedom of personal choice in matters of marriage and family life is one of the liberties protected by the Due Process Clause of the Fourteenth Amendment."); *Wisconsin* v. *Yoder,* 406 U.S. 205, 231-33, 92 S.Ct. 1526, 1541-42, 32 L.Ed.2d 15 (1972); *Stanley* v. *Illinois,* 405 U.S. 645, 651, 92 S.Ct. 1208, 1212, 31 L.Ed.2d 551 (1972); *Ginsberg* v. *New York,* 390 U.S. 629, 639, 88 S.Ct. 1274, 1280, 20 L.Ed.2d 195 (1968).

In related cases, the United States Supreme Court has recognized that the Constitution affords protection to "a right of personal privacy, or a guarantee of certain areas or zones of privacy." *Roe* v. *Wade,* 410 U.S. 113, 152, 93 S.Ct. 705, 726, 35 L.Ed.2d 147 (1973). See also *Carey* v. *Population Services International,* 431 U.S. 678, 684, 97 S.Ct. 2010, 2016, 52 L.Ed.2d 675 (1977) (plurality opinion); *Whalen* v. *Roe,* 429 U.S. 589, 598, 97 S.Ct. 869, 876 (1977); *Griswold* v. *Connecticut, supra* at 485, 85 S.Ct. at 1682. Personal decisions relating to child rearing are within this zone and protected from unwarranted interference by the state. *Carey* v. *Population Services International, supra* at 684, 97 S.Ct. at 2016 (plurality opinion), citing *Pierce* and *Meyer.*

These cases do not, however, support the proposition that the state can never interfere in the parent-child relationship. Indeed, in *Stanley* v. *Illinois, supra,* the United States Supreme Court recognized that the state had not only a right, but a duty to protect minor children. 405 U.S. at 649, 92 S.Ct. at 1212. See also *Prince* v. *Massachusetts, supra* (upholding anti-child labor statute against challenge that it unreasonably infringed upon parent's and child's free exercise of religion and parent's right to educate child in her beliefs). Constitutional restraint on state interference in family matters does not compel the courts to protect parental rights at the expense of ignoring the rights and needs of children. In *Planned Parenthood of Central Missouri* v. *Danforth,* 428 U.S. 52, 96 S.Ct. 2831, 49 L.Ed.2d 788 (1976), the United States Supreme Court rejected the argument that the state's interest in protecting parental authority justified giving parents a veto power over a minor's decision to have an abortion "where the minor and the nonconsenting parent are so fundamentally in conflict and the very existence of the pregnancy has already fractured the family structure." *Id.* at 75, 96 S.Ct. at 2844. See also *Wisconsin* v. *Yoder*, 406 U.S. at 241-49, 92 S.Ct. at 1546-50 (concurring and dissenting opinion of Douglas, J.); *In re Roger S.*, 19 Cal.3d 921, 141 Cal.Rptr. 298, 569 P.2d 1286 (1977) (unconstitutional to permit parent of fourteen year old child to commit the child to a mental institution over the child's objection). In determining whether parental rights should be terminated, the court must recognize the essential needs of the child as well as the rights of the parent.

The source of the state's authority to intervene in family matters to protect minor children has been said to be the doctrine of *parens patriae*, the concept that the sovereign is the father of his country. See, e.g., *Adoption of R.I.*, 468 Pa. at 294, 361 A.2d at 297. Although the doctrine of *parens patriae* has been subject to critical comment in recent years, there is general agreement that the state has the right and the duty to act to protect its weaker members, such as infants, who are unable to protect themselves, and to compel parents and children alike to act in ways beneficial to society. See Kleinfeld, "The Balance of Power Among Infants, Their Parents and the State," 4 *Fam.L.Q.* 320 (1970), 4 *Fam.L.Q.* 410 (1970), 5 Fam.L.Q. 64 (1971). The state's responsibility to protect its weaker members authorizes interference with parental autonomy and decisionmaking in appropriate circumstances. The moral and practical importance of this authority was set forth by Chief Justice Maxey in *Commonwealth ex rel. Children's Aid Society* v. *Gard:*

> Societies which like the relator are entrusted by the sovereign with power over the lives of infants should ever bear in mind that consideration for the sensibilities of children and solicitude for their well-being is the hallmark of an humane individual and of a civilized state.

362 Pa. 85, 99, 66 A.2d 300, 307 (1949).

Parental rights must be accorded significant protection. *Meyer* v. *Nebraska, supra; Pierce* v. *Society of Sisters, supra; Prince* v. *Massachusetts, supra;* and *Wisconsin* v. *Yoder, supra.* The state may, however, constitutionally require the rights of parents to yield to the child's essential health and safety needs. See *Wisconsin* v. *Yoder, supra;* accord, *In the Matter of Petition for Adoption of J.S.R.,* 374 A.2d 860 (D.C. 1977) ("[T]he right of a parent to raise one's child is an essential, but not absolute, one, which can be terminated. . . .''). When, as here, a parent is incapable of meeting the child's essential needs, see section II, *infra,* the state may constitutionally intervene to protect the "physical or mental well-being" of the child. In these circumstances, the interest of the parent in keeping the child conflicts with the interest of the child in its essential physical and emotional needs and the Legislature has constitutionally mandated that the interests of the weaker party, the child, should prevail. This legislative determination must be accorded great deference for "when an issue involves policy choices as sensitive as those implicated by [the involuntary termination of parental rights], the appropriate forum for their resolution in a democracy is the legislature." *Maher* v. *Roe,* 432 U.S. 464, 97 S.Ct. 2376, 2385-86, 53 L.Ed.2d 484 (1977). As Mr. Justice Holmes stated in *Missouri, Kansas and Texas Railway Com-*

pany v. *May,* 194 U.S. 267, 270, 24 S.Ct. 638, 639, 48 L.Ed. 971 (1904): "[L]egisla-
tures are ultimate guardians of the liberties and welfare of the people in quite as great a
degree as the courts."

Therefore, appellants' assertion that "high and substantial misconduct" on the
part of the parent must be shown before parental rights may be constitutionally terminated cannot be accepted. Their contention ignores the state's constitutional interest in
the welfare of the child.

[Section II of the court's opinion where, after a detailed review of the evidence,
the court concluded that the decision of the lower court was supported by competent
evidence, is omitted. Also omitted are the concurring and dissenting opinions.]

NOTES

1. Part of the evidence considered by the court was as follows:

> In January, 1976, appellant, at the request of Children's Services, agreed to be
> interviewed and tested by a psychologist. The psychologist administered a structured
> interview called the Vineland Social Maturity Scale and the standardized Slosson Intelli-
> gence Test. The first test indicated that appellant's social skills and ability to function
> independently were at about the twelve year old level. The intelligence test, which
> measures numerical and verbal reasoning skills, indicated that appellant had an IQ of 43
> and a mental age of six years, ten months. Although appellant testified at the hearing that
> she had completed the seventh grade in school, she told the psychologist that she did not
> know how to read. The psychologist testified that appellant had limited communication
> skills and showed considerable difficulty in comprehending simple ideas concerning
> housework, cooking, and child care. In her psychological evaluation, the psychologist
> concluded that appellant lacked the social maturity and intellectual capability to cope
> with the continuing responsibilities of raising children (At 383 A.2d 1239).

Subsequently, however, the court declared:

> In reviewing whether the evidence supports the orphans' court's decree, we have
> placed only limited reliance on appellant's IQ score. Experts generally agree that so-
> cially and culturally disadvantaged people tend to score lower on standardized intelli-
> gence tests, which suggests that cultural bias may affect the result. See Galliher,
> "Termination of the Parent-Child Relationship: Should Parental I.Q. be an Important
> Factor?," *Law and the Social Order* 855, 865-66 (1973). Moreover, "No Study has ever
> documented the premise that unintelligent parents are unable to give love and affec-
> tion." *Id.* at 871. Consequently, we consider appellant's test score only as a factor
> among many relevant to her incapacity to meet the essential needs of her children (*Id.* at
> 1243 n. 26).

2. In concurring in part and dissenting in part, Justice Nix wrote an opinion in which
he vigorously disagreed with the constitutional reasoning of the majority:

> The majority asserts that "the basis for termination is several years of demonstrated
> parental incapacity, which does not involve parental misconduct." In my judgment this
> premise ignores the record and introduces an insidious and dangerous philosophy com-
> pletely at odds with fundamental American values. First, I take issue with the claim that
> there has been a demonstration of parental incapacity as envisioned in this section. The
> majority relies upon the fact that Marjorie L.'s limited intelligence handicaps her in the
> performance of her parental responsibilities. I would not dispute the possibility that a
> brighter, better trained and more affluent mother might be more proficient in the dis-

charge of parental responsibilities. I do, however, reject the contention that this fact would empower a state to dissolve a maternal relationship and to create an artificial one that the state might deem "more advantageous" [citations omitted].

The example provided by the Nazi Germany Youth Camps should dissuade anyone who might be tempted to opt for such a sterile clinical approach to child rearing. The majority has totally disregarded the wisdom of Judge Woodside in Rinker Appeal, 180 Pa.Super. 143, 117 A.2d 780 (1955), wherein he stated:

> A child cannot be declared "neglected" merely because his condition might be improved by changing his parents. The welfare of many children might be served by taking them from their homes and placing them in what the officials may consider a better home. But the Juvenile Court Law was not intended to provide a procedure to take the children of the poor and give them to the rich, nor to take the children of the illiterate and give them to the educated, nor to take the children of the crude and give them to the cultured, nor to take the children of the weak and sickly and give them to the strong and healthy (*Id.* at 148, 117 A.2d at 783).

By its indifference to law and sound judicial caution, the majority has terminated the parental rights of a mother who did all she could with the few natural attributes that God gave to her.

* * *

The majority construction of section 311(2) in effect means that an involuntary parental incapacity, sustained through no fault of the parent, if found to be irremediable, justifies judicial termination of the incapacitated parent's parental rights. Such a construction raises serious equal protection questions which may very well render section 311(2) invalid.

The construction placed upon section 311(2) by the majority results in the creation of two categories of parents; one consisting of involuntarily incapacitated parents, either physically, mentally, or both, and the other consisting of basically healthy parents. As to those parents in the former category, the majority would apply section 311(2) to terminate their parental rights, whereas those parents in the latter category would not face such a threat without some dereliction on their part. By this judgment they have ordained that the bedridden terminally ill cancer patient, the comatose accident victim, the paralytic, and the contagiously ill patient are all prime subjects for involuntary termination under this section.

* * *

Since the classification drawn by the majority's construction of section 311(2) directly impinges upon involuntarily incapacitated parents' rights to the companionship, care and custody of their children, only a compelling state interest can justify the classification. I have grave doubts that the state's admittedly valid interest in protecting minor children is sufficiently powerful to legitimize the classification. Furthermore, I would submit that even if this state interest is considered to be a "compelling" one, there are less drastic alternatives available (e. g., continued foster home care), short of absolute termination of parental rights, to promote this state interest. The state's interest is that of insuring that the essential needs of the child are met. In cases involving no parental misconduct, such as the instant case, this interest is sufficiently promoted by custody awards (At 383 A.2d 1248-1252).

Is Justice Nix correct when he states that the majority has, by its construction of section 311(2) of the statute, created two groups of parents, those involuntarily incapacitated and those who are healthy, and has discriminated against the former by allowing termination of their parental rights because of their incapacity but requiring that some parental fault be proved in the case of the latter before their rights may be terminated?

Is the majority's conclusion justified in view of the cogent equal protection analysis marshalled by Justice Nix? Does the majority acknowledge the right to raise one's children as fundamental? What compelling state interests justify the majority's conclusion? Does the majority consider any alternatives short of absolute termination?

3. What is the basis of the court's decision to terminate parental rights? Should incapacity to provide parental care based upon mental deficiency but without establishing parental fault be a ground for termination of parental rights? Does the court's decision satisfy substantive due process?

5. Justice Nix, concurring and dissenting, argues that the state may not dissolve a maternal relationship in order to create one it considers materially, culturally, and intellectually more advantageous. His reasoning on this point echoes that of the *McMaster* court, see p. 959n.6, *supra.*

6. Apparently Marjorie L. recognized her intellectual limitations and sought assistance from public agencies. How would the *Lewis* court have considered this factor? Should the *William L.* court have been compelled to find that even provision of supportive services would not have permitted Marjorie L. to adequately care for her children before it terminated her rights? See footnote 5 of the court's opinion.

7. In *Appeal in Maricopa Cty. Juv. Action Nos. JS1308 and JS1412,* 27 Ariz.App. 420, 555 P.2d 679 (1976), the Court of Appeals of Arizona considered a severance of parental rights of a mother described as a "chronic schizophrenic with mental retardation and organic learning disability," who could not even remember her children's names, *id.* at 555 P.2d 681. The court upheld the severance against constitutional challenge, ruling that the challenged statutory scheme for the severance of parental rights was "reasonable." Is this the correct equal protection standard for such a case?

8. *In re Adoption of J.S.R.,* 374 A.2d 860 (D.C.App. 1977), involved a petition for approval of an adoption by foster parents over the objection of the natural mother. The mother was an unmarried woman who had become paraplegic as a result of multiple sclerosis and was allegedly unable to care for her child. The trial court, applying a standard of "the best interest of the child" chose what it termed "the least detrimental alternative," *id.* at 862, and approved the adoption. In upholding the constitutionality of the "best interest" standard, the District of Columbia Court of Appeals declared:

> The right of a natural parent to raise one's child is a fundamental and essential one which is constitutionally protected. *Stanley* v. *Illinois,* 405 U.S. 645, 92 S.Ct.1208, 31 L.Ed.2d 551 (1972). However, it is not an absolute one. The state has both the right and the duty to protect minor children through judicial determinations of their interest. *Id.* To this end, the state has a substantial range of authority to protect the welfare of a child, *Prince* v. *Massachusetts,* 321 U.S. 158, 64 S.Ct. 438, 88 L.Ed. 645 (1944), and the state's legitimate interest in the child's welfare may be implemented by separating the child from the parent, *Stanley* v. *Illinois.*
>
> In *Winter* v. *Director, Department of Welfare,* 217 Md. 391, 143 A.2d 81 (1958), the natural father of a minor challenged the constitutional validity of a Maryland statutory framework, nearly identical to our own, which permitted adoption without parental consent if the court found such consent to be withheld contrary to the best interests of the child. In finding the statute to be constitutionally valid, the Maryland Court of Appeals, recognizing the role of the state as *parens patriae,* stated:

The validity of legislation permitting an adoption without the parents' consent is based upon the fact that a parent has no inherent right of property in a child, and the right that a parent has to the custody and rearing of his children is not an absolute one, but one that may be forfeited by abandonment, unfitness of the parent, or where some exceptional circumstances render the parents' custody of the child detrimental to the best interest of the child. [Id., 217 Md. at 396, 143 A.2d at 84 (citations omitted).]

We find nothing offensive to constitutional mandates in our statutory standard which focuses on the best interest of the child rather than solely on the status or abilities of the natural parent (*Id.* at 863-864).

Is it fair to say that the compelling state interest in *J.S.R.* is the "best interest of the child"? Is this satisfactory equal protection analysis?

The lower court had found that the mother was "a victim of multiple sclerosis with a severely shortened life expectancy," at 374 A.2d 865. Should life expectancy be a factor in determinations of parental fitness?

ALSAGER v. DISTRICT COURT OF POLK COUNTY, IOWA

*United States District Court for the Southern District
of Iowa, Central Division, 1975
406 F.Supp. 10.*

Findings of Fact, Conclusions
of Law and Order for
Judgment

HANSON, Chief Judge.

In May of 1970, the Juvenile Division of the District Court of Polk County entered an order terminating the parental rights of Charles and Darlene Alsager "in and to" five of their six children. In March of 1973, this action was brought attacking the constitutionality of those termination proceedings. The Alsagers seek a declaratory judgment to the effect that Iowa's parent-child termination statute is unconstitutional both on its face, and as it was applied to them. Plaintiffs also complain of alleged procedural defects in the state termination proceedings, and seek monetary damages from the defendants. Their complaint is based on 42 U.S.C. § 1983. This Court has jurisdiction under 28 U.S.C. § 1343(3).

Evidence was presented to this Court, sitting without a jury, in March of 1974. In November, 1974, the Court ruled that the factual situation faced by the plaintiffs was such that federal declaratory relief would be inappropriate. *See* 384 F.Supp. 643. This ruling was greatly influenced by the Court's fervent belief that the interests of the five children involved in this case could be best served by further proceedings, formal or informal, on the state level. On June 17, 1975, the United States Court of Appeals for the Eighth Circuit ruled that this refusal to proceed to the merits of the plaintiffs' constitutional claims was error. 518 F.2d 1160 (8th Cir. 1975). The case was then remanded to this Court for proceedings consistent with that opinion. Accordingly, the Court acts today, under a mandate.

* * *

Before discussing the merits of the Alsagers' constitutional contentions, the Court will reiterate the Findings of Fact made in its prior ruling.

Charles and Darlene Alsager were residing at 614 East 30th Street, Des Moines, Iowa, in the summer of 1969. At that time Mr. Alsager was 36 years old, and Mrs. Alsager was 26 years old. The couple had been married eleven years and were the parents of six children: George, who was 10 in June of 1969; Wanda, who was 8; John, age 7; Charles, Jr., age 6; Michael, age 4; and Albert, who was less than one year old.

The Alsagers began to have contact with the juvenile authorities of the Polk County District Court as early as 1965, when George was adjudicated to be a "neglected child." This adjudication prompted a removal of George from his parents' home, and he was placed in at least two foster homes before he was returned to his parents in 1968.

In the spring and early summer of 1969, the probation department of the Polk County District Court received a number of complaints about the Alsager children from the family's neighbors. On June 13, 1969, Carl Parks, the Chief Probation Officer of the Polk County District Court, wrote a letter to the plaintiffs stating that his office had received a report about their children, and warning the parents that a petition might be filed by the neighbors seeking to remove the children from their custody.

On June 20, 1969, Jane Johnston, a probation officer with the Polk County Juvenile Court, visited the Alsager home. Miss Johnston spent approximately twenty minutes inside the Alsager residence, which at the time was occupied only by Mrs. Alsager and the baby, Albert. Based on her observations inside the house, and without seeing the other five children, Miss Johnston determined that all six children should immediately be removed to the Polk County Juvenile Home. This removal was to be temporary, pending a hearing to determine whether the children were "neglected" as defined by Section 232.2(15) of the Code of Iowa (1973). This hearing was held within one week from the initial removal, on June 26, 1969. As a result of the hearing, Polk County District Judge Don L. Tidrick found the children to be neglected, and ordered that they remain in the custody of the county court pending placement in a foster home or an institution.

Less than one month after the neglect ruling, Chief Probation Officer Parks filed a petition to institute proceedings to terminate the parent-child relationship in Polk County District Court.

This petition alleged that

> the best interests of the children . . . require that the parent-child relationships . . . be terminated by the Court because said parents have substantially and continuously and repeatedly refused to give their children necessary parental care and protection and because said parents are unfit parents by reason of conduct detrimental to the physical or mental health or morals of their children.

Upon a filing of the petition, a guardian *ad litem* was appointed in behalf of the children. A copy of the petition was served upon the parents, who then retained counsel. On September 9, 1969, a termination hearing was held before Judge Tidrick. The parents were present at this hearing, accompanied by their counsel. The children's guardian *ad litem* was also present. On September 29, 1969, Judge Tidrick issued an order pertaining to the termination hearing. The judge stated that "adequate and sufficient cause'' existed to terminate the parent-child relationship, but he declined to do so at that time, stating that "final termination of parental rights should not take place so long as there is any substantial hope that the parents will be able to improve to the extent that they can provide even minimal care." The order then continued the matter of termination of the parental rights. The two eldest children, George and Wanda, were released to the temporary custody of their parents. The four youngest children were ordered to remain in the custody of the court.

The court held a second hearing on the matter of termination on March 19, 1970. One week prior to this hearing the attorney who represented Charles and Darlene Alsager at the September proceedings was appointed to represent them at the March hearing. A final hearing on termination was held on May 22, 1970. On that day, Judge Tidrick issued his final termination order. He ruled that Wanda, who had been returned to her parents in September, would benefit by remaining in her parents' home. The Alsagers' parental rights "in and to" the other five children were terminated. This order of termination was affirmed by the Iowa Supreme Court on October 18, 1972, in a short opinion. *See State* v. *Alsager,* 201 N.W.2d 727 (Iowa 1972). No further proceedings were commenced on the state level subsequent to the decision of the Iowa Supreme Court. This lawsuit was instituted on March 28, 1973.

Conclusions of Law

Plaintiffs' amended complaint asserts that their legal relationship to their children has been terminated pursuant to standards and procedures which violate the First, Ninth, and Fourteenth Amendments to the United States Constitution. The plaintiffs seek a declaratory judgment to the effect that the Iowa statute which permitted the termination of their parent-child relationships is unconstitutional both on its face and as applied. The parental termination statute of the Code of Iowa, § 232.41, provides:

The court may upon petition terminate the relationship between parent and child:

* * *

2.   If the court finds that one or more of the following conditions exist:
   a.   That the parents have abandoned the child.
   b.   That the parents have substantially and continuously or repeatedly refused to give the child necessary parental care and protection.
   c.   That although financially able, the parents have substantially and continuously neglected to provide the child with necessary subsistence, education, or other care necessary for physical or mental health or morals of the child or have neglected to pay for subsistence, education, or other care of the child when legal custody is lodged with others.
   d.   That the parents are unfit by reason of debauchery, intoxication, habitual use of narcotic drugs, repeated lewd and lascivious behavior, or other conduct found by the court likely to be detrimental to the physical or mental health or morals of the child.
   e.   That following an adjudication of neglect or dependency, reasonable efforts under the direction of the court have failed to correct the conditions leading to the termination.

Plaintiffs claim that certain standards of § 232.41 are impermissibly vague in violation of the Due Process Clause of the Fourteenth Amendment to the United States Constitution. Specifically, they challenge the standards embodied in the phrases "refused to give the child necessary parental care and protection," § 232.41(2)(b), and "unfit [parents] by reason of . . . conduct . . . detrimental to the physical or mental health or morals of the child,'' § 232.41(2)(d). Plaintiff's post-trial brief at 26. Plaintiffs also assert that even if the statute were deemed to be sufficiently precise, it would violate their rights to Due Process of law by not requiring a sufficient threshold of harm as a prerequisite to permanent termination. Further, the Alsagers claim that procedural due process was denied them in that (1) adequate notice of the termination proceedings was not given them; (2) the standard of proof employed required a mere preponderance of the evidence rather than clear and convincing evidence; (3) hearsay evidence was admitted; and (4) *ex parte* communications between the judge and witnessing employees of the juvenile court may have occurred.

In order to properly determine the merits of plaintiff's constitutional challenges, it is first essential to examine the nature of the constitutional rights at stake. A plethora of opinions by the United States Supreme Court, addressed to the nature of constitutional interests implicated where various aspects of family life are threatened, indicate that the Alsagers have a fundamental right to family integrity.

In *Meyer* v. *Nebraska,* 262 U.S. 390, 43 S.Ct. 625, 67 L.Ed. 1042 (1923), the Supreme Court upheld the right of parents to have their children taught the German language. The Court determined that the ''liberty'' guaranteed by the Fourteenth Amendment ''without doubt, . . . denotes . . . the right of the individual . . . to marry, establish a home and bring up children.'' *Id.* at 399, 43 S.Ct. at 626. Similarly, in *Pierce* v. *Society of Sisters,* 268 U.S. 510, 45 S.Ct. 571, 69 L.Ed. 1070 (1925), the Court affirmed the enjoining of an Oregon statute which was deemed to interfere ''with the liberty of parents and guardians to direct the upbringing and education of children under their control.'' *Id.* at 534-35, 45 S.Ct. at 573. In *Prince* v. *Massachusetts,* 321 U.S. 158, 64 S.Ct. 438, 88 L.Ed. 645 (1944), the Court noted that ''It is cardinal with us that the custody, care and nurture of the child reside first in the parents, whose primary function and freedom include preparation for obligations the State can neither supply nor hinder. . . . And it is the recognition of this that these decisions (*Meyer* and *Pierce*) have respected the private realm of family life which the state cannot enter.'' *Id.* at 166, 64 S.Ct. at 442.

This ''liberty'' right was similarly recognized in *Skinner* v. *Oklahoma,* 316 U.S. 535, 62 S.Ct. 1110, 86 L.Ed. 1655 (1942), where the Court emphasized the fundamental nature of the constitutionally protected right to marry and to procreate while invalidating a statute allowing the sterilization of habitual criminals. In *May* v. *Anderson,* 345 U.S. 528, 73 S.Ct. 840, 97 L.Ed. 1221 (1953), the Court denied full faith and credit to an *ex parte* custody decree, noting that the Fourteenth Amendment's liberty included a parent's ''immediate right to the care, custody, management and companionship of . . . minor children.'' *Id.* at 533, 73 S.Ct. at 843. More recently, in *Cleveland Board of Education* v. *LaFleur,* 414 U.S. 632, 94 S.Ct. 791, 39 L.Ed.2d 52 (1974), the Court invalidated mandatory leave provisions for pregnant school teachers because they unnecessarily interfered with the decision to raise a family. The Court observed that the ''freedom of personal choice in matters of marriage and family life is one of the liberties protected by the Due Process Clause of the Fourteenth Amendment.'' *Id.,* 94 S.Ct. at 796, 39 L.Ed.2d at 60.

Other decisions, while premised on a ''privacy'' rather than a ''liberty'' rationale, have shown a similar solicitude for the family enclave. *See, e.g., Griswold* v. *Connecticut,* 381 U.S. 479, 85 S.Ct. 1678, 14 L.Ed.2d 510 (1965); *Eisenstadt* v. *Baird,* 405 U.S. 438, 92 S.Ct. 1029, 31 L.Ed.2d 349 (1972). In *Stanley* v. *Illinois,* 405 U.S. 645, 92 Sup.Ct. 1208, 31 L.Ed.2d 551 (1972), the Court acknowledged the right to family integrity in declaring Illinois' dependency statute unconstitutional for depriving unmarried fathers of the care and custody of their natural children on the death of their mother. In the words of the Court, "the integrity of the family unit has found protection in the Due Process Clause of the Fourteenth Amendment, the Equal Protection Clause of the Fourteenth Amendment, and the Ninth Amendment" (citations omitted). *Id.* at 651, 92 S.Ct. at 1213.

Finally, in *Roe* v. *Wade,* 410 U.S. 113, 93 S.Ct. 705, 35 L.Ed.2d 147 (1973), the United States Supreme Court addressed the pertinence of many of its above-mentioned decisions to the abortion context. The Court noted that while privacy is not explicitly mentioned in the Constitution, a right to a "guarantee of certain areas or zones" of privacy has been constitutionally recognized by the Court. In the words of the Court, the guarantee of personal privacy includes only those rights that are "implicit in the concept of ordered liberty," such as "activities relating to marriage . . . procreation . . . contraception . . . family relationships . . . and child rearing and education." *Id.* at 152, 93 S.Ct. at 726 (citations omitted). The Court further stated its belief that the privacy right is "founded in the Fourteenth Amendment's concept of personal liberty." *Id.* at 153, 93 S.Ct. at 727.

The inescapable conclusion arising from the foregoing authorities is that the Alsagers possess a fundamental "liberty" and "privacy" interest in maintaining the integrity of their family unit. *See generally,* Note, *Parental Consent Requirements and Privacy Rights of Minors: The Contraceptive Controversy,* 88 Harv.L.Rev. 1001, 1014-19 (1975). It is this fundamental right to family integrity, protected by the Due Process Clause of the Fourteenth Amendment, which is menaced by Iowa's parental termination statute.

The Alsagers' constitutional arguments will now be considered with the foregoing premises regarding fundamental rights in mind. Plaintiffs challenge the statute as "void for vagueness" and as violative of their rights to substantive and procedural Due Process. While the Court believes the vagueness challenge to be dispositive, it will address the substantive and procedural Due Process issues as well, in order to promote a plenary disposition of this long-running controversy.

Vagueness

Dating back at least to *United States* v. *L. Cohen Grocery Co.,* 255 U.S. 81, 41 S.Ct 298, 65 L.Ed. 516 (1921), federal courts have been called upon to determine whether statutes embody such vague standards as to deny Due Process of Law. While vagueness attacks are made most often in a criminal context, the Supreme Court has held that "civil" statutes are susceptible to vagueness challenges as well. *A.B. Small Co.* v. *American Sugar Ref. Co.,* 267 U.S. 233, 45 S.Ct. 295, 69 L.Ed. 589 (1925). A vagueness attack stems from "the exaction of obedience to a rule or standard which [is] so vague and indefinite as really to be no rule or standard at all." *Id.* at 239, 45 S.Ct. at

297. In *Giaccio* v. *Pennsylvania*, 382 U.S. 399, 86 S.Ct. 518, 15 L.Ed.2d 447 (1966), the Supreme Court reiterated:

> Both liberty and property are specifically protected by the Fourteenth Amendment against any state deprivation which does not meet the standards of due process, and this protection is not to be avoided by the simple label a state chooses to fasten upon its conduct or its statute. So here this state Act whether labeled "penal" or not must meet the challenge that it is unconstitutionally vague. *Id*. at 402, 86 S.Ct. at 520.

In *Giaccio* a jury acquitted the defendant on a misdemeanor indictment but assessed prosecution costs on him, as permitted by Pennsylvania statute, because he was found guilty of "some misconduct" other than that charged. Notwithstanding the state's assertion that the statute merely provided for the collection of costs of a "civil character," the Court found the statute unconstitutionally vague. Accordingly, the State of Iowa cannot avoid a vagueness challenge here by claiming the "civil character" of its parental termination statute. Indeed, the permanent destruction of the family unit—a severe infringement of a fundamental right—is a much more drastic consequence than the imposition of prosecutorial costs.

The United States Supreme Court has identified several dangers inherent in vague laws:

> It is a basic principle of due process that an enactment is void for vagueness if its prohibitions are not clearly defined. Vague laws offend several important values. First, because we assume that man is free to steer between lawful and unlawful conduct, we insist that laws give the person of ordinary intelligence a reasonable opportunity to know what is prohibited, so that he may act accordingly. Vague laws may trap the innocent by not providing fair warning. Second, if arbitrary and discriminatory enforcement is to be prevented, laws must provide explicit standards for those who apply them. A vague law impermissibly delegates basic policy matters to policemen, judges, and juries for resolution on an *ad hoc* and subjective basis, with the attendant dangers of arbitrary and discriminatory application. Third, but related, where a vague statute "abut[s] upon sensitive areas of basic First Amendment freedoms," it "operates to inhibit the exercise of [those] freedoms." Uncertain meanings inevitably lead citizens to " 'steer far wider of the unlawful zone'... than if the boundaries of the forbidden areas were clearly marked" (Footnotes omitted). *Grayned* v. *City of Rockford*, 408 U.S. 104, 108-09, 92 S.Ct. 2294, 2298-2299, 33 L.Ed.2d 222 (1972).

Vague statutes thus carry three dangers: the absence of fair warning, the impermissible delegation of discretion, and the undue inhibition of the legitimate exercise of a constitutional right. An analysis of these dangers in the context of the challenged standards of the Iowa parental termination statute leads the Court to conclude that the portions of the Iowa parental termination statute invoked against the Alsagers are unconstitutionally vague.

The initial danger present in a vague statute is the absence of fair warning. Citizens should be able to guide their conduct by the literal meaning of phrases expressed on the face of statutes. When the standard embodied in a statute is susceptible to multifarious meanings, a person may believe that his actions comply with the law, only to have the law used against him. The standards of "necessary parental care and protection," § 232.41(2)(b), and of "[parental] conduct... detrimental to the physical or mental health or morals of the child," § 232.41(2)(d), are susceptible to multifarious interpretations which prevent the ordinary person from knowing what is and is not prohibited. An examination of these phrases will not inform an ordinary person as to what conduct is required or must be avoided in order to prevent parental termination. For instance, a parent might follow a rigid scheme of "discipline-instilling" corporal punishment believing himself in full compliance with the law, only to learn of his folly at a termination proceeding. The standards challenged here simply fail to give "the person of ordinary intelligence a reasonable opportunity to know what is prohibited."

The second danger present in a vague statute is the impermissible delegation of discretion from the state legislature to the state law enforcement body. The Iowa parental termination standards of "necessary parental care and protection," § 232.41(2)(b), and of "[parental] conduct . . . detrimental to the physical or mental health or morals of the child," § 232.41(2)(d), afford state officials with so much discretion in their interpretation and application that arbitrary and discriminatory parental terminations are inevitable. *Cf. Saia* v. *New York*, 334 U.S. 558, 68 S.Ct. 1148, 92 L.Ed. 1574 (1948). Indeed, the Supreme Court has recently noted that "perhaps the most meaningful aspect of the vagueness doctrine is . . . the requirement that a legislature establish minimal guidelines to govern law enforcement." *Smith* v. *Goguen*, 415 U.S. 566, 574, 94 S.Ct. 1242, 1248, 39 L.Ed.2d 605 (1974). Under Iowa's current scheme, state officials may subjectively determine, on an *ad hoc* basis, what parental conduct is "necessary" and what parental conduct is "detrimental." The termination of the parent-child relationship in any given case may thus turn upon which state officials are involved in the case, rather than upon explicit standards reflecting legislative intent. This danger is especially grave in the highly subjective context of determining an approved mode of child-rearing. The Court finds these standards unconstitutionally vague in that they are permeated with the "dangers of arbitrary and discriminatory application."

The third danger present in a vague statute is the risk that the exercise of constitutional rights will be inhibited. The Iowa parental termination standards of "necessary parental care and protection." § 232.41(2)(b), and of "[parental] conduct . . . detrimental to the physical or mental health or morals of the child," § 232.41(2)(d), serve to inhibit parents in the exercise of their fundamental right to family integrity. Wary of what conduct is required and what conduct must be avoided to prevent termination, parents might fail to exercise their rights freely and fully. The risk that parents will be forced to "steer far wider of the unlawful zone" than is constitutionally necessary is not justified when the state is capable of enacting less ambiguous termination standards. The Court finds the aforementioned standards unconstitutionally vague in that they deter parents from conduct which is constitutionally protected.

Although the Court has found the Iowa parental termination standards of "necessary parental care and protection," § 232.41(2)(b), and of "[parental] conduct . . . detrimental to the physical or mental health or morals of the child," § 232.41(2)(d), to be unconstitutionally vague, this determination in terms of the facial defects of the statute is not necessarily fatal; the Court must next determine whether this vagueness has been cured, either generally, by the Iowa Supreme Court's decisions in other termination cases, or specifically, by the Iowa Supreme Court's opinion in this case. As the United States Supreme Court indicated in *Grayned, supra,* the defect of an enactment's vagueness can be ameliorated by a state court construction restricting the vague standards to constitutionally permissible bounds. In fact, in *Grayned,* the Court concluded that an imprecise phrase in an anti-noise statute had been cured by the Illinois Supreme Court's delimiting construction of a similar phrase in another ordinance. 408 U.S. at 111, 92 S.Ct. 2294. *Grayned* thus suggests that the Iowa standards may be saved from their unconstitutional vagueness if the needed specificity has been supplied by the Iowa Supreme Court. Regrettably, the Iowa Supreme Court has not perfected a general or specific cure of these standards.

The parental termination statute presently under attack was enacted in 1965 by the Sixty-first General Assembly of the State of Iowa. Since then a number of cases brought pursuant thereto have been reviewed de novo by the Iowa Supreme Court. In the great majority of decisions involving an application of the standards of "necessary parental care and protection," and of "[parental] conduct . . . detrimental to the physical or mental health or morals of the child," the Iowa court has simply made a determination as to the "substantiality of the evidence" to support a finding based on those standards. The Iowa court has never attempted a restrictive construction of the termination standards themselves. Moreover, the Iowa courts did not attempt to restrict the scope of the statute while terminating the Alsagers' parent-child relationships. Indeed, the Alsagers were subjected to all the vagueness dangers inherent in the indefinite standards of § 232.41(2)(b) and (d).

The Alsagers were not given fair warning of what was and was not prohibited by the Iowa law. The petition which instituted the termination proceeding against them merely alleged the conclusory language of the statute: "refused to give their children necessary parental care and protection" and "conduct detrimental to the physical or mental health or morals of their children." A reading of the petition and the termination statute would not have given the Alsagers notice of what they were doing wrong. They were not given a factual basis from which to predict how they should modify their past conduct, their "parenting," to avoid termination.

The May 22, 1970 Findings of Fact of the juvenile court, which did catalogue some of the familial deficiencies the state judge felt were most telling, merely incorporated that court's prior legal conclusion that "the allegation that the parents have substantially and continuously and repeatedly refused to give their children necessary care and protection and that they are unfit parents by reason of conduct detrimental to the physical or mental health or morals of their children has been sustained by a preponderance of the evidence." Thus, the Alsagers were once again faced with establishing that their conduct fell outside the potentially boundless scope of § 232.41(2)(b) and (d).

On appeal, the Iowa Supreme Court failed to narrow the statute by specific references to the defective conduct of the Alsagers. Instead, without identifying the statutory basis for affirmance, the Court held that the "material facts" were "identical" to those of *In re McDonald,* 201 N.W.2d 447 (Iowa 1972). This reliance on *McDonald,* which itself contained no narrowing criteria, serves to emphasize the dangers inherent in the vague standards involved. *McDonald* was not only based upon an entirely separate statutory ground than those alleged here, its material facts differed substantially from those of *Alsager*.

McDonald involved a parental termination based upon § 232.41(2)(e): "That following an adjudication of neglect or dependency, reasonable efforts under the direction of the court have failed to correct the conditions leading to the termination." However, § 232.41(2)(e) was not alleged as grounds for the Alsagers' termination. The Iowa Supreme Court has itself held it to be a denial of due process to terminate parental rights on a ground not alleged in the petition to terminate. *In re Robbins,* 230 N.W.2d 489 (Iowa 1975).

Moreover, *McDonald* involved a parent with a clinically tested I.Q. of 47. This fact was heavily relied on by the *McDonald* court in concluding that the parent was unable to care for her children. In contrast, the record here reveals no intelligence testing of the Alsagers. Nor is there any evidence which suggests the Alsagers lacked the mental capacity to perform parental functions. The Iowa court's conclusion claiming an identity of material fact between these two divergent cases is not justified by the record.

The Iowa Supreme Court's failure to cure the vagueness defects of § 232.41, either through a general narrowing construction in prior cases, or by a specific narrowing construction in the Alsagers' own case, leads this Court to conclude that the Alsagers were denied Due Process. The pertinent statutory language is overly vague, both on its face and as applied to the Alsagers. The Iowa court's decision indicates that the Alsagers were found only to have breached these vague standards. In the absence of a showing that the plaintiffs violated a permissibly specific termination standard, their parental termination constitutes a denial of Due Process.

In sum, the Iowa parental termination standards of "necessary parental care and protection" and of "[parental] conduct . . . detrimental to the physical or mental health or morals of the child," are unconstitutionally vague, both on their face and as applied, in that (1) they do not, and did not here, give fair warning of what parental conduct is proscribed, (2) they permit, and permitted here, arbitrary and discriminatory terminations, (3) they inhibit, and inhibited here, the exercise of the fundamental right to family integrity. This Court is not indifferent to the difficulties confronting the State of Iowa when attempting to regulate parental conduct vis-à-vis the child. Nevertheless, Due Process requires the state to clearly identify and define the evil from which the child needs protection and to specify what parental conduct so contributes to that evil that the state is justified in terminating the parent-child relationship.

Substantive Due Process

As an alternative to the vagueness challenge, plaintiffs contend that § 232.41(2)(b) and (d) violate Due Process in that neither subsection requires a showing of a "high and substantial degree of harm to the children" as a prerequisite to termination, nor do they require the state to pursue "less drastic" alternatives prior to resorting to termination.

The United States Supreme Court has provided the following constitutional framework for analyzing statutes which encroach upon protected rights: "Where certain 'fundamental rights' are involved, the Court has held that regulation limiting these rights may be justified only by a 'compelling state interest,' and that legislative enactments must be narrowly drawn to express only the legitimate state interest at stake.'' (citations omitted). *Roe* v. *Wade,* 410 U.S. 113, 155, 93 S.Ct. 705, 728, 35 L.Ed.2d 147 (1973). Accordingly, this Court must determine whether § 232.41(2)(b) and (d) further a "compelling" state interest as justification for parent terminations, and whether these subsections are narrowly drawn so as to express only that compelling interest.

It cannot seriously be disputed that the state seeks to further a legitimate state interest when it sets out to protect the welfare of its citizens of tender age. Indeed, as the Supreme Court recognized in *Stanley* v. *Illinois,* 405 U.S. 645, 92 S.Ct. 1208, 31 L.Ed.2d 551 (1972), the state has the "right" and the "duty" to protect minor children. *Id.* at 649, 92 S.Ct. 1208. *See also Prince* v. *Massachusetts,* 321 U.S. 158, 166, 64 S.Ct. 438, 88 L.Ed. 645 (1944).

The state's interest in protecting children is not absolute, however. It must be balanced against the parents' countervailing interest in being able to raise their children in an environment free from government interference. Moreover, in determining the "compelling" nature of the state's child protection interests when a parental termination is undertaken, an understanding of the mechanics of Iowa law is essential. Even in a case of clear child abuse, Iowa law has vitiated the need for prompt termination action through its child neglect statute, §§ 232.2(15), 232.33, Iowa Code. That law sanctions the immediate, albeit temporary, removal of a child from the parents' home in cases of maltreatment. The Court's ruling today as to the adequacy of Iowa's termination standards is in no way intended to restrict the state's ability to take swift action when necessary to prevent imminent harm or suffering to a child. Once a child has been removed from the risk of harm, however, as well as in cases where the risks of harm are insufficient to justify temporary separation, the state's child protection interests are less compelling. Accordingly, the Court deems that termination proceedings should be distinguished from immediate removal proceedings for purposes of substantive due process analysis. The state's interest in protecting a child from future harm at the hands of his or her parents is clearly less compelling in a situation where the state has already obtained temporary protective custody over the child than in those cases where the supposedly threatened child remains in the parents' home.

It is the Court's conclusion that the evidence urged in this case was wholly insufficient to constitute a "compelling state interest" in terminating the protected parent-child relationship of this already separated family. The evidence reveals that the Alsagers sometimes permitted their children to leave the house in cold weather without winter clothing on, "allowed them" to play in traffic, to annoy neighbors, to eat mush for supper, to live in a house containing dirty dishes and laundry, and to sometimes arrive late at school.

At the time of the termination, Mr. Alsager was a working man who had never been on public welfare rolls. He and his wife lived together, and shared an interest in keeping their family unit intact. The Court cites this evidence not to contradict the findings of the juvenile court, but simply to describe the general nature of the Alsagers' family situation in 1969. The Court accepts the juvenile court's factual findings, but agrees with Dr. Robert Kugel and Dr. Kenneth Berry, plaintiffs' trial experts, who testified that even if all of the evidence harmful to the Alsagers is assumed to be true, their home situation did not justify permanent termination. The probative termination standard to which the Alsagers were subjected in 1969 and 1970 was simply not high enough to ensure that their fundamental parental rights would not be violated. Stated differently, the Alsager family unit was severed on the basis of evidence which was insufficient to give the state a "child-protection interest" compelling enough to require termination.

As plaintiffs concede, the statute's vagueness is a partial cause of its amenability to broad application. Nonetheless, even in the context of a precise and specific enactment, Due Process requires a certain threshold of harm to the child to justify termination. In this regard, the Court accepts plaintiffs' argument that to sustain its compelling interest burden, the state must show that the consequences, in harm to the children, of allowing the parent-child relationship to continue are more severe than the consequences of termination. This burden was clearly not met in the instant case.

The evidence shows the Alsagers to have been affectionate parents, of below average but by no means inadequate intelligence, who lost their children through application of the loose standards, if any, contained within § 232.41(2)(b) and (d). No actual or imminent harm to the children was shown to exist as a prerequisite to termination. This Court has heard much evidence pertaining to the harmful effects which improvident physical separations and final terminations can visit upon young children. If anything has been made clear throughout these proceedings, it is that the area of predicting what will be in the best future interests of the child is a delicate one. Through the benefit of hindsight, this Court can today see no apparent benefit to the 1970 termination. As indicated by plaintiffs' counsel at trial, during the interim from 1969 to 1974, Alsager children John, Charles, Michael and Albert between them experienced some 15 separate foster home placements, and eight juvenile home placements. The uncertainty of post-termination life is further depicted by the fact that when the case was first argued before this Court in March of 1974, plaintiffs' experts recommended that even if the termination proceedings were ruled unconstitutional, two of the children should be permanently placed in their present foster homes. *See* 384 F.Supp. at 651. Some months later, by the time this case was before the Circuit Court of Appeals, the situation had changed in that the two "well-adjusted" boys had apparently rejected their foster homes and were being considered for probationary placements with their parents. 518 F.2d at 1166.

Termination has thus failed to provide the Alsager children with either stable or improved lives. Based on their parents' capabilities, the Court cannot say that separation has benefited the children in any discernible way. In the eyes of plaintiffs' experts, they have been harmed. One lesson emerges clearly from this sad testament. Termination is a drastic, final step which, when improvidently employed, can be fraught with danger. Accordingly, to preserve the best interests of both parents and children, the Court deems that terminations must only occur where more harm is likely to befall the child by staying with his parents than by being permanently separated from them. In such a circumstance, the state does have a compelling interest in curtailing the parents' familial rights. The facts of this case do not rise to that level of harm, however. Accordingly, because the Alsagers' legal relationships to their children were severed in the absence of a compelling state interest, the plaintiffs Due Process rights were violated. Furthermore, § 232.41(b) and (d), to the extent they allow such terminations, clearly "sweep too broadly" by encompassing family situations where no compelling interest exists for termination. Thus, the subsections deny Due Process both on their face and as they were applied in the instant case.[19]

Procedural Due Process

Plaintiffs claim that they were denied procedural Due Process in that (1) the notice given them regarding the termination proceeding was inadequate, (2) the standard of proof employed by the juvenile court required a mere preponderance of the evidence rather than clear and convincing evidence, (3) hearsay evidence was admitted, and (4) *ex parte* communications between the judge and witnessing employees of the juvenile court may have occurred. The Court finds merit in plaintiffs' claims that the notice given them was inadequate and that the standard of proof employed was insufficient. As to the latter two claims, the hearsay evidence admitted was considered only to the extent of its probative value. *See*, Code of Iowa § 232.31. The Court is confident that the juvenile court judge was able to discern probative value absent the safeguards provided by the hearsay rule. Second, the record does not disclose that actual *ex parte* communications occurred. The plaintiffs' assertion that they "may" have occurred is not sufficient to warrant a determination on that issue. Accordingly, the Court finds these two contentions to be without merit.

The plaintiffs argue that the notice given them was insufficient to satisfy Due Process. The Court agrees. The Fourteenth Amendment requires notice in parental termination proceedings to contain both the alleged factual basis for the proposed termination and a statement of the legal standard authorizing termination.

In *In re Gault*, 387 U.S. 1, 87 S.Ct. 1428, 18 L.Ed.2d 527 (1967), the Supreme Court outlined the type of notice which due process requires:

> Notice, to comply with due process requirements, must be given sufficiently in advance of scheduled court proceedings so that reasonable opportunity to prepare will be afforded, and it must "set forth the alleged misconduct with particularity". . . . [P]arents [must] be notified, in writing, of the specific charge or factual allegations. . . .

Although *Gault* involved a juvenile delinquency, the Court deems its exposition of Due Process "notice" to be equally applicable here.

The only written notice the Alsagers received of the grounds for termination was a copy of the petition filed in juvenile court. That petition merely paraphrased the

---

[19]Since the alternatives of providing outside community services to the Alsagers may or may not have existed at the time their parental relationship was terminated, the Court is unable to determine the issue raised by the plaintiffs in regard to requiring the state to pursue the "least drastic" alternative to parental termination. While the Court recognizes that the means employed by the state to achieve its compelling state interest must be narrowly tailored to achieve only that interest, *Shelton* v. *Tucker,* 364 U.S. 479, 81 S.Ct. 247, 5 L.Ed.2d 231 (1960); *Cleveland Board of Education* v. *LaFleur, supra; Lynch* v. *Baxley,* 386 F.Supp. 378, 392 (M.D.Ala. 1974), it is wary of saddling the state with service-oriented responsibilities which its limited resources may not allow. Moreover, the recent Iowa Supreme Court decision of *In re Rice,* filed December 17, 1975, reveals a present awareness in the state courts of the availability and utility of less drastic alternatives in the parent-child context.

vague and conclusory language of the parental termination statute, § 232.41(2)(b) and (d):

> [T]he best interests of the children . . . require that the parent-child relationships . . . be terminated by the Court because said parents have substantially and continuously and repeatedly refused to give their children necessary parental care and protection and because said parents are unfit parents by reason of conduct detrimental to the physical or mental health or morals of their children. (Juvenile Court transcript at 5-6).

The state admits that its petitions for parental termination do not specify allegations of abuse, mistreatment or parental failings. However, the state argues that the "specific charge" language from *Gault* means only that the parents be informed as to what section or subsection of the Code of Iowa will be used to justify termination.

In *Lynch* v. *Baxley,* 386 F.Supp. 378 (M.D.Ala. 1974), a three-judge court applied the *Gault* notice requirements to civil commitment proceedings. There the court concluded that

> such notice should include the date, time and place of the hearing; a clear statement of the purpose of the proceedings and the possible consequences to the subject thereof; the alleged factual basis for the proposed commitment; and a statement of the legal standard upon which commitment is authorized. *Id.* at 388.

Given the nature of the parental rights at stake, and the state's obvious interest in avoiding improvident terminations, the Court is unable to identify any reason why notice in parental termination proceedings should not follow *Baxley* and contain both the alleged factual basis for the proposed termination and a statement of the legal standard authorizing termination. *Cf. Wolff* v. *McDonnell,* 418 U.S. 539, 563-64, 94 S.Ct. 2963, 41 L.Ed.2d 935 (1974).

Plaintiffs argue that they were denied Due Process in that § 232.46 of the Code of Iowa authorizes, and the state court employed, a preponderance of the evidence standard of proof.

In *In re Winship,* 397 U.S. 358, 90 S.Ct. 1068, 25 L.Ed.2d 368 (1970), the Supreme Court looked to the nature of the right at stake in determining what standard of proof should be employed in a juvenile delinquency proceeding. In *Winship,* a child's liberty was at stake, so proof beyond a reasonable doubt was necessary. Similarly, this Court must look to the nature of the right involved in order to determine what standard of proof is required. *Baxley, supra,* held that involuntary civil commitment required at least a standard of clear and convincing evidence. Certainly, the fundamental right to family integrity deserves an equal standard. Moreover, § 232.31 of the Code of Iowa requires clear and convincing evidence in neglect, dependency and delinquency adjudications. The state would not be unduly burdened to treat parental termination adjudications in a similar fashion.

As a final matter, the Court notes that plaintiffs' amended complaint seeks $50,000 in damages for defendants' "willful violation of plaintiffs' constitutional rights." Plaintiffs do not argue that the defendants' actions were outside the scope of the pertinent Iowa statutes. Indeed, they concede that their parenting can be viewed as falling within the statutory language of § 232.41(2)(b) and (d). Their dissatisfaction goes to the potentially boundless scope of those provisions. As the Court noted in its prior Order, "the statute was followed in the state proceedings, and seemingly in good faith." 384 F.Supp. at 651. The Court reaffirms that conclusion here. The evidence is insufficient to justify an award of monetary damages from any of the defendants.

Conclusion

To conclude, the Court today holds that three major constitutional violations occurred in the termination proceedings utilized in 1969 and 1970 to sever the plaintiffs' legal ties with five of their six children. First, the pertinent language of § 232.41(2)(b) and (d) is simply too vague to withstand Fourteenth Amendment analysis. More importantly, however, that language was applied with no discernible narrowing of its broad scope. This Court is well aware of the difficulties inherent in drafting statutes in general, and especially statutes which deal with delicate areas such as familial rights. The Court does not imply by its ruling today the perfect legislative precision must always be obtained. It is the process of a statute's application which is crucial. Subsections (b) and (d), statutes undeniably broad in their scope, were imposed against the plaintiffs with no discernible narrowing of that breadth. Thus, their vagueness was not ameliorated, and plaintiffs' constitutional rights were transgressed. Second, plaintiffs' rights to substantive due process were violated because no compelling state interest was shown for the 1970 termination. The 1969–1970 familial situation of the Alsagers was simply not deficient enough to justify its end. These parents were trying to do the right thing. Under the facts of this case, they should have been allowed to continue to do so. Finally, the Court deems that the notice given the parents and the standard of proof employed in the termination proceedings failed to satisfy due process.

The plaintiffs today receive what they ask for—a declaration of the unconstitutionality of their termination proceedings. In so ruling, the Court is not operating under the delusion that the Alsager family's problems are now ended. The delineation of constitutional protections as it relates to the state, the parent, and the child should and must be approached with extreme caution. Harmony under trying family circumstances requires infinite patience, understanding, and sacrifice. This adjudication of the Alsager parents' constitutional rights regarding termination proceedings touches only one point of the triangle of rights. To state that it will put to rest all the family's difficulties and be a final solution to the problems which began in 1968 and 1969 would be the utmost in judicial conceit.

Accordingly, it is hereby declared that § 232.41(2)(b) and (d), on their face and more particularly as applied to the Alsagers, are unconstitutionally vague;

It is further declared that the Alsagers were denied substantial due process in the 1969 and 1970 termination proceedings, in that no compelling state interest justifying termination was shown;

It is further declared that the notice received by the Alsagers was defective, as was the standard of proof employed against them;

It is further ordered that the plaintiffs' claim for monetary damages, and their procedural due process challenges to hearsay evidence and improper communications to the juvenile court judge are dismissed.

It is further ordered that the above shall constitute the Findings of Fact, Conclusions of Law, and Order for Judgment in accordance with Rule 52(a) of the Federal Rules of Civil Procedure.

IT IS SO ORDERED.

ALSAGER V. DISTRICT COURT OF POLK COUNTY, IOWA

*United States Court of Appeals for the
Eighth Circuit, 1976
545 F.2d 1137*

Before GIBSON, Chief Judge, VAN OOSTERHOUT, Senior Circuit Judge, and HENLEY, Circuit Judge.

PER CURIAM.

The judgment appealed from is affirmed on the basis that plaintiffs were denied substantive due process, in that the State of Iowa failed to exhibit the threshold harm necessary to give the state a compelling interest sufficient to justify permanent termination of the parent-child relationships, and on the further basis that plaintiffs were denied procedural due process, in that they were not given adequate notice of what conduct allegedly warranted such termination, both in violation of the Fourteenth Amendment to the United States Constitution. On these two issues, we approve and adopt the opinion of the district court, the Honorable William C. Hanson, Chief Judge, United States District Court for the Southern District of Iowa, reported at 406 F.Supp. 10 (S.D.Iowa 1975).

Other issues reached by the district court, viz., the vagueness and overbreadth attacks upon the facial validity of *Code of Iowa* § 232.41(2)(b) and (d), 406 F.Supp. at 17-21 and 24, and the appropriate standard of proof at a parental termination hearing, 406 F.Supp. at 25, need not now be resolved in order to effect a plenary disposition of the present controversy between the parties, and we do not reach such issues. *See Garner* v. *Louisiana,* 368 U.S. 157, 162, 82 S.Ct. 248, 7 L.Ed.2d 207 (1961).

Although we decline to resolve whether the statutory provisions cited above are facially unconstitutional, as alternatively held by the district court, we cannot refrain from noting, at minimum, that both the vagueness and overbreadth attacks upon these provisions are serious ones. By declining to affirm on these grounds, however, we afford the Iowa courts an additional opportunity to give the statutory provisions a plainly desirable limiting construction. *See Grayned* v. *City of Rockford,* 408 U.S. 104, 111-12, 92 S.Ct. 2294, 33 L.Ed.2d 222 (1972) (vagueness), and *Broadrick* v. *Oklahoma,* 413 U.S. 601, 613, 93 S.Ct. 2908, 37 L.Ed.2d 830 (1973) (overbreadth). Given the obvious comity concerns at issue, we view such disposition as the one most appropriate.

Since we expressly reserve a ruling on the question of whether the Iowa statutory provisions at issue in this case are facially unconstitutional, there is no collateral estoppel effect to be accorded the district court's resolution of this question in the future. 1B J. Moore, *Federal Practice* ¶ 0.416[2], at 2232 (2d ed. 1974). *See Lathan* v. *Brinegar,* 506 F.2d 677, 691 (9th Cir. 1974).

The judgment appealed from is affirmed insofar as it declares that the termination proceedings against plaintiffs violated their rights to substantive and procedural due process.

NOTES

1.   Under the reasoning of the district court in *Alsager* as to substantive due process, were *Paul, McDonald,* and *Appeal in Maricopa County Juv. Action* cases correctly decided?

2.   If the parents in *Alsager* had been formally diagnosed as mentally ill or mentally retarded would the *Alsager* court have reached a different result? Would it not have had to distinguish any such case from *In re McDonald* in order not to terminate parental rights?

3.   In view of footnote 19 in *Alsager,* would the court have ordered the provision of supportive services to the Alsagers before their rights had been terminated?

4.   Is there a significant difference between the statutes upheld in *In re William L.* and struck down in *Alsager*?

5.   Do the requirements of procedural due process dictate that the child and parent each have a right to independent counsel in a termination proceeding? Generally, it has been held that indigent parents are entitled to court-appointed counsel in such cases. See *Crist* v. *Division of Youth and Family Services,* 128 N.J.Super. 402, 320 A.2d 203 (1974); *In re Adoption of R.I.,* 312 A.2d 601 (Pa. 1973); *In re Friesz,* 190 Neb. 347, 208 N.W.2d 259 (1973); *State* v. *Jamison* 444 P.2d 15 (1968). Provision of independent counsel also has been required for children. See *State ex. rel. Juv. Dept. of Multnomah County* v. *Wade,* 527 P.2d 753 (Oreg. 1974).

ADDITIONAL READING

Anno. 74 A.L.R.2d 1073, "Mental Health of Contesting Parent as Factor in Award of Child Custody."

Note, "Termination of the Parent-Child Relationship: Should Parental I.Q. Be an Important Factor?" *Law and the Social Order* 855, 865-66 (1973).

Comment, "The Indigent Parent's Right to Appointed Council in Actions to Terminate Parental Rights," 43 *Cincinnati L. Rev.* 635 (1974).

Piersma, P., Ganousis, J., and Kramer, P., "The Juvenile Court: Current Problems, Legislative Proposals and a Model Act," 20 *St. Louis U. L.J.* 1 (1975).

Recent Developments, "Parent and Child," 14 *J. Fam. L.* 341 (1975).

Note, "Low Intelligence of the Parent: A New Ground for State Interference with the Parent-Child Relationship?" 13 *J. Fam. L.* 379 (1973-74).

10

CONTRACTS, OWNERSHIP, AND TRANSFERS OF PROPERTY

Robert L. Burgdorf, Jr.

A. CONTRACTS AND CONVEYANCES

1. By Mentally Handicapped Persons

Perhaps no branch of jurisprudence is more tenuous or spectral than that dealing with one's mental capacity to contract. Law books are replete with comments by text- and opinion-writers who have sought, figuratively, to ascertain where the strip of herbage lies "that just divides the desert from the sown"; yet all too often have their labors been in vain.

If the brain has become so affected, irrespective of cause, as to contracept one's power to reason, and in consequence the ordinary affairs of life are not reflected on that mirror called mind, it is generally agreed that the impulse to act, or the absence of impulse, is not the result of intellectual motivation; hence, the attendant infirmity intervenes to protect one so afflicted from the penalty of conduct in respect of which the power to think and to plan reasonably logical sequence are non-existent. *Waggoner* v. *Atkins,* 204 Ark. 264, 162 S.W.2d 55, 58 (1942).

DEXTER V. HALL

Supreme Court of the United States, 1872
82 U.S. (15 Wall.) 9

Mr. Justice STRONG delivered the opinion of the court.

The prominent question in this case is, whether a power of attorney executed by a lunatic is void, or whether it is only voidable. The Circuit Court instructed the jury that a lunatic, or insane person, being of unsound mind, was incapable of executing a contract, deed, power of attorney, or other instrument requiring volition and understanding, and that a power of attorney executed by an insane person, or one of unsound mind, was absolutely void. To this instruction the defendant below excepted, and he has now assigned it for error.

Looking at the subject in the light of reason, it is difficult to perceive how one incapable of understanding, and of acting in the ordinary affairs of life, can make an instrument the efficacy of which consists in the fact that it expresses his intention, or, more properly, his mental conclusions. The fundamental idea of a contract is that it requires the assent of two minds. But a lunatic, or a person *non compos mentis,* has nothing which the law recognizes as a mind, and it would seem, therefore, upon principle, that he cannot make a contract which may have any efficacy as such. He is not amenable to the criminal laws, because he is incapable of discriminating between that which is right and that which is wrong. The government does not hold him responsible for acts injurious to itself. Why, then, should one who has obtained from him that which purports to be a contract be permitted to hold him bound by its provisions, even until he may choose to avoid it? If this may be, efficacy is given to a form to which there has been no mental assent. A contract is made without any agreement of minds. And as it plainly requires the possession and exercise of reason quite as much to avoid a contract as to make it, the contract of a person without mind has the same effect as it would have had he been in full possession of ordinary understanding. While he continues insane he cannot avoid it; and if, therefore, it is operative until avoided, the law affords a lunatic no protection against himself. Yet a lunatic, equally with an infant, is confessedly under the protection of courts of law as well as courts of equity. The contracts of the latter, it is true, are generally held to be only voidable (his power of attorney being an exception). Unlike a lunatic, he is not destitute of reason. He has mind, but it is immature, insufficient to justify his assuming a binding obligation. And he may deny or avoid his contract at any time, either during his minority or after he comes of age. This is for him a sufficient protection. But as a lunatic cannot avoid a contract, for want of mental capacity, he has no protection if his contract is only voidable.

It must be admitted, however, that there are decisions which have treated deeds and conveyances of idiots and lunatics as merely voidable, and not void. In *Beverly's Case* [76 Eng.R. 1118, 4 Co.Rep. 123b (1603)], which was a bill for relief against a bond made by Snow, a lunatic, it was resolved that every deed, feoffment, or grant, which any man *non compos mentis* makes, is avoidable, and yet shall not be avoided by himself, because it is a maxim of law that no man of full age shall be, in any plea to be pleaded by him, received by the law to stultify himself and disable his own person. A second reason given for the rule was, "because when he recovers his memory he cannot know what he did when he was *non compos mentis.*" Neither of these reasons are now accepted, and the maxim no longer exists.

[The remainder of the Court's opinion is omitted.]

NOTES

1. The *Dexter* opinion represents a one hundred eighty degree doctrinal rotation from the principles announced in the venerable *Beverly's Case*. The non-stultification doctrine promulgated in *Beverly's Case* meant that the validity of a contract or conveyance entered into by a mentally ill or mentally retarded person could not be challenged during that person's lifetime; such transactions were, therefore, fully valid in effect. Under the *Dexter* holding, based upon a "meeting of the minds" theory of contracts, however, such transactions were totally void, irrespective of their being challenged by any party.

Prior to the *Dexter* ruling, English courts had already arrived at a moderate position between the extremes of absolute validity and total voidness. In *Molton* v. *Camroux*, 2 Ex. 487, 154 Eng.Rep. 584 (1848), aff'd, 4 Ex. 17, 154 Eng.Rep. 1107

(1849), it was held that the contracts of a person of unsound mind were voidable and that unsoundness of mind could be a defense in an action for enforcement of a contract. In certain circumstances, however, such contracts might not be voidable:

> [W]hen a person, apparently of sound mind, and not known to be otherwise, enters into a contract for the purchase of property which is fair and *bona fide,* and which is executed and completed, and the property, the subject-matter of the contract, has been paid for and fully enjoyed, and cannot be restored so as to put the parties in *status quo,* such contract cannot afterwards be set aside, either by the alleged lunatic, or those who represent him. *Id.* at 154 Eng. Rep. 590.

With minor variations, the principles of *Molton* v. *Camroux* have continued to serve as the applicable standards in such cases in England until the present day.

2. Does the *Dexter* reasoning serve to protect the interests of mentally handicapped people? Of those who make contracts with mentally handicapped persons? What other interests does it serve?

CHARLES MELBOURNE AND SONS, INC. v. JESSET

Court of Appeals of Ohio, Cuyahoga County, 1960
110 Oh.App. 502, 163 N.E.2d 773

SKEEL, Judge.

This appeal comes to this court on questions of law from a judgment for the plaintiff entered in the Municipal Court of Rocky River. The plaintiff, a funeral director, at the request of Mrs. Laura Jesset, on August 5, 1955, entered into a contract with her to conduct the funeral services of her husband and to furnish the necessary material for the sum of $1,054.69. The services were performed as provided by the contract. A claim was made against the estate which was determined to be insolvent and $350 of the estate's assets paid on the claim as the plaintiff's share.

This action was filed against the defendant through her guardian appointed April 15, 1957. The defendant, Laura Jesset, was first adjudged incompetent in the Probate Court of Cuyahoga County after hearing on the affidavit sworn to and filed by William G. Jesset on July 10, 1940. The date of the adjudication was October 29, 1940. She was thereafter discharged from the State Hospital as improved July 31, 1944. On August 12, 1955, her son, William G. Jesset, filed a second affidavit charging mental incompetence against his mother, Laura Jesset, and upon hearing, she was again committed to Hawthornden State Hospital. The second adjudication was dated August 17, 1955. On September 16, 1955, a guardian was appointed for her estate who served until April 15, 1957, and filed his final account. The present guardian, William G. Jesset, son of Laura Jesset, was then appointed guardian of her estate and is still acting in that capacity.

From July 31, 1944, until the date the contract was signed, and from then until August 12, 1955, she was a free agent to act for herself without guardian or any other court supervision. It is also shown by the record that when the contract was signed, Laura Jesset was in the company of her two children, her son, William G. Jesset (now guardian), and her daughter, Joan Supplee, a resident of California, with whom Laura Jesset now resides. Neither of the children suggested anything about the mental history of their mother, nor is there any suggestion that at the time the contract was signed, her conduct was anything other than normal.

The second affidavit was signed by William G. Jesset after the defendant's husband had died, certainly a most disturbing incident in the now incompetent's life, the action being taken when no member of her family was available in this community for her care or companionship except the affiant, William G. Jesset.

Two questions are present: first, is the contract with the plaintiff enforceable, that is, is the adjudication of incompetence in 1940, under the undisputed circumstances here set out, a complete defense, and second, were the services rendered by the plaintiff necessaries which the guardian of the now adjudged incompetent's estate is bound to pay.

* * *

Funeral expenses of a deceased husband are the obligation of the widow, and as to her, are to be characterized as necessaries when the estate of the husband is insolvent, as is shown by the undisputed facts in this case. The public health, as well as the moral well-being of the widow, requires this to be so. The satisfaction of such a debt cannot be measured by the assets of the deceased's estate where the contract of the widow induced the expenditure of monies for the services rendered for her, and for which she agreed to pay.

It is true, as suggested by the defendant, that the amount recoverable for necessaries furnished a minor must be based on reasonable value under the circumstances and not the contract price unless such amount is less than the value determined to be reasonable, which rule has some limited application in the case of an incompetent. Whether the liability of an incompetent for necessaries would represent the only basis for recovery, without deviation, on his contracts, is not so clear. Some qualifications of the rule concerning the liability of persons said to be insane on their executed contracts is to be found in the cases. In the first place, the contract of a person *non compos mentis* is voidable and not void so that the party claiming disability must set up the lack of mental capacity as an affirmative defense and must assume the burden of proof on that issue.

In the case of *Finch* v. *Goldstein,* 1927, 245 N.Y. 300, 157 N.E. 146, the court had for consideration the question of whether the deed of an insane person having been summarily committed to an asylum prior to its execution was void, and whether the insane person's committee could enforce the provisions of the mortgage back. The facts in the case show that on September 16, 1920, Finch was determined to be mentally deranged and committed to the Hudson River State Hospital for the Insane. While there, to the knowledge of the defendant, Goldstein, he executed a deed of a farm, part of the consideration of which was a mortgage back to the incompetent. Thereafter, a committee was appointed for the incompetent and foreclosure brought on the mortgage. The first and third paragraphs of the headnotes of the North Eastern Reporter provide:

> 1.   Deed made by one while confined in the state hospital under a summary commitment by the county judge . . . , and before the appointment of a committee for his person and property . . . , was voidable only, and not void, and the committee on ratifying the conveyance was entitled to foreclose the purchase-money mortgage.

* * *

3. A lunatic retains exclusive possession and control of his property after his commitment to the state hospital by the county judge, . . . , until such time as a committee to take possession of his property may be appointed, ...

The answer in this case, denying all material allegations of the petition prejudicial to the defendant, was in accord with Revised Code, § 2309.20. However, that does not relieve the defendant from the burden of proving his affirmative defenses on the issues which was not done in this case. In the second place, courts have departed from the view that contracts with persons of unsound mind are not enforceable in all events. Where the other party to a contract is ignorant of the lack of mental capacity of the party he is dealing with, and the transaction was fair, and no advantage was taken of the incompetent, and he has received the full benefits of the transaction and cannot put the other contracting party in *status quo,* such contract may be enforced against the incompetent party. Williston in his single volume work on Sales (1909) paragraph 33, page 36, states: "In the leading case of *Molton* v. *Camroux* (2 Ex. 487; 4 Ex. 17), the rule was stated 'The modern cases show that when that state of mind was unknown to the other contracting party, and no advantage was taken of the lunatic, the defense cannot prevail, especially where the contract is not merely executory but executed in the whole or in part and the parties cannot be restored altogether to their original positions.' " And on pages 37 and 38, "in this country the weight of authority certainly supports the rule quoted above from *Molton* v. *Camroux.* . . . . So negotiable paper executed by a lunatic is binding in the hands of an innocent holder for value, if the lunatic received a proper consideration therefor." See *Hosler* v. *Beard,* 1896, 54 Ohio St. 398, 43 N.E. 1040, 35 L.R.A. 161, 56 Am.St.Rep. 720. In the case of *Pichel* v. *Fair Store Co.,* 29 Ohio App. 322, 163 N.E. 511, the court said:

1. Where contract has been entered into with insane person in good faith, without knowledge of insanity, and for fair and adequate consideration, and consideration that passed to insane person cannot be returned, contract can be enforced in favor of the other party.
2. Where insane person entered into contract to pay certain sum in consideration for plaintiff's dismissal of suit on an account for necessaries, and plaintiff acted in good faith, and did not know of insanity, contract was enforceable against deceased insane person's estate, where action was barred on the original account, and thus it was impossible to restore to plaintiff consideration received from it by insane person.

In the case of *Middleton* v. *Bradstreet,* 11 Ohio Law Abst. 413, the first paragraph of the headnotes provides:

1. A contract with an insane person will not be set aside when entered in good faith and without notice of the infirmity unless the parties can be restored to *status quo.*

Under the undisputed facts, as stipulated, not only was the plaintiff completely unaware of any lack of mental capacity on the part of the now supposed incompetent defendant but the conduct of the children, who were fully cognizant of their mother's past history, and who were with her when the funeral was contracted for, did not indicate any possible lack of mental capacity on her part.

This presents the final question as to whether or not the adjudication of mental incompetency on the public records of the Probate Court in 1940, which records also show that she was discharged from the state mental hospital as "improved" in 1944, could charge the plaintiff with knowledge of her then mental condition. In considering the facts, one fact must be kept clearly in mind. Upon the first adjudication of mental incapacity in 1940, the court did not appoint a guardian either of her person or her estate. Upon her release in 1944, until after the death of her husband in 1955, she lived with her husband with no suggestion in the evidence of other than a normal life. It is significant that, as shown by the record, when she was again committed in 1955, a new affidavit was filed by her son (the first affidavit having been signed by her husband) and she was not returned under the first commitment from which the guardian now claims she was not fully released.

Referring again to Williston on Sales, *supra,* at page 42, paragraph 36, after stating that the guardian when appointed must act for his ward, he, the guardian, being vested with the control of the ward's property, and stating further that the guardian alone is capable of dealing with the ward's property, it is stated that any attempt of the ward to contract during guardianship is absolutely void. The author then says "The contrary has, however, been held where the lunatic had regained his reason and the guardianship had been allowed to fall in disuse although not legally terminated." Then, after stating that some cases stress where lunacy has been found by inquisition, and if so, his transactions are void, the author then says "The truth seems to be, however, that the finding merely establishes the fact of insanity, and the legal effect of the transaction is the same as it would be in any case of proved insanity. It is the appointment of a guardian which works the change in the legal power of a lunatic to act for himself."

In the case of *Weeks* v. *Reliance Fertilizer Co.,* 1917, 20 Ga.App. 498, 93 S.E. 152, the second syllabus provides:

> 2.   After the fact of insanity has been established by a court of competent jurisdiction in this state, and after the affairs of the insane person have been vested in a guardian, the power of the ward to contract, while such judgment and appointment remain of force, is gone; but where no guardian has been appointed and a contract is made by one engaged in business in his own behalf, who has been previously adjudged insane, the validity of the contract depends upon whether or not he was actually insane at the time the contract was entered into, and such a previous adjudication furnishes prima facie evidence that such condition continued to exist. The presumption so raised may be rebutted by proof.

The evidence in the instant case clearly rebuts the continuation of the so-called *prima facie* presention suggested as the law of the *Weeks* case. Mrs. Jesset for eleven years was about her neighborhood and circle of friends without claims of incompetency being suggested or that her improvement, which was sufficient to cause her discharge from the institution, did not continue. When recommitment was made after the death of her husband, it was by a new inquest and when the contract was made for the funeral, the man who signed the affidavit of incompetency was with his mother when she signed the contract. Certainly he must have thought she was sufficiently competent to enter into the contract for he did not speak out or suggest that his mother could not be held liable under the funeral contract by reason of insufficient mental capacity formerly established by adjudication or otherwise. We certainly would not want to conclude that

William G. Jesset stood mute, expecting thereby to defeat the right of the undertaker to be paid what was agreed to for the burial of his father.

Also in the case of *Summer* v. *Boyd*, 1951, 208 Ga. 207, 66 S.E.2d 51, 52, in the third paragraph of the headnotes of the South Eastern Reporter, it is said:

> 3. Where one has been adjudged insane by court of competent jurisdiction, but no guardian was appointed, validity of such person's contracts depends upon his sanity at time of execution.

The conclusion must be that the plaintiff dealt with the defendant honestly, without knowledge of any lack of mental capacity, or any indication that such was the fact, that full value was furnished (this question not being denied or the denial supported by evidence), and that any presumption that might be derived from the adjudication of mental incompetence adjudged in 1940, being completely dispelled, that under the stipulated facts of the case, the defendant is liable on her contract with the plaintiff. It must also be concluded that the services of the plaintiff were necessaries, and there being no attempt to show that the charges were unreasonable or unfair, the incompetent's estate is liable for the balance due for such services.

The judgment of the trial court is, therefore, affirmed.

HURD, P. J., and KOVACHY, J., concur.

NOTES

1.   The court's unusual practice of citing to headnotes rather than to the texts of cases notwithstanding, the *Jesset* decision provides an accurate statement of the modern American rule that contracts of mentally incompetent people are voidable. For similar rulings in other states, see, e.g., *Brown* v. *Khoury*, 346 Mich. 97, 77 N.W.2d 336 (1956); *Faber* v. *Sweet Style Manufacturing Corporation*, 40 Misc.2d 212, 242 N.Y.S.2d 763 (1963); *Lawson* v. *Bennett*, 240 N.C. 52, 81 S.E.2d 162 (1954). See generally, Note, "The Mentally Ill and the Law of Contracts," 29 *Temple L.Q.* 380, 383–384 (1956).

2.   Even if the *Jesset* court had ruled that the contract should not have been enforced, since it had found the funeral expenses to be "necessaries," it might have permitted the plaintiff to recover on a *quantum meruit* basis for the services he had rendered. The rules regarding payment for necessaries provided to mentally incompetent persons were succinctly described in *In re Hayes' Guardianship*, 8 Wisc.2d 32, 98 N.W.2d 430 (1959), where an attorney sought payment for legal fees engendered in an unsuccessful attempt to obtain restoration to legal competency. Although recovery of the fees was denied on the facts of the case, the court set out the governing principles:

> When recovery is allowed on the theory of necessaries it is generally done on the rationale that the law implies a contract or a promise to pay by the incompetent or imposes an obligation on him to pay for such necessaries because they are a benefit to him. 44 C.J.S. Insane Persons, Section 115, p. 274. Necessaries are generally considered as what is reasonably necessary for the support, maintenance, care and comfort of the insane person according to his status and condition in life but not necessarily limited to his actual physical wants. A person's liberty and freedom to do what he wishes with his property is a cherished right. An insane person should have reasonable access to legal

services which are required for the benefit of the insane person or necessary for the protection of his property. *In re Dunn,* 1954, 239 N.C. 378, 79 S.E.2d 921: *In re Doyle's Estate,* 1932, 126 Cal.App. 646, 14 P.2d 920. Cases denying recovery for attorney's fees incident to proceedings for judicial determination of mental capacity have found such services not to be necessaries under the facts of that case. *In re Estate of Osts,* 1931, 211 Iowa 1085, 235 N.W. 70. *Id.* at 98 N.W.2d 433.

3. In regard to the prior adjudication of mental incompetency at issue in *Jesset,* the court hedges on whether it is merely *prima facie* evidence or creates a rebuttable presumption of continuing incompetency. What is the difference between these two effects? Most jurisdictions hold that an adjudication of incompetence creates a rebuttable presumption that such mental condition continues to exist, e.g., *Lucas* v. *Parsons,* 23 Ga. 267 (1857); *Mileham* v. *Montagne,* 148 Ia. 476, 125 N.W. 664 (1910); *Herndon* v. *Vick,* 18 Tex.Civ.App. 583, 45 S.W. 852 (1898); *Small* v. *Champeny,* 102 Wis. 61, 78 N.W. 407 (1899). This rule shifts the burden of proof to the party claiming competency and invalidates the usual presumptions of sanity and competency. A few courts have held that a prior adjudication is conclusive proof of continuing incompetence, based upon a rationale that the adjudication gives notice to the world that the individual is incompetent and unable, therefore, to enter into valid contracts; see, e.g., *Pavey* v. *Wintrod,* 87 Ind. 379 (1882); *Gibson* v. *Soper,* 6 Gray 279, 66 Am.Dec. 414 (Mass. 1856); *Thorpe* v. *Hanscom,* 64 Minn. 201, 66 N.W. 1 (1896); *Payne* v. *Burdette,* 84 Mo.App. 332 (1900); *Mainzer* v. *Avril,* 108 Misc. 230, 177 N.Y.Supp. 596 (1919).

ORTELERE v. TEACHERS' RETIREMENT BD. OF NEW YORK

Court of Appeals of New York, 1969
25 N.Y.2d 196, 250 N.E.2d 460

BREITEL, Judge.

This appeal involves the revocability of an election of benefits under a public employees' retirement system and suggests the need for a renewed examination of the kinds of mental incompetency which may render voidable the exercise of contractual rights. The particular issue arises on the evidently unwise and foolhardy selection of benefits by a 60-year-old teacher, on leave for mental illness and suffering from cerebral arteriosclerosis, after service as a public schoolteacher and participation in a public retirement system for over 40 years. The teacher died a little less than two months after making her election of maximum benefits, payable to her during her life, thus causing the entire reserve to fall in. She left surviving her husband of 38 years of marriage and two grown children.

There is no doubt that any retirement system depends for its soundness on an actuarial experience based on the purely prospective selections of benefits and mortality rates among the covered group, and that retrospective or adverse selection after the fact would be destructive of a sound system. It is also true that members of retirement systems are free to make choices which to others may seem unwise or foolhardy. The issue here is narrower than any suggested by these basic principles. It is whether an otherwise irrevocable election may be avoided for incapacity because of known mental illness which resulted in the election when, except in the barest actuarial sense, the system would sustain no unfavorable consequences.

The husband and executor of Grace W. Ortelere, the deceased New York City schoolteacher, sues to set aside her application for retirement without option, in the event of her death. It is alleged that Mrs. Ortelere, on February 11, 1965, two months before her death from natural causes, was not mentally competent to execute a retirement application. By this application, effective the next day, she elected the maximum retirement allowance (Administrative Code of City of New York, § B20-46.0). She thus revoked her earlier election of benefits under which she named her husband a beneficiary of the unexhausted reserve upon her death. Selection of the maximum allowance extinguished all interests upon her death.

Following a nonjury trial in Supreme Court, it was held that Grace Ortelere had been mentally incompetent at the time of her February 11 application, thus rendering it "null and void and of no legal effect." The Appellate Division, by a divided court, reversed the judgment of the Supreme Court and held that, as a matter of law, there was insufficient proof of mental incompetency as to this transaction (31 A.D.2d 139, 295 N.Y.S.2d 506).

Mrs. Ortelere's mental illness, indeed, psychosis, is undisputed. It is not seriously disputable, however, that she had complete cognitive judgment or awareness when she made her selection. A modern understanding of mental illness, however, suggests that incapacity to contract or exercise contractural rights may exist, because of volitional and affective impediments or disruptions in the personality, despite the intellectual or cognitive ability to understand. It will be recognized as the civil law parallel to the question of criminal responsibility which has been the recent concern of so many and has resulted in statutory and decisional changes in the criminal law (e.g., A.L.I. Model Penal Code, § 4.01; Penal Law, § 30.05; *Durham* v. *United States*, 214 F.2d 862).

Mrs. Ortelere, an elementary schoolteacher since 1924, suffered a "nervous breakdown" in March, 1964 and went on a leave of absence expiring February 5, 1965. She was then 60 years old and had been happily married for 38 years. On July 1, 1964 she came under the care of Dr. D'Angelo, a psychiatrist, who diagnosed her breakdown as involutional psychosis, melancholia type. Dr. D'Angelo prescribed, and for about six weeks decedent underwent, tranquilizer and shock therapy. Although moderately successful, the therapy was not continued since it was suspected that she also suffered from cerebral arteriosclerosis, an ailment later confirmed. However, the psychiatrist continued to see her at monthly intervals until March, 1965. On March 28, 1965 she was hospitalized after collapsing at home from an aneurysm. She died 10 days later; the cause of death was "Cerebral thrombosis due to H[ypertensive] H[eart] D[isease]."

As a teacher she had been a member of the Teachers' Retirement System of the City of New York (Administrative Code, § B20-3.0). This entitled her to certain annuity and pension rights, preretirement death benefits, and empowered her to exercise various options concerning the payment of her retirement allowance.

Some years before, on June 28, 1958, she had executed a "Selection of Benefits under Option One'' naming her husband as beneficiary of the unexhausted reserve. Under this option upon retirement her allowance would be less by way of periodic retirement allowances, but if she died before receipt of her full reserve the balance of the reserve would be payable to her husband. On June 16, 1960, two years later, she had designated her husband as beneficiary of her service death benefits in the event of her death prior to retirement.

Then on February 11, 1965, when her leave of absence had just expired and she was still under treatment, she executed a retirement application, the one here involved, selecting the maximum retirement allowance payable during her lifetime with nothing payable on or after death. She also, at this time, borrowed from the system the maximum cash withdrawal permitted, namely, $8,760. Three days earlier she had written the board, stating that she intended to retire on February 12 or 15 or as soon a. she received ''the information I need in order to decide whether to take an option or maximum allowance.'' She then listed eight specific questions, reflecting great understanding of the retirement system, concerning the various alternatives available. An extremely detailed reply was sent, by letter of February 15, 1965, although by that date it was technically impossible for her to change her selection. However, the board's chief clerk, before whom Mrs. Ortelere executed the application, testified that the questions were ''answered verbally by me on February 11th.'' Her retirement reserve totalled $62,165 (after deducting the $8,760 withdrawal), and the difference between electing the maximum retirement allowance (no option) and the allowance under ''option one'' was $901 per year or $75 per month. That is, had the teacher selected ''option one'' she would have received an annual allowance of $4,494 or $375 per month, while if no option had been selected she would have received an annual allowance of $5,395 or $450 per month. Had she not withdrawn the cash the annual figures would be $5,247 and $6,148 respectively.

Following her taking a leave of absence for her condition, Mrs. Ortelere had become very depressed and was unable to care for herself. As a result her husband gave up his electrician's job, in which he earned $222 per week, to stay home and take care of her on a full-time basis. She left their home only when he accompanied her. Although he took her to the Retirement Board on February 11, 1965, he did not know why she went, and did not question her for fear ''she'd start crying hysterically that I was scolding her. That's the way she was. And I wouldn't upset her.''

The Orteleres were in quite modest circumstances. They owned their own home, valued at $20,000, and had $8,000 in a savings account. They also owned some farm land worth about $5,000. Under these circumstances, as revealed in this record, retirement for both of the Orteleres or the survivor of them had to be provided, as a practical matter, largely out of Mrs. Ortelere's retirement benefits.

According to Dr. D'Angelo, the psychiatrist who treated her, Mrs. Ortelere never improved enough to ''warrant my sending her back [to teaching].'' A physician for the Board of Education examined her on February 2, 1965 to determine her fitness to return to teaching. Although not a psychiatrist but rather a specialist in internal medicine, this physician ''judged that she had apparently recovered from the depression'' and that she appeared rational. However, before allowing her to return to teaching, a report was requested from D. D'Angelo concerning her condition. It is notable that the Medical Division of the Board of Education on February 24, 1965 requested that Mrs. Ortelere report to the board's "panel psychiatrist" on March 11, 1965.

Dr. D'Angelo stated "[a]t no time since she was under my care was she ever mentally competent"; that "[m]entally she couldn't make a decision of any kind, actually, of any kind, small or large." He also described how involutional melancholia affects the judgment process: "They can't think rationally, no matter what the situation is. They will even tell you, 'I used to be able to think of anything and make any decision. Now,' they say, 'even getting up, I don't know whether I should get up or whether I should stay in bed.' Or, 'I don't even know how to make a slice of toast any more.' Everything is impossible to decide, and everything is too great an effort to even think of doing. They just don't have the effort, actually, because their nervous breakdown drains them of all their physical energies."

While the psychiatrist used terms referring to "rationality," it is quite evident that Mrs. Ortelere's psychopathology did not lend itself to a classification under the legal test of irrationality. It is undoubtedly, for this reason, that the Appellate Division was unable to accept his testimony and the trial court's finding of irrationality in the light of the prevailing rules as they have been formulated.

The well-established rule is that contracts of a mentally incompetent person who has not been adjudicated insane are voidable. Even where the contract has been partly or fully performed it will still be avoided upon restoration of the *status quo.* (*Verstandig* v. *Schlaffer,* 296 N.Y. 62, 64, 70 N.E.2d 15, 16; *Blinn* v. *Schwarz,* 177 N.Y. 252, 262, 69 N.E. 542, 545; see, also, Ann., Contracts with Incompetent, 95 A.L.R. 1442; Ann., Incompetent—Contract Before Adjudication, 46 A.L.R. 416.)

Traditionally, in this State and elsewhere, contractual mental capacity has been measured by what is largely a cognitive test (*Aldrich* v. *Bailey,* 132 N.Y. 85, 30 N.E. 264; 2 Williston, Contracts [3d ed.], § 256; see 17 C.J.S. Contracts § 133[1], subd. e, pp. 860–862). Under this standard the "inquiry" is whether the mind was "so affected as to render him wholly and absolutely incompetent to comprehend and understand the nature of the transaction" (*Aldrich* v. *Bailey, supra,* at p. 89, 30 N.E. at p. 265). A requirement that the party also be able to make a rational judgment concerning the particular transaction qualified the cognitive test (*Paine* v. *Aldrich,* 133 N.Y. 544, 546, 30 N.E. 725, 726, Note, " 'Civil Insanity': The New York Treatment of the Issue of Mental Incompetency in Non-Criminal Cases," 44 *Cornell L.Q.* 76). Conversely, it is also well recognized that contractual ability would be affected by insane delusions intimately related to the particular transaction (*Moritz* v. *Moritz,* 153 App.Div. 147, 138 N.Y.S. 124, affd. 211 N.Y. 580, 105 N.E. 1090, see Green, "Judicial Tests of Mental Incompetency," 6 *Mo.L.Rev.* 141, 151).

These traditional standards governing competency to contract were formulated when psychiatric knowledge was quite primitive. They fail to account for one who by reason of mental illness is unable to control his conduct even though his cognitive ability seems unimpaired. When these standards were evolving it was thought that all the mental faculties were simultaneously affected by mental illness. (Green, "Mental

Incompetency," 38 *Mich.L.Rev.* 1189, 1197–1202.) This is no longer the prevailing view (Note, "Mental Illness and the Law of Contracts," 57 *Mich.L.Rev.* 1020, 1033–1036).

Of course, the greatest movement in revamping legal notions of mental responsibility has occurred in the criminal law. The nineteenth century cognitive test embraced in the *M'Naghten* rules has long been criticized and changed by statute and decision in many jurisdictions (see *M'Naghten's Case,* 10 Clark & Fin. 200; 8 Eng.Rep. 718 [House of Lords, 1843]; Weihofen, *Mental Disorder as a Criminal Defense* [1954], pp. 65–68; British Royal Comm. on Capital Punishment [1953], ch. 4; A.L.I. Model Penal Code, § 4.01, *supra*; cf. Penal Law, § 30.05).

While the policy considerations for the criminal law and the civil law are different, both share in common the premise that policy considerations must be based on a sound understanding of the human mind and, therefore, its illnesses. Hence, because the cognitive rules are, for the most part, too restrictive and rest on a false factual basis they must be re-examined. Once it is understood that, accepting plaintiff's proof, Mrs. Ortelere was psychotic and because of that psychosis could have been incapable of making a voluntary selection of her retirement system benefits, there is an issue that a modern jurisprudence should not exclude, merely because her mind could pass a "cognition" test based on nineteenth century psychology.

There has also been some movement on the civil law side to achieve a modern posture. For the most part, the movement has been glacial and has been disguised under traditional formulations. Various devices have been used to avoid unacceptable results under the old rules by finding unfairness or overreaching in order to avoid transactions (see, e.g., Green, "Proof of Mental Incompetency and the Unexpressed Major Premise," 53 *Yale L.J.* 271, 298–305).

In this State there has been at least one candid approach. In *Faber* v. *Sweet Style Mfg. Corp.,* 40 Misc.2d 212, at p. 216, 242 N.Y.S.2d 763, at p. 768, Mr. Justice Meyer wrote: "[i]ncompetence to contract also exists when a contract is entered into under the compulsion of a mental disease or disorder but for which the contract would not have been made" (noted in 39 *N.Y.U.L.Rev.* 356). This is the first known time a court has recognized that the traditional standards of incompetency for contractual capacity are inadequate in light of contemporary psychiatric learning and applied modern standards. Prior to this, courts applied the cognitive standard giving great weight to objective evidence of rationality (e.g.,, *Beisman* v. *New York City Employees' Retirement System, Sup.,* 81 N.Y.S.2d, 373, revd. 275 App.Div. 836, 88 N.Y.S.2d 411, affd. 300 N.Y. 580, 89 N.E.2d 876; *Schwartzberg* v. *Teachers' Retirement Bd.,* 273 App.Div. 240, 76 N.Y.S.2d 488, affd. 298 N.Y. 741, 83 N.E.2d 146; *Martin* v. *Teachers' Retirement Bd., Sup.,* 70 N.Y.S.2d 593).

It is quite significant that Restatement, 2d, Contracts, states the modern rule on competency to contract. This is in evident recognition, and the Reporter's Notes support this inference, that, regardless of how the cases formulated their reasoning, the old cognitive test no longer explains the results. Thus, the new Restatement section reads: "(1) A person incurs only voidable contractual duties by entering into a transaction if by reason of mental illness or defect . . . (b) he is unable to act in a reasonable manner in relation to the transaction and the other party has reason to know of his condition.'' (Restatement, 2d, Contracts [T.D. No. 1, April 13, 1964], § 18C.) (See, also, Allen, Ferster, Weihofen, *Mental Impairment and Legal Incompetency*, p. 253 [Recommendation b] and pp. 260–282; and Note, 57 *Mich.L.Rev.* 1020, *supra*, where it is recommended ''that a complete test for contractual incapacity should provide protection to those persons whose contracts are merely uncontrolled reactions to their mental illness, as well as for those who could not understand the nature and consequences of their actions'' [at p. 1036]).

The avoidance of duties under an agreement entered into by those who have done so by reason of mental illness, but who have understanding, depends on balancing competing policy considerations. There must be stability in contractual relations and protection of the expectations of parties who bargain in good faith. On the other hand, it is also desirable to protect persons who may understand the nature of the transaction but who, due to mental illness, cannot control their conduct. Hence, there should be relief only if the other party knew or was put on notice as to the contractor's mental illness. Thus, the Restatement provision for avoidance contemplates that ''the other party has reason to know'' of the mental illness (*id.*).

When, however, the other party is without knowledge of the contractor's mental illness and the agreement is made on fair terms, the proposed Restatement rule is: ''The power of avoidance under subsection (1) terminates to the extent that the contract has been so performed in whole or in part or the circumstances have so changed that avoidance would be inequitable. In such a case a court may grant relief on such equitable terms as the situation requires.'' (Restatement, 2d, Contracts, *supra*, § 18C, subd. [2].)

The system was, or should have been, fully aware of Mrs. Ortelere's condition. They, or the Board of Education, knew of her leave of absence for medical reasons and the resort to staff psychiatrists by the Board of Education. Hence, the other of the conditions for avoidance is satisfied.

Lastly, there are no significant changes of position by the system other than those that flow from the barest actuarial consequences of benefit selection.

Nor should one ignore that in the relationship between retirement system and member, and especially in a public system, there is not involved a commercial, let alone an ordinary commercial, transaction. Instead the nature of the system and its announced goal is the protection of its members and those in whom its members have an interest. It is not a sound scheme which would permit 40 years of contribution and participation in the system to be nullified by a one-instant act committed by one known to be mentally ill. This is especially true if there would be no substantial harm to the system if the act were avoided. On the record none may gainsay that her selection of a ''no option'' retirement while under psychiatric care, ill with cerebral arteriosclerosis, aged 60, and with a family in which she had always manifested concern, was so unwise and foolhardy that a factfinder might conclude that it was explainable only as a product of psychosis.

On this analysis it is not difficult to see that plaintiff's evidence was sufficient to sustain a finding that, when she acted as she did on February 11, 1965, she did so solely as a result of serious mental illness, namely, psychosis. Of course, nothing less serious than medically classified psychosis should suffice or else few contracts would be invulnerable to some kind of psychological attack. Mrs. Ortelere's psychiatrist testified quite flatly that as an involutional melancholiac in depression she was incapable of making a voluntary "rational" decision. Of course, as noted earlier, the trial court's finding and perhaps some of the testimony attempted to fit into the rubrics of the traditional rules. For that reason rather than reinstatement of the judgment at Trial Term there should be a new trial under the proper standards frankly considered and applied.

Accordingly, the order of the Appellate Division should be reversed, without costs, and the action remanded to Special Term for a new trial.

JASEN, Judge (dissenting).

Where there has been no previous adjudication of incompetency, the burden of proving mental incompetence is upon the party alleging it. I agree with the majority at the Appellate Division that he plaintiff, the husband of the decedent, failed to sustain the burden incumbent upon him of proving deceased's incompetence.

The evidence conclusively establishes that the decedent, at the time she made her application to retire, understood not only that she was retiring, but also that she had selected the maximum payment during her lifetime.

Indeed, the letter written by the deceased to the Teachers' Retirement System prior to her retirement demonstrates her full mental capacity to understand and to decide whether to take an option or the maximum allowance. The full text of the letter reads as follows:

February 8, 1965

* * *

Gentlemen:

I would like to retire on Feb. 12 or Feb. 15. In other words, just as soon as possible after I receive the information I need in order to decide whether to take an option or maximum allowance. Following are the questions I would like to have answered:

1. What is my 'average' five-year salary?
2. What is my maximum allowance?
3. I am 60 years old. If I select option four-a with a beneficiary (female) 27 years younger, what is my allowance?
4. If I select four-a on the pension part only, and take the maximum annuity, what is my allowance?
5. If I take a loan of 89% of my year's salary before retirement, what would my maximum allowance be?
6. If I take a loan of $5,000 before retiring, and select option four-a on both the pension and annuity, what would my allowance be?
7. What is my total service credit? I have been on a leave without pay since Oct. 26, 1964.
8. What is the 'factor' used for calculating option four-a with the above beneficiary?

Thank you for your promptness in making the necessary calculations. I will come to your office on Thursday afternoon of this week.

It seems clear that this detailed, explicit and extremely pertinent list of queries reveals a mind fully in command of the salient features of the Teachers' Retirement System. Certainly, it cannot be said that the decedent could possess sufficient capacity to compose a letter indicating such a comprehensive understanding of the retirement system, and yet lack the capacity to understand the answers.

As I read the record, the evidence establishes that the decedent's election to receive maximum payments was predicated on the need for a higher income to support two retired persons—her husband and herself. Since the only source of income available to decedent and her husband was decedent's retirement pay, the additional payment of $75 per month which she would receive by electing the maximal payment was a necessity. Indeed, the additional payments represented an increase of 20% over the benefits payable under option 1. Under these circumstances, an election of maximal income during a decedent's lifetime was not only a rational, but a necessary decision.

Further indication of decedent's knowledge of the financial needs of her family is evidenced by the fact that she took a loan for the maximum amount ($8,760) permitted by the retirement system at the time she made application for retirement.

Moreover, there is nothing in the record to indicate that the decedent had any warning, premonition, knowledge or indication at the time of retirement that her life expectancy was, in any way, reduced by her condition.

Decedent's election of the maximum retirement benefits, therefore, was not so contrary to her best interests so as to create an inference of her mental incompetence.

Indeed, concerning election of options under a retirement system, it has been held: "Even where no previous election has been made, the court must make the election for an incompetent which would be in accordance with what would have been his manifest and reasonable choice if he were sane, and, in the absence of convincing evidence that the incompetent would have made a different selection, it is *presumed that he would have chosen the option yielding the largest returns in his lifetime.*" (*Schwartzberg* v. *Teachers' Retirement Bd.,* 273 App.Div. 240, 242-243, 76 N.Y.S.2d 488, affd. 298 N.Y. 741, 83 N.E.2d 146; emphasis supplied.)

Nor can I agree with the majority's view that the traditional rules governing competency to contract "are, for the most part, too restrictive and rest on a false factual basis."

The issue confronting the courts concerning mental capacity to contract is under what circumstances and conditions should a party be relieved of contractual obligations freely entered. This is peculiarly a legal decision, although, of course, available medical knowledge forms a datum which influences the legal choice. It is common knowledge that the present state of psychiatric knowledge is inadequate to provide a fixed rule for each and every type of mental disorder. Thus, the generally accepted rules which have evolved to determine mental responsibility are general enough in application to encompass all types of mental disorders, and phrased in a manner which can be understood and practically applied by juries composed of laymen.

The generally accepted test of mental competency to contract which has thus evolved is whether the party attempting to avoid the contract was capable of understanding and appreciating the nature and consequences of the particular act or transaction which he challenges. (*Schwartzberg* v. *Teachers' Retirement Bd., supra*; *Paine* v. *Aldrich,* 133 N.Y. 544, 30 N.E. 725; *Beisman* v. *New York City Employees' Retirement System,* 275 App.Div. 836, 88 N.Y.S.2d 411, affd. 300 N.Y. 580, 89 N.E.2d

876.) This rule represents a balance struck between policies to protect the security of transactions between individuals and freedom of contract on the one hand, and protection of those mentally handicapped on the other hand. In my opinion, this rule has proven workable in practice and fair in result. A broad range of evidence including psychiatric testimony is admissible under the existing rules to establish a party's mental condition. (See 2 Wigmore, Evidence [3d ed.], §§ 227–233.) In the final analysis, the lay jury will infer the state of the party's mind from his observed behavior as indicated by the evidence presented at trial. Each juror instinctively judges what is normal and what is abnormal conduct from his own experience, and the generally accepted test harmonizes the competing policy considerations with human experience to achieve the fairest result in the greatest number of cases.

As in every situation where the law must draw a line between liability and nonliability, between responsibility and nonresponsibility, there will be borderline cases, and injustices may occur by deciding erroneously that an individual belongs on one side of the line or the other. To minimize the chances of such injustices occurring, the line should be drawn as clearly as possible.

The Appellate Division correctly found that the deceased was capable of understanding the nature and effect of her retirement benefits, and exercised rational judgment in electing to receive the maximum allowance during her lifetime. I fear that the majority's refinement of the generally accepted rules will prove unworkable in practice, and make many contracts vulnerable to psychological attack. Any benefit to those who understand what they are doing, but are unable to exercise self-discipline, will be outweighed by frivolous claims which will burden our courts and undermine the security of contracts. The reasonable expectations of those who innocently deal with persons who appear rational and who understand what they are doing should be protected.

Accordingly, I would affirm the order appealed from.

Fuld, C. J., and Burke and Bergan, JJ., concur with Breitel, J.

Jasen, J., dissents and votes to affirm in separate opinion in which Scileppi, J., concurs.

Order reversed, without costs, and a new trial granted.

NOTES

1. Contrast the test for competency applied in *Ortelere* to the following statement from *Kelley* v. *Davis,* 216 Ark. 828, 227 S.W.2d 637 (1950):

> The legal test of competency for the purpose here under consideration is fully discussed in *Schuman* v. *Westbrook,* 207 Ark. 495, at page 499, 181 S.W.2d 470, 472, where we said, quoting from *Pulaski County* v. *Hill,* 97 Ark. 450, 134 S.W. 973: "But the question in all such cases, where incapacity arising from defect of the mind is alleged, is, not whether the mind is itself diseased or the person is afflicted with any particular form of insanity, but, rather, whether the powers of the mind have become so affected, by whatever cause, as to render him incapable of transacting business like the one in question. As a general rule, it may be stated that, in order to have that measure of capacity required by law to be of sound mind, a person must have capacity enough to comprehend and understand the nature and effect of the business he is doing, ... " *Id.* at 638–639.

Which is the more workable standard? The *Ortelere* court commented that "nothing less serious than medically classified psychosis should suffice or else few contracts would be invulnerable to some kind of psychological attack." How definite is the standard of medically classified psychosis? Consider criticisms of psychiatric diagnosis by some authorities who contend that psychiatric categories are frequently only a disguised practice for labeling conduct deemed inappropriate, e.g., Szasz, T., *The Myth of Mental Illness* (1961); Torrey, E. F., *The Death of Psychiatry* (1974); Ennis, B., and Litwack, J., "Psychiatry and the Presumption of Expertise: Flipping Coins in the Courtroom," 62 *Cal.L.Rev.* 693 (1974).

2.   Suppose that the retirement system *had* refused to allow Mrs. Ortelere to exercise her right to change her selection of benefit options. Would the system's decision have been susceptible to legal challenge? On what grounds?

Was the *Ortelere* court accurate in declaring that nullification of Mrs. Ortelere's election of options would have no significance to the retirement system other than "the barest actuarial consequences"?

3.   A subsequent New York case that employed the *Ortelere* analytical framework is *Fingerhut* v. *Kralyn Enterprises, Inc.*, 71 Misc.2d 846, 337 N.Y.S.2d 394 (1971). An additional issue raised in *Fingerhut* and in *Faber* v. *Sweet Style Manufacturing Corporation*, 40 Misc.2d 212, 242 N.Y.S.2d 763 (1963), discussed in *Ortelere*, is the notion of ratification, whereby a contract entered into by an incompetent person may be validated if approved or acted upon after the individual regains competence. In *Fingerhut*, the plaintiff sought rescision of a contract for purchase of a golf club entered into while he was in the "manic stage" of a "manic depressive psychosis," *id.* at 337 N.Y.S.2d 395. The evidence showed that after the period of mental incompetence had passed, he wrote a letter to the defendants wherein he elected to postpone passage of title on the property, *id.* at 397. Subsequently, he sought to rescind the transaction. The court held that by the act of postponing the title transfer, he had acknowledged the contract and thereby ratified it:

> The defendant has sustained the burden of proving ratification of the contract. The evidence clearly indicates that plaintiff, without mental disability, ratified the contract. Borrowing from *Faber, supra,* 40 Misc.2d at p. 217, 242 N.Y.S.2d at p. 768, there was "conscious action" on plaintiff's part which recognized the contract at a time when he was not psychotic. In adjourning the closing of title and conduct pertaining thereto, he demonstrated knowledge of the existence of the contract, with confirmation of it as a contractual obligation; and though he regretted its making, he, nevertheless, acted in furtherance of the contract.
>
> While it may be unfortunate that the plaintiff "bit off more than he could chew," the relief he seeks must be denied. *Id.* at 409.

Such "recognition" of the contract, accompanied by regret, seems to mean little more than that the individual remembers the contract after having regained competence. Is a ratification theory based upon memory alone consistent with the rejection in *Ortelere, Fingerhut,* and *Faber* of the cognitive test of contractual capacity?

4.   One of the few cases dealing with the contractual rights of mentally retarded people is an old California case, *Nielsen* v. *Frank*, 117 Cal.App. 117, 3P.2d 607 (1931), which involved an action to recover money paid to an attorney, under a

contract for legal services, by a "mentally deficient" man with a "mentality of ten or twelve years," *id.* at 3 P.2d 608. Despite the fact that the man had been previously adjudicated incompetent and had had a guardian appointed, the California Court of Appeals upheld the trial court's determination that the contract was valid and enforceable. Citing *Hemenway* v. *Abbott,* 8 Cal.App. 450, 97 P. 190 (1908), the court declared:

> It has been held that mere weakmindedness, whether natural or produced by old age, sickness, or other infirmity, unaccompanied by any other inequitable incidents, if a person has sufficient intelligence to understand the nature of the transaction and is left to his own free will, is not sufficient to defeat a contract or set aside an executed agreement or conveyance. *Id.* at 608.

5.   The extent to which mental aberrations interfere with contractual capacity must be examined on the facts of each case. A fairly extreme situation occurred in *Hanks* v. *McNeil Coal Corporation,* 114 Colo. 578, 168 P.2d 256 (1946), where a guardian sought to have a contract, deed, and surface lease pertaining to coal lands set aside on the grounds that his ward was insane and lacked legal capacity to contract. The factual background was described as follows:

> Shortly after 1922 Lee Hanks discovered that he was afflicted with diabetes, and members of his family noticed a progressive change in his physical and mental condition thereafter. He became irritable and easily upset, very critical of his son's work, and increasingly interested in the emotional type of religion. He began to speculate in oil and other doubtful ventures with money needed for payment of debts and taxes. About 1934 he sent his son what he denominated a secret formula for the manufacture of medicine to cure fistula in horses, which was compounded principally of ground china, brick dust, burnt shoe leather and amber-colored glass. If the infection was in the horse's right shoulder, the mixture was to be poured in the animal's left ear, and if on the left shoulder then in the right ear. In 1937 Mr. Hanks started to advertise this medicine through the press under the name of Crown King Remedy. Thereafter he increasingly devoted his efforts and money to the compounding and attempted sale of this concoction, his business judgment became poor and he finally deteriorated mentally to he point that on May 25, 1940, he was adjudicated insane and his son was appointed conservator of his estate. *Id.* at 168 P.2d 258.

In spite of Mr. Hanks' unusual behavior, the Supreme Court of Colorado affirmed the trial court's finding that the transactions were valid, declaring:

> There is always in civil, as well as in criminal, actions a presumption of sanity. *North American Accident Co.* v. *Cavaleri,* 98 Colo. 565, 58 P.2d 756. Insanity and incompetence are words of vague and varying import. Often the definition of the psychiatrist is at variance with that of the law. The legal test of Hanks' insanity is whether "he was incapable of understanding and appreciating the extent and effect of business transactions in which he engaged." *Ellis* v. *Colorado Nat. Bank,* 90 Colo. 489, 10 P.2d 336, 340. The legal rule does not recognize degrees of insanity. It does not presume to make a distinction between much and little intellect. *Fleming* v. *Consolidated Motor Sales Co.,* 74 Mont. 245, 240 P. 376. One may have insane delusions regarding some matters and be insane on some subjects, yet capable of transacting business concerning matters wherein such subjects are not concerned, and such insanity does not make one incompetent to contract unless the subject matter of the contract is so connected with an insane delusion as to render the afflicted party incapable of understanding the nature and effect

of the agreement or of acting rationally in the transaction. *Weller* v. *Copeland,* 285 Ill. 150, 120 N.E. 578.

* * *

Clearly manifested symptoms of senile dementia before a will was made, continuing until the extreme degree of dementia was reached a few months later, is held not conclusive of incapacity to make a will, *Wisner* v. *Chandler,* 95 Kan. 36, 147 P. 849; *Kaleb* v. *Modern Woodmen of America,* 51 Wyo. 116, 64 P.2d 605, nor are senile dementia and improvident expenditures conclusive of lack of capacity to contract. *Gosnell* v. *Lloyd,* 215 Cal. 244, 10 P.2d 45.

Patently Hanks was suffering from insane delusion in 1937 with reference to the efficacy of the horse medicine, but there is no evidence of delusions or hallucinations in connection with this transaction or with his transaction of much of his other business at that time; there is no basis for holding voidable his sale here involved on the ground of his insanity, and the trial court correctly so held. *Id.* at 168 P.2d 260.

RESTATEMENT 2D, CONTRACTS (1964)

§ 18. Capacity to Contract

(1) No one can be bound by contract who has not legal capacity to incur at least voidable contractual duties. Capacity to contract may be partial and its existence in respect of a particular transaction may depend upon the nature of the transaction or upon other circumstances.

(2) A natural person who manifests assent to a transaction has full legal capacity to incur contractual duties thereby unless he is

(a) under guardianship, or

(b) an infant, or

(c) mentally ill or defective, or

(d) intoxicated.

Comment:

a. Total and partial incapacity. Capacity, as here used, means the legal power which a normal person would have under the same circumstances. . . .

b. Types of incapacity. Historically, the principal categories of natural persons having no capacity or limited capacity to contract were married women, infants, and insane persons. Those formerly referred to as insane are included in the more modern phrase "mentally ill," and mentally defective persons are treated similarly.

* * *

f. Necessaries. Persons having no capacity or limited capacity to contract are often liable for necessaries furnished to them or to their wives or children. Though often treated as contractual, such liabilities are quasi-contractual: the liability is measured by the value of the necessaries rather than by the terms of the promise.

§ 18A. Persons Affected by Guardianship

A person has no capacity to incur contractual duties if his property is under guardianship by reason of an adjudication of mental illness or defect.

Comment:

a. Rationale. The reason for appointing a guardian of property is to preserve the property from being squandered or improvidently used. The guardianship proceedings are treated as giving public notice of the ward's incapacity and establish his status with respect to transactions during guardianship even though the other party to a particular transaction may have no knowledge or reason to know of the guardianship: the guardian is not required to give personal notice to all persons who may deal with the ward. The control of the ward's property is vested in the guardian, subject to court supervision; that control and supervision are not to be impaired or avoided by proof that the ward has regained his reason or has had a lucid interval, unless the guardianship is terminated or abandoned.

§ 18C.   Mental Illness or Defect

(1)   A person incurs only voidable contractual duties by entering into a transaction if by reason of mental illness or defect

(a)   he is unable to understand in a reasonable manner the nature and consequences of the transaction, or

(b)   he is unable to act in a reasonable manner in relation to the transaction and the other party has reason to know of his condition.

(2)   Where the contract is made on fair terms and the other party is without knowledge of the mental illness or defect, the power of avoidance under subsection (1) terminates to the extent that the contract has been so performed in whole or in part or the circumstances have so changed that avoidance would be inequitable. In such a case a court may grant relief on such equitable terms as the situation requires.

Comment:

a.   Rationale.   A contract made by a person who is mentally incompetent requires the reconciliation of two conflicting policies: the protection of justifiable expectations and of the security of transactions, and the protection of persons unable to protect themselves against imposition. Each policy has sometimes prevailed to a greater extent than is stated in this Section. At one extreme, it has been said that a lunatic has no capacity to contract because he has no mind; this view has given way to a better understanding of mental phenomena and to the doctrine that contractual obligation depends on manifestation of assent rather than on mental assent. At the other extreme, it has been asserted that mental incompetency has no effect on a contract unless other grounds of avoidance are present, such as fraud, undue influence, or gross inadequacy of consideration; it is now widely believed that such a rule gives inadequate protection to the incompetent and his family, particularly where the contract is entirely executory.

b.   The standard of competency.   It is now recognized that there is a wide variety of types and degrees of mental incompetency. Among them are congenital deficiencies in intelligence, the mental deterioration of old age, the effects of brain damage caused by accident or organic disease, and mental illnesses evidenced by such symptoms as delusions, hallucinations, delirium, confusion and depression. Where no guardian has been appointed, there is full contractual capacity in any case unless the mental illness or defect has affected the particular transaction: a person may be able to understand almost nothing, or only simple or routine transactions, or he may be incompetent only with respect to a particular type of transaction. Even though understanding is complete, he may lack capacity to control his acts in the way that the normal individual can and does control them; in such cases the incapacity makes the contract voidable only if the other party has reason to know of his condition. Where a person has some understanding of a particular transaction which is affected by mental illness or defect, the controlling consideration is whether the transaction in its result is one which a reasonably competent person might have made.

* * *

  c. Proof of incompetency. Where there has been no adjudication of incompetency, the burden of proof is on the party asserting incompetency. . . .

NOTES

1. Examine the language of each of these sections carefully to determine how well they balance the three competing interests at stake: 1) the basic right of mentally handicapped people to enter into contracts, 2) the need to protect mentally incompetent people from being taken advantage of by unfair contractual transactions, and 3) fairness to those who in good faith enter into contracts with mentally handicapped people. Are all three of these interests adequately considered and protected?

2. Competency to enter into contracts is now largely governed by state statutes; see, e.g., Ala. Code Ann. Section 20-206 (1964); C.J.S. "Contracts" Section 133(1) (1966). Few of these statutes, however, have considered that mentally handicapped people may have constitutionally protected rights in the contracts area, which may only be restricted for compelling governmental reasons. For this reason, the "right to contract" seems a likely future frontier for advocates for handicapped people.

ADDITIONAL READING

Weihofen, H., "Mental Incompetency to Contract or Convey," 39 *S.Cal.L.Rev.* 211 (1966).
Alexander, G., and Szasz, T., "From Contract to Status Via Psychiatry," 13 *Santa Clara Lawyer* 537 (1973).

2. By Physically Handicapped Persons

In logic, there is no reason why a physical handicap should affect contractual capacity. Whether viewed under the ancient standard of "meeting of the minds" or through more modern concepts of mutual promises and "reasonable expectations," the process of entering into a contract should be able to be accomplished by anyone having requisite mental ability. Historically, however, this has not always been the case.

  For a lengthy period in English and American jurisprudence, a contractual restriction was applied to persons who could neither hear nor speak, based upon "the old doctrine that a deaf mute was presumed to be an idiot," *Alex* v. *Matzke,* 151 Mich. 36, 115 N.W. 251 (1908). Such persons were "*prima facie* incompetent to make any contract," *Collins* v. *Trotter,* 81 Mo. 275, 282 (1883), and the burden of proof was shifted to the party asserting competency. *Ibid.* Moreover, if such a person were also blind, then the presumption of incapacity to contract was irrebuttable, for the person "would be considered in law as incapable of any understanding, being deficient in those inlets which furnish the human mind with ideas." *Brown* v. *Brown,* 3 Conn. 299, 303, 8 Am.Dec. 187 (1820).

Fortunately, these principles were long ago discarded. As one court described it, "the education and the better discernment of later times have shown the fallacy of ancient theory in this regard." *Brooks* v. *Mason,* 84 Vt. 289, 79 A. 48, 50 (1911). Another court observed: "That period has long passed, and the question as to their legal ability to make a contract is placed on its proper ground—their mental capacity." *Barnett* v. *Barnett,* 54 N.C. 153, 154 (1854).

The modern rule is that no presumption of incompetence is raised by physical disabilities. Physical handicaps affecting communication may necessitate some special efforts in communicating the terms of the contract; see, e.g., *Russell* v. *Rutledge,* 158 Ill.App. 259 (1910), where the court held that a valid contract could be made by the assent of a deaf man in merely nodding his head to signify his agreement. And at least one court has held that persons who enter into contracts with individuals having such handicaps must use "utmost good faith" in their dealings, *Fewkes* v. *Borah,* 376 Ill. 596, 35 N.E.2d 69, 72 (1941). But a physical handicap is no evidence one way or the other of mental competence.

For two cases (reaching opposite results) in which deaf individuals sued to recover payment for years of labor they had rendered to relatives, see *Bunde* v. *Bunde's Estate,* 214 Mich. 469, 183 N.W. 16 (1921), and *Selenak* v. *Selenak,* 150 Ill.App. 399 (1909).

B. WILLS

This section does not attempt to describe the fine points of estate planning and the drafting of wills for handicapped clients or for clients with handicapped children. In regard to such matters, see Effland, R., "Trusts and Estate Planning," *The Mentally Retarded Citizen and the Law* 116 (Kindred, M., Cohen, J., Penrod, D., and Shaffer, T., eds., 1976); Gorman, J., "Planning for the Physically and Mentally Handicapped," 11 *Inst. Estate Planning* 14.1-47 (1977); Comment, "Legal Planning for the Mentally Retarded," 10 *Idaho L.Rev.* 245 (1974). The approach here is a survey of the legal principles and precedents in regard to the more basic question of whether persons with various handicapping conditions can or cannot make a valid will. Thus, rather than examining the content of or draftsmanship involved in wills, this section concentrates on the concept of testamentary capacity—the legal prerequisite to making valid bequests and devises.

1. By Mentally Handicapped Persons

In re Estate of Glesenkamp

Supreme Court of Pennsylvania, 1954
378 Pa. 635, 107 A.2d 731

Before Stern, C. J., and Stearne, Bell, Musmanno and Arnold, JJ.
Allen M. Stearne, Justice.

The Orphans' Court of Allegheny County sustained an appeal from the probate of a will by the Register on the ground that decedent did not possess testamentary capacity. This appeal followed.

Joseph A. Glesenkamp, Jr., the decedent, died December 2, 1951, unmarried, with next of kin consisting of twenty-two first cousins. The probated will is dated October 31, 1951. It was prepared by a lawyer and witnessed by a bank officer and decedent's physician. The will devised and bequeathed his entire estate to Villette O. Carson, the proponent, a first cousin, the appellant. Decedent's attorney was named executor.

The issues presented by the appeal are: (a) testamentary capacity, (b) undue influence and (c) forgery.

* * *

On appeal the function of an appellate court is to determine whether or not the hearing judge's findings of fact and conclusions of law, approved by the court in banc, are sufficiently supported by the evidence.

Judge Cox, with skill and patience, heard the testimony. The printed record, in three volumes, is over 1,850 pages in length. With meticulous care he made an exhaustive analysis of the evidence. After considering the evidence in connection with the applicable principles of law he concluded and found that Joseph A. Glesenkamp, Jr., the decedent, at the date of the execution of the questioned will, did not possess testamentary capacity and sustained the appeal. Upon exceptions, the court in banc affirmed the decree.

Since the hearing judge has so meticulously and at length considered all the evidence and accurately applied the pertinent legal principles, we deem it unnecessary to repeat in detail what has been so amply and ably found and decided. A *summary* will suffice for the present purpose.

The court found that the charge of forgery was not sufficiently proved. The question of undue influence was not decided since decedent was found not to possess testamentary capacity. Decedent was conceded to be weak-minded, with a guardian in charge of his estate. The single question is whether or not decedent had *sufficient* testamentary capacity to make a valid will.

Decedent was the only child of Joseph and Anna Glesenkamp. He was born weak-minded. He was cared for by his parents and was never placed in an institution. The mother died March 24, 1947, at the age of eighty-six years. His father died three weeks later, at the age of eighty-seven years. Decedent was then fifty-five years of age. Upon the death of the mother, Andrew Hess, of West Virginia, came to Pittsburgh and arranged for her burial and later performed the same service for decedent's father. Mr. Hess was the only nephew of the mother. The combined estates of the father and mother and property in decedent's own name totaled approximately $150,000. Upon the death of his parents the decedent required care because of his mental deficiency. In lieu of placing him in an institution Mr. Hess employed Mrs. Carson, the proponent, as housekeeper and companion. Mr. Hess also retained Fred C. Houston, Esq., a lawyer, associated with his son, William McC. Houston, Esq., in the practice of law under the firm name of Houston & Houston. The attorneys arranged for the settlement of the intestate estates of the parents. Being incapable of attending to his own affairs, the attorneys decided to have a guardian appointed for decedent's estate. On May 26, 1947, upon the petition of appellant, the Court of Common Pleas of Allegheny County appointed a guardian for his estate, upon adjudging decedent "to be weak-minded, unable to take care of his estate, . . . and liable to become the victim of designing persons.'' Counsel for appellant stipulated that decedent's mental condition was one of *amentia* and not *dementia*. The former is a permanent absence or deficiency of mind. In the case of *dementia* it is possible to have lucid periods, with the individual *temporarily* freed from mental disease.

Mrs. Carson, the proponent, performed her duties as housekeeper and companion of decedent from the date of the mother's death until that of decedent—a period of four years and eight months. During that period she received a total salary of $13,958.75, a maintenance allowance for her ward of $26,750 and vacation expenses for decedent and herself of $9,300. It is not questioned that Mrs. Carson gave excellent care and attention to decedent and that decedent was more comfortable and happier than if he had been institutionalized.

The will was executed October 31, 1951, while the guardianship was still existing. Decedent died of cancer of the liver one month after the execution of the will. At the date of the execution of the will, while a huge debilitated adult of fifty-nine years, decedent had the mental developments, habits and intellectual attainments of a child of approximately five years. The determinant question is whether or not decedent possessed *sufficient* mental capacity to make a will.

Testamentary capacity has frequently been defined by this Court. Mr. Justice (later Chief Justice) HORACE STERN, in *In re Lewis' Will*, 364 Pa. 225, at page 232, 72 A.2d 80, at page 84, said:

> . . . A decedent possesses testamentary capacity only if he has a full and intelligent knowledge of the act in which he is engaged and of the property he possesses, together with an intelligent perception and understanding of the disposition he wishes to make of his property and of the persons and objects he desires to participate in his bounty. *In re Ash's Will,* 351 Pa. 317, 321, 322, 41 A.2d 620, 622; *In re Dugacki's Will,* 356 Pa. 143, 148, 149, 51 A.2d 627, 630; *In re Patti's Estate,* 133 Pa.Super. 81, 90, 91, 1 A.2d 791, 796.

In *Williams* v. *McCarroll*, 374 Pa. 281, at page 292, 97 A.2d 14, at page 19, Mr. Justice BELL stated the same principle in this language:

> . . . a decedent possesses testamentary capacity ''. . . if he has an intelligent knowledge regarding those who are the natural objects of his bounty, of what his estate consists, and of what he desires done with it, even though his memory has been impaired by age or disease'': *Franz Will,* 368 Pa. 618, 622, 84 A.2d 292, 295; also *In re Sturgeon's Will,* 357 Pa. 75, 53 A.2d 139; *In re Ash's Will,* 351 Pa. 317, 41 A.2d 620; *In re Olshefski's Estate,* 337 Pa. 420, 11 A.2d 487.

In testing the extent of decedent's testamentary capacity, Dr. Hemminger, a psychiatrist, called by the proponent, testified:

> Anxious to determine, if I could, to what extent he was aware of his worldly goods, we went into that to some extent. He had no definite knowledge of his wealth at all. He knew that he had a guardian and that money came from the bank to him, and that he owned the house he lived in, and that he had enough he didn't have to work. I wouldn't feel that beyond that he had much knowledge of his means at all.

Upon this evaluation the doctor was of opinion, as were proponent's other witnesses, that decedent possessed *sufficient* testamentary capacity to make a will *provided* that all decedent was required to know was a *"general"* knowledge of what property he possessed and his next of kin. The witness frankly stated that, if the requirement of such testamentary capacity necessitated a *"full"* knowledge of his estate and kindred, decedent did not have such capacity. Our examination of the evidence convinces us, as it did the learned hearing judge and the court in banc, that the decedent was so mentally deficient that he was incapable of making a valid will. As such he was incapable of possessing, and did not possess, the quantum and quality of knowledge of his estate and the natural objects of his bounty which he was required to possess in order to have testamentary capacity.

Since the testamentary incapacity of decedent was so clearly established we need not discuss the effect of a will drawn by an attorney and witnessed by a physician and a bank officer. Their opinions, under the present circumstances, are of slight, if any, value. Certainly their expressed opinions of decedent's testamentary capacity were contrary to the overwhelming weight of the evidence. We need not, therefore, consider the question of undue influence. We are not favorably impressed, however, with the manner and circumstances under which the will was prepared and executed.

The decree appealed from is affirmed. Costs to be paid out of the estate.

NOTES

1. The legal principles regarding testamentary capacity have changed little in this century. In 1899, the Supreme Court of Missouri outlined the procedures and standards as follows:

> Under the statute of wills, the owner of property is permitted to dispose of it as he chooses after his death. If he makes no disposition of it by will, the statute of descents disposes of it for him. When a will is contested, it devolves upon the proponents to prove the execution of the will, that the testator was of requisite age, and that he was sane. . . . This makes out a *prima facie* case, and it then devolves upon the contestants to establish incompetency or undue influence. By "competency" is meant intelligence sufficient to understand the act he is performing, the property he possesses, the disposition he is making of it, and the persons or objects he makes the beneficiaries of his bounty. Imperfect memory, caused by sickness or old age, forgetfulness of the names of persons he has known, idle questions, or requiring a repetition of information, will not be sufficient to establish incompetency, if he has sufficient intelligence remaining to fulfill the above definition. . . . Mere opinions of witnesses that the testator was "childish," or acted "funny," or was "worse than a child," or that there were "inequalities in the will," unaccompanied by any testimony showing any particular act or fact evidencing incompetency, do not make out a case of incompetency, when the testimony shows that the testator "knew what he was doing and to whom he was giving his property." *Sehr* v. *Lindemann,* 153 Mo. 276, 54 S.W. 537, 540 (1899) (citations omitted).

The definition of *competency* is little different from that applied in *Glesenkamp* or from the wording of a Maryland court in 1962:

> It must appear that at the time of making the will, the testatrix had a full understanding of the nature of the business in which she was engaged, a recollection of the property of which she intended to dispose and the persons to whom she meant to give it, and the relative claims of the different persons who were or should have been the objects of her bounty. *Giardina* v. *Wannen,* 228 Md. 116, 179 A.2d 357, 363 (1962).

2. In *Payton* v. *Shipley,* 80 Okla. 145, 195 P. 125, 128 (1921), subsequently overruled in *In re Nitey's Estate,* 175 Okl. 389, 53 P.2d 215, 220 (1935), the court adopted the following statement of the requisite mental capacity for making a valid will:

> A testator has a sound mind for testamentary purposes when he can understand and carry in mind, in a general way, the nature and situation of his property, and his relations to the persons around him, to those who naturally have some claim to his remembrance, and to those in whom, and the things in which, he has been chiefly interested. He must understand the act which he is doing, and the relation in which he stands to the objects of his bounty and to those who ought to be in his mind on the occasion of making his will.

Compare this with the standard applied in *Glesenkamp,* with particular attention to the words "in a general way" in the *Payton* v. *Shipley* formulation. How well does one have to know the extent of his or her estate?

3. Joseph Glesenkamp's property was left to him by his parents. Because he was unable to manage this property, a guardian was appointed for him. What alternative methods for more effectively providing for their son after their death ought the parents have considered?

4. In some states, will contests may be tried before a jury; in such cases, the question of the standard of testamentary capacity will be raised in the context of jury instructions. One case that has examined the appropriateness of such instructions is *Challiner* v. *Smith,* 396 Ill. 106, 71 N.E.2d 324 (1947). The court declared:

> We are constrained . . . to examine some of the other instructions given on behalf of the plaintiff. In instruction No. 5 the jury was told that to be of sound mind and memory a person making a will must be capable of knowing the property she was to dispose of, who were the natural objects of her bounty, and the effect of the act of executing her will, and it then added: "and if you believe from a preponderance of the evidence, that at the time of the execution of the alleged will, the said Elizabeth Cuchman did not understand the nature or consequence of the execution of said alleged will, then in that case you will find against the validity of the alleged will." This statement is not one of the requirements of testamentary capacity.
>
> In *Yoe* v. *McCord,* 74 Ill. 33, the following instruction was given: "The jury are instructed that the mere fact of the signing, and acknowledgment of the alleged will by the said John McCord does not entitle it to be treated or considered as his will, and that in addition thereto it must appear to the jury, from the evidence, that it is his actual deed, and if they should find, from the evidence, that he did not know each and all of its provisions, then it is not his will." The court said: "The instruction was further wrong in saying that if the testator 'did not know each and all of its provisions' then the instrument was not his will. Most written instruments probably would fail to stand the test of any such rule. Writings are constantly passing from one to another in the every day transactions of business, where the makers are more or less ignorant of their contents, executed often without reading or hearing them read, in trust upon some other person for their being correct, where there may be, in fact, no actual knowledge of what they do contain. A written instrument is not to be defeated by evidence that the maker did not know each and all of its provisions. The idea is inadmissible. Where the testator is shown to have executed an instrument as his will, being in his right mind, and there is nothing of fraud or imposition, it will be presumed that he was aware of its contents."
>
> In *Dowdey* v. *Palmer,* 287 Ill. 42, 122 N.E. 102, 106, an instruction for the contestant contained, among other things, the statement that the testator "Must have had at the time a full comprehension of the surrounding circumstances and of their direct

consequences and probable results,'' in order to have testamentary capacity. This has the same meaning, if not the identical words, as the instruction under consideration in this case. In holding this instruction bad we said, after reviewing earlier authorities: ''Beyond question, instruction 10, because of its misleading character in this regard, should not have been given. No man, even though in full possession of testamentary capacity, can with certainty know that he has full comprehension of the direct consequences and the probable results of his will. He may think he knows, but experience shows that the most farsighted minds are often mistaken as to what they think will be the probable results of actions that they are taking.'' A like instruction was held bad in *Turnbull* v. *Butterfield,* 304 Ill. 454, 136 N.E. 663. *Id*. at 71 N.E.2d 331-332.

How does this holding compare with the standards for testamentary capacity previously discussed?

In re Estate of Teel

Court of Appeals of Arizona, Division I, 1971
14 Ariz.App. 371, 483 P.2d 603

Hathaway, Judge.

This appeal arises out of a will contest that was tried to the court sitting without a jury. The appellant, Frank Teel, brother of decedent and contestant below, appeals from the findings of fact, conclusions of law and judgment entered on March 3, 1970, in the superior court in Maricopa County, in favor of the proponent, Ruth Roberson. The decedent, Marvin Teel, died at the age of 77, on January 5, 1969. He left a will executed on July 6, 1945, bequeathing his entire estate to Ruth Roberson, a half-cousin by marriage and naming her as executrix.

Question Presented for Review

Is a person functioning at the level of a ten to twelve year old child competent to make a will under the law of Arizona? The question is prompted from the finding of fact that the decedent, ''Marvin Teel was mentally retarded. He functioned at an age level of ten to twelve years old.'' The finding of fact further provided:

1. He could drive a car. He could do simple manual tasks. He could assume responsibility for running errands for his family and friends, care of flower gardens and assume the responsibility for driving ladies to and from church meetings and high school students to and from school on a regular basis for sustained periods of time.
2. On July 6, 1945, Marvin Teel executed a will prepared at his own request by an attorney and executed in accordance with the requirements of law.
3. Marvin Teel did not get along well with his brother Frank Teel and there existed a poor relationship between the two over a period of many years. In 1945 Marvin Teel had a fear that his brother was going to take his property or money.
4. Marvin Teel had a close relationship with Ruth Roberson and her family, beginning in 1929 and lasting at least until 1946. Many visits were exchanged, many gifts were exchanged, many favors and much help was given one to another. A meaningful relationship existed. Ruth Roberson helped Marvin Teel's mother in her last years and her last illness. Marvin Teel's mother died at the age of 88 on August 13, 1945.
5. Marvin Teel was perhaps over-protected by his family and over-dependent upon them. He probably did not develop his potential to function more nearly as a normal person even within the limits of his mental retardation.

6. The death of Marvin Teel's mother was a traumatic and distressing experience for him. She represented someone who for 54 years had protected him and had been someone whom he could trust. Marvin Teel's mental condition began to deteriorate significantly after her death.

7. Marvin Teel did, with good reason, want to give his property to Ruth Roberson and have her act as executrix of his will. He did not tell Ruth Roberson of his will; she did not discover the existence of the will until November, 1968.

8. Marvin Teel did on July 6, 1945, have sufficient mental capacity to give his property to Ruth Roberson. He was aware of those who had some claim to benefit from his property. Marvin Teel comprehended generally the kind and nature of his property. He understood the nature and effect of his testamentary act. Finally, he could make disposition of his property according to a plan formed in his mind.

9. There was no evidence of any undue influence on Marvin Teel at the time of the execution of the will.

10. The result of sustaining the will seems just to the Court and a natural disposition of decedent's property.

And based upon the foregoing findings of fact the Court makes the following. . . .

The court admitted the will to probate on the strength of the foregoing findings of facts, dismissed the petition contesting the probate and ordered that letters testamentary issue in favor of Ruth Roberson.

In finding of fact number 8, the court found that the testator was competent, *viz,* he understood the natural objects of his bounty; the kind and character of his property; and the nature of the testamentary act. *In re O'Connor's Estate,* 74 Ariz. 248, 246 P.2d 1063 (1952); *In re Estate of Slater,* 6 Ariz.App. 486, 433 P.2d 666 (1967); *In re Stitt's Estate,* 93 Ariz. 302, 380 P.2d 601 (1963).

Considering the record and the overall findings, we are of the opinion that the conclusion that the decedent "functioned at an age level of ten to twelve years old" is not necessarily inconsistent with the finding of competency as a testator.

> To make a valid will one must be of sound mind though he need not possess superior or even average mentality. *Atkinson on Wills,* p. 232.

> The fact that advanced years are accompanied by mental sluggishness, impairment of memory, childishness, eccentricities and physical infirmity does not show lack of testamentary capacity. *Atkinson on Wills,* p. 250.

> Testamentary capacity is not the same as the ability to transact ordinary business. . . . Testamentary capacity is determined objectively from the standpoint of the purpose to be accomplished. A testator, at the time of executing his will, must have sufficient mental capacity to know the natural objects of his bounty, to comprehend the kind and character of his property, to understand the nature and effect of his act, and to make a disposition of his property according to some plan formed in his mind. 57 *Am.Jur.Wills* § 64 at p. 81.

The record would indicate that the decedent led a very sheltered life, but that his understanding was such that his competency as a testator was established. There was evidence that at one time he carried on a small scale dairy business, including the milking of the cows, processing and separating of the milk, and sale to a dairy of his products. The decedent apparently had very few close friends, but the testimony indicates that he was active as a gardener and worked well with his hands. He was very regular in church affairs and according to his minister made and kept pledges to the church. At least on one occasion at Christmas, he donned a Santa Claus suit and distributed gifts by reading the names on the packages and making the distribution accordingly. He read the newspaper and Sears Roebuck catalog and ordered items from the catalog on occasion. He exchanged gifts and greeting cards. The decedent owned and drove his own automobile and was reportedly a very good driver. He was able to transact business at the grocery store, such as purchasing groceries, and he arranged for the maintenance and repair of his automobile and paid for those services.

Appellant also attempts to infer that decedent did not have the capacity to make a will by pointing out that decedent was declared incompetent and had a guardian appointed for him 10 months after he executed the will. Testator's capacity to make a will will be judged at the time of the execution of the will. *In re Stitt's Estate, supra.* Even if testator had been declared incompetent and had a guardian appointed to him at the time of the will's execution, this does not necessarily preclude testator from having the required mental capacity to execute a valid will. See *In re Thomas' Estate,* 105 Ariz. 186, 461 P.2d 484 (1969).

The evidence shows that the decedent was very close to the beneficiary named under the will and that she thought highly of him and helped care for him. He did not get along well with his brother, the contestant.

The judgment is affirmed.

KRUCKER, C. J., and HOWARD, J., concur.

NOTE

Contrast the result in *Teel's Estate* with that in *Glesenkamp.* What explains the difference?

IN RE HALL'S ESTATE

Supreme Court of Kansas, 1948
165 Kan. 465, 195 P.2d 612

WEDELL, Justice.

Two wills of J. W. Hall were presented for probate at the same time. The first will executed in 1920 devised a life estate in all of the testator's real estate to his wife and the remainder to "... the Presbyterian College, known as the Emporia College, at Emporia, Kansas and to the Park College, of Parkville, Missouri ... " share and share alike. J. W. Hall's wife consented in writing to that will. Mrs. Hall died in August, 1943, while in the same hospital with her husband. The testator's second will was executed December 8, 1943. By it he revoked all former wills and devised all the property he owned, including his ranch in Barber county, Kansas, consisting of approximately 720 acres, to his nephews, Elbert R. Hall and Arden Hall.

The probate court admitted the last will to probate. The two colleges named as beneficiaries under the first will appealed to the district court which sustained the judgment of the probate court. From the latter judgment the colleges appeal.

Appellants contend first, the testator lacked testamentary capacity to make the last will and, second, that it was the result of undue influence. The trial court prepared a rather lengthy memorandum opinion. In it the court analyzed appellants' contentions. It recognized the conflict in the testimony and, in part, said:

It is my opinion that the preponderance of the evidence in this case shows that Mr. Hall was competent to make this will.

The trial court stated the evidence was sufficient to show the testator's compe- years contemplated appellants would receive the property involved after Mrs. Hall's death and, in substance, stated: The testator was sixty-nine years of age when the first will was executed; Mrs. Hall had a very strong influence and much control over her husband; after his wife's death the testator probably felt that his newly acquired freedom similar to that of a colt "when the halter is taken off"; the Halls had no children of their own but Mr. Hall had the two nephews mentioned in his last will; they were his closest kin (the evidence showed he often referred to them as "the boys" and that when he did so friends knew he was referring to those nephews); there were five grandnephews and grandnieces, the surviving children of three predeceased nieces; two nephews and all nieces had predeceased the testator; notwithstanding the testator was ninety-two years of age when he executed the last will he knew he owned the ranch; he clearly knew he had these two nephews; when he was alone in the hospital after his wife's death these nephews and their families visited him frequently; the nephews might have encouraged him to will his property to them but there was no evidence of anything having been said or done by them, or by members of their families, beyond the bounds of propriety.

The court found the preponderance of the evidence showed the making of this particular will was not a complicated matter, the testator knew what property he owned, that he wanted his two nephews to have it and on the day he executed the last will he was competent to make it.

In making the foregoing analysis the court recognized the fact the testator had on occasions been somewhat flighty. The trial court reviewed the testimony of two doctors who expressed their opinion the testator was incompetent to make the will. The court stated it believed the doctors were sincere in their testimony but that the court did not agree their testimony showed the testator, on the date of the last will, did not know what property he owned or to whom he desired to leave it.

The trial court stated the evidence was sufficient to show the testator's compe- tency even though the testimony of the scrivener, testator's attorney, was disregarded. On the basis of that statement appellants ask us to disregard the scrivener's testimony in reaching our conclusion. Whether that statement of the trial court was correct or not, we have no right to, and shall not, disregard the scrivener's testimony. It is a part of the record and strongly supports the conclusion the testator, on the date he made the will, knew what property he had, to whom he desired to leave it and possessed all his mental faculties.

Appellants emphasize certain facts concerning the prior illness of the testator, as follows:

In March, 1942, Mr. Hall was taken to the Achenbach Memorial Hospital in Hardtner, Kansas, in an unconscious condition, which the doctors diagnosed as having been caused by a cerebral hemorrhage and that he was also afflicted with general senility; in January, 1944, C. C. Benefiel, an elder in and the treasurer of the local Presbyterian church at Medicine Lodge, filed a petition in the probate court of Barber county for the appointment of a guardian of Hall's person and estate; the commissioners, two doctors, found Hall was mentally incompetent to transact business as a result of senile sclerosis; that for a period of approximately two years prior to the hearing and since Hall had been in the hospital he had been without lucid intervals; the commissioners' report of February 2, 1944, was approved by the probate court and C. C. Benefiel, the petitioner, was appointed guardian of Hall's person and estate.

Appellants argue a finding of *insanity* is conclusive with respect to the date on which it is made and is prima facie evidence of insanity during the prior period covered by the finding. We have so held. *Fuller* v. *Williams,* 125 Kan. 154, 264 P. 77. See, also, the rule on presumption after adjudication of insanity and discharge from hospital for the insane. *In re Estate of Strohmeier,* 164 Kan. 675, 192 P.2d 181.

We adhere to the rule just stated with respect to an adjudication of insanity. Here there was no finding of insanity but only a finding the testator for approximately two years prior to the hearing for appointment of a guardian on February 2, 1944, was "incompetent to transact business." Manifestly there is quite a distinction in such adjudications. In any event the finding of incompetency to transact business and the appointment of a guardian was not tantamount to a finding the testator lacked testamentary capacity on December 8, 1943, the date of the last will. It has been held a finding of the probate court that an aged person was "feeble-minded and incapable of managing his affairs" and needed a guardian could be rebutted by evidence showing competency to make a will three weeks later. *Mingle* v. *Hubbard,* 131 Kan. 844, 293 P. 513. It is practically a universal rule that the mere fact one is under guardianship does not deprive him of the power to make a will. Anno. 8 A.L.R. 1375. The trial court found the preponderance of the evidence adduced on the hearing for probate of the last will showed testamentary capacity on the date that will was executed.

The time when a will is made is the time of primary importance to be considered in estimating testamentary capacity. Evidence of capacity or lack of capacity before or after that time serves only as an aid to determine the primary question. For example, the fact a person was afflicted with senile dementia before a will was made is not conclusive of his continued incapacity to make a will at a considerably later date. *Wisner* v. *Chandler,* 95 Kan. 36, 147 P. 849. The same rule has been applied in cases involving some other ailments. *Klose* v. *Collins,* 137 Kan. 321, 20 P.2d 494; *Kunkle* v. *Urbansky,* 153 Kan. 117, 109 P.2d 71.

Of course, the testimony of expert witnesses is important in cases involving mental capacity and should always receive proper consideration but the trier of facts is not bound to accept their testimony as true. *Mingle* v. *Hubbard, supra.*

The test of testamentary capacity is not whether a person has capacity to enter into a complex contract or to engage in intricate business transactions. *Kunkle* v. *Urbansky, supra.* Nor is absolute soundness of mind the real test of testamentary capacity. *Kunkle* v. *Urbansky, supra; In re Estate of Crump,* 161 Kan. 154, 157, 166 P.2d 684. The established rule in this state, although not always stated precisely in the same manner, is that one who is able to understand what property he has and how he wants it to go at his death is competent to make a will even though he may be feeble in mind and decrepit in body. *Cole* v. *Drum,* 109 Kan. 148, 197 P. 1105; *Klose* v. *Collins, supra; Anderson* v. *Anderson,* 147 Kan. 273, 76 P.2d 825; *Kunkle* v. *Urbansky, supra.*

Appellants recognize the established rule that appellate courts are concerned only with evidence which supports findings and not with evidence contrary thereto. They contend there was no evidence to support the finding of competency. With that contention we cannot agree. It will serve no useful purpose to delineate and compare the conflicting testimony of the various witnesses.

It must always be borne in mind that on review the question is not what effect the testimony may have on appellate courts but only whether there was substantial testimony which could have convinced the trial court. Where, as here, there is such testimony this court is precluded from disturbing the findings.

What about undue influence? Natural human desire, motive and opportunity to exercise undue influence do not alone authorize the inference it was in fact exercised. Nor is mere suspicion or possibility of parties having induced the making of a will favorable to them as beneficiaries enough to justify a finding of undue influence. *Klose* v. *Collins, supra.*

The test of undue influence, sufficient to destroy a will, is that it must amount to such coercion, compulsion and restraint as to destroy the testator's free agency, and by overcoming his power of resistance, obliges or causes him to adopt the will of another rather than exercising his own. *Anderson* v. *Anderson, supra.*

The burden of establishing undue influence, of course, rests on him who asserts it. *Anderson* v. *Anderson, supra.* A review of the record convinces us we cannot reverse the judgment on the theory the trial court was obliged to believe appellants met that burden.

The judgment is affirmed.

NOTES

1.   The court in *In re Hall's Estate* states the general rule that being under guardianship is no bar to making a valid will. For more recent cases applying this rule, see *Rossi* v. *Fletcher,* 418 F.2d 1169 (D.C. Cir. 1969), cert. denied, 396 U.S. 1009 (1970); *In re Estate of Thomas,* 105 Ariz. 186, 461 P.2d 484 (1969); *In re Estate of O'Laughlin,* 50 Wis.2d 143, 183 N.W.2d 133 (1971). See generally, Annot., 89 A.L.R.2d 1120 (1963).

The related issue of prior adjudications of insanity, held not to be at issue in *Hall's Estate,* was resolved in *In re Armijo's Will,* 57 N.M. 649, 261 P.2d 833 (1953), as follows:

> If a person has so lost touch with reality as to be unable to understand the true uses and meaning of property, then we say that such a person lacks one essential quality constituting testamentary capacity. There remains no true understanding of the extent of the estate. The second factor in this case is the adjudication of insanity which took place only a few moments before decedent executed the purported will. Admitting that this is not conclusive, the better view of the law holds that such an adjudication raises a presumption of incapacity. Page on Wills, Vol. 2, sec. 807, p. 587:
>
> "If the record shows an adjudication of insanity before the execution of the will, the burden of proof is upon the proponent of the will to rebut the presumption or inference of incapacity from such record; and it is said that very clear evidence is required to rebut such presumption."
>
> *Dean* v. *Jordon,* 1938, 194 Wash. 661, 79 P.2d 331, 335:

"The quantum or degree of proof required of the proponent to rebut the presumption of insanity under such circumstances, is variously stated by the authorities and text-writers, but according to the weight of authority, and what we conceive to be a proper and reasonable requirement, the proof in rebuttal of the presumption should be clear and satisfactory to the trier of the fact."

Id. at 261 P.2d 837-838.

Compare this statement of presumptions and evidentiary burdens in the insanity adjudication context with the similar considerations applied in *Hall's Estate* in the context of guardianships. Should there be any differences?

2. The *In re Hall's Estate* decision indicated that testamentary capacity is not equivalent to the ability to enter into a complex contract. Some courts have said that contractual and testamentary capacity are the same, e.g., *Hanks* v. *McNeil Coal Corporation,* 114 Colo. 578, 168 P.2d 256, 260 (1946); others have indicated that less mental capacity is required for the making of a will than for the making of a contract, e.g., *In re Good's Estate,* 274 S.W.2d 900, 902 (Tex.Civ.App. 1955). The weight of modern authority is, however, consistent with the view expressed in *Hall's Estate* that the contractual and testamentary functions are different and cannot be compared quantitatively. See Weihofen, H., "Mental Incompetency to Make a Will," 7 *Natural Resources J.* 89, 91 (1967).

3. The *Hall's Estate* court observed that absolute soundness of mind is not necessary for making a valid will. But what degree of mental unsoundness is sufficient to invalidate a will? A number of courts refer to the concept of "insane delusions." In *In re Good's Estate, supra,* the children of a man, whose nine children received, pursuant to the terms of his will, only $10 each of his $50,000 estate, contested the will on the grounds that their father was laboring under an insane delusion that his children did not care anything about him and had abandoned him. The court, in upholding the father's decision to leave the bulk of his estate to a charity, outlined the following principles:

It has been decided that an insane delusion with reference to an object of bounty renders a testator incompetent on that score. *Stone* v. *Grainger,* Tex.Civ.App., 66 S.W.2d 484. It is therefore necessary to determine if testator here actually had an insane delusion regarding his children. Such a decision is not always easy to make.

* * *

A delusion, to deprive a testator of capacity, must be an *insane delusion.* A mere mistaken belief and erroneous or unjust conclusion is not an insane delusion if there is some foundation in fact or some basis on which the mental operation of the testator may rest, even though the basis may be regarded by others as wholly insufficient. 68 C.J. 433 (30). We do not have, as in the *Grainger* case, *supra,* a sudden termination of long continued affection, replaced by violent hatred. Persons harboring personal dislikes or injured feelings or even sulking without cause deemed sufficient by others are not necessarily suffering from insane delusions. It is the common idea, of course, that children have the right to some of the property of parents, but it is the law of Texas that a citizen of this state may by his will dispose of his property without regard to the ties of nature and relationship, and may do so in defiance of the rules of justice or the dictates of reason, and

"no sentimental considerations of love and affection that should actuate a man in dealing with his own blood can be decisive as to the validity of a will that has been

executed by a person possessing testamentary capacity and without undue influence."
Stolle v. *Kanetzky*, Tex.Civ.App., 220 S.W. 557, 559.

It has been said that the power of disposing of property is an inestimable privilege of the old. It is evident that we must decide here whether the testator harbored an insane delusion or was simply displeased and unhappy with his children. Mere erroneous belief or mistaken ideas are not enough, as was said in *Navarro* v. *Rodriguez*, Tex.Civ.App., 235 S.W.2d 665, 667:

> "Even rational human beings are subject to mistake, prejudice and ill-founded conclusions. 'A delusion, to deprive the testator of capacity, must be an *insame* [sic] delusion. An insane delusion such as will affect testamentary capacity is an idea or belief which has no basis in fact or reason and to which the testator adheres against reason and evidence, or, in other words, it may be stated to be a belief in a state of facts that does not exist and which no rational person would believe to exist. A mere mistaken belief or an erroneous or unjust conclusion is not an insane delusion if there is some foundation in fact or some basis on which the mental operation of the testator may rest, even though the basis may be regarded by others as wholly insufficient.'"

Id. at 902.

A more succinct declaration was made by a California court in similar circumstances: "However mistaken and unreasonable this belief may have been it does not serve to establish that in entertaining the same the decedent was laboring under an insane delusion." *In re Gecht's Estate*, 165 Cal.App.2d 431, 331 P.2d 1019, 1026 (1958).

Moreover, even where the testator is found to have suffered an insane delusion, that fact may not be determinative, for "a delusion is not sufficient evidence to warrant a finding of lack of capacity, unless the will is the product thereof." *Giardina* v. *Wannen*, 228 Md. 116, 179 A.2d 357, 362 (1962).

Contrast the "insane delusion" terminology with the analytical standards applicable where the testator is a mentally retarded person.

2. By Physically Handicapped Persons

In re Estate of McCready

Surrogate's Court, Bronx County, New York, 1975
369 N.Y.S.2d 325

Bertram Gelfand, Surrogate.

In this probate proceeding the proofs pursuant to SCPA 1404 were taken by the Surrogate. The evidence established that the will was executed on August 12, 1954 while the decedent who was blind, was a resident of a home for the blind. The execution of the will was supervised by an attorney who was an attesting witness. He first read the will aloud to the testator in the presence of the two additional attesting witnesses. The testator stated that the said will met with his approval and declared the instrument to be his will. With the assistance of one of the attesting witnesses, the testator made a cross-mark for his signature. This witness wrote on the instrument after the cross-mark "(Joseph McCready) his mark by Lillian T. MacKinnon." At the request of the testator and after the reading aloud of the attestation clause of the will (which recites the facts just stated) the three attesting witnesses signed their names in the presence of the testator. Blindness does not deprive a person from making a will (*Matter of McCabe*, 75 Misc. 35, 134 N.Y.S. 682 and cases cited; Warren's Heaton on Surrogate's Courts (1971) Vol. 2B § 186 C(6)(a)). The law is also well settled that a cross-mark is the signature of the decedent (*Matter of Galvin*, 78 Misc.2d 22, 355 N.Y.S:2d 751, citing *Jackson* v. *Jackson*, 39 N.Y. 153). A signature by mark even with the testator's hand guided is sufficient (*Matter of Stegman*, 133 Misc. 745, 234 N.Y.S. 239 and cases cited in Warren's Heaton, *supra* Vol. 2B § 186-A(4)(d). In the instant case not only did the testator sign with a cross-mark but one of the attesting witnesses signed his name at his request. One of the attesting witnesses was examined by the court. The remaining living attesting witness because of his physical condition is unable to appear in court. His statement was taken pursuant to SCPA 1406.

The propounded instrument appears to have been duly executed in accordance with EPTL 3-2.1. The competency of the decedent to make a will and his freedom from restraint having been established the said instrument is admitted to probate as the will of the decedent.

IN RE FERRIS'S WILL

Prerogative Court of New Jersey, 1934
115 N.J.Eq. 115, 169A. 697, aff'd 117 N.J.Eq. 20, 174 A. 708

BACKES, Vice Ordinary.

One month before she died, Anna Ferris, 80 years of age, feeble and deaf, in charge of a nurse in the home of the nurse's mother, signed a paper writing, giving her estate to the nurse. The paper writing was denied probate by the orphans' court on the ground that it was not declared by the deceased to be her last will and testament to the two attesting witnesses.

The proof is this: The deceased had penned and signed a will, attested by two witnesses, giving her estate to the nurse. By her direction, it was taken to a lawyer for approval, who, upon observing that it contained no attestation clause and appointed no executor, and fearing that it may not have been statutorily executed, suggested that it be redrawn in legal form, and that he be appointed executor. A redraft was immediately typed by the lawyer's secretary, to which she added an attestation clause and her employer's name as executor, and the lawyer and the secretary accompanied the nurse and one of the witnesses to the holograph will back to the home of the deceased for a formal execution. The lawyer conferred privately with the deceased. She read the document. Being too deaf to hear, the lawyer wrote on a piece of paper these four questions:

Do you understand this will?
Do you want me to act as executor?
Do you publish and declare this paper to be your last will and testament?
Do you request Miss McCall and Mrs. Roberts to witness this will?

And having assured himself that the deceased understood the will and she having nodded affirmatively to the first two questions, the witnesses were called into the room where the deceased was sitting at a table with the will before her. Assembled, the lawyer addressed the deceased asking if she "Published and declared this to be her last will and testament and if she requested Miss McCall (secretary) and Mrs. Roberts (witness to the holograph will) to act as subscribing witnesses,'' and being reminded by the nurse that the deceased was deaf and could not hear him, he showed her the last two questions, pointing to them, and upon the deceased nodding affirmatively, he had her sign and the witnesses attest the signature. The lawyer's secretary says she did not know what was written on the paper containing the questions shown the deceased until the next day; that she saw the assenting nod but did not know to what the assent was given. The other witness, Mrs. Roberts, says that the lawyer pointed out and read aloud the last two questions, but that there was no nod, expression, or gesture of assent of any kind.

There is, of course, no question that the deceased and the witnesses individually understood what was being transacted, for the decedent had previously read the document and had written its prototype; the secretary had typed it, and the other witness had attested the holograph will and had procured the redraft. But that the witnesses knew it was the decedent's will they were attesting is not enough. For safe-guarding of decedents' estates, the statute not only requires wills to be in writing and signed by the testator, or his signature acknowledged by him, in the presence of two witnesses, present at the same time, who shall subscribe their names thereto as witnesses, but it is as specific and exacting in this essential: That the testator shall declare to the two witnesses thus present that the writing is his last will and testament. "It is not necessary that the testator should, in express terms, declare the instrument in process of execution to be his will. Another may speak for him. It is a sufficient compliance with the statute when enough is said or done, in the presence and with the knowledge of the testator, to give the witnesses to understand distinctly that the testator desires them to know that the paper is his will and that they are to attest it,'' but the authorities are as one, that the communication of the fact of the will to the attesting witnesses must come to them from the testator, directly or indirectly, at the time of the ceremony of the execution of the will. [Citations omitted.]

Here, the deceased made a declaration which only the lawyer understood. It failed to register with either witness. One of them saw her nod to a paper—the declaration—but was ignorant of its contents; the other heard the declaration read, but saw no nod, although looking. There was no statutory publication.

The decree of the orphans' court will be affirmed.

NOTES

1. The *McCready* and *Ferris* cases demonstrate the two-pronged legal impact of physical handicaps on the process of making a will. On the one hand, as *McCready* illustrates, a physical handicap such as blindness does not interfere with testamentary capacity. On the other hand, as both cases make clear, there may be special problems in ascertaining the testator's intent and in properly preparing and witnessing the document. Thus the Supreme Court of Minnesota has declared: "The decedent was deaf. This did not prevent his making a will. It only added a difficulty to its execution." *In re Eklund's Estate,* 186 Minn. 129, 242 N.W. 467, 468 (1932).

Therefore, special care and safeguards may be required by the attorney in arranging the preparation and execution of wills on behalf of physically handicapped clients. But, where the requisite mental capacity is present and the statutory requirements are followed, there is no reason a physically handicapped person cannot make a valid will, even if unusual techniques must be invoked in its signing and execution. In *Ducasse's Heirs* v. *Ducasse,* 120 La. 731, 45 So. 565 (1908), for example, a will was upheld as to form and substance even though the testator, unable to write because of paralysis, simply touched the pen after a cross had been made to stand as his signature. And in *Lane* v. *Lane,* 95 N.Y. 494, 30 Hun. 230 (1894), paralysis of the testator's vocal cords was held not to impede the validity of a will where intent was shown clearly by signs and acts.

2. In addition to the *McCready* and *Ferris* decisions and the other cases mentioned in Note 1, a number of other courts have held a variety of physical handicapping conditions not to affect testamentary capacity. In *Bodine* v. *Bodine,* 44 S.W.2d 840, 845 (Ky.App. 1931), the court held that epilepsy was not substantive evidence of incapacity to make a will. In *In re Succession of Moody,* 227 La. 609, 80 So.2d 93, 95 (1955), it was held that paresis was not an indicator of testamentary incapacity. Several courts have held that combinations of physical disabilities do not constitute evidence of inability to make a valid will. In *Frazie's Executrix* v. *Frazie,* 186 Ky. 613, 217 S.W. 668, 672 (1919), for example, the court declared:

> Old age alone does not disqualify one from disposing of his property by will. No court has ever so held, yet contestants have little else to entitle their cause to consideration than the extreme old age of the testator and his defective hearing and eyesight, added to his decrepit physical condition, which is largely due to his broken hip or limbs. As one grows older, his sensibilities are dulled, his eyesight dimmed, and his hearing less acute; but this is not mental unsoundness, nor are such facts alone entitled to be considered as tending to prove testamentary incapacity.

Likewise, the Supreme Court of Illinois has declared: "Old age, deafness, and infirmity do not of themselves constitute proof of lack of mental capacity." *Tidholm* v. *Tidholm,* 391 Ill. 19, 62 N.E.2d 473, 477 (1945). And in *Sehr* v. *Lindemann,* 153 Mo. 276, 54 S.W. 537, 541–542 (1899), a case involving a blind, partially deaf man who allegedly acted "funny" and "childish," it was held that there was "no substantial evidence of incompetency" and the court approved a directed verdict on that issue.

In those cases where a physically handicapped person has been held not to have testamentary capacity, e.g., *Payton* v. *Shipley,* 80 Okla. 145, 195 P. 125 (1921), subsequently overruled in *In re Nitey's Estate,* 175 Okl. 389, 53 P.2d 215, 220 (1935), the decision is generally based upon significant evidence of mental incapacity in addition to the person's physical condition.

C. MISCELLANEOUS ISSUES
CONCERNING OWNERSHIP OF PROPERTY

The major way in which many handicapped persons have been denied their right of owning and managing their property is through the process of guardianship, which is examined in detail in Chapter 5. Other limitations upon the exercise of property rights have been discussed in this chapter in regard to contractual rights and the making of wills. There are, however, a few other means worthy of mention by which the property rights of handicapped individuals have sometimes been limited or taken away. One such method is a secondary effect of institutionalization; some residential facilities have made it a practice to deprive new residents of all their items of personal property. Moreover, residents have often not been provided with any place to keep or store any personal belongings. And room searches are conducted during which the staff members seize any "contraband" items that institution rules prohibit. See, Ferleger, D., "Loosing the Chains: In-Hospital Civil Liberties of Mental Patients," 13 *Santa Clara Lawyer* 447, 463–469 (1973). As a result of this problem, some of the major lawsuits resulting in comprehensive standards for the physical plant and operation of large residential institutions, see pp. 630–631, above, have included provisions dealing with maintenance of personal property. The standards in *Wyatt* v. *Stickney,* see pp. 630–631, above, for example, include requirements that each resident be provided "a closet or locker for his personal belongings," at 344 F.Supp. 382 and 344 F.Supp. 404. Likewise, in *Welsch* v. *Likins,* see pp. 630–631, above, the court specified that each resident was entitled to "be provided with, and have access to, individual storage space for personal belongings," Civil No. 4-72-451, slip op. at 5 (D.Minn., Oct. 1, 1974).

A related issue was raised in *In re Matson,* 293 N.Y. 476, 58 N.E.2d 501 (1944). The New York State Department of Mental Health was desirous of searching safety deposit boxes held by state hospital residents to determine if there was property of sufficient value in them to justify obtaining a "committee" to manage (take?) such property. When the department sought a judicial order permitting it to open a safety deposit box, a New York court held that "the relief sought would constitute an unauthorized invasion of this patient's personal rights" and that the court was "without power to grant the order prayed for." *In re Lehr,* 175 Misc. 914, 24 N.Y.S.2d 653 (1940). Subsequently, the Department of Mental Health succeeded in getting a statute passed which gave it the authority to open safety deposit boxes and inventory their contents. The court that had made the *In re Lehr* decision ruled that the new statute was unconstitutional in violation of the search and seizure provision of the state consitution and also as an impairment of the contract between the safe deposit company and its depositor. *In re Matson,* 182 Misc. 389, 49 N.Y.S.2d 598 (1944). On appeal, however, the statute's validity was upheld and the Department's authority to search safety deposit boxes was approved. *In re Matson,* 293 N.Y. 476, 58 N.E.2d 501 (1944).

Another direct attack on the ownership rights of a handicapped person occurred in *Christmas* v. *Mitchell,* 38 N.C. 421 (1845), when a deaf man was challenged as a beneficiary of a will on the ground that he was incapable of managing the property. Although witnesses testified that the man was not capable of doing any business, and the court found that he "has been deaf and dumb from his birth, and is therefore ignorant and uninformed, no efforts having been made to instruct him," *id.* at 426, the court ruled that he should not be deprived of his property, that he had a good mind, and that he was not a lunatic. The court placed the blame for the low state of the man's knowledge on the fact that he had not received an education:

> With the exception of two, all the witnesses agree in the ability of Leonidas to learn, if proper efforts had been made. Formerly, one who was born deaf and dumb, was considered, in presumption of law, an idiot. 1 Hale P.C., 34. This presumption of law,

if it still exists, like every other presumption, yields to proof to the contrary, and Lord Hardwick decreed an estate to one born deaf and dumb, upon his answering, properly, questions put to him in writing. *Dickenson* v. *Blissott,* 1 Dick., 268. But science and benevolence have together rectified the public mind, as to such persons, and it is no longer, in common understanding, any evidence, that an individual is an idiot, because deprived from his birth of the power of speech and hearing. No one, who has witnessed the wonders worked in modern times, in giving instruction to unfortunate persons in this class, would, after hearing the testimony in this case, doubt Leonidas Christmas might have been instructed, not only in the mechanic arts, but that his mind might have been enlightened to receive the high moral obligations of civil life, and the still more profound truths of our holy religion. *Id.* at 426–427.

The implication is that our society had already failed this man by failing to educate him properly, and the court was not going to make matters worse by depriving him of property he had rightfully inherited.

Kany v. *Becks,* 85 So.2d 843 (Fla. 1956), involved the unusual claim by a remainderman that, because the person who had been given a life estate had lost her mental health, she could not use, possess, or enjoy the property and so the title to the property should be "accelerated" to the remainderman. The court did not agree: "A person sent to the state hospital is not to be considered as having died hence as having been divested of an interest in a life estate." *Id.* at 845.

In the absence of guardianship or of a specific proceeding to invalidate a conveyance or a will, the general rule regarding the property of a handicapped person is that "he alone remains in possession of his property and can dispose of it." *Finch* v. *Goldstein,* 245 N.Y. 300, 157 N.E. 146, 147 (1927). And, in all such cases, "it should never be forgotten that the right to control one's property is a sacred right which should not be taken away without urgent reason." *Smith* v. *Smith,* 254 Ala. 404, 48 So.2d 546, 549 (1950).

Vecchione v. Wohlgemuth

United States District Court for the Eastern District of Pennsylvania, 1974
377 F.Supp. 1361, additional proceedings 426 F.Supp. 1297 (E.D.Pa. 1977), aff'd
558 F.2d 150 (2d Cir. 1977), cert. denied sub nom. Beal v. Wohlgemuth,
434 U.S. 943 (1977)

See pp. 554–562, above.

NOTES

1. Footnote 14 to the court's opinion in *Vecchione,* at 377 F.Supp. 1371, not included above, declared:

> The Commonwealth's presumption that all mental patients are incompetent to manage their own financial affairs becomes irrebuttable in some cases. If a mental patient has assets in excess of $2,500, the Revenue Agent. under Section 424(4) of the Act, 50 P.S. Section 4424(4), must request that the Department of Justice seek the appointment of a guardian for that patient, under the Incompetents' Estates Act of 1955. If, however, the court of appropriate jurisdiction declares such patient to be *sui juris* and refuses to appoint a guardian, the Revenue Agent may continue to summarily seize, control and appropriate such patient's assets under Section 424(6) of the Act. 50 P.S. Section 4424(6). We find that this type of irrebuttable presumption is not only factually

unfounded, but also an unconstitutional deprivation of due process rights. Cf. *Bell* v. *Burson,* 402 U.S. 525, 91 S.Ct. 1586, 29 L.Ed.2d 90 (1971) (presumption of fault for class of uninsured motorists); *Stanley* v. *Illinois,* 405 U.S. 645, 92 S.Ct. 1208, 31 L.Ed.2d 551 (1972) (presumption that unmarried fathers are unfit parents); *Vlandis* v. *Kline,* 412 U.S. 441, 93 S.Ct. 2230, 37 L.Ed.2d 63 (1973) (presumption of nonresidence of class of college students).

For another Pennsylvania federal court suit that applied the irrebuttable presumption to discrimination against a handicapped person, in a different context, see *Gurmankin* v. *Costanzo,* pp. 345–350, above.

2. Do the several legal theories espoused in *Vecchione* provide adequate constitutional bases for protecting the property rights of handicapped persons?

11

VOTING AND HOLDING PUBLIC OFFICE

Robert L. Burgdorf, Jr.

A. THE RIGHT TO VOTE

1. Constitutional Status

In *Harper* v. *Virginia Bd. of Elections*, 383 U.S. 663, 667-668 (1966), the Supreme Court traced some of the judicial history of voting rights:

> Long ago in *Yick Wo* v. *Hopkins,* 118 U.S. 356, 370, the Court referred to "the political franchise of voting" as a "fundamental political right, because preservative of all rights." Recently in *Reynolds* v. *Sims,* 377 U.S. 533, 561-562, we said, "Undoubtedly, the right of suffrage is a fundamental matter in a free and democratic society. Especially since the right to exercise the franchise in a free and unimpaired manner is preservative of other basic civil and political rights, any alleged infringement of the right of citizens to vote must be carefully and meticulously scrutinized." There we were considering charges that voters in one part of the State had greater representation per person in the State Legislature than voters in another part of the State. We concluded:
>
>> A citizen, a qualified voter, is no more nor no less so because he lives in the city or on the farm. This is the clear and strong command of our Constitution's Equal Protection Clause. This is an essential part of the concept of a government of laws and not men. This is at the heart of Lincoln's vision of "government of the people, by the people, [and] for the people." The Equal Protection Clause demands no less than substantially equal state legislative representation for all citizens, of all places as well as of all races. *Id.,* at 568.

Subsequently, the status of this right to vote was summarized in *Dunn* v. *Blumstein,* 405 U.S. 330, 336-337 (1972):

> In decision after decision, this Court has made clear that a citizen has a constitutionally protected right to participate in elections on an equal basis with other citizens in the jurisdiction. See, *e.g., Evans* v. *Cornman,* 398 U.S. 419, 421-422, 426 (1970); *Kramer* v. *Union Free School District,* 395 U.S. 621, 626-628 (1969); *Cipriano* v. *City*

of Houma, 395 U.S. 701, 706 (1969); *Harper* v. *Virginia Board of Elections,* 383 U.S. 663, 667 (1966); *Carrington* v. `Rash,* 380 U.S. 89, 93-94 (1965); *Reynolds* v. *Sims, supra.* This "equal right to vote," *Evans* v. *Cornman, supra,* at 426, is not absolute; the States have the power to impose voter qualifications, and to regulate access to the franchise in other ways. See, *e.g., Carrington* v. *Rash, supra,* at 91; *Oregon* v. *Mitchell,* 400 U.S. 112, 144 (opinion of Douglas, J.), 241 (separate opinion of Brennan, White, and Marshall, JJ.), 294 (opinion of Stewart, J., concurring and dissenting, with whom Burger, C. J., and Blackmun, J., joined). But, as a general matter, "before that right [to vote] can be restricted, the purpose of the restriction and the assertedly overriding interests served by it must meet close constitutional scrutiny." *Evans* v. *Cornman, supra,* at 422; see *Bullock* v. *Carter, ante,* p. 134, at 143.

Tennessee urges that this case is controlled by *Drueding* v. *Devlin,* 380 U.S. 125 (1965). *Drueding* was a decision upholding Maryland's durational residence requirements. The District Court tested those requirements by the equal protection standard applied to ordinary state regulations: whether the exclusions are reasonably related to a permissible state interest. 234 F.Supp. 721, 724-725 (Md. 1964). We summarily affirmed *per curiam* without the benefit of argument. But if it was not clear then, it is certainly clear now that a more exacting test is required for any statute that "place[s] a condition on the exercise of the right to vote." *Bullock* v. *Carter, supra,* at 143. This development in the law culminated in *Kramer* v. *Union Free School District, supra.* There we canvassed in detail the reasons for strict review of statutes distributing the franchise, 395 U.S., at 626-630, noting *inter alia* that such statutes "constitute the foundation of our representative society." We concluded that if a challenged statute grants the right to vote to some citizens and denies the franchise to others, "the Court must determine whether the exclusions are *necessary* to promote a *compelling* state interest." *Id.,* at 627 (emphasis added); *Cipriano* v. *City of Houma, supra,* at 704; *City of Phoenix* v. *Kolodziejski,* 399 U.S. 204, 205, 209 (1970). Cf. *Harper* v. *Virginia Board of Elections, supra,* at 670.

NOTE

In recognizing that the right to equality in participation in voting is a fundamental right, requiring application of the compelling state interest test of equal protection, the Supreme Court in *San Antonio School District* v. *Rodriguez,* 411 U.S. 1, 34-35 (1973), observed in footnotes:

> The constitutional underpinnings of the right to equal treatment in the voting process can no longer be doubted even though, as the Court noted in *Harper* v. *Virginia Bd. of Elections,* 383 U.S. at 665, "the right to vote in state elections is nowhere expressly mentioned" (*id.* at 34, n. 74).
>
> Since the right to vote, *per se,* is not a constitutionally protected right, we assume that appellees' references to that right are simply shorthand references to the protected right, implicit in our constitutional system, to participate in state elections on an equal basis with other qualified voters whenever the State has adopted an elective process for determining who will represent any segment of the State's population (*id.* at 35, n. 78).

How can the Court make these statements in light of the fact that the right to vote is expressly mentioned in the Fourteenth, Fifteenth, Nineteenth, Twenty-Fourth, and Twenty-Sixth Amendments to the United States Constitution? *See also* the Seventeenth Amendment. Scrutinize the language of these amendments to see if the *Rodriguez* Court's characterization is accurate.

2. Disqualification for Mental Incapacity

CLARK v. ROBINSON

Supreme Court of Illinois, 1878
88 Ill. 498

Mr. JUSTICE SHELDON delivered the opinion of the Court:

This was a proceeding commenced by the appellant herein, E. E. Clark, in the county court of Coles county, at the December term, 1876, to contest the election held on the 7th day of November, 1876, in that county, for clerk of the circuit court of the county. The cause was heard by the county court at the July term, 1877, and judgment given against appellant, from which this appeal was taken.

* * *

Appellant objects to the five votes of Josh Edington, John Goodwin, Thomas Halbrook, Pant Elkin and George W. Matthews, counted for appellee, that the persons casting them were *non compotes mentis.*

Upon this subject, Judge COOLEY, in his work on Const. Lim. 599, remarks: "In some States, idiots and lunatics are also expressly excluded; and it has been supposed that these unfortunate classes, by the common political law of England and of this country, were excluded with women, minors and aliens, from exercising the right of suffrage, even though not prohibited therefrom by any express constitutional or statutory provision," citing Cushing's Legislative Assemblies, §§ 24, 27.

There is in this State no express exclusion by constitution or statute. Without further remark upon the legal question, we deem it sufficient to say that we do not regard the testimony as bringing these persons within the description of the above named classes. In regard to Thomas Halbrook, who is most obnoxious to the objection, in the amount of adverse professional testimony, there is the testimony of three witnesses, in whose several employ he had been at different times, that he is a good hand at farm work, and in both saw and grist mills; that he needs no instruction about his work, does the same work and receives the same pay as other hands, knows money and its value, makes his own contracts, does his own trading and takes care of his own money, reads, converses freely, talks and laughs like other men, but owing to some disease he had at some time, his speech is imperfect—yet three medical experts, whose opinions we are urged to accept as conclusive, pronounce him an idiot. They differ, in their ideas of an idiot, from Blackstone. He says: "An idiot, or natural fool, is one that hath had no understanding from his nativity, and therefore is, by law, presumed never likely to attain any." "A man is not an idiot, if he have any glimmering of reason, so that he can tell his parents, his age, or the like common matters." 1 Black.Comm. 302, 303. It is but justice, however, that this testimony should be allowed the benefit of the remark in Taylor on Medical Jurisprudence, 743, "but many medico-legal writers apply the term idiot to one who does manifest capacity to receive instruction, although in a low degree."

The only witness testifying against Pont Elkin is a physician, who says that he does not think Elkin insane, but that he does not think him *compos mentis;* that a man vacillating, easily persuaded to do anything, is not properly *compos mentis.*

The testimony with regard to the others, Edington, Goodwin and Matthews, was to much the same effect as that in respect to Halbrook, as regards mental capacity. The evidence shows that for some years Matthews has, at times, labored under some kind of illusion or hallucination, but not to such an extent as to incapacitate him from the general management of his business. This hallucination does not seem to have at all extended to political matters, and the evidence shows that, on the day of election, he conducted himself with entire propriety. As respects the others, witnesses testify to peculiarities and eccentricities indicative of mental deficiency to some extent, but we cannot think that persons possessing the degree of understanding which these are shown to have had, are, on the account of mental incapacity, to be denied the privilege of the exercise of the elective franchise. We can allow to the medical opinions no controlling force, but such weight only as we deem them entitled to in view of the facts in evidence. We find no error in counting these votes for appellee.

[The remainder of the opinion, in which a number of other ballots were challenged for various reasons, is omitted.]

NOTES

1.   In *Sinks* v. *Reese,* 19 Ohio St. 306 (1869), the Supreme Court of Ohio declared:

> We are furthermore of the opinion that the court below erred in counting for the contestor the vote of one Wortz, whom the testimony clearly shows, we think, to be an idiot; and also in refusing to count the vote of an old gentleman of the name of Davidson, who is not shown by the evidence to be either a lunatic or an idiot, but simply a man whose mind is greatly enfeebled by age. This is not a legal disqualification; and the reverence which is due to "the hoary head" ought to have left his vote uncontested (*id.,* at 320).

The *Sinks* v. *Reese* court does not make it clear whether its reasoning is based upon a specific provision of the Ohio Constitution or upon a common law theory of incapacity to vote.

2.   All but four states have specific provisions expressly excluding "idiots" and "insane" persons from the right to vote (Brakel, S., and Rock, R., *The Mentally Disabled and the Law* 308, 333, Table 9.4 (1971)). Some states go further and exclude all those persons under some form of guardianship. Article 7, § 2, 16-101(5) of the Arizona Constitution, for example, provides that "No person under guardianship, *non compos mentis,* or insane, shall be qualified to vote at any election. . . ." In *Harrison* v. *Laveen,* 67 Ariz. 337, 196 P.2d 456 (1948), the state Supreme Court interpreted this provision to disenfranchise any person not "*sui juris,*" i.e., not capable of caring for himself or herself. Other states have similar provisions; see, e.g., Ala. Const., Art VIII, § 182; Ala. Code, Tit. 17, § 3-3 (1977); Idaho Const., Art. VI, § 3; R.I. Const., Art. IX, § 1; *id.,* amend. XXIV, § 1; S.C. Const., Art. 2, §§ 6, 7; *id.,* Art. 17, § 1; Ga. Code Ann. § 89-101(5) (Supp. 1972); Mo. Ann. Stat. § 475.350 (Vernon 1956); Tenn. Code Ann. § 8-2801(7) (1973); 37 *Harv. L. Rev.* 384 (1924). In regard to the validity of such provisions under the United States Constitution, see arguments raised in *Boyd* v. *Board of Reg. of Voters of Belchertown,* pp. 1052–1055, below.

3. The purpose for a New Jersey constitutional provision excluding certain criminals, "paupers," "idiots," and "insane" persons from voting, N.J. Const., Art. II, Par. 6, 7 (1971), has been identified as "to maintain the purity of our elections by excluding those would-be voters whose status was deemed to be inimical thereto," *In re Marino*, 23 N.J.Misc. 159, 42 A.2d 469, 470 (1945). Are there really any legitimate public interests served by restricting the right to vote on grounds of mental incapacity?

3. Architectural Barriers at Polling Places

SELPH v. COUNCIL OF CITY OF LOS ANGELES

United States Disctrict Court for the Central District of California, 1975

390 F.Supp. 58

DAVID W. WILLIAMS, District Judge.

This is a civil rights class action in which the plaintiffs seek to enjoin election officials of the City of Los Angeles from locating polling places in structures containing what the plaintiffs term architectural barriers. The nominal plaintiffs are Jacqueline Selph, who in 1971 received personal injuries which rendered her a paraplegic and resulted in her permanent confinement to a wheelchair; Easter Seal Society for Crippled Children and Adults of Los Angeles County; California Association of the Physically Handicapped, Inc., and California Paralyzed Veterans Association. The City Council of Los Angeles was eliminated as a defendant as not being a "person" within the meaning of 42 U.S.C. § 1983, but the individual members of the City Council remain as defendants as well as those city officials who are responsible for planning and conducting municipal elections in Los Angeles.

The plaintiffs have identified as a class those residents of the City of Los Angeles who are registered voters and who have physical disabilities or who are so advanced in age that their mobility is limited, and who wished to vote in the past, or who wish to vote in future municipal elections; who allege that they were denied the right to vote in person at their assigned polling place because of the location and/or architectural design of their respective polling places such as would deny them physical access to a voting booth.

At the trial the evidence dealt mainly with wheelchair occupants and there was no evidence that addressed itself to the problem of persons who by reason of age or infirmity encountered difficulty entering polling places which have steps or are situated in hillside areas. This opinion therefore shall attempt only to explore the problems of wheelchair occupants.

On May 29, 1973, Los Angeles held a general municipal election to elect a mayor and other officials. On that day Miss Selph, a qualified elector, traveled unassisted to her polling place and learned for the first time that she could not wheel herself inside because the privately-owned residential structure was constructed two steps above the ground. Election officials offered to physically carry her over the steps but plaintiff declined this offer for the reason that she feared they might drop her, causing further personal injury, and for the additional reason that she felt that such an assisted entry would expose her to undue public attention and humiliation. Plaintiff was then offered the right to cast her ballot in the City Clerk's Office in the City Hall or to send her representative to City Hall to obtain a ballot to be cast by her and returned to the City Clerk's Office, but she declined both these offers.

Defendants contend that the criteria for selecting polling places is rational, and neither intentionally nor unintentionally discriminates against plaintiff or any member of the class; that wheelchair occupants are not denied the right to vote; that if their assigned polling places do not have level access the disabled person may vote by the alternative procedure of casting an absentee ballot or he may personally vote on Election Day by casting a ballot in the Office of the City Clerk.

Plaintiffs presented considerable evidence supporting what they characterized as the "stigma" attached to being handicapped. Architectural barriers in the form of steps make many public and private buildings inaccessible to disabled persons. Obtaining a suitable residence or apartment may involve modifications such as ramping or widening of doorways which many landlords find objectionable. Travel and transportation are very difficult problems for the disabled. Buses are almost always totally inaccessible due to their basic design and construction, and even if the wheelchair occupants can gain access, there is no place to secure the chair. Similar observations can be made about trains and taxicabs. Travel by aircraft is discouraged by most carriers and even if allowed presents problems of entry and exit. Unramped hotels with narrow doors present further problems for the disabled traveler. Attendance at theatres is usually an impossibility because fire laws prohibit blocking of aisleways, and the construction of public school buildings causes handicapped children to have to travel long distances to attend special schools built for the disabled. The handicapped adult who is able to perform work skills finds that few employers are willing to overcome problems of accessibility or modify furniture and equipment in order to accommodate this class of employee.

Plaintiffs do not contend that the physically handicapped are totally denied the franchise because they are unable to enter the polls. Rather they allege that the options available to them are inadequate. The absentee ballot is not considered an acceptable substitute because, (a) it does not allow the chance to obtain last minute information about candidates and issues, and (b) it is unavailable unless requested at least five days prior to the date of election which eliminates its use when the disabled person does not discover the inaccessibility of his polling place until Election Day.

Defendants point out that they must provide some 3800 polling places in order to cover the entire City of Los Angeles, and that while they give high priority to soliciting public buildings, there are not enough of these available. At the present time, approximately 65% of all polling places must be in residences to comply with the requirement that polls must be placed as near as possible to the electorate they serve. Defendants further insist that most residences are built above the ground to protect against termites and fungus and that at least two steps are required to reach the floor level. While approximately 100 polling places are located in residential garages, this has proven to be a great problem because the doors must remain open at all times, inadequate interior lighting hampers the work of the staff, and members of the Election

Board are generally reluctant to spend up to 18 hours on Election Day working where no heat or toilet facilities are available.

Plaintiffs present a strong argument to support their contention that many voters either change their minds as to the manner in which they will vote on candidates and issues in the two or three days preceding Election Day or wait until that period to seriously concentrate on the ballot decisions they must make. Mervin Field, the Director of the California Poll, testified that in his 28 years experience researching voter behavior studies and attitudes, he has found that voters make up their minds late in the campaign season except as to major races. Moreover, in elections involving local races and propositions, most voter decisions are reached in the closing days of the campaign. He and another expert witness with experience in managing candidates' campaigns agreed that good strategy calls for spending the greater portion of the advertising budget in the week preceding Election Day for maximum media benefits. This media saturation produces a crescendo of public interest which stimulates discussion of candidates and issues among the voters and often results in last minute changes of mind. Plaintiffs contend that to give disabled persons no better alternative than to vote by absentee ballot is to deprive them of the advantage of the better informed decision that could be made by casting the vote personally on Election Day.

In this case of first impression, the question is whether the location of polling places in these residential and public structures containing architectural barriers is a denial of the handicapped person's right to vote under the Equal Protection Clause of the Fourteenth Amendment, and if so, which Equal Protection test to apply. *Dunn* v. *Blumstein*, 405 U.S. 330, 335, 92 S.Ct. 995, 31 L.Ed.2d 274 (1972).

A handicapped person has a constitutional right to vote, but he has no right to insist that city officials modify all polling places within the city so as to eliminate architectural barriers. The cost of undertaking such a project would be an unfair expenditure of huge amounts of money in order to benefit a small segment of the total population even assuming the city had the ability or right to modify privately-owned structures. Moreover, plaintiffs' demands would call for the modification of many polling places in precincts in which no disabled persons live.

Plaintiffs assert that the failure on the part of defendants to provide polling places accessible to disabled persons amounts to a denial of the right to vote on Election Day, and that such denial calls for the application of the strict scrutiny or compelling state interest test. However, not every limitation or incidental burden on the exercise of voting rights is subject to a stringent standard of review. *McDonald* v. *Board of Election COM of Chicago*, 394 U.S. 802, 89 S.Ct. 1404, 22 L.Ed.2d 739 (1969); *Bullock* v. *Carter*, 405 U.S. 134, 143, 92 S.Ct. 849, 31 L.Ed.2d 92 (1972). In *McDonald*, the Court found that the Illinois Absentee Balloting Statute did not violate the Equal Protection Clause by failing to provide coverage for pretrial jail inmates while including voters unable to go to the polls because of physical incapacity. The Court stated that "there is nothing in the record to indicate that the Illinois statutory scheme has an impact on appellants' ability to exercise the fundamental right to vote. It is thus not the right to vote that is at stake here, but a claimed right to receive absentee ballots. Despite appellants' claim to the contrary, the absentee statutes, which are designed to make voting more available to some groups who cannot easily get to the polls, do not themselves deny appellants the exercise of the franchise." *McDonald*, 394 U.S. at 807, 89 S.Ct. at 1408.

In finding that there was no denial of the franchise, the Court felt that the strict scrutiny test was not applicable and that the traditional standard of a rational relationship to a legitimate state end was a sufficient test. Applying this standard, the Court stated that "a Legislature traditionally has been allowed to take reform 'one step at a time,' addressing itself to the phase of the problem which seems most acute to the legislative mind . . . and a Legislature need not run the risk of losing an entire remedial scheme simply because it failed, through inadvertence or otherwise to cover every evil that might conceivably have been attacked." *McDonald*, 394 U.S. at 809, 84 S.Ct. at 1409.

In the case at bar the City Council has provided the mechanism of the absentee ballot in an attempt to provide a satisfactory solution to the problems faced by disabled persons in voting. While this solution may not be the ideal as envisioned by plaintiff and her class, it is an attempt at reform and does assure plaintiffs of the right to vote. This approach can be seen as a rational alternative to the legitimate state purpose of minimizing the high cost and substantial administrative effort involved in providing more than 3800 accessible polling places.

The Equal Protection guarantee requires that all persons be treated alike under like circumstances and conditions, both in privileges conferred and in the liabilities imposed. *Hartford Steam Boiler Inspection and Ins. Co.* v. *Harrison*, 301 U.S. 459, 57 S.Ct. 838, 81 L.Ed. 1223 (1937).

> A physically incapacitated voter has no more basis to challenge a voting requirement of personal appearance than a blind voter can complain that the ballot is not printed in braille. Nor is it the province of a Court to weigh the relative ease or difficulty with which the state could accommodate its voting procedures to meet the ends of various handicapped voters. These are policy questions to be resolved by legislators. *Whalen* v. *Heimann*, 373 F.Supp. 353, 357 (D.Conn.1974).

The Equal Protection Clause permits some burdens upon the right to vote or upon the right to vote in a manner equal with other voters. In *Smith* v. *Dunn*, 381 F.Supp. 822 (N.D. Tenn. 1974) the Court held that there was no violation of a blind person's Fourteenth Amendment right to a secret ballot by providing that, absent assistance from certain specified relatives, the blind must receive assistance from one election judge while in the presence of a second election judge of a different political affiliation. *Marston* v. *Lewis*, 410 U.S. 679, 93 S.Ct. 1211, 35 L.Ed.2d 627 (1973) and *Burns* v. *Fortson*, 410 U.S. 686, 93 S.Ct. 1209, 35 L.Ed.2d 633 (1973) upheld the right of a state to deny the vote to a person who takes up residence in a district less than 50 days prior to the election. In *Rosario* v. *Rockefeller*, 410 U.S. 752, 93 S.Ct. 1245, 36 L.Ed.2d 1 (1973) the Court upheld denial of the right to vote for persons who failed to comply with the New York Election Law requiring one to register eight months in advance of the election. These cases indicate that the Fourteenth Amendment permits some burdens upon the right to vote or upon the right to vote in a manner equal with other voters. It forbids conduct which results in a total denial of the right to vote on the basis of a class distinction or requirement, or when classes of voters are treated differently. Whereas here, the right is not totally denied and there are reasonable alternatives provided to the person who finds that his polling place is inaccessible to him, the traditional standard of a rational relationship to a legitimate state objective is proper to follow. *San Antonio Independent School District* v. *Rodriquez,* 411 U.S. 1, 17, 93 S.Ct. 1278, 36 L.Ed.2d 16 (1973).

This Court has found that the Constitution does not compel the defendants to modify all its 3800 polling places as requested by the plaintiffs, but some modifications to accommodate the handicapped would seem highly desirable.

Plaintiffs point out that their condition parallels such previously defined "suspect classifications" as race and sex in that these classifications arise for reasons outside the individual's control and cannot be changed by any effort on his part. It may well be that at some future date, a sufficient showing will be made to include the handicapped as a suspect classification.

Regardless of the outcome of subsequent cases, it is important that governmental agencies be at the forefront in the effort to minimize the difficulties faced by the handicapped. It is the mark of an enlightened society that it is sympathetic and cognizant of the needs and desires of the often overlooked members of society such as the aged and the handicapped.

During the trial, several suggestions were offered short of modifying all 3800 polling places. It was suggested that several centrally located, accessible polling places be established for use by the handicapped. Another suggestion involved changing the law which forbids the removal of voting materials from the polling place to allow the handicapped to vote outside if access is physically barred. Another possible solution might involve the absentee ballot, which instead of being returned by mail, might be handed to the election official at the handicapped person's polling place on the day of the election.

All these suggestions would involve a minimal expenditure of public funds, while insuring that the disabled person has access to all last minute information. These suggestions are not intended to be exhaustive or to be put forward as the only practical solution. They are intended only to show that reasonable alternatives are available at a minimal amount of effort and expenditure. The Los Angeles City Council would be well advised to give early consideration to the problems dealt with in this case. It is, however, a legislative matter at this point, and not a task for the Courts.

Judgment is ordered entered for the defendant.

NOTES

1.   In regard to the problem of architectural and transportation barriers, generally, see Chapter 4, this volume.

2.   Some problems with the availability of absentee ballots, viewed by the *Selph* court as a veritable cure-all, are described in Section 4a, below.

3.   Some states have statutes specifically requiring that accessible polling places be available; see, e.g:, Idaho Code § 34-302; Iowa Code Ann. § 49.21 (West); Kan. Stat. § 25-2710.

4. Special Voting Procedures or Assistance

a. Absentee Ballots As the *Selph* case indicates, one option for dealing with the problems of inaccessible polling places and with the difficulties of persons so incapacitated that they cannot go to the polling place even if it is architecturally accessible is to permit persons unable to vote in person to do so by absentee ballots. That legitimate public policies may be served by permitting physically handicapped persons to vote by absentee ballot was indicated by the Supreme Court in *McDonald* v. *Board of Election*, 394 U.S. 802 (1969). *McDonald* involved an equal protection challenge by jail inmates in Illinois to the practice of permitting absentee ballots to be filed by "physically incapacitated" persons but denying such a right to incarcerated persons. At trial in *McDonald*, the plaintiff inmates failed to show that they could not vote by means other than absentee ballots, such as by guarded transportation to the polls or special polling booths at the jails. For this reason, the Court concluded that strict judicial scrutiny under the equal protection clause did not apply:

> [T]here is nothing in the record to indicate that the Illinois statutory scheme has an impact on appellants' ability to exercise the fundamental right to vote. It is thus not the right to vote that is at stake here but a claimed right to receive absentee ballots. . . . Faced as we are with a constitutional question, we cannot lightly assume, with nothing in the record to support such an assumption, that Illinois has in fact precluded appellants from voting. We are then left with the more traditional standards for evaluating appellants' equal protection claims (*id.* at 807-808).

Consequently, the Court rejected the plaintiffs' equal protection claim, ruling there were rational distinctions between jail detainees and physically handicapped persons that justified their differential treatment: "[I]t seems quite reasonable for Illinois' Legislature to treat differently the physically handicapped, who must, after all, present affidavits from their physicians attesting to an absolute inability to appear personally at the polls in order to qualify for an absentee ballot," *id.* at 809.

Moreover, the Court observed that there were many groups other than incarcerated persons, such as persons serving on juries, parents unable to afford babysitters, persons caring for ill relatives, military personnel, doctors on emergency calls, and individuals called away on business, not covered by the absentee provisions, and "for whom voting may be extremely difficult, if not practically impossible," *id.* at 810, n. 8.

In a footnote, the *McDonald* court discussed how absentee ballot provisions in other states compared with the Illinois statute, which permitted the use of absentee ballots by persons who were absent from the county, physically incapacitated, observing a religious holiday, or serving as poll watchers in other precincts:

> Only three other States make provision for election duties, and 14 others for religious observance. Several States have gone further than Illinois, Wisconsin making provision for jury duty, Wis. Stat. § 6.85 (1967), and Alaska, California, and Oregon making provision for inaccessibility of polls, Alaska Stat. § 15.20.010 (1962), Cal. Elections Code § 14620 (1961), Ore. Rev. Stat. §§ 253.010(1)(a), 253.510 (1965). Maine appears to be the only State to allow the absentee ballot for absence from the polls for any "sufficient" reason, Me. Rev. Stat. Ann., Tit. 21, §§ 1251, 1306 (1964).
>
> On the other hand, all States make provisions for the Armed Forces, either expressly or impliedly. All but five States have exended the ballot to the physically disabled, and

only six require absence from the State, rather than county or precinct, as a condition. (*Id.* at 810-811 n. 9.)

WHALEN v. HEIMANN

United States District Court for the District of Connecticut, 1974
373 F.Supp. 353

NEWMAN, District Judge.

This suit raises interesting questions as to whether in certain circumstances the unavailability of absentee ballots impairs constitutionally protected voting rights. Plaintiffs are qualified electors who were unable, by reason of physical disability or absence from the state for business reasons,[1] to appear at the polls to vote in a referendum held in the Town of Trumbull on May 15, 1973. An unincorporated voluntary association of electors in Trumbull is also a plaintiff. The suit challenges the constitutionality of Conn.Gen.Stat. § 9-369 (Supp. 1973) and the constitutionality of Chapter II, § 9 (d), of the Trumbull Town Charter as applied to local referenda. Plaintiffs claim that Conn.Gen.Stat. § 9-369 has a substantial adverse impact upon the right to vote and is unconstitutional because it does not extend absentee balloting to qualified electors who are precluded by personal circumstances from appearing at the polls to vote in local referenda held on a date other than the date of a general election.

Plaintiffs seek a declaratory judgment, pursuant to 42 U.S.C. § 1983, that Conn.Gen.Stat. § 9-369 violates the First and Fourteenth Amendments of the United States Constitution. Defendants urge dismissal of the complaint for failure to state a claim upon which relief can be granted. Fed.R.Civ.P. 12(b)(6). Since, in addition to an offer of proof, affidavits and exhibits have been filed by the parties, this motion to dismiss will be treated as a motion for summary judgment, Fed.R.Civ.P. 12(b), which can appropriately be considered since the parties do not dispute either the truthfulness or the existence of the material facts alleged in these documents.

* * *

Plaintiffs claim that Conn.Gen.Stat. § 9-369 is unconstitutional because it fails to establish absentee balloting procedures for referenda and because election officials have refused to make alternate methods of voting available to qualified electors in referenda who are unable to appear at the designated polling places for health or business reasons. In such circumstances, plaintiffs assert that the denial of absentee ballots in referenda is tantamount to an absolute denial of the right to vote. Therefore, they contend that Conn.Gen.Stat. § 9-369 has a substantial adverse impact upon the right to vote and is unconstitutional in view of the recent decisions in *Goosby* v. *Osser,*

---

[1]Plaintiff Mary S. Whalen alleges that she was unable to vote in the referendum on May 15, 1973, because she was confined to her home by a serious illness and could not appear at the polls. Physical infirmities prevented plaintiff Marie Velgot, a qualified elector in the Town of Trumbull for approximately nineteen years, from using the voting machines at the designated polling place. Plaintiffs Anton Cornell and Silvio Percivalle indicate that they were both in the State of Mississippi on that day negotiating a contract for their employer. They claim that "postponing or delaying these negotiations . . . might have caused serious and adverse financial consequences" to them and to their company. All allege they would have voted to reject the Town Council's appropriation.

409 U.S. 512, 93 S.Ct. 854, 35 L.Ed.2d 36 (1973); *Bullock* v. *Carter,* 405 U.S. 134, 92 S.Ct. 849, 31 L.Ed.2d 92 (1972); *Dunn* v. *Blumstein,* 405 U.S. 330, 92 S.Ct. 995, 31 L.Ed.2d 274 (1972); *McDonald* v. *Board of Election,* 394 U.S. 802, 89 S.Ct. 1404, 22 L.Ed.2d 739 (1969).

Plaintiffs' claim is somewhat different from the claims made in prior cases dealing with absentee ballot provisions. While the claim is said to rest in part on the equal protection clause, plaintiffs do not contend that Connecticut has unconstitutionally distinguished between those elections where absentee ballots are available and those where they are not, *cf. Fidell* v. *Board of Elections,* 343 F.Supp. 913 (E.D.N.Y. 1972) (absentee ballots available in general elections but not in primaries), nor between groups of voters eligible for absentee ballots and groups that are not, *cf. McDonald* v. *Board of Election, supra* (pre-trial detainees incarcerated in the county of their residence denied absentee ballots); *Prigmore* v. *Renfro,* 356 F.Supp. 427 (N.D.Ala. 1972) (absentee ballots denied to those temporarily absent from their resident county for other than specified reasons). The essence of plaintiffs' claim is that their individual circumstances make it impossible (or, for some, difficult) to vote in person, and that voting regulations that require personal attendance to cast a ballot unconstitutionally impair their right to vote. Their equal protection claim rests on a distinction between those who are able to attend the polls in person and those who cannot. Plaintiffs do not claim the existence of a general right to such a ballot, or other alternative, when physical attendance at the polls is impossible and even difficult.

Though prior cases offer some clues to a resolution of plaintiffs' claim, they are not precisely dispositive. No case appears to have faced the issue of whether, without regard to distinctions between elections or between groups entitled to absentee ballots, a person is denied a constitutional right when he is permitted to vote only by a means which for him is physically impossible. *McDonald* never reached this issue because the record in that case failed to indicate that the state would not make some alternative arrangements to permit the pre-trial detainees to vote. Thus, the issue in *McDonald* was simply whether a group, for whom voting was *not* shown to be an impossibility, could complain because they were denied absentee ballots while others obtained them. Applying the traditional rational relationship test, the Court found the classification valid.

The Supreme Court next approached the issue in *Goosby* v. *Osser,* 409 U.S. 512, 93 S.Ct. 854, 35 L.Ed.2d 36 (1973), in which pre-trial detainees sought absentee ballots under circumstances where they alleged state law did prevent them from voting. The Court found *McDonald* not controlling and reversed the lower courts' failure to convene a three-judge court. The Supreme Court held only that the issue raised was not insubstantial, but intimated no view on the merits.

Plaintiffs here analogize their claim to that found substantial in *Goosby.* There is, however, a clear difference. The impossibility of voting that confronted the *Goosby* plaintiffs was far more directly the result of governmental action than what has occurred here. In *Goosby* the state had arrested and incarcerated the plaintiffs and denied or set the terms of their bail, thus preventing them from attending the polls. Here Connecticut has taken no action that impairs plaintiffs' ability to attend the polls. Their inability seems entirely from their personal circumstances. This difference alters, but does not end the inquiry, for Connecticut has not regulated the franchise with complete neutrality with respect to these plaintiffs. After all, it is state law that requires the ballot to be cast in person, in the circumstances of this case, and this is the requirement these plaintiffs are challenging.

Is there anything in the Constitution that prohibits a state from requiring that voting be done by physical attendance at the polls? Surely this is not an arbitrary or unreasonable requirements such as would violate the due process or equal protection clause. A physically incapacitated voter has no more basis to challenge a voting requirement of personal appearance than a blind voter can complain that the ballot is not printed in braille.[6] Nor is it the province of courts to weigh the relative ease or difficulty with which the state could accommodate its voting procedures to meet the needs of various handicapped voters. These are policy questions to be resolved by legislators.

The earlier cases, though distinguishable as to their holdings, all characterized absentee ballots as a remedial device, the type of reform measure that legislatures may generally extend by degrees. *McDonald* v. *Board of Election, supra,* 394 U.S. at 809, 89 S.Ct. 1404; *Prigmore* v. *Renfro, supra,* 356 F.Supp. at 432; *Fidell* v. *Board of Elections, supra,* 343 F.Supp. at 916. One cannot read the Supreme Court's unexcited catalogue of the groups of Illinois voters denied absentee ballots "for whom voting may be extremely difficult, if not practically impossible" without concluding that the Court did not believe their inability to vote denied them any constitutional right. *McDonald* v. *Board of Election, supra,* 394 U.S. at 810 and n.8, 89 S.Ct. at 1409.

Whatever level of justification is needed to validate a requirement of personal attendance at a referendum held on a day other than the day of a general election has been adequately reached by defendants. They point to all of the practical problems testified to before the Connecticut General Assembly that was asked to consider and rejected extension of absentee ballot provisions to precisely the type of referendum at issue here. One of the principal objectives of municipal referenda is the rapid submission of questions to the electorate, an objective that would certainly be impaired by even the slight delays required to prepare, distribute, and validate absentee ballots.

With the rejection of the constitutional challenge by those physically incapacitated from attending the polls in person, the claim of those plaintiffs for whom such attendance is a personal or financial inconvenience falls *a fortiori.*

* * *

NOTES

1. Is the court's use of an "arbitrary or unreasonable" standard appropriate in the context of a voting rights case?

2. The court asserts that a physically handicapped voter has no more basis to challenge a voting requirement of personal appearance at the polls "than a blind voter can

---

[6]Though the Constitution does not require special arrangements to facilitate voting by the physically handicapped, legislatures of course have ample discretion to enact remedial measures for this purpose. See, e.g., Conn.Gen.Stat. § 9-297.

complain that the ballot is not printed in braille." Are the two situations analogous? What constitutional arguments can be constructed in the context of each?

3. While the *Whalen* court reached the conclusion that absentee ballots do not have to be available for referendum elections, in *Fidell* v. *Board of Elections of City of New York*, 343 F.Supp. 913 (E.D.N.Y. 1972), discussed in *Whalen*, the court concluded that absentee ballots are not constitutionally required in primary elections. Significantly, one of the named plaintiffs in *Fidell* was a person who was "incapacitated and physically unable to travel to a polling place," *id.* at 914. The *Fidell* court ruled:

> Since providing for absentee balloting in primaries would be impractical and would require an inordinate amount of time, effort and expense, New York's failure to provide for such ballots must be held to be reasonably related to valid governmental interests and not to constitute a violation of plaintiffs' constitutional rights (*Id.* at 916).

Does this seem to be an appropriate standard in such a case?

4. In regard to absentee ballots for illness, physical disability, and senility, generally, see, 97 A.L.R.2d 278 § 21.

b. Assistance in Marking Ballot

SMITH v. DUNN

United States District Court for the Middle District of Tennessee, Nashville Division,
1974
381 F.Supp. 822

Before PHILLIPS, Chief Circuit Judge, GRAY, Chief District Judge, and MORTON, District Judge.

MORTON, District Judge:

A provision of the Tennessee Election Code has the effect, in certain situations, of requiring persons under disability of blindness to reveal their vote to two election judges in order to receive assistance in marking their ballots at elections. The question presented in this case is whether this state requirement denies blind persons rights protected by the Fourteenth and Fifteenth Amendments to the United States Constitution.

Plaintiffs, individually and as authorized committee members of the organizations they represent, are qualified voters of the State of Tennessee and are persons under the disability of blindness of varying degrees. Defendants are the Governor of Tennessee, Attorney General of Tennessee, and various election officials of the State. Suit is brought under 42 U.S.C. § 1983 and 28 U.S.C. § 2201, with jurisdiction being conferred by 28 U.S.C. § 1343(3), (4) and 28 U.S.C. § 2201. Since plaintiffs seek to enjoin the operation and enforcement of a state statute, a three-judge court has been convened pursuant to 28 U.S.C. §§ 2281, 2284.

Prior to January 15, 1973, T.C.A. § 2-1226 provided that persons blind or otherwise physically disabled could receive voting assistance as follows:

> *Assistance to physically disabled voters.*—Any voter who declares to the officer holding the election that by reason of blindness or other physical disability he is unable to mark his ballot, and who, in the judgment of the officer, is so disabled, shall be permitted,

upon the request of the voter, to have his ballot marked *by any reputable person of the voter's selection.* [Emphasis supplied.]

This statute was repealed by a comprehensive election law enacted by the 1972 Tennessee legislature, and effective January 15, 1973, T.C.A. § 2-716 prescribes assistance to disabled or illiterate voters in the following manner:

A voter who declares that by reason of blindness or other physical disability or illiteracy he is unable to mark his ballot to cast his vote as he wishes and who, in the judgment of the officer of elections, is so disabled or illiterate, may:
(a) Where voting machines are used,
(1) Use a paper ballot, or
(2) If he cannot mark a paper ballot as he wishes, have his ballot marked on a voting machine by his spouse, father, mother, brother, sister, son or daughter or by one (1) of the judges of his choice in the presence of either a judge of a different political party or, if such judge is not available, an election official of a different political party; or
(b) Where voting machines are not used, have his ballot marked by his spouse, father, mother, brother, sister, son or daughter or by one (1) of the judges of his choice in the presence of either a judge of a different political party or, if such judge is not available, an election official of a different political party.
The officer of elections shall keep a record of each such declaration, including the name of the voter and of the person marking the ballot and, if marked by a judge, the name of the judge or other official in whose presence the ballot was marked. The record shall be certified and kept with the poll books on forms to be provided by the coordinator of elections. [Acts 1972 (Adj.S.), ch. 740, § 1.]

Plaintiffs attack the constitutionality of the requirement that voters under disability of blindness who request assistance must, absent being accompanied to the polls by one of the designated relatives, choose an election judge to mark the voter's ballot in the presence of a second election judge or official. Plaintiffs claim that this procedure, which compels them to divulge their vote to persons not of their own choice, violates their right to vote by secret ballot and denies them equal protection of Tennessee law. In addition to seeking to have T.C.A. § 2-716 declared unconstitutional and its operation and enforcement enjoined, plaintiffs also urge the court to reinstate T.C.A. § 2-1226, thereby permitting assistance by "any reputable person of the voter's selection." While the court may find the former provision preferable, nevertheless, regulation of the election process is, within constitutional boundaries hereinafter explored, a purely legislative function. It might be further added that were we to invalidate the current law, Tennessee would be left without a law requiring voter assistance. Should this occur, the blind as well as persons otherwise physically disabled or illiterate might possibly be deprived of their opportunity to vote in elections close at hand.

A long line of Supreme Court decisions has established that the right of suffrage, in both state and federal elections, is a fundamental right protected by the Constitution and exercisable on an equal basis by all qualified citizens within a jurisdiction. *Dunn* v. *Blumstein,* 405 U.S. 330, 92 S.Ct. 995, 31 L.Ed.2d 274 (1972); *Reynolds* v. *Sims,* 377 U.S. 533, 84 S.Ct. 1362, 12 L.Ed.2d 506 (1964); *United States* v. *Classic,* 313 U.S. 299, 61 S.Ct. 1031, 85 L.Ed. 1368 (1941); *Ex parte Yarbrough,* 110 U.S. 651, 4 S.Ct. 152, 28 L.Ed. 274 (1884). The elective franchise was early described as a "fundamental political right, because preservative of all rights." *Yick*

Wo v. *Hopkins,* 118 U.S. 356, 370, 6 S.Ct. 1064, 1071, 30 L.Ed. 220 (1886). More recently the Court has characterized "[t]he right to vote freely for the candidate of one's choice . . . [as] the essence of a democratic society, and any restrictions on that right strike at the heart of representative government." *Reynolds* v. *Sims, supra,* 377 U.S. at 555, 84 S.Ct. at 1378.

Equally clear, however, is the broad power of states to regulate the elective process, and to impose standards which do not unjustly discriminate. *Carrington* v. *Rash,* 380 U.S. 89, 85 S.Ct. 775, 13 L.Ed.2d 675 (1965); *Lassiter* v. *Northampton County Bd. of El.,* 360 U.S. 45, 79 S.Ct. 985, 3 L.Ed.2d 1072 (1959); *Pope* v. *Williams,* 193 U.S. 621, 24 S.Ct. 573, 48 L.Ed. 817 (1904). Thus, while the right to vote is constitutionally protected, it is nevertheless ". . . within the jurisdiction of the state itself, to be exercised as the state may direct, and upon such terms as to it may seem proper, provided, of course, no discrimination is made between individuals, in violation of the Federal Constitution." *Pope* v. *Williams, supra,* 193 U.S. at 632, 24 S.Ct. at 575.

The statute under attack in this case does not impose state regulations which disfranchise a segment of the citizenry, nor does it erect barriers which make the exercise of suffrage more difficult for a particular group. To the contrary, the challenged statute was designed to afford persons blind, otherwise physically disabled, or illiterate an opportunity to exercise the franchise while attempting to minimize the incidence of fraudulent voting practices on the part of those lending assistance. In striving to insure "purity of the ballot box," however, plaintiffs argue that their right to a secret ballot has been infringed, and their right to participate on a nondiscriminatory basis with other voters has been denied.

Secrecy in voting has been called ". . . one of the fundamental civil liberties upon which a democracy must rely most heavily in order for it to survive." *United States* v. *Executive Committee,* 254 F.Supp. 543, 546 (N.D.Ala. 1966). However, the right to vote in secret is nowhere expressly mentioned in the Federal Constitution nor in the Tennessee Constitution. Article 4, § 4 of the Tennessee Constitution provides only that all elections, except those within the General Assembly, "shall be by ballot." The Tennessee Supreme Court, however, has recognized the right to a secret vote by interpreting "ballot" as "designating a method of conducting elections that will guarantee the secrecy and integrity of the ballot." *Mooney* v. *Phillips,* 173 Tenn. 398, 118 S.W.2d 224, 226 (1938). We, therefore, need not reach the question of whether there exists a Federal right to voting secrecy for, even assuming *arguendo* that no such right exists, it still remains that once the right to secret balloting has been made a part of the voting franchise granted by the State, that right may not be withdrawn in ways inconsistent with the equal protection clause of the Fourteenth Amendment. *Cf. Harper* v. *Virginia State Bd. of Elections,* 383 U.S. 663, 86 S.Ct. 1079, 16 L.Ed.2d 169 (1966).

The effect of the legislation in question is to establish two classifications of citizens with respect to voting secrecy. The first class, composed of qualified voters who are able to accomplish the mechanical process of voting, is afforded absolute secrecy. The second class, composed of those physically unable or mentally unable to mark a ballot without assistance, is subjected to a limited intrusion into their right of voting secrecy in order to insure that the voter's selection is accurately recorded on the ballot.

In deciding the constitutionality of this distinction it is, of course, accepted that under the Fourteenth Amendment States need not treat all classes of persons identically. *Reed* v. *Reed,* 404 U.S. 71, 92 S.Ct. 251, 30 L.Ed.2d 225 (1971); *Carrington* v. *Rash, supra; Manson* v. *Edwards,* 482 F.2d 1076 (6th Cir. 1973). The validity of state classifications under the equal protection clause is assessed with reference to one of two established standards of review. The traditional standard, or "rational basis test," "requires that a state classification be upheld unless there is no rational relationship between the classification imposed by the state and the state's reasonable goals." *Robinson* v. *Board of Regents,* 475 F.2d 707, 710 (6th Cir. 1973). In applying this standard courts recognize that "[l]egislatures are presumed to have acted constitutionally . . . and their statutory classifications will be set aside only if no grounds can be conceived to justify them." *McDonald* v. *Board of Election,* 394 U.S. 802, 809, 89 S.Ct. 1404, 1408, 22 L.Ed.2d 739 (1969).

The second and more recent standard, the compelling state interest test, calls for a stricter standard of review where a classification, such as race, is inherently "suspect," or where a fundamental right of the complaining class is at stake. Under this standard a state must go beyond merely showing that its classification has a rational basis and establish that it is justified by a compelling state need. Among the fundamental interests calling for stricter scrutiny are the right to vote, *Dunn* v. *Blumstein, supra;* the right to interstate travel, *Shapiro* v. *Thompson,* 394 U.S. 618, 89 S.Ct. 1322, 22 L.Ed.2d 600 (1969); and the right to procreate, *Skinner* v. *Oklahoma ex rel. Williamson,* 316 U.S. 535, 541, 62 S.Ct. 1110, 86 L.Ed. 1655 (1942).

In choosing the appropriate standard in the instant case, we conclude that the statute under review must be upheld if it can be justified under the rational basis standard of equal protection review. Certainly we do not find the classification of blind persons for voting purposes to be "suspect," and while the right to vote is clearly fundamental, in the circumstances of this case we view the interest of blind persons to do so secretly to be of lesser magnitude.

Unless a state provides means to enable the blind to accomplish the mechanical steps of voting for themselves, and such an obligation on the part of the state is not asserted here, some form of assistance must be offered less the blind be deprived of voting altogether.[3] Tennessee has an obvious and legitimate concern with the manner in which the blind are assisted in marking their ballots at elections. As previously mentioned, in times past Tennessee permitted the blind, along with other disabled persons, to have their ballots marked by any "reputable person" of their choice. Plaintiffs have no quarrel with that limited invasion of their voting secrecy, and further, do not appear to oppose the challenged statute's option for the blind to have their ballots marked by one of the designated family members (spouse, father, mother,

---

[3]Although the right of blind persons to ballot-marking assistance is not in issue here, under the Voting Rights Act of 1965, states have been held to have a duty of providing assistance to persons incapable of performing the mechanics of casting their vote. See, e.g., *Puerto Rican Organization for Political Action* v. *Kusper,* 350 F.Supp. 606 (N.D.Ill. 1972); *Garza* v. *Smith,* 320 F.Supp. 131 (W.D.Tex. 1970); *United States* v. *State of Louisiana,* 265 F.Supp. 703 (E.D.La. 1966).

brother, sister, son or daughter). Rather, it is the new provision that, absent assistance from one of the specified relatives, the blind must receive assistance from one election judge while in the presence of a second of different political affiliation that is assailed as too great an intrusion into plaintiffs' right to a secret vote.

The State justifies the new legislation as being a reasonable regulation enacted to secure the freedom of elections and the purity of the ballot box. Fears voiced in support of the more stringent control of disabled voter assistance relate to the possibility, particularly ripe in the case of the blind or illiterate, that those rendering assistance will not mark the voter's ballot in the way instructed. The State's goal is to preserve the integrity of the election process, and, along with the Tennessee legislature, we have no doubt that loosely supervised voter assistance can open the door to fraudulent voting practices. Whether the potential for voting fraud is sufficiently great to demand the restrictions challenged here is a legislative, not judicial function. Grounds can certainly be conceived to justify the State's fears in this regard, and we are unable to conclude that the statute in question is not rationally related to the State's goal of election integrity.

We further find that, except as relevant in the context of the foregoing discussion, the Fifteenth Amendment has no application in the case at bar.

For these reasons, we hold that T.C.A. § 2-716 is constitutional and that this case must be dismissed. An appropriate order shall be entered.

PHILLIPS, Chief Circuit Judge, concurs in the opinion.

GRAY, Chief District Judge, concurs in the result only.

NOTES

1. Particular attention should be given to footnote 3 of the court's opinion in *Smith* v. *Dunn*. The court indicates that blind persons are legally entitled to assistance in marking their ballots. What other types of disabilities should entitle a person to such assistance?

2. The *Puerto Rican Organization for Political Action* v. *Kusper* and *United States* v. *State of Louisiana* cases cited in footnote 3 in *Dunn* are not especially helpful in regard to the voting rights of handicapped persons. *Kusper* dealt with the question of a constitutional requirement of Spanish versions of election materials, while the *State of Louisiana* case dealt with the rights of illiterate persons to voting assistance under the Voting Rights Act of 1965.

3. *Garza* v. *Smith*, 320 F.Supp. 131 (W.D.Tex. 1970), vacated on other grounds 401 U.S. 1006 (1971), involved a claim by illiterate persons that they were being denied equal protection and due process because they were not provided the same type of voting assistance as was available to those persons having "some bodily infirmity, such as renders [them] physically unable to write or to see," *id.* at 132. The court declared:

> If the "right to vote" consists only of the right to enter the voting booth without hindrance or discrimination, perform the physical act of voting, and have the vote so recorded counted in the total of like votes cast, we cannot say that the challenged provisions have an impact on the illiterate voter's ability to exercise the right. Except for physically disabled or blind illiterates, as to whom the issue is moot, an illiterate voter is capable of performing each element of the "right to vote," as defined above, without

hindrance from the statutes in question. We decide, however, that the "right to vote" additionally includes the right to be informed as to which mark on the ballot, or lever on the voting machine, will effectuate the voter's political choice.

* * *

Absent any voter assistance provisions whatever, a voter would . . . have to be able to do three things at the polling place in order to transform his predetermined political choice into ·a recorded vote. He would have to be capable of (1) visually perceiving the alternatives listed, (2) mentally identifying the alternative that coincides with his predetermined choice, and (3) performing the physical manipulation necessary to record that choice. A physically able voter with unimpaired vision could do all three. A blind voter could mentally identify his choice and manipulate, but could not visually perceive. A physically incapacitated voter could visually perceive and mentally identify his choice, but could not manipulate. An illiterate voter could visually perceive and manipulate, but could not mentally identify the alternatives. We think it clear, therefore, that the voter assistance provisions of the Texas Election Code have a substantial impact on the illiterate voter's ability to exercise his franchise. He is just as surely disabled as the blind or physically incapacitated voter, and therefore equally in need of assistance, yet the statutes forbid anyone to help him.

We think the foregoing analysis also demonstrates adequately the discriminatory nature of the provisions under attack. Two classifications are established: (1) Voters afflicted with some "bodily infirmity" that prevents them from performing the physical act of voting, and (2) all other voters. Voters in the first classification are entitled to assistance; voters in the second classification are not. Illiterate voters, although they possess an infirmity that prevents them from casting their vote, are lumped with all other voters and denied assistance by the statute. The statute thus treats voters in like circumstances differently in respect to their fundamental rights, and is therefore discriminatory (*id*. at 136-137).

Finding no compelling state interest justifying the discriminatory statutory provisions, the court held that they violated the Equal Protection Clause "insofar as they withhold from illiterate voters the assistance they authorize in respect to blind and crippled voters," *id*. at 139. Moreover, the court indicated that the Texas provisions were also in violation of due process:

> We observe that there is an element of fundamental unfairness in a statutory scheme that purports to assist physiologically blind voters but not mentally blind voters, resulting in the effective disenfranchisement of the latter but not the former (*id*. at 139).

4. In *State* v. *Sweeney,* 154 Ohio St. 223, 94 N.E.2d 785 (1950), the Supreme Court of Ohio held that the Ohio Secretary of State did not have legal authority to issue regulations providing for voting assistance to illiterate voters. The court declared:

> Section 6, Article V of the Constitution, disqualifies idiots and insane persons from voting. All other citizens having proper qualifications may vote. The right of citizens to vote may not be denied or abridged, and, clearly, all qualified citizens have a right to vote even though they may suffer physical infirmities, illiteracy, feebleness of mind, ignorance or lack of information. But the ability to mark and cast a ballot rests upon the individual voter.
>
> * * *
>
> The granting to voters handicapped by "physical infirmities" of aid in marking their ballots, although such privilege is not extended to others, is, in the opinion of this court, not unconstitutional legislation. The history of this legislation indicates that such legislation is desirable to preserve the secrecy of the ballot and not encourage the abuse of the

privilege of the aid to the physically infirm voter. The aid is intended to be mechanical in marking the ballot and not informative in the choice of candidates.

* * *

In keeping with the spirit of the statute, the ballot is the instrument through which the voter may express his choice of candidates, and the expression of choice must be exercised by the voter himself and not by another for him. If, by reason of any physical, educational or mental incapacity, he is unable to make such choice, he suffers an inability to vote but is not deprived of the right to vote (*id.* at 94 N.E.2d 789-790).

This result should be contrasted with *Garza* v. *Smith* in n. 3, above.

5. In *Smith* v. *Jones,* 221 Ky. 546, 299 S.W. 170 (1927), the court outlined the difference in voter assistance to be given handicapped and illiterate persons under a Kentucky statute:

> [N]o voter has a right to have the clerk mark his ballot for him on the table, unless he makes oath that he is blind or so physically disabled as to be unable to mark his ballot. In all other cases where the voter is illiterate, the clerk, in the presence of other officers, shall, with a pencil, mark a dot in the appropriate place to indicate the choice of the voter. The clerk shall then fold the ballot and deliver it to the voter, and the voter must retire to the booth and there mark his ballot with the stencil as he may desire. If a person is so devoid of sight that he cannot see the pencil mark made by the clerk, then he is blind within the meaning of this section. But, before the clerk is authorized to mark his ballot, the voter must swear that this is the fact. The voter is not blind within the meaning of this section if he has left his spectacles at home. He should either get his spectacles or borrow a pair for the occasion (*id.* at 299 S.W. 171).

6. In *Rodriguez* v. *Thompson,* 542 S.W.2d 480 (Civ.App.Tex. 1976), the loser of a primary election challenged the counting of (among many others) the vote of a physically disabled, elderly voter whose ballot had been taken to her in a car outside the courthouse where she had voted during absentee voting. Finding no undue influence had been exercised over her, and, indeed, that no one assisted her in the actual voting, the court ruled that her vote was properly submitted and counted, *id.* at 484-485.

5. Voting by Residents of State Institutions

Boyd v. Board of Reg. of Voters of Belchertown

Supreme Judicial Court of Massachusetts, Suffolk, 1975
334 N.E.2d 629

Before Tauro, C. J., and Reardon, Braucher, Hennessey, Kaplan and Wilkins, JJ.

Hennessey, Justice.

In this case we hold that members of the certified class, including the plaintiffs, if otherwise qualified under the Constitution and laws of this Commonwealth, may not be precluded from registering to vote solely because they reside at a State-operated facility for mentally retarded persons.

The case is before us on a statement of agreed facts. The plaintiffs Virginia Boyd and Ida Montufesco are residents of the Belchertown State School (school), a State-run "public medical institution" established pursuant to G.L. c. 19, § 14A. Both are mentally retarded. G.L. c. 123, § 1. G.L. c. 201, § 1. They have resided at the school on a voluntary basis for, in each case, more than thirty years. Neither plaintiff, according to the statement of agreed facts, has ever been "adjudicated incompetent" or placed under guardianship in accordance with the procedures established by G.L. c. 201. On October 4, 1974, the plaintiffs, in the company of a paraprofessional employed by the Mental Retardation Project of Western Massachusetts Legal Services, went to the Belchertown registry of voters for the purpose of applying for registration to vote in general elections and the presidential primary.

Each plaintiff in turn informed the clerk of the board of registrars of voters of her name, age and residence at the school. The clerk refused to register the plaintiffs on the ground that, as residents of the school, they and their fellow residents were "under guardianship" and thus ineligible for enrollment on the town's voter list. Written requests directed to the full board of registrars (board) seeking reconsideration of the position taken by the clerk culminated in a response informing counsel for the plaintiffs that the board "unanimously voted to abide by the previous decision . . . because of the Board's interpretation that . . . [residents of the school] are under guardianship."

The plaintiffs sought review of the board's decision by filing the instant complaint in the county court. They further sought certification as a class of all those in like circumstances. A single justice certified the class and reserved and reported the case to the full court without decision. The full court ordered an expedited hearing of oral argument in the case.

We conclude that our holding need not resolve the due process or equal protection issues raised by the plaintiffs or the Department of Mental Health in its brief as amicus curiae. The defendants contend that, since provisions of the State Constitution and the General Laws preclude registration of "persons under guardianship," mentally retarded persons residing at the State institutions may not register to vote. On the contrary, as we construe the "under guardianship" language of art. 3 of the Amendments to the Constitution of Massachusetts, as amended, and G.L. c. 51, § 1,[3] that language could not have been intended to foreclose competent adults from exercising the franchise. We cannot read the language loosely because to do so would tend to deprive numerous persons of a basic right of citizenship. See *O'Brien* v. *Election Comm'rs of Boston*, 257 Mass. 332, 338, 153 N.E. 553 (1926); *Swift* v. *Registrars of Voters of Quincy*, 281 Mass. 271, 277, 183 N.E. 730 (1932).

Although our decision is based on other grounds, we deem it instructive to summarize the plaintiffs' constitutional arguments. Both counsel for the plaintiffs and the Department of Mental Health as *amicus curiae* advance three contentions founded on perceived violations of our State and Federal Constitutions: (1) the board's action creates a classification which works a disproportionate injustice on the plaintiffs by depriving them of precious rights in violation of the equal protection clause of the Fourteenth Amendment to the United States Constitution; (2) the board's forced categorization of the plaintiffs and members of their class as under guardianship arbitrarily denies them access to the ballot without resort to established judicial procedures

---

[3]The language of the statute parallels the wording of the constitutional amendment, providing in pertinent part that "every citizen eighteen years of age or older, not being a person under guardianship . . . may have his name entered on the list of voters . . . and may vote . . . in any . . . election. . . ."

for doing so in violation of the due process guarantees of the State and Federal Constitutions; and (3) the board's equation of residency at a facility such as the school with incompetency establishes an irrebuttable presumption in violation of due process of law.

The plaintiffs contend, in pressing the equal protection argument, that voting is a fundamental right and that consequently the deprivation of that right mandates strict judicial scrutiny. The plaintiffs fail to see how the board can demonstrate a compelling interest in denying them the right to register and vote. The due process arguments rely on notions of fundamental fairness, attacking the lack of notice, opportunity to be heard, and alleged capriciousness inherent in the board's decision. We do not pass here on the persuasiveness or soundness of these arguments but turn instead to a discussion of the statutory and State constitutional provisions in dispute to determine whether the board's interpretation of them can stand.

1. The voter qualifications originally enumerated in the State Constitution concentrated on the sex, age, duration of residency and landholdings of those seeking to register to vote. See Mass. Const. pt. 2, c. 1, § 2, art. 2; pt. 2, c. 1, § 3, art. 4; pt. 2, c. 2, § 1, art. 3; pt. 2, c. 2, § 2, art 1 (1780). With the adoption of the third article of amendment in 1821, "persons under guardianship," along with other persons not relevant here, were excluded from the ranks of qualified voters.

This third article of amendment superseded the constitutional provisions for voter qualification and although it has been changed in substantial aspects over the years, has always retained the "under guardianship" disqualification. The same exclusion of those "under guardianship" was incorporated in a statute enacted shortly after the constitutional convention adjourned. St.1822, c. 104, § 1 (now G.L. c. 51, § 1).

Although the intent of the delegates to the Constitutional Convention of 1821 and of the Legislature is nowhere expressed in historical documents, we fail to discover any purpose on their part, in disqualifying persons "under guardianship," to propose a new definition for that term to apply solely to voting. Guardianship was then, and is today, a term of art which implies that prescribed statutory procedures will be strictly adhered to before an individual is subjected to the constraints on his person or property which that status connotes. Traditionally, guardianship was viewed as a court-imposed relationship between, usually, a minor or a person of unsound mind and a person or agency entrusted with the power to "control, preserve, and dispose of the property of their wards as these themselves, acting rationally, would do if *sui juris.*" J. G. Woerner, *A Treatise on the American Law of Guardianship of Minors and Persons of Unsound Mind* 2 (1897) (footnote omitted). The relationship followed legal proceedings in courts having jurisdiction of these matters in which the minor or person of unsound mind was declared incompetent to manage himself or his estate. *Id.* at 432. However, incompetence to manage one's affairs or one's estate, which could lead to the appointment of a guardian, was never equated with commitment or admission to a mental health facility.

An early case contrasted the guardianship relationship with commitment in this way: "[T]he [guardianship] decree fixes the *status* of the ward as an insane person 'incapable of taking care of himself.' The statutes give the care and management of his person and estate to the guardian and take from him the capacity to make contracts or to transfer his property. The necessary effect of the decree is that the ward is in law . . . incapable of taking care of himself. . . . But . . . [a commitment order] is not of this character. It does not pretend to declare the person committed to the hospital to be incapable of transacting business. It does not take from him the care and management of his estate. It affords a justification for the restraint of his person, but is not designed to fix his *status*" (emphasis in the original). *Leggate* v. *Clark*, 111 Mass. 308, 310 (1873). Accord, *Dowdell, petitioner*, 169 Mass. 387, 388, 47 N.E. 1033 (1897) (order of commitment as mentally ill not equivalent to appointment of guardian over person committed).

We conclude that this long recognized distinction between placing a person under guardianship and placing him, or allowing him to place himself, in a mental health facility to seek treatment, is even more profound today than when the *Leggate* case was decided. Under modern statutes a mentally retarded person can be placed under guardianship only after adherence to a rigid scheme which incorporates action from the Probate Court and mental health specialists. See G.L. c. 201, § 6A, inserted by St.1974, c. 845, § 4. By contrast, admission to and residence of mentally retarded persons at facilities such as the school are wholly voluntary. See G.L. c. 123, § 10; Code of Human Services Regs., tit. 4, c. 2, § 211.02. The Legislature has indicated in other statutes its general intent to preserve the basic rights of the mentally retarded notwithstanding their admission or commitment to one of these facilities. G.L. c. 123, § 23. G.L. c. 123, § 25. See Walker, "Mental Health Law Reform in Massachusetts," 53 *B.U.L. Rev.* 986, 989 (1973).

We express no opinion as to the validity under the Federal Constitution of the exclusion as voters of persons "under guardianship" even as we have narrowly construed that term in this opinion. That constitutional question is not presented in this case. We do note, however, that the State Constitution and the laws examined here are conspicuously silent on the standard of mental competence demanded of a prospective voter other than to require that he complete a prepared affidavit and sign it or "make his mark." G.L. c. 51, § 44, as appearing in St.1973, c. 1137, § 9. It is true that in the prepared form the affiant is required to swear that he or she is not a person under guardianship, G.L. c. 51, § 36, but this, as we have said, means nothing more than an affirmance that a court has not declared him incapable of managing his own affairs.

2. It follows from all we have said that the defendants are wrong in their contention that persons are ineligible to vote merely because of their residency at the school. The case is remanded to the county court, where a judgment is to enter declaring that the plaintiffs and the members of the certified class are entitled to be registered to vote if they are otherwise eligible to vote.

SO ORDERED.

NOTES

1.   Evaluate the cogency of the plaintiffs' equal protection and due process claims, which the *Boyd* court did not have to reach. Would a plaintiff who was under guardianship prevail on such claims?

2.   For more extended discussion of the nature and effects of guardianship, see Chapter 5, this volume.

CARROLL v. COBB

Superior Court of New Jersey, Appellate Division, 1976
139 N.J.Super. 439, 345 A.2d 355

Before Judges FRITZ, SEIDMAN and MILMED.
The opinion of the court was delivered by SEIDMAN, J. A. D.

These are consolidated appeals by Carol Cobb, Clerk of the Township of Woodland, and the Burlington County Board of Elections from a final judgment entered in the Law Division directing the board to accept and process voter registration forms completed by five of the persons listed in the class of plaintiffs, and to permit them to vote in the November 1974 election; and to allow the remaining 28 persons in the class to register to vote and, if they satisfactorily completed the voter registration form, to vote in the said election.

The named plaintiffs and the class they represent are (or were at the time of the events leading to this litigation) adults living at the New Lisbon State School for the mentally retarded. On September 30, 1974 five of them, accompanied by Gary S. Zambor, the Director of Education at the school, went to Mrs. Cobb's office to apply for registration as voters. It is not controverted that she was authorized to accept such registration under N.J.S.A. 19:31-7. She told them at first that they could not register without a court order; however, after telephoning the county board of elections she said they would be allowed to do so if they could answer the questions on the form but (according to the testimony of Mr. Zambor, and not denied by Mrs. Cobb), she would not process the registrations until she received "clearance from her solicitor." Whether and to what extent the five had any problems with the questionnaire was in dispute at the hearing below; in any event, the forms were filled in and signed.

On October 3 a "busload of people" from the school who came to register were unable to do so because Mrs. Cobb was not available at the time. Later, when someone telephoned her in their behalf, she stated that she had been instructed by "her solicitor" and the county board of elections not to permit those persons to register without a court order.

The Public Advocate then filed a complaint in lieu of prerogative writs and for declaratory relief alleging that of the plaintiffs in the class, all of whom were evaluated pursuant to N.J.S.A. 30:4–25.3 and 25.4 and N.J.S.A. 30:4–165.5 and found not to be mentally deficient or incapable of managing themselves and their affairs, 15 had been evaluated as "dull normal" and the remainder as "mentally retarded." It was further alleged that Mrs. Cobb informed plaintiffs that she had been instructed not to permit the men to fill out the voter registration forms and to void those that had been previously completed, on the ground that they were "idiots or insane persons and thus precluded from exercising their right of suffrage due to the mere fact of their residence at New Lisbon State School." Plaintiffs sought a judgment, among other things, (1) ordering the township clerk and the county board to register all the members of the class and permit them to vote in the November 1974 election; (2) ordering defendants to "cease and desist" from any conduct or act which would "inhibit, impair or discourage" plaintiffs from exercising their right to vote, and (3) declaring the named plaintiffs "to be representatives of the class of all residents present and future of New

Lisbon State School who otherwise qualify to vote and have not been declared to be incompetent.''

An order was obtained directing defendants to show cause why the relief sought in the complaint should not be granted. On the return day of the order, after hearing testimony and considering the arguments of counsel, the trial judge said:

> From what I have heard here, I am firmly convinced that the reason why those men were not permitted to vote was the hostility that the Municipal Fathers and even the County Board of Election had against people who were confined to such a school. I don't think that they really were concerned about their idiocy or their insanity because it hasn't been satisfactorily proven that these persons were in that category at all.

On the further issue of residence, the trial judge, holding that the *Worden* case (*Worden* v. *Mercer Cty. Bd. of Elections,* 61 N.J. 325, 294 A.2d 233 (1972) gave ''all powers to the people in their right to vote,'' resolved the issue in favor of plaintiffs.

The thrust of the municipal clerk's argument on appeal is essentially two-fold: (1) that plaintiffs were ineligible to vote because they were not residents of Woodland Township, and (2) that they were further disqualified by constitutional and statutory provisions denying the right of suffrage to any idiot or insane person.[5]

The county board of elections contends that (1) county boards have the power and the duty to determine whether residents of state schools for the mentally retarded possess the requisite mental competency to vote, and where a county board determines an applicant to be disqualified the burden of proof rests upon the applicant in a subsequent judicial proceeding to establish his right to vote, and (2) persons living at state schools for the retarded who seek to register to vote are required to furnish information sufficient to show they are ''residents'' of the election district within the meaning of the Constitution (N.J.Const. (1947), Art. II, par. 3; and N.J.S.A. 19:14–1).

We intend to decide only those issues projected by the record before us. There are others, presented and argued in the respective briefs, which are of such breadth and importance that their resolution should be put aside to await an appropriate case. The issues which require our consideration in this case are relatively narrow, though by no means unimportant. We shall address ourselves later to the issue of plaintiffs' residence. The threshold problem pertains to the functions and authority of a municipal clerk, under N.J.S.A. 19:31–7, with respect to applicants for permanent voting registration.

N.J.S.A. 19:31–1 *et seq.* provides for the permanent registration of eligible voters,[6] a prerequisite to voting at any election in any municipality in this State. Eligible voters may apply for registration, within the time prescribed by law, to those authorized to receive such applications, or by completing and mailing a registration form (N.J.S.A. 19:31–6.3).

---

[5] ''No idiot or insane person shall enjoy the right of suffrage.'' N.J.Const. (1947), Art. II, par. 6. ''No person shall have the right of suffrage—
(1) Who is an idiot or is insane. . . .'' N.J.S.A. 19:4-1(1).

[6] Every person possessing the constitutional qualifications of citizenship, age (18 years) and residence in the State and county (30 days next before the election) is entitled to vote, N.J.Const. (1947), Art. II, par. 3, unless disqualified by virtue of Art. II, par. 6 (idiocy or insanity), or for the statutory reasons contained in N.J.S.A. 19:14-1.

Applicants appearing in person are required to furnish under oath the information contained in the permanent registration form and to affix their signatures or marks thereto. (In the case of a mark, further identifying information must be given.) N.J.S.A. 19:31-3.

The argument advanced in behalf of the municipal clerk is that she has certain discretionary powers as a registration official, among which is the right to deny registration to any person unable to answer the questions or provide the information required by N.J.S.A. 19:31-3. She maintains, further, that as a registration official she has discretion to determine what individuals "fall within the disqualifying clause of the State Constitution and of N.J.S.A. 19:4-1." More specifically, with reference to these plaintiffs or other like persons, she insists that "the clerk should have some discretion when an individual of this type is produced to determine that this individual is of such limited capacity as would make him ineligible [*sic*] to exercise the franchise."

A municipal clerk, in our view, has a limited function with respect to voter registration. It is simply to assure that an applicant is able to and does complete the form properly under oath and affix thereto either his signature or mark. We have no doubt that if an applicant for registration is unable for any reason to complete the form or to give affirmative answers to the questions concerning age, citizenship and residence, the application may not be received. The trial judge here found, on sufficient credible evidence present in the record, that the five plaintiffs answered the questions on the form. *State* v. *Johnson*, 42 N.J. 146, 162, 199 A.2d 809 (1964). All that remained to be done by the municipal clerk was to comply with the statutory direction to "transmit daily to the commissioner [of registration] all of the filled out forms [s]he may have in [her] office at the time." N.J.S.A. 19:31-7. She was without power to subject "a class to questioning beyond all other applicants." *Cf. Worden* v. *Mercer Cty. Bd. of Elections, supra,* 61 N.J. at 348, 294 A.2d at 245.

The municipal clerk in this case insists, however, that she is vested with discretion to determine whether to reject an applicant for registration who lacks sufficient mental capacity to vote. We deem the contention untenable. While it is true that persons applying for registration who meet the voter requirements of age, citizenship and residence may still not be entitled to register if they are *otherwise disqualified,* N.J.S.A. 19:31-5, and "idiots" and "insane persons" are disqualified from voting, it should be abundantly evident that a lay person is completely unequipped to determine whether an applicant is either an "idiot" or an "insane person," as those terms are used in the Constitution and the statute, and thus disenfranchised. Indeed, we suspect that those imprecise terms may be troublesome to experts in the fields of psychiatry or psychology.

Moreover, we perceive no merit in the attempt to overcome this hurdle, both below and on this appeal, by asserting that a rebuttable presumption of idiocy or incompetency arises "from the determination that an individual is eligible for residential functional services" at an institution for the mentally retarded. Significantly, this position is at variance with the view expressed below by the deputy attorney general who appeared for the county board of elections, that "we would agree with the plaintiffs to the extent that the mere fact of residency in a State Institution does not entitle the Board of Elections to make a final presumption of idiocy."

In fact, the statute dealing with the admission of mentally ill or retarded persons to state hospitals or schools in effect at the times involved in this case, N.J.S.A. 30:4-23 *et seq.*, specifically provided that

> Subject to the general rules and regulations of the facility and except to the extent that the head of the facility determines that it is necessary for the medical care and treatment of the particular individual to impose restrictions, every patient shall be entitled:
>
> (1) to exercise all civil and religious rights provided for under the Constitutions and the laws of the State of New Jersey and the United States, unless he has been adjudicated incompetent and has not been restored to legal capacity; . . . .
>
> For the purpose of a patient's exercising his civil rights there shall be no presumption of his incompetency or unsoundness of mind merely because of his admission to a mental hospital. . . . .[N.J.S.A. 30:4-24.2.]

As for the county board of elections, we are entirely satisfied that it has the responsibility to assure that only properly qualified persons are registered to vote. See *Edelstein* v. *Ferrell*, 120 N.J.Super. 583, 594, 295 A.2d 390 (Law Div. 1972). We need not, however, probe the outermost reaches of the board's broad assertion of its power and duty to determine whether residents of state schools for the mentally retarded possess the requisite mental competency to vote. Nor shall we assess the correctness of its further contention that where a county board determines an applicant to be disqualified, the burden of proof rests upon the applicant in a subsequent judicial proceeding to establish his right to vote. The record in this case does not disclose that the county board of elections here actually made a determination of plaintiffs' disqualification on account of their alleged mental incompetency, or, if it was made, when, on what basis and in what manner it was done. Moreover, especially since the board argues further that the burden rests upon the applicant "in a subsequent judicial proceeding to establish his right to vote," we have no evidence that any of the plaintiffs were notified, formally or otherwise, of their disqualification and the reason therefor, or given an opportunity to be heard thereon.

We do not intend to write a handbook on the subject for the guidance of county boards of elections. But we should say at least this much, that a mentally retarded person need not be an "idiot," and a mentally ill person need not be "insane." We leave for another day the determination of where to draw the line of demarcation, beyond which disenfranchisement results.[12]

---

[12]The ancient inquisition in the nature of a writ *de lunatico inquirendo* required a showing on the return that the individual was so far bereft of reason as to justify his being deprived of power over both his person and his property. A return that a party was an idiot, or a lunatic, or *non compos mentis*, or of unsound mind, was sufficient, because each of those terms imported such a deprivation of sense as rendered the sufferer unfit for control, as well as for the management of his own affairs. *Lindsley's Case*, 44 N.J.Eq. 564, 566, 15 A. 1 (E. & A.1888). An "idiot" has been defined as "a person who has been without understanding from his nativity, and whom the law, therefore, presumes never likely to attain any." *Black's Law Dictionary* (rev. 4, ed. 1968). Medically, the term means a "person congenitally without understanding or ordinary mental capacity." *Stedman's Medical Dictionary* (3d Lawyers ed. 1972). "Insanity" is a "[n]ow outmoded term, more or less synonymous with severe mental illness or psychosis." *Stedman, op. cit.* The laws of this State pertaining to the commitment and admissions of persons to state institutions, speak of "mental illness" and "mental retardation." The former means "mental disease to such an extent that a person so afflicted requires care and treatment for his own welfare, or the welfare of others, or of the community;" the latter, "a state of significant subnormal intellectual development with reduction of social competence in a minor or

Counsel for plaintiffs and the class they represented chose to present evidence at the hearing below relating to their mental capacity. Dr. Bernard White, Deputy Director of the Division of Mental Retardation, Department of Institutions and Agencies, testified that New Lisbon State School was one of seven State schools for the mentally retarded. He said that anyone with an IQ of 35 or more who could care for himself and get along with others was classified as retarded but not mentally deficient, and that anyone not mentally deficient could not be considered an idiot. He mentioned that 30 residents at the Vineland State School and 4 at the Johnstone Training Center were registered to vote. Many of the residents at the schools, he said further, receive educational training and are expected to return to their families and communities. The assistant superintendent of the New Lisbon State School testified that all of the 33 members of the class of plaintiffs were New Jersey residents, none had court appointed guardians, all were competent to manage their own affairs, and none could be considered an idiot.

The trial judge said that

> The whole concern seems to be that these individuals are not qualified either by Statute or by the Constitution in that their mentality is such that they should be permitted to vote, and I don't think that that has been established satisfactorily to me.

A specific finding of fact on the issue would have been preferable since the above excerpt suggests that the result was reached because defendants had the burden of proving that plaintiffs were disqualified from voting and failed to carry that burden, and we do not feel it incumbent upon us to determine now where the burden of proof lies in a situation such as this. However, implicit in the trial judge's remarks is the conclusion that plaintiffs were not so mentally deficient as to be disenfranchised. Our independent evaluation of the transcript satisfies us that such conclusion finds ample support in credible evidence present in the record. *State* v. *Johnson, supra.*

* * *

We direct our attention now to the issue of residence. The municipal clerk urges that plaintiffs and the class they represent are not residents of the Township of Woodland and are, on that account, ineligible to vote. She argues that (1) for these plaintiffs to be eligible for the services offered by the New Lisbon State School, they must have

---

adult person... [which] shall have existed prior to adolescence and is expected to be of life duration.'' N.J.S.A. 30:4-23. ''Mental deficiency'' is defined as ''that state of mental retardation in which the reduction of social competence is so marked that persistent social dependency requiring guardianship of the person shall have been demonstrated or be anticipated.'' *Id.*

In its final report to the Governor and Legislature, the New Jersey Election Law Revision Commission described Title 19 (the Election Law) as a ''relic of the days of horse carts, which has been modernized up to the days of trolley cars.'' 98 N.J.L.J. 401 (May 8, 1975). It proposed to revise N.J.S.A. 19:4-1 by substituting the language, ''who has been adjudged mentally incompetent,'' for ''one who is an idiot or is insane'' in the ancient statute. It said:

> ... [t]he Commission recognizes that its substituted language may not be a complete solution to this troublesome problem, where a fine constitutional balancing of individual rights with a significantly free exercise of the franchise is necessary. Indeed, the final answer may have to await changing judicial conclusions of constitutional construction. In any event, it was decided that the existing language was so imprecise as to require its removal. [*Id.* at 410.]

been evaluated as in need of functional residential services; (2) since such persons still reside at the school "because they have not been able to adjust when they have been sent out into the community," they are patients "within the meaning of the law"; (3) therefore, "this brings the instant case squarely under the doctrine of *Perri* v. *Kisselbach*, 34 N.J. 84 [167 A.2d 377]," and plaintiffs have no right to vote. The county board of elections does not go that far. It reasons that (1) since everyone is deemed to have a domicile at all times, "it may be that even though plaintiffs, as voluntary residents, were free to leave New Lisbon at any time . . . plaintiffs could have demonstrated that they were domiciliaries of Woodland Township"; (2) or "it may be that the relatively short period of time some or all of the plaintiffs lived at New Lisbon, if such was the case, coupled with their continued strong ties to their former communities and a concomitant absence of interest in local affairs in Woodland Township would have precluded their establishing a domicile there;" (3) the fact is that "plaintiffs failed to meet their evidentiary burden of showing they were Woodland residents, and (4) that being so, "the trial court erred in ordering the defendants to allow them to register and vote there."

It thus appears that the municipal clerk seeks to equate the state school with a hospital, so that plaintiffs, as patients therein, would not be capable of forming a legally effective intention to reside indefinitely at the institution. She relies, as indicated above, on *Perri* v. *Kisselbach*, 34 N.J. 84, 167 A.2d 377 (1961). On the other hand, the county board of elections more realistically recognizes the issue to be one of intent on the part of each plaintiff, applying the tests discussed in *Worden* v. *Mercer Cty. Bd. of Elections, supra*. Plaintiffs' position, which seems more responsive to the clerk's arguments than to those presented by the board, is that the mere fact that plaintiffs are residents of a state school "cannot bar them from voting as residents of Woodland Township."

We are in substantial agreement with the concepts of both plaintiffs and the board, although, as to the latter, we do not necessarily conclude therefrom that the trial judge erred in ordering that plaintiffs be allowed to register and vote.

Whatever vitality *Perri* may still have, in light of *Worden*, it does not support the view that these plaintiffs, and the class they represent, cannot under any circumstances be residents of the municipality in which the school is located. *Perri* involved the validity of absentee ballot votes cast by patients in a county tuberculosis sanatorium located in the election district in question. Under applicable statutes, the hospital managers were empowered "to hold and detain any patient . . . when in their judgment it is for the benefit of said patient or for their community that said patient remain there," and were required to "discharge a [tuberculosis] patient whenever cured or whenever further detention would not benefit the patient or the community." The court noted that to acquire a domicile of choice there must be physical presence in the place where domicile is alleged to have been acquired and an intention capable of execution to make that place the home. It said, further, that in order to hold that one "actually resides" in a certain place, "he is required to maintain such a relationship with the place or premises so selected as will entitle him at his will to occupy that place or premises whenever his necessities or pleasure require without having to ask the permission of someone else." The court concluded that the pertinent statute prevented the patients "from forming a legally effective intention to remain indefinitely at the sanatorium." 34 N.J. at 88–89, 167 A.2d at 379.

Viewing the issue as solely one of residence, and setting apart the factor of mental competency to assert a good faith purpose to vote in the community in which their school is situated, we see no substantial reason for not applying to those residents at the New Lisbon State School who would otherwise be eligible to vote, what the court said in *Worden* v. *Mercer Cty. Bd. of Elections*:

> In the light of all of the foregoing there remains little room for doubt that the individual plaintiffs who were *bona fide* campus residents in Mercer County, and others similarly situated, were improperly discriminated against by the Mercer County election officials and were improperly denied the right to register to vote in the communities where their college residences were located. They were subjected as a class to questioning beyond all other applicants, including applicants who were freely registered though their situations indicated that they were comparably short-term residents of their communities; and their applications for registration were rejected though they established that they actually lived at their campus residences, were interested in and concerned with the communities in which their campus residences were located, and asserted in good faith their purpose of voting there and no place else. All this was in violation of the legal principles approvingly expressed in this opinion and clearly called for broad judicial relief. Indeed, under those principles the relief granted below to most resident students should have been granted to all, including (1) those who plan to return to their previous residences, as well as (2) those who plan to remain permanently in their college communities, (3) those who plan to obtain employment away from their previous residences, and (4) those who are uncertain as to their future plans. [61 N.J. at 348, 294 A.2d at 245]

We conclude, therefore, that residence at the New Lisbon State School does not *per se* render one who meets all other voting requirements ineligible to vote. However, we must recognize that the type of institution here involved is obviously vastly different from a college or university. Accordingly, we emphasize the basic premise that the resident who seeks to vote is not disqualified by reason of any "idiocy" or "insanity" thought to spring from that residency alone, and may have "a sufficient subjective attachment" to choose the school community as his sole place for voting and a "sufficient objective attachment" through his physical residence in the school community.

The only proofs submitted below on the issue of whether plaintiffs were *bona fide* residents of the municipality in question for voting purposes were that all 33 members of the class were voluntary residents at the state school, free to leave as they wished, and, in the case of plaintiff Francis Carroll, that he was 47 years of age and had resided at the school for 26 years. The trial judge did not discuss whether the "subjective-objective attachment" tests of *Worden* had been met. He merely commented that "the *Worden* decision could be made applicable to this situation," and that *Worden* seemed to concentrate "more on where you are living" than on "domicile."

We do not mean to imply that the members of the class in this case may not have been *bona fide* residents of Woodland Township. So long as they were properly registered and were not outside the ambit of *Worden*, or otherwise disqualified, they were entitled to vote. But we do not intend to foreclose the county board of elections, on an individual basis and for specifically stated reasons, from reviewing and challenging the voting qualifications of any member of the class, so long as it is done in the manner provided by law.

We iterate that we limit our determination to the 33 persons listed in the complaint, and we express no opinion with respect to any other resident of the school who may also wish to register and vote in Woodland Township.

The judgment is affirmed. No costs.

NOTES

1.   While *Carroll* v. *Cobb* raises some of the same issues as the *Boyd* case, it goes beyond the latter in its consideration of whether institutional residents can vote in the district in which the institution is located rather than the district in which they resided before being institutionalized. This issue can be controversial, for local residents often fear that an influx of votes from large residential facilities may skew election results. An example of backlash against voting by institutional residents occurred in Oklahoma in the early 1970s. Prior to 1971, there were no express limitations upon voting rights of residents of Oklahoma mental health and mental retardation facilities, except, as in *Carroll* v. *Cobb*, a state constitutional prohibition of voting by "idiots and lunatics," Okla. Const., Art. III, § 1. An author of a law review article observed that residents of at least one state facility were taking advantage of their opportunity to vote; one resident told the superintendent that he had always voted in the past, intended to vote in the future, and wondered that there should be any surprise that he was voting (Ginsberg, L., "Civil Rights of the Mentally Disabled in Oklahoma," 20 *Okla. L. Rev.* 117, 118–119 (1967). Unfortunately, however, within a short time after that publication, the Oklahoma Statutes were amended to read as follows:

> . . . Nor shall any person be a qualified elector of this state who is detained in a penal or correctional institution, who is a patient in an institution for mental retardation, or who has been committed by judicial order to an institution for mental illness (Okla. Const., Art III, § 1).

Is such a provision acceptable under the United States Constitution?

2.   In *Brazie* v. *Chiavaroli*, 53 A.D.2d 1057, 385 N.Y.S.2d 953 (1976), six residents of Monroe Community Hospital won their suit seeking to require the county board of elections to permit them to register and vote. However, the plaintiffs were unsuccessful in their attempts to recover attorney's fees in the action, because the court ruled that the defendants had been acting in good faith in refusing their registration.

B.   THE RIGHT TO HOLD PUBLIC OFFICE

IN RE KILLEEN

Supreme Court of New York, Special Term for Motions, Erie County, 1923
121 Misc. 482, 201 N.Y.S. 209

HARRY L. TAYLOR, J. Pursuant to section 80 *et seq.* of our Insanity Law, upon an appropriate verified petition and the affidavits of two qualified physicians, examiners in lunacy, and following the legal requirement as to notice to the person involved, the County Court of Erie County, in October, 1922, adjudged Henry Hofstetter to be insane, and made an order confining him in the Buffalo State Hospital. The statute provides that if either he, or any of his relatives or friends, be or become dissatisfied with such adjudication, a hearing may be had before a jury, and the action of the committing court followed or reversed. No such step has been taken by or on behalf of Hofstetter, although a year has elapsed, less a few days.

Recently a duly executed petition has been presented to the commissioners of elections of the city of Buffalo to place said Hofstetter in nomination for the office of city councilman. As is made clear by our Court of Appeals in Matter of Lindgren, 232 N.Y. 59, 62, 133 N.E. 353, our commissioners of election act purely ministerially. If a petition presented meets the requirements of the law as to its contents and execution, and as to the residence of the petitioner and a few such details, it is the duty of the commissioners to receive the petition and act upon it. It is neither their duty nor their obligation to make any investigations as to the mentality or other qualifications, or lack thereof, of the petitioner.

This proceeding is now instituted to require the commissioners of election to remove the name of Hofstetter from the said list of candidates, and in substance to enjoin them from submitting his candidacy to the people of the city of Buffalo. Two questions arise: (1) Is Mr. Hofstetter a duly adjudicated insane person? (2) Is such an insane person debarred from holding public office?

It is the rule in many of the states of the Union that an insane person cannot have the right of suffrage. Judge Cooley, in his Constitutional Limitations (7th ed. p. 902) says:

> It has been supposed that these unfortunate classes, by the common political law of England and of this country, were excluded ... from ... suffrage, even though not prohibited therefrom by any express constitutional or statutory provision.

And certainly, if such a person cannot have the right of suffrage, he cannot hold public office. It is true that a proceeding is provided in our statute whereby a person may be adjudicated incompetent and a committee appointed over his person or property, or both. It is equally true that a person adjudged insane, as is Mr. Hofstetter, does not lose his property rights, nor most of his individual rights and liberties. However, the right to hold public office is one involving the rights, the welfare, and perhaps the safety, of the public, and it is the invariable rule that, whenever the right of the individual conflicts with the public safety or welfare, such individual right must yield.

As I have stated, Mr. Hofstetter has been confined in the Buffalo State Hospital for practically a year without any effort, so far as I know, on the part of himself or his relatives, to obtain his release or a modification of the order of the County Court. People confined in the Buffalo State Hospital are not so restrained but that they have every opportunity to see their relatives and to make application whenever they may desire to the courts; and it is inconceivable to me that Mr. Hofstetter, if sane, would have remained incarcerated as he has for so long a time, without making some effort to have himself released and adjudged competent. Therefore I cannot help holding that the action of the County Court at present stands as an adjudication, and will so stand until reversed or modified.

Next, can Mr. Hofstetter hold the office of councilman of the city of Buffalo, even though he stand adjudicated insane? I find nothing in the common law of this state holding directly to the contrary, nor is there anything in our Constitution or statutes prohibiting an insane man from holding public office. However, it is clear to me that to permit an insane person to hold important public office would surely tend to jeopardize the public interests, if not the public safety; in short, to permit such a man to hold such an office, or any public office, seems to me preposterous. The citizens surely have a right to hope that their municipal interests may be looked after by people of rational mentality, and they should have the right to vote accordingly, and the courts should bend every effort to bring about such a result.

It is surely good common sense and until the opposite doctrine is laid down by superior authority it is to be the law of this state that a person who stands adjudicated an insane person cannot hold public office. I am not required to and I do not hereby readjudicate Mr. Hofstetter insane; but for the reasons above stated, and in the interest of public policy and the public welfare, I am constrained to hold that the present status of Mr. Hofstetter is such that his name cannot be submitted to the electorate of the city of Buffalo as a candidate for the office of city councilman. Ordered accordingly.

NOTES

1. Notice that Judge Taylor can find no statutory, constitutional, or common law precedent upon which to base his decision. One commentator described the *Killeen* decision as based upon "vague grounds of public policy, an anomalous and dangerous method of approach," 37 *Harv. L. Rev.* 384, 385 (1924).

2. In *In re Carter*, 72 N.Y.S.2d 666 (Supr.Ct.N.Y., Westchester Cty., 1947), a person who had held several public offices was denied retirement benefits because his "continuous and uninterrupted" public service was interrupted by his insanity during the last six months of the requisite 20-year eligibility period. The court declared:

> On April 21, 1937 petitioner was committed to the Harlem Valley State Hospital, an institution for the insane. On July 6, 1937, his wife was judicially appointed committee of his person and property. Upon the happening of one of the foregoing events, petitioner was declared to be insane or incompetent. [Citations omitted.] By such adjudication of insanity or incompetency each of the offices which he had previously held immediately became vacant. Sec. 30(6), Public Officers Law (*Id.* at 668).

Thus, the following conclusion was reached:

> The Court although sympathetic to petitioner's unfortunate situation and fully recognizing his faithful and distinguished public service, nevertheless, for the foregoing reasons, is required to dismiss this proceeding as against the State Retirement System (*Id.* at 669).

Is any public interest served by this result?

3. *Younger* v. *Jordan*, 269 P.2d 616 (Cal. 1954), involved an attempt to remove from the ballot of a primary election the name of a candidate who had been committed to a mental hospital, which, pursuant to California statutes rendered her disqualified to vote or to hold public office. The Supreme Court of California did not, however, reach the merits of the case, because there had been no personal service upon the woman,

whom the court held to be an indispensable party to the action. Consequently, the candidate's name was left on the ballot.

4.   Many states have statutory or constitutional provisions regarding disqualification from public office by reason of mental disabilities, e.g., Ala. Code Pub. Off. § 36-9-3; Ala. Const. 1901 §§ 127,136; Del. Const., Art. III, § 20(b); Fla. Const., Art IV, § 3(b); Idaho Code § 59-917; N.Y. Pub. Off. Law § 30 (McKinney).

State v. Cocking

Supreme Court of Montana, 1923
213 P. 594

Callaway, C. J. This is a proceeding brought by relator to compel the city of Butte and its mayor, treasurer, and clerk to issue to him two warrants in payment of his salary as police judge. He was elected and qualified as police judge of the city of Butte in 1921, and had been drawing his salary without question prior to the time when these officers refused to pay it further.

To the petition praying for a writ of mandate, the respondents answered, setting forth as a defense that the relator was not, when he was elected, and never has been, eligible to hold the office because at all times he has been blind. Upon the hearing the court gave judgment for relator, commanding respondents to issue the warrants, and awarding him the sum of $250—this for attorney's fees, and costs. Respondents have appealed from the judgment.

These questions are presented: (1) Whether a blind man is eligible to hold the office of police judge, and, if he is, (2) whether an attorney's fee should be allowed as damages, and (3) whether these damages and costs should be assessed against the city as well as against its officers.

1. In this state the qualifications for holding office are prescribed either by constitutional provisions or legislative enactments. And this is so generally in the United States. Throop on Public Officers, § 72. Section 11 of article 9 of Montana's Constitution provides:

> Any person qualified to vote at general elections and for state officers in this state, shall be eligible to any office therein except as otherwise provided in this Constitution, and subject to such additional qualifications as may be prescribed by the Legislative Assembly for city offices and offices hereafter created.

The statutory qualifications for one holding a municipal office are prescribed by section 5007 of the Revised Codes of 1921, which reads as follows:

> No person is eligible to any municipal office, elective or appointive, who is not a citizen of the United States, and who has not resided in the town or city for at least two years immediately preceding his election or appointment and is not a qualified elector thereof.

And section 5010 provides:

> All qualified electors of the state who have resided in the city or town for six months and in the ward for thirty days next preceding the election are entitled to vote at any municipal election.

At the time of his election as police judge, relator was a qualified elector under these sections. The office of police judge is a creation of the statute and not of the Constitution. *State ex rel. Working* v. *Mayor*, 43 Mont. 61, 114 Pac. 777.

The Legislature has not prescribed any qualifications for the incumbent of the office of police judge in addition to the statutes above quoted. This policy is consistent with the general rule.

> Where no limitations are prescribed, the right to hold a public office under our political system is an implied attribute of citizenship and is presumed to be coextensive with that of voting at an election held for the purpose of choosing an incumbent for that office; those, and those only, who are competent to select the officer being deemed competent also to hold the office." Mechem on Public Office and Officers, § 67.

Under the common law it was held that unfitness, if gross and palpable, is a disqualification for holding an office. Throop says:

> It is needless to say that the practical application of the doctrine is generally very difficult and, as far as our examination has extended, there is but one case in the United States where it has been applied. That was in New York, where a person ignorant of any foreign language had been appointed interpreter, and it was held that he was incompetent to hold the office." Throop on Public Officers, § 71.

We have not been cited to an instance where a blind man has been declared ineligible to hold an office. No doubt it would be desirable to have as police judge a person perfect physically and mentally, but no such person is to be found in the body of the electorate. It would be desirable, also, to have as police judge a person well educated, learned in the law, a keen student of human nature, possessed of and alert in all his natural faculties. This court, while passing upon the weight of evidence in a lifeless record, has frequently spoken of the advantage possessed by the trial judge who has observed the demeanor of the witness on the stand. Often in the trial court have we observed a witness attempt by words to conceal the truth which the expression of his eye or the lines of his face disclosed. The blind judge is deprived of this advantage; in this respect certainly he is handicapped. But it is suggested that nature somewhat compensates for the loss of the faculty of sight by amplifying his other faculties, and that a blind man, while not able to see the person who speaks, may learn more from what he hears than another who is possessed of all his faculties but fails to use them. Some men have much keener perceptions than others and are truer in the deductions they draw: some possessing all their faculties have little power of observation. So, after all, the difference is one of degree.

It is contended that as the blind judge may not view the appearance of the complaining witness, which is often so material in that court—and sometimes the defendant is a "sight" for those who can see—the judge's disqualification is apparent. This disqualification is further emphasized, say counsel for respondent, by the fact that the police judge in this case personally cannot keep the docket which the law requires, but must intrust that duty to his clerk, and when the judge is called upon to certify to copies of that docket, necessarily he must certify to the verity of something of which he knows nothing except by hearsay. The judge, however, may cause the docket to be kept by his clerk, having what is written therein read to him by the clerk, and may certify to his docket from what is read to him by another. True, there is room for imposition here, but no more so that if the judge were making his will, and testamentary capacity is not affected by the fact that the testator is blind. See *Welch* v. *Kirby*, 255 Fed. 451, 166 C.C.A. 527, 9 A.L.R. 1409, and note on page 1416, in which appears a reference to the fact that the Supreme Court of Louisiana, in *State* v. *Martin*, 2 La. Ann. 667, sustained the will of Francois Xavier Martin, who had served upon the Supreme Court of Louisiana for 31 years, during the last 8 years of which time he was totally blind.

It may be observed that, as to keeping and certifying his docket, a blind man is in no worse situation than one who can neither read nor write. And let it be noted, too, that under the law at present an elector possessed of all his faculties, but unable to read or write, and ignorant to a gross extent, is nevertheless eligible to hold any office in the gift of the people, unless special qualifications for that office are prescribed by the Constitution or the statutes. In this connection it is interesting to recall the fact that a juror is required to be "in possession of his natural faculties, and of ordinary intelligence and not decrepit," and "possessed of sufficient knowledge of the English language." Section 8890, Rev. Codes 1921.

Notwithstanding the disadvantages under which a blind man must labor in the position of police judge, it cannot be said that this misfortune wholly disqualifies him from holding the office. The people of a municipality have the right to select as their police judge any one who comes within the qualifications prescribed by statute. It is their sovereign right to select their own officers. If this rule permits too much latitude, then the question of eligibility cannot be corrected by the courts but must be by the Legislature, in whom the power is reposed. *People* v. *May*, 3 Mich. 598.

[The remainder of the opinion, wherein the defendants are held liable for damages and court costs, is omitted.]

NOTES

1.   What constitutional and statutory arguments can be asserted in support of the result in *State* v. *Cocking*?

2.   In *Sharps* v. *Jones*, 131 S.E.463 (W.Va. 1926), the Supreme Court of Appeals of West Virginia held that an allegation that an individual was "very hard of hearing" was not a sufficient ground for seeking his removal from a board of education, *id*. at 464. Are there any physical conditions that could legitimately be grounds for removal from public office? See, the Twenty-Fifth Amendment to the United States Constitution. Consider the health problems of Justice Earl Warren on the United States Supreme Court.

12

MISCELLANEOUS OTHER RIGHTS

Robert L. Burgdorf, Jr.

This chapter deals with several areas of legal rights of handicapped persons that have not as yet received the amount of judicial and legislative attention afforded the topics discussed in the previous chapters. The matters examined herein are either issues that have only recently begun to be addressed litigatively and legislatively, or issues that have not yet garnered any significant judicial or legislative attention but that seem ripe for action by legal advocates. In either event, it is foreseeable that these issues will be some of the law reform and test case priorities of the legal rights movement for handicapped people in the near future.

A. LICENSES

ORMOND V. GARRETT

Court of Appeals of North Carolina 1970
8 N.C.App. 662, 175 S.E.2d 371

This is a civil action instituted under the provisions of Article 33 of Chapter 143 of the General Statutes of North Carolina to review an order of the North Carolina Driver License Medical Review Board under G.S. § 20-9(g) (4) denying petitioner's application for a driver's license.

The petitioner in this case has a long history of epilepsy dating back to 1951. In 1964, while operating a motor vehicle, he was involved in a single vehicle accident in Pitt County, North Carolina, which apparently was caused by a "blackout" attributed to an epileptic seizure. The petitioner was granted full driving privileges in 1966 and since that time he has driven approximately 75,000 miles per year without an accident. On 8 August 1969, at the request of the Department of Motor Vehicles, the petitioner underwent an extensive examination by Dr. James J. Smith. During this examination the petitioner voluntarily revealed that while in Tennessee on vacation in June 1969 he had a mild blackout in his motel early one morning while dressing. The petitioner told Dr. Smith that this attack occurred without any warning. Dr. Smith, in his report to the Department of Motor Vehicles, stated that he had prescribed an increase in the medication being taken by the petitioner and that in his opinion the petitioner was capable of driving a motor vehicle. Upon receipt of a copy of the results of this examination a panel of medical consultants reviewed his case and recommended on 5 September 1969 that his driving privileges be disapproved and reviewed again on or after June, 1970. On 17 September 1969 the Department of Motor Vehicles suspended his driving privileges and notified him of their decision by letter. The petitioner requested a hearing before the Driver License Medical Review Board and a hearing was set for 8 October 1969. At the hearing evidence was presented to establish the competency of the petitioner to operate a motor vehicle. After hearing the evidence the Medical Review Board rendered its decision which included the following findings of fact and conclusions of law:

Findings of Fact

1. That petitioner is a 37-year-old white male who lives at Greenville, North Carolina.
2. That petitioner's driving privilege was suspended after evaluation of a medical report dated August 20, 1969, signed by Dr. James J. Smith, and Veterans Administration Hospital records from Durham.
3. That petitioner has suffered from epilepsy since 1951.
4. That petitioner has been involved in eight motor vehicle accidents.
5. That petitioner was involved in a motor vehicle accident on September 2, 1964, and the officer's report reveals that petitioner stated, ''He blacked out and left the street and ran into the front loading ramp of the FCX store.''
6. That petitioner's medical report reveals that he experienced his sixth seizure in September 1968.
7. That petitioner experienced his last seizure in June 1969.
8. That petitioner had no warning period prior to the last two seizures.
9. That petitioner's condition is controlled by dilantin and phenobarbital.

Conclusions

It is the collective opinion of this Board that Mr. William Lee Ormond suffers from epilepsy and that his driving privilege should not be restored until he furnishes medical proof, satisfactory to the Department of Motor Vehicles, that he has been free of seizures for a period of twelve months dating from July 1, 1969, and then only after passing a complete license examination to be given by the Department of Motor Vehicles. Further that after restoration of his driving privilege, he should submit to medical and license examinations at twelve-month intervals thereafter for such period of time as the Department of Motor Vehicles should deem necessary in the interest of highway safety. Further that the results of such medical and license examinations should be furnished to the Department of Motor Vehicles as supporting evidence of his continued competency to operate a motor vehicle.

The Board then proceeded to enter its decision and order implementing the conclusions.

The petitioner was notified of the decision of the Medical Review Board on 21 October 1969 and on 18 November 1969 petition was filed in Wake County Superior Court to review the decision of the Medical Review Board.

The matter came on for hearing in the Superior Court of Wake County, and on 13 January 1970, following a hearing, Judge Bailey entered judgment in pertinent part as follows:

(1) That the Decision and Order of the North Carolina Driver License Medical Review Board, dated October 21, 1969, is not supported by the record, including hearings conducted in that there is a finding and evidence to support such finding that petitioner's physical or medical condition is controlled by dilantin and phenobarbitol [sic] and, that the petitioner has driven several hundred thousand miles for the past several years and has not been charged with a motor vehicle violation since 1961.

(2) That there is no finding nor is there any evidence to support such finding that petitioner is afflicted with or suffering from any uncontrolled medical, physical or mental disability which would prevent him from exercising reasonable and ordinary control over a motor vehicle while operating same on the highways of North Carolina.

(3) That the Decision and Order of the North Carolina Driver License Medical Review Board as well as the decision of the respondent in the above matter are unsupported by competent, material and substantial evidence in view of the entire record as submitted and are arbitrary and capricious.

Now, THEREFORE, IT IS ORDERED, ADJUDGED AND DECREED that the Decision and Order of the Respondent, be and the same is hereby reversed.

From the entry of this judgment the respondent appealed to the Court of Appeals assigning error.

HEDRICK, Judge.

The appellant, Joe W. Garrett, North Carolina Commissioner of Motor Vehicles, assigns as error the decision of Judge Bailey reversing the order of the North Carolina Driver License Medical Review Board denying the petition of William Lee Ormond for a North Carolina motor vehicle operator's license. The appellee contends that the findings, inferences, conclusions and decision of the Medical Review Board of the North Carolina Department of Motor Vehicles denying him an operator's license were not supported by competent, material and substantial evidence in view of the entire record as submitted.

An appeal to the Superior Court of Wake County is provided from the denial of a driver's license under G.S. § 143-306 *et seq.* G.S. § 20-9(g) (4) (f). Under the provisions of G.S. § 143–315, the Superior Court of Wake County is given the power to reverse decisions of administrative agencies if the petitioner's substantial rights have been prejudiced because the administrative findings, inferences, conclusions, or decisions are unsupported by competent, material, and substantial evidence in view of the entire record as submitted. *Waggoner* v. *Board of Alcoholic Control,* 7 N.C.App. 692, 173 S.E.2d 548 (1970).

Prior to 1967, G.S. § 20-9(d) prohibited the licensing of anyone who had been diagnosed as having grand mal epilepsy. In 1967 this section was amended to delete the words "grand mal epilepsy".

The Department of Motor Vehicles in finding that the petitioner was incompetent to operate a motor vehicle, and in suspending his driver's license on 17 September 1969, apparently proceeded under G.S. § 20-9(e) which provides:

> The department shall not issue an operator's or chauffeur's license to any person when in the opinion of the Department such person is afflicted with or suffering from such physical or mental disability or disease as will serve to prevent such person from exercising reasonable and ordinary control over a motor vehicle while operating the same upon the highways, ...

The Medical Review Board in the present case found as a fact that the petitioner has been suffering from epilepsy since 1951. All of the evidence received by the Medical Review Board was to the effect that the petitioner's epilepsy was controlled and that he was capable of operating a motor vehicle. The Board, in finding of fact number 9, found that the petitioner's condition was controlled by taking prescribed medication in the form of dilantin and phenobarbital. However, after finding that his condition was controlled medically, the Board proceeded to deny him driving privileges. The decision and order of the Medical Review Board does not contain any finding that the petitioner is afflicted with or suffering from "such physical or mental disability or disease as will serve to prevent such person from exercising reasonable and ordinary control over a motor vehicle while operating the same upon the highways, ... " In the absence of such a finding, it is our opinion that the Board was without authority to deny the petitioner his driving privileges.

The judgment appealed from is affirmed.

Affirmed.

BRITT, J., concurs.

BROCK, J., dissents.

NOTE

The problem of regulating the issuance of driver's licenses in such a manner as to prevent the operation of motor vehicles by persons who will be a safety hazard, while simultaneously making driver's licenses available to all who can drive safely, has not always been dealt with in the most equitable manner. The tendency has often been to be overly exclusive in regard to physical and mental handicaps in developing criteria for eligibility for a license. Epilepsy has been one especially problematic category, and state licensing laws have not always taken into account the great variety of types of seizures and the fact that many epileptic conditions can be controlled by medication. For contrast with the *Ormond* decision, see *Commonwealth* v. *Irwin*, 345 Pa. 504, 29 A.2d 68 (1942). See also *People* v. *Spragney*, 24 Cal.App.3d 333, 100 Cal.Rptr. 902 (1972); *People* v. *O'Neil*, 44 Cal.Rptr. 320, 401 P.2d 928, 931 (1965) (*dicta*); generally, see Fabing, H., and Barrow, R., "Restricted Driver's Licenses to Controlled Epileptics: A Realistic Approach to a Problem of Highway Safety," 2 *U.C.L.A. L. Rev.* 500 (1955); Perr, I., "Epilepsy and the Law," 7 *Clev.-Mar.L.Rev.* 280, 292-296 (1958). See *Rodriguez* v. *Menzagol*, No. 78-194 P (D.N.M. April 11, 1978) reported at 12 *Clearinghouse Rev.* 52 (1978), for a consent judgment in a class action lawsuit challenging a state licensing agency practice of suspending, without prior hearing, the licenses of drivers who have had an epileptic seizure.

FEDERAL MOTOR CARRIER SAFETY REGULATIONS
49 C.F.R. 391.41

(a)   A person shall not drive a motor vehicle unless he is physically qualified to do so and, except as provided in § 391.67, has on his person the original, or a photographic copy, of a medical examiner's certificate that he is physically qualified to drive a motor vehicle.

(b)   A person is physically qualified to drive a motor vehicle if he—

(1)   Has no loss of a foot, a leg, a hand, or an arm, or has been granted a waiver pursuant to § 391.49;

(2)   Has no impairment of the use of a foot, a leg, a hand, fingers, or an arm, and no other structural defect or limitation, which is likely to interfere with his ability to control and safely drive a motor vehicle, or has been granted a waiver pursuant to § 391.49 upon a determination that the impairment will not interfere with his ability to control and safely drive a motor vehicle.

(3)   Has no established medical history or clinical diagnosis of diabetes mellitus currently requiring insulin for control;

(4)   Has no current clinical diagnosis of myocardial infarction, angina pectoris, coronary insufficiency, thrombosis, or any other cardiovascular disease of a variety known to be accompanied by syncope, dyspnea, collapse, or congestive cardiac failure;

(5)   Has no established medical history or clinical diagnosis of a respiratory dysfunction likely to interfere with his ability to control and drive a motor vehicle safely;

(6)   Has no current clinical diagnosis of high blood pressure likely to interfere with his ability to operate a motor vehicle safely;

(7)   Has no established medical history or clinical diagnosis of rheumatic, arthritic, orthopedic, muscular, neuromuscular, or vascular disease which interferes with his ability to control and operate a motor vehicle safely;

(8)   Has no established medical history or clinical diagnosis of epilepsy or any other condition which is likely to cause loss of consciousness or any loss of ability to control a motor vehicle;

(9)   Has no mental, nervous, organic, or functional disease or psychiatric disorder likely to interfere with his ability to drive a motor vehicle safely;

(10)   Has distant visual acuity of at least 20/40 (Snellen) in each eye without corrective lenses or visual acuity separately corrected to 20/40 (Snellen) or better with corrective lenses, distant binocular acuity of at least 20/40 (Snellen) in both eyes with or without corrective lenses, field of vision of at least 70° in the horizontal Meridian in each eye, and the ability to recognize the colors of traffic signals and devices showing standard red, green, and amber;

(11)   First perceives a forced whispered voice in the better ear at not less than 5 feet with or without the use of a hearing aid or, if tested by use of an audiometric device, does not have an average hearing loss in the better ear greater than 40 decibels at 500 Hz, 1,000 Hz, and 2,000 Hz with or without a hearing aid when the audiometric device is calibrated to American National Standard (formerly ASA Standard) Z24.5—1951.

(12)   Does not use an amphetamine, narcotic, or any habit-forming drug; and

(13)   Has no current clinical diagnosis of alcoholism.

NOTES

1.   These regulations promulgated by the Federal Highway Administration prescribe the qualifications of drivers to operate commercial motor vehicles in interstate commerce. Evaluate the practical and legal sufficiency of each of the 13 subparagraphs of part (b), keeping in mind that only the first two have provision for a waiver.

2. In 1976, a request was made to the Federal Highway Administration to amend Section 391.41(b)(11) to permit deaf drivers to operate motor vehicles in interstate commerce. In an opinion dated Dec. 9, 1976, Robert A. Kaye, Director of the Bureau of Motor Carrier Safety, denied this petition and reaffirmed that deaf drivers would not be permitted to operate in interstate commercial service. 41 Fed. Reg. 55898 (Dec. 23, 1976).

This result is consistent with the fact that, even though evidence tends to indicate that deaf drivers have better safety records than persons with normal hearing, the driving privileges of deaf persons have many times been restricted. See, generally, Myers, L., *The Law and the Deaf* 161-170 (1967).

3. While motor vehicle operator's licenses have been the example chosen herein, other activities requiring licenses can give rise to the same types of problems. See, for example, Miss. Code Ann. Section 49-7-19 (1972) (hunting and fishing license); Ind. Code Section 8-9-4-1 (1913) (operation of trains and locomotives). Licensing agencies have all too often been insensitive to the unnecessary deprivations of opportunities to handicapped persons that result from overly restrictive eligibility criteria.

B. INSURANCE

1. Life Insurance

SOUTHARD v. OCCIDENTAL LIFE INSURANCE CO. OF CALIFORNIA

Supreme Court of Wisconsin, 1966
31 Wis.2d 351, 142 N.W.2d 844

This is an appeal by the Occidental Life Insurance Company of California, defendant, from an order denying its motion for summary judgment to dismiss the complaint. The defendant by mail solicitation in the course of its business on October 25, 1963, offered Robert R. Southard, an insurance agent and resident of Wisconsin, an opportunity to become a member of a group-life-insurance plan covering insurance brokers and agents. Robert R. Southard filled out the application form and named the plaintiff James H. Southard the beneficiary. Upon this application the defendant insured Southard for $15,000 under the group-life insurance policy. Some fourteen months later Southard died at the age of 30 on January 3, 1965, and this suit was commenced to recover the principal amount of the policy which the defendant refused to pay. In its answer, the defendant claims the policy is void under sec. 209.06, Stats., because Robert R. Southard made a material misrepresentation in the application which increased the risk and contributed to the loss. Upon this answer and a supporting affidavit the defendant moved for summary judgment.

HALLOWS, Justice.

* * *

In its affidavit in support of its motion, the defendant sets forth the application and states it relied thereon in insuring Southard. The critical question in the application concerning the applicant's health asked, "During the last two years have you had heart disease, diabetes, lung disease, cancer or any other serious illness, or received treatment or medication for blood pressure?'' To this inquiry, Southard answered ''no.''

From the affidavits it is clear and without dispute that Robert R. Southard severed his spine in a swimming accident in June 1954, that as a result he had a nonfunctioning nervous system and was partly paralyzed, that the paralysis affected both his arms and legs, making him a quadriplegic, that he had no control of his normal bladder functions and it was necessary to have a cystotomy tube inserted in his bladder, that this tube caused a chronic cystitis condition which necessitated continual medical treatment for leakage and bleeding around the tube and that from the time of the 1954-swimming accident until his death the applicant was confined to a wheelchair.

The defendant's affidavit claims this condition was a serious illness and thus the answer in the application was a misrepresentation; and on the contrary the plaintiff's affidavit claims such condition was not a serious illness, was not considered so by the applicant, and in spite of his handicap the applicant completed his college education at the University of Wisconsin and the Eau Claire State Teacher's College, established a successful insurance agency in Eau Claire, was president of the Sheltered for Handicapped, Inc., and was chosen Wisconsin's handicapped person for 1960. The cause of death given in the death certificate was ''Pul.[monary] Atelectasis & Pneumonia'' with ''Quadriplegia'' and ''Septicemia'' as significant conditions contributing to death but not related to the terminal disease.

We hold the applicant did not have a serious illness at the time he made the application for group-life insurance coverage. What constitutes a serious illness must be construed in the light of the particular use of the word and in its context. Here, the defendant solicited the application for life insurance by mail and required no physical or medical examination. Only two questions directly relating to insurability were asked. The first inquired whether the applicant had been confined to a hospital or sanitorium within the last two years, to which the applicant answered ''no.'' The second question, claimed to be falsely answered, asked whether ''During the last two years'' the applicant ''had heart disease, diabetes, lung disease, cancer or any other serious illness, or received treatment or medication for blood pressure?'' Under the familiar canon of construction of *ejusdem generis*, ''other serious illness'' would mean an illness of the same general seriousness and classification as cancer, or diabetes, or heart and lung disease. See 17A C.J.S. Contracts § 313 p. 173. These diseases all relate to and seriously affect the general soundness and health of a person and require continuous medical treatment. Quadriplegia is not such an illness, if it is an illness at all. This inquiry in the application relating to insurability is limited and does not cover all illnesses but only serious illnesses of a limited classification. This and the question relating to confinement in a hospital or sanitorium and treatment for blood pressure were all the insurance company was interested in or considered necessary for the type of group-life insurance offered. It does not ask whether the applicant was free from any physical impairment, whether he considered himself in good health, or except for blood pressure whether he had received any medical treatment or advice. Obviously the risks assumed under this group plan are greater than those assumed under individual policies requiring more detailed information and a medical examination and presumably the premiums were related and adjusted to the risks thus assumed.

The inquiry in the application called for a layman's answer, not a medical opinion. An insurer soliciting by mail applications for life insurance from laymen cannot expect medical opinions as answers to inquiries. Conversely, the applicant must make a reasonable use of his faculties in endeavoring to understand and answer the questions asked of him and his answers must be made fairly and in good faith. Nor can an insurer inquire about a few illnesses and expect a complete medical history in response. The questions must "fetch the answer."

It is no doubt true the applicant's condition was material to the risk in the sense it would have influenced an insurance company in its rejection of the application. However, such relationship does not necessarily make the applicant's condition an illness. There can be healthy handicapped people.

True, quadriplegia is a serious physical impairment but so is the loss of a limb, or blindness, or total deafness. But such handicaps are not commonly thought of as illnesses even though they may possibly tend to shorten the span of life by increasing the risk of accidental death. A tube in a bladder to aid its functioning would seem to be a condition or an aid to a physical impairment, not an illness. If the existence of the tube constitutes an illness because it aids the functioning of the human body, then other aids like glasses and hearing aids must be considered *indicia* of an illness, but obviously this is not true.

In *Schneider* v. *Wisconsin Life Ins. Co.* (1956), 273 Wis.2d 105, 76 N.W.2d 586, this court approved the definition of the term "illness" as, "Within the meaning of a statement by an applicant in such respect, the term 'illness' means a disease or ailment which is of such a character as to affect the general soundness and healthfulness of the system seriously, and not a mere temporary indisposition which does not tend to undermine and weaken the constitution." This definition was taken from 29 Am.Jur., Insurance, pages 1005-6, sec. 745. See also Anno., 153 A.L.R. 709, which states "serious illness" or "disease" means only such illnesses or diseases as are likely to be attained by a permanent or material impairment of the health or constitution and do not include such as are merely temporary in duration and the effect of which has entirely passed away. As lay persons use the term "illness," Southard may have been seriously handicapped but he had no serious illness.

Even though the applicant's handicap was not a serious illness, the question arises whether he was under a duty to disclose it because as an insurance man he must have known it was material to the risk. The trial court was of the opinion Southard had a duty to disclose his condition because contracts of insurance are traditionally *uberrimae fidei,* relying on *Stipcich* v. *Insurance Co.* (1928), 277 U.S. 311, 316, 317, 48 S.Ct. 512, 72 L.Ed. 895. We do not agree and also point out no defense was made on the question of concealment. It was pointed out in the *Stipcich* Case, which was cited in *Fjeseth* v. *New York Life Ins. Co.* (1963), 20 Wis.2d 295, 122 N.W.2d 49, that the modern practice of requiring the applicant for life insurance to answer questions prepared by the insurer has relaxed the rule of the duty to disclose known material facts because the information not asked for in such an application is presumed to be unimportant to the insurance company.

This is not a case like *Fjeseth* where the applicant was under a duty to disclose information called for in the insurance application which was subsequently acquired and which made misleading an answer in the application upon which the applicant knew the insurance company was about to rely. Here, no previous answer was made which subsequently but before the issuance of the policy turned out to be false.

A person in a business deal must be under a duty to disclose a material fact before he can be charged with a failure to disclose. The Restatement of the Law of Torts, p. 117, sec. 551(1), states the rule as follows: "One who fails to disclose to another a thing which he knows may justifiably induce the other to act or refrain from acting in a business transaction is subject to the same liability to the other as though he had represented the nonexistence of the matter which he has failed to disclose, if, but only if, he is under a duty to the other to exercise reasonable care to disclose the matter in question." In the specialized field of insurance where a detailed application is used by an insurance company to obtain the information it considers necessary for the writing of the risk, it generally has been considered the applicant's duty has been fulfilled upon making full answers without evasion, suppression, misrepresentation or concealment of the facts within the reasonable scope of the inquiry. 12 Appleman, Insurance Law and Practice, Duty to Disclose, p. 392, sec. 7292. Under this view the applicant is under no duty to volunteer information beyond the scope of the questions asked him. In 9 Couch on Insurance (2d), p. 376, sec. 38:58, it is stated: "The insured is not obligated to volunteer statements of every circumstance which anybody may subsequently deem important as affecting the risk upon his life, for it is requisite only that he answer all questions truly, make no untrue statements, and submit himself to a full examination."

* * *

NOTES

1.   The *Southard* decision typifies the holding of most modern courts that, in order to disclaim liability under an insurance policy, the insurer must prove that there was an intentional misrepresentation by the insured of some material fact that was a contributing factor in the occurrence out of which a claim arises. Thus, to avoid making payments under a life insurance policy, the insurance company must show that an insured person intentionally misrepresented his or her condition, that the misrepresentation was material to the company's issuance of the policy, and that the misrepresented risk did in fact contribute to the insured's death.

2.   It is generally accepted that paraplegia and quadriplegia result in a shortening of life expectancy. Should insurance companies be required to prove such generalizations by appropriate actuarial data before they are permitted to refuse to insure or to charge higher premiums to persons with certain handicapping conditions?

BARGER v. PRUDENTIAL INSURANCE COMPANY OF AMERICA

United States District Court for the Southern District of Illinois, Northern Division,
1969
295 F.Supp. 866

OPINION AND ORDER
ROBERT D. MORGAN, District Judge.
This cause comes before the Court on defendant's motion for summary judg-

ment avoiding a life insurance policy issued to Bruce L. Barger, plaintiff's deceased son, because the insured is claimed to have made material misrepresentations in the application for the policy. This cause was originally filed in the Circuit Court for the Tenth Judicial Circuit of Illinois and was removed by defendant to this court on the ground of diversity of citizenship.

The basic facts out of which this suit arises are not in dispute. On February 15, 1966, the decedent applied for a $10,000 non-medical life insurance policy (physical examination not required) with a supplementary "Accidental Death Benefit" of like amount. The policy was issued on March 15, 1966, with the plaintiff-father as beneficiary. A photocopy of the policy, including the application, is attached to the complaint. Decedent died on April 10, 1967 from causes not fully before the Court and not considered material to the issue here.

"Part 2" of the insurance application asked various questions pertaining to the medical history of the insured. Question 11 asked whether the applicant had "within the past 5 years, ever consulted or been attended by, or been examined by, or had a checkup by any physician or other practitioner?" The answer was "Yes." Question 12 asked if the applicant had "any known indication of any physical disorder, deformity, defect or abnormality not disclosed in the answers to Questions 7 through 11?" The answer was "No." Question 17 asked, "What are the full particulars with respect to each and every part of Questions 6 through 16 to which the answer is 'Yes'?" The application shows the following answer: "11. Bruce: Routine exams required by school. Dr. W. Newcomer, Bartonville, Ill. Last examined Jan. 1966. In good health."

The affidavit of plaintiff establishes that he advised his son to see the family physician, Dr. Newcomer, prior to January 3, 1966, when the son complained of a charley horse-like pain in his left leg, but that this was his son's only complaint at any time other than childhood diseases.

The deposition of Dr. Wilbert S. Newcomer, who examined the decedent on January 3, 1966, just 43 days before the insurance application involved here, shows that he entered on his record a medical history given to him by the decedent as follows:

> Having trouble with jerking of lateral side of left foot and migrates upwards and involves the whole left side of body and into left side of neck. Has happened twice in last week but has had trouble since the eighth grade (duration four years).

It further appears from Dr. Newcomer's deposition that he had seen decedent 7 times previously in 1961 through 1964 for examinations, that none of these examinations disclosed the symptoms related on January 3, 1966; but that he made an examination and a diagnosis on that day "from the history and the exam" that "he was probably subject to petit mal seizures," which the doctor said were an epileptic type of seizure. He prescribed a drug to control the condition, and there is no showing that he told decedent or his parents of the diagnosis or suggested any further course of treatment.

Defendant contends that the failure of the insured to disclose in the answer of Question 17 the symptoms of the complaint which he gave to Dr. Newcomer only 43 days earlier (on an occasion which was not an examination "required by school"), plus the answer to Question 12, which was not true in view of this failure, were material misrepresentations which materially affected the acceptance of the risk by defendant. It further contends that such material misrepresentations render the policy void as a matter of law and hence there is no issue of material fact for trial.

Plaintiff contends that the symptoms disclosed to Dr. Newcomer were not considered serious by his son, that he was not aware of any diagnosis of epilepsy, that there was no intention to deceive, and therefore that the materiality of any application defects is a question of fact for the jury to determine.

The law of Illinois is applicable here. Section 766 of Chapter 73 of the Illinois Revised Statutes, provides in relevant part:

> ... No such misrepresentation or false warranty shall defeat or avoid the policy unless it shall have been made with actual intent to deceive or materially affects either the acceptance of the risk or the hazard assumed by the company....

The Supreme Court of Illinois has made it very clear that any single material misrepresentation which materially affects the appraisal of the risk by the company is grounds for cancelling the policy. *Campbell* v. *Prudential Life Insurance Co.,* 15 Ill.2d 308, 155 N.E.2d 9 (1958). As this court said, on authority there cited, in *Life Insurance Company of North America* v. *Roberson,* 276 F.Supp. 639 (1967) at p. 641:

> The materiality of the misrepresentation would ordinarily, of course, be a question of fact for the jury to decide unless the court finds, as it does here, that "all persons would agree that (it is) material."

This court considers that the materiality of the misrepresentation is equally clear here. The cases differ only in the diseases involved and it is presumably apparent that cancer is more serious than petit mal epilepsy. However, in neither case is it shown that the applicant knew of the diagnosis, so that can have no relevance. In *Roberson,* the failure was to disclose an extended course of treatment. Here, the failure was to disclose a known set of symptoms.

This court cannot conceive impartial questioning of the fact that, had the defendant been informed of the symptoms of four years' standing which were disclosed by the decedent to Dr. Newcomer, it would at least have had a medical examination and evaluation before issuing a policy. The affidavit of its Associate Medical Director asserts that disclosure of these symptoms would have required rejection of the policy under its underwriting rules. Thus this omission, whether careless or intentional, must be said to have materially affected the acceptance of the risk by the defendant. The insured's answer to Question 12 and the answers in Question 17, "Routine exams required by school," and "In good health," can only be described as false and misleading, adding to the material misrepresentations which obviously must have affected the acceptance of the mortality risk by the defendant. This application clearly deprived the insurer of the opportunity to discover and evaluate the true physical condition of the applicant which it needed to evaluate the insurance hazard it was being asked to undertake. See *Rubin* v. *Metropolitan Life Ins. Co.,* 308 Ill.App. 607, 32 N.E.2d 359 (1941).

The Court has considered the affidavits of Lila Vickerman and Thomas L. Hay filed by plaintiff. The first states that life insurance was issued on the life of her son by another company after full disclosure of a long history of "grande mal" epileptic seizures controlled by medication. The second says that the company which issued the Vickerman policy may write epileptics after evaluation of some six different considerations involving the affliction. It is noted that these affidavits either reflect or show the need for a full disclosure of the physical condition of the applicant, and evaluation thereof, before the policy is issued. The avoidance of that opportunity for the insurer is considered the fatal defect here.

Plaintiff relies on *Marshall* v. *Metropolitan Life Ins. Co.*, 405 Ill. 90, 90 N.E.2d 194 (1950). In that case the defendant insurance company sought to avoid a life insurance policy upon discovery that the insured had failed to mention consultation and treatment for a one-day attack of nausea and vomiting after heavy eating and drinking, which the doctor had told him might be a gallbladder attack. The Court rejected that argument because the incident was very short and easily forgotten and there were no clear symptoms of a gallbladder condition. It is the failure to disclose the known unusual symptoms of long standing which distinguish that case and which is considered decisive here.

The case of *LaPenta* v. *Mutual Trust Life Insurance Co.*, 4 Ill.App.2d 60, 123 N.E.2d 165 (1954), relied upon by plaintiff, is also distinguishable on the facts. There the insurance company argued the failure of the insured to mention treatment for gallstones constituted a material misrepresentation. The Court found that the evidence did not establish gallstones at the time of application, and hence, on disputed facts, that a finding of no material misrepresentation was sustainable. In the instant case there are clear symptoms of an unusual physical condition known to the applicant and related by him to his physician, which he failed to mention to the insurance company only 43 days later.

None of the other cases cited by plaintiff are considered inconsistent with or closely in point to the decision here made.

The lack of knowledge on the part of both the decedent and his father-beneficiary of Dr. Newcomer's diagnosis and the fact that Dr. Newcomer did not consider the condition serious enough to refer the decedent to a specialist are clearly not relevant to the question in this case. Neither is being charged with fraud or deliberate misrepresentation. It is the symptoms of which decedent was clearly aware and which he did not disclose, and which clearly were material to the risk, which must relieve the insurer of the risk it did not voluntarily assume. Deceit upon the part of an applicant or beneficiary is not required, by the Illinois statute or the cases, if the insurer was in fact misled in a material way on the risk it was assuming.

Plaintiff filed a motion to strike the affidavit of Dr. Thomas Predey, which was filed in support of the motion for summary judgment. Insofar as said motion to strike is considered to have any merit as to some of the statements in said affidavit, such statements are not relied upon by the Court and the motion to strike is denied.

Accordingly, defendant's motion for summary judgment is allowed and judgment against plaintiff on his complaint is entered, at plaintiff's cost.

NOTES

1. Compare the standards applied in *Barger* with those employed in *Southard*.

The *Barger* court states that the cause of the insured person's death was not before the court and not considered material. Suppose that the decedent died in an airplane crash, from rabies, from heart disease, or from any other cause not related to seizures; should misrepresentation of the fact that he had experienced an apparent seizure permit the insurance company to disclaim liability for death from an unrelated cause? For an older case in which the misstatement by a person with epilepsy that he or she did not have seizures was also held to release the insurance company from liability, see *Westphall* v. *Metropolitan Life Ins. Co.,* 27 Cal.App. 734, 151 P. 159 (1915).

2. Is the existence of epilepsy *per se* actually a material fact in regard to the issuance of a life insurance policy? What kind of actuarial data ought the insurance companies be required to have to justify such a judgment? If an insurance company refuses to insure a person because of epilepsy without such actuarial data, could the company's decision be subject to legal challenge?

3. Should a person who has epilepsy tell the truth on insurance applications and risk being denied insurance, or not tell the truth and risk having coverage voided for misrepresentation? Most policies, often by law, become incontestable after a period of time—frequently two years. How does this affect the question of whether to admit epilepsy or not? Notice that the decedent in *Barger* died a little over a year after the issuance of the policy, before any such incontestability provision would have taken effect.

2. Health and Accident Insurance

FOLLETTE V. UNITED STATES MUTUAL ACCIDENT ASSOCIATION

Supreme Court of North Carolina, 1892
110 N.C. 377, 14 S.E. 923

Appeal from superior court, Durham county; WINSTON, Judge.

Action by A. S. Follette against the United States Mutual Accident Association on a policy of insurance. Verdict and judgment for plaintiff. Defendant appeals.

Affirmed.

AVERY, J. Though in some of its features there are slight differences between the case presented by this appeal and that considered when a new trial was awarded to the plaintiff at September term, 1890, (107 N.C. 240, 12 S.E.Rep. 370), the main question involved is the same. Under the guise of a second appeal, the defendant company insists that this court shall review and overrule its former decision, as if it were a rehearing. There is no branch of the law as to which, in all of its ramifications, there is so much conflict in the rulings of the various courts of appeal, and so great a diversity of opinion among respectable test-writers, as that governing the rights and liabilities of insurers. When the universal custom was that the underwriter sat in his city office, and issued policies of insurance, relying solely upon the representations of the applicant for information, whether as to his own physical state, or as to the value, condition, and surroundings of his buildings, the insurer would have dealt at a great disadvantage with the unreliable class of his customers if a contract procured by false representations had not been declared fraudulent and void, or if the disregard of stipulations intended to insure the observance of ordinary care in the habits of a person or the use of a building had not been held sufficient to defeat a recovery upon the death of the person or the destruction of the property insured. But when, in the new order of things, the active competition between companies brought to every man's door a soliciting agent furnished with instruction and advised as to his duty by the best-trained business men and ablest lawyers in the country, the shrewdest and most unscrupulous of applicants could hope to get no advantage, and the untrained or uneducated among the number labored under a decided disadvantage in answering questions, not always comprehended in all of their hearings, and in receiving subsequently from its chief office, in a distant city, the contract of the company limiting its own liability, and imposing new duties upon the insured by means of conditions never heard of before the issuing of the policy, and often never read or imperfectly understood afterwards. *Ubi eadem ratio, ibi idem jus.* When custom reverses the positions of the parties, it would be strange if the law should undergo no modification. The local agent of the defendant company testifies that, with a knowledge of the deafness of the plaintiff, he filled out his application for an accident policy, signed his own name on the back of it, and forwarded it to the principal office in New York. The policy came in due course of time, and was delivered to the plaintiff, who paid all of the premiums assessed against him, until he was so seriously wounded in his arm by the accidental discharge of a gun in the hands of a friend as to make amputation necessary. The company took a receipt by way of compromise, which, under the findings of the jury, is not evidence of payment, and, as there was no exception to the rulings or charge involving the question of payment or satisfaction, we are brought to the consideration of the leading point. In the application for membership is the following paragraph: ''I have never had nor am I subject to fits, disorders of the brain, . . . or any bodily or mental infirmity, except had an attack of rheumatism six years ago.'' The defendant now contends that the representation by the plaintiff that he was free from bodily infirmity was false and fraudulent, and constituted a material inducement to the defendant to issue the policy. Ordinarily the defendant could avoid the performance of the contract by showing the falsity of a material statement in the application. But the plaintiff, where representations contained in the application are admitted to be untrue, may rebut the presumption of fraudulent intent arising from such admission, by showing that the local agent of the company, with full knowledge of the falsity of the statement, entered the answers of the insured, and forwarded the application approved by his own indorsement. We cannot give the sanction of this court to the doctrine that a local agent may scream into the ear of a deaf person solicitations to apply for an accident policy; write for him an answer, which he knows at the time to be untrue, to a question in the application; procure the policy; receive the premiums as they fall due; and, when the insured becomes prostrate from a wound, stand aside at the bidding of the principal, and allow it, with the premiums in its coffers, to avoid the contract on account of a statement known by the agent to be false when he prepared it for the applicant's signature. The reason which induced the courts to guard the underwriter against misrepresentations, as to facts within the peculiar or exclusive knowledge of applications, no longer exists, when the agent of the insurer, on the ground, has as full knowledge of the truth or falsity of an application prepared by him as has the insured. *Cessante ratione, cessat et ipsa lex.* Where the local agent of a company has actual knowledge of the falsity of an answer to a question in the application which he writes for the insured, the knowledge of the agent will be imputed to the company, and it will not be allowed to avoid the contract on the ground of false warranty. [Citations omitted.]

It is not material whether we say that the conduct of the local agent amounts to a waiver or works an estoppel on the insurer, as the authorities are in conflict upon the point. 1 May, Ins. *supra* § 143; 2 May, Ins. § 498. Certain it is that in such cases the knowledge of the agent is imputed to the principal, and "to deliver a policy with full knowledge of facts upon which its validity may be disputed, and then insist upon those acts as a ground of avoidance, is to attempt a fraud. 2 May, Ins. *supra.* § 497. The agent necessarily discovered, while negotiating with the plaintiff, that the latter was deaf; and it would be as unreasonable to presume that both the agent and the applicant intended to affirm that to be true which they knew to be false, as that such a patent defect as the loss of an eye in a horse did not exist. *Leslie* v. *Insurance Co.,* 5 Thomp. & C. 193; *Insurance Co.* v. *Mahone,* 21 Wall. 152; *Brown* v. *Gray,* 6 Jones, (N.C.) 103; *Fields* v. *Rouse,* 3 Jones, (N.C.) 72. We do not propose to go behind the verdict, and the instruction upon which it was founded, and avoid the reaffirmation of the principles announced on the former hearing of this case by determining what is a bodily infirmity, since, conceding deafness to come under such designation, we think that there was no error in the rulings of the court below. As already intimated, it is immaterial whether we declare that the agent by his conduct waived objection to the inaccurate statement, or that by writing it down, or having full knowledge of the real truth of the matter, his conduct operated to estop the company, since, in view of what occurred when the application was made out and before, the avoidance of liability under the contract because of the infirmity known by the agent to exist would be fraudulent and unjust.

There is no error.

NOTES

1. Even if Mr. Follette *had* expressly declared that he was not deaf, would this misrepresentation have been material to his injury in the circumstances of the case? Can a deaf person be denied insurance as more accident prone?

2. For an Alabama decision reaching an identical result, see *Inter-Ocean Casualty Co.* v. *Ervin,* 229 Ala. 312, 156 So. 844 (1934).

3. In *Colaneri* v. *General Accident Assur. Corp.,* 126 App.Div. 591, 110 N.Y.S. 678 (1908), an applicant for health insurance admitted that he was deaf but failed to disclose that he had had an abscess of the inner ear for which he had required medical treatment within two years prior to the application. When he sought to recover under the terms of the policy for the same type of ear trouble, the court held that a verdict should be directed for the insurance company, because the insured's misrepresentation constituted a breach of his warranty as to his prior physical condition.

3. Automobile Insurance

Harris v. State Farm Mutual Automobile Insurance Co.

United States Court of Appeals for the Sixth Circuit, 1956
232 F.2d 532

Before Simons, Chief Judge, and Allen and McAllister, Circuit Judges.
McAllister, Circuit Judge.

Omer Harris, appellant, while riding as a passenger in an automobile owned by his son, Ralph, was injured when the car went out of control and ran into an embankment. He brought a negligence action against his son and recovered a judgment for personal injuries in the amount of $15,000 in the state court of Tennessee. The son, Ralph, was insured by appellee company against liability to the extent of $10,000. Appellant thereafter sued the insurer for this amount in the state court; and the suit was removed to the district court and tried before the district judge without a jury. The court filed findings of fact, conclusions of law, and entered judgment of dismissal; and from such judgment, Omer Harris appeals.

Appellee insurance company defended the action on several grounds. It contended that the insured was guilty of making false representations in his application for insurance with intent to deceive the insurance company; and, further, that, by reason of such false representation, the risk was increased, and the company thereby damaged. Appellee further defended upon the ground that Ralph Harris, the insured, failed and refused to cooperate with the insurance company, as required by the policy provisions, in order to enable the company to make proper preparation of its case to determine whether there was a genuine defense and in negotiations for settlement.

The false representation claimed to have been made by Ralph Harris in his application for the policy of insurance was that, in reply to a question whether he had any physical defect, he answered, no. Appellee insurance company introduced evidence that he suffered from epilepsy. Appellant contended that epilepsy was not a physical defect but a disease. The insurance company contended that it was a physical defect. After much expert testimony which evaded the real question, the trial judge, during examination of the insurance company's principal expert witness. Dr. R. M. Darnell, went to the crucial point with the question:

> Doctor, in the medical sense, would epilepsy be classified as a physical defect? A. Well, sir, we consider epilepsy as a symptom complex of an illness, and not as a physical defect in itself.

In the light of this expert medical testimony from the insurance company's witness, which was uncontradicted, the fact that Ralph Harris had epilepsy did not render fraudulent or false the answer in his application for insurance, that he had no physical defect.

It appears, however, from the evidence, that some ten years before he applied for the policy of insurance, Ralph Harris had received head injuries in an automobile accident which had resulted in the formation of a scar on his brain tissue. According to the medical witnesses, such a scar, in some cases, affects one's mental condition, and in some cases, it does not, but in the expert opinion of a neurosurgeon who had examined Ralph Harris several times after the accident, the scar on his brain tissue was the cause of a convulsive disorder from which he suffered on repeated occasions. The convulsive disorder was epilepsy. It appeared that a driver's license would not be issued by the state to anyone who was known to be suffering from epilepsy. The injured stated that he had nothing more than "crossed nerves" which had caused him to have "spells." There is no evidence that any physician or anyone else told him that he had crossed nerves, which, as far as the evidence goes, is a nonexistent condition. As to the scar on the brain, it was revealed to the neurosurgeon by an X-ray film. This was a physical defect. But Ralph Harris was never told by anyone that he had a scar on his brain and did not know it.

Section 6126 of Williams' Code of Tennessee provides:

> No written or oral misrepresentation or warranty therein made in the negotiations of a contract or policy of insurance, or in the application therefor, by the assured or in his behalf, shall be deemed material or defeat or void the policy or prevent its attaching, unless such misrepresentation or warranty is made with actual intent to deceive, or unless the matter represented increase the risk of loss.

The district court found that scar tissue on the brain is a physical defect; that it exerts pressure on the brain and causes epilepsy; that the statement in the application for insurance by Ralph Harris setting forth that he had no physical defect was false; that such representation increased the risk of loss under the policy; that Ralph Harris suffered from epileptic seizures; and that the insurance company would not have issued the policy if it had known the true facts.

In *Columbian National Life Ins. Co.* v. *Harrison,* 6 Cir., 12 F.2d 986, Judge Denison, in speaking for the court, held that a false representation in an application for insurance which increased the risk, avoided the policy, under the statute of Tennessee above set forth, even where the representation was made in good faith. In view of circumstances hereinafter discussed, it is to be noted that in the *Harrison* case, *supra,* the express terms of the insurance policy set forth that it was issued in consideration of the statements made in the application, and that such statements were actually copied into, and incorporated in the policy itself, which is contrary to the facts in the instant case. See *Standard Life Ins. Co. of the South* v. *Strong,* 19 Tenn.App. 404, 89 S.W. 2d 367; *Robbins* v. *New York Life Ins. Co.,* 18 Tenn.App. 70, 72 S.W.2d 788; *Insurance Co.* v. *Lauderdale,* 94 Tenn. 635, 30 S.W. 732; *Boyd* v. *Insurance Co.,* 90 Tenn. 212, 16 S.W. 470; *Catron* v. *Tennessee Ins. Co.,* 25 Tenn. 175. Whether a representation results in an increase of risk is a question of law for the court. *Volunteer State Life Ins. Co.* v. *Richardson,* 146 Tenn. 589, 244 S.W. 44, 26 A.L.R. 1270; *Mutual Life Ins. Co.* v. *Dibrell,* 137 Tenn. 528, 194 S.W. 581, L.R.A.1917E, 554. See *American Eagle Fire Ins. Co.* v. *Peoples Compress Co.,* 10 Cir., 156 F.2d 663.

The statement of the insured, in his application for insurance, that he had no physical defect was a misrepresentation which, even though innocently made, increased the risk of loss; and, unless precluded by other considerations, under the provisions of the statutes of Tennessee, above mentioned, would avoid the policy.

However, an insurance policy is a contract, and, as in other contracts, the fundamental question to be determined is what was the real intention of the parties. *Milwaukee Mechanics Ins. Co.* v. *Davis,* 5 Cir., 198 F.2d 441. "Contracts of insurance, like other contracts, are to be construed according to the sense and meaning of the terms which the parties have used, and if they are clear and unambiguous, their terms are to be taken and understood in their plain, ordinary, and popular sense, unless such terms have acquired a different and technical sense in commercial usage or unless it clearly appears from the context that it was the intention of the parties to use such terms in a technical or peculiar sense.'' 29 Am.Jur., Section 159. We are interpreting a contract and are concerned only with the sense in which its words were used. *Aschenbrenner* v. *United States F. & G. Co.*, 292 U.S. 80, 84, 54 S.Ct. 590, 78 L.Ed. 1137. It is our function and duty to ascertain and effectuate the lawful intention of the parties. *New York Life Ins. Co.* v. *Bennion*, 10 Cir., 158 F.2d 260. The application for a policy is not the contract but a mere offer or proposal for a contract of insurance. *Mutual Benefit Life Ins. Co.* v. *Robison*, 8 Cir., 58 F. 723; *Metropolitan Life Ins. Co.* v. *Whitler*, 7 Cir., 172 F.2d 631. The application for a policy of insurance becomes a part of the contract if it is made a part thereof by the express terms of the policy; and in a number of jurisdictions, statutes have been enacted which require a copy of the application to be attached to the policy applied for. In the instant case, the application was not attached to, or incorporated in, or referred to, in the policy. In Tennessee, the applicable statute provides, insofar as here relevant, that every policy of insurance issued to any citizen of the state by any insurance company or association doing business in the state, except fraternal beneficiary associations and mutual insurance companies or associations operating on the assessment plan, or policies of industrial insurance, shall contain the entire contract of insurance between the parties to the contract. Under this statute, an insurance company, unless it is within the exceptions therein specified, cannot take advantage of any breach of the terms of the application when it does not attach the application to, or incorporate it in the policy. *Arnold* v. *New York Life Ins. Co.*, 131 Tenn. 720, 177 S.W. 78. Appellee insurance company, however, is within the exceptions mentioned in the statute, since it is a mutual insurance company.

However, in this case, the express provisions of the contract between the insured and the insurer set forth:

> Declarations. By the acceptance of this policy the named insured agrees that the statements in the declarations are his agreements and representations, that this policy is issued in reliance upon the truth of such representations and that this policy embodies all agreements existing between himself and the company or any of its agents relating to this insurance.

The above provision refers to the heading, ''Declarations,'' on the first page of the policy, which set forth the name of the insured, the type of the automobile insured, the occupation of the insured, and similar information. No reference is made in the policy to the application. The agreement in the insurance contract that ''this policy embodies all agreements existing between [insured] and the company'' is conclusive that it is not based in any way upon the statements in the application. Of course, a fraudulent representation in the application inducing the execution of a policy of insurance can generally be availed of to avoid the policy, just as any contract can be avoided for fraud *ab initio*. And it may well be that under Section 6086 of Williams' Tennessee Code Annotated, above mentioned, the insurance company in this case, if it had not expressly agreed otherwise, could rely, as a defense, upon the statements in the application, which were false but not fraudulent, even though it had not attached the application to, or incorporated it in the policy, in view of the fact that mutual insurance companies are excepted from the requirement that the policy shall contain the entire contract of insurance. But the insurance company, in this case, in its contract of insurance, foreclosed itself from relying on the statements in the application by its stipulation that the policy itself embodied all the agreements between the company and the insured. Mere false representations in an application for insurance, as distinguished from a fraudulent inducement or procurement of a policy of insurance, cannot be relied upon when the insurance contract, by its express terms, provides that the policy itself embodies all the agreements between the parties. The application in this case was no part of the contract of insurance. By the terms of the insurance contract, the policy was issued "in reliance upon the truth of . . . representations" set forth in the policy, and not upon statements in the application. Similarly, in those cases where statutes provide that the policy shall contain the whole contract, a false but not fraudulent representation in an application for insurance cannot be relied upon to avoid a policy where the application is not made a part of the policy. See 29 Am.Jur., Section 173, and cases collated thereunder. It is our conclusion that the application by the insured was never a part of the policy, and because of the express agreement of the parties, no statements therein can be relied upon to avoid the policy.

Appellee insurance company claims that it was relieved from liability under the policy for the reason that Ralph Harris, the insured, failed to cooperate with the insurer, as required by the policy provisions. It contends that a comparison of the insured's written and oral statements before the trial in the state court, with his sworn testimony in that trial, together with his attitude and conduct preceding and during that trial and his deliberate and willful falsification of material facts, shows insured's complete failure to cooperate with the company.

In support of its contention, the company submits that the insured denied having been an epileptic, or having a physical defect, until the trial of the personal injury action in the state court. It appears that, prior to the execution of the policy, the insured was not asked whether he suffered from epilepsy, and such a representation was not included in the application for insurance. As far as a physical defect goes, epilepsy is not, according to the undisputed evidence of the insurance company's witnesses heretofore mentioned, a physical defect. The insurance company shows that in the statement given by Ralph Harris to the claim agent after the accident in which appellant was injured, Ralph stated: "I had . . . my complete facilities about me, and my mind functioning as usual. . . . I must have dropped off to sleep at this very time . . . I have been driving for about fifteen years, and this is the first time I have ever gone to sleep at the wheel of a vehicle. I have never been subject to any spells of drowsiness, or otherwise, at any time." This statement was drawn up by a claim agent of the insurance company and signed by Ralph.

It is claimed by the insurance company that contrary to his written statement, the insured testified thereafter that he had been drowsy and dropped off to sleep. It appears that he had told his physician after he recovered consciousness that he did not know what happened, but that he "reckoned I just went to sleep, I just don't know."

On the witness stand, he testified: "I was sleepy and drowsy that morning." It is insisted that these statements were a willful falsification of the facts and misled the insurance counsel in preparing for trial in that he had previously told him that he had no warning whatever that he was "going to lose consciousness." It appears, then, that the insured told his physician at the hospital, when he first discussed the accident, that he thought he had fallen asleep. He told the claim agent he must have dropped off to sleep. He told counsel for the insurance company before the trial that he suddenly lost consciousness and fell asleep; and he testified on the trial that, as far as he knew, he just went to sleep. As to appellee's claim that the insured had told counsel that he had no warning that he was going to fall asleep, and afterward contradicted this statement by saying that he was a little drowsy, the insured, being pressed on this point, on examination by counsel for the insurance company, testified: "I had no warning whatsoever other than drowsiness and sleepy. Is that warning? What would you say that is?"

From the foregoing, it cannot be said that the insured failed to cooperate by testifying that he was drowsy and had fallen asleep instead of testifying that he had lost consciousness suddenly. Moreover, in spite of the insured's insistence that he did not have spells or epileptic seizures, the insurance company was not prejudiced in introducing the most comprehensive proofs from the doctors who had treated the insured and from the insured's father who was the plaintiff in the personal injury case, that the insured had suffered from epileptic attacks. Thus, in the statement given to the claim agent, Ralph told that Dr. Leigh K. Haynes was the physician who treated him after the accident, and he authorized the counsel for the insurance company to interview and discuss the matter with Dr. Haynes; and, from Dr. Haynes, counsel for the insurance company learned all about the epileptic attacks from which Ralph suffered. He also learned from Dr. Haynes that Dr. Raskind, the neurosurgeon, had treated Ralph; and from Dr. Raskind, counsel further learned of the scar on Ralph's brain tissue and the treatment which was administered for the repeated attacks of epilepsy from which he suffered. On the trial, Ralph's father, appellant herein, testified as to these epileptic seizures. Ralph himself testified that he had spells, but denied that they were epileptic—although he could have had no knowledge as to whether a spell is epileptic or not. During the trial in the state court, counsel for the insurance company, who was also representing Ralph, introduced in evidence the depositions of Dr. Haynes and Dr. Raskind disclosing that Ralph had repeatedly suffered from epilepsy. The defense of the law suit, by the insurance company, was not prejudiced by the need of proof that the insured had epileptic seizures; and this was practically the sole defense relied upon in the state court suit for personal injuries brought by appellant against his son, Ralph. In that suit, the issue was whether, at the time the car ran into the embankment, Ralph suffered an epileptic seizure or fell asleep. If he suffered an epileptic seizure, he would not have been guilty of negligence and no verdict for damages could have been returned. Appellant's claim was based on the theory that the accident happened when Ralph fell asleep. This issue was strenuously contested in the state court.

In the state court case, the trial judge, in his charge to the jury, instructed them that if they found that Ralph Harris had lost control of his automobile by going to sleep and causing the car to crash into the embankment, and if they found that he had omitted to do something that an ordinarily prudent person would have done, that would raise an inference of negligence on his part, and, if unexplained or if no circumstances tending to excuse or justify his conduct were proved, he would be liable. On the other hand, the court instructed the jury that if, immediately before the crash, the insured was suddenly and without warning seized with an attack of epilepsy which made it impossible for him to control the car, and, as a result, the accident occurred, there would be no negligence and no liability. In this regard, the trial court gave the following special instruction:

> I further charge you, gentlemen of the jury, that if you should find that the defendant was an epileptic and that this fact was known to his father, but you should further find that at the time of this accident he went to sleep, not as a result of a sudden seizure of epilepsy, then I charge you that the plaintiff would not be guilty of contributory negligence in this case, if he exercised reasonable care for his own safety. . . .

The issue before the jury, therefore, was whether the accident resulted from the insured's falling asleep or from an epileptic seizure. When the judgment awarded to appellant was appealed by the insurance company to the Tennessee Court of Appeals, that court, in its opinion affirming the judgment, stated:

> The case as presented to the jury, turned almost exclusively on whether the accident happened as the result of the Defendant's having had an epileptic seizure, in which case there would be no liability, or whether it happened as the result of his having fallen asleep at the wheel, in which case there was liability. The jury has found that it occurred as the result of his having fallen asleep at the wheel. As far as this case is concerned, that concludes the matter.

From what we can judge of the record, the insurance company was not prejudiced by anything the insured did in presenting its proof to the jury showing that the insured was a sufferer from epileptic attacks. In fact, the matter was squarely presented during the trial of the instant case when appellant's counsel, during the testimony of the attorney for the insurance company who had taken the stand on behalf of his client, asked:

> Q. Actually, Mr. Nailling, the point I am getting at, . . . defense of that lawsuit was never seriously handicapped at any time by the need of or adequacy of the proof that the boy had these epileptic seizures, was it, just except a little work on the part of the lawyer is all it required, wasn't it? A. I will answer it this way. I was entitled to a full, fair and complete statement of this accident from the insured. I never did get it.

This cannot be said to be proof that any lack of cooperation or discrepancies in statements by the insured were prejudicial in effect. About the only additional proof that appellee company could have adduced in presenting its case was an outright admission from the insured that the accident happened while he had an epileptic seizure; and it is conceded by the medical expert witnesses of the insurance company that the insured would not have been able to remember whether he had fallen asleep or suffered an epileptic attack. "It is well settled that, to relieve the insurer of liability on the ground of lack of cooperation, discrepancies in statements by the insured must be made in bad faith and must be material in nature and prejudicial in effect." *State Automobile Mut. Ins. Co. of Columbus, Ohio* v. *York,* 4 Cir., 104 F.2d 730 733.

In sum, while the question whether the insured fell asleep or suffered an epileptic attack was for the jury in the state court trial, the proofs that the accident resulted from an epileptic seizure were so strong and persuasive and so ably marshalled and advanced by counsel for appellee that we would have had no doubt, had we been the triers of fact, in arriving at a judgment in favor of the appellee. From all of the foregoing, we cannot say that appellee was prejudiced by any statements of the insured, in presenting its proofs, to the effect that the accident happened as the result of an epileptic seizure, for it knew all the facts and circumstances surrounding the susceptibility of the assured to such attacks, before the actual trial of the case.

With regard to the question of the cooperation of the insured with the insurer, there is one disturbing circumstance. When preparing for trial, counsel for the insurance company asked the insured why he had not informed them that he had epilepsy. The insured heatedly replied that he did not have epilepsy and that counsel was "a damn liar." Counsel is an outstanding lawyer of integrity and reputation, as well as ability, as his conduct of the various trials relating to this accident and liability therefore demonstrate, and he was, at all times, engaged in faithfully and honestly representing the interests of his client. The insured seems to have been sensitive on the point of his affliction with epilepsy, which he chose to call spells; but such language by the insured to an honorable member of the bar engaged to defend both the insured and the insurer, is inexcusable and deplorable. Yet the crucial consideration is not whether, on this occasion, there was unjustifiable language used by the insured in speaking to counsel for the insurance company, but whether the insured's conduct prejudiced the company or prevented it from introducing its proofs and fully presenting its case before the jury; and it is our conclusion that it did not.

Other claimed false statements by the insured during preparation for trial were not prejudicial to the insurance company in the presentation of its case to the jury. "The mere inadequacy or untruthfulness of a statement made by the assured to the insurer as to the circumstances of an accident does not of itself necessarily constitute a breach of a cooperation clause." *Rochon* v. *Preferred Accident Ins. Co.*, 118 Conn. 190, 171 A. 429, 98 A.L.R. 1472. And the fact that the insured stated he would never permit his father to settle for the amount of his medical expenses cannot be held to be a failure to cooperate, especially since such an offer was never more than contemplated by the counsel for the insurance company, and no offer was ever made by the company.

On our review of the whole case, it may be said that if epilepsy were a physical defect instead of a disease, the insured's representation that he had no physical defect would have supported a finding of fraudulent misrepresentation to the insurance company, avoiding the policy. If the application wherein the insured innocently stated that he had no physical defect had been made a part of the "Declarations" of the policy of insurance, it would have also avoided the insurance because, though innocent, it was false, and increased the risk. To avail itself of insured's statement that he had no physical defect, the insurance company would either have to show that it was made with intention to defraud, or that such representation was a part of the policy.

If it were not for certain procedures of the insurance company, it would seem strange that no inquiry was made as to whether the applicant was subject to epilepsy or similar afflictions, before issuance of a policy; but it appears that while this is information that is of paramount interest to the insurance company, as is also information with respect to an applicant's drinking habits, whether he is emotionally stable, of sound mind, and of good moral character, no questions are asked with respect to any of these matters, inasmuch as the company generally relies upon the agent and upon a private investigation of each applicant, which was not made in this case. The reasons given why such an investigation was not made were because the mileage—or travel expense—required for the investigation was excessive; and that the agency issuing the insurance had been profitable, it appearing that the company investigates more readily applications made to an agency which has been unprofitable.

It is our conclusion that there was no proof that the insured, by any statement in his application, was guilty of fraudulent misrepresentation inducing the contract of insurance; that the statement that the insured had no physical defect was not a part of the insurance contract relied upon by the insurer; and that there was no failure to cooperate on the part of the insured to the prejudice of the insurance company.

In accordance with the foregoing, the judgment of the district court is reversed and the case remanded for entry of a judgment in favor of appellant, as set forth in the complaint in the district court.

NOTES

1. Compare the holding in *Harris* that epilepsy is a disease and not a physical defect with the ruling in *Southard, supra,* that quadriplegia is a physical impairment but not an illness. How should an insurance company draft the questions on its insurance applications in order to obtain disclosure of such conditions? What underlying policy considerations support court decisions in favor of the insured party in such circumstances?

2. In *Government Employees Insurance Company* v. *Cain,* 226 F.Supp. 589 (D.Md. 1964), a man gave a negative answer to a question in an application form for automobile insurance which inquired whether any operator of the automobile was physically or mentally impaired, giving in parentheses the examples of "one eye, leg, arm, paralysis, etc." *Id.* at 591. In fact, the man's wife had epilepsy and was subsequently involved in an automobile accident as a result of an epileptic seizure. Thereupon, the insurance company sought to disclaim coverage and rescind the policy. Partially in reliance upon *Harris,* the court held that the insurance company was required to honor the policy:

> The court holds that, viewed objectively, Mr. Cain was not reasonably asked to disclose his wife's epilepsy. *Id.* at 593.

C. ENTRY INTO THE UNITED STATES

ADMISSION QUALIFICATIONS FOR ALIENS, 8 U.S.C. SECTION 1182(A)

Excludable Aliens—General Classes

Except as otherwise provided in this chapter, the following classes of aliens shall be ineligible to receive visas and shall be excluded from admission into the United States:

(1)   Aliens who are mentally retarded;

(2)   Aliens who are insane;

(3)   Aliens who have had one or more attacks of insanity;

(4)   Aliens afflicted with psychopathic personality, or sexual deviation, or a mental defect;

* * *

(6)   Aliens who are afflicted with any dangerous contagious disease;

(7)   Aliens not comprehended within any of the foregoing classes who are certified by the examining surgeon as having a physical defect, disease, or disability, when determined by the consular or immigration officer to be of such a nature that it may affect the ability of the alien to earn a living, unless the alien affirmatively establishes that he will not have to earn a living;

* * *

(30)   Any alien accompanying another alien ordered to be excluded and deported and certified to be helpless from sickness or mental or physical disability or infancy . . . whose protection or guardianship is required by the alien ordered excluded and deported;

* * *

NOTE

The categories listed here are in addition to criminals, paupers, vagrants, professional beggars, drug addicts, prostitutes, polygamists, stowaways, anarchists, Nazis and Communists, and other specified classes of undesirables. Quite a pristine "melting pot," is it not?

United States ex rel. Saclarides v. Shaughnessy

United States Court of Appeals for the Second Circuit, 1950
180 F.2d 687

Before L. Hand, Swan and Chase, Circuit Judges.
Chase, Circuit Judge.

A thirteen year old Greek girl, Eleni Saclarides, arrived at the Port of New York on February 5, 1947 accompanied by her father and mother. All were aliens, being native citizens of Greece. They were given a hearing on their applications for admission by a Board of Special Inquiry. A certificate by the examining officers of the United States Public Health Service showed that Eleni was afflicted with a mental deficiency known as mongolism. She was excluded under section 3(d) of the Immigration Act of February 5, 1917, 8 U.S.C.A. § 136(d), and her mother was excluded under section 18 of the same Act, 8 U.S.C.A. § 154, as an alien accompanying an alien who was rejected for a mental defect and required protection or guardianship.

The exclusion of Eleni was based solely upon the medical certificate. The Board of Immigration Appeals affirmed in an appeal by her mother and then the petition for this writ of habeas corpus was granted. The judge, being of the opinion that the relators were entitled at a hearing, before the Board of Special Inquiry, to cross-examine the medical officers who made the certificate and to call a doctor to testify in their behalf, was disposed to dismiss the writ upon condition that this opportunity be made available to them but, upon being informed that the condition would not be met, sustained the writ and this appeal followed.

In *United States ex rel. Johnson* v. *Watkins,* 2 Cir., 170 F.2d 1009, we held that under section 17 of the Immigration Act of 1917, 8 U.S.C.A. § 153, the only evidence of mental defect upon which a Board of Special Inquiry could act was a medical certificate lawfully issued under section 16, 8 U.S.C.A. § 152. Though that decision was reversed upon other grounds, the Supreme Court expressly agreed as to the conclusiveness of the medical certificate in the hearing before the Board of Special Inquiry. *United States ex rel. Johnson* v. *Shaughnessy,* 336 U.S. 806, 809, 69 S.Ct. 921. Nor was there any lack of necessary particularity in the contents of the certificate. It showed that the alien was suffering from the mental affliction, mongolism. That brought the girl within the provisions of the statute under which she was excluded and the suggestion that it did not because the word "deficiency" rather than the statutory word "defective" was used in the certificate requires no comment.

The attack upon the fairness of the hearing before the Board because it did not point out that the medical examiners had to meet statutory qualifications is equally fruitless. Though their qualifications as prescribed do not expressly include two years' experience in the practice of their profession as the relators appear to believe, due to the amendment of section 16 of the Act on July 1, 1944, 58 Stat. 716, that section has always provided that those medical officers who have had "especial training" in the diagnosis of mental defects "shall be detailed for duty or employed at all ports of entry designated by the Attorney General." There is, however, nothing in this record to show that the medical examiners were not so qualified and, absent that, they as public officials will be presumed to have had the power to do the official acts they performed. *Erhardt* v. *Ballin,* 2 Cir., 150 F. 529; *United States ex rel. Petach* v. *Phelps,* 2 Cir., 40 F.2d 500; *Stone ex rel. Colonna* v. *Tillinghast,* 1 Cir., 32 F.2d 447.

Finally, it is argued that the hearing before the Board had to be conducted in accordance with the provisions of the Administrative Procedure Act, 5 U.S.C.A. § 1001 *et seq.* More specifically, the argument seems to be that the provisions of section 7 of the Act, 5 U.S.C.A. § 1006, requiring the agency itself, one of its members or one of the examiners appointed as provided in section 11, 5 U.S.C.A. § 1010, to preside at the taking of evidence, and permitting parties to present rebuttal evidence and to cross-examine, are applicable in such a hearing as this. However, section 7 expressly provides that " . . . nothing in this Act shall be deemed to supersede the conduct of specified classes of proceedings in whole or in part by or before boards or other officers specially provided for by or designated pursuant to statute." We think this provision takes exclusion proceedings out of the requirements as to hearings imposed by the Act, boards of special inquiry being specially provided for by Section 17 of the Immigration Act of 1917, 8 U.S.C.A. § 153, to determine "all cases of immigrants detained at [the various ports of arrival] under the provisions of the law."

Judgment reversed and writ dismissed.

NOTES

1. The *Saclarides* decision is illustrative of the principle that Congress has almost unlimited authority to decide who shall and who shall not be permitted to enter this country. This broad authority has been upheld many times by the United States Supreme Court, most recently in *Fiallo* v. *Bell,* 430 U.S. 787 (1977), where the Court held that a measure that excluded illegitimate children and their fathers from a special preference immigration status afforded to other parents and children was constitutionally permissible. The Court declared:

> At the outset, it is important to underscore the limited scope of judicial inquiry into immigration legislation. This Court has repeatedly emphasized that "over no conceivable subject is the legislative power of Congress more complete than it is over" the admission of aliens. *Oceanic Navigation Co.* v. *Stranahan,* 214 U.S. 320, 339 (1909); accord, *Kleindienst* v. *Mandel,* 408 U.S. 753, 766 (1972). Our cases "have long recognized the power to expel or exclude aliens as a fundamental sovereign attribute exercised by the Government's political departments largely immune from judicial control." *Shaughnessy* v. *Mezei,* 345 U.S. 206, 210 (1953); see, *e.g., Harisiades* v. *Shaughnessy,* 342 U.S. 580 (1952); *Lem Moon Sing* v. *United States,* 158 U.S. 538 (1895); *Fong Yue Ting* v. *United States,* 149 U.S. 698 (1893); *The Chinese Exclusion Case,* 130 U.S. 581 (1889). Our recent decisions have not departed from this long-established rule. Just last Term, for example, the Court had occasion to note that "the power over aliens is of a political character and therefore subject only to narrow judicial review." *Hampton* v. *Mow Sun Wong,* 426 U.S. 88, 101 n. 21 (1976), citing *Fong Yue Ting* v. *United States, supra,* at 713; accord, *Mathews* v. *Diaz,* 426 U.S. 67, 81–82 (1976). And we observed recently that in the exercise of its broad power over immigration and naturalization, "Congress regularly makes rules that would be unacceptable if applied to citizens." *Id.,* at 80. (*Id.* at 792.)

2. Regarding the proper modern terminology of "Down's syndrome" rather than "mongolism" as used in *Saclarides,* see p. 49, above.

3. In *United States ex rel. Duner* v. *Curran,* 10 F.2d 38 (2d Cir. 1925), cert. denied, 271 U.S. 663 (1926), the 15-year-old son of a minister entering the country to carry on his vocation was held validly excluded from entry after being certified as physically defective because of a valvular disease of the heart.

In *United States ex rel. Markin* v. *Curran,* 9 F.2d 900 (2d. Cir. 1925), cert. denied, 270 U.S. 647 (1926), a woman was held properly excluded from the country because of physical defects which included a visual impairment and a syphilitic condition, even though her husband had become a naturalized citizen.

What public policies are served by such results? What public interests are jettisoned?

D. PRIVACY

Various facets of the constitutional right of privacy have been discussed in other chapters of this volume. This section, however, deals with a few miscellaneous privacy issues not addressed elsewhere that are closely related to the condition or status of being handicapped.

DEATON V. DELTA DEMOCRAT PUBLISHING COMPANY

Supreme Court of Mississippi, 1976
326 So.2d 471

Before GILLESPIE, WALKER and BROOM, JJ.

BROOM, Justice:

Unwarranted invasion of their right of privacy was the thesis upon which appellants Deaton (four minor children by their father as next friend) sought damages from appellee, Delta Democrat Publishing Company (the Democrat), in the Circuit Court of Washington County. At trial the suits were consolidated.

For purposes of this appeal, the following allegations contained in the declarations are assumed as facts. The Democrat published a story describing the children as "retarded" and "trainable mentally retarded" in its newspaper featuring a public school special education class for mentally retarded children. Photographs and names identifying the Deaton children as members of the class were made part of the story. The Deatons' declarations also alleged that obtaining the photographs and publishing the story were "done by intentional design" of the Democrat without regard to the rights of privacy of the children and in violation of their "right to the pursuit of happiness."

The Democrat demurred to the appellants' declarations, contending that no cause of action was stated relying upon the First and Fourteenth Amendments to the United States Constitution, and also relying upon Article III, section 13 of the Constitution of the State of Mississippi. Failure of the Deatons to allege in their declarations that the publication "was made by one who had knowledge of its falsity, or with reckless disregard for the truth, or maliciously," according to the demurrer, rendered the publication privileged under the constitutional provisions cited. From judgments sustaining the demurrer the Deatons appealed. We reverse.

Mississippi has by implication judicially recognized the common law right to privacy. *Martin* v. *Dorton,* 210 Miss. 668, 50 So.2d 391 (1951). Although the law of privacy has developed along divergent lines and amid a welter of confusing judicial pronouncements, four distinct theories of the cause of action have been generally recognized: (1) The intentional intrusion upon the solitude or seclusion of another; (2) the appropriation of another's identity for an unpermitted use; (3) the public disclosure of private facts; and (4) holding another to the public eye in a false light. W. Prosser, *Handbook of the Law on Torts* § 117 at 804–14 (4th ed. 1971); *Restatement of Torts,* 2d, § 652A (Tentative Draft No. 21, 1975).

Mississippi Code Annotated section 11-7-35 (1972) provides that declarations shall contain a statement of facts in "ordinary and concise language ... and if it contains sufficient matter of substance for the court to proceed upon the merits of the cause, it shall be sufficient." The section concludes that an objection to maintain an action shall not be based upon "the form thereof. . . . " In our jurisprudence it is the rule that where a demurrer to a declaration raises merely a doubtful question, or where the case is such that justice may be promoted by a trial on the merits, even though the demurrer might be technically sustainable, it must be overruled. *Jacobs* v. *Bodie,* 208

Miss. 779, 45 So.2d 587 (1950); *Goff* v. *Randall,* 206 Miss. 178, 39 So.2d 881 (1949). We also adhere to the rule that facts which are reasonably or necessarily implied from facts stated must on demurrer be considered as true, and when such facts together with express averments, furnish sufficient material of substance for courts to proceed on the merits the demurrer should not be sustained. *Ross* v. *L. & N. R. R.,* 178 Miss. 69, 172 So. 752 (1937). Although the declarations in question may possibly be subject to technical criticism, under our statute (§ 11-7-35) and jurisprudence, they sufficiently state a cause of action upon which the trial court should have heard proof.

This case is not controlled by *Cox Broadcasting Corporation* v. *Cohn,* 420 U.S. 469, 95 S.Ct. 1029, 43 L.Ed.2d 328 (1975), in which the Supreme Court of the United States held that the state may not "impose sanctions on the accurate publication of the name of a rape victim obtained from public records" (court records open to public inspection). In the case before us the facts are opposite to *Cox* in that the information published was not taken from public records, but was by state law made unavailable to the public (Miss.Code Ann. § 37-15-3 (Supp. 1975)). Our holding here is not in conflict with section 652 of Tentative Draft No. 13 of the Second Restatement of Torts which states that there is no liability when the defendant merely publicizes something about someone else which is already public or constitutes matters of public concern.

There is not presented here a case involving a celebrity, public official, or public figure. It is well established that factual reporting of "newsworthy persons and events is in the public interest and is protected." *Time* v. *Hill,* 385 U.S. 374, 87 S.Ct. 534, 17 L.Ed.2d 456 (1967). *Hill* held that in the absence of proof that the defendant published the report with knowledge of its falsity or in reckless disregard of the truth, liability generally cannot be exacted against a publisher. See also, *New York Times Co.* v. *Sullivan,* 376 U.S. 254, 84 S.Ct. 710, 11 L.Ed.2d 686, 95 A.L.R.2d 1412 (1964). However, *Hill,* a New York case, was based at least in part upon a state statute (limited in nature) which allowed invasion of privacy actions only under narrow circumstances. New York jurisprudence apparently does not recognize the common law right of privacy action.

The Democrat relies upon *Cantrell* v. *Forest City Publishing Company,* 419 U.S. 245, 95 S.Ct. 465, 42 L.Ed.2d 419 (1974) as authority for its assertion that the declarations were demurrable for failure to allege actual malice on the part of the Democrat or that it made its publication with knowledge of falsity of the publication or in reckless disregard for the truth. It is also noted that this is not a libel suit brought by a public official as was true in *New York Times Company* v. *Sullivan, supra.*

Cantrell has significant similarity to the instant case: (1) It is a right of privacy action; (2) no "actual malice," as that term is used by appellee, was present or proved; and (3) the publication dealt with a subject of legitimate public interest and concern, but also with private persons who were only incidentally a part of the subject matter. The opinion in *Cantrell* makes it clear that the court was not holding that any kind of malice, or knowledge of falsity or reckless disregard for truth had to be proved in an invasion of privacy case:

The District Judge in the case before us, in contrast with the trial judge in *Time, Inc.* v. *Hill*, did instruct the jury that liability could be imposed only if it concluded that the false statements in the Sunday Magazine feature article on the Cantrells had been made with knowledge of their falsity or in the reckless disregard of the truth. *No objection was made by any of the parties to this knowing-or-reckless-falsehood instruction . . . (Cantrell* v. *Forest City Publishing Co., supra,* at 95 S.Ct. 469) [emphasis supplied]).

From *Cantrell* we perceive that the Supreme Court of the United States has not adopted the view that there is absolute constitutional immunity from liability for a newspaper in a case of the type here presented. We find no case (and none was cited by briefs except *Hill, supra,* which involved a state statute not present here) in which that Court ever said that any kind of malice, knowledge of falsity, or reckless disregard of truth is an essential element in such cases. We do not say, however, that inclusion of such in a plaintiff's declaration would be contrary to principles of good pleading. The fact that a public school offers instruction and assistance to mentally retarded children is a matter of legitimate public interest and may be published under free press guarantees. However, the publication of the names and photographs of the children involved casts the issue into a different legal perspective. It is difficult to conceive that any information can be more delicate or private in nature than the fact that a child has limited mental capabilities or is in any sense mentally retarded. Simply enrolling in a public school does not make one a "public figure" or "personage" to the extent that such person has no right to privacy concerning his mental capabilities or lack of such. Reasonable limitations applied to the right of a free press to expose facts of private concern to individuals do not infringe on the right of the people to be informed of matters properly in the public domain. *Virgil* v. *Time, Inc.,* 527 F.2d 1122 (CA 9 1975).

We recognize that the First Amendment protections relied upon by the Democrat were properly intended to afford this nation and all its citizens the immeasurable benefits which flow from a free and unstifled press. At the same time, to hold that children, situated as were the Deatons, may be publicized, without parental consent, by names and photographs as "mentally retarded" with absolute immunity would run counter to their right to "the pursuit of happiness" as contemplated by those who founded our nation.

Our judgment is that the declarations sufficiently charged a tort, and therefore the judgments of the lower court sustaining the demurrers are reversed and the cause remanded for development of proof.

The case was considered by a conference of the Judges en banc.

Reversed and remanded.

GILLESPIE, C. J., RODGERS, P. J., and PATTERSON, INZER, SMITH, ROBERTSON, SUGG and WALKER, JJ., concur.

NOTE

How applicable is the reasoning of the *Deaton* court to other handicapping conditions? Consider whether the misrepresentation that an individual is mentally retarded would give rise to a cause of action for slander.

COMMONWEALTH v. WISEMAN

Supreme Judicial Court of Massachusetts, Suffolk, 1969
356 Mass. 251, 249 N.E.2d 610

Before WILKINS, C. J., and SPALDING, WHITTEMORE, CUTTER, and SPIEGEL, JJ.
CUTTER, Justice.

This bill seeks, among other relief, to enjoin all showings of a film entitled
"Titicut Follies," containing scenes at Massachusetts Correctional Institution at
Bridgewater (Bridgewater), to which insane persons charged with crime and defective
delinquents may be committed. See G.L. c. 125, § 19, as amended through St. 1967,
c. 619, § 2. The film was made between April 22, and June 29, 1966. Mr. Wiseman
and Bridgewater Film Company, Inc. (BFC) appeal from an interlocutory decree, an
order for a decree, and the final decree which enjoins showing the film "to any
audience" and requires Mr. Wiseman and BFC to deliver up to the Attorney General
for destruction specified films, negatives, and sound tapes. The plaintiffs appeal from
the final decree because it did not order sums realized by various defendants from
showing the film to be held for distribution as the court might direct.

The trial judge made a report of material facts. The evidence (2,556 pages of
proceedings on eighteen trial days and sixty-four exhibits) is reported. The facts,
except as otherwise indicated, are stated on the basis of the trial judge's findings and
certain exhibits. The film has been shown to the Justices participating in this decision.

In 1965, Mr. Wiseman first requested permission from the Superintendent and
from the Commissioner to make an educational documentary film concerning Bridgewater. His first request was denied. On January 28, 1966, permission was granted,
subject to the receipt of a favorable opinion from the Attorney General (that the
officials could grant permission) and to the conditions (a) that "the rights of the
inmates and patients . . . [would be] fully protected," (b) that there would be used only
"photographs of inmates and patients . . . legally competent to sign releases," (c) that
a written release would be obtained "from each patient whose photograph is used in the
film" and (d) that the film would not be released "without first having been . . . approved by the Commissioner and Superintendent." The existence of the final condition
was the subject of conflicting evidence but there was oral testimony upon which the
trial judge could reasonably conclude that it had been imposed.

The then Attorney General (Mr. Brooke) on March 21, 1966, advised that "the
Superintendent may, if he deems it advisable, permit Mr. Wiseman to make his film
at" Bridgewater. Permission was then given.

In April, 1966, Mr. Wiseman and his film crew started work at Bridgewater.
They were given free access to all departments except the treatment center for the
sexually dangerous, whose director made "strong objections" in writing to any photography there without compliance with explicit written conditions. In three months,
80,000 feet of film were exposed. Pictures were made "of mentally incompetent
patients . . . in the nude . . . [and] in the most personal and private situations."

In approaching the Commissioner and the Superintendent, Mr. Wiseman had
indicated that he planned a documentary film about three people: an adult inmate, a
youthful offender, and a correctional officer. It was to be an effort "to illustrate the

various service performed—custodial, punitive, rehabilitative, and medical.'' The judge concluded (a) that the "plain import of [Mr.] Wiseman's representations was that his film was to be . . . non-commercial and non-sensational,'' whereas, in the judge's opinion, it was "crass . . . commercialism''; (b) that, in fact, the film "constitutes a most flagrant abuse[2] of the privilege . . . [Mr. Wiseman] was given''; and (c) that, instead of "a public service project,'' the film, as made, is "to be shown to the general public in movie houses.''

The Superintendent first saw the film on June 1, 1967, and objected, among other things, "to the excessive nudity.'' The then Attorney General (Mr. Richardson) also saw the film in June, 1967, and raised several questions. At a conference on September 21, 1967, Mr. Wiseman and his legal advisers were told by the Attorney General "that in his opinion the film constituted an invasion of the privacy of the inmates shown in the film; that mentally incompetent patients were shown . . . and that the releases, if any, obtained by [Mr.] Wiseman were not valid.'' The Commissioner saw the film "for the first time on . . . September 21, 1967.'' On the next day, he notified Mr. Wiseman "that the film could not be shown 'in its present form.' ''

In September, 1967, Mr. Wiseman made an agreement with Grove for distribution of the film for "showing to the general public . . . throughout the United States and Canada,'' with Mr. Wiseman to receive "50% of the theatrical gross receipts, and 75% from any television sale.'' Grove, for promotion of the film, was to have "complete control of the manner and means of distribution.'' The film was shown privately, and to the public for profit, in New York City in the autumn of 1967.

The trial judge ruled, *inter alia,* (a) that such "releases as may have been obtained [from inmates] are a nullity''; (b) "that the film is an unwarranted . . . intrusion . . . into the . . . right to privacy of each inmate'' pictured, degrading "these persons in a manner clearly not warranted by any legitimate public concern''; (c) that the "right of the public to know'' does not justify the unauthorized use of pictures showing identifiable persons "in such a manner as to . . . cause . . . humiliation''; (d) that "it is the responsibility of the State to protect'' the inmates "against any such . . . exploitation''; and (e) that the Commonwealth is under "obligation . . . to protect the right of privacy of those . . . committed to its . . . custody.''

Reactions to the film set out in the record vary from the adversely critical conclusions of the trial judge to those expressed by witnesses[4] who regarded it as fine journalistic reporting, as education, and as art.[5] The Attorney General (Mr.

---

[2]Among the findings are the following: The film "is a hodge-podge of sequences . . . depicting mentally ill patients engaged in repetitive, incoherent, and obscene rantings. . . . The film is excessively preoccupied with nudity. . . . [N]aked inmates are shown desperately attempting to hide . . . their privates with their hands. . . . There is a scene of . . . [a priest] administering the last rites of the church to a dying patient [and] the preparation of corpse for burial. . . . A . . . patient, grossly deformed by . . . congenital brain damage, is paraded before the camera.''

[4]Witnesses who regarded the film as valuable included a professor of sociology at the Harvard Law School, the film critic for Life (the magazine), the retired director of the Nieman Fellowships at Harvard, the dean of the Boston University School of Public Communication, an associate professor of psychiatry at Tufts Medical School, a professor of law at Yale, and others.

[5]For example the Life review said, in part, "The Bridgewater atmosphere is one of aimless hopelessness. . . . A psychiatrist turns an interview with an inmate into a sadistic baiting, or, with malicious cheerful-

Richardson) testified that the film "was impressive in many ways ... powerful in impact." He, however, expressed concern about the problem of obtaining valid releases, even from those "conceivably competent," since the releases would have been given before the inmates "could have any idea how they would be depicted." There was testimony from experts about the value of the film for instruction of medical and law students, and "exposure of conditions in a public institutions."[6]

    1. We are in as good a position as the trial judge to appraise the film and to determine to what extent (a) its exhibition may invade rights of inmates to privacy or (b) its suppression may interfere with countervailing interests. We may reach our conclusions about the film as documentary evidence, unaffected by findings by the trial judge. [Citations omitted.]

    As to findings based in part upon oral evidence, we decide the case according to our judgment, giving due weight to the judge's findings according to our usual standards of review. [Citations omitted.]

    2. The Commissioner and the Superintendent would have acted wisely if they had reduced any agreement to writing rather than to have risked the misunderstandings possible in oral discussions. They also might have avoided dispute if they had supervised the filming itself much more closely. We, however, need not decide whether the judge on conflicting evidence, largely oral, was plainly wrong in concluding that Mr. Wiseman had agreed to abide completely by the officials' judgment. We think that, in any event, he did not comply adequately with at least two other conditions reasonably imposed upon him before permission to make the film was granted.

    Early in the negotiations, Mr. Wiseman represented in writing that only pictures of inmates "legally competent to sign releases" would be used and that the "question of competency would ... be determined by the Superintendent and his staff." In the 1966 request for the Attorney General's opinion, Mr. Wiseman was quoted as giving assurance that a written release would be obtained "from each ... patient whose photograph is used." The latter assurance was quoted in the opinion (March 21, 1966) stating that the Superintendent had power to permit the film to be made. In the circumstances, the judge reasonably could conclude that these representations were a part of the arrangement.

    The judge was also clearly justified in deciding on the basis of expert tes-

---

ness, forcefeeds a dying old man, while we wonder whether the ash from the doctor's carelessly dangling cigarette is really going to fall into the glop being funneled into the convulsively shuddering throat. A society's treatment of the least of its citizens ... is perhaps the best measure of its civilization. The repulsive reality ... forces us to contemplate our capacity for callousness. No one seeing this film can but believe that reform of the conditions it reports is urgent business ... We cannot forget that ... [the] 'actors' are there to stay, trapped in their own desperate inventions. When a work achieves that kind of power, it must be regarded as art. ... "

    [6]The former director of the division of legal medicine of the State Department of Mental Health, now teaching at the Tufts Medical School, in a letter in evidence, commented, "Even though I was an experienced psychiatrist and had ... worked on violent ... mental hospital wards and maximum security prisons, Bridgewater was the first institution where I ever felt personally in danger. My reaction ... would border on despair each time I went. When I would leave I would quickly put the place out of my mind. ... [T]he film in ... [a] painful way revived the old feelings of depression and ... anger at myself for continuing to ignore the problem. ... [I] n a small way my reactions are a clue to why [such] institutions ... exists. There are some things we prefer not to know about ... not too unlike the Germans who live near Dachau."

timony, that some of sixty-two inmates identified as shown in the film were incompetent to understand a release and, on the basis of a stipulation, that releases were obtained only from eleven or twelve of the numerous inmates depicted. There was ample basis for concluding that Mr. Wiseman had not fulfilled important undertakings clearly designed to assure that the film would show only those consenting in writing to their appearance in the film and competent to understand and to give such consent.

3. The film shows many inmates in situations which would be degrading to a person of normal mentality and sensitivity. Although to a casual observer most of the inmates portrayed make little or no specific individual impression, others are shown in close-up pictures. These inmates are sufficiently clearly exhibited (in some instances naked) to enable acquaintances to identify them. Many display distressing mental symptoms. There is a collective, indecent intrusion into the most private aspects of the lives of these unfortunate persons in the Commonwealth's custody.

We need not discuss to what extent in Massachusetts violation of privacy will give rise to tort liability to individuals. See *Frik* v. *Boyd,* 350 Mass. 259, 264, 214 N.E.2d 460, and cases cited; Restatement 2d: Torts (Tent. draft No. 13, April 27, 1967), §§ 652D-652E. See also Warren and Brandeis, "The Right to Privacy," 4 *Harv.L.Rev.* 193; and (for references to more recent articles) Kalven, "Privacy in Tort Law—Were Warren and Brandeis Wrong?" 31 *Law & Contemp. Prob.* 326. We think, in any event, that Mr. Wiseman's massive, unrestrained invasion of the intimate lives of these State patients may be prevented by properly framed injunctive relief. The Commonwealth has standing and a duty to protect reasonably, and in a manner consistent with other public interests, the inmates from any invasions of their privacy substantially greater than those inevitably arising from the very fact of confinement. See *Ex parte Sturm,* 152 Md. 114, 119-120, 136 A. 312, 51 A.L.R. 356.

There is a "general power of the Legislature, in its capacity as parens patriae, to make suitable provision for incompetent persons." A "comprehensive system for their care and custody" is contained in G.L. c. 123. See Dubois, petitioner, 331 Mass. 575, 578-579, 120 N.E.2d 920. See also *Shapley* v. *Cohoon,* 258 F. 752, 755 (D.Mass.), remanded on other grounds 255 F. 689 (1st Cir.). The Legislature has exercised that power with specific reference to Bridgewater, among other institutions. See G.L. c. 125, § 14 (as amended through St.1957, c. 777, § 5), § 18 (inserted by St.1955, c. 770, § 11), § 19 (as amended through St.1967, C. 619, § 2). These general provisions import all reasonable power, and the duty, to exercise proper controls over the persons confined and the conditions of their custody (cf. *Maas* v. *United States,* 125 U.S.App.D.C. 251, 371 F.2d 348) and to afford the inmates protection and kindness consistent with the terms and rehabilitative purposes of their commitments. See G.L. c. 127, § 32 (as amended through St.1957, c. 777, § 11). The Commissioner and Superintendent, under reasonable standards of custodial conduct, could hardly permit merely curious members of the public access to Bridgewater to view directly many activities of the type shown in the film. We think it equally inconsistent with their custodial duties to permit the general public (as opposed to members of groups with a legitimate, significant, interest) to view films showing inmates naked or exhibiting painful aspects of mental disease. See *York* v. *Story,* 324 F.2d 450, 454-456 (9th Cir.), cert. den. 376 U.S. 939, 84 S.Ct. 794, 11 L.Ed.2d 659. See also *Myers* v.

Afro-Am. Publishing Co. Inc., 168 Misc. 429, 430–431, 5 N.Y.S.2d 223 (Supr.Ct.), affd. 255 App.Div. 838, 7 N.Y.S.2d 662; *Myers* v. *United States Camera Publishing Corp.,* 9 Misc.2d 765, 766–768, 167 N.Y.S.2d 771; 1934 Op.N.Y.Atty.Gen. pp. 374, 375.

These considerations, taken with the failure of Mr. Wiseman to comply with the contractual condition that he obtain valid releases from all persons portrayed in the film, amply justify granting injunctive relief to the Commonwealth. The impracticality of affording relief to the inmates individually also supports granting this collective relief to the Commonwealth as *parens patriae,* in the interest of all the affected inmates. We give no weight to any direct interest of the Commonwealth itself in suppressing the film.

4. The defendants contend that no asserted interest of privacy may be protected from the publication of this film because the conditions at Bridgewater are matters of continuing public concern, as this court has recognized. See *Nason* v. *Commissioner of Mental Health,* 351 Mass. 94, 98, 221 N.E.2d 400; *Nason* v. *Superintendent of Bridgewater State Hosp.,* 353 Mass. 604, 606–614, 233 N.E.2d 908.[8] Indeed, it was concern over conditions at Bridgewater which led various public officials in 1965 and 1966 to consider a documentary film, in the hope that, if suitable, it might arouse public interest and lead to improvement.

Even an adequate presentation to the public of conditions at Bridgewater, however, would not necessitate the inclusion of some episodes shown in the film, nor would it justify (cf. *Travers* v. *Paton,* 261 F.Supp. 110, 116–117 (D.Conn.]) the depiction of identifiable inmates, who had not given valid written consents and releases, naked or in other embarrassing situations. We agree with the trial judge that Mr. Wiseman's wide ranging photography amounted to "abuse of the privilege he was given to make a film" and a serious failure to comply with conditions reasonably imposed upon him.[9] Mr. Wiseman could hardly have fairly believed that officials, solicitous about obtaining consent and releases from all inmates portrayed, could have been expected to approve this type of film for general distribution.

The record does not indicate to us that any inmate shown in the film, by reason of past conduct, had any special news interest as an individual. Each inmate's importance to the film was that he was an inmate of Bridgewater, that he suffered from some form of mental disease, and that he was undergoing in the Bridgewater facilities particular types of custody and treatment. Recognizable pictures of individuals, al-

---

[8]The latter case, decided February 5, 1968, discloses (see pp. 609, esp. fn. 6, and 611, 233 N.E.2d 908) some improvements in conditions at Bridgewater during 1967, the year after the film was made. In the present case, also, there was testimony, for example, that, after the film was completed, thirty-eight officers, fifty-five other persons engaged in rehabilitation, and three doctors had been added to the preexisting Bridgewater staff.

[9]Even if no person portrayed objected to being photographed and even if no pictures were taken of persons who did object, the requirement of releases from persons competent to give them does not seem to us unreasonable. Cf. *Thayer* v. *Worcester Post Co.,* 284 Mass. 160, 163–164, 187 N.E. 292; *Marek* v. *Zanol Prod. Co.,* 298 Mass. 1, 3–4, 9 N.E.2d 393. Indeed, in view of the character of the film, we would not be disposed to give a release (even from an inmate capable of giving one) substantial significance until the inmate giving it had seen the film and fully understood how he was to be portrayed.

though perhaps resulting in more effective photography, were not essential. In the circumstances, there will be no unreasonable interference with any publication of matters of public concern if showing the film to the general public is prevented (a) to protect interests of the inmates in privacy, and (b) because Mr. Wiseman went unreasonably beyond the scope of the conditional permission to enter, and take pictures upon, State owned premises properly not generally open for public inspection and photography. See *Adderley* v. *Florida,* 385 U.S. 39, 41, 47-48, 87 S.Ct. 242, 17 L.Ed.2d 149.

The case is distinguishable from decisions which have permitted publication of newsworthy events where the public interest in reasonable dissemination of news has been treated as more significant than the private interests in privacy. Cf. *Time, Inc.* v. *Hill,* 385 U.S. 374, 380-391. [Additional citations omitted.]

We need not now consider to what extent Mr. Wiseman could have been wholly excluded from making a film at Bridgewater. In this aspect of the case, we hold merely that he violated the permission given to him, reasonably interpreted, and did not comply with valid conditions (cf. note, 73 *Harv.L.Rev.* 1595, 1599-1602), that he obtain written releases.[10]

We are aware, of course, that in *Cullen* v. *Grove Press, Inc.,* 276 F.Supp. 727, 729-731 (S.D.N.Y.), a preliminary injunction against showing the film generally to the New York public was denied when such relief was sought by correction officers at the institution. The then plaintiffs, however, did not represent the inmates as the Commonwealth (as *parens patriae*) does in this case. We, in any event, decline to follow the broad interpretation given in the *Cullen* case to *Time, Inc.* v. *Hill,* 385 U.S. 374, 387-388, 87 S.Ct. 534.

5. That injunctive relief may be granted against showing the film to the general public on a commercial basis does not mean that all showings of the film must be prevented. As already indicated (see e.g. fns. 5, 6), the film gives a striking picture of life at Bridgewater and of the problems affecting treatment at that or any similar institution. It is a film which would be instructive to legislators, judges, lawyers, sociologists, social workers, doctors, psychiatrists, students in these or related fields, and organizations dealing with the social problems of custodial care and mental infirmity. The public interest in having such persons informed about Bridgewater, in our opinion, outweighs any countervailing interests of the inmates and of the Commonwealth (as parens patriae) in anonymity and privacy.

The effect upon inmates of showing the film to persons with a serious interest in

---

[10]The record suggests that Mr. Wiseman, who spent much uncompensated time and about $32,000 in the production, not only was interested in recovering his costs (which he apparently had not done at the time of trial) but also in entering the picture in various cinema art competitions. Mr. Wiseman doubtless desired to produce an effective "documentary," or a work of art which would win awards, or a film which would attract public patronage. In our opinion, no one of these purposes would justify the violation of the conditions or of the proper interests of the inmates. This is not an instance (cf. *Attorney Gen.* v. *The Book Named "Tropic of Cancer,"* 345 Mass. 11, 20, 184 N.E.2d 328) where judges or administrators may be regarded as attempting to be "arbiters of taste" or to determine for a producer what is "unnecessary" to his portrayal of particular scenes. Relief here is granted solely to afford protection to interests entitled to protection.

rehabilitation,[11] and with potential capacity to be helpful, is likely to be very different from the effect of its exhibition merely to satisfy general public curiosity. There is possibility that showings to specialized audiences may be of benefit to the public interest, to the inmates themselves, and to the conduct of an important State institution. Because of the character of such audiences, the likelihood of humiliation, even of identifiable inmates, is greatly reduced. In any event the likelihood of harm seems to us less than the probablity of benefits.

6.   We think that the final decree (unrestricted as it is as to time, geographical scope, and audience) is too sweeping and that more precise and restricted relief against showing the film, and the dissemination of the information contained in it, is necessary. [Citations omitted.] The decree is to be modified to permit (according to standards to be defined in the decree) the showing of the film to audiences of the specialized or professional character already mentioned.

Mr. Wiseman, or those claiming through him, may make a charge for use of the film, so far as showing it may be permitted by the modified decree. In view of the lapse of time since the film was made, the modified decree should fairly require including in the film, for all permitted showings, a brief explanation that changes and improvements have taken place in the institution since 1966.

7.   We perceive no reason for ordering destruction of film footage not included in the film exhibited to us. The decree should be modified to permit preservation of this material at the expense of Mr. Wiseman, if he wishes to save it, provided that no use shall be made of this material without the approval of the Superior Court.

8.   The court shall retain jurisdiction of the case for the granting of such supplemental relief as from time to time may be appropriate under the modified decree.

9.   The trial judge stated that the plaintiffs "do not seek any award of compensatory damages" for the violation of the inmates' rights to privacy. In any event, the present record is not an appropriate basis for a recovery by any particular inmate who may have suffered ascertainable damage. Indeed, the film may indirectly have been of benefit to some inmates by leading to improvement of Bridgewater. Injunctive relief affords the inmates the most effective, and probably the only useful, protection which can be given. We perceive no occasion for imposing, as the Commonwealth urges, a constructive trust upon receipts for past showings of the film.

10.   The interlocutory decree with respect to the demurrer is affirmed. The final decree is reversed in order to permit its modification. A modified decree, consistent with this opinion, is to be entered. The Commonwealth is to have costs of appeal.

So ordered.

NOTE

In light of the interests asserted on behalf of allowing a wide public screening of the movie, how relatively important are the modesty concerns of the patients? Who was

---

[11]The seemingly random and somewhat, incoherent sequence (see fn. 2) of scenes, probably designed to give to the film an impressionistic character, is not likely to confuse seriously interested professional and student audiences. The film, even in its present form, may be highly informative to such specialized audiences.

actually more guilty of invading the privacy of the patients, the institution officials who permitted or caused the patients to run around naked in degrading settings or the filmmakers who recorded such scenes? Is the right to privacy served in such circumstances by keeping the facts of daily degradation a secret?

E. RECREATIONAL AND ATHLETIC PROGRAMS

BORDEN V. ROHR

United States District Court for the Southern District of Ohio, Eastern Division, 1975 No. C 2 75-844, Excerpts of Proceedings, Dec. 30, 1975

ROBERT M. DUNCAN, Judge.

* * *

THE COURT: The Court has listened with interest to the facts in this case, and in order to save everybody a lot of time, I suppose I could make a ruling from the bench.

I think we should first all keep in mind that what we have heard here today is not a hearing on the merits. Regardless of what the Court does with this motion for preliminary relief, the case will have to be tried full scale on the merits if the usual procedures are followed.

The first matter to be evaluated is whether or not the Plaintiff has demonstrated to the Court that he has a great potential for success on the trial of the merits, and in making this kind of a preliminary determination, the Court first must say that I do take judicial notice of the fact that basketball is a contact sport. It seems to me that it would be foreign to just about everything we see in basketball to say otherwise. It is a contact sport. I don't think there is any question about that.

Laying aside and leaving for another day the Plaintiff's statutory claim of jurisdiction in this Court and looking on to the 1983 claim through the Fourteenth Amendment, at this point in time, it appears to the Court that unless the Defendants are able to demonstrate a rational basis for the differentiation that they make to this Plaintiff than those other persons who qualified for junior basketball at Ohio University, then the decision not to let him play must fall unless you demonstrate a rational basis for it, and, of course, here it becomes the real shady, grey, philosophical area we're all dealing with here.

Basically, as I understand the witnesses for the defense, the rational basis is that their physicians, after having considered the American Medical Association Committee's report concerning vital organs, one of which I take it is an eye or the eyes, the American Medical Association has for some reason, which I do not know at this time, but for some reason has concluded that persons with only one vital organ or one eye as we are more specifically concerned with here should not become involved in contact sports. Moreover, the doctors also indicated that they personally believe this to be a wise rule.

But, on the other hand, assuming, and I think it is a good assumption, that there is some additional risk that this Plaintiff must encounter in playing basketball that persons with two well-functioning eyes do not encounter, then it is apparent to me the question is: Is there enough risk to justify him not being allowed to play, so that then we can say that the Defendants have demonstrated there is a rational basis for their action?

And here is where I have a problem, because I have heard no evidence from the Defendants which convinces me that they have evaluated or they know of how much risk is involved in him playing and subsequently losing the sight of an eye through basketball activity, and I suppose you'd argue any risk, any risk would be enough in order to demonstrate a rational basis. I just simply do not at this point believe that, so therefore, it would appear to me that unless there is more evidence coming from the Defendants which would tend to establish a rational basis for a decision at trial, the chance of Mr. Borden prevailing at a trial on the merits in this case is exceedingly good.

Now, that only begins the inquiry to determine whether or not this relief should be granted. The Court must also consider whether or not not being allowed to partici-pate in junior varsity basketball after having made the team at Ohio University is a matter which irreparably harms this Plaintiff, and again, that's not an easy decision.

I suppose, in the order of things in our society, that playing junior varsity basketball at Ohio University may not be one of the most crucial things in the world, but on the other hand, knowing sports activity as I think I gleaned from the Plaintiff's concepts of it and the way he talks about it, it is extremely important to him, extremely. He made a junior varsity college basketball team, and I suppose if you'd look over all young men his age who have had some high school basketball and they had an opportunity to be where he is, they would think that to be a very important station in life.

Now, I don't think that this Plaintiff or I or any one of us here can say what the responsibility is for an enormous attraction that college sports activity has in our society, what the realities are that these attractions are. So we take that away from him, and I think it is taking away a valuable part of his life style, so therefore, if he isn't allowed to play I think even for a short period of time through the month of February, whenever basketball season is, through the month of February, I think you have irreparably harmed this young fellow, coupled with the fact that if he doesn't get to play, he can't go on to the next year, whatever, spring board of the making up of the team will make for him.

The third matter that the Court has to consider on whether or not to issue this relief is the public interest, and again, I do not make light of it, either, because I do think that this director, these physicians and the trainer, the president of this university, do have some great responsibility to see that persons, to the best of their ability, do not suffer mightly, aren't seriously injured, aren't permanently maimed because of their participation in college and athletics. I think in my judgment that concern is valuable, and I'm sure they have it and I hope they continue to have it, but on the other hand, as I look at recent legislation passed by the Congress, as I look at recent legislation passed by the State of Ohio, there is another public interest consideration which is emerging, and that is the regard and the status in this society of those who have some sort of a handicap. This is another emerging concept we're caring more about. We're en-couraging them to fully participate to the best of their ability and the extent of their physical resources in their own personal affairs and the affairs of our social kind of living, so we lend encouragement to them.

On the other hand, we also have a duty, I think, in some instances, to protect. So these are somewhat competing interests, but I do think, in this instance, the public interest, in my judgment, lies with allowing this man to live his own life, risk it, risk his eye to some degree. Again, we don't know how much, but I think the people at the university have done their share. I'm not so sure I wouldn't have done exactly what the director has done if I were in his position, but I am not, I'm in this position, and I think that the values lie, and there are certainly enough to justify to issue this order with allowing this young man to take that risk; and if I have to share it with him, well, that's what I'm going to do. So the monkey's off the back of the Ohio University and it's on that Plaintiff and it's on me until such time as we hear this case on the merits.

This is not an easy decision. Counsel has made some good arguments for the position taken by the University, and I don't discount that good faith on the University, but on the other hand, it is just my judgment today that the way I feel about it, a Plaintiff in the status of this young man, I think he ought to be given the opportunity to play basketball, at least until the case is set down for hearing on the merits, and I will put on an order to that effect.

NOTE

Subsequent to the issuance of the preliminary injunction, the university indicated its willingness to let Michael Borden continue to participate in its basketball program, and the case was settled by agreement between the parties.

KAMPMEIER V. NYQUIST

United States Court of Appeals for the Second Circuit, 1977
553 F.2d 296

Before LUMBARD and OAKES, Circuit Judges, and BRYAN, District Judge.
LUMBARD, Circuit Judge:

Two junior high school students, each with vision in only one eye, and their parents, appeal from an order by Judge Burke in the Western District of New York denying their motion for a preliminary injunction against public school authorities in Pittsford and Canandaigua, New York, who have refused to allow the students to participate in contact sports at school. Plaintiffs contend that the school system's prohibition on participation by one-eyed students in contact sports violates section 504 of the Rehabilitation Act of 1973, 29 U.S.C. § 794, and also deprives them of their fourteenth amendment right to equal protection of the law. Having considered the possible irreparable consequences that may flow from whichever decision the court should choose to make, we conclude that the appellants have not made a sufficient factual showing of likely success of the merits to warrant preliminary relief. Accordingly, we affirm the order of the district court.

In their complaint filed on April 14, 1976, plaintiffs alleged the following: Margaret Kampmeier has a congenital cataract in one eye. As of the beginning of her seventh-grade year in 1975, she was one of the best athletes in her class. Her parents have provided her with protective glasses which have industrial quality safety lenses, wire mesh side shields, and extended ear pieces. The Kampmeiers have also announced their willingness to release the school and its employees from liability for any athletics injury to Margaret's good eye.[1] Steven Genecco is a grade ahead of Margaret. He has been virtually blind in one eye since an injury at age six. Prior to the 1975–76 school year, he had been allowed to participate in all school sports. During 1975 he participated in interscholastic basketball and a community association football league as well as the regular school physical education program. On recommendation by a school physician, each child has now been prohibited from participating in any contact sports at school, solely because of lack of vision in one eye.[2]

In response to plaintiffs' motion for a preliminary injunction, the defendants submitted affidavits explaining that under regulations promulgated by the New York State Commissioner of Education, 8 N.Y.C.R.R.§ 135.4(c)(7)(i)(h), approval from the school medical officer is required before any student may be allowed to participate in interscholastic athletics. Pamphlets distributed to school officials by the Commissioner list blindness in one eye as a disqualifying condition for participation in contact sports, but not noncontact sports.[3] The lists of disqualifications are advisory only: "[t]hese guidelines ... are only guidelines and are not absolute mandates for the school physician."[4] "Some of the disqualifying conditions listed are subject to evaluation by the responsible physician with respect to anticipated risks, the otherwise athletic fitness of the candidate, special protective preventive measures that might be utilized, and the nature of the supervisory control."[5] In *Matter of Spitaleri,* 11 Ed.Dept. Rep. 84 (1972), petition for review dismissed (Sup.Ct. Albany County Special Term, June 15, 1973) (Mahoney, J.), the Commissioner of Education ruled that a school physician's determination against participation in contact sports by a one-eyed child is not reviewable.

Letters from physicians who had examined the children were submitted. Their opinions were divided.[6]

After oral argument based on the foregoing record, Judge Burke on July 28 denied plaintiffs' preliminary injunction motion. He found that plaintiffs had failed to show that they would suffer irreparable harm or that they were likely to succeed on the merits.

The standard for issuance of a preliminary injunction is whether there has been

---

[1]The complaint alleged that the Kampmeiers had attempted to obtain insurance for their daughter, without success.

[2]The schools receive federal and state funds.

[3]American Medical Ass'n, *Medical Evaluation of the Athlete ... a Guide* 7 (rev. ed. 1973); N.Y. State Educ. Dept., *Department Policy Relative to Medical Examinations for Organized Interscholastic Athletic Activities* 4.

[4]*Department Policy, supra* note 3, at 4.

[5]*Medical Evaluation of the Athlete, supra* note 3, at 4.

[6]One of Margaret Kampmeier's doctors wrote that neither he nor her ophthalmologist felt her lack of vision should "be any hinderence [sic] to her full participation in school athletic activities." Another wrote: "I feel that with special protective eye wear the risk to either eye is rather remote. However, there is a risk, and the protective eye wear would by no means guarantee the safety of her eyes." The school physician concluded that contact sports presented an unreasonable risk of injury to Margaret's one good eye.

A doctor who examined Steven Genecco at the request of his school physician wrote: "It is my opinion that the disadvantages of participating in contact sports far outweigh any possible advantages. . . . "

"a clear showing of either (1) probable success on the merits *and* possible irreparable injury, *or* (2) sufficiently serious questions going to the merits to make them a fair ground for litigation *and* a balance of hardships tipping decidedly toward the party requesting the preliminary relief." *Triebwasser & Katz* v. *American Tel. & Tel. Co.,* 535 F.2d 1356, 1358 (2d Cir. 1976); *Sonesta Int'l Hotels Corp.* v. *Wellington Associates,* 483 F.2d 247, 250 (2d Cir. 1973) (emphasis in original). Ordinarily, the grant or denial of a preliminary injunction by a district court is reviewable only for abuse of discretion. See *Triebwasser & Katz* v. *American Tel. & Tel. Co., supra.* However, when—as here—the district court makes no detailed findings in support of his decision, we must engage in a somewhat more searching review. Cf. *Small* v. *Kiley,* No. 76-6162 (2d Cir. March 9, 1977).

Section 504 of the Rehabilitation Act, 29 U.S.C. § 794, provides:

> No otherwise qualified handicapped individual . . . shall, solely by reason of his handicap, be excluded from the participation in, be denied the benefits of, or be subjected to discrimination under any program or activity receiving Federal financial assistance.

In *Lloyd* v. *Regional Transportation Authority,* 548 F.2d 1277, 1284–87 (7th Cir. 1977), the court held that handicapped persons have private rights of action under § 504. Although the circumstances were somewhat different, the reasoning in that opinion is fairly persuasive here. Accord, *Hairston* v. *Drosick,* 423 F.Supp. 180 (S.D.W.Va. 1976). Thus, we think it probable that the plaintiffs do have standing to sue;[7] they are the people in the best position to enforce § 504, which is designed specifically for their protection.[8] See generally *Cort* v. *Ash,* 422 U.S. 66, 78, 95 S.Ct. 2080, 45 L.Ed.2d 26 (1975).

As we read § 504, however, exclusion of handicapped children from a school activity is not improper if there exists a substantial justification for the school's policy. Section 504 prohibits only the exclusion of handicapped persons who are "otherwise qualified." Here, the defendants have relied on medical opinion that children with sight in only one eye are not qualified to play in contact sports because of the high risk of eye injury. The plaintiffs have presented little evidence—medical, statistical, or otherwise—which would cast doubt on the substantiality of this rationale. On the record before us, they have not made a clear showing of probable success on the merits.[9]

Both sides have demonstrated the possibility of irreparable injury. On the one hand, athletics play an important part in the life and growth of teenage children, cf. *Brenden* v. *Independent School District,* 477 F.2d 1292, 1299 (8th Cir. 1973), and the plaintiffs are being deprived of the freedom to participate in sports of their choice. On the other hand, public school officials have a parens patriae interest in protecting the

---

[7]The appellees do not deny that Margaret Kampmeier and Steven Genecco are within the applicable definition of a "handicapped individual" in 29 U.S.C. § 706(6).

[8]We do not need to reach appellants' argument that handicapped individuals are a suspect class and therefore entitled to invoke strict scrutiny analysis under the equal protection clause.

[9]Plaintiffs rely on *Borden* v. *Rohr,* No. C2 75-844 (S.D.Ohio Dec. 30, 1975) (oral decision), wherein a preliminary injunction was granted to allow a one-eyed state university student to play intercollegiate basketball. That case was unlike this one, however, because there the student was old enough to weigh the risks and make the decision for himself.

well-being of their students; the defendants, relying on medical opinion, are concerned about the risk of injury to a child's one good eye.[10] In view of the host of noncontact sports which remain open to the plaintiffs, we conclude that the balance of hardships does not tip decidedly in their favor.

The motion for a preliminary injunction was properly denied. Judgment affirmed.

NOTES

1. Can the results in *Kampmeier* v. *Nyquist* and *Borden* v. *Rohr* be reconciled? Consider the rationale of the Court expressed in footnote 9. What are the ramifications of the age distinction made there?

2. The court notes that the plaintiffs have "presented little evidence—medical, statistical, or otherwise"; what sorts of evidence could and should have been presented?

KAMPMEIER V. HARRIS

Supreme Court of New York, Monroe County, 1978
93 Misc.2d 1032, 403 N.Y.S.2d 638

ELIZABETH W. PINE, Justice.

This special proceeding was commenced pursuant to Education Law § 4409 (L.1977, c. 787), originally known as the "*Spitaleri* bill," to enjoin a school district from prohibiting a student from participating in an athletic program by reason of a physical impairment. It is conceded that the student petitioner is an outstanding athlete and that, at the beginning of her seventh-grade year, she was one of the best athletes in her class. By respondents's admission, petitioner was first "defined as handicapped by the school physician" in October of 1975, and since that time has repeatedly been denied permission to participate in interscholastic contact sports. In January, 1976, this prohibition was expanded in scope so as to exclude petitioner from participation in intramural and gym class contact sports. The statement of respondents' physician, appended to the answer in this proceeding, notes that the school has developed for the student "alternative programs for [her] physical education"which exclude her from all contact sports.

In support of these determinations, respondents have produced undated State Education Department "standards" upon which they rely in excluding petitioner from the regular "physical education" program which the district provides for its pupils (See 8 NYCRR §§ 135.1[f]; 135.4[a]). The undated standards relied upon by respondents recite that they have been adopted to carry out the provisions of 8 NYCRR 135.4(e)(i)(vii), the provision construed in *Matter of Spitaleri,* 12 Ed.Dept.Rep. 84 (1972), petition dism. 74 Misc.2d 811, 345 N.Y.S.2d 878 (Sup. Ct., Spec.Term,

---

[10]The appellees have also expressed fears that athletes lacking depth perception and peripheral vision may be a special hazard to their fellow competitors. However, this claim is not part of the record in the district court, and no evidence has been adduced to support it.

In addition, the defendants say they fear negligence liability should a one-eyed child be injured in contact sports.

Albany Co. 1973). This provision was repealed nearly four years ago, when it was re-enacted as 8 NYCRR 135.4(c)(7)(i)(h).

Since that time, sweeping changes have taken place, at both the federal and state levels, affecting the substantive and procedural rights of the handicapped in general (*e.g.,* Section 504 of the Federal Rehabilitation Act of 1973, 29 U.S.C. § 794; and see 45 C.F.R. Part 84 [42 Fed.Reg. 22676, May 4, 1977]), and those of handicapped students in particular (i.e., the federal Education for All Handicapped Children Act of 1975, Pub.L. 94-142, 20 U.S.C. § 1401 *et seq.,* and regulations thereunder, 45 C.F.R. Part 121a [42 Fed.Reg. 42474, August 23, 1977]; New York's response to this federal mandate was L.1976, c. 853, codified, with some amendments, at Article 89 of the Education Law, § 4401 *et seq.,* with new implementing regulations at 8 NYCRR Part 200).

The *Spitaleri* statute, Education Law § 4409—unlike its companion provisions in Article 89—lacks any genesis in the Education for All Handicapped Children Act of 1975. In accordance with the terms of the *Spitaleri* law, petitioners have provided the court with the affidavits of two licensed physicians—one, a specialist in ophthalmology, and the other, a specialist in pediatrics—both stating that the student is physically capable of participating in the school athletic program, and that it is reasonably safe for her to do so.

Under Education Law § 4409, the court must find not only that it is "reasonably safe," but also that it is in the "best interest" of the student to be allowed to participate in the school's athletic program. The court is puzzled at the need for the "reasonably safe" requirement, since it is difficult to imagine a situation in which participation could possibly not be reasonably safe, and yet somehow be in any student's "best interest." The court, having considered the affidavits of petitioners' physicians and finding none from respondents' physician, and considering the oral and written argument submitted by the parties, does find that petitioner's participation in contact sports, with protective eyewear with which she is already equipped (including industrial quality safety lenses, wire mesh side shields and extended ear pieces) would be reasonably safe within the meaning of the *Spitaleri* statute (Education Law § 4409[3]).

The "best interest" test, however, is more troubling, and the difficulty lies not so much with the medical or social circumstances of the student as with the provisions of the *Spitaleri* law itself. Education Law § 4409(4) provides, rather expansively:

> ... *No school district shall be held liable for any injury sustained* by a student participating pursuant to an order granted under this section in a program as defined in subdivision eight of this section nor for failing to ensure that any prescribed special preventive measures or devices needed to protect the student are employed." [emphasis added.]

It would seem to the court that "relief" under the *Spitaleri* law inures principally to the benefit of the school district rather than to that of the handicapped student. This statutory provision purports to insulate school districts, in advance, from liability for injuries bearing no connection whatever with the student's handicap, and even for gross negligence. The court notes, moreover, that the petitioners might not yet have succeeded in securing, for their daughter, any private insurance coverage to fill the gap. See *Kampmeier* v. *Nyquist*, 553 F.2d 296, 298 § n. 1 (2d Cir. 1977). The court is not surprised, then, that counsel for the State Education Department officially expressed a position of "no opposition" to the enactment of the *Spitaleri* bill, or that the respondents in this proceeding conceded at oral argument that it "might well be" in the student's best interest that this petition be granted under Education Law § 4409.

Though the law was otherwise at the time *Spitaleri* was decided, it is now the law—under the Education for All Handicapped Children Act of 1975 and regulations thereunder, and its state counterpart, Education Law §§ 4401-4407 and regulations thereunder—that a student may not be "classified as handicapped" and provided with "special education," against the wishes of his parents, at the sole discretion of a school physician (as respondents unmistakably admit to having done), subject only to review under Education Law § 310 and the "arbitrary and capricious" standard of CPLR Article 78, as in *Spitaleri*.

There has yet to be a determination, in accordance with the provisions of Education Law §§ 4401-4407 and 8 NYCRR Part 200, that the petitioner is in fact in need of any special education or related services on the basis of physical handicap. Significantly, under these provisions of the Education Law, as under the Education for All Handicapped Children Act of 1975, special education (which includes [45 C.F.R. § 121a.6] physical education, 45 C.F.R. § 121a.14) and related services (45 C.F.R. §121a.13) may be provided on the basis of a physical handicap see 45 C.F.R. § 121a.5[b][11]) only in accordance with integrated and well-articulated procedures which afford, to students and their parents, not only notice and an opportunity to be heard, but an opportunity for a more than peremptory review (See especially 20 U.S.C. § 1415[e][3]).

In view of the broad and virtually irreversible effect of a judgment under Education Law § 4409, and in view of respondents' rather incredible but conceded failure to take any of the measures now required by law *before* a child is classified handicapped or provided special services (and under which broad and lasting immunity from liability is *not* conferred upon a school district) the court finds that judgment under Education Law § 4409 would not be in the best interest of the student under these circumstances. Relief under Education Law § 4409 is accordingly denied without prejudice to the commencement of such a proceeding by petitioners, if so advised, after a final determination of the student's rights under the Education for All Handicapped Children Act of 1975 and Education Law §§ 4401-4407 and regulations thereunder.

Respondents are directed to comply, forthwith, with the notice and hearing and other provisions of Education Law §§ 4401-4407 and regulations thereunder, and with all applicable provisions of the Education for All Handicapped Children Act of 1975 and regulations thereunder and other provisions of federal law. Pending any legally valid identification, evaluation or classification of the petitioner as physically handicapped and in need of special education or related services, respondents are enjoined from excluding the petitioner, solely on account of her visual handicap, from participation in contact sports otherwise available under respondents' physical education program. Education Law § 4404(4.); 8 NYCRR § 200.5(b)(7). See generally 45 C.F.R. § 121a.342.

NOTES

1.   The decision in *Kampmeier* v. *Harris* resulted when the plaintiffs in *Kampmeier* v. *Nyquist,* dissatisfied with the results they were getting in the federal courts, filed a state court action. The contrast between *Harris* and *Nyquist* is also informative as to the impact of the Education for All Handicapped Children Act of 1975 (see pp. 213–244, above) upon the exclusion of handicapped students from school recreational and athletic programs.

2.   The case of *Matter of Spitaleri,* 74 Misc. 2d 811, 345 N.Y.S.2d 878 (1973), discussed in *Harris,* had reached an opposite result under New York law prior to the enactment of the Education for All Handicapped Children Act of 1975. The *Spitaleri* court upheld a decision by the Commissioner of Education that a student with a loss of vision in one eye was medically disqualified from participating in high school football.

3.   A recent decision outside the realm of scholastic sports and recreation programs is *Neeld* v. *National Hockey League,* 594 F.2d 1297 (9th Cir. 1979), where a "one-eyed hockey player," *id.* at 1298, sued the National Hockey League to challenge, as a violation of the Sherman Act, a league by-law that prohibits partially sighted persons from playing on NHL clubs. The court held that the by-law was proper:

> The by-law is not motivated by anticompetitiveness and Neeld does not actually contend that it is. Further, any anticompetitive effect is at most *de minimis,* ... and incidental to the primary purpose of promoting safety, both for Neeld, who lost his eye in a hockey game, and for all players who play with or against him. We take judicial notice that ice hockey is a very rough physical contact sport, and that there is bound to be danger to players who happen to be on Neeld's blind side, no matter how well his mask may protect his one good eye. Also of some importance and legitimate concern to the League and its members is the possibility of being sued for personal injuries to Neeld himself or to others, if Neeld is permitted to play. *Id.* at 1300.

Does this analysis address the sentiments expressed by Judge Duncan in *Borden* v. *Rohr,* that handicapped persons should be permitted to take risks if they knowingly choose to do so?

INDEX